# Fodor's 97
# Caribbean

"When it comes to information on regional history, what to see and do, and shopping, these guides are exhaustive."

—*USAir Magazine*

"Usable, sophisticated restaurant coverage, with an emphasis on good value."

—Andy Birsh, *Gourmet Magazine* columnist

"Valuable because of their comprehensiveness."

—*Minneapolis Star-Tribune*

"Fodor's always delivers high quality...thoughtfully presented...thorough."

—*Houston Post*

"An excellent choice for those who want everything under one cover."

—*Washington Post*

D0107447

Fodor's Travel Publications, Inc.
New York • Toronto • London • Sydney • Auckland
http://www.fodors.com/

# Fodor's Caribbean

**Editors:** Caroline V. Haberfeld, Kristen Perrault

**Contributors:** Pamela Acheson, Robert Andrews, Glen Berger, Robert Blake, Audra Epstein, Janet Foley, Edie Jarolim, Lynda Lohr, JoAnn Milivojevic, Kate Pennebaker, Melissa Rivers, Jonathan Runge, Heidi Sarna, Helayne Schiff, Mary Ellen Schultz, M. T. Schwartzman (Gold Guide editor), Kate Sekules, Jordan Simon, Dinah Spritzer, Simon Worrall, Jane E. Zarem

**Creative Director:** Fabrizio La Rocca

**Cartographer:** David Lindroth

**Cover Photograph:** Catherine Karnow/Woodfin Camp

**Text Design:** Between the Covers

# Copyright

# Special Sales

PRINTED IN THE UNITED STATES OF AMERICA

10 9 8 7 6 5 4 3 2 1

# CONTENTS

## Maps and Plans

# ON THE ROAD WITH FODOR'S

**W**E'RE ALWAYS THRILLED to get letters from readers, especially one like this:

*It took us an hour to decide what book to buy and we now know we picked the best one. Your book was wonderful, easy to follow, very accurate, and good on pointing out eating places, informal as well as formal. When we saw other people using your book, we would look at each other and smile.*

Our editors and writers are deeply committed to making every Fodor's guide "the best one"—not only accurate but always charming, brimming with sound recommendations and solid ideas, right on the mark in describing restaurants and hotels, and full of fascinating facts that make you view what you've traveled to see in a rich new light.

## About Our Writers

Our success in achieving our goals—and in helping to make your trip the best of all possible vacations—is a credit to the hard work of our extraordinary writers and editors.

**Pamela Acheson** spent 18 years in New York City as a publishing executive before heading south to divide her time between Florida and the Caribbean. She writes extensively about both areas and is a regular contributor to *Travel & Leisure*, *Caribbean Travel and Life*, *Florida Travel and Life*, *Fodor's Florida*, *Fodor's Caribbean*, and *Fodor's Virgin Islands*. She is the author of *The Best of the British Virgin Islands* and *The Best of St. Thomas* and is currently working on *The Best of the Bahamas* and several Florida guides.

**Edie Jarolim,** who updated the Trinidad and Tobago chapter, was a senior editor at Fodor's before moving to the sunny southwest. She is a regular contributor to Fodor's guides and her articles have appeared in *American Way, Bride's,* and the *Wall Street Journal*. She enjoys writing but aspires to do more liming—the Trinidad and Tobago term for just hanging out.

**Lynda Lohr** spent the last 12 years as a St. John resident, much of it swimming at her favorite Hawksnest Beach. She's a veteran mainland and U.S. Virgin Islands journalist who works regularly for local, regional, and national publications. She lives with her cat and her boyfriend in a tiny cottage overlooking Cruz Bay.

**JoAnn Milivojevic** is a freelance writer and video producer based in Illinois, whose love affair with the Caribbean began 10 years ago while scuba diving in the Turks and Caicos Islands. She has produced video programs on the Cayman Islands and St. Kitts and Nevis; her articles on the Caribbean have appeared in publications nationwide. She travels regularly to the islands to "wine her waist" to Soca music, collect folktales, and dive the salty blue.

**Melissa Rivers** was married barefoot on a sugary beach in Montego Bay. If she had to plan a honeymoon there today, she'd be hard pressed to choose a place to stay. She also covered the Caymans, and as an avid snorkeler and diver, could not recommend the islands more highly. Melissa travels extensively and has also contributed to *Fodor's Mexico, Fodor's Canada, Fodor's USA, Fodor's Great American Learning Vacations,* and *Fodor's Great American Sports and Adventure Vacations*.

**Jonathan Runge** is the author of *Rum and Reggae, The Insider's Guide to the Caribbean* (Villard Books) as well as *Hot on Hawaii* and *Ski Party!* (St. Martin's Press). He has contributed to *Outside, National Geographic Traveler,* and *Skiing*. He is also a disciple of the Zonker Harris Order of the Perpetual Tan.

**Jordan Simon** has visited nearly every speck of land in the Caribbean for Fodor's, *Caribbean Travel & Life, Modern Bride, Physicians Travel & Meeting Guide, Travel & Leisure,* and *Travelage*. He is the author of *Fodor's Colorado, Fodor's Branson,* and the *USA Today Ski Atlas,* among others.

Husband-and-wife team **Simon Worrall** and **Kate Pennebaker** have years of Caribbean experience between them. Kate Pennebaker first dove when she was dropped off the back of a boat in Dominica with a tank at the age of 10 by her explorer stepfather, Peter Gimbel. She has been going back to the islands, as a diver and photographer, ever since. Simon Worrall is a British-born journalist. His many credits include the *London Sunday Times Magazine, Esquire, Harper's and Queen, Men's Journal,* and *Geo.*

**Jane Zarem** is a freelance writer from Connecticut who travels frequently to the Caribbean. Among the score of islands she has explored, she finds it difficult to pick a favorite—she loves them all. She is a member of the New York Travel Writers' Association and the International Food, Wine & Travel Writers' Association, and has contributed to numerous Fodor's guides, among them *New England USA, Cape Cod, Bahamas,* and *Great American Sports and Adventure Vacations,* as well as *Caribbean.*

## New This Year

### On the Web

Check out Fodor's Web site (http://www.fodors.com/), where you'll find travel information on major destinations around the world and an ever-changing array of travel-savvy interactive features.

### Hurricanes

In September 1995 hurricanes Luis and Marilyn ravaged the western Caribbean. Antigua and St. Martin/St. Maarten bore the brunt of Luis and St. Thomas of Marilyn, but Anguilla, the British Virgin Islands, Montserrat, Saba, and St. Barts were also hit by Luis, and St. Croix and St. John were buffeted by Marilyn; several resorts on these islands sustained serious damage. At this writing, some are still closed for repairs; most should be up and running by the holiday season, although some landscaping and other restoration work may still by under way. If you plan to vacation on any of the afftected islands, make sure that any facilities you want to use will be available when you visit.

## How to Use This Book

### Organization

Up front is the **Gold Guide.** Its first section, **Important Contacts A to Z,** gives addresses and telephone numbers of organizations and companies that offer destination-related services and detailed information and publications. **Smart Travel Tips A to Z,** the Gold Guide's second section, gives specific information on how to accomplish

what you need to in the Caribbean as well as tips on savvy traveling. Both sections are in alphabetical order by topic.

The chapters in this book are listed alphabetically by island; each island's section covers lodging, dining, beaches, outdoor activities and sports, shopping, nightlife and the arts, exploring, and ends with a section called A to Z, which tells you how to get there and get around and gives you important local addresses and telephone numbers.

### Icons and Symbols

★    Our special recommendations
✕    Restaurant
🏠    Lodging establishment
✕🏠    Lodging establishment whose restaurant warrants a detour
⚠    Campgrounds
🦆    Rubber duckie (good for kids)
☞    Sends you to another section of the guide for more info
✉    Address
☎    Telephone number
🕐    Opening and closing times
💰    Admission prices (those we give apply only to adults; substantially reduced fees are almost always available for children, students, and senior citizens)

### Hotel Facilities

We always list the facilities that are available—but we don't specify whether they cost extra: When pricing accommodations, always ask what's included.

### Meal Plans

Assume that hotels operate on the **European Plan** (EP, with no meals) unless we note that they use the **Full American Plan** (FAP, with all meals), the **Modified American Plan** (MAP, with breakfast and dinner daily), the **Continental Plan** (CP, with a Continental breakfast daily), or are **all-inclusive** (all meals and most activities). At the end of each review, we have listed the meal plans the hotel offers.

A Full American Plan may be ideal for travelers on a budget who don't want to worry about additional expenses, but travelers who enjoy a different dining experience each night will prefer to book rooms on the European Plan. Since some hotels insist on the Modified American Plan, particularly during the high season, you might want to find out whether you can exchange dinner for lunch or for meals at neighboring hotels.

The following abbreviations are used: **AE,** American Express; **D,** Discover; **DC,** Diners Club; **MC,** MasterCard; and **V,** Visa.

## Please Write to Us

You can use this book in the confidence that all prices and opening times are based on information supplied to us at press time; Fodor's cannot accept responsibility for any errors. Time inevitably brings changes, so always confirm information when it matters—especially if you're making a detour to visit a specific place. In addition, when making reservations be sure to mention if you have a disability or are traveling with children, if you prefer a private bath or a certain type of bed, or if you have specific dietary needs or any other concerns.

Were the restaurants we recommended as described? Did our hotel picks exceed your expectations? Did you find a museum we recommended a waste of time? If you have complaints, we'll look into them and revise our entries when the facts warrant it. If you've discovered a special place that we haven't included, we'll pass the information along to our correspondents and have them check it out. So send your feedback, positive *and* negative, to the Caribbean Editor at 201 East 50th Street, New York, New York 10022—and have a wonderful trip!

Karen Cure
*Editorial Director*

# The Caribbean

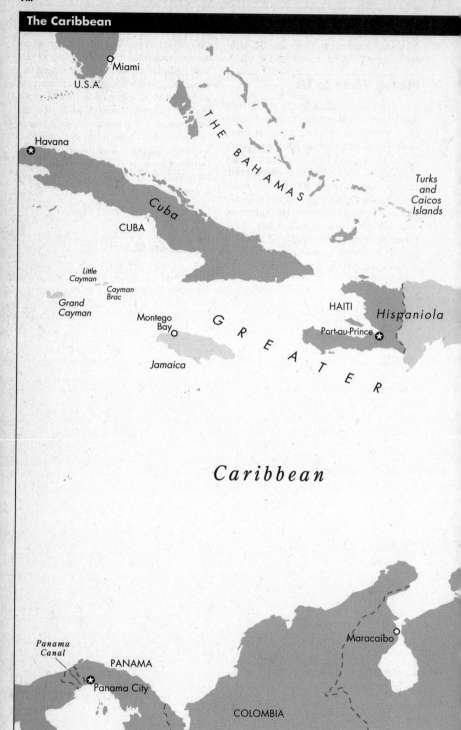

Miami

U.S.A.

THE BAHAMAS

Havana

Cuba

CUBA

Turks
and
Caicos
Islands

Little
Cayman

Cayman
Brac

Grand
Cayman

Montego
Bay

HAITI

Hispaniola

G R E A T E R

Port-au-Prince

Jamaica

*Caribbean*

Panama
Canal

PANAMA

Maracaibo

Panama City

COLOMBIA

0                    200 miles

0                    300 km

N

*ATLANTIC OCEAN*

ks
d
cos
nds

DOMINICAN
REPUBLIC

ola

Santo
Domingo

San Juan

Puerto
Rico

St. Thomas

St. John

St. Maarten/
St. Martin

St.
Croix

Virgin Gorda
Tortola

Anguilla

St. Barth lemy

Saba

St. Eustatius

St. Kitts
Nevis

Montserrat

Guadeloupe

*LEEWARD ISLANDS*

Barbuda

Antigua

Marie
Galante

*WINDWARD ISLANDS*

Dominica

Martinique

St. Lucia

St. Vincent

Barbados

The
Grenadines

Grenada

Tobago

Trinidad

*A N T I L L E S*

*Sea*

*LESSER ANTILLES*

Aruba

Bonaire

Cura ao

Caracas

VENEZUELA

x

Numbers below vertical bands relate each zone to Greenwich Mean Time (0 hrs.).
Local times frequently differ from these general indications,
as indicated by light-face numbers on map.

+11    +12 -    -11    -10    -9    -8    -7    -6    -5    -4    -3    -2

Mecca, **47**
Mexico City, **12**
Miami, **18**
Montréal, **15**
Moscow, **45**
Nairobi, **43**
New Orleans, **11**
New York City, **16**

Ottawa, **14**
Paris, **30**
Perth, **58**
Reykjavík, **25**
Rio de Janeiro, **23**
Rome, **39**
Saigon (Ho Chi Minh City), **51**

San Francisco, **5**
Santiago, **21**
Seoul, **59**
Shanghai, **55**
Singapore, **52**
Stockholm, **32**
Sydney, **61**
Tokyo, **60**

Toronto, **13**
Vancouver, **4**
Vienna, **35**
Warsaw, **36**
Washington, D.C., **17**
Yangon, **49**
Zürich, **31**

# IMPORTANT CONTACTS A TO Z

*An Alphabetical Listing of Publications, Organizations & Companies That Will Help You Before, During & After Your Trip*

## A

### AIR TRAVEL

For information on airports and major airlines serving the Caribbean from the United States, see individual island chapters.

**British Airways** (☎ 0181/897–4000; outside London, 0345/222–111), **British West Indian Airways** (☎ 0181/570–5552), and **Caledonian** (☎ 01293/567–100) are the only airlines with direct flights from London to the Caribbean.

### CARRIERS

For inexpensive, no-frills flights, contact **Carnival Air Lines** (☎ 800/824–7386), which serves the Caicos, Nassau, and Puerto Rico, and **Kiwi International** (☎ 800/538–5494), based in Newark and New York, serving San Juan.

### COMPLAINTS

To register complaints about charter and scheduled airlines, contact the U.S. Department of Transportation's **Aviation Consumer Protection Division** (✉ C-75, Washington, DC 20590, ☎ 202/366–2220). Complaints about lost baggage or ticketing problems and safety concerns may also be logged with the **Federal Aviation Administration (FAA) Consumer Hotline** (☎ 800/322–7873).

### CONSOLIDATORS

For the names of reputable air-ticket consolidators, contact the **United States Air Consolidators Association** (925 L St., Suite 220, Sacramento, CA 95814, tel. 916/441–4166, fax 916/441–3520). For discount air-ticketing agencies, *see* Discounts & Deals, *below.*

### PUBLICATIONS

For general information about charter carriers, ask for the Department of Transportation's free brochure **"Plane Talk: Public Charter Flights"** (✉ Aviation Consumer Protection Division, C-75, Washington, DC 20590, ☎ 202/366–2220). The Department of Transportation also publishes a 58-page booklet, **"Fly Rights,"** available from the Consumer Information Center (✉ Supt. of Documents, Dept. 136C, Pueblo, CO 81009; $1.75).

For other tips and hints, consult the Consumers Union's monthly **"Consumer Reports Travel Letter"** (✉ Box 53629, Boulder, CO 80322, ☎ 800/234–1970; $39 1st yr) and the newsletter **"Travel Smart"** (✉ 40 Beechdale Rd., Dobbs Ferry, NY 10522, ☎ 800/327–3633; $37 per yr).

Some worthwhile publications on the subject are **The Official Frequent Flyer Guidebook,** by Randy Petersen (✉ Airpress, 4715-C Town Center Dr., Colorado Springs, CO 80916, ☎ 719/597–8899 or 800/487–8893; $14.99 plus $3 shipping); **Airfare Secrets Exposed,** by Sharon Tyler and Matthew Wunder (✉ Studio 4 Productions, Box 280400, Northridge, CA 91328, ☎ 818/700–2522 or 800/408–7369; $16.95 plus $2.50 shipping); **202 Tips Even the Best Business Travelers May Not Know,** by Christopher McGinnis (✉ Irwin Professional Publishing, 1333 Burr Ridge Pkwy., Burr Ridge, IL 60521, ☎ 800/634–3966; $11 plus $3.25 shipping); and **Travel Rights,** by Charles Leocha (✉ World Leisure Corporation, 177 Paris St., Boston, MA 02128, ☎ 800/444–2524; $7.95 plus $3.95 shipping).

For information on how to avoid jet lag, read **Jet Lag, A Pocket Guide to Modern Treatment,** by Peter Casano M.D. (✉ MedEd Publications, Box 12415, Columbus, OH 43212, ☎ 614/488–9457; $5.95) and **How to Beat Jet Lag,** by Dan A. Oren (✉ Henry Holt, 115 W. 18th St., New York, NY 10011, ☎ 800/288–2131; $16.95 plus $4 shipping).

Travelers who experience motion sickness or

ear problems in flight should get the brochures **"Ears, Altitude, and Airplane Travel"** and **"What You Can Do for Dizziness & Motion Sickness"** from the American Academy of Otolaryngology (✉ 1 Prince St., Alexandria, VA 22314, ☎ 703/836–4444, FAX 703/683–5100, TTY 703/519–1585).

## B
### BETTER BUSINESS BUREAU

For local contacts in the hometown of a tour operator you may be considering, consult the **Council of Better Business Bureaus** (✉ 4200 Wilson Blvd., Suite 800, Arlington, VA 22203, ☎ 703/276–0100, FAX 703/525–8277).

## C
### CAR RENTAL

For information on car-rental agencies and costs in the Caribbean, *see* individual island chapters.

### RENTAL WHOLESALERS

Contact the **Kemwel Group** (☎ 914/835–5555 or 800/678–0678).

### CHILDREN & TRAVEL

### FLYING

Look into **"Flying with Baby"** (✉ Third Street Press, Box 261250, Littleton, CO 80163, ☎ 303/595–5959; $4.95 includes shipping), cowritten by a flight attendant. **"Kids and Teens in Flight,"** free from the U.S. Department of Transportation's Aviation Consumer Protection Division (✉ C-75, Washington, DC 20590, ☎ 202/366–2220), offers tips on children flying alone. Every two years the February issue of *Family Travel Times* (☞ Know-How, *below*) details children's services on three dozen airlines. **"Flying Alone, Handy Advice for Kids Traveling Solo"** is available free from the American Automobile Association (AAA) (✉ Send legal-size SASE: Flying Alone, Mail Stop 800, 1000 AAA Dr., Heathrow, FL 32746).

### KNOW-HOW

*Family Travel Times,* published quarterly by Travel with Your Children (✉ TWYCH, 40 5th Ave., New York, NY 10011, ☎ 212/477–5524; $40 per yr), covers destinations, types of vacations, and modes of travel.

The *Family Travel Guides* catalog (✉ Carousel Press, Box 6061, Albany, CA 94706, ☎ 510/527–5849; $1 postage) lists about 200 books and articles on traveling with children. Also check *Take Your Baby and Go! A Guide for Traveling with Babies, Toddlers and Young Children,* by Sheri Andrews, Judy Bordeaux, and Vivian Vasquez (✉ Bear Creek Publications, 2507 Minor Ave. E, Seattle, WA 98102, ☎ 206/322–7604 or 800/326–6566; $5.95 plus $1.50 shipping). The Globe Pequot Press (✉ Box 833, 6 Business Park Rd., Old Saybrook, CT 06475, ☎ 203/395–0440) publishes *100 Best Family Resorts in North America,* by Jane Wilford with Janet Tice ($14.95 plus $3 shipping), and eastern and western editions of *50 Great Family Vacations in North America,* by Candyce Stapen ($18.95 plus $3 shipping).

### LODGING

Hotels and resorts that offer special programs for children include:

In Aruba, the **Sonesta Resorts at Seaport Village** (☎ 800/766–3782); in Puerto Rico, the **Hyatt Regency Cerromar Beach** and the **Hyatt Dorado Beach** (☎ 800/233–1234), and the **El San Juan Hotel and Casino** (☎ 800/468–2818); in Jamaica, **Boscobel Beach** (☎ 800/859–7873); and in St. Thomas in the U.S. Virgin Islands, the **Stouffer Grand Beach Resort** (☎ 800/468–3571); in Nevis, **Four Seasons** (☎ 800/332–3442).

### TOUR OPERATORS

Contact **Rascals in Paradise** (✉ 650 5th St., Suite 505, San Francisco, CA 94107, ☎ 415/978–9800 or 800/872–7225).

If you're outdoorsy, look into family-oriented programs run by the **American Museum of Natural History** (✉ 79th St. and Central Park W, New York, NY 10024, ☎ 212/769–5700 or 800/462–8687).

### CRUISING

To find out which ships are sailing where and when they depart, contact the **Caribbean Tourism Organization**

(✉ 20 E. 46th St., 4th floor, New York, NY 10017, ☎ 212/682–0435). The **Cruise Lines International Association** (CLIA) publishes a useful pamphlet entitled "Cruising Answers to Your Questions"; to order a copy send a self-addressed business-size envelope with 52¢ postage to CLIA (✉ 500 5th Ave., Suite 1407, New York, NY 10110).

Cruise lines that operate in the Caribbean include **American Canadian Caribbean Line** (✉ Box 368, Warren, RI 02885, ☎ 401/247–0955 or 800/556–7450), **Carnival Cruise Lines** (✉ Carnival Pl., 3655 N.W. 87th Ave., Miami, FL 33178, ☎ 305/599–2600), **Celebrity Cruises** (✉ 5200 Blue Lagoon Dr., Miami, FL 33126, ☎ 800/437–3111), **Clipper Cruise Line** (✉ 7711 Bonhomme Ave., St. Louis, MO 63105, ☎ 800/325–0010), **Club Med** (✉ 40 W. 57th St., New York, NY 10019, ☎ 800/258–2633), **Commodore Cruise Line** (✉ 800 Douglas Rd., Coral Gables, FL 33134, ☎ 305/529–3000), **Costa Cruise Lines** (✉ World Trade Center, 80 S.W. 8th St., Miami, FL 33130, ☎ 800/462–6782), **Crystal Cruises** (✉ 2121 Ave. of the Stars, Los Angeles, CA 90067, ☎ 800/446–6620), **Cunard Line** (✉ 555 5th Ave., New York, NY 10017, ☎ 800/221–4770), **Dolphin/Majesty Cruise Lines** (✉ 901 South American Way, Miami, FL 33132, ☎ 800/532–7788), **Holland America Line** (✉ 300 Elliott Ave. W, Seattle, WA 98119, ☎ 800/426–0327), **Norwegian Cruise Line** (✉ 95 Merrick Way, Coral Gables, FL 33134, ☎ 800/327–7030), **Premier Cruise Line** (✉ Box 517, Cape Canaveral, FL 32920, ☎ 800/473–3262), **Princess Cruises** (✉ 10100 Santa Monica Blvd., Los Angeles, CA 90067, ☎ 310/553–1770), **Radisson Seven Seas Cruises** (✉ 600 Corporate Dr., Suite 410, Fort Lauderdale, FL 33334, ☎ 800/333–3333), **Renaissance Cruises** (✉ 1800 Eller Dr., Suite 300, Box 350307, Fort Lauderdale, FL 33335, ☎ 800/525–2450), **Royal Caribbean Cruise Line** (✉ 1050 Caribbean Way, Miami, FL 33132, ☎ 800/327–6700), **Royal Olympic Cruises** (✉ 1 Rockefeller Plaza, Suite 315, New York, NY 10020, ☎ 800/872–6400), **Seabourn Cruise Line** (✉ 55 Francisco St., San Francisco, CA 94133, ☎ 800/351–9595), **Seawind Cruise Line** (✉ 1750 Coral Way, Miami, FL 33145, ☎ 800/258–8006), **Silversea Cruises** (✉ 110 E. Broward Blvd., Fort Lauderdale, FL 33301, ☎ 305/522–4477 or 800/722–6655), **Special Expeditions** (✉ 720 5th Ave., New York, NY 10019, ☎ 800/762–0003), **Star Clippers** (✉ 4101 Salzedo Ave., Coral Gables, FL 33146, ☎ 800/442–0551), and **Windstar Cruises** (✉ 300 Elliott Ave. W, Seattle, WA 98119, ☎ 800/258–7245).

## CUSTOMS

### IN THE U.S.

The **U.S. Customs Service** (✉ Box 7407, Washington, DC 20044, ☎ 202/927–6724) can answer questions on duty-free limits and publishes a helpful brochure, "Know Before You Go." For information on registering foreign-made articles, call 202/927–0540 or write U.S. Customs Service, Resource Management, 1301 Constitution Ave. NW, Washington, DC 20229.

COMPLAINTS➤ Note the inspector's badge number and write to the commissioner's office (✉ 1301 Constitution Ave. NW, Washington, DC 20229).

### CANADIANS

Contact **Revenue Canada** (✉ 2265 St. Laurent Blvd. S, Ottawa, Ontario K1G 4K3, ☎ 613/993–0534) for a copy of the free brochure **"I Declare/Je Déclare"** and for details on duty-free limits. For recorded information (within Canada only), call 800/461–9999.

### U.K. CITIZENS

**HM Customs and Excise** (✉ Dorset House, Stamford St., London SE1 9NG, ☎ 0171/

202–4227) can answer questions about U.K. customs regulations and publishes a free pamphlet, **"A Guide for Travellers,"** detailing standard procedures and import rules.

## D
### DISABILITIES & ACCESSIBILITY

### COMPLAINTS

To register complaints under the provisions of the Americans with Disabilities Act, contact the U.S. Department of Justice's **Disability Rights Section** (✉ Box 66738, Washington, DC 20035, ☎ 202/514–0301 or 800/514–0301, FAX 202/307–1198, TTY 202/514–0383 or 800/514–0383). For airline-related problems, contact the U.S. Department of Transportation's **Aviation Consumer Protection Division** (☞ Air Travel, *above*). For complaints about surface transportation, contact the Department of Transportation's **Civil Rights Office** (✉ 400 7th St. SW, Room 10215, Washington, DC 20590, ☎ 202/366–4648).

### LODGING

**Divi Hotels** (☎ 800/367–3484), which has six properties in the Caribbean, runs one of the best dive programs for people with disabilities at its resort in **Bonaire.**

### ORGANIZATIONS

TRAVELERS WITH HEAR-ING IMPAIRMENTS➤ The **American Academy of Otolaryngology** (✉ 1 Prince St., Alexandria, VA 22314, ☎ 703/836–4444, FAX 703/683–5100, TTY 703/519–1585) publishes a brochure, "Travel Tips for Hearing Impaired People."

TRAVELERS WITH MOBIL-ITY PROBLEMS➤ Contact the **Information Center for Individuals with Disabilities** (✉ Box 256, Boston, MA 02117, ☎ 617/450–9888; in MA, 800/462–5015; TTY 617/424–6855); **Mobility International USA** (✉ Box 10767, Eugene, OR 97440, ☎ and TTY 541/343–1284, FAX 541/343–6812), the U.S. branch of a Belgium-based organization (☞ *below*) with affiliates in 30 countries; **Moss Rehab Hospital Travel Information Service** (☎ 215/456–9600, TTY 215/456–9602), a telephone information resource for travelers with physical disabilities; the **Society for the Advancement of Travel for the Handicapped** (✉ 347 5th Ave., Suite 610, New York, NY 10016, ☎ 212/447–7284, FAX 212/725–8253; membership $45); and **Travelin' Talk** (✉ Box 3534, Clarksville, TN 37043, ☎ 615/552–6670, FAX 615/552–1182) which provides local contacts worldwide for travelers with disabilities.

TRAVELERS WITH VISION IMPAIRMENTS➤ Contact the **American Council of the Blind** (✉ 1155 15th St. NW, Suite 720, Washington, DC 20005, ☎ 202/467–5081, FAX 202/467–5085) for a list of travelers' resources or the **American Foundation for the Blind** (✉ 11 Penn Plaza, Suite 300, New York, NY 10001, ☎ 212/502–7600 or 800/232–5463, TTY 212/502–7662), which provides general advice and publishes "Access to Art" ($19.95), a directory of museums that accommodate travelers with vision impairments.

### IN THE U.K.

Contact the **Royal Association for Disability and Rehabilitation** (✉ RADAR, 12 City Forum, 250 City Rd., London EC1V 8AF, ☎ 0171/250–3222) or **Mobility International** (✉ rue de Manchester 25, B-1080 Brussels, Belgium, ☎ 00–322–410–6297, FAX 00–322–410–6874), an international travel-information clearing-house for people with disabilities.

### PUBLICATIONS

Several publications for travelers with disabilities are available from the **Consumer Information Center** (✉ Box 100, Pueblo, CO 81009, ☎ 719/948–3334). Call or write for its free catalog of current titles. The Society for the Advancement of Travel for the Handicapped (☞ Organizations, *above*) publishes the quarterly magazine **"Access to Travel"** ($13 for 1-yr subscription).

The 500-page **Travelin' Talk Directory** (✉ Box 3534, Clarksville, TN 37043, ☎ 615/552–6670, FAX 615/552–1182; $35) lists people and organizations who help travelers with disabilities. For travel agents worldwide, consult the **Directory of Travel Agencies for the Disabled** (✉ Twin Peaks Press, Box 129, Vancouver, WA 98666, ☎ 360/694–2462 or 800/637–2256, FAX 360/

THE GOLD GUIDE / IMPORTANT CONTACTS

696–3210; $19.95 plus $3 shipping).

## TRAVEL AGENCIES & TOUR OPERATORS

The Americans with Disabilities Act requires that all travel firms serve the needs of all travelers. That said, you should note that some agencies and operators specialize in making travel arrangements for individuals and groups with disabilities, among them **Access Adventures** (✉ 206 Chestnut Ridge Rd., Rochester, NY 14624, ☎ 716/889–9096), run by a former physical-rehab counselor; **CareVacations** (✉ 5019 49th Ave., Suite 102, Leduc, Alberta T9E 6T5, ☎ 403/986–8332; in Canada, 800/648–1116), which has group tours and is especially helpful for cruises; and **Tomorrow's Level of Care** (✉ Box 470299, Brooklyn, NY 11247, ☎ 718/756–0794 or 800/932–2012), which offers nursing services and medical equipment.

TRAVELERS WITH MOBILITY PROBLEMS➤ Contact **Accessible Journeys** (✉ 35 W. Sellers Ave., Ridley Park, PA 19078, ☎ 610/521–0339 or 800/846–4537, FAX 610/521–6959), an escorted-tour operator exclusively for travelers with mobility impairments; **Hinsdale Travel Service** (✉ 201 E. Ogden Ave., Suite 100, Hinsdale, IL 60521, ☎ 708/325–1335), a travel agency that benefits from the advice of wheelchair traveler Janice Perkins; and **Wheelchair Journeys** (✉ 16979 Red-

mond Way, Redmond, WA 98052, ☎ 206/885–2210 or 800/313–4751), which can handle arrangements worldwide.

TRAVELERS WITH DEVELOPMENTAL DISABILITIES➤ Contact the nonprofit **New Directions** (✉ 5276 Hollister Ave., Suite 207, Santa Barbara, CA 93111, ☎ 805/967–2841).

## TRAVEL GEAR

The **Magellan's** catalog (☎ 800/962–4943, FAX 805/568–5406), includes a section devoted to products designed for travelers with disabilities.

## DISCOUNTS & DEALS

### AIRFARES

For the lowest airfares to the Caribbean, call 800/FLY–4–LESS.

### CLUBS

Contact **Entertainment Travel Editions** (✉ Box 1068, Trumbull, CT 06611, ☎ 800/445–4137; $28–$53, depending on destination), **Great American Traveler** (✉ Box 27965, Salt Lake City, UT 84127, ☎ 800/548–2812; $49.95 per yr), **Moment's Notice Discount Travel Club** (✉ 7301 New Utrecht Ave., Brooklyn, NY 11204, ☎ 718/234–6295; $25 per yr, single or family), **Privilege Card** (✉ 3391 Peachtree Rd. NE, Suite 110, Atlanta, GA 30326, ☎ 404/262–0222 or 800/236–9732; $74.95 per yr), **Travelers Advantage** (✉ CUC Travel Service, 49 Music Sq. W, Nashville, TN 37203, ☎ 800/548–1116 or 800/648–4037;

$49 per yr, single or family), or **Worldwide Discount Travel Club** (✉ 1674 Meridian Ave., Miami Beach, FL 33139, ☎ 305/534–2082; $50 per yr for family, $40 single).

### STUDENTS

Members of Hostelling International–American Youth Hostels (☞ Students, *below*) are eligible for discounts on car rentals, admissions to attractions, and other selected travel expenses.

### PUBLICATIONS

Consult *The Frugal Globetrotter,* by Bruce Northam (✉ Fulcrum Publishing, 350 Indiana St., Suite 350, Golden, CO 80401, ☎ 800/992–2908; $16.95 plus $4 shipping). For publications that tell how to find the lowest prices on plane tickets, *see* Air Travel, *above*.

Also see Fodor's **Affordable Caribbean** (available in bookstores, or ☎ 800/533–6478; $16.50).

## DIVING

The Caribbean offers some of the best scuba diving in the world. For a list of training facilities where you can earn your diving certification card, write to **PADI** (✉ Professional Association of Diving Instructors, 1251 E. Dyer Rd., #100, Santa Ana, CA 92705). For more information, *see* Diving *in* Chapter 1.

## F

### FURTHER READING

*Caribbean Style* (Crown Publishers) is a coffee-table book with magnificent photographs of the interiors and exteriors of homes and buildings in the Caribbean. Short stories—some dark, some full of laughs—about life in the southern Caribbean made *Easy in the Islands,* by Bob Schacochis, a National Book Award winner. Schacochis has an ear for local patois and an eye for the absurd. To familiarize yourself with the sights, smells, and sounds of the West Indies, pick up Jamaica Kincaid's *Annie John,* a richly textured coming-of-age novel about a girl growing up on Antigua. The short stories in *At the Bottom of the River,* also by Kincaid, depict island mysteries and manners. *Omeros* is Nobel Prize–winning Trinidadian poet Derek Walcott's imaginative Caribbean retelling of the *Odyssey.* Anthony C. Winkler's novels, *The Great Yacht Race, The Lunatic,* and *The Painted Canoe,* provide scathingly witty glimpses into Jamaica's class structure. Another notable chronicle of Caribbean life and customs is the provocative, imaginative novel *Wide Sargasso Sea,* by Jean Rhys. James Michener depicted the islands' diversity in his novel *Caribbean.* To probe island cultures more deeply, read V. S. Naipaul, particularly his *Guerrillas, The Loss of El Dorado* and *The Enigma of Arrival;* Eric William's *From Columbus to Castro;* and Michael Paiewonsky's *Conquest of Eden.*

## G
### GAY & LESBIAN TRAVEL

### ORGANIZATIONS

The **International Gay Travel Association** (✉ Box 4974, Key West, FL 33041, ☎ 800/448–8550, FAX 305/296–6633), a consortium of more than 1,000 travel companies, can supply names of gay-friendly travel agents, tour operators, and accommodations.

### PUBLICATIONS

The premier international travel magazine for gays and lesbians is *Our World* (✉ 1104 N. Nova Rd., Suite 251, Daytona Beach, FL 32117, ☎ 904/441–5367, FAX 904/441–5604; $35 for 10 issues). The 16-page monthly **"Out & About"** (☎ 212/645–6922 or 800/929–2268, FAX 800/929–2215; $49 for 10 issues and quarterly calendar) covers gay-friendly resorts, hotels, cruise lines, and airlines.

### TOUR OPERATORS

Cruises and resort vacations for gays are handled by **R.S.V.P. Travel Productions** (✉ 2800 University Ave. SE, Minneapolis, MN 55414, ☎ 612/379–4697 or 800/328–7787). **Olivia** (✉ 4400 Market St., Oakland, CA 94608, ☎ 510/655–0364 or 800/631–6277) specializes in such bookings for lesbians. For mixed gay and lesbian travel, contact **Atlantis Events** (✉ 9060 Santa Monica Blvd., Suite 310, West Hollywood, CA 90069, ☎ 310/281–5450 or 800/628–5268) and

**Toto Tours** (✉ 1326 W. Albion Ave., Suite 3W, Chicago, IL 60626, ☎ 312/274–8686 or 800/565–1241, FAX 312/274–8695), which offers group tours to worldwide destinations.

### TRAVEL AGENCIES

The largest agencies serving gay travelers are **Advance Travel** (✉ 10700 Northwest Fwy., Suite 160, Houston, TX 77092, ☎ 713/682–2002 or 800/292–0500), **Islanders/Kennedy Travel** (✉ 183 W. 10th St., New York, NY 10014, ☎ 212/242–3222 or 800/988–1181), **Now Voyager** (✉ 4406 18th St., San Francisco, CA 94114, ☎ 415/626–1169 or 800/255–6951), and **Yellowbrick Road** (✉ 1500 W. Balmoral Ave., Chicago, IL 60640, ☎ 312/561–1800 or 800/642–2488). **Skylink Women's Travel** (✉ 2460 W. 3rd St., Suite 215, Santa Rosa, CA 95401, ☎ 707/570–0105 or 800/225–5759) serves lesbian travelers.

## H
### HEALTH

### FINDING A DOCTOR

For its members, the **International Association for Medical Assistance to Travellers** (IAMAT, membership free; ✉ 417 Center St., Lewiston, NY 14092, ☎ 716/754–4883; ✉ 40 Regal Rd., Guelph, Ontario N1K 1B5, ☎ 519/836–0102; ✉ 1287 St. Clair Ave. W, Toronto, Ontario M6E 1B8, ☎ 416/652–0137; ✉ 57 Voirets, 1212 Grand-Lancy, Geneva,

Switzerland, no phone) publishes a worldwide directory of English-speaking physicians meeting IAMAT standards.

## MEDICAL ASSISTANCE COMPANIES

The following companies are concerned primarily with emergency medical assistance, although they may provide some insurance as part of their coverage. For a list of full-service travel insurance companies, see Insurance, below.

Contact **International SOS Assistance** (⊠ Box 11568, Philadelphia, PA 19116, ☎ 215/244–1500 or 800/523–8930; ⊠ Box 466, Pl. Bonaventure, Montréal, Québec H5A 1C1, ☎ 514/874–7674 or 800/363–0263; ⊠ 7 Old Lodge Pl., St. Margarets, Twickenham TW1 1RQ, England, ☎ 0181/744–0033), **Medex Assistance Corporation** (⊠ Box 5375, Timonium, MD 21094-5375, ☎ 410/453–6300 or 800/537–2029), **Traveler's Emergency Network** (⊠ 3100 Tower Blvd., Suite 3100A, Durham, NC 27702, ☎ 919/490–6065 or 800/275–4836, FAX 919/493–8262), **TravMed** (⊠ Box 5375, Timonium, MD 21094, ☎ 410/453–6380 or 800/732–5309), or **Worldwide Assistance Services** (⊠ 1133 15th St. NW, Suite 400, Washington, DC 20005, ☎ 202/331–1609 or 800/821–2828, FAX 202/828–5896).

# I

## INSURANCE

### IN THE U.S.

Travel insurance covering baggage, health, and trip cancellation or interruptions is available from **Access America** (⊠ 6600 W. Broad St., Richmond, VA 23230, ☎ 804/285–3300 or 800/334–7525), **Carefree Travel Insurance** (⊠ Box 9366, 100 Garden City Plaza, Garden City, NY 11530, ☎ 516/294–0220 or 800/323–3149), **Near Travel Services** (⊠ Box 1339, Calumet City, IL 60409, ☎ 708/868–6700 or 800/654–6700), **Tele-Trip** (⊠ Mutual of Omaha Plaza, Box 31716, Omaha, NE 68131, ☎ 800/228–9792), **Travel Guard International** (⊠ 1145 Clark St., Stevens Point, WI 54481, ☎ 715/345–0505 or 800/826–1300), **Travel Insured International** (⊠ Box 280568, East Hartford, CT 06128, ☎ 203/528–7663 or 800/243–3174), and **Wallach & Company** (⊠ 107 W. Federal St., Box 480, Middleburg, VA 22117, ☎ 540/687–3166 or 800/237–6615).

### IN CANADA

Contact **Mutual of Omaha** (⊠ Travel Division, 500 University Ave., Toronto, Ontario M5G 1V8, ☎ 416/598-4083; in Canada, 800/465–0267).

### IN THE U.K.

The **Association of British Insurers** (⊠ 51 Gresham St., London EC2V 7HQ, ☎ 0171/

600–3333) gives advice by phone and publishes the free pamphlet **"Holiday Insurance and Motoring Abroad,"** which sets out typical policy provisions and costs.

# L

## LODGING

### APARTMENT & VILLA RENTAL

Among the companies to contact are **At Home Abroad** (⊠ 405 E. 56th St., Suite 6H, New York, NY 10022, ☎ 212/421–9165, FAX 212/752–1591), **Europa-Let** (⊠ 92 N. Main St., Ashland, OR 97520, ☎ 541/482–5806 or 800/462–4486, FAX 541/482–0660), **Property Rentals International** (⊠ 1008 Mansfield Crossing Rd., Richmond, VA 23236, ☎ 804/378–6054 or 800/220–3332, FAX 804/379–2073), **Rental Directories International** (⊠ 2044 Rittenhouse Sq., Philadelphia, PA 19103, ☎ 215/985–4001, FAX 215/985–0323), **Rent-a-Home International** (⊠ 7200 34th Ave. NW, Seattle, WA 98117, ☎ 206/789–9377 or 800/488–7368, FAX 206/789–9379), **Vacation Home Rentals Worldwide** (⊠ 235 Kensington Ave., Norwood, NJ 07648, ☎ 201/767–9393 or 800/633–3284, FAX 201/767–5510), **Unusual Villas & Island Rentals** (⊠ 101 Tempsford La., Penthouse 9, Richmond, VA 23226, ☎ 804/288–2823 or 800/768–0280, FAX 804/288–2823), **Villas**

**and Apartments Abroad** (✉ 420 Madison Ave., Suite 1003, New York, NY 10017, ☎ 212/759–1025 or 800/433–3020, FAX 212/755–8316), and **Villas International** (✉ 605 Market St., Suite 510, San Francisco, CA 94105, ☎ 415/281–0910 or 800/221–2260, FAX 415/281–0919). Members of the travel club **Hideaways International** (✉ 767 Islington St., Portsmouth, NH 03801, ☎ 603/430–4433 or 800/843–4433, FAX 603/430–4444; $99 per yr) receive two annual guides plus quarterly newsletters and arrange rentals among themselves.

## HOME EXCHANGE

Some of the principal clearinghouses are **HomeLink International/ Vacation Exchange Club** (✉ Box 650, Key West, FL 33041, ☎ 305/294–1448 or 800/638–3841, FAX 305/294–1148; $78 per yr), which sends members five annual directories, with a listing in one, plus updates; and **Intervac International** (✉ Box 590504, San Francisco, CA 94159, ☎ 415/435–3497, FAX 415/435–7440; $65 per yr), which publishes four annual directories.

## M

### MONEY

### ATMS

For specific foreign **Cirrus** locations, call 800/424–7787; for foreign **Plus** locations, consult the Plus directory at your local bank.

## CURRENCY EXCHANGE

If your bank doesn't exchange currency, contact **Thomas Cook Currency Services** (☎ 800/287–7362 for locations). **Ruesch International** (☎ 800/424–2923 for locations) can also provide you with foreign banknotes before you leave home and publishes a number of useful brochures, including a "Foreign Currency Guide" and "Foreign Exchange Tips."

## WIRING FUNDS

Funds can be wired via **MoneyGram$^{SM}$** (for locations and information in the U.S. and Canada, ☎ 800/926–9400) or **Western Union** (for agent locations or to send money using MasterCard or Visa, ☎ 800/325–6000; in Canada, 800/321–2923; in the U.K., 0800/833833; or visit the Western Union office at the nearest major post office).

## P

### PACKING

For strategies on packing light, get a copy of *The Packing Book,* by Judith Gilford (✉ Ten Speed Press, Box 7123, Berkeley, CA 94707, ☎ 510/559–1600 or 800/841–2665, FAX 510/524–4588; $7.95 plus $3.50 shipping).

### PASSPORTS & VISAS

### IN THE U.S.

For fees, documentation requirements, and other information, call the State Department's **Office of Passport Ser-** vices information line (☎ 202/647–0518).

## CANADIANS

For fees, documentation requirements, and other information, call the Ministry of Foreign Affairs and International Trade's **Passport Office** (☎ 819/994–3500 or 800/567–6868).

## U.K. CITIZENS

For fees, documentation requirements, and to request an emergency passport, call the **London Passport Office** (☎ 0990/210410).

### PHOTO HELP

The **Kodak Information Center** (☎ 800/242–2424) answers consumer questions about film and photography. The *Kodak Guide to Shooting Great Travel Pictures* (available in bookstores; or contact Fodor's Travel Publications, ☎ 800/533–6478; $16.50 plus $4 shipping) explains how to take expert travel photographs.

## S

### SAFETY

"Trouble-Free Travel," from the AAA, is a booklet of tips for protecting yourself and your belongings when away from home. Send a stamped, self-addressed, legal-size envelope to Trouble-Free Travel (✉ Mail Stop 75, 1000 AAA Dr., Heathrow, FL 32746).

### SENIOR CITIZENS

### EDUCATIONAL TRAVEL

The nonprofit **Elderhostel** (✉ 75 Federal St., 3rd floor, Boston, MA 02110, ☎ 617/426–

THE GOLD GUIDE / IMPORTANT CONTACTS

THE GOLD GUIDE / IMPORTANT CONTACTS

7788), for people 55 and older, has offered inexpensive study programs since 1975. Courses cover everything from marine science to Greek mythology and cowboy poetry. Costs for two- to three-week international trips—including room, board, and transportation from the United States—range from $1,800 to $4,500.

## ORGANIZATIONS

Contact the **American Association of Retired Persons** (✉ AARP, 601 E St. NW, Washington, DC 20049, ☎ 202/434–2277; annual dues $8 per person or couple). Its Purchase Privilege Program secures discounts for members on lodging, car rentals, and sightseeing.

Additional sources for discounts on lodgings, car rentals, and other travel expenses, as well as helpful magazines and newsletters, are the **National Council of Senior Citizens** (✉ 1331 F St. NW, Washington, DC 20004, ☎ 202/347–8800; annual membership $12) and Sears's **Mature Outlook** (✉ Box 10448, Des Moines, IA 50306, ☎ 800/336–6330; annual membership $14.95).

## PUBLICATIONS

**The 50+ Traveler's Guidebook: Where to Go, Where to Stay, What to Do,** by Anita Williams and Merrimac Dillon (✉ St. Martin's Press, 175 5th Ave., New York, NY 10010, ☎ 212/674–5151 or 800/288–2131; $13.95 plus $4 shipping), offers many useful tips.

**"The Mature Traveler"** (✉ Box 50400, Reno, NV 89513, ☎ 702/786–7419; $29.95), a monthly newsletter, covers all sorts of travel deals.

## STUDENTS

### HOSTELING

In the United States, contact **Hosteling International–American Youth Hostels** (✉ 733 15th St. NW, Suite 840, Washington, DC 20005, ☎ 202/783–6161, FAX 202/783–6171); in Canada, **Hostelling International–Canada** (✉ 205 Catherine St., Suite 400, Ottawa, Ontario K2P 1C3, ☎ 613/237–7884); and in the United Kingdom, the **Youth Hostel Association of England and Wales** (✉ Trevelyan House, 8 St. Stephen's Hill, St. Albans, Hertfordshire AL1 2DY, ☎ 01727/855215 or 01727/845047). Membership (in the U.S., $25; in Canada, C$26.75; in the U.K., £9.30) gives you access to 5,000 hostels in 77 countries that charge $5–$40 per person per night.

### I.D. CARDS

To be eligible for discounts on transportation and admissions, get either the **International Student Identity Card,** if you're a bona fide student, or the **GO 25: International Youth Travel Card,** if you're not a student but under age 26. Each includes basic travel-accident and illness coverage, plus a toll-free travel hot line. In the United States, either card costs $18; apply

through the Council on International Educational Exchange (☞ Organizations, *below*). In Canada, cards are available for $15 each ($16 by mail) from Travel Cuts (☞ Organizations, *below*), and in the United Kingdom for £5 each at student unions and student travel companies.

### ORGANIZATIONS

A major contact is the **Council on International Educational Exchange** (✉ Mail orders only: CIEE, 205 E. 42nd St., 16th floor, New York, NY 10017, ☎ 212/822–2600). The **Educational Travel Centre** (✉ 438 N. Frances St., Madison, WI 53703, ☎ 608/256–5551 or 800/747–5551, FAX 608/256–2042) offers rail passes and low-cost airline tickets, mostly for flights that depart from Chicago.

In Canada, also contact **Travel Cuts** (✉ 187 College St., Toronto, Ontario M5T 1P7, ☎ 416/979–2406 or 800/667–2887).

# T

## TELEPHONES

For local access numbers abroad, contact **AT&T** USADirect (☎ 800/874–4000), **MCI** Call USA (☎ 800/444–4444), or **Sprint** Express (☎ 800/793–1153).

## TOUR OPERATORS

Among the companies that sell tours and packages to the Caribbean, the following are nationally known, have a proven reputation, and offer plenty of options.

## PACKAGES

For independent vacation packages throughout the Caribbean, contact **Adventure Vacations** (✉ 10612 Beaver Dam Rd., Hunt Valley, MD 21030-2205, ☎ 410/785–3500 or 800/638–9040, FAX 410/584–2771), **American Airlines Fly AAway Vacations** (☎ 800/321–2121), **Certified Vacations** (✉ Box 1525, Fort Lauderdale, FL 33302, ☎ 954/522–1440 or 800/233–7260), **Delta Dream Vacations** (☎ 800/872–7786), **Globetrotters** (✉ 139 Main St., Cambridge, MA 02142, ☎ 617/621–9911 or 800/333–1234), and **USAir Vacations** (☎ 800/455–0123). **Funjet Vacations,** based in Milwaukee, Wisconsin, and **Gogo Tours,** based in Ramsey, New Jersey, sell packages only through travel agents. **Club Med** (✉ 40 W. 57th St., New York, NY 10019, ☎ 800/258–2633) sells cruises and packages that include charter air at its family, couples, and singles resorts throughout the Caribbean.

For packages in Antigua, Barbados, St. Lucia, Grenada, Trinidad, and Tobago, contact **BWIA Vacations** (✉ 139 Main St., Cambridge, MA 02142, ☎ 617/621–0099 or 800/333–1234). For packages in Jamaica, Antigua, or the U.S. Virgin Islands, try **Continental Vacations** (☎ 800/634–5555). For packages in Puerto Rico, call **United Vacations** (☎ 800/328–6877). For a greater selection of properties in the Cayman Islands, try **Cayman Airtours** (☎ 800/247–2966).

Regional operators specialize in putting together packages for travelers from their local area. Arrangements may include charter or scheduled air. Contact **Apple Vacations** (✉ 25 N.W. Point Blvd., Elk Grove Village, IL 60007, ☎ 708/640–1150 or 800/365–2775), **Friendly Holidays** (✉ 1983 Marcus Ave., Lake Success, NY 11042, ☎ 800/344–5687), **GWV International** (✉ 300 1st Ave., Needham, MA 02194-2721, ☎ 617/449–5450 or 800/225–5498), **Trans National Travel** (✉ 2 Charlesgate W, Boston, MA 02215, ☎ 617/262–0123 or 800/262–0123, FAX 617/638–3310), and **Travel Impressions** (✉ 465 Smith St., Farmingdale, NY 11735, ☎ 516/845–8000 or 800/284–0044, FAX 516/845–8095).

FROM THE U.K.➤ **Caribbean Connection** (✉ Concorde House, Forest St., Chester CH1 1QR, ☎ 01244/341–131), which publishes a 100-page catalog devoted to Caribbean holidays; **Caribtours** (✉ 161 Fulham Rd., London SW3 6SN, ☎ 0171/581–3517); **Kuoni Travel** (✉ Kuoni House, Dorking, Surrey RH5 4AZ, ☎ 01306/742–222); and **Hayes and Jarvis** (✉ Hayes House, 152 King St., London W6 0QU, ☎ 0181/748–5050).

## THEME TRIPS

ADVENTURE➤ **American Wilderness Experience** (✉ Box 1486, Boulder, CO 80306, ☎ 303/444–2622 or 800/444–3833, FAX 303/444–3999) and **Ocean Voyages** (✉ 1709 Bridgeway, Sausalito, CA 94965, ☎ 415/332–4681, FAX 415/332–7460) offer adventure cruises on motor yachts and catamarans for scuba divers, snorkelers, and kayakers.

GOLF➤ Packages including accommodations, confirmed tee times, and golfing fees and lessons are offered by **Stine's Golftrips** (✉ Box 2314, Winter Haven, FL 33883-2314, ☎ 813/324–1300 or 800/428–1940, FAX 941/325–0384).

HEALTH➤ **Spa-Finders** (✉ 91 5th Ave., #301, New York, NY 10003-3039, ☎ 212/924–6800 or 800/255–7727) represents spas on many Caribbean islands.

HORSEBACK RIDING➤ A one-week package in Jamaica is available from **FITS Equestrian** (✉ 685 Lateen Rd., Solvang, CA 93463, ☎ 805/688–9494 or 800/666–3487, FAX 805/688–2943).

LEARNING➤ **Earthwatch** (✉ Box 403, 680 Mount Auburn St., Watertown, MA 02272, ☎ 617/926–8200 or 800/776–0188, FAX 617/926–8532) recruits volunteers to serve in its EarthCorps as short-term assistants to scientists on research expeditions in an array of scientific fields. Natural history cruises are available from the **National Audobon Society** (✉ 700 Broadway, New York, NY

10003, ☎ 212/979–3066, FAX 212/353–0190). **Natural Habitat Adventures** (✉ 2945 Center Green Ct., Boulder, CO 80301, ☎ 303/449–3711 or 800/543–8917, FAX 303/449–3712) operates tours focused on dolphins and whales. Also contact **Oceanic Society Expeditions** (✉ Fort Mason Center, Bldg. E, San Francisco, CA 94123-1394, ☎ 415/441–1106 or 800/326–7491, FAX 415/474–3395) and **Smithsonian Study Tours and Seminars** (✉ 1100 Jefferson Dr. SW, Room 3045, MRC 702, Washington, DC 20560, ☎ 202/357–4700, FAX 202/633–9250).

SAILING➤ Contact **Annapolis Sailing School** (✉ Box 3334, 601 6th St., Annapolis, MD 21403, ☎ 410/267–7205 or 800/638–9192) for sailing instruction in St. Croix. Also try **Offshore Sailing School** (✉ 16731-110 McGregor Blvd., Fort Meyers, FL 33908, ☎ 813/454–1700 or 800/221–4326, FAX 813/454–1191).

SCUBA DIVING➤ Leading dive packagers to the Caribbean include **Go Diving** (✉ 5610 Rowland Rd. #100, Minnetonka, MN 55343, ☎ 612/931–9101 or 800/328–5285, FAX 612/931–0209), **Rothschild Dive Safaris** (✉ 900 West End Ave., #1B, New York, NY 10025-3525, ☎ 212/662–4858 or 800/359–0747, FAX 212/749–6172), and **Tropical Adventures** (✉ 111 2nd Ave. N, Seattle, WA 98109, ☎ 206/

441–3483 or 800/247–3483, FAX 206/441–5431). For live-aboard dive vacations, try **See & Sea Travel Service** (✉ 50 Francisco St., #205, San Francisco, CA 94133, ☎ 415/434–3400 or 800/348–9778, FAX 415/434–3409).

YACHT CHARTERS➤ For crewed or uncrewed charters, try **Alden Yacht Charters** (✉ 1909 Alden Landing, Portsmouth, RI 02871, ☎ 401/683–1782 or 800/662–2628, FAX 401/683–3668), **Huntley Yacht Vacations** (✉ 210 Preston Rd., Wernersville, PA 19565, ☎ 610/678–2628 or 800/322–9224, FAX 610/670–1767), **Lynn Jachney Charters** (✉ Box 302 Marblehead, MA 01945, ☎ 617/639–0787 or 800/223–2050, FAX 617/639–0216), **The Moorings** (✉ 19345 U.S. Hwy. 19 N, 4th floor, Clearwater, FL 34624-3193, ☎ 813/530–5424 or 800/535–7289, FAX 813/530–9474), **Nicholson Yacht Charters** (✉ 78 Bolton St., Cambridge, MA 02140-3321, ☎ 617/225–0555 or 800/662–6066, FAX 617/661–0554), **Ocean Voyages** (✉ 1709 Bridgeway, Sausalito, CA 94965, ☎ 415/332–4681, FAX 415/332–7460), **Russell Yacht Charters** (✉ 404 Hulls Hwy., Southport, CT 06490, ☎ 203/255–2783 or 800/635–8895), and **SailAway Yacht Charters** (✉ 15605 S.W. 92nd Ave., Miami, FL 33157-1972, ☎ 305/253–7245 or 800/724–5292, FAX 305/251–4408).

### ORGANIZATIONS

The **National Tour Association** (✉ NTA, 546 E. Main St., Lexington, KY 40508, ☎ 606/226–4444 or 800/755–8687) and the **United States Tour Operators Association** (✉ USTOA, 211 E. 51st St., Suite 12B, New York, NY 10022, ☎ 212/750–7371) can provide lists of members and information on booking tours.

### PUBLICATIONS

Contact the USTOA (☞ Organizations, *above*) for its **"Smart Traveler's Planning Kit."** Pamphlets in the kit include the "Worldwide Tour and Vacation Package Finder," "How to Select a Tour or Vacation Package," and information on the organization's consumer protection plan. Also get copy of the Better Business Bureau's **"Tips on Travel Packages"** (✉ Publication 24-195, 4200 Wilson Blvd., Arlington, VA 22203; $2).

### TRAVEL GEAR

For travel apparel, appliances, personal-care items, and other travel necessities, get a free catalog from **Magellan's** (☎ 800/962–4943, FAX 805/568–5406), **Orvis Travel** (☎ 800/541–3541, FAX 703/343–7053), or **TravelSmith** (☎ 800/950–1600, FAX 415/455–0554).

### ELECTRICAL CONVERTERS

Send a self-addressed, stamped envelope to the **Franzus Company** (✉ Customer Service, Dept. B50, Murtha Industrial Park, Box

142, Beacon Falls, CT 06403, ☎ 203/723–6664) for a copy of the free brochure "Foreign Electricity Is No Deep, Dark Secret."

TRAVEL AGENCIES

For names of reputable agencies in your area, contact the **American Society of Travel Agents** (✉ ASTA, 1101 King St., Suite 200, Alexandria, VA 22314, ☎ 703/739–2782), the **Association of Canadian Travel Agents** (✉ 1729 Bank St., Suite 201, Ottawa, Ontario K1V 7Z5, ☎ 613/521–0474, FAX 613/521–0805) or the **Association of British Travel Agents** (✉ 55-57 Newman St., London W1P 4AH, ☎ 0171/637–2444, FAX 0171/637–0713).

# U

## U.S. GOVERNMENT TRAVEL BRIEFINGS

The U.S. Department of State's American Citizens Services office (✉ Room 4811, Washington, DC 20520; enclose SASE) issues **Consular Information Sheets** on all foreign countries.

These cover issues such as crime, security, political climate, and health risks as well as listing embassy locations, entry requirements, currency regulations, and other useful information. For the latest information, stop in at any U.S. passport office, consulate, or embassy; call the interactive hot line (☎ 202/647–5225, FAX 202/647–3000); or, with your PC's modem, tap into the department's computer bulletin board (☎ 202/647–9225).

# V

## VISITOR INFORMATION

Almost all islands have a U.S.–based tourist board, listed with its name and address under the A to Z sections at the end of individual island chapters; they can be good sources of general information, up-to-date calendars of events, and listings of hotels, restaurants, sights, and shops. The **Caribbean Tourism Organization** (✉ 20 E. 46th St., New York, NY 10017-2452, ☎ 212/

682–0435, FAX 212/697–4258) is another resource, especially for information on the islands that have very limited tourist offices in the United States.

**IN THE U.K.**

**Caribbean Tourism Organization** ✉ Vigilant House, 120 Wilton Rd., London SW1V 1JZ, ☎ 0171/233–8382).

# W

## WEATHER

For current conditions and forecasts, plus the local time and helpful travel tips, call the **Weather Channel Connection** (☎ 900/932–8437; 95¢ per minute) from a Touch-Tone phone.

The *International Traveler's Weather Guide* (✉ Weather Press, Box 660606, Sacramento, CA 95866, ☎ 916/974–0201 or 800/972–0201; $10.95 includes shipping), written by two meteorologists, provides month-by-month information on temperature, humidity, and precipitation in more than 175 cities worldwide.

# SMART TRAVEL TIPS A TO Z

*Basic Information on Traveling in the Caribbean &*
*Savvy Tips to Make Your Trip a Breeze*

## A
### AIR TRAVEL

If time is an issue, **always look for nonstop flights,** which require no change of plane. If possible, **avoid connecting flights,** which stop at least once and can involve a change of plane, even though the flight number remains the same; if the first leg is late, the second waits.

For better service, **fly smaller or regional carriers,** which often have higher passenger satisfaction ratings. Sometimes they have such in-flight amenities as leather seats or greater legroom and they often have better food.

### CUTTING COSTS

The Sunday travel section of most newspapers is a good place to look for deals.

MAJOR AIRLINES➤ The least-expensive airfares from the major airlines are priced for round-trip travel and are subject to restrictions. Usually, you must **book in advance and buy the ticket within 24 hours** to get cheaper fares, and you may have to **stay over a Saturday night.** The lowest fare is subject to availability, and only a small percentage of the plane's total seats is sold at that price. It's smart to **call a number of airlines, and when you are quoted a good** price, **book it on the spot**—the same fare may not be available on the same flight the next day. Airlines generally allow you to change your return date for a $25 to $50 fee. If you don't use your ticket, you can apply the cost toward the purchase of a new ticket, again for a small charge. However, most low-fare tickets are nonrefundable. To get the lowest airfare, **check different routings.** If your destination has more than one gateway, **compare prices to different airports.**

FROM THE U.K.➤ To save money on flights, **look into an APEX or Super-Pex ticket.** APEX tickets must be booked in advance and have certain restrictions. Super-PEX tickets can be purchased right at the airport.

CONSOLIDATORS➤ Consolidators buy tickets for scheduled flights at reduced rates from the airlines, then sell them at prices below the lowest available from the airlines directly—usually without advance restrictions. Sometimes you can even get your money back if you need to return the ticket. Carefully read the fine print detailing penalties for changes and cancellations. If you doubt the reliability of a consolidator, **confirm your reservation with the airline.**

CHARTER FLIGHTS➤ Charters usually have the lowest fares and most restrictions. Departures are infrequent and seldom on time, and you can lose all or most of your money if you cancel. (The closer to departure you cancel, the more you lose, although sometimes you can pay only a small fee if you supply a substitute passenger.) The flight may be canceled for any reason up to 10 days before departure (after that, only if it is physically impossible to operate). The charterer may also revise the itinerary or increase the price after you have bought the ticket, but only if the new arrangement constitutes a "major change" do you have the right to a refund. Before buying a charter ticket, **read the fine print** regarding the company's refund policies. Money for charter flights is usually paid into a bank escrow account, the name of which should be on the contract, and if you don't pay by credit card, **make your check payable to the carrier's escrow account** (unless you're dealing with a travel agent, in which case his or her check should be made payable to the escrow account). The U.S. Department of Transportation's Aviation Consumer Protection Division has jurisdiction over charters.

Charter operators may offer flights alone or with ground arrangements that constitute a charter package. Normally, you must book charters through a travel agent.

### ALOFT

AIRLINE FOOD➤ If you hate airline food, **ask for special meals when booking.** These can be vegetarian, low-cholesterol, or kosher, for example; commonly prepared to order in smaller quantities than standard fare, they can be tastier.

SMOKING➤ Smoking is not allowed on flights of six hours or less within the continental United States. Smoking is also prohibited on flights within Canada. For U.S. flights longer than six hours or international flights, **contact your carrier regarding their smoking policy.** Some carriers have prohibited smoking throughout their system; others allow smoking only on certain routes or even certain departures of that route.

### C

### CAMERAS, CAMCORDERS, & COMPUTERS

### CUSTOMS

Before departing, **register your foreign-made camera or laptop with U.S. Customs.** If your equipment is U.S.-made, call the consulate of the country you'll be visiting to find out whether it should be registered with local customs upon arrival.

### IN TRANSIT

Always **keep your film, tape, or disks out of the sun**; never put these on the dashboard of a car. Carry an extra supply of batteries, and **be prepared to turn on your camera, camcorder, or laptop computer for security personnel** to prove that it's real.

### X-RAYS

Always **ask for hand inspection at security.** Such requests are virtually always honored at U.S. airports, and are usually accommodated abroad. Photographic film becomes clouded after successive exposure to airport X-ray machines. Videotape and computer disks are not harmed by X-rays, but **keep your tapes and disks away from metal detectors.**

### CAR RENTAL

### CUTTING COSTS

To get the best deal, **book through a travel agent who is willing to shop around.** Ask your agent to **look for fly-drive packages,** which also save you money, and **ask if local taxes are included** in the rental or fly-drive price. These can be as high as 20% in some destinations. Don't forget to find out about required deposits, cancellation penalties, drop-off charges, and the cost of any required insurance coverage.

Also **ask your travel agent about a company's customer-service record.** How has it responded to late plane arrivals and vehicle mishaps? Are there often lines at the rental counter, and—if you're

traveling during a holiday period—does a confirmed reservation guarantee you a car?

### INSURANCE

When driving a rented car, you are generally responsible for any damage to or loss of the rental vehicle, as well as any property damage or personal injury that you cause. Before you rent, **see what coverage you already have** under the terms of your personal auto insurance policy and credit cards.

If you do not have auto insurance or an umbrella insurance policy that covers damage to third parties, purchasing CDW or LDW is highly recommended.

### LICENSE REQUIREMENTS

For driver's license requirements, see individual island chapters.

### SURCHARGES

Note that some rental agencies charge extra if you return the car before the time specified on your contract. To avoid a hefty refueling fee, **fill the tank just before you turn in the car**—but be aware that gas stations near the rental outlet may overcharge.

### CHILDREN & TRAVEL

Caribbean islands and their resorts are increasingly sensitive to families' needs. Many now have children's programs. Baby food is easy to find, but outside major hotels you may not find such items as high chairs and cribs. When choosing a destination, **consider whether** or not English is spoken **widely**; the language barrier can frustrate children.

When traveling with children, **plan ahead** and **involve your youngsters** as you outline your trip. When packing, **include a supply of things to keep them busy** en route (☞ Children & Travel *in* Important Contacts A to Z). On sightseeing days, try to **schedule activities of special interest to your children,** like a trip to a zoo or a playground. If you **plan your itinerary around seasonal festivals,** you'll never lack for things to do. In addition, **check local newspapers for special events** mounted by public libraries, museums, and parks.

### BABY-SITTING

For recommended local sitters, **check with your hotel desk.**

### DRIVING

If you are renting a car, don't forget to **arrange for a car seat when you reserve.** Sometimes they're free.

### FLYING

As a general rule, infants under two not occupying a seat fly at greatly reduced fares and occasionally for free. If your children are two or older **ask about special children's fares.** Age limits for these fares vary among carriers. Rules also vary regarding unaccompanied minors, so again, check with your airline.

BAGGAGE➤ In general, the adult baggage allowance applies to children paying half or more of the adult fare. If you are traveling with an infant, **ask about carry-on allowances** before departure. In general, for infants charged 10% of the adult fare you are allowed one carry-on bag and a collapsible stroller, which may have to be checked; you may be limited to less if the flight is full.

SAFETY SEATS➤ According to the FAA, it's a good idea to **use safety seats aloft** for children weighing less than 40 pounds. Airline policies vary. U.S. carriers allow FAA-approved models but usually require that you buy a ticket, even if your child would otherwise ride free, since the seats must be strapped into regular seats. However, some U.S. and foreign-flag airlines may require you to hold your baby during takeoff and landing—defeating the seat's purpose. Other foreign carriers may not allow infant seats at all, or may charge a child rather than an infant fare for their use.

FACILITIES➤ When making your reservation, **request children's meals or freestanding bassinets** if you need them; the latter are available only to those seated at the bulkhead, where there's enough legroom. If you don't need a bassinet, **think twice before requesting bulkhead seats**—the only storage space for in-flight necessities is in inconveniently distant overhead bins.

### GAMES

Milton Bradley and Parker Brothers have travel versions of some of their most popular games, including Yahtzee, Trouble, Sorry, and Monopoly. Prices run $5 to $8. Look for them in the travel section of your local toy store.

### LODGING

Children are welcome in all except the most exclusive resorts; many hotels allow children under 12 or 16 to stay free in their parents' room (be sure to **ask the cutoff age** when booking). In addition, several hotel chains have children's programs, and many hotels and resorts arrange for baby-sitting. Representative of the services and activities available are the complimentary "Just Us Kids" program for children ages 5–12 at Aruba's Sonesta Resorts at Seaport Village; the camp available for children ages 5–12 all summer, at Christmastime, and at Easter at Puerto Rico's Hyatt Regency Cerromar Beach and Hyatt Dorado Beach; and the activities program for kids 5–12 at Puerto Rico's El San Juan Hotel and Casino.

Jamaica's all-inclusive Boscobel Beach specializes in families and offers a small army of SuperNannies, a petting zoo, crafts classes, and a disco for teens. On St. Thomas in the U.S. Virgin Islands, the Stouffer Grand Beach Resort has half-day and full-day programs for children ages 3–12. Club Med's St. Lucia and Dominican Republic resorts offer Mini Club programs for children ages 2–11.

Also **consider apartment and villa rentals** (☞ Lodging, *below*). When you book, be sure to **ask about the availability of babysitters,** housekeepers, and medical facilities.

## CRUISES

Cruising the Caribbean is perhaps the most relaxed and convenient way to tour this beautiful part of the world: You get all of the amenities of a Stateside hotel and enough activities to guarantee fun, even on rainy days. Cruising through the islands is an entirely different experience from staying on one island.

Cruise ships usually call at several Caribbean ports on a single voyage but are at each port for only one night. Thus, although you may be exposed to several islands, you don't get much of a feel for any one of them.

As a vacation, a cruise offers total peace of mind. All important decisions are made long before boarding. The itinerary is set, and the total cost of your vacation is known almost to the penny. For details, see Fodor's *Worldwide Cruises and Ports of Call 1997*; the Cruise Primer chapter is particularly helpful if you're cruising for the first time.

To get the best deal on a cruise, **consult a cruise-only travel agency.**

## CUSTOMS & DUTIES

To speed your clearance through customs, **keep receipts for all your purchases abroad** and **be ready to show the inspector what you've bought.** If you feel that you've been incorrectly or unfairly charged a duty, you can **appeal assessments in dispute.** First ask to see a supervisor. If you are still unsatisfied, **write to the port director** of your point of entry, sending your customs receipt and any other appropriate documentation. The address will be listed on your receipt. If you still don't get satisfaction, you can take your case to customs headquarters in Washington.

### IN THE U.S.

You may bring home $400 worth of foreign goods duty-free if you've been out of the country for at least 48 hours and haven't already used the $400 allowance, or any part of it, in the past 30 days. You may bring home $600 worth of foreign goods duty-free if you've been out of the country for at least 48 hours and haven't used the $600 allowance, or any part of it, in the past 30 days. This allowance, higher than the standard $400 exemption, applies to two dozen countries included in the Caribbean Basin Initiative (CBI). If you visit a CBI country and a non-CBI country, such as Martinique, you may still bring in $600 worth of goods duty-free, but no more

than $400 can be from the non-CBI country. Travelers returning from the U.S. Virgin Islands (USVI) are entitled to a $1,200 duty-free allowance. If your travel included the USVI and another country—say, the Dominican Republic—the $1,200 allowance still applies, but at least $600 worth of goods must be from t he USVI.

Travelers 21 or older may bring back 1 liter of alcohol duty-free, provided the beverage laws of the state through which they reenter the United States allow it. In addition, regardless of their age, they are allowed 100 non-Cuban cigars and 200 cigarettes. Antiques, which the U.S. Customs Service defines as objects more than 100 years old, are duty-free. Original works of art done entirely by hand are also duty-free. These include, but are not limited to, paintings, drawings, and sculptures.

Duty-free, travelers may mail packages valued at up to $200 to themselves and up to $100 to others, with a limit of one parcel per addressee per day (and no alcohol or tobacco products or perfume valued at more than $5); on the outside, the package must be labeled as being either for personal use or an unsolicited gift, and a list of its contents and their retail value must be attached. Mailed items do not affect your duty-free allowance on your return.

THE GOLD GUIDE / SMART TRAVEL TIPS

## IN CANADA

If you've been out of Canada for at least seven days, you may bring in C$500 worth of goods duty-free. If you've been away for fewer than seven days but for more than 48 hours, the duty-free allowance drops to C$200; if your trip lasts between 24 and 48 hours, the allowance is C$50. You cannot pool allowances with family members. Goods claimed under the C$500 exemption may follow you by mail; those claimed under the lesser exemptions must accompany you.

Alcohol and tobacco products may be included in the seven-day and 48-hour exemptions but not in the 24-hour exemption. If you meet the age requirements of the province or territory through which you reenter Canada, you may bring in, duty-free, 1.14 liters (40 imperial ounces) of wine or liquor *or* 24 12-ounce cans or bottles of beer or ale. If you are 16 or older, you may bring in, duty-free, 200 cigarettes, 50 cigars or cigarillos, and 400 tobacco sticks or 400 grams of manufactured tobacco. Alcohol and tobacco must accompany you on your return.

An unlimited number of gifts with a value of up to C$60 each may be mailed to Canada duty-free. These do not affect your duty-free allowance on your return. Label the package "Unsolicited Gift— Value Under $60."

Alcohol and tobacco are excluded.

## IN THE U.K.

From countries outside the European Union, including those in the Caribbean, you may import, duty-free, 200 cigarettes, 100 cigarillos, 50 cigars, or 250 grams of tobacco; 1 liter of spirits or 2 liters of fortified or sparkling wine or liqueurs; 2 liters of still table wine; 60 milliliters of perfume; 250 milliliters of toilet water; plus £136 worth of other goods, including gifts and souvenirs.

# D

## DISABILITIES & ACCESSIBILITY

In the Caribbean very few attractions and sights are equipped with ramps, elevators, or wheelchair-accessible rest rooms. However, major new properties are planning with the needs of travelers with disabilities in mind. Wherever possible in our lodging listings, we indicate whether special facilities are available.

When discussing accessibility with an operator or reservationist, **ask hard questions.** Are there any stairs, inside *or* out? Are there grab bars next to the toilet *and* in the shower/tub? How wide is the doorway to the room? To the bathroom? For the most extensive facilities, meeting the latest legal specifications, **opt for newer accommodations,** which more often have been designed with access in mind. Older properties or ships must usually be retrofitted

and may offer more limited facilities as a result. Be sure to **discuss your needs before booking.**

## DISCOUNTS & DEALS

You shouldn't have to pay for a discount. In fact, you may already be eligible for all kinds of savings. Here are some time-honored strategies for getting the best deal.

## LOOK IN YOUR WALLET

When you **use your credit card to make travel purchases,** you may get free travel-accident insurance, collision damage insurance, medical or legal assistance, depending on the card and bank that issued it. Visa and MasterCard provide one or more of these services, so **get a copy of your card's travel benefits.** If you are a member of the AAA or an oil-company-sponsored road-assistance plan, always **ask hotel or car-rental reservationists for auto-club discounts.** Some clubs offer additional discounts on tours, cruises, or admission to attractions. And don't forget that auto-club membership entitles you to free maps and trip-planning services.

## SENIORS CITIZENS & STUDENTS

As a senior-citizen traveler, you may be eligible for special rates, but you should mention your senior-citizen status up front. If you're a student or under 26 can also get discounts, especially if you have an official

ID card (☞ Senior-Citizen Discounts *and* Students on the Road, *below*).

## DIAL FOR DOLLARS

To save money, **look into "1-800" discount reservations services,** which often have lower rates. These services use their buying power to get a better price on hotels, airline tickets, and sometimes even car rentals. When booking a room, always **call the hotel's local toll-free number** (if one is available) rather than the central reservations number—you'll often get a better price. Ask the reservationist about special packages or corporate rates, which are usually available even if you're not traveling on business.

## JOIN A CLUB?

Discount clubs can be a legitimate source of savings, but you must use the participating hotels and visit the participating attractions in order to realize any benefits. Remember, too, that you have to pay a fee to join, so **determine if you'll save enough to warrant your membership fee.** Before booking with a club, **make sure the hotel or other supplier isn't offering a better deal.**

## GET A GUARANTEE

When shopping for the best deal on hotels and car rentals, **look for guaranteed exchange rates,** which protect you against a falling dollar. With your rate locked in, you won't pay more even if the price goes up in the local currency.

## H

### HEALTH

There are few real hazards. The small lizards that seem to have overrun the islands are harmless, and poisonous snakes are hard to find, although you should exercise caution while bird-watching in Trinidad. The worst problem may well be the tiny sand flies known as no-see-ums, which tend to appear after a rain, near wet or swampy ground, and around sunset. You may want to **bring along a good repellent.**

Sunburn or sunstroke can be serious. A long-sleeve shirt, a hat, and long pants or a beach wrap are essential on a boat, for midday at the beach, and whenever you go out sightseeing. **Use sunblock lotion** on nose, ears, and other sensitive areas, **limit your sun time** for the first few days, and be sure to **drink enough liquids.**

Since health standards vary from island to island, inquire about local conditions before you go. No special shots are required for most Caribbean destinations; where they are, we have made note of it.

### DIVERS' ALERT

Scuba divers take note: **Do not fly within 24 hours of scuba diving.**

## I

### INSURANCE

Travel insurance can protect your monetary investment, replace your luggage and its contents, or provide for medical coverage should you fall ill during your trip. Most tour operators, travel agents, and insurance agents sell specialized health-and-accident, flight, trip-cancellation, and luggage insurance as well as comprehensive policies with some or all of these coverages. Comprehensive policies may also reimburse you for delays due to weather—an important consideration if you're traveling during the winter months. Some health-insurance policies do not cover preexisting conditions, but waivers may be available in specific cases. Coverage is sold by the companies listed in Important Contacts A to Z; these companies act as the policy's administrators. The actual insurance is usually underwritten by a well-known name, such as The Travelers or Continental Insurance.

Before you make any purchase, **review your existing health and home-owner's policies** to find out whether they cover expenses incurred while traveling.

### BAGGAGE

Airline liability for baggage is limited to $1,250 per person on domestic flights. On international flights, it amounts to $9.07 per pound or $20 per kilogram for checked baggage (roughly $640 per 70-pound bag) and $400 per passenger for unchecked baggage. Insurance for losses exceeding the terms of your airline ticket can be bought directly from the airline at check-in for about $10 per

*THE GOLD GUIDE / SMART TRAVEL TIPS*

$1,000 of coverage; note that it excludes a rather extensive list of items, shown on your airline ticket.

### COMPREHENSIVE

Comprehensive insurance policies include all the coverages described above plus some that may not be available in more specific policies. If you have purchased an expensive vacation, especially one that involves travel abroad, comprehensive insurance is a must; **look for policies that include trip delay insurance,** which will protect you in the event that weather problems cause you to miss your flight, tour, or cruise. A few insurers will also sell you a waiver for preexisting medical conditions. Some of the companies that offer both these features are Access America, Carefree Travel, Travel Insured International, and TravelGuard (☞ Important Contacts A to Z).

### FLIGHT

You should **think twice before buying flight insurance.** Often purchased as a last-minute impulse at the airport, it pays a lump sum when a plane crashes, either to a beneficiary if the insured dies or sometimes to a surviving passenger who loses his or her eyesight or a limb. Supplementing the airlines' coverage described in the limits-of-liability paragraphs on your ticket, it's expensive and basically unnecessary. Charging an airline ticket to a major credit card often automatically provides you with coverage that

may also extend to travel by bus, train, and ship.

### HEALTH

Medicare generally does not cover health care costs outside the United States; nor do many privately issued policies. If your own health insurance policy does not cover you outside the United States, **consider buying supplemental medical coverage.** It can reimburse you for $1,000–$150,000 worth of medical and/or dental expenses incurred as a result of an accident or illness during a trip. These policies also may include a personal-accident, or death-and-dismemberment, provision, which pays a lump sum ranging from $15,000 to $500,000 to your beneficiaries if you die or to you if you lose one or more limbs or your eyesight, and a medical-assistance provision, which may either reimburse you for the cost of referrals, evacuation, or repatriation and other services, or automatically enroll you as a member of a particular medical-assistance company. (☞ Health *in* Important Contacts A to Z.)

### U.K. TRAVELERS

You can buy an annual travel insurance policy valid for most vacations during the year in which it's purchased. If you are pregnant or have a preexisting medical condition make sure you're covered before buying such a policy.

### TRIP

Without insurance, you will lose all or most of

your money if you cancel your trip regardless of the reason. Especially if your airline ticket, cruise, or package tour is nonrefundable and cannot be changed, it's essential that you **buy trip-cancellation-and-interruption insurance.** When considering how much coverage you need, look for a policy that will cover the cost of your trip plus the nondiscounted price of a one-way airline ticket should you need to return home early. Read the fine print carefully, especially sections that define "family member" and "preexisting medical conditions." Also **consider default or bankruptcy insurance,** which protects you against a supplier's failure to deliver. Be aware, however, that if you buy such a policy from a travel agency, tour operator, airline, or cruise line, it may not cover default by the firm in question.

## L

### LODGING

Plan ahead and **reserve a room well before you travel to the Caribbean.** If you have reservations but expect to arrive later than 5 or 6 PM, tell the management in advance. Unless so advised, some places will not hold your reservations after 6 PM. Also, be sure to **find out what the quoted rate includes**—use of sports facilities and equipment, airport transfers, and the like—and whether the property operates on the European Plan (EP, with no meals), Continental

Plan (CP, with Continental breakfast), Breakfast Plan (BP, with full breakfast), Modified American Plan (MAP, with two meals), or Full American Plan (FAP, with three meals), or is All-inclusive (including three meals, all facilities, and drinks unless otherwise noted). Be sure to **bring your deposit receipt** with you in case questions arise.

Decide whether you want a hotel on the leeward side of the island (with calm water, good for snorkeling) or the windward (with waves, good for surfing). Decide, too, whether you want to pay the extra price for a room overlooking the ocean or pool. Also **find out how close the property is to a beach**; at some hotels you can walk barefoot from your room onto the sand; others are across a road or a 10-minute drive away.

Nighttime entertainment is alfresco in the Caribbean, so if you go to sleep early or are a light sleeper, ask for a room away from the dance floor.

Air-conditioning is not a necessity on all islands, most of which are cooled by trade winds, but it can be a plus if you enjoy an afternoon snooze. Breezes are best in second-floor rooms, particularly corner rooms. If you like to sleep without air-conditioning, make sure that windows can be opened and have screens.

In this book, we categorize properties by price rather than quality.

Prices are intended as a guideline only. Larger hotels with more extensive facilities cost more, but the Caribbean is full of smaller places with charm, individuality, and prices that make up for their lack of activities—which are generally available on a pay-per-use basis everywhere.

### APARTMENT & VILLA RENTAL

If you want a home base that's roomy enough for a family and comes with cooking facilities, **consider taking a furnished rental.** This can also save you money, but not always—some rentals are luxury properties (economical only when your party is large). Home-exchange directories list rentals—often second homes owned by prospective house swappers—and some services search for a house or apartment for you and handle the paperwork. Some send an illustrated catalog; others send photographs only of specific properties, sometimes at a charge; up-front registration fees may apply.

### HOME EXCHANGE

If you would like to find a house, an apartment, or some other type of vacation property to exchange for your own while on holiday, **become a member of a home-exchange organization,** which will send you its updated listings of available exchanges for a year, and will include your own listing in at least one of them. Arrangements for the actual exchange are made by the two parties

involved, not by the organization.

## M

### MEDICAL ASSISTANCE

No one plans to get sick while traveling, but it happens, so **consider signing up with a medical assistance company.** These outfits provide referrals, emergency evacuation or repatriation, 24-hour telephone hot lines for medical consultation, cash for emergencies, and other personal and legal assistance. They also dispatch medical personnel and arrange for the relay of medical records.

### MONEY

#### ATMS

CASH ADVANCES➤ Before leaving home, **make sure that your credit cards have been programmed for ATM use** in the Caribbean. Note that Discover is accepted mostly in the United States. Local bank cards often do not work overseas either; **ask your bank about a Visa debit card,** which works like a bank card but can be used at any ATM displaying a Visa logo.

TRANSACTION FEES➤ Although fees charged for ATM transactions may be higher abroad than at home, Cirrus and Plus exchange rates are excellent, because they are based on wholesale rates offered only by major banks.

#### TRAVELER'S CHECKS

Whether or not to buy traveler's checks depends on where you are

THE GOLD GUIDE / SMART TRAVEL TIPS

headed; **take cash to rural areas and small towns, traveler's checks to cities.** The most widely recognized checks are issued by American Express, Citicorp, Thomas Cook, and Visa. These are sold by major commercial banks for 1%–3% of the checks' face value—it pays to **shop around.** Both American Express and Thomas Cook issue checks that can be countersigned and used by either you or your traveling companion. So you won't be left with excess foreign currency, **buy a few checks in small denominations** to cash toward the end of your trip. Before leaving home, **contact your issuer for information on where to cash your checks** without a incurring a transaction fee. Record the numbers of all your checks, and keep this listing in a separate place, crossing off the numbers of checks you have cashed.

### WIRING MONEY

For a fee of 3%–10%, depending on the amount of the transaction, you can have money sent to you from home through Money-Gram<sup>SM</sup> or Western Union (☞ Money *in* Important Contacts A to Z). The transferred funds and the service fee can be charged to a MasterCard or Visa account.

### P

### PACKING FOR THE CARIBBEAN

Dress on the islands is light and casual. Bring loose-fitting clothes made of natural fabrics to see you through days of heat and humidity. Take a cover-up for the beaches, not only to protect you from the sun but also to wear to and from your hotel room. Bathing suits and immodest attire are frowned upon off the beach on many islands. A sun hat is advisable, but you don't have to pack one, since inexpensive straw hats are available everywhere. For shopping and sightseeing, bring walking shorts, jeans, T-shirts, long-sleeve cotton shirts, slacks, and sundresses. You'll need a light sweater for protection from the trade winds, and at higher altitudes. Evenings are casual, but "casual" can range from really informal to casually elegant, depending on the establishment. A tie is rarely required, but jackets are sometimes de rigueur in fancier restaurants and casinos.

Bring an extra pair of eyeglasses or contact lenses in your carry-on luggage, and if you have a health problem, **pack enough medication** to last the trip or have your doctor write you a prescription using the drug's generic name, because brand names vary from country to country (you'll then need a duplicate prescription from a local doctor). It's important that you **don't put prescription drugs or valuables in luggage to be checked,** for it could go astray. To avoid problems with customs officials, carry medications in the original packaging. Also, don't forget the addresses of offices that handle refunds of lost traveler's checks.

### ELECTRICITY

The general rule in the Caribbean is 110 and 120 volts AC, and the outlets take the same two-prong plugs found in the United States, but there are exceptions, particularly on the French islands and those with a British heritage. Be sure to **check with your hotel** when making reservations. If you are traveling to an island that uses a foreign system, **bring a converter and an adapter.**

If your appliances are dual-voltage, you'll need only an adapter. Hotels sometimes have 110-volt outlets for low-wattage appliances near the sink, marked FOR SHAVERS ONLY; don't use them for high-wattage appliances like blow-dryers. If your laptop computer is older, carry a converter; new laptops operate equally well on 110 and 220 volts, so you need only an adapter.

### LUGGAGE

Airline baggage allowances depend on the airline, the route, and the class of your ticket; ask in advance. In general, on domestic flights and on international flights between the United States and foreign destinations, you are entitled to check two bags. A third piece may be brought on board, but it must fit easily under the seat in front of you or in the overhead compartment.

In the United States, the FAA gives airlines broad latitude regarding carry-on allowances, and they tend to tailor them to different aircraft and operational conditions. Charges for excess, oversize, or overweight pieces vary.

If you are flying between two foreign destinations, note that baggage allowances may be determined not by piece but by weight—generally 88 pounds (40 kilograms) in first class, 66 pounds (30 kilograms) in business class, and 44 pounds (20 kilograms) in economy. If your flight between two cities abroad *connects* with your transatlantic or transpacific flight, the piece method still applies.

SAFEGUARDING YOUR LUGGAGE➤ Before leaving home, **itemize your bags' contents** and their worth, and label them with your name, address, and phone number. (If you use your home address, cover it so that potential thieves can't see it readily.) Inside each bag, **pack a copy of your itinerary.** At check-in, **make sure that each bag is correctly tagged** with the destination airport's three-letter code. If your bags arrive damaged—or fail to arrive at all—file a written report with the airline before leaving the airport.

### PASSPORTS & VISAS

If you don't already have one, **get a passport.** It is advisable that you **leave one photocopy of your passport's** data page with someone at home and keep another with you, separated from your passport, while traveling. If you lose your passport, promptly call the nearest embassy or consulate and the local police; having the data page information can speed replacement.

See individual island chapters for specific requirements.

### IN THE U.S.

Application forms for both first-time and renewal passports are available at any of the 13 U.S. Passport Agency offices and at some post offices and courthouses. Passports are usually mailed within four weeks; allow five weeks or more in spring and summer.

### CANADIANS

Passport application forms are available at 28 regional passport offices, as well as post offices and travel agencies. Whether for a first or a renewal passport, you must apply in person. Children under 16 may be included on a parent's passport but must have their own to travel alone. Passports are valid for five years and are usually mailed within two to three weeks of application.

### U.K. CITIZENS

Some islands require passports; others do not but may require a British Visitor's Passport.

Applications for new and renewal passports are available from main post offices and at the passport offices in Belfast, Glasgow, Liverpool, London, Newport, and Peterborough. You may apply in person at all passport offices, or by mail to all except the London office. Children under 16 may travel on an accompanying parent's passport. All passports are valid for 10 years. Allow a month for processing.

### S

### SENIOR-CITIZEN DISCOUNTS

To qualify for age-related discounts, **mention your senior-citizen status up front** when booking hotel reservations, not when checking out, and before you're seated in restaurants, not when paying the bill. Note that discounts may be limited to certain menus, days, or hours. When renting a car, **ask about promotional car-rental discounts**—they can net even lower costs than your senior-citizen discount.

### STUDENTS ON THE ROAD

The Caribbean is not as far out of a student's budget as you might expect. All but the toniest islands, such as St. Barthélemy, have camping facilities, inexpensive guest houses, or small no-frills hotels. You're most likely to meet students from other countries in the French and Dutch West Indies, where many go on holiday or sabbatical. Puerto Rico, Jamaica, Grenada, and Dominica, among others, have large resident

THE GOLD GUIDE / SMART TRAVEL TIPS

international student populations at their universities.

To save money, **look into deals available through student-oriented travel agencies.** To qualify, you'll need to have a bona fide student ID card. Members of international student groups are also eligible (☞ Students *in* Important Contacts A to Z).

# T

## TELEPHONES

### LONG-DISTANCE

The long-distance services of AT&T, MCI, and Sprint make calling home relatively convenient, but in many hotels you may find it impossible to dial the access number. The hotel operator may also refuse to make the connection. Instead, the hotel will charge you a premium rate—as much as 400% more than a calling card—for calls placed from your hotel room. To avoid such price gouging, travel with more than one company's long-distance calling card—a hotel may block Sprint but not MCI. If the hotel operator claims that you cannot use any phone card, ask to be connected to an international operator, who will help you to access your phone card. You can also dial the international operator yourself. If none of this works, try calling your phone company collect in the United States. If collect calls are also blocked, call from a pay phone in the hotel lobby. Before you go, **find out the local access codes** for your destinations.

## TOUR OPERATORS

A package or tour to the Caribbean can make your vacation less expensive and more hassle-free. Firms that sell tours and packages reserve airline seats, hotel rooms, and rental cars in bulk and pass some of the savings on to you. In addition, the best operators have local representatives available to help you at your destination.

### A GOOD DEAL?

The more your package or tour includes, the better you can predict the ultimate cost of your vacation. Make sure you know exactly what is covered, and **beware of hidden costs.** Are taxes, tips, and service charges included? Transfers and baggage handling? Entertainment and excursions? These can add up.

Most packages and tours are rated deluxe, first-class superior, first class, tourist, or budget. The key difference is usually accommodations. If the package or tour you are considering is priced lower than in your wildest dreams, **be skeptical.** Also, **make sure your travel agent knows the accommodations** and other services. Ask about the hotel's location, room size, beds, and whether it has a pool, room service, or programs for children, if you care about these. Has your agent been there in person or sent others you can contact?

### BUYER BEWARE

Each year a number of consumers are stranded or lose their money

when operators—even very large ones with excellent reputations—go out of business. To avoid becoming one of them, take the time to **check out the operator**—find out how long the company has been in business and ask several agents about its reputation. Next, **don't book unless the firm has a consumer-protection program.** Members of the USTOA and the NTA are required to set aside funds for the sole purpose of covering your payments and travel arrangements in case of default. Non-member operators may instead carry insurance; look for the details in the operator's brochure—and for the name of an underwriter with a solid reputation. Note: When it comes to tour operators, **don't trust escrow accounts.** Although there are laws governing those of charter-flight operators, no governmental body prevents tour operators from raiding the till.

Next, **contact your local Better Business Bureau and the attorney general's offices** in both your own state and the operator's; have any complaints been filed? Finally, **pay with a major credit card.** Then you can cancel payment, provided that you can document your complaint. Always **consider trip-cancellation insurance** (☞ Insurance, *above*).

BIG VS. SMALL➤ Operators that handle several hundred thousand travelers per year can use their purchasing power to give you a good price. Their high volume may also indicate financial stability. But some small companies provide more personalized service; because they tend to specialize, they may also be more knowledgeable about a given area.

## USING AN AGENT

Travel agents are excellent resources. In fact, large operators accept bookings made only through travel agents. But it's good to **collect brochures from several agencies** because some agents' suggestions may be skewed by promotional relationships with tour and package firms that reward them for volume sales. If you have a special interest, **find an agent with expertise in that area**; ASTA can provide leads in the United States. (Don't rely solely on your agent, though; agents may be unaware of small-niche operators, and some special-interest travel companies only sell direct.)

## SINGLE TRAVELERS

Prices are usually quoted per person, based on two sharing a room. If traveling solo, you may be required to pay the full double-occupancy rate. Some operators eliminate this surcharge if you agree to be matched up with a roommate of the same sex, even if one is not found by departure time.

### TRAVEL GEAR

Travel catalogs specialize in useful items that can **save space when packing** and make life on the road more convenient. Compact alarm clocks, travel irons, travel wallets, and personal-care kits are among the most common items you'll find. They also carry dual-voltage appliances, currency converters and foreign-language phrase books. Some catalogs even carry miniature coffeemakers and water purifiers.

# U

## U.S.

### GOVERNMENT

The U.S. government can be an excellent source of travel information. Some of this is free and some is available for a nominal charge. When planning your trip, **find out what government materials are available.** For just a couple of dollars, you can get a variety of publications from the Consumer Information Center in Pueblo, Colorado. Free consumer information is also available from individual government agencies, such as the Department of Transportation or the U.S. Customs Service. For specific titles, see the appropriate publications entry in Important Contacts A to Z, *above*.

# W

### WHEN TO GO

The Caribbean high season has traditionally been winter, usually extending from December 15 to April 14. This is when northern weather is at its worst, not necessarily when Caribbean weather is at its best. In fact, winter is when the Caribbean is at its windiest. It's also the most fashionable, the most expensive, and the most popular time to visit, and most hotels are heavily booked. You have to make your reservations at least two or three months in advance for the very best places (and sometimes a year in advance for the most exclusive spots). Hotel prices drop 20%–50% for summer (after April 15); cruise prices also fall. Saving money isn't the only reason to visit the Caribbean during the off-season. Temperatures are only a few degrees warmer, and more and more hotels and restaurants are staying open year-round, so things aren't as dead-quiet as they used to be. September, October, and November are least crowded, but hotel facilities can be limited and some restaurants may be closed. Singles in search of partners should visit in high season or in summer, or choose a resort with a high year-round occupancy rate.

The flamboyant flowering trees are at their height in summer, and so are most of the flowers and shrubs of the West Indies. The water is clearer for snorkeling, and smoother for sailing in the Virgin Islands and the Grenadines, in May, June, and July. Generally speaking, there's more planned entertainment in winter. The peak of local excitement on many islands, most notably Trinidad, St. Vincent, and the French West Indies, is Carnival.

**THE GOLD GUIDE / SMART TRAVEL TIPS**

## CLIMATE

The Caribbean climate is fairly constant. Average year-round temperature for the region is 78°F–85°F. The extremes of temperature are 65°F low, 95°F high, but as everyone knows, it's the humidity, not the heat, that makes you suffer, especially when the two go hand in hand. You can count on downtown shopping areas being hot at midday any time of the year, but air-conditioning provides some respite. Stay near beaches, where water and trade winds can keep you cool, and shop early or late in the day.

High places can be cool, particularly when the Christmas winds hit Caribbean peaks (they come in late November and last through January). Since most Caribbean islands are mountainous (notable exceptions being the Caymans, Aruba, Bonaire, and Curaçao), the altitude always offers an escape from the latitude. Kingston (Jamaica), Port-of-Spain (Trinidad), and Fort-de-France (Martinique) swelter in summer; climb 1,000 feet or so and everything is fine.

Hurricanes occasionally sweep through the Caribbean in fall, and officials on many islands are not well equipped to warn locals, much less tourists. Check the news daily, and keep abreast of brewing tropical storms by reading Stateside papers if you can get them. The rainy season, usually in fall, consists mostly of brief showers interspersed with sunshine. You can watch the clouds come over, feel the rain, and remain on your lounge chair for the sun to dry you off. A spell of overcast days is "unusual," as everyone will tell you.

# 1 Destination: Caribbean

# THE MANY FACES OF THE ISLANDS

F YOU HAVE SEEN ONE ISLAND you have by no means seen them all. Tiny 5-square-mile Saba has less in common with the vast 19,000-square-mile Dominican Republic than Butte, Montana, has with Biloxi, Mississippi. Butte and Biloxi, however different in terrain and traits, sit in the same country and the citizenry speak more or less the same language. Saba, which is Dutch, and the Dominican Republic, whose roots are in Spain, simply sit in the same sea.

The Caribbean has towering volcanic islands, such as Saba; islands with forests, such as Dominica and Guadeloupe; and some islands, notably Puerto Rico, that have both rain forests and deserts. Glittering discos, casinos, and dazzling nightlife can be found on such islands as Aruba and the Dominican Republic, and throughout the region there are isolated cays with only sand, sea, sun, lizards, and mosquitoes. Some islands, St. Kitts among them, have ancient forts to view, while Puerto Rico and the Caicos Islands have caverns and caves to explore. There are also places like Grand Turk, where the only notable sights to see are beneath the translucent sea.

Different though they are in many ways, the islands are stylistically similar. The style-setter is the tropical climate. Year-round summertime temperatures and a plethora of beaches produce a pace that's known as "island time." Only the trade winds move swiftly. Operating on island time means, "I'll get to it when the spirit moves me."

Similarities are also attributable to the history of the region. The Arawaks paddled up from South America and populated the islands more than 1,000 years ago. In the early 14th century, the cannibalistic Caribs, who gave the area its name, arrived, probably from Brazil or Venezuela, then polished off the peaceful Arawaks and managed, for a time at least, to scare the living daylights out of the Europeans who sailed through in search of gold. (The original name of the Caribs was Galibi, a word the Spanish corrupted to *Canibal*—the origin of the word "can-

nibal.") Christopher Columbus made four voyages through the region between 1492 and 1504, christening the islands while dodging the Carib arrows. He landed on or sailed past all of the Greater Antilles and virtually all of the eastern Caribbean islands.

From the 16th century until the early 19th century, the Dutch, Danes, Swedes, English, French, Irish, and Spanish fought bitterly for control of the islands. Some islands have almost as many battle sites as sand flies. Having gained control of the islands and annihilated the Caribs, the Europeans established vast sugar plantations and brought in Africans to work the fields. With the abolition of slavery in the mid-19th century, Asians were imported as indentured laborers. Today, the Caribbean population is a rich gumbo of nationalities, including Americans and Canadians who have retired to and invested in the islands.

It must be remembered that the Caribbean, like the European continent, is made up of individual countries, each with customs, immigration officials, and, in some instances, political difficulties. Most of the islands have opted for independence; others retain their ties to the mother country. They are developing nations, and many have severe economic and unemployment problems.

Virtually all of the islands depend upon tourism. And, human nature being what it is, many islanders resent their dependency on tourist dollars. Like as not, the person who serves you has stood in a long line, vying with other anxious applicants for the few available jobs. After serving your meals and cleaning your luxurious room, he or she returns to a tiny shack knowing full well that in less than a week you will have shelled out more than an islander makes in a month.

Some visitors object to encountering resentment, when all they seek is a pleasant vacation and they've paid dearly for it. Some feel rather keenly that they'd always like hot water—or at least *some* water—when they turn on the shower; in even the most luxurious resorts there are times when things simply don't work, and that's a fact of Caribbean life. And other visitors simply have no patience with island time.

On the other hand, there are those who travel to the Caribbean year after year. Some return to the same hotel on the same beach on the same island, while the more adventurous try to sample as much as this smorgasbord has to offer.

# WHAT'S WHERE

## Finding Your Own Place in the Sun

The Caribbean Sea, an area of more than a million square miles, stretches south of Florida down to the coast of Venezuela. In the northern Caribbean are the **Greater Antilles**—the islands closest to the United States—composed of Cuba, Jamaica, Haiti, the Dominican Republic, and Puerto Rico. (Haiti and Cuba are not included in this book.) The **Cayman Islands** lie south of Cuba. The **Lesser Antilles**—greater in number but smaller in size than the Greater Antilles—are divided into three groups: the **Leewards** and the **Windwards** in the eastern Caribbean, and the islands in the **southern Caribbean**. The eastern Caribbean islands, from the Virgin Islands in the north all the way south to Grenada, form an arc between the Atlantic Ocean and the Caribbean Sea. Islands in the Leeward chain in order of appearance are the U.S. and British Virgin Islands, Anguilla, St. Martin/St. Maarten, St. Barthélemy, Saba, St. Eustatius, St. Kitts, Nevis, Barbuda, Antigua, Montserrat, Guadeloupe, and Dominica; the Windwards are composed of Martinique, St. Lucia, St. Vincent and the Grenadines, and Grenada. Barbados is just east of this group. In the southern Caribbean, off the coast of Venezuela, Trinidad and Tobago are anchored in the east, while Aruba, Bonaire, and Curaçao (known as the ABC Islands) bathe in the western waters. The **Turks and Caicos Islands,** which lie in the Atlantic Ocean between Florida and the north coast of Hispaniola (Haiti and the Dominican Republic), are part of the Bahamas but are included in this book because of their proximity to and affinity with the Caribbean islands.

# PLEASURES AND PASTIMES

Here are some suggestions on where to go for some of the Caribbean's major pleasures. Consult the Island Finder chart on the following pages to help you choose your destination.

## Boating and Sailing

Whether you charter a yacht with crew or captain a boat yourself, the waters of the Caribbean are excellent for sailing, and the many secluded bays and inlets provide ideal spots to drop anchor and picnic or explore. The marinas on Tortola in the **British Virgin Islands, St. Vincent and the Grenadines,** St. Thomas in the **U.S. Virgin Islands,** and Port la Royale and Oyster Pond in **St. Martin** are the starting points for some of the Caribbean's finest sailing. Yachtsmen also favor the waters around **Antigua** and put in regularly at Nelson's Dockyard, which hosts a colorful regatta in late April or early May.

## Casinos and Nightlife

You can flirt with Lady Luck until the wee small hours in the dazzling casinos of Santo Domingo, **Dominican Republic**; San Juan, **Puerto Rico; St. Maarten;** and **Curaçao. Aruba** is loaded with lively night places, and San Juan's glittering floor shows are legendary. The merengue, born in the **Dominican Republic,** is exuberantly danced everywhere on the island, as is salsa on Puerto Rico. Both **Guadeloupe** and **Martinique** claim to have begun the beguine, and on both islands it is danced with great gusto, although the *zouk* (all-night revelry) is now the rage. The Legislature of **St. Croix** approved six casino hotels in 1995 in hopes of jumpstarting the economy. When builidng will begin is anybody's guess, but insiders expect action by 1997.

## Cuisine

The cuisine on **Martinique** and **Guadeloupe** is a marvelous marriage of Creole cooking and classic French dishes; you'll find much of the same on the other French islands of **St. Martin** and **St. Barts.** You'll also find a fine selection of French wines in the French West Indies. **Grenada,** the spice island, has an abundance of seafood and an incredible variety of fruits and vegetables.

## Island Finder

| | Cost of Island | Number of rooms* | Nonstop flights | Cruise ship port | U.S. dollars accepted | Historic sites | Natural beauty | Lush | Arid | Mountainous | Rain forest | Beautiful beaches | Good roads |
|---|---|---|---|---|---|---|---|---|---|---|---|---|---|
| Anguilla | $$$ | 978 | | | • | | | | • | | | • | |
| Antigua & Barbuda | $$$$ | 3317 | • | • | • | • | • | | • | | • | • | |
| Aruba | $$ | 6150 | • | • | • | | • | | • | | | • | • |
| Barbados | $$ | 5580 | • | • | • | • | | | | | | • | • |
| Bonaire | $$ | 803 | • | | • | | | | | | | • | |
| British Virgin Islands | $$$ | 1224 | | • | • | | • | | | • | • | • | |
| Cayman Islands | $$$$ | 3453 | • | • | • | | | | | • | | • | • |
| Curaçao | $$ | 2200 | • | • | • | • | | | | | | • | |
| Dominica | $ | 757 | | | | | • | • | | • | • | | |
| Dominican Republic | $ | 28,000 | • | | | • | | • | | • | | • | |
| The Grenadines | $ | 500 | | | | | | | | • | • | • | |
| Grenada | $$$ | 1428 | | • | • | • | • | • | | • | • | • | |
| Guadeloupe | $$ | 7798 | | • | • | • | • | • | | • | • | • | |
| Jamaica | $$$ | 18,935 | • | • | • | | • | • | | • | • | • | |
| Martinique | $$$ | 6960 | • | • | | | • | • | | • | • | • | |
| Montserrat | $$ | 710 | | • | • | | • | • | | • | • | | |
| Nevis | $$$ | 400 | | | • | • | • | • | | • | | • | |
| Puerto Rico | $ | 8581 | • | • | • | • | • | • | • | • | • | • | • |
| Saba | $ | 138 | | • | | | • | | | • | | • | |
| St. Barthélemy | $$$$ | 715 | | • | • | | • | | | • | | • | • |
| St. Eustatius | $ | 83 | | • | | • | | | | • | • | | |
| St. Kitts | $$ | 1200 | | • | | | • | • | | • | • | • | |
| St. Lucia | $$ | 2919 | • | • | • | | • | • | | • | • | | |
| St. Martin/St. Maarten | $$$ | 5300 | • | • | • | | | • | | • | | • | • |
| St. Vincent | $$ | 730 | | • | • | • | • | • | | • | • | | |
| Trinidad | $ | 1462 | • | | | | | | | | • | | |
| Tobago | $$ | 1500 | • | | | | | | | • | • | • | |
| Turks and Caicos | $$$ | 1139 | • | | • | | | | • | | | • | |
| U.S. Virgin Islands: | | | | | | | | | | | | | |
| St. Croix | $$ | 1142 | | • | • | • | | • | | • | | • | |
| St. John | $$ | 763 | | • | • | | • | | | • | | • | • |
| St. Thomas | $$ | 3217 | • | • | • | | | | | • | | • | • |

* Figures based on 1995 estimates

| Public transportation | Fine dining | Local cuisine | Shopping | Music | Casinos | Nightlife | Diving and Snorkeling | Sailing | Golfing | Hiking | Ecotourism | Villa rentals | All-inclusives | Campgrounds | Luxury resorts | Secluded getaway | Good for families | Romantic hideaway |
|---|---|---|---|---|---|---|---|---|---|---|---|---|---|---|---|---|---|---|
|  | ● | ● | ● | ● |  |  | ● |  |  |  |  | ● | ● |  | ● | ● |  | ● |
| ● | ● | ● | ● |  | ● | ● | ● | ● | ● |  |  |  | ● |  | ● |  | ● |  |
| ● | ● | ● | ● | ● | ● | ● | ● | ● | ● | ● |  |  | ● |  | ● |  |  | ● |
| ● | ● | ● | ● | ● |  | ● | ● | ● | ● |  |  | ● | ● |  | ● |  |  |  |
|  |  |  |  |  | ● |  | ● | ● | ● | ● | ● |  |  |  |  |  |  |  |
| ● | ● | ● | ● | ● |  | ● | ● | ● | ● |  |  | ● | ● |  | ● |  |  | ● |
|  | ● | ● | ● |  |  | ● | ● | ● |  | ● |  | ● | ● |  | ● |  | ● |  |
| ● | ● | ● |  |  |  | ● | ● | ● | ● |  |  | ● |  |  |  |  | ● |  |
|  |  | ● |  |  |  |  | ● |  |  | ● | ● |  |  |  |  | ● |  | ● |
| ● |  | ● |  |  |  |  | ● |  |  | ● | ● | ● | ● |  | ● |  |  |  |
|  |  | ● |  |  |  |  | ● | ● |  | ● |  |  | ● |  | ● | ● |  | ● |
| ● | ● | ● | ● | ● |  | ● | ● | ● | ● | ● | ● | ● | ● |  | ● | ● | ● | ● |
| ● | ● | ● | ● |  |  | ● | ● | ● | ● | ● | ● | ● |  | ● | ● | ● |  |  |
| ● | ● | ● | ● | ● | ● | ● | ● | ● | ● | ● | ● | ● | ● | ● | ● | ● | ● | ● |
| ● | ● | ● | ● | ● | ● | ● | ● | ● | ● | ● | ● | ● |  | ● | ● |  |  | ● |
| ● | ● | ● |  |  |  |  |  |  |  |  |  |  |  |  |  | ● | ● |  |
|  |  |  |  | ● |  |  |  |  |  |  |  |  |  |  | ● |  |  |  |
| ● | ● | ● | ● |  | ● | ● | ● | ● |  |  | ● | ● | ● | ● | ● | ● | ● | ● |
|  |  | ● |  |  |  |  | ● |  |  | ● | ● | ● |  |  | ● | ● |  | ● |
|  | ● | ● | ● |  |  | ● | ● | ● |  |  |  | ● |  |  |  | ● |  | ● |
|  |  | ● |  |  |  |  | ● |  | ● |  | ● |  |  |  |  | ● |  |  |
|  | ● | ● |  | ● |  | ● | ● | ● | ● | ● | ● | ● |  | ● | ● | ● | ● | ● |
| ● | ● | ● | ● |  | ● | ● | ● | ● | ● | ● | ● |  | ● |  | ● |  | ● | ● |
| ● |  | ● |  | ● |  |  | ● | ● |  | ● | ● |  |  |  | ● | ● | ● | ● |
| ● |  | ● |  | ● |  | ● | ● | ● |  |  |  |  |  |  | ● |  | ● | ● |
|  |  | ● |  | ● |  | ● | ● |  | ● |  |  |  |  |  |  | ● |  |  |
|  |  |  |  |  |  |  | ● | ● |  | ● | ● |  | ● |  | ● |  |  | ● |
|  |  |  |  |  |  |  |  |  |  |  |  |  |  |  |  |  |  |  |
|  |  |  |  |  |  |  |  |  |  |  |  |  |  |  |  |  |  |  |
| ● | ● | ● | ● |  |  | ● | ● |  |  | ● | ● | ● |  |  | ● |  |  |  |
|  | ● | ● |  |  |  |  | ● |  |  | ● | ● | ● |  | ● | ● | ● | ● | ● |
| ● | ● | ● | ● |  |  | ● | ● | ● | ● |  |  | ● | ● |  | ● |  |  |  |

## Diving

Jacques Cousteau named Pigeon Island, off the west coast of **Guadeloupe,** one of the 10 best dive sites in the world. The Wall off Grand Turk in the **Turks and Caicos Islands** is a sheer drop of 7,000 feet and has long been known by scuba divers. The eruption of **Martinique'**s Mt. Pelée at 8 AM on May 8, 1902, resulted in the sinking of several ships. **St. Eustatius** boasts an undersea "supermarket" of ships, as well as entire 18th-century warehouses, somewhat the worse for wear, below the surface of Oranjestad Bay. The waters surrounding all three of the **Cayman Islands** are acclaimed by experts, who also make pilgrimages to **Bonaire'**s 86 spectacular sites. **Tortola** is famous in diving circles for the wreck of the RMS *Rhone.* **Tobago** has a great array of unspoiled coral reefs, and it's the only place in the Caribbean that divers can regularly sight huge manta rays. **Saba** has some of the best advanced diving with its Marine Park and deep dive sites.

## Pointers

While scuba (which stands for self-contained underwater breathing apparatus) looks and is surprisingly simple, *call your physician before your vacation and make sure that you have no condition that should prevent you from diving!* A full checkup is an excellent idea, especially if you're over 30. Since it can be dangerous to travel on a plane after diving, you should schedule both your diving courses and travel plans accordingly.

Learning to dive with a reputable instructor is also a must. In addition to training you how to resurface slowly enough, a qualified instructor can teach you to read "dive tables," the charts that calculate how long you can safely stay at certain depths.

Many resorts offer short courses consisting of two to three hours of instruction on land and time in a swimming pool or waist-deep water to get used to the mouthpiece and hose (known as the regulator) and the mask. A shallow 20-foot dive from a boat or beach, supervised by the instructor, follows.

Successful completion of this introductory course may prompt you to do further coursework to earn a certification card— often called a C-card—from one of the major accredited diving organizations: NAUI (National Association of Underwater Instructors), CMAS (Confederation Mondiale des Activités Subaquatiques, which translates into World Underwater Federation), NASE (National Association of Scuba Educators), or PADI (Professional Association of Diving Instructors). PADI offers a free list of training facilities (☞ Diving *in* Important Contacts A to Z.

## Foreign Culture

AFRICAN➤ **Trinidad** moves with the rhythm of calypso and is the stomping ground of a flat-out, freewheeling Carnival that rivals the pre-Lenten celebrations in Rio and New Orleans. The Trinidadians, whose African heritage has been augmented by many Asian races, have built up one of the most prosperous commercial centers in the Caribbean. Haiti was once another option. (It's now politically volatile and is not covered in this book.)

BRITISH➤ **St. Kitts** is known as the Mother Colony of the West Indies; it was from here that British colonists were dispatched in the 17th century to settle Antigua, Barbuda, Tortola, and Montserrat. If you're a history buff, you won't want to miss Nelson's Dockyard at **Antigua**'s English Harbour or the hunkering fortress of Brimstone Hill on St. Kitts. Sports fans who understand the intricacies of cricket can watch matches between **Nevis** and St. Kitts teams. And the waters around Antigua and the **British Virgin Islands** are a mecca for serious sailors. **Barbados,** with its lovely tradewinds, has cricket, horseracing at Garrison Savannah, and rugby. A British colony from 1627, the island gained independence in 1966.

DUTCH➤ **Saba, St. Eustatius, St. Maarten, Bonaire,** and **Curaçao** all fly the Dutch flag, but there the similarity ends. Saba is a tiny volcanic island known for its beauty, its friendly inhabitants, and its gingerbread-trimmed houses. Curaçao's colorful waterfront shops and restaurants are reminiscent of Amsterdam. Quiet St. Eustatius—affectionately called Statia—has well-preserved historical sites and is famed for being the first foreign nation to salute the new American flag in 1776. The main streets of Philipsburg, the capital of St. Maarten, are lined with colorful Dutch colonial buildings replete with fretwork and verandas. Bonaire is best known for its excellent scuba diving.

FRENCH> **Martinique, Guadeloupe, St. Martin,** and **St. Barthélemy** (often called St. Barts or St. Barths) compose the French West Indies. The language, the currency, the cuisine (the most imaginative in the Caribbean), the culture, and the style are très French. St. Barts is the quietest, Martinique the liveliest, St. Martin the friendliest, and Guadeloupe the lushest. And as an extra added attraction, you can wing over from Guadeloupe to see what life is like on the nearby islands of Les Saintes, Marie Galante, and Désirade.

SPANISH> In the **Dominican Republic,** which occupies the eastern two-thirds of the island of Hispaniola, the language and culture are decidedly Spanish. The Colonial Zone of Santo Domingo is the site of the oldest city in the Western Hemisphere, and its restored buildings reflect the 15th-century Columbus period. One also gets a sense of the past in **Puerto Rico**'s Old San Juan, with its narrow cobblestone streets and filigreed iron balconies.

## Getting Away from It All

If you're looking to back out of the fast lane, you can park at one of the secluded, spartan mountain lodges on **Dominica,** which is one of the friendliest islands in the Caribbean. Or opt for the quiet grandeur of a renovated sugar plantation on **Nevis,** where you can feast in an elegant dining room or enjoy a barbecue on the beach. Tranquil **Anguilla,** with soft white beaches nudged by incredibly clear water, offers posh resorts as well as small, inexpensive, locally owned lodgings. From the low-key **Turks and Caicos Islands,** which lie in stunning blue-green waters, you can boat to more than a score of isolated cays to which even the term "low-key" would imply too fast a pace. **St. Kitts** is another peaceful green oasis, with lovely beaches and upscale, "great house" accommodations in the bargain. **St. Lucia** offers a plethora of places, from the simple to the simply elegant, for "liming" (we call it "hanging out"), the favorite local pastime. On tiny **Saba** there is little to do but tuck into a small guest house, admire the lush beauty of the island, and chat with the friendly Sabans. Nearby **St. Eustatius** is another friendly, laid-back island, as is **Montserrat. St. Vincent and the Grenadines** offer three tiny, private-island luxury resorts: Young Island, Palm Island, and Petit St. Vincent.

## Golf

According to those who have played it, the course at Casa de Campo in the **Dominican Republic** is one of the best in the Caribbean. The course at the Four Seasons Resort on **Nevis** is also challenging (and breathtaking). Golfers on St. Thomas, **U.S. Virgin Islands,** play the spectacular Mahogany Run. There are superb courses in **Puerto Rico,** including four shared by the Hyatt Dorado Beach and the Hyatt Regency Cerromar Beach. **Jamaica** has 10 courses, including top-rated Tryall near Montego Bay, and the new Negril Hills Golf Club. Golf is second only to cricket in **Barbados**; the Royal Westmoreland Golf Club opened its first 18 holes for the 1996 season; another nine holes are under way. The **Cayman Islands** now have an 18-hole championship golf course, The Links at Safehaven, and **Aruba** has its first 18-hole course, Robert Trent Jones–designed Tierra del Sol.

## History

**Antigua**'s well-preserved Nelson's Dockyard is a must for history aficionados. The ancient colonial zones of both Santo Domingo, **Dominican Republic,** and Old San Juan, **Puerto Rico,** should also be high on your "history" list. The Historical Society in **St. Eustatius** (Statia) publishes an excellent walking tour. Brimstone Hill on **St. Kitts** is a well-maintained fortress with several museums full of military memorabilia. **Nevis** has many sugar mills restored as comfortable hotels. Port Royal, outside Kingston, **Jamaica,** was a pirates' stronghold until an earthquake shook things up in 1692.

## Luxury Resorts

A wealth of posh resorts awaits those who seek comfort in the lap of luxury. **Anguilla,** rapidly becoming one of the Caribbean's most popular destinations, has the dazzling Malliouhana and the Moroccan-style Cap Juluca. **Antigua**'s elegant Curtain Bluff has a long list of well-heeled repeat guests. The Four Seasons resort on **Nevis** combines European elegance, state-of-the-art sports facilities, and Caribbean casualness. On **Jamaica** there's the well-established Half Moon Club, Montego Bay. **Puerto Rico**'s El Conquistador Resort and Country Club, with five individual hotels, is a luxurious world unto itself. On French **St. Martin,** La Samanna draws the rich and not-so-famous.

For the ultimate in luxurious privacy, the **British Virgin Islands** has exclusive Necker Island, a 74-acre private island with elegant accommodations. Intimate Le Toiny on **St. Barts** draws worldly personalities. And Caneel Bay resort on **St. John, U.S. Virgin Islands,** has seven beaches and takes up 170 acres inside the Virgin Islands National Park boundaries.

## Music

Calypso was born in **Trinidad; Jamaica** is the home of reggae; the **Dominican Republic** gave the world the merengue; and both **Martinique** and **Guadeloupe** claim to be the cradle of the beguine. The music of **Barbados** ranges from that heard during the Crop-Over Festival (mid-July–early August) to the hottest jazz. Salsa reigns in **Puerto Rico.** Steel drums, limbo dancers, and jump-ups are ubiquitous in the Caribbean. Jump-up? Simple. You hear the music, jump up, and dance.

## Nature

**Dominica,** laced with rivers and streams, is a ruggedly beautiful island with arguably the lushest, most untamed vegetation in the Caribbean. **Puerto Rico**'s luxuriant 28,000-acre El Yunque is the only rain forest in the U.S. forestry system. Little **Saba** is awash with giant vegetation, and the island's Mt. Scenery is justly named. **Guadeloupe**'s 74,000-square-acre Natural Park boasts dramatic waterfalls, cool pools, and miles of hiking trails. Majestic Mt. Pelée, a not entirely dormant volcano, towers over **Martinique**'s rain forest; on **St. Eustatius,** adventurers can crawl down into a jungle cradled within a volcanic crater; and on **St. Lucia** you can drive right into a volcano.

## Snorkeling

Snorkeling requires no special skills, and most hotels that rent equipment have a staff member or, at the very least, a booklet offering instruction in snorkeling basics.

As with any water sport, it's never a good idea to snorkel alone, especially if you're out of shape. You don't have to be a great swimmer to snorkel, but occasionally currents come up that require stamina. The four dimensions as we know them seem altered underwater. Time seems to slow and stand still, so wear a water-resistant watch and let someone on land know when to expect you back.

Remember that taking souvenirs—shells, pieces of coral, interesting rocks—is forbidden. Many reefs are legally protected marine parks, where removal of living shells is prohibited because it upsets the ecology.

## Snuba

Not quite ready for scuba diving? Not to worry. For those kept from diving by poor health or claustrophobia, there is snuba, a combination of snorkeling and scuba diving. The snuba system consists of an inflatable raft that supports a tank of compressed air and a 20-foot air hose for one or two persons. The raft not only warns boats of your presence, but also provides a convenient resting place when you're tired. (There is even a clear window in the raft so you can still have an underwater view while taking a break.) The rental cost is approximately $45 an hour, and it takes only about an hour to become a certified snuba user.

## Sunbathing

Just plain basking is one of the great pleasures of a Caribbean vacation, but before abandoning yourself to the tropics, you would be well advised to take precautions against the ravages of its equatorial sun. Be sure to use a sunscreen with a sun-protection factor, or SPF, of at least 15; if you're engaging in water sports, be sure the sunscreen is waterproof. At this latitude, the safest hours for sunbathing are 4–6 PM, but even then it is wise to limit exposure during your first few days to 15–20 minutes. Keep your system plied with fruit juices and water, and avoid coffee, tea, and alcohol.

## Swimming

The calm, leeward, Caribbean side of most islands has the safest and most popular beaches for swimming. There are no big waves, there is little undertow, and the salt water—which buoys the swimmer or snorkeler—makes staying afloat almost effortless.

The windward, or Atlantic, side of the islands, however, is a different story: Even strong, experienced swimmers should exercise caution here. The ocean waves are powerful and can be dangerous; unseen currents, strong undertows, and uneven, rocky bottoms may scuttle the novice. Some beaches post signs or flags daily to alert swimmers to water conditions. Pay attention to them! Where there are no flags, stick to wading and sunbathing.

Few beaches or pools in the Caribbean—even those at the best hotels—are protected by lifeguards, so you and your children swim at your own risk.

## Waterskiing

Some large hotels have their own water-skiing concessions, with special boats, equipment, and instructors. Many beaches (especially those in Barbados), however, are patrolled by private individuals who own boats and several sizes of skis; they will offer their services through a hotel or directly to vacationers or can be hailed like taxis. Ask your hotel staff or other guests about their experiences with these entrepreneurs. Be *sure* they provide life vests and at least two people in the boat: one to drive and one to watch the skier at all times.

## Windsurfing

Windsurfing is as strenuous as it is exciting, so it may not be the sport to try on your first day out, unless you're already in excellent shape. Always windsurf with someone else around who can go for help if necessary.

# NEW AND NOTEWORTHY

A decade ago some Caribbean islands put more emphasis on tourism than others did. St. Maarten and the Virgin Islands actively sought tourists, while St. Lucia relied on its banana crop and Guadeloupe on sugarcane for revenue. Now, however, the scramble for tourists and the dollars they bring is fast becoming the primary focus of all the Caribbean islands.

Although the competition for tourists hasn't led to lower prices—in fact, some governments have been increasing tourist taxes to pay for advertising—it has created more travel options. New hotels open all the time, old hotels are renovated, and ways to get to and from the islands are multiplying.

Airline service to and from the Caribbean is expanding. **American Airlines** now covers most of the islands with either direct flights from the mainland or with connecting flights through San Juan on its subsidiary, American Eagle. American also has plans to build its own wing at the **Donald Sangster International Airport** in Montego Bay, Jamaica, although construction had not begun by press time. **ALM**, the Antillean airline, is also becoming a major carrier to many of the islands, with departures from Atlanta and Miami as well as interisland flights. Renovations of Trinidad's **Piarco Airport** have been completed, and Tobago has started direct air service from the United States via **BWIA.** Changes in the customs area of the **Las Américas International Airport** in the Dominican Republic may succeed in reducing baggage problems and keeping taxi hustlers at bay. Dominica has a new cruise-ship dock, making it twice as accessible to travelers.

Anyone who has driven on **St. Lucia** will be pleased to know that the West Coast road has opened between Castries and Soufrière. It still winds through the mountains, with hairpin turns and fabulous vistas—but so far, it is pothole-free.

Hotel and resort development continues with megaresorts in the ABC's, including Aruba's big **Aruba Marriott Resort & Stellaris Casino** and Bonaire's **Harbour Village Beach Resort,** with a new spa that opened and a golf course and casino on the horizon. In Puerto Rico, the **Wyndham Old San Juan Hotel and Casino** is scheduled to open in late 1996 as is the newly renovated **Gran Hotel El Convento.** The **Horned Dorset Primavera** plans to establish a second boutique hotel in a historic house in Old San Juan. The Grand Cayman **Westin Casuarina Resort** opened in December 1995 and is one of the few hotels there actually on the beach. Meanwhile, on Jamaica, Superclubs has introduced **Breezes,** a line of moderately priced all-inclusive resorts, and they are popping up in towns across the island.

# FODOR'S CHOICE

## Beaches

★ **Shoal Bay, Anguilla.** This 2-mile L-shape beach of talcum-powder-soft white sand may get crowded, but that's only because it's one of the prettiest in the Caribbean.

⭐**Green Cay, British Virgin Islands.** Sail to this little piece of heaven, off the shore of Jost Van Dyke, and pretend you were shipwrecked (while you drink a rum punch). There's absolutely nothing here, just intensely blue water, a couple of palm trees, and soft white sand.

⭐**Seven Mile Beach, Grand Cayman.** It's actually 5½ miles of powdery white sand, litter- and peddler-free, and headquarters for the island's water sports concessions.

⭐**Grand Anse Beach, Grenada.** Clear, gentle surf laps the gleaming sand of this 2-mile beach. To the north, you can see the narrow mouth of St. George's Harbour and the pastel houses, with their fish-scale tile rooftops, that climb the surrounding hillsides.

⭐**Negril, Jamaica.** Although it's no longer untouched by development, this 7-mile stretch of sand is still a beachcomber's Eden. Nude beach areas are found along sections where no hotel or resort has been built.

⭐**Macaroni Beach, Mustique.** Surfy swimming (be careful!), powdery white sand, a few palm huts and picnic tables, and very few people are the draws here.

⭐**Anse du Gouverneur, St. Barthélemy.** This beautiful, secluded spot offers good snorkeling and views of St. Kitts, Saba, and St. Eustatius.

## Diving/Snorkeling

⭐**Reefs around Bonaire.** An enormous range of coral, parrotfish, surgeon fish, angelfish, eels, snappers, and grouper are just some of the creatures you may see in the Bonaire Marine Park. The park encompasses the entire coastline around Bonaire and Klein Bonaire and includes more than 80 dive sites.

⭐**Wreck of the *Rhone*, British Virgin Islands.** A Royal Mail Ship sunk by a hurricane in 1867, and still well preserved, makes for magnificent diving.

⭐**Stingray City, Cayman Islands.** These islands are a diver's paradise, and this is one of their most unique sites. Dozens of unusually tame stingrays swim and twist around divers in the shallow waters.

⭐**Scotts Head, Dominica.** Dramatic underwater walls and sudden drops line the coast here.

⭐**Saba's Marine Park.** Encircling the entire island, the marine park features submerged pinnacles of land (at about the 70-foot depth mark), where all kinds of sea creatures rendezvous.

⭐**Turks and Caicos Island's reefs.** More than 200 square miles of reefs surround these islands.

## Hotels

⭐**Cap Juluca, Anguilla.** This spectacular 179-acre resort wraps around the edge of Maunday's Bay and almost 2 miles of sugary white-sand beach. $$$$

⭐**Curtain Bluff, Antigua.** The setting is breathtaking—high on a bluff between the wild Atlantic and calm Caribbean. The ambience is pure country-club elegance. $$$$

⭐**Hyatt Regency Aruba Resort & Casino, Aruba.** With central public areas styled after a Spanish grandee's villa, this is the top-flight luxury resort on the island. $$$$

⭐**Sandy Lane Hotel, Barbados.** Rooms are nothing short of spectacular, bathrooms are vast and luxurious, the beach is one of the best on the island, and the staff treats you like royalty. $$$$

⭐**Biras Creek, Virgin Gorda, British Virgin Islands.** A former guest bought this resort and completely renovated it, from building a new kitchen to lining the beach with magnificent palm trees; it's now a spectacular hideaway. $$$$

⭐**Spice Island Inn, Grenada.** The spacious suites, fabulous bathrooms, and private plunge pools or in-room whirlpools are great, but it's actually the location right on beautiful Grand Anse Beach that steals the show. $$$$

⭐**Sans Souci Lido, Jamaica.** As if the decorative luxury of this pastel cliffside palace weren't enough, a free spa session is also offered. $$$$

⭐**Habitation Lagrange, Martinique.** Experience the old-world charms of Martinique's plantation house society at this beautiful 19th-century manor house. The restaurant also boasts one of the best chefs on the island. $$$$

★**Four Seasons, Nevis.** This model chain property strikes just the right balance between posh and casual; it also boasts a superb Robert Trent Jones II–designed championship golf course, a fine family program, and the sensuous Pinney's Beach at your doorstep. $$$$

★**Horned Dorset Primavera, Puerto Rico.** The emphasis here is on privacy and relaxation. The pounding of the surf and the squawk of the resident parrot are the only sounds you'll here as you lounge on the beach. $$$$

★**The Golden Lemon, St. Kitts.** St. Kitts and its sister island are beloved by Caribbean aficionados for their impeccably restored plantation inns (and their often eccentric owners); Arther Leaman, a former design editor of *House and Garden,* has fashioned a jewel with an equally eclectic, international, refined decor and clientele. $$$$

★**Anse Chastanet Hotel, St. Lucia.** Rooms were designed to meld into the tropical mountainside, with louvered wooden walls open to stunning Piton and Caribbean vistas or to the deep shady green of the forest. $$$–$$$$

★**La Samanna, St. Martin.** This luxurious, secluded hotel overlooks the ravishing Baie Longue beach and offers accommodations that are perfect right down to their fresh flowers and potpourri. $$$$

★**Young Island, St. Vincent.** On its own private island a stone's throw from shore, these luxury cottages are halfway between Swiss Family Robinson's tree house and the Ritz. $$$$

★**Grace Bay Club, Providenciales, Turks and Caicos.** Enjoy the views from your suite of Grace Bay's stunning turquoise waters, and take advantage of the expertly pampering service. $$$

## Restaurants

★**Malliouhana, Anguilla.** Sparkling crystal and fine china, exquisite service, and a spectacularly romantic, candlelit, open-air setting are the perfect match for this restaurant's exceptional haute French cuisine. $$$$

★**Julian's, Antigua.** Everything about this cozy eatery is stylish, from the simple yet striking decor to the chef's sophisticated takes on traditional dishes. $$$

★**Gasparito Restaurant, Aruba.** Tasty local cuisine is served in the refined gallery atmosphere of an authentic country house. $$

★**Sandy Bay, Barbados.** Each morning a van is sent to scour the island for the freshest produce and seafood: The results—succulent grilled dolphin and lobster, lamb dressed with thyme and wild rosemary—are heavenly. $$$

★**Hemingway's, Grand Cayman.** Enjoy the breezes on Seven Mile Beach while sipping a Seven Mile Meltdown (dark rum, peach schnapps, pineapple juice, and fresh coconut) and savoring grouper stuffed with sweet corn and crab. $$–$$$

★**Château de Feuilles, Guadeloupe.** A bit of a trip, but velvety sea urchin pâté, kingfish fillet with vanilla, and pineapple flan are worth every mile. $$$

★**Le Fromager, Martinique.** From its perch above St-Pierre this beautiful restaurant offers views of the town's red roofs and the sea beyond, as well as delectable crayfish colombo, marinated octopus, and sole pecheur in a Creole sauce. $$

★**Carl Gustaf, St. Barthélemy.** Sweeping views of Gustavia harbor and delectable classic French cuisine with an island accent are the draws here. $$$$

★**Top Hat, St. Croix.** Both the wonderful Danish menu and the Danish owners are reminders of St. Croix's colonial past. Try the *frikadeller* (meatballs in a tangy sauce) and fried Camembert with ligonberries. $$$

★**The Royal Palm, St. Kitts.** Pamela Yahn studied her craft at the Culinary Institute of America, a hotbed of gastronomic subversion; her sublime food, a feast for the eye as well as the palate, deftly fuses classic preparations and indigenous ingredients, redefining the new Caribbean cuisine. $$$$

★**Chez Martine, St. Martin.** Chef Thierry de Launay studied under Joël Robuchon; his fois gras claims a loyal following. $$$$

⭐**Veni Mange, Trinidad.** Allyson Hennessey, a Cordon Bleu–trained chef with a local TV talk show, cooks up the best Creole lunches in town. *$$*

⭐**Anacaona, Providenciales, Turks and Caicos.** This is a true gourmet dining experience, minus the attitude. Traditional French recipes are combined with Caribbean fruits, vegetables, and spices. *$$–$$$*

⭐**Virgilio's, St. Thomas, U.S. Virgin Islands.** Come here for some of the best northern Italian cuisine in the islands, and don't leave without having a Virgilio's cappuccino, a chocolate-and-coffee drink so rich it's dessert. *$$$$*

# FESTIVALS AND SEASONAL EVENTS

Regardless of when Carnival season starts on each island, it always means days and nights of continuous partying. There's a celebration going on from January through August, it's just a matter of being on the right island.

The first Carnival of the season is also the longest. **Martinique**'s Carnival begins in early January and lasts through the first day of Lent, in mid-February. **Guadeloupe**'s Carnival starts a day later and also continues until Lent, finishing with a parade of floats and costumes on Mardi Gras and a huge bash on Ash Wednesday. **Curaçao**'s Carnival season lasts from late January to early February. All of these Carnivals feature music, dance, and a costumed parade.

February brings a flood of Carnival events, including those on **Bonaire, Dominica, Puerto Rico, St. Lucia, St. Martin** (the French side of the island), **St. Barthélemy,** and **Trinidad and Tobago,** all of which combine feasting, dancing, music, and parades. During Carnival on **Trinidad and Tobago,** adults and children alike are swept up in the excitement of Playing Mas'—the state of surrendering completely to the rapture of fantastic spectacle, parades, music, and dancing.

Spring brings the **St. Thomas (U.S. Virgin Islands)** and the **Sint Maarten** (Dutch side of the island) Carnivals in April and the **Cayman Islands'** Carnival, which

begins on Grand Cayman in May. In July, the season reaches **Saba** and the **Dominican Republic,** whose popular 10-day Merengue Festival features entertainment from outdoor bands and orchestras and the best cuisine from local hotel chefs. **Anguilla** and the **British Virgin Islands** start Carnival in early August with street dancing, calypso competitions, the Carnival Queen Coronation, and sumptuous beach barbecues. The **Turks and Caicos** islands finish the string of festivals during the last days of the month.

Many other festivals celebrate the islands' rich local cultures. Barbados's **Holetown Festival** commemorates the first settlement of Barbados on February 17, 1627, with a week of fairs, street markets, and revelry. The Historical and Cultural Foundations organize the **St. Martin Food Festival** in May. During the **Tobago Heritage Festival** in July, each village on Trinidad and Tobago mounts a different show or festivity. Beginning in July and continuing through August, Barbados celebrates the **Crop-Over Festival,** a monthlong cheer for the end of the sugarcane harvest. Calypsonians battle for the coveted Calypso Monarch award, and Bajan cooking abounds at the massive Bridgetown Market street fair. On a Sunday in early August, Guadeloupe holds a **Fête des Cuisinières** and celebrates the masters of Creole cuisine with a five-hour banquet that is

open to the public. The **Hatillo Festival of the Masks,** held in December in Puerto Rico, is a carnival featuring folk music and dancing, as well as parades in which islanders don brightly colored masks and costumes.

Sports enthusiasts, tourists, and islanders enjoy the many regattas. Grenada's **New Year Fiesta Yacht Race** in late January is highlighted by the Around Grenada sailing contest.

Antigua's **Sailing Week** in April brings together more than 300 yachts from around the world. The British Virgin Islands' **Spring Regatta,** the **Curaçao Regatta,** the **Grenada Easter Regatta,** and the U.S. Virgin Islands' **International Rolex Cup Regatta** take place in April. Boat racing is the national sport in Anguilla, and the most important competitions take place on **Anguilla Day,** May 30. Also in May, the St. Croix Yacht Club hosts the **Mumm's Cup Regatta.** Just about every type of competition that can be held on or in water constitutes the weeklong **Aqua Action Festival** held in St. Lucia at the end of June. Canoe racing, Sunfish sailing, windsurfing, sportfishing, waterskiing, and a non-mariners race are some of the main attractions. The British Virgin Islands host the **Hook In and Hold On Boardsailing Regatta** in June and July. In July, windsurfers from across the Caribbean gather at the **Caribbean Boardsailing Championships** in St. Thomas.

Martinique hosts the **Tour des Yoles Rondes** point-to-point yawl race in early August, and the annual **Sailing Regatta** in Bonaire takes place in October. The **Route du Rosé**, a transatlantic regatta of tall ships that set sail from St-Tropez in early November, is welcomed to St. Barts in December with a round of festivities. The **Thanksgiving Regatta** in St. John is a chance for local sailors to compete against each other, culminating in a celebration at Skinny Leg's Bar.

Music lovers should also take note of several other annual events. In January, St. Barthélemy is host to an international collection of soloists and musicians as part of the **Annual St. Barts Music Festival.** The **Barbados Caribbean Jazz Festival** in Bridgetown features performances of original compositions and traditional jazz for three days at the end of May. At the end of June, the **Aruba Jazz and Latin Music Festival** is held in Oranjestad, offering well-known entertainers performing Latin, pop, jazz, and salsa music at Mansur Stadium. And the **August Reggae Sunsplash International Music Festival** is getting hotter every year, as the best, brightest, and newest of the reggae stars gather to perform in open-air concerts in MoBay on Jamaica.

# 2 Anguilla

Updated by
Pamela
Acheson

**B**EACH LOVERS BECOME GIDDY when they first spot Anguilla (rhymes with vanilla) from the air and see the blindingly white sand and lustrous blue and aquamarine waters that rim this scrubby piece of land. The island's star attractions are its dozens and dozens of gorgeous, soft-sand beaches. An inspirational setting for sunbathers, the island also possesses exceptionally clear waters and coral reefs just offshore which mean good snorkeling can be found almost everywhere. If you don't like the sand, you won't find a lot to do here. There are no glittering casinos or nightclubs and no duty-free shops stuffed with irresistible buys (although you're only about 30 watery minutes away from the bustle of St. Martin/St. Maarten's resorts and casinos). Peace, quiet, and pampering account for the island's popularity among travelers searching for a Caribbean getaway. Times are slowly changing, however, and there are now six traffic lights on the island instead of the solitary signal of years past.

This is the most northerly of the Leeward Islands, lying between the Caribbean Sea and the Atlantic Ocean. Stretching from northeast to southwest, this dry, limestone isle is about 16 miles long and only 3 miles across at its widest point. The highest spot is 213 feet above sea level, and there are neither streams nor rivers, only saline ponds used for salt production. The island's name, a reflection of its shape, is most likely a derivative of *anguille,* which means "eel" in French. Archaeological evidence indicates that the island was inhabited as many as 2,000 years ago by the Arawak Indians who named the island Malliouhana, a more mellifluous title that's been adopted by some of the island's shops and resorts.

In 1631, the Dutch built a fort here, but no one has been able to locate its site. English settlers from St. Kitts colonized the island in 1650, and, except for a brief period of independence with St. Kitts–Nevis in the 1960s, Anguilla has remained a British colony ever since.

From the early 1800s various island units and federations were formed and disbanded, with Anguilla all the while simmering over its subordinate status and enforced union with St. Kitts. Anguillans twice petitioned for direct rule from Britain, and twice were ignored. In 1967, when St. Kitts, Nevis, and Anguilla became an associated state, the mouse roared, kicked St. Kitts policemen off the island, held a self-rule referendum, and for two years conducted its own affairs. A British "peacekeeping force" then parachuted down to the island, squelching Anguilla's designs for autonomy, but helping a team of royal engineers stationed there to improve the port and build roads and schools. Today Anguilla elects a House of Assembly and its own leader to handle internal affairs, while a British governor is responsible for public service, the police, and judiciary and external affairs.

The territory of Anguilla includes a few islets or cays, such as Scrub Island to the east, Dog Island, Prickly Pear Cays, Sandy Island, and Sombrero Island. The island's population numbers about 8,000, predominantly of African descent but also including descendants of Europeans, especially Irish. Historically, because the limestone land was hardly fit for agriculture, attempts at enslavement and colonization never lasted long; consequently Anguilla doesn't bear the scars of slavery found on so many Caribbean islands. Because the island couldn't be farmed successfully (although cotton was produced here for a while), Anguillans became experts at making a living from the sea and are known for their boatbuilding and fishing skills. Tourism is the growth industry of the island's stable economy, but the government is determined to keep expansion at a slow and cautious pace to protect the island's natural resources and beauty. New hotels—scattered throughout Anguilla—are being kept small, select, and casino-free. The island has chosen to emphasize its high-quality service, serene surroundings, and friendly people.

## Lodging

Anguilla has a wide range of accommodations. There are grand and sumptuous resorts, apartments and villas from the deluxe to the simple, and small, cozy, locally owned guest houses. Because Anguilla has so many beautiful and uncrowded beaches, it is not necessary (the way it is on some other islands) for beach lovers to choose a particular property because of its beach. If calling to reserve a room in a resort, be sure to inquire about special packages. Meal plans are available, but the particulars vary from resort to resort.

| CATEGORY | COST* |
|---|---|
| $$$$ | over $400 |
| $$$ | $275–$400 |
| $$ | $150–$275 |
| $ | under $150 |

*All prices are for a standard double room for two, excluding 8% tax and a service charge, which is typically 10%.*

### Hotels

**$$$$** ★ **Cap Juluca.** This spectacular 179-acre resort wraps around the edge of Maunday's Bay, encompassing almost 2 miles of sugary white-sand beach. Its sparkling white, Moorish-style, two-story villas with domes, arches, and turrets are some of the most luxurious and oversized accommodations in the Caribbean. Rooms are minimally but elegantly decorated, with Moroccan fabrics, Brazilian hardwood, and built-in, plumply cushioned seating areas. The immense bathrooms vary, but many lead out to private sunporches or gardens and two-person soaking tubs. At the end of the bay is Chatterton's, the hotel's casual Mediterranean-style grill, which overlooks the water and is open for lunch and dinner. Dinners are also served at the elegant adjoining restaurant, Pimms (☞ Dining, *below*). Well-organized tennis and water-sports programs are offered. ⊠ *Box 240, Maunday's Bay,* ☎ *809/497–6666, 809/497–6779, or 800/235–3505;* FAX *809/497–6617. 98 units, 7 private villas. 3 restaurants, bar, room service, pool, golf privileges at Mullet Bay Resort on St. Maarten (½ hr away by boat), putting green, 3 tennis courts, croquet, fitness center, water sports, boutique, library, VCRs and cassettes for rent, laundry service. AE, V. CP, MAP.*

**$$$$** ★ **Malliouhana.** This ultrasophisticated resort, Anguilla's classiest, sits on 25 lush tropical acres on a promontory that juts out between two exquisite beaches. The lobby entrance, boutique, restaurants, and bar are in a grand, multitiered, open-air building with tile floors and beautifully maintained mahogany walls. Accommodations are sleekly decorated, with white walls and tile floors, rattan furniture, and Haitian prints; marble bathrooms have oversize tubs. The restaurant is the most elegant on the island. Also, children will like the small beachfront playground. ⊠ *Box 173, Meads Bay,* ☎ *809/497–6111 or 800/372–1323,* FAX *809/497–6011. 20 doubles, 15 junior suites, 15 1-bedroom suites, 4 2-bedroom suites. Restaurant, bar, 3 pools, beauty salon, massage, 4 tennis courts, exercise room, water-sports center, drugstore, boutique, playground. No credit cards. EP, MAP.*

**$$$** ★ **Cinnamon Reef Beach Club.** Low-key luxury sets the tone at this small, appealing resort. Most of the whitewashed, split-level villas are nestled

# Anguilla

0 — 4 miles

0 — 6 km

N

Flat Cap Point

⑩ Little Bay
⑪
⑫
❸ The Valley
⑬ ❷ ⑨

Sandy Island
⑯ – ⑳
Road Bay
North Hill
Sandy Ground
⑭ Wallblake Airport
Sandy Ground ❶
⑮

Long Bay ㉑
㉒
㉓
Meads Bay ㉔
㉙ ㉚
㉛ ㉜
㉞ Little Harbour

Barnes Bay
Rendezvous Bay
㉘
Blowing Point Harbour
㉝

West End
Maunday's Bay
Cove Bay
㉕
㉖ ㉗

Anguillita Island
Shoal Bay West

**Exploring**
Crocus Hill Prison, **3**
Island Harbour, **4**
Sandy Ground, **1**
The Valley, **2**

**Dining**
Aquarium, **31**
Arlo's, **15**
Blanchard's, **21**
Cafe at Cove Castles, **25**
Casablanca, **26**
Cora's Pepperpot, **11**

Cross Roads, **10**
Ferryboat Inn, **33**
La Fontana, **8**
Hibernia, **5**
Johnno's, **17**
Koal Keel, **9**
Lucy's Harbour View Restaurant, **32**

Malliouhana, **23**
Old House, **14**
Palm Court, **34**
Paradise Cafe, **26**
Le Petit Patissier, **9**
Pimms, **27**
Pizzazz, **20**

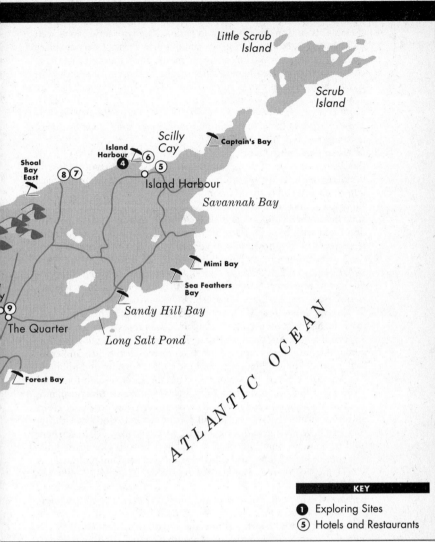

Little Scrub
Island

Scrub
Island

Scilly
Cay

Captain's Bay

Island
Harbour
**4**  **6**

**5**

Shoal
Bay
East

**8** **7**

Island Harbour

Savannah Bay

Mimi Bay

Sea Feathers
Bay

**9**

The Quarter

Sandy Hill Bay

Long Salt Pond

Forest Bay

ATLANTIC OCEAN

**KEY**

**1** Exploring Sites
**5** Hotels and Restaurants

Riviera Bar &
Restaurant, **16**
Roy's, **13**

**Lodging**
Arawak Beach
Resort, **6**
Cap Juluca, **27**
Cinnamon Reef Beach
Club, **34**
Ferryboat Inn, **33**
Fountain Beach, **8**

Frangipani Beach
Club, **24**
Inter-Island Hotel, **12**
Malliouhana, **23**
Mariners, **18**
Pineapple Beach
Club, **29**
Rendezvous Bay
Hotel, **30**

Shoal Bay Villas, **7**
La Sirena, **22**
Sonesta Beach
Resort, **28**
Syd-an's, **19**

among the palm trees along the narrow beach, while five are tucked on a bluff. Each casually decorated villa has a living room, raised bedroom, dressing room, sunken shower, and patio, along with little extras such as a hammock, built-in hair dryer, and minibar. This is a friendly place with a gracious staff and lots of repeat guests. The restaurant chefs have won a number of the Anguilla Chefs of the Year awards, and the Friday-night barbecue is an island favorite. Meal plans and packages are available. ✉ *Box 141, Little Harbour,* ☎ *809/497–2727 or 800/223–1108; in Canada, 416/485–8724;* ℻ *809/497–3727. 14 studios, 8 1-bedroom suites. Restaurant, lounge, room service, pool, 2 tennis courts, water sports. AE, MC, V. EP, MAP.*

$$$ ⊞ **Frangipani Beach Club.** This splashy, inviting spot on brilliant Meads
★   Bay beach consists of pink, multilevel, Spanish Mediterranean–style buildings with archways, stone balustrades, wrought-iron railings, and roofs of red clay tiles. Grounds are lushly landscaped with colorful tropical flowers and greenery. Each one-, two-, or three-bedroom suite has arched windows and exposed beam ceilings and is tastefully decorated with blond rattan furniture and colorful fabrics. All units have marble-tiled bathrooms and doors that open out to spacious terraces or balconies; many have full kitchens. ✉ *Box 328, Meads Bay,* ☎ *809/497–6442 or 800/892–4564. 8–24 units (varies depending on number of bedrooms being used by 1 unit), luxury penthouse. Restaurant, 2 bars, pool, water sports. AE. EP.*

$$$ ⊞ **Sonesta Beach Resort.** This pink and green Moorish beachside fantasia, formerly known as the Casablanca, was recently taken over by Sonesta Resorts. Although it's by far the gaudiest-looking hotel on Anguilla, the glitz of the architecture is tempered by the lush and carefully tended tropical plantings, and the staff is friendly and obliging. The way to reception, the restaurants, and the 1,200-square-foot pool is through a long, domed, open-air hallway of authentic Moroccan mosaics past a long reflecting pool. The rooms are done in pastel green and pink prints, pale green rattan furniture, and Moroccan throw rugs and have marble bathrooms with capacious tubs. The beach here used to be quite small, but is now sizable thanks to Hurricane Luis. The restaurant, which is still called Casablanca (☞ *Dining, below*), is excellent. ✉ *Box 444, Rendezvous Bay West,* ☎ *809/497–6999 or 800/766–3782,* ℻ *809/497–6899. 88 rooms and suites. 2 restaurants, bar, piano bar, pool, 2 tennis courts, health club, water sports, bicycles, shops, library. AE, D, MC, V. EP, BP, MAP.*

$$–$$$ ⊞ **Arawak Beach Resort.** Built on the site of an ancient Arawak village, this waterfront resort is one of the first in the Caribbean to showcase the Amerindian heritage of the region. Hexagonal, breezy, two-story villas are furnished with hand-carved replicas of Amerindian furniture. The restaurant serves Caribbean and Amerindian food, utilizing cassava, papaya, plantains, and other traditional island crops, some of which grow right in the restaurant's courtyard. A small museum displays artifacts uncovered during construction. In addition to the usual water sports, canoes are available. Although the hotel beach is not one of Anguilla's best, Scilly Cay and its beautiful beaches are just a minute away by launch. This is a no-smoking property, and alcoholic beverages are not served, although you may bring your own. ✉ *Box 98, Island Harbour,* ☎ *809/497–4888,* ℻ *809/497–4898. 10 rooms, 3 junior suites, 1 luxury suite. Restaurant, pool, water sports, museum, boutique. AE. EP.*

$$–$$$ ⊞ **Fountain Beach.** The family who owns this tiny, delightful property
★   along beautiful Shoal Bay is of Italian descent, and their heritage is evident in the resort's Mediterranean-style white stucco buildings. Each unit comes with a fully equipped kitchen, a large bathroom with an open sunken shower, and a view of the sea. Furnishings are rattan and

colorfully painted wicker, and Haitian art decorates the walls. Despite the long bumpy road to the hotel, guests from all over the island head to La Fontana (☞ Dining, *below*), the hotel's Italian restaurant, for dinner. ✉ *Box 474, Shoal Bay,* ☎ 📠 *809/497–3491. 10 1-bedroom suites, 2 junior suites. Restaurant, 2 pools, 2 tennis courts. AE, MC, V. EP, MAP. Closed Sept.*

**$$–$$$** 🏨 **Mariners.** Honeymooners and businesspeople on retreat make up much of the clientele of this popular casual resort. It's set at the far end of the beach at Sandy Ground, Anguilla's busiest stretch of sand, and is just a short stroll from a number of beach bars and restaurants. The pervasive West Indian style of the Mariners includes the charm of 19th-century gingerbread cottages, as well as the occasional annoyance of service that, while friendly, is so laid-back it verges on lackadaisical. Accommodations vary considerably in size and price range, from deluxe two-bedroom, two-bath cottages with full kitchens to small rooms with twin beds, minibars, and shower baths. All units are light and airy, with tile floors, white rattan, and bright prints. Charter the resort's Boston whaler for picnics, snorkeling, and fishing trips. The Thursday-night barbecue and Saturday West Indian night in the beachfront restaurant are popular island events. ✉ *Box 139, Sandy Ground,* ☎ *809/497–2815, 809/497–2671, or 800/223–0079;* 📠 *809/497–2901. 32 1-bedroom suites, 35 studios. 2 restaurants, 2 bars, pool, hot tub, tennis court, water sports, boutique, laundry service. AE, MC, V. EP, MAP, FAP, all-inclusive (drinks not included).*

**$$–$$$** 🏨 **Pineapple Beach Club.** Rooms here are in white West Indian–style bungalows strung along the edge of Rendezvous Bay, one of Anguilla's longest beaches. From a chaise on your charming veranda, the view of the ocean is framed by vine-covered trellises and gingerbread trim. Most bungalows have five rooms and each room has mahogany furnishings, hand-embroidered linens, a huge tile shower, and ceiling fans (no air-conditioning). ✉ *Box 157, Rendezvous Bay,* ☎ *809/497–6061 or 800/223–0079,* 📠 *809/497–6019. 27 rooms. Restaurant, pool, gym, water sports, gallery/boutique. AE, MC, V. All-inclusive.*

**$$–$$$** 🏨 **Shoal Bay Villas.** This small condominium hotel is tucked in a grove of palm trees on 2 miles of splendid sand. Units are brightly decorated in pink and blue, with painted rattan furniture; all but the poolside doubles have fully equipped kitchens. There's no air-conditioning, but all rooms have ceiling fans. The Reefside Beach Bar is an informal open-air restaurant open for breakfast, lunch, and dinner. All water sports can be arranged, and meal and room packages can be tailored to fit your needs. Children are not allowed during the winter. ✉ *Box 81, Shoal Bay,* ☎ *809/497–2051 or 800/722–7045; in NY, 212/535–9530; in Canada, 416/283–2621;* 📠 *809/497–3631. 2 studios, 2 2-bedroom units, 7 1-bedroom units, 2 poolside doubles. Restaurant, bar, pool. AE, MC, V. EP, BP, MAP.*

**$$**
★ 🏨 **La Sirena.** You'll find one of the island's best values at this personable, well-run hotel set among tropical greenery overlooking Meads Bay. La Sirena doesn't have the chic elegance of Malliouhana, but it lets you stay just down the beach for about a third of the cost. Choose one of the five spacious villas or one of the 20 guest rooms. Buildings are white stucco with red tile roofs and lots of balconies and terraces. The interior decor is typical Caribbean—rattan furniture and pastel-printed fabrics. Rooms are cooled by ceiling fans. The restaurant, which serves a variety of French and Caribbean cuisine, is on the second floor and open to the sea breezes. ✉ *Box 200, Meads Bay,* ☎ *809/497–6827 or 800/331–9358; in NY, 212/251–1800;* 📠 *809/497–6829. 20 rooms, 5 villas. Restaurant, bar, picnic supplies, 2 pools, snorkeling equipment, car rental. AE, MC, V. EP, MAP.*

**$–$$**  🏨 **Rendezvous Bay Hotel.** Opened in 1972, Anguilla's first resort sits amid 60 acres of coconut groves on the fine white sand of Rendezvous Bay, just a mile from the ferry dock. The main building is simple and rather undecorated and has a breezy, broad front patio. Owner Jeremiah Gumb has turned the lounge into a showcase for his elaborate electric train set, complete with tunnels and multiple tracks. The original guest rooms are about 100 yards from the beach and are quite spare, with one double and one single bed, a private shower bath, Haitian art on the walls, and ceiling fans (no air-conditioning). Much newer two-story villas along the shore contain spacious, air-conditioned, one-bedroom suites with refrigerators or kitchenettes. These are decorated with natural wicker and pastel prints and can be joined to form larger suites. There's a wide sand beach and also a rocky stretch of coast that is great for snorkeling. ✉ *Box 31, Rendezvous Bay,* ☎ *809/497–6549; in the U.S., 908/738–0246 or 800/274–4893; in Canada, 800/468–0023;* FAX *809/497–6026. 20 rooms, 24 1-bedroom villa suites. Restaurant, lounge, 2 tennis courts, water sports, game and TV room. AE, MC, V. EP, MAP.*

**$**  🏨 **Ferryboat Inn.** The spacious apartments at this small family-run complex are a bargain. Each is simply decorated with white or pastel fabrics and has a full kitchen, dining area, cable TV, and ceiling fans. It's on a small beach and just a short walk from the ferry dock. The two-bedroom beach house is air-conditioned. All rooms and the open-air restaurant look out across the water toward hilly, more-populated St. Martin, which is gorgeous at night with its host of sparkling lights. ✉ *Box 189, Blowing Point,* ☎ *809/497–6613,* FAX *809/497–3309. 6 1- and 2-bedroom apartments, 1 beach house (air-conditioned). Restaurant, bar. AE, MC, V. EP.*

**$**  🏨 **Inter-Island Hotel.** Rooms and two small one-bedroom apartments at this modest establishment are simply furnished with wicker and rattan. There is no air-conditioning, but some rooms have a breezy open balcony. Most rooms have refrigerators and all have cramped shower bathrooms that define the term "water closet." The homey restaurant serves hearty breakfasts and offers heaping servings at its West Indian dinners. The nearest beach is a two-minute drive away. ✉ *Box 194, The Valley,* ☎ *809/497–6259 or 800/223–9815; in Canada, 800/468–0023;* FAX *809/497–5381. 12 rooms, 2 1-bedroom apartments. Restaurant, bar, TV lounge, transportation to beach ½ mi away. AE, D, MC, V. EP.*

**$**  🏨 **Syd-an's.** These pleasant, clean efficiencies are a true bargain. Each has a kitchenette and shower bath and is comfortably furnished. Road Bay, with all its bustling activity, is just across the street. ✉ *Sandy Ground,* ☎ *809/497–3180,* FAX *809/497–2332. 6 studios. Gift shop. AE, MC, V. EP.*

## Villas and Condominiums

The tourist office has a complete listing of vacation rentals. You can also contact **Sunshine Villas** (✉ Box 142, Blowing Point, ☎ 809/497–6149, FAX 809/497–6021), the **Anguilla Connection** (✉ Island Harbour, ☎ 809/497–4403, FAX 809/497–4402), or **Select Villas of Anguilla** (✉ Box 256, George Hill, ☎ 809/497–5810, FAX 809/497–5811), all of which offer one- to three-bedroom houses for rent. Apartments for rent on the island are plentiful and well organized. The following are a selection.

**$$$$**  🏨 **Cove Castles Villa Resort.** These glistening white, futuristic sculp-
**★**    tures on one of Anguilla's prettiest beaches are actually luxuriously comfortable, very elegant and private apartments. Each is decorated with custom-made wicker furniture, raw silk cushions, and hand-embroidered sheets. Balconies are wide and secluded, and the kitchens are state-of-the-art. Some units are air-conditioned. ✉ *Box 248, Shoal Bay*

West, ☎ 809/497–6801 or 800/348–4716; in Canada, 800/468–
0023; FAX 809/497–6051. 4 3-bedroom villas, 8 2-bedroom villas.
Restaurant, tennis court, boutique. AE, MC, V.

$$$ 🏨 **Paradise Cove.** Two-story buildings rimmed with balconies and pa-
tios and set amidst beautiful tropical landscaping house this group of
luxury apartments. The units are spacious and charming and overlook
a large pool. It is a very short walk to quiet Cove Beach. One- and two-
bedroom units are furnished in rattan and wicker and decorated with
colorful tropical print fabrics. All have fully equipped kitchens and pri-
vate laundry facilities. Maid service and private cooks are available.
✉ Box 135, Cove Beach, ☎ 809/497–2259 or 800/553–4939,
FAX 809/497–2149. 14 units. Restaurant, pool bar, pool, croquet court,
boutique, playground. AE, MC, V.

$$$ 🏨 **Sea Grape Beach Club.** The attractive white stucco and red-tile-
roofed buildings of this complex on Meads Bay contain luxurious
2,000-square-foot, two-bedroom condominiums. A blue-trimmed arched
doorway in each unit leads to an airy common room, where enormous
windows offer spectacular views of the beach. Each condo has three
bathrooms, king-size beds, huge closets, and a very private deck. ✉ Box
65, The Valley, ☎ 809/497–6433 or 809/497–6541, FAX 809/497–6410.
6 condos. Restaurant, bar, water sports, satellite TV. AE, MC, V.

$$ 🏨 **Blue Waters.** These glistening white, Moorish-style buildings sit at
★ one end of a spectacular beach and are within walking distance of sev-
eral excellent restaurants. Sunny one- and two-bedroom units are ap-
pealingly decorated with pastel fabrics and have white tile floors,
separate dining areas, full kitchens, and comfortable balconies or ter-
races. ✉ Box 69, Shoal Bay West, ☎ 809/497–6292, FAX 809/497–
3309. 9 apartments. AE, MC, V.

$$ 🏨 **Easy Corner Villas.** These modest one-, two-, and three-bedroom
apartments are adequately furnished and have well-equipped kitchens
with microwaves. Only three of the units have air-conditioning. Number 10 is a deluxe two-bedroom villa. The location, on a bluff overlooking Road Bay, means you have to walk five minutes to the beach,
but the price is right. ✉ Box 65, South Hill, ☎ 809/497–6433 or
809/497–6541, FAX 809/497–6410. 10 units. AE, MC, V.

$$ 🏨 **Rainbow Reef.** Three seaside acres provide a dramatically beauti-
ful setting for this small group of villas. Each self-contained unit has
two bedrooms, a fully equipped kitchen, a spacious dining and living
area, and a large gallery overlooking the sea. A gazebo with beach fur-
niture and barbecue facilities is perched right above the beach. ✉ Box
130, Sea Feather Bay, ☎ 809/497–2817 or 708/325–2299. 4 villas.
No credit cards.

$$ 🏨 **Skiffles Villas.** These self-catering villas, perched on a hill overlooking
★ Road Bay, are usually booked a year in advance. The one-, two-, and
three-bedroom apartments have fully equipped kitchens, floor-to-ceiling windows, and pleasant porches. ✉ Box 82, Lower South Hill, ☎
809/497–6619, 219/642–4855, or 219/642–4445; FAX 809/495–6110.
5 units. Pool. No credit cards.

# Dining

Anguilla's eateries range from the truly elegant to down-home seaside
shacks. Most restaurants are open to the breezes and many have terraces where you can eat under the stars. Even very expensive restaurants can be in simple (although usually very well- decorated) open-air
structures. Call ahead—in the winter to make a reservation, and in the
late summer and fall to confirm if the place you've chosen is open. Restaurants not affiliated with a hotel often tack on an additional 5% to the
service charge if you pay by credit card.

## What to Wear

During the day, casual clothes are widely accepted: Shorts will probably be fine, although many establishments don't allow cover-ups over bathing suits. In the evening, shorts are acceptable at the extremely casual eateries; but elsewhere, sundresses or nice casual pants for women and long pants for men are appropriate. Some hotel restaurants expect a degree of formality and may have a jacket requirement in high season; ask when you make your reservation.

| CATEGORY | COST* |
|----------|-------|
| $$$$ | over $45 |
| $$$ | $35–$45 |
| $$ | $25–$35 |
| $ | under $25 |

*per person, excluding drinks, service, and 8% sales tax*

$$$$ ✕ **Cafe at Cove Castles.** Elegant, intimate dinners are served here overlooking beautiful Shoal Bay. Each season a new menu of consistently excellent dishes combines the best of Caribbean and French cooking. Past favorites include West Indian chicken stew, lobster medallions with ginger sauce, veal chops in truffle cream sauce, and fresh pasta with julienned vegetables. ⊠ *Shoal Bay West,* ☎ *809/497–6801. AE, MC. Closed Sept.–Nov. No lunch.*

$$$$ ✕ **Casablanca.** Multiarched ceilings covered with pastel Moroccan mosaics, and nighttime views of the lights of St. Martin twinkling across the water, lend an air of the dramatic to this favored dining spot. Grouper steamed with pepper and lime and served with cornmeal pancakes, Cornish hen roasted with almonds and raisins, and filet mignon with an onion and marsala compote are a few of the entrées found on the eclectic menu. Pistachio crème brûlée may sound a bit unorthodox, but it's the hit of the dessert list. ⊠ *Rendezvous Bay,* ☎ *809/497–6999. AE, MC, V.*

$$$$ ✕ **Malliouhana.** Sparkling crystal and fine china, exquisite service,
★ and a spectacularly romantic, candlelit, open-air setting are the perfect match for this restaurant's exceptional haute French cuisine. Michel Rostang, renowned for his Paris boîte, created the menu and is still the consulting chef. Try the goat cheese wrapped in fresh salmon or warm stewed lobster with pumpkin and French corn salad, then segue into lobster medallions with seasoned polenta or chicken breasts from Bresse stuffed with asparagus. Don't pass up desserts, especially the roast pear in Sauternes with walnut brioche and cinnamon ice cream. The wine cellar contains nearly 25,000 bottles. ⊠ *Meads Bay,* ☎ *809/497–6111. Reservations essential. AE, MC, V. Closed Sept.–Oct.*

$$$$ ✕ **Pimms.** You expect Rudolph Valentino to sweep in beneath the domes, arches, and billowing canvas of this Arabian Nights setting on the edge of a half-moon bay. Water laps almost unnervingly close to the outer tables, but from them you can see brightly colored tropical fish swim up for a spare bit of your roll. French chefs prepare picture-perfect plates of mostly Continental-style items with a touch of Creole or West Indian flavor. Entrées include grilled Black Angus sirloin and fresh lobster or grouper in a spicy tomato sauce. ⊠ *Cap Juluca, Maunday's Bay,* ☎ *809/497–6666. Reservations essential. AE, MC, V.*

$$$ ✕ **Blanchard's.** At restaurateurs Bob and Melinda Blanchard's popu-
★ lar spot, set amidst lush tropical greenery on beautiful Mead's Bay, your meal might include elements of Cajun, Caribbean, and Asian cooking. After a drink at the stunning mahogany-and-coral bar in the lounge, the green chili corn cakes, wild mushroom ragout, or Indonesian beef satay make good starters and can be followed by swordfish stuffed with leeks and fontina cheese or red snapper brushed with a balsamic mango glaze. Fish is the house specialty, but you can also order Black Angus

hand-cut steaks, free-range chicken, or one of the daily pasta specials. Desserts are tempting, especially the cappuccino brownies and a remarkable gingerbread box filled with warm bananas and cinnamon cream. There is also a 2,000-bottle wine cellar and a selection of fine Armagnacs and cognacs. ⊠ *Long Bay,* ☎ *809/497–6100. AE, MC, V. Closed Sun. No lunch.*

$$$ ✗ **Hibernia.** One of the island's most creative menus is served in this delightful wood-beamed cottage restaurant. Unorthodox yet delectable culinary pairings—inspired by French, Thai, Vietnamese, and Burmese dishes—include duck breast with grilled almonds and passion-fruit sauce, fricassee of lobster in mustard cinnamon sauce, and breast of chicken cooked with honey and mild chilies. There is also an unusual Thai-inspired bouillabaisse of assorted local seafood. For dessert, try the talked-about prunes in Armagnac chocolate sauce with homemade chestnut ice cream. ⊠ *Island Harbour,* ☎ *809/497–4290. AE, D, MC, V. Closed Mon.*

$$$ ✗ **Koal Keel.** This restaurant, in a restored 18th-century great house
★ that was once part of a sugar and cotton plantation, provides a nice contrast to the island's ubiquitous beachfront eateries. The dining room is furnished with richly upholstered period furniture, and the original handwrought stone walls are broken by window-size open spaces, creating a cool, breezy atmosphere. A replica of the house's original rock oven is used to bake fresh breads and to roast chickens and racks of lamb. The chefs make abundant use of local ingredients like fresh fish, mangoes, coconut, and pigeon peas and have dubbed their cuisine "EuroCaribe," reflected in such dishes as the Anguilla pea soup, lobster crepes, smoked grouper on a bed of leeks, and grilled breast of duck. ⊠ *The Valley,* ☎ *809/497–2930. Reservations essential in season. AE, MC, V. Closed Sept.–mid-Oct.*

$$$ ✗ **Palm Court.** This stylish eatery in the Cinnamon Reef Beach Club
★ is a long palm-lined corridor with red terra-cotta tile floors, Haitian furniture, a beautiful mural of the many varieties of local fish, and huge arched picture windows fronting the Caribbean. Frenchman Didier Rochat and Anguillan Vernon Hughes collaborate in the creation of an exciting nouvelle Caribbean menu. Char-grilled tuna with cinnamon tomato raisin sauce, queenfish roasted in phyllo and served with saffron cappellini, and swordfish steak in passion-fruit salsa are house specialties. The mango puffs in caramel sauce are justly famous. ⊠ *Cinnamon Beach Club, Little Harbour,* ☎ *809/497–2727. AE, MC, V. Closed mid-Sept.–mid-Oct.*

$$$ ✗ **Paradise Cafe.** Seductive aromas from the kitchen and the tinkling of wind chimes waft through this informal, breezy, beachfront restaurant overlooking Shoal Bay. The chef draws from French and Asian influences in the preparation of seafood, chicken, and beef. Among the standouts are West Indian bouillabaisse, rack of lamb in a Chinese black bean sauce, and rockfish fillet flash-fried in peanut oil and served with a sake and tamarind sauce. Hamburgers, salads, soups, and individual pizzas round out the lunch menu. ⊠ *Shoal Bay West,* ☎ *809/497–6010. AE, MC, V. Closed Mon.*

$$ ✗ **Ferryboat Inn.** Just a short walk from the Ferry Dock at Blowing
★ Point is this charming waterside restaurant. Tables are open to the breezes, and the nighttime view of St. Martin's glimmering lights lends a romantic atmosphere. The French onion and black bean soups, grilled lobster, lobster thermidor (the house specialty), and *entrecôte du vin au poivre* (a house version of steak au poivre with a red wine sauce) are all delicious. There are also veal and chicken dishes, hamburgers, and omelets. ⊠ *Cul de Sac Rd., Blowing Point,* ☎ *809/497–6613. AE, MC, V. No lunch Sun.*

**$$** ✕ **La Fontana.** Northern Italian dishes at this small restaurant have spicy island touches, thanks to the Rastafarian chef. Pasta possibilities include *fettuccine al limone* (with a sauce of black olives, lemon, parmesan, and butter), pasta with lobster and fresh herbs, and a daily Rasta pasta special, such as linguine with tomatoes and shrimp. Also on the menu are grilled duck, steak, fish, and chicken and a fantastic lobster dish cooked with black olives, capers, and tomatoes. ⊠ *Fountain Beach hotel, Shoal Bay,* ☎ *809/497–3492. AE, MC, V. Closed Wed. and Sept.*

**$$** ✕ **Lucy's Harbour View Restaurant.** A swinging gate forms the entrance to this terrace restaurant. Sweeping sea views and Lucy's delicious whole red snapper are the specialties here; curried and Creole dishes, such as conch and goat, are also favored selections. Be sure to try the sautéed potatoes (but be cautious with the table-side hot sauce!). A reggae band plays on Wednesday and Friday nights. ⊠ *South Hill,* ☎ *809/497–6253. No credit cards. Closed Sun.*

**$$** ✕ **Pizzazz.** Two Cape Cod restaurateurs opened this appealing spot on busy Sandy Ground (where Ripples used to be) and found immediate popularity. The menu features a variety of veal, seafood, chicken, and pasta dishes including fresh mussels and clams, osso buco, and lobster fra diavolo. The olive bread comes straight from their oven and is delicious. The intimate candlelit dining room also has the rare Anguillan distinction of being air-conditioned. ⊠ *Sandy Ground,* ☎ *809/497–2386. MC, V. No lunch.*

**$$** ✕ **Riviera Bar & Restaurant.** The chef here has created an unusual menu of French, Creole, and Asian specialties—French cheeses, homemade pâté, sushi, oysters sautéed in soy sauce and sake, and conch in a spicy Creole sauce are typical offerings. The grilled lobster and fish soup à la Provençale are highly recommended. There are also several prix fixe three-course selections. The beachside setting is relaxed and informal, and there's a very happy Happy Hour from 6 to 7 daily. Live bands play here frequently in season. ⊠ *Sandy Ground,* ☎ *809/497–2833. AE, V.*

**$–$$** ✕ **Arlo's.** This popular Italian restaurant, on a hilltop overlooking the
★ sea, serves the best pizza on the island. If you don't want pizza as a main course, share one as an appetizer, then choose from a list of entrées that includes spaghetti Bolognese, lasagna, tortellini du jour, various preparations of fettuccine, and veal or chicken parmigiana. There's always a nightly appetizer and entrée special. ⊠ *South Hill,* ☎ *809/497–6810. MC, V. Closed Sun. and Sept.–Oct. No lunch.*

**$–$$** ✕ **Old House.** Guests enjoy the relaxing atmosphere at this lovely
★ restaurant on a hill near the airport. Tables are covered with white and green tablecloths and are decorated with fresh flowers, even at breakfast, when regulars know to order the island fruit pancakes. For lunch or dinner try the conch simmered in lime juice and wine, curried local lamb with pigeon peas and rice, or Anguillan pot fish cooked in a sauce of limes, garlic, and tomatoes. ⊠ *George Hill,* ☎ *809/497–2228. AE, D, MC, V.*

**$** ✕ **Aquarium.** An upstairs terrace, the Aquarium is all gussied up with gingerbread trim, bright blue walls, and red tablecloths. For lunch, there are sandwiches and burgers. Stewed lobster, curried chicken, barbecued chicken, and mutton stew are offered at night. This is a popular spot with locals. ⊠ *South Hill,* ☎ *809/497–2720. No credit cards. Closed Tues. and Sun.*

**$** ✕ **Cora's Pepper Pot.** Cora Richardson's small eatery in the center of town serves some of the best rotis on the island. These Trinidadian specialties are made of boneless chicken, *tania* (a local vegetable), celery, pepper, onion, garlic, and peas, all wrapped in dough and baked. Dumpling dinners, lobster, whelk, and conch are also good choices. ⊠ *The Valley,* ☎ *809/497–2328. No credit cards.*

**$ ✕ Cross Roads.** Millie Philip's roadside bar is a great place to get a hearty breakfast. At lunch, seafood salads, fish, and chicken are served. ⊠ *Wallblake, The Valley,* ☎ *809/497–2581. No credit cards.*

**$ ✕ Johnno's.** Performances by the island band Dumpa and the AnvVibes make this *the* place to be on Sunday afternoons, but the grilled or barbecued lobster, kingfish, snapper (all of which Johnno catches himself), and chicken are good anytime. This is a classic Caribbean beach bar, attracting a funky eclectic mix, from locals to movie stars. ⊠ *Sandy Ground,* ☎ *809/497–2728. No credit cards.*

**$ ✕ Le Petit Patissier.** Espresso and cappuccino plus just-baked pastries, breads, and cakes are served from morning to night indoors or on the small balcony of this café above the well-known restaurant **Koal Keel** (☞ *above*). ⊠ *The Valley,* ☎ *809/497–2930. AE, MC, V. Closed Sept.–mid-Oct.*

**$ ✕ Roy's.** The dainty pink-and-white-covered deck belies the rowdy reputation of Roy and Mandy Bosson's pub, an Anguillan mainstay and one of the island's best buys. The menu's most popular items are Roy's fish-and-chips, cold English beer, pork fricassee, and a wonderful chocolate rum cake. Sunday's lunch special is roast beef and Yorkshire pudding. A faithful clientele gathers in the lively bar. ⊠ *Crocus Bay,* ☎ *809/497–2470. MC, V. Closed Mon. No lunch Sat.*

# Beaches

Renowned for their beauty, the dazzling white-sand beaches here are the best reason to come to Anguilla, and each one is different. You'll find long beaches that are great for walking, deserted beaches, and beaches lined with bars and restaurants, accompanied by surf ranging from wild to super-calm.

## Northeast Coast

**Captain's Bay** rewards you with peaceful isolation for making the grueling, four-wheel-drive-only trip along the inhospitable dirt road that leads to the northeastern end of the island toward Junk's Hole. The surf here slaps the sands with a vengeance, and the undertow is quite strong—wading is the safest water sport.

The mostly calm waters of **Island Harbour** are surrounded by a long, slender beach. For centuries Anguillans have put out from these sands in colorful, handmade fishing boats to seek the day's catch. There are several beach bars and restaurants, and this is the departure point for the three-minute boat ride to **Scilly Cay.** From this boat, you can get snorkeling equipment, but at times the waters are too rough to see much. A beach bar on Scilly Cay serves drinks and grilled seafood.·

## Northwest Coast

**Barnes Bay** is a superb spot for windsurfing and snorkeling. The elegant Coccoloba Plantation perches above and offers a poolside bar. In high season this beach can get a bit crowded with day-trippers from St. Martin.

At **Little Bay,** sheer cliffs embroidered with agave and creeping vines rise up behind a small gray-sand beach, usually accessible only by water (it's a favored spot for snorkeling and night dives). Virtually assured of total privacy, the hale and hearty can also clamber down the cliffs by rope to explore the caves and surrounding reef.

The clear blue waters of **Road Bay** beach are usually dotted with yachts. The Mariners resort, several restaurants, a water-sports center, and lots of windsurfing and waterskiing activity make this area (often referred to as Sandy Ground) an active and commercial one. It's a typical Caribbean scene daily, as fishermen set out in their boats and goats

ramble the littoral at will. The snorkeling is not very good here, but
the bay does specialize in glorious sunset vistas.

**Sandy Island,** nestled in coral reefs about 2 miles offshore from Road
Bay, first appears to be no more than a tiny speck of sand and a few
spindly palm trees. From the distance it has the look of a classic "deserted island," but it's got the modern-day comforts of a beach boutique, beach bar, and restaurant, and the use of snorkeling gear and
underwater cameras is free. There is a ferry that heads there every hour
from Sandy Ground.

### Southeast Coast
**Mimi Bay** is a difficult-to-reach, isolated, ½-mile-long beach east of Sea
Feathers Bay. The trip is worth it. When the surf is not too rough, the
barrier reef makes for great snorkeling.

Not far from Sea Feathers Bay is **Sandy Hill,** a base for fishermen. Here
you can buy fresh fish and lobster right off the boats and snorkel in the
warm waters. Don't plan to sunbathe—the beach is quite narrow here.

Unfortunately it's no longer a secret that **Shoal Bay East** (⌧ Shoal Bay,
via Shoal Bay Rd.) is one of the prettiest beaches in the Caribbean. But
this 2-mile L-shape beach of talcum-powder-soft white sand is definitely
still worth a visit. There are beach chairs, umbrellas, a backdrop of
sea-grape and coconut trees, and for seafood and tropical drinks there's
Trader Vic's, Uncle Ernie, and the Round Rock. Souvenir shops for T-
shirts, suntan lotion, and the like abound. There's good snorkeling in
the offshore coral reefs, and the water-sports center here can arrange
diving, sailing, and fishing trips.

### Southwest Coast
The good news and the bad news about **Cove Bay** is the same—it's virtually deserted. There are no restaurants or bars, just calm waters, coconut trees, and soft sand that stretches down to Maunday's Bay.

One of the most popular beaches, wide, mile-long **Maunday's Bay** is
known for good swimming and snorkeling; you can rent water-sports
gear at Tropical Watersports (☞ Water Sports, *below*). Try Pimms at
Cap Juluca for fine food and drink.

**Rendezvous Bay** is 1½ miles of pearl-white sand. Here the water is calm,
and there's a great view of St. Martin. The Pineapple Beach Club's open-
air beach bar is handy for snacks and frosty island drinks.

Adjacent to Maunday's Bay is **Shoal Bay West,** a dazzling beach with
several striking villa complexes, including the sculpturelike Cove Castles. Stop for lunch at the Paradise Cafe (☞ Dining, *above*), and ask
someone there to point out the best snorkeling spots. Beachcombers
may find lovely conch shells here.

## Outdoor Activities and Sports
### Cycling
There are plenty of flat stretches, making wheeling pretty easy. Bikes
can be rented from **Multiscenic Tours** (☎ 809/497–5810), which rents
mountain bikes at George Hill and the Blowing Point Ferry Terminal.

### Deep-Sea Fishing
Albacore, dolphin, and kingfish are among the sea creatures angled after
off Anguilla's shores. Trips can be arranged through **Sandy Island
Deep Sea Fishing** in Sandy Ground (☎ 809/497–6395); or you can
head to Sandy Ground and see which of the many locals who provide
trips is available. Fishing tackle, diving gear, and other sports equip-

ment is available at the **Tackle Box Sports Center** (⌂ The Valley, ☎ 809/497–2896).

## Diving
Seven sunken wrecks and a long barrier reef offer excellent diving opportunities. **Tamariain Watersports** (☎ 809/497–2020), the only full service dive operator on the island, is a PADI 5-Star Training Center.

## Fitness
Lest you go flabby lolling about on the beach, you'll find exercise equipment, aerobics, and martial arts instruction at **Highway Gym** (⌂ George Hill Rd., ☎ 809/497–2363).

## Horseback Riding
Ride English or Western at **El Rancho–Del Blues** (☎ 809/497–6164). Two rides are scheduled daily and both end with an afternoon swim at one of Anguilla's many fine beaches.

## Sea Excursions
Picnic, swimming, and diving excursions to Prickly Pear, Sandy Island, and Scilly Cay are available through **Sandy Island Enterprises** (☎ 809/497–6395). **Anguilla Sails Ltd.** (☎ 809/497–2253) offers day sails, sunset sails, and moonlight cruises. *Chocolat* (☎ 809/497–3394) is a 35-foot catamaran that is available for private charter and also has scheduled day, sunset, and evening excursions to various nearby cays. **BING!** (☎ 809/497–6395) specializes in day, evening, and overnight trips for two to four people in a 37-foot sailboat.

## Tennis
Peter Burwash International, highly respected for its tennis programs, manages several courts on the island, including those at Coccoloba Plantation, Malliouhana, and Cap Juluca. There are two lighted courts at **Coccoloba Plantation** (☎ 809/497–6871); two courts at the **Carimar Beach Club** (☎ 809/497–6881); four Laykold (hard) courts at **Malliouhana** (☎ 809/497–6111); three (hard) courts at **Cap Juluca** (☎ 809/497–6666); two Deco Turf tournament courts at **Cinnamon Reef** (☎ 809/497–2727); two courts at the **Fountain Beach and Tennis Club** (☎ 809/497–6395) and **Rendezvous Bay** (☎ 809/497–6549); and a single tennis court at **Cove Castles** (☎ 809/497–6801), the **Mariners** (☎ 809/497–2671), **Sea Grape** (☎ 809/497–6433), and **Spindrift Apartments** (☎ 809/497–4164).

## Water Sports
The major resorts offer complimentary Windsurfers, paddleboats, and water skis to their guests. If your hotel has no water-sports facilities, you can get in gear at **Tamariain Watersports** (☎ 809/497–2020). Tamariain Watersports also has PADI instructors, short resort courses, and more than a dozen dive sites; also, *Sundancer,* Tamariain's 30-foot powerboat, is available for charters. **Tropical Watersports** (☎ 809/497–6666) rents Sunfish and Hobie Cats. Sailboats and speedboats can be rented at **Sandy Island Enterprises** (☎ 809/497–6395).

# Shopping

Shopping tips can be found in the informative free publications *Anguilla Life* and *What We Do in Anguilla,* but you have to be a truly dedicated shopper to peel yourself off the beach and poke around in Anguilla's few shops. For a better selection, catch the ferry to Marigot on St. Martin and spend the day in chic boutiques showcasing the latest in Italian and French fashion. For local arts and crafts, many artists will hold open studios in addition to showing their work in the shops listed below; the tourist office can provide brochures.

## Good Buys

### CLOTHES

**Beach Stuff** (⊠ Back St., South Hill, ☎ 809/497–6814), in its brightly painted building, attracts the younger crowd with bathing suits and cover-ups, sunglasses, T-shirts, and other sportswear.

**Boutique at Malliouhana** (⊠ Meads Bay, ☎ 809/497–6111) is the most upscale shop on Anguilla, selling such designer specialties as jewelry by Oro De Sol, La Perla swimwear, Go Silk resort wear, and Robert LaRoche sunglasses.

**Caribbean Fancy** (⊠ George Hill Rd., ☎ 809/497–3133) features cotton resort wear and also sells books, coffees and spices, and gift items.

**Caribbean Style** (⊠ Rendezvous Bay, ☎ 809/497–6717) has a small but eclectic collection of everything from sandals to jewelry to furniture.

**Java Wraps** (⊠ George Hill Rd., ☎ 809/497–5497), a small outpost of the Caribbean chain, carries superb batik clothing for the whole family.

**Objets D'Art Collectibles** (⊠ Warden's Place, The Valley, ☎ 809/497–2787) is a gallery that also sells "wearable art," sandals, jewelry, and fabrics.

**Oluwakemi's Afrocentric Boutique** (⊠ Lansome Rd., The Valley, ☎ 809/497–5411) sells books, sandals, umbrellas, jewelry, T-shirts, hats, and a variety of other garments. You can also choose from an array of fabrics and have virtually any item of apparel custom-made.

**La Romana** (⊠ Meads Bay, ☎ 809/497–6181), a miniversion of the well-known international specialty boutique, is the place to go for swimwear, Fendi fashions and fine luggage.

**La Sirena Boutique** (⊠ Meads Bay, ☎ 809/467–6827) is bursting with colorful dresses, slacks, belts, and other accessories.

**Sunshine Shop** (⊠ South Hill, ☎ 809/497–6964) stocks cotton *pareos* (Polynesian-style wraps), silk-screen items, cotton resort wear, and hand-painted Haitian wood items.

**Valley Gap** (⊠ Shoal Bay Beach, ☎ 809/497–2754) sells a selection of local crafts, plus T-shirts and swimwear.

**Vanhelle Boutique** (⊠ Sandy Ground, ☎ 809/497–2965) is a little shop with an appealing selection of gift items, as well as Brazilian swimsuits for men and women.

**Whispers** (⊠ Cap Juluca, ☎ 809/497–6666) carries Caribbean handcrafts and stylish resort wear for men and women.

### FOOD TO GO

If you plan to picnic (on the beach or in your room), try the **Fat Cat** (⊠ George Hill, ☎ 809/497–2307), for escargots to go, as well as takeout quiche, soups, chili, chicken, and conch dishes.

**Amy's Bakery** (⊠ Blowing Point, ☎ 809/497–6775) turns out homemade pies, cakes, tarts, cookies, and breads.

### LOCAL ARTS AND CRAFTS

**Alicea's Place** (⊠ The Quarter, ☎ 809/497–3540), a small boutique, sells locally made ceramics and pottery and lifelike wooden flowers from Bali.

**Anguilla Arts and Crafts Center** (⊠ The Valley, ☎ 809/497–2200) carries a wide selection of island crafts.

**Cheddie's Carving Shop** (⊠ The Cove, ☎ 809/497–6027), just down the road from Coccoloba Plantation, showcases Cheddie's own fanciful creatures crafted out of wonderfully textured woods, including mahogany, walnut, and driftwood. Even the whimsically carved desk and balustrade in his studio testify to his vivid imagination.

**Devonish Cotton Gin Art Gallery** (⊠ The Valley, ☎ 809/497–2949) purveys the wood, stone, and clay creations of Courtney Devonish, an internationally known potter and sculptor, as well as works by other prominent local artists.

**Michéle R. Lavalette Art Studio** (✉ North Hill, ☎ 809/497–5668) displays original oils, pastels, and watercolors.

**Mother Weme** (✉ The Valley, ☎ 809/497–4504) is an internationally known artist who paints charming montages of Anguillan and general Caribbean life, incorporating homes, churches, marketplaces, and people. Call for an appointment.

**New World Gallery** (✉ The Valley, ☎ 809/407–5950) has frequent exhibits of local art and sells artwork, jewelry, textiles, and antiquities.

**Scruples Gift Shop** (✉ Social Security Bldg., ☎ 809/497–2800) offers simple gift items such as shells, handmade baskets, wood dolls, hand-crocheted mats, lace tablecloths, and bedspreads.

## Nightlife

Most of the major hotels feature some kind of live entertainment almost nightly in season. A Calypso combo plays most nights at **Cinnamon Reef Beach Club** (✉ Little Harbour, ☎ 809/497–2727). The **Mariners** (✉ Sandy Ground, ☎ 809/497–2815 or 809/497–2671) has regularly scheduled Thursday-night barbecues and Saturday-night West Indian parties, both with live entertainment by local groups. During high season, **Pimms** and **Chatterton's** (✉ Cap Juluca, ☎ 809/497–6666) have live music at dinner. Things are pretty loose and lively at **Johnno's** beach bar (☎ 809/497–2728) in Sandy Ground, which has live music and alfresco dancing Wednesday and Saturday nights and Sunday afternoons, when it feels as if the entire island population is in attendance. **Dragon's Disco** (✉ South Hill, no phone) is a hot spot on weekends after midnight. For soft dance music after a meal, go to **Lucy's Palm Palm** (☎ 809/497–2253) at Sandy Ground; there is usually a live band on Tuesday and Friday evenings. **Uncle Ernie's** (✉ Shoal Bay, no phone) often has music and a lively crowd heads here almost every night. **Round Rock** (✉ Shoal Bay, ☎ 809/497–2076) is a popular nightspot. At **Smitty's** (✉ Island Harbour, ☎ 809/497–4300) the crowd swings all day and well into the night. Be on the lookout for **Bankie Banx,** Anguilla's own reggae superstar. He has his own group called New Generations. If you're lucky, you'll catch him playing solo at **Malliouhana** (✉ Meads Bay, ☎ 809/497–6111) during cocktail hours. He's a true talent—no electronics, just a remarkable voice and great guitar playing. Other local groups include Keith Gumbs and the Mellow Tones, Spraka, Megaforce, Joe and the Invaders, Dumpa and the AnvVibes, and Sleepy and the All-Stars, a string-and-scratch band. Steel Vibrations, a pan band, often entertains at barbecues and West Indian evenings. The **Mayoumba Folkloric Theater,** a group made up of the best performers in the Anguilla Choral Circle, performs song-and-dance skits depicting Antillean and Caribbean culture with African drums and a string band. They appear every Thursday night at **La Sirena** (✉ Meads Bay, ☎ 809/497–6827).

## Exploring Anguilla

Exploring on Anguilla is mostly about checking out the spectacular beaches and classy resorts. There are only a few roads on the island, and none of them are marked, so it's fairly easy to get lost your first time out. Having a map, and checking it frequently against passing landmarks, is essential. If you didn't get a map at the airport, the ferry dock, or your hotel, head to the tourist office in The Valley (☞ Visitor Information, *below*).

*Numbers in the margin correspond to points of interest on the Anguilla map.*

SIGHTS TO SEE

❸ **Crocus Hill Prison.** On the highest point in Anguilla—213 feet above sea level—the historical building is pretty much in ruin, but the view is outstanding. ⊠ *Valley Rd. at Crocus Hill.*

❹ **Island Harbour.** Anguillans have been fishing for centuries in the brightly painted, simple, handcrafted fishing boats that line this shore. It's hard to believe, but skillful pilots take these little boats out to sea as far as 50 or 60 miles. Late afternoon is the best time to see the day's catch—piles of wriggling lobster and local fish. ⊠ *Island Harbour, at northwest end of island, facing Island Harbour Bay.*

The **Amerindian Mini-Museum** showcases a small display of objects used by the Arawak Indians that inhabited Anguilla centuries ago. There is also a 4-by-8-foot oil painting suggesting what Big Springs, a nearby Amerindian ceremonial ground, might have looked like when Amerindians still lived there. ⊠ *Arawak Beach Resort, Island Harbour,* ☎ *809/497–4888.*

❶ **Sandy Ground.** By far the most active and most developed of the island's beaches, almost everyone who comes to Anguilla stops by here at least one afternoon or evening. Little open-air bars and restaurants line the shore and there are several little boutiques, a dive shop, and a small commercial pier. This is where you catch the ferry for tiny **Sandy Island,** which is just 2 miles offshore. Not far from Sandy Ground, at South Hill, is the **Road Methodist Church.** An excellent example of skillful island stonework can be found in the walls of this charming little building, which also has some colorful stained-glass windows.

❷ **The Valley.** A number of Anguillan administrative offices, banks, markets, and a few boutiques, guest houses, and eateries are located here, as well as some historic sites.

For many years the cotton that was grown on Anguilla and imported to England was ginned in the **Old Factory,** a beautiful historic building that is now the home of the Cotton Gin Art Gallery. Much of the original ginning machinery is intact and on display here.

On Wallblake Road, just north of the roundabout, is **Wallblake House,** a plantation house built in 1787 by Will Blake (Wallblake is probably a corruption of his name). High living, invasions by the French in 1796, and legends of murders pervade the atmosphere here. Now owned and actively used by the Catholic Church, the estate has spacious rooms, with ceilings edged with handsome carving. On the grounds are an ancient vaulted stone cistern and an outbuilding called the Bakery (which wasn't used for bread making at all but for baking turkeys and hams). Call Father John (☎ 809/497–2405) to make an appointment to tour the plantation.

**Warden's Place,** a former sugar plantation great house, was built in the 1790s and is one of the two oldest buildings on Anguilla. Now the location of the Koal Keel restaurant, for many years it served as the residence of the chief administrator of the island, who also doubled as the only medical practitioner! The building is a fine example of island stonework.

# Anguilla A to Z

## Arriving and Departing

### BY BOAT

Ferryboats run frequently between Anguilla and St. Martin. They leave from Blowing Point on Anguilla every half hour from 7:30 to 5 and from Marigot on St. Martin every half hour from 8 to 5:30. There are also evening ferries that leave from Blowing Point at 6 and 9:15 and from Marigot at 7 and 10:45. You pay the $9 one-way fare ($11 evenings) on board and a $2 departure tax before boarding. Don't buy a round-trip ticket, because it restricts you to the boat on which it is purchased. On very windy days the 20-minute trip can be bouncy, and if you suffer from motion sickness, you may want medication. An information booth outside the customs shed in Blowing Point is usually open daily from 8:30 to 5, but sometimes the attendant wanders off.

### FROM THE DOCKS

Taxis are always waiting to pick passengers up at the Blowing Point landing. It costs $12 to get to the Malliouhana Hotel, $15 to the Cap Juluca Hotel, and $17 to the most distant hotels.

### BY PLANE

**American Airlines** (☎ 800/433–7300) is the major airline with non-stop flights from the continental United States to its hub in San Juan, from which the airline's **American Eagle** flies three times daily (twice daily off-season) to Anguilla. **Windward Islands Airways** (Winair; ☎ 809/775–0183) wings in daily from St. Thomas and at least three times a day from St. Maarten's Juliana Airport. **LIAT** (☎ 809/465–2286) comes in from Antigua, Nevis, St. Kitts, St. Maarten, and St. Thomas. **Air Anguilla** (☎ 809/497–2643) offers several flights daily from St. Maarten, the U.S. Virgin Islands, and the British Virgin Islands and provides air-taxi service on request from neighboring islands. **Tyden Air** (☎ 809/497–2719) has scheduled flights four times a week to both St. Thomas and St. Kitts from Anguilla and offers charter day trips to many neighboring islands.

### FROM THE AIRPORT

At **Wallblake Airport** you'll find taxis lined up to meet the planes. A trip from the airport to Sandy Ground will cost about $8, to west-end resorts between $14 and $20.

## Currency

Legal tender here is the Eastern Caribbean dollar (E.C.), but U.S. dollars are widely accepted. (You'll often get change in E.C. dollars.) The E.C. dollar is fairly stable relative to the U.S. dollar, hovering between E.C.$2.60 and $2.70 to U.S.$1. Credit cards are not always accepted, and it's hard to predict where you'll need cash. Some resorts will only settle in cash; a few will also accept personal checks. Be sure to carry lots of small bills; change for a $20 bill is often difficult to obtain. Note: Prices quoted are in U.S. dollars unless indicated otherwise.

## Emergencies

**Police** and **fire:** ☎ 911; for nonemergencies, ☎ 809/497–2333.

**Hospital:** There is a 24-hour emergency room at the **Princess Alexandra Hospital** (✉ Stoney Ground, ☎ 809/497–2551).

**Ambulance:** ☎ 809/497–2551.

**Pharmacies:** The **Government Pharmacy** (✉ The Valley, ☎ 809/497–2551) is in Princess Alexandra Hospital; the **Paramount Pharmacy** (✉ Waterswamp, ☎ 809/497–2366) is open Monday–Saturday 8:30–8:30 and has a 24-hour emergency service.

## Getting Around

CAR RENTALS

This is your best bet for maximum mobility if you're comfortable driving on the left and don't mind some jostling. Anguilla's roads are generally paved (in a manner of speaking), but those that are not can be incredibly rutted, even those leading to a fancy hotel. Observe the 30 miles-per-hour speed limit, and watch out for the four-legged creatures—goats, sheep, and cows—that amble across the road. To rent a car you'll need a valid driver's license and a local license, which can be obtained for $6 at any of the car-rental agencies. Among the island's agencies are **Avis** (☎ 809/497–6221 or 800/331–1212), **Budget** (☎ 809/497–2217 or 800/472–3325), **Connors (National)** (☎ 809/497–6433 or 800/328–4567), and **Island Car Rental** (☎ 809/497–2723). Count on $35 to $45 per day's rental, plus insurance. Motorcycles and scooters are available for about $30 per day from **R & M Cycle** (☎ 809/497–2430).

TAXIS

Taxi rates are regulated by the government, and there are fixed fares from point to point. Fares, which are government regulated, should be listed in brochures the drivers carry. Posted rates are for one or two people; each additional passenger adds $3 to the total. Tipping is welcome.

## Guided Tours

A round-the-island tour by taxi will take about 2½ hours and will cost $40 for one or two people, $5 for each additional passenger. **Bennie's Tours** (✉ Blowing Point, ☎ 809/497–2788) and **Malliouhana Travel and Tours** (✉ The Valley, ☎ 809/497–2431) put together personalized package tours of the island.

## Language

English, with a strong West Indian lilt, is spoken here.

## Opening and Closing Times

Banks are open Monday to Thursday 8–3 and Friday 8–5. Shopping hours vary. No two shops seem to have the same hours, but many are certainly open between 10 and 4. Call the shop, or ask at the tourist office for opening and closing times, or adopt the island way of doing things: If they're not open when you stop by, stop by again.

## Passports and Visas

U.S. and Canadian citizens need proof of identity. A passport is preferred (even one that has expired within the last five years). Also acceptable is a photo ID, such as a driver's license, *along with* a birth certificate (with raised seal), voter registration card, or naturalization papers. All visitors must also have a return or ongoing ticket. Visitor's passes are valid for stays of up to three months. British citizens must have a passport.

## Precautions

The manchineel tree, which resembles an apple tree, shades many beaches. The tree bears poisonous fruit, and the sap from the tree causes painful blisters. Avoid sitting beneath the tree, because even dew or raindrops falling from the leaves can blister your skin.

Be *sure* to take along insect repellent—mosquitoes can be pesky in the late afternoon.

Anguilla is a quiet, relatively safe island, but there's no point in tempting fate by leaving your valuables unattended in your hotel room, on the beach, or in your car.

## Taxes and Service Charges

The government imposes an 8% tax on accommodations. The departure tax is $10 at the airport, $2 if you leave by boat. A 10% service charge is added to all hotel bills and most restaurant bills. If you're not certain about the restaurant service charge, ask. If you are particularly pleased with the service, you can certainly leave a little extra. Tip taxi drivers 10% of the fare.

## Telephones and Mail

To call Anguilla from the United States, dial area code 809 + 497 + the local four-digit number. International direct dial is available on the island. To make a local call on the island, just dial the four-digit number. **Cable & Wireless** (⊠ Wallblake Rd., ☎ 809/497–3100) is open weekdays 8–6, Saturday 9–1, Sunday and holidays 10–2 and sells Caribbean Phone Cards ($5, $10, $20 denominations) for use in specially marked phone booths. The card can be used for local calls and calls to other islands. You can also use the card to call the United States and, in this case, bill the call to a MasterCard or Visa. Inside the departure lounge at the Blowing Point Ferry and at the airport, there is an AT&T USADirect access telephone for collect or credit-card calls to the United States.

Airmail letters to the United States cost E.C.60¢; postcards, E.C.25¢.

## Visitor Information

You can get very helpful information through the **Anguilla Tourist Information and Reservation Office** (⊠ c/o Medhurst & Associates, 775 Park Ave., Huntington, NY 11743, ☎ 516/271–2600 or 800/553–4939, FAX 516/425–0903). In the United Kingdom, contact the **Anguilla Tourist Office** (⊠ 3 Epirus Rd., London SW6 7UJ, ☎ 0171/937–7725).

On Anguilla, the **Anguilla Tourist Office** (⊠ Social Security Bldg., The Valley, ☎ 809/497–2759) is open weekdays 8–noon and 1–4.

# 3 Antigua

**Updated by
Jordan Simon**

**O**NE COULD SPEND AN ENTIRE YEAR exploring Antigua's beaches; the island has 366 of them, many with snow-white sand. All the beaches are public, some absolutely deserted and others with resorts stretching right along the water's edge and offering sailing, diving, windsurfing, and snorkeling. This is an island with hotels to please travelers of all kinds, from those seeking refined elegance, to those in search of casual beachfront merriment or quiet beachside snoozing, to those charmed by beautifully restored historic inns.

Antigua (An-*tee*-ga), the largest of the British Leeward Islands (108 square miles), is an island with a strong sense of national identity and rich, historic inheritance. Its cricketers, like the legendary Viv Richards (arguably the greatest batsman the game has ever seen), are famous throughout the Caribbean. Its people are known for their sharp, commercial spirit (a typically revealing—and disarming—sign reads "Diane's Boutique and Car Parts"); their wit; and, unfortunately at the government level, their corruption.

In the colonial era, Antigua was the headquarters of Lord Horatio Nelson's fleet. English Harbour, in the southeast of the island, is steeped in the history of that time. At its center is Nelson's Dockyard, now a national park. It is Antigua's answer to Williamsburg, Virginia—a carefully restored gem of British Georgian architecture. Accommodations here are generally in smaller, inn-type hotels. For Anglophiles and those interested in history, English Harbour and the surrounding villages and historic sites will be immensely rewarding.

Those in search of good beaches, plenty of nightlife, and a wide choice of restaurants will want to head to the northwestern end of the island, where resorts and hotels are scattered from Five Islands Harbour, south of St. John, to Dickenson Bay and the northwest shore. If you like to walk from one beach bar and restaurant to another, then Dickenson Bay and its long sliver of white sand is the spot for you.

One of the least-developed parts of the island is in the southwest, in the shadow of Antigua's highest mountain, Boggy Peak. At beaches like Fry's Bay and Darkwood Beach, visitors will find long, unspoiled scimitars of sand.

The original inhabitants of Antigua were a people called the Siboney. They lived here as early as 4,000 years ago and disappeared mysteriously, leaving the island unpopulated for about 1,000 years. When Columbus arrived in 1493, the Arawaks had set up housekeeping. The English took up residence 139 years later in 1632. After 30-odd years of bloody battles involving the Caribs, the Dutch, the French, and the English, the French ceded the island to the English in 1667. Unlike many other Caribbean islands, which spent centuries being reflagged like political Ping-Pong balls, Antigua remained under English control until achieving full independence, with its sister island Barbuda (26 miles to the north), on November 1, 1981.

The combined population of the two islands is about 90,000, only 1,200 of whom live on Barbuda. Tourism is the main industry here—there has been a recent building boom in tourism properties, with the construction of condominiums and the extensive renovation and expansion of the major hotels—and the government is seeking to broaden its monetary resources by reintroducing agriculture and manufacturing into the economy.

# Lodging

Scattered along Antigua's fine sandy beaches and tropical hillsides are resorts of all kinds, from exclusive, elegant hideaways and romantic restored inns to casual go-barefoot-everywhere places and all-inclusive hot spots for couples. Pick a spot near St. John's—anywhere between Dickenson Bay and Five Islands Harbour—if you want to be close to restaurants and shopping or want lots of action. If you stay right on Dickenson Bay you can easily walk to quite a few restaurants, beach bars, and resorts. English Harbour, though far from St. John's, has the best collection of inns, several excellent restaurants, and is the hangout for the yachting crowd. The resorts scattered elsewhere on the island tend to cater more to guests who want to stay put or are seeking seclusion. Though many properties sustained some damage during the 1995 hurricanes, most have since completed renovations (many much-needed before Luis and Marilyn); in some cases they gave management an excuse to institute dramatic—and welcome—changes. The price categories below reflect the room cost during high season.

| CATEGORY | COST* |
| --- | --- |
| $$$$ | over $350 |
| $$$ | $250–$350 |
| $$ | $150–$250 |
| $ | under $150 |

*All prices are for a standard double room for two, excluding 7% tax and 10% service charge.*

$$$$   ★   **Curtain Bluff.** Howard Hulford built this resort more than 30 years ago, and he's still very active in its management. You're likely to see him puttering around his beloved gardens or tasting a new wine for his legendary cellar of nearly 15,000 bottles. The resort is named for its spectacular setting, on a bluff bordered on one side by the wild Atlantic Ocean and on the other by the calm Caribbean. Spacious standard rooms are in two-story beachfront buildings facing the Caribbean, with terraces or balconies. They have wicker furnishings and a teal-and-white color scheme. The suites zigzag their way up the bluff on the Atlantic side and are some of the finest accommodations on Antigua—huge split-level apartments with two large balconies offering spectacular views, a large, tastefully decorated living room, and, up a flight of steps, a spacious and inviting bedroom. All accommodations have a safe and a phone. Swiss chef Reudi Portmann, who has ruled the kitchen here since the resort opened, prepares the meals served in the greenery-filled open-air restaurant. Jacket and tie are required for dinner, except on Wednesday and Sunday. Curtain Bluff's exceptional service, casual elegance, and country-club ambience appeal to a select, more mature crowd who return annually. ⊠ *Box 288, St. John's,* ☎ *268/462–8400; in NY, 212/289–8888;* ℻ *268/462–8409. 61 rooms and suites. 2 restaurants, lounge, in-room safes, putting green, 4 tennis courts, croquet, exercise room, squash, water-sports center, pro shop. AE. Closed mid-May–mid-Oct. FAP.*

$$$$   ★   **Jumby Bay.** Just five minutes by taxi and another 10 minutes by launch from Antigua is this exclusive, 330-acre, private island retreat. Spanish-style white stucco buildings with cedar-shingled roofs line the beach. Rooms are in the two-story Pond Bay House and in individual rondavels (circular bungalows) and cottages spread around the property. All are spacious, and even those not labeled suites have separate sitting areas. Some bathrooms open out to small areas filled with tropical greenery. The 1995 hurricanes gave management the excuse to thoroughly refurbish the property; new fabrics were individually chosen for each unit, and the decor schemes—ranging from Laura Ashley to

Forbidden Palace-meets-the-Caribbean—dazzle with their casual opulence. For an extra $600 per day, you can rent an expansive and well-furnished two-bedroom villa with a kitchen-dining room and a small swimming pool that's shared with several other villas. The new chef, Rex Hale, has lightened and brightened the cuisine with his boldly flavored yet sensuously textured dishes. He plans to import celebrity chefs like Jeremiah Tower and Wolfgang Puck for a week each during high season. There are lots of walking trails, and everything is spread out, so if you hate to walk or bicycle, you might want to stay elsewhere. No children under age eight are permitted during high season. There is occasional jet noise from the nearby airport. ⊠ *Box 243, St. John's,* ☎ *268/462–6000 or 800/421–9016,* 𝖥𝖠𝖷 *268/462–6020. 38 suites, 18 villas. 2 restaurants, 3 bars, 4 tennis courts, croquet, sailing, water-sports center, bicycles. AE, MC, V. All-inclusive (including liquor and wine).*

$$$$ ★ **K Club.** K stands for Krizia, the famed Italian designer; her dramatic style and touch animate every nook and cranny of her super-deluxe Barbuda hideaway, a member of the Leading Hotels of the World. The public spaces gleam with white tiles and columns, natural wicker furnishings with oversize sea-foam-and-white striped cushions, and striking cloth-and-bronze sculptures. All rooms and cottages open onto the dazzling champagne-color beach. The decor is chic and cool: white wicker and tile livened by turquoise and mint fabrics, wonderful wooden chairs whimsically carved with pineapples, speckled ceramic lamps, bamboo mats, towering fruit sculptures, showers submerged in vegetation, and amusing paintings (for example, a sole pair of ruby-red stiletto pumps on a beach). Each has its own kitchenette on a private veranda. The cuisine, under the creative hand of Anacleta Brizzola, is as elegantly simple, an innovative fusion of Tuscan grilling and Caribbean ingredients. It may seem steep at $1,100 per couple and up, but the utmost privacy and discretion are assured. No children under 12 allowed. ⊠ *Coco Point, Barbuda,* ☎ *268/460–0300,* 𝖥𝖠𝖷 *268/460–0305. 39 units. Restaurant, bar, grill, pool, hot tub, 9-hole golf course, 2 tennis courts, snorkeling, windsurfing, waterskiing, fishing, game/TV room. AE, MC, V. MAP, FAP.*

$$$$ **St. James's Club.** This out-of-the-way hotel is on the 100-acre spit of land that helps form Mamora Bay. Rooms and one-bedroom suites are in the main buildings at the water's edge on the tip of the peninsula. Units are nicely furnished and painted in pastel colors; some have romantic canopy beds. You enter past the "villa village," a group of tightly clustered two-bedroom villas that rest on the top of the hills that spill down toward the main hotel. Although also well decorated, these villas include views of your neighbor's roof. You can dine at the three restaurants in the main building: the Rainbow Garden, an elegant spot for dinner; the Docksider Cafe, with an elegant menu but casual alfresco setting; or the Poolside Reef Deck, a breakfast and lunch spot. Also part of the resort is the French restaurant Chez Pascal (☞ Dining, *below*). Overall, the St. James tends to live off its *renommé* (it is affiliated with other like-named resorts in London, Paris, and Los Angeles), rather than what it delivers. After all, the resort started life as a Holiday Inn, and it shows. The casino is a hoot, filled with brass and tacky red-fringed lamp shades that a bordello might reject. That said, the beaches and extensive sports facilities—and such amenities as a hotel helicopter that can be chartered for sightseeing—make this a fine, if overpriced, full-service resort. ⊠ *Box 63, St. John's,* ☎ *268/460–5000 or 800/274–0008,* 𝖥𝖠𝖷 *268/460–3015. 178 units. 3 restaurants, 5 bars, room service, 3 pools, beauty salon, hot tub, massage, golf privileges, 7 tennis courts, croquet, exercise room, horseback riding, scuba diving, dive shop, ma-*

**40**

Antigua (and Barbuda)

Pineapple Beach
Club, **48**
Rex Halcyon Cove
Beach Resort, **18**
Royal Antiguan
Resort, **33**
St. James's Club, **46**
Sandals, **20**
Siboney Beach
Club, **19**
Yepton Beach
Resort, **32**

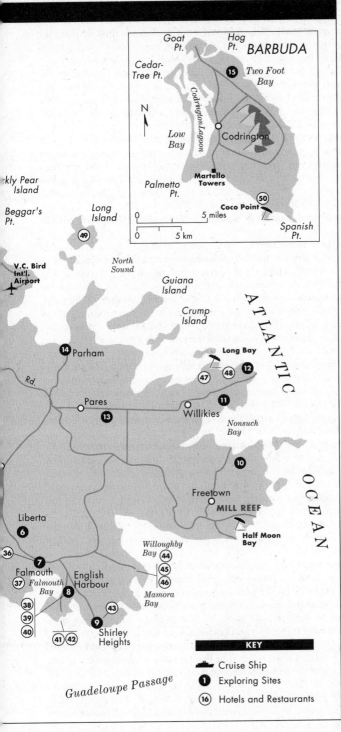

Goat
Pt.

Hog
Pt.  **BARBUDA**

Cedar-
Tree Pt.

15  Two Foot
Bay

N

Low
Bay

Codrington

Palmetto
Pt.

**Martello
Towers**

**Coco Point**  50

Spanish
Pt.

0          5 miles
0          5 km

kly Pear
Island

Beggar's
Pt.

Long
Island

49

**V.C. Bird
Int'l.
Airport**

North
Sound

Guiana
Island

Crump
Island

14  Parham

Rd

Pares

13

Willikies

47  48  12

11

**Long Bay**

Nonsuch
Bay

10

Freetown

**MILL REEF**

**Half Moon
Bay**

Liberta

6

36

7  Falmouth
37  Falmouth
Bay

English
Harbour

8

Willoughby
Bay  44

45
46

Mamora
Bay

38
39
40

43

41  42

9  Shirley
Heights

**KEY**

🚢  Cruise Ship

❶  Exploring Sites

⑯  Hotels and Restaurants

Guadeloupe Passage

rina, snorkeling, windsurfing, sailing, waterskiing, shops, casino, night-club, playground. AE, MC, V. EP, MAP.

$$$–$$$$   🏨 **Pineapple Beach Club.** A broad stone walk leads directly from the reception area to the beach of this bustling, beachside, all-inclusive resort. All rooms are on or very near the beach, but some have only partial ocean or garden views. Though the property was hit hard by the 1995 hurricanes, management has taken advantage of the opportunity to freshen everything, adding redwood louvered windows, terra-cotta floors in the rooms, and new, more vivid Caribbean colors. There are no phones or TVs in rooms, but fax and phone service is available at the front desk. This is an activity-oriented place with a full array of water sports, nightly entertainment, and an electronic casino, but it does quiet down soon after midnight. Be sure to bring the letter confirming your reservation; the hotel has a bad habit of overbooking or losing reservation information. ✉ Box 54, St. John's, ☎ 268/463–2006 or 800/345–0356, FAX 268/465–2452. 125 rooms. Restaurant, bar, pool, 4 tennis courts, croquet, horseshoes, volleyball, kayaking. AE, MC, V. All-inclusive.

$$$   🏨 **Hawksbill Beach Hotel.** Thirty-seven acres of the bucolic Five Islands peninsula, including five beaches of fine tan sand (you can bathe in the buff at one), make up the grounds of this sprawling resort. The main building, reception area, and dining room are on a small bluff that commands a sweeping view of the sea and Montserrat beyond, set off by the restored ruins of a sugar mill in the foreground. Deluxe rooms are in gingerbread-trimmed, West Indian–style cottages surrounded by grass lawns and facing the sea, with a decor of wicker, tile floors, and light floral pastels. The less expensive rooms are in cottages with garden views. Most of these actually have restricted beach views and are the same size as the pricier beachfront units. Bedrooms, even in the deluxe category, are quite small, but guests here spend most of their time outside. There is no air-conditioning, TV, or phone. The classiest accommodations aren't the cottage guest rooms but the three-bedroom West Indian Great House, an old, colonial-style building with king-size beds, tile floors, wicker furniture, and kitchenette. Men are requested not to wear short sleeves into the dining room after 7 PM. And though children are more welcome than they used to be ("screamers" not included), Hawksbill is more a place for young couples and singles. Breakfast and the use of most water-sports facilities are complimentary. ✉ Box 108, St. John's, ☎ 268/462–0301 or 800/223–6510; in Canada, 416/622–8813; FAX 268/462–1515. 90 rooms. 2 restaurants, 2 bars, pool, tennis court, water-sports center. AE, DC, MC, V. BP, MAP.

$$$   🏨 **Hodges Bay Club.** A great snorkeling beach and proximity to both the airport and St. John's are good reasons to stay at this condominium property on the prestigious north shore, facing Prickley Pear Island. Connected, air-conditioned one- and two-bedroom villas line the beach or overlook the pool. All are spacious, comfortably decorated, and have fully equipped kitchens, king-size beds, balconies, and daily maid service. Each bedroom has a private bath and can be closed off for rental as a hotel room. The Pelican Club restaurant here is considered one of the best hotel dining rooms on the island. ✉ Box 1237, St. John's, ☎ 268/462–2300 or 800/432–4229; in NY, 212/535–9530; FAX 268/462–1962. 4 1-bedroom villas, 22 2-bedroom villas. Restaurant, pool, air-conditioning, full kitchens, 2 tennis courts, water-sports center. AE, DC, MC, V. EP.

$$$   🏨 **Rex Halcyon Cove Beach Resort.** Many European and American tour groups patronize this large, somewhat impersonal hotel on beautiful Dickenson Bay, so it's typically crowded, and your neighbor may be paying a third of what you are. Accommodations are in two- and

three-story flat-roofed buildings scattered around the courtyard or along the beach. They have white tile floors and are decorated with blond wood and mint fabrics. All have air-conditioning and a private balcony or patio, but only higher-grade accommodations have full bath, TV, and refrigerator. A water-sports center on the busy beach offers excursions on a glass-bottom boat and waterskiing, in addition to the other usual water sports. The Warri Pier restaurant is set on stilts over the ocean and serves fine seafood and grilled items all day long. While you're on the walkway that connects it to the beach, be sure to look into the water—it's filled with schools of colorful fish. Thanks to the hurricanes, this place had a major face-lift, making it look a lot more inviting than it did before the storms. ⊠ *Box 251, St. John's,* ☎ *268/462–0256,* FAX *268/462–0271. 194 rooms, 16 1-bedroom suites. 2 restaurants, 4 bars, ice-cream parlor, air-conditioning, pool, beauty salon, 4 tennis courts, shops, water-sports center, car rental. AE, D, DC, MC, V. EP, MAP.*

$$–$$$ 🏨 **Dickenson Bay Cottages.** There are only 13 units at this small, pleasant development on Marble Hill, just above Dickenson Bay. The two-story black- or gray-and-white villa-style buildings are surrounded by gardens and elegantly furnished with high-quality painted rattan, blond woods, and soft pastel fabrics. Downstairs is a well-equipped kitchen and a large living room area with a TV. The bedroom and bathroom are up a flight of stairs. Larger units have two bedrooms upstairs and a large veranda overlooking the ocean. One annoyance is the lack of a cross breeze, which obliges you to keep the air conditioner on. Guests have beach privileges at the excellent but busy beach at Halcyon Cove, just a five-minute walk away, and the resort has an arrangement for the use of the tennis and water-sports facilities there at a 20% discount. Several other resorts nearby give you a selection of entertainment and restaurants. ⊠ *Box 1379, St. John's,* ☎ *268/462–4940,* FAX *268/462–4941. 13 rooms. Air-conditioning, kitchens, pool. AE, DC, MC, V. EP.*

$$–$$$ 🏨 **Inn at English Harbour.** The reception area, bar and dining room, ★ and six of the guest rooms of this inn sit atop a hill with stunning views of English Harbour. The bar, with its green leather chairs, wooden floors, stone walls, and maritime prints, is one of the most pleasant on the island; and the flagstone terrace dining room offers an unparalleled romantic ambience and dependable Continental fare. Off to the side of the main house are the hilltop rooms, in individual, cottage-style units nestled amid typical English gardens. Down the steep hill, right on the beach, are 22 additional rooms in two-story wooden buildings surrounded by hibiscus and bougainvillea. The superior rooms are slightly larger, but all rooms have phones, wall safes, refrigerators, and hair dryers and are attractively furnished with rattan furniture and tropical or floral fabrics. Also on the beach is a second bar-restaurant that stays open until 6 PM. A shuttle bus runs guests up and down the hill. The beach, like all those in English Harbour, is not the best. During high season only MAP bookings are accepted. An air of quiet, laidback refinement is cultivated by amiable second-generation owner Paul Deeth. ⊠ *Box 187, St. John's,* ☎ *268/460–1014 or 800/223–6510; in Canada,* ☎ *800/424–5500;* FAX *268/460–1603. 28 rooms. 2 restaurants, 2 bars, in-room safes, refrigerators, snorkeling, windsurfing, boating, sailing. AE, MC, V. EP, MAP.*

$$–$$$ 🏨 **Royal Antiguan Resort.** This nine-story, high-rise hotel, possibly the island's ugliest, is set on the waterside a few miles south of St. John's. The hotel caters to groups and conventions and is by far the most "stateside-like" hotel on Antigua. Rooms and suites are air-conditioned, with minibars and TVs, and there are numerous facilities: three restaurants, three bars, a huge ballroom used for meetings and cocktail parties, a shopping arcade, and a 5,500-square-foot casino with blackjack,

roulette, craps, baccarat, and 130 slot machines, all played by Atlantic City rules. It has been taken over by the Pineapple Beach Club management, which is investing several million dollars in a complete renovation. The initial stage calls for brightening the drab decor. Thus far it just looks like a superficial cosmetic job done by a recent beauty school grad. ✉ *Deep Bay, St. John's,* ☎ *268/462–3733 or 800/228–9898,* 𝖥𝖠𝖷 *268/462–3732. 300 rooms. 3 restaurants, 4 bars (including swimup pool bar), air-conditioning, minibars, pool, golf privileges at nearby 18-hole Cedar Valley course, 5 tennis courts, snorkeling, windsurfing, boating, waterskiing, certified dive master, fishing, casino, minicrafts market. AE, D, MC, V. EP.*

**$$–$$$**    🏨 **Sandals.** Pool competitions and beach volleyball, aerobics sessions,
★    and evening social events, including all kinds of group games, are just a few of the things going on at this couples-only resort. The schedule of events is organized by a "play maker," who will cajole (but not force) you to join in the fun; but you can still enjoy the place if you just want to read and relax. Everything, from the tennis coaching to the pedal boats, the scuba diving to the swim-up pool-bars, discos, and meals, is included in the price. For a little extra, you can even get married in front of a miniature waterfall. Rooms, facing the beach or the garden, and rondavels facing the beach are spacious. All units are air-conditioned and have phone, coffeemaker, TV, safe, and hair dryer. Many have four-poster or frilly beds, and all are light and fresh in pastels and/or bright floral fabrics; all were thoroughly refurbished after the 1995 hurricanes. You have a choice of four restaurants offering Continental, Italian, Japanese, and southwestern fare. Public areas are handsome, especially the vast colonnaded reception area. ✉ *Box 147, St. John's,* ☎ *268/462–0267; U.S. reservations, 800/726–3257;* 𝖥𝖠𝖷 *268/462–4135. 191 rooms and suites. 4 restaurants, 4 bars, air-conditioning, in-room safes, 5 pools, 5 hot tubs, spa, 2 tennis courts, scuba diving, snorkeling, windsurfing, sailing, waterskiing, gift shop, nightclub. AE. All-inclusive.*

**$$–$$$**    🏨 **Siboney Beach Club.** When Tony Johnson arrived in Antigua in the
★    late '50s, he planned to stay just a few weeks. Instead, he ended up building or refurbishing some of the island's finest resorts, and eventually opened his own small gem set in an exquisite tropical garden on Dickenson Bay. Each suite has a small bedroom, a cleverly designed Pullman kitchen, a modestly furnished living room, and a plant-filled patio or balcony that looks out to tropical greenery. Decor varies slightly, but all feature rattan and rich tropical fabrics. Most units are air-conditioned. Room 9 is for those who revel in sea views, but the soothing sound of the surf permeates even those with partial views. A few yards away is an excellent, although often busy, calm-water beach and the Coconut Grove (☞ Dining, *below*), where guests can enjoy great breakfasts and lunches as well as candlelight dinners at the water's edge. The staff is exceptionally friendly, and Tony and his Trinidadian wife, Ann, are always available to offer advice and good cheer, making Siboney your home away from home. ✉ *Box 222, St. John's,* ☎ *268/462–0806 or 800/533–0234,* 𝖥𝖠𝖷 *268/462–3356. 12 suites. Restaurant, bar, pool. AE, MC, V. EP, MAP.*

**$$**    🏨 **Copper and Lumber Store Hotel.** Overlooking the marina at English Harbour, this former supply store for Nelson's Caribbean fleet and fine example of Georgian British architecture has been beautifully transformed into a gracious inn. The warm brick, hardwood floors, timbered ceilings, and burgundy leather, button armchairs and sofas give it an Old World charm unique in the West Indies. Each of the 14 suites is meticulously decorated with authentic Georgian period furnishings, including antique washstands, secretaries, and four-poster canopy beds; many include such touches as wrought-iron chandeliers, old sailing prints, mahogany steamer trunks, brass sinks, and faux gas lamps. All suites have showers, and although they lack air-conditioning, ceiling fans capture nice breezes. Unfortunately, many rooms have become a bit frayed around the edges and could use a face-lift. A ferry service shuttles guests to a beach on the other side of English Harbour. Be warned that the hotel sits inside a national park and visitors stream through the area during the day. ⊠ *Box 184, St. John's,* ☎ *268/460–1058 or 800/275–0877; in Canada, 800/463–0877;* FAX *268/460–1529. 14 suites. 2 restaurants, pub, fans. AE, MC, V. EP, MAP.*

**$$** ⊡ **Yepton Beach Resort.** This Swiss-designed, full-service, all-suites resort is set on Hog John Bay on the Five Islands peninsula, not far from St. John's. The Mediterranean-style white-stucco buildings are situated so that accommodations have views on one side of the resort's own attractive beach and on the other side of a lagoon dotted with pelicans and egrets. Some of the rooms are two-room suites, with a bedroom and large living-room-cum-kitchenette. Others are studios, with a folding Murphy bed and kitchenette. By putting together a double bedroom and a studio, one can also make an apartment that sleeps four. All rooms are air-conditioned. Many different packages are available. ⊠ *Box 1427, St. John's,* ☎ *268/462–2520 or 800/361–4621,* FAX *268/462–3240. 38 units. Restaurant, air-conditioning, kitchenettes, pool, 2 tennis courts, snorkeling, boating. AE, MC, V. EP, MAP.*

**$** ⊡ **Admiral's Inn.** This lovingly restored 18th-century Georgian inn is
★ the centerpiece of the magnificent Nelson's Dockyard complex. Once the engineers' office and warehouse (the bricks were originally used as ballast for British ships), the Admiral's Inn reverberates with history. The best rooms, upstairs in the main building, have the original timbered ceilings, complete with iron braces, hardwood floors, and massive whitewashed brick walls. Straw floor mats from Dominica and views through wispy Australian pines to the sunny harbor beyond complete the effect. The rooms in the garden annex are smaller and a bit airless. The Loft, which used to be the dockyard's joinery, has two big bedrooms, an enormous kitchen, and a magnificent view from the timbered living room onto the busy harbor. Be aware that this inn sits smack in the middle of a bustling daytime tourist attraction. ⊠ *Box 713, St. John's,* ☎ *268/460–1027, 800/223–5695, or 800/223–9815;* FAX *268/460–1534. 14 rooms, 1 2-bedroom apartment. Restaurant, pub, complimentary beach shuttle and use of water sports at Falmouth Beach Apts. AE, MC, V. EP, MAP.*

**$** ⊡ **Banana Cove.** These one- and two-bedroom self-contained apartments are set in a relatively secluded part of Antigua, near Devil's Bridge. The units are airy and appealing, with hardwood floors, island prints, and bright pastel fabrics. Each has a complete kitchen and bath, a small terrace, and remarkably large closets. The best buys are the two-bedroom suites with pool views (ocean view is nearly twice as expensive). The beach is a small spit of land, but Long Bay is a short drive. ⊠ *Dian Bay, Box 1389,* ☎ *268/463–2003 or 800/223–9815,* FAX *268/463–2425. 30 units. Restaurant, bar, kitchens, pool. AE, MC, V. EP.*

**$** ⊡ **Catamaran Hotel.** This plantation-style house, with attractive apricot, white, and black trim and a wraparound veranda supported on white, classical-style pediments, retains its historical ambience. The property sits on the water at Falmouth Harbour, on a beach lined with palm and almond trees. The best rooms are the eight first-floor suites, with four-poster beds, full baths, kitchenettes, and private balconies. None of the rooms has air-conditioning, TV, or telephone. English Harbour is only 2 miles away. There's also a restaurant (under different management), Captain Bruno's, serving à la carte meals and good pizzas. For those who want a low-key, low-priced, tranquil resort, this offers excellent

value. ⊠ *Box 958, Falmouth,* ☎ *268/460–1036,* ℻ *268/460–1506.*
*16 rooms. Restaurant, bar, kitchenettes, marina, shops. AE, MC, V. EP.*

**$** 🏨 **Falmouth Beach Apartments.** This is the sister hotel of the Admi-
ral's Inn at English Harbour. The best accommodations are in an attractive colonial-style house at the water's edge on the hotel's own small
palm-lined beach. These quiet, simple units are basically one large room—
a bedroom-living-room-kitchenette combination—and a bathroom
with a shower. All open onto the house's timbered wraparound veranda
with a view of the water and the hilly peninsula opposite. Since the
beach is very sheltered, it is perfect for toddlers and small children who
are learning to swim. There is no air-conditioning and no telephones
or TVs. (The upstairs units catch the breezes better.) Other rooms are
located in four modern buildings perched on the hillside and have a
separate kitchen, a bedroom with twin beds, and a bathroom with
shower. Decor is the standard rattan and beige tiles, jazzed up by old
maps or striking artwork. All apartments have daily maid service.
⊠ *Box 713, Falmouth Harbour,* ☎ *268/460–1094 or 800/223–5695,*
℻ *268/460–1534. 28 rooms. Water-sports center (Sunfish and paddleboats included in price). AE, MC, V. EP.*

**$** 🏨 **Lord Nelson Beach Hotel.** This small, weathered mom-and-pop re-
★ sort is run by the Fullers, expatriate Americans who have been here
since 1949. As they have a vast, extended family of their own, it's a
perfect place for children to scamper about and explore. If you don't
mind a bit of chipped paint and organized chaos, you'll love it, too (as
did Eugene Fodor when he once stayed here). An extensive collection
of windsurfing boards, easy access to the water, and a dedicated pro
have also made it a mecca for windsurfers. The best rooms are in a
two-story, apricot-colored building looking directly onto the property's
own horseshoe-shape beach. Each room is a slightly different hodge-
podge (one has beautiful tiled floors and an ornately carved bed from
Dominica that is so high you almost need to be a pole-vaulter to get
into it). Several others have four-poster beds, antique armoires, and
vivid local still lifes. Guests eat in the timbered dining room, draped
with fishnets and dominated by a replica of the boat in which Captain
Bligh was cast off from the *Bounty*; expect hearty dishes such as stuffed
pork chops, wahoo, and snapper. Because the resort is fairly isolated
(5 miles from St. John's), figure an extra E.C.$25 into your budget for
cab fare to any meal you have elsewhere. ⊠ *Box 155, St. John's,* ☎
*268/462–3094,* ℻ *268/462–0751. 16 rooms. Restaurant, bar, maid
service, dive shop, windsurfing. AE, MC, V. EP, MAP, FAP. Closed Sept.*

## Dining

Antigua has a wide variety of restaurants, and you can find excellent
food whether you feel like dressing up or dressing down. There are elegant Continental and French restaurants, casual waterfront bistros,
and barefoot beach bars. It's impossible not to find fresh seafood on
the menu, and virtually every chef incorporates local ingredients and
elements of West Indian and Creole cuisine. Alas, the food is often over-
cooked, even in the tonier establishments.

Most menus list prices in E.C. dollars, but you should make sure
which currency you're dealing with. It's also a good idea to ask if credit
cards are accepted. Prices below are in U.S. dollars. Dinner reservations are needed during high season.

### What to Wear

Perhaps because of the island's British heritage, Antiguans tend to
dress more formally for dinner than is the custom on many of the other
Caribbean islands. A few places, which will be noted, require a jacket.

Wraps and shorts (no beach attire) are de rigueur for lunch, except at local hangouts.

| CATEGORY | COST* |
| --- | --- |
| $$$$ | over $50 |
| $$$ | $35–$50 |
| $$ | $20–$35 |
| $ | under $20 |

*per person, excluding drinks, service, and 7% sales tax*

**$$$** ✕ **Alberto's.** ★ Set above Willoughby Bay on Antigua's southeast side, this superior Italian restaurant is a bit out of the way but popular nevertheless. The ebullient owner, Alberto, taught his culinary secrets to his English wife, Vanessa, and the two turn out delicious seafood prepared with an Italian accent. Try fresh island lobster (perhaps grilled with basil and garlic); cockles Alberto; the chef's creation of the evening (you're in luck if it's baked grouper in pine-nut crust or snapper *marechiaro,* in a tomato, olive, and caper sauce); or more traditional dishes such as eggplant parmigiana, osso buco, or linguine with clams. The ravioli in creamy walnut sauce and breadfruit in garlic parsley butter are sheer heaven. Tables line a balcony open to the breezes and hung with bougainvillea; marvelous painted china graces the walls (check out the octopuses and squids on the plates by the bar). ⊠ *Willoughby Bay,* ☎ *268/460–3007 or via VHF 68. Reservations essential. AE, D, MC, V. Closed Mon. and July–Oct. No lunch.*

**$$$** ✕ **Chez Pascal.** This top-notch bistro recently relocated, but has retained its distinctive ambience and refined menu. Cool jazz and French pop (Piaf, Montand, et al.) waft through the open-air beachfront space, adorned with boldly colored Haitian paintings, copper pots, and a virtual jungle of potted plants, flowers, and dangling vines. Savor Pascal Milliat's refined classic Lyonnaise cuisine. You might start with the sublime *croustade de fruits de mer* (seafood puff pastry), chilled leek and breadfruit soup, or grouper marinated in lime, olive oil, and fines herbes. Entrées might include a marvelous rack of lamb in its own juice, grouper in red wine, snapper in a caper-lime sauce, or shrimp in tomato *coulis* (a sauce of pureed tomatoes) and garlic butter. Pascal's sauces are delicate, while his pairings provide the perfect counterpoint of flavor and texture. Finish with an unimpeachable *tarte aux pommes* (apple tart) or profiteroles. The wine list is excellent, if overpriced. ⊠ *St. James Club, Mamora Bay,* ☎ *268/462–3232. AE, MC, V. Closed Sun. No lunch.*

**$$$** ✕ **Coconut Grove.** Coconut palms grow up through the roof of this open-air thatched restaurant, candles flicker gently in lanterns, and waves lap the white-coral sand a few feet away. For a romantic evening, head here when there's a full moon and reserve table 1, closest to the water and under the stars. The menu always includes freshly grilled local lobster and choices of other fresh fish, plus lamb, steak, a vegetarian dish, and marinated and grilled chicken breast. New management has significantly improved the service and the kitchen, which now complement the unparalleled setting. ⊠ *Siboney Beach Club, Dickenson Bay,* ☎ *268/462–1538. MC, V.*

**$$$** ✕ **Colombo's.** This open-air restaurant is on a small bay in English Harbour, with views of palm trees, historic cannons, and the water in the distance. Various pennants draped around the bar attest that this is a big yachtie hangout. The extensive menu is condensed during the off-season, but you can still order such creative dishes as grouper carpaccio, *gamberoni Antigua* (shrimp flamed in rum in ginger sauce), lobster in basil sauce, and veal with wild mushrooms. At lunchtime there are also light salads, hamburgers, and sandwiches. On Wednesday nights a reggae band entertains. ✉ *Galleon Beach Club, English Harbour,* ☎ *268/460–1452. AE, MC, V.*

**$$$** ✕ **Julian's.** You enter this new restaurant—Antigua's finest—through
★ a lovely historic courtyard. The reception area strikes an immediate
note of elegance, with vibrant islandscapes contrasting with stark
white walls and wood beams. The intimate dining room (only eight
tables) has olive straw-and-rattan chairs, lime-green shutters, and
black-and-white napery. Chef and co-owner Julian Waterer creates mas-
terpieces with a brilliant counterpoint of flavors and colors. Even
something as straightforward as lentil soup is perfectly textured. Other
choices on the rotating menu might include blackened brie with grape-
fruit, asparagus, and honey; wild mushroom, leek, and feta strudel in
onion compote; or roast breast of duck with pear *coulis* (a sauce made
from pureed pears) over field greens. There is an excellent selection of
wines by the glass from the well-considered list. ✉ *Corn Alley and
Church La., St. John's,* ☎ *268/462–4766. AE, D, MC, V. Closed
Mon. No lunch Sun.*

**$$$** ✕ **La Perruche.** The plant-filled patio here is a pleasure, with pretty
green-and-white trim, trellises crawling with creepers, crystal glasses,
and a profusion of painted wooden parrots that hang everywhere—
hence, the restaurant's name. Careful division of the eating area gives
the large space an intimate feel. Regrettably, the new owners have sim-
plified everything, from the whimsically baroque decor to the complex
fusion of flavor and textures that were the trademark of the previous
chef. Nonetheless, La Perruche remains the best bet for French food
(with island touches) in English Harbour, with dependable offerings
including blackened shrimp in raspberry cream sauce and medallions
of lobster in mango sauce. ✉ *English Harbour,* ☎ *268/460–3040. AE,
MC, V. Closed Sun. and Sept. No lunch.*

**$$–$$$** ✕ **Lobster Pot.** A fishing boat sits in the center of this beachfront
★ restaurant's flagstone dining room, and sea breezes sweep in through
the open gallery. The owners restored the restaurant impeccably after
Hurricane Marilyn's devastation. The best seats are those right on the
water. The long (seven pages!) and diverse menu is a mix of fresh seafood,
pasta, and Creole- and Caribbean-style dishes. Starters include lobster
and pineapple phyllo with tamari and chili dips and grilled baby eggplant stuffed with cheese and herbs. Follow these with coconut-milk
curry shrimp; baked breast of chicken stuffed with goat cheese, broc-
coli, and sun-dried tomatoes; herb-encrusted swordfish in tomato
sauce; or of course, succulent lobster. For dessert try the apple crepes
in honey and island spice sauce. The wine list is well considered and
very fairly priced, with most selections in the $20s. ✉ *Runaway Bay,*
☎ *268/462–2856. D, MC, V.*

**$$–$$$** ✕ **Wardroom Restaurant.** An atmosphere of Olde England pervades
in this restaurant on the ground floor of the beautifully restored Copper and Lumber Store. The dining room, with massive brick walls and
stained wood beams, opens out to a charming courtyard hung with
bougainvillea and to views of the floodlit battlements of English Harbour. The menu is international, mixing dishes such as West African
peanut soup with lobster in puff pastry, a good selection of local fish
dishes, and even lamb cutlets. ✉ *Nelson's Dockyard,* ☎ *268/460–1058.
AE, DC, MC, V. Closed Wed. No lunch.*

**$$** ✕ **Admiral's Inn.** Known as the Ad to yachtsmen around the world,
★ this historic inn, in the heart of English Harbour, is a must for Anglophiles
and mariners. At the bar inside, you can sit and soak up the centuries
under dark, timbered wood (the bar top even has the names of sailors
from Nelson's fleet carved into it), but most guests tend to sit on the
terrace under shady Australian gums to enjoy the splendid views of the
harbor complex and Clarence House opposite. Specialties include cur-

ried conch, fresh snapper with equally fresh limes, and lobster thermidor. The pumpkin soup is not to be missed. ⊠ *Nelson's Dockyard,* ☎ *268/460–1027. Reservations essential. AE, MC, V.*

**$$** ✕ **Commissioner's Grill.** The gaudy exterior—in raspberry, mango, blueberry, and lavender—of this 19th-century tamarind warehouse seems edible itself. The interior is more restrained, with white tile floors, powder-blue chairs, floral tablecloths, and nice local touches like bronze wind chimes, Antiguan pottery, conch shells, and historic maps. The day's specials are scrawled on a blackboard, and might include whelks in garlic butter, snapper in lobster sauce, marinated conch, or shrimp Creole. Fresh seafood prepared with local flair is the obvious choice, although beef and poultry are also reliable. ⊠ *Commissioner Alley and Redcliffe St., St. John's,* ☎ *268/462–1883. AE, DC, MC, V.*

**$$** ✕ **Home.** When Carl Thomas came back to his native Antigua after years in New York, he decided to open a restaurant in his boyhood home, a '50s bungalow in a quiet suburb of St. John's. So he completely refurbished the original house, knocked down walls to create one large space, and planted an herb and vegetable garden. Modern, unfinished pine furniture and polished wood floors give the place an airy atmosphere. Unusual ceramic candlesticks adorn the tables, and walls are hung with African and Caribbean art. The menu, which Carl dubs "Caribbean haute cuisine," is ambitious for Antigua. Unfortunately, the quality is quite uneven. Carl could use a stronger hand with his seasonings. Grouper in herb sauce and other simpler offerings are more successful than such intriguing dishes as molasses pepper steak. Don't miss the smoked fish, a house specialty, and bread pudding with whiskey sauce. ⊠ *Gambles Terr., St. John's,* ☎ *268/461–7651. AE, MC, V. Closed Sun. No lunch weekdays.*

**$$** ✕ **Lemon Tree.** This air-conditioned, art-deco restaurant, on the second floor of a historic building in the old part of St. John's, is a smart, upbeat eating place, popular with cruise-ship guests. There's live music every night, varying from soft classical piano to funky reggae. The menu is eclectic, mixing minipizzas and ribs with beef Wellington, Cornish hen, lobster, vegetarian crepes, very spicy Cajun garlic shrimp, and pasta dishes. For those who like Mexican food, the Lemon Tree offers unbeatable burritos, as well as chili, nachos, and fajitas. ⊠ *Long and Church Sts., St. John's,* ☎ *268/462–1969. AE, DC, MC, V. Closed Sat. No lunch Sun.*

**$$** ✕ **Redcliffe Tavern.** Every item on the tavern's part northern Italian,
★ part Continental, part Creole menu is wonderfully fresh. The dinner menu includes delicious pastas, marinated grilled chicken, fresh local lobster, spicy Creole crab puffs, and a smoked salmon and shellfish terrine in lime mousseline. The lunch menu also lists salads, sandwiches, and hamburgers. The dining room is on the second floor of a beautifully restored colonial warehouse set amid the courtyards of Redcliffe Quay. Brick and stone walls are decorated with antique water-pumping equipment still bearing the original English maker's crests. Salvaged from all over the island, the beautiful old machines, with their flywheels and pistons, have been imaginatively integrated into the restaurant's structure (one supports the buffet bar, for instance). You can also dine on the treetop-level terrace. ⊠ *Redcliffe Quay, St. John's,* ☎ *268/461–4557. AE, MC, V.*

**$$** ✕ **Shirley Heights Lookout.** This restaurant is set in an 18th-century fortification high on a bluff, with a breathtaking view of English Harbour below. The first-floor pub opens onto the lookout point. Upstairs, there's a cozy, windowed dining room with hardwood floors and beamed ceilings. Pub offerings include burgers, sandwiches, and barbecue, while upstairs you can order the likes of pumpkin soup and lobster in lime sauce. If you like to be at the center of things, come here Sunday around 3 PM or Thursday around 3:30 PM, when locals, yachters, and visitors troop up the hill for the barbecue. Livened by steel-band and reggae music, it lasts well into the evening. ⊠ *Shirley Heights,* ☎ *268/463–1785. Reservations essential in season in dining room. AE, MC, V.*

**$–$$** ✕ **Calypso.** The St. John's professional set frequents this cheerful outdoor spot. At lunchtime it is packed with smartly dressed lawyers and government functionaries smoking cigars and chatting over traditional Caribbean food. Tables are arranged under green umbrellas on a sunny trellised patio dominated by the remains of a brick kiln. Specials change every day, but you can usually count on stewed lamb, grilled lobster, and baked chicken served with rice, dumplings, and *fungi,* a pastelike vegetable dish made of cornmeal and okra. ⊠ *Redcliffe St., St. John's,* ☎ *268/462–1965. AE, MC, V. Closed Sun. No dinner except Fri.*

**$–$$** ✕ **La Dolce Vita.** This Italian/French hybrid in Redcliffe Quay is a cool semi-alfresco oasis with crisp peach and white napery, old gas lamps, and a charming polished wood bar. There's nothing wildly innovative here, just good, solid standards like pasta carbonara, bolognaise, and Alfredo; chicken or veal milanese; and yummy pizzas (try the unusual tuna or lobster). The bountiful salads are also reliable. The new French chef, who studied with masters like Bocuse and Troisgros, has introduced more sophisticated dishes such as snapper with shrimp sauce scented with anise, or kingfish baked in salt. ⊠ *Redcliffe Quay 16,* ☎ *268/462–2016. AE, D, MC, V.*

**$–$$** ✕ **Russell's.** Russell Hodge, the vivacious owner, had the brilliant idea of restoring a part of Fort St. James, with its gorgeous views of the bay and headlands, and converting it into an open-air restaurant. Potted plants and faux-Victorian gas lamps lend a romantic aura to the cool stone-and-wood terrace. The menu—all delectable local specialties with an emphasis on seafood—is listed on the blackboard. You might start with definitive conch fritters or whelks in garlic butter, then try an excellent snapper Creole. Live jazz is a lure Sunday nights. Russell's sister Valerie owns the estimable Shirley Heights Lookout (☞ *above*), and sister Patsy operates the delightful Pumpkin Runner, a fast-food van dispensing savory local dishes every night in St. John's. The Hodges might well be Antigua's first family of food. ⊠ *Fort James,* ☎ *268/462–5479. AE, DC.*

**$** ✕ **Big Banana-Pizzas on the Quay.** This tiny, often crowded spot is ★ tucked into one side of a beautifully restored warehouse with broad plank floors and stonework archways. It serves some of the best pizza on the island, topped with traditional and not-so-traditional items. You can also enjoy delectable specials like conch salad. It's a busy lunch and dinner spot, and there is live entertainment some evenings. ⊠ *Redcliffe Quay, St. John's,* ☎ *268/462–2621. AE, MC, V.*

## Beaches

All of Antigua's beaches are public, and many are dotted with resorts that provide water-sports-equipment rentals and a place to grab a cool drink. Sunbathing topless or in the buff is strictly illegal except on one of the small beaches at Hawksbill Beach Club, where allover tans are possible. Beware that on the one or two days a week that cruise ships dock in St. John's (check with your hotel for specific dates), buses drop off loads of cruise-ship passengers on virtually all the west-coast beaches. Choose this day to tour the island by car, visit one of the more remote east end beaches, or take a day trip to Barbuda.

## Antigua

**Carlisle Bay** has a large coconut grove and two long snow-white beaches over which the estimable Curtain Bluff resort sits. Standing on the bluff of this peninsula, you can see the almost-blinding blue waters of the Atlantic Ocean drifting into the Caribbean Sea. **Dickenson Bay** has a lengthy stretch of powder-soft white sand and exceptionally calm water. Here you'll find small and large hotels, supercasual beach bars, and beachfront restaurants. Water-sports equipment can be rented at the Halcyon Cove. **Five Islands Peninsula** has four secluded beaches (including one for bathing in the buff) of fine tan sand and coral reefs for snorkeling. The Hawksbill Beach Hotel is here. **Half Moon Bay** is a ¾-mile crescent of sand, a prime area for snorkeling and windsurfing. It is on the Atlantic side of the island and can be quite rough at times. **Johnson's Point** is a deliciously deserted beach of bleached white sand on the southwest coast. **Long Bay,** on the far eastern coast, has coral reefs in water so shallow that you can actually walk out to them. Along the lovely beach are the Long Bay Hotel and the rambling Pineapple Beach Club. **Pigeon Point**, near English Harbour, is a fine white-sand beach with very calm water. There are several restaurants and bars nearby. **Runaway Beach** is home to the Barrymore Beach Hotel and the Runaway Beach Hotel, so it's stretch of white sand can get crowded. Refresh yourself with hot dogs and beer at the Barrymore's Satay Hut.

## Barbuda

**Coco Point,** on Barbuda, is an uncrowded 8-mile stretch of white sand. Barbuda, encircled by reefs and shipwrecks, is great for scuba diving.

# Outdoor Activities and Sports

Almost all the resort hotels can provide fins and masks, Windsurfers, Sunfish, catamarans, and other water-related gear (☞ Lodging, *above*).

## Bicycling

Try **Sun Cycles** (✉ Nelson Dr., Hodges Bay, ☎ 268/461–0324) for short- or long-term leases.

## Boating

**Halcyon Cove Watersports** (✉ Dickenson Bay, ☎ 268/462–0256) offers waterskiing and other water rides and rents small boats. **Nicholson Yacht Charters** (☎ 800/662–6066) are real professionals. A long-established island family, they can charter you anything from a 20-foot ketch to a giant schooner. **Sea Sports** (✉ Dickenson Bay, ☎ 268/462–3355) rents Jet Skis and Sunfish and offers parasailing and waterskiing trips. The atmosphere here can be hectic.

## Fitness Center

**Benair Fitness Club** (✉ Country Club Rd., Hodges Bay, ☎ 268/462–1540) has fitness equipment, Jacuzzi, aerobics classes, and a juice bar. **Fitness Shack** (✉ Dickenson Bay, ☎ 268/462–5223) has extensive fitness equipment and aerobics classes. **Lotus Health Centre** (✉ Dickenson Bay, ☎ 268/462–2231) offers spa treatments, including Swedish massage, foot reflexology, and various kinds of facials.

## Golf

**Cedar Valley Golf Club** (✉ Friar's Hill, northeast of St. John's, ☎ 268/462–0161) has an 18-hole course.

## Horseback Riding

**Spring Hill Riding Club** (✉ Falmouth, ☎ 268/460–1333) offers trail rides on the beach or through the bush.

## Sailing

**Antigua School of Sailing** (✉ St. John's, ☎ 268/462–2026) offers short resort courses.

## Scuba Diving

With all the wrecks and reefs, there are lots of undersea sights to see.

**Dive Antigua** (☎ 268/462–3483) offers certification courses and day and night dives from two separate locations: the St. James's Club (☎ 268/460–5000) and the Royal Antiguan (☎ 268/462–3733). **Dockyard Divers** (☎ 268/464–8591, FAX 268/460–1179) is in the English Harbour area. Owned by British ex–merchant seaman Captain A. G. Fincham, it's one of the oldest established outfits on the island, and offers diving and snorkeling trips, PADI (Professional Association of Diving Instructors) courses, and dive packages with accommodations.

## Sea Excursions

**Jolly Roger** (☎ 268/462–2064) cruises, on a real pirate ship, come complete with "pirate" crew, limbo dancing, plank walking, and other pranks. **Kokomo Cats** (☎ 268/462–7245) runs several different cruises including one to deserted beaches, one to English Harbour, and one to gaze at the sunset. **Paradise I** (☎ 268/462–4158), a 45-foot Beneteau yacht, offers both lunch or sunset cruises. **Splish Splash** (☎ 268/462–3483) is a glass-bottom boat offering two-hour snorkeling trips to Paradise Reef (landlubbers get almost as good a view from the boat). **Titi I** (☎ 268/460–1452), a 34-foot motorboat powered with twin 300 Evinrudes, will take you to nearby islets, remote beaches, or out for specially tailored snorkeling trips. They're based in Falmouth Harbour but will pick you up almost anywhere. **Wadadli Cats** (☎ 268/462–4792) offers various cruises, including a circumnavigation of the island, on its three sleek catamarans.

## Spectator Sports

For information about sports events, contact **Antigua Sports and Games** (☎ 268/462–1925).

### CRICKET

Practically the only thing most Americans know about this game is that there's something called a sticky wicket. Here, as in Britain and all the West Indies, the game is a national passion. Youngsters play on makeshift pitches, which apparently are comparable to sandlots, and international matches are fought out in the stadium on Independence Avenue in St. John's.

## Tennis

The **Temo Sports Complex** (✉ Falmouth Bay, ☎ 268/463–1781) has two floodlit tennis courts, three glass-backed squash courts, showers, a sports shop, and snack bars. Many of the larger resorts have their own tennis courts. The **St. James's Club** (☎ 268/460–5000) has seven (five lighted for night play); **Sandals** (☎ 268/462–0267) has two; **Rex Halcyon Cove Beach Resort** (☎ 268/462–0256) four (lighted); and **Curtain Bluff** (☎ 268/462–8400) four Har-Tru and a grass court. Guests have top priority. For nonguests, court fees are about $30 an hour.

## Waterskiing

**Halcyon Cove Watersports** (☎ 268/462–0256) and **Sea Sports** (☎ 268/462–3355), both at Dickenson Bay, will take you waterskiing.

## Windsurfing

Most major hotels offer windsurfing equipment.

The **High Wind Centre** (✉ Lord Nelson Beach Hotel, ☎ 268/462–3094) is the spot for serious board sailors, run by expert Patrick Scales.

**Halcyon Cove Watersports** (☎ 268/462–0256) offers rentals and instruction.

# Shopping

Antigua's duty-free shops are at Heritage Quay; they're the reason so many cruise ships call here. Bargains can be found on perfumes, liqueurs and liquor (including, of course, Antiguan rum), jewelry, china, and crystal. As for local items, look for straw hats, baskets, batik, pottery, and hand-printed cotton clothing.

## Shopping Areas

**Redcliffe Quay,** on the waterfront at the south edge of St. John's, is by far the most appealing shopping area. Here several restaurants and over 30 boutiques, many with interesting one-of-a-kind items, are set around landscaped courtyards shaded by colorful trees. **Heritage Quay,** also in St. John's, has some 35 shops—including many that are duty-free— that cater primarily to the cruise ship crowd that docks almost at its doorstep. Outlets here include Benetton, the Body Shop, Polo, Gucci, and Oshkosh B'Gosh. The main tourist shops in St. John's are along **St. Mary's, High,** and **Long streets.**

## Good Buys

### BOOKS AND MAGAZINES

**Flower Basket** (⌧ Nevis St.—on the left, keep going, it's really there; ☎ 268/462–0411) is not only a flower shop, but also has the latest U.S. magazines, newspapers, and best-selling paperback books. **Map Shop** (⌧ St. Mary's St., ☎ 268/462–3993) has a "must" buy for those interested in Antiguan life: the paperback *To Shoot Hard Labour: The Life and Times of Samuel Smith, an Antiguan Workingman.* Also check out any of the books of Jamaica Kincaid, whose works on her native Antigua have won international, albeit controversial, acclaim.

### CIGARS, LIQUOR, AND LIQUEURS

**Cigar Shop** (⌧ Heritage Quay, ☎ 890/462–2677) sells Cuban cigars, but remember that it's illegal to bring them back to the United States. **Manuel Diaz Liquor Store** (⌧ Long and Market Sts., ☎ 268/462–0440) has a wide selection of Caribbean rums and liqueurs. **The Warehouse** (⌧ St. Mary's St., ☎ 268/462–0495) offers bargains on imported wines and liquor.

### CHINA AND CRYSTAL

**Little Switzerland** (⌧ Heritage Quay, ☎ 268/462–3108) houses pricey buys in a luxurious, and air-conditioned, setting. **Norma's Duty-Free Shop** (⌧ Heritage Quay Shopping Center and the Halcyon Cove, ☎ 268/462–0172) offers the usual range of delicate sets, from Lladro to Limoges. **Specialty Shoppe** (⌧ St. Mary's St., ☎ 268/462–1198) has wares that make impressive presents.

### CLOTHING AND FABRICS

**Base** (⌧ Redcliffe Quay, ☎ 268/460–2500) is the brainchild of English designer Steven Giles, whose striped cotton-and-Lycra beach-wear is now all the rage on the island. **CoCo Shop** (⌧ St. Mary's St., ☎ 268/462–1128) is a favorite source for Sea Island cotton designs, Daks clothing, and Liberty of London fabrics, along with the shop's own designs for the country-club set. **Galley Boutiques** (⌧ Main shop in English Harbour, ☎ 268/460–1525; St. James's Club, ☎ 268/460–1333) is where Janie Easton sells her original designs at reasonable prices. **Jacaranda** (⌧ Redcliffe Quay, ☎ 268/462–1888) sells batiks, sarongs, and swimwear. **Noreen Phillips** (⌧ Redcliffe St. and Friendly Alley, ☎ 268/462–3127) creates glitzy appliquéd and beaded evening wear inspired by the colors of the sea and sunset. **A Thousand Flowers** (⊠ Redcliffe Quay, ☎ 268/462–4264) sells resort wear made of comfortable silks, linens, and batiks from all over the world and has many unusual items.

## JEWELRY

**Colombian Emeralds** (⊠ Heritage Quay, ☎ 268/462–2086) is the largest retailer of Colombian emeralds in the world. **The Goldsmitty** (⊠ Redcliffe Quay, ☎ 268/462–4601) is Hans Smit, an expert goldsmith who turns gold, black coral, and precious and semiprecious stones into one-of-a-kind works of art. (Be aware that environmental groups discourage tourists from purchasing corals that are designated as endangered species, because the reefs are often harvested carelessly.)

**Norma's Duty-Free Shop** (⊠ Heritage Quay Shopping Center and the Halcyon Cove, ☎ 268/462–0172) has jewelry bargains.

## LOCAL ART AND CRAFTS

**Craft Originals Studio** (⊠ Coast Rd., ☎ 268/463–2519) is where Trinidadian Natalie White sells her sculptured cushions and wall hangings, all hand-painted on silk and signed. **Decibels** (⊠ Redcliffe, Quay, ☎ 268/462–3955) offers a United Nations of craftwork, from Creole houses to Mexican raku pottery. **Handicraft Centre** (⊠ High and Thames Sts., St. John's, ☎ 268/462–0639) specializes in island products—straw bags, mahogany warri boards, pottery, and hand-painted T-shirts and sundresses. **Harmony Hall** (⊠ At Brown's Bay Mill, near Freetown, ☎ 268/460–4120) is the Antiguan sister to the original Jamaica location. In addition to "Annabella Boxes," books, and cards, there are pottery and ceramic pieces, carved wooden fantasy birds, and an ever-changing roster of exhibits. **Island Arts Galleries** (⊠ Alton Pl., Sandy La., behind Hodges Bay Club, ☎ 268/461–3332; Heritage Quay, ☎ 268/462–2787; and St. James's Club, ☎ 268/460–5000), run by artist-filmmaker Nick Maley and his wife, Gloria, is a melting pot for Caribbean artists, with prices ranging from $10 to $15,000. **Mimosa** (⊠ Heritage Quay, ☎ 268/462–2923) sells hand-painted wind chimes and porcelain clowns in island dress. **Seahorse Studios** (⊠ At Cobbs Cross, en route to English Harbour, ☎ 268/463–1417), opened by John and Katie Shears, presents the works of good artists in a bucolic setting.

## PERFUME

**CoCo Shop** (⊠ St. Mary's St., ☎ 268/462–1128) stocks exotic island fragrances. **Little Switzerland** (⊠ Heritage Quay, ☎ 268/462–3108) has an extensive selection of European scents for men and women. **La Parfumerie** (⊠ Heritage Quay, ☎ 268/462–2601) offers high-priced imported scents. **Scent Shop** (⊠ High St., ☎ 268/462–0303) in downtown St. John's offers scent-sational buys in perfumes and cosmetics.

# Nightlife

Most of Antigua's evening entertainment centers on the resort hotels, which feature calypso singers, steel bands, limbo dancers, and folkloric groups on a regular basis. Check with the Department of Tourism for up-to-date information.

**Colombo's** (⊠ Galleon Beach Club, English Harbour, ☎ 268/460–1452) is the place to be on Wednesday night for live reggae. **Crazy Cactus Cantina** (⊠ All Saints Rd., ☎ 268/462–1183) holds frequent Latin nights, when the sensuous rhythms of live merengue and salsa hold sway. **Jolly Roger** (⊠ Dickenson Bay, ☎ 268/462–2064) gets a boisterous group for its Saturday-night cruises. Head out on this replica of a pirate ship for a four-hour sail under the stars with a barbecue, open bar,

and dancing to live island music. **Lemon Tree** (✉ Long and Church Sts.,
St. John's, ☎ 268/461–1969) restaurant swings every night but Sunday in season until at least 11 PM. **Millers by the Sea** (✉ Runaway Beach,
☎ 268/462–2393) draws a crowd that spills over onto the beach for
its ever-popular happy hour and live nightly entertainment. This is the
place to come and dance on the beach way into the night. **Russell's**
(✉ Fort James, ☎ 268/462–5479) presents live jazz combos on Sunday nights. **Shirley Heights Lookout** (✉ Shirley Heights, ☎ 268/463–
1785) does Sunday-afternoon barbecues that continue into the night
with music and dancing. It's *the* place to be Sunday afternoons and
Thursday evenings, when local residents, visitors, and the yachting crowd
gather for boisterous fun and to exchange the latest gossip. **The Verandah**
(✉ St. Mary's St., St. John's, ☎ 268/462–5677) attracts an appreciative
local crowd for live music Friday and Saturday nights.

### Casinos

There are four major casinos on Antigua, as well as several holes-in-
the-wall that feature mainly one-armed bandits. Hours vary depending on the season and whether or not cruise ships are in, so it's best to
inquire upon your arrival to the island. The "world's largest slot machine" as well as gaming tables are at the **King's Casino** (✉ Heritage
Quay, ☎ 268/462–1727). The **St. James's Club** (✉ Mamora Bay, ☎
268/463–1113) has a rather flamboyant casino with a European ambience. The casino at the **Royal Antiguan Resort** (☎ 268/462–3733)
is a model of those in Atlantic City, New Jersey.

### Discos

**Ribbit** (✉ Donovans, Green Bay, ☎ 268/462–7996) attracts a lively
mix of locals and tourists who dance the night away (no shorts allowed).
It's open Wednesday–Saturday from 10:30 PM. **The Web** (✉ Old
Parham Rd., St. John's, ☎ 268/462–3186) and **Grasshopper** (✉ Airport Rd., no phone) attract a somewhat rowdier, more heavily local
crowd.

## Exploring Antigua

Before you start, study your map for a minute or two. Road names
are not posted, so you will need to have a sense of where you are heading if you hope to find it. The easiest way to get to anything is to see
if a popular restaurant is near it, since easy-to-spot signs leading the
way to restaurants are posted all over the island. (You'll see tons of
them nailed to a post at every crossroad.) If you start to feel lost along
the way, don't hesitate to ask anyone you see for directions. Bear in
mind that locals generally give directions in terms of landmarks that
may not seem much like landmarks to you (turn left at the yellow house,
or right at the big tree). All major hotels provide free maps and island
brochures, or, if you happen to be in St. John's, stop in at the Tourist
Bureau, at the corner of Long and Thames streets. It's a good idea to
wear a swimsuit under your clothes while you're sightseeing—one of
the sights to strike your fancy may be an enticing secluded beach. Be
sure to bring your camera along. There are some picture-perfect spots
around the island.

*Numbers in the margin correspond to points of interest on the Antigua
(and Barbuda) map.*

SIGHTS TO SEE

**❸ Betty's Hope.** Just outside the village of Pares a marked dirt road leads
to the village of Betty's Hope, Antigua's first sugar plantation, founded
in 1650. You can tour the twin windmills and view exhibits on the is-

land's sugar era. It isn't much now, but the private trust overseeing the restoration has ambitious plans.

**⑤ Curtain Bluff.** At the tip of a tiny outcropping of land, between Carlisle Bay and Morris Bay, Curtain Bluff offers dramatic views of the wonderful color contrasts where waters of the Atlantic Ocean meet those of the Caribbean Sea. From here, the main road skirts the southwest coast, dancing in and out of hardwood trees and offering tantalizing glimpses of lovely beaches and spectacular views. The road then veers away from the water and goes through the villages of Bolans and Jennings.

**⑫ Devil's Bridge.** This natural formation, sculpted by the crashing breakers of the Atlantic at Indian Creek, is now a national park. Blowholes have been carved by the waves. They may be hard to spot at first, but just wait until a wave bursts through!

**⑧ English Harbour.** The most famous of Antigua's attractions lies on the coast, just south of Falmouth. In 1671, the governor of the Leeward Islands wrote to the Council for Foreign Plantations in London pointing out the advantages of this landlocked harbor, and by 1704 English Harbour was in regular use as a garrisoned station.

In 1784, 26-year-old Horatio Nelson sailed in on HMS *Boreas* to serve as captain and second in command of the Leeward Island Station. Under his command was the captain of HMS *Pegasus,* Prince William Henry, duke of Clarence, who was to ascend the throne of England as William IV. The prince was Nelson's close friend and acted as best man when Nelson married the young widow Fannie Nisbet on Nevis in 1787.

When the Royal Navy abandoned the station at English Harbour in 1889, it fell into a state of decay. The Society of the Friends of English Harbour began restoring it in 1951, and on Dockyard Day, November 14, 1961, **Nelson's Dockyard** was opened with much fanfare.

The dockyard is reminiscent, albeit on a much smaller scale, of Williamsburg, Virginia. Within the compound there are crafts shops, hotels, and restaurants. It is a hub for oceangoing yachts and serves as headquarters for the annual Sailing Week Regatta. A lively community of mariners keeps the area active in season. Beach lovers tend to stay elsewhere on the island, but visitors who enjoy history and who are part of (or like being around) the nautical scene often choose one of the hotels in the area of English Harbour. If you'd like to get a look at the area from the water, board the *Horatio Nelson* for a 20-minute guided cruise (☞ Guided Tours *in* Antigua A to Z, *below*).

The **Admiral's House Museum** displays ship models, a model of English Harbour, silver trophies, maps, prints, and Nelson's very own telescope and tea caddy. ⊠ *English Harbour,* ☎ *268/463–1053 or 268/463–1379.* ⊠ *$2.* ⊙ *Daily 8–6.*

On a ridge overlooking the dockyard is **Clarence House** (☎ 268/463–1026), built in 1787 and once the home of the duke of Clarence. Princess Margaret and Lord Snowdon spent part of their honeymoon here in 1960, and Queen Elizabeth and Prince Philip have dined here. It is now used by the governor-general as a country home; visits are possible when he is not in residence. The place is decorated pretty much as it was in the 18th century and is definitely worth a visit.

NEED A        Cool off with the yachting crowd on the terrace of the **Admiral's Inn**
BREAK?        (⊠ English Harbour, ☎ 268/460–1027), where the deeply tanned
              crews can keep an eye on their multimillion-dollar babies offshore—and

on each other. The people-watching is first-rate, and so are the banana daiquiris (with or without Antiguan rum).

**❼ Falmouth.** This town sits on a lovely bay backed by former sugar plantations and sugar mills. **St. Paul's Church** was rebuilt on the site of a church once used by troops during the Nelson period.

**❹ Fig Tree Drive.** This road takes you through the rain forest, which is rich in mangoes, pineapples, and banana trees (*fig* is the Antiguan word for banana). This is also the hilliest part of the island—**Boggy Peak,** to the west, is the highest point, rising to 1,319 feet.

**❻ Fort George.** East of **Liberta,** one of the first settlements founded by freed slaves, on Monk's Hill, this fort was built from 1689 to 1720. It wouldn't be of much help to anybody these days, but among the ruins you can make out the sites for its 32 cannons, its water cisterns, the base of the old flagstaff, and some of the original buildings.

**❷ Fort James.** Named after King James II, this fort was constructed between 1704 and 1739 as a lookout point for the city and St. John's Harbour. The ramparts overlooking the small islands in the bay are in ruins, but 10 cannons still point out to sea.

**❿ Harmony Hall.** Northeast of Freetown (follow the signs), is this interesting art gallery. A sister to the Jamaican gallery near Ocho Rios, Jamaica, Harmony Hall is built on the foundation of a 17th-century sugar-plantation great house. Artists Graham Davis and Peter and Annabella Proudlock, who founded the Jamaican gallery, teamed up with local entrepreneur Geoffrey Pidduck to create an Antiguan art gallery specializing in high-quality West Indian art. A large gallery is used for one-man shows, and another exhibition hall displays watercolors. A small bar and an outside restaurant under the trees are open in season. ✉ *Brown's Mill Bay,* ☎ *268/463–2057.* ☉ *Daily 10–6.*

**⓫ Indian Town.** This is a national park where archaeological digs have revealed evidence of Carib occupation.

**❸ Megaliths of Greencastle Hill.** It's an arduous but rewarding climb to these eerie rock slabs. Some say the megaliths were set up by humans for the worship of the sun and moon; others believe they are nothing more than unusual geological formations.

**⓮ Parham.** This tiny village is a splendid, sleepy example of a traditional colonial settlement. **St. Peter's Church,** built in 1840 by Thomas Weekes, an English architect, is an octagonal Italianate building whose facade was once richly decorated with stucco, though it suffered considerable damage during the earthquake of 1843.

**❶ St. John's.** Antigua's capital, home to some 40,000 people (nearly half the island's population), lies at sea level at the inland end of a sheltered bay on the northwest coast of the island. The city has seen better days, but it is in the midst of a face-lift, and there are some notable historic sights, pleasant shopping areas, and good restaurants. Although much of the city looks shabby, it is definitely worth a visit. Most of the gift stores and restaurants are near the waterfront. Up the hill is Antigua's downtown, with stores carrying major appliances, plumbing supplies, and other goods unlikely to be of interest to tourists.

The **Museum of Antigua and Barbuda** offers a true "hands-on history" opportunity. Signs say PLEASE TOUCH, with the hope of welcoming both citizens and visitors into Antigua's past. Try your hand at the educational video games. Exhibits interpret the history of the nation from its geological birth to its political independence in 1981. There are fossil and coral remains from some 34 million years ago, a life-size replica of an Arawak house, models of a sugar plantation and a wattle-and-daub house, and a minishop with handicrafts, books, historical prints, and paintings. The colonial building that houses the museum is the former courthouse, which dates from 1750. ⊠ *Church and Market Sts.,* ☎ *268/462–1469.* 🎟 *Free.* ⊙ *Weekdays 8:30–4, Sat. 10–1.*

At the south gate of the **Anglican Cathedral of St. John the Divine,** there are figures of St. John the Baptist and St. John the Divine said to have been taken from one of Napoléon's ships and brought to Antigua. The original church was built in 1681, replaced by a stone building in 1745, and destroyed by an earthquake in 1843. The present building dates from 1845. With an eye to future earthquakes, the parishioners had the interior completely encased in pitch pine, hoping to forestall heavy damage. The church was elevated to the status of cathedral in 1848. ⊠ *Between Long and Newgate Sts.,* ☎ *268/461–0082.*

Shopaholics head directly for **Heritage Quay,** a continually expanding multimillion-dollar shopping complex. Two-story buildings showcase stores specializing in duty-free goods, sportswear, T-shirts, imports from down-island (paintings, T-shirts, straw baskets), and local crafts, plus several restaurants and a casino. Cruise-ship passengers disembark here from the 500-foot-long pier. ⊠ *High and Thames Sts.*

**Redcliffe Quay,** set at the water's edge just south of Heritage Quay, is the most appealing part of St. John's. Attractively restored buildings in a riot of cotton-candy colors house shops, restaurants, and boutiques and are linked by courtyards and landscaped walkways. This is the shopping area favored by both residents and return guests. There are no duty-free shops, but there are many other interesting choices. There are also cafés where you can sit and ponder the scene of two centuries ago, when slaves were held here prior to being sold.

NEED A      At **Hemingway's** (⊠ Jardine Court, ☎ 268/462–2763), a historic clap-
BREAK?      board house in the center of St. John's, you can sit on the upstairs ve-
            randa and drink papaya and mango juice or have breakfast and watch
            the bustling life of the streets below.

At the far south end of town, where Market Street forks into Valley Road and All Saints Road, a whole lot of haggling goes on every Friday and Saturday, when locals jam the public **marketplace** to buy and sell fruits, vegetables, fish, and spices. Be sure to ask before you aim a camera; expect the subject of your shot to ask for a tip. This is shopping the old-time Caribbean way, a jambalaya of sights, sounds, and smells.

**⑨ Shirley Heights.** This bluff affords a spectacular view of English Harbour. The heights are named for Sir Thomas Shirley, the governor who fortified the harbor in 1787. Not far from Shirley Heights is the **Dows Hill Interpretation Centre,** where observation platforms provide still more sensational vistas of the whole English Harbour area. There's a multimedia presentation on the island's history and culture, from the days of the Amerindians to the present. ⊠ *For information, call National Parks Authority at 268/460–1053.* 🎟 *E.C.$15.* ⊙ *Daily 9–5.*

## Barbuda

**⑮ Barbuda.** Twenty-six miles north of Antigua is Barbuda—a flat, 62-square-mile coral atoll with 17 miles of stunning pinkish white-sand beaches. Almost all the island's 1,200 people live in **Codrington.** Barbuda's 8-mile **Coco Point Beach** lures beachcombers, and the island is ringed by wrecks and reef, which makes it a great draw for divers and snorkelers. Ornithologists and bird lovers come here, too. The **Bird Sanctuary,** a wide mangrove-filled lagoon, is home to an estimated 170 species of birds, including frigate birds with 8-foot wingspans.

The sole historic ruin here is **Martello Tower,** which is believed to have been a lighthouse built by the Spaniards before the English occupied the island. LIAT (☞ Arriving and Departing *in* Antigua A to Z, *below*) has regularly scheduled daily flights from Antigua to Barbuda (with departure times just right for day-trippers); air and boat charters are also available (contact the Department of Tourism). Those wishing to overnight here can choose from two superluxury resorts and several guest houses.

## Antigua A to Z

### Arriving and Departing

BY PLANE

**American Airlines** (☎ 800/433–7300) has daily direct service from New York and Miami, as well as several flights from San Juan that connect with flights from more than 100 U.S. cities. **BWIA** (☎ 800/327–7401) has nonstop service from New York, Miami, and Toronto. **Air Canada** (☎ 800/776–3000) has nonstop service from Toronto. **British Airways** (☎ 800/247–9297) has nonstop service from London. **Lufthansa** (☎ 800/645–3880) has nonstop service from Frankfurt. **LIAT** (☎ 268/462–0701) has daily flights from Antigua to Barbuda, 15 minutes away, as well as to and from many other Caribbean islands. At press time, **Continental** was in the midst of negotiations to initiate service from several North American gateways.

**V. C. Bird International Airport** is, on the tiniest of scales, to the Caribbean what O'Hare is to the Midwest. It's a major hub for traffic between Caribbean islands, and it is always busy with tiny planes taking off and landing.

FROM THE AIRPORT

Taxis meet every flight, and drivers will offer to guide you around the island. The taxis are unmetered, but rates are posted at the airport and drivers are required to carry a rate card with them. The fixed rate from the airport to St. John's is $12 in U.S. currency (although drivers have been known to *quote* Eastern Caribbean dollars) and from the airport to English Harbour, $21.

### Currency

Local currency is the Eastern Caribbean dollar (E.C.$), which is tied to the U.S. dollar and fluctuates only slightly. At hotels, the rate is E.C.$2.60 to U.S.$1; at banks, it's about E.C.$2.70. American dollars are readily accepted, although you will usually receive change in E.C. dollars. Be sure you understand which currency is being used, since most places quote prices in E.C. dollars. Most hotels, restaurants, and duty-free shops take major credit cards, and all accept traveler's checks. It's a good idea to inquire at the tourist office or your hotel about current credit-card policy. Note: Prices quoted are in U.S. dollars unless indicated otherwise.

### Emergencies

**Police:** ☎ 268/462–0125. **Fire:** ☎ 268/462–0044. **Ambulance:** ☎ 268/462–0251. **Hospital:** There is a 24-hour emergency room at the 210-bed **Holberton Hospital** (✉ Hospital Rd., St. John's, ☎ 268/462–0251, 268/462–0252, or 268/462–0253). **Pharmacies: City Pharmacy** (✉ St. Mary's St., St. John's, ☎ 268/462–1363) and **Health Pharmacy** (✉ Redcliffe St., St. John's, ☎ 268/462–1255).

## Getting Around

### BUSES

You'll see two bus stations in St. John's, near the Botanical Gardens and near Central Market, but don't expect to see many buses. Bus schedules here epitomize what is called "island time," which is to say they roll when the spirit (infrequently) moves them.

### CAR RENTALS

To rent a car, you'll need a valid driver's license and a temporary permit ($12), which is available through the rental agent. Rentals average about $50 per day in season, with unlimited mileage. You'll probably get a better daily rate if you rent for several days. Most agencies rent automatic, stick-shift, and right- and left-hand-drive vehicles, as well as Jeeps ($55 per day). Although these four-wheel-drive vehicles will get you more places and are refreshingly open, beware that the roads are full of potholes, and a day in a Jeep can leave you feeling as if you've been through a paint-mixing machine! Remember to drive on the left (pay particular attention getting in and out of rotaries and making turns), and know that virtually all roads are unmarked. Fortunately, you will not have to deal with the incredibly steep curves that are on so many Caribbean islands.

Among the agencies are **Budget** (⊠ St. John's, ☎ 268/462–3009 or 800/472–3325), **National** (⊠ St. John's, ☎ 268/462–2113 or 800/328–4567), **Thrifty** (⊠ Airport, ☎ 268/462–0976), **Hertz** (⊠ St. John's, also Jolly Harbour, ☎ 268/462–4114), **Dollar** (⊠ St. John's, ☎ 268/462–0362), and **Avis** (⊠ At the airport or the St. James's Club, ☎ 268/462–2840).

### TAXIS

If you're uncomfortable about driving on the left or prone to getting lost, a taxi is your best bet, although fares mount up quickly. Taxis are unmetered, but rates are fixed from here to there, and drivers are required to carry a rate card at all times. They'll even take you from the St. John's area to English Harbour and wait for a "reasonable" amount of time (about a half hour) while you look around for about $40.

## Guided Tours

Virtually all taxi drivers double as guides, and you can arrange an island tour with one for about $20 an hour. Every major hotel has a cabbie on call and may be able to negotiate a discount, particularly off-season.

**Alexander, Parrish Ltd.** (⊠ St. John's, ☎ 268/462–0387) specializes in island tours and can also arrange overnight stays. **Antours** (⊠ St. John's, ☎ 268/462–4788) gives half- and full-day tours of the island. Antours is also the American Express representative on the island. **Bryson's Travel** (⊠ St. John's, ☎ 268/462–0223) offers personalized tours of the island, as well as cruises and deep-sea-fishing trips. **Estate Safari Adventure** (☎ 268/462–4713) offers tours to the "wilds" of Antigua's interior, where there are few marked trails and roads are rough. You'll see deserted plantation houses, rain-forest trails, and ruined sugar mills and forts. The luxuriant tropical forest around the island's highest point, Boggy Peak, is especially worth seeing. The cost of the tour (about $60 per person) includes lunch and snorkeling at a secluded beach. **Horatio Nelson** (⊠ Dockyard Divers, ☎ 268/464–8591) provides a good view of English Harbour from the water; hop on board for the 20-minute guided cruise. The tour costs $6 per person, and the boat leaves every half hour from 9 to 5 daily. **Tropikelly** (☎ 268/461–0383) offers an off-road adventure in a jeep, allowing participants to appreciate the island's topography. Hiking is involved, though not strenuous. The tour visits the island's plantation houses, forts, and rain forests.

## Language
Antigua's official language is English.

## Opening and Closing Times
Although some stores still follow the tradition of closing for lunch, most shops, especially in season, are open Monday–Friday 9–5 and Saturday 8–noon or 8–3. Hours vary from bank to bank, but generally they are open Monday–Thursday 8–2 and Friday 8–4.

## Passports and Visas
U.S. and Canadian citizens need proof of identity. A valid passport is most desirable, but a birth certificate is acceptable provided it has a raised or embossed seal and has been issued by a county or state (not a hospital) *and* provided that you also have some type of photo identification, such as a driver's license. A driver's license by itself is *not* sufficient. British citizens need a passport. All visitors must present a return or ongoing ticket.

## Precautions
Some beaches are shaded by manchineel trees, whose leaves and applelike fruit are poisonous to touch. Most of the trees are posted with warning signs and should be avoided; even raindrops falling from them can cause painful blisters. If you should come in contact with one, rinse the affected area and contact a doctor.

Throughout the Caribbean, incidents of petty theft are increasing. Leave your valuables in the hotel safe-deposit box; don't leave them unattended in your room or on the beach. Also, the streets of St. John's are fairly deserted at night, so it's not a good idea to wander out alone.

## Taxes and Service Charges
Hotels collect a 7% government room tax and usually add a 10% service charge to your bill. In restaurants, a 10% service charge is usually added to your bill, and it is customary to leave another 5% if you are pleased with the service. Taxi drivers expect a 10% tip. The departure tax is $10.

## Telephones and Mail
To call Antigua from the United States, dial 1, then area code 268, then the local seven-digit number. Few hotels have direct-dial telephones, but connections are easily made through the switchboard. The Caribbean Phone Card, available in $5, $10, and $20 amounts, can be used for local and long-distance calls and for access to AT&T USA Direct lines. There are now quite a few phones that accept the phone cards, and they work much better than the regular pay phones. You can purchase the card from most hotels or from a post office. Some phone-card booths can now access Sprint and MCI. In addition, there are several Boatphones scattered throughout the island at major tourist sites; simply pick up the receiver and the operator will take your credit-card number (any major card) and assign you a PIN (personal identification number). Calls using your PIN are then charged to that credit card.

To place a call to the United States, dial 1, the appropriate area code, and the seven-digit number, or use the phone card or one of the AT&T USA Direct phones, which are available at several locations including the airport departure lounge, the cruise terminal at St. John's, and the English Harbour Marina. To place an interisland call, dial the local seven-digit number.

In an emergency, you can make calls from Cable & Wireless (WI) Ltd. (✉ 42–44 St. Mary's St., St. John's, ☎ 268/462–9840; ✉ Nelson's Dockyard, English Harbour, ☎ 268/463–1517).

Airmail letters to North America cost E.C.80¢; postcards, E.C.60¢. The post office is at the foot of High Street in St. John's.

## Visitor Information

Before you go, contact the **Antigua and Barbuda Tourist Offices** in the United States (✉ 610 5th Ave., Suite 311, New York, NY 10020, ☎ 212/541–4117; ✉ 25 S.E. 2nd Ave., Suite 300, Miami, FL 33131, ☎ 305/381–6762), in Canada (✉ 60 St. Clair Ave. E, Suite 304, Toronto, Ontario M4T 1N5, ☎ 416/961–3085), and in the United Kingdom (✉ Antigua House, 15 Thayer St., London W1M 5LD, England, ☎ 0171/486–7073).

Once on Antigua, visit the **Antigua and Barbuda Department of Tourism** (✉ Thames and Long Sts., St. John's, ☎ 268/462–0480), open Monday–Thursday 8–4:30, Friday 8–3. There is also a tourist-information desk at the airport, just beyond the immigration checkpoint. The tourist office gives limited information. You may have more success with the **Antigua Hotels Association** (✉ Long St., St. John's, ☎ 268/462–3703), which also provides assistance.

# 4 Aruba

Updated by
Melissa Rivers

**I**MAGINE ARUBA AS ONE BIG LOVE BOAT CRUISE. Most of its 38 hotels sit side by side down one major strip along the southwestern shore, with restaurants, exotic boutiques, fiery floor shows, and glitzy casinos right on their premises. Nearly every night there are organized theme parties, treasure hunts, beachside barbecues, and fish fries with steel bands and limbo dancers.

The "A" in the ABC Islands, Aruba is small—only 19.6 miles long and 6 miles across at its widest point. Once a member of the Netherlands Antilles, Aruba became an independent entity within the Netherlands in 1986, with its own royally appointed governor, a democratic government, and a 21-member elected Parliament. With education, housing, and health care financed by an economy based on tourism, the island's population of 70,337 recognizes visitors as valued guests. The national anthem proclaims, "The greatness of our people is their great cordiality," and this is no exaggeration. Waiters serve you with smiles, English is spoken everywhere, and hotel hospitality directors appear delighted to serve your special needs. Direct air service from the United States makes Aruba an excellent choice for even a short vacation.

The island's distinctive beauty lies in its countryside—an almost extraterrestrial landscape full of rocky deserts, divi-divi trees, cactus jungles, secluded coves, and aquamarine vistas with crashing waves. With its low humidity and average temperature of 82°F, Aruba has the climate of a paradise; rain comes mostly during November. Sun, cooling trade winds, friendly and courteous service, modern and efficient amenities, new golf and tennis clubs, and 11 modern casinos are Aruba's strong suit and help fill its more than 7,000 hotel rooms.

## Lodging

Hotels are fairly expensive in Aruba. To save money, go during low season (summer) or take advantage of the packages that American Airlines and other tour operators offer, and the hotel packages, which are considerably less expensive than the one-night rate. Most of the hotels are west of Oranjestad along L. G. Smith and J.E. Irausquin boulevards and are miniresort complexes, with their own drugstores, boutiques, fitness centers, beauty parlors, casinos, restaurants, pool bars, and gourmet delis. Daily activities (beach bingo or volleyball, aquacise or aerobics, craft classes, even Papiamento lessons) are usually part of the package. At family resorts, children often get free accommodation in their parents' room; check with the property for age qualifications. Hotel restaurants and clubs are open to all guests on the island, so you can visit other properties no matter where you're staying. Most hotels, unless specified, do not include meals in their room rates. The meal plans offered are optional and incur an additional per-day expense. Off-season rates are discounted approximately 40%.

| CATEGORY | COST* |
|---|---|
| $$$$ | over $300 |
| $$$ | $225–$300 |
| $$ | $150–$225 |
| $ | under $150 |

*All prices are for a standard double room for two during high season, excluding 5% government tax and 11% service charge.

$$$$  ⊞ **Americana Aruba Beach Resort & Casino.** Teeming activity surrounds the clover leaf–shape pool with a waterfall and two hot tubs in its center. The buzz is indicative of the atmosphere in general: A so-

cial director is always cajoling you to participate in everything from beer-drinking contests to bikini shows. Children can be kept equally busy in the free daily children's activities program. In the guest rooms, white bamboo and bleached-wood furniture are complemented by tropical blue, green, and peach fabrics; balconies are narrow step-outs. Suites are oddly laid out and therefore not recommended. Americans and Canadians, mostly in tour groups, make up 80% of the clientele. The staff can be a tad lackadaisical. ✉ *J.E. Irausquin Blvd. 83, Palm Beach,* ☎ *297/8–24500 or 800/447–7462; in NY, 212/223–2848;* ℻ *297/8–23191. 419 rooms. 3 restaurants, 3 bars, refrigerators, room service, pool, barbershop, beauty salon, 2 outdoor hot tubs, 2 tennis courts, exercise room, Ping-Pong, volleyball, beach, water-sports center, casino, video games, baby-sitting, children's program (4–13), laundry service and dry cleaning, business services, travel services, car rental. AE, DC, MC, V. EP, MAP, All-inclusive.*

**$$$$** 🏨 **Aruba Marriott Resort and Stellaris Casino.** Aruba's newest—and most expensive—luxury high-rise resort opened on Palm Beach close to the Tierra del Sol golf course in the summer of 1995. You'll hear the sound of water everywhere, whether it's the trickling of streams and waterfalls in the elegant marble lobby and around the tropically landscaped free-form pool or the beating of the surf. The rooms are spacious and attractively appointed (crisp, clean forest-green-on-white decor softened by floral bedspreads and pastel watercolor paintings), and all have an ocean view and a balcony. Well-planned amenities include minibars, hair dryers, robes, and double sinks in the bathrooms. In fact, everything here is top notch: gorgeous grounds and beach, an enormous casino, gourmet dining, a complete health spa, and an array of land- and water-oriented activities. ✉ *L. G. Smith Blvd. 101,* ☎ *297/8–69000 or 800/223–6388,* ℻ *297/8–60649. 413 rooms, 18 suites. 3 restaurants, 5 bars, café, in-room safes, minibars, no-smoking floors, refrigerators, room service, pool, barbershop, beauty salon, indoor hot tub, outdoor hot tub, massage, saunas, spa, 3 tennis courts, aerobics, health club, horseshoes, volleyball, beach, water-sports center (including scuba diving), shops, casino, art gallery, baby-sitting, children's program (5–12), laundry service and dry cleaning, concierge floor, business services, meeting rooms, travel services, car rental. AE, D, DC, MC, V. EP, MAP, FAP, All-inclusive.*

**$$$$** 🏨 **Hyatt Regency Aruba Resort & Casino.** This $57-million resort, a
★ favorite among Aruba's luxury properties, looks like a Spanish grandee's palace with art deco–style flourishes and a multilevel pool with waterfalls, a two-story waterslide, and a lagoon stocked with tropical fish and black swans. Beyond that is a white-sand beach dotted with palms. The rooms, decorated with southwestern motifs, are all the same spacious size, so the view determines their price. Tiny step-out balconies are nothing special, but extras in the room—coffee/tea setup, voice mail, and an oversize bathroom—make up for it. The top floor houses the hedonistic Regency Club rooms, each with two huge his-and-her marble bathrooms loaded with every amenity, plus a private-floor lounge where free breakfast, afternoon tea, and happy-hour drinks are served. Camp Hyatt keeps children ages 3 to 12 busy. Four excellent restaurants are on the premises, among them Olé and Ruinas del Mar. Their design is exquisite: stone and marble "ruins" surrounded by moats, waterfalls, and splashing fountains. The food is equally luscious. The extensive facilities, a host of well-managed services, plus a fine staff have turned this property into the top luxury resort on the island. It is a truly romantic resort, a top choice for honeymooners. ✉ *J.E. Irausquin Blvd. 85, Palm Beach,* ☎ *297/8–61234 or 800/236–1234,* ℻ *297/8–61682. 325 rooms, 18 suites. 4 restaurants, 4 bars, snack bar, in-room safes, minibars, no-smoking floor, room service, pool, beauty*

# Aruba

California Pt.

California
Sand Dunes

Malmok Beach

Fisherman's Hut

Mt. Altovista

Bushiribana

Noord

Palm Beach

Eagle Beach

Paradera

Santa Cruz

Manchebo Beach

Divi Beach

Druif
Bay

Oranjestad

Reina Beatrix
International
Airport

N

0          4 miles
0          6 km

**Exploring**
Alto Vista Chapel, **8**
California
Lighthouse, **9**
Frenchman's Pass, **3**
Guadirikiri/Fontein
Caves, **5**
Hooiberg (Haystack
Hill), **2**
Malmok, **10**
Natural Bridge, **7**

Oranjestad, **1**
Rock Formations
(Ayo and Casiban), **6**
San Nicolas, **4**

**Dining**
Boonoonoonoos, **35**
Brisas del Mar, **40**
Buccaneer
Restaurant, **20**
Charlie's Restaurant
& Bar, **41**
Chez Mathilde, **36**
Gasparito Restaurant
and Art Gallery, **21**
Kowloon, **37**

Old Cunucu
House, **15**
Old Mill, **25**
La Paloma, **22**
Papiamento, **23**
Le Petit Café, **38**
Talk of the Town
Restaurant, **39**
Valentino's, **24**
Ventanas del Mar, **11**

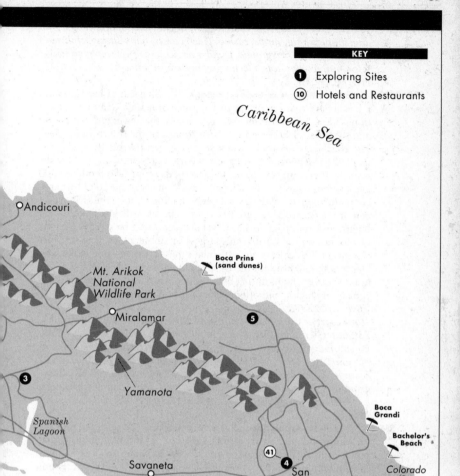

KEY
- ❶ Exploring Sites
- ⑩ Hotels and Restaurants

*Caribbean Sea*

○ Andicouri

Boca Prins
(sand dunes)

Mt. Arikok
National
Wildlife Park

○ Miralamar

❺

❸

Yamanota

Spanish
Lagoon

Boca
Grandi

Bachelor's
Beach

Savaneta ○

㊶

❹ San
Nicolas

Colorado
Pt.

○ Seroe
Colorado

㊵

Rodger's
Beach

Baby Beach

**Lodging**

Americana Aruba
Beach Resort &
Casino, **16**

Amsterdam
Manor Beach
Resort, **27**

Aruba Blue Village
Suites, **30**

Aruba Marriott
Resort & Stellaris
Casino, **12**

Aruba Palm Beach
Hotel & Casino, **18**

Bucuti Beach
Resort, **29**

Bushiri Beach
Resort, **33**

La Cabana All Suite
Beach Resort &
Casino, **28**

Divi Aruba Beach
Resort, **31**

Holiday Inn Aruba
Beach Resort &
Casino, **13**

Hyatt Regency Aruba
Resort & Casino, **14**

Mill Resort, **26**

Radisson Aruba
Caribbean Resort &
Casino, **17**

Sonesta Resorts at
Seaport Village, **34**

Tamarijn Aruba, **32**

Wyndham Aruba
Beach Resort and
Casino, **19**

salon, 2 outdoor hot tubs, massage, sauna, steam rooms, 2 tennis courts, health club, volleyball, beach, dock, water-sports center with dive shop, fishing, shops, casino, video games, baby-sitting, children's program (3–12), playground, laundry service and dry cleaning, concierge floor, business services, meeting rooms, travel services, car rental. AE, DC, MC, V. EP, MAP.

$$$–$$$$  🏨 **Sonesta Resorts at Seaport Village.** If rolling out of bed and onto
  ★       a beach isn't that important to you, then Sonesta's Oranjestad location is ideal. The resort includes two hotels: the newer one with suites and the older (1992) high-rise with rooms. In the resort lobby, sleek low couches wrap around pink stucco pillars; parrots fly free in the tropical garden atrium; and guests board motor skiffs headed for the resort's 40-acre private island—perfect for day trips. The combined 300 guest rooms and suites with tropical decor in gemstone colors are spacious and modern, with tiny balconies that look out on the atrium garden or the ocean. There are free casino classes, volleyball, and beach bingo, and the neighboring Crystal Casino, Aruba's only 24-hour casino, houses the Caribbean's largest $1 slot machine. The gourmet restaurant, L'Escale, is one of Aruba's most creative—and expensive. Dancers should head for the Desires Lounge, where there's live entertainment every night during high season. This lively property is a top choice for singles, and offers plenty for families, too. ✉ *L. G. Smith Blvd. 9,* ☎ *297/8–36000 or 800/766–3782,* 📠 *297/8–34389. Sonesta Resort & Casino, 285 rooms, 15 suites; Sonesta Suites & Casino, 250 suites. 4 restaurants, 4 bars, in-room safes, kitchenettes, minibars, no-smoking floor, room service, 2 pools, beauty salon, massage, tennis court, aerobics, exercise room, hiking, volleyball, beach, shops, 2 casinos, nightclub, baby-sitting, children's program (4–12), playground, coin laundry, laundry service and dry cleaning, concierge, business services, convention center, travel services, car rental. AE, DC, MC, V. EP, MAP, FAP.*

$$$      🏨 **Wyndham Aruba Beach Resort and Casino.** The price tag thus far for this Wyndham resort (formerly the Hilton) is $42 million. Grand public areas are dazzling in size and scope. The rooms are done in dusty rose, peach, and sea-foam green; all have an ocean-view balcony. Fountains splash playfully into the free-form pool, and the Casablanca Casino has Rick's Place in mind. A full-service spa, with all the muds and rubs, and a Red Sail water-sports facility on the beach have launched the project with vigor. There is a fee for use of the health club. ✉ *J.E. Irausquin Blvd. 77, Palm Beach,* ☎ *297/8–64466 or 800/996–3426,* 📠 *297/8–68217. 378 rooms, 66 suites. 4 restaurants, 4 bars, deli, in-room safes, minibars in some rooms, room service, pool, wading pool, beauty salon, massage, sauna, steam room, tennis court, health club, Ping-Pong, volleyball, beach, water-sports center with dive shop, shops, billiards, casino, video games, baby-sitting, children's program (4–12), playground, concierge, business services, meeting rooms, travel services, car rental. AE, DC, MC, V. EP, CP, MAP, FAP.*

$$–$$$   🏨 **Holiday Inn Aruba Beach Resort & Casino.** This is one of the larger properties on Palm Beach, but its size is cleverly camouflaged. Three buildings of seven stories each are set apart from each other along the shore, nicely landscaped with palm trees. Rooms, in shades of teal and mauve, are clean and fairly spacious. Restaurants, bars, and the Grand Holiday Casino keep the night lights shining. Daytime activities include swimming, tennis, windsurfing, and other water sports, as well as shopping. Children's activities are organized during high season, so it's a reliable choice for families. ✉ *J.E. Irausquin Blvd. 230,* ☎ *297/8–63600 or 800/465–4329,* 📠 *297/8–65165. 600 rooms. 3 restaurants, 3 bars, in-room safes, no-smoking rooms, refrigerators on request, room*

*service, pool, barbershop, beauty salon, massage, 6 tennis courts, boccie, exercise room, Ping-Pong, beach, dock, water-sports center (including dive shop), shops, casino, video games, baby-sitting, children's program (5–12), coin laundry, laundry service and dry cleaning, concierge, business services, meeting rooms, travel services, car rental. AE, DC, MC, V. EP, MAP, FAP.*

**$$–$$$** 🏨 **Mill Resort.** Two-story red-roof buildings flank the open-air common areas of this small condominium hotel. Unlike time-share resorts, this hotel sells each unit to an individual, who then leases the unit back to the resort for use as a hotel room, so there's none of the usual time-share sales pitch. The decor is soft country French, with a delicate rose-and-white color scheme. The junior suites have a king-size bed, sitting area, and kitchenette. Studios have a full kitchen, but only a queen-size convertible sofa bed, a tiny bathroom, and no balcony; different kinds of suites can be created by connecting units. This resort is popular with couples seeking a quiet getaway and with families vacationing with small children. There is a small poolside bar and grill on the premises, and the Old Mill restaurant is next door (☞ Dining, *below*). There are also (to the relief of many guests) no casino and no organized evening activities. Action can be found at the nearby large resorts, and the beach is only a five-minute walk away. ⊠ *J.E. Irausquin Blvd. 330,* ☎ *297/8–67700,* 🖷 *297/8–67271. 200 apartment-style rooms. Bar/grill, grocery, in-room safes, kitchenette or refrigerator, pool, wading pool, sauna, 2 tennis courts, exercise room, baby-sitting, children's program (2–12), coin laundry, laundry service and dry cleaning, travel services, beach shuttle, car rental. AE, DC, MC, V. EP.*

**$$–$$$** 🏨 **Radisson Aruba Caribbean Resort & Casino.** Called La Grande Dame of the Caribbean, this resort was the first high-rise on the island. Liz Taylor used to stay here when she was married to Eddie Fisher, so the staff is used to filling special needs. A comprehensive renewal has brought flowers, artwork, and a generally festive air to the lobby. Of the sunny air-conditioned rooms, 72 have a full-ocean view; all have a balcony and were scheduled for top-to-bottom renovations to be completed by early 1997. The fitness center near the tennis courts offers a Universal weight system and aerobics classes. There's a new activities program to keep the littlest ones (two- to seven-year-olds) entertained. ⊠ *J.E. Irausquin Blvd. 81, Palm Beach,* ☎ *297/8–66555 or 800/333–3333,* 🖷 *297/8–63260. 353 rooms, 19 suites. 3 restaurants, 4 bars, café, ice-cream parlor, in-room safes, no-smoking rooms, room service, refrigerators, pool, beauty salon, massage, 4 tennis courts, aerobics, boccie, basketball, exercise room, shuffleboard, volleyball, beach, water-sports center (including scuba diving), casino, baby-sitting, children's program (2–7), playground, laundry service and dry cleaning, business services, meeting rooms, travel services, car rental. AE, D, DC, MC, V. EP, MAP. All-inclusive.*

**$$** 🏨 **Bucuti Beach Resort.** The small, European-style Bucuti Beach is a
★ refreshingly peaceful antidote to the impersonal feel of some larger, bustling resorts. Hacienda-style buildings house enormous rooms with bright floral decor, sparkling tile floors, and terrace or balcony with ocean view. In-room extras include hair dryers, minibar, microwave, and coffeemaker. The resort has an enviable beach location. The breezy oceanfront Pirate's Nest restaurant, which looks like a beached galleon, is known islandwide for its excellent theme dinners. ⊠ *J.E. Irausquin Blvd. 55-B, Eagle Beach,* ☎ *297/8–36141 or 800/528–1234,* 🖷 *297/8–25272. 63 rooms. Restaurant, bar, in-room safes, minibars, refrigerators, pool, exercise room, volleyball, beach, bicycles, laundry service and dry cleaning, travel services. AE, D, DC, MC, V. CP, MAP.*

**$$** ⊞ **Bushiri Beach Resort.** Two long, low buildings—built around three outdoor hot tubs surrounded by lush foliage and situated on a wide expanse of beach—make up Aruba's first all-inclusive resort. These buildings are old and nondescript, and although the rooms were renovated in 1995, they remain ordinary. But the Bushiri is a hotel-training school, a factor that shows in the enthusiastic staff. The best rooms are in the West Wing, including the "deluxe" rooms, which are the largest and have minifridges, safe-deposit boxes, and balconies that face the ocean. Where this resort shines is in its full daily activities program for adults. Snorkeling (with instruction and equipment), tennis, sailing, windsurfing, pool volleyball, and casino gambling classes are among the offerings. Kids are kept busy with their own daylong supervised program. A sightseeing tour around the island, three meals daily, a poolside barbecue, and a midnight buffet, as well as all beverages, are included in the single tab—and it still remains in the moderate category. In other words, this is quite a bargain. ⊠ *L. G. Smith Blvd. 35, Oranjestad,* ☎ *297/8–25216, 800/462–6867, or 800/462–6868;* FAX *297/8–26789. 154 rooms. Restaurant, 2 bars, beach grill, in-room safes, some refrigerators, pool, wading pool, beauty salon, 3 outdoor hot tubs, 2 tennis courts, exercise room, Ping-Pong, beach, dive shop, boating, fishing, billiards, baby-sitting, children's program (4–12), laundry service, travel services, car rental, shuttle to La Cabana for casino and dinner shows. AE, DC, MC, V. All-inclusive.*

**$$** ⊞ **Divi Aruba Beach Resort.** The motto at this popular Mediterranean-style low rise, taken over by Doral Resorts in 1993, remains "barefoot elegance," which means you can streak through the lobby in your bikini. The main section of the resort has standard guest rooms, beachfront lanai rooms, and casitas (garden bungalows) that look out onto individual courtyards; most are only steps away from the beach. Note that the original rooms are on the island's water system (which means the water is cooled and heated by Mother Nature, which can take some getting used to). A newer section, Divi Dos, contains luxury rooms and a bridal suite, all with refrigerators and whirlpool bathtubs. At press time, rooms were scheduled for much needed face-lifts, which will bring beige and red tropical prints over crisp white tile floors. There is a daily activities program and theme dinners each night; the recently renovated Red Parrot restaurant offers romantic beachside dining. If you book the all-inclusive package here, you'll also get to use the facilities at the Tamarijn Aruba Beach Resort, a sister property just down the beach. There's no casino on the property, so it remains thankfully quiet, but if you want action, the Alahambra Casino is next door. ⊠ *L. G. Smith Blvd. 93, Divi Beach,* ☎ *297/8–23300 or 800/554–2008,* FAX *297/8–31940. 203 rooms. 2 restaurants, 2 bars, in-room safes, refrigerators, 2 pools, barbershop, beauty salon, outdoor hot tub, tennis court, shuffleboard, volleyball, beach, water-sports center (with scuba diving), mountain bikes, shops, baby-sitting, laundry service, travel services, car rental. AE, D, DC, MC, V. EP, MAP, FAP, All-inclusive.*

**$$** ⊞ **La Cabana All Suite Beach Resort & Casino.** At the top end of Eagle Beach, across the road from the sand, is Aruba's largest time-sharing condominium-hotel complex. The original four-story building faces the beach and forms a horseshoe around a huge free-form pool complex with a water slide, poolside bar, outdoor café, and water-sports center. One-third of the rooms have a full sea view; two-thirds have a partial view. All the oddly configured, but comfortable, rooms—studio suites or one-bedroom suites—come with a fully-equipped kitchenette, a small balcony, and a whirlpool bath for two. Suites have interconnecting doors so that three may be linked together to form two- and three-bedroom units. Shuttle buses run guests over to the upscale casino, where the hotel has a theme restaurant and the Tropicana nightclub, with comedians and dance reviews. The gracious staff makes the resort seem one-third its size. ⊠ *J.E. Irausquin Blvd. 250,* ☎ *297/8–39000 or 800/835–7193; in NY, 212/251–1710;* ℻ *297/8–37208. 803 suites. 4 restaurants, 3 bars, ice-cream parlor, grocery, in-room safes, kitchenettes, room service, whirlpool bathtubs, 3 pools, barbershop, beauty salon, massage, 3 outdoor hot tubs, sauna, aerobics, basketball, health club, racquetball, shuffleboard, squash, volleyball, beach, water-sports center (including dive shop), shops, billiards, nightclub, video games, baby-sitting, children's program (5–12), playground, coin laundry, laundry service and dry cleaning, chapel, concierge, business services, car rental. AE, DC, MC, V. EP, MAP, All-inclusive.*

**$$** 🏨 **Tamarijn Aruba.** This all-inclusive resort on Bravo Beach features all oceanfront rooms in a series of low-rise buildings stretched along the property. The spacious rooms have a casual feel, with woven fiber mats on dark tile floors, light rattan and wood furnishings, and patios or balconies. The all-inclusive package here covers meals and snacks, all beverages, nightly entertainment (including theme nights), tickets to the Bon Bini Festival, a sunset cruise, and an array of activities including mountain biking, snorkeling, sailing, and windsurfing (lessons are included as well). It's a low-key, active place catering primarily to singles and couples. ⊠ *J.E. Irausquin Blvd. 41,* ☎ *297/8–24150 or 800/554–2008,* ℻ *297/8–31940. 236 rooms. 3 restaurants, 3 bars, snack bar, in-room safes, refrigerators, 2 pools, barbershop, beauty salon, 2 tennis courts, Ping-Pong, shuffleboard, volleyball, beach, water-sports center (with scuba diving at additional cost), fishing, mountain bikes, shops, billiards, baby-sitting, laundry service and dry cleaning, travel services, car rental. AE, D, DC, MC, V. All-inclusive.*

**$–$$** 🏨 **Amsterdam Manor Beach Resort.** This attractive, gabled, russet- and mustard-colored hotel looks like part of a Dutch Colonial village. Rooms are furnished either in Dutch modern or provincial style and range from smallish studios with a balcony and whirlpool bathtub to deluxe two-bedroom suites with peaked ceilings, whirlpool bathtub and shower, and full kitchen. Alas, this cozy enclave and its lovely pool with a waterfall are intruded upon by the noise of traffic from Palm Beach Road. At least that glorious beach is just across the street. ⊠ *J.E. Irausquin Blvd. 252,* ☎ *297/8–71492 or 800/766–6016,* ℻ *297/8–71463. 72 units. Restaurant, bar, in-room safes, kitchenettes, refrigerators, pool, snorkeling, baby-sitting, playground, travel services, car rental. AE, MC, V. EP.*

**$–$$** 🏨 **Aruba Palm Beach Hotel & Casino.** Formerly a Sheraton, this pink, eight-story Moorish palazzo has pink-swaddled palm trees dotting its drive. The lobby is a haze of pink and purple and cool marble. The large backyard sunning ground is a well-manicured tropical garden, with a fleet of vociferous parrots guarding the entrance. The oversize guest rooms are cheerfully decorated in plaids and tropical prints. Each has a large walk-in closet and a postage stamp balcony that overlooks the ocean, the pool, or the gardens. For a peaceful meal, eat alfresco in the rock-garden setting of the Seawatch Restaurant. For live music, try the Players Club lounge. A limbo and steel-band show is scheduled one night a week. ⊠ *J.E. Irausquin Blvd. 79, Palm Beach,* ☎ *297/8–63900 or 800/345-2782,* ℻ *297/8–61941. 202 rooms. 2 restaurants, 2 bars, deli, refrigerators, room service, pool, wading pool, beauty salon, 2 tennis courts, volleyball, beach, water-sports center (including scuba diving), shops, casino, laundry service and dry cleaning, travel services, car rental. AE, DC, MC, V. EP, MAP.*

**$** 🏨 **Aruba Blue Village Suites.** If a plumper wallet is more important to you than a beachfront location, this comfortable enclave tucked away from the hotel strip in a residential area is the answer. The single-story apartments form an open-ended rectangle around one of two pools;

each basic but tidy apartment has a fully equipped kitchen, sparse Dutch-style furnishings, and air-conditioned bedroom(s). Studios are a fine budget option for a family of four, and there's a playground and pool area for the little ones. If you want to go to the beach, though, you'll need a car to get there. ⊠ *Cunucu Abao 37,* ☎ *297/8–78618,* ℻ *297/8–70081. 56 studios, 1- and 2-bedroom suites. Bar, in-room safes, kitchenettes, 2 pools, sauna, exercise room, poolside barbecue, beach shuttle. AE, DC, MC, V. EP.*

# Dining

Aruba's restaurants serve a cosmopolitan variety of cuisines, although most menus are specifically designed to please American palates—you can get fresh surf and New York turf almost anywhere. Make the effort to try Aruban specialties—*pan bati* is a delicious beaten bread that resembles a pancake, plantains are similar to cooked bananas though not as sweet, and *keshi yena* is a marvelous baked concoction of gouda cheese stuffed with spices and meat.

For better or worse, fast food has arrived in Aruba. For those who are homesick, there's McDonald's, Kentucky Fried Chicken, Burger King, and Wendy's. For breakfast and lunch, the restaurants in the hotels tend to be more expensive than the ones in town. Most hotels offer several food plans, which you can purchase either in advance or upon arrival. But before you purchase a Full American Plan (FAP), which includes breakfast, lunch, and dinner, remember that Aruba has numerous excellent and reasonably priced restaurants from which to choose. Nonetheless, most resorts here do offer better-than-average hotel dining; for more information consult the lodging listings. On Sunday, it may be difficult to find a restaurant outside of the hotels that's open for lunch. Good hotel options, though, are the extensive buffet at the Holiday Inn or the wonderful champagne brunch at the Hyatt.

## What to Wear

Dress ranges from casual at less expensive restaurants to elegant in more expensive establishments and resort dining rooms. However, even the finest restaurants require at the most only a jacket for men and a sundress for women. The air-conditioning does get cold, so don't go bare-armed. And anytime you plan to eat in the open air, remember to douse yourself first with insect repellent—the mosquitoes can get unruly, especially in July and August, when the winds drop and November through January (the rainy season).

| CATEGORY | COST* |
|---|---|
| $$$ | over $30 |
| $$ | $20–$30 |
| $ | under $20 |

*per person for a main course only, excluding drinks and 10%–15% service charge.*

$$$  ✕ **Chez Mathilde.** This elegant restaurant occupies one of the last surviving 19th-century houses in Aruba. Ask to sit in the swooningly romantic Pavilion Room, which has an eclectic mix of turn-of-the-century Italian and French decor, ivy-covered walls, and curtained nooks and crannies for privacy. Then sit back and enjoy the high culinary standards of the French-style menu, which is constantly being re-created by the Dutch chef. Feast on artfully presented baked escargots with herbs and garlic, bouillabaisse with garlic croutons and cream and Cognac to taste, grilled Canadian salmon with a delicate Balsamic dressing, or filet mignon in signature pepper sauce prepared table-side. The chef has a deft touch with sauces. Then, too, there's crêpes suzette and

a chocolate gâteau to tempt the taste buds. ⊠ *Havenstraat 23, Oranjestad,* ☎ *297/8–34968. Reservations essential. AE, MC, V. No lunch Sun.*

**$$$** ✕ **Valentino's.** The airy two-level dining room here is invitingly dressed in sparkling white and shades of rose. The tables are placed comfortably far apart, and the service is attentive without being overbearing. The Italian menu has knockouts such as the *gamberoni di teresa* (shrimp sautéed in garlic and fresh tomatoes) and fettuccine in smoked salmon cream sauce. A festive atmosphere makes the restaurant popular with celebrating Arubans. You'll find their gaiety infectious. ⊠ *Caribbean Palm Village, Noord 43E,* ☎ *297/8–62700. AE, DC, MC, V. Closed Sun. No lunch.*

**$$** ✕ **Buccaneer Restaurant.** Imagine you're in a sunken ship—fishnets and turtle shells hang from the ceiling, and through the portholes you see live sharks, barracudas, and groupers swimming by. That's the Buccaneer, a virtual underwater grotto snug in an old stone building, flanked by heavy black chains. Add to that a fantastic 5,000-gallon saltwater aquarium, plus 12 more porthole-size tanks. The surf-and-turf cuisine is prepared by the chef-owners with European élan. Order the fresh catch of the day or more exotic fare, such as shrimps with Pernod; smoked pork cutlets with sausage, sauerkraut, and potatoes; or the turtle steak with a light cream sauce. Go early (around 5:45 PM) to get a booth next to the aquariums. ⊠ *Gasparito 11-C, Noord,* ☎ *297/8–66172. AE, MC, V. Closed Sun. No lunch.*

**$$** ✕ **Gasparito Restaurant and Art Gallery.** As the name states, this
★ charming restaurant also serves as a gallery showcasing the works of local artists on softly lit, creamy white walls. It's set in an authentic *cunucu* (country house) in Noord not far from the hotel strip. The Aruban specialties—pan bati, keshi yena, fish croquettes, conch stew with hot Aruban pepper, stewed chicken, Creole-style fish fillet—are also works of art, so it comes as no surprise that Gasparito's chefs walk away with top awards in Caribbean culinary competitions. Service is discreet and very accommodating (they'll stay open if guests come for a late dinner). ⊠ *Gasparito 3,* ☎ *297/8–67044. AE, MC, V. Closed Sun. No lunch.*

**$$** ✕ **Old Mill** (De Olde Molen). A gift from the queen of Holland, this real Dutch mill was shipped brick by brick to Aruba in 1920 and reassembled here. For starters, try the seafood crepe Neptune, nestled in a delicate cheese bed. Also excellent are the shrimp with spinach and cream sauce and the Dutch fries—crunchy little nuggets of potato. Order the ice cream with chocolate liqueur and take the bottle home as a souvenir of Aruba's oldest restaurant. There are two dinner seatings, at 6:30 and 9. ⊠ *330 J.E. Irausquin Blvd., off Palm Beach,* ☎ *297/8–62060. Reservations essential. AE, DC, MC, V. Closed Sun.*

**$$** ✕ **Papiamento.** Longtime restaurateurs Lenie and Eduardo Ellis de-
★ cided Aruba needed a bistro that was cozy yet elegant, intimate, and always romantic. So they converted their 130-year-old home into just such a spot. Guests can feast sumptuously indoors surrounded by antiques, or outdoors in a patio garden decorated with enormous ceramics (designed by Lenie) and filled with ficus and palm trees adorned with lights. The chef utilizes flavors from both Continental and Caribbean cuisines to produce favorites that include seafood and meat dishes. Try the Dover sole, the Caribbean lobster, shrimp and red snapper cooked table-side on a hot marble stone, or the "claypot" for two—a medley of seafoods prepared in a sealed clay pot. ⊠ *Washington 61, Noord,* ☎ *297/8–64544. AE, MC, V. Closed Mon. No lunch.*

**$$** ✕ **Talk of the Town Restaurant.** Here you'll find candlelight dining and some of the best steaks in town: The owner comes from a family of Dutch butchers. Chateaubriand and flaming desserts are prepared with flair at your table. Seafood specialties, such as the crabmeat crêpes and the *escargots à la bourguignonne,* are popular, too. Saturday night is all-you-can-eat prime rib night ($18.95). The restaurant adjoins the Best Western Talk of the Town Resort, between the airport and Oranjestad, where rates are quite reasonable. The poolside grill stays open until 2 AM. This fine restaurant is also a member of the elite honorary restaurant society, Chaîne de Rotisseurs. ⊠ *L. G. Smith Blvd. 2, Oranjestad,* ☎ *297/8–23380. AE, DC, MC, V. Closed Mon.*

**$$   ✕ Ventanas del Mar.** The name means windows on the sea, which couldn't be more appropriate considering the setting above the Tierra del Sol Golf Course at the northern tip of the island. This quietly elegant restaurant features floor-to-ceiling windows that look out across the back nine holes and the rolling sand dunes to the sea. Sandwiches, salads, conch fritters, nachos, and quesadillas fill the midday menu; at night the focus is on seafood (roasted red snapper, crab cakes, grilled garlic shrimp, panfried oysters) and meat (prime rib, veal chop in rosemary demi-glace, herbed half chicken). ⊠ *Tierra del Sol Golf Course, Malmokweg,* ☎ *297/8–67800. AE, MC, V.*

**$–$$   ✕ Boonoonoonoos.** The name—say it just as it looks!—means extraordinary, a bit of hyperbole for this Austrian-owned Caribbean bistro in the heart of Oranjestad, but in the fiercely competitive Aruban restaurant business, you gotta have a gimmick. The specialty here is Pan-Caribbean cuisine. The decor is simple, but the tasty food, served with hearty portions of peas and rice and plantains, makes up for the lack of tablecloths, china, and crystal. The roast chicken Barbados is sweet and tangy, marinated in pineapple and cinnamon and simmered in fruit juices. The Jamaican jerk ribs (a 300-year-old recipe) are tiny but spicy, and the satin-smooth hot pumpkin soup drizzled with cheese and served in a pumpkin shell may as well be dessert. Avoid the place when it's crowded, since the service and the quality of the food deteriorate. ⊠ *Wilhelminastraat 18A,* ☎ *297/8–31888. AE, MC, V. No lunch Sun.*

**$–$$   ✕ Brisas del Mar.** This friendly 18-table place overlooking the sea makes
★   you feel as if you're dining in an Aruban home. Old family recipes use traditional indigenous ingredients like the aromatic *yerbiholé* leaf and the sizzling Mme. Jeanette pepper. Try the smashing steamy fish soup (which would do a Marseillais proud), *keri keri* (shredded fish kissed with annatto seed), or some of the best pan bati on the island. Fresh catch of the day cooked Aruban-style (panfried and covered in a tangy Creole sauce) has drawn a crowd here for over 20 years. It's so good, it justifies the taxi ride needed to reach it—10 miles east of Oranjestad in the town of Savaneta. ⊠ *Savaneta 222A,* ☎ *297/8–47718. AE, D, MC, V. Closed Mon.*

**$–$$   ✕ Old Cunucu House.** On a small estate in a residential neighborhood, three minutes from the high-rise hotels, this 75-year-old white stucco home with slanting roofs, wood beams, and a terra-cotta courtyard filled with bougainvillea has been converted to a seafood-and-international restaurant of casual élan. Dine on red snapper, almond-fried shrimp with lobster sauce, Cornish hen, New York sirloin, or beef fondue à deux. An Aruban trio sings and plays background music every Friday, and on Saturday evening a mariachi band serenades the patrons. ⊠ *Palm Beach 150,* ☎ *297/8–61666. AE, MC, V. No lunch.*

**$   ✕ Charlie's Restaurant & Bar.** Now an institution, Charlie's has been
★   a San Nicolas hangout for more than 50 years. During the oil-refinery days, it was a hopping bar for all kinds of rough-and-scruffs. Now tourists flock here to gawk at the decor: License plates, hard hats, baseball pennants, intimate apparel, and credit cards cover and crowd every inch of the walls and ceiling. The house specialty is "shrimps—jumbo and dumbo." You'll have to peel the shell off, but needing to wash up

afterwards gives you a reason to go check out the incredible "decor" in the rest room. And don't leave before trying Charlie's special "honeymoon sauce" (so called because it's really hot). ⊠ *Zeppenfeldstraat 56,* ☎ *297/8–45086. No credit cards. Closed Sun.*

$ ✕ **Kowloon.** In addition to many Chinese provinces, Indonesia is also represented on the menu here. Try the *bami goreng,* a noodle-based dish with shreds of shrimp, pork, vegetables, and an Indonesian blend of herbs and spices. The modern Asian decor blends easily with the island's palms and sands. ⊠ *Emmastraat 11, Oranjestad,* ☎ *297/8– 24950. AE, MC, V.*

$ ✕ **La Paloma.** "The Dove" is a no-frills, low-key joint decorated with hanging plants and chianti bottles, and it's usually packed. The cuisine is international and Italian, but you can order conch stew with pan bati and fried plantains. Caesar salad and minestrone soup are house specialties. This is not the place for a romantic interlude; come for the family atmosphere, simple Italian food, and reasonable prices. ⊠ *Noord 39,* ☎ *297/8–74611. AE, MC, V. Closed Tues. No lunch.*

$ ✕ **Le Petit Café.** The motto here is "Romancing the Stone"—referring to tasty cuisine cooked on hot stones. The low ceiling and hanging plants make this an intimate lunch spot for shoppers. Alfresco dining in the bustling square lets diners keep an eye on things, but fumes from nearby traffic tend to spoil the meal. Jumbo shrimps, sandwiches, ice cream, and fresh fruit dishes are light delights. ⊠ *Emmastraat 1, Oranjestad,* ☎ *297/8–26577. AE, DC, MC, V. No lunch Sun.*

# Beaches

Beaches in Aruba are legendary in the Caribbean: white sand, turquoise waters, and virtually no garbage, for everyone takes the "no littering" sign—NO TIRA SUSHI—very seriously, especially with an AFl500 fine. The influx of tourists in the past decade, however, has crowded the major beaches, which back up to the hotels along the southwestern strip. These beaches are public, and you can make the two-hour hike from the Holiday Inn to the Bushiri Beach Hotel free of charge and without ever leaving sand. If you go strolling during the day, make sure you are well protected from the sun—it scorches fast, and the trade winds can make it feel deceptively cooler. Luckily, there's at least one covered bar (and often an ice-cream stand) at virtually every hotel you pass. If you take the stroll at night, you can hotel-hop for dinner, dancing, gambling, and late-night entertainment. On the northern side of the island, heavy trade winds make the waters too choppy for swimming, but the vistas are great and the terrain is wonderfully suited to sunbathing and geological explorations.

**Baby Beach.** On the island's eastern tip, this semicircular beach borders a bay that is as placid as a wading pool and only 4–5 feet deep—perfect for tots and terrible swimmers. Thatched shaded areas are good for cooling off. You may occasionally find topless sunbathers here.

**Bachelor's Beach.** To the north of San Nicolas, this gorgeous beach is perfect for advanced windsurfing.

**Boca Grandi.** Just west of Bachelor's Beach, on the northwest coast (near the Seagrape Grove and the Aruba Golf Club), Boca Grandi is excellent for wave jumping and windsurfing. Strong swimming skills are a must here.

**Boca Prins.** Near the Fontein Cave and Blue Lagoon, this beach is about as large as a Brazilian bikini, but with two rocky cliffs and tumultuously crashing waves, it's as romantic as you get in Aruba. This is not a swimming beach, however. Boca Prins is famous for its backdrop of enor-

mous vanilla sand dunes. You'll need a jeep to make the trek here. Bring
a picnic lunch, a beach blanket, and sturdy sneakers.

**Eagle Beach.** Across the highway from what is quickly becoming
known as Time-Share Lane is Eagle Beach on the southern coast. Not
long ago, it was a nearly deserted stretch of pristine sands dotted with
the occasional thatched picnic hut. Now that the time-share resorts are
completed, this beach is one of the more hopping on the island.

**Fisherman's Hut.** Next to the Holiday Inn, this beach is a windsurfer's
haven. Take a picnic lunch (tables are available) and watch the elegant
purple, aqua, and orange sails struggle in the wind.

**Malmok Beach.** On the northwestern shore, this lackluster beach, also
known as Boca Catalina, borders shallow waters that stretch out 300
yards from shore, making it perfect for beginners learning to windsurf.
Right off the coast here is a favorite haunt for divers—the wreck of
the German ship *Antilla,* scuttled in 1940.

**Manchebo Beach** (formerly Punta Brabo Beach). In front of the
Manchebo Beach Resort, this impressively wide stretch of white powder is where officials turn a blind eye to topless sunbathers. Going topless is not permitted in Aruba (though officials rarely enforce the ban
here or at Baby Beach).

**Palm Beach.** Once called one of the 10 best beaches in the world by
the *Miami Herald,* this is the stretch behind the Americana Aruba, Aruba
Hilton Hotel and Casino, Aruba Palm Beach, and Holiday Inn hotels.
It's the center of Aruban tourism, offering the best in swimming, sailing, and fishing. During high season, however, it's a sardine can.

**Rodger's Beach.** Next to Baby Beach on the eastern tip of the island,
this is a beautiful curving stretch of sand only slightly marred by the
view of the oil refinery at the far side of the bay.

## Outdoor Activities and Sports

### Bowling

The **Eagle Bowling Palace** (⊠ Pos Abou, ☎ 297/8–35038) has 12 lanes,
a cocktail lounge, and a snack bar; it's open 10 AM to 2 AM.

### Deep-Sea Fishing

With catches including barracuda, kingfish, bonito, and black and yellow tuna, deep-sea fishing is great sport on Aruba. Many charter boats
are available for a half- or full-day sail. **De Palm Tours** (☎ 297/8–24400
or 297/8–24545) can arrange trips for up to six people, in a variety
of boat sizes and styles. Half-day tours, including all equipment, are
around $250. Private yachts, manned by independent sea captains, can
also be chartered. Check with the Aruba Tourism Authority or your
hotel. Half-day tours run about $250, full-day about $500. **Pelican Tours**
(☎ 297/8–31228 or 297/8–24739) and **Red Sail Sports** (☎ 297/8–
61603) also arrange deep-sea fishing charters.

### Golf

An 18-hole par-71 golf course, **Tierra del Sol** (⊠ Malmokweg, ☎
297/8–67800), opened in 1995 on the northwest coast near the California Lighthouse. Designed by Robert Trent Jones, the course combines Aruba's native beauty, such as the flora, cacti, and rock formations,
with the lush greens of the world's best courses. The costly installa-
tion of a water-irrigation system on this arid isle allows 600,000 gallons of recycled refuse water to be distributed throughout the course
each night. The $115 greens fee includes a golf cart. Club rentals are
$25–$40. Four lighted tennis courts were recently added, and, at press
time, there was talk of initiating half-day golf clinics for about $30.
The charming Ventanas del Mar restaurant in the clubhouse is worth
a visit in it's own right.

**Aruba Golf Club** (✉ Golfweg 82, near San Nicolas, ☎ 297/8–42006) has a nine-hole course with 25 sand traps, roaming goats, and lots of cacti. There are 11 AstroTurf greens, making 18-hole tournaments a possibility. The clubhouse contains a bar, and men's and women's locker rooms. The course's official U.S. Golf Association rating is 67; greens fees are $7.50 for 9 holes, $10 for 18 holes. Caddies and club rentals are available.

Two elevated 18-hole minigolf courses surrounded by a moat are available at **Joe Mendez Adventure Golf** (✉ Sasakiweg, ☎ 297/8–76625). There are also paddleboats and bumper boats, a bar, and a snack stand. A round of minigolf is $14. It's open from 4 PM–11 PM.

## Hiking
There are no marked trails through the **Arikok National Wildlife Park,** but that doesn't mean you can't blaze your own. Watch for snakes in this arid landscape, and carry water with you. Wild donkeys, goats, rabbits, parakeets, and a plethora of lizards (even the occasional iguana) will be your companions. The park is crowned by 577-foot Mt. Arikok, so climbing is also a possibility.

**De Palm Tours** (✉ L. G. Smith Blvd. 142, ☎ 297/8–24400 or 297/8–24545) offers a guided three-hour trip to remote sites of unusual natural beauty accessible only on foot. The fee is $25 per person, including refreshments and transportation; a minimum of four people is required.

## Horseback Riding
One-hour jaunts ($15) arranged through **Rancho El Paso** (✉ Washington 44, ☎ 297/8–63310) or **De Palm Tours** (✉ L. G. Smith Blvd. 142, ☎ 297/8–24400 or 297/8–24545) will take you through countryside flanked by cacti, divi-divi trees, and aloe vera plants; two-hour trips ($30) also go to the beach. Remember to wear a hat and take lots of suntan lotion.

## Land Sailing
Carts with a Windsurfer-type sail are rented at **Aruba SailCart** (✉ Bushiri 23, ☎ 297/8–35133) at $15 (single seater) and $20 (double seater) for 30 minutes of speeding back and forth across a dirt field. The sport is new to Aruba and thrilling for landbound sailors. Anyone can learn the rudiments of driving the cart in just a few minutes. Rentals are available from 10 AM to 7 PM; food and drinks are served until 10 PM.

## Parasailing
Motorboats from Eagle and Palm beaches tow people up and over the water for about 15 minutes ($40 for a single seater, $70 for a tandem).

## Snorkeling and Scuba Diving
With visibility up to 90 feet, Aruban waters are excellent for snorkeling in shallow waters, and scuba divers will discover exotic marine life and coral. Certified divers can go wall diving or reef diving—or explore wrecks sunk during World War II. The *Antilla* shipwreck—a German freighter sunk off the northwest coast of Aruba near Palm Beach—is a favorite spot with divers and snorkelers.

**Aruba Pro Dive** (✉ Ponton 88, ☎ 297/8–25520) offers resort courses, daily one-tank dives, two-tank dives, and night dives. Other reputable dive operators offering daily one- and two-tank dives are **Charlie's S.E.A. Scuba** (✉ San Nicolas, ☎ 297/8–34877) and **Mermaid Sports Divers** (✉ Manchebo Beach Resort, ☎ 297/8–35546).

**De Palm Tours** (⊠ L. G. Smith Blvd. 142, ☎ 297/8–24400 or 8–24545, FAX 297/8–23012) offers daily snorkeling and scuba-diving trips. However, its rates ($25–$45) are the most expensive on the island.

**Pelican Watersports** (⊠ J. G. Emanstraat 1, Oranjestad, ☎ 297/8–31228 or 297/8–24739) offers snorkeling and scuba diving, as well as scuba instruction and certification.

**Red Sail Sports** (⊠ L. G. Smith Blvd. 83, ☎ 297/8–61603) offers scuba packages, resort courses, PADI-certification courses, night diving, and underwater camera rental.

## Tennis

Aruba's winds add a certain challenge to the best of swings, but world-class tennis has just arrived, at the **Aruba Racquet Club** (☎ 297/8–60215). The $1.4 million club was designed by Stan Smith Design International and is near the Aruba Marriott. There are eight tennis courts (six lighted) as well as a swimming pool, aerobics center, and a restaurant on the grounds.

## Windsurfing

**Pelican Watersports** (⊠ J. G. Emanstraat 1, ☎ 297/8–31228) rents equipment and offers instruction with a certified Mistral instructor. Stock boards and custom boards rent for $35 per two hours, $60 per day. Pelican offers lessons every morning at 10.

**Red Sail Sports** (⊠ L. G. Smith Blvd. 83, ☎ 297/8–61603) offers two-hour beginner lessons for $45 (or two people for $60). It also offers Fanatic board and regular windsurfing board rentals by the hour, day, and week.

Windsurfing instruction and board rental are also available through **Carib Asurf** (⊠ Manchebo Beach Resort, ☎ 297/8–23444), **Sailboard Vacation** (⊠ L. G. Smith Blvd. 462, ☎ 297/8–61072), **Roger's Windsurf Place** (⊠ L. G. Smith Blvd. 472, ☎ 297/8–61918), and **De Palm Tours** (⊠ L. G. Smith Blvd. 142, ☎ 297/8-24400 or 297/8–24545).

# Shopping

Caya G. F. Betico Croes—Aruba's chief shopping street—makes for a pleasant diversion from the beach and casino life. *Duty-free* is a magic word here. Major credit cards are welcome virtually everywhere, U.S. dollars are accepted almost as often as local currency, and traveler's checks can be cashed with proof of identity. Shopping malls have arrived in Aruba, so when you finish walking the main street, stop in at a mall to browse through the chic boutiques.

Aruba's souvenir and crafts stores are full of Dutch porcelains and figurines, as befits the island's Netherlands heritage. Dutch cheese is a good buy (you are allowed to bring up to 1 pound of hard cheese through U.S. customs), as are hand-embroidered linens and any products made from the native aloe vera plant—sunburn cream, face masks, and skin refreshers. Since there is no sales tax, the price you see on the tag is the price you pay. But one word of warning: Don't try to bargain. Arubans consider it rude to haggle.

## Specialty Shops

Crafts can be found at several stores. At **Artesania Aruba** (⊠ L. G. Smith Blvd. 178, ☎ 297/8–37494) you'll find charming Aruban

home-crafted pottery, silk-screened T-shirts and wall hangings, and folklore objects. There's a kiosk in the shopping district on Betico Croes as well. The **Artistic Boutique** (⊠ Caya G. F. Betico Croes 25, ☎ 297/8–23142, with branches at the Aruba Hilton, ☎ 297/8–64466, ext. 3508; Seaport Village Mall, ☎ 297/8–32567; and the Holiday Inn, ☎ 297/8–33383) sells Aruban hand-embroidered linens, gold and silver jewelry, Persian carpets and dhurries, porcelain and pottery from Spain, and lots of antiques. **Art and Tradition Handicrafts** (✉ Caya G. F. Betico Croes 30, ☎ 297/8–22078) sells intriguing items that look hand-painted but aren't. Buds from the mopa mopa tree are boiled to form a resin, to which artists add vegetable colors. This resin is then stretched by hand and mouth. Tiny pieces are cut and layered to form intricate designs on wooden shapes—truly unusual gifts. **Creative Hands** (✉ Socotorolaan 5, Oranjestad, ☎ 297/8–35665) sells porcelain and ceramic *cunucu* houses and divi-divi trees, but the store's real draw is its exquisite Japanese dolls.

For duty-free perfumes and cosmetics, stop in at **Aruba Trading Company** (✉ Caya G. F. Betico Croes 12, ☎ 297/8–22602), whose

name is synonymous with old-fashioned reliability. ATC offers internationally known brand names at discounts, but you have to hunt for them. Perfumes and cosmetics are on the first floor, jewelry and men's and women's fashions on the second.

Clothing is also sold at **Wulfsen & Wulfsen** (✉ Caya G. F. Betico Croes 52, ☎ 297/8–23823). One of the highest-rated stores in the Netherlands Antilles for 25 years—and for much longer in Holland—Wulfsen's offers Italian, French, German, and Dutch fashions for both sexes. The Dutch-line Mexx is a favorite of hip teens; Betty Barkley and Mondo are popular for women. Men's clothes range from the conservative to the wild.

**J. L. Penha & Son's** (✉ Caya G. F. Betico Croes 11, ☎ 297/8–24161), another venerated name in Aruban merchandising, also sells clothes, perfumes, and cosmetics and features Boucheron, Lanvin, Dior, and Cartier for women and Givenchy and Pierre Cardin for men.

For jewelry and watches, stop in at **Gandelman's Jewelers** (✉ Caya G. F. Betico Croes 5-A, ☎ 297/8–34433) for Gucci and Swatch watches at reasonable prices, gold bracelets, pink and red coral, and a full line of Gucci accessories, from key chains to handbags. They have a customer service office in Connecticut (☎ 203/325–9786). **Little Switzerland** (✉ Caya G. F. Betico Croes 14, ☎ 297/8–21192), the St. Thomas–based giant, has china, crystal, and fine tableware and offers good buys on Omega and Rado watches, Swarovski silver, Baccarat crystal, and Lladro figurines. If you don't see what you want, ask and they'll ship it to you.

Cuban cigars are available at **La Bonbonniere** (✉ Havenstraat 6, ☎ 297/8–20297) in the Holland Aruba Mall.

## Shopping Malls

**Seaport Village Mall** (✉ L. G. Smith Blvd. across from the harbor, ☎ 297/8–36000) is landmarked by the Crystal Casino Tower. This covered mall is only five minutes away from the cruise terminal. It has more than 130 stores, boutiques, and perfumeries, with merchandise to meet every taste and budget. The arcade is lined with tropical plants and caged parrots, and there is a casino at the top of the escalator. **Arti** has period-clad china dolls in a rainbow of skin tones. Made in Holland, the dolls stand 12 to 18 inches tall. Clown dolls in satin and lace and a very unusual tiny clay orchestra are collector's items. **Les Accessoires** sells purses made in Florence and exclusive leather designs, with prices ranging from $85 to $600. Their Venezuelan pareus come in handy as pool cover-ups. If green fire is your passion, **Colombian Emeralds** is located just over the inside and outside bridges to the mall.

**Tropical Wave** has, in the back behind the junk, some nice Indonesian sculpture and handwoven duffel bags and sweaters from Ecuador.

There are several other shopping malls in Oranjestad, all of which are worth visiting. The **Holland Aruba Mall** (⊠ Havenstraat 6, right downtown) houses a collection of smart shops and eateries. Nearby are the **Strada I** and **Strada II,** two small complexes of shops in tall Dutch buildings painted in pastels. Strada II is home to **Fendi,** whose Etrusco striped vinyl luggage is available at a 45% discount.

**Port of Call Marketplace** (⊠ L. G. Smith Blvd. 17, ☎ 297/8–36706) features fine jewelry, perfumes, duty-free liquors, batiks, crystal, leather goods, and fashionable clothing.

# Nightlife

## Casinos

Casinos are all the rage in Aruba. At last count there were 11. The crowds seem to flock to the newest of the new: Marriott's 10,700 square foot **Stellaris Casino** (⊠ L. G. Smith Blvd. 101, ☎ 297/8–69000) is the latest dazzler on the high-roller scene. Prior to it's opening, Sonesta's 24-hour **Crystal Casino** (⊠ L. G. Smith Blvd. 82, ☎ 297/8–36000) enjoyed the business until the Hyatt Regency opened the ultramodern **Copacabana Casino** (⊠ J.E. Irausquin Blvd. 85, ☎ 297/8–61234), a 10,000-square-foot complex with a Carnival in Rio theme and live entertainment. Then it was the wildly popular **Royal Cabana Casino**—largest in the Caribbean—in La Cabana All Suite Beach Hotel (⊠ J.E. Irausquin Blvd. 250, ☎ 297/8–79000) with its sleek interior, multi-theme three-in-one restaurant, and showcase Tropicana nightclub. Smart money's on the just-opened **Wyndham Casablanca Casino,** quietly elegant with a Bogart theme (⊠ J.E. Irausquin Blvd. 77, ☎ 297/8–64466). One place where you'll always find some action is the **Alhambra Casino** (⊠ L. G. Smith Blvd. 47, Oranjestad, ☎ 297/8–35000), where a "Moorish slave" gives every gambler a hearty handshake upon entering. The **Holiday Inn**'s casino (⊠ J.E. Irausquin Blvd. 230, ☎ 297/8–63600) is open 19 hours a day. The **Americana Aruba Beach Resort & Casino** (⊠ J.E. Irausquin Blvd. 83, ☎ 297/8–64500) opens daily at 1 PM for slots, 5 PM for all games. The **Aruba Palm Beach Hotel Casino** (⊠ J.E. Irausquin Blvd. 79, ☎ 297/8–63900) opens at 10 AM for slots, 6 PM for all games. Low-key gambling can be found at the waterside **Seaport Casino** (⊠ L. G. Smith Blvd. 9, ☎ 297/8–35027).

## Discos and Dancing

Arubans usually start partying late, and action doesn't start till around midnight, mostly on the weekends. At the **Cellar** (⊠ Klipstraat 2, ☎ 297/8–26490) live bands perform Monday, Wednesday, Friday, and Saturday; it may be blues, jazz, funk, reggae, or rock. For fresh air, head to the **Penthouse** bar area and dance floor on the roof. Another popular nightclub is **Cheers Café Bistro** (⊠ L. G. Smith Blvd. 17, ☎ 297/8–30838) in the Port of Call Marketplace near the pier. The dance floor is usually so packed that you can barely wiggle, and the party typically spills out onto the side porch.

Jazz lovers may prefer the quiet piano bar atmosphere of **La Nota** (⊠ Elleboogstraat 1, ☎ 297/8–32739), which gets lively from around 10 PM until closing at 2 AM.

One truly different evening out is **Bonbini Chiva Parranda** (☎ 297/8–35353), which means "bus out on the town." Every Tuesday and Thursday at 6:30 PM, this nightlife tour boards up to 40 people on a wooden, hand-painted 1947 Ford bus and whisks them off to the five hot local nightspots and a restaurant. The $49.50-per-person price includes a drink at each rum shop and a three-course dinner. You're picked up (and poured off) at your hotel. As your affable host remarks, "I finally learned how to cash in on being a party animal." Party animals can prowl farther now, with the **Cucunu,** a bus that offers them the chance to taste the pleasures of country bars. No dinner, but a snack and "jungle juice" are served aboard, for $29.50. It takes place Tuesday and Saturday from 8 till midnight. You're picked up and (fortunately, we'd guess) dropped off after the country crawl.

## Specialty Theme Nights

One of the unique things about Aruba's nightlife is the number of specialty theme nights offered by the hotels: At last count there were more than 30. Each "party" features dinner and entertainment, followed by dancing. Best bets are **Aruban Folkloric** on Monday at the Radisson and **Caribbean Carnival Royale** on Friday at La Cabana. For a complete list, contact the Aruba Tourism Authority (☎ 297/8–60242).

An Aruban must is the **Bon Bini Festival,** held every Tuesday evening from 6:30 to 8:30 PM in the outdoor courtyard of the Fort Zoutman Museum. *Bon Bini* is Papiamento for "welcome," and this tourist event is the Aruba Institute of Culture and Education's way of introducing you to all things Aruban. Stroll by the stands of Aruban foods, drinks, and crafts, or watch Aruban entertainers perform Antillean music and folkloric dancing. A master of ceremonies explains the history of the dances, instruments, and music. It's a fun event, and a good way to meet other tourists. Look for the clock tower. ✉ *Oranjestraat,* ☎ *297/8–22185.* 🎫 *$3.*

## Theater

**Tropicana** (✉ J.E. Irausquin Blvd. 250, ☎ 297/8–69806), La Cabana All Suite's cabaret theater and nightclub, features first-class Las Vegas–style reviews and a special comedy series every weekend. The **Wyndham Aruba** (✉ J.E. Irausquin Blvd. 77, ☎ 297/8–64466) showcases an entertaining Cuban review from 11 to 12:30 PM Tuesday through Saturday in their theater.

**Twinklebone's House of Roast Beef** (✉ Noord 124, ☎ 297/8–26780) does serve succulent prime rib and the like. But it's best known for the fun cabaret put on by the staff every night but Sunday. Customers eat it up.

# Exploring Aruba

Oranjestad, the capital of Aruba, is good for shopping by day and dining by night, but the "real Aruba"—what's left of a wild, untamed beauty—can be found only in the countryside. Rent a car, take a sightseeing tour, or hire a cab for $30 an hour (for up to four people). The main highways are well paved, but on the windward side of the island some roads are still a mixture of compacted dirt and stones. Although a car is fine, a Jeep will allow you to explore the unpaved interior. Traffic is sparse, and you can't get lost. If you do lose your way, just follow the divi-divi trees (because of the direction of the trade winds, the trees are bent toward the leeward side of the island, where all the hotels are). Signs leading to sights of interest are often small and hand lettered, so watch closely.

Few beaches outside the hotel strip have refreshment stands, so take your own food and drink. And one more caution: Note that there are *no* public bathrooms—anywhere—once you leave Oranjestad, except in the infrequent restaurant.

*Numbers in the margin correspond to points of interest on the Aruba map.*

SIGHTS TO SEE

**8  Alto Vista Chapel.** Alone near the northwest corner of the island sits the scenic little Alto Vista Chapel. The wind whistles through the simple mustard-colored walls, eerie boulders, and looming cacti. Along the side of the road back to civilization are miniature crosses painted with depictions of the Stations of the Cross and hand-lettered signs exhorting PRAY FOR US, SINNERS, and the like—a primitive yet powerful evocation of faith. To get there, follow the rough, winding dirt road that loops around the northern tip of the island, or from Oranjestad take Boerhaavestraat across the island.

**9  California Lighthouse.** At the far northern end of the island stands the closed lighthouse. It is surrounded by huge boulders that look like extraterrestrial monsters; in this stark landscape, you'll feel as though you've just landed on the moon.

**5  Caves.** Anyone looking for geological exotica should head for the northern coast, driving northwest from San Nicolas. Stop at the two old Indian caves **Guadirikiri** and **Fontein.** Both were used by the native Indians centuries ago, but you'll have to decide for yourself whether the "ancient Indian inscriptions" are genuine—rumor has it they were added by a European film company that made a movie here years ago. You may enter the caves, but there are no guides available, and bats are known to make appearances. Wear sneakers and take a flashlight or rent one from the soda vendor who has set up shop here. Just before the Fontein and Guadirikiri caves lies the **Tunnel of Love,** a heart-shape tunnel containing naturally sculpted rocks that look just like the Madonna, Abe Lincoln, even a jaguar. The climb through the tunnel is strenuous and should not be attempted by anyone not in good physical condition. It's definitely not recommended for elderly people or young children. Remember, admission is free to all three caves—don't be deterred by the occasionally pushy vendors.

**3  Frenchman's Pass.** A bit of history can be found along this dark, luscious stretch of highway arbored by overhanging trees. Local legend claims that the French and native Indians warred here during the 17th century for control of the island. To get there, drive east on L. G. Smith Boulevard past a shimmering vista of blue-green sea toward San Nicolas, on what is known as the Sunrise side of the island. Turn left where you see the drive-in theater (a popular hangout for Arubans), drive to the first intersection, turn right, and follow the curve to the right. Gold was discovered on Aruba in 1824, and nearby you'll find the cement ruins of the **Balashi Gold Smelter Ruins** (take the dirt road veering to the right)—a lovely place to picnic, listen to the parakeets, and contemplate the towering cacti. A magnificent gnarled divi-divi tree guards the entrance.

**2  Hooiberg.** Translated to mean Haystack Hill, this 541-foot peak is inland just past the airport. If you have the energy, climb the 562 steps up to the top for an impressive view of the city. To get there from Oranjestad, turn onto Caya C.F. Croes (shown on island maps as 7A) toward Santa Cruz; the peak will be on your right.

**10  Malmok.** On the drive to the northern tip of the island you'll pass through Malmok, where Aruba's wealthiest families reside. Jutting above the water not far off Malmok Beach, one of the finest spots for shelling, snorkeling, and windsurfing, are parts of the wreck of the German ship *Antilla,* scuttled here in 1940.

**❼ Natural Bridge.** This bridge, at the midway mark on the windward coast, was sculpted out of coral rock by centuries of raging wind and sea. To get to it, follow the main road inland (Hospitalstraat) and then signs that lead the way. All along, you'll pass the massive ruins of the Bushiribana Gold Smelter, which resembles a crumbling fortress, and a section of coastline called Boca Mahose where local restaurateurs bring scraps to feed sharks (thereby encouraging them to stay on the windward side of the island). Near the natural bridge is a café overlooking the water and a souvenir shop stuffed with trinkets, T-shirts, and postcards for reasonable prices.

**❶ Oranjestad.** Aruba's charming Dutch capital is best explored on foot. There are many shopping malls with boutiques and shops. The palm-lined thoroughfare in the center of town runs between pastel painted buildings, old and new, of typical Dutch design.

At the **Archeology Museum** you'll find two rooms chockablock with fascinating Indian artifacts, farm and domestic utensils, and skeletons. Across the street you'll see the handsome Protestant Church. ⊠ *Zoutmanstraat 1,* ☎ *297/8–28979.* 🎫 *Free.* ⊘ *Weekdays 8–noon and 1–4:30.*

One of the island's oldest buildings, **Fort Zoutman** was built in 1796 and used as a major fortress in the skirmishes between British and Curaçao troops. The Willem III Tower, named for the Dutch monarch of that time, was added in 1868. The fort's Historical Museum displays centuries' worth of Aruban relics and artifacts in an 18th-century Aruban house. ⊠ *Oranjestraat,* ☎ *297/8–26099.* 🎫 *$1.25.* ⊘ *Weekdays 9–noon and 1:30–4:30.*

Tiny **Numismatic Museum,** next to St. Francis Roman Catholic Church, displays coins and paper money from more than 100 countries. ⊠ *Zuidstraat 27,* ☎ *297/8–28831.* 🎫 *Free.* ⊘ *Weekdays 7:30–noon and 1–4:30.*

**❻ Rock Formations.** The massive boulders at Ayo and Casibari are said to be a mystery since they don't match the geological makeup of the island. Mystery or no, you can climb to the top for fine views of Aruba's arid countryside or snapshots of brown or blue lizards as you hike among the towering cactus surrounding the formations. Climbing is not recommended for children or older visitors—there are no handrails on the way up and you must climb through tunnels and on narrow steps and ledges to reach the top. Access is via the Tanki Leendert Highway (4A); watch carefully for the turn-off signs near the center of the island on the way to the windward side.

**❹ San Nicolas.** During the heyday of the Exxon refineries, Aruba's oldest village was a bustling port; now it's dedicated to tourism, with the main-street promenade full of interesting kiosks. The **China Clipper Bar** on Main Street used to be a famous "red-light" bar frequented by sailors docked in port. Another institution is **Charlie's Bar** (⊠ Zeppenfeldstraat 56, ☎ 297/8–41513 or 297/8–45086), a San Nicolas hangout for more than 50 years (☞ Dining, *above*). Stop in for a drink and advice on what to see and do on this section of the island.

# Aruba A to Z

## Arriving and Departing

BY PLANE

Aruba is 2½ hours away from Miami and four hours from New York. Flights leave daily to Aruba from New York area airports and Miami International Airport with easy connections from most American cities.

**Air Aruba** (☎ 297/8–23151 or 800/882–7822), the island's official airline, flies nonstop to Aruba daily from Miami and Newark. Twice-weekly service has begun from Baltimore. **American Airlines** (☎ 800/433–7300 or 297/8–22006) offers daily nonstop service from both Miami and New York. **ALM** (☎ 800/327–7230 or 297/8–23546), the major airline of the Dutch Caribbean islands, flies six days a week non-stop from Miami to Aruba. Air Aruba and ALM also have connect-ing flights to Caracas, Bonaire, Curaçao, and St. Maarten as well as other Caribbean islands. ALM also offers a "Visit Caribbean Pass" for interisland travel. From Toronto and Montréal, you can fly to Aruba on American Airlines via San Juan. American also has connecting flights from several U.S. cities via San Juan. **Viasa,** the Venezuelan car-rier (☎ 297/8–36526 or 800/468–4272), flies direct from Houston.

## Currency

Arubans happily accept U.S. dollars virtually everywhere, so there's no real need to exchange money, except for necessary pocket change (cigarettes, soda machines, or pay phones). The currency used, how-ever, is the Aruban florin (AFl), which at press time exchanged to the U.S. dollar at AFl1.77 for cash, AFl1.79 for traveler's checks, and to the Canadian dollar at AFl1.51. The Dutch Antillean florin (used in Bonaire and Curaçao) is not accepted in Aruba. Major credit cards and traveler's checks are widely accepted, but you will probably be asked to show identification when cashing a traveler's check. Prices quoted here are in U.S. dollars unless otherwise noted.

## Emergencies

**Police:** ☎ 1000. **Hospital:** ✉ Horacio Oduber, ☎ 74300. **Pharmacy:** ✉ Botica del Pueblo, ☎ 22154.

**Ambulance** and **Fire:** ☎ 115. All hotels have house doctors on call 24 hours a day. Call the front desk.

## Getting Around

Remember, the island's winding roads are poorly marked, if at all. The major tourist attractions are fairly easy to find; others you'll happen upon only by sheer luck (or with an Aruban friend).

### BUSES

Buses run hourly trips between the beach hotels and Oranjestad. Round-trip fare is $1.50, and exact change is preferred. Buses also run down the coast from Oranjestad to San Nicolas for the same fare. Con-tact the Aruba Tourism Authority (☎ 297/8–21019) for a bus sched-ule, or inquire at the front desk of your hotel.

### CAR RENTALS

You'll need a valid U.S. or Canadian driver's license to rent a car, and you must be able to meet the minimum age requirements of each rental service, implemented for insurance reasons. **Budget Rent-A-Car** (☎ 800/472–3325) requires drivers to be between 25 and 65, **Avis** (☎ 800/331–1212) requires drivers to be between 23 and 70, and **Hertz** (☎ 800/654–3131) requires drivers to be older than 21. A deposit of $500 (or a signed credit-card slip) is required. Rental rates are between $35–$70 per day. Insurance is available starting at $10 per day, and all companies offer unlimited mileage. Local car-rental companies gen-erally have lower rates.

Local addresses and phone numbers for the rental agencies are **Avis** (✉ Kolibristraat 14, ☎ 297/8–28787; ✉ airport, ☎ 297/8–25496), **Budget Rent-A-Car** (✉ Kolibristraat 1, ☎ 297/8–28600; ✉ airport, ☎ 297/8–25423; ✉ Divi resorts, ☎ 297/8–35000), **Hertz, De Palm Car Rental** (✉ L. G. Smith Blvd. 142, Box 656, ☎ 297/8–24545; ✉

airport, ☎ 297/8–24886), **Dollar Rent-a-Car** (✉ Grendeaweg 15, ☎ 297/8–22783; airport, ☎ 297/8–25651; ✉ Manchebo, ☎ 297/8–26696), **National** (✉ Tanki Leendert 170, ☎ 297/8–21967; ✉ airport, ☎ 297/8–25451; ✉ Holiday Inn, ☎ 297/8–23768), **Thrifty** (✉ Balashi 65, ☎ 297/8–55300; ✉ airport, ☎ 297/8–35335), and **Hedwina Car Rental** (✉ Bubali 93A, ☎ 297/8–76442; ✉ airport, ☎ 297/8–30880). Dollar and National require drivers to be at least 23 years old.

### MOTORCYCLES

Rates vary according to the make of the vehicle. For Yamaha scooters ($27–$29 per day), contact **George's Cycle Center** (✉ L. G. Smith Blvd. 136, ☎ 297/8–25975). Other moped, scooter, and motorcycle rental companies are **Ron's Motorcycle Rental** (✉ Bakval 17A, ☎ 297/8–62090), **Nelson Motorcycle Rental** (✉ Gasparito 10A, ☎ 297/8–66801), and **Semver Cycle Rental** (✉ Noord 22, ☎ 297/8–66851). If you're feeling hoggish, you can rent a Harley Davidson for $100 per day (insurance is included) from **Melcor Cycle Rental** (✉ Tanki Leendert 170A, ☎ 297/8–234480).

### TAXIS

A dispatch office is located at the airport (☎ 297/8–21906); you can also flag down taxis on the street. Since taxis do not have meters, rates are fixed and should be confirmed before your ride begins. Add $1 to the fare after midnight and on holidays. All Aruba's taxi drivers have participated in the government's Tourism Awareness Programs and have received their Tourism Guide Certificate. An hour's tour of the island by taxi will run you about $35, for a maximum of four people per car. A taxi from the airport to most hotels will run $8–$14.

## Guided Tours

Aruba's **#1 Hotline** (☎ 297/8–25353) offers all major tours on the island at discounted rates.

### BOAT CRUISES

If you try a cruise around the island, know that trimarans give a much smoother ride than monohull boats on choppy waters stirred up by the trade winds. Sucking on lemon or lime candy may help a queasy stomach; avoid going with an empty stomach. The most popular and reputable sailing cruises are offered by **De Palm Tours** (☎ 297/8–24400 or 297/8–24545), **Mi Dushi** (☎ 297/8–28919), **Red Sail Sports** (☎ 297/8–24500), **Pelican Watersports** (☎ 297/8–31228), and **Wave Dancer** (☎ 297/8–25520).

Moonlight cruises offer stunning views and cost about $25 per person. (Be prepared to sail with a lot of sappy honeymooners.) There are also a variety of snorkeling, dinner and dancing, and sunset party cruises to choose from priced from $25 to $60 per person. Contact **Red Sail Sports** (☎ 297/8–24500), **Pelican Watersports** (☎ 297/8–31228), or **De Palm Tours** (☎ 297/8–24400 or 297/8–24545). One favorite is the four-hour snorkel, sail, open-bar, and lunch cruise aboard the *Mi Dushi*, a beautifully restored 1925 Swedish sailboat. This two-masted wooden vessel is captained by Mario Maduro and a fun crew who act as lifeguards, snorkel instructors, bartenders, galley staff, deckhands, and storytellers. Two stops are made for snorkeling; save your energy for the second one at the wreck of the *Antilla*. Cost is $30.

### ORIENTATION TOURS

Aruba's highlights can be seen in a day. Although most highways are in excellent condition, signs and directions are haphazard, making a guided tour your best option for exploring if you have only a short time. **De Palm Tours** (✉ L. G. Smith Blvd. 142, ☎ 297/8–24400, 297/8–24545, or 800/766–6016; FAX 297/8–23012) has a near monopoly on the Aruban sightseeing business; reservations may be made through its general office or at hotel tour-desk branches. The basic 3½-hour tour hits the high spots of the island, including popular spots that are difficult to find on your own, such as the Ayo and Casibari rock formations (Jeep tours). Wear tennis or hiking shoes (there'll be optional climbing) and note that the air-conditioned bus can get cold. The tour, which begins at 9:30 AM, picks you up in your lobby and costs $17.50 per person. De Palm also offers full-day tours of Caracas, Venezuela ($240, passport required), and Curaçao ($200). Prices include round-trip airfare, transfers, sightseeing, and lunch; there is also free time for shopping. **Aruba Friendly Tours** (⊠ Cumana 20, Oranjestad, ☎ 297/8–39922) also offers tours of Aruba's main sights.

SPECIAL-INTEREST TOURS

For a three-in-one tour of prehistoric Indian cultures, volcanic formations, and natural wildlife, contact archaeologist Eppie Boerstra of **Marlin Booster Tracking, Inc.,** at Charlie's Bar (☎ 297/8–41513 or 297/8–45086). The fee for a six-hour tour is $35 per person, including a cold picnic lunch and beverages. Tours can be given in English, Dutch, German, and French.

Hikers will enjoy a guided three-hour trip to remote sites of unusual natural beauty accessible only on foot. The fee is $25 per person, including refreshments and transportation; a minimum of four people is required. Contact **De Palm Tours** (☎ 297/8–24400 or 297/8–24545).

You can now explore an underwater reef teeming with marine life without getting wet. **Atlantis Submarines** (⊠ Seaport Village Marina, ☎ 297/8–36090) operates a 65-foot, modern, air-conditioned sub that takes 46 passengers 95–150 feet below the surface along Aruba's Barcadera Reef. The 50-minute plunge costs $64 for adults, $29 for children 4 to 16. If you are not a scuba diver, the hour in the submarine is the next best thing to being down among the fish and coral. Another option is the **Seaworld Explorer** (☎ 297/8–24400), a semisubmersible that allows passengers to sit and view the Aruba's marine habitat from 5 feet below the surface. Cost is $29.

## Opening and Closing Times

Shops are generally open between 8 AM and 6 PM, Monday through Saturday. Most stores stay open through the lunch hour, noon–2 PM. Many stores open when cruise ships are in port on Sundays and holidays. Nighttime shopping at the Alhambra Bazaar runs 5 PM–midnight. Bank hours are weekdays from 8 to noon and 1:30 to 4. The Aruba Bank at the airport is open on Saturday from 9 to 4 and on Sunday from 9 to 1.

## Passports and Visas

U.S. and Canadian residents need only show proof of identity—a valid passport, birth certificate, naturalization certificate, green card, valid nonquota immigration visa, or a valid voter registration card. All other nationalities must submit a valid passport.

## Precautions

Aruba is a party island, but only up to a point: A police dog sniffs for drugs at the airport.

It's a safe island, but common sense rules still apply. Don't leave things in a rental car, and lock the car when you leave it. You needn't be afraid to stop and ask anyone for directions on Aruba.

Mosquitos can be bothersome during the rainy season (November through January), so pack some repellant. The strong trade winds are a relief in the subtropical climate, but don't hang your bathing suit on a balcony—it will probably blow away. Help Arubans conserve water and energy: Turn off air-conditioning when you leave your room, and keep your faucets turned off.

## Taxes and Service Charges

Hotels collect a 5% government tax and usually add an 11% service charge to room bills. Restaurants usually add a 10%–15% service charge to your bill. The departure tax is $20. There is no sales tax.

## Telephones and Mail

To dial direct to Aruba from the United States, dial 011–297–8, followed by the number in Aruba. Local and international calls in Aruba can be made via hotel operators or from the Government Long Distance Telephone, Telegraph, and Radio Office, SETAR, in the post office building in Oranjestad. When dialing locally in Aruba, simply dial the five-digit number. To reach the United States, dial 001, then the area code and number.

Telegrams and telexes can be sent through SETAR, at the Post Office Building in Oranjestad or via your hotel. There is also a SETAR office in front of the Hyatt Regency hotel, adjacent to the hotel's parking lot (☎ 297/8–67138).

You can send an airmail letter from Aruba to the U.S. and Canada for AFl1.40, a postcard for AFl.0.60, to Europe AFl.1.50 and AFl.0.70.

## Visitor Information

Contact the **Aruba Tourism Authority,** ✉ 1000 Harbor Blvd. (Ground Level), Weehawken, NJ 07087, ☎ 201/330–0800 or 800/862–2782, FAX 201/330–8757; in Miami, ✉ 2344 Salzedo St., Miami, FL 33134, ☎ 305/567–2720, FAX 305/567–2721; in Canada, ✉ 86 Bloor St. W, Suite 204, Toronto, Ontario, M5S 1M5, ☎ 416/975–1950. In Aruba, the **Aruba Tourism Authority** (✉ L. G. Smith Blvd. 172, Eagle Beach, Aruba, ☎ 297/8–23777) has free brochures and information officers who are ready to answer any questions.

# 5  Barbados

**B**ARBADOS HAS A LIFE OF ITS OWN that continues after the tourists have packed up their sun oils and returned home. The government is stable, business operations are sophisticated, and unemployment is relatively low, so the difference between haves and have-nots is less marked—or at least less visible—than on some islands. The 260,000 Bajans (Barbadians) are a warm, friendly, and hospitable people. They are genuinely proud of their country and welcome visitors as privileged guests. Barbados is a good spot for people who want nothing more than to offer their bodies to the sun, yet travelers who want to discover Caribbean island life and culture will also find it ideal.

Updated by
Jane E. Zarem

Barbados, the most easterly of all the Caribbean islands, lies partially in the Atlantic Ocean and partially in the Caribbean Sea. It is 21 miles long, 14 miles wide, and relatively flat; the highest point, Mt. Hillaby, has an elevation of 1,115 feet. Most people live in the urban area surrounding Bridgetown, the capital—between Speightstown on the northwest coast and Oistins in the south. The rest of the population resides in tiny hamlets scattered around the island.

Beaches along the tranquil West Coast—in the lee of the northwest trade winds—are backed by first-class resorts. More hotels stretch along the beaches on the South Coast. British and Canadian visitors often favor the posh hotels of St. James Parish. Americans (couples more often than singles) tend to congregate at the large South Coast resorts. Because the beaches of Barbados are open to the public, they lack the privacy that some visitors seek; but the beaches are lovely.

To the northeast are rolling hills and valleys covered by impenetrable acres of sugarcane. The Atlantic surf pounds gigantic boulders along the rugged East Coast, where the Bajans themselves have vacation homes. Elsewhere on the island, linked by almost 900 miles of good roads, are small villages, historic plantation houses, stalactite-studded caves, a wildlife preserve, and the Andromeda Gardens, one of the most attractive small tropical gardens in the world.

No one is sure whether the name Los Barbados ("the bearded ones") refers to the beardlike root that hangs from the island's fig trees or to the bearded natives who greeted the Portuguese "discoverer" of the island in 1536. The name Los Barbados was still current almost a century later when the British landed—by accident—in what is now Holetown in St. James Parish. They colonized the island in 1627 and the British rule remained uninterrupted until the island achieved independence in 1966.

Barbados has retained a very British atmosphere. Afternoon tea is a ritual at numerous hotels. Cricket is the national sport (a religion, some say), and Barbados produces some of the world's top players. Polo is played in winter. The British tradition of dressing for dinner is firmly entrenched; a few luxury hotels request tie and jacket at dinner in season, and in fine restaurants most women will consider themselves inappropriately dressed in anything less formal than a cocktail dress. (A daytime stroll in a swimsuit is as inappropriate in Bridgetown as it would be on New York's 5th Avenue.) Yet the island's atmosphere is hardly stuffy. When the car you ordered for noon doesn't arrive until 12:30, the cheerful driver is just operating on "Caribbean time."

**Exploring**

**Dining**

**Lodging**

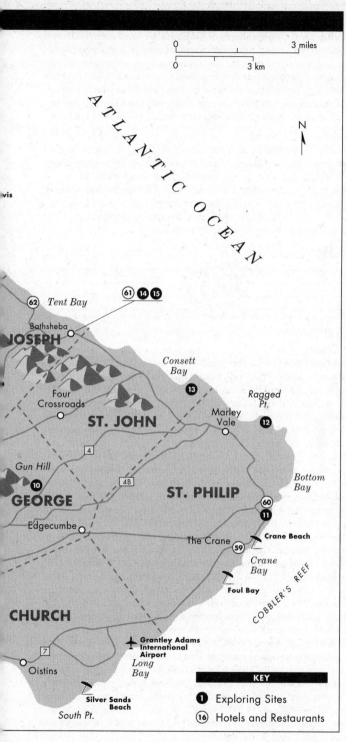

Benston Windsurfing
Club Hotel, **58**

Casuarina Beach
Club, **55**

Club Rockley
Barbados, **46**

Cobblers Cove
Hotel, **64**

Coconut Creek
Club, **33**

Coral Reef Club, **26**

Crane Beach Hotel, **59**

Discovery Bay
Hotel, **30**

Divi Southwinds Beach
Resort, **53**

Glitter Bay, **27**

Grand Barbados
Beach Resort, **41**

Little Bay Hotel, **50**

Marriott's Sam Lord's
Castle, **60**

Ocean View, **44**

Royal Pavilion, **28**

Sandridge, **66**

Sandy Beach Island
Resort, **47**

Sandy Lane Hotel, **34**

Sichris Hotel, **48**

Southern Palms, **54**

Treasure Beach, **35**

# Lodging

The southern and western shores of Barbados are lined with hotels and resorts of every size and price, offering a variety of accommodations ranging from private villas and elegant hotels to modest but comfortable rooms in simple inns. At the same time, apartment and home rentals and time-share condominiums have become widely available and are growing increasingly popular among visitors to the island. A few hotels are all-inclusive, though most still offer either EP or MAP meal plans.

The location of your hotel is important. Hotels to the north of Bridgetown, in the West Coast parishes of St. Peter, St. James, and St. Michael, tend to be self-contained resorts with stretches of empty road between them that discourage strolling to a neighborhood bar or restaurant. Along the South Coast, in Christ Church Parish, many of the hotels cluster near or along the busy strip known as St. Lawrence Gap, where dozens of small restaurants, bars, and nightclubs are close by. Hotels listed here are grouped by parish.

| CATEGORY | COST* |
| --- | --- |
| $$$$ | over $350 |
| $$$ | $250–$350 |
| $$ | $150–$250 |
| $ | under $150 |

*All prices are for a standard double room, excluding 5% government tax and 10% service charge.*

## West Coast

$$$$   🏨 **Coral Reef Club.** Guests here spend their days relaxing on the white-sand beach or around the pool, taking time out for the hotel's superb afternoon tea. The public areas ramble along the beach and face the Caribbean Sea, and small coral-stone cottages are scattered over the surrounding 12 flower-filled acres. (The cottages farthest from the beach are a bit of a hike to the main house.) The accommodations are spacious, each with air-conditioning and ceiling fans, a small patio, and fresh flowers. The restaurant, under the direction of Bajan chef Graham Licorish, is noted for its inventive cuisine that combines local cooking with European flair. Most guests are on an MAP plan that includes a complimentary buffet lunch. Another convenience is the free shuttle into Bridgetown. ⊠ *Porters,* ☎ *246/422–2372,* 𝐅𝐀𝐗 *246/422–1776. 68 rooms. Restaurant, pool, air-conditioning. AE, MC, V. EP, MAP.*

$$$$   🏨 **Glitter Bay.** In the 1930s, Sir Edward Cunard, of the English shipping family, bought this estate, built the main Great House and a beach house similar to his palazzo in Venice, and began hosting famous parties in honor of visiting aristocrats and celebrities, making Glitter Bay synonymous with grandeur. Today, buildings angled back from the beach house 81 one- to three-bedroom suites with full kitchens, and the beach house has been transformed into five garden suites. Manicured, landscaped gardens separate the reception area and large, comfortable tea lounge from the pool, the alfresco dining room where evening entertainment is held, and a half mile of beach. Glitter Bay is more casual and family oriented than its next-door sister property, the Royal Pavilion (☞ *below*); but they share facilities, including complimentary water sports. Guests at either resort have dining privileges at both. ⊠ *Porters,* ☎ *246/422–4111,* 𝐅𝐀𝐗 *246/422–3940. 74 rooms. Restaurant, pool, air-conditioning, golf course nearby, 2 tennis courts, water sports center. AE, DC, MC, V. EP, MAP.*

$$$$   🏨 **Royal Pavilion.** Of the 75 rooms here, 72 are oceanfront suites; the
★      remaining three are nestled in a garden villa. The ground-floor oceanfront rooms allow guests simply to step through sliding doors, cross

their private patio, and walk onto the sand. Second- and third-floor rooms, however, have the advantage of an elevated view of the sea. Breakfast and lunch are served alfresco along the edge of the beach. Afternoon tea and dinner are in the Palm Terrace (☞ Dining, *below*). The Royal Pavilion attracts sophisticated guests who want serenity (bringing children under the age of 12 is discouraged during the winter months). Recreational facilities are shared with the adjoining and more informal sister hotel, Glitter Bay. ⊠ *Porters,* ☎ *246/422–4444,* FAX *246/422–3940. 75 rooms. 2 restaurants, 2 bars, pool, beach, air-conditioning, golf course nearby, 2 tennis courts, water-sports center, beauty parlor. AE, DC, MC, V. EP.*

$$$$ ★ 🏨 **Sandy Lane Hotel.** This prestigious hotel has set a standard for elegance and style since 1961. Set on one of the best beaches in Barbados, with acres of well-tended grounds, Sandy Lane is one of the most impressive hotels in the Caribbean. The white coral structure, finished with Zandobbio marble throughout, with a staircase leading to the beach shaded with mahogany trees, will remind you of the *Great Gatsby.* All rooms overlook the sea and have private balconies for eating breakfast and watching magnificent sunsets. Rooms are nothing short of spectacular; bathrooms are vast and luxurious. Afternoon tea, fine dining, and personalized service all add to the charm. You'll be treated like royalty—in fact, royalty stays here when they visit Barbados. Plan to dress up, particularly in season—no jeans or shorts after 7 PM. ⊠ *Hwy. 1,* ☎ *246/432–1311,* FAX *246/432–2954. 90 rooms, 30 suites. 3 restaurants, 5 bars, pool, beach, air-conditioning, health club, 18-hole golf course and club, 5 tennis courts, fitness facility, water sports center, Tree Top club for children, beauty parlor, baby-sitting. AE, DC, MC, V. EP, MAP.*

$$$ 🏨 **Coconut Creek Club.** A luxury cottage colony, the Coconut Creek Club is set on handsomely landscaped grounds with a small private beach and a bar pavilion for entertainment and dancing. The atmosphere here is casual. Set on a low bluff, the hotel overlooks the ocean, and steps lead down to two secluded coves. Some rooms have ocean views; others overlook the garden or pool. Televisions are available on request for a small fee. ⊠ *Reservations: Box 249, Bridgetown; Hwy. 1,* ☎ *246/432–0803,* FAX *246/422–1726. 53 rooms. Dining room, bar, pool, beach, air-conditioning, water sports center, baby-sitting. AE, DC, MC, V. EP, MAP.*

$$$ 🏨 **Discovery Bay Hotel.** In historic Holetown, site of the British "discovery" and settlement of the island, this quiet hotel—with a grand, white-columned, plantation-style entrance—is surrounded by 4½ acres of tropical gardens and bordered by a broad strand of Caribbean beach. Deluxe rooms have ocean views; others open onto a central lawn and pool area. A shuttle to Bridgetown is available to guests on weekdays. ⊠ *Hwy. 1, Holetown,* ☎ *246/432–1301,* FAX *246/422–1726. 87 rooms. Restaurant, pool, beach, air-conditioning, Ping-Pong, boutique. AE, D, DC, MC, V. EP.*

$$$ 🏨 **Treasure Beach.** Most of the one-bedroom suites of this compact resort face the small garden and pool, although some have sea views, and all are just steps from the beach. Suites are spacious, with kitchenettes and sitting rooms that open onto large patios or verandas with louvered, full-length shutters for privacy. The atmosphere is quiet and pleasant, and the staff is equally so. ⊠ *Payne's Bay,* ☎ *246/432–1346,* FAX *246/432–1094. 24 1-bedroom, suites; 1 2-bedroom penthouse suite. Restaurant, pool, beach, air-conditioning, water sports. AE, DC, MC, V. EP, MAP.*

$$–$$$ 🏨 **Almond Beach Club.** In this hotel, everything is included in the price of the room—all you want to eat and drink (including wine and liquor), water sports, boat trips, tennis, Bajan beach picnic, shopping excur-

sions to Bridgetown, departure transportation to the airport, and service and taxes. Accommodations are in one-bedroom suites with balconies, two-bedroom duplex suites, and individual poolside or garden-view rooms. The food is excellent, from the breakfast buffet and a four-course lunch to the afternoon tea and pastries and the extensive dinner menu. The menus offer plenty of choice, but if your stay is seven days or more, the Almond Beach Club offers a dine-around program—dinner or lunch at a number of area restaurants with round-trip transportation included. There's an exchange program, which includes golf privileges, with Almond Beach Village (☞ *below*); shuttle service is provided. The Almond Beach Club doesn't have the enforced-activity, "whistle-blowing" atmosphere of some all-inclusives. ⊠ *Vauxhall*, ☎ *246/432–7840 or 800/425–6663*, ℻ *246/432–2115. 151 rooms. 2 restaurants, 4 bars, 3 pools, beach, air-conditioning, 1 tennis court, sauna, squash, water sports center, boutique. AE, MC, V. All-inclusive.*

## St. Peter Parish

**$$$$**   🏨 **Cobblers Cove Hotel.** This all-suite resort, 12 miles up the West Coast
★          from Bridgetown, combines comfort and informal elegance in an English-style country house. The pink-and-white hotel building and the tropical gardens are bounded on three sides by stone walls, giving the property a self-contained ambience. This fine retreat overlooking the sea is part of the Relais & Châteaux organization, the only member in Barbados. The atmosphere is casual and smart. There's an excellent gourmet restaurant, a clublike lounge/library, and the bar becomes the evening gathering spot. For all-out luxury, you can stay in the new Colleton Suite or the Camelot Suite. Designed by renowned Prue Lane Fox, whose work graces aristocratic British homes, the Colleton Suite has a large living room with enormous windows opening out to a patio and private plunge pool. The sumptuous Camelot Suite has a four-poster bed, bathroom with Jacuzzi, large sitting area, and private plunge pool and wet bar on its own roof-top terrace. Guests enjoy special rates and guaranteed tee times at the nearby Royal Westmoreland Golf Course. ⊠ *Hwy. 1*, ☎ *246/422–2291 or 800/890–6060*, ℻ *246/422–1460. 40 suites. Restaurant, snack bar, bar, pool, tennis court, water sports center, baby-sitting (but no children under 12 allowed late Jan.–late Mar.). AE, MC, V. CP, MAP.*

**$$$**   🏨 **Almond Beach Village.** The 30-acre property that used to be Heywoods is the sister hotel to Almond Beach Club (☞ *above*) in St. James. Renovated to the tune of $12 million, all rooms were gutted and completely redecorated. Pools were added, and the golf course was upgraded. Accommodations are in seven low-rise complexes that stretch along a mile of beach. A 70-suite family section has junior and one-bedroom suites, a family restaurant, play area, kiddy pool, and children's program. All meals (including beverages), activities, and departure transfers are included in the rates. ⊠ *Hwy. 1*, ☎ *246/422–4900 or 800/425–6663*, ℻ *246/422–1581. 288 rooms, including 70-suite family section. 4 restaurants, 5 bars, 9 pools, 9-hole golf course, 5 tennis courts, squash, fitness center, water sports center, boutique. AE, MC, V. All-inclusive.*

**$$**   🏨 **Sandridge.** Six new waterfront suites and a new dining room with lounge have been added to this fashionable beachfront property near Speightstown. Guest rooms have been restyled in bright colors with tropical furnishings; some rooms have kitchenettes. Ground floor accommodations have wide doors and ramps, allowing easy access for guests with disabilities. A supervised children's program makes this property particularly attractive to families. The resort's second pool has been remodeled to include a dramatic waterfall and deck of coral stone.

✉ *Road View,* ☎ *246/422–2361,* FAX *246/422–1965. 58 rooms. 2 restaurants, 2 bars, 2 pools, beach, water sports center, baby-sitting. AE, DC, MC, V.*

## St. Michael Parish

**$$$** 🏨 **Grand Barbados Beach Resort.** A mile from Bridgetown on Carlisle Bay, this convenient hotel has comfortable rooms and suites. The white-sand beach is lapped by a surprisingly clear sea, despite the oil refinery close by. The Aquatic Club executive floor has rooms whose rates include a Continental breakfast and secretarial services. Nightly live music, a dance floor, and a 260-foot-long pier that's perfect for romantic walks add to the enjoyment of a stay here. ✉ *Box 639, Bridgetown,* ☎ *246/426–0890,* FAX *246/436–9823. 133 rooms. 2 restaurants, pool, beach, air-conditioning, barbershop, beauty salon, sauna, 1 tennis court, whirlpool, exercise room, shopping arcade. AE, DC, MC, V. EP.*

**$$–$$$** 🏨 **Barbados Hilton.** This large resort, just five minutes from Bridgetown, bustles with activity from the people who come to attend seminars and conferences. You may detect an odor from the nearby oil refinery. Attractions here include an atrium lobby, a 1,000-foot-wide man-made beach with full water sports, and lots of shops. All rooms and suites have balconies. ✉ *Needham's Point,* ☎ *246/426–0200,* FAX *246/436– 8946. 184 rooms. Restaurant, 2 bars, lounge, pool, beach, air-conditioning, 4 tennis courts, health club. AE, DC, MC, V. EP.*

## Christ Church Parish

**$$** 🏨 **Casuarina Beach Club.** This luxury apartment hotel consists of five clusters of Spanish-style buildings in 7½ acres of gardens. The hotel takes its name from the casuarina pines that surround it. The quiet setting provides a dramatic contrast to that of other South Coast resorts. The bar and restaurant are on the beach—900 feet of pink sand. A reception area includes small lounges where you can get a dose of TV— there aren't any in the bedrooms. Rooms have kitchenettes and large balconies. Scuba diving, golf, and other activities can be arranged. The Casuarina Beach is popular with those who prefer self-catering holidays in a secluded setting, yet want to be close to nightlife and shopping. ✉ *St. Lawrence Gap,* ☎ *246/428–3600 or 800/223–9815,* FAX *246/428–1970. 134 rooms. Restaurant, bar, pool, beach, 2 tennis courts, squash, shop. AE, DC, MC, V. EP.*

**$$** 🏨 **Club Rockley Barbados.** Some of these time-share condominiums have been transformed into an all-inclusive resort with air-conditioned one- and two-bedroom accommodations with balcony or patio. On 65 acres near one of the most popular beach areas in Barbados, the resrot offers an extensive list of guest amenities and an excellent location for golfers and tennis players. ✉ *Hastings, Christ Church,* ☎ *246/435–7880,* FAX *246/435–8015. 288 rooms. 2 restaurants, 3 bars, 7 pools, air-conditioning, 5 tennis courts, 9-hole golf course, squash, beauty salon, shops. AE, DC, MC, V. All-inclusive.*

**$$** 🏨 **Divi Southwinds Beach Resort.** In this resort, on 20 lush acres, the toss-up is whether to take one of the one-bedroom suites, with a balcony and kitchenette overlooking the gardens and pool, or one of the smaller and older-looking rooms, just steps from the white sandy beach. Though all the rooms are pleasant, the buildings themselves are rather plain. Guests come here for a rollicking good time that includes making full use of the scuba and water-sports facilities. ✉ *St. Lawrence,* ☎ *800/367–3484,* FAX *246/428–4674. 166 rooms. 2 restaurants, 3 pools, beach, putting green, 2 tennis courts, shops. AE, MC, V. EP, MAP.*

**$$** 🏨 **Sandy Beach Island Resort.** On a wide, sparkling white beach, this comfortable hotel has a popular poolside bar and the Beachfront Restaurant, which serves a West Indian buffet Tuesday and Saturday nights.

The accommodations have been reconfigured and upgraded to include large one-bedroom suites, the restaurant has been enlarged, and a boardwalk gazebo, roof garden, and spectacular free-form pool have been added to the grounds. Scuba-diving certification, deep-sea fishing, harbor cruises, and catamaran sailing can be arranged. It's also a convenient walk to St. Lawrence Gap for other restaurants and entertainment. ⊠ *Worthing,* ☎ *246/435–8000,* FAX *246/435–8053. 89 units. Restaurant, bar, pool, beach, air-conditioning. AE, DC, MC, V. EP.*

**$$** 🏨 **Southern Palms.** A plantation-style hotel on a 1,000-foot stretch of pink sand near the Dover Convention Center, Southern Palms is a convenient businessperson's hotel and a good choice for active guests wanting to be near the Gap's shops and restaurants. You may choose from standard bedrooms, deluxe oceanfront suites with kitchenettes, and a four-bedroom penthouse. Each wing of the hotel has its own small pool. ⊠ *St. Lawrence,* ☎ *246/428–7171,* FAX *246/428–7175. 93 rooms. 2 restaurants bar, 2 pools, beach, air-conditioning, miniature golf, tennis court, water sports, duty-free shop, conference center. AE, DC, MC, V. EP.*

**$** 🏨 **Benston Windsurfing Club Hotel.** A small hotel that began as a gathering place for windsurfing enthusiasts, the Benston Windsurfing Club is now a complete school and center for the sport. The rooms are spacious and sparsely furnished to accommodate the active and young crowd who choose this bare-bones hotel right on the beach. The bar and restaurant overlook the water. All sports can be arranged, but windsurfing (learning, practicing, and perfecting it) is king. ⊠ *Maxwell Main Rd.,* ☎ *246/428–9095,* FAX *246/435–6621. 14 rooms. Restaurant, bar, beach. AE, MC, V. EP.*

**$** 🏨 **Little Bay Hotel.** This small hotel is a find for anyone who wants to go easy on the wallet and yet sleep to the sounds of the sea. Each room has a private balcony, bedroom, small lounge, and kitchenette. Ceiling fans will keep you cool, but there are no TVs in the rooms—you can catch up on the news and watch sports in the small lounge next to the popular restaurant, Southern Accents. ⊠ *St. Lawrence Gap,* ☎ *246/435–7246,* FAX *246/435–8574. 10 rooms. Restaurant, bar, lounge, beach. AE, MC, V. EP.*

**$** 🏨 **Ocean View.** Possibly the best-kept secret in the Caribbean, the 40 ★ rooms and suites of this individualistic hideaway are home to celebrities on their commute to private villas in Mustique. The rooms vary considerably, and their charm depends on whether you appreciate the eclectic furnishings. Although it lacks modern amenities, bear in mind that this is an old colonial building and enjoy it for that. Owner John Chandler places his personal collection of antiques throughout his three-story grande dame nestled against the sea, adds great bouquets of tropical flowers everywhere, and calls it home. In season, the downstairs Club Xanadu presents very good, off-off-Broadway revues. ⊠ *Hastings,* ☎ *246/427–7821,* FAX *246/427–7826. 40 rooms. Restaurant, bar, pool, beach, air-conditioning. AE, MC, V. EP.*

**$** 🏨 **Sichris Hotel.** The Sichris is a real find. More attractive inside than seen from the road, it's a comfortable and convenient self-contained resort. Just minutes from the city, the air-conditioned one-bedroom suites all have kitchenettes and private balconies or patios. It's a walk of two or three minutes to the beach. ⊠ *Worthing,* ☎ *246/435–7930,* FAX *246/435–8232. 24 rooms. Restaurant, bar, pool. AE, DC, MC, V. EP.*

## St. Philip Parish

**$$$** 🏨 **Crane Beach Hotel.** This remote hilltop property on a cliff overlooking ★ the dramatic Atlantic coast remains one of the special places of Barbados. The Crane Beach has suites and one-bedrooms. Rooms are decorated with four-poster beds and antique furniture; rates vary depending on the view. Corner suite 1 is one of the nicest rooms, with its two walls of windows and patio terrace. The Roman-style pool with columns separates the main house from the dining room. To reach the beach, you walk down some 200 steps onto a beautiful stretch of sand thumped by waves that are good for both bodysurfing and swimming. ⊠ *Crane Bay,* ☎ *246/423–6220,* FAX *246/423–5343. 18 rooms. Restaurant, bar, 2 pools, beach, 4 tennis courts. AE, DC, MC, V. EP, MAP.*

$$ 🏨 **Marriott's Sam Lord's Castle.** Set on the Atlantic coast about 14 miles east of Bridgetown, Sam Lord's Castle is not a castle with moat and towers but a sprawling great house surrounded by 72 acres of grounds, gardens, and beach. The seven rooms in the main house have canopied beds; downstairs, the public rooms have furniture by Sheraton, Hepplewhite, and Chippendale—for admiring, not for sitting. Additional guest rooms in surrounding cottages have conventional hotel furnishings. The beach is a mile long, the Wanderer Restaurant offers Continental cuisine, and there are even a few slot machines, as befits a pirate's lair. A special tennis package includes unlimited court time, airport transfers, and a Thursday Shipwreck party. ⊠ *Long Bay,* ☎ *246/423–7350,* FAX *246/423–5918. 234 rooms. 3 restaurants, 3 pools, beach, air-conditioning, 7 tennis courts. AE, D, DC, MC, V. EP, MAP.*

## St. Joseph Parish

$ 🏨 **Atlantis Hotel.** The Atlantis provides a warm, pleasant atmosphere in a pastoral location overlooking a majestically rocky Atlantic coast. The hotel is modest, yet the congeniality and the Bajan food more than make up for that. ⊠ *Bathsheba,* ☎ *246/433–9445. 16 rooms. Dining room, bar, beach. AE. EP.*

### Villas and Condominiums

Villas, private homes, and condos are available for rent south of Bridgetown in the Hastings–Worthing area, along the coast of St. James Parish, and in St. Peter Parish. As an example, two-to-three bedroom condos near the beach start at $800–$1,000 per week in the summer months—double that in winter. Rentals are also available through Barbados realtors. Among the realtors to contact are **Alleyne, Aguilar & Altman** (⊠ Rosebank, St. James, ☎ 246/432–0840), **Bajan Services** (⊠ St. Peter, ☎ 246/422–2618), and **Ronald Stoute & Sons Ltd.** (⊠ St. Philip, ☎ 246/423–6800). The **Barbados Tourism Authority** (☎ 246/427–2623, FAX 246/426–4080) has a listing of apartments and rates. In the United States, contact **At Home Abroad** (☎ 212/421–9165) or Jan Pizzi at **Villa Vacations** (☎ 617/593–8885 or 800/800–5576).

# Dining

The better hotels and restaurants of Barbados have employed chefs trained in New York and Europe to attract and keep their sophisticated clientele. Gourmet dining here usually means fresh seafood, beef, or veal with finely blended sauces.

The native West Indian cuisine offers an entirely different dining experience. The island's West African heritage brought rice, peas, beans, and okra to its table, the staples that make a perfect base for slowly cooked meat and fish dishes. Many side dishes are cooked in oil (the pumpkin fritters can be addictive). And be cautious at first with the West Indian seasonings; like the sun, they are hotter than you think.

Most menus include dolphinfish, kingfish, snapper, and flying fish prepared every way imaginable. Flying fish is a Bajan delicacy—so popular it has become a national symbol. Shellfish abound; so does steak. For breakfast and dessert you'll find mangoes, soursop, papaya (pawpaw), and, in season, "mammy apples," a softball-size, thick-skinned fruit with giant seeds.

**Buljol** is a cold salad of codfish, tomatoes, onions, sweet peppers, and celery, marinated and served raw.

**Callaloo** soup is made from okra, crabmeat, the spinachlike vegetable that gives the dish its name, and seasonings.

**Christophines** and **eddoes** are tasty, potatolike vegetables that are often served with curried shrimp, chicken, or goat.

**Conkies** are a mixture of cornmeal and coconut, pumpkin, raisins, sweet potatoes, and spices served wrapped in a banana leaf.

**Cou-cou** is a mix of cornmeal and okra with a spicy Creole sauce made from tomatoes, onions, and sweet peppers; it is often served with steamed flying fish. A version served by the Brown Sugar restaurant, called "red herring," is smoked herring and breadfruit in Creole sauce.

**Pepper-pot stew,** a hearty mix of oxtail, beef chunks, and "any other meat you may have," simmered overnight, is flavored with *cassareep,* an ancient preservative and seasoning that gives the stew its dark, rich color.

Among the liquid refreshments of Barbados, in addition to the local and omnipresent Banks Beer and Mount Gay rum, there are **falernum,** a liqueur concocted of rum, sugar, lime juice, and almond essence, and **mauby,** a refreshing nonalcoholic beerlike drink made by boiling bitter bark and spices, straining the mixture, and sweetening it.

### What to Wear
Barbados's British heritage and large resident population keep the island's dress code modest. This can mean a tie and jacket for gentlemen and a cocktail dress for ladies in the fanciest restaurants. Other places are less formal, although you'll find jeans, shorts, and beach shirts are frowned upon at dinnertime.

| CATEGORY | COST* |
|---|---|
| $$$ | over $40 |
| $$ | $25–$40 |
| $ | under $25 |

*per person, excluding drinks and 10% service charge*

$$$ ✕ **Bagatelle Great House.** Occupying a converted plantation house in
★ a hilly area, Bagatelle Great House gives diners an impression of colonial life. The terrace allows intimate dining at tables for two, while inside the castlelike walls there are much larger round tables. The superb ambience is somewhat more memorable than the expensive Continental dishes. Upstairs is a gallery of Caribbean art. ⊠ *St. Thomas Parish,* ☎ *246/421–6767. Reservations essential. AE, MC, V.*

$$$ ✕ **Carambola.** Candlelight and a cliffside setting overlooking the
★ Caribbean make this alfresco restaurant in St. James Parish one of the most romantic on the island. It also happens to serve some of the best food in Barbados. The menu is a mix of Thai and Continental dishes, all prepared with a Caribbean touch. Start with a spicy, Caribbean-style crab tart, served with hollandaise sauce on a bed of sweet pepper coulis. For an entrée try fillet of kingfish broiled with ginger, coriander, and spring onions, or sliced duck breast with a wild mushroom fumet served with stuffed tomatoes and *gratin dauphinoise* (potatoes au gratin). When you think you can't eat another bite, the *citron gâteau* (lime mousse on a bed of lemon coulis) makes a wonderfully light finish. ⊠ *Derricks, St. James Parish,* ☎ *246/432–0832. Reservations essential. AE, MC, V. Closed Sun. No lunch.*

**$$$** ✕ **La Cage aux Folles.** The restored Summerland Great House and its 2 acres of tropical gardens are the setting for one of the island's most acclaimed restaurants. The exotic five-course menu of international cuisine includes fresh fish with orange and Cointreau, sweet-and-sour shrimp, Malaysian satay, and sesame prawn pâté. ✉ *Prospect, St. James Parish,* ☎ *246/424–2424. Reservations essential. Jacket and tie. AE, D, DC, MC, V. Closed Tues. No lunch.*

**$$$** ✕ **Palm Terrace.** The Palm's young British chef, who came here from London's Le Gavroche, applies his talents to combine Barbadian produce with top-quality imports. The result is modern European creations, such as mille-feuille of home-smoked chicken with tomato, chives, and carrots in a light mustard cream sauce. Fresh mint accents New Zealand rack of lamb, and panfried crab becomes a stuffing for the breast of chicken entrée. Widely spaced tables, comfortable chairs, and indoor palms swaying under floor-to-ceiling arches create an ambience that is formal yet relaxed, as you dine facing the Caribbean Sea. ✉ *Royal Pavilion, Porters, St. James Parish,* ☎ *246/422–4444. AE, D, DC, MC, V. No lunch.*

**$$$** ✕ **Sandy Bay Restaurant.** The renowned Sandy Lane Hotel is the per-
★ fect place for an elegant meal overlooking one of the best beaches on the island. Munich-born chef Hans Schweitzer, formerly of the Midsummer House in Cambridge, England, has modernized the cuisine by introducing "art culinair" to this historic resort. His new dishes are mostly light fare, elegantly dressed with silky sauces, and accented with fresh vegetables. Grilled dolphinfish; lobster and shrimp tempura; and lamb with honey, thyme, and wild rosemary are among the entrées. To ensure that the best produce is used, a van is sent out every morning to scour the island for the freshest vegetables and fish. Desserts are French, creamy, and delicious. Be sure to dress for the occasion. ✉ *Sandy Lane Hotel and Golf Club, St. James Parish,* ☎ *246/432–1311. AE, MC, V.*

**$$** ✕ **Brown Sugar.** A special-occasion atmosphere prevails at Brown Sugar, set in a restored West Indian wooden house across the road from the Grand Barbados Beach Resort outside Bridgetown. Dozens of ferns and hanging plants decorate the breezy multilevel restaurant. An extensive and authentic West Indian lunch buffet (noon to 2:30)—everything from cou-cou to pepper-pot stew—is popular with local businessmen. The dinner menu adds entrées such as char-broiled ginger beef, Creole orange chicken and homemade desserts, including angel food chocolate mousse cake, passion fruit or nutmeg ice cream, and lime cheesecake with guava sauce. ✉ *Aquatic Gap, Bay St., St. Michael Parish,* ☎ *246/426–7684. AE, DC, MC, V. No lunch Sat.*

**$$** ✕ **Fathoms.** The newest property of veteran restaurateurs Stephen and Sandra Toppin is open seven days a week for lunch and dinner, with 22 well-dressed tables scattered from the inside dining rooms to the patio's ocean edge. Dinner may bring a grilled lobster, local rabbit, jumbo baked shrimp, or cashew-crusted kingfish. Fathoms is casual by day, candlelit by night. ✉ *Payne's Bay, St. James Parish,* ☎ *246/432– 2568. AE, MC, V.*

**$$** ✕ **Ile de France.** French owners Martine (from Lyon) and Michel
★ (from Toulouse) Gramaglia have adapted the pool and garden areas of the Windsor Arms Hotel and turned them into an island "in" spot. White latticework opens to the night sounds, soft taped French music plays, and a single, perfect hibiscus dresses each table. Specialties include foie gras, tournedos Rossini (with foie gras and truffles in Madeira), lobster-and-crepe flambé, and filet mignon with a choice of pepper, béarnaise, or champignon sauce. If you yearn for classic French cuisine while in Barbados, this is the place to be. ✉ *Windsor Arms Hotel,*

*Hastings, Christ Church Parish, ☎ 246/435–6869. Reservations essential. No credit cards. Closed Mon. No lunch.*

**$$**  **✕ Josef's.** Swede Nils Ryman successfully created a menu from the un-
**★**  usual combination of Caribbean and Scandinavian fare. Blackened fish,
rolled in Cajun spices and seared in oil, and toast Skagen, made from
diced shrimp blended with mayonnaise and fresh dill, are menu favorites.
Stroll around the garden before moving to the alfresco dining room
downstairs or to the simply decorated room upstairs for a table that
looks out over the sea. ⊠ *Waverly House, St. Lawrence Gap, Christ
Church Parish, ☎ 246/435–6541. AE, DC, MC, V.*

**$$**  **✕ La Maison.** The elegant atmosphere in the colonial-style Balmore
**★**  House is created by English country furnishings and a paneled bar open-
ing onto a seaside terrace for dining. The award-winning gourmet cuisine is nothing less than terrific. A French chef from the Loire Valley
creates seafood specials, including a flying-fish parfait appetizer. Passion-fruit ice cream is a dessert special. ⊠ *Holetown, St. James Parish,
☎ 246/432–1156. AE, DC, MC, V. Closed Mon.*

**$$**  **✕ Ocean View Hotel.** Among Barbados's oldest restaurants, the din-
ing room of this elegant pink grande dame hotel is dressed in fresh fab-
rics, with great bunches of equally fresh flowers and sparkling crystal
chandeliers. Bajan dishes are served for lunch and dinner, and the Sun-
day-only Planter's Luncheon Buffet offers course after course of tra-
ditional dishes—callaloo, cou-cou, flying fish, and more. There's a cabaret
and dancing on weekend evenings. ⊠ *Hastings, Christ Church Parish,
☎ 246/427–7821. AE, MC, V.*

**$$**  **✕ Pisces.** Fish is the way to go at this excellent waterfront restaurant
**★**  in lively St. Lawrence Gap. Flying fish, dolphinfish, crab, kingfish, shrimp,
prawns, and lobster are prepared any way from charbroiled to sautéed.
There are also some chicken and beef dishes. Other items include
conch fritters, tropical gazpacho, and seafood terrine with a mango
sauce. The homemade rum raisin ice cream is a top choice for dessert.
Enjoy your meal in a contemporary setting filled with hanging tropical plants and twinkling white lights. ⊠ *St. Lawrence Gap, Christ Church
Parish, ☎ 246/435–6564. AE, MC, V. No lunch.*

**$$**  **✕ Plantation.** The Bajan buffet and entertainment on Wednesday, Fri-
day, and Saturday are big attractions here. The Plantation is in a ren-
ovated Barbadian residence surrounded by spacious grounds above the
Southwinds Resort. French and Barbadian cuisine is served either in-
doors or on the terrace. ⊠ *St. Lawrence Gap, Christ Church Parish,
☎ 246/428–5048. AE, MC, V. No lunch.*

**$$**  **✕ Rose and Crown.** A variety of fresh seafood is served in this casual
eatery, but it's the local lobster that's high on diners' lists. Indoors is a
paneled bar; outdoors are tables on a wraparound porch. ⊠ *Prospect,
St. James Parish, ☎ 246/425–1074. AE, MC, V. Closed Sat. No lunch.*

**$$**  **✕ Witch Doctor.** The interior of the Witch Doctor is decorated with
pseudo-African art that gives a lighthearted, carefree atmosphere to
this casual hangout across the street from the sea. The sensible menu
includes traditional Barbadian dishes, such as steamed flying fish with
rice and vegetables, as well as American fare and seafood. Prices are
reasonable. ⊠ *St. Lawrence Gap, Christ Church Parish, ☎ 246/435–
6581. MC, V. No lunch.*

**$**  **✕ Atlantis Hotel.** Although the surroundings may be simple, the seem-
ingly endless buffet and the magnificent ocean view make this restau-
rant a real find. Under the direction of owner-chef Enid Maxwell, the
staff serves up an enormous Bajan buffet daily, where you're likely to
find pickled souse (marinated pig parts and vegetables), pumpkin
fritters, spinach balls, pickled breadfruit, fried "fline" (flying) fish, roast
chicken, pepper-pot stew, and West Indian–style okra and eggplant.
After that, move on to one of the homemade pies—apple and a dense

coconut among them. ⊠ *Bathsheba, St. Joseph Parish,* ☎ *246/433–9445. AE.*

$ ✕ **Bonito Beach Bar & Restaurant.** When you tour the rugged East Coast, plan to arrive in Bathsheba at lunchtime and stop at Mrs. Enid Worrell's Bonito Bar for a wholesome West Indian meal. The view of the Atlantic coast from the second-floor dining room of this rather plain restaurant is magnificent. Lunch might be a choice of fried fish, baked chicken, or beef stew, accompanied by vegetables and salads fresh from the family garden. If your timing is right, Mrs. Worrell may have homemade cheesecake for dessert. Be sure to try the fresh fruit punch—with or without rum. The Bajan luncheon buffet, on Sunday from 1 to 3, is popular with residents and visitors alike. ⊠ *Coast Rd., Bathsheba, St. Joseph Parish,* ☎ *246/433–9034. No credit cards.*

$ ✕ **David's Place.** Come here for first-rate food in a first-rate location—a black-and-white Bajan cottage overlooking St. Lawrence Bay. Waves slap against the pilings of the open-air deck, providing a rythmic accompaniment to your meal. Baxters Road chicken, local flying fish, pepper-pot stew, curried shrimp, and other entrées are served with homemade cheese bread. Dessert might be banana pudding, coconut-cream pie, carrot cake with rum sauce, or a homemade cake-like dessert called cassava pone. ⊠ *St. Lawrence Main Rd., Worthing, Christ Church Parish,* ☎ *246/435–6550. AE, MC, V. No lunch Sat.–Mon.*

$ ✕ **Waterfront Cafe.** On the Careenage, a sliver of sea in Bridgetown, this is the perfect place to enjoy a drink, snack, or meal. Locals and tourists gather at outdoor café tables for sandwiches, salads, fish, casseroles, and steak-and-kidney pie. The panfried flying-fish sandwich is especially tasty. In the evening, from the brick and mirrored interior, you can gaze through the arched windows, enjoy the cool trade winds, and let time pass. ⊠ *Bridgetown, St. Michael Parish,* ☎ *246/427–0093. MC, V. Live music nightly. Closed Sun.*

# Beaches

**Barbados beaches** are all open to the public. Although nonguests may not always have immediate access to hotel beaches, you can walk onto almost any beach from an adjacent one. Beaches on the West Coast and much of the South Coast have gentle Caribbean surf and are dotted with tall palms and shaded by leafy mahogany trees. On East Coast beaches, the Atlantic Ocean surf can be rough with a strong undertow, so swimming and surfing is risky there.

## West Coast Beaches

The West Coast has the stunning coves and white-sand beaches that are dear to postcard publishers—plus calm, clear water for snorkeling, scuba diving, and swimming. **West Coast beaches** continue almost unbroken from Almond Beach Village in the north down to Bridgetown. Elegant private homes and luxury hotels take up most of the beachfront property in this area, which is why this stretch of sand is called Barbados's Gold Coast.

Although West Coast beaches are seldom crowded, they are not the place to find isolation. Owners of private boats stroll by, offering waterskiing, parasailing, and snorkel cruises. There are no concession stands, but hotels welcome nonguests for terrace lunches (wear a cover-up). Picnic items and necessities can be bought at the Sunset Crest shopping center in Holetown. The afternoon clouds and sunsets are breathtaking from any of the West Coast beaches.

Just north of Bridgetown, **Brighton Beach** is popular with locals.

**Mullins Beach,** south of Speightstown at Mullins Bay, is a good place for a swim. There's easy parking on the main road; and when you want a break from the sun, Mullins Beach Bar has snacks and drinks.

**Paynes Bay,** south of Holetown, is the site of a number of luxury hotels. It's a very pretty area with plenty of beach to go around.

## South Coast Beaches

**South Coast beaches** are much busier than those on the West Coast and generally draw a younger, more active crowd. The quality of the beach itself is consistently good; the reef-protected waters are safe for swimming and snorkeling.

The cove at **Bottom Bay,** north of Sam Lord's Castle, is lovely. Follow the steps down the cliff to a strip of white sand lined by coconut palms and faced by an inviting aquamarine sea. There's even a cave to explore. It's out of the way and not near restaurants, so bring a picnic lunch.

**Casuarina Beach,** at the Casuarina Beach Club in the St. Lawrence Gap area, is a beach with lots of breeze and a fair amount of surf.

Where the South Coast meets the Atlantic side of the island, the waves roll in bigger and faster. **Crane Beach** has for years been a popular swimming beach, and the waves are a favorite with bodysurfers. Remember, though, that this is the rougher ocean, not the Caribbean, and exercise caution.

**Foul Bay** is ruggedly attractive and lives up to its name only for sailboats; for swimmers and alfresco lunches, it's perfect.

**Greaves End Beach,** south of Bridgetown at Aquatic Gap, between the Grand Barbados Beach Resort and the Barbados Hilton in St. Michael Parish, is a good spot for swimming.

**Needham's Point,** with its lighthouse, is one of Barbados's best beaches, crowded with locals on weekends and holidays.

In Worthing, next to the Sandy Beach Hotel, **Sandy Beach** has shallow, calm waters and a picturesque lagoon. It's an ideal location for families, with beach activities on weekends. There are plenty of places nearby to buy food or drink.

**Silver Sands Beach** is close to the southern most point of the island. It's a beautiful expanse of white sand beach, with a stiff breeze that appeals to windsurfers.

## East Coast Beaches

With secluded beaches and crashing ocean waves on one side, rocky cliffs and verdant landscape on the other, the windward side of Barbados won't disappoint anyone who seeks dramatic views. But be cautioned: Swimming at East Coast Beaches is treacherous and *not* recommended. The waves are high, the bottom tends to be rocky, and the currents are unpredictable. Limit yourself to enjoying the view and watching the surfers—who have been at it since they were kids.

Miles of beach follow the wild coast at **Bathsheba and Cattlewash,** where the pounding surf of the Atlantic is mesmerizing. This is an area where native Barbadians spend holidays; some have second homes here. Swimming in these waters, however, can be extremely dangerous even for strong swimmers. Bring a picnic or have lunch at the Bonito Beach Bar.

A worthwhile, little-visited beach for those who don't mind trekking about a mile off the beaten path, **Morgan Lewis Beach** is on the coast—east of Morgan Lewis Mill, the oldest intact windmill on the island.

Turn east on the small road that goes to the town of Boscobelle (between Cherry Tree Hill and Morgan Lewis Mill), but instead of going to the town, take the even less-traveled road (unmarked on most maps; you will have to ask for directions) that goes down the cliff to the beach. What awaits is more than 2 miles of unspoiled, uninhabited white sand and sweeping views of the Atlantic coastline. You may see a few Barbadians swimming, sunning, or fishing, but for the most part you'll have privacy.

# Outdoor Activities and Sports

## Fishing
**Blue Jay Charters** (☎ 246/422–2098) has a 45-foot, fully equipped fishing boat, with a crew that knows the waters where blue marlin, sailfish, barracuda, and kingfish play.

## Golfing
Barbadians love golf, and golfers love Barbados. All **golf courses** are open to nonguests. Greens fees range from $12.50 for 9 holes at Belair to $145 for 18 holes at Royal Westmoreland Golf Club.

**Almond Beach Village** (☎ 246/422–4900), on the northwest corner of the island, has a nine-hole course. The **Belair Par-3** (☎ 246/423–4653) course is on the rugged East Coast, near Sam Lord's Castle. **Club Rockley Barbados** (☎ 246/435–7873), on the South Coast, has a challenging nine-hole course. The $400 million **Royal Westmoreland Golf Club** (☎ 246/422–4653), with a challenging Robert Trent Jones Jr. 18-hole course. The course meanders through the 480-acre Westmoreland Sugar Estate and overlooks the scenic West Coast. Nine additional holes are underway. Future construction is planned to add private villas and restaurants. The prestigious **Sandy Lane Club** (☎ 246/432–1145) has a challenging 18-hole championship course. The dramatic 7th hole is famous for both its elevated tee and its incredible view.

## Hiking
Hilly but not mountainous, the interior of Barbados is ideal for hiking. The **Barbados National Trust** (✉ No. 2, 10th Ave., Belleville, St. Michael, ☎ 246/426–9033) sponsors free 5-mile walks year-round on Sunday, from 6:30 AM to about 9:30 AM and from 3:30 PM to 5:30 PM, as well as special moonlight hikes when the heavens permit. Newspapers announce the time and meeting place (or you can call the Trust).

## Horseback Riding
The **Caribbean International Riding Center** (✉ St. Joseph, ☎ 246/433–1246) offers one-hour to half-day rides that range in price from $27.50 to $187.50, which includes transportation to and from your hotel. On the West Coast, **Brighton Stables** (☎ 246/425–9381) offers one-hour rides along beaches and palm groves for $27.50, including transportation.

## Parasailing
Parasailing is available, wind conditions permitting, on the beaches of St. James and Christ Church. **Skyranger Parasail** (☎ 246/432–2323) operates at the Casuarina Hotel, in Christ Church, and at Holetown, in St. James. Just flag down the speedboat, though the operator may find you first. Rates are $30–$45 per flight.

## Sailing Excursions
For around $55, Lunchtime and cocktail hour catamaran cruises are available on *Tiami* or *Spirit of Barbados* (☎ 246/425–5800) and on *Irish Mist* (☎ 246/436–9201).

The West Coast is the area for lunch-and-rum cruises on the red-sailed *Jolly Roger* "pirate" party ship (Fun Cruises, ☎ 246/436–6424; $52).

## Scuba Diving

Certified divers can explore several **dive sites**—reefs, wrecks, and the walls of "blue holes," the huge circular depressions in the ocean floor. Underwater visibility is generally 80–90 feet. Not to be missed is the *Stavronikita*, a 368-foot Greek freighter that was deliberately sunk at about 125 feet; hundreds of butterfly fish hang out around its mast, and the thin rays of sunlight that filter down through the water make exploring the huge ship a wonderfully eerie experience. A one-tank dive runs about $40–$45; two-tank, $50–$55.

Many dive shops provide **instruction** in scuba diving—a three-hour beginner's "resort" course (about $75) or a weeklong certification course (about $350), followed by a shallow dive—usually on Dottin's Reef.

Barbados has a **decompression chamber,** based at the Barbados Defence Force Dive Accident Unit (✉ St. Ann's Fort, St. Michael, ☎ 246/436–6185), available to divers on a 24-hour basis.

**Dive Boat Safari** (✉ Barbados Hilton, St. Michael, ☎ 246/427–4350) offers full diving and instruction services.

The **Dive Shop, Ltd.** (✉ Aquatic Gap, near Grand Barbados Beach Resort, St. Michael, ☎ 246/426–9947) has one- or two-tank dive trips or you can purchase a six-dive package.

**Exploresub Barbados** (✉ St. Lawrence Gap, Christ Church, ☎ 246/435–6542) is a PADI five-star training facility that offers a full range of daily dives.

Through **Willie's Watersports** (✉ Colony Club, St. James, ☎ 246/422–2335; ✉ Sunset Crest, St. James, ☎ 246/432–7090), experienced divers can participate in deep dives to old wrecks to look for bottles and other artifacts (and you can usually keep what you find).

## Snorkeling

Gear for **snorkeling** can be rented for a small charge from nearly every hotel. Snorkelers can usually accompany dive trips for about $20 for a two-hour trip (☞ Scuba Diving, *above,* for operators).

## Squash

Squash courts can be reserved at the **Club Rockley Barbados** (✉ Rockley, Christ Church, ☎ 246/435–7880) for $10 per hour.

At the **Barbados Squash Club** (✉ Marine House, Christ Church, ☎ 246/427–7913), squash courts can be reserved at the rate of $9 for 45 minutes.

## Submarining

Minisubmarine voyages are enormously popular with families and those who enjoy watching fish without getting wet.

The great-for-kids, 28-passenger *Atlantis* turns the Caribbean into a giant aquarium. The 45-minute trip aboard the Canadian-built, 50-foot submarine takes you to wrecks and reefs as deep as 150 feet below the surface for a look at what even sport divers rarely see. The nighttime dives, using high-power searchlights, are spectacular. Classical music plays while an oceanography specialist informs during both day or night dives, either of which last about 90 minutes. ☎ 246/436–8929 or 246/436–8932. Cost: $70.

Children will love the *Atlantis SEATREC* (Sea Tracking and Reef Exploration Craft), which allows passengers to "snorkel without getting wet! On the 46-passenger *SEATREC* you sit 6 feet underwater to view near-shore reefs off the coast. The craft has large viewing windows or you can stay on deck. ☎ *246/436–8929 or 246/436–8932. Cost: $29.50.*

## Surfing

The best **surfing** is available on the East Coast, and most wave riders congregate at the Soup Bowl, near Bathsheba. An annual international surfing competition is held on Barbados every October.

## Tennis

Most hotels have tennis courts that can be reserved day and night. Be sure to pack your whites, as appropriate dress is expected on the court. Public courts are available at **Folkestone Park,** in Holetown.

## Waterskiing

Waterskiing is offered through **Blue Reef Watersports** at the Royal Pavilion Hotel, St. James (☎ 246/422–4444). **Willie's Watersports** offers waterskiing in St. James through its facilities at the Colony Club (☎ 246/422–2335) and at Sunset Crest (☎ 246/432–7090). **Private speedboat owners** troll along the waterfront in St. James and Christ Church, but you water-ski at your own risk.

## Windsurfing

The best place to windsurf is at **Silver Sands and Silver Rock Beach,** on the southeast coast of the island, where local and international windsurfing competitions are held. Barbados ranks as one of the best locations in the world for windsurfing—part of the World Cup Windsurfing Circuit.

Windsurfing boards and equipment are often guest amenities at the larger hotels and can be rented by nonguests. The **Benston Windsurfing Club Hotel** (✉ Maxwell Main Rd., Christ Church, ☎ 246/428–9095) caters specifically to windsurfing aficionados.

## Spectator Sports

### CRICKET

The island is mad for cricket, and you can sample a match at almost any time of year. Although the season is June through late December, test matches are usually played from January through April. The newspapers give the details of time and place. Tickets to **cricket matches at Kensington Oval** range from $2.50 to $15.

### HORSE RACING

Horse racing takes place on alternate Saturdays, from January to April and August to November, at the **Garrison Savannah** in Christ Church, about 3 miles south of Bridgetown. Appropriate dress might be described as "casual elegance." ✉ *Christ Church,* ☎ *246/426–3980.* 🎟 *$5.* ☉ *1:30 on race days.*

### POLO

Polo, the sport of kings, is played seriously in Barbados. Matches are held at the **Polo Club** in Trents, St. James, on Wednesday and Saturday from September to March. Hang around the club room after the match. That's where the lies, the legends, and the invitations happen. Cost: About $2.50.

### RUGBY

The rough-and-tumble game of rugby is played at the Garrison Savannah; schedules are available from the **Barbados Rugby Club.** Contact Victor Roach (☎ 246/435–6543).

SOCCER

The "football," or soccer, season runs from January through June at National Stadium. For game schedules write to the **Barbados Football Association,** Box 1362, Bridgetown, Barbados.

# Shopping

Traditionally, **Broad Street** and its side streets in Bridgetown have been the center for shopping action. Hours are generally weekdays 9–5 and Saturday 8–1. The **Quayside Shopping Center** (⊠ Rockley in Christ Church, ☎ 246/428–2474) is small and has a group of exclusive shops, such as Coconut Junction and Lazy Days, which has top-quality beachwear, beach accessories, and beach equipment—including surf and boogie boards. The mall-like **Sheraton Centre** (⊠ Sargeant's Village in Christ Church, ☎ 246/435–8115) has toys for tots, togs for teens, and temptations for all.

### Antiques

Barbadian and British antiques and fine memorabilia are the stock of **Greenwich House Antiques** (⊠ Greenwich Village, Trents Hill, St. James Parish, ☎ 246/432–1169). It's a whole plantation house full of antique Barbadian mahogany furniture, crystal, silver, china, and pictures and is open daily from 10:30 AM to 6 PM.

**Antiquaria** (⊠ Spring Garden Hwy., St. Michael's Row, next to the Anglican cathedral, Bridgetown, ☎ 246/426–0635), a pink Victorian house, sells antique silver, brass ware, mahogany furniture, and maps and engravings of Barbados. It's open every day but Sunday.

### Boutiques

Hidden in separate corners of Barbados are some very upscale, little-known shops that would be able to hold their own in New York or London. Carol Cadogan's **Cotton Days Designs** at Ramsgate Cottage (⊠ Lower Bay St., ☎ 246/427–7191) and on the Wharf in Bridgetown sets the international pace with all-cotton collage creations that have been declared "wearable art." These are fantasy designs, with prices that begin at $250. Fortunately, she takes credit cards.

Another shop worth a visit on the Wharf is **Origins—Colours of the Caribbean** (☎ 246/436–8522), where original hand-painted and batik clothing, imported cottons, linens and silks for day and evening, and handmade jewelry and accessories are the order of the day. The hand-painted T-shirt dresses, priced at about $100, are fabulous.

At **Sunny Shoes Inc.** (⊠ Cave Shepherd's Broad St. store, ☎ 246/431–2121) concessionaire DeCoursey Clarke will make a pair of women's strap sandals while you wait—in any color(s) you wish—for about $26.

### Duty-Free Luxury Goods

Bridgetown's **Broad Street stores** offer values on luxury goods, such as fine bone china, crystal, cameras, stereo and video equipment, jewelry, perfume, and clothing. In order to purchase items duty-free, visitors must produce ongoing travel tickets or a passport.

**Cave Shepherd,** the island's largest department store, offer a wide selection of tax-free luxury goods at many locations, including Broad Street, the airport, and the Cruise Ship Terminal.

**DaCosta's Mall,** on Broad St., has several fine stores. Among them are Louis Bayley, which sells Waterford crystal and Wedgwood china at duty-free prices.

**De Lima's** is the centerpiece of its own small mall and stocks high-quality imports. Among the specialty stores here are several jewelry stores and a few crafts stores.

**Harrison's** is a department store with 14 locations on the island, including a large store on Broad Street.

## Handicrafts

Island handicrafts are everywhere: woven mats and place mats, dresses, dolls, handbags, shell jewelry.

**Best 'n the Bunch** (⊠ St. Lawrence Gap, ☎ 246/428–2474) is a wildly colored chattel house at the Chattel House Village and its own best advertisement. Here the expert jewelry of Bajan David Trottman is sold at reasonable prices.

The **Best of Barbados** shops (⊠ Mall 34, Broad St., Bridgetown, ☎ 246/436–1416, and 6 other locations) offer the highest-quality artwork and crafts, both "native style" and modern designs. A resident artist, Jill Walker, sells her watercolors and prints here.

**Coffee & Cream Gallery** (⊠ Paradise Village, St. Lawrence Gap, ☎ 246/428–2708) displays and sells local artwork of all types.

The **Pelican Village Handicrafts Center,** on the Princess Alice Highway near Bridgetown Harbour (☎ 246/426–4391), offers bargains from local craftsmen. In a cluster of open-air, conical shops, you can watch goods and crafts being made before you purchase them. Locally made handbags and leather goods, coconut shell accessories, mahogany items, grass rugs and mats made from pandanus, and khuskhus are good buys.

For native Caribbean arts and crafts, including items from Barbados and elsewhere in the region, visit the **Verandah Art Gallery** (⊠ Broad St., Bridgetown, ☎ 246/426–2605).

# Nightlife and the Arts

## The Arts

**Barbados Art Council.** The gallery shows drawings, paintings, and other art, with a new show about every two weeks. ⊠ *2 Pelican Village, Harbour Rd., Bridgetown,* ☎ *246/426–4385.* ✆ *Free.* ☉ *Weekdays 10–5, Sat. 9–1.*

A selection of private art galleries offer Bajan and West Indian art at collectible prices. The **Studio Art Gallery** (⊠ Fairchild St., Bridgetown, ☎ 246/427–5463) exhibits local work (particularly that of Rachael Altman) and will frame purchases. The **Natural Cultural Foundation Gallery** (⊠ Queen's Park, Bridgetown, ☎ 246/427–2345), the island's largest gallery, is run by the National Culture Foundation and presents changing, month-long exhibits.

## Nightlife

When the sun goes down, the musicians come out, and folks go limin' in Barbados (anything from hanging out to a chat-up or jump-up). Competitions among reggae groups, steel bands, and calypso singers are major events, and tickets can be hard to come by—but give it a try.

Most of the large resorts have weekend shows for visitors, and there is a selection of dinner shows. The dinner show at the **Sherbourne Centre,** Barbados's new convention center, is called "1627 and All That." It has a 17th-century Barbados theme and is performed by the energetic dancers of the Barbados Dance Theater. ⊠ *Two Mile Hill, east* *of Bridgetown, St. Michael,* ☎ *246/431–7600. Cost: $50 for dinner, show, and open bar; $25 show only.*

Island residents have their own favorite nightspots. The most popular one is still **After Dark** (⊠ St. Lawrence Gap, Christ Church, ☎ 246/435–6547), with the longest bar on the island, a jazz-club annex, and an outdoor area where headliners appear live.

On Wednesdays, Thursdays, and Friday evenings at Plantation Restaurant and Garden Theater, the **Barbados Tropical Spectacular** calypso cabaret show features dancing, fire-eating, limbo, steel-band music, and the award-winning sounds of Spice & Company. The cost for dinner and the show is $50. ⊠ *St. Lawrence Rd., Christ Church Parish,* ☎ *246/428–5048. AE, DC, MC, V.*

A late-night (after 11) excursion to **Baxter Road,** "the street that never sleeps," is de rigueur for midnight Bajan street snacks, local rum, great gossip, and good storytelling. Enid & Livy's and Collins are just two of the long-standing favorite haunts.

**Club Xanadu** is a mid-December through April cabaret. On Thursday and Friday nights, it's the hottest ticket in town. David McCarty, who danced on Broadway and with the New York City Ballet, has joined forces with chanteuse Jean Emerson; along with local strutters, they put on a great show. Dinner—served in the upstairs flower-decked dining room—and show cost $44; cabaret admission only, approximately $12.50. ⊠ *Ocean View Hotel, Hastings,* ☎ *246/427–7821. Reservations essential.*

Stop in for an evening of jazz at **Cobbler's Cove** (⊠ Hwy. 1, St. Peter, ☎ 246/422–2291).

Another "in" spot, **Front Line** (⊠ Wharf St., ☎ 246/429–6160) at the Wharf in Bridgetown, attracts a young crowd for its reggae music.

**Harbour Lights** claims to be the "home of the party animal," and most any night features live reggae and soca music with dancing under the stars. ⊠ *Marine Villa, Bay St., Bridgetown, St. Michael,* ☎ *246/436–7225.*

For a more refined evening, enjoy dancing to a steel band or a string quartet at Sandy Lane Hotel's **Starlight Terrace** (⊠ Hwy. 1, St. Peter, ☎ 246/432–1311).

BARS AND INNS

Barbados supports the rum industry in more than 1,600 "rum shops," simple bars where people (mostly men) congregate to discuss the world's ills, and in more sophisticated inns, where you'll find world-class rum drinks made with the island's renowned Mount Gay and Cockspur rums. The following cocktail bars offer welcoming spirits: **Ship Inn,** a friendly pub (⊠ St. Lawrence Gap, Christ Church Parish, ☎ 246/435–6961), **Coach House** (⊠ Paynes Bay, St. James Parish, ☎ 246/432–1163), and **Harry's Oasis** (⊠ St. Lawrence, Christ Church Parish, no phone). **Bert's Bar** at the Abbeville Hotel (⊠ Rockley, Christ Church Parish, ☎ 246/435–7924) serves the best daiquiris in town . . . any town. Also try the **Boat Yard** (⊠ Bay St., Bridgetown, ☎ 246/436–2622), **Waterfront Cafe** (⊠ Bridgetown, ☎ 246/427–0093), and **Boomers Restaurant & Lounge** (⊠ St. Lawrence Gap, Christ Church Parish, ☎ 246/428–8439).

# Exploring Barbados

The island is divided into 11 parishes. The terrain and vegetation changes dramatically as you wander from parish to parish. So does the pace and ambience of each area. Bridgetown is a busy and sophisticated city. Gold Coast resorts and private homes ooze luxury, while the small villages and plantations scattered throughout the rest of Central Barbados mark the island's history. The remote East Coast, with its cliffs and heavy surf, has been designed by the Atlantic Ocean. The North is called Scotland, because that's what it looks like. And along the South Coast, the activity continues day and night.

The Barbados National Trust, headquartered at 10th Avenue, Belleville, St. Michael (☎ 246/426–2421), has designed the **Heritage Passport,** a 50% discounted admission to Barbados's most popular attractions and historic sites. A Full Passport includes 16 sites and costs $35; a Mini-Passport includes five sites and costs $18. Children under 12 are admitted free if accompanied by a Passport holder (maximum two children per passport). Passports may be purchased at hotels, Trust headquarters, or at the sites.

## Bridgetown

❶ **Bridgetown** is a bustling city and a major Caribbean duty-free port. The principal shopping area is Broad Street, which leads west from Trafalgar Square. The city is complete with rush hours and traffic congestion. Sightseeing will take only an hour or so, and the shopping area is compact.

SIGHTS TO SEE

*Numbers in the margin correspond to points of interest on the Bridgetown map.*

❾ **Barbados Museum.** This intriguing museum has artifacts dating from Arawak days (around 400 BC) and mementos of military history and everyday life in the 19th century. Here you'll see cane-harvesting implements, lace wedding dresses, ancient (and frightening) dentistry instruments, and slave sale accounts kept in a spidery copperplate handwriting. Wildlife and natural history exhibits, a well-stocked gift shop, and a good café are also here, in what used to be the military prison. ✉ *Hwy. 7, Garrison Savannah,* ☎ *246/427–0201.* ✆ *BDS$10.* ☉ *Mon.–Sat. 9–5, Sun. 2–6.*

❽ **The Careenage.** The finger of sea that made early Bridgetown a natural harbor and a gathering place is where working schooners were careened (turned on their sides) to be scraped of barnacles and repainted. Today the Careenage serves mainly as a berth for pleasure yachts and charter boats. The two bridges over the Careenage are the Chamberlain Bridge and the Charles O'Neal Bridge.

❺ **Harry Bayley Observatory.** Built in 1963, this is the headquarters of the Barbados Astronomical Society. It's located off Highway 6, in Clapham, and is rather unique in the Caribbean. The observatory is equipped with a 14-inch reflector telescope. ☉ *Fri. 8:30 AM–11:30 PM.* ✆ *$2.50.*

❻ **House of Assembly and Parliament.** The buildings that house the third oldest Parliament of the British Commonwealth are adjacent to Trafalgar Square. A series of stained-glass windows depicting British monarchs from James I to Queen Victoria adorn these Victorian government buildings. Like so many smaller buildings in Bridgetown, they stand beside a growing number of modern office buildings.

❷ **Jewish Synagogue.** This is the oldest synagogue in the Western Hemisphere. It dates back to 1654 and has recently been restored to its original purpose as a house of prayer. ✉ *Synagogue La.,* ☎ *246/ 426–5792.*

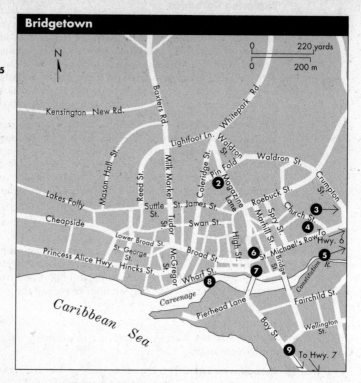

**3 Queen's Park.** Northeast of Bridgetown, Queen's Park is the site of one of the largest trees in Barbados, an immense baobab more than 10 centuries old. The historic Queen's Park House, former home of the commander of the British troops, has been converted into a theater, with an exhibition room on the lower floor and a restaurant. ⊘ Daily 9–5.

**4 St. Michael's Cathedral.** Although no one has proved it conclusively, George Washington, on his only visit outside the United States, is said to have worshiped at St. Michael's Cathedral, east of Trafalgar Square. The structure was nearly a century old when Washington visited in 1751, and it has since been destroyed by hurricanes and rebuilt twice, in 1780 and 1831.

**7 Trafalgar Square.** In the center of town overlooking the picturesque harbor known as the Careenage, its monument to Lord Horatio Nelson predates Nelson's Column in London's Trafalgar Square by 36 years.

## Central Barbados

Holetown and Speightstown, are the island's other major towns (after Bridgetown, the capital). Holetown is the center of the Gold Coast resort area and the place where Captain John Powell landed in 1625 and claimed the island in the name of King James. The port city of Speightstown is more characteristically West Indian with its 19th-century architecture (undergoing restoration) and quaint shops and restaurants. The natural history of Barbados is also represented in the central parishes by fascinating caves, a mile-long gully, and beautiful tropical vegetation.

*Numbers in the margin correspond to points of interest on the Barbados map.*

SIGHTS TO SEE

**18** **Flower Forest.** Enjoy meandering through 8 acres of fragrant flowering bushes, canna and ginger lilies, puffball trees, and more than a hundred other species of flora in a tranquil setting. From this area, you can also have a beautiful view of Mt. Hillaby. ⊠ *Richmond Plantation, St. Joseph,* ☎ *246/433–8152.* ☜ *$6.* ☉ *Daily 9–5.*

**25** **Folkestone Marine Park & Visitor Centre.** There's a land museum of marine life here and an underwater snorkeling trail around Dottin's Reef (glass-bottom boats are available for nonswimmers). A dredge barge sunk in shallow water is the home to myriad fish, and it and the reef are popular with scuba divers. Huge sea fans, soft coral, and the occasional giant turtle are sights to see. ⊠ *Holetown, St. James,* ☎ *246/422–2314.* ☜ *50¢. Closed Mon.*

**10** **Gun Hill Signal Station.** The view from Gun Hill is so pretty it seems almost unreal. Shades of green and gold cover the fields all the way to the horizon, the picturesque gun tower is surrounded by brilliant flowers, and the white limestone lion behind the garrison is a famous landmark. Military invalids were once sent here to convalesce. ⊠ *St. George,* ☎ *246/429–1358.* ☜ *$4.*

**16** **Harrison's Cave.** This series of beautiful, pale-gold, limestone caverns, complete with stalactites, stalagmites, subterranean streams, and a 40-foot waterfall, is considered to be among the finest cave systems in the world. Open since 1981, the caves are so extensive that the one-hour tours are made by electric tram (hard hats are provided, but all that may fall on you is a little dripping water). ⊠ *Hwy. 2, St. Thomas,* ☎ *246/438–6640.* ☜ *$7.50. Reservations advised.* ☉ *Daily 9–6.*

**17** **Welchman Hall Gully.** Part of the National Trust in St. Thomas, here's another chance to commune with nature. Acres of labeled flowers and trees stretch along in a ¾-mile natural gully, with the occasional green monkey showing itself and great peace and quiet. ⊠ *St. Thomas,* ☎ *246/438–6671.* ☜ *$5.* ☉ *Daily 9–5.*

## The East Coast

The Atlantic Ocean crashes dramatically against the Eastern Coast of Barbados where, over eons, the waves have eroded the shoreline into caves, arches, cliffs, and sea rocks that look like giant mushrooms. Narrow roads weave among the ridges, and small villages cling to hillsides that slide into the sea. Local people come to the coastal areas called Bathsheba and Cattlewash to spend weekends and holidays.

SIGHTS TO SEE

**14** **Andromeda Gardens.** A fascinating collection of unusual and beautiful plant specimens from around the world are cultivated in beds set into the cliffs overlooking the sea. The plants were collected by the late horticulturist Iris Bannochie and are now administered by the Barbados National Trust. ⊠ *Bathsheba, St. Joseph,* ☎ *246/433–9384.* ☜ *$5.* ☉ *Daily 9–5.*

**24** **Animal Flower Cave.** Displays of small sea anemones, or sea worms, resemble jewel-like flowers when they open their tiny tentacles. For a small fee you can explore inside the cavern while waves break just outside. ⊠ *North Point, St. Lucy,* ☎ *246/439–8797.* ☜ *$1.50.* ☉ *Daily 9–4.*

**15** **Atlantis.** The view is phenomenal from this Bathsheba lodging, one of the oldest hotels in Barbados—where you may need help getting up from the table after sampling the lunch buffet.

**(19) Barclay's Park.** Just north of Bathsheba, this park was given to the people of Barbados by Barclay's Bank. It offers a gorgeous view of the ocean, plus picnic facilities. At the nearby **Chalky Mount Potteries,** you'll find craftspersons making and selling their wares.

**(23) Pie Corner.** This tiny community in the far northeast of the island is known not for baked goods but for artifacts left by the Carib and Arawak tribes who once lived here.

## Northern Barbados

The northern reaches of the island, St. Peter and St. Lucy parishes, provide a range of terrain. Between the tiny fishing towns along the northwestern coast and the sweeping views out to the Atlantic Ocean on the corresponding coast are areas of forest and farm, moor and mountain. Most guides include this loop on a daylong island tour—it's a beautiful drive.

SIGHTS TO SEE

**(21) Barbados Wildlife Reserve.** The reserve is home to herons, land turtles, a kangaroo, screeching peacocks, innumerable green monkeys, geese, brilliantly colored parrots, and a friendly otter. The fauna are not in cages, so step carefully and keep your hands to yourself. The preserve has been much improved in recent years with the addition of a giant walk-in aviary and natural-history exhibits. Terrific photo opportunities are everywhere. ⊠ *Farley Hill, St. Peter,* ☎ *246/422–8826.* ☑ *$10.* ☉ *Daily 10–5.*

**(20) Farley Hill.** At this national park in northern St. Peter Parish, the imposing ruins of a once-magnificent plantation great house are surrounded by gardens, lawns, an avenue of towering royal palms, and gigantic mahogany, whitewood, and casuarina trees. Partially rebuilt for the filming of *Island in the Sun,* the structure was later destroyed by fire. This part of Barbados is called the Scotland area because of the rugged landscape. ⊠ *St. Peter.* ☑ *$1.50 per car; walkers free.* ☉ *Daily 8:30–6.*

**(22) St. Nicholas Abbey.** This property was named for a former owner, a prominent farmer with no religious connection to St. Nicholas. It is the oldest (circa 1650) great house in Barbados and is well worth visiting for its stone-and-wood architecture—one of only three original houses in the Jacobean style still standing in the Western Hemisphere. It has Dutch gables, finials of coral stone, and an herb garden in a medieval design. Fascinating home movies, made by the present owner's father, record scenes of Bajan town and plantation life in the 1920s and 1930s. ⊠ *Near Cherry Tree Hill, St. Lucy,* ☎ *246/422–8725.* ☑ *$2.50.* ☉ *Weekdays 10–3:30.*

## The South Coast

The heavily traveled south coast of Christ Church Parish is much more built up than the St. James Parish coast in the west. Here you'll find condos, high-rise hotels, beach parks, many places to eat and shop, and the traffic (including public transportation) that serves them.

Many chattel houses, the property of tenant farmers and typically Barbadian in style, are farther out along the south coast. These ever-expandable houses were built to be dismantled and moved when necessary.

SIGHTS TO SEE

**(13) Codrington Theological College.** In the eastern corner of St. John Parish, the coral-stone buildings and serenely beautiful grounds of Codrington Theological College (☎ 246/433–1274) founded in 1745, stand on a cliff overlooking Consett Bay.

⑫ **Ragged Point Lighthouse.** Appropriately named, this is where the sun first shines on Barbados and its dramatic Atlantic seascape.

⑪ **Sam Lord's Castle.** The Regency house built by the buccaneer is considered by many to be the finest mansion in Barbados. Built in 1820 and now part of a resort owned by Marriott (☞ Lodging, *above*), the opulent estate features double verandas on all sides and magnificent plaster ceilings created by Charles Rutter, who crafted the ceilings in England's Windsor Castle. Most of the rooms are furnished with the fine mahogany furniture and gilt mirrors Sam Lord is reputed to have acquired from passing ships that he lured onto treacherous reefs by hanging lanterns in palm trees to simulate harbor lights. ⊠ *Long Bay, St. Philip,* ☎ *246/423–7350,* ⌑ *$3.50, hotel guests free.* ☉ *Daily 10–4.*

# Barbados A to Z

## Arriving and Departing

### BY BOAT

Bridgetown's Deep Water Harbour is on the northwest side of Carlisle Bay. Barbados is a popular cruise port—half of the annual visitors to the island are cruise passengers. Up to eight cruise ships can dock at one time at the snazzy **Cruise Ship Terminal.** Passengers can buy duty-free goods at more than a dozen retail shops in the terminal's attractive shopping arcade; vendors display their handcrafts in colorful reproductions of chattel houses just outside the building. Downtown Bridgetown is a half-mile walk from the pier; a taxi costs about $1.50 each way.

### BY PLANE

**American Airlines** (☎ 800/433–7300) and **BWIA** (☎ 800/538–2942) both have nonstop flights between New York and Grantley Adams Airport in Barbados and direct flights between Miami and Barbados. American serves Barbados from other U.S. cities with connecting flights through San Juan. From Canada, **Air Canada** (☎ 800/776–3000) flies nonstop from Toronto. From London, **British Airways** (☎ 800/247–9297) has nonstop service and BWIA connects through Trinidad.

Flights to St. Vincent, St. Lucia, Martinique, Trinidad, and other islands are scheduled on **LIAT** (☎ 246/495–1187), **Carib Express, Air Martinique,** and BWIA; **Air St. Vincent/Air Mustique** links Barbados with St. Vincent and the Grenadines.

### FROM THE AIRPORT

**Airport taxis** are not metered. A large sign at the airport announces the fixed rate to each hotel or parish, stated in both Barbados and U.S. dollars (about $20 to West Coast hotels, $13 to South Coast ones). A highway bypasses Bridgetown, which saves time getting to the West Coast.

## Currency

One **Barbados dollar** (BDS$1) equals about U.S.50¢. Because the value of the Barbados dollar is pegged to that of the U.S. dollar, the ratio remains constant. Both currencies are accepted everywhere on the island. Prices quoted throughout this chapter are in U.S. dollars unless noted otherwise.

## Emergencies

**Emergency and Police:** ☎ 112. **Ambulance:** ☎ 115. **Fire department:** ☎ 113. **Scuba diving accidents:** Divers' Alert Network (DAN; ☎ 246/684–8111 or 246/684–2948). **24-hour decompression chamber:** Barbados Defence Force, St. Ann's Fort, Garrison, St. Michael Parish, ☎ 246/436–6185.

## Getting Around

### BUSES

Blue buses with a yellow stripe are public, yellow buses with a blue stripe are private, and private maxitaxis may be any color. They all travel constantly along Highway 1 (St. James Road) and are inexpensive (BDS$1.50 for any destination, exact change appreciated), plentiful, reliable, and usually packed. **Buses and maxitaxis** provide a great opportunity to experience local color, and your fellow passengers will be eager to share their knowledge.

### CAR RENTALS

It's a pleasure to explore Barbados by car, provided you take the time to study a map and don't mind asking directions frequently. The more remote roads are in good repair, yet few are well lighted at night—and night falls quickly at about 6 PM. Even in full daylight, the tall sugarcane fields lining a road can make visibility difficult. Use caution: Pedestrians are everywhere. Remember: drive on the left.

To rent a car you must have an international driver's license or **Barbados driving permit,** obtainable at the airport and major car-rental firms for $5 if you have a valid driver's license.

More than 40 offices rent **minimokes** (open-air vehicles) for $35–$60 a day plus insurance (about $215 a week), usually with a three-day or four-day minimum; cars with automatic shift are $65–$70 a day, or approximately $250–$275 a week. Gas costs about $3 a gallon. The speed limit, in keeping with the pace of life, is 37 miles per hour (60 kilometers per hour) in the country, 21 miles per hour (40 kilometers per hour) in town.

Among car-rental firms are **National** (⊠ Bush Hall, St. Michael, ☎ 246/426–0603), **Dear's Garage** (⊠ Christ Church, ☎ 246/429–9277 or 246/427–7853), **Sunny Isle** (⊠ Worthing, ☎ 246/435–7979), **Sunset Crest Rentals** (⊠ St. James, ☎ 246/432–1482), and **P&S Car Rentals** (⊠ St. Michael, ☎ 246/424–2052).

### SCOOTER AND BICYCLE RENTALS

Scooters rent for about $31 a day, with a $100 refundable deposit. Bicycles rent for about $10 a day, or $50 per week, with a $50 refundable deposit.

### TAXIS

**Taxis** operate at a fixed hourly rate of BDS$32. For short trips, the rate per mile (or part thereof) should not exceed BDS$2.50. Settle the rate before you start off, and be sure you agree on whether it's in U.S. or Barbados dollars. Most drivers will cheerfully narrate a tour.

## Guided Tours

Barbados has a lot to see. A half- or full-day bus or taxi tour is a good way to get your bearings and can be arranged by your hotel. The price varies according to the number of attractions included; an average full-day tour (4½ to 6 hours) costs about $50 per person and generally includes lunch and admissions.

**Bajan Helicopters** (⊠ The Wharf, Bridgetown, ☎ 246/431–0069) offers an eagle's-eye view of Barbados. Price per person ranges from $65 for a 20-minute half-island tour to $100 for a 30-minute full-island trip.

Every Wednesday afternoon, from mid-January through mid-April, the **Barbados National Trust** (☎ 246/426–2421 for reservations) offers a bus tour of both historical great houses and modern private homes that are open for public viewing. The cost: $17.50 per person, which includes admissions to the houses and transportation from your hotel.

**Highland Outdoor Tours** (✉ Canefield, St. Thomas Parish, ☎ 246/438–8069) specializes in adventure trips to the island's seldom-seen natural wonders. Visitors have the option of half-day or full-day horseback treks (including a bareback ride in the surf), scenic hiking expeditions, and tractor-drawn jitney rides through some of Barbados's great plantations. Prices range from $25 per person for a short, two-hour plantation tour by open jitney to $100 per person for the 7-mile Horseback Trek. A 5-mile Scenic Safari Hike is $70. All tour include refreshments and transportation to and from your hotel.

**L. E. Williams Tour Co.** (☎ 246/427–1043) offers an 80-mile island tour for about $50. A bus picks you up between 8:30 and 9:30 AM and takes you through Bridgetown, the St. James beach area, past the Animal Flower Cave, Farley Hill, Cherry Tree Hill, Morgan Lewis Mill, the East Coast, St. John's Church, Sam Lord's Castle, Oistin's fishing village, and to St. Michael Parish, with drinks along the way and a West Indian lunch at the Atlantis Hotel in Bathsheba.

Sally Shearn operates **VIP Tours** (✉ Hillcrest Villa, Upton, St. Michael Parish, ☎ 246/429–4617) and personalizes tours to suit your taste. Bajan-born Ms. Shearn knows her island well and provides a swim at her favorite beach. She picks up her clients in an air-conditioned Mercedes-Benz and charges $30 per hour for four people, with a minimum of five hours.

## Language
English is spoken everywhere, often accented with the phrases and lilt of a Bajan dialect.

## Opening and Closing Times
Stores are open weekdays 9–5, Saturday 8–1. Some supermarkets are open daily 8–6 or later. Banks are open Monday to Thursday 8–3, Friday 8–5.

## Passports and Visas
To enter Barbados, U.S. and Canadian citizens need proof of citizenship and a return or ongoing ticket. Acceptable proof of citizenship is a valid passport or an original birth certificate and a photo ID; a voter registration card or baptismal certificate is not acceptable. British citizens need a valid passport.

## Precautions
Take normal precautions: Don't leave valuables unattended on the beach or in plain sight in your room, and don't pick up hitchhikers.

Insects aren't much of a problem on Barbados, but if you plan to hike or spend time on secluded beaches, it's wise to use insect repellent.

The little green apples that fall from the large branches of the manchineel tree may look tempting, but they are poisonous to eat and toxic to the touch. Even taking shelter under the tree when it rains can give you blisters. Most manchineels are identified with signs. If you do come in contact with one, go to the nearest hotel and have someone there phone for a physician.

The water on the island is plentiful and safe to drink in both hotels and restaurants. It is naturally filtered through 1,000 feet of pervious coral.

## Taxes and Service Charges
At the airport you must pay a departure tax of BDS$25 (about U.S.$12.50) in either currency before leaving Barbados; no charge for

children 12 and under. A 5% government tax is added to hotel bills; a 10% service charge is added to hotel bills and to most restaurant checks. Any additional tip recognizes extraordinary service. When no service charge is added, tip maids $1 per room per day, waiters 10% to 15%, taxi drivers 10%. Airport porters and bellboys expect U.S.50¢–$1 per bag.

## Telephones and Mail

The area code for Barbados is 246. Except for emergency numbers (☞ Emergencies, *above*) all phone numbers have seven digits and begin with 42 or 43.

An airmail letter from Barbados to the United States or Canada costs BDS90¢ per half ounce; an airmail postcard costs BDS65¢. Letters to the United Kingdom are BDS$1.10; postcards are BDS70¢.

## Visitor Information

For information before you go, contact the **Barbados Tourism Authority,** ✉ 800 2nd Ave., 2nd floor, New York, NY 10017, ☎ 212/986–6516 or 800/221–9831, FAX 212/573–9850; ✉ 2442 Hinge St., Troy MI 48083, ☎ 810/740–7835, FAX 810/740–9434; ✉ 3440 Wilshire Blvd., Suite 1215, Los Angeles, CA 90010, ☎ 213/380–2198, FAX 213/384–2763. **In Canada:** ✉ 5160 Yonge St., Suite 1800, N. York, Ontario M2N–6L9, ☎ 416/512–6569 or 800/268–9122, FAX 416/512–6581. **In the United Kingdom:** ✉ 263 Tottenham Court Rd., London W1P 0LA, England, ☎ 0171/636–9448, FAX 0171/637–1496.

In Barbados, the **Barbados Tourism Authority** is on Harbour Road in Bridgetown (☎ 246/427–2623, FAX 246/426–4080). Hours are 8:30–4:30 weekdays. Information booths, staffed by Tourism Authority representatives are located at Grantley Adams International Airport ☎ 246/428–0937) and at Bridgetown's Cruise Ship Terminal (☎ 246/4426–1718).

# 6 Bonaire

**I**F ARUBA IS FOR THE HIGHEST ROLLERS, Bonaire is for the deepest divers—not to exclude the snorkelers, of course. Divers come to Bonaire as pilgrims to their holy land. Diving is learned here, photographed, and perfected. Even the license plate says "A Diver's Paradise." The luxuriant reefs that encircle Bonaire have remained miraculously free of exploitation. The government, way back in 1979, when green was just becoming a color to be dealt with, designated all surrounding waters as a marine park and threw in a ban on spearfishing and coral collecting. The underwater park includes, roughly, the entire coastline, from the high-water tidemark to a depth of 200 feet, all protected by strict laws. Because the Bonairians desperately want to keep their paradise intact, any diver with a reckless streak is firmly requested to go elsewhere. Thanks to their foresight, the world can enjoy Bonaire's bounty.

Updated by
Melissa Rivers

Bonaire, on land, is a stark desert island, perfect for the rugged individualist who is turned off by the overcommercialized high life of the other Antillean islands. The island boasts a spectacular array of exotic wildlife—from fish to fowl to flowers—that will keep nature watchers awestruck for days. It's the kind of place where you'll want to rent a Jeep and go dashing off madly in search of the wild flamingo, the wild iguana, or even the wild yellow-winged parrot named the Bonairian lora.

This little (112 square miles) island is not for connoisseurs of gourmet cuisine (though options are improving), shopping maniacs, or lounge lizards. The island itself may be lacking in "resort splendor", but what lies off its shores keeps divers enthralled, and its unhurried pace pleases all in search of uninterrupted relaxation. With only 14,000 inhabitants, the island has the feeling of a small community with a gentle pace. As the locals say, folks simply come here to dive, eat, dive, sleep, and dive.

## Lodging

Hotels on Bonaire, with the exception of Harbour Village, cater primarily to avid divers who spend their days underwater and come up for air only for evening festivities. Hence, hotel facilities tend to be modest with small swimming pools and limited service. Groomed sandy beaches are not a requisite for a hotel, but an efficient dive shop is. Many resort accommodations have fully equipped kitchens. Although the larger hotels offer a variety of meal plans, most are on the European Plan. As a general rule, hotel restaurants can be significantly more expensive than restaurants in town. There are, however, all-inclusive packages available at an extra per-day charge at many properties. Divers can take advantage of very good prices by comparing the packages offered by the hotels. Ask the tourist office for a listing by calling 800/826–6247.

The **Bonaire Government Tourist Office** (☎ 800/826–6247) can help you find suitable guest houses and smaller rental apartments in Bonaire. Rental apartments are also available through **Bonaire Sunset Villas** (☎ 800/223–9815, FAX 599/7–8118), **Sunset Oceanfront Apartments** (☎ 800/223–9815, FAX 599/7–8865), **Club Laman Caribe** (☎ 599/7–6840, FAX 599/7–7741), or **Black Durgon Inn Properties** (☎ 599/7–5736; in the U.S., 800/526–2370; FAX 599/6–8846).

| CATEGORY | COST* |
|----------|-------|
| $$$$ | over $225 |
| $$$ | $150–$225 |
| $$ | $100–$150 |
| $ | under $100 |

*All prices are for a standard double room for two in high season, excluding a $4.50 per-person, per-night, government room tax and 10%–15% service charge.

**$$$$** ★ **🏠 Harbour Village Beach Resort.** This is the resort for divers who want both an upscale resort and a dive vacation. If Armani designs a scuba mask, it will sell here. Wide walkways bordered by lush foliage and blooming tropical flowers separate nine low-rise, southwestern-style buildings, with Moorish arches, red barrel-tile roofs, and a pastel color scheme. The palm tree–lined beach is wide and inviting. Although not as impressive as the grounds or building exteriors, the pleasant rooms and suites are done in dusty rose and aqua and have French doors leading to a terrace or patio (except for second-story courtyard rooms), white tile floors, and natural wood furniture. Each room also has a hair dryer, amenity package including robes, and television hidden in an armoire. Price category is determined by view—garden courtyard, marina, or ocean. There is a full-service dive shop and a water-sports concession that offers sailing, windsurfing, kayaking, and powerboat rentals at the resort's marina. A fitness center offers an air-conditioned state-of-the-art workout. A full service spa offering every body treatment and an array of physical activities was added in 1995 and a casino and Peter Burwash International tennis program in 1996; a nine-hole golf course was poised to open in 1997. There will soon be no reason to go elsewhere. It's so well run that even seekers of the quiet life will be satisfied. There is an organized program of activities for children, and kids under 12 stay free in their parents' room. ✉ Box 312, ☎ 599/7–7500 or 800/424–0004, 📠 599/7–7507. 64 rooms, 8 oceanfront suites, 40 condominium units. 3 restaurants, 2 bars, spa café, in-room safes, refrigerator, room service, pool, outdoor hot tub, sauna, steam room, 4 tennis courts, aerobics, aquacise, health club, horseback riding, beach, marina, water-sports center with dive shop, water taxi to Klein Bonaire, bicycles, shopping arcade, casino, library, baby-sitting, children's program (5–12), laundry service and dry cleaning, concierge, business services. AE, DC, MC, V. EP, MAP, FAP.

**$$$–$$$$** ★ **🏠 Captain Don's Habitat.** Since its expansion and massive renovation, the Habitat, once a sort of extended home of Captain Don Stewart, the island's wildest sharpshooting personality, can no longer pass itself off as a mere guest house for divers. Stewart's Curaçaoan partners have poured money into this resort, adding a set of upscale rooms (junior suites) and then a long row of private villas (the Hamlet section) that rank among the island's best: All are spacious, with ocean-view verandas, full kitchens, and stylish appointments. The updated original 11 cottages have fully stocked kitchens, wicker furnishings, and garden views. The atmosphere at the Habitat is laid-back and easy-going (no rooms have TVs), with the emphasis on 24-hour diving. This is also one of few dive resorts that welcome families; children 12 and under stay free with their parents. The beachfront property units—with glorious views of Klein Bonaire—are spaced widely apart, and the grounds have been landscaped with rocks and cacti. Be sure to meet Captain Don, who shows up once a week to present a slide show, shoot the breeze, and tell his incredible tales, most of which are actually true. A full dive center with seven boats, complete with a resident photo pro, rounds out the picture. ✉ Kaya Gobrenador Debrot 103, Box 88, ☎ 599/7–8290. U.S. representative: Habitat North American, ☎ 800/327–

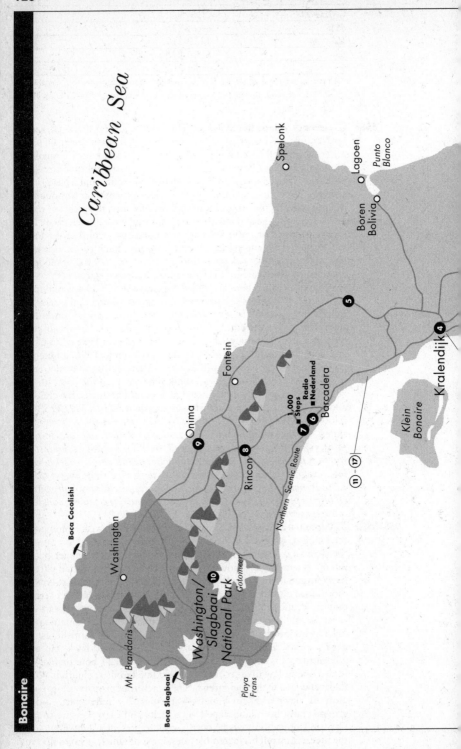

**Bonaire**

*Caribbean Sea*

Spelonk

Lagoen

*Punto Blanco*

Boren Bolivia

Kralendijk ④

*Klein Bonaire*

⑤

Fontein

Onima

⑨

Rincon ⑧

Radio
■ Nederland
1,000
Steps
⑦ ⑥ Barcadera

*Northern Scenic Route*

⑪ — ⑰

Washington

Boca Cocolishi

Washington/
Slagbaai
National Park

⑩

*Gotomeer*

Mt. Brandaris

Boca Slagbaai

*Playa
Frans*

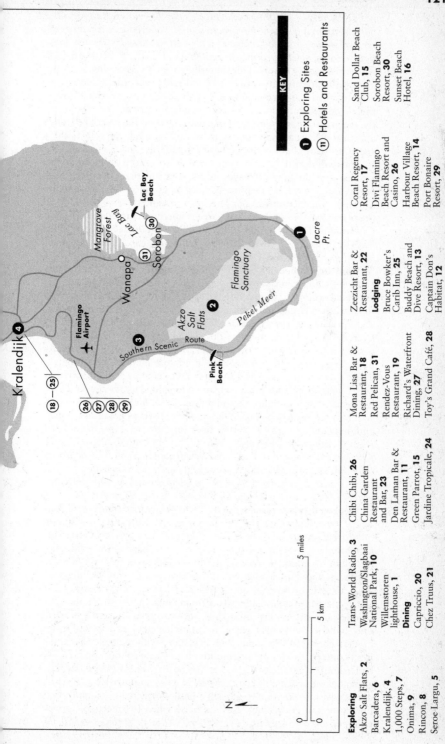

**KEY**

● Exploring Sites

⑪ Hotels and Restaurants

0 ─── 5 miles
0 ─── 5 km

N ←

**Exploring**
Akzo Salt Flats, **2**
Barcadera, **6**
Kralendijk, **4**
1,000 Steps, **7**
Onima, **9**
Rincon, **8**
Seroe Largu, **5**

Trans-World Radio, **3**
Washington/Slagbaai National Park, **10**
Willemstoren lighthouse, **1**

**Dining**
Capriccio, **20**
Chez Truus, **21**

Chibi Chibi, **26**
China Garden Restaurant and Bar, **23**
Den Laman Bar & Restaurant, **11**
Green Parrot, **15**
Jardine Tropicale, **24**

Mona Lisa Bar & Restaurant, **18**
Red Pelican, **31**
Rendez-Vous Restaurant, **19**
Richard's Waterfront Dining, **27**
Toy's Grand Café, **28**

Zeezicht Bar & Restaurant, **22**

**Lodging**
Bruce Bowker's Carib Inn, **25**
Buddy Beach and Dive Resort, **13**
Captain Don's Habitat, **12**

Coral Regency Resort, **17**
Divi Flamingo Beach Resort and Casino, **26**
Harbour Village Beach Resort, **14**
Port Bonaire Resort, **29**

Sand Dollar Beach Club, **15**
Sorobon Beach Resort, **30**
Sunset Beach Hotel, **16**

*6709,* FAX *599/7–8240. 11 cottages, 11 villas, 24 suites. Restaurant, 2 bars, in-room safes, some kitchenettes, pool, volleyball, beach, dive center and shop, photo lab, bicycles, baby-sitting, laundry service, business services, meeting room, car rental. AE, D, MC, V. EP, MAP, FAP.*

**$$$**  🏨 **Coral Regency Resort.** This time-share resort's 28 studios and one- and two-bedroom suites are in 10 coral-pink, two-story buildings set around a quadrangle containing a small pool and sunbathing area—there's no beach for lounging. As a result, for privacy, the rooms on the second floor are more desirable than those on the first. The studio apartments have a small but complete kitchen, while the suites have a spacious living room with overhead fan, a large balcony looking out to sea (wonderful for morning breakfasts), and a fully equipped kitchen—including microwave and blender. The plain but clean bedrooms are compact, but their marble-tiled bathrooms (with shower only) are large. The Oceanfront Bar & Restaurant and the dive shop add to the offerings. Kids under 12 stay free in their parents' room. ⊠ *Kaya Gobrenador, Debrot 90, Box 380,* ☎ *599/7–5580; in the U.S.,* ☎ *800/ 327–8150;* FAX *599/7–5680. 28 units. Restaurant, bar, kitchenettes, pool, beach, dive center. AE, DC, MC, V. CP, MAP, FAP.*

**$$$**  🏨 **Sand Dollar Beach Club.** These spacious time-share apartments combine a European design with a tropical rattan decor, though this varies according to the individual owner's taste. Each has cable TV, a full kitchen, a large bathroom, a couch that turns into a queen-size bed, and a private patio or terrace that looks out to the sea (though the views from the ground-floor units are obstructed by foliage). This American enclave is popular with serious divers and their families. There's daily maid service, and the maids will even do your laundry for $4 a load. There's an on-premise PADI five-star dive center, a limited activities club for children (additional fee), and two lighted tennis courts. There is a beach, but it's minuscule and disappears at high tide. The resort's waterfront Green Parrot (☞ Dining, *below*) serves breakfast, lunch, and dinner, and there's a grocery store for those who like to cook. ⊠ *Kaya Gobrenador Debrot 79,* ☎ *599/7–8738 or 800/228–4773,* FAX *599/7–8760. 75 studio, 1-, 2-, and 3-bedroom units and 8 2-bedroom town houses. Restaurant, bar, ice-cream parlor, in-room safes, pool, 2 tennis courts, beach, dive center, photo lab, baby-sitting, children's program (5–15), car rental. AE, D, DC, MC, V. EP, BP, MAP, FAP.*

**$$$**  🏨 **Sorobon Beach Resort.** Here's the perfect place for acting out all your *Swept Away* fantasies. The Sorobon is a secluded cluster of cottages on a lovely private sandy beach at Lac Bay, on the southeast shore. This delightfully unpretentious small resort is for "naturalists" who take its "clothing-optional" motto literally. Guests are a fair mix of older European and American couples. The chalets are arranged in a "V" shape to give the resort more openness and access to the beach. Each chalet consists of two small one-bedroom units, each with simple light-wood Scandinavian furnishings, an older-style kitchen, and a shower-only bath. New owners added a swimming pool and several more modern chalets in 1995 and 1996. In keeping with the get-away-from-it-all concept, there's no air-conditioning, TV, telephone, or radio. A daily shuttle will take you to town. The heady windsurfing in Lac Bay, a result of the unbeatable combo of shallow bay and strong trade winds, draws raves. Restaurant, bar, even a nature-oriented book and video library are all convenient. But act blasé when the manager arrives wrapped in a towel. ⊠ *Box 14,* ☎ *599/7–8080 or 800/828–9356,* FAX *599/7–5363. 30 rooms in 15 chalets. Restaurant, bar, in-room safes, fans, kitchenettes, beach, sailboats, snorkel gear, library, laundry service, airport and downtown shuttles. AE, MC, V. EP.*

**$$–$$$**  🏨 **Divi Flamingo Beach Resort and Casino.** This plantation-style resort consists of the hotel and the Club Flamingo studio apartments, which have the newest and nicest rooms. It's the oldest hotel on the island—a former internment camp for German POWs during World War II, and even those rooms that have been "renovated" still cry out for new furnishings and another coat of fresh paint. Though the resort is definitely showing signs of age, because of its dive facility and upbeat activities programs it still receives a fair share of repeat guests. Dive Bonaire was founded by world-class expert Peter Hughes and features some of the best photo labs in the Caribbean. Several rooms (those in the former POW barracks) are accessible to travelers using wheelchairs, and the dive operation even has specially trained masters who teach scuba diving to individuals with disabilities and dive with them. No matter which hotel you're staying at, reserve a table at the Chibi Chibi restaurant (☞ Dining, *below*), where you can hear ocean waves pounding beneath the floorboards. The all-inclusive package offers great value for the price. Kids under 16 stay free with their parents. ✉ *40 J. A. Abraham Blvd.,* ☎ *599/7–8285. U.S. representative: Divi Hotels,* ☎ *800/367–3484,* 𝖥𝖠𝖷 *599/7–8238. 105 rooms, 40 time-share units. 2 restaurants, 2 bars, in-room safes, kitchenettes in studios, 2 pools, outdoor hot tub, tennis court, beach, 2 dive shops, photo shop, casino, dry cleaning and laundry service, meeting room, car rental. AE, D, MC, V. EP, MAP, All-inclusive.*

**$$–$$$**  🏨 **Port Bonaire Resort.** Opened at the end of 1994, Port Bonaire is a group of luxury apartments, penthouses, and beach houses, all with patios or balconies that look out on the ocean. The overall design, with tile roofs and pastel exteriors, is called Dutch Mediterranean. Families will find the fully equipped kitchens handy; they even have microwaves and dishwashers. Daily maid service and a room safe are also welcome. There are no facilities to speak of on property, but guests can use those at the new Bonaire Plaza Resort next door. ✉ *Box 269, Kaya International,* ☎ *599/7–5636,* 𝖥𝖠𝖷 *599/7–5639. 26 units. In-room safes, kitchenettes, pool. AE, DC, MC, V. EP.*

**$$**  🏨 **Sunset Beach Hotel.** In 1990 a group of businessmen purchased this hotel (then called the Bonaire Beach Hotel) and began renovations. Age, however, has its drawbacks, and here the drawback is the location of the original buildings: They are all set back from the shore, giving even the best rooms only garden views. Rooms were gutted in 1996, replacing old wooden floors, funky colored furniture, and plumbing fixtures with tidy white tile floors, rattan furnishings, tropical print curtains and bedspreads, and all new plumbing. The hotel's 12 acres encompass one of the island's better hotel beaches (in contrast to the tiny swimming pool), a water-sports concession, and a thatch-roof seaside restaurant where the popular Bonairian Theme night (including native buffet, folkloric dance show, steel band, and dancing waitresses) takes place on Saturday nights. Up to two children under 12 stay free in their parents room (except during winter season when a $10 per night fee is charged). At press time there was talk of adding 46 apartments. ✉ *Kaya Gobrenador Debrot 75, Box 333,* ☎ *599/7–8448,* 𝖥𝖠𝖷 *599/7–8118. U.S./Canada representative:* ☎ *800/333–1212, 800/344–4439, or 800/223–9815. 142 rooms, 3 1-bedroom suites. 2 restaurants with bars, in-room safes, refrigerators, pool, 3 outdoor hot tubs, 2 tennis courts, Ping-Pong, shuffleboard, volleyball, beach, dive center, water-sports center, water taxi to Klein Bonaire, game room with billiard and darts, dry cleaning and laundry service, travel services, car rental. AE, D, DC, MC, V. EP, FAP, MAP.*

**$–$$**  🏨 **Bruce Bowker's Carib Inn.** American diver Bruce Bowker started his
★  small diving lodge out of a private home, continually adding onto and refurbishing the air-conditioned inn, about a mile from the airport. Rat-

tan furnishings, cable TVs, completely renovated kitchens, and a family-style atmosphere have turned his homey hostelry into one of the island's best bets, albeit one that gets booked far in advance by repeat guests. Bowker knows everybody by name and loves to fill special requests. The two units with no kitchen have a refrigerator and electric kettle, but for more involved dining, you'll have to leave the premises—there's no restaurant. (Richard's Waterfront Restaurant is right next door.) Those who prefer to cook can shop for supplies at the grocery store just across the street. Nervous virgin divers will enjoy Bowker's small scuba classes (one or two people); PADI certification is available. The beach is just a sliver, but fine for shore entries. ⊠ *Box 68*, ☎ *599/7–8819*, ℻ *599/7–5295. U.S. representative: ITR*, ☎ *212/545–8649 or 800/223–9815. 10 units. Kitchenettes, refrigerator, pool, beach, dive center, retail dive shop. AE, MC, V. EP.*

**$–$$** 🏨 **Buddy Beach and Dive Resort.** Those who eschew luxury, requiring only basic amenities with matching rates, enjoy this growing complex situated on the beach. The original 10 apartments, given a face-lift and air-conditioning in 1995, are small but clean, with a kitchenette, tile floors, twin beds, a sleep sofa, and a shower-only bathroom. There are also four three-story buildings with studios, one-, two-, and three-bedroom apartments to choose from; all have sea views, TV, air-conditioned bedrooms, full kitchen, plus dishwasher and microwave. A dive operation and two pools are also on the premises. ⊠ *Kaya Gobrenador Debrot, Box 231*, ☎ *599/7–5080 or 800/786–3483*, ℻ *599/ 7–8647. 40 studio and 1- to 3-bedroom condominium units. Restaurant, swim-up bar, in-room safes, kitchenettes, 2 pools, beach, dive shop, car rental. AE, D, MC, V. EP.*

# Dining

Gourmets have not been sneaking off to Bonaire for five-star cuisine, but with a healthy variety of dining experiences, visitors should not go home hungry.

### What to Wear

Dress on the island is casual but conservative. Most restaurants don't allow beachwear; even casual poolside restaurants prefer a sarong or cover-up.

| CATEGORY | COST* |
| --- | --- |
| $$$ | over $25 |
| $$ | $15–$25 |
| $ | under $15 |

*per person, excluding drinks and service (there is no sales tax)*

**$$$** ✕ **Chez Truus.** Seekers of a romantic tête-à-tête flock to this air-conditioned oasis of green and white, where soft jazz plays, tables are intimate and candlelit, and the service is unobtrusive. More casual, café-style dining can be found outside on the terrace, where you can watch the strolling passersby. There's an à la carte menu, imaginatively blending Caribbean influences with Continental standards such as pork tenderloin stuffed with olives and pine nuts in mango sauce or dorado (a tasty white fish) fillet with brie in a light mustard sauce. Look for the landmark red British phone booth that sits outside the door. ⊠ *Kaya C.E.B. Hellmund 5*, ☎ *599/7–8617. AE, MC, V. Closed Mon. No lunch.*

**$$$** ✕ **Jardine Tropicale.** The only elevator on the island whisks diners to
★ this rooftop restaurant. It's a charming spot, with ivy and dichondria vining across the ceiling above windows framing views of the twinkling town lights below; it's also enclosed and air-conditioned, so come to relax over a leisurely meal. The menu is French, built around seasonal

produce, seafood, and meat. Salad with chicken, mango, and coconut or Dutch smoked salmon and eel are good starters. Follow up with the catch of the day prepared as you like, filet of sole with souffle of lobster, or filet mignon with red wine and heavy cream sauces. It wouldn't be a French restaurant without sinful desserts, so save some room for the fresh daily offering. ⊠ *La Terraza Shopping Center, Kaya Grandi,* ☎ *599/7–5718. MC, V. Closed Mon. No lunch.*

**$$$** ✕ **Red Pelican.** Near the far southern end of the island, the Red Pelican presents a harmonious blend of terra-cotta tile floors, heavy wood beams, comfortable rattan furnishings, and coral pink napery, all accented by constantly changing art exhibits. Here you have the stuff of a most civilized evening out. The Dutch chefs weave together traditional Brazilian and European fare. The crab cocktail, spicy pastas, and seasonal fish are fresh and light. ⊠ *Kaminda Sorobon 64, Lac Bay,* ☎ *599/7–5686. AE, MC, V.*

**$$–$$$** ✕ **Capriccio.** Classic Italian finally made it's way to Bonaire with the
★ opening of Capriccio in late 1994. The pastas are handmade daily, and there's a true climate-controlled wine cellar at this wonderful Italian-run eatery. You'll have a choice of casual à la carte dining on the terrace or a romantic, candlelit dinner in the tonier, air-conditioned dining room. If your appetite is hearty, go for the six-course, prix-fixe "tour of the menu." Otherwise, sure bets are the smoked fish appetizer, prosciutto with hearts of palm salad, pumpkin ravioli with sage and Parmesan, gnocchi al pesto, lamb with mustard sauce, and (surprisingly) turkey breast in sweet-and-sour sauce with stewed cabbage. Pizza, calzone, and other standards are of course available. ⊠ *Kaya Isla Riba 1,* ☎ *599/7–7230. AE, MC, V. Closed Tues. No lunch Sun.*

**$$–$$$** ✕ **Mona Lisa Bar & Restaurant.** Here you'll find Continental fare, along with a few authentic Dutch and Indonesian dishes. The most famous plate is the pork tenderloin *sate* drizzled with a peanut-butter sauce. Somehow, Mona Lisa has become renowned for fresh vegetables, though who knows where they come from, since nearly everything in Bonaire has to be imported. Lunch prices are more reasonable than those on the dinner menu. This is also a late-night hangout for local schmoozing and light snacks or fresh catch of the day, served until about 2 AM in the colorful bar adorned with various team and business baseball-style caps. The intimate dining room, presided over by a copy of the famous painting of the smiling lady, is decorated with brick-and-iron grillwork, lace curtains, and whirring ceiling fans. ⊠ *15 Kaya Grandi,* ☎ *599/7–8718. AE, MC, V. Closed weekends.*

**$$** ✕ **Chibi Chibi.** In an unusual, open-air, beach-facing wooden structure—with balustrade and open planking—the Chibi Chibi is praised for its menu of local, American, and Continental fare. Try the fettuccine Flamingo (this is one of the Divi Flamingo Resort's restaurants) or the *keshi yena* (baked gouda cheese stuffed with meat and spices). Fish is also a specialty. ⊠ *Divi Flamingo Beach Resort, 40 J. A. Abraham Blvd.,* ☎ *599/7–8285. AE, D, MC, V. No lunch.*

**$$** ✕ **Den Laman Bar & Restaurant.** A 6,000-square-foot aquarium provides the backdrop to this casual, nautically decorated, sea-breeze-cooled restaurant. Eat indoors next to the glass-enclosed "ocean show" (request a table in advance) or outdoors on the noisier patio overlooking the sea. Pick a fresh Caribbean lobster from the tank, or order red snapper Creole, a hands-down winner. Homemade cheesecake is a draw as is the live entertainment each Saturday night. ⊠ *77 Gobrenador Debrot, next to Sunset Beach Hotel,* ☎ *599/7–8955. AE, MC, V. No lunch.*

**$$** ✕ **Rendez-Vous Restaurant.** The terrace of this café, draped with a canopy of electric stars, is the perfect place to watch the world of Bonaire go by as you fill up on warm freshly baked French bread with garlic butter, hearty homemade soups, seafood, steaks, and vegetarian specialties. The Dutch pea soup, sautéed veggies baked in puff pastry, and sautéed squid, shrimp, or conch are favorites here. ⊠ *3 Kaya L. D. Gerharts,* ☎ *599/7–8454. AE, MC, V. Closed Sun.*

**$$**   ✕ **Richard's Waterfront Dining.** Animated and congenial owner Richard
★   Beady's alfresco eatery on the water is casually romantic and has become the most recommended restaurant on the island—a reputation that's well deserved. Richard, originally from Boston, sets the tone by personally checking on every table. The fresh daily menu is listed on large blackboards, and the food is consistently excellent, catering to American palates with flavorful, not spicy, preparations. Among the best dishes are conch *alajillo* (fillet of conch with garlic and butter), shrimp primavera, and grilled wahoo. For a touch of seafood, start with the fish soup, a tasty broth with chunks of the catch of the day. Filet mignon béarnaise satisfies the palette already sated with creatures of the deep. The wine list is printed on the label of the wine bottle on each table. A new pier lets you arrive by boat. The Sunset Happy Hour is popular with locals. ⊠ *60 J. A. Abraham Blvd.,* ☎ *599/7–5263. MC, V. Closed Mon. No lunch.*

**$$**   ✕ **Toy's Grand Café.** Restaurants don't come much more playful than this hip Dutch paean to high camp. Murals of everyone from Elvis to Chaplin to Mickey Mouse enliven the walls. Toy trains and crazy puppets jut out from the walls, and jack-in-the-boxes seem poised for assault at any minute. Potted plants engulf the wicker chairs. The food is equally eclectic: French, barbecue, or Indonesian. Try the snails in garlic sauce, the *nasi goreng* (fried rice), or the pork medallions in mushroom sauce. ⊠ *J. A. Abraham Blvd., Kralendijk,* ☎ *599/7–6666. MC, V. No lunch.*

**$–$$**   ✕ **Green Parrot.** This family-run restaurant, on the dock of the Sand Dollar Beach Club, features the biggest hamburgers and the best strawberry margaritas on the island. Try the onion string appetizer, which consists of onion rings shaped into a small bread loaf. Chargrilled steaks, Creole fish, and barbecued chicken and ribs are also served. Transplanted Englishman Kirk Gosden, who manages the place, has added theme dinner nights; his Monday night Italian fare is very tasty. This is where you'll find both the American expatriates and tourists hanging out. It's also a good place for viewing the setting sun. ⊠ *Sand Dollar Beach Club, Kaya Gobrenador Debrot 79,* ☎ *599/7–5454. AE, MC, V.*

**$–$$**   ✕ **Zeezicht Bar & Restaurant.** Zeezicht (pronounced *zay-zeekt* and meaning sea view) is one of the better restaurants in town that are open for three meals a day. At breakfast and lunch you'll get basic American fare with an Antillean touch, such as a fish omelet. Dinner is either on the terrace overlooking the harbor or in the homey, rough-hewn main room. Locals are dedicated to this hangout, especially for the ceviche, conch sandwiches, and the Zeezicht special soup with conch, fish, shrimps, and oysters. ⊠ *10 Kaya Corsow, across from Karel's Beach Bar,* ☎ *599/7–8434. AE, MC, V.*

**$**   ✕ **China Garden Restaurant and Bar.** Despite its name, this place has an everything-you-could-ever-want menu, from American sandwiches to shark's-fin soup, T-bone steaks, lobster, even omelets to Indonesian *bami goreng.* But Cantonese dishes are still the specialty. Try the goat Chinese-style, anything in black-bean sauce, or one of the sweet-and-sour dishes. Lots of locals turn up between 5 and 7 PM to have a drink and watch the latest in sports on the bar's cable TV. The decor is brightened with Chinese lanterns and scarlet tablecloths. Take-out is available. ⊠ *47 Kaya Grandi,* ☎ *599/7–8480. AE, DC, MC, V. Closed Tues.*

# Beaches

Beaches in Bonaire are not the island's strong point. Don't come expecting Aruba-length stretches of glorious white sand. The island's beaches are smaller, and though the water is indeed blue (several shades of it, in fact), the sand is not always white. You can have your pick of beaches in Bonaire according to color: pink, black, or white. The best hotel beaches are found at Harbour Village, Sunset Beach, and Sorobon (the only clothing optional beach on the island, reserved for the exclusive use of hotel guests).

Hermit crabs can be found along the shore at **Boca Cocolishi,** a black-sand beach in Washington/Slagbaai National Park on the northeast coast. The dark hues of tiny bits of dried coral and shells form the basin and beach, giving the sand an unusual look. This beach gives new meaning to the term windswept: Cooling breezes whip the water into a frenzy as the color of the sea changes from midnight blue to aquamarine. This being the windward side of the island, the water is too rough for anything more than wading; however, the spot is perfect for an intimate picnic *à deux*. To get there, take the Northern Scenic Route to the park, then ask for directions at the gate.

Inside Washington/Slagbaai Park is **Boca Slagbaai,** a beach of coral fossils and rocks with interesting coral gardens that are good for snorkeling just offshore. Bring scuba boots or canvas sandals to walk into the water, because the coral "beach" is rough on bare feet. The gentle surf makes it an ideal place for picnicking or swimming, especially for children. The exquisite ocher-and-russet building here was constructed by the first plantation owner and included a customs office and slaughterhouse. Today it houses a restaurant serving fine lunches Thursday–Sunday.

**Lac Bay Beach** adjacent to the Sorobon Resort Beach is *the* spot for windsurfing on Bonaire. There's a restaurant/bar at the far end near the bay entrance, and a couple of windsurfing equipment rental outfits along the beach.

As the name suggests, the sand at **Pink Beach** boasts a pinkish tint that takes on a magical shimmer in the late-afternoon sun. The water is suitable for swimming, snorkeling, and scuba diving. Take the Southern Scenic Route on the western side of the island, past the Trans-World Radio station, close to the slave huts. A favorite hangout for Bonairians on the weekend, it is virtually deserted during the week.

**Playa Funchi,** a Washington Park beach, is notable for the lagoon on one side where flamingos nest, and the superb snorkeling on the other, where iridescent green parrot fish swim right up to shore.

# Outdoor Activities and Sports

## Deep-Sea Fishing

Captain Bob of **It's About Time Fishing Charters** (☎ 599/7–7070, FAX 599/7–7071) offers deep-sea charters for those in search of wahoo, marlin, tuna, swordfish, and sailfish. His rates, which cover bait, tackle, and refreshments, average $325 for a half day, $500 for a full day. **Piscatur Charters** (☎ 599/7–8774) offers light-tackle angler reef fishing for jacks, barracudas, and snappers from a 15-foot skiff. Rates are $200 for a half day, $300 for a full day. The 30-foot sportfisherman *Piscatur* is available for charter at $350 for a half day, $500 for a full day.

## Sailing Cruises

The Siamese sailing junk *Samur* (☎ 599/7–5433), the privateer's ketch *Mistress* (☎ 599/7–8330), the sailing yacht *Lady Curzon* (☎ 599/7–2050), and the trimaran *Woodwind* (☎ 599/7–8285) offer a variety of cruises for snorkeling, picnicking, and watching the sunset. Prices range from $25 to $50 per person. A private day's cruise on the sailboat *Oscarina* (☎ 599/7–8290 or 599/7–8988) is $350 for a party of four. Glass-bottom-boat trips are offered on the *Bonaire Dream* (☎ 599/7–8239 or 599/7–4514). The 1½-hour trip costs $15 and leaves daily, except Sunday, from the Harbour Village Marina. They also offer a night trip utilizing submarine lights to bring out the brilliant colors.

## Scuba Diving

Bonaire has some of the best reef diving this side of Australia's Great Barrier Reef. In fact, the island is unique primarily for its incredible dive sites; it takes only 5–25 minutes to reach your site, the current is usually mild, and although some reefs have very sudden, steep drops, most begin just offshore and slope gently downward at a 45° angle. General visibility runs 60 to 100 feet, except during surges in October and November. An enormous range of coral can be seen, from knobby brain and giant brain coral to elkhorn, staghorn, mountainous star, gorgonian, and black coral. You're also likely to encounter schools of parrot fish, surgeonfish, angelfish, eels, snappers, and groupers. Beach diving is excellent just about everywhere on the leeward side of the island, so night diving is highly popular. There are dive sites here suitable for every skill level, from beginner to deep open-water to advanced wreck divers.

The well-policed Bonaire Marine Park, which encompasses the entire coastline around Bonaire and Klein Bonaire, remains an underwater wonder because visitors take the rules here seriously. Do not even think about (1) spearfishing; (2) dropping anchor; or (3) touching, stepping on, or collecting coral. Divers must pay an admission charge of $10, for which they receive a colored plastic tag (to be attached to an item of scuba gear) entitling them to one calendar year of unlimited diving in the Marine Park. The fees are used to maintain the underwater park. Tags are available at all scuba facilities and from the marine park headquarters in the Barcadera (☎ 599/7–8444). Check-out dives—diving first with a master before going out on your own—are required on the island and can be arranged through any dive shop. All dive operations on Bonaire now offer free buoyancy-control, advanced buoyancy-control, and photographic buoyancy-control classes. Check with any dive shop for the schedule.

There is a hyperbaric decompression chamber located next to the hospital in Kralendijk (☎ 599/7–8187 or 599/7–8900 for emergencies).

### DIVE OPERATIONS

Bonaire hotels frequently offer dive packages, which include accommodations, boat trips, shore diving, air, and use of tanks. Ask the Bonaire tourist office for a brochure describing the various packages. Organized tours are not necessary on Bonaire, as many dive sites are easily accessible from shore and clearly marked by yellow stones on the roadside. Most of the hotels listed in this guide have dive centers. The competition for quality and variety is fierce. Before making a room reservation, inquire about specific dive/room packages that are available. Many of the dive shops also have boutiques where you can purchase T-shirts, color slides showing underwater views, postcards, and tropical jewelry.

**Peter Hughes Dive Bonaire** (✉ Divi Flamingo Beach Resort, ☎ 599/7–8285 or 800/367–3484), **Sand Dollar Dive and Photo** (✉ Sand Dol-

## Bonaire Diving

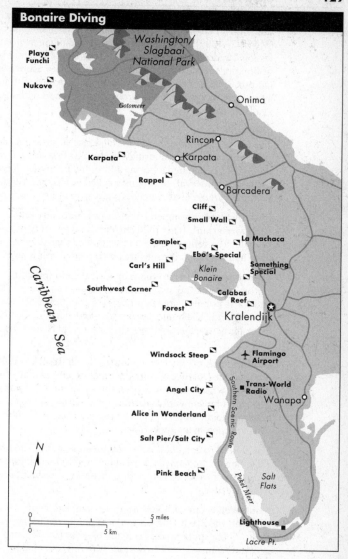

Washington/
Slagbaai
National Park

Playa
Funchi

Nukove

Gotomeer

○ Onima

Rincon ○

Karpata ◻

○ Karpata

Rappel ◻

Barcadera ○

Cliff ◻

Small Wall ◻

Sampler ◻

Ebo's Special ◻

◻ La Machaca

Carl's Hill

Klein
Bonaire

Something
Special

Southwest Corner ◻

Forest ◻

Calabas
Reef ◻

Kralendijk

*Caribbean Sea*

Windsock Steep ◻

✈ Flamingo
Airport

Angel City ◻

■ Trans-World
Radio

Wanapa ○

Alice in Wonderland ◻

*Southern Scenic Route*

Salt Pier/Salt City ◻

N

Pink Beach ◻

*Pekel Meer*

Salt
Flats

0 _____ 5 miles
0 _____ 5 km

Lighthouse ■

*Lacre Pt.*

lar Beach Club, Kaya Gobrenador Debrot 79, ☎ 599/7–5252), and
**Habitat Dive Center** (✉ Captain Don's Habitat, Kaya Gobrenador
Debrot 103, ☎ 599/7–8290) are all PADI (Professional Association
of Diving Instructors) five-star dive facilities qualified to offer both PADI
and NAUI (National Association of Underwater Instructors) certification
courses. Sand Dollar Dive and Photo is also qualified to certify dive
instructors. Other centers include **Bonaire Scuba Center** (✉ Black Durgon Inn, ☎ 599/7–5736; in the U.S., ✉ Box 775, Morgan, NJ 08879,
☎ 908/566–8866 or 800/526–2370), **Buddy Dive Resort** (✉ Kaya Gobrenador N., Debrot 85, ☎ 599/7–5080), **Dive Inn** (✉ close to South
Pier, Kaya C.E.B. Hellmund, ☎ 599/7–8761), **Bon Bini Divers** (✉
Coral Regency Resort, Kaya Gobrenador Debrot 90, ☎ 599/7–5580
or 800/327–5425), **Great Adventures at Harbour Village** (✉ Harbour
Village Beach Resort, ☎ 599/7–7500 or 800/424–0004), and **Bruce
Bowker's Carib Inn Dive Center** (✉ Bruce Bowker's Carib Inn, ☎ 599/
7–8819, FAX 599/7–5295).

Americans Jerry Schnabel and Suzi Swygert of **Photo Tours N.V.** (✉ Captain Don's Habitat, Kaya Gobrenador Debrot 103, ☎ 599/7–5390, FAX 599/7–4089) specialize in teaching and guiding novice-through-professional underwater photographers. They also offer land-excursion tours of Bonaire's birds, wildlife, and vegetation. **Dee Scarr's Touch the Sea** (✉ Box 369, ☎ 599/7–8529) is a personalized (two to four people at a time) diving program that provides interaction with marine life; it is available to certified divers.

### DIVE SITES

The *Guide to the Bonaire Marine Park* lists 44 sites that have been identified and marked by moorings. In the past few years, however, an additional 42 designated mooring and shore diving sites have been added through a conservation program called Sea Tether. Guides associated with the various dive centers can give you more complete directions.

It's difficult to recommend one site over another because all have lush coral formations, fairly mild currents, and an array of fascinating marine life. The following are a few popular sites to whet your appetite; these and selected other sites are pinpointed on our Bonaire Diving map.

Take the track down to the shore just behind the Trans-World Radio station; dive in and swim south to **Angel City,** one of the shallowest and most popular sites in a two-reef complex that includes Alice in Wonderland. The boulder-size green-and-tan coral heads are home to black margates, Spanish hogfish, gray snappers, and large purple tube sponges.

**Calabas Reef,** off the Divi Flamingo Beach Resort, is the island's busiest dive site. All divers using the hotel's facilities make their warm-up dive here where they can inspect the wreck sunk for just this purpose. The site is replete with Christmas-tree worms, sponges, and fire coral adhering to the ship's hull. Fish life is frenzied, with the occasional octopus putting in an appearance.

You'll need to catch a boat to reach **Forest,** a dive site off the coast of Klein Bonaire, so named for the abundant black-coral forest found there. This site gets a lot of fish action, including a resident spotted eel that lives in a cave.

**Small Wall** is one of Bonaire's three complete vertical wall dives. Located off the Black Durgon Inn, it is one of the island's most popular night-diving spots. Access is made by boat (Black Durgon guests can access it from shore). The 60-foot wall is frequented by squid, turtles, tarpon, and barracudas and has dense hard and soft coral formations; it also allows for excellent snorkeling.

**Rappel** is one of the most spectacular dives, near the Karpata Ecological Center. The shore is a sheer cliff, and the lush coral growth is home to an unusual variety of marine life, including occasional orange sea horses, squid, spiny lobsters, and spotted trunkfish.

**Something Special,** just south of the entrance of the marina, is famous for its garden eels, which wave about from the relatively shallow sand terrace looking like long grass in a breeze.

**Windsock Steep,** situated in front of the small beach opposite the airport runway, is an excellent shore dive ranging from 20 to 80 feet and a popular place for snorkeling close to town. The current is moderate, the elkhorn coral profuse; you may also see angelfish and rays here.

## Snorkeling

Don't consider snorkeling the cowardly diver's sport; in Bonaire the experience is anything but elementary because the surface water tends to be choppy due to the trade winds. For only $6–$11 per day, you can rent a mask, fins, and snorkel at any hotel with a water-sports center (☞ Lodging, *above*). The better spots for snorkeling are on the leeward side of the island, where you have shore access to the reefs.

## Swimming

Beaches good for swimming can be found anywhere along the western coast of the island. Excellent sites are **Pink Beach** and **Boca Cai.** The best resort beaches are found at **Harbour Village Beach Resort, Sunset Beach Hotel,** and **Divi Flamingo Beach Resort and Casino.** Or take a water taxi ($12 round-trip) to **Klein Bonaire,** an islet where you can spend the day playing king of the dune. Except for a few forgotten sneakers, there is absolutely *nothing* on Klein Bonaire, so remember to take some food and drink along. And don't miss the boat back home.

## Tennis

Tennis is available for free to the guests at the **Sunset Beach Hotel, Divi Flamingo Beach Resort,** and the **Sand Dollar Beach Club.** Nonguests can play for free during the day at the **Divi Flamingo Beach Resort.** At night, there's an hourly charge. Plan to play in the early morning or evening hours to avoid the worst of the day's heat.

## Waterskiing

To stay above the water—with luck—learn to water-ski. **Club Nautico** (☎ 599/7–5800) can make the arrangements for you.

## Windsurfing

Lac Bay, a protected cove on the east coast, is ideal for windsurfing. Novices will find it especially comforting since there's no way to be blown out to sea. **Windsurfing Bonaire,** known locally as "Jibe City" (☎ FAX 599/7–5363; U.S. representative, 800/748–8733), offers courses for beginning to advanced board sailors. Lessons cost $20; board rentals start at $20 an hour, $40 for a half day. There are regular pickups at all the hotels at 9 AM and 1 PM; ask your hotel to make arrangements.

# Shopping

You can get to know all the shops in Bonaire in a matter of a few hours, but sometimes there's no better way to enjoy some time out of the sun and sea than to go shopping, particularly if your companion is a dive fanatic and you're not. Almost all the shops are situated on the Kaya Grandi or in adjacent streets and tiny malls. There are several snazzy boutiques worth a browse. One word of caution: Buy as many flamingo T-shirts as you want, but don't take home items made of goatskin or tortoiseshell; they are not allowed into the United States.

## Cigars, Havana Style

Cigar smokers will find friends at **Little Holland** (✉ Harborside Mall, ☎ 599/7–5670) as they breathe in the smoky splendor of Havana cigars. Montecristo, H. Upmann, Romeo & Juliet, and Cohiba are in residence. Far from being banished to the porch, cigar smokers will be welcomed into a special acclimatized Cedar Cigar Room.

## Clothing

**Benetton** (✉ 19 Kaya Grandi, ☎ 599/7–5107) has added Bonaire to its list of franchises in the Caribbean and makes the claim that prices here are 30% less than in New York. Colorful cotton resort wear is available at **Bye-Bye Bonaire** (✉ Harbourside Mall, ☎ 599/7–7578). Visit **Boutique Gina** (✉ Harbourside Mall, ☎ 599/7–2923) for chic designer swimsuits and beach cover-ups.

## Perfume and Cosmetics

**Sparky's** (✉ Harborside Mall, ☎ 599/7–5288) sells name-brand, duty-free perfumes and makeup from Lancôme, Clinique, Estée Lauder, Chanel, Nina Ricci, and Ralph Lauren, to name a few.

## Souvenirs and Crafts

The **Bonaire Art Gallery** (✉ 10 Kaya L. D. Gerharts, ☎ 599/7–7120) showcases the works (paintings, etchings, and jewelry) of local artists. **Donzie** (✉ Kaya Bonaire across from Zeezicht restaurant, ☎ 599/7–7642) offers unique jewelry created from island odds and ends (shiny beads, sun-bleached bones, and sea-polished colored glass) as well as local art, second-hand clothing, and antiques. Island tunes are available at **Mundo Musical** (✉ 13 Kaya Grandi, ☎ 599/7–8174). **Littman Gifts** (✉ 35 Kaya Grandi, ☎ 599/7–8091) is the place for batik cloth by the yard, European costume jewelry, T-shirts, framed underwater pictures, wooden divers, and glass flamingos. **Caribbean Arts and Crafts** (✉ 38-A Kaya Grandi, ☎ 599/7–5051) offers unique Mexican onyx, papier-mâché clowns, woven wall tapestries, painted wooden fish and parrots, straw bags, and handblown glass vases. **Things Bonaire** (✉ Kaya Grandi 38C, ☎ 599/7–8423) offers T-shirts, shorts, colorful earrings, batik dresses, souvenirs, and guidebooks. A government-funded crafts center, **Fundashon Arte Industri Bonairiano** (✉ J. A. Abraham Blvd., Kralendijk, catercorner to post office, no phone), sells locally made necklaces of black coral, hand-painted shirts and dresses, and the "fresh craft of the day."

# Nightlife and the Arts

## Nightlife

Most divers are exhausted after they finish their third, fourth, or fifth dive of the day, which probably explains why there are so few discos in Bonaire. Nevertheless, **E Wowo** (✉ Kaya Grandi 38A, ☎ 599/7–8998) is usually packed in high season, so get there early. The name E Wowo means "eye" in Papiamento and is illustrated with two flashing op-art eyes on the wall. Recorded music is loud, and the large circular bar seats a lot of action. **Fantasy Disco** (✉ Kaya L. D. Gerharts 11, ☎ 599/7–6345) is the island's newest disco. It's spacious, features big screen TVs and taped merengue, jazz, rock, reggae and occasional live performances.

The popular bar **Karel's** (✉ Kaya J.N.E. Craane 12, ☎ 599/7–8434), on the waterfront across from the Zeezicht Restaurant, sits on stilts above the sea and is *the* place for mingling with islanders, dive pros, and tourists, especially Friday and Saturday nights, when there's live island and pop music.

**Mi Ramada** (✉ Rincon, ☎ 599/7–6338) is a hopping joint, splashed with neon colors and adorned with everything from license plates to creatively carved driftwood, that serves fine local Creole food to the accompaniment of top bands from all three ABC islands. Friday and Saturday nights are party time, when Bonairians gather along the main street of Kralendijk to dance to informal bands that set up on the sidewalk. However, it's open irregularly, so call ahead to make sure there's something on the schedule before you make the drive out.

For years the island had only one casino, the **Divi Flamingo Beach Casino,** which opens at 8 PM and is closed on Sunday. However, at press time the **Plaza Resort Bonaire** and the **Harbour Village Beach Resort** were both on the verge of opening small but luxurious casinos.

## The Arts

Slide shows of underwater and above-water scenes keep both divers and nondivers fascinated in the evenings. Dee Scarr, a dive guide, presents the fascinating "Touch the Sea" show Monday night at 8:45, from the beginning of November to the end of June, at **Captain Don's Habitat** (☎ 599/7–8290). Check with the Habitat for other shows (Bonaire Above and Below, Sea Turtles, Adventure's of Captain Don, etc.) throughout the week. **Sunset Beach Hotel** (☎ 599/7–8448) offers slide shows on identifying sea critters Tuesday nights at 8:45 and on the island's flora and fauna Thursday night at 8:15. Check out the list of Bonaire's Weekly Happenings at the tourist information office or inquire at the front desk of your hotel.

Top performers on the island, including guitarist **Cai-Cai Cecelia,** the **Kunuku Band,** and **Duo Flamingo,** migrate among the island's top resorts to entertain throughout the week. For times and locations, check the list of Bonaire's Weekly Happenings at the tourist information office or inquire at the front desk of your hotel. Don't miss the Bonairian folklore nights, with live island music and dancing along with typical local foods, Tuesday night at **Captain Don's Habitat** (☎ 599/7–8290) on Tuesday at 8 and the **Sunset Beach Hotel** (☎ 599/7–8448) on Saturday at 7:30.

# Exploring Bonaire

Two routes, north and south from Kralendijk, the island's small capital, are possible on the 24-mile-long island; either one will take from a few hours to a full day, depending upon whether you stop to snorkel, swim, dive, or lounge.

*Numbers in the margin correspond to points of interest on the Bonaire map.*

## Kralendijk

❹ Bonaire's capital city of **Kralendijk** (population: 2,500) is five minutes from the airport and a short walk from Bruce Bowker's Carib Inn and the Divi Flamingo Beach Resort. There's really not much to explore here, but there are a few sights worth noting in this small, very tidy city.

Kralendijk has one main drag, J. A. Abraham Boulevard, which turns into **Kaya Grandi** in the center of town. Along it are most of the island's major stores, boutiques, restaurants, duty-free shops, and jewelry stores (☞ Shopping, *above*).

Across Kaya Grandi, opposite the Littman jewelry store, is Kaya L. D. Gerharts, with several small supermarkets, the ALM office, a handful of snack shops, and some of the better restaurants. Walk down the narrow waterfront avenue called Kaya C.E.B. Hellmund, which leads straight to the **North and South piers.** In the center of town, the Harbourside Mall has 13 chic boutiques. Along this route you will see **Fort Oranje,** with cannons pointing to the sea. From December through April, cruise ships dock in the harbor once or twice a week. The elegant white structure that looks like a tiny Greek temple is the **Fish Market;** local fishermen no longer bring their catch here to sell (they sell out of their homes these days), but you'll find plenty of fresh vegetables and fruits.

## South Bonaire

The trail south from Kralendijk is chock-full of icons—both natural and man-made—that tell the minisaga of Bonaire. Rent a Jeep (a car will do, but during the rainy months the roads can become muddy, making traction difficult) and head south along the Southern Scenic Route. The roads wind through otherworldly desert terrain, full of organ-pipe cacti and spiny-trunk mangroves—huge stumps of saltwater trees that rise out of the marshes like witches. Watch for long-haired goats and lizards of all sizes.

**2** **Akzo Salt Flats.** When touring the southern section of the island, you can't miss the salt flats, voluptuous white drifts that look something like huge mounds of vanilla ice cream. Harvested once a year, the "ponds" are owned by the Akzo Salt Antilles N.V. company, which has reactivated the 19th-century salt industry with great success. (One reason for that success is that the ocean on this part of the island is higher than the land—which makes irrigation a snap.) Keep a look-out for the three 30-foot obelisks—white, blue, and red—that were used to guide the trade boats coming to pick up the salt. Look also in the distance across the pans to the abandoned solar salt works that are now designated **flamingo sanctuary.** With the naked eye, you might be able to make out a pink-orange haze just on the horizon; with binoculars you will see a sea of bobbing pink bodies. The sanctuary is completely protected, and no entrance is allowed, but if luck is on your side, somewhere along the far southern route you'll find some flamingos close enough to the road to hear and see more clearly.

**Slave Huts.** The gritty history of the salt industry is revealed in Rode Pan, the site of two groups of tiny slave huts. The white grouping is on the right side of the road opposite the Akzo Salt Works; the second grouping, called the red slave huts (though they appear yellow) stretches across the road a bit farther on toward the southern tip of the island. During the 19th century, the salt workers, imported slaves from Africa, worked the fields by day, then crawled into these huts at night to sleep. Each Friday afternoon, they walked seven hours to Rincon to weekend with their families, returning each Sunday to the salt pans. In recent years, the government has restored the huts to their original simplicity. Only very small people will be able to go inside, but take a walk around and put your head in for a look.

**3** **Trans-World Radio.** The first landmark you'll come to on the Southern Scenic Route is an unexpected symbol of modernism—the towering 500-foot antennas of one of the most powerful stations in Christian broadcasting. From here, evangelical programs and gospel music are transmitted daily in five languages to all of North, South, and Central America, as well as the entire Caribbean.

**1** **Willemstoren Lighthouse.** At the southern tip of the island, Bonaire's first lighthouse was built in 1837 and is now automated, but closed to visitors. Take some time to explore the beach and notice how the waves, driven by the trade winds, play a crashing symphony against the rocks. Locals make a habit of stopping here to collect pieces of driftwood in spectacular shapes and to build fanciful pyramids from found objects washed ashore.

## North Bonaire

The Northern Scenic Route takes you right into the heart of Bonaire's natural wonders—desert gardens of towering cacti (*kadushi,* used to prepare soup, and the thornier *yatu,* used to build cactus fencing), tiny coastal coves, dramatically shaped coral grottoes, and plenty of fantastic panoramas. The road also weaves through spectacular eroded pink-and-black limestone walls and eerie rock formations with fanciful names like the Devil's Mouth and Iguana Head (you'll need a vivid imagination and sharp eye to recognize them).

A snappy excursion with the requisite photo stops will take about 2½ hours, but if you pack your swimsuit and a hefty picnic basket (forget about finding a Burger King), you could spend the entire day exploring this northern sector, including a few hours snorkeling in Washington/Slagbaai Park. Head out from Kralendijk on the Kaya Gobrenador

N. Debrot until it turns into the Northern Scenic Route. Note that once you pass the Radio Nederland radio towers, you cannot turn back to Kralendijk. The narrow road becomes one-way until you get to Land-huis Karpata, and you will have to follow the cross-island road to Rin-con and return via the main road through the center of the island.

SIGHTS TO SEE

**❻ Barcadera.** Once used to trap goats, this cave is one of the oldest in Bonaire; there's even a tunnel that looks intriguingly spooky. It's the first sight along the northern route; watch closely for a yellow marker on your left before you reach the towering Radio Nederland anten-nas. Pull off across from the entrance to the Bonaire Caribbean Club, and you'll discover some stone steps that lead down into a cave full of stalactites and vegetation.

**Goto Meer.** This saltwater lagoon near the northern end of the island is a popular **flamingo hangout.** Bonaire is one of the few places in the world where pink flamingos nest. The spindly legged creatures—af-fectionately called "pink clouds"—at first look like swizzle sticks. But they're magnificent birds to observe—and there are about 15,000 of them in Bonaire. The best time to catch them at home is January through June, when they tend to their gray-plumed young. For the best view of these shy birds, take the newly paved access road running along-side the lagoon through the jungle of cacti to the parking and obser-vation area on the rise overlooking the lagoon and Washington/Slagbaai Park beyond.

**Landhuis Karpata.** This mustard-color building was the landhouse of an aloe plantation. Notice the rounded outdoor oven where aloe was boiled down before exporting the juice. At press time, the Bonairian government was considering making Karpata a rest stop and drink stand since there is nothing of the sort in this section of the island. We can only hope!

**❼ 1,000 Steps.** Once you've passed the Radio Nederland towers on the main road headed to the north end of the island, watch closely for a short yellow marker on the opposite side of the road to locate 1,000 Steps, a limestone staircase carved right out of the cliff. If you take the trek down them, you'll discover a lovely coral beach and protected cove to snorkel and scuba dive. Actually, you'll climb only 67 steps, but it feels like 1,000 when you walk up them carrying scuba gear.

**❾ Onima.** Small signposts direct the way to the **Indian inscriptions** found on a 3-foot limestone ledge that juts out like a partially formed cave entrance. Look up to see the red-stained designs and symbols inscribed on the limestone, said to have been the handiwork of the Arawak In-dians when they inhabited the island centuries ago. The pictographs were recently dated—they're at least 500 years old—and new de-scriptive placards were being erected at press time. To reach Onima, pass through Rincon on the road that heads back to Kralendijk, but take the left-hand turn before Fontein.

**❽ Rincon.** The original Spanish settlement on the island, Rincon became home to the slaves brought from Africa to work on the plantations and salt fields. Superstition and voodoo lore still have a powerful impact here, more so than in Kralendijk, where they work hard at suppress-ing the old ways. Rincon is now a well-kept cluster of pastel cottages and century-old buildings that constitute Bonaire's oldest village. Watch your driving here—both goats and dogs often sit right in the middle of the main drag. There are a couple of local eateries, but the real temptation is **Prisca's Ice Cream** (☎ 599/7–6334), to be found at her house on Kaya Komkomber (watch for the hand-lettered road sign).

⑤ **Seroe Largu.** Just off the main road, is the highest point on the northern of the island. During the day, a winding path leads to a magnificent view of Kralendijk's rooftops and the island of Klein Bonaire; at night, the twinkling city lights below make this a romantic stop. The road was recently paved, making the drive much easier.

⑩ **Washington/Slagbaai National Park.** Once a plantation producing divi-divi trees (whose pods were used for tanning animal skins), aloe (used for medicinal lotions), charcoal, and goats, the Park is now a model of conservation, designed to maintain fauna, flora, and geological treasures in their natural state. Visitors may easily tour the 13,500-acre tropical desert terrain along the dirt roads. As befits a wilderness sanctuary, the well-marked, rugged roads force you to drive slowly enough to appreciate the animal life and the terrain. A four-wheel-drive is a must. (Think twice about coming here if it rained the day before—the mud you may encounter will be more than inconvenient.) If you are planning to hike, bring a picnic lunch, camera, sunscreen, and plenty of water. There are two different routes: The long one, 22 miles (about 2½ hours), is marked by yellow arrows; the short one, 15 miles (about 1½ hours), is marked by green arrows. Goats and donkeys may dart across the road, and if you keep your eyes peeled, you may catch sight of large iguanas, camouflaged in the shrubbery.

Bird-watchers are really in their element here. Right inside the park's gate, flamingos roost on the salt pad known as **Salina Mathijs,** and exotic parakeets dot the foot of **Mt. Brandaris,** Bonaire's highest peak at 784 feet. Some 130 species of colorful birds fly in and out of the shrubbery in the park. Keep your eyes open and your binoculars at hand. (For choice beach sites in the park, ☞ Beaches, *above.*) Swimming, snorkeling, and scuba diving are permitted, but visitors are requested not to frighten the animals or remove anything from the grounds. There is absolutely no hunting, fishing, or camping allowed. A useful guidebook to the park is available at the entrance for about $6. ☎ 599/7–8444. ⌧ $5. ⊙ Daily 8–5, but you must enter before 3.

# Bonaire A to Z

## Arriving and Departing

### BY PLANE

**ALM** (☎ 800/327–7230 or 599/7–7400) and **Air Aruba** (☎ 800/882–7822 or 599/7–8300) will get you to Bonaire. ALM has two nonstop flights a week from Miami, daily flights via Curaçao from Miami, and two flights a week from Atlanta tied in with Delta. ALM also flies to Aruba, Curaçao, Jamaica, and St. Maarten, as well as other Caribbean islands, using Curaçao as its Caribbean hub. Air Aruba flies six days a week from Newark and daily from Miami to Aruba with connecting service to Bonaire. **American Airlines** (☎ 800/433–7300) offers daily flights from New York to Bonaire via Aruba and daily flights from Miami via Curaçao. ALM also offers a Visit Caribbean Pass, which allows easy interisland travel. **Avia Air** (☎ 599/7–30178) also offers scheduled service to Aruba and Curaçao.

### FROM THE AIRPORT

Bonaire's Flamingo Airport is tiny, but you'll appreciate its welcoming ambience. The customs check is perfunctory if you are arriving from another Dutch isle; otherwise you will have to show proof of citizenship, plus a return or ongoing ticket. Rental cars and taxis are available at the airport, but try to arrange the pickup through your hotel. A taxi will run between $8 and $12 (for up to four people) to most hotels.

## Currency

The great thing about Bonaire is that you don't need to convert your American dollars into the local currency, the NAf guilder. U.S. currency and traveler's checks are accepted everywhere, and the difference in exchange rates is negligible. Banks accept U.S. dollar banknotes at the official rate of NAf1.78 to the U.S. dollar, traveler's checks at NAf1.80. The rate of exchange at shops and hotels ranges from NAf1.75 to NAf1.80. The guilder is divided into 100 cents. Note: Prices quoted here are in U.S. dollars unless indicated otherwise.

## Emergencies

**Police and Fire:** For emergency assistance call ☎ 599/7–80004. **Ambulance:** ☎ 599/7–8900. **Hospital: St. Franciscus Hospital,** Kralendijk (☎ 599/7–8900); there is a hyperbaric chamber for diving emergencies. **Pharmacies: Botika Bonaire** (☎ 599/7–8905) or **Botika Korona** (☎ 599/7–7552).

## Getting Around

You can zip about the island in a car or a Suzuki Jeep. Scooters and bicycles, which are also available, are less practical but can be fun, too. Just remember that there are miles of unpaved road (though several leading to sights of interest on the northern end of the island were paved in late 1995); the roller-coaster hills at the national park require a strong stomach; and during the rainy season, mud—called Bonairian snow—is unpleasant. All traffic stays to the right, and, delightfully, there is yet to be a single traffic light. Signs or green arrows are usually posted to leading attractions; if you stick to the paved roads and marked turnoffs, you won't get lost.

### BICYCLES

**Bonaire Bicycle & Motorbike Rental** (☎ 599/7–8226), **Hot Shot Rentals** (☎ 599/7–7166), and **Harbour Village Beach Resort** (☎ 599/7–7500) rent regular, hybrid, or Dutch touring bikes. For mountain bikes, try **Captain Don's Habitat** (☎ 599/7–8290 or 599/7–8913) or **Cycle Bonaire** (☎ 599/7–7558). Rates average around $15 per day, and a credit-card chit or cash deposit is usually required.

### CAR RENTALS

**Budget** rents cars, Suzuki minivans, and Jeeps at its six locations, but reservations can be made only at the head office (☎ 599/7–8300, ext. 225). Pickups are at the airport (☎ 599/7–8315) and at several hotels. It's always a good idea to make advance reservations (FAX 599/7–8865; in the U.S., ☎ 800/472–3325). Prices range from $35 a day for a Suzuki minivan to $60 a day for an automatic, air-conditioned four-door sedan. Other agencies are **Avis** (☎ 599/7–5795, FAX 599/7–5791), **Dollar Rent-A-Car** (☎ 599/7–8888; at the airport, ☎ 599/7–5588, FAX 599/7–7788), **Sunray** (☎ FAX 599/7–4888), and **AB Car Rental** (☎ 599/7–8980 or 599/7–5410, FAX 599/7–5034). There is a government tax of $2 per day per car rental.

### SCOOTERS

Scooters are available from **Bonaire Bicycle & Motorbike Rental** (☎ 599/7–8226), **Avanti Scooters** (☎ 599/7–5661), **Hot Shot Rentals** (☎ 599/7–7166), and **S. F. Wave Touch** (☎ 599/7–4246). Single seaters cost around $26 per day or $130 per week, while double seaters run $32 per day or $175 per week.

### TAXIS

Taxis are unmetered; they have fixed rates controlled by the government. A trip from the airport to your hotel will cost between $8 and $12 for up to four passengers. A taxi from most hotels into town costs between $5 and $8. Fares increase from 7 PM to midnight by 25% and from midnight to 6 AM by 50%. Taxi drivers are usually knowledgeable enough about the island to conduct half-day tours; they charge about $60 for a northern-route tour and $40 for a southern-route tour. Call **Taxi Central Dispatch** (☎ 599/7–8100 or dial 10), or inquire at your hotel.

## Guided Tours

If you don't like to drive, **Bonaire Sightseeing Tours** (☎ 599/7–8778, FAX 599/7–4890) will chauffeur you around the island on various tours, among them a two-hour Northern Island Tour ($15) that visits the 1,000 steps; Goto Lake; Rincon, the oldest settlement on the island, and Indian inscriptions at Onima; and a two-hour Southern Island Tour ($15) that covers Akzo Salt Antilles N.V., a modern salt-manufacturing facility where flamingos gather; Lac Bay; and the oldest lighthouse on the island. A half-day tour ($20) visits sites in both the north and south. For $35, you can take a half-day tour of Bonaire's Washington/Slagbaai National Park (entrance fee included), 13,500 acres of majestic scenery, wildlife, unspoiled beaches, and tropical flora. A full-day tour of the park costs $55. **Branca Tours** (☎ 599/7–5636) offer similar tours at slightly less cost. **Ayubi's Tours** (☎ 599/7–5338) also offers several half- and full-day island tours.

## Language

The official language is Dutch, but few speak it, and even then only on official occasions. The street language is Papiamento, a mixture of Spanish, Portuguese, Dutch, English, African, and French—full of colorful Bonairian idioms that even Curaçaoans sometimes don't get. You'll light up your waiter's eyes, though, if you can remember to say *Masha danki* (thank you). English is spoken by most people working at the hotels, restaurants, and tourist shops, but a Spanish phrase book may come in handy.

## Opening and Closing Times

Stores in the Kralendijk area are generally open Monday through Saturday 8–noon and 2–6 PM. On Sundays and holidays, and when cruise ships arrive, most shops open for a few extra hours. Most restaurants are open for lunch and dinner, but few not affiliated with hotels are open for breakfast. Banks stay open from 8 to 4 Monday through Friday.

## Passports and Visas

U.S. and Canadian citizens need offer only proof of identity, so a passport, notarized birth certificate, or voter registration card will suffice. British subjects may carry a British Visitor's Passport, available from any post office; all other visitors must carry an official passport. In addition, any visitor who steps onto the island must have a return or ongoing ticket and is advised to confirm that reservation 48 hours before departure.

## Precautions

Because of violent trade winds pounding against the rocks, the windward (eastern) side of Bonaire is much too rough for diving. The *Guide to the Bonaire Marine Park* (available at dive shops around the island) specifies the level of diving skill required for 44 sites, and it knows what it's talking about. No matter how beautiful a beach may look, heed all warning signs regarding the rough undertow.

During Bonaire's "rainy season" (November–April), the mosquitos can be fierce. Smart, happy people douse themselves, including their arms, legs, and face, with repellent and also spray their hotel room before going to bed. Open-air restaurants usually have a can of repellent handy for patron use.

Get an orientation on what stings underwater and what doesn't. As the island's joke goes, you won't appreciate Bonaire until you've stepped on a long-spined urchin, but by then, you won't appreciate the joke.

Bonaire used to have a reputation for being the friendliest and safest island in the Caribbean, but lately, even residents are locking their car doors. Don't leave your camera in an open car, and leave your money, credit cards, jewelry, and other valuables in your hotel's safety-deposit box.

## Taxes and Service Charges

Hotels charge a room tax of $4.50 per person, per night, and many hotels (not all) add a 10%–15% maid service charge to your bill. Most restaurants add a 10% service charge to your bill. There's no sales tax on purchases in Bonaire. Departure tax when going to Curaçao is $5.75. For all other destinations it's $10.

## Telephones and Mail

It's difficult for visitors to Bonaire to get involved in dramatic, heart-wrenching phone conversations or *any* phone discussions requiring a degree of privacy: Only about one-third of the major hotels have phones in their rooms, so calls must be made from hotel front desks or from the central telephone company office in Kralendijk. Telephone connections have improved, but static is still common. To call Bonaire from the United States, dial 011–599–7 + the local four-digit number. When making interisland calls, dial the local four-digit number. Local phone calls cost NAf25¢.

Airmail postage rates to the United States and Canada are NAf1.75 for letters and NAf.90¢ for postcards; to Britain, NAf2.50 for letters and NAf1.25 for postcards.

## Visitor Information

Contact the **Bonaire Government Tourist Office** (⊠ 10 Rockefeller Plaza, Suite 900, New York, NY 10020, ☎ 212/956–5911 or 800/826–6247, FAX 212/956–5913) for advice and information on planning your trip. Ask about diving packages, either including accommodations or not. In Bonaire, stop by the **Bonaire Tourist Board** (⊠ Kaya Simon Bolivar 12, ☎ 599/7–8322 or 599/7–8649, FAX 599/7–8408) office for a map and list of weekly events.

# 7 The British Virgin Islands

*Tortola, Virgin Gorda, and Outlying Islands*

Updated by
Pamela
Acheson

**T**HE BRITISH VIRGIN ISLANDS consist of about 50 islands, islets, and cays that are serene, seductive, and spectacularly beautiful. Although at some points they lie only a mile or so from the U.S. Virgin Islands, the B.V.I. have managed to retain their quiet, friendly, and very laid-back character. It's true that the last five years have seen a huge increase in the number of automobiles and the construction of a cruise-ship dock, but for the most part the B.V.I. still remain happily free of the runaway development that has detracted from the charm of so many West Indian islands.

The pleasures to be found here are of the understated sort—sailing around the multitude of tiny, nearby islands; diving to the wreck of the RMS *Rhone,* sunk off Salt Island by a nasty hurricane in 1867; snorkeling in one of hundreds of wonderful spots; walking empty beaches; seeing some spectacular views from the island's peaks; and settling down on some breeze-swept terrace to admire the sunset.

One reason the B.V.I. have retained this sense of blissful simplicity is their strict building codes. No building can rise higher than the surrounding palms—two stories is the limit. The lack of direct air flights from the mainland United States also helps the British islands retain the endearing qualities of yesteryear's Caribbean. One first has to get to Puerto Rico, 60 miles to the west, or to nearby St. Thomas in the United States Virgin Islands and catch a small plane to the little airports on Beef Island/Tortola and Virgin Gorda. Many of the travelers who return year after year prefer arriving by water, either aboard their own ketches and yawls or on one of the convenient ferryboats that cross the turquoise waters between St. Thomas and Tortola. The B.V.I. government recently approved a major expansion of the Beef Island airport. Although it will be four to five years before the construction is completed, those seeking the simplicity of the B.V.I. might want to head here soon.

Tortola, about 10 square miles, is the largest of the islands, and Virgin Gorda, with 8 square miles, ranks second. The islands scattered around them include Jost Van Dyke, Great Camanoe, Norman, Peter, Salt, Cooper, Ginger, Dead Chest, and Anegada, among others. Tortola is the most populated of the B.V.I. and has the largest number of hotels, restaurants, and shops. Virgin Gorda offers a limited number of restaurants and shops and resorts on the island are mostly self-contained. Jost Van Dyke has become a major charter boat anchorage and although little bars now line the beach at Great Harbour, there are few places to stay overnight on the island. The other islands are either uninhabited or have a single hotel or resort.

Sailing has always been a popular activity in the B.V.I. The first arrivals here were a romantic seafaring tribe, the Siboney Indians. Christopher Columbus was the first European to visit, in 1493. Impressed by the number of islands dotting the horizon, he named them *Las Once Mil Virgines* (The 11,000 Virgins) in honor of the 11,000 virgin-companions of Saint Ursula, martyred in the 4th century.

In the ensuing years, the Spaniards passed through these waters fruitlessly seeking gold. Then came the pirates, who found the islands' hidden coves and treacherous reefs an ideal base from which to prey on passing galleons crammed with Mexican and Peruvian gold, silver, and spices. Among the most notorious of these predatory men were Blackbeard Teach; Bluebeard; Captain Kidd; and Sir Francis Drake, who lent his name to the channel that sweeps through the two main clusters of the B.V.I.

In the 17th century, these colorful cutthroats were replaced by the Dutch, who, in turn, were soon sent packing by the British. It was the British who established a plantation economy, and for the next 150 years developed the sugar industry. African slaves were brought in to work the cane fields while the plantation owners and their families reaped the benefits. When slavery was abolished in 1838, the plantation economy quickly faltered, and the majority of the white population returned to Europe.

The islands dozed, a forgotten corner of the British empire, until the early 1960s. In 1966, a new constitution, granting greater autonomy to the islands, was approved. Although the governor is still appointed by the queen of England, his limited powers concentrate on external affairs and local security. Other matters are administered by the legislative council, consisting of representatives from nine island districts. General elections are held every four years. The arrangement seems to suit the British Virgin Islanders just fine: The mood is serene, with none of the occasional political turmoil found on other islands. Having had tacit control over their destinies for more than a century and a half, local residents now have no reason to feel that visitors are more than welcome guests.

In the 1960s Laurance Rockefeller and American-expatriate Charlie Cary brought the beginnings of tourism to the B.V.I. In 1965 Rockefeller set about creating the Little Dix resort on Virgin Gorda. A few years later, Cary and his wife, Ginny, established the Moorings marina complex on Tortola, and sailing in the area burgeoned. Today the majority of jobs on the islands are tourism-related. British Virgin Islanders love their unspoiled tropical home and are determined to maintain its easygoing charms, for both themselves and the travelers who are their guests.

# TORTOLA

## Lodging

The number of rooms available in the B.V.I. is small compared with that at other destinations in the Caribbean; what is available is also often in great demand, and the prices are not low. The top-of-the-line resorts here are among the most expensive in the Caribbean and are sometimes difficult to book even off-season. Even the more moderately priced hotels command top dollar during the season; off-season, however, they are legitimate bargains at about half the price. In addition, many of the hotels offer rates that include all three meals.

| CATEGORY | COST* |
|---|---|
| $$$$ | over $300 |
| $$$ | $200–$300 |
| $$ | $100–$200 |
| $ | under $100 |

*All prices are for a standard double room in high season, excluding 7% hotel tax and 10% service charge.*

$$$ ★ 🏨 **Long Bay Beach Resort.** This is Tortola's finest hotel. The mile-long arc of white sand from which this resort gets its name graces the front of many a B.V.I. postcard. A wide variety of accommodations includes 32 deluxe beachfront rooms, with two queen-size beds or one king-size four-poster bed, marble-top wet bars, and showers with Italian tiles. There are also smaller beach cabanas, 10 rustic, tropical hideaways set on stilts at the water's edge. Hillside choices include small but adequate rooms, studios with a comfortable seating area, and roomy one- and

two-bedroom villas; all have balconies with lovely views. The Beach restaurant, which has been expanded and now has a charming upper-level deck, offers all-day dining. The Garden restaurant serves gourmet dinners in a romantic, candlelit setting. There are two brand-new tennis courts. There is also a new conference room that can seat 150 people. ⊠ *Box 433, Road Town,* ☎ *809/495–4252 or 800/729–9599,* FAX *809/495–4677. 105 rooms. 2 restaurants, 2 bars, commissary, pool, putting green, 2 tennis courts, beach, boutique, meeting room. AE, MC, V. EP, MAP.*

**$$$** 🏨 **Sugar Mill Hotel.** The owners of this small, out-of-the-way hotel, Jeff and Jinx Morgan, opened it over two decades ago after becoming well-established travel and food writers. The reception area, bar, and restaurant are in the ruins of a centuries-old sugar mill and are decorated with bright Haitian artwork. Rather plain guest houses are scattered on the hillside; the rooms are furnished in soft pastels and rattan and have ceiling fans but no air conditioners. (Light sleepers may be disturbed by the roosters, who start crowing long before dawn.) There's a circular swimming pool set into the hillside and a tiny beach where lunch is served on a shady terrace. The Sugar Mill Restaurant is well known on the island (☞ Dining, *below*). ⊠ *Box 425, Road Town,* ☎ *809/495–4355,* FAX *809/495–4696. 20 rooms. 2 restaurants, 2 bars, fans, pool, small beach, snorkeling. AE, MC, V. EP, MAP.*

**$$–$$$** 🏨 **Prospect Reef Resort.** This sprawling resort overlooking Sir Francis Drake Channel is painted in bright pinks, purples, blues, and yellows. There are 11 types of units, including variously sized rooms with kitchenettes and two-story, two-bedroom units with private interior courtyards. All have a balcony, patio, or both and may face either the water or the hotel's gardens. There are 7 acres of neatly manicured grounds with creative rock paths and a network of lagoons. In addition to a large swimming pool and diving pool, Prospect Reef has a saltwater pool sectioned off from the sea with large rocks and a narrow, artificial beach. The resort also has its own harbor, where sailboats are available for day trips or longer excursions. The resort offers a special camp for kids. ⊠ *Box 104, Road Town,* ☎ *809/494–3311,* FAX *809/494–5595. 131 rooms. 2 restaurants, 2 bars, beachside snack bar, commissary, 3 pools, children's splash pool, beauty salon, putting green, 6 tennis courts, beach, dive shop, snorkeling, gift shop, beachwear shop, convention center. AE, MC, V. EP.*

**$$** 🏨 **Fort Recovery.** The appealing one- to four-bedroom bungalows here
★  are built around the remnants of a Dutch fort, along a small beach facing Sir Francis Drake Channel. The grounds are bright with tropical flowers; a large swimming pool was added in 1995. All units have patios, kitchens, and equally excellent views. Although there's no restaurant, there is a dinner menu, and three-course meals—delivered course by course—can be served to you in your living room or on your terrace. Yoga classes, exercise classes, massages, and fitness packages are available. ⊠ *Box 239, Road Town,* ☎ *809/495–4467,* FAX *809/495–4036. 10 units. Commissary, kitchens, pool, beach. AE, MC, V. EP.*

**$$** 🏨 **Moorings-Mariner Inn.** Headquarters for the Moorings Charter operation and popular with yachting folk who find its full-service facilities convenient and the companionship of fellow "boaties" congenial, this is also a good choice for those who want to be within easy walking distance of town. The atmosphere is a combination of laid-back and lively, and the rooms, including four suites, are large and comfortable. Rooms have peach tile floors and bright, tropical-print bedspreads and curtains; all also have a small kitchenette (with sink, refrigerator, and two-burner stove) and a balcony. Most rooms face the water, except for eight, which overlook the pool or the tennis court. ⊠ *Box 139, Road Town,* ☎ *809/494–2331,* FAX *809/494–2226. 40 rooms. Restau-*

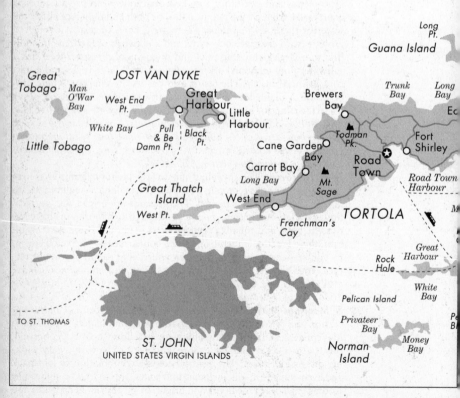

*A T L A N T I C*

Long
Pt.

Guana Island

Trunk
Bay

Long
Bay

*Great
Tobago*

*Man
O'War
Bay*

*JOST VAN DYKE*

West End
Pt.

Great
Harbour

Brewers
Bay

*White Bay*

*Little
Harbour*

Ec

*Little Tobago*

Pull
& Be
Damn Pt.

*Black
Pt.*

Cane Garden
Bay

Todman
Pk.

Fort
Shirley

*Road Town
Harbour*

Carrot Bay

Road
Town

*Great Thatch
Island*

*Long Bay*

*Mt.
Sage*

**TORTOLA**

West Pt.

West End

*Frenchman's
Cay*

*Great
Harbour*

*Rock
Hole*

*White
Bay*

*Pelican Island*

TO ST. THOMAS

*Privateer
Bay*

*Money
Bay*

Pe
B

**ST. JOHN**
UNITED STATES VIRGIN ISLANDS

*Norman
Island*

West End Pt.

Bones Bight

Flamingo Pond

Red Pond

Loblolly Bay

Table Bay

The Settlement

**ANEGADA**
(15 miles north of Necker Is.)

Lower Bay

Budrock Pond

Horse Shoe Reef

White Bay

*O C E A N*

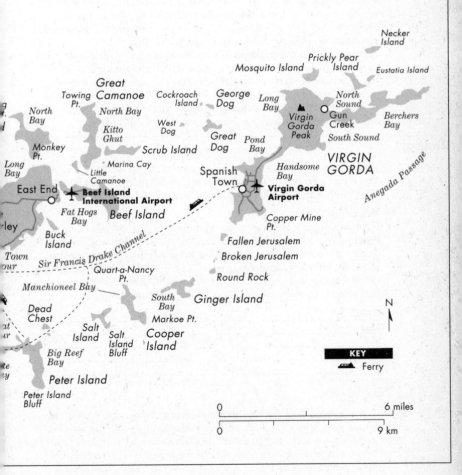

Necker Island

Prickly Pear Island

Mosquito Island

Eustatia Island

**Great Camanoe**

Towing Pt.

Cockroach Island

George Dog

Long Bay

North Sound

North Bay

North Bay

Kitto Ghut

West Dog

Great Dog

Pond Bay

*Virgin Gorda Peak*

Gun Creek

Berchers Bay

Monkey Pt.

Scrub Island

South Sound

**VIRGIN GORDA**

Long Bay

Marina Cay

Little Camanoe

Spanish Town

Handsome Bay

*Anegada Passage*

**East End**

**Beef Island International Airport**

**Virgin Gorda Airport**

Fat Hogs Bay

**Beef Island**

Copper Mine Pt.

Buck Island

*Sir Francis Drake Channel*

Fallen Jerusalem

Town

Quart-a-Nancy Pt.

Broken Jerusalem

Manchioneel Bay

Round Rock

Dead Chest

South Bay

**Ginger Island**

Salt Island

Markoe Pt.

Salt Island Bluff

**Cooper Island**

Big Reef Bay

**Peter Island**

N

Peter Island Bluff

| 0 | | 6 miles |
|---|---|---|
| 0 | | 9 km |

*rant, bar, kitchenettes, pool, tennis court, volleyball, dive shop, gourmet shop. AE, MC, V. EP.*

**$$** ⊞ **Sebastian's on the Beach.** Airy white rooms, simply decorated with
★ floral-print curtains and bedspreads, have either terraces or balconies, some with great ocean views. There is no air-conditioning, but ceiling fans and louvered windows keep the rooms cool, and you are lulled to sleep by the sound of the ocean. Bathrooms have only stall showers. There are nonbeachfront rooms across the street, which lack views and can be noisy, but they are just as big and are quite a bit cheaper than the beachfront rooms. The restaurant here is excellent. ⊠ *Box 441, Road Town,* ☎ *809/495–4212,* FAX *809/495–4466. 26 rooms. Restaurant, bar, commissary, fans, beach, snorkeling. AE. EP.*

**$$** ⊞ **Treasure Isle Hotel.** Bright shades of lemon, violet, and mango-pink cover the exterior of this pretty hillside property, which overlooks the harbor. The proximity of Road Town and several marinas makes this hotel a handy base. The air-conditioned rooms are spacious and accented with fabrics printed with Matisse-like patterns. Open to the breezes and the heady aroma of tropical flowers, the Spy Glass Bar with its comfortable lounge is the perfect place to relax and look out at a stunning view of the harbor and islands in the distance. There is daily transportation to Cane Garden Bay. ⊠ *Box 68, Road Town,* ☎ *809/494–2501,* FAX *809/494–2507. 40 rooms. Restaurant, 2 bars, air-conditioning, pool, scuba diving, boating. AE, MC, V. EP.*

**$** ⚠ **Brewer's Bay Campground.** If you care to camp, both prepared and bare sites are located on Brewer's Bay, one of Tortola's prime snorkeling spots. Check out the ruins of the distillery that gave the bay its name. There are public bathrooms but no showers. ⊠ *Box 185, Road Town,* ☎ *809/494–3463. 10 prepared and 18 bare sites. Restaurant, bar, commissary, beach, windsurfing, baby-sitting. No credit cards.*

# Dining

The most popular choices in B.V.I. restaurants are seafood dishes. You'll find a greater range of eateries on Tortola than on more remote Virgin Gorda and the other islands, where most hotels offer a meal plan.

## What to Wear

Casual but neat is the way to go on both Tortola and Virgin Gorda. Beachwear is a bit too casual, but nice shorts are fine during the day. At the very casual restaurants, shorts are acceptable to wear in the evening but at the nicer restaurants long pants for men and sundresses or chic resort wear for women are considered the norm. Resort dining rooms may require a jacket; ask when you make your reservations.

| CATEGORY | COST* |
|----------|-------|
| **$$$$** | over $35 |
| **$$$** | $25–$35 |
| **$$** | $15–$25 |
| **$** | under $15 |

*\*per person for three courses, excluding drinks and service; there is no sales tax in the B.V.I.*

**$$$** ✕ **Brandywine Bay.** For the best in romantic dining, don't miss this
★ hillside gem, where candlelit alfresco tables have a sweeping view of neighboring islands. Italian owner-chef Davide Pugliese prepares food the Tuscan way—grilled with lots of fresh herbs. The remarkable menu, which hostess Cele Pugliese describes tableside, can include homemade mozzarella, grilled portobello mushrooms, grilled local wahoo, and grilled veal chops with ricotta and sun-dried tomatoes. Roast duck, a house specialty, is always served with an exotic sauce such as berry, mango, orange-and-ginger, or passion fruit. The lemon tart and

the *tiramisù* are irresistible. There's also an excellent wine list. ⊠ *Sir Francis Drake Hwy., east of Road Town,* ☎ *809/495–2301. AE, MC, V. Closed Sun. No lunch.*

**$$$** ✕ **Skyworld.** You'll want to arrive early for dinner at this mountain-top aerie; the sunset views are breathtaking. Watch the western horizon become ablaze with color, then settle back in the casually elegant dining room to feast on some delectable offerings. Try the veal in lemon caper sauce, the local swordfish with sun-dried-tomato pesto, or the passion-fruit sorbet. This is also a special place for lunch. Not only are the sandwiches on home-baked bread delicious, but both the restaurant and the observation tower above offer the B.V.I.'s highest (and absolutely breathtaking) 360-degree view of numerous islands and cays. Even St. Croix (40 miles away) and Anegada (20 miles away) can be seen on a clear day. ⊠ *Ridge Rd.,* ☎ *809/494–3567. AE, MC, V.*

**$$$** ✕ **Sugar Mill Restaurant.** The candles gleam and the background music is pleasingly mellow in this well-known restaurant. The lovely stone dining room is built in the ruins of a centuries-old sugar mill. The copper cauldron that is now a bubbling fountain was once used for the mill's rum production. Well-prepared selections on the à la carte menu include pasta and vegetarian entrées. House favorites are the spicy Caribbean sausage with Creole sauce, the glazed duck with sesame noodles, and fresh fish in banana leaves with herb butter. Although the setting is romantic, service here can be a bit on the speedy side. ⊠ *Apple Bay,* ☎ *809/495–4355. AE, MC, V. No lunch.*

**$$$** ✕ **The Upstairs.** Ask for a window table here and you'll be bathed in
★ gentle tropical breezes as you gaze out at the stars. Excellent service and food are hallmarks of this elegant and romantic restaurant overlooking a small marina. For a truly exceptional meal, try the filet mignon served with peaches and an outstanding port-wine sauce. Other specialties include a delicious lobster au gratin appetizer, grilled local fish, roast duck, and key lime pie. A 10% service charge is included in the bill. ⊠ *On Prospect Reef Resort grounds (turn left just after the entrance), Road Town,* ☎ *809/494–2228. AE, MC, V.*

**$$–$$$** ✕ **Pusser's Landing.** Yachters flock to the two-story home of this popular waterfront restaurant. Downstairs, belly up to the large, outdoor mahogany bar or choose a waterside table for drinks, sandwiches, or a light dinner. Head upstairs for quieter alfresco dining and a delightfully eclectic menu that includes homemade black bean soup, freshly grilled local fish, pasta, and such pub favorites as shepherd's pie. The air-conditioned Dinner Theater, with its 15-foot screen, features fixed-price, three-course meals and showings of movies and sports events. ⊠ *Soper's Hole,* ☎ *809/495–4554. AE, MC, V.*

**$$** ✕ **The Apple.** This small, inviting restaurant is in a West Indian house. Soft candlelight creates a relaxed atmosphere for diners as they sample fish steamed in lime butter, conch or whelks in garlic sauce, and other local seafood dishes. There is a traditional West Indian barbecue and buffet every Sunday evening from 7 to 9, and coconut chips and conch fritters are served at Happy Hour which runs from 5 to 7 on weekdays. The excellent lunch menu includes a variety of sandwiches, meat and vegetarian lasagna, lobster quiche, seafood crepes, and croissants with ham and Swiss or spinach and feta. ⊠ *Little Apple Bay,* ☎ *809/495–4437. AE, MC, V.*

**$$** ✕ **C and F Restaurant.** Just outside Road Town, on a side street past the Moorings, is one of the island's most popular restaurants. Crowds head here for the best barbecue in town (chicken, fish, and ribs), fresh local fish prepared any way you wish, and excellent curries. Sometimes you have to wait for a table, but it is worth it. ⊠ *Purcell Estate,* ☎ *809/494–4941. Reservations not accepted. AE, MC, V. No lunch.*

**$$**  ✕ **The Fishtrap.** Dine alfresco at this restaurant, which serves grilled local fish, steaks, and chicken plus Mexican and Asian selections. Friday and Saturday there's a barbecue with a terrific salad bar; prime rib is the special on Sunday. The lunch menu includes burgers and salads. ⊠ *Columbus Centre, Wickham's Cay, Road Town,* ☎ *809/494–2636. AE, MC, V. No lunch Sun.*

**$$**  ✕ **Spaghetti Junction.** This funky spot is a hit with the boating crowd. Nightly specials like penne with a spicy tomato sauce or capellini with shellfish complement the tasty and traditional Italian menu (veal or chicken parmigiana, pastas, etc.), and sun-dried tomatoes in the Caesar salad is a nice twist. Check out the gorilla in the rest room. ⊠ *Waterfront Dr., Road Town,* ☎ *809/494–4880. No credit cards. Closed holidays and Sept. No lunch.*

**$$**  ✕ **Virgin Queen.** The sailing and rugby crowd and locals gather here
★    to play darts, drink beer, and eat Queen's Pizza (some say it's the best pizza in the Caribbean) or some of the excellent West Indian and English fare. The delicious menu includes saltfish, barbecued ribs with beans and rice, bangers and mash (sausages and mashed potatoes), shepherd's pie, and chili. ⊠ *Fleming St., Road Town,* ☎ *809/494–2310. No reservations. No credit cards. Closed Sun.*

**$-$$**  ✕ **Capriccio di Mare.** The owners of the well-known Brandywine Bay
★    restaurant (☞ *above*) also run this authentic Italian café. You can stop by for cappuccino and a fresh pastry (it's open for breakfast), or have a delicious meal of toast Italiano (grilled ham and Swiss cheese sandwiches), perfectly cooked linguine or penne with a variety of sauces, or crispy-crust tomato-and-mozzarella pizza topped with hot Italian sausage or fresh grilled eggplant. Try the Mango Bellini, a mango and Italian sparkling wine mixture that's a variation on the famous Bellini Cocktail served by Harry's Bar in Venice. ⊠ *Waterfront Dr., Road Town,* ☎ *809/494–5369. Reservations not accepted. No credit cards. Closed Sun.*

**$-$$**  ✕ **Fort Wine Gourmet.** Tables are positioned to provide views through the French doors of this charming spot, which doubles as a gourmet deli. It's open all day and is a great spot for an espresso or a cappuccino, a fresh pastry, or a tasty salad or sandwich. ⊠ *Main St., Road Town,* ☎ *809/494–3036. Reservations not accepted. AE, MC, V.*

## Beaches

Beaches in the B.V.I. are less developed than, say, on St. Thomas or St. Croix. You'll also find fewer people. Try to get out on a boat at least one day during your stay in these islands, whether a dive-snorkeling boat or a day-trip sailing vessel. It's sometimes the best way to get to the most virgin Virgin beaches (some have no road access).

Tortola's north side has a number of postcard-perfect, palm-fringed white-sand beaches that curl luxuriantly around turquoise bays and coves. Nearly all are accessible by car (preferably with four-wheel drive), albeit down bumpy roads that corkscrew precipitously. Facilities range from none to several beach bars with rest rooms.

**Apple Bay,** which includes **Little Apple Bay** and **Cappoon's Bay,** is the spot to go if you want to surf; good waves are never a sure thing, but January and February are usually high times here. The beach itself is pretty narrow. Sebastian's, the very appealing hotel here, caters especially to those in search of the perfect wave. **Brewers Bay** is good for snorkeling. There's a campground here, but in the summer you'll find almost nobody around. The beach and its old sugar mill and rum-distillery ruins are just north of Cane Garden Bay (up and over a steep hill), just past Luck Hill. **Cane Garden Bay** rivals St. Thomas's Magens Bay in beauty but is Tortola's most popular beach (it's the closest beach to Road Town—one steep up- and down-hill drive) and one of the B.V.I.'s best-known anchorages. It's a grand beach for jogging if you can resist staying out of that translucent water. You can rent sailboards and such, and for noshing or sipping you have a choice of going to Stanley's Welcome Bar; Rhymer's; The Wedding; Myett's; or Quito's Gazebo, where local recording star Quito Rhymer sings island ballads four nights a week. For true romance, nothing beats an evening of stargazing from the bow of a boat, listening to Quito's love songs drift across the bay. **Josiah's Bay** is a favorite place to hang-10. The beach is wide, very often deserted, and a nice place to come for a quiet picnic. **Long Bay (East)** on Beef Island offers scenery that draws superlatives and is visited only by a knowledgeable few. The view of Little Camanoe and Great Camanoe islands is appealing, and if you walk around the bend to the right, you can see little Marina Cay and Scrub Island. Long Bay is also a good spot for interesting seashell finds. Take the Queen Elizabeth II Bridge to Beef Island and watch for a small dirt turnoff on the left before the airport. Follow the road that curves along the east side of the dried-up marsh flat—don't drive directly across the flat. **Long Bay (West)** is a stunning mile-long stretch of white sand, and the road that leads to it offers panoramic views of the bay (bring your camera). Long Bay Beach Resort sits along part of it, but the whole beach is open to the public. The water is not as calm as that at Cane Garden or Brewer's Bay, but it is still very swimmable. **Smuggler's Cove** is on Lower Belmont Bay. After bouncing your way to this beautiful beach, you'll really feel as if you've found a hidden paradise (although don't expect to be alone on weekends). Have a beer or a toasted cheese sandwich, the only items on the menu, at the *extremely casual* snack bar. There is a fine view of the island of Jost Van Dyke, and the snorkeling is good. **Trunk Bay** is directly north of Road Town, midway between Cane Garden Bay and Beef Island. About the only thing you'll find moving here is the surf. You'll have to hike down a *ghut* (gully) from the high Ridge Road.

## Outdoor Activities and Sports

### Horseback Riding

Equestrians should get in touch with **Shadow Stables** (☎ 809/494–2262) or Mr. Thomas at his **Ellis Thomas Riding School** (☎ 809/494–4442).

### Sailboarding

One of the best spots for sailboarding is at Trellis Bay on Beef Island. **Boardsailing B.V.I.** (✉ Trellis Bay, Beef Island, ☎ 809/495–2447) has rentals, private lessons, and group rates.

### Sailing and Boating

The B.V.I. offer some of the finest sailing waters in the world, with hundreds of boats available for charter—with or without crew—as well as numerous opportunities for day sails.

**The Moorings** (✉ 1305 U.S. 19 S, Suite 402, Clearwater, FL 34624, ☎ 800/535–7289), based in Road Town, is the largest operator in the Caribbean and offers sailboats in a wide range of sizes, with or without crew. **Virgin Island Sailing** (✉ Box 146, Road Town, Tortola, B.V.I., ☎ 800/382–9666), a top brokerage house, is who to contact for help in chartering a boat and crew for an extended trip.

### Scuba Diving and Snorkeling

Divers and snorkelers will find sites at Brewer's Bay and Frenchman's Cay on Tortola. In addition to renting equipment, many of the dive operators here also offer instruction, hotel-dive packages, and snorkeling excursions. Contact **Baskin-in-the-Sun** (⊠ Box 108, Road Harbour, ☎ 809/494–2858 or 800/233–7938) or **Underwater Safaris Ltd.** (⊠ Box 139, Road Town, ☎ 809/494–3235 or 800/537–7032).

### Sportfishing
A number of companies can transport and outfit you for fishing. On Tortola try **Miss Robbie Charter Fishing** (⊠ Fort Burt Marina, ☎ 809/494–3193).

### Tennis
Several resorts on Tortola have tennis courts for guests' use. For a fee, nonguests may use courts at **Prospect Reef** (⊠ Road Town, ☎ 809/494–3311).

## Shopping

The British Virgins are not known as a shopping haven, but there are interesting finds, particularly artwork. Don't be put off by an informal shop entrance. Some of the best finds in the B.V.I. lie behind a shop-worn door.

### Shopping Districts
Most of the shops and boutiques on Tortola are clustered on and off Road Town's **Main Street** and at **Wickham's Cay** shopping area, adjacent to the Marina. There is also an ever-growing group of art, jewelry, clothing, and souvenir stores at **Soper's Hole** on Tortola's West End.

### Specialty Stores
ART AND ANTIQUES

**Caribbean Fine Arts Ltd.** (⊠ Main St., Road Town, ☎ 809/494–4240) is a small shop that carries a wide range of Caribbean art, including original watercolors, oils, and acrylics, as well as signed prints, limited-edition serigraphs, and turn-of-the-century sepia photographs. **Collector's Corner** (⊠ Columbus Centre, Wickham's Cay, ☎ 809/494–3550) carries antique maps, watercolors by local artists, gold and silver jewelry, coral, and larimar, a pale blue Caribbean gemstone. **Courtyard Gallery** (⊠ Main St., Road Town, no phone) is worth visiting for its exclusive Carinia Collection, delicate crushed-coral sculptures created on the premises and depicting hummingbirds, angelfish, pelicans, and flowers. **Islands Treasures** (⊠ Soper's Hole Marina, ☎ 809/495–4787) is the place to find watercolors, paintings, pottery, sculpture, model ships, coffee-table books on the Caribbean, and prints of Caribbean maps and scenes. **Sunny Caribbee Art Gallery** (⊠ Main St., Road Town, ☎ 809/494–2178) has one of the largest displays of paintings in the Caribbean, along with a sizable selection of island spices and sauces and bath products made from natural ingredients.

CLOTHING

**Bonker's Gallery** (⊠ Main St., Road Town, ☎ 809/494–2535) is a trendy shop that carries resort wear for women, including cotton and washable-silk tops and bottoms and cover-ups. There is also a small collection of pants and shirts for men. **Sea Urchin** (⊠ Columbus Centre, Road Town, ☎ 809/494–2044; Waterfront Dr., Road Town, ☎ 809/494–6234; Soper's Hole Marina, ☎ 809/495–4850) has a great selection of island-living designs: print shirts and shorts, slinky swimsuits, sandals, and T-shirts, plus books and maps of the B.V.I. **Violet's** (⊠ Wickham's Cay I, ☎ 809/494–6398) stocks beautiful silk lingerie and a small line of designer dresses.

FOOD AND DRINK

**Ample Hamper** (⊠ Village Cay Marina, Wickham's Cay, ☎ 809/494–2494; Soper's Hole Marina, ☎ 809/495–4684) sells cheeses, wines, fresh fruits, and canned goods from the United Kingdom and the United States. It will provision yachts and rental villas. **Fort Wine Gourmet** (⊠ Main St., Road Town, ☎ 809/494–3036), a café-cum-store, carries a remarkably sophisticated selection of gourmet items and fine wines, including Petrossian caviars and Hediard goods from France. **Gourmet Galley** (⊠ Wickham's Cay II, Road Town, ☎ 809/494–6999) stocks a fine selection of wines, cheeses, and fresh fruits and vegetables and provides full provisioning for yachtspeople and villa renters.

### GIFTS

**J. R. O'Neal, Ltd.** (⊠ Main St., Road Town, ☎ 809/494–2292) carries fine crystal, Royal Worcester china, a wonderful selection of hand-painted Italian dishes, hand-blown Mexican glassware, ceramic housewares from Spain, and woven rugs and tablecloths from India. **Pink Pineapple** (⊠ Prospect Reef Resort, ☎ 809/494–3311) has a remarkable array of gift items, from wearable artwork and hand-painted jewelry to watercolors and batik fabric. **Pusser's Company Store** (⊠ Main St. and Waterfront Rd., Road Town, ☎ 809/494–2467; Soper's Hole Marina, ☎ 809/495–4603) draws crowds with its selection of nautical memorabilia, an entire line of clothes and gift items bearing the Pusser's logo, and handsome decorator bottles of Pusser's rum. **Sunny Caribbee Herb and Spice Company** (⊠ Main St., Road Town, ☎ 809/494–2178), located in a brightly painted West Indian house, packages its own herbs, teas, coffees, herb vinegars, hot sauces, natural soaps, skin and suntan lotions, Caribbean art, and hand-painted decorative accessories. A small branch of this store is located at the Skyworld restaurant (☞ Dining, *above*). **Turtle Dove Boutique** (⊠ Flemming St., Road Town, ☎ 809/494–3611) is among the best in the B.V.I. for French perfume, international swimwear, and silk dresses, as well as gifts and accessories for the home.

### JEWELRY

**Felix Gold and Silver Ltd.** (⊠ Main St., Road Town, ☎ 809/494–2406) may not be much to look at from the outside, but inside jewelers handcraft exceptionally fine jewelry. Choose from island or other themes, or have something custom made; in some cases, the shop will make it for you within 72 hours. **Samarkand** (⊠ Main St., Road Town, ☎ 809/494–6415) specializes in handmade gold and silver pendants, earrings, bracelets, and pins.

### LOCAL CRAFTS

**Caribbean Handprints** (⊠ Main St., Road Town, ☎ 809/494–3717) creates silk-screened fabrics, which you can buy by the yard or fashioned into dresses, shirts, pants, bathrobes, beach cover-ups, and beach bags.

### TEXTILES

**Zenaida** (⊠ Frenchman's Cay, ☎ 809/495-4867) displays the fabric finds of Argentinean Vivian Jenik Helm, who travels through South America, Africa, and India in search of batiks, hand-painted and hand-blocked fabrics, and interesting weaves. You can choose from her fabulous pareus and wall hangings, unusual bags, belts, sarongs, scarves, and ethnic jewelry.

## Nightlife

Check the weekly *Limin' Times* for current schedules.

**Bomba's Shack** (⊠ Apple Bay, ☎ 809/495–4148) draws crowds to hear live bands on Sunday, Wednesday, and every full moon. **Jolly Rodger** (⊠ West End, ☎ 809/495–4559) has live music Friday and Saturday. **Pusser's Landing** (⊠ Soper's Hole, ☎ 809/494–4554) hosts live bands from Thursday through Sunday. **Quito's Gazebo** (⊠ Cane Garden Bay, ☎ 809/495–4837) is where B.V.I. recording star Quito Rhymer sings his own island ballads Sunday, Tuesday, Thursday, and Friday nights, starting at 8:30. **Sebastian's** (✉ Apple Bay, ☎ 809/495–4214) is where to go on Saturday and Sunday for live music. **Stanley's Welcome Bar** (✉ Cane Garden Bay, ☎ 809/495–4520) gets rowdy when crews stop by to party.

## Exploring Tortola

The drives on Tortola are dramatic, with dizzying roller-coaster dips and climbs and glorious views. Leave plenty of time to negotiate the hilly roads and drink in the irresistible vistas at nearly every hairpin turn. Distractions are the real danger here, from the glittering mosaic of azure sea, white skies, and emerald islets to the ambling cattle and grazing goats roadside.

*Numbers in the margin correspond to points of interest on the Tortola map.*

### SIGHTS TO SEE

**❺ Belmont Point.** This sugar-loaf promontory has been described as "a giant, green gumdrop." It's at the west end of **Long Bay**, a mile-long stretch of white sand, home to the Long Bay Beach Resort, one of Tortola's more appealing resorts. The large island visible in the distance is Jost Van Dyke.

NEED A BREAK?
After you've had a swim or a walk on the beach, stop at the beach restaurant at **Long Bay Beach Resort** (☎ 809/495–4252), where you can dine inside in an old sugar mill or outside around the beachfront pool, which you are welcome to swim in if you dine there.

**❻ Bomba's Shack.** One of the Caribbean's most famous bars is on the north shore of Tortola, and it's worth a look even if you generally skip bars. The shack, which took a beating from Hurricane Luis in 1995, has been rebuilt, and is festooned with everything from license plates to crepe-paper leis to colorful graffiti. It's hard to believe that this ramshackle place is one of the liveliest nightspots on Tortola and home of the famous Bomba Shack "Full Moon" party. Every full moon, bands play here all night long and people flock here from all over Tortola and from other islands. ✉ *North Coast Rd.,* ☎ *809/495–4148.* ☾ *Daily 11-11 or later.*

**❼ Cane Garden Bay.** Its crystalline water and silky stretch of sand make this enticing beach one of Tortola's most popular getaways. Its existence is no secret, however, and it can get crowded, especially when cruise ships are in Road Harbour.

**❸ Fort Recovery.** The unrestored ruins of this 17th-century Dutch fort, 30 feet in diameter, sit amidst a profusion of tropical greenery on the grounds of Fort Recovery villas. There are no guided tours, but the public is welcome to stop by. ✉ *Waterfront Dr.,* ☎ *809/485–4467.* ☐ *Free.*

**❹ Frenchman's Cay.** On this little island, connected by a causeway to Tortola's West End, there's a marina and a captivating complex of pastel-hued West Indian–style buildings with shady second-floor balconies, colonnaded arcades, shuttered windows, and gingerbread trim that showcase art galleries, boutiques, and restaurants. **Pusser's Landing** is a lively place where you can stop for a cold drink (many are made with Pusser's famous rum) and a sandwich and watch the boats come and go from the harbor.

**❽ Queen Elizabeth II Bridge.** This narrow bridge connects Tortola and Beef Island, and you'll have to pay a toll to cross (50¢ for passenger cars, $1 for vans and trucks). It's worth it if only for the sight of the toll taker extending a tin can attached to the end of a board through your car window to collect the fee.

❶ **Road Town.** The laid-back capital of the British Virgin Islands is on the south coast of Tortola and looks out over Road Town Harbour. **Main Street** and the **waterfront** have shops and traditional pastel-painted West Indian buildings with high-pitched, corrugated tin roofs, bright shutters, and delicate fretwork trim.

**Sir Olva Georges Square,** across from the ferry dock and customs office, is open to the harbor on its eastern side, and a handful of Tortolans can generally be found enjoying the breeze that sweeps in from the water here. The General Post Office is at the opposite end of the square. The hands of the clock atop this building permanently point to 10 minutes to 5, rather appropriate in this drowsy town, where time does seem to be standing still.

Founded in 1983, the **British Virgin Islands Folk Museum** has a large collection of artifacts from the Arawak Indians, some of the early settlers of the islands. Of particular interest are the triangular stones called *zemis,* which depict the Arawak gods Julihu and Yuccahu. The museum also has a display of a number of bottles, bowls, and plates salvaged from the wreck of the RMS *Rhone,* a British mail ship sunk off Salt Island in a hurricane in 1867. ⊠ *Main St., no phone.* 🎫 *Free.* ☉ *Mon., Tues., Thurs., Fri. 10–4; Sat. 10–1, though hrs may vary.*

**Wickham's Cay** provides broad views of the wide harbor, home of countless sailing vessels and yachts and a base of the well-known yacht-chartering enterprise, the Moorings. Along with banks, a post office, and stores and boutiques, there's also a **B.V.I. Tourist Board** office here that can provide sightseeing brochures and the latest information on everything from taxi rates to ferry boat schedules. ⊠ *Wickham's Cay I,* ☎ *809/494–3134.* ☉ *Mon.–Fri. 9–5.*

The 2.8-acre **J. R. O'Neal Botanic Gardens** showcases lush gardens of tropical plant life. There are sections devoted to prickly cacti and succulents, hothouses for ferns and orchids, gardens of medicinal herbs, plants that bloom around Christmas, and plants and trees indigenous to the seashore. ⊠ *Station Ave.,* ☎ *809/494–4557.* 🎫 *Free.* ☉ *Mon.–Sat. 8–4, Sun. noon–5.*

The most intact historic ruin on Tortola, **Fort Burt** was built by the Dutch in the early 17th century to safeguard Road Town Harbour. It sits on a hill on the western edge of town and is now the site of a small hotel and restaurant. The foundations and magazine remain, and the structure offers a commanding view of Road Town. ⊠ *Waterfront Dr., no phone.* 🎫 *Free.* ☉ *Daily, dawn–dusk.*

❷ **Sage Mountain National Park.** At 1,716 feet, Tortola's Sage Mountain is the highest peak in the B.V.I. The best unobstructed views up here are from the top. From the parking area, a trail will lead you in a loop not only to the peak itself but also to the island's small rain forest, sometimes shrouded in mist. Most of the island's forest was cut down over the centuries to clear land for sugarcane, cotton, and other crops, as well as pastureland and timber. But in 1964 this park was established to preserve the remaining rain forest. Up here you can see mahogany trees, white cedars, mountain guavas, elephant-ear vines, mamey trees, and giant bulletwoods, to say nothing of such birds as mountain doves and thrushes. Take a taxi from Road Town or drive up Joe's Hill Road and make a left onto Ridge Road toward Chalwell and Doty villages.

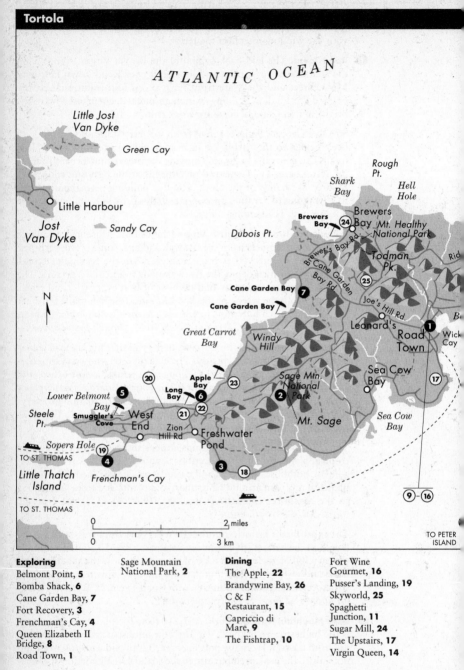

*ATLANTIC OCEAN*

Little Jost
Van Dyke

Green Cay

Little Harbour

Jost
Van Dyke          Sandy Cay          Dubois Pt.

Rough
Pt.

Shark
Bay          Hell
Hole

Brewers
Bay ⓐ          Brewers
Bay   Mt. Healthy
National Park

Cane Garden Bay ⑦

Cane Garden Bay

Todman
Pk.

Rid

㉕

Joe's Hill Rd.

Great Carrot
Bay          Windy
Hill          Leonard's

Road
Town ①          Wick
Cay

Apple
Bay
⑥          ㉓          Sage Mtn.
National
Park
②          Sea Cow
Bay

㉖

Long
Bay

Lower Belmont
Bay ⑤

Smuggler's
Cove          West
End          ㉑          ㉒

Steele
Pt.          Zion
Hill Rd.          Freshwater
Pond          Mt. Sage          Sea Cow
Bay

Sopers Hole          ⑲

TO ST. THOMAS          ④          ③          ⑱          ⑰

Little Thatch
Island          Frenchman's Cay          ⑨ ⑯

TO ST. THOMAS

N

0          2 miles
0          3 km

TO PETER
ISLAND

**Exploring**
Belmont Point, **5**
Bomba Shack, **6**
Cane Garden Bay, **7**
Fort Recovery, **3**
Frenchman's Cay, **4**
Queen Elizabeth II
Bridge, **8**
Road Town, **1**

Sage Mountain
National Park, **2**

**Dining**
The Apple, **22**
Brandywine Bay, **26**
C & F
Restaurant, **15**
Capriccio di
Mare, **9**
The Fishtrap, **10**

Fort Wine
Gourmet, **16**
Pusser's Landing, **19**
Skyworld, **25**
Spaghetti
Junction, **11**
Sugar Mill, **24**
The Upstairs, **17**
Virgin Queen, **14**

**KEY**

🚢 Ferry

❶ Exploring Sites

⑨ Hotels and Restaurants

**Lodging**

Brewer's Bay
Campground, **24**

Fort Recovery, **18**

Long Bay Beach
Resort, **20**

Moorings-Mariner
Inn, **12**

Prospect Reef
Resort, **17**

Sebastian's on the
Beach, **21**

Sugar Mill Hotel, **23**

Treasure Isle
Hotel, **13**

The road dead-ends at the park. ⊠ *Ridge Rd., no phone (contact the tourist office for information).* ⊠ *Free.*

# VIRGIN GORDA

## Lodging

For price information on hotels, *see* the price chart *in* the Lodging section of Tortola, *above.*

**$$$$**  ⭐ 🏨 **Biras Creek Hotel.** A longtime guest purchased Biras Creek in 1995 and turned it into one of the classiest resorts in the B.V.I. Virtually everything is brand new: The bedroom/living room units were gutted and now have handsome Mexican tile floors, louvered windows, comfortable furniture, and expanded decks; the pool was retiled; and the tennis courts were replaced. Even the beach was redone: Tons of sand were added to the formerly grassy beach, and majestic palm trees were planted. The new general manager, Jamie Holmes, brings years of Caribbean hotel experience to this secluded 150-acre hideaway. The hilltop open-air bar and restaurant area is made of stonework and offers stunning views of North Sound. ⊠ *Box 54, North Sound,* ☎ *809/494–3555,* �℻ *809/494–3557. 34 rooms. Restaurant, bar, pool, 2 lighted tennis courts, hiking trails, 2 beaches, snorkeling, boating, marina, biking trails. AE, MC, V. FAP.*

**$$$$**  🏨 **Bitter End Yacht Club and Marina.** Stretching along the coastline of North Sound, the BEYC enjoys panoramic views of the sound, Leverick Bay, and nearby islands. Accommodations range from exceptionally comfortable and appealing hillside or beachfront villas and chalets to live-aboard yachts. Also inviting about this property is the friendly, unpretentious welcome the staff extends to all its guests. The resort organizes daily snorkeling and diving trips to nearby reefs, windsurfing lessons, and excursions to local attractions, but the BEYC is most touted for its Nick Trotter Sailing School. Judged by many to offer the best sailing instruction in the Caribbean, the school helps both seasoned salts and beginners sharpen their skills. When the sun goes down, the festivities continue at either the elegant Carvery, where themed buffets are served on special occasions, or at the Clubhouse, an open-air restaurant overlooking the sound. The hotel's character is one of the liveliest and most convivial in the B.V.I. ⊠ *Box 46, North Sound,* ☎ *809/494–2746,* ⍰ *809/494–3557. 100 rooms. 2 restaurants, bar, pool, beach, marina. AE, MC, V. FAP.*

**$$$$**  ⭐ 🏨 **Little Dix Bay.** The luxury resort that first set the standards for understated elegance in the B.V.I. has been a Rosewood Resort since 1993 and refurbishing continues. Rooms have telephones (although you can request to have yours removed) and air-conditioning has been added to many rooms. Dining in the open, peak-roofed Pavilion restaurant is a memorable experience. There are beautifully manicured lawns, the reef-protected beach is long and silken, and tennis, water sports, and bicycling are included in the rate. The newer, garden rooms can be noisy. Nonetheless, the accommodations are superb, the service is thoughtful and attentive, and the setting is unforgettable. ⊠ *Box 70,* ☎ *809/495–5555,* ⍰ *809/495–5661. 102 rooms. 3 restaurants, 2 bars, 7 tennis courts, beach, snorkeling, waterskiing, sailing, marina, bicycles, boutique. AE, MC, V. EP, MAP, FAP.*

**$$**  🏨 **Guavaberry Spring Bay Vacation Homes.** These unusual hexagonal cottages are perched on stilts. You'll feel like you're in a tree house, amid the swaying branches and chirping birds. One- and two-bedroom units are situated on a hill, a short walk from a tamarind-shaded beach and not far from the mammoth boulders and cool basins of the famed

Baths. ⊠ *Box 20, Virgin Gorda,* ☎ *809/495–5227,* FAX *809/495–7367. 16 units. Commissary, beach. No credit cards. EP.*

**$$**   🏨 **Leverick Bay Resort.** The 16 hillside rooms of this small hotel are decorated in pastels and hung with original artwork. All rooms have refrigerators, balconies, and lovely views of North Sound. Four two-bedroom condos are also available. A Spanish colonial–style main building houses a restaurant operated by Pusser's of Tortola. ⊠ *Box 63,* ☎ *809/495–7421,* FAX *809/495–7367. 20 rooms. Restaurant, bar, commissary, pool, beauty salon, beach, dive shop, snorkeling, marina, shops, coin laundry. AE, D, MC, V. EP.*

**$$**   🏨 **Olde Yard Inn.** Owners Charlie Williams and Carol Kaufman have
★   cultivated a refreshingly unique atmosphere at this quiet retreat just outside Spanish Town. Classical music plays in the small bar; a large and varied collection of books lines the walls of the octagonal library cottage. The restaurant's French-accented menu is lovingly prepared and served with style in the high-ceilinged dining rooms. The guest rooms are cozy and simply furnished. There's a large pool, a lunch restaurant that overlooks the pool, and a health club where you can work out, take exercise classes, and have massages. The inn is not on the beach; Savannah Bay and Pond Bay are a 20-minute walk away. You may want to request one of the air-conditioned rooms; the hotel's location in the Valley means trade winds are less noticeable here. ⊠ *Box 26, Spanish Town,* ☎ *809/495–5544,* FAX *809/495–5986. 14 rooms. Restaurant, bar, pool, health club, library. AE, MC, V. EP, MAP.*

**$**   🏨 **The Wheelhouse.** You won't find any frills at this hotel, but it certainly is easy on the pocketbook, and it's conveniently close to the Virgin Gorda marina and shopping center. The cinder-block building has rooms that are air-conditioned and decorated with pastel print bedspreads and curtains. However, the rooms are small and the restaurant and bar can get noisy. ⊠ *Box 66,* ☎ *809/495–5230. 12 rooms. Restaurant, bar, air-conditioning. AE, MC, V. CP.*

## Dining

For price information on restaurants, *see* the price chart in the Dining section of Tortola, *above.*

**$$$**   ✕ **Biras Creek.** This hilltop restaurant, with its signature turret roof,
★   is one of the most stunning settings for a meal in all of the B.V.I. Broad stairs lead to an open-air lounge and restaurant with beautiful views of North Sound. The Biras Creek Resort was taken over in 1995 by a longtime guest, who built a new kitchen and hired several new chefs. The menu is still being refined, but the dining experience promises to match the view. ⊠ *North Sound,* ☎ *809/494–3555. Reservations essential. AE, MC, V.*

**$$$**   ✕ **Drake's Anchorage.** You come by boat (provided free) to this serene and romantic candlelit spot right at the water's edge. Dine on lobster *dorado* (encrusted with bananas and bread crumbs), rack of lamb, or steak au poivre. ⊠ *North Sound,* ☎ *809/494–2252. Reservations essential. AE, MC, V.*

**$$$**   ✕ **Olde Yard Inn.** Dinner here is a civilized and charming affair. The intimate dining room is suffused with gentle classical melodies and the scent of herbs. A cedar roof covers the breezy, open-air room decorated with old-style Caribbean charm. The French-accented cuisine includes lamb chops with mango chutney, chicken breast in a rum cream sauce, garlic shrimp, grilled local fish and lobster, and steaks. For great chili, burgers, or tortellini salad at lunch, stop by the poolside **Sip and Dip Grill.** ⊠ *The Valley, north of the marina,* ☎ *809/495–5544. AE, MC, V.*

$$ ✕ **Bath and Turtle.** You can really sit back and relax at this informal
★ patio tavern with its friendly staff. Choose from the simple menu's burg-
ers, well-stuffed sandwiches, pizzas, pasta dishes, and daily specials.
Live entertainment is presented on Wednesday and Sunday nights. ⊠
*Virgin Gorda Yacht Harbour,* ☎ *809/495–5239. MC, V.*

$–$$ ✕ **Crab Hole.** Callaloo soup, saltfish, stewed goat, rice and peas, green
bananas, curried chicken roti, and other West Indian specialties are the
draw at this homey hangout. ⊠ *The Valley,* ☎ *809/495–5307. No credit
cards.*

$–$$ ✕ **Mad Dog's.** Piña coladas are the specialty at this breezy bar just
outside of The Baths. The all-day menu includes BLTs, hot dogs, and
burgers. ✕ *The Valley,* ☎ *809/495–5830. Reservations not accepted.
MC, V.*

## Beaches

The best beaches are most easily reached by water, although they are
accessible on foot, usually after a moderately strenuous hike of 10 to
15 minutes.

**Bercher's Beach** and its windswept surf is reached on foot from Biras
Creek or Bitter End. **The Crawl,** north of The Baths, is a good place to
experience swimming or snorkeling among unique boulder formations—a must for visitors to Virgin Gorda. Although The Baths are
usually crowded, The Crawl—just a short walk or swim from The
Baths—is a quieter spot to catch some rays. **Deep Bay,** a calm, well-
protected swimming beach, is reached by footpaths from Bitter End
and foot and bike paths from Biras Creek. **Hay Point Beach,** on
Mosquito Island, is a broad band of white sand accessible only by boat
or by path from the dock at Drake's Anchorage resort. **Leverick Bay**
is a small, busy beach-cum-marina that fronts a resort restaurant and
pool. Don't come here to be alone or to jog but do come if you want
a lively little place and a break from the island's noble quiet. The view
of Prickly Pear Island is an added plus, and there's a dive facility right
here to motor you out to beautiful Eustatia Reef just across North Sound.
**Long Bay,** near Virgin Gorda's northern tip, past the Diamond Beach
Club, is worth visiting for the snorkeling (Little Dix Bay resort has outings here). The drive takes about half an hour after the turnoff from
North Sound Road; part of the route is dirt road. **Savannah Bay** is a
wonderfully private beach close to Black Rock. It may not always be
completely deserted, but it's a lovely long stretch of white sand. **Spring
Bay** beach is a gem, and is easily reached from The Baths on foot or
by swimming. It is less crowded than The Baths, and also has unique
boulder formations that draw snorkelers. **Vixen Point Beach,** on Prickly
Pear Island, is a calm swimming beach.

## Outdoor Activities and Sports

### Sailboarding
**Nick Trotter Sailing School** (⊠ Bitter End Yacht Club, North Sound,
☎ 809/494–2746) has beginner and advanced courses.

### Scuba Diving and Snorkeling
For snorkelers, perhaps the most popular spot in the B.V.I. is at the
famed Baths on Virgin Gorda. Dive and snorkel sites can be found near
the North Sound area of Virgin Gorda. Contact **Dive BVI** (⊠ Virgin
Gorda Yacht Harbour, ☎ 809/495–5513 or 800/848–7078).

### Sportfishing
On Virgin Gorda contact **Captain Dale** (☎ 809/495–5225), who operates the 38-foot Bertram *Classic* out of Biras Creek.

**Tennis**

Nonguests can use the courts at **Biras Creek** (☎ 809/494–3555) for a fee.

# Shopping

## Shopping Districts

On Virgin Gorda there is a cluster of shops at the bustling yacht harbor in Spanish Town and also boutiques located within the individual hotel complexes. Several of the best are at **Little Dix Bay, Bitter End Yacht Club, Biras Creek,** and **Olde Yard Inn.** There is also a small collection of shops at Leverick Bay.

## Specialty Stores

### CLOTHING

**Next Wave** (✉ Virgin Gorda Yacht Harbour, ☎ 809/495–5623) has bathing suits, T-shirts, and canvas tote bags. **Pelican's Pouch Boutique** (✉ Virgin Gorda Yacht Harbour, ☎ 809/495–5599) has a large selection of swimsuits plus cover-ups, beach hats, T-shirts, and accessories.

### FOOD AND DRINK

**Bitter End's Emporium** (✉ Bitter End Yacht Club, North Sound, ☎ 809/494–2745) is a great place to stop for such edible treats as local fruits, bakery goods, and cheeses. **Virgin Island Bakery** (✉ Virgin Gorda Yacht Harbour, no phone) is the place to stop for freshly baked loaves, rolls, muffins, and cookies, and sandwiches and sodas to go. You get a whiff of the fresh breads before you even get in the door.

### GIFTS

**Palm Tree Gallery** (✉ Leverick Bay, ☎ 809/495–7421) has an excellent selection of books about the B.V.I., good maps, handcrafted jewelry, and local artwork. **Pusser's Company Store** (✉ Leverick Bay, ☎ 809/495–7369) sells its famous rum, as well as various sundries with the Pusser's logo.

### LOCAL CRAFTS

**Tropical Gift Collections** (✉ Top of The Baths Shops, ☎ 809/495–5374) sells locally made spices, hats, handbags, and pottery. **Virgin Gorda Craft Shop** (✉ Virgin Gorda Yacht Harbour, ☎ 809/495–5137) displays the work of local artists. Choose among West Indian jewelry and crafts styled in straw, shells, and other local materials, or pick up clothing and paintings by Caribbean artists.

# Nightlife

Consult the *Limin' Times,* which is published weekly, for current schedules.

**Andy's Chateau de Pirate** (✉ Fischer's Cove Beach Hotel, The Valley, ☎ 809/495–5252) has live music and dancing on the weekends. **Bath and Turtle** (✉ Virgin Gorda Yacht Harbour, ☎ 809/495–5239) hosts local bands Wednesday and Sunday evenings.

# Exploring Virgin Gorda

For great views of nearby islands and of Virgin Gorda's own eccentric shape, just drive or take a taxi on North Sound Road, which runs across Virgin Gorda's hilly center. You'll notice nary a dwelling nor sign of mundane civilization up here, only a green mountain slope on your left (if you're driving north) and a spectacular view down to South Sound on the right. From here, too, you can also look back and get a wonderful sense of Virgin Gorda's stringy, crooked shape: Back there, looking flat and almost like a separate island, is the Valley. Because of this shape, Virgin Gorda is one of those places where you can get a bird's-eye (or map's-eye) view of things from right inside your car.

*Numbers in the margin correspond to points of interest on the Virgin Gorda map.*

SIGHTS TO SEE

**❷ The Baths.** This is Virgin Gorda's most celebrated site. Giant boulders, brought to the surface eons ago by a vast volcanic eruption, are scattered about the beach and in the water. Some are almost as large as small houses and form remarkable grottoes. Climb between these rocks to swim in the many pools. Early morning and late afternoon are the best times to visit, since the Baths and the beach here are usually crowded with cruise-ship passengers and day-trippers visiting from Tortola. (If it's privacy you crave, follow the shore north for a few hundred yards to reach several quieter bays—Spring, the Crawl, Little Trunk, and Valley Trunk—or head south to Devil's Bay. These beaches have the same giant boulders as those found at the Baths.) It's a 35-yard walk from the parking lot to the beach. ⊠ *Lee Rd., no phone.* 🎫 *Free.*

**❹ Black Rock.** A thin neck of land connecting Virgin Gorda's southern extension to the larger northern half is marked by two pristine stretches of sand, **Savannah Bay** and **Pond Bay.** The view from this scenic elbow, called Black Rock, is of the Sir Francis Drake Channel to the northeast and the Caribbean Sea to the southwest.

**❸ Copper Mine Point.** Here you will discover a tall, stone shaft silhouetted against the sky and a small stone structure overlooking the sea. These are the ruins of a copper mine established here 400 years ago and worked first by the Spanish, then by English miners until the early 20th century. This is one of the few places in the B.V.I. where you won't see islands along the horizon. ⊠ *Copper Mine Rd., no phone.* 🎫 *Free.*

**❺ Leverick Bay. Leverick Bay Resort** is here, plus a cozy beach and marina, a restaurant, a cluster of shops, and some luxurious hillside villas to rent. This is also where a launch picks up passengers for Drake's Anchorage, a resort on nearby **Mosquito Island.** You can view the island from the top of one of the narrow hillside roads; the hunk of land straight ahead is **Prickly Pear,** which has been named a national park to protect it from development. At the neck of land to your right is **Biras Creek Hotel,** and around the bend to the north of that you'll see the Danish-roof building of the **Bitter End Yacht Club and Marina.** Between the Bitter End and Prickly Pear you should be able to make out **Saba Rock,** home of one of the Caribbean's best-known diving entrepreneurs, Bert Kilbride—a colorful character who knows where all the wrecks are and who is recognized and commissioned by the queen of England as Honorary Keeper of the Wrecks. That magical color change in the sea near Prickly Pear reveals **Eustatia Sound** and its extensive reef. Beyond that are Horseshoe Reef, Necker Island, and the flat coral island of Anegada some 20 miles north, where most of those wrecks are and where bareboaters are not permitted to sail because of the perilous reefs. But you can easily take a boat to Biras Creek, the Bitter End, or Drake's Anchorage. In fact, that's the only way you can get there.

**❶ Spanish Town.** Virgin Gorda's main settlement, located on the island's southern wing, is a peaceful village so tiny that it barely qualifies as a town at all. Also known as the Valley, Spanish Town is home to a marina, a small cluster of shops, and a couple of car-rental agencies. Just north of town is the ferry slip. At the **Virgin Gorda Yacht Harbour** you can enjoy a stroll along the dock front or do a little browsing in the shops there.

**⑤ Virgin Gorda Peak National Park.** A small sign on North Sound Road marks the trail up to the 265-acre National Park and the island's summit at 1,359 feet. (Sometimes the sign is missing, so keep your eyes open for a set of stairs that disappears into the trees.) It's about a 15-minute hike up to a small clearing, where you can climb a ladder to the platform of a wood observation tower. If you're keen for some woodsy exercise or just want to stretch your legs, go for it. Unfortunately, the view at the top is somewhat tree-obstructed. ⊠ *North Sound Rd., no phone.* ☎ *Free.*

# OUTLYING ISLANDS

## Lodging

For price information on hotels, *see* the price chart *in* the Lodging section of Tortola, *above.*

### Anegada

**$$$** 🏨 **Anegada Reef Hotel.** This hotel is away from it all in every sense of the phrase: It's the only hotel on Anegada, and the island itself is off the beaten path. Rooms are motel-like and rustic, but people come here for peace rather than luxury. Snorkeling and diving are as good here as anywhere else in the islands. Bonefishing in the flats is a favorite activity, and deep-sea fishing trips can be arranged. If you favor true laid-back living and absolutely no schedules, this is the spot for you. ⊠ *Anegada,* ☎ *809/495–8002,* FAX *809/495–9362. 16 rooms. Restaurant, bar, beach, dive shop, snorkeling, gift shop. MC, V. FAP.*

### Guana Island

**$$$$** 🏨 **Guana Island Club.** Fifteen extremely comfortable guest rooms, each with its own living room area, are spread among seven houses scattered along the top of a hillside on this totally private island. The units are simply decorated in Caribbean style, with rattan furniture and ceiling fans, and each has a porch. The island's many trails make it a favorite spot for hikers, there are great beaches to walk to, and it's a bird-watching paradise. ⊠ *Box 32, Road Town, Tortola,* ☎ *809/494–2354,* FAX *914/967–8048. 15 rooms. Restaurant (open to guests of the hotel only), fans, 2 tennis courts, croquet, hiking, wildlife sanctuary, beach, snorkeling, boating. No credit cards. FAP.*

### Jost Van Dyke

**$$** 🏨 **Sandcastle.** This tiny, four-cottage hideaway (with a staff of five) is on a half mile of white beach on remote White Bay. There's "nothing" to do here, except maybe snooze in a hammock, read, gaze, walk, swim, rest, and savor sophisticated cuisine by candlelight. Arrangements can be made for diving, sailing, and sportfishing trips. ⊠ *White Bay,* ☎ *809/775–5262,* FAX *809/775–5262. 4 cottages. Restaurant, bar, beach. No credit cards. FAP.*

**$$** 🏨 **Sandy Ground Estates.** Tucked into the foliage along the edge of one of Jost Van Dyke's East End beaches is this collection of eight privately owned one- and two-bedroom houses. Each one is architecturally different, and interiors range from spartan to stylish. Kitchens are fully equipped and can be pre-stocked (you'll want to do this, since supplies are limited on the island), and there are four very casual restaurants within walking distance. ⊠ *Sandy Ground, East End of Jost Van Dyke,* ☎ *809/495–3391. 8 1- and 2-bedroom houses. Kitchens, beach. No credit cards. EP.*

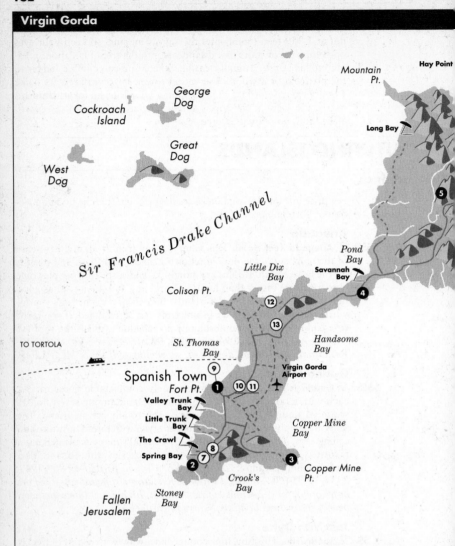

**Exploring**
The Baths, **2**
Black Rock, **4**
Copper Mine Point, **3**
Leverick Bay, **6**
Spanish Town, **1**
Virgin Gorda Peak
National Park, **5**

**Dining**
Bath and Turtle, **9**
Biras Creek, **16**
Crab Hole, **10**
Drake's
Anchorage, **14**
Mad Dog's, **7**
Olde Yard Inn, **13**

**Lodging**
Biras Creek, **16**
Bitter End Yacht Club
and Marina, **17**
Guavaberry Spring
Bay Vacation
Homes, **8**
Leverick Bay
Resort, **15**

Little Dix Bay, **12**
Olde Yard Inn, **13**
The Wheelhouse, **11**

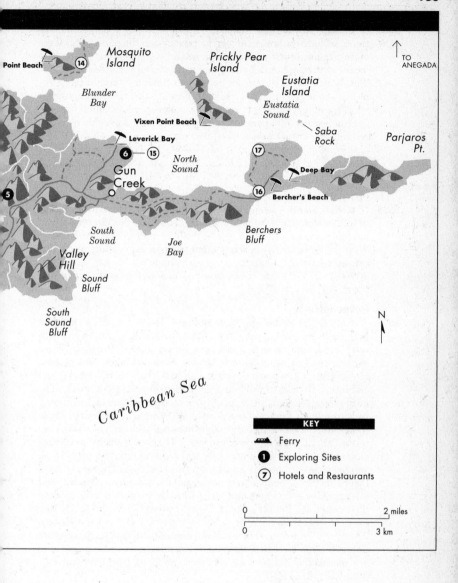

Point Beach

(14)

Mosquito
Island

Prickly Pear
Island

Eustatia
Island

TO
ANEGADA

Blunder
Bay

Eustatia
Sound

Saba
Rock

Parjaros
Pt.

Vixen Point Beach

Leverick Bay

(6)—(15)

North
Sound

(17)

Gun
Creek

(16)

Deep Bay

Bercher's Beach

(5)

South
Sound

Joe
Bay

Berchers
Bluff

Valley
Hill

Sound
Bluff

South
Sound
Bluff

N

Caribbean Sea

**KEY**

🚢 Ferry

❶ Exploring Sites

⑦ Hotels and Restaurants

0   2 miles

0   3 km

## Mosquito Island

**$$$$** ⬛ **Drake's Anchorage.** Manager Albert Wheatley ensures that this
★ small, secluded getaway offers true privacy and the pampering of the
more elegant resorts without the formality. Changing for dinner here
means switching from a bathing suit to comfortable cottons. The three
West Indian–style, waterfront bungalows contain 10 comfortably furnished rooms, including two suites. There are also two fully equipped
villas for rent. There are hiking trails, water-sports facilities, four delightful beaches with hammocks here and there, and a highly regarded
restaurant—a truly peaceful, rejuvenating experience. ⊠ *Box 2510,
North Sound, Virgin Gorda,* ☎ FAX *809/494–2254 or* ☎ *800/624–6651.
10 rooms in 3 bungalows, 2 villas. Restaurant, bar, hiking, 4 beaches,
snorkeling, boating, gift shop. AE, MC, V. FAP.*

## Necker Island

**$$$$** ⬛ **Necker Island.** You and 19 of your closest friends can rent this whole
island. In fact, that's the only way you can stay at this ultraexpensive,
ultrachic getaway, vacation spot of the likes of Princess Di and Oprah
Winfrey. There are five beaches, many walks, a tennis court, and a luxurious villa with 20 spacious guest rooms. ⊠ *Necker Island,* ☎
*809/494–2757. Villa. Tennis court, 5 beaches, several sportfishing
boats. AE, MC, V. FAP.*

## Peter Island

**$$$$** ⬛ **Peter Island Resort and Yacht Harbour.** This luxury resort includes
both an elegant and a casual restaurant, five beaches, a stunning freshwater pool, tennis courts, and a Peter Burwash tennis program. There
are also small sailboats, Sunfish, kayaks, mountain bikes, Windsurfers,
Hobie Cats, a 20-station fitness trail, a basketball court, a small exercise room, 10 miles of walking trails, a dive shop, and a masseuse. The
most desirable rooms are in quadriplex cottages that are tucked among
beds of radiant tropical flowers right at the edge of the beach. These
rooms are spacious and comfortably furnished (although the fabrics are
on the dark side) and have excellent views. The pool-, garden-, and ocean-
view rooms are a bit run down and could use some refurbishment. Those
seeking seclusion should be aware that the resort's beaches are on bays
that happen to be popular anchorages and the restaurants, beaches, and
hiking trails can be somewhat hectic with day-trippers and the charter-
boat crowd. ⊠ *Box 211, Road Town, Tortola,* ☎ *809/494–2561 or
800/346–4451,* FAX *809/494–2313. 50 rooms, 2 villas. 2 restaurants,
2 bars, pool, massage, 4 lighted tennis courts, basketball, exercise room,
fitness trail, 5 beaches, 5-star PADI dive facility, dive shop, windsurfing, marina (limited services), sailing, 2 gift shops, helicopter pad. AE,
MC, V. EP, MAP, FAP.*

## Pusser's Marina Cay

**$$** ⬛ **Pusser's Hotel.** Pusser's Marina Cay is home to Pusser's Restaurant,
Pusser's Store, and this hotel. Six units are available—four rooms and
two suites. Rooms are on the small side but are comfortably furnished
and perched above the water's edge. The islet is quite small, and there's
not much to do but relax. It's a great place to lie on the beach, get some
sun, and snorkel. But if you want to explore, you can easily get to Tor-
tola or Virgin Gorda. There's free (and frequent) ferry service to the
dock on Beef Island. ⊠ *Pusser's Marina Cay,* ☎ *809/494–2174. 6 units.
Restaurant, beach. AE, MC, V. EP.*

# Beaches

Beaches on outlying islands, reachable only by boat, include Jost Van
Dyke's **Great Harbour** and **White Bay**; **Marina Cay**; Peter Island's **Big
Reef Bay**, **White Bay**, and **Dead Man's Bay**; Mosquito Island's **Lime-**

tree Beach, Long Beach, and **Honeymoon Beach**; and Cooper Island's **Manchioneel Bay.** Farther off, and reachable by plane as well as by boat, is beach-ringed, reef-laced **Anegada.**

## Outdoor Activities and Sports

### Scuba Diving and Snorkeling

The famed wreck of the RMS *Rhone,* off Salt Island, is reason enough to dive during your B.V.I. stay. Dive and snorkel sites also abound near the smaller islands of Norman, Peter, Cooper, Ginger, the Dogs, and Jost Van Dyke, and in the wreck-strewn waters off Anegada. A branch of **Dive BVI** (☞ Outdoor Activities and Sports, Virgin Gorda, *above*) is located on Peter Island.

## Shopping

### Gifts

**Pusser's Company Store** (⊠ Marina Cay, ☎ 809/494–2174), on a Pusser's-dominated islet, stocks its own brand of rum, plus a line of clothes and other items bearing the company's logo.

## Nightlife

### Jost Van Dyke

One of the busiest nocturnal spots in the B.V.I. is little Jost Van Dyke. Check out **Rudy's Mariner Rendezvous** (☎ 809/495–9282), **Foxy's Tamarind** (☎ 809/495–9258), and **Sydney's Peace and Love** (☎ 809/495–9271).

## Exploring Outlying Islands

Just across the channel from Road Town on Tortola is **Peter Island,** an 1,800-acre island known for its exclusive resort. **Jost Van Dyke,** the sizable island north of Tortola's western tip, is a good choice for travelers in search of isolation and good hiking trails; it has a small hotel, a cluster of rental villas, and two campgrounds, but only two small settlements, few cars, and limited electricity. Guests of the resort on **Guana Island** also enjoy the nature trails and wildlife sanctuary on this private island just above the eastern tip of Tortola. **Pusser's Marina Cay** is a snug 6-acre islet near Great Camanoe, just north of Beef Island, east of Tortola, with a Pusser's Store, Restaurant, and Hotel. **Cooper Island** is a green, hilly island on the south side of Sir Francis Drake Channel. It has a restaurant and a 12-room hotel and has long been a popular anchorage. **Necker** is a private island just north of Virgin Gorda with accommodations for 20 that can only be rented as a block. **Anegada,** about 16 miles north of Virgin Gorda's North Sound, is a flat mass of coral 11 miles long and 3 miles wide with a population of only about 160 and a single hotel. Visitors are chiefly scuba divers, snorkelers, lovers of deserted beaches, and fishermen, some of whom come for the bonefishing here. (For more information on these islands, *see* Lodging, *above*.)

# THE BRITISH VIRGIN ISLANDS A TO Z

### Arriving and Departing

BY BOAT

Various ferries connect St. Thomas, U.S.V.I., with Tortola and Virgin Gorda. **Inter-Island Boat Services'** *Sundance II* (☎ 809/776–6597) connects St. John and West End on Tortola daily. **Native Son, Inc.** (☎ 809/495–4617), operates three ferries—(**Native Son, Oriole,** and **Voyager Eagle**)—and offers service between St. Thomas and Tortola (West

End and Road Town) daily. **Smiths Ferry Services** (☎ 809/494–4430 or 809/494–2355) carries passengers between downtown St. Thomas and Road Town and West End on Monday through Saturday, offers daily service between Red Hook on St. Thomas and Tortola's West End, and travels between St. Thomas and Spanish Town Tuesday, Thursday, and Sunday. **Speedy's Ferries** (☎ 809/495–5240) runs between Virgin Gorda, Tortola, and St. Thomas on Tuesdays, Thursdays, and Saturdays.

BY PLANE

No nonstop service is available from the United States to the B.V.I.; connections are usually made through San Juan, Puerto Rico, or St. Thomas, U.S.V.I. Airlines serving both San Juan and St. Thomas include **American** (☎ 800/433–7300), **Continental** (☎ 800/231–0856), and **Delta** (☎ 800/241–4141). **American Eagle** (☎ 800/433–7300) flies from San Juan to Tortola. Regularly scheduled service between the B.V.I. and most other Caribbean islands is provided by **Leeward Islands Air Transport (LIAT)** (☎ 809/495–1187). Many Caribbean islands can also be reached via **Gorda Aero Service** (✉ Tortola, ☎ 809/495–2271), a charter service.

## Currency
British though they are, the B.V.I. have the U.S. dollar as the standard currency.

## Emergencies
**Police:** ☎ 999. **Medical emergency:** ☎ 999. **Hospital:** On Tortola there is **Peebles Hospital** in Road Town (☎ 809/494–3497). Virgin Gorda has two clinics, one in Spanish Town (☎ 809/495–5337) and one at North Sound (☎ 809/495–7310). **Pharmacies:** in Road Town, **J. R. O'Neal Drug Store** (☎ 809/494–2292) and **Lagoon Plaza Drug Store** (☎ 809/494–2498).

## Further Reading
Vernon Pickering's *Concise History of the British Virgin Islands* is a wordy but worthy guide to the events and personalities that shaped the region. Look for copies of *A Place Like This: Hugh Benjamin's Peter Island,* a charming, eloquent, and very personal tale by Hugh Benjamin, a Kittitian who has spent the last 20 years living in the British Virgin Islands.

For linguists, *What a Pistarckle!* by Lito Valls gives the origins of the many expressions you'll be hearing, and historians will enjoy *Eyewitness Accounts of Slavery in the Danish West Indies* by Isidor Paiewonsky. *Conquest of Eden* by Michael Paiewonsky includes excerpts from the logs of Christopher Columbus and journals of noblemen, and is beautifully illustrated with woodcuts. For sailors, Simon Scott has written a *Cruising Guide to the Virgin Islands.* If you happen to be traveling with children, be sure to pick up a copy of *Visiting the Virgin Islands with the Kids* by Richard B. Myers.

On the B.V.I., the *Island Sun* and the *BVI Beacon* are the best local papers for everything from entertainment listings to local gossip. The *Welcome Tourist Guide,* which is published every other month, is comprehensive and available free at airports and larger hotels.

## Getting Around
BOATS

**Speedy's Fantasy** (☎ 809/495–5240) and **Smith's Ferry** (☎ 809/494–4430) both make the run between Road Town, Tortola, and Spanish Town, Virgin Gorda, daily. Running daily between Virgin Gorda's North Sound (Bitter End Yacht Club) and Beef Island, Tortola, are **North**

**Sound Express** (☎ 809/494–2746) boats. There are also daily boats between Peter Island's private dock on Tortola just east of Road Town and Peter Island. **Jost Van Dyke Ferry Service** (☎ 809/495–2997) makes the run between Jost Van Dyke and Tortola's West End several times a day via the **When** ferry.

BUSES
For information about rates and schedules on Tortola, call **Scato's Bus Service** (☎ 809/494–2365).

CAR RENTALS
Driving on Tortola and Virgin Gorda is not for the timid. Roller-coaster roads with breathtaking ascents and descents and tight turns that give new meaning to the term "hairpin curves" are the norm. It's a challenge well worth trying, however; the ever-changing views of land, sea, and neighboring islands are among the most spectacular in the Caribbean. Most people will strongly recommend renting a four-wheel-drive vehicle. Driving is on the left side of the road. It's easy to become accustomed to it if you drive slowly, think before you make a turn, and pay attention when driving in and out of the occasional traffic circle, locally called a "roundabout." Speed limits are 30–40 mph outside town and 10–15 mph in residential areas. A valid B.V.I. driver's license is required and can be obtained for $10 at car-rental agencies. You must be at least 25 and have a valid driver's license from another country to get one.

On Tortola, car rentals are available from **Avis** (☎ 809/494–3322), **Budget** (☎ 809/494–2639), **Hertz** (☎ 809/495–4405), and **National** (☎ 809/494–3197). On Virgin Gorda, try **Mahogany Rentals** (☎ 809/495–5469) or **Andy's Taxi and Jeep Rental** (☎ 809/495–5252).

TAXIS
Your hotel staff will be happy to summon a taxi for you. On Tortola, there are B.V.I. Taxi Association stands in Road Town near the ferry dock (☎ 809/494–2875) and Wickham's Cay I (☎ 809/494–2322); there's one on Beef Island at the airport (☎ 809/495–2378). You can also usually find a taxi at the Soper's Hole ferry dock, West End, where ferries from St. Thomas arrive. On Virgin Gorda, Mahogany and Andy's (☞ *above*) also provide taxi service.

## Guided Tours

If you'd like to do some chauffeured sightseeing on Tortola, get in touch with the **B.V.I. Taxi Association** (three-person minimum, ☎ 809/494–2875, 809/494–2322, or 809/495–2378), **Style's Taxi Service** (☎ 809/494–2260 during the day or 809/494–3341 at night), or **Travel Plan Tours** (☎ 809/494–2872). **Scato's Bus Service** (☎ 809/494–2365), in Road Town, provides public transportation, special tours with group rates, and beach outings. Guided tours on Virgin Gorda can be arranged through **Andy's Taxi and Jeep Rental** (☎ 809/495–5252) or **Mahogany Rentals and Island Tours** (☎ 809/495–5469).

## Language

British English, with a West Indian inflection, is the language spoken.

## Opening and Closing Times

Stores are generally open from 9 to 5 Monday through Saturday. Bank hours are Monday through Thursday 9–2:30 and Friday 9–2:30 and 4:30–6.

## Passports and Visas

Upon entering the B.V.I., U.S. and Canadian citizens are required to present some proof of citizenship—if not a passport, then a birth certificate or voter-registration card with a driver's license or photo ID.

## Precautions

Although there are generally no perils from drinking the water in these islands, it is a good idea to ask if the water is potable when you check into your hotel.

Animals in the B.V.I. are not dangerous, but they can be road hazards. Give goats, sheep, horses, and cows the right of way.

Mosquitoes are not usually a problem in these breeze-blessed isles, but it is always a good idea to bring some repellent along. Beware, however, of the little insects called "no-see-ums." They're for real and are especially pesky at twilight near the water. So if you're going for an evening stroll on the beach, apply some type of repellent liberally. No-see-um bites itch worse than mosquito bites and take a lot longer to go away. Prevention is the best cure, but witch hazel (or a dab of gin or vodka) offers *some* relief if they get you.

## Taxes and Service Charges

Hotels collect a 7% accommodations tax, which they will add to your bill along with a 10% service charge. Restaurants may put a similar service charge on the bill, or they may leave it up to you. For those leaving the B.V.I. by air, the departure tax is $8; by sea it is $5.

## Telephones and Mail

The area code for the B.V.I. is 809. To call anywhere in the B.V.I. once you've arrived, dial only the last five digits: Instead of dialing 494–1234, just dial 4–1234. A local call from a public pay phone costs 25¢. Coin-operated pay phones are frequently on the blink, but phones that use the **Caribbean Phone Card,** available in $5, $10, and $20 denominations, are a handy alternative. The cards are sold at most major hotels and many stores and can be used in special Phone Card telephones. You can call anywhere in the world with them (although rates to the U.S. are cheaper if you use AT&T). For credit-card or collect long-distance calls to the United States, look for special USA DIRECT phones that are linked to an AT&T operator, or dial 111 from a pay phone and charge the call to your MasterCard or Visa. USA DIRECT and pay phones can be found at most hotels and in towns.

There are post offices in Road Town on Tortola and in Spanish Town on Virgin Gorda. Postage for a first-class letter to the United States is 35¢ and for a postcard 20¢. (It might be noted that postal efficiency is not first class in the B.V.I.) For a small fee, **Rush It** in Road Town (☎ 809/494–4421) or Spanish Town (☎ 809/495–5821) offers most U.S. mail and UPS services via St. Thomas the next day.

## Visitor Information

Before you go, contact the **British Virgin Islands Tourist Board** (✉ 370 Lexington Ave., Suite 313, New York, NY 10017, ☎ 212/696–0400 or 800/835–8530) or at the **British Virgin Islands Information Office** (✉ 1804 Union St., San Francisco, CA 94123, ☎ 415/775–0344 or 800/232–7770). British travelers can write or visit the **BVI Information Office** (✉ 110 St. Martin's La., London WC2N 4DY, ☎ 0171/2404259).

On Tortola there is a **B.V.I. Tourist Board Office** (✉ Box 134, Road Town, Tortola, ☎ 809/494–3134) at the center of Road Town near the ferry dock, just south of Wickham's Cay I. For all kinds of useful information about these islands, including rates and phone numbers, get a free copy of the *Welcome Tourist Guide,* available at hotels and many restaurants and stores.

# 8 Cayman Islands

**T**HE VENERABLE OLD SATURDAY EVENING POST dubbed them "the islands that time forgot." No longer: The Cayman Islands, a British Crown colony that includes Grand Cayman, Cayman Brac, and Little Cayman, are now one of the Caribbean's hottest destinations, world-renowned for two offshore activities: banking and scuba diving. The former pays dividends in the manicured capital of George Town, bulging as it does with some 554 offshore banks. The latter is on vivid display in the translucent waters and the colorful variety of marine life protected by the government, which has created a marine parks system in all three islands.

Updated by
Jordan Simon

Why do metropolis-weary visitors trek 480 miles south of Miami, filling the hotels and condominiums that line famed Seven Mile Beach, even during the slow summer season? Their dollars certainly go farther in other Caribbean destinations, for in Grand Cayman—which positively reeks of suburban prosperity (residents joke that the national flower is the satellite dish)—the U.S. dollar is worth 80 Cayman cents, and the cost of living is 20% higher than in the United States.

Effective advertising accounts for some visitors, but the secret is word-of-mouth testimonials. The Cayman Islanders—the population is around 31,000, almost all of it residents of Grand Cayman—are renowned for the courteous and civil manners befitting their British heritage. Visitors will find no hasslers or panhandlers and no need to look apprehensively over their shoulder on dark evenings, for the colony enjoys a very low crime rate. Add to that permanent political and economic stability, and you have a fairly rosy picture.

Columbus is said to have sighted the islands in 1503, but he didn't stop off to explore. He did note that the surrounding sea was alive with turtles, so the islands were named Las Tortugas. The name was later changed to Cayman.

The islands stayed largely uninhabited until the late 1600s, when Britain took over the Cayman Islands and Jamaica from Spain under the Treaty of Madrid. Cayman attracted a mixed bag of English, Dutch, Spanish, and French settlers, pirates, refugees from the Spanish Inquisition, shipwrecked sailors, and deserters from Oliver Cromwell's army in Jamaica. Today's Caymanians are the descendants of those nationalities.

The caves and coves of the islands—still fascinating to explore—were a perfect hideout for pirates like Blackbeard and Sir Henry Morgan, who plundered Spanish galleons hauling riches from the New World of South America to Spain. Many a ship also fell afoul of the reefs surrounding the islands, often with the help of the Caymanians, who lured the vessels to shore with beacon fires. Some of the old pioneer homes on the islands were made from the remains of those galleons.

The legend of the Wreck of the Ten Sails was to have a lasting effect on the Caymanians. In 1794, a convoy of 10 Jamaican ships bound for England foundered on the reefs, but the islanders managed to rescue everyone. Royalty was purportedly aboard, and a grateful George III decreed that Caymanians should forever be exempt from conscription and never have to pay taxes; however, research completed in 1994 shows this tale to be purely fictional.

The Cayman Islands are still a British colony. A governor appoints three official members to the Legislative Assembly and has to accept the advice of the Executive Council in all matters except foreign affairs, defense, internal security, and civil-service appointments.

# Lodging

The success of the Cayman Islands as a resort destination means you should book ahead for holidays. Most lodgings require a seven- or 14-day minimum stay at Christmastime. During the summer season, it's possible to find suitable lodging even on short notice. If you choose to stay in a condominium, you can book on a daily basis and stay any length of time. While about a third of the visitors come for the diving, a growing number are young honeymooners. There are few accommodations in the economy range, so guests must be prepared for resort prices.

Most of the larger hotels along Seven Mile Beach don't offer meal plans. The smaller properties that are more remote from the restaurants usually offer MAP or FAP. The rates for most hotels on Cayman Brac and Little Cayman include meals, and in some cases drinks and diving as well, making them a better value than their prices reveal at first glance. (In general, the food is far better at Little Cayman properties than at the Brac hotels.) Much cozier and more intimate than their Grand Cayman counterparts, hoteliers treat guests like family; indeed many divers create whimsical artwork fashioned from driftwood, dead coral, and artifacts they pick up underwater to splash the hotel dining rooms and bars with color and originality. Over half the Caymans' rooms are rental condos and villas; all are equipped with fully stocked kitchens, telephones, satellite television, air-conditioning, living and dining areas, patios, and are individually decorated (most following a pastel tropical scheme). **Cayman Islands Reservation Service** (☎ 800/327–8777) can describe and book most condominiums and villas on the islands.

| CATEGORY | COST* |
|----------|-------|
| **$$$$** | over $260 |
| **$$$** | $200–$260 |
| **$$** | $145–$200 |
| **$** | under $145 |

*All prices are for a standard double room for two in winter, excluding 6% tax and 10% service charge. To estimate rates for hotels offering MAP/FAP, add about $40 per person per day to the average price ranges above.*

## Grand Cayman

HOTELS

**$$$$**
★  🔝 **Hyatt Regency Grand Cayman.** Painted sky blue and white and set amid gorgeous grounds, the Hyatt is adjacent to the Britannia Golf Course. The rooms, moderate in size and renovated in 1995, have a marble entranceway, oversize bathtub, minibar, French doors, and a veranda. Regency Club accommodations include complimentary Continental breakfast, early-evening hors d'oeuvres, and 24-hour concierge service. Across the street on Seven Mile Beach, the Hyatt's beach club offers every water sport imaginable, as does the new club at Rum Point (a ferry runs regularly). At Camp Hyatt, kids 3–12 can participate in a supervised activities program for a cost of around $50 a child per day. Though it's by far the poshest lodging in the Cayman Islands, rates are comparably outrageous, especially for the so-called deluxe rooms, which differ only in that you can see a sliver of ocean beyond the parking lot. ✉ Box 1698, Grand Cayman, ☎ 809/949–1234 or 800/233–1234, FAX 809/949–8528. 225 rooms, 10 suites; 44 rooms in Regency Club; 35 1-, 2-, 3-, and 4-bedroom villas. 3 restaurants, 4 bars, 4 pools, beauty salon, hot tub, massage, golf course, 4 tennis courts, croquet, dive shop, marina, water-sports center, boutiques, car rental, conference rooms. AE, D, DC, MC, V. EP, BP, MAP.

# Grand Cayman

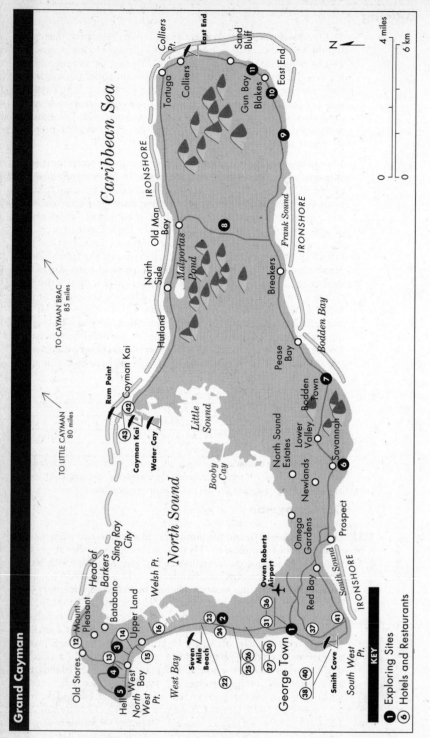

Caribbean Sea

TO CAYMAN BRAC
85 miles

TO LITTLE CAYMAN
80 miles

Colliers Pt.
East End
Colliers
Sand Bluff
Tortuga
**11**
Gun Bay
**10**
East End
Blakes
**9**
IRONSHORE

Old Man Bay
North Side
**8**
Malportas Pond
Hutland
Breakers
Frank Sound
IRONSHORE

Rum Point
**42**
Cayman Kai
**43**
Water Cay
Little Sound

North Sound

Booby Cay

Head of Barkers
Sting Ray City
Batabano
Mount Pleasant
Old Stores
**12**
**13**
**14**
**3**
**15**
Hell
**4**
West Bay
**5**
North West Pt.
Upper Land
Welsh Pt.
**16**
West Bay

Seven Mile Beach
**23**
**2**
**24**
**25**
**26**
**22**

Pease Bay
Bodden Bay
Bodden Town
**7**
Savannah
**6**
Lower Valley
Newlands
North Sound Estates

Omega Gardens
Prospect
Red Bay
South Sound
IRONSHORE

Owen Roberts Airport
**36**
**31**
**30**
**27**
**1**
George Town
**37**
**41**
**38**
**40**
Smith Cove
South West Pt.

0  4 miles
0  6 km

N

KEY
**1** Exploring Sites
**6** Hotels and Restaurants

# Cayman Brac and Little Cayman

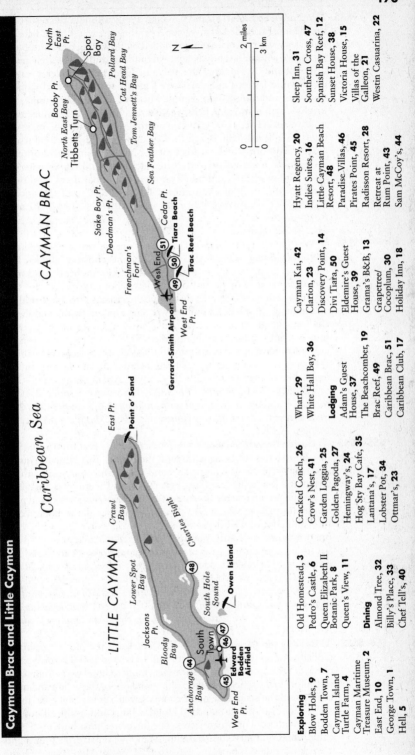

*Caribbean Sea*

**LITTLE CAYMAN**

**CAYMAN BRAC**

North East Pt.
Spot Bay
Booby Pt.
Pollard Bay
Cat Head Bay
North East Bay
Tibbetts Turn
Tom Jennett's Bay
Sea Feather Bay
Stake Bay Pt.
Deadman's Pt.
Cedar Pt.
Frenchman's Fort
Tiara Beach
West End
Brac Reef Beach
West End Pt.
Gerrard-Smith Airport

East Pt.
Point o' Sand
Crawl Bay
Charles Bight
South Hole Sound
Owen Island
Lower Spot Bay
Jacksons Pt.
Bloody Bay
South Town
Anchorage Bay
West End Pt.
Edward Bodden Airfield

N

0        2 miles
0        3 km

**Exploring**
Blow Holes, 9
Bodden Town, 7
Cayman Island Turtle Farm, 4
Cayman Maritime Treasure Museum, 2
East End, 10
George Town, 1
Hell, 5

Old Homestead, 3
Pedro's Castle, 6
Queen Elizabeth II Botanic Park, 8
Queen's View, 11

**Dining**
Almond Tree, 32
Billy's Place, 33
Chef Tell's, 40

Cracked Conch, 26
Crow's Nest, 41
Garden Loggia, 25
Golden Pagoda, 27
Hemingway's, 24
Hog Sty Bay Cafe, 35
Lantana's, 17
Lobster Pot, 34
Ottmar's, 23

Wharf, 29
White Hall Bay, 36

**Lodging**
Adam's Guest House, 37
The Beachcomber, 19
Brac Reef, 49
Caribbean Brac, 51
Caribbean Club, 17

Cayman Kai, 42
Clarion, 23
Discovery Point, 14
Divi Tiara, 50
Eldemire's Guest House, 39
Grama's B&B, 13
Grapetree/ Cocoplum, 30
Holiday Inn, 18

Hyatt Regency, 20
Indies Suites, 16
Little Cayman Beach Resort, 48
Paradise Villas, 46
Pirates Point, 45
Radisson Resort, 28
Retreat at Rum Point, 43
Sam McCoy's, 44

Sleep Inn, 31
Southern Cross, 47
Spanish Bay Reef, 12
Sunset House, 38
Victoria House, 15
Villas of the Galleon, 21
Westin Casuarina, 22

$$$$  🏨 **Spanish Bay Reef.** Grand Cayman's only all-inclusive resort is by far the most secluded of any property along the west shore. Pale pink two-story stucco units are surrounded by flowering trees and bushes on their own small sandy beach. An outdoor dining-bar area around the pool and overlooking the ocean includes tables under a semicircular white-latticed arcade. There's also a spacious, coral-stone indoor bar and dining area. Simple but comfortable guest units, with bright Caribbean print bedspreads and curtains, are connected by boardwalks. The resort is on the northwest tip of the island, several miles past Seven Mile Beach in West Bay. Spanish Bay Reef itself is a deep drop-off, which means superior beach diving and snorkeling; instruction in both is offered. Rates include round-trip transfers, all taxes and gratuities, unlimited shore diving, boat dives, and use of bicycles (not in mint condition). ✉ *Box 903, Grand Cayman,* ☎ *809/949–3765 or 800/482–3483,* 🖷 *809/949–1842. 50 units. Restaurant, bar, pool, hot tub, dive shop, fishing charters. AE, D, MC, V. All-inclusive.*

$$$$  🏨 **Westin Casuarina Resort.** This new property, which opened in late 1995, is bidding to become Grand Cayman's choicest lodging. It already has an advantage in that it's actually on the beach, and many rooms have at least partial ocean view (standards boast the same amenities but have "island" view, which translates into the parking lot and main drag). Over $1 million was spent on landscaping alone, including a jungle of palms, fountains, and cascading waterfalls. Decor ranges from subdued mountain colors and desert pastels to brighter jade, ultramarine, and pearl-gray tones, with white rattan furnishings. Every conceivable amenity has been included, from safe and minibar to marble vanities. ✉ *Box 30620, Grand Cayman,* ☎ *809/945–3800 or 800/228–3000,* 🖷 *809/949–5825. 351 rooms, 5 suites. 2 restaurants, 2 bars, beach grill, pool with swim-up bar, beauty salon, 2 hot tubs, 2 tennis courts, fitness canter, dive shop, shopping arcade. AE, D, MC, V. EP.*

$$$–$$$$  🏨 **Clarion Grand Pavilion.** While it is across the street from Seven Mile
★     Beach (it shares the beach club with the Hyatt), this intimate, quietly luxurious property is wrapped around a beautiful courtyard with waterfall and fountains cascading into the pool. The lobby is august but welcoming, with marble floors, teardrops chandeliers, teak, and plush leather furnishings. Rooms in teal and peach offer all the modern comforts and a lot of well-thought-out extras you won't find at the other bustling resorts—daily newspaper, coffee/tea machine, minibar, bathrobes, an amazing array of toiletries, pants press, nightly turndown, even an in-room fax on request. The service is impeccable. ✉ *Box 30117, Grand Cayman,* ☎ *809/947–5656 or 800/252–7466,* 🖷 *809/947–5353. 88 rooms, 5 2- and 3-bedroom suites. Restaurant, bar, pool bar, café, cocktail lounge, pool, hot tub, sauna, golf privileges at Safe Haven, fitness room, water-sports center, gift shop, laundry facilities. AE, D, DC, MC, V. EP.*

$$$–$$$$  🏨 **Holiday Inn Grand Cayman.** This hotel was the pioneer resort establishment on the beach, and it's still loose and fun. The property is cheerful yet unpretentious, a sprawling modern hotel with bright tropical colors in the spacious public rooms and one of the widest and nicest beaches on the strip. The guest rooms, given a fresh new face during a 1994 renovation, are standard Holiday Inn: comfortable, if not luxurious, with pool or ocean views. The huge breakfast buffet is a good value, and don't miss the "Barefoot Man," who performs four nights a week outside on the patio. ✉ *Box 904, Seven Mile Beach, Grand Cayman,* ☎ *809/947–4444 or 800/421–9999,* 🖷 *809/947–4213. 215 rooms. 3 restaurants, 2 bars, ice-cream parlor, pool, dive shop, water-*

*sports center, nightclub, conference facilities, car rental. AE, DC, MC, V. EP, BP, MAP.*

**$$$** ⊞ **Indies Suites.** Cayman's first and only all-suite hotel is attractive,
★ comfortable, and across the road from the beach at the quieter north
end of the Seven Mile stretch. One- or two-bedroom suites are done
in cream and burnt orange, with contemporary wood furniture. Each
has a fully equipped modern kitchen with a microwave oven, a living-
dining room (with a sleeper sofa), a terrace, and a storeroom for dive
gear. Free Continental buffet breakfast daily, a complimentary sunset
cruise once a week, and a live band that entertains in the lushly land-
scaped courtyard twice a week are nice extras. The lobby itself is spec-
tacular, with vintage 1930s Fords on display. ⊠ *Box 2070 GT, Seven
Mile Beach, Grand Cayman,* ☎ *809/947–5025 or 800/654–3130,* ☏
*809/947–5024. 38 suites. Poolside bar, snack bar, pool, hot tub,
snorkeling, convenience shop, dive shop, water-sports shop, laundry
facilities, maid service, conference facilities. AE, MC, V. CP.*

**$$$** ⊞ **Radisson Resort Grand Cayman.** This is a five-story luxury prop-
★ erty on Seven Mile Beach, just 1 mile from George Town. Designed in
colonial style with arched doorways, the hotel's airy pale yellow and
marble lobby opens onto a plant-filled courtyard. Families like the large
adjoining rooms done in bright tropical colors; all have balconies facing either the ocean or a garden court. There's an inviting beach bar
near the pool, a dive shop offering every possible water sport, a full-
service spa, and a good snorkeling reef just 50 feet offshore. Since it
also boasts the top conference center on island, it's predictably popular for convention and incentive travel. ⊠ *Box 30371, Seven Mile Beach,
Grand Cayman,* ☎ *809/949–0088 or 800/333–3333,* ☏ *809/949–
0288. 315 rooms, 4 suites. Restaurant, bar, snack bar, pool, beauty salon,
hot tub, spa, dive shop, water-sports center, boutiques, car rental. AE,
D, DC, MC, V. EP.*

**$$** ⊞ **Cayman Kai Resort.** Nestled next to a coconut grove, each sea lodge
has a full kitchen, dining room, immaculate if spartan white living area,
and a screened-in porch overlooking the ocean. The hotel is on a beach
at the north-central tip of the island—quite remote. You need a car to
get anywhere, but many guests are content to stay put and dive. Not
all rooms have air-conditioning, so be sure to request it if it's impor-
tant to you. ⊠ *Box 201, North Side,* ☎ *809/947–9055 or 800/223–
5427,* ☏ *809/947–9102. 16 units. Restaurant, 2 bars. AE, MC, V. EP.*

**$$** ⊞ **Sleep Inn.** This two-story Choice Hotels affiliate is a quick stroll from
★ Seven Mile Beach, close to the airport, and just a mile from George Town's
shops, making it excellent value. Air-conditioned rooms are motel-
modern, with peaches-and-cream pastels and modern wood furnishings.
The Dive Inn dive shop is here, as are tours and car and motorcycle rentals.
⊠ *Box 30111, Grand Cayman,* ☎ *809/949–9111,* ☏ *809/949–6699.
124 rooms. Poolside bar and grill, pool, whirlpool, dive center, water-
sports center, boutique. AE, D, MC, V. EP.*

**$–$$** ⊞ **Sunset House.** Low-key and laid-back describe this resort with
sparse, motel-style rooms on the ironshore south of George Town, 4
miles from Seven Mile Beach. A congenial staff, popular bar, and
seafood restaurant are pluses, but it's the diving and dive packages that
attract most guests. Full dive services include free waterside lockers,
two- and three-tank dives at the better reefs around the island, and Cathy
Church's U/W Photo Center. It's a five-minute walk to a sandy beach,
10 minutes to George Town. ⊠ *Box 479, S. Church St., Grand Cayman,* ☎ *809/949–7111 or 800/854–4767,* ☏ *809/949–7101. 59
rooms. Restaurant, bar, 2 pools, whirlpool, dive shop and underwater photo center. AE, D, DC, MC, V. EP, BP, MAP.*

CONDOMINIUMS AND VILLAS

**Cayman Islands Department of Tourism** provides a complete list of condominiums and small rental apartments in the **$$** range. Many of these are multibedroom units that become affordable when shared by two or more couples. Rates are higher during the winter season, and there may be a three- or seven-night minimum, so check before you book. The following complexes bear a marked similarity to one another: All are equipped with fully stocked kitchens, telephones, satellite television, air-conditioning, living and dining areas, and patios, and are individually decorated (most following a pastel tropical scheme). Differences arise in property amenities and proximity to town. All are well maintained and directly on the beach, though you will need a car for grocery shopping. **Cayman Islands Reservation Service** (✉ 6100 Blue Lagoon Dr., Suite 150, Miami, FL 33126, ☎ 800/327–8777), **Cayman Villas** (✉ Box 681, Grand Cayman, ☎ 809/947–4144 or 800/235–5888, FAX 809/949–7471), **and Hospitality World Ltd.** (✉ Box 30123, Grand Cayman, ☎ 809/949–8098 or 800/232–1034, FAX 809/949–7054) can also make reservations.

**$$$$**   🏨 **The Beachcomber.** Set in the middle of Seven Mile Beach, each of the simply furnished apartments in this older condo community has a view of the ocean from a private, screened patio. There is a grocery store just across the street and countless shopping and dining outlets within walking distance, so once you're here, you don't really need a car. The Beachcomber reef is just offshore for snorkeling, and palapas on the beach provide shade when the sun gets a bit too warm. ✉ *Box 1799, Seven Mile Beach, Grand Cayman,* ☎ *809/947–4470 or 800/327–8777,* FAX *809/947–5019. 23 units. Grills, pool, beach huts, laundry facilities. AE, MC, V.*

**$$$$**   🏨 **Caribbean Club.** Eighteen one- and two-bedroom villas (six on the beach) make up this quiet island condominium getaway. All units were renovated in 1994. While secluded, these units are not quite on a par with the truly deluxe properties on the island. Children under age 11 are not allowed in the winter season. ✉ *Box 30499, Seven Mile Beach, Grand Cayman,* ☎ *809/947–4099 or 800/327–8777,* FAX *809/947–4443. 18 villas. Restaurant, bar, tennis court, maid service. AE, MC, V. EP, MAP.*

**$$$$**   🏨 **Discovery Point Club.** At the quiet, far north end of Seven Mile Beach in West Bay, 6 miles from George Town, this complex offers the same lovely beach with more peace and seclusion and is within walking distance of great snorkeling in the protected waters of Cemetery Reef. Tennis courts, a hot tub, and a pool for relaxation are part of the appeal here. Kids 12 and under stay for free during the off-season (April–December). ✉ *Box 439, West Bay, Grand Cayman,* ☎ *809/947–4724 or 800/327—8777,* FAX *809/947–5051. 45 units. Grills, pool, hot tub, 2 tennis courts, laundry facilities. AE, MC, V.*

**$$$$**   🏨 **Victoria House.** The one-, two-, and three-bedroom units in this squarish white building have white tile floors and white walls and are decorated with muted Caribbean prints and rattan furniture. You may choose from a range of activities, including tennis and water sports. The Victoria is 3 miles north of town on a quiet stretch of Seven Mile Beach; if you're an early riser, you may catch a glimpse of giant sea turtles on the sand. ✉ *Box 30571, Seven Mile Beach (near West Bay), Grand Cayman,* ☎ *809/947–4233,* FAX *809/947–5328. 25 units. Tennis, scuba, snorkeling, laundry facilities. AE, MC, V.*

**$$$$**   🏨 **Villas of the Galleon.** The exteriors of these deluxe stucco cottages look somewhat shabby, but the units themselves are lovely and beautifully maintained. Each duplex one- or two-bedroom unit has full kitchen, terrace, enormous closets (a big plus for families) and individual decor running toward eggshell tile floors, pastels, and rattan furnishings. The location couldn't be better: perched on the widest section of Seven-Mile Beach, just across from the Jack Nicklaus–designed Links Golf Club. ✉ *Box 1797, Grand Cayman,* ☎ *809/947–4433,* FAX *809/947–4705. 74 units. Grills. AE, MC, V.*

$$$–$$$$  ⊞ **Grapetree/Cocoplum.** A half mile from George Town on Seven Mile Beach, these sister condos are adjacent to one another. Grapetree's two-bedroom, two-bath units are carpeted, with traditional wicker furnishings and a beige and brown decor. Cocoplum's units are similar, with Caribbean pastel prints; its grounds have more plants and trees. The two share two pools and tennis courts. ✉ *Box 1802, Seven Mile Beach, Grand Cayman,* ☎ *809/949–5640 or 800/635–4824,* FAX *809/949–0150. 51 units. Grills, 2 pools, tennis courts. AE, MC, V.*

$$$–$$$$  ⊞ **Retreat at Rum Point.** It has its own narrow beach with casuarina trees, far from the madding crowd on the north-central tip of Grand Cayman, 27 miles from town. Up to six people can rent a two-bedroom villa here. Two or three people are comfortable in the one-bedroom units. Spacious rooms have blue-lavender upholstered furniture. There are dive facilities nearby, where you can take advantage of superb offshore diving, including the famed North Wall. You'll be stranded without a car; it's a 35-minute drive to George Town or the airport. ✉ *Box 46, North Side, Grand Cayman,* ☎ *809/947–9135,* FAX *809/947–9058. 23 units. Restaurant, bar, pool, sauna, tennis courts, exercise room, racquetball court, laundry facilities. MC, V.*

GUEST HOUSES AND B&BS

Away from the beach and short on style and facilities, these lodgings nevertheless offer rock-bottom prices (all fall well below our $ category), a friendly atmosphere, and your best shot at getting to know the locals. Rooms are clean and simple, often with cooking facilities, and most have private bathrooms. Many establishments have outdoor grills and picnic tables for guest use. A rental car is recommended. These establishments do not accept personal checks or credit cards but do take reservations through the **Cayman Islands Reservation Service** (☎ 800/327–8777).

**Grama's Bed & Breakfast** (✉ Box 198, Crescent Close of Town Hall Crescent, West Bay, Grand Cayman, ☎ 809/949–3798), 8 miles from town and the airport, has five rooms and a pool. **Adam's Guest House** (✉ Box 312, on Melnac Ave. near the Seaview Hotel, Grand Cayman, ☎ 809/949–2512, ☎ FAX 809/949–0919), a mile south of George Town and 4 miles from the beach, also has five rooms, all with kitchenette. **Eldemire's Guest House** (✉ Box 482, on South Church St., Grand Cayman, ☎ 809/949–5387, FAX 809/949–6987), Grand Cayman's first guest house, has seven rooms and is a 15-minute drive to Seven Mile Beach, but less than a mile south of pretty Smith Cove Bay.

## Cayman Brac

HOTELS

$$–$$$$  ⊞ **Brac Reef Beach Resort.** This resort lures divers and vacationers who come to savor the special ambience of this tiny island. The recently (1994) renovated but already worn rooms have private balconies, but still resemble a '50s strip motel in earth tones and, surprisingly, none has a water view. The pool, pretty beach, snorkeling, guest bicycles, dive shop, and two-story covered dock (whose gazebo is glorious on a star-filled night, when you can see brilliantly hued fish darting about) are additional reasons to stay here. The modest all-inclusive package rates include three buffet meals daily, all drinks, airport transfers, and taxes and service charges. There's even an all-inclusive dive package. ✉ *Box 56, Cayman Brac,* ☎ *809/948–7323; in FL, 813/323–8727 or 800/327–*

*3835;* ℻ *809/948–7207. 40 rooms. Restaurant, bar, pool, hot tub, tennis court, dive shop, bicycles. AE, D, MC, V. EP, MAP, FAP, All-inclusive.*

\$\$–\$\$\$    ⊞ **Divi Tiara Beach Resort.** This older resort is dedicated to divers. It has a top-quality diving facility complemented by the Divi chain's standards: tile floors, bright tropical prints, rattan furniture, louvered windows, balconies, and ocean views (from most rooms; standards have neither view nor TV). Some of the more expensive rooms have whirlpool bathtubs. A shuttle takes guests across the island to a great snorkeling spot. Kids 16 and under stay free in their parents' room. ✉ *Box 238, Cayman Brac,* ☎ *809/948–1553; in the U.S., 919/419–3484 or 800/801–5550;* ℻ *809/948–7316 or 919/419–2075 in the U.S. 70 rooms. Restaurant, bar, pool, tennis court, volleyball, snorkeling, fishing, dive shop, water-sports center, underwater photo shop, gift shop. AE, MC, V. EP, MAP, FAP, All-inclusive.*

CONDOMINIUMS AND VILLAS

\$\$    ⊞ **Caribbean Brac Beach Village.** This small condo complex built in
★    1992 enjoys the same pretty beach as the other resorts, but for the money you get a two-bedroom, 2½-bath fully furnished apartment right on the beach. Kids 11 and under stay free with their parents, making this a family money saver. Beige walls and rattan furniture, white tile floors, and pastel floral prints give the units a bright, airy look. With advance notice, the management company will stock your kitchen with groceries and arrange for dive packages, rental cars, and maid service (each at minimal additional cost). A pool, restaurant, bar, and gift shop were added during a 1995 expansion. ✉ *Box 4, Stake Bay, Cayman Brac,* ☎ *809/948–2265 or 800/791–7911,* ℻ *809/948–2206. 16 rooms. Pier, laundry room. MC, V. EP.*

## Little Cayman

HOTELS

\$\$–\$\$\$    ⊞ **Little Cayman Beach Resort.** Considerably less rustic than those of
★    other Little Cayman resorts, the air-conditioned rooms in this two-story property, have modern furnishings in jewel-tone tropical colors. Only Rooms 115, 116, 215, and 216 boast a water view—for the same rate! The elegant (for Little Cayman) dining room overlooking the bar area seats 50 for family-style buffet meals. Double hammocks are slung under beach palapas. The resort offers diving and fishing packages and also caters to bird-watchers and soft-adventure ecotourists. Paddleboats, sailboats, kayaks, a complete dive operation, tennis, and free bicycles provided for exploring the island keep guests busy. All-inclusive packages are available for both divers and nondivers and include three meals daily, all alcoholic and soft drinks, airport transfers, taxes, and gratuities. ✉ *Blossom Village, Little Cayman,* ☎ *809/948–1033 or 800/327–3835,* ℻ *809/948–1045. 32 rooms. Restaurant, bar, pool, hot tub, tennis court, dive packages, deep-sea fishing charters, bicycles, dive shop, gift shop. AE, D, MC, V. EP, MAP, FAP. All-inclusive.*

\$\$–\$\$\$    ⊞ **Pirates Point Resort.** The guest-house feel of this comfortably in-
★    formal resort generates almost instant camaraderie among the guests, and many come back year after year. The charming, individually decorated rooms have tiled floors, white rattan and wicker furnishings, ceiling fans, and louvered windows. But Pirates Point is most notable for its flamboyant owner, Texan Gladys Howard, whose warm down-home welcome belies her upscale meals (she trained at Cordon Bleu with Julia Child, James Beard, and Jacques Pepin). She'll also personally guide guests along the Salt Rocks Nature Trail, discoursing on everything from botany to history. "Relaxing" rates (for nondivers) include the mouthwatering meals and wine; all-inclusive rates include meals, alcoholic beverages, two daily boat dives, fishing, and picnics on un-

inhabited Owen Island. Sunset wine-and-cheese parties are held weekly on the beachside dock. ⊠ *Little Cayman,* ☎ *809/948–1010 or 800/654–7537,* FAX *809/948–1011. 10 rooms. Restaurant, bar, dive operation, fishing, bicycles, complimentary airport transfers. MC, V. FAP, All-inclusive.*

**$$–$$$** ⊞ **Southern Cross Club.** Three family-style meals a day are included in the rates at this older retreat that caters to fishers and divers. The rooms, in cottages spread along a pretty beach, have a simple white-on-white decor with wicker furniture, ceiling fans (no air-conditioning), and painted cement floors. Diving and fishing (deep-sea, light-tackle, bottom, and bonefishing) are the draw here. A motorboat makes trips to uninhabited Owen Island nearby. There's been a lot of turnover in staff and management lately, and service is suffering for it. ⊠ *Little Cayman,* ☎ *809/948–1099 or 800/899–2582; in the U.S., 317/636–9501;* FAX *317/636–9503. 10 rooms. Restaurant, beach bar, dive packages, snorkeling, fishing packages, bicycles, complimentary airport transfers. No credit cards. FAP.*

**$$** ⊞ **Sam McCoy's Diving and Fishing Lodge.** Be prepared for an ultra-★ casual experience: This is an ordinary family house with very simple but cheerful bedrooms and baths in royal and powder blues. There's no bar or restaurant per se; guests just eat at a few tables outdoors or with Sam and his family in the thatched dining room, draped with fishing nets, diving artifacts, and guests' artwork. Fans like it for its owner's infectious good nature, the superb diving and snorkeling just offshore, and the family atmosphere. "Relaxing" rates (for nondivers) include three meals a day and airport transfers; all-inclusive rates also include beach and boat diving. Sam's son, Chip, is the most experienced local fishing guide on the island; his bonefishing trips are around $20 an hour. ⊠ *Little Cayman,* ☎ *800/626–0496,* ☎ FAX *809/948–0026. 6 rooms. Beach barbecue, pool. No credit cards. FAP, All-inclusive.*

CONDOMINIUMS AND VILLAS

**$–$$** ⊞ **Paradise Villas.** If you're looking for cozy one-bedroom self-catering units, all with kitchens, air-conditioning, and terrace opening onto the beach, look no further. The 12 units are sunny, breezy, simply but immaculately appointed with rattan and muted abstract fabrics. ⊠ *Little Cayman,* ☎ *809/948–0004. 12 units. Pool, dive shop. AE.*

# Dining

Grand Cayman's restaurants satisfy every palate and pocketbook. Gourmet Continental cuisine is available to the high rollers; ethnic food can be had at moderate prices. West Indian fare in dining spots serving locals is the best in taste and value.

Seafood, not surprisingly, appears on most restaurant menus. Fish—including grouper, snapper, dolphin, tuna, wahoo, and marlin—is served either simply (baked, broiled, steamed) or Cayman-style, with peppers, onions, and tomatoes. Conch, the meat of a large pink mollusk, is ubiquitous in stews and chowders and as fritters or panfried ("cracked"). Caribbean lobster is available but is often quite expensive, and other shellfish are in short supply in local waters. The only traditional culinary treat of the islands is turtle soup, stew, or steak, but fewer restaurants carry it these days.

All the restaurants reviewed below are on Grand Cayman, because there are few to none on the sister islands (visitors eat at the resorts and guest houses). Dining out here can be expensive, so replenish your billfold, because some places do not accept plastic. Many restaurants add a 10%–15% service charge to the bill, so check before leaving an additional tip.

## What to Wear

Smart casual wear (slacks and sundresses) is acceptable throughout the Caymans for dinner in all but a few places. The nicer resorts and more expensive restaurants may require a jacket, especially in high season; ask when making reservations. Shorts are usually acceptable during the day, but unless you're going to an ultracasual beach bar, beachwear (bathing suits, cover-ups, tank tops, etc.) is a no-no. Most restaurants have an alfresco dining section, and if you plan to dine under the stars, ask for bug spray they provide—the mosquitoes are fierce after sunset.

| CATEGORY | COST* |
|----------|-------|
| $$$ | over $30 |
| $$ | $20–$30 |
| $ | under $20 |

*per person, excluding drinks and service charge*

$$$  ✕ **Chef Tell's Grand Old House.** TV celebrity chef Tell Erhardt's menu features Continental entrées and a few local specialties. Among the spicier appetizer choices is fried coconut shrimp with mustard apricot sauce. On the milder side are entrées such as lobster "The Chef's Way," dipped in egg batter and sautéed with shallots, mushrooms, and white wine, and coffee-lacquered duck with fresh pear chutney. The oceanside gazebos, surrounded by palms and cooled by ceiling fans, are the liveliest and best spots for dining. The excellent service adds to this gracious dining experience. ⊠ *S. Church St.,* ☎ *809/949–9333. Reservations essential for dinner. DC, MC, V. Closed Sun. No lunch Sat.*

$$$  ✕ **Garden Loggia Cafe.** The Hyatt's indoor-outdoor café opens onto the most beautifully landscaped garden courtyard on the island. The Caribbean decor includes pastel colors, ceiling fans, and marble-top tables. The restaurant, serving Italian and Oriental cuisine, opens for dinner only during high season (mid-December–May), but it's the weekly Sunday champagne brunch, featuring everything from fresh seafood to waffles and custom-made omelets, that draws a crowd. Reserve a seat as early as possible to avoid disappointment. ⊠ *Hyatt Regency Grand Cayman, West Bay Rd.,* ☎ *809/949–1234. Reservations essential. AE, D, DC, MC, V.*

$$$  ✕ **Ottmar's.** This quietly elegant restaurant is styled after a West In-
★    dian great house. Jade carpeting, peach walls, linen, trickling fountain, mahogany furniture, and glass chandeliers create an attractive setting for the excellent service. Favorites on the international menu include bouillabaisse, chicken breast Oscar (topped with crab, asparagus, and hollandaise), French pepper steak (flamed in cognac and doused with green peppercorn sauce and crème fraîche), Florida red snapper (broiled, poached, panfried, or Provençal), and Indonesian rijsttafel (platter of seafood and rice in curry sauce with traditional condiments). ⊠ *Clarion Grand Pavilion, West Bay Rd.,* ☎ *809/941–5879 and 809/947– 5882. Reservations essential. AE, D, DC, MC, V. No lunch.*

$$$  ✕ **The Wharf.** Stylishly decorated in blue and white, the Wharf looks onto a veranda and the nearby sea. On the surf-and-turf menu are conch fritters, home-smoked salmon, "Seafood a L'aneth" (lobster and scallops in dill sauce), veal scallopini, and steak fillet béarnaise; anything on the fresh daily menu is recommended. Live Paraguayan music entertains diners. The Ports of Call bar is a perfect spot from which to watch the sun set, and tarpon feeding off the deck is a nightly (9 PM) spectacle here. ⊠ *West Bay Rd.,* ☎ *809/949–2231. AE, D, MC, V. No lunch weekends.*

$$–$$$  ✕ **Hemingway's.** Sea views and breezes attract diners to this classy open-
★    air restaurant on Seven Mile Beach. In the evening, candlelight and a guitarist (except Sunday) complete the romantic atmosphere. Nouvelle

Caribbean and seafood dishes include pumpkin-coated mahimahi with mango jus, macadamia-crusted pork loin, and grouper stuffed with crab and sweet corn in a jerk cream sauce. Portions are large, and service is superb. For a tropical drink, try the Seven Mile Meltdown, with dark rum, peach schnapps, pineapple juice, and fresh coconut. ⊠ *West Bay Rd. across from the Hyatt,* ☎ *809/949–1234, ext. 2009. AE, D, DC, MC, V.*

**$$–$$$** ✕ **Lantana's.** Alfred Schrock, longtime chef at the Wharf Restaurant,
★ now creates excellent American-Caribbean lunches and dinners here. Enjoy lobster quesadillas, house-made lamb sausage, or blackened king salmon over cilantro linguine with banana fritters and cranberry relish. If you come for nothing else, *don't* miss the incredible roasted garlic soup and the apple pie. The decor of the bi-level restaurant— potted plants, teak furniture, painted wooden fish—is as imaginatively authentic as the food. ⊠ *Caribbean Club, West Bay Rd.,* ☎ *809/947–5595. AE, D, MC, V. No lunch weekends.*

**$$–$$$** ✕ **Lobster Pot.** The second-floor terrace of this cozy restaurant overlooks the bay downtown, so the sunsets are an extra attraction. The menu includes both Continental dishes and such Caribbean specialties as conch chowder, seafood curry, shrimp Diane, and, of course, lobster. This place is popular, and the constant turnover creates a rather frenzied atmosphere. If you can't make it for dinner, drop by the pub and have a frozen banana daiquiri. ⊠ *N. Church St.,* ☎ *809/949–2736. AE, D, MC, V.*

**$$** ✕ **Crow's Nest.** This secluded seafood restaurant, about a 15-minute drive south of George Town, is set in a rustic West Indian Creole cottage set amid overgrown foliage and flowering shrubs right on the beach (diners often go snorkeling after lunch); sit on the enclosed terrace, draped in fishnets, for the best breezes. The shark du jour, herb-crusted dolphin with lobster sauce, swordfish with jerk mayo, and shrimp and conch dishes are excellent, as is the chocolate fudge rum cake. ⊠ *South Sound Rd.,* ☎ *809/949–9366. AE, MC, V. No lunch Sun.*

**$$** ✕ **Golden Pagoda.** The well-known Chinese restaurant in the Caymans features Hakka-style cooking (similar to using a hibachi). Among its specialties are moo goo gai pan, butterfly shrimp, and chicken in black-bean sauce. Takeout (takie-outie, they call it) is now available, as are showy Japanese teppanyaki dinners (minimum two persons) Tuesday through Saturday night. ⊠ *West Bay Rd.,* ☎ *809/949–5475. Reservations essential for Japanese dinner. AE, MC, V. No lunch weekends.*

**$$** ✕ **White Hall Bay.** This popular local hangout occupies a charming traditional Caymanian waterfront home, hung with gourds, straw bags, and marvelous black-and-white photos of old-timers. The food is equally charming and traditional, from sultry turtle and pepper-pot stews (both seeming to have bubbled for years) to luscious yam cake and coconut cream pie. ⊠ *N. Church St.,* ☎ *809/949–8670. AE, D, MC, V.*

**$–$$** ✕ **Cracked Conch.** Specialties of this popular, often-crowded seafood
★ restaurant, the originator of cracked (tenderized and panfried) conch, include conch fritters, conch chowder, spicy Cayman-style snapper, turtle steak, and other seafood offerings. The key lime and coconut pies are definitive and divine. Locals flock here on weekdays for the low-priced lunch buffet—hot entrée, soup, and salad for C.I.$7.50. The bar, a prime local hangout, has karaoke, dive videos, and great happy-hour specials. Regrettably, at press time the owners had been forced out of their original location, adorned with owner Suzy Soto's marvelous seascape murals and shell lamps, but she promised the new semi-open-air beachfront location would be just as fancifully decorated with her artwork and hubby Bob Soto's antique diving equipment. ⊠ *West Bay Rd. near Turtle Bay Farm,* ☎ *809/947–5217. MC, V.*

**$–$$**  ✕ **Hog Sty Bay Cafe.** Lots of socializing goes on in the casual atmosphere of this English-style café on the harbor in George Town. A simple menu of sandwiches, hamburgers, and Caribbean dishes will satisfy you for lunch and dinner. This is the classic Caribbean hangout, with hand-painted wooden fish hanging everywhere, an invigorating mix of zany residents and curious tourists. Many believe the conch fritters served here are the best in town. Come and watch the sun set from the seaside patio or for the weekday happy hour. ✉ *N. Church St.,* ☎ *809/949–6163. AE, MC, V.*

**$**  ✕ **Almond Tree.** Looking for authentic island atmosphere in modern Grand Cayman? This eatery combines architecture from the South Seas isle of Yap with bones, skulls, and bric-a-brac from Africa, South America, and the Pacific. Sample good-value seafood entrées, including turtle steak and fresh grouper, with "All-U-Can-Eat" entrées for C.I.$12 on Wednesday and Friday. ✉ *N. Church St.,* ☎ *809/949–2893. AE, MC, V. Closed Sun.*

**$**  ✕ **Billy's Place.** Billy's, the yellow and blue diner in the Kirk Supermarket parking lot surprises in many ways. In addition to hearty servings of jerk chicken, pork, goat, shrimp, conch, fish, lobster, and burgers, you can order Indian *pakoras* (vegetable fritters), tandoori chicken or shrimp, and several curried selections. Service tends to be abrupt, but the crowds don't seem to mind. Calypso and reggae throb in the background, as colorful as the vividly hued underwater photos adorning the walls. And there's always Billy, a native Jamaican, wandering about, ensuring everything's fine—sometimes inviting himself to sit down and relate fascinating anecdotes (some of them unprintable) about his life in the islands. ✉ *N. Church St.,* ☎ *809/949–0470. AE, D, MC, V. Closed Sun.*

# Beaches

## Grand Cayman

You may read or hear about the "dozens of beaches" of these islands, but that's more exaggeration than reality. Grand Cayman's west coast, the most developed area of the entire colony, is where you'll find its famous **Seven Mile Beach** (actually 5½ miles long) and its expanses of powdery white sand. The beach is litter-free and sans peddlers, so you can relax in an unspoiled, hassle-free (if somewhat crowded) atmosphere. This is also Grand Cayman's busiest vacation center, and most of the island's accommodations, restaurants, and shopping centers are on this strip. You'll find headquarters for the island's aquatic activities in various places along the strip (☞ Outdoor Activities and Sports, *below*).

Grand Cayman has several smaller beaches that may better be called coves, including **Smith Cove,** off South Church Street, south of the Grand Old House—a popular bathing spot with residents on weekends.

The best shore-entry snorkeling locations are off the ironshore south of George Town, at **Eden Rock** (☎ 809/949–7243) and **Parrot's Landing** (☎ 809/949–7884); north of town, at the reef just off the **West Bay Cemetery** on Grand Cayman's west coast; and in the reef-protected shallows of the island's north and south coasts, where coral and fish life are much more varied and abundant.

The best windsurfing is just off the beaches in **East End,** at Colliers, by Morritt's Tortuga Club. The beach can be lovely if it's kept clean of seaweed tossed ashore by trade winds, but the windsurfing is the real draw here. Seldom discovered by visitors unless they're staying here are the beautiful beach areas of **Cayman Kai** (which was undergoing some development at press time), **Rum Point,** and, even more isolated and unspoiled, **Water Cay.** These are favored hideaways for residents and popular Sunday picnic spots.

## Cayman Brac

The accommodations on the **southwest coast** have fine small beaches, better for sunning than for snorkeling because of the abundance of turtle grass in the water. Excellent snorkeling can be found immediately offshore of the now-defunct **Buccaneer's Inn** on the north coast.

## Little Cayman

The beaches **Point o' Sand,** on the eastern tip, and **Owen Island,** off the south coast, are isolated patches of powder that are great for sunbathing and worth every effort to reach by car, bike, or boat.

# Outdoor Activities and Sports

## Deep-Sea Fishing

If you enjoy action fishing, Cayman waters have plenty to offer—blue and white marlin, yellowfin tuna, sailfish, dolphin, and wahoo. Bonefish and tarpon are also plentiful off Little Cayman. Some 25 boats are available for charter, offering fishing options that include deepsea, reef, bone, tarpon, light-tackle, and fly-fishing. Grand Cayman charter operators to contact are **Charter Boat Headquarters** (☎ 809/947–4340), **Crosby Ebanks** (☎ 809/947–4049), **Island Girl** (☎ 809/947–3029), and **Bayside Watersports** (☎ 809/949–3200). Little Cayman operators are **Sam McCoy's Fishing & Diving** (☎ 809/949–2891 or 800/626–0496) and **Southern Cross Club** (☎ 800/899–2582). In 1984 June was dubbed Million Dollar Month; registered anglers can win cash and vacation prizes by landing record-breaking catches. Five tournaments are held, each with its own rules, records, and entrance fees. For information and applications, write to the Million Dollar Month Committee (✉ Box 878 GT, Grand Cayman, Cayman Islands, B.W.I.).

## Diving and Snorkeling

To call the Cayman Islands a scuba diver's paradise is not overstating the case. Jacques Cousteau named Bloody Bay (off Little Cayman) one of the world's top dives, and the famed Cayman Wall, off Grand Cayman, ranks up there as well. Pristine water (often exceeding 100-foot visibility), breathtaking coral formations, and plentiful and exotic marine life await divers. A host of top-notch dive operations offer a variety of services, instruction, and equipment. A Grand Cayman must-see for adventurous souls is **Stingray City,** which has been called the best 12-foot dive (or snorkel) in the world. Here are dozens of unusually tame stingrays who, accustomed to being fed first by fishermen and now by divers, suction squid off divers' outstretched palms and gracefully swim and twist around the divers in the shallow waters.

Divers are required to be certified and possess a "C" card or take a short resort or full certification course. A certification course, including classroom, pool, and boat sessions as well as checkout dives, takes four to six days and costs $350–$400. A short resort course usually lasts a day and costs about $80–$100. It introduces the novice to the sport and teaches the rudimentary skills needed to make a shallow, instructor-monitored dive.

All dive operations on Cayman are more than competent; among them are **Aquanauts** (☎ 809/945–1990 or 800/357–2212), **Bob Soto's** (☎ 809/947-4631 or 800/262–7686), **Don Foster's** (☎ 809/949–5679 or 800/833–4837), **Eden Rock** (☎ 809/949–7243), **Parrot's Landing** (☎ 809/949–7884 or 800/448–0428), **Red Sail Sports** (☎ 809/949–8745 or 800/255–6425), and **Sunset Divers** (☎ 809/949–7111 or 800/854–

4767). Request full information on all operators from the Department of Tourism (☞ Cayman Islands A to Z, *below*). A single-tank dive averages $45; a two-tank dive, about $55. Snorkel-equipment rental runs from $5 to $15 a day.

On Cayman Brac, **Brac Aquatics** (☎ 809/949–1429 or 800/544–2722) and **Divi Tiara** (☎ 809/948–1553 or 800/367–3484) offer scuba and snorkeling. On Little Cayman, contact **Paradise Divers** (☎ 809/948–0004 or 800/450–2084), **Reef Divers** (☎ 809/948–1033), **Sam McCoy's Fishing & Diving** (☎ 809/949–2891 or 800/626–0496), or the **Southern Cross Club** (☎ 800/899–2582). Each hotel also has its own instructors.

Most operations can rent all diving gear, including equipment for underwater photography; Bob Soto's, Don Foster's, and Cathy Church's U/W Photo (in Sunset House) have facilities for film processing and underwater photo courses.

One-week live-aboard dive cruises are available aboard the 110-foot **Cayman Aggressor III** (☎ 800/348–2628) and the luxury yacht **Little Cayman Diver II** (☎ 800/458–2722).

## Fitness

Most hotels and resorts offer fitness facilities. **Nautilus Fitness Center** (✉ Seven Mile Beach, Grand Cayman, ☎ 809/949–5132) has machines, weights, a sauna, and a whirlpool. Daily membership is $10; weekly, $25.

## Golf

The **Grand Cayman–Britannia** golf course (☎ 809/949–8020), next to the Hyatt Regency, was designed by Jack Nicklaus. The course is really three in one—a 9-hole par-70 regulation course, an 18-hole par-57 executive course, and a Cayman course (played with a Cayman ball that goes about half the distance of a regulation ball). Greens fees range from $40 to $80. Golf carts ($15–$25) are mandatory.

Windier, and therefore more challenging, is the **Links at Safe Haven** (☎ 809/949–5988), Cayman's first 18-hole championship golf course, set amid a virtual botanical garden of indigenous trees, plants, and flowering shrubs. The Roy Case–designed par-71, 6,519-yard course also has an aqua driving range (the distance markers and balls float), a two-story clubhouse, locker rooms, a pro shop, a patio bar with live jazz happy hours on weekends, and a fine restaurant serving Continental and Caribbean cuisine daily for lunch and dinner. Greens fees run to $60. Golf carts ($15–$20 per person) are mandatory.

## Hiking

Nature trails abound on all three islands (on the sister islands, it's best to ask locals for directions: they'll literally take you to the small clearing in the bush you looked right through). Guided nature walks are available at the National Trust's Mastic Trail on Grand Cayman (✉ Off Frank Sound Rd., ☎ 809/949–1996, tours by appointment 10–3 daily, $30 per person), a rugged 2-mile slash through pristine woodlands, mangrove swamps, and ancient rock formations.

## Tennis

Most hotels and condo complexes have tennis courts for guests.

## Water Sports

Water skis, Windsurfers, Hobie Cats, and Jet Skis are available at many of the aquatic shops along Seven Mile Beach (☞ Diving and Snorkeling, *above*). **Sailboards Caribbean** (☎ 809/949–1068) offers windsurfing rentals, lessons for beginners, and a full gamut of courses through high-wind advanced levels. **Cayman Windsurf** (☎ 809/947–

7492) offers windsurfing lessons and rentals at the East End of the island at Morritt's Tortuga Club and on North Sound by Safe Haven.

# Shopping

Grand Cayman has two money-saving attributes—duty-free merchandise and the absence of a sales tax. Prices on imported merchandise—English china, Swiss watches, French perfumes, and Japanese cameras and electronic goods—are often lower than elsewhere, but not always. To make sure you get a bargain, come prepared with a price list of items you are thinking of buying and comparison shop. The main shopping areas are **Elizabethan Square, Cardinal Avenue,** and the chic **Kirk Freeport Plaza,** known for its fine jewelry, plus duty-free china, crystal, Gucci items, perfumes, and fine cosmetics. Unusual jewelry can also be found, ranging from authentic sunken treasure and ancient coins made into necklaces and pins to relatively inexpensive rings and earrings made from semiprecious stones, coral, and seashells. **Tortuga Rum Company's** (☎ 809/949–7701, 809/949–7866, or 809/949–7867) scrumptious rum cake makes a great souvenir.

## Good Buys
### ARTS AND CRAFTS
Debbie van der Bol runs an arts-and-crafts shop called **Pure Art** (☎ 809/949–9133) on South Church Street and at the Hyatt Regency (☎ 809/947–5633). She sells watercolors, wood carvings, and lacework by local artists, as well as her own sketches and cards. Original prints, paintings, and sculpture with a tropical theme are found at **Island Art Gallery** (☎ 809/949–9861) in the Anchorage Shopping Center in George Town. The **Kennedy Gallery** (☎ 809/949–8077), in West Shore Center and on Fort Street in George Town, features primarily limited-edition pastel watercolors of typical Cayman scenes by Robert E. Kennedy.

The **Heritage Crafts Shop** (☎ 809/949–7093), near the harbor in George Town, sells local crafts and gifts. The **West Shore Shopping Center,** on Seven Mile Beach near the Radisson, offers good-quality island art, beachwear, ice cream, and more. The **Queen's Court Shopping Center,** on Seven Mile Beach close to town, offers an array of souvenirs, crafts, and gifts. **Calico Jack's** (⊠ West Bay Rd., George Town, ☎ 809/949–4373) is a good source for local T-shirts, casual resort wear, and dive gear (truly self-contained, it also operates a dive shop and pub).

### BLACK CORAL
Black coral products are exquisite and a popular choice. However, environmental groups discourage tourists from purchasing any coral that is designated as endangered species, because the reefs are not always harvested carefully. If you feel differently, there are a number of local craftsmen who create original designs and finish their own work. The coral creations of **Bernard Passman** (⊠ Fort St., George Town, ☎ 809/949–0123) won the approval of the English royal family. Beautiful coral pieces are also found at **Richard's Fine Jewelry** (⊠ Harbour Dr., George Town, ☎ 809/949–7156), where designers Richard and Rafaela Barile attract their fair share of celebrities. **Carey Cayman Coral** (⊠ South Sound Rd., no phone) is a workshop run by Carey Hurlstone. Carey, a gentle bear of a man covered with tattoos, professes he was a biker with the Hell's Angels before coming home to Cayman to work as a craftsman. He makes black coral jewelry and figurines and carves glass. Carey's workmanship is superb, and his prices are quite reasonable for the quality.

# Nightlife

Each of the island hot spots attracts a different clientele. The **Holiday Inn** (☎ 809/947–4444) offers something for everyone: **Coconuts** (☎ 809/947–5757), the hotel's original comedy club, features young American stand-up comedians who entertain year-round every Wednesday through Sunday. Crowds also gather poolside, where the island-famous "Barefoot Man" sings and plays four nights a week. Dancing is spontaneous and welcome, and it's a great spot to people-watch.

**Long John Silver's Nightclub** (☎ 809/949–7777), at the Treasure Island Resort, is a spacious, tiered club that is usually filled to capacity when the island's top bands play there. **Island Rock Nightclub** (✉ Falls Shopping Center, Seven Mile Beach, ☎ 809/947–5366), a popular disco and bar with occasional live bands, had been converted to a teen club at press time but may revert to an adult club during high season; call to check before venturing out. Latest to hit the hot-spot list is **Rumheads** (☎ 809/949–7169), featuring nightly drink specials, live entertainment, and theme nights; the youngish crowd can get pretty rowdy, and brawls aren't exactly out of the ordinary here.

Locals and visitors frequent the **Cracked Conch** (✉ West Bay Rd., near the Turtle Farm, ☎ 809/947–5217) for karaoke, classic dive films, and a great happy hour with hors d'oeuvres Tuesday–Friday evenings.

For current entertainment, look at the freebie magazine, *What's Hot,* or check the Friday edition of the *Caymanian Compass* for listings of music, movies, theater, and other entertainment possibilities.

# Exploring Grand Cayman

There are three main sightseeing areas on Grand Cayman. The first, the historic capital of George Town, is easily explored on foot and conveniently perched on one side of Seven Mile Beach. The West End is noted for its quixotic jumble of affluent colonial neighborhoods and rather tawdry tourist attractions. The less developed East End contains many natural attractions, from blowholes to botanical gardens, as well as the remains of the original settlements. Figure a whole day to explore the lengthy island—including a stop at a beach for a picnic or swim.

*Numbers in the margin correspond to points of interest on the Grand Cayman map.*

## George Town

❶ **George Town.** Begin exploring the capital by strolling along the waterfront, Harbour Drive. The circular gazebo is where visitors from the cruise ships disembark. Diagonally across the street is the **Elmslie Memorial United Church,** named after Scotsman James Elmslie, the first Presbyterian missionary to serve in the Caymans. The church was the first concrete block building built in the Cayman Islands. Its vaulted ceiling, wood arches, and sedate nave reflect the quietly religious nature of island residents. Along your rambles, you'll come across **Fort Street,** a main shopping street where you'll also notice the small clock tower dedicated to Britain's King George V and the huge fig tree manicured into an umbrella shape. Here, too, is a statue (unveiled in 1994) of national hero James Bodden, the father of Cayman tourism. Across the street is the **Cayman Islands Legislative Assembly Building,** next door to the 1919 **Peace Memorial Building.**

On Edward Street, you'll find the charming **library,** built in 1939; it has English novels, current newspapers from the United States, and a small reference section. It's worth a visit just for the Old World atmosphere and a look at the shields depicting Britain's prominent institutions of learning that decorate the ceiling beams. Across the street is the **courthouse.** Down the next block is the financial district, where banks from all over the world have offices.

Straight ahead is the **General Post Office,** also built in 1939, with its strands of decorative colored lights and some 2,000 private mailboxes on the outside. (Mail is not delivered on the island.) Behind the post office is **Elizabethan Square,** a shopping and office complex on Shedden Road that houses various food, clothing, and souvenir establishments. The courtyard, with benches around a pleasant garden and fountain, is a good place to rest your feet.

Built in 1833, the **Cayman Islands National Museum** was used as a courthouse, a jail (now the gift shop), a post office, and a dance hall before being reopened in 1990 as a museum. It is small but fascinating, with excellent displays and videos illustrating the history of Cayman plant, animal, human, and geological life. Pick up a walking-tour map of George Town at the museum gift shop before leaving. ⊠ *Harbour Dr.,* ☎ *809/949–8368.* ☜ *$5.* ⊘ *Weekdays 9–5, Sat. 10–4.*

NEED A BREAK?
Follow your nose north on Harbour Drive, which becomes North Church Street to the **Wholesome Bakery and Café** (☎ 809/949-7588), which adds the homey smell of baking bread to the sea breezes off George Town Harbour. Stop in here for the delectable meat patties, generous slices of pie, and coconut or rum raisin ice cream.

❷ **Cayman Maritime Treasure Museum.** Just outside of George Town is this "treasure." Dioramas here show how Caymanians became seafarers, boatbuilders, and turtle breeders. An animated figure of Blackbeard the Pirate spins salty tales about the pirates and buccaneers who "worked" the Caribbean. Since the museum is owned by a professional treasure-salvaging firm, it's not surprising that there are a lot of artifacts from shipwrecks. ⊠ *West Bay Rd., near Hyatt Regency,* ☎ *809/947–5033.* ☜ *$5.* ⊘ *Mon.–Sat. 9–5.*

## The Outer Districts

To see the rest of the island, rent a car or scooter, or take a guided tour (☞ Cayman Island A to Z, *below*). A full-day guided tour (sufficient to see the major sites) is comparable in cost to a single day of car rental. The flat road that circles the island is in good condition, with clear signs. Venturing away from the Seven Mile Beach strip, you'll encounter the more down-home character of the island.

WEST END
❹ **Cayman Island Turtle Farm.** Started in West Bay in 1968, this is the most popular attraction on the island today, with some 200,000 visitors a year. There are turtles of all ages, from Ping-Pong-ball-size eggs to day-old hatchlings to huge 600-pounders that can live to be 100 years old. The Turtle Farm was set up both as a conservation and a commercial enterprise; it releases about 5% of its stock back out to sea every year, harvests turtles for local restaurants, and exports the byproducts. (Note: U.S. citizens cannot take home any turtle products because of a U.S. regulation banning their import.) In the adjoining café, you can sample turtle soup or turtle sandwiches while looking over an exhibit about turtles. ⊠ *West Bay Rd.,* ☎ *809/949–3893.* ☜ *$5.* ⊘ *Daily 8:30–5.*

❺ **Hell.** This tiny village is little more than a patch of incredibly jagged rock formations called ironshore. The big attraction here is a small post office, which sells stamps and postmarks cards from Hell (a postcard of bikini-clad beauties emblazoned "When Hell freezes over" tells you what to expect), and lots of T-shirt and souvenir shops. Almost unbelievably, a nearby nightclub, called the Club Inferno, is run by the McDoom family.

**❸ Old Homestead.** Formerly known as the West Bay Pink House, this is probably the most photographed home in Grand Cayman. The picturesque pink-and-white Caymanian cottage was built in 1912 of wattle and daub around an ironwood frame, and tours, led by cheery Mac Bothwell, who grew up in the house, present a nostalgic and touching look at life in Grand Cayman before the tourism and banking boom. ⊠ *West Bay Rd.,* ☎ *809/949–7639.* ▦ *$5.* ☉ *Mon.–Sat. 8–5.*

EAST END

**❾ Blow Holes.** These make the ultimate photo opportunity as crashing waves force water into caverns and sending geysers shooting up through the ironshore (calcified coral ledge).

**❼ Bodden Town.** In the island's original capital you'll find an old cemetery on the shore side of the road. Graves with A-frame structures are said to contain the remains of pirates, but, in fact, they may be those of early settlers. There are also the ruins of a fort and a wall erected by slaves in the 19th century for defense. A curio shop serves as the entrance to what's called the **Pirate's Caves,** partially underground natural formations that are more hokey (decked out with fake treasure chests and mannequins in pirate garb) than spooky.

**❿ East End.** The first recorded settlement on the island, its major claim to fame these days is that it's where a renowned local musician called the Fiddle Man, a.k.a. Radley Gourzong, lives and occasionally performs his distinctive form of music (more akin to Louisiana's backwater zydeco than reggae) with his band, the Happy Boys.

**❻ Pedro's Castle.** Built in 1780, this modest burgher's home hardly qualifies for palatial status, but lays claim to being the oldest structure on the island. Legends linked to the structure abound, but what is known is that the building was struck by lightning in 1877 and left in ruins until bought by a restaurateur in the 1960s. Gutted once again by fire in 1970, the building was purchased by the government in 1991 for restoration as a historic landmark. ⊠ *East End, South Sound Rd., Savannah, no phone.* ▦ *Free.*

NEED A
BREAK?

The large and airy **Lighthouse at Breakers Restaurant** (⊠ Breakers, ☎ 809/947–2047) has booth seating around spectacular waterfront windows and offers seafood and Italian cuisine.

**❽ Queen Elizabeth II Botanic Park.** This 60-acre wilderness preserve showcases the variety of habitats and plants native to the islands. Interpretive signs identify the flora along the walking trail. Halfway along the trail is a walled compound housing the rare blue iguana found only in remote sections of the Caymans. You will also see native orchids and, if you're lucky, the brilliant green Cayman parrot. ⊠ *Frank Sound Rd.,* ☎ *809/947–9462.* ▦ *$3.* ☉ *Daily 7:30–5:30.*

**⓫ Queen's View.** This functions as both a lookout point and a monument dedicated by Queen Elizabeth in 1994 to commemorate the legendary **Wreck of the Ten Sails,** which took place just offshore.

# Exploring Cayman Brac

Brac, the Gaelic word for "bluff," aptly identifies this island's most distinctive feature, a rugged limestone cliff that runs down the center of the island's 12-mile length and soars to 140 feet at its eastern end. Lying 89 miles northeast of Grand Cayman, accessible via Cayman Airways and Island Air, Cayman Brac is a spelunker's paradise: You can explore the island's **large caves (namely Peter's, Great, Bat, and Rebeka's)**, some of which are still used for hurricane protection. Wear sneakers for exploring, not flip-flops; some of the paths to the caves are steep and rocky.

Only 1,200 people live on this island, in communities such as Watering Place and Spot Bay. In addition to displaying the implements used in the daily lives of Bracers in the 1920s and 1930s, the two-room **Cayman Brac Museum** (✉ Old Government Administration Bldg., Stake Bay, ☎ 809/948-2622), open weekdays 9-noon and 1-4 and Saturday 9-noon, showcases a few oddities, such as a 4,000-year-old Viking ax. The variety of Brac flora includes unusual orchids, mangoes, papaya, agave, and cacti. The endangered Cayman Brac parrot is most easily spotted in the **Parrot Preserve** on Major Donald Drive (also known as Lighthouse Road); this 6-mile dirt road also leads to ironshore cliffs that offer the best panoramic view of North East Point and the open ocean. Parts of the island are unpopulated, so you can explore truly isolated areas both inland and along the shore. Two hotels catering to divers and a rental condo complex are located on the southwest coast. Swimming is possible, but unlike at Seven Mile Beach, the bottom is rocky and clogged with turtle grass.

## Exploring Little Cayman

Only 7 miles away from Cayman Brac is Little Cayman Island, which has a population of about 50 (only 20 or so full-timers) on its 12 square miles. This is a true hideaway: few phones, fewer shops, no nightlife— just spectacular diving, great fishing, and laid-back camaraderie. Visitor accommodations are mostly in small lodges. In addition to privacy, the real attractions of Little Cayman are diving in spectacular **Bloody Bay,** off the north coast, and fishing, which includes angling for tarpon and bonefish. You can also go birding at the **Governor Gore Bird Sanctuary**, established in 1994 and home to 5,000 pairs of red-footed boobies (the largest colony in the Western Hemisphere) and 1,000 magnificent frigate birds. Nature abounds, from the eerie waterscape of **Tarpon Pond,** where silvery tarpon pirouette in the sun amid a maze of gnarled, knobby mangrove trees to bird preserves where red-footed boobies, black frigates, and snowy egrets compete for lunch in dramatic dive-bombing battles.

And if Little Cayman ever gets too busy, there is one final retreat— **Owen Island,** which is just 200 yards offshore. Accessible by rowboat, it is in the middle of a blue lagoon and has a sandy beach. Take your own picnic if you plan to spend the day.

## Cayman Islands A to Z

### Arriving and Departing
BY PLANE

**Cayman Airways** (☎ 800/422-9626) flies nonstop to Grand Cayman from Miami two or three times daily, from Tampa four times a week, from Orlando three times a week, and from Houston and Atlanta three times a week. **American Airlines** (☎ 800/433-7300) has daily nonstop flights from both Miami and Raleigh/Durham, North Carolina. **Northwest** (☎ 800/447-4747) has regularly scheduled nonstop flights from Miami. **USAir** (☎ 800/428-4322) flies daily nonstop from Tampa and three times a week from Pittsburgh and Charlotte, North Carolina. **American Trans Air** (☎ 800/225-2995) is a charter service offering direct weekly flights from Indianapolis and Cincinnati. **Cayman Air-tours** (☎ 800/247–2966) offers package deals. Air service from Grand Cayman to Cayman Brac and Little Cayman is offered via Cayman Airways and **Island Air** (☎ 809/949–5152 or 800/922–9606). Flights land at Owen Roberts Airport, Gerrard-Smith Airport, or Edward Bodden Airfield. **Airport Information:** For flight information, call 809/949–5252.

Upon arrival, some hotels offer free pickup at the airport. Taxi service and car rentals are also available.

## Currency

Although the American dollar is accepted everywhere, you'll save money if you go to the bank and exchange U.S. dollars for Cayman Island (C.I.) dollars, which are worth about $1.20 each. The Cayman dollar is divided into a hundred cents with coins of 1¢, 5¢, 10¢, and 25¢ and notes of $1, $5, $10, $25, $50, and $100. There is no $20 bill. Prices are often quoted in Cayman dollars, so it's best to ask. All prices quoted here are in U.S. dollars unless otherwise noted.

## Emergencies

**Police and Hospitals:** ☎ 911. **Ambulance:** ☎ 555. **Pharmacy:** Island Pharmacy (☎ 809/949–8987) in West Shore Centre on Seven Mile Beach. **Divers' Recompression Chamber:** Call 809/949–4234 or 555.

## Getting Around

If your accommodations are along Seven Mile Beach, you can walk or bike to the shopping centers, restaurants, and entertainment spots along West Bay Road. George Town is small enough to see on foot. If you're touring Grand Cayman by car, there's a well-maintained road that circles the island; it's hard to get lost. If you want to see the sights or simply get away from the resort, you'll need a rental car or moped on Little Cayman and Cayman Brac; your hotel can make the arrangements for you. Otherwise, airport transfers are included in most resort rates, and many resorts offer bicycles for local sightseeing.

### BICYCLES AND SCOOTERS

When renting a motor scooter or bicycle, don't forget the sunblock and that driving is on the left. Bicycles ($10–$15 a day) and scooters ($25–$30 a day) can be rented from **Bicycles Cayman** (☎ 809/949–5572), **Cayman Cycle** (☎ 809/947–4021), and **Soto Scooters** (☎ 809/947–4363).

### CAR RENTALS

Grand Cayman is relatively flat and fairly easy to negotiate if you're careful of the traffic. To rent a car, bring your current driver's license and the car-rental firm will issue you a temporary permit ($5). Most firms have a range of models available, from compacts to Jeeps to minibuses. Rates range from $35 to $55 a day. The major agencies have offices in a plaza across from the airport terminal, where you can pick up and drop off vehicles. Just remember, driving is on the left.

Car-rental companies are **Ace Hertz** (☎ 809/949–2280 or 800/654–3131), **Budget** (☎ 809/949–5605 or 800/472–3325), **Cico Avis** (☎ 809/949–2468 or 800/331–1212), **Coconut** (☎ 809/949–4377 or 800/262–6687), **Economy** (☎ 809/949–9550), **Soto's 4X4** (☎ 809/945–2424), and **Thrifty** (☎ 809/949–6640 or 800/367–2277).

### TAXIS

Taxis offer island-wide service. Fares are determined by an elaborate rate structure set by the government, and although it may seem pricey for a short ride (fare from Seven Mile Beach for four people to the airport ranges from $10 to $15), cabbies rarely try to rip off tourists. Ask to see the chart if you want to double-check the quoted fare. **A.A. Trans-**

portation (☎ 809/949–7222), **Cayman Cab Team** (☎ 809/947–1173), and **Holiday Inn Taxi Stand** (☎ 809/947–4491) offer 24-hour service.

## Guided Tours

Money-saving packages (everything from honeymoon trips to air-hotel deals) are offered through hotels and through **TourScan, Inc.** (☎ 800/962–2080 or 203/655–8091) and **Cayman Airtours** (☎ 800/247–2966).

### AIR TOURS

**Cayman Helicopter Tours** (☎ 809/949–4400) operates a six-passenger, air-conditioned helicopter that makes quick work of taking in the geographical features of Grand Cayman. The waters around the island are so clear that you can see shipwrecks, stingrays, and shallow reefs from the air. Fares start at around $150 per person. **Seaborne Flightseeing Adventures** (☎ 809/949–6029) offers a 25-minute narrated "flightseeing" tour for $56 per person.

### LAND TOURS

Guided day tours of the island can be arranged with **A.A. Transportation Services** (☎ 809/949–7222; ask for Burton Ebanks), **Majestic Tours** (☎ 809/949–7773), **Reids Premier Tours** (☎ 809/949–6531), **Rudy's Travellers Transport** (☎ 809/949–3208), and **Tropicana Tours** (☎ 809/949–0944). Half-day tours average $30–$50 a person and generally include a visit to the Turtle Farm and Hell in West Bay, drives along Seven Mile Beach and through George Town, and time for shopping downtown. In addition to those stops, full-day tours, which average $55–$75 per person and include lunch, also visit Bodden Town to see pirate caves and graves and the East End to see blowholes on the ironshore and the site of the famous Wreck of the Ten Sails.

### WATER TOURS

The most impressive sights are underwater. Don't miss a trip on **Atlantis Submarines** (☎ 809/949–7700), which takes 48 passengers, a driver, and a guide down along the Cayman Wall to depths of up to 100 feet for close-up views of the abundant, colorful marine life. This $2.8 million submarine has entertained hundreds of thousands of passengers, has all sorts of safety features, including a constantly circling surface monitor boat, and is air-conditioned. Through its large windows, you can see huge barrel sponges, corals in extraterrestrial-like configurations, strange eels, and schools of beautiful and beastly fish. Night dives are quite dramatic, because the artificial lights of the ship make the colors more vivid than they are in daytime excursions. Costs range from around $60 to $80 per person for trips from an hour to an hour and a half in length. The company also operates private trips on a research submersible that reaches depths of 800 feet. In the *Seaworld Explorer* (☎ 809/949–8534), passengers sit before windows in the hull of the boat just 5 feet below the surface, observing divers who swim around with food, attracting fish to the craft. The cost of this hour-long trip is $29.

Guided snorkeling trips, available through **Charter Boat Headquarters** (☎ 809/947–4340), **Captain Eugene's Watersports** (☎ 809/949–3099), and **Kirk Sea Tours** (☎ 809/949–6986), usually include stops at Stingray City Sandbar, Coral Garden, and Conch Bed, the top snorkel sites. Full-day trips include lunch prepared on the boat or onshore and cost under $40 per person; half-day trips average $25. Glass-bottom-boat trips also cost around $25 and are available through **Aqua Delights** (☎ 809/947–4786), **Cayman Mermaid** (☎ 809/949–8100), and **Kirk Sea Tours** (☎ 809/949–6986).

Sunset sails, dinner cruises, and other themed (dance, booze, pirate, etc.) cruises are available aboard the *Jolly Roger* (☎ 809/949–8534), a replica of a 17th-century Spanish galleon; *Blackbeard's Nancy* (☎ 809/949–8988), a 1912 topsail schooner; and the *Spirit of Ppalu* (☎ 809/949–1234), a 65-foot glass-bottom catamaran. Party cruises typically run $20–$50 per person.

## Language
English is spoken everywhere; local publications are also in English.

## Opening and Closing Times
Banking hours are generally Monday–Thursday 9–2:30 and Friday 9–1 and 2:30–4:30. Shops are open Monday–Friday 9–5, and on Saturday in George Town from 10 to 2; in outer shopping plazas, from 10 to 5. Shops are usually closed on Sunday except in hotels.

## Passports and Visas
American and Canadian citizens do not have to carry passports, but they must show some proof of citizenship, such as a birth certificate or voter registration card, plus a return ticket. British and Commonwealth subjects do not need a visa but must carry a passport. Visitors to the islands cannot be employed without a work permit.

## Precautions
Locals zealously conserve fresh water, so don't waste a precious commodity. Caymanians also strictly observe and enforce laws that prohibit collecting or disturbing endangered animal, marine, and plant life and historical artifacts found throughout the islands and surrounding marine parks; simply put, take only pictures and don't stand on reefs.

Penalties for drug and firearms importation and possession of controlled substances include large fines and prison terms.

Theft is not widespread, but be smart: Lock up your room and car and secure valuables as you would at home. Outdoors, marauding blackbirds called "ching chings" have been known to carry off jewelry if it is left out in the open.

Poisonous plants on the island include the maiden plum, the lady hair, and the manchineel tree. If in doubt, don't touch. The leaves and apple-like fruit of the manchineel are poisonous to touch and should be avoided; even raindrops falling from them can cause painful blisters.

## Taxes and Service Charges
Hotels collect a 10% government tax and add a 10% service charge to your bill. Many restaurants add a 10%–15% service charge. At press time, the departure tax was C.I.$8. (U.S. $10).

## Telephones and Mail
For international dialing to Cayman, the area code is 809. To call outside, dial 0 + 1 + area code and number. You can call anywhere, anytime, through the cable and wireless system and local operators. To make local calls, dial the seven-digit number. To place credit-card calls, dial 110. AT&T USA Direct (☎ 800/872–2881) and MCI Direct (☎ 800/624–1000) can be used from any public phone and most hotels.

Beautiful stamps are available at the main post office in downtown George Town and at the philatelic office in West Shore Plaza. Both are open weekdays from 8:30 to 3:30 and Saturday from 8:30 to 11:30. Sending a postcard to the United States, Canada, the Caribbean, or Central America costs C.I.20¢. An airmail letter is C.I.30¢ per half ounce. To Europe and South America, the rates are C.I.25¢ for a postcard and C.I.40¢ per half ounce for airmail letters.

## Visitor Information

For the latest information on activities and lodging, write or call any of the offices of the **Cayman Islands Department of Tourism:** ✉ 6100 Waterford Bldg., 6100 Blue Lagoon Dr., Suite 150, Miami, FL 33126-2085, ☎ 305/266–2300; ✉ 2 Memorial City Plaza, 820 Gessner, Suite 170, Houston, TX 77024, ☎ 713/461–1317; ✉ 420 Lexington Ave., Suite 2733, New York, NY 10170, ☎ 212/682–5582; ✉ 9525 W. Bryn Mawr Ave., Suite 160, Rosemont, IL 60018, ☎ 708/678–6446; ✉ 3440 Wilshire Blvd., Suite 1202, Los Angeles, CA 90010, ☎ 213/738–1968; ✉ 234 Eglinton Ave. E, Suite 306, Toronto, Ontario M4P 1K5, ☎ 416/485–1550; ✉ Trevor House, 100 Brompton Rd., Knightsbridge, London SW3 1EX, ☎ 0171/581–9960.

The main office of the **Department of Tourism** is in the Pavilion, (✉ Cricket Sq. and Elgin Ave., ☎ 809/949–0623). Information booths are at the airport (☎ 809/949–2635); in the George Town Craft Market, on Cardinal Avenue, open when cruise ships are in port (☎ 809/949–8342); and in the kiosk at the cruise-ship dock in George Town (no phone). There is also an islandwide tourist hot line (☎ 809/949–8989). You can also contact the **Tourist Information and Activities Service** (☎ 809/949–6598, FAX 809/947–6222) day or night for complete tourist information and free assistance in booking island transportation, tours, charters, cruises, and other activities.

# 9 Curaçao

**C**URAÇAO IS AN ISLAND FOR EXPLORERS. Its charming Dutch capital, underwater park, Seaquarium, floating market, and dozens of little cove beaches give it a taste of everything, and it is apt to please most tastes. Thirty-five miles north of Venezuela and 42 miles east of Aruba, Curaçao, at 38 miles long and 2–7½ miles wide, is the largest of the islands in the Netherlands Antilles. The sun smiles down on the island, but it's never stiflingly hot: The gentle trade winds refresh. Water sports attract enthusiasts from all over the world, and some of the best reef diving is here. Though the island claims 38 beaches, it doesn't have long stretches of silky sand; rather, beaches are rocky stretches of washed-up coral that eventually breaks down into smooth white or pink sand. The island is dominated by an arid countryside, rocky coves, and a sprawling capital situated around a natural harbor. Until recently, the economy was based not on tourism but on oil refining and catering to offshore corporations seeking tax hedges. Although tourism has become a major economic force in the past decade, with millions of dollars invested in restoring old colonial landmarks and modernizing hotels, Curaçao's atmosphere remains comparatively low-key—offering an appealing alternative to the commercialism of many other islands.

Updated by
Melissa Rivers

As seen from the Otrabanda of Willemstad by the first-time visitor, Curaçao's "face" will be a surprise—spiffy rows of pastel-color town houses that look transplanted from Holland. Although the gabled roofs and red tiles show a Dutch influence, the absurdly gay colors of the facades, as novelist Christopher Isherwood once described them, are peculiar to Curaçao. It is said that a popular governor suffered from migraines, a condition irritated by the color white, so all the houses were painted in colors. Government funding has allowed for a tremendous boost in restoration of these houses, so you'll notice bright new coats of paint. The dollhouse look of the *landhuizen* (plantation houses) makes a cheerful contrast to the stark cacti and the austere shrubbery dotting the countryside.

The history books still cannot agree on who discovered Curaçao—one school of thought believes it was Alonzo de Ojeda, another says it was Amerigo Vespucci—but they seem to agree that it was around 1499. The first Spanish settlers arrived in 1527. In 1634, the Dutch came via the Netherlands West India Company. They promptly shipped off the Spaniards and the few remaining Indians—survivors of the battles for ownership of the island, famine, and disease—to Venezuela. Eight years later, Peter Stuyvesant began his rule as governor, which lasted until he left for New York around 1645. Twelve Jewish families arrived from Amsterdam in 1651, and by 1732 there was a synagogue; the present structure is the oldest synagogue still in use in the Western Hemisphere. Over the years, the city built massive fortresses to defend against French and British invasions—many of those ramparts now house unusual restaurants and hotels. The Dutch claim to Curaçao was finally recognized in 1815 by the Treaty of Paris. In 1954, Curaçao became an autonomous part of the Kingdom of the Netherlands, with a governor appointed by the queen, an elected parliament, and an island council.

Today Curaçao's population is derived from more than 50 nationalities in an exuberant mix of Latin, European, and African roots and a Babel of tongues, resulting in superb restaurants and an active cultural scene. The island, like its Dutch settlers, is known for its religious tolerance, and tourists are warmly welcomed.

# Lodging

If you're a business traveler, you'll appreciate the modest Van Der Valk Plaza, Otrabanda, and Porto Paseo, with easy access to the city center, but you'll have a long trek to the beach. Guests at the sophisticated Avila Beach, Sonesta Beach, Curaçao Caribbean, Princess Beach, and Holiday Beach hotels enjoy their own beaches, but they're a 10-minute drive from town. The Curaçao Caribbean and the Sonesta Beach Hotel are across the road from the International Trade Center. Most hotels offer free shuttle bus services to downtown. They also either include a Continental breakfast or offer a large buffet breakfast at a reasonable price. Full American Plans are not popular because of the abundance of good restaurants.

At press time, **Dive Resort Habitat** (☎ 599/9–607263 or 800/327–6709), a sister to the highly popular Captain Don's Habitat in Bonaire, was under construction, scheduled to open in August 1996. The 56 rooms are junior suites with kitchenettes, and there's a five-star PADI dive center on the property. Initial reports have been good.

Many rentals are available. Contact the **Curaçao Tourism Development Foundation** (✉ Box 3266, Curaçao, Netherlands Antilles, ☎ 599/9–616000, FAX 599/9–612305) at least two months in advance for a list of available properties.

| CATEGORY | COST* |
| --- | --- |
| $$$ | over $225 |
| $$ | $150–$225 |
| $ | under $150 |

*All prices are for a standard double room for two, including 7% government tax and 12% service charge.*

**$$$** 🏨 **Curaçao Caribbean Hotel and Casino.** This five-story complex is self-contained, with one of the best organized activities programs on the island, including rum-swizzle parties, volleyball, T-shirt painting contests, Papiamento lessons, walking tours, and special theme nights. The lovely champagne-color coves can become crowded, but the lounging area above them is perfect for sunbathing. Water sports include everything imaginable. Guest rooms on the first four floors are less than striking, but are very spacious and tidy. The top floor is dedicated to business guests. All the hotel rooms have small balconies; half face the sea. ✉ *Box 2133, Piscadera Bay, Willemstad,* ☎ *599/9–625000 or 800/344–1212,* FAX *599/9–625846. 181 rooms, 15 suites. 3 restaurants, 2 bars, coffee shop, room service, pool, barbershop, beauty salon, 2 tennis courts, exercise room, shuffleboard, volleyball, beach, dive shop, marina, water-sports center, shops, casino, baby-sitting, playground, laundry service and dry cleaning, concierge floor, business services, meeting rooms. AE, D, DC, MC, V. EP, MAP.*

**$$$** 🏨 **Kadushi Cliffs.** If you're staying for a week or more, you might want to rent a condo, in the beautifully lush western part of the island. The modern two-bedroom villas here are all beautifully furnished. A pool and a restaurant are the only real facilities (there's a tiny beach), but this keeps the noise level down. A car is required. ✉ *Westpunt,* ☎ *599/9–640200 or 800/448–8355,* FAX *599/9–640282. 22 villas. Restaurant, bar, in-room safes, kitchens, refrigerators, whirlpool bathtub, in-room VCRs on request, pool, tennis court, volleyball, beach, aviary, baby-sitting, playground, business services, meeting rooms, travel services. AE, DC, MC, V. EP.*

**$$$** 🏨 **Sonesta Beach Hotel & Casino.** Curaçao's newest resort is a sprawl-
★     ing, burnished-ocher low rise, built to blend in with the surrounding Dutch Colonial–style architecture. The approach, through lushly land-

scaped grounds brimming with oleander, hibiscus, and gently swaying palms, is impressive; the beach is one of Curaçao's finest. The tasteful accommodations have a muted tropical pastel color scheme and either a terrace or a balcony. Striking contemporary art adorns the walls. Price is determined solely by view, though all rooms boast at least a partial ocean vista. There's also an array of daily activities and nightly entertainment for adults. ⊠ *Box 6003, Piscadera Bay,* ☎ *599/9–368800 or 800/766–3782,* FAX *599/9–627502. 212 rooms, 32 suites. 3 restaurants, 2 bars (including swim-up), minibar, no-smoking rooms, refrigerators, room service, whirlpool bathtub and private sunning terrace in top suites, pool, wading pool, 2 outdoor hot tubs, massage, saunas, steam rooms, 2 tennis courts, aerobics, health club, volleyball, beach, private island, water-sports and dive center, shopping arcade, casino, baby-sitting, children's program (5–12), laundry service and dry cleaning, concierge, business services, meeting rooms, travel services, car rental. AE, D, DC, MC, V. EP, MAP, FAP.*

**$$** 🖼 **Holiday Beach Hotel and Casino.** This former–Holiday Inn is a four-story, U-shape, aquamarine-colored building surrounding a pool. Rooms have a beige, emerald, and rose color scheme, with bleached wood and rattan furniture. Half the rooms face the parking lot; most of the others face the pool area; a few have sea views. The air-conditioned lobby is spacious to permit the assembly of tour groups, and one of the island's largest casinos, Casino Royale, is off the lobby. The crescent beach is quite large for Curaçao and dotted with palm trees. There's also a water-sports concession and a tiki-hut beach bar. The daily selection of activities is voluminous. The lobby bar happy hour is one of the most popular on the island. Although this is an older property, the renovation, along with the friendly service, makes it a good choice if you want good value on a middle-of-the-road budget. ⊠ *Box 2178, Otrabanda, Pater Euwensweg, Willemstad,* ☎ *599/9–625400 or 800/223–9815,* FAX *599/9–624397. 200 rooms. 2 restaurants, 2 bars, refrigerators on request, room service, pool, beauty salon, 2 tennis courts, Ping-Pong, shuffleboard, volleyball, beach, water-sports center with dive shop, casino, video games, baby-sitting, playground, dry cleaning and laundry service, business services, meeting rooms, travel services, shopping shuttle, car rental. AE, DC, MC, V. EP.*

**$$** 🖼 **Princess Beach Resort and Casino.** You can't beat the location of this Holiday Inn Crowne Plaza property: You're on one of the most beautiful beaches in Curaçao and right in front of the Underwater Marine Park. Most guest rooms are huge, with breathtaking ocean or garden views. The pathway to the rooms is through lush, tropical grounds. The casino is one of the more exciting in Curaçao. This is a high-energy place, with lively happy hours, popular theme buffet dinners, and a slew of sports activities and nightly entertainment. This is also one of the few hotels on the island to offer designated no-smoking rooms, and rooms accessible to people with disabilities. ⊠ *Martin Luther King Blvd. 8,* ☎ *599/9–367888 or 800/327–3286,* FAX *599/9–614131. 341 rooms. 3 restaurants, 4 bars (including swim-up and piano bars), in-room safes, minibar, no-smoking rooms, refrigerators, room service, 2 pools, beauty salon, exercise room, volleyball, beach, dive shop, dock, water-sports center, shops, casino, baby-sitting, children's program (4–12), laundry service and dry cleaning, business services, meeting rooms, travel services, car and scooter rental. AE, DC, MC, V. EP, CP, MAP, FAP.*

**$–$$** 🖼 **Avila Beach Hotel.** The royal family of Holland and its ministers stay ★ at this 200-year-old mansion overlooking the ocean for three good reasons: the privacy, the personalized service, and the peacefulness. The reception area is cooled by whirring fans and graced with a baby grand. The original guest rooms are charmingly adorned in locally made

# Curaçao

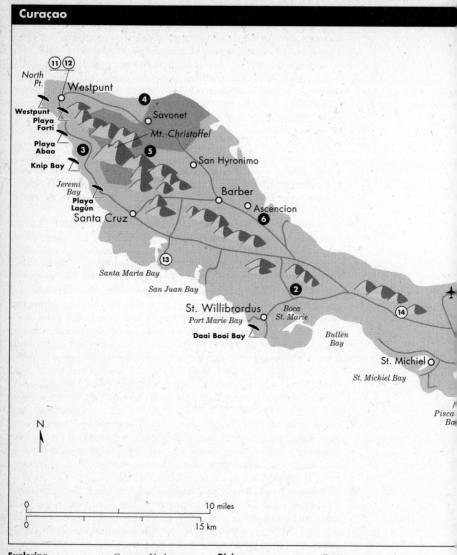

**Exploring**
Boca Tabla, **4**
Christoffel Park, **5**
Curaçao House
Museum, **6**
Curaçao
Seaquarium, **10**

Curaçao Underwater
Marine Park, **9**
Hato Caves, **7**
Landhuis
Brievengat, **8**
Landhuis Jan Kok, **2**
Landhuis Knip, **3**
Willemstad, **1**

**Dining**
L'Alouette, **28**
Bistro Le
Clochard, **18**
Cactus Club, **32**
Fort Nassau
Restaurant, **30**

Fort
Waarzaamreid, **20**
Golden Star
Restaurant, **29**
Jaanchi's
Restaurant, **11**
L'Orangerie, **25**
La Pergola, **22**

**KEY**
🚢 Cruise Ship
❶ Exploring Sites
⑪ Hotels and Restaurants

Pirates, **15**
Rijstaffel Indonesia
Restaurant, **31**
Seaview, **24**
Le Taveerne, **33**

**Lodging**
Avila Beach Hotel, **27**
Coral Cliff Resort
and Beach Club, **13**
Curaçao Caribbean
Hotel and Casino, **15**
Holiday Beach Hotel
and Casino, **17**

Kadushi Cliffs, **12**
Landhaus Daniel, **14**
Lions Dive Hotel &
Marina, **26**
Otrabanda Hotel &
Casino, **19**
Porto Paseo Hotel
and Casino, **21**

Princess Beach Resort
and Casino, **25**
Sonesta Beach Hotel
& Casino, **16**
Van Der Valk Plaza
Hotel and Casino, **23**

furniture and art, but are still basic-looking, with hardwood or tile floors and small baths with showers and sun-warmed water only. Most guests prefer the newer La Belle Alliance section, on its own beach adjacent to the main property. These Mediterranean-style yellow-and-gold low-rise buildings, with Dutch red-gabled roofs and lighted walkways, have either balconies or patios with sea views. Although they lack the Old World ambience of the original structure, the accommodations are larger and have more modern amenities. The restaurant has a unique outdoor dining area shaded by an enormous tree. The Danish chefs, who specialize in a Viking pot, local dishes, and weekly smorgasbord, also smoke their own fish and bake their own bread. A shaded terrace with Adirondack chairs (referred to on the island as Avila chairs) overlooks the two crescent beaches and the pier bar where live jazz takes center stage Thursday and Saturday evenings. Many consider this quiet, family-owned-and-operated hotel the best buy on the island. ⊠ *Box 791, Penstraat 130134, Willemstad,* ☎ *599/9–614377 or 800/448–8355,* 𝙵𝙰𝚇 *599/9–611493. 107 rooms, 8 suites. 2 restaurants, 2 bars, kitchenettes, refrigerators, tennis court, beach, baby-sitting, laundry service and dry cleaning, business services, conference center, car rental, shuttle bus to city center. AE, DC, MC, V. EP, MAP.*

$ ⛱ **Coral Cliff Resort and Beach Club.** Seclusion and rustic simplicity are everything here. A 45-minute ride from the center of Willemstad, the resort boasts a beach so alluring that it attracts even native islanders seeking a weekend retreat. (The only clothing-optional beach on the island, it's open to the public for a charge.) The resort feels very European—wood beams accent the lavender, mint, olive, cream, and teal colors in bi-level suites—and is very popular with Dutch tourists. If you're used to luxurious resorts, you may find the standard rooms stark and in need of modernizing. However, the deluxe rooms are comfortable and attractive, with balconies. At press time, construction was under way on a new pool. ⊠ *Box 3782, Santa Marta Bay,* ☎ *599/9–642666 or 800/223–9815,* 𝙵𝙰𝚇 *599/9–641781. 62 units. Restaurant, bar, kitchenettes, pool, tennis court, miniature golf, minizoo, horseback riding, Ping-Pong, beach, dive shop, dock, billiards, casino, baby-sitting, playground, coin laundry, laundry service, meeting room, downtown shuttle. AE, D, DC, MC, V. EP, BP, MAP, FAP.*

$ ⛱ **Landhaus Daniel.** Dating back to 1630, this plantation house was never a farm, but it served as an inn for travelers going east or west on the island. The property, situated near the narrow center of the island, has a restaurant, a pool, and a dive center. Rooms are tiny but clean, with basic, functional furnishings. All have private bathrooms with showers; only two are air-conditioned (the rest have ceiling fans), but the trade winds usually take care of excessive heat at night. This is a fine budget option and has the fun atmosphere of a youth hostel. ⊠ *Wegnaar Westpunt,* ☎ *599/9–648400. 8 rooms. Restaurant, bar, pool, dive center, billiards, darts, TV room. AE, MC, V. EP, MAP.*

$ ⛱ **Lions Dive Hotel & Marina.** This rose-and-green caravansary is a hop, skip, and plunge away from the Seaquarium, next to a quarter mile of private beach. Rooms are airy, modern, and light-filled, with tile floors, large bathrooms (showers only), and lots of windows. A pair of French doors leads out to a spacious balcony or terrace, and every room has a view of the sea. The Sunday-night happy hour is especially festive, with a local merengue band playing poolside. By midnight, however, the only sound to be heard is the whir of your room's air conditioner. Pluses include a young staff who are eager to please and a top-notch scuba center. Dive packages are offered with Underwater Curaçao, and most, if not all, of the guests are dive enthusiasts. ⊠ *Bapor Kibra, Curaçao,* ☎ *599/9–618100 or 800/223–9815,* 𝙵𝙰𝚇 *599/9–618200. 72 rooms. Restaurant, bar, in-room safes, pool, exercise room, beach, dock,* *water-sports center and dive shop, laundry service. AE, DC, MC, V. CP, EP.*

$ ▦ **Otrabanda Hotel & Casino.** Built in 1991, this little city hotel—superior value—is across the harbor from downtown Willemstad, in the historic Otrabanda section. Rooms are cramped but appealing, with smashing harbor views, rattan furnishings, and paintings of country scenes. The most attractive and roomiest are those tucked under the peaked roof. At press time, plans were under way to add a swimming pool. ⊠ *Breedestraat, Otrabanda,* ☎ *599/9–627400,* FAX *599/9–627299. 42 rooms, 3 suites. Restaurant, bar, coffee shop, casino, baby-sitting, dry cleaning and laundry service, car rental. AE, MC, V. CP.*

$ ▦ **Porto Paseo Hotel and Casino.** This charming property on the Otra-
★ banda side of the harbor recalls a typical landhouse, with its tropical gardens, a lamp-lit flagstone courtyard, rock walls, and mustard-color bungalow-style buildings with red-tile roofs. At its center is the hotel, a restored 17th-century building. It's a remarkably peaceful, private place amid the city's bustle. Squawking white cockatoos preside over the entrance to an open-air bar splashed with murals depicting island life and overlooking Santa Anna Bay. The unadorned but pleasant rooms shimmer in silver, mauve, and ecru; all have showers. At press time there was talk of expanding the casino. ⊠ *De Rouvilleweg 47, Willemstad,* ☎ *599/9–627878 or 800/287–2226,* FAX *599/9–627969. 45 rooms, 4 suites. Restaurant, bar, kitchenettes, pool, casino, baby-sitting, laundry service. AE, DC, MC, V. EP.*

$ ▦ **Van Der Valk Plaza Hotel and Casino.** "Please don't touch the passing ships" is the slogan of the Van Der Valk Plaza, the island's first high-rise hotel, and the only hotel in the world with marine-collision insurance. The ships do come close; since the structure is built right into the massive walls of a 17th-century fort at the entrance of Willemstad's harbor. At the Plaza, you give up beachfront (you have beach privileges at Seaquarium, however) for walking access to the city's center. Consequently, it's a business traveler's oasis. The ramparts rising from the sea offer a fantastic evening view of the twinkling city lights. The lobby is a vision in marble, with handsomely upholstered furniture and a winding lagoon and waterfall. There's a casino on the property. Rooms are scheduled for renovation; many have a sea view and some have balconies. ⊠ *Box 229, Plaza Piar, Willemstad,* ☎ *599/9–612500 or 800/447–7462,* FAX *599/9–616543. 236 rooms, 18 suites. 2 restaurants, 3 bars, snack bar, in-room safes, refrigerators on request, room service, pool, beach shuttle, casino, baby-sitting, dry cleaning and laundry service, business services, meeting rooms, travel services, car rental. AE, DC, MC, V. CP.*

## Dining

Dine under the boughs of magnificent old trees, in the romantic gloom of wine cellars in renovated landhouses, or on the ramparts of 18th-century forts. Curaçaoans partake of some of the best Indonesian food in the Caribbean, and they also have access to fine French, Swiss, Dutch, and Swedish fare.

### What to Wear

Dress in restaurants is almost always casual (though beachwear is generally not acceptable). Some of the resort dining rooms and nicer restaurants require that men wear jackets, especially in high season; ask when you make reservations. Do take a wrap or a light sweater with you—most restaurants keep air conditioners going full blast.

| CATEGORY | COST* |
|----------|-------|
| $$$$ | over $40 |
| $$$ | $30–$40 |
| $$ | $15–$30 |
| $ | under $15 |

*per person, excluding drinks and service charge*

$$$$  ✕ **Le Taveerne.** From the intricate detail of its antiques and brickwork
★  to its impressive Continental menu, this restaurant is the most elegant,
romantic spot on the island. Dining is in the whitewashed wine cellar
of a magnificent renovated octagonal country estate, built in the 1800s
by an exiled Venezuelan revolutionary. The best appetizer is the salmon
carpaccio with laurel bay dressing en brioche. The entrées are rich and
decadent: velvety lobster bisque finished with Armagnac, sautéed goose
liver in plum sauce, smoked eel with horseradish. Finish with the unforgettable broiled pears, topped with vanilla ice cream and drenched
with Curaçao chocolate liqueur. ⊠ *Landhuis Groot Davelaar, on
Silena, near Promenade Shopping Center,* ☎ *599/9–370669. AE, D,
DC, MC, V. Closed Sun. No lunch Sat.*

$$$–$$$$  ✕ **L'Alouette.** With only eight tables, this cozy space defines intimate.
★  Tasteful touches include stained glass, fanciful stemware, art-deco
lamps, and severe black-and-white tables that provide a stunning con-
trast to the peach walls and voluminous, lushly folded drapery. Maria
Eugenia Saban's cooking is equally subtle and sophisticated, wonder-
fully textured; everything is carefully prepared. You might begin with
two cheese flans (goat cheese–leek and Gruyère-mushroom), or a
seafood sausage in lobster velouté. Your entrée might be the sublime
salmon in lime and chive sauce. The exquisite presentations and cre-
ative counterpoints are infallible. You'll feel underdressed here in jeans
and sneakers. ⊠ *Orionweg 12,* ☎ *599/9–618222. AE, DC, MC, V.
Closed Sun. No lunch Sat.*

$$$–$$$$  ✕ **Bistro Le Clochard.** This romantic gem is built into the 18th-century
Rif Fort—an oasis of arched entryways, exposed brickwork, wood
beams, and lace curtains. Cocktails and hors d'oeuvres are served on
the Waterside Terrace, with its merry view of the floating bridge and
harbor. The French and Swiss dishes are consistently well prepared,
though pricey. Try the fresh-fish platters or the veal in mushroom
sauce. Savor the fondue and let yourself get carried away by the un-
usual setting; save room for the chocolate mousse. Avoid weekends,
when an inexplicably hokey duo plays, but you might enjoy the com-
plimentary snacks of Friday's Hungry Hour 5-to-7. ⊠ *On the Otra-
banda Rif Fort,* ☎ *599/9–625666. AE, DC, MC, V. Closed Sun. No
lunch Sat.*

$$$–$$$$  ✕ **L'Orangerie.** A romantic setting and gourmet Continental cuisine
await you at this new restaurant at the Princess Beach Resort (☞
Lodging, *above*). Favorites from the à la carte menu include the salad
of smoked salmon, creamy cucumber, and potato rösti; sautéed jumbo
shrimp in lobster sauce—but don't make your selection until you hear
the daily specials. The $28 prix-fixe option offers savings. ⊠ *Princess
Beach Resort, Martin Luther King Blvd. 8,* ☎ *599/9–655955. AE, DC,
MC, V. Closed Mon. No lunch.*

$$$  ✕ **Fort Nassau Restaurant.** This is *the* place to view twinkling Curaçao
at night. High on a hilltop overlooking Willemstad, the restaurant is
built into an 18th-century fort and gives a 360-degree view. Go for a
drink in the breezy, Battery Terrace bar or dine in air-conditioned comfort in front of the huge bay windows. The menu is diverse, from duck
with molasses sauce to lightly broiled fish (ask the waiter what's fresh—
and not on the menu). Stay away from the enticing yet overly complex
stabs at innovative cuisine: The simple selections are best here. Dinner

seatings are at 7 and 9 PM. ✉ *Near Juliana Bridge,* ☎ *599/9–613086. Reservations essential. AE, D, DC, MC, V. No lunch weekends.*

$$$ ✗ **La Pergola.** Built into the stuccoed walls of the Waterfort, with huge picture windows fronting the rambunctious sea and a pretty pink-and-white arbor wound with bunches of grapes, La Pergola offers creative variations on Italian standards. Try the smoked salmon drizzled with olive oil and studded with cloves or the grouper siciliana with capers, olives, anchovies, tomatoes, and garlic. ✉ *Waterfort Arches, Willemstad,* ☎ *599/9–613482. AE, D, DC, MC, V. No lunch Sun.*

$$–$$$ ✗ **Pirates.** A friendly and efficient wait staff delivers dish after dish of superb seafood, including oyster soup, seviche, paella, and conch. The sea bass Creole-style is delicious, as is the red snapper in almond sauce. The decor is nautical, with an anchor, a watch tower, and, of course, a mermaid. ✉ *Curaçao Caribbean Hotel,* ☎ *599/9–628500. AE, DC, MC, V.*

$$ ✗ **Fort Waarzaamreid.** High on a hill overlooking Willemstad and the harbor, this fort was captured by Captain Bligh of HMS *Bounty* two centuries ago. Now it is controlled by an Irishman, Tom Farrel, who operates an open-air restaurant and bar in the evening. The atmosphere is informal, and the food is primarily barbecued seafood and steaks decorated with your own makings from a salad bar. You will be equally well greeted if you go just for cocktails and snacks—and the sunsets are magnificent. ✉ *Off main highway on Otrabanda side of suspension bridge, Seru Domi, Willemstad,* ☎ *599/9–623633. AE, D, MC, V. Closed Tues. No lunch.*

$$ ✗ **Rijstaffel Indonesia Restaurant.** An antique rickshaw guarding the entrance sets the mood in this tranquil spot. No steaks or chops here, just one dish after another of exotic delicacies that make up the traditional Indonesian banquet called rijstaffel, where some 16 to 25 dishes are set buffet-style around you. You can also order from an à la carte menu, which includes fried noodles, fresh jumbo shrimp in garlic, and combination meat-and-fish platters. Desserts are nearly mystical: The coconut ice cream comes packed in a coconut shell. The walls are hung with beautiful Indonesian puppets ($25–$40) that make stunning gifts. ✉ *Mercurriusstraat 13–15, Salina,* ☎ *599/9–612606. AE, DC, MC, V. No lunch Sun.*

$$ ✗ **Seaview.** This casual terrace eatery is nestled snugly in the corner of the Waterfort Arches, where the surf pounds against the rocks—you expect the sea to drench you at any minute. Try the tender pepper fillet or the tangy *salpicon de mariscos,* a version of seviche that includes everything from octopus to shrimp vinaigrette. The chef can also surprise with such specialties as green-and-white asparagus en brioche. It's a marvelous place to watch the pyrotechnics of the sun at dusk. ✉ *Waterfort Arches, Willemstad,* ☎ *599/9–616688. AE, DC, MC, V. No lunch Sun.*

$ ✗ **Cactus Club.** A veritable grove of aloe and cacti greets you in the courtyard of this Caribbean version of Bennigan's. The inside is surprisingly subdued: faux Tiffany lamps, hanging plants, whirring ceiling fans. Food is cheap and filling, including fettuccine Alfredo, fajitas, buffalo wings, Cajun snapper, and burgers. It's predictably popular with both locals and homesick Americans. ✉ *Mahaai,* ☎ *599/9–371600. D, MC, V.*

$ ✗ **Golden Star Restaurant.** This place looks and feels more like a friendly roadside diner, but the native food here is among the best in town. Owner Marie Burke turns out such Antillean specialties as *bestia chiki* (goat stew), shrimp Creole, and delicately seasoned grilled conch, with generous heaps of rice, fried plantains, and avocado. Steaks and

chops can be had for the asking. ⊠ *Socratestraat 2,* ☎ *599/9–654795.*
*AE, DC, MC, V.*

$ ✕ **Jaanchi's Restaurant.** Tour buses stop regularly at this open-air
★ restaurant for lunches of mouthwatering native dishes. The main-
course specialty is a hefty platter of fresh-caught fish, conch, or shrimp
with potatoes or *funchi* (cornbread) and vegetables on the side. Curaçaoans joke that Jaanchi's "iguana soup is so strong it could resur-
rect the dead"—truth is, it tastes just like chicken soup, only better.
But Jaanchi Jr. says, if you want iguana, you should order in advance
"because we have to go out and catch them." He's not kidding. He
usually closes at 6:30 PM but will stay open later if you call ahead to
reserve a spot. ⊠ *Westpunt 15,* ☎ *599/9–640126. AE, DC, MC, V.*

# Beaches

Curaçao has some 38 beaches, but unfortunately some are rocky and
litter-strewn. The best way to find "your" beach is to rent a Jeep, motor
scooter, or heavy-treaded car. Ask your hotel to pack a picnic basket
and go exploring. Getting lost and ending up in some undiscovered cove
is half the fun. Curaçao doesn't have Aruba's long stretches of sand;
instead, you'll discover the joy of inlets: tiny bay openings to the sea
marked by craggy cliffs, exotic trees, and scads of interesting pebbles.
Imagine a beach that's just big enough for two. Beware of thorns and
keep an eye out for flying fish. They propel their tails through the water
until they reach a speed of 44 mph, then spread their fins and soar.

Hotels with the best beaches include the Sonesta Beach Hotel (impressively long), the Princess Beach (impressively sensuous), and the
Coral Cliff Resort (impressively deserted). No matter where you're staying, beach hopping to other hotels can be fun. Nonguests are supposed
to pay the hotels a beach fee, but often there is no one to collect.

**Daai Booi Bay** is a sandy shore dotted with thatched shelters. The road
to this public beach (follow signs from the church of St. Willibrordus)
is a small paved highway flanked on either side by thick lush trees and
huge organ-pipe cacti. The beach is curved, with shrubbery rooted into
the side of the rocky cliffs—a great place for swimming. **Knip Bay** has
two parts: Big (Groot) Knip and Little (Kleine) Knip. Only Little Knip
is shaded with trees, but these are manchineels, so steer clear of them.
Also beware of cutting your feet on beer-bottle caps. Both beaches have
alluring white sand, but only Big Knip has changing facilities. Big
Knip also has several tiki huts for shade and calm turquoise waters that
are perfect for swimming and lounging. The protected cove, flanked
by sheer cliffs, is usually a blast on Sundays, when there is live music.
To get there, take the road to the Knip Landhouse, then turn right. Signs
will direct you. **Playa Forti,** just south of Westpunt (the island's northwest point), is a double cove of beige sand with a splendid view of Westpunt Church, colorful fishing boats bobbing in the turquoise water, and
a little café in the shade where you can watch local boys dive from the
cliffs on weekends. **Playa Lagun,** southeast of Playa Forti, is dotted with
powder-blue camping huts and caught between towering gunmetal gray
cliffs. Cognoscenti know this is one of the best places to snorkel—you
may even go nose to nose with the resident giant squid. **Santa Barbara,**
a popular family beach on the eastern tip, is reached by driving through
one of Curaçao's toniest neighborhoods, Spanish Water, where gleaming white yachts replace humble fishing fleets. The beach has changing facilities and a snack bar but charges a small admission fee, usually
around $3.35 per car. Around the bend, **Caracas Bay** is a popular dive
site, with a sunken ship so close to the surface that snorkelers can view
it clearly.

# Outdoor Activities and Sports

## Fitness Centers

**Ooms Sports Institute** (⊠ Lions Dive Hotel, ☎ 599/9–618100) is open to nonguests for a fee. It schedules exercise classes and is equipped with the latest fitness equipment. **Sundance Health & Fitness Center** (⊠ John F. Kennedy Blvd. at Rif Recreation Area, ☎ 599/9–627740) has all the gentle luxuries, including Turkish bath, sauna, whirlpool, massage, and beauty treatments. Professional medical staff is on tap.

## Golf

**Curaçao Golf and Squash Club** (⊠ Emmastad, ☎ 599/9–373590, ☉ 8–12:30) welcomes visitors. The nine-hole course offers a challenge because of the stiff trade winds and the sand greens.

## Horseback Riding

**Ashari's Ranch** (☎ 599/9–690315) is the only stable to offer romps to the beach.

## Jogging

**Rif Recreation Area,** locally known as the *corredor,* stretches from the water plant at Mundo Nobo to the Sonesta Beach Hotel along the sea. It consists of more than 1.2 miles of palm-lined beachfront, a wading pond, and a jogging track with an artificial surface, as well as a big playground. There is good security and street lighting along the entire length of the beachfront.

## Sailing

**Sail Curaçao** (⊠ Yachtclub Asiento, Spanish Water, ☎ 599/9–676003) offers day sails, sailing instruction, snorkeling trips, and windsurfing.

## Tennis

Most hotels (including Sonesta Beach, Curaçao Caribbean, Las Palmas, Princess Beach, and Holiday Beach) offer well-paved courts, illuminated for day and night games. These courts are usually occupied by guests of the hotels. Your best bet if you're not staying at one of these properties is the **Santa Catherina Sports and Country Club** (☎ 599/9–677028), where 45 minutes of court time costs $10 during the day, $15 after 6 PM.

## Water Sports

Curaçao has facilities for all kinds of water sports, thanks to the government-sponsored **Curaçao Underwater Marine Park** (☎ 599/9–618131), which includes almost a third of the island's southern diving waters. Scuba divers and snorkelers can enjoy more than 12½ miles of protected reefs and shores, with normal visibility from 60 to 80 feet (up to 150 feet on good days). With water temperatures ranging from 75° to 82°F, wet suits are generally unnecessary. No coral collecting, spearfishing, or littering is allowed. An exciting wreck to explore is the SS *Oranje Nassau,* which ran aground more than 80 years ago and now hosts hundreds of exotic fish and unusually shaped coral.

Most hotels either offer their own program of water sports or will be happy to make arrangements for you. An introductory scuba resort course usually runs about $50–$65.

**Coral Cliff Diving** (☎ 599/9–642822) offers an open-water certification course ($330) and a full schedule of dive and snorkeling trips to Curaçao's southwest coast. It also rents pedal boats, Hobie Cats, and underwater cameras. **Peter Hughes Divers** (☎ 599/9–367888, ext. 5047), at the Princess Beach Resort, rents equipment (including underwater camera) and conducts diving and snorkeling trips. Two-tank boat dives run $55, while three days of unlimited shore diving costs $33. Also available is a cabin cruiser for half- or full-day deep-sea fishing excursions. **Seascape** (☎ 599/9–625000, ext. 6056, or 599/9–625905), at the Curaçao Caribbean Hotel and Casino, specializes in snorkeling and scuba-diving trips to reefs and underwater wrecks in every type of water vehicle—from pedal boats, kayaks, and water scooters to waterskis and Windsurfers. A six-dive package costs $165 and includes unlimited beach diving plus one boat dive per day and one night dive. Snorkeling gear costs about $10 a day to rent. Die-hard fishermen with companions who prefer to suntan will enjoy the day trip to Little Curaçao, the "clothes optional" island between Curaçao and Bonaire, where the fish are reputed to be lively: Plan on $50 per person. Deep-sea fishing for a maximum of four people can also be arranged; it costs $350 for a half day, $560 for a full day. **Underwater Curaçao** (☎ 599/9–618131) offers complete vacation-dive packages in conjunction with the Lions Dive Hotel & Marina. Its fully stocked dive shop, located between the Lions Dive Hotel and the Curaçao Seaquarium, offers equipment for both sale and rental. Personal instruction and group lessons are conducted on state-of-the-art dive boats personally designed by "Dutch" Schrier. One dive will run you $33; dive-only packages are available. Take a dive-snorkeling trip on the *Coral Sea,* a 40-foot twin diesel yacht-style dive boat. Landlubbers can see beneath the sea aboard *The Coral View,* a monohull flat-top glass-bottom boat that makes four excursions a day.

## Spectator Sports

**Centro Deportivo** (✉ Bonamweg 49, ☎ 599/9–376620, ⊙ Daily 9:30–12:30 and 1–6), a modern and comfortable stadium located about 10 minutes from town, holds soccer matches and baseball games from March through October.

# Shopping

Curaçao has long enjoyed the reputation of having some of the best shops in the Caribbean, but don't expect posh Madison Avenue boutiques. With a few exceptions (such as Benetton, which recently moved into the Caribbean with a vengeance), the quality of women's fashions here lies along the lines of sales racks, although not paying a VAT or other taxes sweetens any purchase. Be aware that many shops are closed on Sunday.

If you're looking for bargains on Swiss watches, cameras, crystal, perfumes, or electronic equipment, do some comparison shopping back home and come armed with a list of prices. Willemstad is no longer a free port.

## Shopping Areas

Most of the shops are concentrated in Willemstad's Punda within about a six-block area. The main shopping streets are Heerenstraat, Breedestraat, and Madurostraat. Heerenstraat and Gomezplein are pedestrian malls, closed to traffic, and their roadbeds have been raised to sidewalk level and covered with pink inlaid tiles. The hippest shopping area lies under the Waterfort Arches, along with a variety of restaurants and bars.

## Good Buys

**Bamali** (✉ Waterfort Arches, ☎ 599/9–612258) sells Indonesian batik clothing, leather bags, and charming handicrafts. **Boolchand's** (✉ Heerenstraat 4B, ☎ 599/9–616233) handles an interesting variety of merchandise behind a facade of red-and-white-checked tiles. Stock up here on French perfumes, British cashmere sweaters, Italian silk ties, Dutch dolls, Swiss watches, and Japanese cameras. **Clarisa & Laura Kemper** (✉ Waterfort Arches, ☎ 599/9–618313) specializes in exquisite leather and silk creations. **Julius L. Penha & Sons** (✉ Heerenstraat 1, ☎ 599/9–612266), in front of the Pontoon Bridge, sells French perfumes, Hummel figurines, linen from Madeira, delftware, and handbags from Argentina, Italy, and Spain. The store also has an extensive cosmetics counter. **Little Switzerland** (⊠ Breedstraat 44, ☎ 599/9–612111) is the place for duty-free shopping; here you'll find perfumes, jewelry, watches, crystal, china, and leather goods at significant savings.

CLOTHING

**Benetton** (⊠ Madurostraat 4, ☎ 599/9–614619, and other addresses) has winter stock in July and summer stock in December; all stock is 20% off the retail price. **Boutique Aquarius** (⊠ Breedestraat 9, ☎ 599/9–612618) sells Fendi merchandise for 25% less than in the United States. Fendi fanatics can stock up on belts, shoes, pocketbooks, wallets, and even watches. **Boutique Liska** (⊠ Schottegatweg Oost 191-A, ☎ 599/9–613111) is where local residents shop for smart women's fashions. **Clog Dance** (⊠ De Rouvilleweg 9B, ☎ 599/9–623280) is where to go if you long for Dutch clogs, tulips, delftware, Dutch fashions, or chocolate. **Crazy Look** (⊠ Madurostraat 6, ☎ 599/9–611440) has French, Italian, and Dutch fashions with a hip Eurotrash look, as well as trendy sweatshirts and baggy pants.

DELICACIES

**Toko Zuikertuintje** (⊠ Zuikertuintjeweg, ☎ 599/9–370188), a supermarket built on the original 17th-century Zuikertuintje Landhuis, is where most of the local elite shop. Enjoy the free tea and coffee while you stock up on all sorts of European and Dutch delicacies. Shopping here for a picnic is a treat in itself.

JEWELRY AND WATCHES

**Gandelman** (⊠ Breedestraat 35, ☎ 599/9–611854 and Sonesta Beach Hotel, ☎ 599/9–628386) has watches by Cartier and Piaget, leather goods by Prima Classe, and Lallique, Baccarat, and Daum crystal. **La Zahav N.V.** (⊠ Curaçao International Airport, ☎ 599/9–689594) is one of the best places to buy gold jewelry—with or without diamonds, rubies, and emeralds—at true discount prices. The shop is located in the airport transit hall, just at the top of the staircase.

LINENS

**New Amsterdam** (⊠ Gomezplein 14, ☎ 599/9–612469) is the place to price hand-embroidered tablecloths, napkins, and pillowcases. Tablecloths begin at $32, double bedspreads at $100.

LOCAL CRAFTS

**Arawak Craft Factory** (⊠ Cruise Terminal, Otrabanda, ☎ 599/9–627249) has a factory showroom of native-made crafts. You can purchase a variety of tiles, plates, pots, and tiny replicas of landhouse. **Black Coral** (⊠ Princess Beach Hotel, ☎ 599/9–614944) is owned by Dutch-born artisan Bert Knubben, one of Curaçao's true characters. For the past 30 years, he's been designing and sculpting the most exciting black-coral jewelry in the Caribbean—and he even dives for the coral himself, with special permission from the government. Dolphin pendants and twiglike earrings finished in 14-karat gold are excellent buys. Call before you drop by. **Fundason Obra di Man** (⊠ Bargestraat 57, ☎ 599/9–612413) stocks native crafts and curios. Particularly impressive are the posters of Curaçao's architecture. **Gallery 86** (⊠ In Bloksteeg (Punda) opposite Bank of the Netherlands Antilles, ☎ 599/9–613417) features the works of local artists and occasionally those of South Americans and Africans. **Landhuis Groot Santa Martha** (☎ 599/9–641323) is where artisans with disabilities fashion handicrafts of varying types.

# Nightlife and the Arts

## Nightlife

Friday is the big night out, with rollicking happy hours—most with live music—at several hotels, most notably the Holiday Beach and Avila Beach (☞ Lodging, *above*). The once-a-month open house at Landhuis Brievengat (☞ Exploring, *below*) is a great way to meet interesting locals—it usually offers a folkloric show, snacks, and local handicrafts. Every Friday night the landhouse holds a big party with two bands. Check with the tourist board for the schedule of folkloric shows at various hotels. The Sonesta Beach, Van Der Valk Plaza, Curaçao Caribbean, Holiday Beach, Otrabanda, and Princess Beach hotels all have casinos that are open 1 PM–4 AM.

### BARS

**Blues** (⊠ Avila Beach Hotel, Penstraat 130, ☎ 599/9–614377) focuses on live jazz Thursday and Saturday. The bar is at the end of the pier; magnificent sunset views are guaranteed. **Rum Runners** (⊠ Otrobanda Waterfront, De Rouvilleweg 9, ☎ 599/9–623038) is a casual hot spot. This well-lit indoor-outdoor bar and eatery serves up tapas in an atmosphere that's reminiscent of a college fraternity hall. There's music nightly.

### DISCOS

The Salina district is the spot for clubbing: You'll find everything from merengue to house.

**L'Aristocrat** (⊠ Lindbergweg, Salina, ☎ 599/9–617939) attracts the more mature crowd seeking late-night pleasures, and on Saturday night the line to get in stretches down the block. Inside, the trendy clientele gyrates to a heavy beat while silent large-screen TVs flash sensual images. **Façade** (⊠ Lindbergweg 32, Salina, ☎ 599/9–614640) is a hip Curaçao dance spot. It's dark and cool, with huge bamboo chairs for lounging. There are two disco floors with flashing lights and an intense aural assault, sometimes from a live band. **The Jail** (⊠ Keukenplein, ☎ 599/9–656810), newest on the dance scene, comes complete with a warden, caged or chained dancers, jailhouse graffiti lit by black light, and, on the mellower second floor, individual "cells" for private rendezvous. **The Pub** (⊠ Salina 144A, ☎ 599/9–612190) is a crowded, energetic dancing-and-drinking club. It's the place for the loud, the hip, the young, and the wanna-bes checking on the latest Curaçao fads.

## The Arts

The **Curaçao Museum,** housed in a century-old former plantation house, is filled with artifacts, paintings, and antique furnishings that trace the island's history. This is also the venue for art exhibitions that visit the island. ⊠ *Leeuwenhoekstraat,* ☎ *599/9–623873.* 🖭 *$2.* ☉ *Tues.–Fri. 9–noon and 2–5, Sun. 10–4.*

# Exploring Curaçao

Willemstad, the capital, is cut in two by Santa Anna Bay. There are three ways to make the crossing from one side to the other: (1) drive or take a taxi over the Juliana Bridge, (2) traverse the Queen Emma Pontoon Bridge on foot, or (3) ride the free ferry, which runs when the bridge is open for passing ships. All the major hotels outside of town offer free shuttle service to town once or twice daily. Shuttles coming from the Otrabanda side leave you at Rif Fort. From there it's a short walk north to the foot of the Pontoon Bridge. Shuttles coming from the Punda side leave you near the main entrance to Fort Amsterdam. The road through the village of Soto that leads to the northwest tip of the island winds through landscape that Georgia O'Keeffe might have painted—towering cacti, flamboyant dried shrubbery, and aluminum-roof houses. Throughout this *cunucu,* or countryside, you'll see native fishermen hauling in their nets, women pounding cornmeal, and an occasional donkey blocking traffic. Landhouses, large plantation houses from centuries past, dot the countryside, though most are closed to the public. Their facades, though, can often be glimpsed from the highway. To explore the eastern side of the island, take the coastal road—Martin Luther King Boulevard—from Willemstad about 2 miles to Bapor Kibra. Here you'll find the Seaquarium and the Underwater Park.

*Numbers in the margin correspond to points of interest on the Curaçao map.*

SIGHTS TO SEE

**❹ Boca Tabla.** At Boca Tabla, the sea has carved a magnificent grotto. Safely tucked in the back, you can watch and listen to the waves crashing ferociously against the rocks. ⌂ *Westpunt Hwy., just past village of Soto.*

**❺ Christoffel Park.** This fantastic 4,450-acre (1,860 hectares) garden and wildlife preserve has the towering Mt. Christoffel at its center. Open to the public since 1978, the park consists of three former plantations with individual trails that take about 1 to 1½ hours each to traverse. You may drive your own car (if it has heavy-treaded wheels) or rent a Jeep with an accompanying guide (around $90 for up to four passengers). Start out early (by 10 AM the park starts to feel like a sauna), and if you're going solo, first study the *Excursion Guide to Christoffel Park* that's sold at the front desk of the elegant, if dilapidated, Landhuis Savonet (the plantation house turned Natural History Museum); it outlines the various routes and identifies the flora and fauna found here. No matter what route you take, you'll be treated to interesting views of hilly fields full of prickly pear cacti, divi-divi trees, bushy-haired palms, and exotic flowers that bloom unpredictably after April showers. There are also caves—the strong at heart will revel in the rustling of bat wings and the sight of scuttling scorpion spiders (scary but not poisonous)—and ancient Indian drawings.

As you drive through the park, keep a lookout for tiny deer, goats, and other small wildlife that might suddenly dart in front of your car. The whip snakes and minute silver snakes you may encounter are not poisonous. White-tail hawks may be seen on the green route, white orchids and crownlike passionflowers on the yellow route. Climbing the 1,239-foot Mt. Christoffel on foot is an exhilarating experience and a definite challenge to anyone who hasn't grown up scaling the Alps. The guidebook claims the round-trip will take you one hour, and Curaçaoan adolescent boys do make a sport of racing up and down, but it's really more like two (sweaty) hours from the foot of the mountain for a reasonably fit person who's not an expert hiker. And the last few feet are deadly. The view from the peak, however, *is* thrilling—a panorama of the island, including Santa Marta Bay and the tabletop mountain of St. Hironimus. On a clear day, you can even see the mountain ranges of Venezuela, Bonaire, and Aruba. ⌂ *Savonet,* ☎ *599/9–640363.* 🎫 *Park and museum $9, natural history museum $3.* ⊙ *Mon.–Sat. 8–4, Sun. 6–3; last tour departs 1 hr before closing.*

**❻ Curaçao House Museum.** This thatch-roof cottage is a living museum demonstrating country life as it was in the 19th century. It's filled with antique furniture, farm implements, and clothing typical of colonial life on the island. Out back is a minifarm with vegetable garden, penned donkeys, and caged parrots, eagles, and iguana. Look closely at the fence—it's made of living cacti. There's also a snack bar. A festival featuring live music and local crafts takes place here on the first Sunday of each month. ⊠ *Dokterstuin 27,* ☎ *599/9–642742.* 🎫 *$2.* ⊙ *Tues.–Fri. 9–4, weekends 9–5.*

⤴ **⑩** **Curaçao Seaquarium.** The Seaquarium is *the* place to see the island's underwater treasures without getting your feet wet. It's now more fun than ever, thanks to the *Seaworld Explorer,* a semisubmersible submarine that leaves from near the Seaquarium entrance to take its daily hour-long tour of the coral reefs and submerged wrecks offshore, with their kaleidoscope of fish who are happy to emerge when the diver empties their daily meal into the water. Queen angelfish, yellowtail snapper, porcupine fish, and the ever-popular barracuda are among the denizens. The craft, with a barge top that submerges only 5 feet underwater, has wide glass windows in the submerged section, which extends down to about 100 feet. Call for reservations and tour times 24 hours in advance, and get your ticket before going into the Seaquarium.

Don't neglect the Seaquarium itself. It's the world's only public aquarium where sea creatures are raised and cultivated totally by natural methods. Where else can you hand-feed a shark (or watch a diver do it)? The section called **Animal Encounters** consists of a broad, 12-foot-deep open-water enclosure that brings you face to face with a variety of jaws. If you want to snorkel among them, you're welcome; snorkelers and divers swim freely with stingrays, tarpon, groupers, and such. Diving instruction and equipment are part of the package; it's a thrilling introduction to the sport in a controlled environment, and, in fact, up to 75% of participants have never tried diving before. The highlight for most is the variety of sharks in one section of the enclosure safely divided off by mesh fencing and thick plexiglass; divers and snorkelers can feed the sharks by hand in perfect safety through holes in the plexiglass that separates diver and shark. If shark feeding isn't your cup of tea, there is an underwater observatory where you can watch. The cost is $50 for divers, $30 for snorkelers, which includes admission to the Seaquarium, training in snorkeling and scuba diving, use of equipment, and food for the sharks. Reservations for Animal Encounters must be made 24 hours in advance.

You can spend several hours in Seaquarium, mesmerized by the 46 freshwater tanks full of more than 400 varieties of exotic fish and vegetation found in the waters around Curaçao, including sharks, lobsters, turtles, corals, and sponges. Look out for the more than 5-foot-long mascot, Herbie the lugubrious jewfish. One outdoor enclosure houses a sea lion and a sea bear (yes, they're different, like a horse and a mule). A snack bar and a restaurant are on the grounds in case you get hungry. There are also glass-bottom-boat tours, fun feeding shows, and a viewing platform overlooking the wreck of the steamship SS *Oranje Nassau,* which sank in 1906 and now sits in 10 feet of water. A nearby 495-yard man-made beach of white sand is well suited to novice swimmers and children, and bathroom and shower facilities are available. A souvenir shop sells some of the best postcards and coral jewelry on the island. ⊠ *Bapor Kibra.* Seaworld Explorer, ☎ *599/7–628833.* 🎫 *$29. Seaquarium,* ☎ *599/9–616666 or 599/9–616670,* 🎫 *$12.50.* ⊙ *Daily 8:30 AM–10 PM.*

❾ **Curaçao Underwater Marine Park.** About 12½ miles of untouched coral reefs have been granted the status of national park. Mooring buoys have been placed at the most interesting dive sites on the reef to provide safe anchoring and to prevent damage to the reef. Several sunken ships lie awaiting visitors in the deep. The park stretches along the south shore from the Princess Beach Hotel in Willemstad to the eastern tip of the island. ⊠ *Off southeast shore,* ☎ *599/9–618131.*

**❼ Hato Caves.** Hour-long guided tours wind down into the various chambers to the water pools, voodoo chamber, wishing well, fruit bats' sleeping quarters, and Curaçao Falls, where a stream of silver joins with a stream of gold (they're colored by lights) and is guarded by a limestone "dragon" perched nearby. Hidden lights illuminate the limestone formations and gravel walkways. This is one of the better Caribbean caves open to the public, but keep in mind that the cave is dank and hot, and the pathway rough in spots. ⊠ *Head northwest toward airport, take right onto Gosieweg, follow loop right onto Schottegatweg, take another right onto Jan Norduynweg, a final right onto Rooseveltweg, and follow signs,* ☎ *599/9–68037.* ☞ *$4.* ⊙ *Daily 10–5.*

**❽ Landhuis Brievengat.** This mustard-colored plantation house is a fine example of the island's past. You can see the original kitchen still intact, the 18-inch-thick walls, fine antiques, and the watch towers once used for lovers' trysts. The restaurant, which is open only on Wednesday and Friday, serves a fine *rijstaffel* (Indonesian smorgasbord). Every Friday night a party is held on the wide wraparound terrace, with two bands and plenty to drink. On the last Sunday of the month (from 10 AM to 3 PM), this old estate holds an open house with crafts demonstrations and folkloric shows. ⊠ *10-min drive northeast of Willemstad, near Centro Deportivo sports stadium,* ☎ *599/9–378344.* ☞ *$1.* ⊙ *Mon.–Sat. 9:15–12:15 and 3–6.*

**❷ Landhuis Jan Kok.** For a splendid view, and some unusual island tales of ghosts, visit this mid-17th-century plantation house overlooking the salt pans. Since the hours are irregular, be sure to call ahead to arrange a tour of this reputedly haunted house, or stop by on Sunday mornings, when the proprietor occasionally opens the small restaurant behind her home and serves delicious Dutch pancakes. ⊠ *Weg Naar San Willibrordus,* ☎ *599/9–648087.* ⊙ *Call ahead to arrange tour.*

**❸ Landhuis Knip.** In terms of the number of slaves held, this was the largest plantation on the island in it's prime. It therefore comes as no surprise that the slave revolt took place here in 1795. The renovated plantation house near the western tip of the island is filled with period furnishings, clothing, and other household goods. You can also walk around the extensive stables and barns used in the operation of this maize plantation. ⊠ *Weg Naar Santa Cruz,* ☎ *599/9–640244.* ☞ *$2.* ⊙ *Sun.–Fri. 9–noon and 2–4.*

## Willemstad

**❶** What does **Willemstad,** the capital of Curaçao, have in common with New York City? Broadway, for one. Here it's called Breedestraat, but the origin is the same. Dutch settlers came here in the 1630s, the same period when they sailed through the Narrows to Manhattan, bringing with them original red-tile roofs, first used on the trade ships as ballast and later incorporated into the architecture of Willemstad.

Willemstad is a favorite cruise stop for two reasons: The shopping is considered among the best in the Caribbean, and a quick tour of most of the downtown sights can be managed within a six-block radius. Santa Anna Bay slices the city down the middle: On one side is the Punda, and on the other is the Otrabanda (literally, the "other side"). Think of the Punda as the side for tourists, crammed with shops, restaurants, monuments, and markets. Otrabanda is less touristy, with lots of narrow winding streets full of private homes notable for their picturesque gables and Dutch-influenced designs.

SIGHTS TO SEE

**Floating Market.** Each morning dozens of Venezuelan schooners laden with tropical fruits and vegetables arrive at this bustling market on the Punda side of the city. Fresh mangoes, papayas, and exotic vegetables vie for space with freshly caught fish and herbs and spices. It's probably too much to ask a tourist to arrive by 6:30 AM, when the buying is best, but there's plenty of action to see throughout the afternoon. Any produce bought here, however, should be thoroughly washed before eating. Note: At press time the floating market was temporarily located across Waaigat Channel while the city renovated the dock area, but it should be back on Sha Caprileskade by late 1996. ⊠ *Sha Caprileskade.*

**Fort Amsterdam.** Take a few steps through the archway and enter another century. The entire structure dates from the 1700s, when it was actually the center of the city and the most important fort on the island. Now it houses the governor's residence, the Fort Church, the ministry, and several other government offices. Outside the entrance a series of majestic gnarled *wayaka* trees are fancifully carved with a dragon, a giant squid, and a mermaid—the work of noted local artist Mac Alberto, who can be seen strolling the streets impeccably garbed in blinding white suits, a courtly boutonniere in his lapel. ⊠ *Foot of Queen Emma Bridge.*

**Mikveh Israel-Emanuel Synagogue.** This synagogue was dedicated in 1732 by the Jewish community that came from Amsterdam in 1651 to establish a new congregation. Jews from Portugal and Brazil, fleeing persecution, soon joined them, and by the early 1700s more than 2,000 Jews were in residence. This temple, the oldest still in use in the Western Hemisphere, is one of the most important sights in Curaçao and draws 20,000 visitors a year. Enter through the Spanish-tiled courtyard around the corner from Columbusstraat on Hanchi Di Snoa, and ask the front office to direct you to the guide on duty. A unique feature is the brilliant white sand covering the synagogue floor, a remembrance of Moses leading his people through the desert and of the Diaspora. The Hebrew letters on the four pillars signify the names of the Four Mothers of Israel: Sarah, Rebecca, Rachel, and Leah. The fascinating **Jewish Cultural Museum** (☎ 599/9–611633, 🖅 $2) in the back displays Jewish antiques (including a set of circumcision instruments) and artifacts from Jewish families collected from all over the world. The gift shop near the gate has excellent postcards and commemorative medallions. ⊠ *Hanchi Di Snoa 29,* ☎ *599/9–611067.* 🖅 *Small donation expected.* ☉ *Weekdays 9–11:45 and 2:30–5 (closing time depends on schedule of services). English and Hebrew services conducted by an American rabbi are held Fri. at 6:30 PM and Sat. at 10 AM. Jacket and tie required at services.*

**Old Market (Marche).** Behind the post office is where you'll find local women preparing hearty Antillean lunches at the Old Market. For $4–$6 you can enjoy such Curaçaoan specialties as *funchi* (corn bread), *keshi yena* (Gouda cheese stuffed with meat), goat stew, fried fish, peas and rice, and fried plantains. ⊠ *De Ruyterkade.*

**Plaza Piar.** This plaza, next to Fort Amsterdam, was dedicated to Manuel Piar, a native Curaçaoan who fought for the independence of Venezuela under the liberator Simon Bolívar. On one side of the plaza is the **Waterfort,** a bastion dating from 1634. The original cannons are still positioned in the battlements. The foundation, however, now forms the walls of the Van Der Valk Plaza Hotel. One of the most delightful shopping areas on the island was recently built under the **Waterfort Arches** (☞ Shopping, *above*).

**Queen Emma Bridge.** This bridge is affectionately called the Swinging Old Lady by the natives. If you're standing on the Otrabanda side, take a few moments to scan Curaçao's multicolored "face" on the other side of Santa Anna Bay. If you wait long enough, the bridge will swing open (at least 30 times a day) to let the seagoing ships pass through. The original bridge, built in 1888, was the brainchild of the American consul Leonard Burlington Smith, who made a mint off the tolls he charged for the bridge. Initially, the charge was 2¢ per person for those wearing shoes, free to those crossing barefoot. Today it's free to everyone.

**Queen Juliana Bridge.** This 1,625-foot-long bridge, to the north of the Queen Emma Bridge, was completed in 1974 and stands 200 feet above water—a great vantage point for photos of the city. It's the bridge you drive over to cross to the other side of the city, and although the route is time-consuming (and more expensive if you're going by taxi), the view from the bridge is worth it. At every hour of the day, the sun casts a different tint over the city, creating an ever-changing panorama; the nighttime view, rivaling Rio's, is breathtaking.

**Scharloo.** The Wilhelmina Drawbridge connects Punda with the once-flourishing district of Scharloo, where the early Jewish merchants first built stately homes. The end of the district closest to Kleine Werf is now a red-light district and is pretty run down, but the rest of the area is well worth a visit. The architecture along Scharlooweg (much of it dating to the 17th century) is intriguing, and, happily, many of the structures that had become dilapidated have been meticulously renovated.

# Curaçao A to Z

## Arriving and Departing

BY PLANE

**American Airlines** (☎ 800/433–7300 or 599/9–687008) flies direct daily from Miami. **ALM** (☎ 800/327–7230 or 599/9–695533), Curaçao's national airline, maintains frequent service from Miami and Atlanta. For Atlanta departures, ALM has connecting services (through-fares) to most U.S. gateways with Delta. ALM also offers a Visit Caribbean Pass, allowing easy interisland travel. **Air Aruba** (☎ 800/882–7822 or 599/9–683777) has daily direct flights to Curaçao (flights make brief stops in Aruba) from both Miami and Newark airports. Air Aruba also has regularly scheduled service to Curaçao from Baltimore, and to Aruba and Bonaire. **Guayana Air** (☎ 599/9–613033 or 599/9–695533) now offers nonstop service from New York. Service from Europe is available through **British Airways** (☎ 599/9–617187). **KLM** (☎ 599/9–652747) offers service from Europe. **E Liner Airways** (☎ 599/9–697270 or 599/9–604773) has interisland service, including sightseeing and a beach tour of Aruba and Bonaire.

## Currency

U.S. dollars—in cash or traveler's checks—are accepted nearly everywhere, so there's no need to worry about exchanging money. However, you may need small change for pay phones, cigarettes, or soda machines. The currency in the Netherlands Antilles is the guilder, or florin, as it is also called, indicated by an fl. or NAf. on price tags. The U.S. dollar is considered very stable; the official rate of exchange at press time was NAf1.77 to U.S. $1. Note: Prices quoted here are in U.S. dollars unless indicated otherwise.

## Emergencies

**Police** or **fire:** ☎ 114. **Hospitals:** For medical emergencies, call **St. Elis-abeth's Hospital** (☎ 599/9–624900 or 599/9–625100) or an ambu-lance (☎ 112). **Pharmacies: Botica Popular** (✉ Madurostraat 15, ☎ 599/9–611269), or ask at your hotel for the nearest one. After nor-mal business hours, dial ☎ 2222 to see which pharmacy has the night rotation.

## Getting Around

### BICYCLES, SCOOTERS, MOPEDS, AND MOTORCYCLES

**Easy Going** (☎ 599/9–695056) rents scooters ($20), mopeds ($15), and bikes ($12.50). **Motor Salon Caribbean** (☎ 599/9–603882) rents motorcycles, including Harley Davidsons, for $50 per day.

### CAR RENTALS

You can rent a car from **Budget** (☎ 599/9–683466 or 800/472–3325), **Avis** (☎ 599/9–611255 or 800/331–1212), **Dollar** (☎ 599/9–690262), or **National Car Rental** (☎ 599/9–683489 or 800/328–4567) at the airport or have one delivered free to your hotel. Rates typically range from about $50 a day for a Toyota Starlet to about $75 for a four-door sedan. If you're planning to do country driving or rough it through Christoffel Park, a Jeep is best. All you'll need is a valid U.S. or Canadian driver's license.

### TAXIS

Taxi drivers have an official tariff chart, with fares from the airport vicin-ity to Willemstad and the nearby beach hotels running about $10–$15. Taxis tend to be moderately priced, but since there are no meters, you should confirm the fare with the driver before departure. There is an additional 25% surcharge after 11 PM. Taxis are readily available at hotels; in other cases, call Central Dispatch at ☎ 599/9–690747.

## Guided Tours

A guided tour can save you time and energy, though it is easy to cover the island yourself in a rented car. Most hotels have tour desks where arrangements can be made with reputable tour operators.

**Casper Tours** (☎ 599/9–653010 or 599/9–616789) has very personal, amiable service. For around $25 per person, you'll be escorted around the island in an air-conditioned van, with stops at the Juliana Bridge, the salt lakes, Knip Bay for a swim, the grotto at Boca Tabla, and the Jaanchi Restaurant—famous for its native cuisine—for lunch. **Cur-ven Tours** (☎ 599/9–379806) offers island tours and special pack-ages to Venezuela. **Old City Tours** (☎ 599/9–613554) has walking tours led by Anko van der Woude, which allow you to see Willem-stad with an architect's eye. He takes you to the old sections, Otra-banda (on Thursday, $6) and Punda (on Friday, $8.50, including admission to mansion). He points out the similarities of street names with New Amsterdam (New York), which was being created at about the same time. **Seaworld Explorer** (☎ 599/9–628833), a semisub-mersible, runs hour-long tours of beautiful coral reefs; cost is $30. **Taber Tours** (☎ 599/9–376637) offers a 2½-hour East Tour ($12.50) that includes visits to the Curaçao Liqueur factory at Landhuis Chobolobo, the Curaçao Museum, and the Bloempot shopping cen-ter. An array of countryside and snorkeling tours and day trips to Aruba and Bonaire are also available. **Willemstad Trolley Train Tour** (☎ 599/9–653513) passes all the major downtown sights in an hour, costs only $15, and is a fine way to get your bearings before exploring on your own.

## Language
Dutch is the official language, but the vernacular is Papiamento—a mixture of Dutch, Portuguese, Spanish, and English. Developed during the 18th century by Africans, Papiamento evolved in Curaçao as the mode of communication between landowners and their slaves. These days, however, English, as well as Spanish, and, of course, Dutch, are studied by schoolchildren. Anyone involved with tourism—shopkeepers, restaurateurs, and museum guides—speaks English. But a Spanish phrase book may help.

## Opening and Closing Times
Most shops are open Monday–Saturday 8–noon and 2–6. Banks are open weekdays 8–3:30 or 8–11:30 and 1:30–4.

## Passports and Visas
U.S. and Canadian citizens traveling to Curaçao need only proof of citizenship and a valid photo ID. A voter's registration card or a notarized birth certificate (not a photocopy) will suffice—a driver's license will *not*. British citizens must produce a passport. All visitors must show an ongoing or return ticket.

## Precautions
Mosquitoes on Curaçao do not seem as vicious and bloodthirsty as they do on Aruba and Bonaire, but that doesn't mean they don't exist, at least during the rainy season. The bad news is the rainy season falls between November and April, which coincides with the tourist high season. To be safe, keep perfume to a minimum, be prepared to use insect repellent before dining alfresco (most restaurants have a can of spray for the asking), and spray your hotel room at night—especially if you've opened a window.

If you plan to go into the water, beware of long-spined sea urchins, which can cause pain if you come in contact with them.

Do not eat any of the little green applelike fruits (they even smell like apples) of the manchineel tree: They're poisonous. In fact, steer clear of the trees altogether; raindrops or dewdrops dripping off the leaves can blister your skin. If contact does occur, rinse the affected area with water and, in extreme cases, get medical attention. Usually, the burning sensation won't last longer than two hours.

Curaçao is relatively safe, but common-sense rules should apply. Lock rental cars, use the theft deterrent device if provided by the rental firm, and do not leave valuables in the car. Joy riding is the leading cause of missing vehicles.

## Taxes and Service Charges
Hotels collect a 7% government tax and add a 12% service charge to the bill; restaurants add 10%–15%. The airport departure tax is NAf122.50 (about U.S. $13).

## Telephones and Mail
Phone service through the hotel operators in Curaçao is slow, but direct-dial service, both on-island and to the United States, is fast and clear. Hotel operators will put the call through for you, but if you make a collect call, do check immediately afterward that the hotel does not charge you as well. To call Curaçao direct from the United States, dial 011–599–9 plus the number in Curaçao. To place a local call on the island, dial the six-digit local number. An airmail letter to the U.S. and Canada costs NAf2.00, a postcard NAf1.00.

## Visitor Information

Contact the **Curaçao Tourist Board** (✉ 475 Park Ave. S, Suite 2000, New York, NY 10016, ☎ 212/683–7660 or 800/270–3350, ℻ 212/683–9337; ✉ 330 Biscayne Blvd., Suite 808, Miami, FL 33132, ☎ 305/374–5811 or 800/445–8266, ℻ 305/374–6741) for information.

In Curaçao, the **Curaçao Tourism Development Foundation** has three offices on the island where multilingual guides are ready to answer questions. You can also pick up maps, brochures, and a copy of *Curaçao Holiday*. The main office is located in Willemstad at Pietermaai No. 19 (☎ 599/9–616000); other offices are in the Waterfort Arches (☎ 599/9–613397), across from the Van Der Valk Plaza Hotel, and at the airport (☎ 599/9–686789).

# 10 Dominica

**T**HE NATIONAL MOTTO emblazoned on the coat of arms of the Commonwealth of Dominica reads *"Après Bondi, c'est la ter."* It is a French-Creole phrase meaning "After God, it is the land." On this unspoiled isle, the land is indeed the main attraction: It turns and twists, towers to mountain crests, then tumbles to falls and valleys. They say that if Christopher Columbus were to come back today, Dominica (pronounced dom-in-ee-ka) would be the only island in the Caribbean that he would recognize. Much of the interior is still covered by a luxuriant rain forest and remains inaccessible by road: a wild place straight out of Conan Doyle's *Lost World.* The Smithsonian has called Dominica a giant plant laboratory, unchanged for 10,000 years. This exotic spot is home to such unusual critters as the Sisserou (or Imperial) parrot and the red-necked (or Jacquot) parrot, neither of which can be found anywhere else in the world. The rugged northwest of the island is also home to the last survivors of the region's original inhabitants, the Caribs.

Updated by
Simon Worrall

Wedged between two rich French islands, Guadeloupe to the north and Martinique to the south, Dominica has always been something of an anomaly. Its most famous sons have been daughters: Jean Rhys, the novelist, and Dame Eugenia Charles,"Iron Lady" of the Caribbean—the only woman to have headed a government in this part of the world. Its official language is English, its family and place-names French, its religion predominantly Catholic. Driving is on the left. It is only 29 miles long and 16 miles wide, has a population less than that of Huntington, Long Island, but is an independent commonwealth with a seat at the United Nations. Unusual for the Caribbean, its economy is still based on agriculture. Bananas, not tourist dollars, are the largest money-earner.

Nature has always been Dominica's greatest enemy. It had too many mountains to make the cultivation of sugar profitable. It had too many rivers to make an effective road network viable. It rained too much. Throughout its history, Dominica has also been sorely tried by hurricanes: by David in 1979, by Hugo in 1989, and by Marilyn in 1995. But today nature is also Dominica's greatest asset. There may not be casinos or gourmet restaurants, but if you want to hike in the rain forest or scuba dive, bird-watch, or explore volcanic lakes, this is the best place to do it. And Dominica has only just begun to discover its vast potential. Mountain lodges are being built. Life is being breathed back into old plantation houses. There are plans for a hiking trail that will traverse the island from north to south. This, combined with a slow, easygoing pace of life and an immensely friendly people will make it a perfect refuge from an ever more abrasive world. The whales evidently already think so. Orca and humpback whales are regularly seen in Dominican waters. The island is now one of the most important sites in the world for sperm whales. Come now, and you will have it all to yourself.

## Lodging

Most hotels here are locally owned, and standards are often not up to what seasoned Caribbean travelers expect. On the plus side, prices are low, and staffs are usually friendly and down-to-earth. It pays to compare rates and call for hotel brochures, as everything from bare-bones motels to charming hilltop retreats is comparably priced here.

The only beachfront hotels are in the Portsmouth area, the one exception being the Castaways on Mero Beach. Roseau's seaside facilities have splendid Caribbean views but are beachless. Beaches are not what Dominica is about, however. The most interesting accommodations are found at the mountain lodges, nature retreats, and refurbished plantation houses that are springing up all over the island.

Most hotels offer a MAP plan; considering the uniformity of Dominica's restaurants and the difficulty of getting around, this option makes sense. Dominican hoteliers seldom differentiate between high and low season—though a few have caught on.

| CATEGORY | COST* |
|---|---|
| **$$$** | over $100 |
| **$$** | $65–$100 |
| **$** | under $65 |

*All prices are for a standard double room for two, excluding 5% tax, 3% sales tax, and 10%–15% service charge.

## Hotels

**$$$** ⊞ **Fort Young Hotel.** Once the island's main military installation, Fort
★ Young is now Roseau's top downtown hotel. The fort was built in the late 1700s, and decorative features from that era, like the canons at the entrance, flagstone floors, and massive walls, convey a sense of history. The cliffside setting offers dramatic views and keeps you away from the mosquitos. It's worth paying extra for a room facing the ocean. Rooms have small balconies, air-conditioning, ceiling fans, shower baths, cable TV, and modern furnishings. The Marquis de Bouille restaurant (☞ Dining, *below*) is one of the best on the island. ⊠ *Box 519, Roseau,* ☎ *809/448–5000,* 𝔽𝔸𝕏 *809/448–5006. 73 rooms. Restaurant, bar, air-conditioning, fans, pool, disco. AE, MC, V. EP, MAP, FAP.*

**$$$** ⊞ **Garraway Hotel.** The owner proudly compares Dominica's first international, standard business hotel to a Ramada or Marriott. It's an apt comparison, though the Garraway, which is situated in downtown Roseau by the waterfront, is unusually tasteful and elegant for a business hotel. Rooms are large and decorated mainly in soft seashell colors like sea foam, coral, and powder blue; all have direct-dial phones, cable TV, and air-conditioning. Suites have sitting rooms of varying sizes and sofa beds. The higher floors survey a colorful jumble of rooftops that seems straight from a Chagall canvas. Local paintings and vetiver mats add a distinctive touch to the decor of the public spaces. The restaurant specializes in creative Creole cuisine and the downstairs bar has the best view on the island. ⊠ *Bay Front, Box 789, Roseau,* ☎ *809/449–8800,* 𝔽𝔸𝕏 *809/449–8807. 20 rooms, 11 suites. Restaurant, bar, air-conditioning, hot tub, conference room. AE, DC, MC, V. EP.*

**$$$** ⊞ **Lauro Club.** From the dining room's bright linen napery, cheerful
★ wall mural, and fresh flowers to the cottages' bold colors and contemporary furniture, the Lauro Club has a neat European feel that, oddly enough, works well in the Caribbean. Each unit has a sitting area, a daybed, and a kitchenette on a large veranda, but none has a TV or air-conditioning. Six units have direct sea views; the other four are up the hill a bit but still catch a glimpse of the water. Below are a swimming pool and a sandy beach area; a long wooden staircase twists down to the ocean. The Club is in Salisbury, between Roseau and Portsmouth and about 13 miles from each, so you'll probably need to rent a car. ⊠ *Box 483, Roseau,* ☎ *809/449–6602,* 𝔽𝔸𝕏 *809/449–6603. 10 units. Restaurant, bar, kitchenettes, pool, beach. AE, MC, V. EP, MAP.*

**$$$** ⊞ **Petit Coulibri Guest Cottages.** You need a four-wheel-drive vehicle
★ to reach this aerie, perched high above Soufrière at the end of one of the worst access roads in the Caribbean. It's worth it: Once there on top of the world, you won't want to come down. Loye and Barney Barnard (she's from Savannah, he's a Yankee from the Berkshires) have

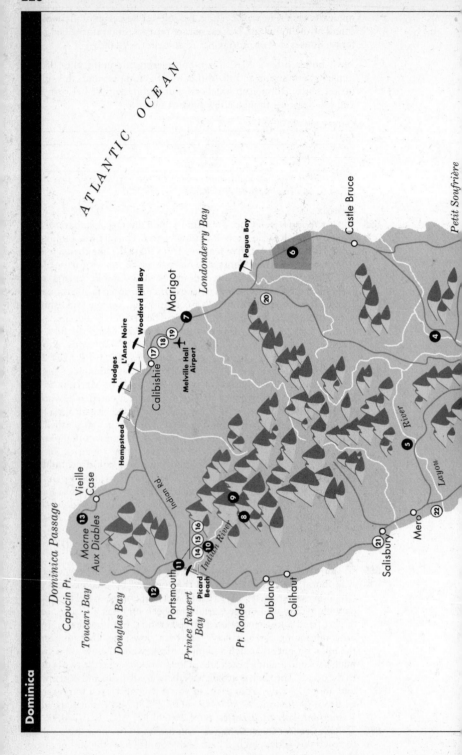

ATLANTIC OCEAN

Dominica Passage

Capucin Pt.

Toucari Bay

Douglas Bay

Vieille Case

Morne Aux Diables **13**

**12**

Portsmouth **11**

Prince Rupert Bay

Picard Beach

Pt. Ronde

**14** **15** **16**

**10**

Indian River

Indian Rd.

Dublanc

Colihaut

**21** Salisbury

Mero

**22**

Layou

River

**5**

**8**

**9**

Hampstead

Hodges

L'Anse Noire

Woodford Hill Bay

Calibishie **17** **18** **19**

Melville Hall Airport

Marigot **7**

**20**

Londonderry Bay

Pagua Bay **6**

Castle Bruce

Petit Soufrière

**4**

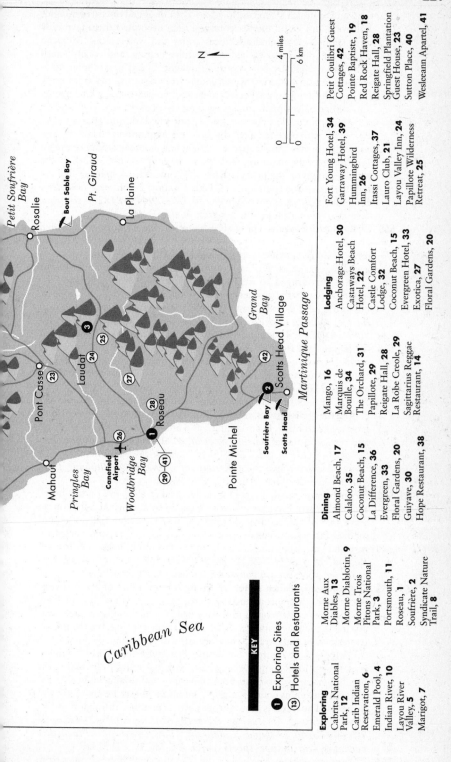

Caribbean Sea

Petit Soufrière Bay

Bout Sable Bay

Rosalie

Pt. Giraud

La Plaine

Pont Casse

Laudat

Mahaut

Pringles Bay

Canefield Airport

Woodbridge Bay

Roseau

Pointe Michel

Grand Bay

Soufrière Bay

Scotts Head

Scotts Head Village

Martinique Passage

N

0        4 miles
0      6 km

**KEY**

① Exploring Sites

⑬ Hotels and Restaurants

**Exploring**
Cabrits National Park, **12**
Carib Indian Reservation, **6**
Emerald Pool, **4**
Indian River, **10**
Layou River Valley, **5**
Marigot, **7**
Morne Aux Diables, **13**
Morne Diablotin, **9**
Morne Trois Pitons National Park, **3**
Portsmouth, **11**
Roseau, **1**
Soufrière, **2**
Syndicate Nature Trail, **8**

**Dining**
Almond Beach, **17**
Calaloo, **35**
Coconut Beach, **15**
La Difference, **36**
Evergreen, **33**
Floral Gardens, **20**
Guiyave, **30**
Hope Restaurant, **38**
Mango, **16**
Marquis de Bouille, **34**
The Orchard, **31**
Papillote, **29**
Reigate Hall, **28**
La Robe Creole, **29**
Sagittarius Reggae Restaurant, **14**

**Lodging**
Anchorage Hotel, **30**
Castaways Beach Hotel, **22**
Castle Comfort Lodge, **32**
Coconut Beach, **15**
Evergreen Hotel, **33**
Exotica, **27**
Floral Gardens, **20**
Fort Young Hotel, **34**
Garraway Hotel, **39**
Hummingbird Inn, **26**
Itassi Cottages, **37**
Lauro Club, **21**
Layou Valley Inn, **24**
Papillote Wilderness Retreat, **25**
Petit Coulibri Guest Cottages, **42**
Pointe Baptiste, **19**
Red Rock Haven, **18**
Reigate Hall, **28**
Springfield Plantation Guest House, **23**
Sutton Place, **40**
Wesleeann Apartel, **41**

created Dominica's choicest lodging. They designed the three individual stone-and-wood duplex cottages, then decorated them tastefully with stained-glass windows, local crafts and watercolors, Mexican serapes, maple beds swathed in mosquito netting, and ceramic-and-straw lamps. This is an ecotourist's delight: Everything is solar-powered or run on batteries, water comes from cisterns, and trees grow through the living room. Each cottage has two bedrooms, a kitchenette, and a huge balcony affording sweeping views of the sea. Travelers on a budget might consider the studio, but it's dark and spartan. The Barnards (who once ran a nearby aloe vera plantation and factory) can suggest many hikes in the rugged surrounding mountains. Save one night for dinner in the main house. Loye's a marvelous cook, much of the food is grown on the property, and the conversation sparkles like the lights on far-off Martinique. ⊠ *Petit Coulibri Estate near Soufrière, Box 331, Roseau,* ☎ *809/446–3150,* FAX *809/449–8182. 3 cottages, 1 studio. Dining room, kitchenettes, pool. AE, MC, V. EP.*

$$$    🏨 **Red Rock Haven.** These stylish self-contained cottages perched
★     above the Atlantic are the perfect place to get away from it all. All have terrace and ocean view, and are charmingly furnished with local crafts and designer linens. Well-stocked bookshelves are a wonderful bonus (you're encouraged to make a contribution when you leave). The beach, arguably the prettiest on the island, is within walking distance, but you'll need a car to reach everything else. ⊠ *Pointe Baptiste, Calibishie; mailing address: Box 71, Roseau,* ☎ *809/448–2181,* FAX *809/448–5787. 3 cottages. Bar, pool, sauna, gift shop. AE, MC, V. EP.*

$$$    🏨 **Reigate Hall Hotel.** It was once the fanciest hotel in Dominica. The setting, high on a steep wooded cliff with spectacular views of the ocean, is as grand as ever, but, sadly, in recent years the service and standards at Reigate Hall have deteriorated, and the property is not what it was. Rooms have locally made furnishings, air-conditioning, and private balconies; the higher-priced rooms 17 and 18 have sea views. Some rooms have exposed brick, beam ceilings, and antiques; others have wet bars and refrigerators. ⊠ *Reigate, Roseau,* ☎ *809/448–4031; in the U.S., 800/223–9815; in Canada, 800/468–0023;* FAX *809/448–4034. 14 rooms, 2 suites, 1 apartment. Restaurant, 2 bars, air-conditioning, pool, sauna, 2 tennis courts. AE, MC, V. EP, MAP.*

$$–$$$    🏨 **Anchorage Hotel.** Years of wear have taken their toll on this hotel, although it still becomes an active scene in season. Make sure you reserve one of the renovated rooms, which have clay-tile floors and madras fabrics, in the two-story galleried section. Despite recent refurbishment, other units remain rather dark and lifeless. ⊠ *Box 34, Roseau,* ☎ *809/448–2638,* FAX *809/448–5680. 36 rooms. Restaurant, bar, pool, squash court. AE, D, MC, V. EP, MAP, FAP.*

$$–$$$    🏨 **Castaways Beach Hotel.** A young crowd, most of them divers, flocks to this beachfront hotel in Mero, 11 miles north of Roseau. Daytime activity centers on its mile-long beach, which, unfortunately, was eroded in the hurricane season of 1995. In the evening, the focus is on the restaurant and terrace, which are attractive, although the food leaves something to be desired. The festive Sunday brunch with live music packs them in. Rooms are spacious, with balconies overlooking the beach, but are rather dingy. Some have air-conditioning and cable TV. Though the tennis court is in poor condition, guests are charged extra to use it. The hotel is closed from early September through mid-October. ⊠ *Box 5, Roseau,* ☎ *809/449–6245 or 800/742–4276,* FAX *809/449–6246. 27 rooms. Restaurant, 2 bars, tennis court, beach, dive packages, scuba, water-sports center. AE, MC, V. EP, MAP.*

$$–$$$    🏨 **Evergreen Hotel.** The newer annex at this small hotel, 2 miles from downtown Roseau, may be somewhat lacking in authentic island charm, but make sure you request a room here. It includes six bright,

modern, air-conditioned rooms with bright print fabrics, rattan fur-nishings, cable TV, large shower baths, and balconies with lovely sea views, as well as an airy bar and restaurant with terrace. Other addi-tions include a pool, Italian ceramic tiles in the public areas, and a small garden. The older building, a stone-and-wood structure with a red roof, has more character, and rooms here are less expensive, but they are plain and lack sea views. Public rooms contain paintings and wood carv-ings by noted local artist Carl Winston. The restaurant is excellent. ✉ *Box 309, Roseau,* ☎ *809/448–3288,* 🖷 *809/448–6800. 16 rooms. Restaurant, bar, pool. AE, D, MC, V. CP, MAP.*

**$$–$$$** 🏨 **Sutton Place Hotel.** The Harris family has sunk their life savings—
★ and then some—into refurbishing this small, historic hotel in the heart of Roseau. Everything, from the wrought-iron gates at the entrance (bought in Trinidad) to the tauroniro wood floors (from South Amer-ica), suggests that no expense has been spared. Steps lead from the street (one of the hotel's many strong points is that there is a 24-hour secu-rity guard) to a pleasant reception area decorated with antiques. The house was built in the 1890s and some of the original stonework can still be seen in the large, ground-floor restaurant, which serves good Creole and East Indian food. Standard rooms on the second floor are attractively furnished with fabrics and fittings imported from New York. The three suites on the top floor are some of the nicest rooms in Do-minica: Spacious, with two queen beds or a four-poster bed, they have fully equipped kitchenettes, antique furnishings, teak louvered windows, and polished wood floors. All rooms have air-conditioning as well as ceiling fans, cable TV, and phones. The whole family is involved in run-ning the hotel: One daughter was the decorator, another is the man-ager, the brother is the builder—and, so far, they are doing a superb job. ✉ *25 Old St., Roseau,* ☎ *809/448–8700,* 🖷 *809/448–3045. 7 rooms, 3 suites. Restaurant, bar, air-conditioning, fans. AE, D, MC, V. CP, MAP.*

**$$–$$$** 🏨 **Wesleeann Apartel.** As the name implies, this is an apartment-style hotel. From the outside, it looks like a French apartment block plunked down on the edge of the Caribbean. The spacious one-, two-, or three-bedroom apartments are ideal for business travelers on a longer stay. It will take awhile before this brand new complex acquires the patina of use. Apartments have a balcony with a sea view, cable TV, phone, air-conditioning, a breakfast room, and a kitchenette with microwave oven, fridge, and utensils. White tile floors, white rattan, and floral chintz fabrics decorate the rooms. The restaurant serves Italian and Creole food. ✉ *Box 1764, Roseau,* ☎ *809/449–0419,* 🖷 *809/449–2473. 12 apartments, 1 suite. Restaurant, bar, exercise room. AE, MC, V.*

**$$** 🏨 **Coconut Beach Hotel.** No sooner had it received a much-needed face-lift in 1994 than Hurricane Marilyn devastated this beachfront hotel near Portsmouth in 1995. Undeterred, the management rebuilt the re-sort, which will be open for the 1997 season (call ahead). The new rooms, set back 50 feet from the beach, have private bath, satellite television, and a kitchenette but no phone. Most have air-conditioning. Plans are under way to build 12 new suites. The setting, on Picard, Dominica's finest beach, is as delightful as ever. Unchanged, too, is the friendli-ness of the staff. ✉ *Box 37, Roseau,* ☎ *809/445–5393,* 🖷 *809/445–5693. 20 rooms. Restaurant, bar. AE, D, MC, V. EP, MAP.*

**$** 🏨 **Papillote Wilderness Retreat.** Lush greenery abounds at this moun-
★ tain retreat, geese and guinea fowl ramble the grounds, a nearby river beckons you to take a dip, and 200-foot Trafalgar Falls is a short hike from your room. As if this weren't enough, there's also owner Anne Jean-Baptiste's botanical garden: a mind-boggling assortment of plants and flowers, which she may graciously use to brew you a soothing herbal infusion—*bergamot* to combat insomnia or *l'oiselles* for a cold. Rooms

are not as spectacular as their surroundings; they're low-ceilinged and somewhat dark, with a rustic, log-cabin feel. And, sadly, the island's main hydroelectric plant is only a stone's throw away. In some rooms the hum of electricity is louder than the croaking of tree frogs. That said, Papillote remains a special place, imbued with the energy and commitment of its owner and staffed by some of the friendliest personnel on the island. The terrace-style restaurant, which has fine views of the surrounding mountains, serves good, moderately priced meals. ⊠ *Box 67, Roseau,* ☎ *809/448–2287,* ℻ *809/448–2286. 10 rooms. Restaurant, bar, gift shop. AE, DC, MC, V. EP, MAP.*

## Guest Houses and Lodges

$$$    ⊞ **Exotica.** Fae and Atherton Martin, a prominent local couple (he is president of the Dominica Conservation Association), built five chalet-style houses in 1995. Getting here is an adventure in itself. You corkscrew up the mountainside through vegetation that grows lusher with every turn, until you reach a property covered in flowers and fruit trees, perched 1,600 feet above the ocean. The chalets—made of treated wood and stone, with red galvanized roofs fitted with solar panels—are less spectacular, but pleasant enough. The interiors, with their wood paneling, pitched ceilings, and tile floors, contain a bedroom with two (extra long) double beds, a living room plus kitchenette, bathroom, phone, and TV. There are plans for a café, but at the moment—particularly since Roseau is 5 miles away—self-catering is the rule, though the owners can arrange for a local cook. A nearby river (a five-minute walk away) is a good spot for swimming. Nature lovers will enjoy the many birds to be spotted (nature trails are planned). The views, of Morne Anglais and the ocean, are breathtaking. If you're really lucky, you might even see a whale spouting, right from your veranda. ⊠ *Box 109, Roseau,* ☎ *809/448–7895,* ℻ *809/448–3855. 8 chalets. AE, MC, V.*

$$$    ⊞ **Pointe Baptiste.** Alec Waugh wrote a book here. Noel Coward was
★    a visitor. Princess Margaret stayed during her honeymoon. And it's easy to see why. This weathered plantation house exudes old-world charm. The setting, above a beautiful beach, is divine, the antiques-filled interior, patrician. There are three rooms in the main house, which also contains a superb library. A whitewashed cottage straight out of a Ralph Lauren catalog contains an additional room. That said, this is not a place for the smart set: It's an old house, with antiquated fittings, and guests are expected to "do" for themselves (though a local cook can be provided by arrangement). As the main house can only be rented in its entirety, and you will need a car to do anything, a stay here is not for all pocketbooks, either. For those wanting something more affordable, the family also runs D'Auchamps Apartments, an attractive property on the other side of the island, near Trafalgar Falls. ⊠ *c/o Mrs. Geraldine Edwards, Calibishie Village,* ☎ *809/445–7322,* ℻ *809/445–8343. 3 rooms and cottage. No credit cards.*

$$    ⊞ **Castle Comfort Lodge.** This small dive lodge, sandwiched between the Anchorage and Evergreen hotels and run by the enthusiastic Derek and Ginette Perryman, wins a loyal following for its first-rate dive shop and excellent-value dive packages. Rooms are nothing special, although the five oceanfront units are more modern and cheerful than many you will find on the island. The back rooms are smaller but have cable TV and phone. As a bonus, the home-cooked meals are bountiful and delicious. The Perrymans can also arrange inland adventures and nature walks. The restaurant is open to nonguests by reservation. ⊠ *Box 63, Roseau,* ☎ *809/448–2188,* ℻ *809/448–6088. 10 rooms. Restaurant, dive shop. AE, MC, V. EP, MAP.*

$$    ⊞ **Hummingbird Inn.** This simple hilltop retreat is just a short drive
★    from Roseau and Canefield Airport. Two hillside bungalows with out-

standing Caribbean views hold 10 rooms. Interiors are simple—white walls, terra-cotta-tile floors, and peaked wooden ceilings. Varnished wooden hurricane windows can be left open all night to let in fresh breezes and the sounds of tree frogs and the ocean a few hundred yards below. There's no air-conditioning, TV, or phones, but rooms do come with ceiling fans. Other nice touches include handmade quilts, hammocks slung strategically on the wraparound terraces, and tables fashioned out of the trunks of local gommier trees. One large suite also has a four-poster bed and kitchen. The Hummingbird's cook is perhaps the best of any guest house on Dominica, and nonguests can arrange for dinner here if they call a day in advance. ⊠ *Box 20, Roseau,* ☎ 𝖥𝖠𝖷 *809/449–1042. 9 rooms, 1 suite. Restaurant, bar, fans. AE, MC, V. EP, MAP.*

**$–$$** 🍴 **Floral Gardens.** It's a surprise to find a Swiss chalet-style hotel, complete with latticed windows and flower boxes, on the edge of a rainforest reserve; owner O. J. Seraphin, a former prime minister and full-time human dynamo, is probably the only person who could carry it off. The hotel has grown bit by bit over the years, something that is reflected in the higgledy-piggledy layout and variable quality of the rooms. The oldest rooms are in the main building; although they are decorated with island crafts and homey fabrics, they have a slightly claustrophobic feel. Larger units are located across the road and overlook the Layou River. A further 12 rooms—including three suites—were added in 1995. The restaurant here (☞ *Dining, below*) is one of the best on the island and the hotel's location is convenient for river bathing, hiking, and relaxing on the beaches of the northeast coast. Hurricane Marilyn did considerable damage in 1995, but this merely gave the irrepressible O. J. an excuse to undertake further renovations and expansions. He's already added a waterfall pool and botanical garden. At press time, he was overseeing the building of a minimall, comprising six boutiques, each one showcasing a different island craft or product. ⊠ *Concord,* ☎ *809/445–7636,* 𝖥𝖠𝖷 *809/445–7636. 18 rooms. Restaurant, gift shop. AE, MC, V. EP, MAP.*

**$–$$** 🍴 **Itassi Cottages.** Run by the same family who own the excellent Sut-
★ ton Place Hotel (☞ *above*), these three self-contained cottages pretty well live up to the promise in the brochure: ". . . for discerning travelers who are not necessarily loaded." They can each house two to six people, and are much homier than most island lodgings, with a mix of antiques, straw mats, beautiful handmade floral bedspreads, calabash lamps, and wraparound porches with hammocks and sweeping views of Roseau, Scotts Head, and the Caribbean. Ideal for long-term stays, each cottage has a kitchen, ceiling fans, and cable TV, and there is a shared laundry facility. Grounds are beautifully landscaped and include a tennis court. ⊠ *Box 319, Roseau,* ☎ *809/448–4313,* 𝖥𝖠𝖷 *809/448–3045. 3 cottages. Fan, kitchens, tennis court, laundry service. AE, MC, V.*

**$–$$** 🍴 **Layou Valley Inn.** Tamara Holmes and her late husband built this tasteful house in the foothills of the national park, under the peaks of Morne Trois Pitons. She's a Russian who once translated for NASA but now devotes her talents to the kitchen, where she whips up excellent Creole food, as well as the occasional French or Russian specialty—coq au vin or chicken Kiev. The rooms are simple and clean, and the sunken lounge (an oasis of hand-hewn mosaics, stone floors, exquisite wood carvings, and hanging plants) and glass-fronted dining area are comfortable, attractive places where guests mingle. The surroundings of lush rain forest and mountains are superb. If you're lucky, you might even spot a Sisserou parrot. ⊠ *Box 196, Roseau,* ☎ *809/449–6203,* 𝖥𝖠𝖷 *809/448–5212. 10 rooms. Restaurant, bar, swimming in nearby rivers. AE, MC, V. EP, MAP.*

**$–$$** ⊞ **Springfield Plantation Guest House.** This 19th-century plantation house, built on a 200-acre property festooned with lush vegetation, feels like something out of Jean Rhys' *Wide Sargasso Sea*. It's a bit gloomy and run-down, but is full of character. The wood-paneled dining room displays antique furniture, a piano, hat stands, and pictures of clipper ships, and a portrait of King George V hangs on the wall. Most of the rooms are upstairs in the main house; Room 16, which has a four-poster bed and antique furniture, is especially imposing. The other rooms are split between a guest cottage and a long, wooden building across the courtyard. The ancient ovens and fridges in some of the rooms suggest that time has, indeed, stood still here. The property also serves as the Centre for Environmental Protection, so you may find yourself surrounded by the Birkenstock brigade. If you don't mind the company, if fixtures from another era don't phase you, and if you're a nature lover (there are 2 miles of trails right on the property), then you'll love this place. The restaurant serves Creole food, much of it prepared with organic vegetables grown on the estate. ✉ *Box 456, Roseau,* ☎ *809/449–1401,* 𝔽𝔸𝕏 *809/449–2160. 15 rooms. Restaurant, bar, swimming in nearby rivers, nature trails. AE, MC, V. EP, CP, MAP, FAP.*

# Dining

Dominica may only be a few miles from Martinique and Guadeloupe, the culinary capitals of the Caribbean, but don't expect gourmet dining or excellent wines here. Look, instead, for Creole fare utilizing the cornucopia of fresh vegetables that grow in the fertile Dominican soil. There are sweet green plantains, *kushkush* yams, breadfruit, and dasheen (a tuber similar to the potato called taro elsewhere)—these and other staples are known as ground provisions. You'll find fresh fish on virtually every menu, and occasionally mountain "chicken"—a euphemism for a large frog called *crapaud*. Two rare delicacies for the intrepid diner are *manicou* (a small opossum) and the tender, gamey *agouti* (a large, indigenous rodent)—both are best smoked or stewed. You will not find fast-food restaurants or a variety of ethnic options, but the local cuisine is delicious.

## What to Wear

Dominica is far from the chic fashion world. Clothes here are practical and traditional—for dinner it's shirt and trousers for men and modest dresses for women. During the day, nice shorts are acceptable at most places, but beach attire is frowned upon.

| CATEGORY | COST* |
|---|---|
| $$$ | over $35 |
| $$ | $15–$35 |
| $ | under $15 |

*per person, excluding drinks, service charge, and 3% tax*

**$$$** ✕ **Reigate Hall.** The setting at this stylish but rustic restaurant, with an old-fashioned waterwheel, green linen napery, and formal place settings—a rarity in Dominica—is as pleasant as ever, but in recent years the quality of the food and service has considerably deteriorated. Although some low-fat, low-cholesterol dishes have been added, favored specialties remain mountain chicken in champagne sauce and coq au vin. ✉ *Reigate Hall Hotel, Roseau,* ☎ *809/448–4031. AE, MC, V.*

**$$$** ✕ **La Robe Creole.** This is the best restaurant in Roseau, housed in a
★ pretty building near the cathedral. Take your pick from an eclectic à la carte menu. Callaloo and crab soup, made with dasheen and coconut, is a specialty. Other tasty options include lobster and conch crepes, charcoal-grilled fish and meats, barbecued chicken, and a selection of salads. The dining room is a cozy place, with wood rafters, ladder-back

chairs, and colorful madras tablecloths. The downstairs take-out annex, the Mouse Hole, is an inexpensive place to stock up for your picnic. The restaurant also makes its own delicious mango chutney, which can be bought in local shops. ✉ *3 Victoria St., Roseau,* ☎ *809/448–2896. AE. Closed Sun.*

**$$** ✕ **Evergreen.** Enjoy a relaxing meal on a large airy terrace overlooking the sea. It's decorated with bright tropical prints, crystal teardrop chandeliers, and a striking art deco–style bar in stark gray, black, and white. Delicious dinners include a choice of soup and salad; the entrées of chicken, fish, and beef are served with local fruits and vegetables, such as kushkush and plantains. Homemade desserts include fresh fruit, cake, and ice cream. ✉ *Evergreen Hotel, Roseau,* ☎ *809/448–3288. AE, MC, V.*

**$$** ✕ **Floral Gardens.** You may feel as if you're dining in a private home at
★ this warm, welcoming restaurant, particularly if owner O. J. Seraphim is around. Wood paneling, rough-hewn timber beams, and vetiver mats create a rustic atmosphere. Tables are laid out in an L-shape in the main building, and there are more tables in a gallery-style building across the road, overlooking the river. The food is delectable; sample local specialties, such as crapaud, agouti, or crayfish caught by the local Carib Indians, whose reservation adjoins the property. There are also vegetarian dishes. Finish with luscious homemade coconut or rum raisin ice cream. ✉ *Floral Gardens Hotel, Concord,* ☎ *809/445–7636. AE, MC, V.*

**$$** ✕ **Guiyave.** This popular lunchtime restaurant in the center of Roseau is actually two businesses in one. Downstairs is a patisserie, where owner Hermina Astaphan makes chicken patties, spicy *rotis* (Caribbean burritos), and a scrumptious selection of pies, tarts, and cakes. These can also be ordered at the upstairs restaurant (run by her son), along with more elaborate fare such as spareribs, mountain chicken, steamed fish, and chicken in a sweet-and-sour sauce. You may dine in the green and white wood-paneled dining room, which has a bar at one end, or on the sunny balcony perched above Roseau's colorful streets—the perfect spot to indulge in one of the fresh-squeezed tropical juices. ✉ *15 Cork St., Roseau,* ☎ *809/448–2930. AE, MC, V. No dinner.*

**$$** ✕ **Mango.** Locals frequent this unassuming restaurant, with its vases overflowing with fresh flowers and beautiful mural depicting the Indian River. Diners enjoy both the comparatively refined ambience and Peter Pascal's solid home cooking. The *lambi* (conch) is tender as can be, the goat *colombo* (curry) has quite a kick, and the mountain chicken is succulent. This is one of the few places where you can find breego, a tiny flavorful conch. ✉ *Bay St., Portsmouth,* ☎ *809/445– 3099. No credit cards.*

**$$** ✕ **Marquis de Bouille.** The upscale, attractive, candlelit dining room
★ at the historic Fort Young Hotel, with its stone walls and wood-raftered ceiling, is one of the better restaurants on the island. The Indian chef adds a touch of his homeland cuisine to Continental and Dominican dishes (the special may be mountain chicken tandoori). The menu also includes callaloo and pumpkin soup, grilled lobster, and blue marlin in a lime sauce. ✉ *Fort Young Hotel, Roseau,* ☎ *809/448–5000. AE, MC, V.*

**$$** ✕ **The Orchard.** A spacious, unadorned dining room opens onto a pleasant, covered courtyard, surrounded by latticework. Chef Joan Cools-Lartique whips up Creole-style coconut shrimp, lobster, black pudding, mountain chicken, callaloo soup with crabmeat, and other island delicacies, as well as an assortment of sandwiches, for the changing menu. ✉ *31 King George V St., Roseau,* ☎ *809/448–3051. AE, D, MC, V.*

**$$** ✕ **Papillote.** Anne Jean-Baptiste's stone-and-tile restaurant boasts
★ botanical gardens right outside, a bubbling hot-spring pool (just the spot to savor a lethal rum punch before or after dinner), and is just as

popular with birds, butterflies—and tour groups—as ever. Try the bracing callaloo soup, dasheen puffs, chicken rainforest (marinated with papaya and wrapped in banana leaves), and, if they're on the menu, the succulent *bouk* (tiny, delicate river shrimp). ⊠ *Papillote Wilderness Retreat,* ☎ *809/448–2287. AE, D, MC, V.*

**$–$$** ✕ **Almond Beach Restaurant & Bar.** If you're visiting one of the island's northeast beaches, stop here for a lunch of callaloo soup, lobster, or octopus. Select from tantalizing fruit juices, including guava, passion fruit, tangerine, soursop, and papaya, or one of the bewitching spice rums steeped for more than two months in various herbs and spices. Try the *pweve* (patois for pepper), the aniselike *nanie,* or *lapsenth,* a violet-scented pick-me-up and digestive. The setting and ambience are delightful: Murals painted by local artists adorn the back wall, and you dine in a series of gazebos overlooking the Atlantic. The genial owners, Mr. and Mrs. Joseph, are experts on local culture and custom and sometimes arrange a traditional belé dance or jing ping (a type of folk music) concert on busy weekends. ⊠ *Calibishi,* ☎ *809/445–7783. AE, D, MC, V.*

**$–$$** ✕ **Calaloo Restaurant.** Mrs. Marge Peters is the vivacious hostess of this small, informal eatery. She takes great pride in age-old cooking traditions and uses only the freshest local produce. (What she does with breadfruit alone—roasted slabs, puffs, creamy velouté, juice, pie—could fill a cookbook.) Changing lunch and dinner specials, served with heaping helpings of provisions such as pumpkin, plantain, yams, and yucca, might include pepper-pot soup, curried conch, or the signature crab callaloo, fragrant with cumin, coconut cream, lime, clove, and garlic. Most everything here is homemade, including juices (try the sea moss—"puts lead in your pencil") and ice cream (the soursop is marvelous). ⊠ *63 King George V St., Roseau,* ☎ *809/448–3386. No credit cards.*

**$–$$** ✕ **La Difference.** The first sign of a halfway decent restaurant is that it has solid wood furniture, not white plastic. It is no surprise that owner Frank De Smet, who used to be the chef at Reigate Hall, has insisted on this detail in his new bistro in the center of Roseau. The restaurant is up a flight of stairs and is decorated with ocher walls and lace curtains. Low lighting makes it hard to see the food, which is a shame, because Frank knows how to cook. Mountain chicken, fried to a crisp with garlic, or chicken Creole with rice and local vegetables like dasheen and christophine, are just two of the dishes he creates. ⊠ *27 Marlborough St., Roseau,* ☎ *809/448–7365. No credit cards. Closed Sun.*

**$** ✕ **Coconut Beach.** This casual, low-key beachfront restaurant and bar is popular with visiting yacht owners, expatriate medical students from the nearby school, and anyone interested in an afternoon on a stretch of white-sand beach. Fresh tropical drinks and local seafood dishes are the specialty here; sandwiches and rotis are also served. Unfortunately, the property was devastated by Hurricane Marilyn in 1995. At press time, rebuilding was in progress; call ahead. ⊠ *Coconut Beach Hotel, Portsmouth,* ☎ *809/445–5393. AE, D, MC, V.*

**$** ✕ **Hope Restaurant.** The owners did their best to cheer up the unprepossessing interior, painting the walls a bright turquoise and strewing fresh flowers around the three cramped dining rooms. But you don't come here for the ambience. You come for genuine Creole cooking at rock-bottom prices. Mountain chicken (E.C.$35) and agouti (E.C.$25) are served with generous sides of provisions—for barely half the price charged at fancier restaurants. Savory pork, goat, and chicken are even cheaper. Hope provides local flavor in every sense of the phrase: It's filled with old men playing dominoes and cabbies whose runs have just ended (they always know a good deal). It's open every day for breakfast, lunch, and dinner. ⊠ *15 Steber St., Roseau,* ☎ *809/448–2019. No credit cards.*

**$** ✕ **Sagittarius Reggae Restaurant.** Astrological paraphernalia covers the walls of this place. The johnnycakes have Egg McMuffins beat by a country mile, and the fruit juices are sublime. Weekends, a disc jockey blasts reggae and soca, transforming the restaurant into a hopping club. ✉ *Portsmouth, no phone. No credit cards.*

## Beaches

If you want to hang out at the beach, there are plenty of better places to do it than Dominica. Travel-poster beaches do exist, but mostly you'll find dark-sand beaches, evidence of the island's volcanic origins. The best beaches are around Portsmouth or in the northeast of the island. The hurricane season of 1995 rearranged most of them, particularly around Portsmouth, but by the time this book goes to press they will probably have been restored to normal.

### Northeast Coast
**Pagua Bay,** a quiet, secluded beach of dark sand, is on the Atlantic and is best suited to strong swimmers. **Woodford Hill Bay, Hampstead, L'Anse Noir,** and **Hodges,** are some of the most beautiful beaches on the island and are excellent for snorkeling and scuba diving, though all this wind-tossed beauty can be dangerous to swimmers, since there are strong underwater currents as well as whipped-cream waves. From these beaches you can see the French island of Marie Galante in the distance.

### Northwest Coast
**Picard Beach,** on the northwest coast, is the island's best beach. Great for windsurfing and snorkeling, it's a 2-mile stretch of brown sand fringed with coconut trees. The Picard Beach Cottage Resort and Coconut Beach hotel are along this beach.

### Southeast Coast
In the southeast, near La Plaine, **Bout Sable Bay** is not much good for swimming, but the surroundings are stirringly elemental: Towering red cliffs challenge the rollicking Atlantic.

### Southwest Coast
The beaches south of Roseau are not great, but the snorkeling and scuba diving are excellent because of the dramatic underwater walls and sudden drops. At **Scotts Head** and **Soufrière Bay,** you will find some of the finest snorkeling and scuba diving in the world. At one spot, volcanic vents puff steam into the sea; the experience has been described as "swimming in champagne."

## Outdoor Activities and Sports
### Boating
Motorboat and sailing trips can be arranged through **Dominica Tours** (☎ 809/448–2638) and the **Castaways Beach Hotel** (☎ 809/449–6245).

### Hiking
Dominica is rightly renowned for its superb hiking. Majestic mountains, clear rivers, and lush, green vegetation all combine to make rambling about a great pleasure. The island is, in fact, crisscrossed by ancient footpaths, some created by the "Nègres Marron," escaped slaves (including some Carib Indians) who established camps in the mountains. There are now ambitious plans to incorporate these old trails into a path which would traverse the island from north to south. Existing trails range from easygoing to arduous. For the former, all you'll need are sturdy, rubber-soled shoes and an adventurous spirit. For both, bring insect repellent.

For the hike to **Boiling Lake** or the climb up **Morne Diablotin** you will need hiking boots, a guide, and water. Guides will charge about $30–$35 per person and can be contacted through the Dominica Tourist Office or the Forestry Division (☎ 809/448–2401 or 809/448–2638).

## River Swimming

With 365 rivers—one for every day of the year—it's not surprising that river swimming is one of the most popular pastimes on Dominica. All the rivers are clean, but the best one for swimming and inner-tubing is the **Layou River.** In some places, you can sunbathe and picnic on its banks.

## Scuba Diving

"Amazing! Incredible! Fantastic!" These are some of the words people use when they surface after a dive in Dominica. Voted one of the top ten dive destinations in the world by *Skin Diver* magazine, Dominica is a paradise for divers and snorkelers alike. The diving is especially good in the southeast of the island, around Soufrière Bay, the site of a submerged volcanic crater. Within half a mile of the shore, the water drops almost vertically to 800 feet and thence 1,500 feet. Visibility frequently extends to 100 feet. There are not so many large fish as on some islands (they are not fed here), but marine life is abundant. Shoals of several thousand boga fish, Creole wrasse, or blue cromis are not uncommon, and you might even see a spotted moray eel or honeycomb cowfish. Crinoids (rare elsewhere) are also abundant, as are giant barrel sponges. The opportunities for underwater photography, particularly macro-photography, are unparalleled. The going rate is about $60–$65 for a two-tank dive or $80–$90 for a resort course with two open-water dives.

**Castaways Beach Hotel** (☎ 809/449–6245 or 800/934–3483), 11 miles north of Roseau, has diving at its water-sports center. **Dive Dominica** (✉ Castle Comfort, ☎ 809/448–2188 or 800/544–7631, FAX 809/448–6088) has three boats and is one of the oldest dive shops on the island. Owners Derek and Ginette Perryman, NAUI-approved instructors, offer snorkeling and resort dives for beginners and, for the advanced set, dives on drop-offs, walls, and pinnacles—by day or night. **Dominica Dive Resorts, Waitukubuli** (✉ Anchorage Hotel, ☎ 809/448–2638; ✉ Portsmouth Beach Hotel, ☎ 809/445–5142) are run by PADI-certified owners and offer both resort courses and full certification. **Nature Island Dive** (✉ Soufrière, ☎ 809/449–8181) is an excellent operation run by two friendly, Generation-X couples, one Canadian and one British/American. They also offer sea kayaking and mountain bike tours, as well as packages with their own cottage on the beach or with nearby hotels.

## Snorkeling

Major island operators rent equipment: **Anchorage Hotel** (☎ 809/448–2638), **Castaways Beach Hotel** (☎ 809/449–6245), **Coconut Beach Hotel** (☎ 809/445–5393), **Picard Beach Cottage Resort** (☎ 809/445–5131), and **Sunshine Village** (☎ 809/445–5066).

## Windsurfing

Contact **Anchorage Hotel** (☎ 809/448–2638), **Castaways Beach Hotel** (☎ 809/449–6245), or **Picard Beach Cottage Resort** (☎ 809/445–5131).

# Shopping

## Gift Ideas

The distinctive handicrafts of the Carib Indians include traditional baskets made of dyed *larouma* reeds and waterproofed with tightly woven *balizier* leaves. These crafts are sold on the reservation, as well as in

Roseau's shops. Dominica is also noted for its spices (especially saffron), hot peppers, bay rum, and coconut-oil soap; its vetiver-grass mats are sold all over the world. Cafe Dominique, the local equivalent of Jamaican Blue Mountain coffee, is an excellent buy. Dominican rum is stronger, and rougher, than French brands—try Macoucherie. Proof that the old ways live on in Dominica can be found in the number of herbal doctors setting up shop in the streets of Roseau. One stimulating memento of your visit is rum steeped with Bois Bandé (scientific name Richeria Grandis), a tree whose bark is reputed to have aphrodisiacal properties. You can find it at Tropicrafts (☞ *below*) and in the supermarkets (try **Whitchurch** on Kennedy Ave.).

**Arnold and Roberta Toulon** (⊠ 54 Queen Mary St., ☎ 809/448–3740), siblings who work out of their studio-home, hand-paint T-shirts that sell so well, stock is always limited. They will, however, make up a special order within two days. Arnold's canvases of fine art are also on display.

**Balisier** (⊠ 35 Great George St., no phone) is the spot for charming sunbonnets, carnival dolls, island jewelry, and hand-painted T-shirts.

**Caribana Handcrafts** (⊠ 31 Cork St., Roseau, ☎ 809/448–2761) sells ceramics, wood carvings, and baskets.

**Dominica Pottery** (⊠ Bayfront St. and Kennedy Ave., Roseau, no phone) is run by a local priest, whose products are fashioned with various local clays and glazes.

**Fadelle's** (⊠ 28 Kennedy Ave., Roseau, ☎ 809/448–2686) sells straw and woodwork, as well as soaps, sauces, and perfumes.

**NDFD Small Business Mini Mall** (⊠ 9 Great Marlborough St., Roseau, ☎ 809/448–0412) was opened with the help of the government, which actively encourages local artisans. Among the more notable booths are **Linx Jewelry,** where Dyanna hand-paints T-shirts and creates unusual African-influenced earrings and pins from coconut husks, seashells, clay, wood and pods; **Caribbean Perfumes,** fragrant with teas, scents, and potpourri; and the **Blow Kalbass Healing Center,** which sells natural products touted to cure everything from acne to rheumatism (locals swear by the skin creams, clay baths, and hair pomade).

**Papillote Wilderness Retreat** (⊠ Roseau, ☎ 809/448–2287 has a gift shop with an excellent selection of wood carvings from Haiti.

**Starbrite Industries** (⊠ Canefield Industrial Estate, ☎ 809/449–1006) makes great candles, including some in the shape of the Dominican parrot, cupids, and trees.

**Tropicrafts** (⊠ 41 Queen Mary St., Roseau, ☎ 809/448–2747; ⊠ Bay St., Portsmouth, ☎ 809/445–5956) has a back room where you can watch the local ladies weaving. Here you'll find wood carvings, rum, hot sauces, and local perfumes, in addition to traditional Carib baskets, hats, and woven mats.

# Nightlife

When the moon comes up, the Dominicans go out to party. The Fortress Disco, at the Fort Young Hotel, is popular. So, too, are the steel bands and calypso groups that play at most of the larger hotels—the Castaways, Anchorage, Garraway, and Reigate Hall. Music to be heard elsewhere includes reggae, ska, calypso, and jing ping, a type of folk music featuring the accordion, the *quage* (a kind of washboard instrument), drums, and a boom boom (a percussive instrument).

**Carib 2000** (⊠ Prevo Cinemall, Roseau, ☎ 809/448–1677) serves seafood and cocktails to an upscale crowd. On Friday and Saturday nights there are live steel bands and jazz.

**Club Coconuts** (✉ 3 mi north of Roseau, ☎ 809/449–1489), at Rockaway Beach, has live ska, reggae, and R&B.

**Night Box** (✉ Goodwill Rd., ☎ 809/448–8887) is a disco that attracts a rowdier clientele.

**Roxy's Mountain Lodge** (✉ Laudat, ☎ 809/448–4845) is the place to go if you want to get high (we're talking altitude here); it has taped music and an excellent selection of rums.

**Shipwreck** (✉ In the Canefield industrial area, ☎ 809/449–1059) has live reggae and taped music on weekends and a Sunday bash that starts at noon and continues into the night.

**Warehouse** (✉ Outside Roseau toward airport, ☎ 809/449–1303) is a local disco where the locals go on weekends.

**Wykie's La Tropical** (✉ 51 Old St., Roseau, ☎ 809/448–8015) is a classic Caribbean hole-in-the-wall and gathering spot for the island's movers and shakers, especially during Friday's happy hour, when they nibble on stewed chicken or black pudding, then stay on for a local calypso band or some jing ping.

## Exploring Dominica

Despite the small size of this almond-shape island, it can take a couple of hours to get between many of the island's popular destinations; roads are in poor shape and travel is relatively slow. The amount of time you spend hiking, mountain climbing, bird-watching, or just enjoying the scenery will determine how much you can see during one round-the-island trip. It takes about four days of solid trekking to take in the whole of Dominica. The highways ringing most of the island's perimeter have been upgraded in recent years; but more remote destinations remain somewhat inaccessible, and it's wise to hire a car and driver or to take an escorted tour (☞ Guided Tours *in* Dominica A to Z, *below*).

*Numbers in the margin correspond to points of interest on the Dominica map.*

SIGHTS TO SEE

⑫ **Cabrits National Park.** Just north of the town of Portsmouth, this 250-acre park is, along with Brimstone Hill in St. Kitts, Shirley Heights in Antigua, and Fort Charlotte in St. Vincent, one of the most significant historic sites in the Caribbean. The heart of the park is the **Fort Shirley** military complex. Built by the British between 1770 and 1815, it once comprised 50 major structures, including batteries, powder magazines, and storehouses, as well as barracks and officers quarters to house 500 men. With the help of the Royal Navy (who send sailors ashore to work on the site each time a ship is in port) and local volunteers, historian Lennox Honychurch has restored the fort. There is also a small museum that highlights the natural and historic aspects of the park. The cruise-ship facility offers a cooperative crafts shop, a continuously screened film about Fort Shirley, and occasional live dance or music performances. The herbaceous swamps nearby are an important site for several species of rare plants, including the cachiman marron and the white mangrove.

⑥ **Carib Indian Reservation.** A fierce, warrior race who sprinkled newborn, male babies with their fathers' blood, the Caribs were, for centuries, the implacable enemies of the colonists. For this they were hunted down and exterminated. Finally, in 1903, they were granted these 3,700 acres of land, and their chief was allowed to call himself "King" and was endowed with an annual allowance of 6 sterling. Don't expect a lot in the way of ancient culture and costume. The folks who gave the Caribbean its name live pretty much like other West Indians, as fishermen and farmers. They have maintained their traditional skills of wood carving and basket weaving, and their wares are displayed at stands along the roadside. A point of interest on the reservation is **L'Escalier Tête Chien** ("trail of the snake staircase" in Creole patois)—a hardened lava flow that juts down to the ocean. The Atlantic here is particularly fierce and roily, the shore marked with countless coves and inlets; according to Carib legend, nearby Londonderry Islets metamorphose at night into grand canoes to take the spirits of the dead out to sea. Look for the altar at the reservation's Roman Catholic church at Salibia; it was once a canoe. The Caribs still build their own canoes—long, elegant crafts scooped from the trunk of a single gommier tree. If you are lucky, you can watch this being done on the beach at **Castle Bruce**, a few miles to the south of the reservation.

NEED A BREAK?

Stop for lunch or a cold drink at the **Carib Territory Guesthouse** (☎ 809/445-7256), owned by Caribs Charles and Margaret Williams. They offer half- or full-day walks through the territory. For those who want to stay overnight, there are eight basic rooms. A good selection of Carib crafts is sold here.

**④ Emerald Pool.** It's only a 20-minute walk down a trail to this swirling, fern-bedecked basin into which a 50-foot waterfall splashes. Lookout points along the way provide sweeping views of the windward (Atlantic) coast and the forested interior.

NEED A BREAK?

Peter Kaufmann and his friendly dogs will welcome you at the **Emerald Bush Hotel–Nature Park** (☎ 809/446-0300). Stop for a glass of fresh juice or a rum punch, wander along a lush trail, or spend the night in an A-frame cottage. This is one of the most beautiful settings in Dominica—but be prepared to rough it. The bar and restaurant are open only until about sundown.

**⑩ Indian River.** Portsmouth is the place to embark for a canoe or rowboat ride up this lazy, tropical river that snakes through lush rain forest thick with mangrove trees and exotic bird life. The guides here are notoriously overeager (they will try and get you into a powerboat, which will scare off all the birds), so choose carefully or ask your hotel to recommend someone. If you don't want to do the canoe ride, take the road along the Indian River valley northeast to the Atlantic, considered by many to be one of the prettiest roads of the island. Twisting through embankments of red clay festooned with ferns, coconut trees, and bananas, you pass villages with French names like Dos D'Ane and Paix Bouche, which proudly announce their populations (300 is a megalopolis) as you enter them, and where brightly painted shanties vie with the flowers for color.

**⑤ Layou River Valley.** Rich with bananas, cacao, citrus fruits, and coconuts, this is one of the most pleasant spots on the island. The river is the island's longest and largest, with deep gorges, quiet pools, beaches, waterfalls, and rapids—a great place for a full day's swimming and shooting the rapids, or just sunning and picnicking. The remains of Hillsborough Estate, once a rum-producing plantation, are also here.

**⑦ Marigot.** The largest settlement on the east coast (population: 5,000) is not a particular point of interest, but it is a good jumping-off point to explore the northeast coast, with its steep cliffs, dramatic reefs, and rivers swirling down through forests of mangroves and fields of coconut. The nearby beaches of Woodford Hill Bay, Hampstead, L'Anse Noir, and Hodges are excellent for snorkeling and scuba diving.

⑬ **Morne Aux Diables.** In the far north of Dominica is this peak, which soars 2,826 feet above sea level and slopes down to Toucari Bay and Douglas Bay on the west coast, where you'll find long stretches of dark-sand beach.

⑨ **Morne Diablotin.** At 4,747 feet, it is the island's highest summit. It takes its name from a bird, known in English as the black-capped petrel, which was prized by hunters in the 18th-century. There aren't many left today, but Dominica is still a birders' paradise: 135 species live or migrate here, including bananaquits, exotic flycatchers and fluorescent hummingbirds. Morne Diablotin, situated in the northern forest reserve, is a good place to see them, though the hike to the top is not one that you should attempt alone. You'll need a good guide (☞ Hiking, *above*), sturdy shoes, a warm sweater, and firm resolve.

③ **Morne Trois Pitons National Park.** Dedicated as a national park in 1975, this 17,000-acre swath of lush, mountainous land in the south central interior of the island is the Crown Jewels of the "Nature Island." Named after one of the highest (4,600 ft.) mountains on the island, it contains bubbling volcanos, majestic waterfalls, and cool mountain lakes. For naturalists, there are four different types of vegetation zones to browse through. Ferns grow 30 feet tall and wild orchids sprout from trees. Sunlight leaks through green canopies and a gentle mist rises over the jungle floor. A system of trails has been developed in the park but shortage of funds, excessive rainfall, and the profusion of vegetation all make them hard to maintain. Access to the park is possible from most points of the compass, though the easiest approach is via the small, mountaintop village of Laudat, 7 miles from Roseau.

About 5 miles out of Roseau, the Wotton Waven Road branches off toward **Sulphur Springs,** where you'll see the belching, sputtering, and gurgling release of hot springs along a river and nearby field—evidence of the area's restless volcanic activity. At the base of Morne Micotrin, you'll find two crater lakes: The first, at 2,500 feet, is **Freshwater Lake,** which was believed to be haunted by a vindictive mermaid and a monstrous serpent with a gemlike carbuncle on its forehead. Farther on is **Boeri Lake,** which is fringed with greenery and has purple hyacinths floating on its surface. But the undisputed highlight of the park is **Boiling Lake.** The world's second-largest boiling lake, it is a cauldron of gurgling gray-blue water, 70 yards wide, of unknown depth, with water temperatures from 180°F to 197°F. It is believed that the lake is not a volcanic crater but a flooded fumarole—a crack through which gases escape from the molten lava below. The hike up to the lake is challenging and you will be slipping and sliding the whole way up. You should go only with a guide (☞ Hiking, *above*) and will have to leave at about 8 AM for this all-day, 7-mile (round-trip) trek. Guides keep small groups of hikers (usually six to eight maximum) under a watchful eye at all times. You will return exhausted, covered with mud, nicks, and scrapes, but glowing with satisfaction that you've seen one of the wonders of the world. On your way to the lake, you'll pass through the **Valley of Desolation,** a sight that definitely lives up to its name. Harsh sulfuric fumes have destroyed virtually all the vegetation in what was once a lush forested area. Stay on the trail to avoid breaking through the crust that covers the hot lava below, unless you want to make your own journey to the center of the earth.

Also in the National Park are the island's three highest waterfalls: Sari Sari, Middleham, and the spectacular Trafalgar Falls. All three falls are more than 150 feet high. If you're in decent shape and possess agility and balance, it's worth hiking up the riverbed to the cool pools at the bases of the twin **Trafalgar Falls.** The taller of the two is where hot, orange-colored sulfuric and ferric waters mix with the crash of cold river water; taking a dip is an exhilarating experience; sadly, in 1995, Hurricane Marilyn caused a landslide that buried the base of this waterfall. At press tim, the Army Corps of Engineers was scheduled to help the government dislodge thousands of tons of rubble.

**NEED A BREAK?** **Roxy's Mountain Lodge** (☎ 809/448–4885) sits at 2,500 feet near the village of Laudat. It's a good place to rest weary feet and dry off over a cup of tea or a shot of rum from the bar's wide selection. Snacks and light meals are also available.

⓫ **Portsmouth.** The past of this rather drab town is more illustrious than its present. It was once intended to be the capital of Dominica, thanks to its superb natural harbor on **Prince Rupert Bay.** In its heyday, as many as 400 ships docked here at one time. In 1782 it was also the site of one of the most decisive naval engagements between the French and the English, the Battle of Les Saintes. The English won that one, but lost the much tougher fight against the mosquitoes breeding in the nearby swamps. As a result, Roseau, not Portsmouth, is today the capital. Maritime traditions are continued here by the yachting set and there are more than 2 miles of good, sandy beaches fringed with coconut trees and a few small hotels. Unfortunately, this part of the island was particularly hard hit by Hurricane Marilyn in 1995.

**NEED A BREAK?** The bar in the **Purple Turtle Guest House** (✉ Portsmouth, ☎ 809/445–5296) is a fine place for a rum punch before or after a tour of Portsmouth, especially at sunset.

➊ **Roseau.** With a population of only 20,000, Roseau (pronounced rose-oh) must be one of the smallest capital cities in the world. You are more likely to see goats and chickens than statues and fountains. But if you give it a chance, you will make friends with this slow-moving Caribbean town, with its wood-and-stone shanties, bright colored roofs, and bustling marketplace. The locals are so helpful that, even before you have a chance to ask them directions, they will be shepherding you through the streets. Then they will probably follow you to see that you have gone the right way! New developments at **Bayfront** have brightened up the waterfront. The old court house now houses the excellent new **Dominica Museum,** labor of love of local writer and historian, Lennox Honychurch. The **Fort Young Hotel,** built as a British fort in the 18th century, is also worth a visit. The state house, public library, and Anglican Cathedral are all nearby.

The 40-acre **Botanical Gardens,** founded in 1891 as an annex of Kew Gardens, in London, has extensive collections of tropical plants and trees. Don't miss the remains of a giant baobab tree that came down during Hurricane David. The school bus it crushed is still there, as a memento of David's fury. The **national park office** is also here. It can provide tour guides and a wealth of printed information. ✉ *National Park Office,* ☎ *809/448–2401, ext. 417.* ☉ *Mon. 8–1 and 2–5, Tues.–Fri. 8–1 and 2–4. Dominica Museum, no phone.* ▨ *$1.* ☉ *Weekdays 9–5, Sat. 9–1.*

**NEED A BREAK?** Sit in the garden of the late Jean Rhys, the Dominican-born novelist who wrote *Wide Sargasso Sea.* The garden has been turned into an informal garden eatery, the **World of Food** (✉ Queen Mary St. and Field's La., ☎ 809/448–6125). If you've never read Rhys, stop off at **Paperbacks** (✉ 6 Cork St., ☎ 809/448–2370), which carries a wide selection of her works.

**②  Soufrière.** This lazy, sunbaked village at the southernmost tip of the island was first settled by French lumbermen in the 17th century. The Frenchness of Soufrière (the name comes from the nearby sulphur springs) can still be felt in the Roman Catholic church. Built of volcanic stone, with red and blue trim, it is the prettiest on the island. Today, Soufrière is, literally, the jumping-off point for some of the finest diving and snorkeling in the Caribbean (☞ Outdoor Activities and Sports, *above*). From Scotts Head, a narrow peninsula that encircles the bay, there are wonderful views of Martinique.

**❽  Syndicate Nature Trail.** The road at the bend near Dublanc that leads to the Syndicate Estate also leads to the 200-acre site of **Project Sisserou.** This protected site, which includes the Syndicate Nature Trail, has been set aside with the help of some 6,000 schoolchildren, each of whom donated 25¢ for the land where the endangered Sisserou parrot (found only in Dominica) flies free. At last estimate, there were only about 60 of these shy and beautiful birds, covered in rich green feathers with a mauve front.

# Dominica A to Z

## Arriving and Departing

### BY FERRY

**Atlantika** (✉ c/o Trois Pitons Travel, ☎ 809/448–6977) runs jet catamarans from Guadeloupe to Martinique, with stops at Les Saintes and Dominica, on Wednesday, Friday, Saturday, and Sunday. **Caribbean Express** (✉ c/o Whitchurch Shipping & Tours, ☎ 809/448–2181) has scheduled service Monday, Wednesday, Friday, and Saturday from Guadeloupe in the north to Martinique in the south, with stops at Les Saintes and Dominica. The crossing, in a jet catamaran, takes approximately three hours and offers superb views of the other islands.

### BY PLANE

**American Eagle** (☎ 800/433–7300) flies four times weekly from San Juan. **LIAT** (☎ 809/462–0700) connects with flights from the United States on Antigua, Barbados, Guadeloupe, Martinique, St. Lucia, St. Maarten, and San Juan. **Air Martinique** (☎ 809/448–2181) flies from Fort de France. **Air Guadeloupe** (☎ 809/448–2181) flies from Pointe-à-Pitre. **Air BVI** (☎ 809/774–6500) connects from Tortola, BVI. **BWIA** (☎ 809/462–0262) connects from Antigua. **Winair** (☎ 809/448–2181) connects from St. Maarten. The newest service, **Cardinal Airlines** (☎ 809/449–0600), connects from both Antigua and St. Maarten.

### FROM THE AIRPORT

**Canefield Airport** (about 3 miles north of Roseau) handles only small aircraft and daytime flights; landing here can be a hair-raising experience for those uneasy about flying. Cab fare is about $8 to Roseau. **Melville Hall Airport,** on the northeast coast, handles larger planes; although interesting, the 90-minute drive through the island's rain forest to Roseau is bumpy, exhausting, and costs about $50 by private taxi or $17 per person by co-op cab.

## Currency

The official currency is the Eastern Caribbean dollar (E.C.$). Figure about E.C.$2.60 to U.S.$1. U.S. dollars are readily accepted, but you'll usually get change in E.C. dollars. Major credit cards are widely accepted, as are traveler's checks. Prices quoted here are in U.S. dollars unless indicated otherwise.

## Emergencies

**Police, fire, and ambulance:** ☎ 999. **Hospital: Princess Margaret Hospital** (✉ Federation Dr., Goodwill, ☎ 809/448–2231 or 809/448–2233). **Pharmacy: Jolly's Pharmacy** (✉ 12 King George V St., Roseau, ☎ 809/448–3388).

## Getting Around

### CAR RENTALS

If it doesn't bother you to drive on the left on potholed mountainous roads with hairpin curves, rent a car and strike out on your own. Daily car-rental rates begin at $35 (weekly about $190), plus collision damage insurance at $6 a day and personal accident insurance at $2 a day, and you'll have to put down a deposit and purchase a visitor's driving permit for E.C.$20. You can rent a car from **Avis** (✉ 4 High St., Roseau, ☎ 809/448–2481), **Wide Range Car Rentals** (✉ 79 Bath Rd., Roseau, ☎ 809/448–2198), **Valley Rent-A-Car** (✉ Goodwill Rd., Roseau, ☎ 809/448–3233), or **Anselm's Car Rental** (✉ 3 Great Marlborough St., Roseau, ☎ 809/448–2730). **Budget Rent-A-Car** (✉ Canefield Industrial Estate, ☎ 809/449–2080) offers daily rates, three-day specials, and weekly and monthly rates.

### TAXIS

Taxis are available at the airports and in Roseau. The rates are fixed by the government, but prices can usually be negotiated. **Mally's Tour & Taxi Service** (☎ 809/448–3114) and **Julius John's** (☎ 809/449–1968) are two of the better operators.

Taxi drivers are also happy to offer their services as guides at the cost of $18 an hour, per car of four, with tip extra. It's a good idea to get a recommendation from your hotel manager or the Dominica Division of Tourism (☞ Visitor Information, *below*) before selecting a guide and driver.

### VANS

This is a cheap, though not always dependable, means of transportation. Minivans cruise the island and, like taxis, will stop when hailed. You can also catch a minivan in Roseau by the bridges crossing the Roseau River.

## Guided Tours

**Dominica Tours** (☎ 809/448–2638) conducts a wide variety of hiking and photo safari tours in sturdy four-wheel-drive vehicles. Prices range from $15 to $100 per person, depending upon the length of the trip and whether picnics and rum punches are included. There are also boat tours, which include snorkeling, swimming, and rum or fruit drinks. The latest rage in Dominica is whale-watching; the knowledgeable diver-photographer Fitzroy Armour leads three- to four-hour expeditions from November through April, when surprisingly graceful schools of sperms, humpbacks, and orcas patrol the surrounding waters. **Ken's Hinterland Adventure Tours** (✉ ☎ 809/448–4850) are the best tours on the island. Ken's provides vans with knowledgeable guides and can design expeditions to fit your needs. One of the most exciting tours is a hike down the dramatic Layou River Gorge. If you're uneasy about some of the more dangerous hikes, Ken's is the best choice: They use two-way radios at all times, which you'll appreciate if ever there's an emergency. Ken's also offers sea kayaking, a wonderful opportunity to challenge the crashing surf and explore the scalloped coast. **Rainbow Rover Tours** (☎ 809/448–8650) are conducted in air-conditioned Land Rovers. You can take in the island for a half or full day at a cost of $30–$60, which includes food and drink.

## Language

The official language is English, but most Dominicans also speak a French-Creole patois.

## Opening and Closing Times

Business hours are weekdays 8–1 and 2–4, Saturday 8–1. Banks are open Monday–Thursday 8–3, Friday 8–5.

## Passports and Visas

U.S. and Canadian citizens must present a driver's license or passport and a return or ongoing ticket. British citizens must show a passport.

## Precautions

Bring insect repellent. If you are susceptible to motion sickness, be sure to bring along some medication, as the roads twist and turn dramatically, and the local drivers barrel down them at dizzying speeds. If you plan on hiking even the simplest trail, bring along extra clothing and hiking boots or athletic sneakers to change into; trails are very rugged and often very muddy. Note: Unlike neighboring Martinique and Guadeloupe, topless bathing is not en vogue on Dominica. A note in the government tourist guide also states that swimsuits may not be worn in the street.

## Taxes and Service Charges

Hotels collect a 5% government tax, restaurants a 3% tax. The departure tax is $10 or E.C.$25. All hotels and restaurants add a 10% service charge to your bill. Tipping is welcomed.

## Telephones, Electricity, and Mail

To call Dominica from the United States, dial area code 809 and the local access code, 44, followed by the five-digit local number. On the island, you need to dial only the five-digit number. The island has efficient direct-dial international service. All pay phones are equipped for local and overseas dialing.

Electric voltage is 220/240 AC, 50 cycles. American appliances require an adaptor.

First-class (airmail) letters to the United States and Canada cost E.C.95¢; postcards cost E.C.50¢.

## Visitor Information

Before you go, contact the **Caribbean Tourism Organization** (✉ 20 E. 46th St., New York, NY 10017, ☎ 212/682–0435). In the United Kingdom, contact the **Dominica Tourist Office** (✉ 1 Collingham Gardens, London SW5 0HW, ☎ 0171/835–1937 or 0171/370–5194).

Once on Dominica, contact the main office of the **Division of Tourism** (✉ National Development Corp., Valley Rd., Box 293, Roseau, ☎ 809/448–2045). The tourist desk at the **post office** (✉ Bay St., no phone) is open weekdays 8–4, Saturday 9–1. The office at **Canefield Airport** (☎ 809/449–1242) is open weekdays 6:15–11 AM and 2–5:30 PM. The office at **Melville Hall Airport** (☎ 809/445–7051) is open weekdays 6:15–11 AM and 2–5:30 PM.

# 11 Dominican Republic

**S**PRAWLING OVER TWO-THIRDS OF THE ISLAND of Hispaniola, the Dominican Republic is the spot where European settlement of the Western Hemi-

Updated by
Jonathan Runge

sphere really began. Santo Domingo, its capital, is the oldest continuously inhabited city in this half of the globe, and history buffs who visit have difficulty tearing themselves away from the city's 16th-century Colonial Zone. Sunseekers head for the beach resorts of Puerto Plata, Barahona, Samaná, Bavaro, Punta Cana, and La Romana. The highest peak in the West Indies is here: Pico Duarte (10,128 feet) lures hikers to the central mountain range. Ancient sunken galleons and coral reefs divert divers and snorkelers.

Columbus happened upon this island on December 5, 1492, and on Christmas Eve his ship, the *Santa María,* was wrecked on the Atlantic shore. He named it La Isla Española ("the Spanish island"), established a small colony, and sailed back to Spain on the *Pinta.* A year later he returned, only to find that the Spanish colony had been destroyed by the Taino Indians, the island's original inhabitants. But Columbus established another colony nearby, leaving his brother Bartholomew in charge. Santo Domingo, which is located on the south coast where the Río Ozama spills into the Caribbean Sea, was founded in 1496 by Bartholomew Columbus and Nicolás de Ovando and during the first half of the 16th century became the bustling hub of Spanish commerce and culture in the New World.

Hispaniola (a derivation of *La Isla Española*) has had an unusually chaotic history, replete with bloody revolutions, military coups, yellow-fever epidemics, invasions, and bankruptcy. In the 17th century, the western third of the island was ceded to France. A slave revolt in 1804 resulted in the establishment there of the first black republic, Haiti. Dominicans and Haitians battled for control of the island on and off throughout the 19th century. The Dominicans declared themselves independent from Haiti in 1844 and from Spain in 1865. The country was, however, bankrupt by the turn of the century. The United States helped to administer the island's finances, and eventually U.S. Marines occupied the country from 1916 to 1924, until a new Dominican constitution was signed. Rafael Trujillo ruled the Dominican Republic with an iron fist from 1930 until his assassination in 1961. A short-lived democracy was overthrown soon thereafter, followed by another occupation by the U.S. Marines in 1965. The country has been relatively stable since the early 1970s, and administrations have been staunch supporters of the United States.

American influence looms large in Dominican life. If Dominicans do not actually have relatives living in the United States, they know someone who does; and many speak at least rudimentary English. Still, it is a vibrantly Latin country, and the Latino flavor contrasts sharply with the culture of the British, French, and Dutch islands in the Caribbean. All one has to do is listen to one of the country's most famous exports, the fast-paced merengue, to feel the energy, dynamism, and vitality of the Dominicans.

Dominican towns and cities are generally not quaint, neat, or particularly pretty. Poverty is everywhere, but the country is also alive and chaotic, sometimes frenzied, sometimes laid-back. Dominicans love their music—there is dancing in the streets every summer at Santo Domingo's Merengue Festival—and they have a well-deserved reputation for being one of the friendliest people in the region. This is a tropical country; there is less urgency to get things done, and tempers don't flare up quickly.

Blackouts, for instance, are a daily occurrence in much of the country, but this does not cause much discomfort for visitors, since most major hotels have emergency generators.

In recent years, tourism has played an increasingly important role in the government's scheme of things. Like Puerto Rico, its cousin to the east across the Mona Channel, the Dominican Republic used the 500th anniversary of its "discovery" by Christopher Columbus to give the tourist industry a much-needed boost. Its tourist zones are incredibly varied and include extravagant Casa de Campo (where many rich Santo Domingans have villas), the package-tour hotels of Playa Dorada, Santo Domingo's exquisite Colonial Zone, the neglected streets of Jarabacoa in its gorgeous mountain setting, and the world-weary beauty of the Samaná peninsula.

## Lodging

Your options here vary from the New World's first hotel to some of the world's newest and poshest resorts. An ambitious development plan continues, especially on the north coast. The Dominican Republic has the largest hotel inventory (28,000 rooms and growing) in the Caribbean. Puerto Plata alone has 9,000 rooms and hosts 250,000 tourists a year. There are already so many adjoining resorts that when you go out for a stroll you have to flag landmarks to find your way back to the one where your luggage is. The fierce competition translates into some of the best hotel buys in the Caribbean. Be sure to inquire about special packages when you call to reserve; arranging your room as a package through a tour operator will cost considerably less. Be aware that many hotels, especially on the north coast, turn their water supply off at midnight as a conservation measure. Rooms are air-conditioned unless otherwise noted.

Hotels in Santo Domingo base their tariffs on the EP and maintain the same room rates through the year. In contrast, resorts have high winter and low summer rates, with the low rate reducing the room prices by as much as 50%. All-inclusive properties are concentrated along the north coast. More and more hotels are turning all-inclusive, but those that haven't offer EP or MAP. Our prices, in U.S. dollars, are based on a double room during the high season. For meal plans, add $20–$30 per person to the room-only rate listed below; for all-inclusive, add $40–$45 per person.

| CATEGORY | COST* |
| --- | --- |
| $$$$ | over $175 |
| $$$ | $125–$175 |
| $$ | $75–$125 |
| $ | under $75 |

*All prices are for a standard double room for two, excluding 15% service charge and 8% tax.*

### Boca Chica/Juan Dolio

**$$$** ⬚ **Hamaca Beach Hotel.** This large, all-inclusive resort is a half hour east of Santo Domingo and just a few minutes from Las Américas Airport. The impressive reception area has terra-cotta floors, wicker furnishings, and water walls; its teal and yellow decor is picked up beautifully by huge floral arrangements. Guest rooms have full baths and cable TV and are furnished in painted rattan and dark woods. Floral linens coordinate with pale green tile floors. There's a lovely champagne-color beach. The food at the restaurants, although good, is mostly standard Continental fare. ✉ *Boca Chica Beach,* ☎ *809/523-4611 or 800/472-3985,* ℻ *809/566-2436. 464 rooms. 4 restaurants,*

# Dominican Republic

Cofresi Beach
Luperón Beach
Montecristi
Playa Dorada
18 - 23
25 - 28
16 17
Puerto Plata
12 24 13
Sosúa
Cabarete Beach
29
Guayubin
11
Dajabón
La Unión International Airport
Santiago de los Caballeros
10
Moca
San Francisco de Macorís
9
HAITI
7
8 Jarabacoa
Bánica
San Juan
Lago Enriquillo
Neiba
Azua
6
Duvergé
Bani
Pedernales
Barahona 5
Bahia de Ocoa
HISPANIOLA
Oviedo
Isla Beata    Cabo Beata

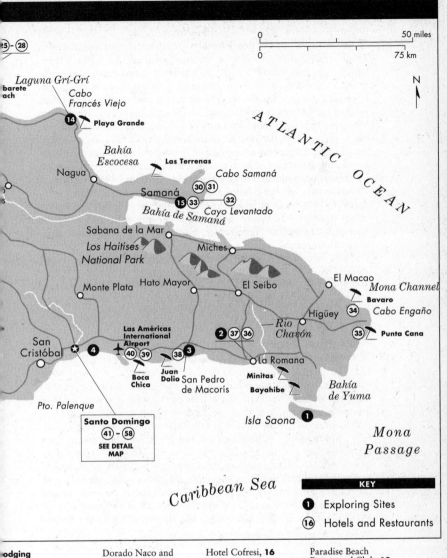

**KEY**

**1** Exploring Sites

**16** Hotels and Restaurants

odging
Bavaro Beach Resort, **34**
Bayside Hill Resort and Beach Club, **17**
Cabarete Beach Hotel, **29**
Caribbean Village Club and Resort, **21**
Casa de Campo, **37**
Cayo Levantado, **32**
Club Marina, **28**

Dorado Naco and Playa Naco, **18**
Flamenco Beach Resort, Villas Doradas, and Playa Dorada Beach Resort, **24**
Gran Hotel Lina and Casino, **43**
Hamaca Beach Hotel, **40**
Hostal Palacio Nicolás de Ovando, **52**

Hotel Cofresi, **16**
Hotel El Embajador and Casino, **51**
Hotel Gran Bahía, **31**
Hotel Hispaniola, **58**
Hotel Santo Domingo, **41**
Inter-Continental Hotel V Centenario, **53**
Jaragua Renaissance Resort and Casino, **50**

Paradise Beach Resort and Club, **19**
Puerto Plata Beach Resort and Casino, **20**
Punta Cana Beach Resort, **35**
Renaissance Capella Beach Resort, **38**
Sand Castle, **26**
Santo Domingo Sheraton Hotel and Casino, **42**
Villa Serena, **30**

*3 bars, grill, 2 tennis courts, archery, horseback riding, scuba diving, snorkeling, windsurfing, sailing, bicycles, transportation to Santo Domingo casinos. AE, MC, V. All-inclusive.*

**\$\$–\$\$\$**   ⊡ **Renaissance Capella Beach Resort.** This deluxe resort, popular with Americans, opened in 1994 on a section of Juan Dolio Beach it ostentatiously calls Villas Del Mar, and is striving to become the top southern-coast destination, with the exception, of course, of Casa de Campo. It's built on a grand scale, with beautiful tile and mosaic work in the elegant public spaces and a hodgepodge of architectural styles from Victorian (white colonnaded porticoes) to Moorish (arches and red-tile roofs) to South Pacific (two of the restaurants sit in cathedralesque thatched huts). Rooms are large and handsomely appointed with ceramic lamps, pictures of local plants, and pink and mint-green fabrics. Most have balconies and huge walk-in closets; some have ocean views. Unfortunately, service does not yet meet exacting international standards, food is not as good as it might be, and the property already requires upkeep (bathrooms seem rather cheaply done and elevators have stained carpets). Nonetheless, the vast array of amenities and facilities is bound to please travelers seeking something a cut above most Dominican resorts, especially at the surprisingly reasonable rates. ⊠ *Villas Del Mar, Box 4750, Santo Domingo,* ☎ *809/526–1080 or 800/468–3571,* ℻ *809/526–1088. 261 rooms, 22 suites. 3 restaurants, 3 bars, 2 pools, massage, sauna, 2 tennis courts, health club, watersports center (including dive shop and 46-ft' yacht), shops, recreation room, nightly entertainment. AE, D, MC, V. EP, MAP.*

### The Amber Coast

**\$\$\$**   ⊡ **Paradise Beach Resort and Club.** Of the 12 hotels in the Playa Do-
**★**   rada complex, this hotel stands out on two counts: It is one of the few that front the beach and it has a unique design. Its cluster of low-rise buildings with white-tile roofs and latticed balconies and windows follows winding paths through palms, birds-of-paradise, and hibiscus from the reception area down to the beach. Rooms are decorated in a carefully chosen palette of pastel greens and blues. Standard rooms have one double or two twin beds; some of the one-bedroom apartments have kitchens. In the center of the resort is a free-form pool, with a water channel that winds its way from the pool to the beach. Two of the resort's three restaurants (not the gourmet Italia) are open-air and on the beach. ⊠ *Box 337, Playa Dorada,* ☎ *809/586–3663 or 800/752–9236,* ℻ *809/320–4858. 436 rooms, 174 suites. 3 restaurants, 3 bars, 18-hole golf course, 2 tennis courts, horseback riding, water-sports center, bicycles, scooters, shops, dance club. AE, DC, MC, V. All-inclusive.*

**\$\$–\$\$\$**   ⊡ **Bayside Hill Resort and Beach Club.** Part of the Costambar development—a 15-hotel complex including a nine-hole golf course, residential community, and supermarket—this hotel is an adroit blend of classic and contemporary elements: modern artwork and Corinthian columns, marble floors and metal sculptures. The centerpiece is a split-level pool and Jacuzzi with waterfalls and cavorting mermaid statuary. The Cafemba restaurant is highly respected for its innovative Continental cuisine. The rooms, decorated in olive, yellow, and peach, have tile floors, cable TV, and a small terrace or balcony. They are pleasant enough but disappointing compared to the public areas. The best rooms are those with stunning panoramic vistas of Puerto Plata. A free shuttle runs guests from the hillside development to the beach. Costambar is pleasantly quiet compared to Playa Dorada. ⊠ *Costambar, Puerto Plata,* ☎ *809/586–5260 or 800/322–2388,* ℻ *809/586–5545. 150 rooms. 3 restaurants, 4 bars, 3 pools, beauty salon, 9-hole golf* *course, beach club and water-sports center, gift shop, dance club. AE, MC, V. All-inclusive.*

**$$–$$$**
**★** 🎫 **Flamenco Beach Resort, Villas Doradas,** and **Playa Dorada Beach Resort.** Guests can use the facilities at all three of these hotels that are lined up one after the other on the mile-long white-sand beach. They're all known for their lively nightlife and variety of social and sports programs, but the similarities end there. Rooms at the older, all-inclusive Playa Dorada are dowdy and sadly in need of refurbishment. Service is efficient but unenthusiastic. Villas Doradas, also all-inclusive, is a step up. Rooms are decorated in earth tones (a refreshing change of pace) and hung with abstract paintings, and all have cable TV, safe, and minibar. The Chinese restaurant here is surprisingly good. The newer Flamenco is the nicest spot in the complex. The glorious public spaces include cobblestone and Andalusian brick floors, hand-painted tiles, stuccoed walls, and antique carved doors. There are four above-average restaurants including Via Veneto, a lively trattoria, and gourmet Spanish El Cortijo. The main free-form pool (with swim-up bar) is designed to resemble a lake, complete with waterfall and lapping waves. Rooms and suites have tasteful hardwood furnishings, terra-cotta floors, bright floral upholstery, minibar, cable TV, and a balcony or terrace. Club Miguel Angel is a hotel within a hotel offering premium concierge service. The only thing missing at the Flamenco is an ocean view. ⊠ *Flamenco: Playa Dorada, Puerto Plata,* ☎ *809/320–5084,* FAX *809/320–6319. 585 units. 4 restaurants, 3 bars, pizzeria, 2 pools, 2 tennis courts, water-sports center, shops. Villas Doradas: Box 1370, Puerto Plata,* ☎ *809/320–3000,* FAX *809/320–4790. 207 rooms. 5 restaurants, 2 bars, pool, 3 tennis courts, water-sports center, car rental. Playa Dorada: Box 272, Puerto Plata,* ☎ *809/586–3988 or 800/423–6902,* FAX *809/320–1190. 252 rooms, 1 suite. 4 restaurants, 2 bars, ice-cream parlor, pool, 18-hole golf course, tennis courts, horseback riding, jogging, water-sports center, bicycles, casino, dance club. AE, DC, MC, V. EP, MAP, FAP (Flamenco), All-inclusive (Playa and Villas Doradas).*

**$$–$$$** 🎫 **Sand Castle.** The name says it all. This resort is a bizarre fantasy of curves, balconies, and balustrades set high above coral cliffs. Royal palms rise majestically from the beachside gardens. Badly in need of a facelift, rooms are simple and comfortable in muted green and yellow pastels; some have a stained-glass window or decorative stained-glass above the bathroom door. All rooms have cable TV. Your stay here will be more enjoyable if you have a room with a view, especially of the small curving beach below. Though the hotel is by itself on a peninsula, lots of organized activities and the nearby village of Sosúa keep guests busy. Service is polite but distant. ⊠ *Puerto Chiquito, Sosúa,* ☎ *809/571–2420 or 800/446–5963,* FAX *809/571–2000. 240 rooms. 3 restaurants, 5 bars, 2 pools, horseback riding, water-sports center, dive shops, bicycles, shops, dance club, convention center. AE, MC, V. EP, MAP.*

**$$** 🎫 **Caribbean Village Club and Resort.** Rooms in the newer Royale building have kitchenettes and cable TV and are simply decorated in peach tones. The older Tropicale is a series of small houses with connecting skywalks. Rooms here are more like miniapartments, perfect for families, all with terrace or balcony, kitchenette, small sitting area, marble floors, and light pastel decor. One free-form pool has a swim-up terrace. The beach is a 10-minute hike away, but there's free shuttle service. The hotel's La Tortuga restaurant, a snack bar, and water-sports facilities are right on the sand. Nightly entertainment and dancing take place in the patio lounge and lobby bar. The staff genuinely works hard to compensate for the off-beach location. ⊠ *Playa Dorada,* ☎ *809/586–5350,* FAX *809/320–5386. 336 rooms, 26 suites. 3 restaurants, 3 bars/lounges, grill, kitchenettes, pool, 18-hole golf course, 2 tennis courts,* *beach club and water-sports center, minimart, shops, dance club, baby-sitting, medical clinic. AE, MC, V. CP, MAP.*

$$ **Dorado Naco** and **Playa Naco.** These two sister hotels make up a sprawling complex. Dorado Naco is a cluster of villas containing spacious, carpeted one- and two-bedroom apartments. In the living and dining area are a sofa bed, cable TV, two phones, dining table that seats four, and a counter bar. Each apartment has a large patio or terrace surrounded by tropical flowers and plants. The larger, more expensive rooms have views of the pool and the restaurants that surround it (there are no ocean views here). Hacienda-style Playa Naco went all-inclusive in 1994. The main lobby and standard hotel rooms overlook the pool and tennis courts and are a five-minute walk from the sands. More expensive one- and two-bedroom units are in two-story buildings along the path to the beach. The pleasing decor includes tile floors and mauve, lavender, and olive tones. The bustling free-form pool has several waterfalls. ⊠ *Box 162, Playa Dorada. Dorado Naco:* ☎ *809/320–2019,* FAX *809/320–3608. Playa Naco:* ☎ *809/320–6226,* FAX *809/320–6225. U.S. reservations for both,* ☎ *800/322–2388. 496 units. 6 restaurants, 3 bars, coffee shop, pub, 2 pools, beauty salon, 3 hot tubs, 18-hole golf course, 4 tennis courts, horseback riding, beach club and water-sports center, bicycles, minimarket, shops, dance club, recreation room, convention center, car rental. AE, DC, MC, V. EP, MAP, FAP (Dorado Naco), All-inclusive (Playa Naco).*

$$ **Puerto Plata Beach Resort and Casino.** More of a village than a resort, Puerto Plata's 7 acres hold cobblestone pathways, colorful gardens, and suites in 23 porticoed two- and three-story buildings. Accommodations have terra-cotta floors and a primarily mint and jade decor, with cable TV, minifridge, and balcony or terrace. An activities center sets up water-sports clinics, arranges horseback rides, and so forth. The resort also caters to the little ones, with children's games and enclosures for them at the shallow end of the pool. La Lechuza is the glitzy disco. Ylang-Ylang, named after the evening flower that blooms here, is a highly rated gourmet restaurant and catering service. The Neptune restaurant across the road on the beach is good for seafood. This resort is just outside of town and a ways from Playa Dorada, which will be an added attraction to some. ⊠ *Box 600, Av. Malecón, Puerto Plata,* ☎ *809/586–4243 or 800/223–9815,* FAX *809/586–4377. 216 units. 4 restaurants, bar, pool, outdoor hot tub, 4 tennis courts, horseback riding, water-sports center, casino, nightclub. AE, MC, V. MAP, All-Inclusive.*

$–$$ ★ **Cabarete Beach Hotel.** This delightful small hotel is set right on a tantalizing curve of golden sand ideal for windsurfing and swimming (the surrounding reef protects it from fierce breakers). Deluxe rooms—recommended—are those with full ocean view and air-conditioning. Standards (some with air-conditioning) are slightly smaller and noisier. All rooms are decorated with bright framed prints and blond woods and have charming touches such as rocking chairs. The lovely terrace restaurant is known for its bountiful breakfast buffets of luscious homemade breads, muffins, and pastries. The Tropical Bar—a riot of painted gourds and coconuts, colorful murals, and thatching—prides itself on its eight fresh fruit juices daily and more than 50 exotic libations. The BIC Windsurf Center (though not part of the hotel) is right next door. The staff is unfailingly helpful and courteous. ⊠ *Cabarete,* ☎ *809/571–0755,* FAX *809/571–0831. 24 rooms. Restaurant, bar, gift shop. AE, MC, V. EP, MAP.*

$–$$ **Hotel Cofresi.** Rooms here are rather basic and somewhat cramped, but the staff is courteous and the setting is breathtaking. The resort is built on the reefs along the Atlantic, and the sea spritzes its waters into the peaceful man-made lagoon and pools along the beach. Most rooms have cable TV, hair dryer, safe, and kitchenette. There are jogging and exercise trails, paddleboats for the lagoon, scuba-diving clinics, and evening entertainment, including a disco. The restaurants specialize in flavorful Dominican fare. ⊠ *Box 327, Costambar,* ☎ *809/586–2898,* FAX *809/586–8064. 237 rooms, 5 suites. 2 restaurants, 2 bars, 3 pools (1 saltwater), tennis court, horseback riding, water-sports center, paddleboats, bicycles, dance club, recreation room. AE, MC, V. All-inclusive.*

$ ▦ **Club Marina.** This charming beige stucco and red tile hotel is owned by the beachfront Casa Marina resort, and although you're paying only half as much as guests there, you get the use of all its facilities! Eduardo de Lora, a master stained-glass craftsman, designed the Club and everything displays his creative touch: The pool is landscaped with rocks, giving it a natural grotto feel, and spiral staircases are embedded with shards of glass (there are no exposed edges!). The rooms themselves are plain but impeccably neat, with a well-worn integrity. The blue-and-white tiles, lilac bedspreads, and closets painted jade green brighten them up. All units have cable TV, private bath, and a small balcony. The beach is a five-minute walk away. ⊠ *Alejo Martínez St., Sosúa,* ☎ *809/571–3939. 50 rooms. Restaurant, pool. AE, MC, V. MAP.*

## La Romana

$$$$ ▦ **Casa de Campo.** "House in the country" is an interesting appella-
★  tion for this deluxe resort, which sprawls over 7,000 acres and accommodates some 3,000 guests. Indeed, many wealthy Dominicans have luxurious second homes here. The complex includes 350 casitas (double rooms) and 150 one-, two-, and three-bedroom villas with fully equipped kitchens. For many, the main attractions are the two 18-hole golf courses: One of them, called Teeth of the Dog, has seven holes that skirt the sea and is rated the best in the Caribbean. Casa de Campo is also a sportsperson's paradise, with 13 tennis courts, horseback riding, polo, archery, trapshooting, and every imaginable water sport. Minibuses provide free transportation around the resort, but you can also rent electric golf carts, scooters, and bicycles (villa renters are provided with golf carts). An excellent children's program (including "kid's night out," where children spend the evening at a center with games, videos, and supervision), is great for families. Oscar de la Renta helped design much of the resort, owns a villa, and has a boutique in Altos de Chavón, the re-created medieval, Mediterranean village and art colony on the property. Some rooms and villas are decorated in Laura Ashley style, others with bolder, more abstract touches. The resort is—in a word—awesome. The advantage of staying here is that the resort has its own airport. American Airlines flies in daily from Miami and American Eagle flies in twice a day from San Juan. The disadvantage is that there are few attractions in the vicinity of the hotel other than the hotel's own campus—not that most guests mind. Although the resort's Minitas Beach is not the island's prettiest, daily excursions to the beach on Catalina Island help compensate. ⊠ *Box 140, La Romana,* ☎ *809/523–3333 or 800/877–3643,* FAX *809/523–8548. 350 rooms, 150 2- to 4-bedroom villas. 9 restaurants, 8 bars, 13 pools, hot tub, sauna, 2 18-hole golf courses, 13 tennis courts, exercise room, shooting and archery ranges, polo fields, horseback riding, marina, shops, airstrip. AE, DC, MC, V. EP, MAP.*

## Punta Cana

$$$ ▦ **Bavaro Beach Resort.** This huge, sprawling, four-star luxury resort,
★  actually a complex of five low-rise hotels, is situated on the glorious 20-mile stretch of Punta Cana beach. Each room has a private balcony or terrace, cable TV, and refrigerator. The biggest rooms are at the Bavaro Beach Hotel, with hemp and wood furnishings and bright striped upholstery. The Bavaro Gardens is decorated in vivid primary colors. The

Bavaro Casino Hotel has several duplex suites ideal for families. All of the accommodations at the Bavaro Golf Hotel are suites with kitchenettes—a real money saver if you're willing to cook. The Bavaro Palace is the most refined and subdued, with such touches as marble vanities. A social director coordinates a wide variety of daily activities, and there is nightly entertainment at each hotel. The resort has an aloof air about it, but this has more to do with the clientele than the staff, which is very friendly. Most important, the beach is fabulous and among the best in the Dominican Republic. ⊠ *Higüey,* ☎ *809/682– 2162 or 800/858–0606,* 🗚 *809/682–2169. 1,359 rooms. 9 restaurants, 14 bars, 7 pools, beauty salon, 18-hole golf course, 6 tennis courts, archery, horseback riding, water-sports center, bicycles, shops, casino, 2 dance clubs, nightclub, medical center. AE, MC, V. MAP, FAP.*

**$$$**   📠 **Punta Cana Beach Resort.** Several pretty coral-and-aquamarine
  ★     buildings dot the lush grounds of this rambling resort. The handsome lobby sets a civilized tone with Dominican crafts, birdcages, and lots of plants. Rooms are spare but pleasant, primarily in jade, coral, and cream, with wicker furnishings. Fifty-four deluxe rooms, all with balconies, were recently added in the new Cocotal building. The half-mile private beach is gorgeous, and there are nature walks on a marked and guided eco-trail into the mahogany forest, where you can take a dip in several, natural freshwater pools. There are lots of activities here, too, including nightly musical entertainment by the friendly staff. A 36-hole golf course and a 450-room hotel are scheduled to open in 1998. ⊠ *Punta Cana Beach,* ☎ *809/221–2262 or 800/972–2139,* 🗚 *809/687–8745. Write to Box 1083, Santo Domingo. 395 units. 5 restaurants, 3 bars, pool, beauty parlor, 4 tennis courts, water-sports center, minimart, gift shop, dance club, baby-sitting, children's programs, playground, resident doctor. AE, DC, MC, V. MAP.*

## Samaná

**$$–$$$**   📠 **Hotel Gran Bahia.** Overdevelopment has not yet reached the pretty water's edge where this small, all-inclusive resort sits. The modern colonial Victorian has graceful verandas and balconies looking out over the pool and the sea beyond; you can see schools of whales frolicking offshore during the winter. The superb views make breakfast on your room's private terrace or balcony a treat. Guest rooms are large, with cheerful floral prints, tiled floors, and pastel watercolor paintings. The grand yet welcoming reception area and three-story white colonnaded atrium surround a spectacular fountain flanked with numerous cozy nooks for cocktails or reading. Dining alfresco is pleasant, although the food leaves much to be desired, and remember—this is an all-inclusive resort. It is also a staple hotel for travelers on cheap package tours; the local staff is overworked, and the result is a lack of the usual Dominican friendliness and hospitality. ⊠ *Box 2024, Santo Domingo,* ☎ *809/538–3111 or 800/372–1323,* 🗚 *809/538–2764. 110 rooms. 2 restaurants, bar, pool, beauty salon, 9-hole golf course, 2 tennis courts, archery, exercise room, whale watching arranged. AE, MC, V. All-inclusive.*

**$$**   📠 **Cayo Levantado.** This tranquil hotel is tucked into the lush greenery of the tiny island national park just off the Samaná coast. The exquisite fringe of pearly white beach is overrun weekends with daytrippers, and if you've traveled all the way to this remote outpost for a party atmosphere, you won't mind the makeshift stalls hawking T-shirts, paintings, beer, and delicious grilled items. There's another, smaller beach on the other side of the island for the romantically inclined. The rooms, either in the main building or bungalows, are simple and appealing, with writing desks, wicker furnishings, and bright pastel fabrics. There are no TVs or phones. The food is good, solid

Creole: a fortunate thing, since the hotel now operates as an all-inclusive. ⊠ *Cayo Levantado,* ☎ *809/538–3141. 44 rooms. Restaurant, bar, pool, snorkeling, boating, fishing, boutique. AE, MC, V. All-inclusive.*

**$$**   🏨 **Villa Serena.** Tucked away in a remote corner of the island in un-
★ spoiled Samaná, this little-known, 11-room hotel is a gem. Located down the beach from the tiny fishing village of Las Galeras, it is literally at the end of the long road from Puerto Plata, a three-hour, scenic drive by car. Croatian expatriates Natasha Despotovic and Kresimir Zovko have created an intimate place where each of the rooms is individu-ally decorated to provide different moods. All have lanais overlook-ing the Bahía de Rincón. Some of the rooms are air-conditioned; those that aren't have ceiling fans. A restaurant serves the best food on the peninsula, and a large veranda provides an excellent spot for a cock-tail. Two of Samaná's prettiest and most deserted beaches, Playa Col-orado and Playa de Rincón, are easily reached by water taxi, horseback, or hike from the hotel. The hotel has a small, private beach in front, as well as a small, free-form pool. ⊠ *Apartado Postal 51–1, Las Galeras, Samaná,* ☎ *809/696–0065,* 🆇 *809/538–2545. 11 rooms. Restaurant, bar, pool, horseback riding, snorkeling, diving, boat trips. AE, MC, V. MAP.*

## Santo Domingo

**$$$–$$$$**   🏨 **Jaragua Renaissance Resort and Casino.** Fourteen acres of gar-
★ dens, waterfalls, and fountains surround this pink, ultramodern com-plex. Top-name entertainers are booked into the 800-seat La Fiesta Showroom, master chefs from four countries tend to the cuisine, great massages are available at affordable prices in the spa, and the casino covers 20,000 square feet. Spacious rooms have three phones, 21-channel satellite TV, minibar, and hair dryer. Each floor has a differ-ent decor, one in peach and burgundy, another apricot and mint. Penthouse suites have their own hot tubs. Rates are based on view (gar-den, pool, or ocean). Twelve cabanas surround the Olympic-size free-form pool—an oasis in the middle of this bustling, chaotic city. The friendly and courteous staff makes you feel welcome. ⊠ *Av. George Washington 367, Santo Domingo,* ☎ *809/221–2222 or 800/468–3571,* 🆇 *809/686–0528. 300 rooms and suites. 5 restaurants, 4 bars, mini-bars, pool, hot tubs, saunas, European spa with exercise/diet pro-grams, golf privileges, 4 clay tennis courts, casino, dance club. AE, MC, V. EP, MAP, FAP.*

**$$$**   🏨 **Inter-Continental Hotel V Centenario.** Santo Domingo's newest five-
★ star hotel opened in late 1992 on the Malecón. Marble floors and pil-lars give the reception area a crisp, fresh feel. The rooms are a refreshing change, furnished in attractive earth tones, Dominican handicrafts, and burnished rattans. Each has a minifridge, cable TV, and an electronic safe. You can try your luck at the casino or take time out to relax in the lounge-bar area with its subdued lighting and enticing easy chairs. The cellar tapas bar has become a favorite after-work hangout for lo-cals. A casual coffee shop looks out over the Caribbean, and the pool shares a terrace with a bar and an alfresco seafood restaurant. At press time a sauna and gym were under construction. ⊠ *Av. George Washington 218, Santo Domingo,* ☎ *809/221–0000,* 🆇 *809/221–2020. 200 rooms, 26 suites. 3 restaurants, 2 bars, in-room safes, re-frigerators, pool, tennis court, squash, shops, casino, free parking. AE, MC, V. EP, MAP, FAP.*

**$$$**   🏨 **Santo Domingo Sheraton Hotel and Casino.** This 11-story modern hotel is on Avenida George Washington in the center of the Malecón action. Rooms are average in size and decorated in taupe and teal; many have French balconies (more like a ledge) overlooking the sea, and all have minibar and cable TV. Sixty-nine of the rooms are designated no-smoking. The three restaurants are superior in all respects: Antoine's for gourmet Continental fare in a romantic setting, the cozy Canasta for expertly prepared Dominican specialties, and La Terraza for cafeteria-style breakfast, lunch, and dinner. This Sheraton's service is disorganized, but the staff tries to be helpful. ⊠ *Box 1493, Santo Domingo,* ☎ *809/686–6666 or 800/325–3535,* FAX *809/687–8150. 242 rooms, 16 suites. 3 restaurants, 3 bars, minibars, no-smoking rooms, pool, beauty salon, 2 tennis courts, health club, shops, casino, dance club. AE, DC, MC, V. EP, MAP, FAP.*

**$$–$$$** 🏨 **Hotel Hispaniola.** Catering to a younger crowd, the Hispaniola has 165 rooms, an active pool, a trendy and modern disco, and a casino filled with striking paintings, stained glass, and towering floral arrangements. There are two restaurants here, Las Cañas and La Pizetta, as well as the Hispaniola Bar—it's very dark, very intimate, and very, very red—which has a small dance area. Guest rooms, refurbished in 1994, are spacious and furnished mostly in chintz, wicker, and blond woods. All have balconies, minibars, and cable TV. Guests here have privileges at the Hotel Santo Domingo across the street. ⊠ *Av. Independencia and Abraham Lincoln, Box 2112, Santo Domingo,* ☎ *809/221–7111 or 800/877–3643,* FAX *809/535–4050. 165 rooms. 2 restaurants, bar, minibars, pool, 3 tennis courts available at the Santo Domingo, casino, dance club, conference rooms. AE, MC, V. EP, MAP, FAP.*

**$$–$$$** 🏨 **Hotel Santo Domingo.** Located on 14 delicately manicured acres over-
**★** looking the Caribbean, this hotel is favored by businessmen and diplomats. Many VIPs check into the Excel Club for extra perks. Dominican-born Oscar de la Renta helped design the interiors, incorporating such touches as black- and red-lacquered hall lamps, conchshell mirrors, bold colors, and handcrafted Dominican furniture. The rooms have balconies and cable TVs, and most have double beds. The elegant Alcázar restaurant serves excellent Continental meals in de la Renta's romantic Moorish dining room. The regular merengue combo at dimly lit Las Palmas makes it a local favorite for music and dancing. The hotel is at the western edge of the Malecón—often more convenient for businesspeople who want to be close to the commercial section of town than for tourists who prefer being closer to the historic area. ⊠ *Av. Independencia and Abraham Lincoln, Box 2112, Santo Domingo,* ☎ *809/221–7111 or 800/877–3643,* FAX *809/535–4050. 220 rooms. 3 restaurants, 2 bars, pool, sundeck, sauna, 3 tennis courts, conference rooms, helipad. AE, MC, V. EP, MAP, FAP.*

**$$** 🏨 **Gran Hotel Lina and Casino.** The whitewashed modern cinder-block structure of this hotel gives little hint of its stylish, exquisite interior, which gleams with marble floors, mirrored brass colonnades, and striking modern artwork. The rather plain rooms, mostly in dusky rose, are air-conditioned with double beds, minifridges, huge marble baths, and cable TVs and exude a staid secure ambience. The staff is friendly and helpful. ⊠ *Box 1915, Santo Domingo,* ☎ *809/563–5000 or 800/858–0606,* FAX *809/686–5521. 214 rooms, 4 suites. Restaurant, coffee shop, piano bar, 2 pools including wading pool, sauna, 2 tennis courts, health club, casino, nightclub. AE, DC, MC, V. EP, MAP, FAP.*

**$$** 🏨 **Hotel El Embajador and Casino.** This hotel radiates an air of faded gentility; it seems caught in a '50s time warp—Hollywood's idea of a top hotel in an exotic locale. But though the exterior needs sprucing up, the public rooms are imposing by Dominican standards. The bedrooms are spacious but spare, with tatty carpeting, old-fashioned desks and wardrobes, and bare walls. All have minibar, cable TV, and private balcony with either a mountain or an ocean view (choose the latter). An executive concierge floor is good for business travelers. The Jardin de Jade serves marvelous Chinese food. The pool is open to the public and is a popular weekend gathering place for resident foreigners. You can try your luck at the casino, or just listen to the live bands that play there throughout the day and night. ⊠ *Av. Sarasota 65, Santo Domingo,* ☎ *809/221–2131 or 800/457–0067,* FAX *809/532– 4494. 304 rooms, 12 suites. 2 restaurants, 2 bars, minibars, pool, 4 tennis courts, shops, casino. AE, DC, MC, V. EP, MAP.*

**$** ⊞ **Hostal Palacio Nicolás de Ovando.** The oldest hotel in the New World,
★ and one of the few in the Colonial Zone, was home to the first governor in the early 1500s. The decor is Spanish, with carved mahogany doors, beamed ceilings, tapestries, arched colonnades, and three courtyards with splashing fountains. The spartan rooms are reminiscent of monks' cells but have views of the port, the pool, or the Colonial Zone. Dominican specialties are served in the restaurant. This is Santo Domingo's only hotel with the charm of antiquity. Its disadvantage is its location: At night, the area can be deserted and unpleasant for walking alone. ⊠ *Calle Las Damas 44, Apdo. 89-2, Santo Domingo,* ☎ *809/687–3101,* FAX *809/686–5170. 55 rooms. Restaurant, bar, pool. AE, MC, V. EP.*

# Dining

Most restaurants begin serving dinner around 6 PM, but the locals don't generally turn up until 9 or 10. There are Spanish, French, Italian, and Chinese restaurants, as well as those serving traditional Dominican fare. (Regrettably, many local restaurants in heavily touristed areas like the Amber Coast are closing, victims of the all-inclusive craze.) Hotel restaurants uniformly range from fair to good; consult lodging listings for additional recommendations. Some favorite local dishes you should sample are paella, *sancocho* (a thick stew usually made with five different meats, though sometimes as many as seven), *arroz con pollo* (rice with chicken), *plátanos* (plantains) in all their tasty varieties, and *tortilla de jamón* (spicy ham omelet). Country snacks include *chicharrones* (fried pork rinds or chicken pieces) and *galletas* (flat biscuit crackers). Many a meal is topped off with *majarete,* a tasty cornmeal custard. Presidente, Bohemia, and Quisqueya are the local beers, Barceló, Bermúdez, and Brugal the local rums. Wine is on the expensive side because it has to be imported. It also doesn't travel well as it often gets exposed to tropical heat.

## What to Wear

In resort areas, shorts and beach wraps are acceptable at lunch; for dinner, especially at gourmet restaurants, long pants, skirts, and collared shirts are the norm. Dress tends to be more formal in Santo Domingo, both at lunch and dinner, with long pants required for men and dresses suggested for women. Ties are not required anywhere.

| CATEGORY | COST* |
| --- | --- |
| $$$ | over $30 |
| $$ | $20-$30 |
| $ | under $20 |

*per person, excluding drinks, 10% service charge, and 8% sales tax*

## Boca Chica

**$–$$** ✕ **Neptuno's Club.** This breezy seaside eatery is little more than a shack perched above the water, seemingly held together by the barnacles of marine memorabilia. While you can order good local preparations of chicken and pork, it goes without saying that seafood reigns supreme. Try the Neptuno's fish casserole in coconut water or kingfish in béchamel sauce. ⊠ *Boca Chica Beach,* ☎ *809/523–4703. MC, V. Closed Mon.*

## La Romana

**$$$** ✕ **Casa del Rio.** Look out over the virtual jungle of the banks of the
★ Rio Chavón while you dine in the ultraromantic, candlelit stone cel-
lar of a 16th century–style castle. The elegant decor is a mere back-
drop for the imaginative creations put forth by chef Philippe Mongereau.
His new Caribbean cuisine is a combination of classic French meth-
ods of preparation and savory indigenous ingredients and culinary tra-
ditions. The seasonally changing menu may include such standouts as
leg of lamb baked in Creole marmalade, lobster tail glazed with vanilla
vinaigrette, and mango Napoleon on a bed of julienne shrimp and ar-
tichoke hearts. Mongereau experiments with Asian ingredients like
lemongrass, coriander, and garam masala, and the subtle counterpoint
of textures and flavors is truly heavenly. The restaurant's success is mea-
sured not only by the heavy repeat clientele but by the capitaleños who
swear it's worth the two-hour drive from Santo Domingo. ✉ *Altos de
Chavón,* ☎ *809/523–3333, ext. 2345. Reservations essential. Jacket
required. AE, DC, MC, V. No lunch.*

## The Amber Coast

**$$–$$$** ✕ **De Armando.** You may feel that you're dining in a proper old rela-
tive's dining room in this charmingly old-fashioned eatery. In a pretty
aqua-and-white house, the dining room has high-backed embroidered
chairs, crisp white napery, and dark-wood tables. Steak, seafood, and
Continental dishes are all served to the tune of a guitar trio. Try the
snapper in green peppercorn sauce or sea bass in champagne mush-
room velouté. ✉ *Av. Mota 23, at Av. Separación,* ☎ *809/586–3418.
Reservations essential. MC, V.*

**$–$$** ✕ **Caribae.** Aquariums teeming with all kinds of sea creatures decorate the dining room of this warm, unassuming spot. You can choose
your own lobster, shrimp, and oysters for the barbecue. Costs are low,
because the restaurant raises its own shrimp at a farm and grows its
own 100% organic vegetables. ✉ *Camino Libre 70, Sosúa,* ☎ *809/571–
3138. MC, V.*

**$** ✕ **Guajiro's Caribbean Cafe.** Visit this casual Sosúa eatery for some
of the best inventive local cuisine in the area. Try the green plantain
soup or *yuca* (an island tuber) in *mojo* (a lime, garlic, and olive oil marinade) to start, then *pollo à la merengue* (sweet and spicy coriander
chicken) or *filetillo saltado* (catch of the day, usually kingfish, in
*sofrito,* a savory sauce of garlic and green pepper rouged with tomato).
For a filling meal, order the cubano sandwich, bursting with roast pork,
ham, cheese, and pickles. Thatching, nautical paraphernalia dangling
from the rafters, rough-hewn wood tables and chairs, and traditional
hats, shirts, and machetes hanging on the walls give the place a rustic
country feel. Latin Jazz nights are scheduled regularly and draw a rollicking crowd. ✉ *Calle Pedro Clisande, El Batey, Sosúa,* ☎ *809/571–
2161. Reservations not accepted. AE, MC, V.*

**$** ✕ **Roma II.** Surprisingly delicious pizzas, cooked in a wood-burning
oven, come from this unassuming wood shack. The pizza dough and
pasta are made fresh daily. Other specialties include *spaghetti con
pulpo* (octopus), *filete chito* (steak with garlic), and there's a host of
other pastas and sauces. ✉ *Corner of Calle E. Prudhomme and Calle
Beller,* ☎ *809/586–3904. Reservations not accepted. No credit cards.*

## Samaná

**$$** ✕ **Café de France.** Local aficionados swear the beef here is among the
best in the Dominican Republic—try the fillet in mushroom or pep-
percorn sauce. Seafood here is also dependable: One standout is shrimp
(or grouper) in garlic-coconut sauce. The small bistro is on the waterfront
and is simply decorated, with white stucco walls and red tablecloths.

An even more casual annex serves knockout pizzas. ✉ *Malécon, Samaná, no phone. MC, V.*

$$ ✕ **Villa Serena.** Literally at the end of the long road from Puerto Plata
★ is this lovely small hotel and restaurant. Located on the beach and the Bahía del Rincón at the tiny village of Las Galeras, the restaurant is in an open-air pavilion facing the trade winds. Specialties include fresh fish caught by local fishermen and delicious homemade desserts. ✉ *Las Galeras, Samaná,* ☎ *809/696–0065. MC, V.*

## Santo Domingo

$$$ ✕ **Pappalapasta.** Delicious Italian food and a location around the cor-
★ ner from the Presidential Palace combine to make this eatery popular with politicians, diplomats, and the businessmen seeking favors from them. A series of intimate dining rooms are handsomely decorated with rattan and polished hardwood furnishings, abstract artwork, richly colored Tiffany-style lamps, and cut-glass windows. Start with a classic selection of antipasto—carpaccio, eggplant Parmesan, and tuna with capers. Pumpkin ravioli in almond-amaretto butter, gnocchi al pesto, and spaghetti with lobster sauce are standouts in the pasta selection. You may also opt for the sublime sea bass *à la meunière* (breaded and topped with butter, parsley, and lemon juice), snapper *chiaro di mare* (with olives, capers, garlic, tomato, and peppers), or the unimpeachable fillet in cognac mushroom sauce. The service, although attentive, is surprisingly leisurely; maybe they're waiting discreetly for your deal to be consummated. ✉ *Dr. Baez 23,* ☎ *809/689–4849. Jacket required. AE, MC, V. Closed Mon.*

$$$ ✕ **Vesuvio.** Capital-city denizens flock to this superb Italian restaurant
★ and institution, where everything on the lengthy menu is either freshly caught, homemade, or homegrown. On most islands it's a struggle to get (and keep) things fresh, and the crisp vegetables here are nothing short of miraculous. Vesuvio has spent 40 years as the best in its business, yet refuses to rest on its laurels. Part of the restaurant's appeal is the lively ambience created by well-heeled Dominican families relishing their meal. The chef doesn't shy away from combining strong, bold flavors. Start with antipasti—kingfish carpaccio dancing in zesty capers, onions, and basil-infused olive oil or *calamares al vino blanco* (squid in white-wine sauce)—then segue into *scaloppina al tarragon* (veal with tarragon), or, if they have it, succulent river crayfish grilled simply with butter and garlic. The pièce de résistance is the dessert cart. (**Vesuvio II** is at Av. Tiradentes 17, ☎ 809/562–6060.) ✉ *Av. George Washington 521,* ☎ *809/221–3333. Reservations not accepted. Jacket required. AE, DC, MC, V.*

$$–$$$ ✕ **La Briciola.** The owners of this upscale Milan restaurant chain combined three venerable eateries housed in adjoining 16th-century colonial buildings to create this stunner. They did an exemplary job of modernizing the interiors while preserving their architectural integrity. The arch-ceilinged stone-and-brick main dining room and more casual piano bar/pizzeria overlook an interior courtyard whose trees are romantically illuminated at night. Cerise upholstery, mahogany furnishings, wooden chandeliers, and Italian tile work create a warm atmosphere. Excellent fresh pastas include velvety *gnocchi fume* (with Scamorze cheese, ham, and cream), tortellini al salmone, and *maccheroni capriccio* (in a tomato sauce enlivened by capers, pine nuts, and parsley). The risotto *dell'oza,* (with salmon caviar and vodka), is superb. Meat dishes take a backseat to the deftly prepared seafood, such as grouper al limone, tuna in balsamic vinegar, and salmon in three sauces (mayonnaise, tartar, and mint). Delicious *tiramisù* and zabaglione complete the feast (but save room for the gratis cherry marzipan and lemon or chocolate cookies offered with the bill). The all-Italian wine

list is extensive and fairly priced. ✉ *Calle Arzobispo Merino 152-A at Padre Bellini,* ☎ *809/688–5055. Jacket required. AE, DC, MC, V. Closed Mon.*

**$$–$$$** ✗ **El Caserio.** An extensive menu lists such specialties as paella *valenciana* (rice casserole with chicken, seafood, and sausage), seafood *zarzuela* (a mix of fish and shellfish in a green herbal sauce), bluefish with anchovies, and leg of lamb Segovia. For dessert, forget your diet and order chocolate cake Caserio. Adjacent to the formal dining room and reminiscent of a whitewashed Andalusian cottage is **Aranjuez,** a bistrolike place that serves an appetite-whetting range of tapas (appetizers). ✉ *Av. George Washington 459,* ☎ *809/685–3392. Reservations essential. Jacket required. AE, DC, MC, V.*

**$$–$$$** ✗ **Lina.** Lina was the personal chef of Trujillo, and she taught her se-
★ cret recipes to the chefs of this stylish contemporary restaurant, still a favorite of Santo Domingo movers and shakers. Brass columns, mirrored ceiling, planters, art naïf, Villeroy & Boch china, and a pianist tickling the ivories set the elegant tone. The extensive menu favors Continental and haute Dominican dishes. Paella is the best-known specialty, but other offerings include filet mignon Roquefort, red snapper in coconut or almond cheese sauce, and a casserole of mixed seafood flavored with Pernod. ✉ *Gran Hotel Lina, Av. Máximo Gómez at Av. 27 de Febrero,* ☎ *809/686–5000. Reservations essential. Jacket required. AE, DC, MC, V.*

**$$–$$$** ✗ **Mesón de la Cava.** The capital's most unusual restaurant (and a tourist trap) is more than 50 feet below ground in a natural cave complete with stalagmites and stalactites. You must descend a circular staircase, ducking rock protrusions, to dine on Continental standards like prime fillet with Dijon flambé, and tournedos Roquefort. Seafood preparations tend to be more adventurous, such as red snapper poached in white wine and served with coconut sauce, but the food takes a backseat to the spectacular setting. There is live music and dancing nightly until 1 AM, although sometimes you may wish they'd stop playing Jackson Five renditions and allow a majestic silence to fall over the cathedralesque grotto. ✉ *Av. Mirador del Sur,* ☎ *809/533–2818. Reservations essential. Jacket required. AE, DC, MC, V.*

**$$** ✗ **Café St. Michel.** The decor is rather odd, sort of a contemporary indoor take on a gazebo, but the menu of French bistro–style dishes and local fare keeps diners coming back. Cream of pumpkin soup and steak tartare are specialties. Desserts include a prizewinning chocolate torte and spectacular soufflés. ✉ *Av. Lope de Vega 24,* ☎ *809/562–4141. Jacket required. AE, MC, V.*

**$$** ✗ **Fonda de la Atarazana.** Dinner and dancing on the brick patio of a 17th-century building in the Colonial Zone make for a very romantic evening. Try the kingfish, shrimp, or *chicharrones de pollo* (bits of fried chicken). ✉ *La Atarazana 5,* ☎ *809/689–2900. AE, MC, V.*

**$** ✗ **La Bahía.** The catch of the day is always tops at this unpretentious spot. Try the kingfish in coconut sauce. The conch, which appears in a variety of dishes, is also good. For starters, try the *sopa palúdica,* a thick soup made with fish, shrimp, and lobster and served with tangy garlic bread. The decor strikes a nautical note, with fishing nets and seashells. ✉ *Av. George Washington 1,* ☎ *809/682–4022. Reservations not accepted. AE, MC, V.*

**$** ✗ **El Conuco.** Conuco means countryside—and it's hard to believe that
★ this open-air thatched hut, alive with hanging plants, hibiscus, and frangipani and decorated with basketry, sombreros, license plates, and graffiti, is smack in the center of Santo Domingo. This is a superb place to sample typical Dominican cuisine, from *la bandera* (white rice, kidney beans, and stewed beef duplicating the colors of the flag) to a magnificent, delicately flaky *bacalao de la comai* (cod in white cream sauce

with garlic and onions). The ambience is always celebratory; waiters occasionally take to makeshift drum sets to accompany the merengue tapes. ⊠ *152 Casimiro de Moya,* ☎ *809/221–3231. MC, V.*

$ ✕ **Ludovino's** and **Joaquin's.** Shacks and stands serving cheap eats for
★ people on the run are a Dominican tradition, as much a part of the culture and landscape as the Colonial Zone. Two such shacks have become legends in Santo Domingo; both are located in working-class districts outside the normal tourist loop. El Palacio de los Yaniqueques (everyone calls it Ludovino's after the nutty owner) is famed for its johnnycakes—fried dough stuffed with everything from chicken to seafood. You pay the cashier when you order and get a free thimbleful of strong, sweet coffee while you wait for your food. Joaquin's serves up the best pork sandwich—laden with onions, tomatoes, pickles, and seasonings— in the Western world. The price for a filling meal? Two bucks at either. ⊠ *Ludovino's: 19 Summer Wells, no phone.* ⊙ *Daily 7 AM–8 PM. Joaquin's: Av. Abraham Lincoln and Max Henríquex Ureña St., no phone.* ⊙ *Nightly 7 PM–2 AM.*

# Beaches

The Dominican Republic has more than 1,000 miles of beaches, including the Caribbean's longest strip of white sand—Punta Cana/Bavaro. Many beaches are accessible to the public and may tempt you to stop for a swim. Be careful: Some have dangerously strong currents.

**Boca Chica** is the beach closest to Santo Domingo (2 miles east of Las Américas Airport, 21 miles from the capital), and it's crowded with city folks on weekends. This beach was once a virtual four-lane highway of fine white sand. "Progress" has since cluttered it with plastic beach tables, chaise longues, pizza stands, and beach cottages for rent. But the sand is still fine, and you can walk far out into clear blue water, which is protected by natural coral reefs that help keep the big fish at bay. **Cabarete Beach,** on the north coast, has ideal wind and surf conditions that have made it an integral part of the international windsurfing circuit. **Juan Dolio** is a narrow beach of fine white sand located about 20 minutes east of Boca Chica (☞ *above*). The Metro Hotel and Marina, the all-inclusive Decameron, Villas del Mar Hotel, and Punta Garza Beach Club are on this beach. **Luperón Beach,** about an hour west of Puerto Plata, is a wide white-sand beach fit for snorkeling, windsurfing, and scuba diving. The Luperón Beach Resort is handy for rentals and refreshments. **Playa Grande,** on the north coast, is a long stretch of powdery sand that is slated for development. The Playa Grande Hotel has already disturbed the solitude. With this exception, the entire northeast coast seems like one unbroken golden stretch, unmaintained and littered with kelp, driftwood, and the occasional beer bottle. If you don't mind the lack of facilities and upkeep, you have your pick of deserted beaches. **Puerto Plata,** still developing on the north Amber Coast, is about to outdo San Juan's famed Condado strip—especially the Playa Dorada area. The beaches are of soft beige or white sand, with lots of reefs for snorkeling. The Atlantic waters are great for windsurfing, waterskiing, and fishing expeditions. **Punta Cana,** the gem of the Caribbean, is a 20-mile strand of pearl-white sand shaded by trees and coconut palms. Located on the easternmost coast, it is the home of several top resorts. **La Romana** is the home of the 7,000-acre Casa de Campo resort, so you're not likely to find any private place in the sun here. The area is home to miniature **Minitas beach** and lagoon, and the long, white-sand, palm-lined crescent of **Bayahibe beach,** which is accessible only by boat. **Sosúa** has a lovely beach where calm waters gently lap at long stretches of soft white sand. Unfortunately the backdrop here is a string of tents, with hawkers pushing cheap souvenirs. You can, however, get snacks and rent water-sports equipment from the vendors. **Las Terrenas,** on the north coast of the Samaná peninsula, looks like something from *Robinson Crusoe*: Tall palms list toward the sea, away from the mountains; the beach is narrow but sandy; and best of all, there is nothing man-made in sight—just vivid blues, greens, and yellows. Two adjacent hotels are right on the beach at nearby Punta Bonita.

## Outdoor Activities and Sports

Although there is hardly a shortage of outdoor activities here, the resorts have virtually cornered the market on sports, including every conceivable water sport. In some cases, facilities may be available only to guests. You can check with the tourist office for more details. Listed below is a mere smattering of the island's athletic options.

### Bicycling

Pedaling is easy on pancake-flat beaches, but there are also steep hills in the Dominican Republic. Bikes are available at **Dorado Naco** (⊠ Dorado Beach, ☎ 809/320–2019), **Jack Tar Village** (⊠ Puerto Plata, ☎ 809/586–3800), **Hotel Cofresi** (⊠ Puerto Plata, ☎ 809/586–2898), and **Villas Doradas** (⊠ Playa Dorada, Puerto Plata, ☎ 809/320–3000).

### Boating

Hobie Cats and pedal boats are available at **Heavens** (⊠ Playa Dorada, ☎ 809/586–5250). Check also at **Casa de Campo** (⊠ La Romana, ☎ 809/523–3333) and **Club Med** (⊠ Punta Cana, ☎ 809/567–5228).

### Deep-Sea Fishing

Marlin and wahoo are among the fish that folks angle for here. Arrangements can be made through **Casa de Campo** (⊠ La Romana, ☎ 809/523–3333) or **Actividas Acuaticás** (⊠ Playa Dorada, ☎ 809/586–3988). Fishing is best between January and June.

### Golf

**Casa de Campo** has two 18-hole Pete Dye courses that are open to the public and a third for the private use of villa owners. The **Bávaro Beach** resort complex shares an 18-hole course. The **Playa Dorada** hotels have their own 18-hole Robert Trent Jones–designed course; there is also a 9-hole course nearby at the **Costambar** complex. Guests in Santo Domingo hotels are usually allowed to use the 18-hole course at the **Santo Domingo Country Club** on weekdays—*after* members have teed off. There is a 9-hole course outside of town, at Lomas Lindas. A new Pete Dye course is at the **Metro Country Club,** east of Santo Domingo on the road to La Romana.

### Horseback Riding

**Casa de Campo** (⊠ La Romana, ☎ 809/523–3333) has a dude ranch on its premises, saddled with 2,000 horses. You can even arrange for polo lessons (it's a major stop on the international circuit). In Puerto Plata, **Gran Chapparal** (☎ 809/320–4250) offers beach rides.

### Sailing

Sailboats are available at **Club Med** (Punta Cana) and **Casa de Campo** (La Romana).

### Scuba Diving

Ancient sunken galleons, undersea gardens, and offshore reefs are the lures here. For equipment and trips, contact **Dominican Adventures Dive Center** (⊠ Santo Domingo, ☎ 809/472–1718). Most resorts have dive shops on the premises or can arrange trips for you. Be sure to ask when making reservations.

## Spectator Sports

### BASEBALL

Baseball is the national pastime and passion. Major leaguers hone their skills in the Professional Winter League, which plays from late October through January. Call **Liga de Béisbol** (☎ 809/567–6371) for details on the five teams and their schedule of play. You can also consult newspaper listings, or your hotel can reserve tickets. You may not reach an English-speaking representative at Liga de Béisbol.

### HORSE RACING

There are races year-round at the **Hipódromo V Centenario.** ⊠ *Av. Las Americas, Santo Domingo,* ☎ *809/687–6060.* 🎫 *Free.* ☉ *Daily 8* AM–*2:45* PM.

### POLO

The ponies pound down the field at **Sierra Prieta** (Santo Domingo) and at **Casa de Campo** (La Romana). The season runs from October through May. For information about polo games, call 809/565–6880.

## Tennis

There must be a million nets laced around the island, and most of them can be found at the large resorts.

## Windsurfing

Between June and October, **Cabarete Beach** offers what many consider to be optimal windsurfing conditions: wind speeds at 20–25 knots and 3- to 15-foot waves. The Professional Boardsurfers Association has included Cabarete Beach in its international windsurfing slalom competition. The novice is also welcome to learn and train on modified boards stabilized by flotation devices. **Carib BIC Center** (⊠ Cabarete Beach, ☎ 809/571–0640, FAX 809/571–0649) offers accommodations, equipment, and professional coaching and instruction.

# Shopping

The hot ticket in the Dominican Republic is amber jewelry. This island has the world's largest deposits of amber, and the prices here for the translucent, semiprecious stones, which range in color from pale lemon to dark brown, are unmatched. The most valuable stones are those in which tiny insects or small leaves are embedded. (Don't knock it till you've seen it.) When buying amber, beware of fakes, which are especially prevalent with street vendors. Visit a reputable dealer or store and ask how you can tell the difference between real amber and imitations.

The Dominican Republic is the homeland of designer Oscar de la Renta, and you may want to stop at some of the chic shops that carry his creations. In the crafts department, hand-carved wood rocking chairs are big sellers, and they are sold unassembled and boxed for easy transport. La Vega is famous for its *diablos cojuelos* (devil masks) and Santiago for its cigars, which rival the best Havanas. Look also for the delicate ceramic lime figurines that symbolize the Dominican culture.

Bargaining is both a game and a social activity in the Dominican Republic, especially with street vendors and at the stalls in El Mercado Modelo. Vendors are disappointed and perplexed if you don't haggle. They also tend to be tenacious, so unless you really have an eye on buying, don't even stop to look—you may get stuck buying a souvenir just to get rid of an annoying vendor.

## Shopping Districts

**El Mercado Modelo** in Santo Domingo is a covered market in the Colonial Zone bordering Calle Mella. The restored buildings of **La Atarazana** (⊠ across from the Alcázar in the Colonial Zone) are filled with shops, art galleries, restaurants, and bars. One of the main shopping streets in the Colonial Zone is **Calle El Conde,** which has been transformed into an exclusively pedestrian thoroughfare. Some of the best shops on **Calle Duarte,** a main shopping street in the Colonial Zone, are north of the Colonial Zone, between Calle Mella and Avenida de Las Américas. **Plaza Criolla** (⊠ corner of Av. 27 de Febrero and Av. Anacaona) is filled with shops that sell everything from scents to nonsense.

One major commercial mall in Santo Domingo is **Unicentro** (⊠ 406 Av. Abraham Lincoln). **Plaza Central** (⊠ Avs. Bolívar and 27 de Febrero), a mall in Santo Domingo, includes such top boutiques as **Jenny Polanco, Nicole B,** and **Benetton,** which includes a coffeehouse on its second level with rotating exhibit by up-and-coming young artists.

In Puerto Plata, the seven showrooms of the **Tourist Bazaar** (⊠ Calle Duarte 61) are in a wonderful old galleried mansion with a patio bar. Another cluster of shops is at the **Plaza Shopping Center** (⊠ Calle Duarte at Av. 30 de Marzo). A popular shopping street for jewelry and local souvenirs is **Calle Beller.**

In **Altos de Chavón,** art galleries and shops are grouped around the main square.

## Good Buys

### AMBER

**Ambar Tres** (⊠ La Atarazana 3, Colonial Zone, Santo Domingo, ☎ 809/688–0474) carries a wide selection of the Dominican product.

### DOMINICAN ART

In Santo Domingo, the **Arawak Gallery** (⊠ Av. Pasteur 104, ☎ 809/685–1661) specializes in pre-Columbian artifacts and contemporary pottery and paintings. **Galería de Arte Nader** (⊠ Hotel Nicolás Nader, Colonial Zone, ☎ 809/687–6674) showcases top Dominican artists in a variety of medias. **Novo Atarazana** (⊠ Atarazana 21, ☎ 809/685–0582) has an assortment of local artwork.

Visit the stalls of **El Mercado Modelo** in the Colonial Zone for a dizzying selection of Dominican crafts. **El Conde Gift Shop** (⊠ Calle El Conde 153, Santo Domingo, ☎ 809/682–5909) is the spot for exquisite mahogany carvings.

In Puerta Plata, **Macaluso's** (⊠ Calle Duarte 32, and in Plaza Turisol, ☎ 809/586–3433) specializes in Dominican and Haitian paintings and wood carvings. The **Collector's Corner Gallery and Gift Shop** (⊠ Plaza Shopping Center, Calle Duarte at Av. 30 de Marzo, no phone) offers a wide range of souvenirs, including amber.

In Santiago, try **Artesanía Lime** (⊠ Autopista Duarte, Km 2½, Santiago, ☎ 809/582–3754) for mahogany carvings as well as Carnival masks.

Check out the Dominican fashions at **Jenny Polanco's** boutiques in the Santo Domingo Sheraton (☎ 809/686–6666, ext. 2270), Plaza Central (☎ 809/541–5929), and the Paradise Beach Resort and Club in Playa Dorada (☎ 809/586–3663, ext. 314).

### DUTY FREE

Duty-free shops selling liquors, cameras, and the like are at the **Centro de los Héroes** (Av. George Washington), the **Hotel El Embajador,** the **Santo Domingo Sheraton,** and at **Las Américas Airport.**

# Nightlife and the Arts

Get a copy of the magazine *Vacation Guide* and the newspaper *Touring,* both of which are available free at the tourist office and at hotels, to find out what's happening around the island. Also look in the *Santo Domingo News* and the *Puerto Plata News* for listings of events. The monthly *Dominican Fiesta!* also provides up-to-date information.

## Cafés

**Café Atlántico** (⌧ J.A. Aybar at Abraham Lincoln, ☎ 809/565–1841) is responsible for bringing happy hour and Tex-Mex cooking to the Dominican Republic. (Its sister restaurants of the same name are hot spots in Washington, D.C. and Miami Beach.) Usually young, very lively, and very friendly, the late-afternoon yuppie crowd comes for the music, the food, the exotic drinks, and the energetic atmosphere. **Grand Café** (⌧ Av. Lope de Vega 26, ☎ 809/562–4141), an annex to the Café St. Michel, attracts a relaxed local crowd. You can escape the music by going upstairs to the Tree House. The menu is informal and generally light, but try the Creole oxtail served with crabmeat patties. **Museo del Jamon** (⌧ La Atarazana 9, ☎ 809/688–9644) is a casual boîte (with displays on curing ham, hence the name) that is popular Thursday and Sunday evenings after 10 for its folkloric dance shows, with the brilliantly lit Alcazar as a thrilling backdrop.

## Casinos

Most of the casinos are concentrated in the larger hotels of Santo Domingo, but there are others here and there, and all offer blackjack, craps, and roulette. Casinos are open daily 3 PM–4 AM. You must be 18 to enter, and jackets are required. In Santo Domingo, the most popular casinos are in the **Embajador** (⌧ Av. Sarasota, ☎ 809/533–2131), the **Gran Hotel Lina** (⌧ Av. Máximo Gómez, ☎ 809/563–5000), the **Hispaniola** (⌧ Av. Independencia, ☎ 809/221–7111), the **Jaragua** (⌧ Av. Independencia, ☎ 809/686–2222), and the **Naco Hotel** (⌧ Av. Tiradentes 22, ☎ 809/562–3100).

## Clubs and Discos

You'll soon discover that there is no such thing as last call in the Dominican Republic. Customers usually decide when closing time will be.

**La Aurora** (⌧ Av. Hermanos Deligne, ☎ 809/685–6590) is where the capitaleños go when all the partying is over. This lush after-hours supper club is set in a rustic garden. Savor typical dishes, even sancocho, at 4 in the morning. Here you'll see not only party goers but also the musicians who entertained them. It's a spot of preference for Santo Domingo's hottest band, 4:40. **Bachata Rosa** (⌧ Colonial Zone, 9 La Atarazana, ☎ 809/688–0969 or 809/682–7726) is the disco for capitaleños. Named after a popular song by the Dominican merengue megastar Juan Luis Guerra (he is part-owner), this is *the* place of the moment. There's live music on many nights. **Disco Free** (☎ Av. Ortega y Gaset, ☎ 809/565–8100) is Santo Domingo's gay club. The music is a mix of merengue, salsa, and New York house. Tables and a balcony surround the dance floor. It's open Thursday to Sunday. **Guácara Taína** (⌧ 655 Rómulo Betancourt Ave., ☎ 809/530–2666), a cultural center/disco set in a cave, hosts folkloric dances during the early evening and transforms into one of the city's hottest nightspots later on. The world's only disco grotto, it boasts two dance floors, three bars, and lots of nooks and crannies. **Las Palmas** (⌧ Hotel Santo Domingo, Av. Independencia at Abraham Lincoln, ☎ 809/221–7111) has a happy hour from 6 to 8 PM. Happy hours are joyous indeed at Santo Domingo's top hotels, thanks to two-for-one drinks and energetic bands. This one's a favorite of locals for its performances by local merengue bands.

**Pyramid** (✉ Corner of Pedro Clisante and Dr. Rosen, Sosúa, no phone), in the heart of El Batey, is a disco with the best sound and lights in town. **Tops** (✉ Plaza Hotel, Av. Tiradentes, ☎ 809/541–6226), the most appealing dance club in Puerto Plata, is on the 12th floor of the Plaza Hotel, and offers excellent views of the city. The multilevel, mirrored and metal space also hosts a variety of special events, from lingerie fashion shows to the latest bands.

Nearly every hotel in Puerto Plata has a disco and frequent live entertainment. **Crazy Moon** (✉ Paradise Beach Resort and Club, ☎ 809/320–3663) is a lively disco where Latin music is mixed with American and Euro dance tunes. **Andromeda** (✉ Heavens, ☎ 809/586–5250) is a dance club and video bar that gets going late (after 1 AM).

# Exploring the Dominican Republic

## Santo Domingo

Spanish civilization in the New World began in the 12-block area of Santo Domingo called the Colonial Zone. This historical area is now a bustling, noisy district with narrow cobbled streets, shops, restaurants, residents, and traffic jams. Ironically, all the noise and congestion make it somehow easier to imagine this old city as it was when the likes of Columbus, Cortés, Ponce de León, and pirates sailed in and out and colonists were settling themselves in the New World. Tourist brochures boast that "history comes alive here"—a surprisingly truthful statement.

A quick taxi tour of the old section takes about an hour, but if you're interested in history, you'll want to spend a day or two exploring the many old "firsts," and you'll want to do it in the most comfortable shoes you own. Wearing shorts, miniskirts, and halters in churches is considered inappropriate. Men in Santo Domingo never wear shorts, even in the soggy heat of summer. (Note: Hours and admission charges are erratic; check with the tourist office for up-to-date information.)

Parque Independencia separates the old city from the new. Avenidas 30 de Marzo, Bolívar, and Independencia traverse the park and mingle with avenues named for George Washington, John F. Kennedy, and Abraham Lincoln. Modern Santo Domingo is a sprawling, noisy city with a population of close to 2 million.

*Numbers in the margin correspond to points of interest on the Santo Domingo map.*

SIGHTS TO SEE

**㉖ Acuario Nacional.** The largest aquarium in the Caribbean, with an impressive collection of tropical fish and dolphins, its construction was a controversial public expenditure. ✉ *In the Sans Souci district on Av. de las Américas,* ☎ *809/592–1509.* ⛶ *Free.* ☉ *Weekdays 8–5, Sat. 8–4, Sun. 9–12:30.*

**Agua Splash Caribe.** This aquapark across from the aquarium (☞ *above*) features the usual water slides, "river rapids," and wave pools. A schedule of spectacular water revues is planned for the evenings. ✉ *Av. Espana,* ☎ *809/591–5927.* ⛶ *R.D.$50 Tues.–Fri., R.D.$80 weekends.* ☉ *Tues.–Sun. 10–7.*

**❺ Alcázar de Colón.** The castle of Don Diego Colón, built in 1514, was painstakingly reconstructed and restored in 1957. Forty-inch-thick coral limestone walls were patched and shored with blocks from the original quarry. The Renaissance structure, with its balustrade and double row of arches, has strong Moorish, Gothic, and Isabelline influences. There are 22 rooms, furnished in a style to which the viceroy

# Santo Domingo

Acuario Nacional, **26**
Alcázar de Colón, **5**
La Atarazana, **2**
Calle Las Damas, **12**
Capilla de los
Remedios, **7**
Casa de Bastidas, **13**
Casa de Tostado, **16**
Casa del Cordón, **4**
Catedral Santa María
la Menor, **15**

Concepción
Fortress, **20**
El Faro a Colón, **27**
Hospital de San
Nicolás de Bari, **8**
Hostal Palacio
Nicolás de
Ovando, **10**
La Iglesia de Regina
Angelorum, **18**
Iglesia y Convento
Domínico, **17**

Jardín Botánico
Nacional Dr. Rafael
M. Moscoso, **19**
Malecón, **24**
Montesina, **23**
Museo de las
Casas Reales, **6**
National
Pantheon, **9**
Parque Colón, **11**
Parque
Independencia, **21**

Plaza de la
Cultura, **25**
Puerta de la
Misericordia, **22**
San Francisco
Monastery, **3**
Santa Bárbara
Church, **1**
Torre del
Homenaje, **14**

of the island would have been accustomed—right down to the dishes and the viceregal shaving mug. Many of the period paintings, statues, tapestries, and furnishings were donated by the University of Madrid. ⊠ *On Plaza de España (just off Calle Emiliano Tejera at the foot of Calle Las Damas),* ☎ *809/687–5361.* ☞ *R.D.$10.* ☉ *Mon. and Wed.–Fri. 9–5, Sat. 9–4, Sun. 9–1.*

**②** **La Atarazana.** The Royal Mooring Docks was once the colonial commercial district, where naval supplies were stored. There are eight restored buildings, the oldest of which dates from 1507. It now houses crafts shops, restaurants, and art galleries. ⊠ *Calle La Atarazana.*

NEED A BREAK? If you wind up near La Atarazana by midday, join the Reserve Bank and Telecom staff at the **Café Montesinos** (⊠ Calle La Atarazana 23, ☎ 809/689–0580) for a typical Dominican noonday meal. For R.D.$90 you can try fish or beef in a succulent Creole sauce, a tasty bean soup with plantains, or one of the other hearty dishes on the menu. If you happen to be in the area in the late afternoon, stop in for a pizza and a drink at **Drake's Pub** (⊠ Calle La Atarazana 25, ☎ 809/687–8089). There's a fine view of the Alcázar from here, and the place fills up with congenial locals and foreigners.

**⑫** **Calle Las Damas.** The New World's oldest street, the "Street of the Ladies" was named after the elegant ladies of the court who, in the Spanish tradition, promenaded in the evening. Here you'll see a sundial dating from 1753 and the **Casa de los Jesuitas,** which houses a fine research library for colonial history as well as the Institute for Hispanic Culture. ☞ *Free.* ☉ *Weekdays 8–4:30.*

**❼** **Capilla de los Remedios.** The Chapel of Our Lady of Remedies was originally built in the 17th century as a private chapel for the family of Francisco de Dávila. Early colonists also worshiped here before the completion of the cathedral. Its architectural details, particularly the lateral arches, are evocative of the Castilian-Romanesque style. ⊠ *Calle Las Damas, at the foot of Calle de Las Mercedes, no phone.* ☞ *Free.* ☉ *Mon.–Sat. 9–6; Sun. masses begin at 6 AM.*

**⑬** **Casa de Bastidas.** There is a lovely inner courtyard here with tropical plants and temporary exhibit galleries. ⊠ *Calle Las Damas, just off Calle El Conde, no phone.* ☞ *Free.* ☉ *Tues.–Sun. 9–5.*

**⑯** **Casa de Tostado.** The house was built in the first decade of the 16th century and was the residence of writer Don Francisco Tostado. Its twin Gothic windows are the only ones that are still in existence in the New World. It now houses the **Museo de la Familia Dominicana** (Museum of the Dominican Family), which features exhibits on the well-heeled Dominican family in the 19th century. ⊠ *Calle Padre Bellini, near Calle Arzobispo Meriño,* ☎ *809/689–5057.* ☞ *R.D.$10.* ☉ *Thurs.–Tues. 9–2.*

**❹** **Casa del Cordón.** This house, built in 1503, is the Western Hemisphere's oldest surviving stone house. It's recognizable by the sash of the Franciscan order carved in stone over the arched entrance. Columbus's son Diego Colón, viceroy of the colony, and his wife lived here until the Alcázar was finished. It was in this house, too, that Sir Francis Drake was paid a ransom to prevent him from totally destroying the city. The house is now empty, having been vacated by Banco Popular. However, you can still peek inside to check out the architecture. ⊠ *Corner of Calle Emiliano Tejera and Calle Isabel la Católica, no phone.* ☞ *Free.* ☉ *Weekdays 8:30–4:30.*

**⑮** **Catedral Santa María la Menor.** The coral limestone facade of the first cathedral in America towers over the south side of the Parque Colón

(☞ *below*). Spanish workmen began building the cathedral in 1514 but left off construction to search for gold in Mexico. The church was finally finished in 1540. Its facade is composed of architectural elements from the late Gothic to the plateresque style. Inside, the high altar is made of beaten silver, and in the treasury there is a magnificent collection of gold and silver. Some of its 14 lateral chapels serve as mausoleums for noted Dominicans, including Archbishop Meriño, who was once president of the Dominican Republic. Of interest is the Chapel of Our Lady of Antigua, which was reconsecrated by John Paul II in 1984. In the nave are four baroque columns, carved to resemble royal palms, which for more than four centuries guarded the magnificent bronze and marble sarcophagus containing (say Dominican historians) the remains of Christopher Columbus, whose last wish was to be buried in Santo Domingo. The sarcophagus was most recently moved to the Columbus Memorial Lighthouse—only the latest in the Great Navigator's posthumous journeys. ⊠ *Calle Arzobispo Meriño,* ☎ *809/689–1920.* ☞ *Free.* ☉ *Mon.–Sat. 9–4; Sun. masses begin at 6* AM.

❷⓿ **Concepción Fortress.** Within the old city walls, this fortress was the northwest defense post of the colony. ⊠ *Calle Palo Hincado at Calle Isidro Duarte, no phone.* ☞ *Free.* ☉ *Tues.–Sun. 9–6.*

🖐 ㉗ **El Faro a Colón** (Columbus Memorial Lighthouse). This striking—if not exactly architecturally significant—lighthouse monument and museum dedicated to the Great Navigator is shaped like a pyramid cross (although from ground level it looks like a giant concrete casket). The lighthouse complex was completed in 1992, its inauguration coinciding with the 500th anniversary of Christopher Columbus's landing on the island. Along with its showpiece laser-powered lighthouse, the complex holds the tomb of Columbus (moved there after 400 years in the Catedral Santa María la Menor) and six museums featuring exhibits related to Columbus and early exploration of the New World. One museum focuses on the long, rocky, and often controversial history of the lighthouse memorial itself and another on the Great Navigator's posthumous peregrinations (Cuba, Spain, and the Dominican Republic have all laid claim to—and hosted—his remains, which even today are a subject of controversy). ⊠ *Av. España,* ☎ *809/591–1492.* ☞ *R.D.$10.* ☉ *Tues.–Sun. 10–5.*

❽ **Hospital de San Nicolás de Bari.** Ruins are all that remain of the first hospital in the New World, which was built in 1503 by Nicolás de Ovando. ⊠ *Calle Hostos, between Calle de Las Mercedes and Calle Luperon, no phone.*

❿ **Hostal Palacio Nicolás de Ovando.** Now a highly praised hotel, this was once the residence of Nicolás de Ovando, one of the principal organizers of the colonial city. ⊠ *Calle Las Damas 44,* ☎ *809/687–3101.*

⓲ **La Iglesia de Regina Angelorum.** The Church of Regina Angelorum dates from 1537. The church was damaged during the Haitian regime, from 1822 to 1844, but you can still appreciate its Baroque dome, Gothic arches, and traceries. ⊠ *Corner of Calle Padre Bellini and Calle José Reyes,* ☎ *809/682–2783.* ☞ *Free.* ☉ *Mon.–Sat. 9–6.*

⓱ **Iglesia y Convento Dominico.** This graceful building with the rose window is the Dominican Church and Convent, founded in 1510. In 1538, Pope Paul III visited here and was so impressed with the lectures on theology that he granted the church and convent the title of university, making it the oldest institution of higher learning in the New World. ⊠ *Calle Padre Bellini and Av. Duarte,* ☎ *809/682–3780.* ☞ *Free.* ☉ *Tues.–Sun. 9–6.*

⑲ **Jardín Botánico Nacional Dr. Rafael M. Moscoso.** The Dr. Rafael M. Moscoso National Botanical Garden, the largest garden in the Caribbean, is north of town in the Arroyo Hondo district. Its 445 acres include a Japanese garden, a great ravine, a glen, a gorgeous display of orchids, and an enormous floral clock. You can tour the gardens by train, boat, or horse-drawn carriage. ✉ *Av. República de Colombia at Av. de los Proceres,* ☎ 809/687–6211. 🎟 *R.D.$10.* ☉ *Tues.–Sun. 9–5.*

☾ In the 320-acre **Parque Zoológico Nacional** (National Zoological Park), not far from the botanical gardens, animals roam free in natural habitats. There is an African plain, a children's zoo, and what the zoo claims is the world's largest birdcage. ✉ *Av. Máximo Gómez at Av. de los Proceres,* ☎ 809/562–2080. 🎟 *R.D.$5.* ☉ *Tues.–Sun. 9–6.*

㉔ **Malecón.** Avenida George Washington, which is lined with tall palms and Las Vegas–style tourist hotels, breezes along the Caribbean Sea. The Parque Litoral de Sur, better known as the Malecón, borders the avenue from the colonial city to the Hotel Santo Domingo, a distance of about 3 miles. The seaside park, with its cafés and places to relax, is a popular spot, but beware of pickpockets.

㉓ **Montesina.** One of the first things you'll see as you approach the Colonial Zone is this statue, only slightly smaller than the Colossus of Rhodes, staring out over the Caribbean Sea. Montesina was the Spanish priest who came to the Dominican Republic in the 16th century to appeal for human rights for Indians.

➏ **Museo de las Casas Reales.** The Museum of the Royal Houses has collections displayed in two early-16th-century palaces that have been altered many times over the years. Exhibits cover everything from antique coins to replicas of the *Niña,* the *Pinta,* and the *Santa María.* There are statue and cartography galleries, coats of armor and coats of arms, coaches and a royal court room, gilded furnishings, and Indian artifacts. The first room of the former Governor's Residence has a wall-size map marking the routes sailed by Columbus's ships on expeditions beginning in 1492. ✉ *Calle Las Damas, corner Calle de Las Mercedes,* ☎ 809/682–4202. 🎟 *R.D.$10.* ☉ *Tues.–Sat. 9–4:45, Sun. 10–1.*

➒ **National Pantheon.** The building, which dates from 1714, was once a Jesuit monastery and later a theater. Trujillo had it restored in 1955 with an eye toward being buried there. (He is buried instead at Père Lachaise in Paris.) An allegorical mural of his assassination is painted on the ceiling above the altar, where an eternal flame burns. The impressive chandelier was a gift from Spain's Generalissimo Franco. ✉ *Calle Las Damas, near the corner of Calle de Las Mercedes, no phone.* 🎟 *Free.* ☉ *Mon.–Sat. 10–5.*

⓫ **Parque Colón.** The huge statue of Columbus here dates from 1897 and is the work of French sculptor Gilbert. On the west side of the square is the **old town hall** and, on the east, the **Palacio de Borgella,** residence of the governor during the Haitian occupation of 1822–44 and presently the seat of the Permanent Dominican Commission for the **Fifth Centennial of the Discovery and Evangelization of the Americas.** Gallery spaces house architectural and archaeological exhibits pertaining to the fifth centennial.

㉑ **Parque Independencia.** Independence Park, on the far western border of the Colonial Zone, is a big city park dominated by the marble and concrete **Altar de la Patria.** The impressive mausoleum was built in 1976 to honor the founding fathers of the country (Duarte, Sánchez, and Mella).

㉕ **Plaza de la Cultura.** Landscaped lawns, modern sculptures, and sleek buildings make up the Plaza de la Cultura. Among the buildings are the

National Theater (☎ 809/687–3191), which stages performances in Spanish; the **National Library** (☎ 809/688–4086), in which the written word is Spanish; and museums and art galleries, whose notations are also in Spanish. The **Museum of Dominican Man** (☎ 809/687–3623) traces the migrations of Indians from South America through the Caribbean islands. The **Museum of Natural History** (☎ 809/689–0106) examines the flora and fauna of the island. In the **Gallery of Modern Art** (☎ 809/682–8260), the works of 20th-century Dominican and foreign artists are displayed. ⊠ *Museums R.D.$10 each.* ☉ *Tues.–Sat. 10–5.*

㉒ **Puerta de la Misericordia.** The Gate of Mercy is part of the old wall of Santo Domingo. It was here on the plaza, on February 27, 1844, that Ramón Mata Mella, one of the country's founding fathers, fired the shot that began the struggle for independence from Haiti. ⊠ *Calle Palo Hincado at Calle Arzobispo Portes.*

❸ **San Francisco Monastery.** Constructed between 1512 and 1544, the monastery contained the church, chapel, and convent of the Franciscan order. Sir Francis Drake's demolition squad significantly damaged the building in 1586, and in 1673 an earthquake nearly finished the job, but when it's floodlit at night, the majestic ruins of the old monastery are indeed a dramatic sight. ⊠ *Calle Hostos at Calle Emiliano.*

❶ **Santa Bárbara Church.** This combination church and fortress, the only one of its kind in Santo Domingo, was completed in 1562. ⊠ *Av. Mella, between Calle Isabel la Católica and Calle Arzobispo Meriño, no phone.* ⊡ *Free.* ☉ *Weekdays 8–noon; Sun. masses begin at 6 AM.*

⑭ **Torre del Homenaje.** You won't have any trouble spotting the Tower of Homage in the Fort Ozama. The fort sprawls two blocks south of the Casa de Bastidas, with a brooding crenellated tower that still guards the Ozama River. The fort and its tower were built in 1503 to protect the eastern border of the city. The sinister tower was the last home of many a condemned prisoner. ⊠ *On Paseo Presidente Bellini, overlooking Río Ozama, no phone.* ⊡ *R.D.$10.* ☉ *Tues.–Sun. 8–7.*

## The East Coast

Las Américas Highway (built by the dictator Trujillo as a place for his son to race his sports cars) runs east along the coast from Santo Domingo to La Romana—about a two-hour drive. All along the highway are small resort-hotel complexes where you can find refreshments or stay overnight.

East of La Romana are Punta Cana and Bavaro, glorious beaches on the sunrise side of the island. Along the way is Higüey, an undistinguished collection of ramshackle buildings notable only for its controversial church and shrine (someone apparently had a vision of the Virgin Mary), consecrated by Pope John Paul II in 1984, which resembles a pinched, concrete McDonald's arch.

*Numbers in the margin correspond to points of interest on the Dominican Republic map.*

SIGHTS TO SEE

❷ **Altos de Chavón.** The two big businesses around La Romana used to be cattle and sugarcane. That was before Gulf & Western created (and subsequently sold) the Casa de Campo resort, which is a very big business, indeed, and Altos de Chavón, a re-creation of a 16th-century Mediterranean village and art colony on the resort grounds. It sits on a bluff overlooking the Río Chavón, about 3 miles east of the main facility of Casa de Campo. You can drive there easily enough, or you can take one of the free shuttle buses from the resort. There are cobblestone streets lined with lanterns, wrought-iron balconies, and court-yards swathed with bougainvillea. More than a museum piece, this village is a place where artists live, work, and play. There is an art school, affiliated with New York's Parsons School of Design; a disco; an archaeological museum; five restaurants; and a 5,000-seat outdoor amphitheater (used about four times a year), where Frank Sinatra and Julio Iglesias have entertained. The focal point of the village is **Iglesia St. Stanislaus**, which is named after the patron saint of Poland in tribute to the Polish pope John Paul II, who visited the Dominican Republic in 1979 and left some of the ashes of St. Stanislaus behind.

**Boca Chica Beach.** About 20 minutes east of Santo Domingo, this beach is popular because of its proximity to the capital; it's absolutely mobbed on weekends.

**❶ Isla Saona.** Just off the east coast of Hispaniola lies this island, now a national park inhabited by sea turtles, pigeons, and other wildlife. Caves on the island were once used by Indians. The beaches are beautiful, and legend has it that Columbus once strayed ashore here.

**❹ Parque de los Tres Ojos.** About 1½ miles outside the capital is the Park of the Three Eyes. The "eyes" are cool blue pools peering out of deep limestone caves, and it's actually a four-eyed park. If you've a mind to, you can look into the eyes more closely by climbing down into the caves.

**❸ San Pedro de Macorís.** The national sport and the national drink are both well represented in this city, an hour or so east of Santo Domingo. Some of the country's best *béisbol* games are played in **Tetelo Vargas Stadium**. Many major-league players in the States have roots here. The grander homes in the area most likely belong to Dominican baseball stars like George Bell. The **Macorís Rum distillery** is on the eastern edge of the city. Outside town is **Juan Dolio**, a beach and resort area popular with *capitaleños* and German tourists.

## The Southwest

**❺ Barahona.** The latest area to be developed in the Dominican Republic is still wild and pristine. Here mountains carpeted with emerald rain forests and laced with silvery streams slope down into sugary white stretches of sand. The best places to stay are the intimate country inn, **Casa Bonita** (☎ 809/685–5184), **Hotel Riviera Beach** (☎ 809/524–5111), and the deluxe **Bohoruco Beach Resort** (☎ 809/685–5184).

**❻ Lago Enriquillo.** The largest lake in the Antilles is near the Haitian border. The salt lake is also the lowest point in the Antilles: 114 feet below sea level. It encircles wild, arid, and thorny islands that serve as sanctuary to such exotic birds and reptiles as the flamingo, the iguana, and the caiman—the indigenous crocodile.

## The Cibao Valley

The heavily trafficked road north from Santo Domingo, known as the Autopista Duarte (slated to be opened as a four-lane divided highway in 1997), cuts through the lush banana plantations, rice and tobacco fields, and royal poinciana trees of the Cibao Valley. All along the road there are stands where, for a few centavos, you can buy ripe pineapples, mangoes, avocados, chicharrones (either fried pork rinds or chicken pieces), and fresh fruit drinks.

**❽ Jarabacoa.** Nature lovers should consider a trip to Jarabacoa, in the mountainous region known rather wistfully as the Dominican Alps. There is little to do in the town itself but eat and rest up for excursions

on foot, horseback, or by motorbike taxi to the surrounding waterfalls and forests—quite incongruous in such a tropical country. Accommodations in the area are rustic but comfortable. Recommended
are **Alpes Dominicanos** (☎ 809/581–1462), which offers both hotel
rooms with kitchenettes and individual self-service cottages, and the
hacienda-style motel **Pinar Dorado** (☎ 809/574–2820).

**❼ Pico Duarte.** At 10,128 feet, this is the highest peak in the West Indies.

**❿ Santiago de los Caballeros.** This industrial city sits about 90 miles northwest of Santo Domingo. A massive monument honoring the restoration of the republic guards the entrance to the city. Many past presidents
were born in Santiago, and it is currently a center for processing tobacco leaf. You can gain an appreciation of the art and skill of Cuban
cigar making with a tour of **E. Leon Jiménez Tabacalera** (☎ 809/563–
1111 or 809/535–5555). The best hotel in town is the **Gran Almirante**
(☎ 809/580–1992).

**❾ La Vega Vieja.** In the heart of the Cibao is La Vega. Founded in 1495
by Columbus, it is the site of one of the oldest settlements in the New
World. The inquisitive will find the tour of the ruins of the original
settlement, the Old La Vega, a rewarding experience. About 3 miles
north of La Vega is **Santo Cerro** (Holy Mount), site of a miraculous
apparition of the Virgin and therefore many local pilgrimages. The **Convent of La Merced** is there, and the views of the Cibao Valley are breathtaking. The new town boasts a remarkable church of its own, **Concepcíon
de la Vega**, constructed in 1992 to commemorate the 500th anniversary of the discovery (and evangelization) of América. The unusual modern Gothic style—all curvaceous concrete columns, arches, and
buttresses—is striking indeed.

La Vega is also celebrated for its Carnival, featuring the haunting, disturbing devil masks. These papier-mâché creations are incredibly intricate, fanciful gargoyle demons painted in surreal colors with real cow's
teeth contributing eerie authenticity. The skill is usually passed down
for generations; several artisans work in dark cramped studios throughout the area. The studio closest to downtown is that of José Luis Gomez.
Ask any local (tip them 10–20 pesos) to guide you to his atelier (no
phone). José speaks no English but will show you the stages of mask
development. He sells the masks, which make extraordinary wall hangings, for U.S.$50–$60, a great buy considering the craftsmanship.

## The Amber Coast
The Autopista Duarte ultimately leads (in three to four hours from Santo
Domingo) to the Amber Coast, so called because of its large, rich, and
unique deposits of amber. The coastal area around Puerto Plata is a
region of splashy resorts and megadevelopments like Costambar and
Playa Dorada. The north coast boasts more than 70 miles of beaches,
with condominiums and villas going up fast. The farther east from Puerto
Plata and Sosúa you get, the prettier and less spoiled the scenery becomes. The Autopista runs past Cabarete, a neat little village that's a
popular windsurfing haunt, and Playa Grande. The powdery white beach
remains miraculously undisturbed and unspoiled by development.

SIGHTS TO SEE
**⓮ Laguna Grí-Grí.** This swampland, smack out of the Louisiana bayou
country, has the added attraction of a cool blue grotto that almost out-
does the Blue Grotto of Capri. Laguna Grí-Grí is only about 90 minutes west of Puerto Plata, in Río San Juan (ask your hotel concierge
for directions off the Autopista).

**⑪  Mt. Isabel de Torres.** Southwest of Puerto Plata, this mountain soars 2,600 feet above sea level. On the mountain there is a botanical garden, a huge statue of Christ, and a spectacular view. You can take a cable car (when it is working) to the top. The cable was first laid in 1754, although rest assured that it's been replaced since then. Lines can be long, and once on top of the mountain you will wonder if it was worth the time. Don't eat at the restaurant at the top—the food is awful. ✉ *Follow the signs from the Autopista, no phone.* 🎟 *R.D.$20 round-trip.* ☉ *Cable car operates Tues., Thurs., Fri., Sat., and Sun. 8–6.*

**⑫  Puerto Plata.** Although now quiet and almost sleepy, this was a dynamic city in its heyday. You can get a feeling for this past in the magnificent Victorian **Glorieta** (Gazebo) in the central **Parque Independencia.** Next to the park, the **Catedral de San Felipe** recalls a simpler, colonial past. On Puerto Plata's own Malecón, the **Fortaleza de San Felipe** protected the city from many a pirate attack and was later used as a political prison. The fort is most dramatic at night.

Puerto Plata is also the home of the **Museum of Dominican Amber,** a lovely galleried mansion and one of several tenants in the Tourist Bazaar. The museum displays and sells the Dominican Republic's national stone. Semiprecious, translucent amber is actually fossilized pine resin that dates back about 50 million years, give or take a few millennia. The north coast of the Dominican Republic has the largest deposits of amber in the world (the only other deposits are found in Germany and the former U.S.S.R.), and jewelry crafted from the stone is the best-selling item on the island. ✉ *Calle Duarte 61,* ☎ *809/586–2848.* 🎟 *R.D.$15.* ☉ *Mon.–Sat. 9–5.*

**⑮  Samaná.** Back in 1824, a sailing vessel called the *Turtle Dove,* carrying several hundred escaped American slaves from the Freeman Sisters' underground railway, was blown ashore in Samaná. The escapees settled and prospered, and today their descendants number several thousand. The churches here are Protestant; the worshipers live in villages called Bethesda, Northeast, and Philadelphia; and the language spoken is an odd 19th-century form of English—although you're more likely to hear Spanish.

The wealth of marine life in the surrounding waters is beginning to attract more specialty tourists. Sportfishing at Samaná is considered to be among the best in the world. In addition, about 3,000 humpback whales winter off the coast of Samaná from December to March. Major whale-watching expeditions like those out of Massachusetts are being organized and should boost the region's economy without scaring away the world's largest mammals.

Samaná makes a fine base for exploring the area's natural splendors. Most hotels on the peninsula arrange tours to the **Los Haitises National Park,** a remote unspoiled rain forest with limestone knolls, crystal lakes, mangrove swamps teeming with aquatic birds, and caves stippled with Taino petroglyphs. **Las Terrenas,** a remote stretch of beautiful, nearly deserted beaches on the north coast of the Samaná peninsula, is barely known to North American tourists, although French Canadians and Europeans, especially Germans, have begun making the long trek to this latter-day hippie haven that also attracts surfboarders and windsurfers. There are several modest seafood restaurants (the best is **Boca Fina,** no phone), a dusty main street in the town of Las Terrenas, a small airfield, the comparatively grand all-inclusive **El Portillo Beach Club** (☎ 809/688–5785), and several congenial hotels right on the beach at Punta Bonita. If you're seeking tranquillity and are happy just hanging out drinking beer and soaking up sun, this is the place for you. The road from Samaná, even though it is longer and not paved, is a lot less strenuous than coming over the hills from Sanchez.

**⑬ Sosúa.** This small community was settled during World War II by 600 Austrian and German Jews. After the war, many of them returned to Europe or went to the United States, and most of those who remained married Dominicans. Only a few Jewish families reside in the community today, and there is only one small one-room synagogue. The flavor of the town is decidedly Spanish. (Note: The roads off the Autopista are horribly punctured with potholes and ruts. The city has been laying down water mains, and road repair may happen sometime before the end of the century.)

Sosúa has become one of the most frequently visited tourist destinations in the country, favored by French Canadians and Europeans. Hotels and condos are going up at breakneck speed. It actually consists of two communities, **El Batey,** the modern hotel development, and **Los Charamicos,** the old quarter, separated by a cove and one of the island's prettiest beaches. The sand is soft and white, the water, crystal clear and calm. The walkway above the beach is packed with tents filled with souvenirs, pizzas, and even clothing for sale—a jarring note in this otherwise idyllic setting.

NEED A
BREAK?

**P.J.'s International Pub Café** (✉ Calle Pedro Clisante, no phone), in the center of Sosúa, is a shack seemingly glued together by old license plates, business cards, beer posters, and yellowing calendars. Fifteen pesos will buy you a pint of draft. The ambience, courtesy of colorful expatriates and scruffy young Europeans, is free.

# Dominican Republic A to Z
## Arriving and Departing
### BY PLANE

The Dominican Republic has two major international airports: **Las Américas International Airport,** about 20 miles outside Santo Domingo, and **La Unión International Airport,** about 15 miles east of Puerto Plata on the north coast. **American Airlines** (☎ 800/433–7300) has the most extensive service to the Dominican Republic. It flies nonstop from New York and Miami to Santo Domingo, Puerto Plata, and La Romana and offers connections to both Santo Domingo and Puerto Plata from San Juan, Puerto Rico. **American Eagle** (☎ 809/542–5151 or 800/433–7300) has a daily flight to Santo Domingo, two flights a day from San Juan to La Romana, and several flights weekly to Punta Cana. **Carnival** (☎ 800/824–7386) offers daily service to Santo Domingo from New York, Miami, and Orlando. **Continental** (☎ 800/231–0856) flies nonstop from Newark to Puerto Plata and Santo Domingo. **TWA** (☎ 800/221–2000) flies nonstop to Santo Domingo from New York/Kennedy. **APR International Air** (☎ 718/341–5000, 305/599–1299, or 809/547–2727) flies nonstop from Miami and New York/Kennedy. Minneapolis-based **TransGlobal Tours** (☎ 800/338–2160) offers weekly charters during the winter season from the Twin Cities to Puerto Plata.

Several regional carriers serve neighboring islands. **ALM** (☎ 800/327–7230) connects Santo Domingo to St. Maarten and Curaçao. There is also limited domestic service available from La Herrera Airport in Santo Domingo to smaller airfields in La Romana, Samaná, and Santiago.

The Barahona International Airport handles large jet aircraft, mostly charters and domestic flights.

The remodeled and enlarged Las Américas (Santo Domingo) and La Unión (Puerto Plata) facilities are sophisticated by Latin American standards. Still, overworked customs and immigration officials are often less than courteous, and luggage theft is rife. Try to travel with carry-on luggage, and keep a sharp eye on it. Be prepared for a daunting experience as you leave customs. However, some order is being imposed—taxis now line up and, for the most part, charge the official established rates. If you have arranged for a hotel transfer, a representative should be waiting for you in the immigration hall.

FROM THE AIRPORT

Taxis are available at the airport, and the 25-minute ride into Santo Domingo averages R.D.$250 (about U.S.$21). Taxi fares from the Puerto Plata airport average R.D.$200.

## Currency

The coin of the realm is the Dominican peso, which is divided into 100 centavos. It is written R.D.$ and fluctuates relative to the U.S. dollar. At press time, U.S.$1 was equivalent to R.D.$13.40. Always make certain you know in which currency any transaction is taking place (any confusion will probably not be to your advantage). Although all transactions are required by law to be in pesos, there is a growing black market for hard currency; be wary of offers to exchange U.S. dollars at a rate more favorable than the official one. Prices quoted here are in U.S. dollars unless noted otherwise.

## Emergencies

**Police:** In Santo Domingo, ☎ 711; in Puerto Plata, ☎ 586–2804; in Sosúa, ☎ 571–2233. However, do not expect too much from the police, aside from a bit of a hassle and some paperwork that they will consider the end of the matter. In general, the police and government bureaucrats take a hostile approach to visitors.

**Hospitals:** Santo Domingo emergency rooms that are open 24 hours are **Centro Médico Universidad Central del Este** (UCE) (⊠ Av. Máximo Gómez 68, ☎ 809/221–0171), **Clínica Abreu** (⊠ Calle Beller 42, ☎ 809/688–4411), and **Clínica Gómez Patino** (⊠ Av. Independencia 701, ☎ 809/685–9131). In Puerto Plata, you can go to **Clínica Dr. Brugal** (⊠ Calle José del Carmen Ariza 15, ☎ 809/586–2519). In Sosúa, try the **Centro Médico Sosúa** (⊠ Av. Martinez, ☎ 809/571–3949).

**Pharmacies:** Pharmacies that are open 24 hours a day are, in Santo Domingo, **San Judas Tadeo** (⊠ Av. Independencia 57, ☎ 809/689–6664); in Puerto Plata, **Farmacia Deleyte** (⊠ Av. John F. Kennedy 89, ☎ 809/586–2583).

## Getting Around

BUSES

*Públicos* are small blue-and-white or blue-and-red cars that run regular routes, stopping to let passengers on and off. The fare is R.D.$2. Competing with the públicos are the *conchos* or *colectivos* (privately owned buses), whose drivers tool around the major thoroughfares, leaning out of the window or jumping out to try to persuade passengers to climb aboard. It's a colorful, if cramped, way to get around town. The fare is about R.D.$1. Privately owned air-conditioned buses make regular runs to Santiago, Puerto Plata, and other destinations. Avoid night travel, because the country's roads are full of potholes. You should make reservations by calling **Metro Buses** (⊠ Av. Winston Churchill; in Santo Domingo, call 809/566–7126; in Puerto Plata, 809/586–

6062; in Santiago, 809/587–4711) or **Caribe Tours** (✉ Av. 27 de Febrero at Leopoldo Navarro, ☎ 809/221–4422). One-way bus fare from Santo Domingo to Puerto Plata is R.D.$75 (U.S.$6). *Voladoras* ("fliers") are vans that run from Puerto Plata's Central Park to Sosúa and Cabarete a couple of times each hour for R.D.$10. They don't run on a reliable schedule and are not always labeled with their destination.

### CAR RENTALS

You'll need a valid driver's license from your own country and a major credit card and/or cash deposit. Cars can be rented at the airports and at many hotels. Among the known names are **Avis** (☎ 809/535–7191), **Budget** (☎ 809/562–6812), **Hertz** (☎ 809/221–5333), and **National** (☎ 809/562–1444). Rates average U.S.$70 and up per day, depending upon the make and size of the car. Some local outfits, like **Nelly Rent-A-Car** (☎ 809/544–1800 or, from the U.S., 800/526–6684), may give you better rates. Driving is on the right. Many Dominicans drive recklessly, often taking their half of the road out of the middle, but they will flash their headlights to warn against highway patrols. The first-time visitor to the island may marvel how some cars can drive at all, as they look like they will fall to pieces at any second.

It is strongly suggested that—with the exception of driving within the major cities—you do not drive at night. If for some unavoidable reason you must drive at night, especially on the narrow, unlighted mountain roads, exercise extreme caution. Many local cars are without headlights or taillights. Bicyclists do not have lights, cows and goats wander onto the pavement, and there is always pedestrian traffic on the sides of the road. Traffic and directional signs are less than adequate, and unseen potholes (some 5 to 6 feet wide and more than a foot deep) can easily break a car's axle. At press time, the road between Santo Domingo and Santiago, the major commercial road in the country, was thankfully being expanded into a four-lane divided highway. It should be fully open in 1997. Beware of the road between Santiago and Puerto Plata—it can feel like maneuvering on a lunar landscape. Surprisingly, many of the more scenic secondary roads are in good shape. Be sure to talk to someone at your hotel before embarking on a driving tour. Keep in mind that gas stations are few and far between in some of the remote regions. Finally, the 80-kilometer-per-hour (50-mile-per-hour) speed limit is strictly enforced. If you drive anywhere outside the city limits of Santo Domingo, there is more than a good chance you will be pulled over for speeding, even if you weren't. You will be expected to pay a bribe of about R.D.$40 (about U.S.$3). Pay it, smile, and gripe later. The hassles encountered if you don't are just not worth it. The police count on these payoffs to augment their meager incomes (low-level public servants make very little here).

### MOTORBIKE TAXIS

Known as *motoconchos,* these bikes are a popular and inexpensive way to get around such tourist areas as Puerto Plata, Sosúa, and Jarabacoa. Bikes can be flagged down both on the road and in town; rates vary from R.D.$3 to R.D.$20 per person, depending upon distance. Be careful: No helmets are provided, and they drive like maniacs!

### PLANE

Incredibly, there is no local scheduled airline service between Santo Domingo and Puerto Plata, Samaná, or Punta Cana. If you lack the time to travel overland, you can charter a small plane for trips around the island and to neighboring countries, and for surprisingly inexpensive rates. Contact Jimmy or Irene Butler at **Air Taxi** (✉ Núñez de Cáceres 2, Santo Domingo, ☎ 809/227–8333 or 809/567–1555).

TAXIS

Taxis, which are government regulated, line up outside hotels and restaurants. The taxis are unmetered, and the minimum fare within Santo Domingo is about R.D.$50 (U.S.$4), but you can bargain for less if you order a taxi away from the major hotels. Hiring a taxi by the hour and with any number of stops is R.D.$125 (U.S.$10) per hour with a minimum of two hours. Be sure to establish the time that you start; drivers like to advance the time a little. You should also be certain that it is clearly understood in advance which currency is to be used in the agreed-upon fare. Taxis can also drive you to destinations outside the city. Rates are posted in hotels and at the airport. Sample fares are R.D.$1,000 (U.S.$80) to La Romana and R.D.$1,900 (U.S.$150) to Puerto Plata. If you're negotiating, the going rate is R.D.$5 per kilometer. Round-trips are considerably less than twice the one-way fare. Call **El Conde Taxi** (☎ 809/563–6131) or **Tecni-Taxi** (☎ 809/567–2010 in Santo Domingo, 809/320–7621 in Puerto Plata).

In a separate category are radio taxis, which are convenient if you'd like to schedule a pickup—and a wise choice if you don't speak Spanish. The fare is negotiated over the phone when you make the appointment. The most reliable company is **Apolo Taxi** (☎ 809/541–9595). The standard charge is R.D.$100 per hour during the day, R.D.$120 at night, no minimum, with as many stops as you like.

Avoid unmarked street taxis—there have been numerous incidents of assaults and robberies, particularly in Santo Domingo.

## Guided Tours

**Apolo Tours** (☎ 809/586–5329) offers a full-day tour of Playa Grande and tours to Santiago (including a casino tour) and Sosúa. It will also arrange transfers between your hotel and the airport, day sightseeing tours, and custom and small-group tours along the north coast, which include stops along the way for swimming and an overnight stay at Samaná. **Cafemba Tours** (☎ 809/586–2177) runs various tours of the Cibao Valley and the Amber Coast, including Puerto Plata, Sosúa, and Río San Juan. **Caribbean Jeep Safaris** (☎ 809/571–1924) is an English-speaking outfit that runs Jeep tours in the mountains behind Puerto Plata and Sosúa, ending up at the Cabarete Adventure Park, where you can swim in an underground pool and explore caves with Taino rock paintings. Buffet lunch and unlimited drinks are included in the R.D.$600 price. **Ecoturisa** (☎ 809/221–4104) arranges ecological tours and cultural and scientific expeditions, many of them tailored to the clients' needs. **Prieto Tours** (☎ 809/685–0102) operates Gray Line of the Dominican Republic. It offers half-day bus tours of Santo Domingo, nightclub tours, beach tours, tours to Cibao Valley and the Amber Coast, and a variety of other tours. **Turinter** (☎ 809/685–4020) tours include dinner and a show or casino visit, a full-day tour of Samaná, and specialty tours (museum, shopping, fishing).

## Language

Before you travel to the Dominican Republic, you should know at least a smattering of Spanish. Guides at major tourist attractions and front-desk personnel in the major hotels speak a fascinating form of English, though they often have trouble understanding tourists. Traffic signs and restaurant menus, except at popular tourist establishments, are in Spanish. Using smiles and gestures will help, but a nodding acquaintance with the language or a phrase book is more useful.

## Opening and Closing Times

Regular office and shop hours are weekdays 8–12:30 and 2:30–5, Saturday 8–noon. Government offices are open weekdays 7:30–2:30. Banking hours are weekdays 8:30–4:30.

## Passports and Visas

U.S. and Canadian citizens must have either a valid passport or proof of citizenship, such as an original (not photocopied) birth certificate, and a tourist card. Legal residents of the United States must have an alien registration card (green card), a valid passport, and a tourist card. British citizens need only a valid passport; no entry visa is required. The requisite tourist card costs $10, and you should be sure to purchase it at the airline counter when you check in and then fill it out on the plane. You can purchase the card on arrival at the airport, but you may encounter long lines. Be advised that only U.S. cash (not traveler's checks) is acceptable. Keep the bottom half of the card in a safe place because you'll need to present it to immigration authorities when you leave. There is also a U.S.$10 departure tax (payable only in U.S. dollars).

## Precautions

Beware of the *buscones* at the airports. They offer to assist you, and do so by relieving you of your luggage and disappearing with it. Also avoid the black marketers, who will offer you a tempting rate of exchange for your U.S. dollars. If the police catch you changing money on the street, they'll haul you off to jail (the *calabozo*)—and you do not *ever* want to visit one here. Also, buy amber only from reputable shops. The attractively priced piece offered by the street vendor is more than likely plastic. Guard your wallet or pocketbook in Santo Domingo, especially around the Malecón (waterfront boulevard), which teems with pickpockets. If you elect to rent a car, be sure to have some kind of stress-reducing techniques available. Getting behind the wheel here makes the streets of Rome or Paris seem like peaceful, country lanes.

## Taxes and Service Charges

Hotels and restaurants add a service charge (15% in hotels, 10% in restaurants) and 8% government tax. It is customary to leave a dollar per day for the hotel maid. At restaurants and nightclubs you may want to leave an additional 5%–10% tip for a job well done. Taxi drivers expect a 10% tip. Skycaps and hotel porters expect at least R.D.$5 per bag. U.S. visitors must buy a $10 tourist card before entering the Dominican Republic, and all foreign visitors must pay a $10 departure tax. Both must be paid in U.S. dollars.

## Telephones and Mail

To call the Dominican Republic from the United States, dial area code 809 and the local number. Connections are clear and easy to make. Remember that English is not widely spoken. Fortunately, service from the Dominican Republic is much improved. There is direct-dial service to the United States; just dial 1, followed by the area code and number.

Airmail postage to North America for a letter or postcard costs R.D.$2, to Europe, R.D.$4, and may take up to three weeks to reach the destination.

## Visitor Information

Before you go, contact the **Dominican Republic Department of Tourism** (✉ Dominican Consulate, 1 Times Sq., 11th floor, New York, NY 10036, ☎ 212/768–2480; ✉ 2355 Salzedo Ave., Suite 305, Coral Gables, FL 33134, ☎ 305/444–4592; ✉ 1464 Crescent St., Montréal, Québec,

Canada H3A 2B6, ☎ 514/933–6126). The best source of information is the **Dominican Tourist Information Center** (☎ 800/752–1151) in Santo Domingo. Be prepared to wait at least two weeks to get requested material sent to you.

In the Dominican Republic, the **Secretary of Tourism** (✉ Officinas Guberbamentales Bldg. D, ☎ 809/221–4660, FAX 809/682–3806) is in Santo Domingo in a complex of government offices at the corner of Avenida Mexico and Avenida 30 de Marzo. Unless you are seeking special assistance, it is not worth making the trek here for the limited material offered to tourists. The **tourist office** (✉ Playa Long Beach, ☎ 809/586–3676) is in Puerto Plata. Both offices are open weekdays 9–2:30, but the Puerto Plata office often opens late and closes early.

# 12 Grenada

Updated by
Jane E. Zarem

**G**RENADA, A JEWEL OF AN ISLAND only 21 miles long and 12 miles wide, is bordered by 45 beaches and countless secluded coves, crisscrossed by nature trails, and filled with spice plantations, tropical forests, and select hotels that cling to hillsides and overlook the sea.

If the Irish hadn't beaten them to the name, Grenadians might very well have called their land the Emerald Isle, for the lush rain forests and the thick vegetation on the hillsides give it a great, green beauty that few places in the world can match. Located in the Eastern Caribbean 12 degrees north of the equator, Grenada is the most southerly of the Windward Islands. Three inhabited islands and a few uninhabited islets comprise the nation: Grenada island is the largest of the three, with 120 square miles and a population of about 96,000 people; Carriacou, 16 miles north of Grenada, has 13 square miles and a population of about 5,000; and Petit Martinique, 5 miles northeast of Carriacou, has just 486 acres and a population of 700. Although Carriacou and Petit Martinique are popular for day trips or fishing and snorkeling excursions, most of the tourist action is on Grenada. This is also where you'll find the nation's capital, St. George's, and it's eponymous harbor—the largest and busiest on Grenada.

Until 1983, when the United States/Eastern Caribbean intervention catapulted tiny Grenada into the forefront of international news, it was a relatively obscure island providing a quiet hideaway for those who love fishing, snorkeling, or simply lazing in the sun. Today, Grenada is a safe and secure vacation spot with enough good shopping, restaurants, and pubs to make it a regular port of call for major cruise lines and plenty of beaches and coves for those who want to scuba dive, snorkel, or just sit and watch the waves.

Known as the Isle of Spice, Grenada is also a major producer of nutmeg, cinnamon, mace, cocoa, and many other common spices. The pleasant aroma of spices fills the air: at the outdoor markets where they're sold from large burlap bags, in restaurants where chefs believe in using them liberally, and in pubs where nutmeg is sprinkled on rum punches.

Grenada's popularity as a vacation destination continues to increase each year, as more and more travelers seek new and exotic sunny climates. To protect the native charm that keeps Grenada somewhat unique, any expansion of the tourism industry is carefully controlled. No building can stand taller than a coconut palm, and new construction on the beaches must be at least 165 feet from the high-water mark. Hotels, resorts, and restaurants remain, for the most part, small and family-owned, run by people who get to know their guests and pride themselves on giving personalized service. They're typical of the islanders as a whole—friendly and hospitable.

Grenada was sighted by Columbus in 1498. Although he never set foot on the island, he gave it the name Concepción. Throughout the 17th century, it was the scene of bloody battles between the indigenous Carib Indians and the French. The Caribs finally lost to the French in 1651, committing mass suicide by leaping off a cliff rather than submitting to their captors. The French, however, lost the island to the British in 1762, thus beginning the seesaw of power between the two nations that became a familiar tale on many of the Windward Islands.

In 1967, Grenada became part of the British Commonwealth. Seven years later, it was granted total independence. The New Jewel Movement (NJM) seized power in 1979, formed the People's Revolutionary Government, and named as prime minister Maurice Bishop, who established controversial ties with Cuba. Bishop's prime ministry lasted until 1983, when a coup d'état led to his execution, along with that of many of his supporters. NJM Deputy Prime Minister Bernard Coard and Army Commander Hudson Austin then took over the government. U.S. troops invaded the island on October 25, 1983, and evacuated the American students who were attending St. George's University Medical School. Coard and Austin were arrested, and resistance to the invasion was quickly quelled.

Herbert A. Blaize was elected prime minister in December 1984. With many millions of dollars in U.S. and Canadian aid, his government began reorganizing Grenada's economy to focus on agriculture, light manufacturing, and tourism. The country started to rebuild roads and installed a direct-dial telephone system. Grenada's modern Point Salines International Airport, which opened in 1984, enabled jets to land on the island and allowed night landings. It still has one of the longest runways in the Caribbean.

The election in June, 1995, of the New National Party, under the leadership of Dr. Keith Mitchell, continues the peaceful progress of this island nation.

## Lodging

Grenada's accommodations are primarily located on or around Grand Anse Beach. They range from simply furnished kitchenette apartments to suites of overwhelming Caribbean-style elegance. Many of the hotels are owned and operated by Grenadians; those that aren't are usually run by British or American expatriates who thrive on the simplicity of Grenadian life. The hotels tend to be small and intimate, with friendly managers and owners.

Most posted daily room rates at Grenadian hotels are quoted in U.S. currency and represent the room rate only, without meals. Visitors can often opt for CP or MAP, depending on the season. Only one hotel on the island is all-inclusive. The plans specified in the individual listings below apply year-round unless otherwise noted. Prices during the summer are discounted by up to 40%.

| CATEGORY | COST* |
|----------|-------|
| $$$$ | over $200 |
| $$$ | $150–$200 |
| $$ | $100–$150 |
| $ | under $100 |

*All prices are for a standard double room for two during high season, excluding 8% government tax and 10% service charge.*

### Hotels

GRENADA

$$$$ 🏨 **The Calabash.** Rooms in this all-suite hotel are scattered over 8 acres of tropical gardens overlooking a curved beach, a yacht harbor, and charter-boat anchorage in "Prickly Bay," L'Anse aux Epines, a few minutes away from the hotel row of Grand Anse. Fourteen suites have whirlpool baths, and eight suites each have a private pool. All have air-conditioning and a veranda, where breakfast is delivered. You'll have to live with the noise generated by the nearby Point Salines International Airport: Early-morning flights can bounce you out of bed. ⊠ *Box 382, St. George's,* ☎ *809/444–4234,* �📠 *809/444–4804. 28 suites. Restaurant, beach bar-restaurant, air-conditioning, pool, tennis, water-sports center. AE, MC, V. BP, MAP.*

## Grenada (and Carriacou)

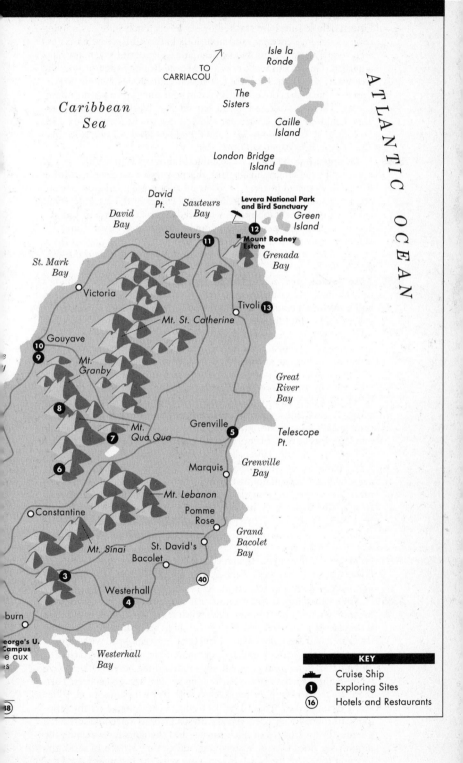

**$$$$**   ⊞ **Mahogany Run.** Just over the hill from Grand Anse Beach, this colony of Mediterranean-style buildings slopes down to Morne Rouge Beach. Fifteen deluxe suites are stacked on six levels. Each suite has a living room, kitchen, bedroom, and luxurious bath. All have either a covered veranda or patio, providing dramatic views of the bay; many have a garden. Guests can walk down to Morne Rouge Beach or take the free water shuttle to Dr. Groom's Beach Club. Rates include airport transfers, breakfast cooked and served in your suite, and a private housekeeper. There's a restaurant and bar on site. Weekly rates are available. Children under 12 are not allowed. ⊠ *Morne Rouge, Box 730, St. George's,* ☎ *809/444–3171,* 𝖥𝖠𝖷 *809/444–3172. 15 suites. Restaurant, bar, beach, beach club. AE, MC, V.*

**$$$$**   ⊞ **Mariposa Beach Resort.** Adjacent to Mahogany Run (☞ *above*) and operated by the same management, this new resort overlooking Morne Rouge Bay opened in early 1996. Its 32 rooms are piled atop one another to resemble a hillside Mediterranean village by the sea. Each room and bathroom has Italian tiles, a covered veranda or garden, and can accommodate two persons. All rooms have water views. Rates include breakfast and dinner. ⊠ *Morne Rouge, Box 730, St. George's,* ☎ *809/444–3171,* 𝖥𝖠𝖷 *809/444–3172. 32 rooms. Restaurant, bar, beach, beach club. AE, MC, V. MAP.*

**$$$$**   ⊞ **La Source.** Just minutes from Point Salines airport is Grenada's only all-inclusive resort. A louvered wood-and-stained-glass reception hall leads into a courtyard around which spa treatment rooms, an excellent restaurant (dine on the mint-and-raspberry colonnaded terrace or in the colonial teak and plush Great Room), piano bar, and pool are arranged. The bedrooms have Persian rugs on Italian marble floors, Jamaican mahogany furniture and woodwork, high ceilings, balconies, and marble bathrooms with hair dryers and illuminated makeup mirrors. Rooms are in several four-story buildings on or above the main beach. Be prepared to walk up and down lots of stairs to get to your room. Rates seem steep at first glance, but they include *everything*— three meals, snacks, drinks at the bar, wine with dinner, tipping (it's banned), sports, plus, of course, spa treatments at The Oasis. Massages and facials are augmented by creams and oils made from lemons, limes, papayas, or whatever's in season. Body treatments and saunas are scheduled for you upon arrival. The array of sports facilities is impressive—the best in Grenada. You're truly supposed to be getting away from it all: There's no television on the property. ⊠ *Pink Gin Beach, Box 852, St. George's,* ☎ *809/444–2556 or 800/544–2883,* 𝖥𝖠𝖷 *809/444–2561. 100 rooms. 2 restaurants, poolside bar service, piano bar, air-conditioning, pool, beauty salon, hot tub, sauna, spa, 9-hole golf course, 2 tennis courts, aerobics, archery, fencing, Ping-Pong, volleyball, yoga, 2 beaches, scuba diving, snorkeling, sailing, windsurfing, waterskiing, cabaret, piano. AE, MC, V. All-inclusive.*

**$$$$**   ⊞ **Spice Island Inn.** If you want luxurious accommodations in the best
  ★        location Grenada has to offer, this stylish resort on Grand Anse beach is the place to go. There are three types of suites here, all spacious, brightly decorated with the colors of sand and coral, and equipped with air-conditioning, ceiling fan, phone, hair dryer, minibar, vast mirrored closets, and a patio. Some suites are, literally, right on the beach. Others have white-ballustraded terraces overlooking garden, sea, and sunset. Then there are the private pool suites, each with its own plunge pool. What really distinguishes Spice Island from the pack, though, are the fabulous bathrooms. They're equipped with spa Jacuzzis that could submerge a family of four, heaps of thick towels, and skylights for watching the moon rise. Since Grand Anse is Grenada's prime stretch of sand, the location is perfect for beach lovers. And with the restaurant (☞ Dining, *below*) and bar at the edge of the sand in the center of the com-

plex, your feet need never touch concrete. ⊠ *Box 6, Grand Anse, St. George's,* ☎ *809/444–4258 or 800/223–9815,* ⅢX *809/444–4807. 39 whirlpool suites and 17 private-pool suites. Restaurant, bar, air-conditioning, fans, minibars, golf privileges, tennis court, exercise room, water-sports center, boutique, cabaret. AE, D, DC, MC, V. CP, MAP.*

**$$$–$$$$** ▥ **Grenada Renaissance Resort.** The location (across from the Grand Anse Shopping Center) is convenient, the grounds are lush and beautiful, the rooms are comfortable, and the list of amenities is long. The ceilings are low, however, and the rooms less spacious than those at competing resorts. Still, all rooms have king-size or large twin beds, satellite TV, and hair dryers. And the hotel is located right on Grand Anse Beach. ⊠ *Box 441, Grand Anse, St. George's,* ☎ *809/444–4371,* ⅢX *809/444–4800. 184 doubles, 2 luxury suites. 2 restaurants, lounge, pool, barbershop, beauty salon, 2 tennis courts, 2 gift shops. AE, DC, MC, V. EP, MAP.*

**$$$** ▥ **Coyaba Beach Resort.** Coyaba means "heaven" in the Arawak Indian language. Situated right on Grand Anse Beach, certainly a heavenly spot, Coyaba is comfortable, popular, and a terrific value. Three buildings were added in 1995, nearly doubling the size of the resort; other rooms were refurbished. Leading off the lawns are tennis and volleyball courts, a sizable pool with swim-up bar, and a bamboo-walled terrace restaurant. Table tennis, volleyball, and shuffleboard are permanent fixtures on the grounds. Rooms are located in several peachy-pink two-story buildings, which surround beautifully landscaped lawns and gardens and a sizable pool with swim-up bar. The beach is a short amble through the grounds, and most rooms have a water view. Each room is attractively decorated with spreads and drapes in tropical colors, natural wood furniture, and Arawak-inspired folk art. Rooms all have air-conditioning, satellite TV, phone, hair dryer, and either a balcony or strip of grass with lounge chair. Meal plans are available, and the food in the restaurant is quite good. Entertainment is provided most nights. ⊠ *Box 336, Grand Anse, St. George's,* ☎ *809/444–4129 or 800/223–9815,* ⅢX *809/444–4808. 70 rooms. Restaurant, bar, air-conditioning, pool, tennis court, water-sports center, boutique. AE, D, DC, MC, V. EP, CP, BP, MAP, FAP.*

**$$–$$$** ▥ **Rex Grenadian.** You're likely to be vacationing alongside a convention group at this massive British-owned resort near the airport. The resort is also very popular with European tour groups. The central building is a faux-Palladian white palace of lofty, pink-limed oak ceilings, vast arched windows, trellised walkways, and tiled terraces. The snazziest rooms and suites are the ones conveniently located adjacent to the central building. Other rooms are in eight two-story cliffside blocks of buildings with either a garden or ocean view. All rooms are decorated in robin's-egg blue and taupe with rattan furniture, king or large twin beds, and balconies. Basic garden-view rooms are equipped with a fan and shower. For an extra $25 you can have air-conditioning, tub, and hair dryer. Enthusiastic landscaping includes a lake and fountain, which many rooms overlook, and a pool terrace with restaurant and bar above one of two beaches. All manner of activity is laid on—water sports, rainy-day programs (bingo, local dialect classes, dance lessons), evening shows, happy hours. ⊠ *Point Salines, Box 893, St. George's,* ☎ *809/444–3333 or 800/255–5859,* ⅢX *809/444–1111. 212 rooms. 3 restaurants, beach bar, café, lounge, piano bar, pool with bar-restaurant, sauna, 2 tennis courts, health club, 2 beaches, scuba diving, snorkeling, sunfish sailing, windsurfing, waterskiing, entertainment, executive lounge, conference facilities. AE, D, DC, MC, V. EP.*

**$$** ▥ **Blue Horizons Cottage Hotel.** Spice Island Inn's sister hotel is an es-
★ pecially good value. Each comfortable, air-conditioned suite has a kitchenette, private terrace, TV, phone, and hair dryer. Handsome ma-

hogany furniture is set off by white walls and cool, tiled floors. Palms stud the large, sunny lawn around the swimming pool. Grand Anse beach, where the Spice Island Inn sprawls along 1,600 feet of sand, is a short walk down the hill. Guests may eat at Blue Horizon's La Belle Creole or at Spice Island (☞ *above*). Water sports (at Spice Island) are complimentary for guests of either hotel. ⊠ *Box 41, Grand Anse, St. George's,* ☎ *809/444–4316 or 809/444–4592; in the U.S., 800/223– 9815;* ⒻⒶⓍ *809/444–2815. 26 deluxe and 6 superior suites. Restaurant, 2 bars, air-conditioning, lounge, pool, water sports at Spice Island. AE, MC, V. EP, CP, MAP.*

$$ 🏨 **Flamboyant Hotel and Cottages.** Not just a good value, the friendly Flamboyant is also home of the famous Monday-night crab-racing spectacular. The rooms and suites of this Grenadian-owned hotel/self-catering resort have one of the island's best views, sweeping over the entire Grand Anse Bay to St. George's. All rooms are simply furnished with air-conditioning, minibar, satellite TV, phone, and balcony. One-bedroom suites and two-bedroom cottages each have a kitchen and lounge. You can take a dip in the freshwater pool or enjoy the beach. Be prepared to climb stairs: The rooms are built into a rather steep hill at the southern end of Grand Anse Beach, and the stairway to the beach is at least 100 steps; the pool, restaurant, and cabana bar are midway down the stairs. ⊠ *Box 214, St. George's,* ☎ *809/444–4247,* ⒻⒶⓍ *809/444–1234. 16 rooms, 20 suites, and 2 cottages. Restaurant, bar, beach bar, air-conditioning, minibars, pool, snorkeling. AE, D, MC, V. EP, BP, MAP.*

$ 🏨 **La Sagesse Nature Center.** This secluded getaway is on a lovely bay 10 miles east of Point Salines International Airport. The grounds include a salt-pond bird sanctuary, thick growths of mangroves, and several hiking trails. The main guest house has two high-ceilinged suites with kitchenettes, ceiling fans, and hot-water baths. There is also a two-bedroom beach cottage, and two less-expensive rooms are tucked in behind the restaurant. Mike Meranski, the cheerful American owner-manager, will run guests into town for grocery supplies and shopping. ⊠ *Box 44, St. David's,* ☎ *809/444–6458,* ⒻⒶⓍ *809/444–6458. 6 double rooms. Restaurant, bar (with satellite TV). MC, V. EP.*

$ 🏨 **True Blue Inn.** Although the "blue" in the inn's name comes from the history of the residential area that was once an indigo plantation, the title could just as easily have come from the beautiful views of blue Prickly Bay. Four spacious one-bedroom apartment units are perched cliffside, among the trees, each with a private veranda overlooking the sea. Three two-bedroom island cottages, nestled in private seaside gardens, are air-conditioned and have ceiling fans. Kitchens in both the apartments and the cottages are large and fully equipped. You can swim in the pool or the bay. Sunsets are spectacular from Indigo's, the inn's deck restaurant. Boaters frequently come for dinner, tying up at the inn's private dock. For a special treat, you can book a day sail on the owner's yacht. ⊠ *True Blue Inn, Box 308, St. George's (Old Mill Ave., True Blue),* ☎ *809/444–2000 or 800/742–4276,* ⒻⒶⓍ *809/444–1247. 7 units. Restaurant, bar, pool, dock, yacht charter, dinghy service, full maid/laundry service daily. AE, MC, V.*

### CARRIACOU

$$ 🏨 **Silver Beach Resort.** Stretches of pristine beach surround this 18-room hotel on Carriacou, Grenada's sister isle. All rooms have private patios and ocean views (but no TVs). The scuba facilities here are the biggest in the Grenadines. The open-air restaurant by the water is the best place on the island for a hearty, early-morning breakfast. Day trips to offshore islets can be arranged. ⊠ *Silver Beach,* ☎ *809/443–7337,* ⒻⒶⓍ *809/443–7165. 12 doubles (2 with kitchenettes),*

*6 cottages. Restaurant, dock, scuba certification course, snorkeling, spearfishing, windsurfing, moorings, showers and garbage disposal for yachts, boutique, gift shop, island bus service, car rental. AE, MC, V. EP, CP, MAP.*

## Apartment Hotels

These fully equipped units often represent a great budget alternative, especially for families. Contact the tourist office for additional listings.

**$$–$$$** ⊞ **Twelve Degrees North.** Eight top-of-the-line (and most expensive) one- and two-bedroom apartments come with maid service (which includes cooking your breakfast and lunch and doing your laundry), private beach, pool, and tennis. A minimum stay of one week is required during high season, and children under 12 are not allowed. ⊠ *Box 241, L'Anse aux Epines, St. George's,* ☎ *809/444–4580,* FAX *809/444–4580. 8 apartments. Pool, tennis court, beach, scuba diving, snorkeling, windsurfing, boating. AE, V. EP.*

**$** ⊞ **Wave Crest Holiday Apartments.** Owner-manager Joyce DaBreo runs a tight ship. She and her husband take great pains to keep all 20 air-conditioned, sunny rooms and apartments, some of which are self-catering, spotless and well maintained. Grand Anse beach is only a five-minute walk away. ⊠ *Box 278, St. George's,* ☎ *809/444–4116,* FAX *809/444–4847. 14 1-bedroom apartments, 2 2-bedroom apartments, 4 double rooms. Air-conditioning. AE, D, MC, V.*

## Villa and Private-Home Rentals

Several local agencies handle rentals of villas and private homes: The most reliable is **Villas of Grenada** (⊠ Box 218, St. George's, ☎ 809/440–1896, FAX 809/444-4529). In-season rates range from about $600 a week for a two-bedroom home with a pool to about $3,500 for a six-bedroom home on the beach.

# Dining

Unlike many Caribbean islands, which have a scarcity of fresh produce and must rely on imports, Grenada has everything from cabbages and tomatoes to bananas, mangoes, papaya (called pawpaw), plantains, melons, callaloo (similar to spinach), breadfruit, oranges, tangerines, limes, christophines (similar to squash), and avocados—the list is endless. And all the dishes are enhanced by the wide range of spices grown here. Be sure to try one of the exotic ice creams made from guava or nutmeg.

Fresh seafood of all kinds, including lobster and oysters, is also plentiful. Conch, known here as *lambi,* is popular and appears on most menus in some form, often curried or as a stew. Almost all Grenadian restaurants have seafood on the menu and serve at least some native dishes.

Rum punches are served everywhere, but no two places make them exactly alike—except that nutmeg is always grated on top. Carib, the local beer, is also very popular and quite good.

## What to Wear

Dining in Grenada is a casual experience. Collared shirts and casual sundresses are apropos; even the fanciest restaurants don't require gentlemen to wear a jacket.

| CATEGORY | COST* |
| --- | --- |
| $$$ | over $40 |
| $$ | $20-$40 |
| $ | under $20 |

**per person, excluding drinks, service, and 8% government tax*

GRENADA

**$$$** ✕ **La Belle Creole.** Creative West Indian cuisine and a wraparound view
★ of Grand Anse are the claims to fame of this romantic hillside restau-
rant. The lunch and fixed-price dinner menus are always changing, but
reappearing favorites include Grenadian caviar (roe of the white sea
urchin), soursop mousse, and lobster-egg flan on the appetizer list and
entrées of baked stuffed rainbow runner, lobster à la Creole, and
callaloo quiche. On Sunday, a local band plays at the lunchtime pool-
side barbecue. The graciousness of the staff is bound to impress even
the most jaded traveler. ⊠ *Blue Horizons Cottage Hotel, Morne Rouge,
St. George's,* ☎ *809/444–4316. Reservations essential for nonhotel
guests. AE, MC, V.*

**$$$** ✕ **Le Bistro.** A touch of Paris in Grenada is the idea here. Located at
Ross Point, close to St. George's, the restaurant has beautiful views of
sparkling lights from both the harbor and Grand Anse. The fine French
cuisine created by owner Frederic DuBourg and chef Bruno Gallou will
make your mouth water. The à la carte menu might include fillet of
fish with finely minced *herbes de provence* or roast duck with Port wine
sauce. A special *menu dégustation,* allowing you to sample the chef's
specialties, is priced at $40. Le Bistro has only 40 seats. ⊠ *Ross Point,*
☎ *809/444–0191. AE, MC, V. Closed Sun.*

**$$$** ✕ **Canboulay.** Trinidadians Erik and Gina-Lee Johnson put Canboulay
★ on the map with their exciting reconfigurations of local cuisine. The
menu changes often, but regular items include crab crepes with a puree
of callaloo, breadfruit vichyssoise, grilled tuna steak with citrus-pep-
per sauce, African *bobotie* (spiced, raisin-studded ground beef topped
with a baked custard), and five-star versions of the ubiquitous *roti* (cur-
ried meat, potatoes, and beans wrapped in a giant tortilla) and nut-
meg ice cream. The frozen chocolate-mocha cheesecake has broken
hearts, and anything the Johnsons do with shrimp—coconut-beer-bat-
ter-it, or peanut-sauce-it—is memorable. Wednesday nights feature
fresh seafood specialties. Canboulay is high on a hill overlooking
Grand Anse, and the dining room's shutters open to hilltop breezes and
a grand view. ⊠ *Morne Rouge, St. George's,* ☎ *809/444–4401. Reser-
vations essential. AE, D, MC, V. Closed Sun. No lunch.*

**$$$** ✕ **Cicely's.** The open-air restaurant at the Calabash hotel, named for
award-winning chef Cicely Roberts, is small and pretty, surrounded
by palms and tropical flowers. The prix fixe dinner is a good deal; past
menus have included fillet of kingfish with roast potatoes, mixed vegetables, and fried plantains and chicken with ginger and chive sauce,
accompanied by a salad and cauliflower in mustard sauce. Cheese and
English-style biscuits with coffee, tea, or cocoa top off your meal.
There's nightly cabaret and piano entertainment. ⊠ *Prickly Bay,
L'Anse aux Epines,* ☎ *809/444–4234. AE, MC, V.*

**$$$** ✕ **Spice Island Inn.** Diners tend to dress for the five-course, fixed-price
★ evening meal at this open-air, hotel dining room (reservations for non-
hotel guests are limited). The ivy-hung terrace is separated from Grand
Anse beach by the narrowest of paths. Roast beef or calves' liver are
as likely to appear on the menu as local fare, of which the unlikely sound-
ing grapefruit consommé is a sublime example. Lobster usually appears
in some form, taking the title role at the Saturday "Seafood Night"
buffet, upstaged only by a dessert table loaded with pineapple pie, nut-
meg ice cream, chocolate truffle torte, and the like. Wednesday is
"Grenadian Night," when crab back, sea egg, roast suckling pig, and
all the trimmings are on the table, followed by dancing under the
stars. Fridays feature an equally festive barbecue and steel-band music.
⊠ *Grand Anse,* ☎ *809/444–4258 or 809/444–4423. Reservations es-
sential in season. AE, D, MC, V.*

**$$** ✕ **The Boatyard.** Embassy personnel and expatriates fill this lively restaurant, which sits smack in the middle of a marina. Burgers, fish-and-chips, and deep-fried shrimp are served at lunchtime. At dinner you may order club steaks, lobster, and different types of meat and seafood brochettes. In season there's a steel band on Saturday nights. ✉ *Spice Island Marina, L'Anse aux Epines,* ☎ *809/444–4662. MC, V. Closed Mon.*

**$$** ✕ **Coconut's Beach, the French Creole Restaurant.** Take local seafood, add butter, wine, and Grenadian herbs, and you have excellent French Creole cuisine. Throw in a beautiful setting at the northern end of Grand Anse Beach, and this West Indian cottage becomes a delightful spot for lunch or dinner. Lambi curry is a hit. Lobster is a specialty and may be wrapped in a crepe, dipped in garlic butter, or added to spaghetti. In season, there's a beach barbecue with live music each Wednesday, Friday, and Sunday night. It's open daily from 10 AM to 10 PM, and free transportation can be arranged. ✉ *Grand Anse Beach,* ☎ *809/444–4644. AE, MC, V.*

**$$** ✕ **The Nutmeg.** Fresh seafood, homemade West Indian dishes, great hamburgers, and the view of the harbor are reasons why local residents and visitors like The Nutmeg. It's on the second floor, and you can watch the harbor traffic through the large open windows as you eat. Try the grilled turtle steaks, lobster, or shrimp, or just stop by for a drink or a chicken roti. ✉ *The Carenage, St. George's,* ☎ *809/440–2539. AE, D, MC, V.*

**$$** ✕ **Red Crab.** Average, somewhat overpriced food hasn't kept this pub from being a favorite meeting and eating spot, especially on Saturday night. The curried lambi and shrimp crepes keep the regulars coming back. Seafood, particularly lobster, and steak are the staples of the menu; hot garlic bread comes with all orders. You can eat inside or under the trees and stars. There's live music Monday and Friday in season. ✉ *L'Anse aux Epines (near the Calabash),* ☎ *809/444–4424. AE, MC, V. Closed Sun.*

**$$** ✕ **Rudolf's.** This informal pub offers fine West Indian fare, as well as fish-and-chips, sandwiches, and burgers. Skip the attempts at haute cuisine "Viennoise" or "Parisienne," and enjoy the crab back, lambi, and delectable nutmeg ice cream. This is *the* place for eavesdropping on local gossip. Even for Grenada, the rum punches are lethal. It's open from 10 AM to midnight for lunch and dinner. ✉ *The Carenage, St. George's,* ☎ *809/440–2241. MC, V. Closed Sun.*

**$$** ✕ **Tabanca at Journey's End.** Alfresco dining on a terrace at the edge of the sea, with spectacular views of the Grand Anse waterfront and St. George's Harbour, is the lure for those wanting a touch of romance with their terrific seafood dinner. The fillet of kingfish topped with a poached egg wins raves, as does the fresh broiled grouper. Carib beer is on tap, and the special rum punch hits the spot. ✉ *Grand Anse Beach,* ☎ *809/444–1300. AE, D, DC, MC, V. Closed Tues. No lunch.*

**$** ✕ **La Boulangerie.** This French bakery and coffee shop, handy to the Grand Anse hotels, is a great place for breakfast or a light meal. You can order a French croissant, baguette, *pain au chocolat,* and other special breads and pastries. They also serve espresso, juices, sandwiches, and roasted chicken. It's open from 8 AM to 8 PM daily except Sunday, when it closes at 2 PM. ✉ *Le Marquis Shopping Complex, Grand Anse,* ☎ *809/444–1131. AE, MC, V.*

**$** ✕ **Cot Bam.** "Club on the Beach at Morne Rouge" is on Grand Anse Beach, next to the Coyaba Beach Resort and within walking distance of all the Grand Anse hotels. The casual atmosphere of this bar-restaurant-nightclub, with its tin roof and tile floor, makes it a great place to kick back and relax. It's open for breakfast, lunch, and dinner. Stroll in from the beach onto the outdoor terrace for a Carib beer and

a chicken roti with coleslaw. Or come in the evening for the special
lambi curry or other native dishes served inside at Papa Hall's Fine Creole Restaurant, and eat, dance, or chat the night away. ⊠ *Grand Anse,*
☎ *809/444–2050. AE.*

$  ✕ **Mamma's.** Mamma's has been a fixture for years. One of Mamma's
daughters will set generous helpings of local specialties before you—
roast turtle, lobster salad, callaloo soup, christophine salad, cabbage
salad, or fried plantain, as well as such exotica as *tatou* (armadillo),
*manicou* (opossum), and sea urchin. There is no menu. Some 21 native dishes are served family style at a fixed E.C.$45 per person. You
will not leave hungry. ⊠ *Lagoon Rd., St. George's,* ☎ *809/440–1459.
Reservations essential. No credit cards.*

$  ✕ **La Sagesse.** A perfect spot to soothe the most frazzled of souls, this
open-air restaurant and beach bar is on a secluded cove 20 minutes
from Grand Anse. Come for a swim, hike, and a meal—or just a meal!
Select from sandwiches, salads, or lobster for lunch. Lambi, smoked
marlin or dolphinfish, fillet of grouper, and tuna steak are joined on
the dinner menu by a daily vegetarian special. Entrées range from
E.C.$15 for a burger to E.C.$30 for lobster salad. Transportation to
and from your hotel is provided. ⊠ *La Sagesse Nature Center, St.
David's,* ☎ *809/444–6458. AE, MC, V.*

CARRIACOU

$  ✕ **Callaloo Restaurant & Bar.** Right on Main Street, this quaint restau-
rant has extraordinary views of Sandy Island and Hillsborough Bay.
Be sure to sample the callaloo soup. Excellent seafood dishes, including lobster thermidor, are reasonably priced. ⊠ *Hillsborough,* ☎
*809/443–8004. AE, MC, V. Closed Sept.*

$  ✕ **Scraper's.** Good things are happening at Tyrrel Bay. Scraper's serves
up lobster, conch, and an assortment of fresh catches, along with a simple spirit and decor seasoned with occasional calypsonian serenades
(owner Steven Gay "Scraper" is a pro). Order a rum punch and exercise your right to do nothing. ⊠ *Tyrrel Bay,* ☎ *809/443–7403. AE,
D, MC, V.*

## Beaches

Grenada has some 80 miles of coastline, 65 bays, and 45 white-sand
beaches—many in secluded little coves. All the beaches are public. Most
beaches are on the Caribbean, south of St. George's in the Grand Anse
and L'Anse aux Epines areas, where the majority of the hotels are also
clustered. Virtually every hotel, apartment complex, and residential area
has easy access to a beach or tiny cove.

**Grand Anse,** about a 10-minute ride from St. George's, is the loveliest and most popular beach on Grenada. It's a gleaming, 2-mile semi-
circle of sand lapped by clear, gentle Caribbean surf. Brilliant rainbows
frequently spill a spectrum of color into the aquamarine sea or the high
green mountains that frame St. George's Harbour to the north. Mature sea-grape trees provide shady areas to escape the midday sun. Vendors selling spices, palm hats and baskets, hair-braiding services,
T-shirts, and coral jewelry punctuate a day on this beach. These vendors are, for the most part, licensed, and their wares are worth a look.
**Morne Rouge Beach** is on the Caribbean, about 1 mile south of Grand
Anse Bay and 3 miles south of St. George's Harbour. The beach forms
a half-mile-long crescent and has a gentle surf that is excellent for swimming. A small café serves light meals during the day. In the evening,
there's a disco, Fantazia 2001 (☞ Nightlife, *below*).

# Outdoor Activities and Sports

## Bicycling

Level ground is rare in Grenada, but that doesn't stop the aerobically primed. What's more, 15-speed mountain bikes are available for a much more reasonable rate than are four-wheel-drive vehicles. You can rent bikes at **Ride Grenada** (L'Anse aux Epines, ☎ 809/444–1157). Caution: Roads are narrow and winding, and sharing lanes with fast-moving vehicles can be hazardous.

## Fishing

Deep-sea fishing around Grenada is excellent, with marlin, sailfish, yellowfin tuna, and dolphinfish topping the list of good catches. The annual **Spice Island Game Fishing Tournament** is held in late January. Half-day and full-day sportfishing excursions on *Xiphias Seeker,* a 35-foot Bertram Sport Fisherman, are available through **Evans Chartering Services** (☎ 809/444–4422 or 809/444–4217).

## Golf

**Grenada Golf and Country Club** (☎ 809/444–4128), near Grand Anse, has a nine-hole course and is open to visitors. Greens fees are E.C.$7. Your hotel will make arrangements for you.

## Jogging

At 4 PM on alternate Saturdays throughout the year, **Hash House Harriers** (☎ 809/440–3343) welcome not-so-serious runners and walkers for exercise and fun in the countryside.

## Sailing

**Moorings' Club Mariner Watersports Center** (☎ 809/444–4439 or 809/444–4549), at the Secret Harbour Hotel on the southeast shore, has half- and full-day charter yachts and a range of Shore 'n' Sail programs, developed by America's Cup racer Steve Colgate, for beginning and experienced sailors. **Seabreeze Yacht Charters** (☎ 809/444–4924; from the U.S., 800/387–3998) at the Spice Island Marine Centre rents sailing or power yachts, with or without crew. **Starwind Enterprise** (☎ 809/440–3678 or 809/440–2508) offers day, half-day, and sunset sailing trips along Grenada's southwest coast.

## Scuba Diving and Snorkeling

Diving in this area is excellent, with visibility as far as 200 feet. Hundreds of varieties of fish and more than 40 species of coral await underwater explorers. The best snorkeling is found around Carriacou's offshore islands. A superb spot for scuba diving is at the site of what is sometimes dubbed the *Titanic* of the Caribbean. The *Bianca C,* a 600-foot cruise ship that caught fire and sank in 1961, settled in waters more than 100 feet deep and is now home to giant turtles, spotted eagle rays with 15-foot wingspans, and a 350-pound grouper that lives in the ship's smokestack.

**Dive Grenada** (✉ At Cot Bam on Grand Anse Beach and the Calabash Hotel at Lance aux Epines, ☎ 809/444–1092 or 809/444–5875 in the evening, ℻ 809/440–6699) offers scuba and snorkeling trips to reefs and shipwrecks, including night dives and special excursions to the *Bianca C.* PADI-certified diving instruction, ranging from a resort course for novices to a dive master program, is available. **Grand Anse Aquatics, Ltd.** (✉ At Coyaba Beach Resort on Grand Anse Beach, ☎ 809/444–4129) offers scuba and snorkeling trips and diving instruction, including resort courses for novices. Single dives are $45; *Bianca C* dives, $60; snorkeling trips, $20. **SCUBA World** (✉ At Rex Grenadian Resort in Point Salines, ☎ 809/444-3333, ext. 584; ✉ Grenada Renaissance Resort on Grand Anse Beach, ☎ 809/444–4371, ext. 638;

⊠ Secret Harbour Resort, ☎ 809/444–4504) offers professional instruction to beginners and advanced divers alike, has a complete inventory of modern equipment, and runs daily excursions to the best dive sites on Grenada. **Silver Beach Diving** (⊠ On Carriacou near Hillsborough, ☎ 809/443–7882) is a fully equipped, PADI-certified dive center. Dive trips, including night dives, visit Carriacou's virgin reefs, spectacular underwater walls, and mysterious caves. **Tanki's Watersport Paradise, Ltd.** (⊠ On L'Esterre Bay, ☎ 809/443–8406) offers scuba diving at more than 20 sites, including trips to Sandy Island. Night dives can be arranged.

## Tennis

Several hotels have tennis courts that are free to their guests: **Calabash** (☎ 809/444–4234), **Secret Harbour** (☎ 809/444–4548), **Coyaba Beach Resort** (☎ 809/444–4129), **Spice Island Inn** (☎ 809/444–4258), **Grenada Renaissance** (☎ 809/444–4371), **Coral Cove** (☎ 809/444–4217), **La Source** (☎ 809/444–2556), **Rex Grenadian** (☎ 809/444–3333), and **Twelve Degrees North** (☎ 809/444–4580). Visitors may also play on public courts in Grand Anse and at the Tanteen Tennis Club courts in St. George's. Your hotel desk clerk can contact them for you.

## Triathlon

Each January, triathletes from around the world compete in Grenada's annual **International Triathlon.** The two-day competition starts and finishes at Grand Anse Beach. Participants compete in a 1.5-kilometer swim, a 25-kilometer cycling race, and a 5-kilometer run on the first day. A three-person relay takes place on the second day. Teams must include at least one female and have a combined age of at least 100 years.

## Water Sports

The major hotels on Grand Anse Beach have water-sports centers where you can rent small sailboats, Windsurfers, and Sunfish. The centers are located on the beach in front of the hotels. Your hotel can make arrangements for you, or you can call one of the major hotels for information.

# Shopping

The best souvenirs of Grenada are little spice baskets filled with cinnamon, nutmeg, mace, bay leaf, vanilla, turmeric, and ginger. You can buy them for as little as $2 in practically every shop, at the market, or from vendors who stroll the beach in Grand Anse. Beach vendors also sell fabric dolls, T-shirts, coral jewelry, seashells, and hats and baskets woven from green palm fronds.

## Good Buys

ST. GEORGE'S

**Art Fabrik** (⊠ Young St., ☎ 809/440–0568) is a batik studio, where you can watch artisans create the designs by painting fabric with hot wax. The dyeing room is on the first floor; as likely as not, you'll see lengths of batik hanging out to dry in the courtyard. You can buy batik by the yard ($22–$27, depending on the width) or fashioned into dresses, shirts, shorts, hats, scarves, and more. **Gifts Remembered** (⊠ Cross St., ☎ 809/440–2482; ⊠ Coyaba Beach Resort, ☎ 809/444–4129) is crammed with wonderful, inexpensive stuff, including brightly painted ceramic boats and buses laden with fruit and smiling islanders, interesting T-shirts, hand-painted masks made from calabash halves, spices, and sundries. **Marketing & National Importing Board** (⊠ Young St., ☎ 809/440–1791) stocks fresh fruits and vegetables, spices, hot sauces, molasses, nutmeg, and other local food products. **The open-air mar-**

**ket** (⊠ Market Sq., no phone) is open weekday mornings, but Saturday morning is the best—and busiest—time to go. Vendors sell fruits and vegetables from their own gardens, coconut water, and spices—a feast for the eyes as well as for the stomach. You'll also find clothing, leather sandals, and handcrafted items for sale. **Spice Island Perfumes** (⊠ On the Carenage, ☎ 809/440–2006) is a treasure trove of local perfumes, body oils, and natural extracts of spices and herbs. Best of all are its tiny wooden pots of solid fragrances, including bitter orange, jasmine, or spice for around $8. **Tikal** (⊠ Young St., ☎ 809/440–2310), a long-established boutique, is well known for its exquisite handicrafts, baskets, artwork, jewelry, carvings, batik items, and fashions, both locally made and imported from Africa and Latin America. **Turbo Charge Records & Tapes** (⊠ St. John's St., ☎ 809/440–0586) is where to go for the latest reggae, calypso, soca, and steel-band music. **White Cane Industries** (⊠ At far end of the Carenage, ☎ 809/444–2014) stocks bargain baskets, hats, and spectacularly colored rag rugs, all handwoven locally by blind craftspeople. Credit cards are not accepted here. **Yellow Poui Art Gallery** (⊠ At intersection of Cross St. and the Esplanade, ☎ 809/440–3001), displays artwork from Grenada, Jamaica, Trinidad, and Guyana and canvases by expatriate British, German, and French artists.

GRAND ANSE

**Gift Shop** (⊠ Grand Anse Shopping Centre, ☎ 809/444–4408) is an outlet for imported luxury items such as watches, leather goods, fine jewelry, crystal, and china, at duty-free prices. **Imagine** (⊠ Grand Anse Shopping Centre, ☎ 809/444–4028) specializes in island handicrafts, including batik fabrics. **United Artists Art Gallery** (⊠ Le Marquis Complex, ☎ 809/444–5022) displays a unique collection of top-quality artwork. You'll find wood and stone carvings, painted masks, paintings, furniture, and other objets d'art created by artists from Grenada, Carriacou, and Petit Martinique.

CARRIACOU

In L'Esterre on Carriacou, hand-painted signs announce "This way to the great artist," **Canute Calliste.** If you get lost, one of his many (more than 20) grandchildren will lead the way. Works by Calliste, colorful watercolors of island scenes, are also available at the Carriacou Museum.

# Nightlife

Grenada's nightlife is centered mainly on the resort hotels. During winter, Spice Island Inn, the Calabash, Coyaba, Rex Grenadian, and the Grenada Renaissance have steel band or other entertainment several nights of each week (☞ Lodging, *above*). Your hotel or the tourist information office will have information about where various bands are performing on a given night.

**Beachside Terrace** (⊠ Flamboyant Hotel, Grand Anse, ☎ 809/444–4247) is casual and unpretentious and draws an international set for crab racing on Monday nights, a live steel band on Wednesdays, and a beach barbecue with calypso music on Friday evenings. **Boatyard** (⊠ Prickly Bay, L'Anse aux Epines, ☎ 809/444–4662), at the Marina, is the place to be on Friday night from 11 PM till sun up, when international discs are spun by a smooth-talkin' local DJ. **Cot Bam** (⊠ Grand Anse Beach, ☎ 809/444–2050) hits the spot for visitors who want something simple, lively, and friendly for little money. Dancing, dining, and socializing take place nightly. The place is open until 3 AM on Friday and Saturday. **Fantazia 2001** (⊠ Gem Apartments premises, Morne Rouge, ☎ 809/444–4224 or 809/444–1189) is a popular disco on the beach, where soca and reggae are played, along with international favorites, from 9:30 PM until the wee hours. Wednesday is Golden Oldie's Night. It's dark and loud and fun, with a mix of locals and tourists. Transportation is available. There is a small cover charge (E.C.$5) on Friday and Saturday nights. **Hillsborough Bar** (⊠ Carriacou, ☎ 809/443–7932) is a small, white, flat-topped structure on the main street of the island's seat of government, a town populated by no more than about 600 citizens, including owner Edward Primus. Brave the twin otter (small airplane) to Carriacou, then buy yourself a drink—the rum flows freely. **Rhum Runner** (⊠ On the Carenage, St. George's, ☎ 809/440–2198), a 60-foot twin-deck catamaran, leaves from the fire station jetty at 7:30 PM each Friday and Saturday night for a moonlit cruise in the waters around St. George's and Grand Anse, returning about midnight. Tickets are E.C.$20, and reservations are recommended. **Rhum Runner II**, a 72-foot sister ship, operates sunset dinner cruises on Wednesday evenings from 6 to 9 PM. Enjoy a buffet dinner, steel-band music, and unlimited free bar for $40 per person. Transportation from hotels is provided. **Le Sucrier** (⊠ Sugar Mill, Grand Anse, ☎ 800/444–1068) is open on Wednesday, Thursday, Friday, and Saturday from 9 PM to 3 AM and attracts a young crowd with local comedy and a disco on Thursday and "oldies" night on Wednesday.

## Exploring Grenada

It may be hard to pull yourself away from the beach to see the rest of this lovely island, but a day or so of exploring is worth the effort. St. George's is a picturesque capital city, with a busy harbor, interesting shops, and several historic sites. A trip into the countryside and a visit to a spice plantation and a nutmeg processing plant will help you see what makes Grenada tick. Along the scenic coast road, you're likely to come across a group of strapping young fishermen in a tug-of-war with the sea, pulling in an enormous fishing net; it's an all-day job, and a share of the catch is the reward. Passing through tiny villages, you'll receive waves from locals perched on the verandas of colorful cottages, and see women carrying baskets of laundry on their heads. A guide can take more adventurous sightseers hiking into the thick of the rain forest or for a swim under a waterful in lush, Eden-like surroundings. Touring Grendada is a treat for the senses—the scenery is eye-popping, and the scent of nutmeg fills the air.

Carriacou, Petit Martinique, and a handful of uninhabited specks that are included in the nation of Grenada are north of Grenada island and part of the Grenadines, an archipelago of 32 tiny islands and cays. You can fly into Carriacou's Lauriston Airport from Grenada or come by sea. Schooners leave from St. George's Harbour twice a week, ferrying cargo and passengers on a 4½-hour voyage.

*Numbers in the margin correspond to points of interest on the Grenada (and Carriacou) map.*

SIGHTS TO SEE

**⑥ Annandale Falls and Visitors' Centre.** A mountain stream cascades 50 feet into a pool surrounded by exotic tropical flora, such as liana vines and elephant ears. This is a good spot for swimming and picnicking. ⊠ *Main interior road, 15 mins east of St. George's,* ☎ *809/440–2452.* ☉ *Daily 9–5.*

**③ Bay Gardens.** Just outside St. George's is a private horticultural paradise where 450 species of flowers and plants that grow on the island are cultivated in patterns mimicking their growth in the wild. Eight acres of paths are open to visitors. Bay Gardens is in the suburb of St. Paul's, a short drive into the countryside from town. Taxi drivers and tour guides know the way. ✉ *St. Paul's,* 🔳 *$1.* ☉ *Daily during daylight hrs.*

⓫ **Carib's Leap.** At Sauteurs (the French word for leapers), at the north-ernmost tip of the island, Carib's Leap (also called Leapers Hill) is the 100-foot cliff from which Carib Indians flung themselves in 1651, pre-ferring to die rather than submit to the French invaders.

⓮ **Carriacou.** This little island (13 square miles) packs a lot of punch—rum punch, that is! With more than a hundred rum shops and only one gas station, Carriacou will bring the fastest metabolism down to a quiet purr. This island hideaway exudes the kind of ebullient spirit and goodwill that you want to find in a Caribbean retreat but usually find only in a travel brochure. Come here if you want peace. Don't bother if you want luxurious amenities or if you would suffer coldly a parrot on your breakfast table!

Hillsborough is Carriacou's main town. Rolling hills cut a wide swath through the island's center, from Gun Point in the north to Tyrrel Bay in the south. In February, fun lovers are drawn to Carriacou for Car-nival festivities. In August, the **Carriacou Regatta**—the largest sail-ing event in the Grenadines—attracts yachts and sailboats from throughout the Caribbean for three days of races between Grenada and Carriacou. The annual event has been celebrated for more than three decades. Festivities include cultural activities and Big Drum dance performances.

Carriacou's colonial past parallels Grenada's, although its tiny size has restricted its political role to a minor part in the area's history. The only museum in the eastern Caribbean that is owned by the people, not the government, is the **Carriacou Museum** (✉ Paterson St., Hillsborough), located in Hillsborough behind Gramma's Bakery. Housed in an old cotton ginnery, it has displays of unearthed Amerindian, European, and African artifacts and features a gift shop loaded with locally made items. The museum is open daily 9:30–4; admission is $2.

**Sandy Island,** just offshore opposite Silver Beach Resort, is a gorgeous spot of sand punctuated by a stand of palm trees. For a few dollars, a local fellow with a motorboat will transport you back and forth. Bring your snorkeling gear.

❽ **Concord Falls.** The coast road north from St. George's winds past soar-ing mountains and valleys covered with banana and breadfruit trees, palms, bamboo, and tropical flowers. Off the road, about 8 miles north of St. George's, are the Concord Falls, with a small visitor cen-ter, a viewing platform, and a changing room for donning a bathing suit. During the dry months, when the currents aren't too strong, you can take a dip under the cascades. If you're up to it, hike 2 miles through tropical forest to a second, spectacular waterfall which thunders down over huge boulders and creates a small swimming pool. The path is clear, but it's smart to use a guide. The boulders, as well as the path, are slippery as you get close to the falls, and maneuvering can be tricky. ✉ *Coast Rd.* 🔳 *$1 for changing room.*

❾ **Dougaldston Estate.** Just south of Gouyave, this estate has a spice fac-tory where you can see cocoa, nutmeg, mace, cloves, cinnamon, and other spices laid out on giant racks to dry in the sun. One of the work-ers will be glad to explain the process. You can purchase a bag of cin-namon bark, cloves, bay leaves, mace, or nutmeg for about $2 each. ✉ *Gouyave, no phone.* 🔳 *$1.* ☉ *Weekdays 9–4.*

❷ **Grand Anse.** Most of the island's hotels and nightlife are in Grand Anse or the adjacent community of L'Anse aux Epines, which means Cove of Pines. St. George's University Medical School, located directly on Grand Anse Beach, is sandwiched between Spice Island Inn and Coyaba Beach Resort. Rumor has it that the university is planning to vacate this prime location, consolidating the school at its facility in True Blue, a residential area set in a picturesque cove, so-named because it used to be an indigo plantation.

A short walk from the resorts of Grand Anse is the **Grand Anse Shopping Centre,** which includes a supermarket/liquor store, clothing store, bank, fast-food restaurant, and several small gift shops with good-quality souvenirs and such luxury items as English china and Swedish crystal. The **Marquis Complex,** across the street, has restaurants, shops, an art gallery, and tourist services (☞ Shopping, *above*).

**❼ Grand Etang National Park.** In the middle of lush, mountainous Grenada is a bird sanctuary and forest reserve, with miles of hiking trails and streams for fishing. Visit the informative Welcome Center to view displays on the local flora and fauna. A forest manager is on hand to answer questions. Crater Lake, in the crater of an extinct volcano, is a 13-acre glasslike expanse of cobalt blue water. ⊠ *Main interior road, between Grenville and St. George's,* ☎ *809/440–6160.* 🎟 *$1.* ⊙ *Daily 8:30–4.*

**❺ Grenville.** The island's second-largest city is reminiscent of a French market town. Saturday is market day, and the town fills with local people doing their weekly shopping. Schooners set sail from Grenville for the outer islands. The local spice-processing factory is open to the public.

**⓬ Levera National Park and Bird Sanctuary.** This portion of Grenada's protected parkland encompasses 450 acres at the northeastern tip of the island, where the Caribbean Sea meets the Atlantic Ocean. Facilities include a visitor center, changing rooms, a small amphitheater, and a gift shop. The first islet of the Grenadines is visible in the distance. The thick mangroves provide food and protection for nesting seabirds and seldom-seen tropical parrots. Some fine Arawak ruins and petroglyphs can be seen, as well.

**⓾ Nutmeg Processing Cooperative.** Gouyave is the center of Grenada's nutmeg industry. A tour of the Nutmeg Processing Cooperative in the center of town makes a fragrant and fascinating half hour. Workers in the three-story plant, which turns out 3 million pounds of Grenada's most famous export per year, sort nutmegs by hand and pack them in burlap bags for shipping world-wide. ⊠ *Gouyave, no phone.* 🎟 *$1.* ⊙ *Weekdays 10–1 and 2–4.*

NEED A
BREAK?

**Mount Rodney Estate** (☎ 809/442–9420), just 1 mile from Sauteurs, was built in the 1870s and has a magnificent view of the Grenadines. Lunches are served in the breezy gazebo on weekdays from noon to 3 PM. Afterward, take a leisurely tour of the home and 6 acres of gardens. Reservations are essential, as lunch is limited to 30 guests per day.

**⓯ Petit Martinique.** Five miles northeast of Carriacou is Petit Martinique, the smallest of Grenada's inhabited islands. Like Carriacou and Grenada, Petit Martinique was settled by the French. Most visitors to Petit Martinique come on fishing trips; the island does not really have tourist facilities.

**⓭ River Antoine Rum Distillery.** At this local operation, which is kept open primarily as a museum, rum is produced by the same methods used since the distillery opened in the mid-1700s. The result is a potent over-proof rum that will knock your socks off! ⊠ *River Antoine Estate, St. Patrick's.* ⊠ *Free.* ⊙ *Guided tours daily 9–4.*

**❶** **St. George's.** Grenada's capital city and major port is one of the most picturesque and authentic West Indian towns in the Caribbean. Pastel-painted buildings with orange-tile roofs cling to the curving shore along horseshoe-shape **St. George's Harbor.** Small, rainbow-color houses rise up from the waterfront and disappear into steep green hills. On weekends, a windjammer is likely to be anchored in the harbor, giving the entire scene a 19th-century appearance.

**The Carenage,** the road and walkway around St. George's Harbor, is the capital's main thoroughfare. Warehouses, small shops, and restaurants face the water. At the southern side of the Carenage, near the Grenada Board of Tourism office, is the pier where cruise ships dock. **Young Street,** a steep up-and-down hill that also is a main shopping street, starts at the northern side of the Carenage and descends to the marketplace.

The **Grenada National Museum,** (⊠ Young and Monckton Sts., ☎ 809/440–3725), a couple of blocks off the Carenage, is set in the foundation of an old French army barracks and prison built in 1704. The small museum has exhibits of news items, photos, and proclamations regarding the intervention, along with memorabilia depicting various other periods in Grenada's history—replicas of posters advertising the sale of "slaves . . . of good character," the young Josephine Bonaparte's marble bathtub, 18th-century rum-making equipment, shells and artifacts, and a Miss World 1970 portrait. The museum is open weekdays 9–4:30 and Saturday 10–1:30; admission is $1.

On the bay side of St. George's, facing the sea and separated from the harbor by the Sendall Tunnel, the **Esplanade** is the location of the open-air meat and fish markets. At high tide, waves sometimes crash against the seawall. This area is also the terminus of the minibus route.

Don't miss picturesque **Market Square,** a block from the Esplanade at Granby Street. It's open weekday mornings but really comes alive Saturdays from 8 AM to noon. The scene is colorful, noisy, and exciting. Vendors sell baskets, spices, brooms, clothing, knickknacks, coconut water, and fresh produce, including tropical fruit you can eat on the spot. Market Square is also where parades and political rallies take place—and the beginning of the minibus routes to outer areas of the island.

St. George's has several fine old churches that are worth visiting. **St. Andrew's Presbyterian Church,** built in 1830, is at the intersection of Halifax and Church streets. Also known as Scots' Kirk, it was built with the help of the Freemasons. **St. George's Anglican Church,** on Gore Street, was built in 1828. It's a beautiful stone and pink stucco building filled with statues and plaques depicting Grenada in the 18th and 19th centuries. **St. George's Methodist Church,** on Green Street near Tyrrel Street, was built in 1820 and is the oldest original church in the city. The tower of **St. George's Roman Catholic Church** dates from 1818, but the current church building was built in 1884.

On Church Street, **York House,** built around 1800, is home to Grenada's Houses of Parliament and Supreme Court. It and the neighboring Registry building, built in 1780, are fine examples of early Georgian architecture.

**Marryshow House** (⊠ Tyrrel St., near Bain Alley, ☎ 809/440–2451), built in 1917, combines Victorian and West Indian architecture. It's home to the Marryshow Folk Theatre, Grenada's first cultural center. Plays, West Indian dance and music, and poetry readings are presented here on occasion. The house is open weekdays 8:30–4:30 and Saturday 9–1; admission is free.

**Fort George** (✉ Church St., no phone) is high on the hill at the southern tip of Church Street. The fort, rising above the entrance to the harbor, was built by the French in 1705 to defend the harbor. No shots were ever fired from the fort until October 1983, when Prime Minister Maurice Bishop and some of his followers were assassinated in the courtyard. The fort now houses Grenada's police headquarters but is open to the public daily during daylight hours; admission is free. The 360-degree view from here is spectacular.

On Richmond Hill, high above St. George's and the harbor, historic **Fort Frederick** provides a magnificent view. The fort was completed in 1791; it was the headquarters of the People's Revolutionary Government during the infamous intervention of 1983. Today, visitors can get a bird's-eye view of the prison, on top of an adjacent hill, where the perpetrators of that event are incarcerated.

In St. Paul's, five minutes outside St. George's, **de la Grenade Industries** (✉ Box 788, St. George's, ☎ 809/440–3241) is a local spice-processing plant that began in 1960 as a small cottage industry and today manufacturers award-winning products made from nutmeg and other homegrown fruits and spices: syrups, jams and jellies, and liqueur. Visitors are welcome to watch the process—each day it may be a different product—and purchase gift items from the small retail operation on site. The plant is open weekdays 8–5 and Saturday 9–12:30; admission is free.

❹ **Westerhall.** This residential area about 5 miles southeast of St. George's is known for its beautiful villas, gardens, and panoramic views. A great deal of pricey development is happening here: European and North American retirees and local business people are building elegant homes with striking views of the sea.

## Grenada A to Z

### Arriving and Departing

#### BY PLANE

**American Airlines** (☎ 800/433–7300 or 809/444–2222) has daily flights into Grenada's Point Salines International Airport from major U.S. and Canadian cities via its San Juan hub. **BWIA** (☎ 800/327–7401, 800/538–2942 in Miami, or 809/444–4134) flies direct from New York and Miami. **Air Canada** (☎ 800/776–3000) flies from Toronto via Barbados. **British Airways** (☎ 800/247–9297 or 809/440–2796) flies from London twice a week.

**LIAT** (Leeward Islands Air Transport, ☎ 809/440–2796 or 809/440–2796), **Carib Express** (☎ 809/444–3549), **Region Air** (☎ 809/444–1117), **Airlines of Carriacou** (☎ 809/444–3549 or 809/444–1479), and **HelenAir** (809/444–4101, ext. 2090) each have scheduled service between Grenada and Carriacou's Lauriston Airport and also serve various other Caribbean islands. Renovations to Carriacou's Lauriston Airport, completed in late 1994, included expanding the runway and adding lights for night landings.

#### FROM THE AIRPORT

No bus service is available between the Point Salines airport and hotels, but taxis are readily available. Fares to St. George's and the hotels of Grand Anse and L'Anse aux Epines are $10–$12. Rides taken between 6 PM and 6 AM incur a $2.50 surcharge. From Carriacou's Lauriston Airport to Hillsborough, the fare is $2.50.

## Currency

Grenada uses the Eastern Caribbean (E.C.) dollar. At press time, the exchange rate was fixed at E.C.$2.67 to U.S.$1. Money can be exchanged at any bank or hotel. U.S. currency and traveler's checks are widely accepted. Prices are usually quoted in E.C. dollars, but be sure to ask which currency is referred to when you make purchases and business transactions. Hotels are unable by law to give foreign currency in change or on departure. Most hotels, major restaurants, and shops accept credit cards.

## Emergencies

**Police and fire:** ☎ 911. **Ambulance:** In St. George's, Grand Anse, and L'Anse aux Epines, ☎ 434. In St. Andrew's, ☎ 724. For other areas, check with your hotel. **Hospitals:** St. George's Hospital (☎ 809/440–2051); St. Andrew's Hospital (☎ 809/442–7251); Carriacou Hospital (☎ 809/443–7400). **Pharmacies: Gitten's** (✉ Halifax St., St. George's, ☎ 809/440–2165; after hrs 809/440–2340) is open weekdays and Saturday 9–8, Sunday and public holidays 9–noon. **Gitten's Drugmart** (✉ Main Rd., Grand Anse, ☎ 809/444–4954; after hrs 809/440–2340) is open weekdays and Saturday 9–8, Sunday and public holidays 9–noon. **Parris' Pharmacy Ltd.** (✉ Victoria St., Grenville, ☎ 809/442–7330), on the windward side of the island, is open Monday–Wednesday and Friday 9–4:30, Thursday 9–1, and Saturday 9–7.

## Getting Around

### BUSES

Privately owned 15-passenger minivans ply the winding road between St. George's and Grand Anse Beach, where many of the hotels are located. Hail one anywhere along the way, pay E.C.$1, and hold on to your hat. They pass by frequently from about 6 AM to 8 PM daily except Sundays and public holidays. You can get anywhere on the island via these minivans for E.C.$1–E.C.$5 per person—a bargain by any standard—but be prepared for packed vehicles, unpredictable schedules, and some hair-raising maneuvers on mountainous roads and byways.

### CARS

Roads are mountainous and winding once you get beyond the Grand Anse area, and driving is to the left (English style). To rent a car, you will need a valid driver's license with which you may obtain a local permit from the traffic department (at the fire station on the Carenage) or some car-rental firms at a cost of E.C.$30. Rental cars cost $45–$60 a day or $220–$285 a week with unlimited mileage. A Jeep or automatic-drive car runs about $60 a day and $285 a week. Gas costs about $2.60 per gallon. Your hotel can arrange a rental for you.

Car-rental agencies in St. George's are numerous. **David's** (☎ 809/444–3399 or 809/444–3038, FAX 809/444–4404) maintains four offices: Point Salines International Airport, Grenada Renaissance Resort, Rex Grenadian Hotel, and the Limes in Grand Anse. **Dollar Rent-a-Car** (☎ 809/444–4786, FAX 809/444–4788) is at Point Salines Airport. **Avis** (☎ 809/440–3936 or 809/440–2624, FAX 809/440–4110; after hours ☎ 809/444–4563) is at Spice Isle Rental on Paddock and Lagoon roads in St. George's. In the True Blue area, call **McIntyre Bros. Ltd.** (☎ 809/444–3944 or 809/440–2901, FAX 809/444–2899; after hours ☎ 809/443–5319).

### TAXIS

Taxis are plentiful and rates are set by the government. The trip between Grand Anse and St. George's costs about E.C.$20. An E.C.$10 surcharge is added to all fares for rides taken between 6 PM and 6 AM. Taxis are often waiting for fares at hotels, at the cruise passenger Welcome Center, and on the Carenage.

## Guided Tours

On at least one day of your stay in Grenada, be sure to get off the beach and out into the countryside to experience the magnificent scenery that nature has bestowed on this island. Guided tours regularly take individuals or small groups on sightseeing excursions in and around St. George's, to Grand Etang National Park, to spice plantations in Gouyave, hiking in the rain forest, and on day trips to Carriacou.

TOUR OPERATORS

**Amerindian Tours** (☎ 809/440–9686) offers interesting and innovative tours of Grenada's waterfalls, spice plantations, old forts, and historical sites. **Arnold's Tours** (☎ 809/440–0531 or 809/440–2213, FAX 809/440–4118) offers several land, sea, and "Lan-Sea" combination tours. Prices typically range from $25 for an island tour, hiking trip, or sunset cruise to $140 for an all-day cruise to Carriacou. Dennis Henry of **Henry's Safari Tours** (☎ 809/444–5313, FAX 809/444–4847) knows Grenada like the back of his hand. He offers a program of adventurous hikes and Jeep safaris, or you can design your own tour. Depending on the size of the group, a full-day island tour, including lunch, costs $40–$55 per person; a six-hour hike to Concord Falls is $30–$45 per person. **Spiceland Tours** (☎ 809/440–5180) offers several five- and seven-hour island tours, from an "Urban/Suburban" tour of St. George's and the South Coast to an "Emerald Forest Tour" highlighting Grenada's natural beauty. Some other reputable operators who offer similar guided tours are **Sunshine Tours** (☎ 809/444–4296), **Sunsation Tours** (☎ 809/444–1594), and **Caribbean Horizons** (☎ 809/444–1555).

## Language

English is the official language of Grenada.

## Opening and Closing Times

Stores are generally open from 8 AM–4 or 4:30 PM weekdays, 8 AM–1 PM on Saturday. Most are closed Sunday. Banks in St. George's are open Monday–Thursday 8 AM–1:30 or 2 PM, Friday 8 AM–5 PM. The main post office, on Lagoon Road in St. George's, is open 8 AM–3:30 PM weekdays.

## Passports and Visas

Passports are not required of U.S., Canadian, or British citizens, provided visitors have two proofs of citizenship (one with photo) and a return air ticket. A passport, even an expired one, is the best proof of citizenship. A driver's license with photo *and* an original birth certificate or voter registration card will also suffice.

The **U.S. Embassy** (☎ 809/444–1173 or 809/444–1179) is located in Point Salines. The **British High Commission** (☎ 809/440–3536) is at 14 Church Street, in St. George's.

## Precautions

Secure your valuables in the hotel safe. Avoid walking alone late at night in the Grand Anse/L'Anse aux Epines hotel districts; it's dark enough to bump into things, maybe even into one of the cows that graze silently by the roadside in Grand Anse. Starving mosquitoes adore tourists, especially after heavy rains, and on the beach, tiny sand fleas begin to bite after 4 PM; bring repellent.

## Taxes and Service Charges

Hotels and restaurants add an 8% government tax. Many hotels and restaurants add an additional 10% service charge to your bill. If not, a 10%–15% gratuity should be added for a job well done.

The departure tax is E.C.$35 for adults and E.C.$17.50 for children ages 5 to 11. Children under five are exempt. A surcharge of E.C.$10 is levied when departing Carriacou.

## Telephones and Mail

Grenada can be dialed directly from the United States and Canada. The area code is 809. Long-distance calls from Grenada can be dialed directly from pay phones and most hotel rooms, as well.

Airmail rates for letters to the United States and Canada are E.C.75¢ for a half-ounce letter and E.C.35¢ for a postcard.

## Visitor Information

The **Grenada Board of Tourism** (☎ 809/440–2001, FAX 809/440–6637) office—located on the south side of the Carenage, in St. George's — distributes maps, brochures, and information on accommodations, tours, and other services.

For information before leaving home, contact the **Grenada Board of Tourism** in the United States (✉ 820 2nd Ave., Suite 900D, New York, NY 10017, ☎ 212/687–9554 or 800/927–9554, FAX 212/573–9731), in Canada (✉ Suite 820, 439 University Ave., Toronto, Ontario M5G 1Y8, ☎ 416/595–1339, FAX 416/595–8278), or in the United Kingdom (✉ 1 Collingham Gardens, Earl's Court, London SW5 0HW, ☎ 0171/370–5164 or 0171/370–5165, FAX 0171/370–7040).

Hotel reservations may be made at any of the hotels that are members of the **Grenada Hotel Association** by calling 800/223–9815 in the United States or Canada, 212/545–8469 in New York State.

# 13 Guadeloupe

Updated by
Simon Worrall

**I**T'S A STEAMY HOT SATURDAY in August. There may be a tropical depression brewing somewhere to the west—it's that time of year. But the mood in Pointe-à-Pitre, Guadeloupe's commercial center, is anything but depressing. Amid music and laughter, women adorned with gold jewelry and dressed in clothes made of the traditional madras and foulard parade through the streets. Balanced on their heads are huge baskets decorated with miniature kitchen utensils and filled with mangoes, papayas, breadfruits, christophines, and other island edibles. The procession wends its way to the Cathédrale de St-Pierre et St-Paul, where a high mass is celebrated. A five-hour feast with music, song, and dance will follow.

The Fête des Cuisinières (Cooks' Festival) takes place annually in honor of St. Laurent, patron saint of cooks. The parading *cuisinières* are the island's women chefs, an honored group. This festival gives you a tempting glimpse of one of Guadeloupe's stellar attractions—its cuisine. The island's more than 200 restaurants serve some of the best food in the Caribbean.

But there is more here than meets the palate. Night owls and nature enthusiasts, hikers and bikers, scuba divers, sailors, mountain climbers, beachcombers, and hammock potatoes all can indulge themselves in Guadeloupe.

An old saying of the French Caribbean refers to *"Les Grands Seigneurs de la Martinique et les Bons Gens de la Guadeloupe"* (the lords of Martinique and the bourgeoisie of Guadeloupe). And though there are few aristocrats left on Martinique these days, the saying still holds some truth in Guadeloupe. Look about you in the restaurants or at the beach, and you will see the faces of middle-class France. They come here to swim and sunbathe, to scuba dive and sightsee. Most come on package tours. But sugar, not tourism, is still Guadeloupe's primary source of income. Currently, only about 10% of the workforce is employed in the tourism industry. At harvesttime in January, the fields teem with workers cutting cane and the roads are clogged with trucks taking the harvest to distilleries.

During *la saison,* roads are clogged with zippy little cars ferrying scantily clad Parisians to *le beach.* Everything about Guadeloupe—from the ubiquitous franglais (*le topless, le weekend, le snack-bar*) to the yellow car headlights, helter-skelter driving, and joie de vivre—is French, through and through. If you are sensitive to cigarette smoke, be forewarned: Whether in the hotel corridors or on the beach, at breakfast or on a dive boat, cigarette smoke is as much a part of the ambience as the tropical breeze. Efforts have been made in recent years to teach hotel and restaurant staff some rudimentary English, but to really feel at home here, some *français* is indispensable. Even then, you will sometimes receive a bewildered response, as the Guadeloupeans' Creole patois greatly affects their pronunciation.

Columbus "discovered" Guadeloupe on November 4, 1493, when he landed at Ste-Marie on the southern shore of Basse-Terre. He named the island for Santa Marie de Guadeloupe de Estremadura. The Carib inhabitants, who had already polished off the peaceful Arawaks, had no intention of relinquishing the land they called Karukéra (Island of Beautiful Waters), and the Spaniards gave up on the island in 1604. In 1635, the French laid claim to it. They ran the Caribs off and brought in African slaves to work their sugar plantations, and in 1674 Guadeloupe was annexed by France. During the French Revolution, battles

Chez Jackye, **44**
Chez Violetta-
La Creole, **63**
Le Corsaire, **69**
Le Côte Jardin, **59**
El Dorado, **50**
L'Endroit, **71**
Le Flibustier, **72**
Folie Plage, **86**
Les Gommiers, **45**
La Grande Pizzeria, **58**
Le Karacoli, **42**
La Louisiane, **83**
Nilce's Bar, **54**
Les Oiseaux, **75**
La Plantation
Ste-Marthe, **73**
Le Rocher de
Malendure, **47**
La Saladerie, **49**
La Table Creole, **68**
Le Touloulou, **87**

**Lodging**
L'Anse des Rochers, **76**
Auberge de la
Distillerie, **55**
Auberge de la
Vieille Tour, **61**
L'Auberge les Petits
Saints aux
Anacardies, **52**
Bois Joli, **53**
Canella Beach
Residence, **67**
Cap Sud Caraïbes, **66**
Club Méditerranée
La Caravelle, **73**
La Cocoteraie, **78**
La Créole Beach
Hotel, **64**
Domaine de
Petite Anse, **46**
Fleur d'Epée
Novotel/Marissol, **60**
Fort Royal
Touring Club, **43**
Golf Marine Club
Hotel, **81**
Grand Anse Hotel, **48**
Hamak, **80**
Le Méridien
St. François, **79**
L'Orchidée, **65**
La Plantation
Ste-Marthe, **82**
Relais des Sources, **56**
Relais du Moulin, **74**
La Sucrerie du
Comté, **41**
Tropical Club
Hotel, **84**
Village Creole, **51**

broke out between royalists and revolutionaries on the island. In 1794, Britain responded to the call from Guadeloupe royalists to come to their aid, and that same year France dispatched Victor Hugues to sort things out. (In virtually every town and village you'll run across a "Victor Hugues" street, boulevard, or park.) After his troops banished the British, Hugues issued a decree abolishing slavery and guillotined recalcitrant planters. The ones who managed to keep their heads fled to Louisiana or hid in the hills of Grande-Terre, where their descendants now live. Hugues—who quickly became known as the "Robespierre of the Isles"—was soon relieved of his command, slavery was reestablished by Napoléon, and the French and English continued to battle over the island. The 1815 Treaty of Paris restored Guadeloupe to France, and in 1848, due largely to the efforts of Alsatian Victor Schoelcher, slavery was permanently abolished. The island has been a *département* of France since 1946, and in 1974 it was elevated to a *région,* administered by a prefect appointed from Paris.

Guadeloupe looks like a giant butterfly resting on the sea between Antigua and Dominica. Its wings—Basse-Terre and Grande-Terre—are the two largest islands in the 659-square-mile Guadeloupe archipelago. The Rivière Salée, a 4-mile seawater channel flowing between the Caribbean and the Atlantic, forms the "spine" of the butterfly. Smaller, flatter Grande-Terre (218 square miles) is dry, flat, and sandy. It was once sugarcane country, but today survives on intensively developed tourism. It has the best beaches, restaurants, casinos, resorts, and clubs. Basse-Terre ("low land") is wild, wet, and mountainous, and is not so developed; there are fewer tourists here. Its lush, precipitous west coast is as beautiful as any place in the Caribbean. Guadeloupe offers a third type of landscape and culture: On Les Saintes, La Désirade, Marie-Galante, and the other islands of the archipelago, you will find little-explored places that have remained largely untouched by the world.

## Lodging

Guadeloupe doesn't have the selection of elegant, tasteful hotels found on Martinique, but you can opt for a splashy hotel with a full complement of resort activities or head for a small inn called a Relais Creole. If French is not your forte, you'll fare better in the large hotels. Gosier and Bas-du-Fort have been the main venues for resort hotels, but the areas around Ste-Anne and St-François also have their fair share of resorts. There are also small hotels throughout Basse-Terre and on Iles des Saintes and Marie-Galante. Most hotels include buffet breakfast in their rates. Prices decline 25% to 40% in the off-season.

For information about villas, apartments, and private rooms in modest houses, contact **Gîtes de France** (☎ 590/91–64–33). For additional information about apartment-style accommodations, contact the **ANTRE Association** (☎ 590/88–53–09).

CATEGORY COST*

| CATEGORY | COST* |
|---|---|
| $$$$ | over $300 |
| $$$ | $225–$300 |
| $$ | $150–$225 |
| $ | under $150 |

*All prices are for a standard double room for two, excluding* taxe de séjour, *which varies from hotel to hotel, and 10%–15% service charge.*

$$$$    ☒ **La Cocoteraie.** You get the most luxury the island has to offer here,
  ★     and you pay for it—between $300 and $600 a night. This very private annex to Le Méridien consists of 52 suites. Each has a private balcony with a view of either the marina or the pool. Large bathrooms have a

round tub and separate shower. The decor is a handsome blend of bright pastels (lavender, mauve, turquoise, and taupe), mahogany furnishings, glazed ceramic lamps, and madras upholstery. A restaurant, two tennis courts, an extravagantly large multilevel pool surrounded by columns and enormous Chinese vases, and a very small beach are all for the exclusive use of La Cocoteraie guests, and you have full use of the facilities of Le Méridien (☞ *below*). The only drawback is a management that caters to the French—the booking office is in Paris—and expresses little interest in attracting English-speaking guests. ✉ *Ave. de l'Europe, St-François 97118,* ☎ *590/88–79–81 or 800/543–4300,* FAX *590/88–78–33. 52 suites. Restaurant, pool, minibars, in-room safes, 2 tennis courts, access to Le Méridien's facilities. AE, DC, MC, V. CP, MAP.*

$$$$ ⊞ **Hamak.** Five landscaped acres, a private white-sand beach, and at-
★ tentive service make this one of the smartest places on Guadeloupe, a perennial favorite of Americans. Golfers will be delighted that Guadeloupe's municipal golf course is across the street, and gardeners will appreciate the hotel's array of flowers and shrubs. One-bedroom suites are in bungalows; each unit has a private rear patio with outdoor freshwater shower, and a front terrace with a hammock. All are air-conditioned, with twin beds, hair dryers, and international direct-dial phones. Some have small kitchenettes with hand stenciling. TVs and videos are available. Blond wood and wicker furnishings are accented by local artwork. You pay a high price for the bungalows, which have small rooms, bathrooms no bigger than closets, and a tiny and crowded beach, but the pampering service and seclusion compensate. ✉ *St-François 97118,* ☎ *590/88–59–99 or 800/633–7411,* FAX *590/88–41–92. 56 units. Restaurant, 2 bars, air-conditioning, hot tub, tennis court, watersports center. AE, MC, V. BP, MAP.*

$$$–$$$$ ⊞ **Auberge de la Vieille Tour.** This property was extensively reno-
★ vated in the winter of 1995, making it one of the premiere resorts in the French West Indies. The most important addition is a two-story building perched on the hillside, housing 32 new suites. The suites are spacious and furnished with reproduction antiques, but their most spectacular feature is the view: From your bed or your bath you have an uninterrupted view of the ocean. The majority of the remaining rooms are down a flight of steps, on either side of the pool, in town houses decorated in a contemporary style. The bar and gourmet restaurant have been remodelled; the bar now overlooks the Ilet de Gosier and its red-and-white striped lighthouse. Breakfast, lunch, and barbecues are served at the poolside terrace restaurant. A third restaurant serves Creole dishes in the evening. Water-sports equipment and diving tours are available for guests at the Auberge's sister hotels, the Fleur d'Epée and Marissol, a bit farther along the beach. The resort's own beach is rather small. ✉ *Montauban Gosier 97190,* ☎ *590/84–23–23 or 800/223–9862,* FAX *590/84–33–43. 160 rooms. 3 restaurants, bar, pool, 2 tennis courts, boutiques. AE, DC, MC, V. BP, MAP.*

$$$ ⊞ **La Créole Beach Hotel.** Ten acres of tropical greenery and two beaches are the lush setting for this hotel. Rooms are spacious and have sliding glass doors that open onto a balcony. Decor is dominated by vivid jungle fabrics. Mazelike corridors and pathways can be somewhat confusing. The water-sports center offers excursions to Ilet du Gosier. ✉ *Box 19, Gosier 97190,* ☎ *590/90–46–46 or 800/755–9313,* FAX *590/90–46–66. 156 rooms, 6 duplexes. 2 restaurants, bar, air-conditioning, pool, 2 tennis courts, boating, water-sports center, car rental. AE, DC, MC, V. CP, EP, MAP.*

$$–$$$ ⊞ **Club Méditerranée La Caravelle.** This version of the well-known club chain has air-conditioned twin-bed rooms, some with balconies, and 50 secluded acres at the western end of a magnificent white-sand

beach. Nice extras include a volleyball court, calisthenics classes, and a French-English language lab where you can take French classes and use a tape recorder and headphones to practice. The property draws a fun-loving, younger crowd, most of whom are from France, and serves as the home port for Club Med's sailing cruises. ⊠ *Ste-Anne 97180,* ☎ *590/88–21–00 or 800/258–2633,* FAX *590/88–06–06. 310 rooms. Restaurant, pub, air-conditioning, pool, 6 tennis courts (with pro), beach, water-sports center. AE, MC, V. All-inclusive (drinks extra).*

**$$–$$$** 🏨 **Fleur d'Epée Novotel/Marissol.** "If you can't beat them, join them" could be the motto for the merger of these two hotels on a cove in Bas-du-Fort. Once competitors, they have joined forces under the banner of the giant Groupe Accord. Mike Niang, manager at Novotel, is a human dynamo who keeps the staff on their toes. Tour groups from France are still the primary clientele, and when both hotels are full, the narrow strip of sand they share can get rather crowded. Rooms at the Fleur d'Epée are rather cramped, but the powder-blue fabrics and white tiles give them a pleasant, fresh look. All rooms have a terrace, most with views of the sea. An extensive renovation of both properties is planned. ⊠ *Bas-du-Fort 97190,* ☎ *590/90–40–00,* FAX *590/90–99–07. 400 rooms. 4 restaurants, bar, air-conditioning, minibars, pool, water-sports center. AE, D, DC, MC, V. CP, MAP.*

**$$–$$$** 🏨 **Le Méridien St. François.** You couldn't pack more activity into one vacation than is offered by this hotel. The 150-acre resort puts out its own *A to Z Leisure Guide* and broadcasts from Télé Méridien to let you know what's going on. The activities director organizes everything from boccie to book lending. The beach hut is a busy place even off-season (partly because the Air France crews use the hotel). The spacious, breezy lobby has a trompe l'oeil mural of an arcade and is filled with Haitian artwork and fresh flowers. Standard rooms are modest, and wear and tear has taken its toll, but all have balconies, about half of which face the sea. Odd-numbered rooms have the best views. Decor is standard to the Méridien chain, right down to the mint-and-orange fabrics and boxy configuration. This one at least sports a few individual touches, such as flowerpots on the balconies. ⊠ *St-François 97118,* ☎ *590/88–51–00 or 800/543–4300,* FAX *590/88–40–71. 267 rooms, 10 suites. 2 restaurants, 2 bars, air-conditioning, pool, spa, 2 tennis courts, water-sports center, shops, disco, car rental. AE, D, MC, V. CP, MAP.*

**$$–$$$** 🏨 **La Plantation Ste-Marthe.** You are a few miles inland from the coast
★     here, among gently rolling hills and fields, but the 7 acres of grounds are lovely, the ocean can be seen from some guest rooms, and there is shuttle service to the beach. If the place has one drawback, it is that it lacks atmosphere. Though bits of machinery from the old sugar refinery have been cleverly incorporated into the grounds, this is a modern, designer version of a plantation house. But it is sumptuous. The august, almost baroque reception area has columns of pale blue and mango, vast murals, a winding, polished-wood double staircase, and black-and-white patterned marble floors. The rooms are housed in four three-story Creole-style buildings, with spacious terraces that overlook the large pool. They are large and elegant. Twenty-four duplex suites have loft-style bedrooms looking down upon a salon. Throughout the hotel, tasteful furniture is a unique modern adaptation of French period pieces that incorporate cane work. Mahogany beds and aquamarine and coral tile work contribute to the refined aura. The restaurant, one of the best on the island, is by the large free-form pool, which is designed to resemble a lake. ⊠ *St-François 97118,* ☎ *590/93–11–11 or 800/333–1970,* FAX *590/88–72–47. 96 rooms, 24 duplexes. Restaurant, bar, air-conditioning, in-room safes, minibars, pool, conference rooms. AE, MC, V. EP, MAP.*

**$$** 🖭 **L'Anse des Rochers.** The 27 acres of this resort are spread along the coast a few miles from St-François. Rooms are either in Creole-style buildings or in 34 villas that climb the rise behind them. All rooms have terra-cotta floors, rich russet-patterned bedspreads, ceramic lamps, and original touches like antique radios. Bathrooms are merely functional, but terraces and kitchenettes are pluses. The formal restaurant offers à la carte dining, but most evenings, guests attend the theme buffet dinner at the Blanc Mangé restaurant, where performers entertain on the large piazza. Across the piazza is an open-sided disco, good for late-night revelry. The complex is so large that the trek to the man-made beach at one end can prompt you to use the car. L'Anse des Rochers may not have the best beach on the island, but it does boast the largest swimming pool. Dramatically designed, the pool creates the effect of water cascading into the sea. Your travel agent should be able to obtain discounted rates for you. ⊠ *Anse des Rochers, St-François 97118,* ☎ *590/93–90–00,* FAX *590/93–91–00. 356 rooms. 2 restaurants, beach snack bar, pool, 2 tennis courts, archery, minimart, gift shop, disco, meeting rooms, car rental. MC, V. EP, MAP.*

**$$** 🖭 **Canella Beach Residence.** In this 146-room resort built to resemble a Creole village, you have a choice of single-level and duplex studios and junior and duplex suites. Each has its own terrace or balcony with a small kitchenette. Ask for a room on the top floor for the best views. Decor is a pleasant departure from pastels, with earth tones complementing the white tile floors and rattan furnishings. Unlike the other Pointe de la Verdure hotels, the Canella Beach enjoys its own semiprivate cove. Water sports are free, and there is a beach bar for refreshments. Set back from the beach are the swimming pool and tennis courts. The staff, with inspiration from Jean-Pierre Reuff, the general manager, is enthusiastic (though sometimes disorganized) and enjoys speaking English. Another plus is the Verandah restaurant, where you can dine indoors in air-conditioning or enjoy the sea breezes outdoors. The menu includes Creole and French dishes; the salad with warm goat cheese makes an excellent light meal or appetizer. Excursions can be arranged to nearby islands. ⊠ *Pointe de la Verdure, Gosier 97190,* ☎ *590/90– 44–00 or 800/223–9815; in NY, 212/251–1800;* FAX *590/90–44–44. 146 rooms. Restaurant, pool, 4 tennis courts, snorkeling, windsurfing, waterskiing, boating, fishing. AE, DC, MC, V. EP, MAP.*

**$$** 🖭 **Cap Sud Caraïbes.** This is a tiny Relais Creole on a country road between Gosier and Ste-Anne, just a five-minute walk from a quiet beach. The staff does its best to make you feel at home. Each individually decorated room has a balcony and either a shower or an enormous bath. ⊠ *Gosier 97190,* ☎ *590/85–96–02,* FAX *590/85–80–39. 12 rooms. Bar, air-conditioning, pool, snorkeling, dry cleaning, laundry service, airport shuttle. MC, V. CP.*

**$$** 🖭 **Fort Royal Touring Club.** This is by far the most elegant, comfortable lodging on Basse-Terre. The modern white structure overlooks two pristine beaches. Spacious rooms all have a terrace or balcony with sea views, tile floors, handsome wicker and rattan furnishings, and mahogany beds. The hotel offers tours into the national park and plenty of activities, most of them beach-related. ⊠ *Pointe du Petit Bas-Vent, Deshaies 97126,* ☎ *590/25–50–00,* FAX *590/25–50–01. 120 rooms, including 78 bungalows. Restaurant, bar, air-conditioning, 2 pools, miniature golf, 4 tennis courts, dive shop, water-sports center. AE, MC, V. EP, CP, MAP.*

**$$** 🖭 **Golf Marine Club Hotel.** Near the town's newer shops and restaurants, this small hotel offers a more moderately priced alternative to Hamak and Le Méridien. But the hotel's name overpromises: It is not a club, the municipal golf course is across the street, and it has neither marina nor beach. You must walk two blocks to the nearest public beach.

The rooms, however, are pristine and pleasingly decorated in soft blues. Each has a balcony, but those facing the street tend to be noisy, so reserve one overlooking the gardens. A third of the rooms are called mezzanine suites and have loft bedrooms and a roll-out couch in the lounge. These are pleasant for two people, and a small family can squeeze in. On the patio terrace facing the small pool is a relaxed, informal restaurant where meals are served. ⊠ *Ave. de l'Europe, B.P. 204, St-François 97118,* ☎ *590/88–60–60,* ℻ *590/88–68–98. 74 rooms, including 29 duplexes and 15 bungalows. Restaurant, pool, 2 tennis courts. AE, MC, V. CP, MAP.*

**$$** 🏨 **L'Orchidée.** Right in the center of Gosier, this hotel is perfect for the businessperson who does not need resort facilities or a beach. Its spotless studios have balconies. The decor consists of dark-wood furnishings, teal fabrics, and sparkling white tile floors. On the ground floor a small shop serves morning coffee. Owner-manager Madame Karine Chenaf speaks English and can help you arrange your day. ⊠ *32 blvd. Général de Gaulle, Gosier 97190,* ☎ *590/84–54–20,* ℻ *590/84–54–90. 18 studios. Dining room, air-conditioning, kitchenettes, free membership in local recreation center with pool, boutique. MC, V. EP.*

**$$** 🏨 **Relais du Moulin.** A restored windmill serves as the reception room for this Relais Creole tucked in Châteaubrun, near Ste-Anne. A spiral staircase leads up to a TV/reading room, from which there is a splendid view. Accommodations are in bungalows. Rooms are immaculate but claustrophobic, somehow managing to pack in twin beds, small terraces, and kitchenettes. The hotel is on a small hill, and there is usually a pleasant, cooling breeze. The restaurant overlooks the restored windmill; by day, sunlight floods through large windows, while at night candlelight flickers on crisp white cloths. Try the house specialty: grouper and lobster served with Creole sauce or stuffed with fresh homemade pâté. Crème caramel in coconut sauce is among the sumptuous desserts. A *menu dégustation* for 220F offers seven courses and is a good way to sample Creole cooking. The beach is a 10-minute hike away. It's best to have your own rental car. ⊠ *Châteaubrun, Ste-Anne 97180,* ☎ *590/88–23–96 or 800/223–9815,* ℻ *590/88–03–92. 40 rooms. Restaurant, bar, air-conditioning, kitchenettes, pool, tennis court, archery, bicycles. AE, DC, MC, V. CP, MAP.*

**$$** 🏨 **Tropical Club Hotel.** Great windsurfing and swimming are big draws for this hotel on the northeastern coast of Grand-Terre. The golden beach catches cooling trade winds from the Atlantic, but a reef about 100 yards offshore keeps the waves gentle. Set back from the beach is an almond-shape pool, adjacent to an open-sided dining room that serves French and Creole fare. The guest rooms are in three buildings on a rise at the back of the main hotel building. Each room has a double bed and two bunk beds, which are in an entrance annex—ideal for children (those under 21 stay free). The bathroom has a shower only, and the toilet is in a separate area. Every room has a private balcony with a small kitchenette, table and chairs, and a view of the sea. The best views are from the rooms on the top (third) floor. The decor, in tired rattan and sea-foam colors, won't win any awards, and the setting is remote, but the property compensates with a host of activities and an energetic staff. ⊠ *Le Moule, 97160,* ☎ *590/93–97–97,* ℻ *590/93–97–00. 72 rooms. Restaurant, bar, air-conditioning, fans, kitchenettes, pool, 3 tennis courts nearby, boccie, exercise room, windsurfing, boutique. AE, MC, V. CP, MAP.*

**$–$$** 🏨 **Relais des Sources.** This newly opened Relais Creole is one of the better inns on Basse-Terre. The hotel is set in the foothills of Grosse Montagne, only a few hundred yards from the Ravine Chaude thermal baths, in a typically Guadeloupean landscape of sugarcane fields and sleepy villages. There are five (rather dark) rooms in the main building and 10 bungalows dotted about the shady property. The bungalows come with kitchenette, phone, air-conditioning, and TV. There is a good restaurant, which makes use of spices and organically grown vegetables from the garden. The (extremely young) staff will take care of your every need—from baby-sitting to airport transfers. On the downside, you might mistake the swimming pool for a birdbath, and the nearest beach is about 9 miles away. ⊠ *Lamentin, 91729,* ☎ *590/25–31–04,* FAX *590/25–30–63. 5 rooms, 10 bungalows. Restaurant, bar, pool, boutique, tours. AE, MC, V. CP, MAP.*

$ ★ 🏨 **Auberge de la Distillerie.** This is one of the best Relais Creole on the island: a homey country inn ideal for those who want to be close to the national park. The 12 rooms in the 19th-century house are individually decorated, with wicker furnishings, tile floors, wood beams, ceramic lamps, and local artwork; the color scheme includes such tones as apricot, mint, olive, silver, and rose. Each has a terrace; some have a fridge. The slightly larger bungalows have larger terraces and open onto the extravagantly overgrown gardens. There's also a rustic wood chalet that sleeps two to four people. The restaurant, noted for its delectable Creole cuisine, is built around the partially enclosed pool. Boat trips on the Lézarde River can be arranged; you can also swim in the river. ⊠ *Vernou 97170, D23, Petit-Bourg,* ☎ *590/94–25–91 or 800/223–9815,* FAX *590/94–11–91. 14 rooms. Restaurant, bar, air-conditioning, pool, bakery. AE, MC, V. CP, MAP.*

$ 🏨 **Domaine de Petite Anse.** Another Relais Creole, the ocher, red-roofed buildings of this resort spill down lushly landscaped hills overlooking the ocean. The location is perfect: You're near a beach and close to the national park. Accommodations are either in hotel rooms or bungalows and are decorated with dark rattan and bright floral fabrics. Rooms are simple and small, but well equipped. Be sure to request one with a balcony and sea view (they're the same price). Bungalows have a terrace, full bath, and kitchenette in addition to the amenities listed above. This is one of Guadeloupe's premier spots for an active vacation, and very popular with young French couples and families. The resort is noted for its dive shop and nature tours. The staff, although friendly, speaks limited English. ⊠ *Plage de Petite Anse, Monchy, Bouillante 97125,* ☎ *590/98–78–78,* FAX *590/98–80–28. 135 rooms, 40 bungalows. Restaurant, bar, air-conditioning, in-room safes, refrigerators, pool, archery, volleyball, boating, dive shop, water-sports center, boutique. AE, DC, MC, V. EP.*

$ 🏨 **Grand Anse Hotel.** Less than a mile from a black-sand beach, and offering spectacular mountain views, this Relais Creole is a good choice for nature lovers. It's also near the ferry to Les Saintes. Bungalows have small balconies. The heavy polished wood furnishings should achieve antique status in a few years. Water sports and nature hikes can be arranged. ⊠ *Trois-Rivières 97114,* ☎ *590/92–90–47,* FAX *590/92–93–69. 16 bungalows. Restaurant, bar, air-conditioning, refrigerators, pool. MC, V. CP, MAP.*

$ ★ 🏨 **La Sucrerie du Comté.** The ruins and rusting equipment (including a locomotive) of a 19th-century sugar factory litter the lawns and gardens here like hulking abstract sculptures. In fact, it is the historically significant grounds, along with the attractive public areas, that are the main attraction of this resort. The interiors of the fine restaurant and bar re-create gracious plantation living, with wood beams, stone walls, lace lamp shades, and towering floral arrangements. Twenty-six bungalows duplicate the gingerbread architecture of the turn of the century. Inside, the air-conditioned rooms are small but pretty. The nearest beach is a 10-minute stroll through a tangle of greenery. The enthusiastic French owner, Monsieur Girard Jean-Luc, will have you speaking French in no time, as you try the homemade fruit punches lined up in great jars on the bar in the evening. ⊠ *Comté de Lohéac, Ste-Rose 97115*, ☎ *590/28–60–17*, FAX *590/28–65–63. 50 rooms. Restaurant, bar, pool, tennis court. AE, DC, MC, V. CP, MAP.*

### Iles des Saintes

$–$$  ⊡ **Village Creole.** Baths by Courrèges, dishwashers, freezers, satellite
★     TV, and videos are among the amenities in this apartment hotel. Somewhat isolated, it appeals to the likes of models and high-powered business titans looking for a peaceful retreat. Units are decorated simply but chicly, with white tile floors, unvarnished rattan, and framed posters. Ghyslain Laps, the English-speaking owner and would-be chef, will help you whip up meals in the kitchen. If you'd prefer not to cook, he can provide you with a cook and housekeeper for an extra charge. A sailboat is available for excursions to Marie-Galante and Dominica. The small beach is too rough for swimming. ⊠ *Pte. Coquelet 97137, Terre-de-Haut,* ☎ *590/99–53–83,* FAX *590/99–55–55. 22 duplexes. Water-sports center, scooter and boat rentals, daily maid service, convention center, airport shuttle. MC, V. EP.*

$    ⊡ **L'Auberge les Petits Saints aux Anacardies.** This is one of the most
★    distinctive properties in the archipelago. Ten rooms are tucked into this inn, which is trimmed with trellises and topped by dormers. Each room has twin beds and casement windows that open to a splendid view of gardens, hills, and the bay. Some also have sea views (Room 2's is extraordinary), and most have a private bath. A glorious clutter greets you in the reception area, which is crammed with antiques and objets d'art culled from owners Jean-Paul Coles and Didier Spindler's world travels—porcelain lions, birdcages, cigar-store Indians. Furnishings are a similarly odd assortment of antiques. There's a one-bedroom bungalow next to the main house. The restaurant is one of the best on the island. The hotel's private boat makes excursions around the islands. ⊠ *La Savane 97137, Terre-de-Haut,* ☎ *590/99–50–99,* FAX *590/99–54–51. 10 rooms (9 with private interior bath). Restaurant, bar, air-conditioning, pool, sauna. MC, V. CP, MAP.*

$    ⊡ **Bois Joli.** A beautiful setting, right on the bay, is the attraction here. Most of the rooms, either in the inn or one of the bungalows, are air-conditioned but rather drab. The hotel restaurant serves wonderful clams in Creole sauce on a terrace that overlooks the sea. Water sports can be arranged, and the Anse Crawen nudist beach is a five-minute walk away. Pets are allowed. ⊠ *Terre-de-Haut 97137,* ☎ *590/99–50–38 or 800/223–9815,* FAX *590/99–55–05. 21 rooms, 8 bungalows. Restaurant, bar, pool, airport shuttle. MC, V. CP, MAP.*

## Dining

Along with Martinique, Guadeloupe is one of the culinary epicenters of the Caribbean. Many of the restaurants here feature seafood (shellfish is a great favorite), often flavored with rich herbs and spices à la Creole. Favorite appetizers are *accras* (codfish fritters), *boudin* (highly seasoned pork sausage), and *crabes farcis* (stuffed land crabs). Christophines, a type of vegetable pear, are prepared in a variety of ways. Plantains, served as a side dish, are considered a vegetable banana. *Blaff* is a spicy fish stew. Lobster, turtle steak, and *lambi* (conch) are often among the main dishes, and homemade coconut ice cream is a typical dessert. The island boasts more than 700 restaurants, including those serving classic French, Italian, African, Indian, Vietnamese, and South American fare. But they are not cheap. Even the simplest Creole fare costs $20–$25. For a good meal you can expect to pay $50–$70. The local libation of choice is the *petit punch* ("tee poonch," as it is pronounced)—a heady concoction of rum, lime juice, and sugarcane syrup. The innocent-sounding little punch packs a powerful wallop.

## What to Wear

Dining is casual at lunch, but beach attire is a no-no. Except at the more laid-back marina and beach eateries, dinner is slightly more formal. Long pants, collared shirts, and skirts or dresses are appreciated, although not required.

| CATEGORY | COST* |
|---|---|
| $$$ | over $40 |
| $$ | $25–$40 |
| $ | under $25 |

*per person, excluding drinks

## Grande-Terre

$$$ ✕ **Auberge de la Vieille Tour.** This restaurant was extensively re-
★ designed in 1995. Guests now sit at tables grouped around the historic, whitewashed sugar mill that gives the resort its name, and there is a new, conservatory-style extension at the front, with views up into lighted trees. Lionel Péan's cuisine is as good as ever. It's hard to choose from the constantly changing menu, with entrées such as smoked swordfish with a two-pepper mousse and blinis, noisettes of lamb in honey and lime, and sea bream kissed with passion-fruit vinegar. You may want to opt for the *menu dégustation,* for a representative sampling of Péan's work. There is an extensive (and expensive) wine list. A band plays cool jazz Wednesday–Saturday evenings. ⊠ *Gosier,* ☎ 590/84–23–23. *AE, DC, MC, V.*

$$$ ✕ **Auberge de St-François.** Claude Simon's country home is set in an orchard, and his tables are set with Royal Doulton china and fine crystal. Dining is indoors or on one of the flower-filled patios, with a superb view of Marie-Galante and Pointe des Châteaux. The house specialty is crayfish prepared in several ways (the unusual fricassee with bacon and scallops is a standout). The brochette of smoked shark with a pepper sauce and the conch dishes are also good. A *menu touriste* (180F) of three courses, each with a choice of three dishes, is an affordable alternative to the à la carte offerings. Monsieur Simon has a superior cellar of vintage wine and champagne to complement his cuisine. ⊠ *St-François,* ☎ 590/88–51–71. *MC, V. Closed Sun. and Mon.*

$$$ ✕ **Le Balata.** This commanding restaurant sits high on a bluff above the
★ main Gosier Bas-du-Fort highway. If you're traveling from Gosier in the direction of Fort-de-France, you'll find the winding, pitted entrance road off the highway, at the Elf gas station. Pretty flowered linens and trellises woven with hanging vines create a pastoral setting. Madame Guynamant presents classic French cuisine and a selection of good French wines at reasonable prices. A fixed menu, including wine, is available at 155F. Choose a table by the window (reserve early) and enjoy the magnificent view of Fort Fleur d'Epée. ⊠ *Rte. de Labrousse, Gosier,* ☎ 590/90–88–25. *AE, MC, V. Closed Sun. and Aug. No lunch Sat.*

$$$ ✕ **La Canne à Sucre.** A favorite over the years for its innovative Cre-
★ ole cuisine, La Canne à Sucre has a reputation for being the best restaurant in Pointe-à-Pitre. It has a commanding position on the quay, in the complex adjacent to the cruise-ship terminal, and hulking ships cast a shadow over the terrace. Take time to admire the lovely murals of a sugarcane harvest that adorn the building. There are two dining rooms with separate menus. Meals upstairs are more elaborate and twice as expensive (a jacket is required for dinner here). Try the *foie gras frais de canard au vieux rhum* (fresh duck liver in old rum) or red snapper in a cucumber *coulis* (a sauce made from pureed cucumber). The views here are wide-ranging. In the main-floor Brasserie, you can order such

classic bistro dishes as duck à l'orange, grouper in red wine butter, and a puff pastry of skate with saffron sauce. ⊠ *Quai No. 1, Port Autonome, Pointe-à-Pitre,* ☎ *590/82–10–19. AE, MC, V. No lunch Sat.*

**$$$**  ✕ **Château de Feuilles.** This restaurant is worth a special trip. You will
★ savor no finer luncheon than one served by Martine and Jean-Pierre Dubost in this relaxed, stylish country setting. While waiting for your meal you can take a dip in the pool or stroll around the 2-acre farm. For an aperitif, about 20 different punch concoctions are made with different juices and flavors: Sample all if you dare. The changing menu may include goose *rillettes* (pâté), velvety sea urchin pâté, kingfish fillet with vanilla, swordfish with sorrel, or the deep-sea fish *capitan* grilled with lime and green pepper. For dessert, try the pineapple flan. The estate is 9 miles from Le Moule on the Campêche road, between Gros-Cap and Campêche. ⊠ *Campêche,* ☎ *590/22–30–30. MC, V. Closed Mon. No dinner (except for groups of 10 or more by reservation).*

**$$$**  ✕ **Chez Deux Gros.** The name is a play on one of France's most famous restaurants, Chez Trois Gros; though the food is not quite of that standard, you will eat extremely well at this unusual restaurant, which is also an antiques shop, or what the French call *une brocante*. If you fancy taking home the mahogany table at which you ate or the 19th-century armoire in the corner, that's not a problem. But as the antiques are imported from Paris, they are not exactly cheap. Culinary specialties include shrimp ravioli in saffron butter, marinated raw fish à la Gaugin, and salmon in a honey and vanilla sauce. The restaurant is built on a steep, plant-hung incline, with tables set in tiled alcoves and terraces. Floral tablecloths, delicate lighting, and jazz music give this place a lot of character. Sadly, what was once a small, country road is now the main drag to Gosier and Ste-Anne; it's loud and passes just below the restaurant. Make sure you ask for a table in the room at the back—it's also got the best antiques. ⊠ *Gosier,* ☎ *590/84–16–20. MC, V. No lunch.*

**$$$**  ✕ **Le Côte Jardin.** The marina between Bas-du-Fort and Pointe-à-Pitre is a lively evening venue with a dozen restaurants, bar lounges, and shops around the quay. You can take your pick from pizzas to hamburgers, but for something more formal, try the creative cuisine at Le Côte Jardin. The plant-filled restaurant is very pretty indeed, with white lace curtains, wicker peacock chairs, and coral and white napery. A menu of haute French Creole lists dishes that range from basic lamb Provençal and baked red snapper to more exotic *escargots de la mer* with garlic butter. Unfortunately, the staff has a tendency to behave like prima donnas. ⊠ *La Marina,* ☎ *590/90–91–28. AE, MC, V.*

**$$$**  ✕ **La Louisiane.** The owner, chef Daniel Hogon, who hails from the
★ Carlton in Cannes, prepares such traditional favorites as duck-liver confit with raspberry vinaigrette or smoked fish as starters, then crayfish flambé, fillet of beef in green pepper sauce, or roast rack of lamb. For dessert, try the charlotte of exotic fruits. The Menu Creole at 120F is a fine buy. The dozen tables of this small restaurant are on a terrace decorated with paintings and flower-filled hanging pots. The restaurant is on the road to Ste-Marthe, about 2 miles from St-François, and Monsieur Hogon will send a car for you upon request. You'll receive far better service if you speak adequate French. ⊠ *St-François,* ☎ *590/88–44–34. MC, V. Closed Mon.*

**$$$**  ✕ **La Plantation Ste-Marthe.** Housed in the ritziest resort on the island
★ (☞ Lodging, *above*), this restaurant serves exceptionally good French food. For starters, try the *salade auchoise,* a green salad with duck, or the *carpaccio de filet de boeuf,* thin slices of raw beef with aromatic herbs. Then move on to a bouillabaisse Creole or noisettes of lamb with thyme. The three-chocolate mousse for dessert is a killer. The wine list is extensive. ⊠ *St-François,* ☎ *590/93–11–11. AE, MC, V. EP, MAP.*

**$$–$$$** ✕ **Le Flibustier.** The word is French for buccaneer, and this rustic hill-top farmhouse plays on the theme for all its worth. Waiters are dressed like extras from *Hook*. Roasting sides of meat are the backdrop for lots of piratical carrying-on. It's particularly lively after 8 PM, when the G.O.'s (*general organisateurs*—the staffers who force you to limbo) from the neighboring Club Med come in to hold court, smoke up a storm, and serenade attractive guests with ribald ditties. You can order a complete dinner—mixed salad, grilled lobster, coconut ice cream, petit punch, and half a pitcher of wine—or à la carte off the blackboard menu. ✉ *La Colline, Fonds Thézan (between Ste-Anne and St-Felix),* ☎ *590/ 88–23–36. No credit cards. Closed Mon. No lunch Sun.*

**$$–$$$** ✕ **Les Oiseaux.** The delights of this restaurant begin with its setting,
★ a stucco-and-stone house nestled amid a tangle of gardens overlook-ing the sea. The dining room is filled with potted plants and dressed with colorful madras linens and local crafts. Owner-chefs Claudette and Arthur Rolle have developed a menu of such dishes as *entrecôte Roquefort* (shark steak with coconut) and *marmite de Robinson* (a stew of dorado, kingfish, tuna, shrimp, and local vegetables). Shellfish afi-cionados should try *cassoulet de fruits de mer* (seafood casserole). Ask Claudette to show you her book of local remedies. If your French is *very* good she might even prepare a special infusion for your particu-lar complaint. Even if it isn't, be sure to sample a homemade *digestif* (after-dinner liqueur) such as *rhum d'amour,* which aids the circula-tion, helps sweat out colds, and improves *"la force, pour marcher le sexe,"* as Claudette slyly comments. ✉ *Anse des Rochers,* ☎ *590/88– 56–92. Reservations essential. AE, MC, V. Closed Oct. No lunch Mon.–Wed.*

**$$** ✕ **La Grande Pizzeria.** Open late and very popular, this simple seaside spot serves pizza, pasta, salads, and some Milanese, Bolognese, and other Italian seafood specialties, including a smashing seafood risotto and tagliatelle with shrimp scampi. Plastic tables and chairs are set on the terrace and spruced up with colorful napery. ✉ *Bas-du-Fort,* ☎ *590/90–82–64. MC, V. No lunch.*

**$–$$** ✕ **Chez Violetta–La Creole.** The late Violetta Chaville established this restaurant's à la carte Creole menu when she was head of Guadeloupe's association of *cuisinières* (female chefs). Her brother has carried on her cooking traditions, dishing up specials such as red snapper in Belle Doudou sauce, a Creole mix of onions, tomatoes, peppers, and spices. The food, although still good, has been eclipsed by other island kitchens, but the restaurant remains a stop on many tourist itineraries and is pop-ular with American visitors. ✉ *Eastern outskirts of Gosier Village,* ☎ *590/84–10–34. AE, MC, V.*

**$–$$** ✕ **Le Corsaire.** Restaurants on Gosier's main drag and the Route des Hôtels leading to the Pointe de la Verdure vie with one another to offer the best-value menus. Family-run Le Corsaire rates highly, thanks not only to its fine fare at finer prices but also to its fun-loving ambience. The wait staff affects a piratical look with ponytails, earrings, and goa-tees. A *vivier* (lobster tank) and a flamboyant mural of a buccaneer and his ship dominate the decor. Maman is a sweetie, singing out *"C'est bon?"* from the kitchen and nodding approvingly as you eat. For 99F you get a set menu, which might start with a conch tart or stuffed crab, then segue into beef brochette, octopus fricassee, or chicken *colombo* (curry). The King Creole menu at 120F nets you a large lobster. You can also order pizzas for 40F–52F. ✉ *Rte. des Hô-tels, Gosier,* ☎ *590/84–17–39. AE, MC, V. No lunch Mon.*

**$–$$** ✕ **La Table Creole.** Carmélite Jeanne rules the kitchen of this little ter-
★ race eatery, turning out dazzling Creole cuisine that is deceptively mild yet will heat you up like the noonday sun. Sea urchin gratin, succulent kingfish and snapper blaff, and goat colombo are among her memo-

rable specialties. The menus at 80F and 100F are fabulous bargains. Sprays of fresh flowers are everywhere, and Madame Jeanne usually dresses colorfully to match. ⊠ *St. Félix, outside Gosier,* ☎ *590/84–28–28. MC, V. No dinner Sun.*

$   ✕ **L'Endroit.** This popular pizzeria and cocktail bar is the most pleasant of the low-priced restaurants lining the road into Gosier. Thirty-five types of pizza, cooked in an oven at the back of the veranda, plus salads and pasta dishes, are on the menu. For a budget restaurant, the ambience is surprisingly pleasant. At the front, the veranda overlooks a floodlit garden. Inside, white wood and stucco walls, lots of plants, and candles give the place a light, airy feel. For pool and billiards fans, there are three good tables in the rear. ⊠ *Montauban, Gosier,* ☎ *590/ 84–46–57. MC, V.*

$   ✕ **Folie Plage.** This lovely spot, north of Anse-Bertrand, is especially popular with families on weekends. Prudence Marcelin prepares reliable Creole food; superb court bouillon and imaginative curried dishes are among the specialties. There is a children's wading pool here. ⊠ *Anse Laborde,* ☎ *590/22–11–17. No credit cards.*

## Basse-Terre

$–$$   ✕ **Chez Clara.** Clara Laseur, who gave up a jazz-dancing career in Paris
★   to run her family's seaside restaurant with her mother, dishes out delicious Creole meals. Seating is on the inviting terrace of a gorgeous Creole house adorned with lacy gingerbread trim. Clara takes the orders (her English is excellent), and the place is often so crowded with her friends and fans that you may have to wait at the octagonal wooden bar before being seated. The food is worth the wait, however—check the daily specials listed on the blackboard, for example the succulent octopus or sublime ginger carambola sorbet. ⊠ *Ste-Rose,* ☎ *590/28–72–99. MC, V. Closed Wed. and Oct. No dinner Sun.*

$–$$   ✕ **Le Karacoli.** With her flowing white dress and flamboyant style, Lu-
★   cienne Salcede, the owner of this pleasant seaside restaurant, looks as though she walked off the set of *Showboat*. The restaurant's entrance, along a rather scruffy lane by a campground, doesn't bode well, but this is one of the best restaurants on the spectacular west coast of Basse-Terre. There are two dining areas: inside, at dark, wood tables or outside, on the terrace, where all you will hear are the splash of the waves and the rustling of coconut palms. The food is solid Creole fare: goat colombo, boudin, court bouillon. For dessert, try the banana flambé, heavily perfumed with rum, followed by a homemade *digestif* (after-dinner liqueur). By then, you'll be ready to stretch out on the chaise longues that Lucienne sets out just for that purpose. When you wake up, she'll even lend you a beach towel for a swim. If that's not your idea of heaven, what is? ⊠ *Grande-Anse, north of Deshaies,* ☎ *590/ 28–41–17. MC, V. No dinner.*

$–$$   ✕ **Le Rocher de Malendure.** Tables at this bistro, perched on a lush hill-side on Guadeloupe's rugged west coast, are set out on airy verandas built around a Creole-style house; from here are spectacular views of Pigeon Island. Specialties include "souchy" Antillean (a local fish), smoked swordfish, conch, and prawns. For dessert, try the banana flambé in an orange sauce. If you want to catch fish, as well as eat them, owner Ghiseline Nouy will be happy to arrange a deep-sea fishing trip for you after lunch. ⊠ *Bouillante,* ☎ *590/98–70–84. DC, MC. Closed early–mid-Sept. No dinner Sun.*

$   ✕ **Chez Jackye.** Jacqueline Cabrion serves Creole and African dishes in her cheerful, plant-filled, seaside restaurant. Creole boudin is a house specialty, as are lobster (grilled, vinaigrette, or fricassee), fried crayfish, clam blaff, and goat in port sauce. There's also a wide selection of omelets, sandwiches, and salads. For dessert, try peach melba or banana flambé. The 120F menu will have you waddling out happily. ⊠ *Anse Guyonneau, rue de la Bataille, Pte. Noire,* ☎ *590/98–06–98. DC, MC, V. Closed Sun.*

**$**   ✕ **Les Gommiers.** A changing menu here may list crayfish soup, octopus fricassee, pork chops with banana, goat colombo, seafood paella, and grilled entrecôte. Banana splits and profiteroles are on the dessert list. For lunch, salade Niçoise and other light dishes are offered. Fixed menus at 70F and 100F are sensational values. Lovely peacock chairs grace the bar, and polished wood furnishings and potted plants fill the dining room. ⊠ *Rue Baudot, Pte. Noire,* ☎ *590/98–01–79. MC, V. No dinner Sun.–Tues.*

## Iles des Saintes, Terre-de-Haut

**$–$$**   ✕ **L'Auberge les Petits Saints aux Anacardies.** The restaurant of the island's prettiest inn is also open to nonguests. You sit out on an airy veranda overlooking the ocean. There is only one main dish per day; specialties include steak au poivre, grilled lobster, or smoked local fish. The wine list is excellent. ⊠ *La Savane,* ☎ *590/99–50–99. MC, V. Closed mid-Sept.–mid-Oct.*

**$–$$**   ✕ **El Dorado.** This is one of the best bets on Les Saintes. A plant-filled, Creole-style house with a double veranda, on Bourg's delightful main square, is the setting for dishes prepared by Roselle Zeline, chef and co-owner, a local woman steeped in the traditions of Creole cooking. There is a three-course Creole menu for 75F. The pizza, which is only served at night, is made on the premises, the beef for the BBQ steaks is imported from France, and there is a decent wine list. ⊠ *Bourg, Terre-de-Haut,* ☎ *590/99–54–31. MC. Closed Sun.*

**$–$$**   ✕ **Nilce's Bar.** This piano bar and restaurant in a large, Creole-style house right on the waterfront, is *the* place for Terre-de-Haut's barefoot crowd. Owners Jacques and Odette Chan, who used to run the popular Banc de Sable, serve tapas, salads, and a wide selection of ice creams in the upstairs dining room. Downstairs, local musicians perform Brazilian, French, and Creole music. Dogs and children wander about—it's very casual and informal. The later it gets, the raunchier it gets, so come early. ⊠ *Bourg, Terre-de-Haut,* ☎ *590/99–56–80. MC, V. No lunch.*

**$–$$**   ✕ **La Saladerie.** This delightful seaside terrace restaurant serves a so-
**★**   phisticated mélange of Creole and Continental dishes. Begin with rillettes of smoked fish, crabes farcis, or a warm crepe filled with lobster, conch, octopus, and fish. House specialties include an assortment of smoked fish served cold and stuffed fish fillet served in a white-wine sauce. The wine list is pleasantly varied. This is the place for a light meal served with a great view. ⊠ *Anse Mirre,* ☎ *590/99–50–92. MC, V.*

## Marie-Galante

**$**   ✕ **Le Touloulou.** The ultracasual Le Touloulou, on the curve of Petite Anse beach, serves sumptuous seafood at down-to-earth prices. Chef Patrice Pillet's standouts include conch *feuilleté* (in puff pastry) with yams and the very local *bébélé* (tripe with breadfruit, plantains, and dumplings). There are set menus for 60F, 90F, and 140F. ⊠ *Petite Anse,* ☎ *590/97–32–63. MC, V. Closed Mon. and mid-Sept.–mid-Oct.*

# Beaches

Guadeloupe's beaches are not spectacular. They are generally rather narrow (particularly since the hurricane season of 1995) and tend to be cluttered with cafés and impromptu parking lots in the sand. But they are all free and open to the public. For a small fee, hotels allow nonguests to use changing facilities, towels, and beach chairs. Some of the island's best beaches of soft white sand lie on the coast of

Grande-Terre from Ste-Anne to Pointe des Châteaux. All along the western shore of Basse-Terre you'll see signposts to small beaches. The sand starts turning gray as you reach Pigeon Island; it becomes volcanic black as you work your way farther south. There are several nudist beaches (noted below), and topless bathing is commonplace throughout the island. Note that the Atlantic waters on the northeast coast of Grande-Terre are too rough for swimming.

**Anse de la Gourde** is a beautiful stretch of sand that becomes very popular on weekends. It's located between St-François and Pointe des Châteaux. **Caravelle Beach,** just outside the town of Ste-Anne, is one of the longest and prettiest stretches of beach on Grande-Terre, though there are rather dilapidated shacks and cafés scattered about the area. Protected by reefs, the beach makes a fine place for snorkeling. Club Med occupies one end of this beach. **La Grande Anse,** just outside of Deshaies, on the northwest coast of Basse-Terre, is a secluded beach of soft beige sand sheltered by palms. There's a large parking area but no facilities other than the Karacoli restaurant (☞ Dining, *above*). **Ilet du Gosier** is a little speck off the shore of Gosier where you can bathe in the buff. Take along a picnic for an all-day outing. The beach is closed on weekends. **Malendure** beach lies on the west coast of Basse-Terre, across from Pigeon Island. Jacques Cousteau called it one of the 10 best diving places in the world. Several scuba operations are based here (☞ Outdoor Activities and Sports, *below*). There are also glass-bottom-boat trips for those who prefer keeping their heads above water. **Petit-Anse,** on Marie-Galante, is a long gold-sand beach crowded with locals on weekends. During the week it's quiet, and there are no facilities other than the little seafood restaurant, Le Touloulou (☞ Dining, *above*). **Place Crawen,** Les Saintes's quiet, secluded beach for skinny-dipping, is a half mile of white sand on Terre-de-Haut. **Pointe Tarare** is a secluded strip of sand just before the tip of Pointe des Châteaux, and is one of the most popular nudist beaches on Guadeloupe. There is a small bar-café located in the parking area, a four-minute walk from the beach. **Les Pompierres,** a palm-fringed stretch of tawny sand, is a popular Les Saintes beach. **Souffleur,** on the west coast of Grande-Terre, north of Port-Louis, has brilliant flamboyant trees that bloom in the summer. There are no facilities on the beach, but you can buy the makings of a picnic from nearby shops.

## Outdoor Activities and Sports

### Bicycling

The French are mad about *le cyclisme,* so if you want to feel like a native, take to two wheels. Pedal fever hits the island in August every year, when hundreds of cyclists take to the tarmac for the 10-day Tour de Guadeloupe. You can rent bikes in Pointe-à-Pitre at **Velo Tout Terrain** (☎ 590/97–85–40), which also offers mountain-bike tours in Basse-Terre and Marie-Galante. In St-François you can rent from **Espace VTT** (☎ 590/88–79–91).

### Boating

If you plan to sail these waters, you should be aware that the winds and currents of Guadeloupe tend to be strong. There are excellent, well-equipped marinas in Pointe-à-Pitre, Bas-du-Fort, Deshaies, St-François, and Gourbeyre. Bareboat or crewed yachts can be rented in Bas-du-Fort at **Moorings** (☎ 590/90–81–81), **Star Voyages Antilles** (☎ 590/90–86–26), and **ATM Yachts** (☎ 590/90–92–02). Most beachfront hotels rent Hobie Cats, Sunfish, pedal boats, motorboats, and water skis.

## Deep-Sea Fishing

Half- and full-day trips in search of bonito, dolphin, captain fish, barracuda, kingfish, and tuna can be arranged through **Le Rocher de Malendure** (⊠ Pigeon, Bouillante, ☎ 590/98–70–84) and **Caraibe Peche** (⊠ Marina, Bas-du-Fort, ☎ 590/90–97–51). Count on about 3,500F for a half-day's boat charter and 4,500F for a full day.

## Fitness

**Gym Tropic** (⊠ Marissol hotel, Bas-du-Fort, ☎ 590/90–84–44) offers gym space for calisthenics and stretching, water exercise classes in the pool or the sea, yoga classes, and beauty care. **Viva Forme** (⊠ Bas-du-Fort, ☎ 590/90–98–74) has two squash courts and weights and machines for muscle toning.

## Flying

ULMs (Ultra Léger Motorisés) are popular with European tourists. The extremely lightweight seaplanes soar along the coast at approximately 100 feet. Go for a ride at **Holywind** (⊠ Canella Beach Residence, Pointe de la Verdure, Gosier, ☎ 590/90–44–00). The cost is 170F for 10 minutes.

## Golf

**Golf Municipal Saint-François** (⊠ St-François, ☎ 590/88–41–87) has an 18-hole Robert Trent Jones course, an English-speaking pro, a clubhouse, a pro shop, and electric carts for rental. The greens fee is 250F.

## Hiking

Basse-Terre's national park is laced with fascinating trails, many of which should be attempted only with an experienced guide. Trips for up to 12 people are arranged by **Organisation des Guides de Montagne de la Caraïbe** (⊠ Maison Forestière, Matouba, ☎ 590/94–29–11).

## Horseback Riding

Beach rides, picnics, and lessons are available through **Le Criolo** (⊠ St-Felix, Gosier, ☎ 590/84–04–06). On Basse Terre, contact **La Manade** (⊠ Saint-Claude, ☎ 590/81–52–21).

## Scuba Diving

Cousteau called the dive off Pigeon Island, on the west coast of Basse-Terre, one of the 10 best dives in the world. But when you compare it to other famous sites—even neighboring Dominica—Cousteau's claim falls a bit short. The main diving area, at the Cousteau Underwater Park, a 10-minute boat ride from the mainland, offers fairly simple dives to 60 feet—no canyons, no caves, no volcanic ridges. Numerous glass-bottomed boats and day-trippers also make the site feel a bit like a crowded marine car-park. That said, the fish are spectacular. Guides and instructors here are certified under the French CMAS rather than PADI or NAUI. To explore the wrecks and reefs, contact **Chez Guy et Christian** (⊠ Malendure, ☎ 590/98–82–43). This outfit also arranges dives elsewhere around Guadeloupe and weekly packages that include accommodations in bungalows. Other leading operations include **Caraïbes Plongées** (⊠ Gosier, ☎ 509/90–44–90), **Les Heures Saines** (⊠ Malendure, ☎ 590/98–86–63), and **Marine Anse Plongée** (⊠ Bouillante, ☎ 590/98–78–78). On Isle des Saintes, the **Centre Nautique des Saintes** (⊠ Plage de la Coline, Terre-de-Haut, ☎ 590/99–54–25) and **Espace Plongé Caraïbes** (⊠ Bourg, ☎ 590/99–51–84) arrange dives.

## Snorkeling and Sea Excursions

Most hotels rent snorkeling gear and post information about excursions. The *King Papyrus* (⊠ Marina Bas-du-Fort, ☎ 590/90–92–98) is a catamaran you can snorkel from that offers full-day outings replete with rum, dances, and games, as well as moonlight sails. **Nautilus Club** (⊠ Plage de Malendure, ☎ 590/98–89–08) offers glass-bottom-boat tours and snorkeling.

### Tennis
Courts are located at many hotels, including **Auberge de la Vieille Tour** (two courts), **Caravelle/Club Med** (six courts), **La Créole Beach** (two courts), **Golf Marine Club Hotel** (two courts), **Hamak** (one court), **Le Méridien St. François** (two courts), and **Relais du Moulin** (one court). You can also play at the **Marina Club** (☎ 590/90–84–08) in Pointe-à-Pitre and at the **Tennis League of Guadeloupe** (☎ 590/90–90–97) at the Centre Lamby-Lambert Stadium in Glosier.

### Windsurfing
Windsurfing is immensely popular here. Rentals and lessons are available at all beachfront hotels. Windsurfing buffs congregate at the **UCPA Hotel Club** (☎ 590/88–64–80) in St-François. You can also rent a *planche-à-voile* (Windsurfer)—try the **Callinago** (⊠ Gosier, ☎ 590/84–25–25).

## Shopping

If shopping is your goal and you want to do it on a French island, head for Martinique—selection is better and you are more likely to be understood. But shopping can be fun in Pointe-à-Pitre at the street stalls around the harbor quay, in front of the tourist office, and at the market. Moreover, numerous small boutiques selling unique designs have opened in town. The more touristy shops are down at the St-John Perse cruise terminal, where an attractive mall is home to two dozen shops. Get an early start, because it gets very hot and sticky around midday.

Many stores offer a 20% discount on luxury items purchased with traveler's checks or, in some cases, major credit cards. You can find good buys on anything French—perfumes, crystal, china, cosmetics, fashions, scarves. As for local handcrafted items, you'll see a lot of junk, but you can also find wood carvings, madras table linens, island dolls dressed in madras, finely woven straw baskets and hats, and salako hats made of split bamboo. Of course there's the favorite Guadeloupean souvenir—rum.

### Shopping Areas
In Pointe-à-Pitre the main shopping streets are rue Schoelcher, rue de Noizières, and rue Frébault, the liveliest street in the city. Bas-du-Fort's two shopping districts are the Mammouth Shopping Center and the Marina, where there are 20 or so boutiques and several restaurants. In St-François there are also several shops surrounding the marina. Many of the resorts have fashion boutiques. There are also a number of duty-free shops at Raizet Airport.

### Good Buys
#### CHINA, CRYSTAL, AND SILVER
**Rosebleu** (⊠ 5 rue Frébault, Pointe-à-Pitre, ☎ 590/82–93–43; also at the airport) sells crystal and silver by top lines, including Christofle. **Selection** (⊠ Rue Schoelcher, Pointe-à-Pitre, no phone) stocks Baccarat, Lalique, Porcelaine de Paris, Limoges, and other upscale tableware.

#### COSMETICS AND LINGERIE
**Soph't** (⊠ 41, Immeuble Lesseps, Centre St-John Perse, Pointe-à-Pitre, ☎ 590/83–07–73) is the place to buy delicate, fanciful, and very French lingerie. **Vendome** (⊠ 8–10 rue Frébault, Pointe-à-Pitre, ☎ 590/83–42–84) is Guadeloupe's exclusive purveyor of Stendhal and Germaine Monteil.

LOCAL CRAFTS

**L'Atelier de l'Art** (⊠ Gosier, Rte. des Hotels, no phone) offers fanciful creations of wood and straw. **Au Caraibe** (⊠ 4 rue Frébault, Pointe-à-Pitre, no phone) sells dolls, straw hats, baskets, and madras table linens. **Boutique de la Plage** (⊠ Blvd. Général de Gaulle, Gosier, ☎ 590/84–52–51) offers a mind-boggling jumble ranging from tacky tchotchke like "fertility" sculptures to sublime art naif canvases for as little as $20. **La Case à Soie** (⊠ Ste-Anne, ☎ 590/88–11–31) creates flowing silk dresses and scarves in Caribbean colors. **Centre d'Art Haitien** (⊠ Rue Delgres, Pointe-à-Pitre, ☎ 590/82–54–46, and 65 Montauban, Gosier, ☎ 590/84–32–60) is the place to buy imaginative art. **Centre de Broderie** (⊠ Vieux Fort, ☎ 590/92–04–14) is in the small town of Vieux Fort, on the southern coast of Basse-Terre, renowned for its lacework. The Centre is built into the ruins of Fort L'Olive, and you can watch local ladies at work tatting intricate tablecloths, napkins, and place mats, according to traditions passed down over generations. This kind of stitchery is rare; unfortunately with the devaluation of the dollar, prices are *très cher*: $30 for a doily. **Floral Antilles** (⊠ 80 rue Schoelcher, ☎ 590/82–18–63) packages anthuriums and other plants that pass muster at U.S. customs. **José Beaujour** (⊠ Terre-de-Bas, ☎ 590/99–80–20) is who to contact for an authentic salako hat. **Maogany Artisanat** (⊠ Bour, Terre-de-Haut, ☎ 590/99–50–12) sells Yves Cohen's batik and hand-painted T-shirts in luminescent seashell shades. **Pascal Foy** (⊠ Rte. à Pompierres, ☎ 590/99–52–29) produces stunning homages to traditional Creole architecture: painted houses incorporating collage and *objets trouvés* that make marvelous wall hangings. Prices begin at $90 and are well worth it. **Tim Tim** (⊠ 15 rue Henri IV, ☎ 590/83–48–71) is a nostalgia shop with elegant (and expensive) antiques ranging from Creole furniture to maps.

PERFUMES

**L'Artisan Parfumeur** (⊠ Rue Schoelcher, Pointe-à-Pitre, no phone) sells both top French and American brands and tropical scents. **Au Bonheur des Dames** (⊠ 49 rue Frébault, Pointe-à-Pitre, ☎ 590/82–00–30) offers an array of cosmetics and skin-care products, in addition to its perfumes. **Phoenicia** (⊠ Bas-du-Fort, Gosier, ☎ 590/90–85–56; 8 rue Frébault, Pointe-à-Pitre, ☎ 590/83–50–36; and 121 bis rue Frébault, Pointe-à-Pitre, ☎ 590/82–25–75) sells various perfumes.

RUM AND TOBACCO

**Comptoir sous Douane** (⊠ Raizet Airport, ☎ 590/82–22–76) has a good selection of island rums and tobacco. **Delice Shop** (⊠ 45 rue Achille René-Boisneuf, Pointe-à-Pitre, ☎ 590/82–98–24) is the spot for island rums and gourmet items from France, from cheese to chocolate.

# Nightlife

Cole Porter notwithstanding, Guadeloupeans maintain that the beguine began here (the Martinicans make the same claim for their island). Discos come, discos go, and the current music craze is "zouk," but the beat of the beguine remains steady. Many of the resort hotels feature dinner dancing, as well as entertainment by steel bands and folkloric groups.

## Bars and Nightclubs

**Au Bar du Minuit** (⊠ Montauban, Gosier, ☎ 590/84–53–77) is a popular hangout. **La Belle Epoque** (⊠ Bas-du-Fort, no phone) has live music. **Cafe de la Marina** (☎ 590/99–53–78) is where the locals congregate after the day-trippers leave; there's always someone playing the Santois version of a bagpipe. **Le Figuier Vert** (⊠ Mare Galliard, Gosier, ☎ 590/85–85–51) offers live jazz Friday and Saturday nights. **Le**

**Jardin Brésilien** (⊠ Bas-du-Fort, ☏ 590/90−99−31), at the Marina, has live music. **Lele Bar** (⊠ Le Méridien, St-François, ☏ 590/88−51−00) draws locals and tourists alike. **Nilce's Bar** (⊠ Bourg, Terre-de-Haut, no phone), right at the pier in Bourg, is where sultry Brazilian chanteuse Nilce Laps holds sway nightly. This charming waterfront bistro is decorated with assorted authentic bistro antiques.

### Casinos

There are two casinos on the island. Both have American-style roulette, blackjack, and chemin de fer. Admission is $10. The legal age is 21, and you'll need a photo ID. Tie and jacket are not required, but "proper attire" means no shorts.

**Casino de Gosier** (⊠ Gosier, ☏ 590/84−18−33) has a bar and restaurant and is open Monday–Saturday 9 PM–dawn. Slot machines open at 10 AM. **Casino de St-François** (⊠ Marina, St-François, ☏ 590/88−41−31) has a snack bar and nightclub and is open Tuesday–Sunday 9 PM–3 AM.

### Discos

A mixed crowd of locals and tourists frequents the discos. Night owls should note that carousing is not cheap. Most discos charge a cover of at least $8, which includes one drink (drinks cost about $5 each). Some of the enduring hot spots are the very Parisian **Elysée Matignon** (⊠ Rte. des Hôtels, Bas-du-Fort, ☏ 590/90−89−05), **Le Caraibe** (⊠ Salako, Gosier, ☏ 590/84−22−22), **Caraïbes 2** (⊠ Carrefour de Blanchard, Bas-du-Fort, ☏ 590/90−97−16), **La Victoria** (⊠ Rte. de Bas-du-Fort, ☏ 590/90−97−76), and **New Land** (⊠ Rte. Riviera, Gosier, ☏ 590/84−34−91). The only disco of note on Basse-Terre is **Chez Vaneau** (⊠ Mahaut, ☏ 590/98−25−72).

# Exploring Guadeloupe

There is a lot to see on Guadeloupe, and the island is one of the larger ones in the region. The capital, Pointe-à-Pitre, can be visited in half a day. To see each "wing" of the butterfly, you'll need to budget at least one day. Grande Terre, which has better roads and is much easier to negotiate, has pretty villages all along its south coast; don't miss the spectacular Pointe des Châteaux. Rugged and mountainous Basse Terre presents a challenge; getting about takes much longer. If time is a problem, head straight to the spectacular west coast; you could easily spend a day traveling its length, taking time to stop for a bit of sightseeing, lunch, and a swim. For the outlying islands, budget more time and more money, as you will probably have to fly there. Iles des Saintes, the most developed of them, is well worth an overnight stay.

*Numbers in the margin correspond to points of interest on the Guadeloupe map.*

### Grande-Terre

**⓭ Anse Bertrand.** The northernmost village in Guadeloupe lies 4 miles south of La Pointe de la Grande Vigie. It was the last refuge of the Caribs and prosperous in the days of sugar. Most of the excitement these days takes place in the St-Jacques Hippodrome, where horse races and cockfights are held. The beach at nearby Anse Laborde is good for swimming.

**❷ Bas-du-Fort.** The main attraction here is the **Fort Fleur d'Epée**, an 18th-century fortress that hunkers on a hillside behind a deep moat. This was the scene of hard-fought battles between the French and the English. You can explore the well-preserved dungeons and battlements and, on a clear day, take in a sweeping view of Iles des Saintes and Marie-Galante.

**⑩ Edgar-Clerc Archaeological Museum.** Three miles to the north of Le
Moule, archaeologists uncovered the remains of Arawak and Carib settlements. This museum contains Amerindian artifacts from the personal
collection of Edgar-Clerc, a well-known archaeologist and historian.
There are several rooms with displays pertaining to the Carib and Arawak
civilizations. ⊠ *La Rosette,* ☎ *590/23–57–57.* ☜ *Free.* ☉ *Thurs.–Tues.*
*9–12:30 and 2–5.*

NEED A    **Château de Feuilles** (☎ 590/22–30–30), between Le Moule and Cam-
BREAK?    pêche (nearer Gros-Cap), is an absolutely superb place for a long
          lunch. A mini-estate, the château has style and excellent cuisine. Bring
          your swimming togs and use the pool while lunch is being prepared (☞
          Dining, *above*).

**④ Gosier.** This pretty village, with red-roofed villas perched above the sea,
is reminiscent of a small town on the Côte d'Azur. People stroll about
with baguettes under their arms, or sit at sidewalk cafés reading *Le
Monde* and drinking "planteurs," the local rum punch. It is the island's
major tourist center, with hotels and inns, nightclubs, shops, a casino,
and a long stretch of sand.

**③ Guadeloupe Aquarium.** This aquarium is one of the Caribbean's largest
and ranked fourth in all of France. ⊠ *Place Créole, off Rte. N4,* ☎
*590/90–92–38.* ☜ *35F.* ☉ *Daily 9–7.*

**⑮ Morne-à-l'Eau.** This agricultural city of about 16,000 people is home
to an amphitheater-shape cemetery, with black-and-white checkerboard
tombs, elaborate epitaphs, and multicolored (plastic) flowers. It's the
most spectacular cemetery on the island, and one of the finest in the
French West Indies. On All Saints' Day it is the scene of a moving (and
photogenic) candlelight service. Just south of Morne-à-l'Eau are the villages of **Jabrun du Sud** and **Jabrun du Nord,** which are inhabited by
the descendants of the "Blancs Matignon," the whites who hid in the
hills and valleys of the Grands Fonds after the abolition of slavery.

**⑨ Le Moule.** This port city of about 17,000 people was once the capital
of Guadeloupe. It was bombarded by the British in 1794 and 1809 and
by a hurricane in 1928. Canopies of flamboyants hang over narrow
streets, where colorful vegetable and fish markets do a brisk business.
The small buildings are of weathered wood with shutters, balconies,
and bright awnings. The town hall, with graceful balustrades, and a
small 19th-century neoclassical church are on the main square. Le Moule
also has a beautiful crescent-shape beach where Atlantic waves roll into
the shore. A mile to the east is another beach protected by a reef, making it perfect for windsurfing.

**⑫ La Pointe de la Grande Vigie.** This is the northernmost tip of the island. Park your car and walk along the paths that lead right out to the
edge. There is a splendid view of Porte d'Enfer from here. On a clear
day you can also see Antigua, 35 miles away.

**⑦ Pointe des Châteaux.** This is the Land's End of Guadeloupe, the easternmost point of the island where the Atlantic and the Caribbean are
hurled together to crash against huge rocks, carving them into pyra-
midlike shapes. The jagged, majestic cliffs are reminiscent of the headlands of Brittany. The only human contribution to this elemental scene
is a massive concrete cross, visible from several miles. From this point
there are spectacular views of the south and east coasts of Guadeloupe
and the island of La Désirade. A St-John Perse poem, inscribed on a
panoramic map, conjures the magic of the place. On weekends locals
come in large numbers to walk their dogs, surf, or romance.

NEED A
BREAK?     **Paillote** (☎ 590/88–63–61) is a tiny roadside stand right on the *pointe* where you can get libations and light bites, such as lobster and fish grilled on a wood fire.

⑭ **Port Louis.** This fishing village of about 7,000 is best known for the Souffleur beach. It was once one of the island's prettiest, but it has become a little shabby. Still, the sand is fringed by flamboyant trees and though the beach is crowded on weekends, it's blissfully quiet during the week. There are also spectacular views of Basse-Terre.

NEED A
BREAK?     **Poisson d'Or** (☎ 590/22–88–75), on rue Sadi Carnot in Port-Louis, is a rustic seaside restaurant that serves spicy Creole dishes.

⑪ **Porte d'Enfer.** The Gate of Hell, 1½ miles north of Campêche, marks a dramatic point on the coast where two jagged cliffs are stormed by the wild Atlantic waters. One legend has it that a Madame Coco strolled out across the waves carrying a parasol and vanished without a trace.

❻ **St-François.** This town was once a simple little village primarily involved with fishing and tomatoes. The fish and tomatoes are still here, but so are some of the island's ritziest hotels. This is the home of the Hamak and Le Méridien's extension, La Cocoteraie, two very plush properties. Avenue de l'Europe runs between the well-groomed 18-hole Robert Trent Jones municipal golf course and the man-made marina. On the marina side, a string of shops, hotels, and restaurants cater to tourists.

❺ **Ste-Anne.** In the 18th century, this town, about 8 miles east of Gosier, used to be a major sugar-exporting center. But only a few ruined sugar mills remain from those days. Sand has replaced sugar as the town's most valuable asset. La Caravelle and the other soft white-sand beaches here are among the best in Guadeloupe. On a more spiritual note, Ste-Anne has a lovely cemetery with stark-white aboveground tombs.

❽ **Zévalos.** Four miles north of St-François is this handsome colonial mansion that was once the manor house of the island's largest sugar plantation.

## Pointe-à-Pitre

❶ **Pointe-à-Pitre.** This city of some 100,000 people in the southwest of Grande-Terre is not the capital of Guadeloupe (that honor goes to the much smaller Basse-Terre), but it is the commercial and industrial hub of the island. It's bustling, noisy, and hot; a place of honking horns and traffic jams. The pulse is faster than in many other Caribbean capitals, though at night the streets are almost deserted.

Life has not been easy for Pointe-à-Pitre. The city has suffered severe damage over the years as a result of earthquakes, fires, and hurricanes. The most recent damage was done in 1979 by Hurricane Frederick, in 1980 by Hurricane David, and in 1989 by Hurricane Hugo. Standing on the rue Frébault, you can see on one side the remaining French colonial structures and on the other, the modern city. However, downtown is rejuvenating itself while maintaining its old charm. Completion of the Centre St-John Perse has meant the transformation of old warehouses into a cruise-terminal complex that consists of a hotel (the Hotel St-John), three restaurants, space for 80 shops, and the headquarters for Guadeloupe's Port Authority.

Rues Noizières, Frébault, and Schoelcher are Pointe-à-Pitre's main shopping streets. Rue Achille René-Boisneuf is the best street to see traditional, Creole-style houses. But the heart of the old city is the **Place de la Victoire**, surrounded by wood buildings with balconies and shutters. Many sidewalk cafés have opened up on this revitalized square, making it a good place for lunch or light refreshments. At the southern edge of the square, you can watch the busy life of the harbor. Place de la Victoire was named in honor of Victor Hugues's 1794 victory over the British. The sandbox trees in the park are said to have been planted by Hugues the day after the victory. During the French Revolution, Hugues expressly ordered the guillotine to be set up in the square so that the public could witness the bloody end of 300 recalcitrant royalists. Today the large palm-shaded park is a popular gathering place, with stalls selling everything from clothes to kitchen utensils, and gaggles of colorfully dressed women selling fruits and vegetables.

Even more colorful is the bustling **marketplace,** between rues St-John Perse, Frébault, Schoelcher, and Peynier. It is a cacophonous and colorful place where housewives bargain for papayas, breadfruits, christophines, tomatoes, and a bright assortment of other produce.

Anyone with an interest in French literature and culture won't want to miss the **Musée St-John Perse,** on rue Achille René-Boisneuf. It is dedicated to Guadeloupe's most famous son, and one of the giants of world literature, Alexis Léger, better known as St-John Perse, winner of the Nobel Prize for literature in 1960. Some of his finest poems are inspired by the history and landscape of his beloved Guadeloupe—above all, the sea. Before you go to the museum, look for his birthplace at No. 54 rue René-Boisneuf. The museum, which is housed in a restored colonial "Steamboat Gothic" house, contains a complete collection of his poetry, as well as some of his personal belongings. There are also works written about him and various mementos, documents, and photographs. ⊠ *Corner rues Noizières and Achille René-Boisneuf,* ☎ *590/90–07–92.* ⊇ *10F.* ☉ *Thurs.–Tues. 8:30–12:30 and 2:30–5:30.*

Guadeloupe's other famous son is celebrated at the **Musée Schoelcher** at the corner of rues Schoelcher and Peynier. Victor Schoelcher, a high-minded abolitionist from Alsace, fought against slavery in the French West Indies during the 19th century. The museum contains many of his personal effects, and exhibits trace his life and work. ⊠ *24 rue Peynier,* ☎ *590/82–08–04.* ⊇ *10F.* ☉ *Weekdays 8:30–11:30 and 2–5.*

For fans of French ecclesiastical architecture, there is the imposing **Cathédrale de St-Pierre et St-Paul,** on rue Alexandre Isaac. Built in 1807, it has been terribly battered by hurricanes and is now reinforced with iron pillars and ribs that look like leftovers from the Tour Eiffel. Hurricane Hugo destroyed many of the upper windows and shutters. But the fine stained-glass windows and Creole-style upper balconies still make it well worth a visit.

## Basse-Terre

Yellow butterflies—clouds of them—are the first thing you see when you arrive on Basse-Terre. Rugged, green, and mysterious, this half of Guadeloupe is a place of mountain trails, lakes, waterfalls, and hot springs. It is also the home of the Old Lady, as the Soufrière volcano is called locally, as well as of the capital, also called Basse-Terre. It has always been poorer and less developed than Grande-Terre, and the hurricane season of 1995 didn't help. Many villages in the south, which was especially hard hit, have a gloomy, run-down feeling. But the northwest coast, between Bouillante and Grand Anse, is anything but gloomy. The road twists and turns up steep hills smothered in tropical vegetation, skirting scalloped bays before dropping down to colorful little seaside towns. Constantly changing light, towering clouds, and frequent rainbows only add to the beauty. J. M. W. Turner would have loved it. For hikers, the Parc National is crisscrossed by numerous trails, many of them following the old *traces,* routes that porters took across the mountains in historic times.

**㉟ Allée du Manoir.** There's no trace of the manor house, but this magnificent tunnel of century-old royal palms, near the village of Capesterre, is still here. Soaring to as much as 100 feet, the palms have survived both hurricanes and the telephone company, which used to nail the telegraph wires into them.

**㉛ Basse-Terre.** The capital and administrative center of Guadeloupe is an active city of about 15,000 people. Founded in 1640, it has had even more difficulties than Pointe-à-Pitre. The capital has endured not only foreign attacks and hurricanes but sputtering threats from La Soufrière as well. More than once it has been evacuated when the volcano began to hiss and fume. The last major eruption was in the 16th century. But the volcano seemed active enough to warrant the evacuation of more than 70,000 people in 1975. In spite of its troubles, Basse-Terre has retained far more of its old-world charm than Pointe-à-Pitre, with imposing government buildings and town houses.

A good place to start exploring the city is imposing 17th-century **Fort Louis Delgrès.** There is also a small museum, which gives a good outline of Basse-Terre's history. The **Cathedral of Our Lady of Guadeloupe,** to the north across the Rivière aux Herbes, is also worth a short visit. On Boulevard Felix Eboué you can see the impressive colonial buildings housing the government offices. Two main squares, both with gardens, **Jardin Pichon** and **Champ d'Arbaud,** give you a feel for how the city used to be. Not far away are the **botanical gardens.**

**㉖ Bouillante.** The name, literally translated, means "boiling," and so it is no surprise that the main attraction here is the hot springs. At the Source de Thomas, a few minutes' walk up the old Thomas Road, there is a natural bathing spa where you can loll around in hot, smelly water. The Geothermal Power Station nearby is the only one of its kind in the West Indies, and France.

**㉒ Cascade aux Ecrevisses.** Part of the ☞ **Parc National de la Guadeloupe,** Crayfish Falls is one of the loveliest spots on the island. There is a marked trail (walk carefully—the rocks along the trail can be slippery) leading to the splendid waterfall dashing down into the Corossol River— a good place for a dip, though you probably won't have it to yourself. This is one of the most popular sights on the island.

**㉞ Chutes du Carbet.** Carbet Falls are the most spectacular waterfalls on Guadeloupe. Three of them, which drop from 65 feet, 360 feet, and 410 feet, can be reached by following a long, steep path from the village of Habitueé. On the way up, you'll pass the **Grand Etang** (Great Pond), a volcanic lake surrounded by interesting plant life. For Dracula fans there is also the curiously named **Etang Zombi.**

| NEED A BREAK? | After hiking around the falls, you can have a hearty lunch of Creole chicken, curried goat, or crayfish at **Chez Dollin-Le Crepuscule** (✉ Habitueé Village, ☎ 590/86–34–56). There's also a four-course menu. |
| --- | --- |

**㉚ Etang As de Pique.** Reaching this lake, 2,454 feet above the town of Gourbeyre, is a challenge for hikers, but you can also get to it in an hour by car via paved Palmetto Road. The 5-acre lake, formed by a lava flow, is named after its shape, an *as de pique*—French for "ace of spades."

**⑳ Les Mamelles.** Two mountains—Mamelle de Petit-Bourg at 2,350 feet and Mamelle de Pigeon at 2,500 feet—rise in the ☞ **Parc National de**

la Guadeloupe. *Mamelle* means "breast," and when you see the mountains you'll understand why they are so named. From here, trails ranging from easy to arduous lace up into the surrounding mountains. There's a glorious view from the lookout point 1,969 feet up Mamelle de Pigeon. If you're a climber, you'll want to spend several hours exploring this area.

**㉘ Matouba.** This village was settled by East Indians whose descendants still practice ancient rites, including animal sacrifice. If you've an idle 10 hours or so, take off from Matouba for a 19-mile hike on a marked trail through the Monts Caraïbes to the east coast.

**㉝ Parc Archéologique des Roches Gravées.** Situated in the town of Trois-Rivières, this is the principal site in the Lesser Antilles containing rocks engraved and carved by the Arawaks. The park, which is set in a lovely botanical garden full of giant, moss-covered boulders, stairways cut into the rock, and lush plants, is a haven of tranquillity. ⌧ *Bord de la Mer, Trois-Rivières,* ☎ *590/92–91–88.* ⌦ *4F.* ☉ *Daily 9–5.*

**Parc National de la Guadeloupe.** This 74,100-acre park was recently elevated to the status of a recognized Biosphere Reserve by UNESCO, of which there are only 325 worldwide. For the ecotourist, this is the place to come. Before going, pick up a *Guide to the National Park* from the tourist office, which rates the hiking trails according to difficulty. Note: The majority of mountain trails are in the southern half. The park is bisected by the **Route de la Traversée** (La Traversée), a 16-mile-long paved road lined with masses of thick tree ferns, shrubs, flowers, tall trees, and green plantains. It is the ideal point of entry to the park. Wear rubber-soled shoes, and take along both swimsuit and sweater, and perhaps food for a picnic. Try to get an early start to remain ahead of the hordes of cruise-ship passengers that descend on La Traversée and the park for the day. The park's top attractions include ☞ **Cascade aux Ecrevisses,** ☞ **Les Mamelles,** ☞ **Parc Tropical de Bras-David,** and the ☞ **Zoological Park and Botanical Gardens.** ⌧ *Administrative Headquarters, Basse-Terre,* ☎ *590/80–24–25.*

**㉑ Parc Tropical de Bras-David.** This part of the ☞ **Parc National de la Guadeloupe** is where you can park and explore various nature trails. The **Maison de la Forêt** has a variety of displays that describe (for those who can read French) the flora, fauna, and topography of the national park. It's open daily 9–5; admission is free. There are three marked botanical trails and picnic tables where you can enjoy an alfresco lunch.

**㉔ Petit-Bourg.** The highlight here is the Domaine de Valombreuse, a floral park not far from the town. Three hundred species of flowers, spice gardens, and numerous bird species make this a pleasant place for a stroll. There is also a restaurant in the gardens. ⌧ *Petit-Bourg,* ☎ *590/95–50–50.* ⌦ *38F.* ☉ *Daily 9–5.*

**㉕ Pigeon Island.** This tiny, rocky island, a few hundred yards off the coast of Malendure, is the site of the Jacques Cousteau Marine Reserve, the best scuba and snorkeling site on Guadeloupe (☞ **Outdoor Activities and Sports,** *above*). Les Heures Santes and Chez Guy, both on the attractive Malendure Beach, conduct diving trips, and the glass-bottom *Aquarium* and *Nautilus* make daily trips to this spectacular site.

NEED A BREAK? There are several snack wagons at the Malendure beach, but the place to go is **Chez Toulouse** (no phone), a bar and café above the sand.

**⑱ Pointe-Noire.** This town has two small museums devoted to local products. **La Maison du Bois** offers a glimpse into the traditional use of wood on the island. Superbly crafted musical instruments and furnishings are on sale. Just across the road is **La Maison du Cacao,** a working cocoa plantation. Point Noire is a good jumping-off point to explore the little visited **northwest coast** of Basse-Terre. A magnificent coastal road skirts cliffs and tiny coves, dancing in and out of thick stands of mahogany and gommier trees, and weaving through unspoiled fishing villages with boats and ramshackle houses as brightly colored as a child's finger painting. One of the most attractive villages is **Deshaies.** The northwest coast also encompasses the excellent beaches of Grande-Anse, Riflet, La Perle, and Ferry. ✉ *La Maison du Bois,* ☎ *590/98–17–09.* 🎫 *5F.* ☉ *Tues.–Sun. 9:30–5:30. La Maison du Cacao,* ☎ *590/98–21–23.* 🎫 *25F.* ☉ *Daily 9–5.*

🔟 **Ravine Chaude.** It's not Vichy, but this modest spa is a good place to soak after tackling the trails. It draws upon the area's healthful geothermal waters and caters almost entirely to locals, though efforts are being made to upgrade it for an international clientele. Massage, sauna, algae masks, and hydrotherapy are some of the available treatments. The surrounding landscape, in the foothills of Grosse Montagne, with its cane fields, country lanes, and colorful little villages, is very pleasant, in an undramatic kind of way. ✉ *Lamentin,* ☎ *590/25–75–92.* 🎫 *20F.* ☉ *Daily 8–8.*

🔞 **St-Claude.** This village lies on the western slopes of La Soufrière, with good views of "The Old Lady," as the volcano is called. It erupted in 1695 and 1797, and is still quite active, occasionally rumbling and letting off steam. You can get a closer look at it by driving up to the Savane à Mulets. From there leave your car and hike (with an experienced guide) the strenuous two-hour climb to the summit at 4,813 feet, the highest point in the Lesser Antilles. Here, sulphurous fumaroles and solidified lava flows make for an impressive scene. When you get back down, head for **La Maison du Volcan** (☎ 590/80–33–43), a museum that will tell you everything you need to know about volcanoes.

🔟 **Ste-Rose.** As well as a sulphur bath, there are two good beaches, Amandiers and Clugny, and several interesting, small museums in Ste-Rose. **Le Domaine de Severin** is a historic rum distillery with a working paddle wheel; the restaurant in a restored colonial house is well known for its accras and colombos. The nearby **Musée du Rhum** is a bit of a tourist trap. It features the usual exhibits on the history of rum distillation and a collection of insects from the grotesque to the luminous, but at 40F a pop, it's overpriced. ✉ *Le Domaine de Severin,* ☎ *590/28–91–86.* 🎫 *Free.* ☉ *Daily 8:30–12:30. Musée du Rhum, Bellevue,* ☎ *590/28–70–04.* 🎫 *40F.* ☉ *Mon.–Sat. 9–1.*

🔟 **Vernou.** Many of the old mansions you'll see in this area remain in the hands of the original aristocratic families, the Bekés (whites in Creole), who can trace their lineage to before the French Revolution. Traipsing along a path that leads beyond the village through the lush forest you'll come to the waterfall at **Saut de la Lézarde** (Lizard's Leap).

🔟 **Vieux Fort.** In 1980, 40 local lace makers got together to preserve—and display—the ancient tradition of lace making. At the **Centre de Broderie** (☞ Shopping, *above*) you can always see one of them at work. There are handkerchiefs, tablecloths, doilies, and even negligees for sale.

🔟 **Vieux-Habitants.** Several good beaches, a restored coffee plantation and the oldest church on the island (1650), make this village well worth a stop.

🔟 **Zoological Park and Botanical Gardens.** You don't have to be much of a hiker to climb the stone steps leading from the road to this sight in the ☞ **Parc National de la Guadeloupe.** Titi the Raccoon is the mascot of the park. There are also cockatoos, iguanas, and turtles. The cramped cages are a sorrowful sight (you'll want to liberate the residents immediately), but the setting and views are stunning. A snack bar is open for lunch daily except Monday. ✉ *La Traversée,* ☎ *590/98–83–52.* ☑ *25F.* ☉ *Daily 9–4.30.*

## Iles des Saintes

**㊲** **Fort Napoléon.** A relic from the period when the French fortified these islands against the Caribs and the English, nobody has ever fired a shot at or from this fort. Inside is a museum whose galleries hold a collection of 250 modern paintings, heavily influenced by Cubism and Surrealism and hung at odd angles, and an exhaustive exhibit on the important naval Battle of Les Saintes (history buffs may recall Admiral de Grasse from the American Revolution). You can also visit the well-preserved barracks and prison cells and admire the surrounding botanical gardens, which specialize in cacti of all sizes and descriptions. From the fort you can see Fort Josephine across the channel on the Ilet à Cabrit. ✉ *Bourg, no phone.* ☑ *15F.* ☉ *Daily 9–12:30.*

**㊱** **Les Saintes.** The eight-island archipelago of Iles des Saintes, usually referred to as Les Saintes, dots the waters off the south coast of Guadeloupe. The islands are Terre-de-Haut, Terre-de-Bas, Ilet à Cabrit, Grand Ilet, La Redonde, La Coche, Le Pâté, and Les Augustins. Columbus discovered the islands on November 4, 1493, and christened them Los Santos in honor of All Saints' Day.

Of the islands, only Terre-de-Haut and Terre-de-Bas are inhabited, with a combined population of 3,260. Many of les Saintois, as the islanders are called, are fair-haired, blue-eyed descendants of Breton and Norman sailors. Fishing is the main source of income for les Saintois, and the shores are lined with their fishing boats and *filets bleus* (blue nets dotted with burnt-orange buoys). The fishermen wear hats called *salakos,* which look like inverted saucers or coolie hats. They are patterned after a hat said to have been brought here by a seafarer from China or Indonesia.

With 5 square miles and a population of about 1,500, **Terre-de-Haut** is the largest island and the most developed for tourism. Its "big city" is Bourg, which boasts one street and a few bistros, cafés, and shops. Clutching the hillside are trim white houses with bright red or blue doors, balconies, and gingerbread frills.

Getting to Terre-de-Haut is an exhilarating affair, whether by land or sea. Air Guadeloupe has regularly scheduled flights, and your whole life may flash before your eyes as you soar down to the tiny airstrip. However, the flight is mercifully brief, and you may prefer it to the choppy 35-minute ferry crossing from Trois-Rivières or the 60-minute ride from Pointe-à-Pitre. Ferries leave Trois-Rivières at about 8:30 AM (7:30 AM on Sunday) and return about 3 PM. From Pointe-à-Pitre the usual departure time is 8 AM, with return at 4 PM. The round-trip fare from either point is 160F. Check with the tourist office for up-to-date ferry schedules.

Terre-de-Haut's ragged coastline is scalloped with lovely coves and beaches, including the nudist beach at Anse Crawen. The beautiful bay, complete with sugarloaf, has been called a mini Rio. This is a quiet, peaceful getaway, but it may not remain unspoiled. Tourism is increasing and now accounts for 50% of the economy. Although government plans call for a total of only 250 hotel rooms, the tourist-related industries are making a major pitch for more facilities for tourists. Although it makes a great day trip, you'll really get a feel for Les Saintes only if you stay over.

There are three paved roads on the island, but don't even think about driving here. The roads are ghastly, and backing up is a minor art form, choreographed on those frequent occasions when two vehicles meet on one of the steep, narrow roads. The four minibuses that transport passengers from the airstrip and the wharf double as tour buses. However, the island is so small you can get around by walking. It's a mere five-minute stroll from the airstrip and ferry dock to downtown Bourg.

For such a tiny place, Terre-de-Haut offers a variety of hotels and restaurants. For details, ☞ Dining and Lodging, *above.* There are also the **Centre Nautique des Saintes** (⊠ Plage de la Coline, ☎ 590/99–54–25) and **Espace Plongé Caraïbes** (⊠ Bourg, ☎ 590/99–51–84), should you wish to scuba dive off the islands.

### Marie-Galante

Columbus sighted this flat island on November 3, 1493, the day before he landed at Ste-Marie on Basse-Terre. He named it for his flagship, the *Maria Galanda,* and sailed on.

The ferry departs from Pointe-à-Pitre at 8 AM, 2 PM, and 5 PM with returns at 6 AM, 9 AM, and 3:45 PM. (Schedules often change, especially on the weekends, so check them at the tourist office or the harbor offices.) The round-trip costs 160F. You'll put in at Grand Bourg, the major city, with a population of about 8,000. A plane will land you 2 miles from Grand Bourg. If your French or phrase book is good enough, you can negotiate a price with the taxi drivers for touring the island.

**㊳** **Marie-Galante.** Covering about 60 square miles, this is the largest of Guadeloupe's islands. It is dotted with ruined 19th-century sugar mills, and sugar is still one of its major products—the others are cotton and rum. One of the last refuges of the Caribs when they were driven from the mainland by the French, the island is now a favorite retreat of Guadeloupeans, who come on weekends to enjoy the beach at Petit-Anse.

You'll find dramatic coastal scenery, with soaring cliffs holding an angry ocean at bay, such as the Gueule Grand Gouffre (Mouth of the Giant Chasm) and Les Galeries (where millennia of erosion have sculpted a natural arcade), and enormous sun-dappled grottoes like Le Trou à Diable, whose underground river can be explored with a guide. Don't miss the **Château Murat** (☎ 590/97–03–79), a restored 17th-century sugar plantation and rum distillery that houses exhibits on the history of rum making and sugarcane production, as well as the admirable Ecomusée, whose displays celebrate local crafts and customs. The château is open daily 9:15–5; admission is 10F. And do visit the distilleries, especially **Père Labat,** whose rum is considered one of the finest in the Caribbean and whose atelier turns out lovely pottery.

There are several places near the ferry landing where you can get an inexpensive meal of seafood and Creole sauce. If you want to stay over, you can choose from Au Village de Ménard (5 bungalows, ☎ 590/97–77–02) in St-Louis, Auberge de l'Arbre à Pain (7 rooms, ☎ 590/97–73–69) in Grand Bourg, or Hotel Hajo (6 rooms, ☎ 590/97–32–76) in Capesterre. An entertainment complex in Grand Bourg called El Rancho has a 400-seat movie theater, a restaurant, terrace grill, snack bar, disco, and a few double rooms.

### La Désirade

**㊴** **La Désirade.** According to legend, this is the "desired land" of Columbus's second voyage. He spotted it on November 3, 1493. The 8-square-mile island, 5 miles east of St-François, was for many years a leper colony. Most of today's 1,600 inhabitants are fishermen. The main settlement is Grande-Anse, where there is a pretty church and a hotel called L'Oasis (10 rooms, ☎ 590/20–02–12). The restaurant is not fancy, but it serves excellent seafood.

There are good beaches here, notably Souffleur and Baie Mahault, and there's little to do but loll around on them. The island is virtually unspoiled by tourism and is likely to remain so in the foreseeable future.

Three or four minibuses meet the flights and ferries, and you can negotiate with one of them to get a tour. Ferries depart from St-François daily at 8 and 4. The return ferry departs daily at 3:30. However, be sure to check schedules.

# Guadeloupe A to Z

## Arriving and Departing

### BY BOAT

Major cruise lines call regularly, docking at berths in downtown Pointe-à-Pitre about a block from the shopping district. **Trans Antilles Express** (☎ 590/83–12–45) and **Transport Maritime Brudey Frères** (☎ 590/90–04–48) provide ferry service to and from Marie-Galante and Les Saintes. The *Jetcat* and *Madras* ferries depart daily from the pier at Pointe-à-Pitre for Marie-Galante starting at 8 AM (check the schedule). The trip takes one hour, and the fare is 160F round-trip. For Les Saintes, Trans Antilles Express connects daily from Pointe-à-Pitre at 8 AM and from Terre-de-Haut at 4 PM. The trip takes 45 minutes and costs 160F round-trip. The *Socimade* (☎ 590/88–48–63) runs between La Désirade and St-François, departing daily at 8 AM and 4 PM. Return ferries depart daily at 3:30 PM. These schedules are subject to change and should be verified through your hotel or at the tourist office. The **Caribbean Express** (☎ 590/83–04–43) operates from Guadeloupe's Pointe-à-Pitre to Dominica and Martinique. The fare to Dominica is 450F, and the ride takes 2½ hours; the fare to Martinique is 450F and takes four hours. The ferry departs from Pointe-à-Pitre at 8 AM four days a week, but check the schedules because they frequently change.

### BY PLANE

**American Airlines** (☎ 800/433–7300) is usually the most convenient, with year-round daily flights from more than 100 U.S. cities direct to San Juan and nonstop connections to Guadeloupe via American Eagle. **Air Canada** (☎ 800/776–3000) flies direct from Montréal and Toronto. **Air France** (☎ 800/237–2747) flies nonstop from Paris and Fort-de-France and has direct service from Miami and San Juan. **Air Guadeloupe** (☎ 590/82–28–35) flies daily from St. Martin and St. Maarten, St. Barts, Marie-Galante, La Désirade, and Les Saintes. **LIAT** (☎ 212/251–1717 or 590/82–00–84) flies from St. Croix, Antigua, and St. Maarten in the north and is your best bet from Dominica, Martinique, St. Lucia, Grenada, Barbados, and Trinidad.

### FROM THE AIRPORT

You'll land at La Raizet International Airport, 2½ miles from Pointe-à-Pitre. Cabs are lined up outside the airport. The metered fare is about 60F to Pointe-à-Pitre, 90F to Gosier, and 200F to St-François. Fares go up 40% on Sundays and holidays and from 9 PM to 7 AM nightly. For 5F, you can take a bus from the airport to downtown Pointe-à-Pitre.

## Currency

Legal tender is the French franc, which is equal to 100 centimes. At press time, U.S.$1 bought 4.65F and £1 bought 6.90F, but currencies fluctuate daily. Check the current rate of exchange around the time of your departure. Some places accept U.S. dollars, but it's best to change your money into the local currency. Credit cards are accepted in most major hotels, restaurants, and shops, less so in smaller places and in the countryside. There are two ATMs at the airport and at some banks which accept Visa and MasterCard, but not Cirrus. Prices are quoted here in U.S. dollars unless otherwise noted.

## Emergencies

**Police:** In Pointe-à-Pitre (☎ 590/82–13–17), in Basse-Terre (☎ 590/81–11–55). **Fire:** In Pointe-à-Pitre (☎ 590/83–04–76), in Basse-Terre (☎ 590/81–19–22). **SOS ambulance:** ☎ 590/82–89–33. **Hospitals:** There is a 24-hour emergency room at the main hospital, **Centre Hopitalier de Pointe-à-Pitre** (✉ Abymes, ☎ 590/89–10–10). There are 23 clinics and five hospitals located around the island. The tourist office or your hotel can assist you in locating an English-speaking doctor. **Pharmacies:** Pharmacies alternate in staying open around the clock. The tourist office or your hotel can help you locate the one that's on duty.

## Getting Around

### BICYCLES

If you opt to tour the island by bike, you won't be alone. Biking is a major sport here (☞ Outdoor Activities and Sports, *above,* for rental information).

### BUSES

Modern public buses run from 5 AM to 6 PM. They stop along the road at bus stops and shelters marked ARRET-BUS, but you can also flag one down along the route.

### CAR RENTALS

Your valid driver's license will suffice for up to 20 days, after which you'll need an international driver's permit. Guadeloupe has 1,225 miles of excellent roads (marked as in Europe), and driving around Grande-Terre is relatively easy. On Basse-Terre it will take more effort to navigate the hairpin bends that twist through the mountains and around the eastern shore. Guadeloupeans are skillful drivers, but they do like to drive fast. Cars can be rented at **Avis** (☎ 590/82–33–47 or 800/331–1212), **Budget** (☎ 590/82–95–58 or 800/472–3325), **Hertz** (☎ 590/82–00–14 or 800/654–3131), **Thrifty** (☎ 590/91–42–17), and **Eurorent** (☎ 590/91–42–16). There are rental offices at the airport as well as at the major resort areas. Car rentals cost a bit more on Guadeloupe than on the other islands: Count on about $60 a day for a small rental car. Insist on a Peugeot or Ford rather than a Citroën, which seem to break down more easily on rutted roads and in the rain forest.

To rent RVs, contact **Antilles Locap Soleil** (☎ 590/90–95–72) or **Alligator Vacance** (☎ 590/26–72–71; on Basse-Terre, ☎ 590/28–52–25).

### HITCHHIKING

Surprisingly, hitchhiking is legal throughout the archipelago. Be aware that there's not a lot of traffic on Basse-Terre.

### TAXIS

Taxis are metered and fairly pricey. During the day you'll pay about 60F from the airport to Pointe-à-Pitre, about 90F to Gosier, and about 200F to St-François. On Sundays, holidays, and between 9 PM and 7 AM, fares increase 40%. If your French is in working order, you can contact radio cabs at 590/82–00–00, 590/83–09–55, and 590/20–74–74. On Basse-Terre call 590/81–79–70.

### VESPAS

Vespas (motorbikes) can be rented at **Vespa Sun** (many locations in Pointe-à-Pitre, ☎ 590/91–30–36) and **Equator Moto** (✉ Gosier, ☎

590/90−36−77). A scooter generally costs 200F per day including insurance. You'll need to put down a 1,000F deposit.

## Guided Tours

There are set fares for taxi tours to various points on the island. The tourist office or your hotel can arrange for an English-speaking taxi driver and even organize a small group for you to share the cost of the tour.

**George-Marie Gabrielle** (✉ Pointe-à-Pitre, ☎ 590/90−04−82) offers half- and full-day excursions around the island. A modern bus with an English-speaking guide will pick you up at your hotel. **Guides de Montagne de la Caraibe,** O.G.M.C. (✉ Maison Forestière, Matouba, ☎ 590/80−05−79), provides guides for hiking tours in the mountains. **Norbert Noel Robert** (✉ Pointe-à-Pitre, ☎ 590/82−97−86) speaks excellent English, loves to talk, knows *everybody,* and is a font of information (practical or not). **Organisation des Parfum d'Aventure** (✉ Ste-Anne, ☎ 590/88−47−62) offers adventure excursions in Basse-Terre, including canyoning, canoeing on the Lézarde, sea kayaking, four-wheel drives, and hikes—from easy to grueling.

## Language

The official language is French. Everyone also speaks a Creole patois, which you won't be able to understand even if you're fluent in French. In the major tourist hotels, most of the staff knows some English. However, communicating may be more difficult in the smaller hotels and restaurants in the countryside. Some taxi drivers speak a little English. Arm yourself with a phrase book, a dictionary, patience, and a sense of humor.

## Opening and Closing Times

Banks are open weekdays 8−noon and 2−4. Credit Agricole, Banque Populaire, and Société Générale de Banque aux Antilles have branches that are open Saturday. During the summer most banks are open 8− 3. Banks close at noon the day before a legal holiday that falls during the week. As a rule, shops are open weekdays 8 or 8:30−noon and 2:30− 6, but hours are flexible when cruise ships are in town.

## Passports and Visas

U.S. and Canadian citizens need only proof of citizenship. A passport is best (even one that expired up to five years ago). Other acceptable documents are a notarized birth certificate with a raised seal (not a photocopy) or a voter registration card accompanied by a government-authorized photo ID. A free temporary visa, good only for your stay in Guadeloupe, will be issued to you upon your arrival at the airport. British citizens need a valid passport, but no visa. In addition, all visitors must hold an ongoing or return ticket.

## Precautions

Put your valuables in the hotel safe. Don't leave them unattended in your room or on the beach. Keep an eye out for motorcyclists riding double, as they sometimes play the notorious game of veering close to the sidewalk and snatching shoulder bags. It isn't a good idea to walk around Pointe-à-Pitre at night, because it's almost deserted after dark. If you rent a car, always lock it with luggage and valuables stashed out of sight.

The rough Atlantic waters off the northeast coast of Grande-Terre are dangerous for swimming.

Ask permission before taking a picture of an islander, and don't be surprised if the answer is a firm "No." Guadeloupeans are also deeply religious and traditional. Don't offend them by wearing short shorts or swimwear off the beach.

## Taxes and Service Charges

The *taxe de séjour* varies from hotel to hotel but never exceeds $1.50 per person, per day. Most hotel prices include a 10%–15% service charge; if not, it will be added to your bill.

Restaurants are legally required to include a 15% gratuity in the menu price, and no additional gratuity is necessary. Tip skycaps and porters about 5F. Many cab drivers own their own cabs and don't expect a tip. You won't have any trouble ascertaining if a 10% tip is expected.

## Telephones and Mail

To call from the United States, dial 011–590, then the local number. (To call person-to-person, dial 01–590.) It is not possible to place collect or credit-card calls to the United States from Guadeloupe. Coin-operated phones are rare but can be found in restaurants and cafés. If you need to make many calls outside of your hotel, purchase a Tele-carte at the post office or other outlets marked "Telecarte en Vente Ici." Telecartes look like credit cards and are used in special booths labeled "Telecom." Local and international calls made with the cards are cheaper than operator-assisted calls.

To call the United States from Guadeloupe, dial 19 + 1 + the area code and phone number. To dial locally in Guadeloupe, simply dial the six-digit phone number.

Postcards to the United States cost 3.70F; letters up to 20 grams, 4.60F. Stamps can be purchased at the post office, *café-tabacs*, hotel newsstands, and souvenir shops. Postcards and letters to the United Kingdom cost 3.60F.

## Visitor Information

For information contact the **French West Indies Tourist Board** by calling France-on-Call at 900/990–0040 (50¢ per minute 9 AM–7 PM EST). You may write to the U.S. branches of the **French Government Tourist Office** (⊠ 444 Madison Ave., New York, NY 10022; ⊠ 9454 Wilshire Blvd., Beverly Hills, CA 90212; ⊠ 645 N. Michigan Ave., Chicago, IL 60611) and write or call the branches in Canada and the United Kingdom (⊠ 1981 McGill College Ave., Suite 490, Montréal, Québec H3A 2W9, ☎ 514/288–4264; ⊠ 30 St. Patrick St., Suite 700, Toronto, Ontario M5T 3A3, ☎ 416/593–6427; ⊠ 178 Piccadilly, London W1V 0AL, ☎ 0171/499–6911).

In Guadeloupe, The **Office Départemental du Tourism** has an office in Pointe-à-Pitre (⊠ 5 Square de la Banque B.P. 1099, 97181 Cedex, ☎ 590/82–09–30). The office is open weekdays 8–5, Saturday 8–noon. There is also a tourist information booth at the airport.

# 14 Jamaica

**T**HE THIRD-LARGEST ISLAND in the Caribbean (after
Cuba and Puerto Rico), the English-speaking nation
of Jamaica enjoys a considerable self-sufficiency
based on tourism, agriculture, and mining. Its physical attractions include jungle mountaintops, clear waterfalls, and unforgettable beaches,
yet the country's greatest resource may be the Jamaicans themselves.
Although 95% of the population trace their bloodlines to Africa,
their national origins lie in Great Britain, the Middle East, India,
China, Germany, Portugal, South America, and many of the other islands in the Caribbean. Their cultural life is a wealthy one; the music,
art, and cuisine of Jamaica are vibrant, with a spirit easy to sense but
as hard to describe as the rhythms of reggae or a flourish of the street-
wise patois.

Updated by
Melissa Rivers

In addition to its north-coast pleasure capitals—Montego Bay and Ocho
Rios—Jamaica has a real capital in Kingston. For all its congestion and
for all the disparity between city life and the bikinis and parasails to
the north, Kingston is the true heart and head of the island. This is the
place where politics, literature, music, and art wrestle for acceptance
in the largest English-speaking city south of Miami, its actual population of nearly 1 million bolstered by the emotional membership of
virtually all Jamaicans.

The first people known to have reached Jamaica were the Arawaks,
Indians who paddled their canoes from the Orinoco region of South
America about a thousand years after the death of Christ. Then, in 1494,
Christopher Columbus stepped ashore at what is now called Discovery Bay. Having spent four centuries on the island, the Arawaks had
little notion that his feet on their sand would mean their extinction within
50 years.

What is now St. Ann's Bay was established as New Seville in 1509 and
served as the Spanish capital until the local government crossed the island to Santiago de la Vega (now Spanish Town). The Spaniards were
never impressed with Jamaica; their searches found no precious met-
als, and they let the island fester in poverty for 161 years. When 5,000
British soldiers and sailors appeared in Kingston Harbor in 1655, the
Spaniards did not put up a fight.

The arrival of the English, and the three centuries of rule that followed,
provided Jamaica with the surprisingly genteel underpinnings of its
present life—and the rousing pirate tradition fueled by rum that en-
livened a long period of Caribbean history. The British buccaneer
Henry Morgan counted Jamaica's governor as one of his closest friends
and enjoyed the protection of His Majesty's government no matter what
he chose to plunder. Port Royal, once said to be the "wickedest city
of Christendom," grew up on a spit of land across from present-day
Kingston precisely because it served so many interests. Morgan and
his brigands were delighted to have such a haven, and the people of
Jamaica profited by being able to buy pirate booty at terrific bargains.

Morgan enjoyed a prosperous life; he was knighted and made lieutenant
governor of Jamaica before the age of 30, and, like every good bureaucrat,
he died in bed and was given a state funeral. Port Royal fared less well.
On June 7, 1692, an earthquake tilted two-thirds of the city into the
sea, the tidal wave that followed the last tremors washed away millions in pirate treasure, and Port Royal simply disappeared. In recent
years divers have turned up some of the treasure, but most of it still

lies in the depths, adding an exotic quality to the water sports pursued along Kingston's reefs.

The very British 18th century was a time of prosperity in Jamaica. This was the age of the sugar baron, who ruled his plantation great house and made the island the largest sugar-producing colony in the world. Because sugar fortunes were built on slave labor, however, production became less profitable when the Jamaican slave trade was abolished in 1807 and slavery was ended in 1838.

As was often the case in colonies, a national identity came to supplant allegiance to the British in the hearts and minds of Jamaicans. This new identity was given official recognition on August 6, 1962, when Jamaica became an independent nation with loose ties to the Commonwealth. The island today has a democratic form of government led by a prime minister and a cabinet of fellow ministers.

# Lodging

The island has a variety of destinations to choose from, each of which offers its own unique expression of the Jamaican experience.

**Kingston** is the most culturally active place in Jamaica. Some of the island's finest business hotels are here, and those high towers are filled with rooftop restaurants, English pubs, serious theater and pantomime, dance presentations, art museums and galleries, jazz clubs, upscale supper clubs, and disco dives.

**Mandeville,** 2,000 feet above the sea, is noted for its cool climate and proximity to secluded south-coast beaches. Most accommodations don't have air-conditioning (it's simply not needed) but are close to golf, tennis, horseback riding, and bird-watching areas.

**Montego Bay** has miles of hotels, villas, apartments, and duty-free shops. Although lacking much in the way of cultural stimuli, MoBay presents a comfortable island backdrop for the many conventions it hosts.

**Negril,** some 50 miles west of Montego Bay, was long a sleepy bohemian retreat. In the last decade the town has bloomed considerably and added a number of classy all-inclusive resorts (Sandals Negril, Grand Lido, and Swept Away), with a few more on the drawing board. Negril itself is only a small village, so there isn't much of historical significance to seek out. Then again, that's not what brings the sybaritic singles and couples here. The crowd is young, hip, laid-back, and here for the sun, the sand, and the sea.

**Ocho Rios,** on the northeast coast halfway between Port Antonio and Montego Bay, is hilly and lush, with rivers, riotous gardens, and a growing number of upscale resorts, many of which are all-inclusive. Ocho Rios's hotels and villas are all within short driving distance of shops and one of Jamaica's most scenic attractions, Dunn's River Falls.

**Port Antonio,** described by poet Ella Wheeler Wilcox as "the most exquisite port on earth," is a seaside town nestled at the foot of verdant hills toward the east end of the north coast. The two best experiences to be had here are rafting the Rio Grande and a stop at the Trident, one of the island's classiest resorts. Today, Port Antonio enjoys the reputation of being Jamaica's most favored out-of-the-way resort.

**Runaway Bay,** the smallest of the resort areas, has a handful of modern hotels and an 18-hole golf course.

Jamaica was the birthplace of the Caribbean all-inclusive, the vacation concept that took the Club Med idea and gave it a lusty, excess-in-the-

Mahoe Bay

Cornwall Beach
Doctor's Cave Beach
Walter Fletcher Beach
Donald Sangster International Airport

Falmouth

Puerto Seco Beach
Duncans

Runaway Bay

34 – 38

41

39

A1

B11

Brown's Town

Pedro Pt.

Lucea

A1

Sandy Bay

B8

1 Montego Bay

Clark's Town

2

Green Island

Montpelier

15

Albert Town

Alexandria

Glasgow

B6

B3

Long Bay

Negril Beach
Hedonism II Beach

Savanna-la-Mar

Balaclava

Christiana

16 Negril

A2

B6

Southwest Pt.

Bluefields Beach

Bluefields

Middle Quarters

Santa Cruz

Mandeville

14

17 – 31

Black R.

Black River

A2

32 33

A2

Crane Beach

Treasure Beach

Alligator Pond

Treasure Beach

Great Pedro Bluff

Old Woman's Pt.

Long Bay

N

0 ——— 10 miles
0 ——— 15 km

**Exploring**
Blue Mountains, **10**
Cockpit Country, **15**
Crystal Springs, **6**
Firefly, **5**
Golden Eye, **4**
Kingston, **11**
Mandeville, **14**
Martha Brae River, **2**
Montego Bay, **1**
Negril, **16**
Ocho Rios, **3**
Port Antonio, **8**

Port Royal, **12**
Rio Grande River, **9**
Somerset Falls, **7**
Spanish Town, **13**

**Dining**
Almond Tree, **43**
Blue Mountain Inn, **60**
Cafe au Lait, **18**
Cosmo's Seafood Restaurant and Bar, **26**

Double V Jerk Centre, **56**
Evita's, **44**
Hot Pot, **62**
Hotel Four Seasons, **64**
Ivor Guest House, **68**
Jade Garden, **65**
Palm Court, **63**
Paradise Yard, **20**
Peppers, **61**
Rick's Cafe, **17**
The Ruins, **45**

Sweet Spice, **21**
Tan-ya's, **24**
La Trattoria, **67**

**Lodging**
Astra Country Inn & Restaurant, **32**
Bonnie View Plantation Hotel, **71**
Boscobel Beach, **54**
Braco Village Resort, **38**
Breezes Runaway Bay, **34**

**KEY**

- ● Exploring Sites
- ⑰ Hotels and Restaurants

Charela Inn, **23**
Chukka Cove, **39**
Ciboney, Ocho Rios, **58**
Club Caribbean, **36**
Club Jamaica Beach Resort, **47**
Comfort Suites, **55**
Couples, **53**
Devine Destiny, **19**
Dragon Bay, **70**
Enchanted Garden, **42**

FDR, Franklyn D. Resort, **37**
Goblin Hill, **75**
Grand Lido, **30**
H.E.A.R.T. Country Club, **35**
Hedonism II, **29**
Hibiscus Lodge, **48**
High Hope Estate, **41**
Hotel Mocking Bird Hill, **74**
Jamaica Grande, **46**
Jamaica Inn, **51**

Jamaica Palace, **73**
Jamaica Pegasus, **55**
Mandeville Hotel, **33**
Morgan's Harbour Hotel, Beach Club, and Yacht Marina, **59**
Negril Cabins, **31**
Negril Gardens, **22**
Plantation Inn, **50**
Poinciana Beach Resort, **27**
Sandals Dunn's River, **40**

Sandals Negril, **28**
Sandals Ocho Rios, **49**
Sans Souci Lido, **57**
Shaw Park Beach Hotel, **52**
Strawberry Hill, **69**
Swept Away, **25**
Terra Nova, **66**
Trident Villas and Hotel, **72**
Wyndham New Kingston, **62**

tropics spin. The all-inclusive resort has become the most popular vacation option in Jamaica, offering incredible values with rates from $145 to $350 per person per night. Rates include airport transfers; hotel accommodations; three meals a day plus snacks; all bar drinks, often including premium liquors; wine, beer, and soft drinks; a plethora of land and water sports, including instruction and equipment; and all gratuities and taxes. The only surcharges are usually for such luxuries as massages, souvenirs, sightseeing tours, and weddings or vow-renewal ceremonies (though these are often included at any of the high-end all-inclusives). At times they may feel a bit like Pleasure Island, as all of your needs and most of your wants are taken care of. The all-inclusives have branched out, some of them courting families, others going after an upper crust that would not even have picked up a brochure a few years ago. Most require a three-night minimum stay.

If you're the exploring type who likes to get out and about, you may prefer an EP property. Many places offer MAP or FAP packages that include extras like airport transfers and sightseeing tours. Even if you don't want to be tied down to a meal plan, it pays to inquire, because the savings can be considerable. Rooms at most hotels come equipped with cable or satellite TV, air-conditioning, direct-dial phone, clock radio, and, in many cases, a safe. Larger properties usually have no-smoking rooms and rooms accessible to travelers with disabilities, as well room service, a beauty parlor, a tour desk, and car rentals.

Please note that the price categories listed below are based on winter rates. As a general rule, rates are reduced anywhere from 10% to 30% from April 30 to December 15. The **Jamaica Reservation Service** (☎ 800/526–2422 in the U.S. and Canada) can book resorts, hotels, and guest houses throughout the country.

At press time, the family-oriented, all-inclusive **Vista Ambassador** (⊠ MoBay, ☎ 809/952–4703), with separate spas for the kids and the adults, was just about to open. We were unable to visit the property in fully operational state, but initial reports have been good. Other welcome additions to Jamaica's lodging scene include **Breezes,** a new line of moderately priced all-inclusives introduced by SuperClubs (☎ 800/859–7873); the flagship Breezes took over Jamaica- Jamaica in Runaway Bay, and there's a newly constructed Breezes on Doctors Cave Beach in MoBay and a Breezes scheduled to open in Negril by 1997.

| CATEGORY | COST EP/BP* | COST MAP** | COST AI*** |
|---|---|---|---|
| $$$$ | over $245 | over $250 | over $275 |
| $$$ | $175–$245 | $190–$250 | $225–$275 |
| $$ | $105–$175 | $130–$190 | $175–$225 |
| $ | under $105 | under $130 | under $175 |

*EP prices are for a standard double room for two in winter, excluding 10% tax and any service charge. Many hotels either include breakfast in the tariff or offer a BP price which includes breakfast as their minimum plan.*

**MAP prices include breakfast and dinner for two daily in winter. Often MAP packages come with use of nonmotorized water sports and other benefits.*

***All-inclusive (AI) winter prices are per person, double occupancy, and include tax, service, gratuities, all meals, drinks, facilities, lessons, and airport transfers. Motorized water sports and scuba are sometimes included; ask if it's important to you.*

## Kingston

$$$$    🏨 **Stawberry Hill.** One of many island properties owned by Chris
★    Blackwell, head of Island Records, this Blue Mountains retreat 45 minutes north of Kingston offers refined luxury and absolute peace. Au-

thors, musicians, and screenwriters come here for extended periods to relax, rejuvenate the creative juices, and get some serious work done, encouraged by the remote, peaceful setting so removed from the workaday world. The food is top notch, as are the staff and the accommodations—elegant Georgian-style villas appointed with mahogany furnishings and roomy balconies overlooking grand vistas. There's no air-conditioning here, simply because it's not needed at 3,100 feet above sea level. Sunday brunch, featuring an enormous Jamaican buffet, is an affair to remember, but reserve a spot early because it's a favored event among Kingston's movers and shakers. ✉ *Irishtown, Box 590, Liguanea, St. Andrew,* ☎ *809/944–8400 or 800/688–7678,* FAX *809/944–8404. 12 1-, 2-, and 3-bedroom villas. Restaurant, bar, in-room CD players, 1 villa with outdoor hot tub, refrigerators, room service, plunge pool, sauna, croquet, CD and video library, laundry service, business services, meeting room, travel services, airport shuttle. AE, MC, V. BP.*

**$$$** ☷ **Jamaica Pegasus.** The Jamaica Pegasus is one of two business-class hotels in the New Kingston area. The 17-story complex near downtown has an efficient and accommodating staff, Old World decor, and a newly renovated lobby. Other advantages here include an excellent business center, duty-free shops, and 24-hour room service. Guests on the business floors can check out complimentary cellular phones for use during their stay. The rooms, all with balcony, coffee/tea setups, and voice mail, were scheduled to have desperately needed face-lifts in 1996. ✉ *81 Knutsford Blvd., Box 333, Kingston,* ☎ *809/926–3690 or 800/225–5843,* FAX *809/929–5855. 334 rooms, 16 suites. 2 restaurants, 2 bars, coffee shop, in-room safes, minibars, no-smoking floors, room service, pool, wading pool, beauty salon, 2 tennis courts, basketball, exercise room, jogging track, boutiques, baby-sitting, playground, dry cleaning and laundry service, concierge, business services, meeting rooms, travel services. AE, DC, MC, V. EP, MAP.*

**$$–$$$** ☷ **Wyndham New Kingston.** The high-rise Wyndham New Kingston
★ is the best of Kingston's business hotels. The expansive marble lobby leads to the well-appointed guest rooms. The concierge floors include complimentary cocktails, hors d'oeuvres, and Continental breakfast. Lots of extras include secured-access elevators, an American Airline's service desk, and in-room coffee/tea setup. Rates include admission to Jonkanoo, the hotel's hot nightclub (☞ Nightlife, *below*). ✉ *Box 112, Kingston,* ☎ *809/926–5430 or 800/526–2422,* FAX *809/929–7439. 284 rooms, 13 suites, 6 1- and 2-bedroom housekeeping units. 2 restaurants, 3 bars, in-room modem lines, in-room safes, no smoking floors, refrigerators on request, pool, beauty salon, massage, sauna, 2 tennis courts, health club, shopping arcade, gaming room, art gallery, dry cleaning and laundry service, concierge, business services, meeting rooms, travel services. AE, DC, MC, V. EP, MAP.*

**$$** ☷ **Morgan's Harbour Hotel, Beach Club, and Yacht Marina.** A favorite of the sail-into-Jamaica set, this small property has 22 acres of beachfront at the very entrance to the old pirate's town. Done in light tropical prints, the rooms are very basic, but many have a balcony and minifridge; the suites with loft bedrooms are the nicest. Ask for one in the newer wing. Because the hotel is so close to the airport, passengers on delayed or canceled flights are often bused here to wait. ✉ *Port Royal, Kingston,* ☎ *809/924–8464 or 800/526–2422,* FAX *809/924–8562. 44 rooms, 6 suites. Restaurant, bar, refrigerators, room service, pool, volleyball, dive center, water-sports center, full-service marina, fishing, billiards, disco, laundry service, business services, travel services, airport shuttle. AE, MC, V. EP.*

**$$** ☷ **Terra Nova.** Set in the quieter part of New Kingston, 1 mile from the commercial district and within walking distance of Devon House, is the intimate Terra Nova hotel. Guest rooms are decked out in clas-

sical mahogany furniture and fine art. The El Dorado restaurant offers international cuisine and reasonably priced buffets. You'll also find
formal high tea service here on Thursdays. ⊠ *17 Waterloo Rd.,
Kingston 10, ☎ 809/926–9334, ᖴᴀX 809/929–4933. 35 rooms. Restaurant, coffee shop, lounge, snack bar, in-room safes, no-smoking rooms,
room service, pool, baby-sitting, laundry service, business services,
meeting rooms. AE, DC, MC, V. EP.*

## Mandeville

$   🏨 **Astra Country Inn & Restaurant.** Country is the key word in the name
of this retreat, which is 2,000 feet up in the mountains. The low price
reflects the nature of the very basic rooms here: They define spartan
but are immaculately clean. There is no air-conditioning, but you
shouldn't miss it this high in the mountains. The small restaurant is
open from 7 AM to 9 PM and serves snacks in addition to breakfast,
lunch, and dinner. The food is billed as "home cooking" and emphasizes fresh produce—lots of vegetables and fruit juices. ⊠ *Ward Ave.,
Box 60, Mandeville, ☎ 809/962–3265 or 800/526–2422, ᖴᴀX 809/962–
1461. 20 rooms, 2 housekeeping suites. Restaurant, bar, kitchenettes,
pool, sauna, laundry service. AE, MC, V. EP.*

$   🏨 **Mandeville Hotel.** Tropical gardens wrap around the building, and
flowers spill onto the terrace where breakfast and lunch are served.
Rooms are simple and breeze-cooled; suites have full kitchens. You'll
need a car to get around town, go out for dinner, and get to the beach,
which is an hour away. ⊠ *Box 78, Mandeville, ☎ 809/962–2460 or
800/233–4582, ᖴᴀX 809/962–0700. 46 rooms; 17 1-, 2-, and 3-bed-
room housekeeping suites. Restaurant, bar, coffee shop, kitchenettes,
refrigerator, pool, golf privileges, baby-sitting, laundry services, meeting room, travel services. AE, MC, V. EP.*

## Montego Bay

$$$$   🏨 **Round Hill Hotel and Villas.** The Hollywood set frequents this peace-
★   ful resort, 8 miles west of town on a hilly peninsula. Twenty-seven villas housing 74 suites are scattered over 98 acres, and there are 36 hotel
rooms in Pineapple House, a two-story building overlooking the sea.
Rooms are done in a refined Ralph Lauren style, with mahogany furnishings and terra-cotta floors. The villas are leased back to the resort
by private owners and vary in decor, but jungle motifs are a favorite.
All come with a personal maid and a cook to make your breakfast (for
an extra charge), and several have private pools. The restaurant's good
food and elegant presentation make feasting in the dining room, or better yet on the seaside terrace, a memorable treat. ⊠ *Box 64, Montego
Bay, ☎ 809/952–5150 or 800/237–3237, ᖴᴀX 809/952–2505. 36
rooms, 27 housekeeping villas. Restaurant, pool, room service, beauty
salon, massage, 5 tennis courts, aerobics, exercise room, jogging, nature trails, beach, water-sports center, shops, baby-sitting, laundry service, concierge, business services, meeting rooms, car rental, helipad.
AE, DC, MC, V. EP, MAP, FAP, All-inclusive.*

$$$$   🏨 **Tryall Golf, Tennis, and Beach Club.** Part of a posh residential development 13 miles west of Montego Bay, Tryall clings to a hilltop overlooking a golf course and the Caribbean. You choose between rooms
in the former great house of a 2,200-acre island plantation and one of
the private villas dotting the landscape, each with its own pool and
full staff (butler, cook, maid, laundress, and gardener). You provide
the grocery list, and the villa staff will do all the food preparation. All
accommodations are individually and plushly decorated. There are two
fine dining rooms at the great house: The one inside is elegant and serves
Continental and Jamaican cuisine, and the other, out on the terrace overlooking the ocean, serves more casual fare. The beautiful seaside golf
course is one of this resort's more memorable features. It's also reputed

**Montego Bay Dining and Lodging**

to be one of the meanest courses in the world and as such hosts big-money tournaments. ⊠ *Box 1206, Montego Bay,* ☎ *809/956–5660, 809/956–5667, or 800/742–0498;* 𝔽𝔸𝕏 *809/956–5673. 47 rooms, 57 villas. 2 restaurants, 2 bars, in-room safes, refrigerators on request, room service, pool, beauty salon, massage, driving range, 18-hole golf course, 9 tennis courts, jogging, beach, water-sports center, art gallery, shops, baby-sitting, laundry service, business services, meeting rooms, car rental. AE, DC, MC, V. EP, MAP, FAP, All-inclusive.*

**$$$–$$$$** 🏨 **Coyaba Beach Resort and Club.** Owners Joanne and Kevin Robert-
**★** son live on the property, interacting with guests daily, giving this $4 million oceanfront retreat the feel of an intimate and inviting country inn. Coyaba is also very family friendly. The plantation-style great house, just east of Montego Bay, is a successful blend of modern amenities and Old World grace: Guest rooms are decorated with lovely Colonial prints and hand-carved mahogany furniture, and sunshine from the tall windows pours over terra-cotta floors and potted plants.

Ocean-view rooms are considerably more expensive than those with a mountain view. Airport transfers, banana cake and rum baskets, afternoon tea, and Continental breakfast are part of the package. Kids under 12 stay free in their parents' room. ⊠ *Little River,* ☎ *809/953–9150 or 800/237–3237,* 𝔽𝔸𝕏 *809/953–2244. 50 rooms. 2 restaurants, 2 bars, room service, pool, outdoor hot tub, massage, golf packages, tennis court, exercise room, volleyball, water-sports center, scuba diving, fishing, gift shop, laundry service, business services, meeting rooms, airport shuttle. MC, V. EP, MAP, All-inclusive.*

**$$$–$$$$** ⊞ **Half Moon Golf, Tennis, and Beach Club.** For over four decades the
★          400-acre Half Moon Club resort has been a destination unto itself with a reputation for doing the little things right. Although it has mushroomed from 30 to more than 300 units, it has maintained its intimate, luxurious feel. The rooms, suites, and villas, whether in modern or Queen Anne style, are decorated in exquisite taste, with such flourishes as Oriental throw rugs and antique radios. Several villas—which come with a cook, butler, housekeeper, and rental car or golf cart—have private pools, and the mile-long stretch of beach is just steps away from every guest room. There's also an upscale shopping mall, 20 more luxury villas with pools, and a nature reserve. Further expansion in 1996 included 11 luxurious new villas. Kids under 12 are given a 50% discount on meal plans. ⊠ *Box 80, 7 mi east of Montego Bay,* ☎ *809/953–2211 or 800/227–3237,* 𝔽𝔸𝕏 *809/953–2731. 50 individual rooms, 291 rooms in housekeeping suites and villas. 7 restaurants, 3 bars, 39 pools, outdoor hot tub, sauna, spa, 18-hole golf course, minigolf, 13 tennis courts, aerobics, croquet, exercise room, horseback riding, Ping-Pong, squash, water-sports center, bicycles and golf carts, shops, theater, library, baby-sitting, children's program (ages 3–10), playground, play room, business services, convention facilities, travel services, airport shuttle. AE, DC, MC, V. EP, MAP, FAP, All-inclusive.*

**$$$–$$$$** ⊞ **Wyndham Rose Hall.** The veteran Wyndham Rose Hall, a self-contained resort built on the 400-acre Rose Hall Plantation, mixes recreation with a top-flight conference setup. A bustling business hotel popular with groups, it has all the resort amenities: tennis courts, golf course, three interconnected pools, a nightclub, a water-sports center, and a shopping arcade. Rooms in shades of beige, deep blue, and rose are comfortable but somewhat sterile. A "Kid's Klub" with daily supervised activities is included in the rates; kids under 12 stay and eat free from May through September. The thin crescent of beach is good for sailing and snorkeling. Indoor and outdoor restaurants serve Continental, Italian, and Jamaican fare. ⊠ *Box 999, Montego Bay,* ☎ *809/953–2650 or 800/996–3426,* 𝔽𝔸𝕏 *809/953–2617. 470 rooms, 19 suites. 4 restaurants, 3 bars, in-room safes, room service, 3 pools, beauty salon, massage, 6 tennis courts, golf privileges, aerobics, basketball, exercise room, volleyball, water-sports center, shopping arcade, baby-sitting, children's program (ages 5–12), playground, laundry service, business services, meeting rooms, travel services. AE, DC, MC, V. EP, MAP, All-inclusive.*

**$$$** ⊞ **Sandals Royal Jamaican.** Another all-inclusive resort for couples only, the Royal Jamaican is distinguished by Jamaican-style architecture arranged in a semicircle around attractive gardens. It's a sister in both theme and quality to other Sandals resorts. Although sportive and activity-laden, this property is a bit quieter and more genteel than the other Sandals and draws a nicely mixed international crowd. Standard rooms have lacquered furniture in light colors and mauve carpeting and bedspreads; bathrooms are small. The deluxe oceanfront rooms and suites are more elegant and inviting, with mahogany four-poster beds and floral print fabrics. All accommodations are air-conditioned, but the breezes that come in the slat windows do a nice job of keeping things cool. A colorful "dragon boat" carries guests across to Sandals's private island to dine at the Indonesian restaurant. ✉ *Box 167, Montego Bay,* ☎ *809/953–2231 or 800/726–3257,* ℻ *809/953–2788. 190 rooms. 4 restaurants, 4 bars, in-room safes, minibar in suites, 4 pools, beauty salon, 5 outdoor hot tubs, saunas, golf privileges and transfers, 3 tennis courts, aerobics, croquet, exercise room, horseshoes, lawn chess, Ping-Pong, shuffleboard, volleyball, beach, private offshore island, water-sports center, game room with billiards and darts, library, laundry service and dry cleaning, concierge, business services, meeting room, travel services, airport shuttle. 3-night minimum stay. AE, DC, MC, V. All-inclusive.*

**$$–$$$** 🏨 **Holiday Inn Sunspree Resort.** The hotel chain has done much to raise a run-down campground to the level of a full-service property, with activities day and night and many tour facilities (and large tour groups as well). Although the rooms are cheerful enough, the hotel is big and noisy. Hallways and public areas, once dark and drab, were perked up with better lighting and brighter decor during a major renovation in 1995. The quietest rooms are those farthest from the pool. The beach is just a palm-shaded sliver. Kids under 12 stay and eat free. ✉ *Box 480, Montego Bay,* ☎ *809/953–2485 or 800/352–0731,* ℻ *809/953–2840. 516 rooms. 2 restaurants, 2 snack bars, 4 bars, in-room safes, no-smoking rooms, whirlpool bathtub in family suites, pool, golf privileges, 4 tennis courts, aerobics, exercise room, basketball, shuffleboard, volleyball, beach, water-sports center, billiards, gaming room with slot machines, Ping-Pong, shops, baby-sitting, children's program (ages 3–17), playground, kids disco/movie room, laundry service, concierge, business services, meeting rooms, airport and shopping shuttles. AE, DC, MC, V. All-inclusive.*

**$$–$$$** 🏨 **Sandals Montego Bay.** The largest private beach in Montego Bay is
★ the spark that lights Sandals Montego Bay, one of the most popular couples resorts in the Caribbean. The all-inclusive format includes airport transfers, all taxes and tips, a plethora of water and land sports, including scuba diving, all sports equipment and lessons, aerobics classes, meals, theme parties, and other entertainment. It's a bit like a cruise ship that remains in port, with rooms overlooking the bay. The revelers don't seem to mind the zooming planes (the airport is next door), and the atmosphere here remains one of a great big fun party. Even the staff seem happy as they hum or sing their way through the workday. Rooms are comfortable enough, but the revelers here are seldom in them because there is so much to do. The Oleandor Restaurant is probably the best fine-dining outlet in the Sandals chain. ✉ *Box 100, Montego Bay,* ☎ *809/952–5510 or 800/726–3257,* ℻ *809/952–0816. 243 rooms. 4 restaurants, 4 bars, snack bar, in-room safes, minibar in suites, 2 pools, 4 plunge pools, beauty salon, 3 outdoor hot tubs, saunas, golf privileges and transfers, 3 tennis courts, aerobics, basketball, boccie, croquet, exercise room, horseshoes, lawn chess, Ping-Pong, racquetball, shuffleboard, volleyball, beach, water-sports center, game room with billiards and darts, library, laundry service and dry cleaning, concierge, business services, meeting room, travel services, airport shuttle. 3-night minimum stay. AE, DC, MC, V. All-inclusive.*

**$$** 🏨 **Atrium at Ironshore.** Fifteen moderately priced, fully furnished apartments make up this small complex. Decor varies, but each of the charming units has pastel floral and plaid prints, cool white tile floors, beige rattan furniture, a patio or balcony, and a private housekeeper/cook on call. Large saltwater tanks full of tropical fish brighten the alfresco dining terrace near the waterfall-fed pool, and you'll often find lively games of darts or skittles under way in the English-style pub. A shopping mall with supermarket, cinema, and several boutiques is within walking distance, but you'll have to take a shuttle to the beach. Children under 12 stay free with their parents. ✉ *1084 Morgan Rd., Box 604,* ☎ *809/953–2605,* FAX *809/953–3683. 15 1½-, 2-, and 3-bedroom housekeeping suites. Restaurant, pub, kitchenettes, refrigerator, pool, coin laundry, meeting room, beach and shopping shuttle. AE, DC, MC, V. EP.*

**$–$$**  🏨 **Sandals Inn.** If you're willing to do without a private beach (there's
  ★     a public one across the street), you can stay here for much less than at the other couples-only Sandals resorts. The inn is more intimate and far quieter than the other Sandals; it's managed more as a small hotel than a large resort. The charming rooms are compact; most have balconies facing the pool. Dark carpet contrasts with white lacquered furniture and tropical print fabrics. There's plenty to do here, and you can get in on the action at the other two MoBay Sandals by hopping aboard the free hourly shuttle. The in-town location makes the inn convenient to shopping and tours. ✉ *Box 412, Montego Bay,* ☎ *809/952–4140 or 800/726–3257,* FAX *809/952–6913. 52 rooms. 2 restaurants, 2 bars, in-room safes, pool, beauty salon, outdoor hot tub, golf privileges and transfers, tennis court, basketball, croquet, darts, exercise room, horseshoes, Ping-Pong, shuffleboard, volleyball, nearby beach club, water-sports center, library, laundry service and dry cleaning, concierge, business services, meeting room, travel services, airport shuttle. 3-night minimum stay. AE, DC, MC, V. All-inclusive.*

**$**    🏨 **Richmond Hill Inn.** The hilltop Richmond Hill Inn, a quaint, 200-year-old great house originally owned by the Dewars clan, enjoys spectacular views of the Caribbean and a great deal of peace, compared with MoBay's hustle. Decor tends toward the dainty and is a bit dated, with frilly lace curtains and doilies, lots of lavenders and mauves, and crushed-velvet furniture here and there. A free shuttle will take you to shopping and beaches, about 10–15 minutes away. ✉ *Union St., Box 362, Montego Bay,* ☎ *809/952–3859 or 800/423–4095. 15 rooms, 4 suites. Bar, dining room, coffee shop, pool, laundry service, MoBay shuttle. AE, MC, V. MAP, FAP.*

## Negril

**$$$$**  🏨 **Grand Lido.** The dramatic entrance of marble floors and columns,
  ★      filled with Jamaican artwork, sets a tone of striking elegance at this SuperClubs all-inclusive property geared to the upper-income bracket. Well-appointed oceanfront and garden rooms are split-level and are some of the most spacious and stylish accommodations of the all-inclusives. Eighteen one-bedroom suites with two balconies, a dining/sitting room, and equipped with a VCR and CD player, were added in 1995. For some, the pièce de résistance is a sunset cruise on the resort's 147-foot yacht, *Zien,* which was a wedding gift from Aristotle Onassis to Prince Rainier and Princess Grace of Monaco. Grand Lido attracts a slightly more mature and settled crowd than does the usual Negril resort. The gourmet restaurant, Piacere, is one of Jamaica's best, and an atmosphere of cool elegance prevails throughout. Children under 16 are not accepted at this romantic resort. ✉ *Box 88, Negril,* ☎ *809/957–4010 or 800/859–7873,* FAX *809/957–4317. 182 rooms, 18 suites. 3 restaurants, 9 bars, in-room safes, room service, 2 pools, 5 outdoor hot tubs, beauty salon, massage, golf package, 4 tennis courts, aerobics, exercise room, volleyball, clothed and nude beaches, water-sports center, bicycles, nature walks, cooking classes, dance classes, mixology classes, art gallery, disco, billiards, Ping-Pong, recreation room, video and book library, video theater, complimentary laundry and dry cleaning and pressing service, concierge, business services, meeting rooms, travel services, airport shuttle, complimentary sightseeing tours, complimentary weddings. 3-night minimum stay. AE, DC, MC, V. All-inclusive.*

**$$$$** ⊞ **Swept Away.** Fitness and health-conscious couples are the target market for this all-inclusive, which emphasizes sports and healthy cuisine. Twenty-six cottages containing 134 suites are spread along half a mile of drop-dead gorgeous beach. Each cottage has a private inner-garden atrium. The 10-acre sports complex across the road outclasses the competition by a long shot. The Feathers Continental Restaurant is open to nonguests. The compound's chefs concentrate on healthful dishes with lots of fish, white meat, fresh fruits, and vegetables. Guests must be at least 18 years of age. ⊠ *Long Bay, Negril,* ☎ *809/957–4040 or 800/545–7937,* FAX *809/957–4060. 134 suites. 2 restaurants, 4 bars, air-conditioning, fans, in-room safes, pool, beauty salon, 2 outdoor hot tubs, massage, spa, 2 steam rooms and saunas with plunge pools, golf privileges, 10 tennis courts, aerobics room, health club, jogging track, racquetball, squash, yoga classes, water-sports center, laundry service, business services, meeting rooms, airport shuttle. AE, DC, MC, V. All-inclusive.*

**$$$–$$$$** ⊞ **Poinciana Beach Resort.** The management here has created all-inclusive packages with families in mind. A stay at Poinciana includes a "FunPass" to Anancy Park across the street, a supervised children's activity program, a playground, and baby-sitting during meal hours. Up to two children under 14 (one per parent) can stay free. One- and two-bedroom housekeeping suites with kitchens are a good choice for families. Rooms and suites have tile floors, and Jamaican prints adorn the walls. One of Jamaica's prettiest palm-speckled sandy beaches awaits, along with a water-sports center (scuba diving costs extra). There are French, Italian, and Jamaican restaurants on the property in addition to a beach grill and a special kids restaurant. ⊠ *Box 44, Negril,* ☎ *809/957–4100 or 800/468–6728,* FAX *305/749–6794 in FL. 135 rooms including studios and 1- and 2-bedroom housekeeping suites. 4 restaurants, grill, 2 bars, 2 pools, beauty salon, outdoor hot tub, massage, golf package, 2 tennis courts, croquet, exercise room, lawn chess, Ping-Pong, shuffleboard, volleyball, beach, water-sports center with dive shop, duty-free shop, game room, billiards, slot machines, disco, library, coin laundry, baby-sitting, children's program (no age limit), playground, business services, meeting room, travel services, airport shuttle. AE, MC, V. All-inclusive.*

**$$–$$$$** ⊞ **Negril Gardens.** Towering palms and well-tended gardens surround the pink and white buildings of this hotel. Half of the rooms are beachside, half across the street overlooking the pool; all are attractive, with tile floors and rattan furniture in light colors (no telephones or televisions). Water sports are available at the beach. ⊠ *Box 58, Negril,* ☎ *809/957–4408 or 800/752–6824,* FAX *809/957–4374. 65 rooms. Restaurant, 2 bars, in-room safes, pool, tennis court, exercise room, water-sports center, bicycles, game room, laundry facilities, travel services, airport shuttle (on All-inclusive plan only). AE, MC, V. EP, MAP, FAP, All-inclusive.*

**$$$** ⊞ **Hedonism II.** Here is the resort that introduced the Club Méd–style all-inclusive to Jamaica years ago. Still wildly successful, Hedonism appeals mostly to single (60% of guests are), uninhibited vacationers who like a robust mix of physical activities. You can try everything from scuba diving to a trampoline clinic. Wood-trimmed public areas are filled with potted plants (and scantily clad guests). Handsome guest rooms have modern blond wood furniture; you'll also find mirrored ceilings above the king-size (or twin, depending on the set up requested) bed. Wooden floors in the hallways tend to echo traffic as the party atmosphere continues into the wee hours. If you come alone, expect to pay a single supplement or get an assigned roommate. ⊠ *Box 25, Negril,* ☎ *809/957–4200 or 800/859–7873,* FAX *809/957–4289. 280 rooms. 2 restaurants, 2 beach grills, 5 bars, pool, 2 outdoor hot tubs, 6 tennis* courts, aerobics, badminton, basketball, exercise room, horseback riding, Ping-Pong, shuffleboard, squash, trapeze and trampoline clinics, volleyball, clothed and nude beaches, water-sports center with scuba diving, bicycles, billiards, game room, laundry service, business services, meeting rooms, airport shuttle, complimentary sightseeing tours, complimentary weddings. AE, DC, MC, V. All-inclusive.

$$$ ☎ **Sandals Negril.** One of the best and longest stretches of Negril's 7-mile beach is a tempting reason to choose this Sandals resort. Couples looking for an upscale, sportive getaway and a casual atmosphere (you can wear dressy shorts to dinner) flock here. Water sports, including scuba diving, are emphasized; and the capable staff is happy both to teach neophytes and take out guests who are already certified. One pool is designated for scuba training. There's an offshore island, a huge swim-up pool bar, and a range of spacious accommodations. Both rooms and staff are sunny and appealing. ⊠ Box 10, Negril, ☎ 809/957–4216 or 800/726–3257, FAX 809/957–4338. 215 rooms. 4 restaurants, 4 bars (including swim-up, piano, and disco), in-room safes, minibar in suites, 3 pools, beauty salon, 2 outdoor hot tubs, saunas, golf privileges, 4 tennis courts, aerobics, basketball, croquet, exercise room, horseshoes, lawn chess, Ping-Pong, racquetball, shuffleboard, squash, volleyball, beach, water-sports center, game room, billiards, darts, slot machines, laundry service and dry cleaning, concierge, business services, meeting room, travel services, airport shuttle. 3-night minimum stay. AE, DC, MC, V. All-inclusive.

$$–$$$ ☎ **Negril Cabins.** These elevated timber cottages are nestled amid lush vegetation and towering royal palms. Rooms are open and airy, with floral bedspreads, gauzy curtains, natural wood floors, and high ceilings. Only "superior" rooms have air-conditioning; other rooms are cooled by ceiling fans and the breezes that come through the slatted windows. Televisions and bathtubs are also found only in the superior rooms (the other rooms have shower stalls); because these rooms are so popular, 38 more were added in 1996. The gleaming beach across the road is the site of a festive party once a week (there's also a poolside Calypso party once a week). A most convivial place, this property is popular with young Europeans. Reasonably priced dive packages are available, and kids under 16 stay free in their parents' room. ⊠ Norman Manley Blvd., Box 118, Negril, ☎ 809/957–4350 or 800/382–3444, FAX 809/957–4381. 88 rooms. 3 restaurants, 3 bars, in-room safes, room service, pool, outdoor hot tub, sauna, tennis court, exercise room, beach, water-sports center, dive shop, recreation room, gift shop, baby-sitting, children's program (ages 3–12), playground, coin laundry, meeting room, travel services, downtown shuttle. 3-night minimum stay. AE, MC, V. EP, MAP.

$$ ☎ **Charela Inn.** Each quiet, elegantly appointed room here has a private balcony or a covered patio. The owners' French-Jamaican roots find daily expression in the kitchen, and there's an excellent selection of wines. The small beach here is part of the glorious 7-mile Negril crescent. Kids under 10 stay free with parents, but they aren't allowed in deluxe rooms. ⊠ Box 33, Negril, Westmoreland, ☎ 809/957–4277 or 800/423–4095, FAX 809/957–4414. 39 rooms. Restaurant, bar, pool, beach, sailboats, windsurfing, day cruise, laundry service. 5-night minimum stay. AE, MC, V. EP, MAP.

$ ☎ **Devine Destiny.** Lush tropical forest surrounds this terra-cotta tile-roofed resort set 500 yards from the West End cliffs, well removed from the bustle and traffic of town. Spacious guest rooms have no telephones, radios, or televisions. Some rooms have kitchenettes and air-conditioning; be sure to state your preferences when making reservations. Most rooms overlook what the resort claims is the largest pool in Negril. Whether or not this is true matters little, for the free-form pool with graceful arched bridges, half-moon swim-up bar, and dining terrace is lovely. Up to two children under 12 stay free with their parents, and there's a game room to keep them occupied. The beach is 20 minutes away on foot, but a daily shuttle makes it easily accessible. ⊠ *Summerset Rd., Box 117, West End, Negril,* ☎ FAX *809/957–9184. 44 rooms. 2 restaurants, bar, air-conditioning or fans, refrigerators, room service, pool, sundeck, game room, TV room, laundry service, travel services, beach shuttle to beach club with restaurant and bar. AE, MC, V. EP.*

## Ocho Rios

**$$$$** 🏨 **Boscobel Beach.** This is a parent's dream of a Jamaican vacation,
★ an all-inclusive that makes families feel welcome. Everybody is kept busy all week for a single package price, and everyone leaves happy. The cheery day-care centers group children by age and offer an extensive array of entertaining and educational activities. Thoughtfully, there is an adults-only section of the resort (for when the kids want to get away). Up to two children (one per parent) under 14 stay free in their parents' room. Bedspreads in bright sea-life motifs or soothing pastel florals spice up the white tile floors and creamy walls of the rooms and suites. Only the adults can dine at Allegro, a romantic Italian restaurant (kids get a supervised dinner in their own restaurant). Families can dine together at the Pavillion restaurant, which has a Continental menu. You can have your vacation here videotaped (for a minimal fee) for posterity rather than use your vacation time shooting your own family movies. ⊠ *Box 63, Ocho Rios,* ☎ *809/975–7330 or 800/859–7873,* FAX *809/975–7370. 207 rooms, half of them junior suites. 5 restaurants, 5 bars (including disco, piano, and pool bars), in-room safes, refrigerators, 2 pools, wading pool, beauty salon, massage, 2 outdoor hot tubs, 4 tennis courts, golf privileges (greens fees) and transportation, aerobics, basketball, exercise room, Ping-Pong, volleyball, beach, water-sports center with scuba diving, bicycles, game room, baby-sitting, children's programs (no age limit), nursery, playground, petting zoo, laundry service, business services, meeting room, travel services, airport shuttle, complimentary sightseeing tours, complimentary weddings. 3-night minimum stay. AE, DC, MC, V. All-inclusive.*

**$$$$** 🏨 **Sans Souci Lido.** This pastel-pink cliffside fantasyland looks and
★ feels like a dream. Romantic oceanfront suites are equipped with oversize whirlpool tubs. Soothing, light colors are the base of the decor; blond wood furniture, cool tile floors, and sheer curtains are accented by pastel watercolors and Jamaican prints on the walls. The Caribbean and Continental cuisine at the Casanova Restaurant delights, as does the pampering guests receive at Charlie's Spa in the form of a complimentary massage, body scrub, reflexology session, facial, manicure, and pedicure (book treatments as soon as you arrive, if not before). A stay here is a wonderfully luxurious experience and a hands-down favorite in Jamaica. Children under 16 are not allowed. ⊠ *Box 103, Ocho Rios,* ☎ *809/974–2353 or 800/859–7873,* FAX *809/974–2544. 13 rooms, 98 suites. 3 restaurants, beach grill, 4 bars (including beach and piano bars), in-room safes, minibars, room service, freshwater and mineral pools, mineral whirlpool tub, beauty salon, massage, full-service spa, golf privileges (greens fees) and transportation, 4 tennis courts, aerobics, badminton, basketball, boccie, croquet, darts, exercise room, shuffleboard, volleyball, yoga, beach, water-sports center including scuba diving, game room, library, complimentary laundry and dry cleaning and pressing service, concierge, business services, meeting rooms, travel services, airport shuttle, complimentary sightseeing tours, complimentary weddings. 3-night minimum stay. AE, DC, MC, V. All-inclusive.*

**$$$–$$$$** 🏨 **Ciboney, Ocho Rios.** A Radisson Villa, Spa, and Beach Resort, this stately plantation property has 38 rooms in its great house and 264 spacious one-, two-, and three-bedroom villa suites on 45 lush hillside acres. It is operated as a luxury all-inclusive geared toward affluent adults, both singles and couples; no children under the age of 16 are allowed. Outstanding features are the European-style spa and four signature restaurants, including the Orchids restaurant, whose menu was developed by the Culinary Institute of America. Every villa has an attendant and a pool, giving guests the ultimate in privacy and pampering. A casual contemporary decor is found throughout—light-colored rattan, tile floors, and pastel fabrics. All guests receive complimentary massage, manicure, and pedicure: Book your treatments early (even before you arrive) if you want to get a spot on the spa's roster. If there's a drawback here it's how busy the place is. The bustle creates a crowded feel. The private beach is a shuttle ride away. ⊠ *Box 728, Main St., Ocho Rios,* ☎ *809/974–1027 or 800/333–3333,* ℻ *809/974–5838. 264 1-, 2-, and 3-bedroom suites, 38 rooms. 4 restaurants, 7 bars (including disco and 2 swim-ups), in-room safes, kitchenettes, minibars, refrigerators, room service, in-room VCRs, 2 public pools, 90 private pools, beauty salon, 1 indoor and 5 outdoor hot tubs, 2 saunas, 2 cold plunges, spa, 2 steam rooms, golf privileges (greens fees) and transportation, 6 tennis courts, aerobics, basketball, croquet, health club, horseback riding, jogging, lawn chess, shuffleboard, squash, volleyball, beach, water-sports center (scuba diving at additional cost), bicycles, art gallery, shops, gaming room, laundry service, concierge, business services, meeting rooms, travel services, airport and beach shuttles, car rental. AE, DC, MC, V. All-inclusive.*

$$$–$$$$   🏨 **High Hope Estate.** If you prefer a secluded location and personal attention to the frenetic activity of large beachfront resorts, High Hope is the answer. Families and groups can book the entire villa on an all-inclusive package, but rooms are also available on a bed-and-breakfast basis at this luxurious, 15th-century-style villa, set on 40 lush acres in the trade-wind-cooled hills of St. Ann's Bay, 7 miles west of Ocho Rios. The tranquility here is undisturbed, the vista of 20 miles of Caribbean coastline superb. One of several homes built for wealthy socialite Kitty Spence (granddaughter of William Jennings Bryan), the estate features Italian marble floors, graceful arches, carved mahogany doors, and trim, sweeping verandas overlooking manicured lawns. A fascinating collection of antiques sets a refined tone. The small staff provides attentive, warm service, and owner Dennis Rapaport is a charming host full of fascinating stories. A governess is available for those traveling with children, who are warmly welcomed here. There are no planned activities, no disco, no bustling beach (it's 10 minutes away by car); come for the peace, to explore the hibiscus and orchid-dotted lawns, to listen to the twittering of tropical birds, and to watch the fireflies and falling stars. ⊠ *Box 11, St. Ann's Bay,* ☎ *809/972–2277,* ℻ *809/972–1607. 6 rooms. Fans, pool, tennis court, library, babysitting, laundry service. MC, V. EP, All-inclusive.*

$$$–$$$$   🏨 **Jamaica Grande.** This Ramada property is the largest conference hotel in Jamaica. The property attracts families (kids under 12 stay free with parents), couples, singles (there are special singles activities, and no added singles supplement), and conference attendees. Even though it's a beachfront resort, the focal point is definitely the tiered and winding pool with waterfall, swaying bridge, and swim-up bar. Accommodations in the south building are a bit roomier, whereas those in the north have slightly better views. The staff is quite friendly for such a large and rather overwhelming property. Kids are kept busy in the daily Club Mongoose activity program (included in the rates). The hotel's disco, Jamaica Me Crazy (☞ Nightlife, *below*), is *very* popular. ⊠ *Box 100, Ocho Rios,* ☎ *809/974–2201 or 800/228–9898,* ℻ *809/974–5378. 706 rooms, 14 suites. 5 restaurants, 9 bars, in-room*

safes, minibars in suites, room service, 3 pools, beauty salon, massage, 2 outdoor hot tubs, 4 tennis courts, aerobics, exercise room, beach, water-sports center, shops, game room with slot machines, kid's game room, baby-sitting, children's program (ages 2–12), nursery, playground, laundry service and dry cleaning, concierge, business services, convention center, travel services, airport shuttle. AE, DC, MC, V. EP, MAP, All-inclusive.

**$$$–$$$$** **⊡ Sandals Dunn's River.** Twenty-three acres of gardens surround this
**★** luxury couples-only all-inclusive. The Continental-Italian masterpiece, set on a wide sugary beach, is the finest of Sandals' Jamaican resorts. The rooms are larger than at most Sandals and are decorated in light pink, blue, turquoise, and cream. Most have a balcony or patio overlooking the sea or the lush grounds. Oceanfront suites have four-poster beds. There are Italian, West Indian, Continental, and even a Japanese teppanyaki restaurant to choose from, in addition to the buffet dining for breakfast and lunch on the terrace. The resort draws a well-heeled crowd in their thirties and forties and prides itself on catering to every guest's every whim. ⊠ *Box 51, Ocho Rios,* ☎ *809/972–1610 or 800/726–3257,* 𝔽𝔸𝕏 *809/972–1611. 246 rooms, 10 suites. 4 restaurants, 7 bars, in-room safes, minibar in suites, 2 pools, beauty salon, 3 outdoor hot tubs, saunas, steam rooms, putting green, golf privileges, 4 tennis courts, aerobics, basketball, croquet, exercise room, horseshoes, jogging, lawn chess, Ping-Pong, racquetball, shuffleboard, squash, volleyball, beach, water-sports center, game room, billiards, darts, slot machines, laundry service and dry cleaning, concierge, business services, meeting room, travel services, airport shuttle. 3-night minimum stay. AE, DC, MC, V. All-inclusive.*

**$$$** **⊡ Sandals Ocho Rios.** The Sandals concept follows its successful formula at yet another couples-only, all-inclusive resort, this one on 12½ acres of beachfront property. The white- and sand-colored buildings contrast nicely with the vegetation and the sea. The accommodations are airy, but generic and somewhat impersonal (not that it matters, with all the activities to draw you outside). Guests enjoy meandering paths through lush foliage, hammocks for two strung between trees, and cozy benches nestled amid flower beds for private stargazing. ⊠ *Ocho Rios,* ☎ *809/974–5691 or 800/726–3257,* 𝔽𝔸𝕏 *809/974–5700. 237 units. 4 restaurants, 4 bars, in-room safes, minibar in suites, 3 pools, beauty salon, 2 outdoor hot tubs, saunas, golf privileges and transfers, 2 tennis courts, aerobics, basketball, croquet, exercise room, horseshoes, lawn chess, Ping-Pong, shuffleboard, volleyball, beach, water-sports center, game room with billiards and darts, laundry service and dry cleaning, concierge, business services, meeting room, travel services, airport shuttle, complimentary sightseeing tour. 3-night minimum stay. AE, DC, MC, V. All-inclusive.*

**$$–$$$** **⊡ Couples.** No singles, no children: The emphasis at Couples is on ro-
**★** mantic adventure for just the two of you, and the all-inclusive concept eliminates the decision making that can intrude on social pleasure. One-bedroom suites are designed for romance, with two-person hot tubs in the bathroom that peek through a window at the four-poster king-size bed. Continental breakfast is served in bed. The favorite dining spot is Bayside, an open-air restaurant with seating in graceful gazebos that stretch out over the water on stilted platforms. There's a lovely white beach for relaxation or water sports, and a private island where you can sunbathe in the buff. Couples has one of the highest occupancy rates of any resort on the island—and perhaps the most suggestive logo as well. There may be a correlation. No guests under 18 accepted. ⊠ *Tower Isle, St. Mary,* ☎ *809/975–4271 or 800/268–7537,* 𝔽𝔸𝕏 *809/975–4439. 161 rooms, 11 suites. 4 restaurants, 4 bars, in-room safes, whirlpool bathtubs and minibars in suites, room service, in-*

room CD players, pool, beauty salon, 5 outdoor hot tubs, massage, sauna, golf privileges (greens fees) and transfers, 5 tennis courts, aerobics, basketball, exercise room, horseback riding, lawn chess, Ping-Pong, squash, volleyball, beach, island for nude sunbathing, water-sports center, fishing, bicycles, shopping arcade, game room, billiards, slot machines, video games, arts and crafts center, laundry service, complimentary sightseeing tours and sunset cruise, travel services, meeting room, airport shuttle, complimentary weddings. 3-night minimum stay. AE, DC, MC, V. All-inclusive.

**$$–$$$** ⚅ **Plantation Inn.** This plantation actually looks like one—the Deep South variety à la *Gone with the Wind*. The whole place conjures up an existence as soft as a southern drawl. All the big, breezy rooms have big private balconies, and each has a dramatic view down to the sea. Jamaican cuisine is served at the popular restaurant, where dining and dancing by candlelight round out the romantic experience. Up to two children under 12 stay free in their parents' room. ⊠ *Box 2, Ocho Rios,* ☎ *809/974–5601 or 800/752–6824,* ℻ *809/974–5912. 59 rooms, 17 suites (including 2 villas). Restaurant, 2 bars, minibars and refrigerator in suites, room service, pool, beauty salon, massage, sauna, golf packages, 2 tennis courts, croquet, exercise room, Ping-Pong, volleyball, beach, water-sports center, dive shop, library, baby-sitting, children's program (ages 5–12), laundry service, travel services, meeting room. AE, DC, MC, V. EP, MAP, All-inclusive.*

**$$** ⚅ **Comfort Suites.** Families on a budget planning an extended stay might consider booking a suite at Comfort; the fully stocked kitchens here can help keep the dining bills down. This is also one of the few places you'll find designated no-smoking rooms (but be sure to specify no-smoking when making your reservation). Each unit, with typical white tile floors, rattan furniture, and tropical floral prints, is spacious and immaculately tidy. The two-bedroom suite has an open bathroom (it's only divided from the main room by a screen) with whirlpool tub in the lofted master bedroom. It's not on the beach (though it's close enough to walk, and a shuttle is provided), but suites in "A" block do have a partial ocean view. ⊠ *17 Da Costa Dr., Ocho Rios,* ☎ *809/974–8050 or 800/221–2222,* ℻ *809/974–8070. 60 1- and 2-bedroom suites. Restaurant, 2 bars, in-room safes, kitchenettes, refrigerators, no-smoking rooms, room service, outdoor hot tub, 2 tennis courts, baby-sitting, laundry service, car rental, travel services, airport and beach shuttles. AE, DC, MC, V. EP, MAP, FAP.*

**$$** ⚅ **Jamaica Inn.** A combination of class and quiet attracts a discerning crowd to this vintage property. There are weeks in season when every single guest is on at least his or her second visit. Each room has its own veranda (larger than most hotel rooms) on the private cove's powdery champagne-color beach. The colonial decor is on the dark side, with mahogany furniture, terrazzo floors, and walls hung with oil paintings. There are no TVs or radios. Jacket and tie are de rigueur after 7 PM during high season (December–April). No children under 14 are permitted. ⊠ *Box 1, Ocho Rios,* ☎ *809/974–2514 or 800/837–4670,* ℻ *809/974–2449. 44 rooms, 1 suite with private pool. Restaurant, 2 bars, room service, pool, croquet, exercise room, beach, snorkeling, boating, library, gift shop. AE, MC, V. MAP, All-inclusive.*

**$$** ⚅ **Shaw Park Beach Hotel.** Another popular property, Shaw Park offers an alternative to downtown high-rises. Hallways are dimly lit and uninviting, and rooms are fairly non-descript but comfortable enough. The grounds are colorful and well tended, and the Silks disco is a favorite for late-night carousing. The 1,500-foot beach is dotted with almond and palm trees. Rates here include breakfast, and up to two children under 12 stay free in their parents' room. ⊠ *Cutlass Bay, Box 17, Ocho Rios,* ☎ *809/974–2552 or 800/243–9420,* ℻ *809/974–5042. 119* rooms. *Restaurant, 3 bars, pool, beauty salon, massage, golf privileges, exercise room, beach, water sports center, dive shop, game/TV room, library, baby-sitting, playground, laundry service, business services, meeting room, airport shuttle. AE, DC, MC, V. BP, All-inclusive.*

$ 🏨 **Club Jamaica Beach Resort.** This intimate all-inclusive has only 95
★ rooms, ensuring guests plenty of personal attention from the young, cheerful staff. The rooms are refreshing, with gleaming white tile floors, comfortable modern furnishings, and gem-tone color schemes; more than half look out on the ocean. Guests, identified by their plastic, hospital-style bracelets, tend to be active middle-agers and can be seen participating in the resort's daily activities (including nonmotorized water sports on the public beach) and dancing the night away to live entertainment. The Ocho Rios craft market is adjacent to the resort. Children under 12 are not allowed. ✉ *Box 342, Turtle Beach, Ocho Rios,* ☎ *809/974–6632 or 800/818–2964,* FAX *809/974–6644. 95 rooms. Restaurant and dining terrace, 3 bars, in-room safes, pool, beauty salon, outdoor hot tub, exercise room, public beach, water-sports center, shops, laundry service, travel services, business services, meeting room, airport shuttle. AE, DC, MC, V. All-inclusive.*

$ 🏨 **Enchanted Garden.** Twenty stunning acres of gardens, filled with tropical plants and flowers and punctuated with a dramatic series of streams and waterfalls, certainly are enchanting. There is an aviary and a seaquarium where you can enjoy a delicatessen lunch or tea surrounded by tanks of fish and hanging orchids. The futuristic cream-color villas seem somewhat incongruous amid the natural splendor, but the rooms are comfortable, if somewhat small, and you're never far from the soothing sound of rushing water. Don't miss the guided garden tour, just one of dozens of activities here. There's a free shuttle to the beach, which is several minutes away. Guests must be at least 16. ✉ *Box 284, Ocho Rios,* ☎ *809/974–5346 or 800/323–5655,* FAX *809/974–5823. 113 villa rooms and suites (some housekeeping units). 5 restaurants, 4 bars, minibar in suites, 40 private plunge pools, room service, 2 pools, beauty salon, outdoor hot tub, spa, sauna, Turkish bath, 2 tennis courts, aerobics, basketball, croquet, tai chi, volleyball, yoga, public beach, water-sports center, game room with billiards, library, laundry service, travel services, beach and shopping shuttles, airport shuttle. AE, MC, V. All-inclusive.*

$ 🏨 **Hibiscus Lodge.** This gleaming white building with a blue awning sits amid beautifully manicured lawns laced with trellises and adorned by peacocks, not too far from its tiny private beach. The impeccably neat, cozy rooms all have at least a partial sea view, terrace, and shower-bath but no phone. Air-conditioning and televisions were added in 1995. This Swiss- and Jamaican-run property may be Ocho Rios' best bargain, attracting a lot of repeat guests. There are two reefs just off the beach, so the snorkeling is great here. ✉ *Box 52, Ocho Rios,* ☎ *809/974–2676 or 800/526–2422,* FAX *809/974–1874. 27 rooms. Restaurant, bar, air-conditioning, pool, outdoor hot tub, tennis court, TV room, laundry service. AE, DC, MC, V. BP, MAP.*

## Port Antonio

$$$–$$$$ 🏨 **Trident Villas and Hotel.** If a single hotel had to be voted the most
★ likely for coverage by *Lifestyles of the Rich and Famous*, this would have to be it. Peacocks strut the manicured lawns, colonnaded walkways wind through whimsically sculpted topiary dotting the 14 acres, and the pool—buried in a rocky bit of land jutting out into crashing surf—is a memory unto itself. The luxurious Laura Ashley–style rooms, many with turrets, bay windows, and balconies or verandas, are awash in mahogany and local art; they do not have TVs or clocks. The truly gracious living and white-gloved dining will transport you back to the

days of Empire. Cocktail parties are occasionally held at the opulent castle at the far end of the property near the new water-sports center (when the suites there are not rented out to high-flying groups). ⊠ *Box 119, Port Antonio,* ☎ *809/993–2602 or 800/237–3237,* ℻ *809/993–2590. 8 rooms, 4 suites, 14 villas, 8 suites in castle. Restaurant, bar, in-room safes, minibars, room service, pool, massage, 2 tennis courts, aerobics, croquet, nature trail, beach, water-sports center, boating, library/TV room, baby-sitting, laundry service, chapel, concierge, travel services, helipad. AE, MC, V. EP, BP, MAP, All-inclusive.*

$$–$$$     ▦ **Goblin Hill.** This lush 12-acre estate is set atop a hill overlooking San San Bay. Each attractively appointed villa comes with its own dramatic view, plus a housekeeper-cook to do the grocery shopping, cleaning, and cooking for you. The villas are not equipped with phones or TVs. The beach is a 10-minute walk away. Excellent villa and car-rental packages are available. ⊠ *Box 26, Port Antonio,* ☎ *809/925–8108 or 800/472–1148,* ℻ *809/925–6248. 28 housekeeping villas. Bar, in-room safes, kitchenettes, pool, putting green, 2 tennis courts, nature trail, beach, scuba diving, snorkeling, sailing, windsurfing, library/game room, baby-sitting, playground, laundry service, meeting room. AE, MC, V. EP.*

$$     ▦ **Dragon Bay.** Set on a scenic private cove (you may remember seeing it, and the beach bar, in Tom Cruise's movie, *Cocktail*), Dragon Bay is an idyllic grouping of individually decorated villas surrounded by tropical gardens. Villa 35 has a private pool, a large living room, and two bedrooms with separate sitting rooms that have sofa beds. This place is very popular with German and Italian tour groups. ⊠ *Box 176, Port Antonio,* ☎ *809/993–3281 or 809/993–3283,* ℻ *809/993–3284. 30 1-, 2-, and 3-bedroom villas. 2 restaurants, 2 bars, refrigerators, room service, pool, massage, 2 tennis courts, aerobics, exercise room, volleyball, beach, water-sports center, dive shop, baby-sitting, laundry service, travel services. AE, MC, V. EP, MAP, All-inclusive.*

$$     ▦ **Hotel Mocking Bird Hill.** With dogs running around the hillside property and only 10 rooms overlooking the sea and the Blue Mountains, Mocking Bird Hill feels more like a cozy bed-and-breakfast than a hotel. Owners Barbara Walker and Shireen Aga run an extremely environmentally sensitive operation: They've used bamboo instead of hardwood for furniture, solar panels to heat water, ceiling fans instead of ozone-depleting air-conditioning systems, local produce for meals in their Mille Fleurs dining terrace (which is open to the public as well), locally produced toiletries and stationary sets, and natural landscaping on their 7 acres. They also offer an array of eco-tour options in conjunction with other like-minded community members. The tasteful blue-on-white rooms do not have phones or televisions; most are designated no-smoking. Children under 10 stay free. ⊠ *Box 254, Port Antonio,* ☎ *809/993–3370,* ℻ *809/993–7133. 10 rooms. Restaurant, bar, in-room safes, no-smoking rooms, room service, pool, massage, nature trail, art studio with classes, TV room, baby-sitting, laundry service, meeting room, travel services. MC, V. EP, BP, MAP.*

$$     ▦ **Jamaica Palace.** Built to resemble a 17th-century Italian Colonial mansion, this imposing and somewhat impersonal property rises in an expanse of white-pillared marble, with a black-and-white theme continued on the interior, including black lacquer and gilded oversize furniture. Each room has a semicircular bed on a concrete base, and original European objets d'art and Oriental rugs; some are more lavish than others. None are equipped with televisions, but they are available for rent. Although the hotel is not on the beach, there is a 114-foot swimming pool shaped like Jamaica. ⊠ *Box 227, Port Antonio,* ☎ *809/993–2021 or 800/423–4095,* ℻ *809/993–3459. 24 rooms, 56 suites. 3 restaurants, 2 bars, in-room safes, room service, pool, mas-*

*sage, golf packages, garden chess, shops, baby-sitting, laundry service, meeting room, helipad, beach shuttle. AE, MC, V. EP, BP, MAP.*

$ ⬚ **Bonnie View Plantation Hotel.** Accommodations here are spartan, mattresses are a tad lumpy, and the furnishings a bit frayed. But the hotel certainly lives up to its name: Guests come for the sublime views and air of tranquillity. The nicest rooms (more expensive) are those with private verandas. But you can open your window for a burst of invigorating mountain air or hang out in the restaurant and savor the unparalleled water panoramas. Beachcombers are forewarned: It's a 25-minute drive to the ocean. ⊠ *Box 82, Port Antonio,* ☎ *809/993–2752 or 800/423–4095,* Ⅲ *809/993–2862. 20 rooms. Restaurant, pool, horseback riding, gift shop, laundry service. AE, MC, V. EP.*

## Runaway Bay

$$$ ⬚ **FDR, Franklyn D. Resort.** Jamaica's first all-suite, all-inclusive resort for families, this is the answer to parents' prayers. Upscale yet unpretentious, the pink buildings house spacious and well-thought-out one-, two-, and three-bedroom villas and are grouped in a horseshoe around the swimming pool. Best of all, a "girl Friday" is assigned to each suite, filling the role of nanny, housekeeper, and (when desired) cook. She'll even baby-sit at night for a small charge. Most parents are so impressed that they wish they could take their girl Friday home with them when they leave. Children and teens are kept busy with daylong supervised activities and sports, although parents are free to join in, lounge around the pool, play golf, go scuba diving, or just enjoy uninterrupted time together. Kids under 16 stay and play free with their parents. ⊠ *Box 201, Runaway Bay, St. Ann,* ☎ *809/973–3067 or 800/654–1337,* ⅢX *809/973–3071. 76 suites. 2 restaurants, 4 bars, kitchens, refrigerators, pool, tennis court, exercise room, clothed and nude beaches, watersports center, bicycles, game room, gift and crafts shops, baby-sitting, children's program (no age limit), laundry service, travel services, airport shuttle. AE, MC, V. All-inclusive.*

$$–$$$ ⬚ **Braco Village Resort.** Situated just west of Runaway Bay (a 15-minute drive), near the quaint town of Rio Bueno, this new all-inclusive, sister resort to FDR (☞ *above*) feels like a local version of Disney's Epcot Center, focusing on the cultural heritage, crafts, music, people, and food of Jamaica in a gingerbread and Georgian-styled village. Boutiques, an art shop, and several restaurants including a jerk grill, a pastry shop, and a sidewalk café fan out from the pretty central fountain in the "town square." The sidewalks are alive with local craft vendors demonstrating and selling their wares, and carts with typical Jamaican treats such as jelly coconuts, tropical fruits, and sugarcane. The meandering pool next to the white sand beach is one of the largest in the country. Rooms, done in citron, pink, and other bright tropical colors, are generously sized and all but a few with garden views are steps from the 2,000-foot beach or have a great view of the ocean from the patio. It's an all-adult (age 16 and over) property, but a family phase, complete with "girl Fridays" to watch the kids, is scheduled for completion in 1997. ⊠ *Rio Bueno, Trelawny,* ☎ *809/954–0000 or 800/654–1337,* ⅢX *809/954–0020. 174 rooms, 6 suites. 3 restaurants, 3 bars, café, in-room safes, minibars in suites, room service, pool, beauty salon, outdoor hot tub, 9-hole golf course, 2 tennis courts, aerobics, exercise room, game room, hiking trails, jogging, Ping-Pong, soccer, clothed and nude beaches, water-sports center, bicycles, boutiques, art studio, billiards, disco, theater, TV room, laundry service, business services, meeting rooms, travel services, airport shuttle. AE, DC, MC, V. EP, MAP, FAP, All-inclusive.*

$$ ⬚ **Breezes Runaway Bay.** Formerly known as Jamaica, Jamaica, this ★ moderately priced SuperClubs all-inclusive emphasizes an active, sports-oriented vacation, from golf, tennis, and horseback riding to an array

of water sports, including a Mistral windsurfing school. Expert instruction and top-rate equipment is part of the package. Extensively renovated in 1995, rooms now have white tile floors, cozy love seats, televisions, carved wooden headboards in the shape of palm trees, and big marble bathrooms. Guests—often Germans, Italians, and Japanese—flock here for the psychedelically colored reef just off the beach, as well as the superb golf school. Children under 16 are not allowed. ⊠ *Box 58, Runaway Bay,* ☎ *809/973–2436 or 800/859–7873,* FAX *809/973–2352. 238 rooms, 4 suites. 2 restaurants, 4 bars, beach grill, in-room safes, minibars in suites, swimming pool, lap pool, misting pool, beauty salon, 3 outdoor hot tubs, massage, 18-hole golf course with golf school nearby, 2 tennis courts, aerobics, croquet, exercise room, horseback riding, carriage rides, Ping-Pong, shuffleboard, volleyball, clothed and nude beaches, water-sports center, scuba diving, fishing, bicycles, shops, billiards, disco, nightclub, recreation room, laundry service, business services, meeting room, travel services, airport shuttle, complimentary sightseeing tours and sunset cruise, complimentary weddings. AE, DC, MC, V. All-inclusive.*

$$    🏨 **Club Caribbean.** This all-inclusive markets itself to families on a budget. A series of typically Caribbean cottages, many with kitchenette, lines the long but narrow beach. The rooms are simple and clean, with rattan furnishings, and floral print fabrics, but no telephone or TV; all should be fully air-conditioned by 1997. For more space, ask for one of the garden suites (with telephone and TV) added in late 1995. The place is very popular with European families. Children under 12 stay free, and many cottages feature bunk beds. Swings provide seating in the gazebo bar, a popular hangout around sunset. ⊠ *Box 65, Runaway Bay,* ☎ *809/973–3507 or 800/223–9815,* FAX *809/973–3509. 134 rooms, 19 suites. Restaurant, 3 bars, in-room safes, minibars in suites, pool, massage, 2 tennis courts, aerobics, exercise room, volleyball, clothed and nude beaches, water-sports center, gift shop, billiards, baby-sitting, children's program (ages 4–12), playground, laundry service, travel services. AE, MC, V. All-inclusive.*

$$    🏨 **H.E.A.R.T. Country Club.** It's a shame more visitors don't know about this place, perched above Runaway Bay and brimming with Jamaica's true character. While training young islanders interested in the tourism industry—H.E.A.R.T. stands for Human Employment And Resource Training—it also provides a quiet and pleasant stay for guests. The employees make an effort to please. Rooms were redecorated in 1995 and have either an ocean or pretty garden view. The tranquil restaurant serves delicious local and Continental specialties. Rates here include breakfast, and kids under 12 stay free with their parents. An excellent beach is a 20-minute hike (uphill coming back) or a 5- to 10-minute drive away. ⊠ *Box 98, St. Ann,* ☎ *809/973–2671,* FAX *809/973–2693. 20 rooms. Restaurant, piano bar, massage, baby-sitting, laundry service, meeting room, beach shuttle. AE, MC, V. BP, MAP.*

# Dining

Sampling the island's cuisine introduces you to virtually everything the Caribbean represents. Every ethnic group that has made significant contributions on another island has made them in Jamaica, too, adding to a Jamaican stockpot that is as rich as its melting pot. So many Americans have discovered the Caribbean through restaurants owned by Jamaicans that the very names of the island's dishes have come to represent the region as a whole. Jamaican food represents a true cuisine, organized, interesting, and ultimately rewarding. It would be a terrible shame for anyone to travel to the heart of this complex culture without tasting several typically Jamaican dishes. Here are a few:

**Ackee and Saltfish.** Salted fish was once the best islanders could do between catches, so they invented this incredibly popular dish that joins saltfish (in Portuguese, *bacalao*) with ackee, a vegetable (introduced to the island by Captain Bligh of Bounty fame) that reminds most people of scrambled eggs.

**Curry Goat.** Young goat is cooked with spices and is more tender and has a gentler flavor than the lamb for which it was substituted by immigrants from India.

**Jerk Pork.** Created by the Arawaks and perfected by the Maroons, jerk pork is the ultimate island barbecue. The pork (the purist cooks the whole pig) is covered with a paste of hot peppers, pimento berries (also known as allspice), and other herbs and cooked slowly over a coal fire. Many think that the "best of the best" jerk comes from Boston Beach in Port Antonio.

**Patties.** These spicy meat pies elevate street food to new heights. Although they in fact originated in Haiti, Jamaicans can give patty lessons to anybody.

**Pepper Pot.** The island's most famous soup—a peppery combination of salt pork, salt beef, okra, and the island green known as callaloo—it is green, but at its best it tastes as though it ought to be red.

**Rice and Peas.** This traditional dish is known also as Coat of Arms and is similar to the *moros y christianos* of Spanish-speaking islands: white rice cooked with red beans, coconut milk, scallions, and seasoning.

Where restaurants are concerned, Kingston has the widest selection; its ethnic restaurants offer Italian, French, Rasta natural foods, Cantonese, German, Thai, Indian, Korean, and Continental fare. There are fine restaurants as well in all the resort areas, and the list includes many that are in large hotels. Most of the restaurants outside the hotels in MoBay and Ocho Rios will provide complimentary transportation.

## What to Wear

Dress is casual chic (just plain casual at the local hangouts), except in Kingston and at the top resorts, some of which require semiformal wear in the evening during high season. People tend to dress up a little for dinner—just because they feel like it—so you may feel more comfortable in nice slacks or a sundress. Ask about the dress code when making your reservations.

| CATEGORY | COST* |
|---|---|
| $$$$ | over $40 |
| $$$ | $30–$40 |
| $$ | $20–$30 |
| $ | Under $20 |

*per person, excluding drinks, service charge, and tip*

## Kingston

$$$–$$$$ ✕ **Blue Mountain Inn.** The elegant Blue Mountain Inn is a 30-minute
★ taxi ride from New Kingston and worth every penny of the fare. On a former coffee plantation, the antique-laden inn complements its English Colonial atmosphere with Continental cuisine. All the classics of the beef and seafood repertoires are here, including chateaubriand béarnaise and lobster thermidor. ⊠ *Gordon Town Rd.,* ☎ *809/927–1700 or 809/927–2606. Reservations essential. Jacket required. AE, MC, V. Closed Sun. No lunch.*

$$–$$$ ✕ **Palm Court.** Nestled on the mezzanine floor of the Wyndham New Kingston, the elegant Palm Court is open for lunch and dinner (lunch is noon to 3 PM; dinner from 6 PM). The menu is Continental; the rack

of New Zealand lamb, sautéed snapper almondine, and grilled Chilean salmon are very tasty, but save room for the signature pumpkin cheese-cake. ⊠ *Wyndham New Kingston,* ☎ *809/926–5430. AE, DC, MC, V. No lunch weekends.*

**$$** ✕ **Hotel Four Seasons.** The Four Seasons has been pleasing local res-idents for more than 25 years with cuisine from the German and Swiss schools as well as local seafood and Jamaican fare. The setting tries to emulate Old World Europe without losing its casual island character. ⊠ *18 Ruthven Rd.,* ☎ *809/926–8805. AE, DC, MC, V.*

**$$** ✕ **Ivor Guest House.** This elegant yet cozy restaurant has an incredi-ble view of Kingston from 2,000 feet above sea level. Go for dinner, when the view is dramatically caught between the stars and the glit-tering brooch of Kingston's lights. International cuisine with Jamaican flare is served in prix fixe four-course dinners that average $35 per per-son. Owner Helen Aitken is an animated and cordial hostess. After-noon tea here is a treat. ⊠ *Jack's Hill,* ☎ *809/977–0033 or 809/927–1460. Reservations essential. AE, MC, V. Closed Sept.*

**$$** ✕ **Jade Garden.** On the third floor of the Sovereign Centre, the Jade Garden, with its shiny black lacquer chairs and views of the Blue Mountains, garners rave reviews for its Cantonese and Thai menu. Fa-vorites include steamed fish in black-bean sauce, black mushrooms stuffed with shrimp, and shrimp with lychee. There is an inexpensive lunch buffet every Friday afternoon and dim sum on the last Sunday of each month. ⊠ *106 Hope Rd.,* ☎ *809/978–3476 or 809/978–3479. AE, MC, V.*

**$$** ✕ **La Trattoria.** The Old World setting is as suitable for a business lun-
★ cheon as for a romantic dinner for two. The Northern Italian fare is classic—lasagna, manicotti, and spaghetti bolognaise are all on the menu—but a few interesting twists include linguine with jerk chicken in a cream sauce and the restaurant's signature dish, Pasta Carnival, pasta of the day tossed with cheese, local vegetables, olive oil, garlic, shrimp, and chicken. This Swiss-run restaurant is a delightful addition to Kingston's bountiful dining scene. ⊠ *29½ Munroe Rd.,* ☎ *809/977–1379. AE, MC, V. Closed Sun.*

**$** ✕ **Hot Pot.** Jamaicans love the Hot Pot for breakfast, lunch, and din-
★ ner. Fricassee chicken is the specialty, along with other local dishes, such as mackerel run-down (salted mackerel cooked down with coconut milk and spices) and ackee and salted cod. The restaurant's fresh juices "in season" are the best—tamarind, sorrel, coconut water, soursop, and cucumber. ⊠ *2 Altamont Terr.,* ☎ *809/929–3906. Reservations not accepted. MC, V.*

**$** ✕ **Peppers.** This casual outdoor bar is the "in" spot in Kingston. It's slow during weekday afternoons, but frenetic all weekend—especially Friday nights. Sample the grilled lobster or jerk pork and chicken with the local Red Stripe beer. ⊠ *31 Upper Waterloo Rd.,* ☎ *809/925–2219. MC, V.*

## Montego Bay

**$$$–$$$$** ✕ **Georgian House.** A landmark restaurant in the heart of town, the Georgian House occupies a restored 18th-century building set in a shady garden courtyard. An extensive wine cellar complements the Continental and Jamaican cuisines, the best of which are the steaks and the dishes made with the local spiny lobster. Don't miss the gallery of Jamaican art. ⊠ *2 Orange St.,* ☎ *809/952–0632. Reservations essential. AE, DC, MC, V.*

**$$$** ✕ **Julia's Italian Restaurant.** Couples flock to this romantic Italian restau-rant set up in the hills overlooking the twinkling lights of MoBay. Din-ers choose from an à la carte or five-course fixed-price menu ($33–$45 per person, depending on the entrée) that includes homemade soups and pastas; entrées of fish, chicken, and veal; and scrumptious desserts.

Don't expect the meal to equal the stupendous view, and you won't be disappointed. ⊠ *Bogue Hill,* ☎ *809/952–1772 or 809/979–0744. Reservations essential. AE, MC, V.*

$$$ ✕ **Sugar Mill.** Seafood is served with flair at this terrace restaurant set
★ on the manicured grounds of the Half Moon Golf Course. Caribbean specialties, steak, and lobster are usually offered in a pungent sauce that blends Dijon mustard with Jamaica's own Pickapeppa sauce. Otherwise, choices are the daily à la carte specials and anything flamed. Live music and a well-stocked wine cellar round out the experience. ⊠ *At Half Moon Golf Course,* ☎ *809/953–2228. Reservations essential for dinner. AE, DC, MC, V.*

$$–$$$ ✕ **Day-O Plantation Restaurant.** Transport yourself back in time with a fine meal served on the garden terrace of this Georgian-style plantation house. Start with smoked marlin, segue into seafood ragout or beef fillet with béarnaise sauce, and sweeten things up with one of the traditional Jamaican deserts (rum pudding, sweet cakes, or fruit salad). ⊠ *Barnett Estate Plantation, Fairfield,* ☎ *809/952–1825. AE, MC, V. Closed Mon.*

$$–$$$ ✕ **Norma at the Wharf House.** This sister property to creative chef and entrepreneur Norma's successful Kingston restaurant has gathered rave reviews as a supper club. The setting is a converted 300-year-old stone sugar warehouse on the water, decorated in blue and white. Innovative Jamaican cuisine ranges from Caribbean lobster steamed in Red Stripe beer to jerk chicken with mangoes flambé. ⊠ *10 mins west of MoBay in Reading,* ☎ *809/979–2745. Reservations essential for dinner. MC, V. Closed May–Aug. No lunch Mon.–Wed.*

$$–$$$ ✕ **Pier 1.** Pier 1 writes the book daily on waterfront dining. After tropical drinks at the deck bar, you'll be ready to dig into the international variations on fresh seafood, the best of which are the grilled lobster and any preparation of island snapper. Several party cruises leave from the marina here, and the restaurant is mobbed by locals who come to dance on Friday night. ⊠ *Just off Howard Cooke Blvd.,* ☎ *809/952–2452. AE, MC, V.*

$$ ✕ **Town House.** Most of the rich and famous who have visited Jamaica over the decades have eaten at the Town House. You will find specials of the day and good versions of standard ideas (red snapper papillote is the specialty, with lobster, cheese, and wine sauce), along with many Jamaican favorites (curried chicken with breadfruit and ackee). The 18th-century Georgian house is adorned with original Jamaican and Haitian art. There's alfresco dining on the stone patio. ⊠ *16 Church St.,* ☎ *809/952–2660. Reservations essential for dinner. AE, DC, MC, V. No lunch Sun.*

$ ✕ **Le Chalet.** Don't let the French name fool you. This Denny's look-
★ alike, set in a nondescript shopping mall, serves heaping helpings of some of the best Chinese and Jamaican food in MoBay. Tasty lobster Cantonese costs only $9. ⊠ *32 Gloucester Ave.,* ☎ *809/952–5240. AE, MC, V. No lunch Sun.*

$ ✕ **Pork Pit.** This open-air hangout, across the street from popular
★ Walter Fletcher Beach and not far from the airport, must introduce more travelers to Jamaica's fiery jerk pork than any other place on the island. The Pork Pit is a local phenomenon down to the Red Stripe beer, yet it's accessible in both location and style. Plan to arrive around noon, when the jerk begins to be lifted from its bed of coals and pimento wood. ⊠ *Gloucester Ave., across from Walter Fletcher Beach,* ☎ *809/952–1046. Reservations not accepted. No credit cards.*

## Negril

$$ ✕ **Cafe au Lait.** The proprietors of Cafe au Lait are French and Jamaican, and so is the cuisine. Local seafood and produce are prepared with del-

icate touches and presented in a setting overlooking the sea. ⊠ *Mirage Resort on Lighthouse Rd.,* ☎ *809/957–4471. MC, V.*

**$$** ✕ **Tan-ya's.** This alfresco restaurant is on the edge of the beach at the Seasplash hotel. Jamaican delicacies with an international flavor are served for breakfast, lunch, and dinner. Try the excellent deviled crab backs or the snapper Florentine stuffed with callaloo. ⊠ *Seasplash Hotel, Norman Manley Blvd.,* ☎ *809/957–4041. AE, DC, MC, V.*

**$–$$** ✕ **Rick's Cafe.** Here it is, the local landmark complete with cliffs, cliff divers, and powerful sunsets, all perfectly choreographed. Most folks come for the drinks and the renowned sunset party, since the standard pub menu seems pricey. In the sunset ritual, the crowd toasts Mother Nature with rum drinks, shouts and laughter, and ever-shifting meeting and greeting. When the sun slips below the horizon, there are more shouts, more cheers, and more rounds of rum. ⊠ *Lighthouse Rd.,* ☎ *809/957–4335. No credit cards.*

**$** ✕ **Cosmo's Seafood Restaurant and Bar.** Owner Cosmo Brown has made
★ this seaside open-air bistro a pleasant place to spend the afternoon— and maybe stay on for dinner. The fresh fish is the main attraction, and the conch soup that's the house specialty is a meal in itself. There's also lobster (grilled or curried), fish-and-chips, and a catch-of-the-morning. Customers often drop cover-ups to take a dip before coffee and dessert and return later to lounge in chairs scattered under almond and sea-grape trees. (There's an entrance fee for the beach alone, but it's less than $1.) ⊠ *Norman Manley Blvd.,* ☎ *809/957–4330. Reservations not accepted. AE, MC, V.*

**$** ✕ **Paradise Yard.** Locals enjoy this alfresco restaurant on the Savanna-La-Mar side of the roundabout in Negril. Sit back and relax in the casual atmosphere while eating Jamaican dishes or the house special Rasta Pasta. It's open for breakfast, lunch, and dinner. ⊠ *White Hall Rd.,* ☎ *809/957–4006. Reservations not accepted. MC, V.*

**$** ✕ **Sweet Spice.** When Paradise Yard (☞ *above*) is full (it happens) turn to Sweet Spice, immediately next door. This open-air mom-and-pop diner run by the Whytes serves inexpensive, generous plates of conch steak, fried or curried chicken, fresh-catch fish, oxtail in brown stew sauce, and other down-home specialties. The fresh juices are quite satisfying. Drop by for breakfast, lunch, or dinner. ⊠ *1 White Hall Rd.,* ☎ *809/957–4621. Reservations not accepted. MC, V.*

## Ocho Rios

**$$–$$$** ✕ **Almond Tree.** One of the most popular restaurants in Ocho Rios,
★ the Almond Tree has a menu of Jamaican and Continental favorites: pumpkin and pepper-pot soups, many wonderful preparations of fresh fish, veal piccata, fondue. The swinging rope chairs of the terrace bar and the tables perched above a lovely Caribbean cove are great fun. ⊠ *83 Main St., Ocho Rios,* ☎ *809/974–2813. Reservations essential for dinner. AE, DC, MC, V.*

**$$** ✕ **The Ruins.** A 40-foot waterfall dominates the open-air Ruins restaurant, and in a sense it dominates the food as well. Surrender to local preference and order the Lotus Lily Lobster, a stir-fry of the freshest local shellfish, then settle back and enjoy the tree-shaded deck and the graceful footbridges that connect the dining patios. There's live entertainment on weekends. ⊠ *DaCosta Dr.,* ☎ *809/974–2442. AE, MC, V.*

**$–$$** ✕ **Evita's.** The setting here is a sensational, nearly 100-year-old gin-
★ gerbread house high on a hill overlooking Ocho Rios Bay (but also convenient from MoBay). Large, open windows provide cooling mountain breezes and stunning views of city and sea. More than 30 kinds of pasta are served here, ranging from lasagna Rastafari (vegetarian) and firey "jerk" spaghetti to rotelle *Colombo* (crabmeat with white sauce and noodles). There are also excellent fish dishes—sautéed fillet of red

snapper with orange sauce, scampi and lobster in basil cream sauce, red snapper stuffed with crabmeat—and several meat dishes, among them a tasty grilled sirloin with mushroom sauce. Kids 12 and under eat for half price, and light eaters will appreciate half-portion orders. ✉ *Mantalent Inn, Ocho Rios,* ☎ *809/974–2333. AE, MC, V.*

**$** ✕ **Double V Jerk Centre.** This open-air eatery is a good place to park yourself for frosty Red Stripe beer and fiery jerk pork or chicken. It's lively at lunch, when you can tour the adjacent minizoo, with fish and tropical birds. ✉ *109 Main St.,* ☎ *809/974–2084. AE, MC, V. Closed Sun.*

## Beaches

Jamaica has 200 miles of beaches, some of them still uncrowded. The beaches listed below are public places (there is usually a small admission charge), and they are among the best Jamaica has to offer. In addition, nearly every resort has its own private beach, complete with towels and water sports. Some of the larger resorts sell day passes to nonguests. Generally, the farther west you travel, the lighter and finer the sand.

### Discovery Bay
**Puerto Seco Beach** is frequented primarily by locals.

### Kingston Area
There are no good beaches in Kingston. Beachgoers can travel outside of the city, but the beaches there, as a rule, are not as beautiful as those in the resort areas.

**Fort Clarence,** a beach in the Hellshire Hills area southwest of the city, has changing facilities and entertainment. **Hellshire Beach,** in Bridgeport, about a 20- to 30-minute drive from Kingston, is the most popular stretch of sand. Here you'll find food and drink vendors, changing rooms, and plenty of (recorded) music. **Lime Cay** can be reached by boat (they can be hired from Morgan's Harbor Marina at Port Royal for a small fee). This island, just beyond Kingston Harbor, is perfect for picnicking, sunning, and swimming. **Lyssons Beach,** in Morant Bay, sometimes lures Kingstonians 32 miles east of the city to its lovely golden sand.

### Montego Bay
**Cornwall Beach** is lively, with lots of food and drink available, as well as a water-sports concession. **Doctor's Cave Beach** shows a tendency toward population explosion, attracting Jamaicans and tourists alike; at times it may resemble Fort Lauderdale at spring break. The 5-mile stretch of sugary sand has been spotlighted in so many travel articles and brochures over the years that it's no secret to anyone. On the bright side, Doctor's Cave is well fitted for all its admirers with changing rooms, colorful if overly insistent vendors, and a large selection of snacks. **Rose Hall Beach Club,** east of central MoBay near Rose Hall Great House, recently opened and is a secluded area (far less crowded than beaches in town) with changing rooms and showers, a water-sports center, volleyball and other beach games, and a beach bar and grill. **Walter Fletcher Beach,** near the center of town, offers protection from the surf on a windy day and therefore unusually fine swimming; the calm waters make it a good bet for children, too.

### Negril
**Negril Beach** was, not too long ago, a beachcomber's vision of Eden. Today much of the 7 miles of white sand is fronted by modern resorts, although the 2 miles of beach fronting Bloody Bay remain relatively untouched. The nude beach areas are found mostly along sections of the beach where no hotel or resort has been built, such as the area ad-

jacent to Cosmo's (☞ Dining, *above*). A few resorts have built accommodations overlooking their nude beaches, thereby adding a new dimension to the traditional notion of "ocean view."

### Ocho Rios
**Ocho Rios public beach,** stretching behind Jamaica Grande and Club Jamaica, is the busiest beach in Ocho Rios. **Turtle Beach** is where the islanders go to swim in Ocho Rios.

### Port Antonio
**Boston Bay,** approximately 11 miles east of Port Antonio, beyond the Blue Lagoon, is a small, intimate beach. It's a good place to buy the famous peppery delicacy, jerk pork, available at any of the shacks spewing scented smoke along the beach. **San San Beach,** about 5 miles east of Port Antonio, has beautiful blue waters and is used mainly by area villa/hotel owners and their guests.

### South Coast
Those who seek beaches off the main tourist routes will want to explore Jamaica's unexploited south coast.

**Bluefields Beach,** near Savanna-La-Mar, south of Negril, is nearest to "civilization." **Crane Beach,** at Black River, has retained its natural beauty and has—so far—remained undiscovered by most tourists. **Treasure Beach** has to be the best that the south shore has to offer. Set by a quaint, quiet fishing village, the beach is undeveloped and is dotted with coves that are ideal for snorkeling.

## Outdoor Activities and Sports

The tourist board licenses all operators of recreational activities, which should ensure you of fair business practices as long as you deal with companies that display the decals.

### Fishing
Deep-sea fishing can be great around the island. Port Antonio gets the headlines with its annual Blue Marlin Tournament, and Montego Bay and Ocho Rios have devotees who talk of the sailfish, yellowfin tuna, wahoo, dolphinfish, and bonito. Licenses are not required. Boat charters can be arranged at your hotel.

### Golf
The best courses are found around Montego Bay at **Tryall** (☎ 809/956–5681), **Half Moon** (☎ 809/953–2560), **Rose Hall** (☎ 809/953–2650), and **Ironshore** (☎ 809/953–2800). Good courses are also found at **Caymanas** (☎ 809/926–8144) and **Constant Spring** (☎ 809/924–1610) in Kingston and at **SuperClubs Runaway Bay** (☎ 809/973–2561) and **Sandals Golf and Country Club** (☎ 809/974–2528) in Ocho Rios. A 9-hole course in the hills of Mandeville is called **Manchester Club** (☎ 809/962–2403). Great golf, rolling hills, and a "liquor mobile" go hand in hand at the **Negril Hills Golf Club** (☎ 809/957–4638) in Negril, which opened all 18 holes in 1995. **Prospect Plantation** (☎ 809/974–2058) in Ocho Rios and the **Anancy Family Fun and Nature Park** (☎ 809/957–4100) in Negril have 18-hole minigolf courses.

### Horseback Riding
Jamaica is fortunate to have the best equestrian facility in the Caribbean, **Chukka Cove** (☎ 809/972–2506, ℻ 809/972–0814), near Ocho Rios. The resort, complete with stylishly outfitted villas, offers instruction in riding, polo, and jumping, as well as hour-long trail rides, three-hour beach rides, and six-hour mountain-to-sea rides. Weekends, in season, this is the place for hot polo action and equally hot social action. **Rocky Point Stables** (☎ 809/953–2286), just east of the Half Moon Club in

Montego Bay, **Rhodes Hall Plantation Ltd.** (☎ 809/957–4258), between Green Island and Negril, and **Prospect Plantation** (☎ 809/974–2058) in Ocho Rios also offer rides.

## Tennis

Many hotels have tennis facilities that are free to their guests, but some will allow nonguests to play for a fee. The sport is a highlight at **Tryall** (☎ 809/956–5660), **Round Hill Hotel and Villas** (☎ 809/952–5150), **Sandals Montego Bay** (☎ 809/952–5510), and **Half Moon Club** (☎ 809/953–2211) in Montego Bay; **Swept Away** (☎ 809/957–4040) in Negril; **Sandals Dunn's River** (☎ 809/972–1610), **Sans Souci Lido** (☎ 809/974–2353), and **Ciboney, Ocho Rios** (☎ 809/974–1027) in Ocho Rios; and **Breezes Runaway Bay** (☎ 809/973–2436) in Runaway Bay.

## Water Sports

The major areas for swimming, windsurfing, snorkeling, and scuba diving are Negril in the west and Port Antonio in the east. All the large resorts rent equipment for a deposit and/or a fee. Diving is perhaps the only option that requires training, because you need to show a C-card in order to participate. However, some dive operators on the island are qualified to certify you. Jamaica Tourist Board–licensed dive operators include **Resort Divers** (✉ Montego Bay, ☎ 809/952–4285; Ocho Rios, ☎ 809/974-5338), **Sundivers** (✉ Negril, ☎ 809/957–4069), **Garfield Diving Station** (✉ Ocho Rios, ☎ 809/974–5749), **Dolphin Divers** (✉ Negril, ☎ 809/957–4944), **North Coast Marine** (✉ Montego Bay, ☎ 809/953–9266), and **Sandals Beach Resort Watersports** (✉ Montego Bay, ☎ 809/979–0104). All of these operators offer certification courses and dive trips. Most all-inclusive resorts offer free scuba diving to their guests. **Lady Godiva** (✉ San San Beach, Port Antonio, ☎ 809/993–3281) offers scuba diving, snorkeling, windsurfing, a glass-bottom boat, and sailing; excursions start at $25 per person.

# Shopping

Shopping in Jamaica goes two ways: things Jamaican and things imported. The former are made with style and skill; the latter are duty-free luxury finds. Jamaican crafts take the form of resort wear, hand-loomed fabrics, silk screens, wood carvings, paintings, and other fine arts. Jamaican rum is a great take-home gift. So is Tia Maria, Jamaica's world-famous coffee liqueur. The same goes for the island's prized Blue Mountain and High Mountain coffees and its jams, jellies, and marmalades. Some bargains, if you shop around, include Swiss watches, Irish crystal, jewelry, cameras, and china. The top-selling French perfumes are also available alongside Jamaica's own fragrances.

## Shopping Areas

KINGSTON

A shopping tour of the Kingston area should begin at Constant Spring Road or King Street. No matter where you begin, keep in mind that the trend these days is shopping malls, and in Jamaica they caught on with a fever. The ever-growing roster includes Twin Gates Plaza, New Lane Plaza, the New Kingston Shopping Centre, Tropical Plaza, Manor Park Plaza, the Village, the Springs, and the newest (and some say nicest), Sovereign Shopping Centre.

A day at **Devon House** (✉ 26 Hope Rd., Kingston, ☎ 809/929–6602) should be high on your shopping list. This is the place to find old and new Jamaica. The great house is now a museum with antiques and furniture reproductions and the Lady Nugent's Coffee Terrace outside. There are boutiques in what were once the house's stables: a branch of Things Jamaican, Jacaranda for leather finds, fine lace at the Battenburg Lace Shop, and some of the best tropical-fruit ice cream (mango, guava, pineapple, and passion fruit) at I-Scream.

Although you should not rule out a visit to the "crafts market" on Market Street in MoBay, you should consider first how much you like pandemonium and haggling over prices and quality. The crafts markets in Ocho Rios are less hectic unless a cruise ship is in port, and the crafts markets in Port Antonio and Negril are good fun. You'll find a plethora of T-shirts; straw hats, baskets, and place mats; carved wood statues; colorful Rasta berets; and cheap jewelry.

If you're looking to spend money, head for City Centre Plaza, Half Moon Village, Miranda Ridge Plaza, Montego Bay Shopping Center, St. James's Place, and Westgate Plaza in Montego Bay; in Ocho Rios, the shopping plazas are Pineapple Place, Ocean Village, the Taj Mahal, Coconut Grove, and Island Plaza. It's also a good idea to chat with salespeople, who can enlighten you about the newer boutiques and their whereabouts.

## Specialty Shops

ARTS AND CRAFTS

**Caribatik** (⊠ A-1, 2 mi east of Falmouth, ☎ 809/954–3314), the studio of the late Muriel Chandler, stocks silk batiks, by the yard or made into chic designs. Drawing on patterns in nature, Chandler translated the birds, seascapes, flora, and fauna into works of art. **Gallery of West Indian Art** (⊠ 1 Orange La., MoBay, ☎ 809/952–4547 and at Round Hill, ☎ 809/952–5150) is the place to find Jamaican and Haitian paintings. A corner of the gallery is devoted to hand-turned pottery (some painted) and beautifully carved and painted birds and jungle animals. **Harmony Hall** (⊠ An 8-min drive east on A1 from Ocho Rios; ☎ 809/975–4222), a restored great house, is where Annabella Proudlock sells her unique wood Annabella Boxes. The covers feature reproductions of Jamaican paintings. Larger reproductions of paintings, lithographs, and signed prints of Jamaican scenes are also for sale, along with hand-carved wood combs—all magnificently displayed. Harmony Hall is also well known for its art shows by local artists. **Images Art Gallery** (⊠ Half Moon Club, ☎ 809/953–9043) showcases a fine collection of Jamaican art, from colorful works on canvas and paper to carefully hewn wooden sculptures. **Ital-Craft** (⊠ Shop 8, Upper Manor Park Shopping Plaza, 184C Spring Rd., Kingston, ☎ 809/931–0477) sells belts, bangles, and beads from it's factory location. Although Ital-Craft's handmade treasures are sold in boutiques throughout Jamaica, we recommend a visit to the factory for the largest selection of the belts, made of spectacular shells, combined with leather, feathers, or fur. (The most ornate belts sell for about $75.) You'll also find some intriguing jewelry and purses here (many made from reptile skins). **Things Jamaican** (⊠ Devon House, 26 Hope Rd., Kingston, ☎ 809/929–6602, and 44 Fort St., MoBay, ☎ 809/952–5605) has two outlets and two airport stalls that display and sell some of the best native crafts made in Jamaica, with items that range from carved wood bowls and trays to reproductions of silver and brass period pieces.

BIKINIS

**Vaz Enterprises, LTD.** (⊠ 77 East St., Kingston, ☎ 809/922–9200), the manufacturing outlet of designer Sonia Vaz, sells teeny-weeny bikinis. They're also for sale at Sandals, and other resorts.

JEWELRY

**L. A. Henriques** (⊠ Shop 11, Upper Manor Park Plaza, Kingston, ☎ 809/931–0613) sells high-quality jewelry made to order.

RECORDS

Reggae tapes by world-famous Jamaican artists, such as Bob Marley, Ziggy Marley, Peter Tosh, and Third World, can be found easily in U.S. or European record stores, but a pilgrimage to **Randy's Record Mart** (⌧ 17 N. Parade, Kingston, ☎ 809/922–4859) should be high on the reggae lover's list. Also worth checking are the **Record Plaza** (⌧ Tropical Plaza, Kingston, ☎ 809/926–7645), **Record City** (⌧ 14 King St., Port Antonio, ☎ 809/993–2836), **De Muzic Shop** (⌧ Island Plaza, Ocho Rios, ☎ 809/974–9500), and **Top Ranking Records** (⌧ Westgate Plaza, MoBay, ☎ 809/952–1216).

SANDALS

Cheap sandals are good buys in shopping centers throughout Jamaica. Although workmanship and leathers don't rival the craftsmanship of those found in Italy or Spain, neither do the prices (about $20 a pair). In Kingston, **Lee's Fifth Avenue Shoes** (⌧ Tropical Plaza, ☎ 809/926–7486) is a good place to sandal-shop, as is **Jacaranda** (⌧ Devon House, ☎ 809/929–6602), a leather shop at Devon House. In Ocho Rios, the **Pretty Feet Shoe Shop** (⌧ Ocean Village Shopping Centre, ☎ 809/974–5040) is a good bet. In Montego Bay, try **Westgate Plaza.**

## Gift Ideas

CIGARS

Fine Macanudo handmade cigars make great gifts and are easily carried. They can be bought on departure at Montego Bay airport (☎ 809/925–1082 for outlet information).

COFFEE

Blue Mountain coffee can be found at **John R. Wong's Supermarket** (⌧ 1–5 Tobago Ave., Kingston, ☎ 809/926–4811). The **Sovereign Supermarket** (⌧ Sovereign Center, 106 Hope Rd., ☎ 809/978–1254) has a wide selection of coffee and other goods. **Magic Kitchen Ltd.** (⌧ Village Plaza, Kingston, ☎ 809/926–8894) sells the magic beans. If the stores are out of Blue Mountain, you may have to settle for High Mountain coffee, the natives' second-preferred brand.

## Rum

Jamaican-brewed rums and Tia Maria can be bought at either the Kingston or MoBay airports before your departure. As a general rule, only rum factories, such as Sangster's, are less expensive than the airport stores, and if you buy at the airport there's no toting of heavy, breakable bottles from your hotel.

# Nightlife

Jamaica—especially Kingston—supports a lively community of musicians. For starters there is reggae, popularized by the late Bob Marley and the Wailers and performed today by son Ziggy Marley, Jimmy Tosh (the late Peter Tosh's son), Gregory Isaacs, Third World, Jimmy Cliff, and many others. If your experience of Caribbean music has been limited to steel drums and Harry Belafonte, then the political, racial, and religious messages of reggae may set you on your ear; listen closely and you just might hear the heartbeat of the people. Those who already love reggae may want to plan a visit in mid-July to August for the Reggae Sunsplash. The four-night concert at the Bob Marley Performing Center (a field set up with a temporary stage), in the Freeport area of Montego Bay, showcases local talent and attracts such performers as Rick James, Gladys Knight and the Pips, Steel Pulse, Third World, and Ziggy Marley and the Melody Makers.

## Discos and Clubs

For the most part, the liveliest late-night happenings throughout Jamaica are in the major resort hotels. Some of the all-inclusives offer a dinner and disco pass from about $50.

### KINGSTON

The most popular spots in Kingston are **Godfather's** (⊠ Knutsford Blvd., ☎ 809/929–5459), **Mingles** (⊠ Courtleigh, ☎ 809/929–5321), **Illusions** (⊠ New Lane Plaza, ☎ 809/929–2125), **Jonkanoo** (⊠ Wyndham New Kingston, ☎ 809/929–3390), and the trendy disco, **Mirage** (⊠ Sovereign Centre, ☎ 809/978–8557).

### MONTEGO BAY

The hottest places in Montego Bay are **Sir Winston's Reggae Club** (⊠ Kent Ave., ☎ 809/952–2084), **Walter's** (⊠ 39 Glouchester Rd., ☎ 809/952–9399), and the **Rhythm Nightclub** (⊠ Holiday Inn Sunspree Resort, ☎ 809/953–2485). After 10 PM on Friday nights, the crowd gathers at **Pier 1** (⊠ Howard Cooke Blvd., ☎ 809/952–2452) opposite the straw market.

### NEGRIL

Some of the best music will be found in Negril at **Alfred's** (☎ 809/957–4735), **De Buss** (☎ 809/957–4405), and at the hot, hot spot, **Kaiser's Cafe** (☎ 809/957–4070), as well as the disco at **Hedonism II** (☎ 809/957–4200).

### OCHO RIOS

The principal clubs in Ocho Rios are **Jamaica Me Crazy** (⊠ Jamaica Grande, ☎ 809/974–2201), **Acropolis** (⊠ 70 Main St., ☎ 809/974–2633), **Silks** (⊠ Shaw Park Beach Hotel, ☎ 809/974–2552), and the **Little Pub on Main Street** (☎ 809/974–2324), which produces Caribbean revues.

### PORT ANTONIO

In Port Antonio, if you have but one night to disco, do it at the **Roof Club** (⊠ 11 West St., no phone). On weekends, from elevenish on, this is where it's all happening. An alternative for Port Antonio nightlife is the dance scene at **Shadows** (⊠ 40 West St., ☎ 809/993–3823) or the live jazz performances on Saturday evenings at the **Blue Lagoon Restaurant** (⊠ Fairy Hill, ☎ 809/993–2752).

# Exploring Jamaica

Jamaica can be both thrilling and extremely frustrating to tour, primarily due to the infrastructure of the country. Roads are, for the most part, full of potholes and, during the rainy season, can be entirely washed out (*always* check road conditions prior to heading out on your own to do any sightseeing). Primary roads that loop around and across the island are two lanes, signs are not prevalent, numbered addresses are seldom used outside of major townships, locals drive aggressively, and people and animals seem to have a particular talent for appearing out of nowhere before your vehicle. That said, Jamaica's natural scenery should not be missed. The solution? Stick to guided tours wherever possible—both for safety's sake and to avoid the virtually guaranteed frustration of navigating the island on your own.

*Numbers in the margin correspond to points of interest on the Jamaica map.*

### SIGHTS TO SEE

**❿ Blue Mountains.** Lush, with deep valleys and soaring peaks that climb into the clouds, the Blue Mountains rise to the north of Kingston. Admirers of Jamaica's wonderful coffee may wish to visit **Pine Grove**, a working coffee farm that doubles as an inn. It also has a restaurant that serves owner Marcia Thwaites's Jamaican cuisine. Another spot worth a visit is **Mavis Bank** and its Jablum coffee plant. Mavis Bank is delightfully primitive—especially considering the retail price of the beans it processes. A half-hour guided tour is available for $5; inquire when you arrive at the main office. Stop in World's End for a free tour of **Dr. Sangster's Rum Factory** (call ahead, ☎ 809/926–8888), open weekdays 9–4. The small factory produces wonderful liqueurs flavored with local coffee beans, oranges, coconuts, and other Jamaican produce; samples are part of the tour.

---

**NEED A BREAK?**

On your way up (or back) from World's End, stop by Gloria Palomino's café-restaurant, **The Gap** (☎ 809/923–5617 or 809/997–3032), open daily for breakfast and lunch. It's set 4,200 feet above sea level and is adjacent to several well-defined nature walking trails. Her gift shop sells the coveted Blue Mountain coffee.

---

Unless you are traveling with a local, do not rent a car and go to the Blue Mountains on your own, as the mountain roads wind and dip, hand-lettered signs blow away, and a tourist can easily get lost—not just for hours, but for days. Another way to see the Blue Mountains is by the downhill bicycle tour offered by **Blue Mountain Tours** (☞ Guided Tours *in* Jamaica A to Z, *below*).

**⑮ Cockpit Country.** Fifteen miles inland from Montego Bay is one of the most primitive areas in the West Indies, a terrain of pitfalls and potholes carved by nature in limestone. For nearly a century after 1655 it was known as the Land of Look Behind because British soldiers rode their horses back-to-back in pairs, looking out for the savage freedom fighters known as Maroons. Fugitive slaves who refused to surrender to the invading English, the Maroons eventually won a treaty of independence and continue to live apart from the rest of Jamaica in the Cockpit Country. The government leaves them alone, untaxed and virtually ungoverned by outside authorities.

**❻ Crystal Springs.** About 18 miles west of Port Antonio, Crystal Springs has more than 15,000 orchids, and hummingbirds dart among the blossoms, landing on visitors' outstretched hands. Hiking and camping are available here. ✉ *Buff Bay,* ☎ *809/993–2609 or 809/996–1400.* ✆ *J$100.* ☉ *Daily 9–5.*

**❺ Firefly.** Located about 20 miles east of Ocho Rios in Port Maria, Firefly was once Sir Noël Coward's vacation residence and is now preserved in all its hilltop wonder by the Jamaican National Heritage Trust. Coward used to entertain jet-setters and royalty in the surprisingly spartan digs in an Eden-like setting. He wrote *High Spirits, Quadrille,* and other plays here. Coward's simple grave is on the grounds next to a small stage where his plays are occasionally performed. Recordings of Coward singing of mad dogs and Englishmen echo over the lawns. Guided tours include time in the photo gallery and a walk through the house and grounds, the viewing of a biographical video on Coward, and a drink in the gift shop. ✉ *Port Maria,* ☎ *809/997–7201,* FAX *809/974–5830.* ✆ *J$10.* ☉ *Daily 8:30–5:30.*

**❹ Golden Eye.** Between Oracabessa and Port Maria, east of Ocho Rios on the main coast road, Golden Eye was used in wintertime by Ian Fleming, the creator of James Bond, from 1946 until his death in 1964. Later Golden Eye served as home to reggae legend Bob Marley and to the founder of Island Records, Chris Blackwell. Today it can be seen only by those who can afford to rent it from the record company. It's an airy complex of deep-blue buildings, walls, and bookcases bursting with Bond memorabilia, and a private cove reached by stone steps that would have delighted 007.

**⑪  Kingston.** The reaction of most visitors to the capital city, situated on the southeast coast of Jamaica, is anything but love at first sight. In fact, only a small percentage of visitors to Jamaica see it at all. Kingston, for the tourist, may seem as remote from the resorts of Montego Bay as the loneliest peak in the Blue Mountains. Yet the islanders themselves can't seem to let it go. Everybody talks about Kingston, about their homes or relatives there, about their childhood memories. More than the sunny havens of the north coast, Kingston is a distillation of the true Jamaica. Parts of it may be dirty, crowded, often raucous, yet it is the ethnic cauldron that produces the cultural mix that is the nation's greatest natural resource. (Note, however, that when the sun sets even Kingstonians beat a quick path out of downtown Kingston, which is considered unsafe after dark.) Kingston is a cultural and commercial crossroads of international and local movers and shakers, art-show openings, theater (from Shakespeare to pantomime), and superb shopping. Here, too, the University of the West Indies explores Caribbean art and literature, as well as science. As one Jamaican put it, "You don't really know Jamaica until you know Kingston."

The first-time business or pleasure traveler may prefer to begin with New Kingston, which glistens with hotels, office towers, apartments, and boutiques. Newcomers may feel more comfortable settling in here and venturing forth from comfort they know will await their return.

Kingston's colonial past is very much alive away from the high-rises of the new city. **Devon House,** built in 1881 and bought and restored by the government in the 1960s, is filled with period furnishings. Shoppers will appreciate Devon House, for the firm Things Jamaican has converted portions of the space into some of the best crafts shops on the island. On the grounds you'll find one of the few mahogany trees to survive Kingston's ambitious but not always careful development. ✉ *26 Hope Rd.,* ☎ *809/929–7029.* 🎟 *J$100.* ☉ *Tues.–Sat. 9:30–5. Shops open Mon.–Sat. 10–6.*

Once you have accepted the fact that Kingston doesn't look like a travel poster—too much life goes on here for that—you may see your trip here for precisely what it is, the single best introduction to the people of Jamaica. Near the waterfront, the **Institute of Jamaica** is a museum and library that traces the island's history from the Arawaks to current events. The charts and almanacs here make fascinating browsing; one example, famed as the Shark Papers, is made up of damaging evidence tossed overboard by a guilty sea captain and later recovered from the belly of a shark. ✉ *12 East St.,* ☎ *809/922–0620.* 🎟 *Free.* ☉ *Mon.–Thurs. 9–5, Fri. 9–4.*

Jamaica's rich cultural life is evoked at the **National Gallery,** which was once at Devon House and can now be found at Kingston Mall near the reborn waterfront section. The artists represented here may not be household names in other nations, yet the paintings of such intuitive masters as John Dunkley, David Miller, Sr., and David Miller, Jr., reveal a sensitivity to the life around them that transcends academic training. Among other highlights from the 1920s through the 1980s are works by Edna Manley and Mallica Reynolds, better known as Kapo. Reggae fans touring the National Gallery will want to look for Christopher Gonzalez's controversial statue of Bob Marley. ✉ *12 Ocean Blvd.,* ☎ *809/922–1563.* 🎟 *Fees charged for special exhibits.* ☉ *Weekdays 11–4:30.*

Reggae fans will want to see the **Bob Marley Museum.** Painted in Rasta-farian red, yellow, and green, this recording studio was built by Mar-ley at the height of his career. The museum gives guided tours of the medicinal herb garden, the room where Marley was shot, his bedroom, and rooms wall-papered with magazine and newspaper articles chron-icling his rise to stardom. The tour includes a 20-minute biographical film on his life; there's also a reference library if you want to learn more. Certainly there is much here to help the outsider understand Marley, reggae, and Jamaica itself. The Ethiopian flag is a reminder that Ras-tas consider the late Ethiopian emperor Haile Selassie to be the Mes-siah, a descendant of King Solomon and the Queen of Sheba. A striking mural by Jah Bobby, *The Journey of Superstar Bob Marley,* depicts the hero's life from its beginnings in a womb shaped like a coconut to en-shrinement in the hearts of the Jamaican people. ⊠ *56 Hope Rd.,* ☎ *809/927–9152.* ⊒ *J$180.* ⊙ *Mon., Tues., Thurs., and Fri. 9:30–5, Wed. and Sat. 12:30–6.*

| | |
|---|---|
| NEED A BREAK? | After touring the museum, stop to rest your feet and sip fresh fruit juice at the **Queen of Sheba** (no phone), an Ethiopian restaurant on the museum grounds. If you're hungry, you can sample local Jamaican dishes such as rice and peas or Ethiopian fare (strictly vegetarian) here as well. |

There is also a fine **statue** of Bob Marley on Arthur Wint Drive across from the **National Stadium.**

Although no longer lovingly cared for, the **Royal Botanical Gardens at Hope** is a nice place to picnic or while away an afternoon. Donated to Jamaica by the Hope family following the abolition of slavery, the garden consists of 50 acres filled with tropical trees, plants, and flow-ers, most clearly labeled for those taking a self-guided tour. Free con-certs are given here on the first Sunday of each month. ⊠ *Hope Rd.,* ☎ *809/927–1085.* ⊒ *J$10.* ⊙ *Weekdays 10–5, weekends 10–5:30.*

Another good picnic spot is the **Rockfort Mineral Baths.** Named for the stone fort built above Kingston Harbour in 1694 by the British to guard against invasion, and for the natural mineral spring that emerged following a devastating earthquake in 1907, this complex was listed on the Jamaica National Heritage Trust after being restored by the Caribbean Cement Company. It draws Kingstonians who come to cool off in the invigorating spring water in the public swimming pool or to unwind tense muscles in private whirlpool tubs. You can also have a massage and visit the juice bar or the cafeteria before staking out your picnic spot on the landscaped grounds. ⊠ *Kingston (on A-1, just out-side town),* ☎ *809/938–5055.* ⊒ *Pool J$50; private baths start at J$300.* ⊙ *Weekdays 6:30–6, weekends 8–6.*

**⑭** **Mandeville.** More than a quarter of a century after Jamaica achieved its independence from Great Britain, Mandeville seems like a hilly tribute to all that is genteel and admirable in the British character. At 2,000 feet above sea level, 70 miles southeast of Montego Bay, Man-deville is considerably cooler than the coastal area 25 miles to the south. Its vegetation is more lush, thanks to the mists that drift through the mountains. The people of Mandeville live their lives around a village green, a Georgian courthouse, tidy cottages and gardens, even a parish church. The entire scene could be set down in Devonshire, were it not for the occasional poinciana blossom or citrus grove.

Mandeville is omitted from most tourist itineraries even though its res-idents are increasingly interested in showing visitors around. It is still much less expensive than any of the coastal resorts, and its diversions include horseback riding, cycling, croquet, hiking, tennis, golf, bird-watching, and people-meeting.

The town itself is characterized by its orderliness. You may stay here several days, or a glimpse of the lifestyle may satisfy you and you'll scurry back to the steamy coast. **Manchester Club** (☎ 809/962–2403) features tennis, nine holes of golf, and well-manicured greens; Mrs. Stephenson conducts photographic tours of her **Gardens** (☎ 809/962–2328), an arboretum filled with lovely orchids and fruit trees; and the natural **Bird Sanctuary at Marshall's Penn Great House** (☎ 809/963–8569) is visited by more than 25 species indigenous to Jamaica. Tours of this bird sanctuary are by appointment only and are led by owner Robert Sutton, one of Jamaica's leading ornithologists. Other sites worth visiting are **Lover's Leap,** where legend has it that two slave lovers leapt off the 1,700-foot-high cliff rather than be recaptured by their plantation owner, and the **High Mountain Coffee Plantation** (☎ 809/963–4211) in nearby Williamsfield, where free tours (by appointment only) show how coffee beans are turned into one of America's favorite morning drinks.

**➋** **Martha Brae River.** One of the most popular excursions in Jamaica is rafting on this river. The gentle waterway takes its name from that of an Arawak Indian who killed herself because she refused to reveal the whereabouts of a local gold mine to the Spanish. According to legend, she finally agreed to take them there and, on reaching the river, used magic to change its course, drowning herself along with the greedy Spaniards. Her duppy (ghost) is said to guard the mine's entrance to this day. **Martha Brae River Rafting** (☞ Guided Tours *in* Jamaica A to Z, *below*) leads trips down the river. The ticket office, gift shops, a bar-restaurant, and swimming pool are at the top of the river. Bookings can be made through hotel tour desks.

**➊** **Montego Bay.** The number and variety of its attractions make Montego Bay, on the island's north coast, the logical place to begin an exploration of Jamaica. Confronting the string of high-rise developments that crowd the water's edge, you may find it hard to believe that little of what is now Montego Bay (the locals call it MoBay) existed before the turn of the century. Today many explorations of Montego Bay are conducted from a reclining chair on Doctor's Cave Beach, with a table nearby to hold frothy drinks.

Led by a charming guide in period costume who recites poetry and sings songs of the period, the tour of the **Barnett Estates** is one of the best you'll find in Jamaica. The Kerr-Jarrett family has held the land here for 11 generations, and still grow coconut, mango, and sugarcane on 3,000 acres; you'll get samples during the plantation tour by jitney. ✉ *Granville Main Rd.,* ☎ *809/952–2382,* FAX *809/952–6342.* ✍ *$30 (includes lunch).* ☉ *Call ahead for tour times.*

**Rose Hall Great House,** perhaps the greatest in the West Indies in the 1700s, enjoys its popularity less for its architecture than for the legend surrounding its second mistress, Annie Palmer, who was credited with murdering three husbands and a plantation overseer who was her lover. The story is told in two novels sold everywhere in Jamaica: *The White Witch of Rose Hall* and *Jamaica White.* There's a pub on site. ✉ *East of Montego Bay, just across hwy. from Rose Hall resorts,* ☎ *809/953–2323.* ✍ *$15.* ☉ *Daily 9–6.*

**Greenwood Great House** has no spooky legend to titillate visitors, but it's much better than Rose Hall at evoking the atmosphere of life on a sugar plantation. The Barrett family, from which the English poet Elizabeth Barrett Browning was descended, once owned all the land from Rose Hall to Falmouth, and built several great houses on it, including Greenwood. (The poet's father, Edward Moulton Barrett, "the Tyrant of Wimpole Street," was born at Cinnamon Hill, currently the private estate of country singer Johnny Cash.) Highlights of Greenwood include oil paintings of the Barretts, china made especially for the family by Wedgwood, a library filled with rare books printed as early as 1697, fine antique furniture, and a collection of exotic musical instruments. There's a pub on site. ⊠ *15 mi east of Montego Bay,* ☎ *809/953–1077.* 🖾 *J$10.* ☻ *Daily 9–6.*

**⑯ Negril.** Situated 55 miles southwest of Montego Bay on the winding coast road, Negril is no longer Jamaica's best-kept secret. In fact, it has begun to shed some of its bohemian, ramshackle atmosphere for the attractions and activities traditionally associated with Montego Bay. Applauding the sunset from Rick's Cafe may still be the highlight of a day in Negril, yet increasingly the hours before and after have come to be filled with conventional recreation.

One thing that has not changed around this west-coast center (whose only true claim to fame is a 7-mile beach) is the casual approach to life. As you wander from lunch in the sun to shopping in the sun to sports in the sun, you'll find that swimsuits are common attire. Want to dress for a special meal? Slip a caftan over your bathing suit.

Negril stretches along the coast south from the horseshoe-shape **Bloody Bay** (named during the period when it was a whale-processing center) along the calm waters of **Long Bay** to the Lighthouse section and the landmark **Rick's Cafe** (☎ 809/957–4335). Sunset at Rick's is a Negril tradition. Divers spiral downward off 50-foot-high cliffs into the deep green depths as the sun turns into a ball of fire and sets the clouds ablaze with color.

Even though you may be staying at one of the charming smaller inns in Negril, you may enjoy spending a day at **Hedonism II** (☞ Lodging, *above*), a kind of love poem to health, Mother Nature, and good (mostly clean) fun. The owners love to publicize the occasional nude volleyball game in the pool at 3 AM, but most of the pampered campers are in clothes and in bed well before that hour. And what if Hedonism II is not the den of iniquity it likes to appear to be? What it is, and what your day pass ($50) gets you, is a taste of the spirit as well as the food and drink—and participation in water sports, tennis, squash, and daily activities. Next to Hedonism II is a sister resort, the **Grand Lido** (☞ Lodging, *above*), that offers a night pass for nonguests that includes dinner at the Cafe Lido, live entertainment, and dusk-to-dawn dancing. The price is a hefty $70, and reservations are a must.

Negril's newest attraction is the **Anancy Family Fun & Nature Park** (☎ 809/957–4100), just across the street from the family-oriented Poinciana Beach Resort. Named after the mischievous spider character in Jamaican folktales, the 3-acre site features an 18-hole miniature golf course, go-cart rides, a minitrain, a fishing pond, a nature trail, and three small museums (craft, conservation, and heritage).

Around sunset, activity centers on **West End Road,** Negril's main (and only) thoroughfare, which comes to life in the evening with bustling bistros and ear-splitting discos. West End Road leads to the town's only building of historical significance, the **Lighthouse.** All anyone can tell you about it, however, is that it's been there for a while. Even historians find it hard to keep track of the days in Negril.

What is known of the island's history is that, in the 18th century, Negril was where the English ships assembled in convoys for the dangerous ocean crossing. Not only were there pirates in the neighborhood, but the infamous Calico Jack and his crew were captured right here, while they guzzled the local rum. All but two of them were hanged on the spot; Mary Read and Anne Bonney were pregnant at the time, and their execution was delayed.

❸ **Ocho Rios.** Perhaps more than anywhere else in Jamaica, Ocho Rios—67 miles east of Montego Bay—presents a striking contrast of natural beauty and recreational development. The Jamaicans can fill the place by themselves, especially on a busy market day, when cars and buses from the countryside clog the heavily traveled coastal road that links Port Antonio with Montego Bay. Add a tour bus or three and the entire passenger list from a cruise ship, and you may find yourself mired in a considerable traffic jam.

Yet a visit to Ocho Rios is worthwhile, if only to enjoy its two chief attractions—Dunn's River Falls and Prospect Plantation. A few steps away from the main road in Ocho Rios are waiting some of the most charming inns and oceanfront restaurants in the Caribbean. Lying on the sand of what will seem to be your private cove or swinging gently in a hammock with a tropical drink in your hand, you'll soon forget the traffic that's only a brief stroll away.

The dispute continues as to the origin of the name Ocho Rios. Some claim it's Spanish for "eight rivers"; others maintain that the name is a corruption of *chorreras*, which describes a seemingly endless series of cascades that sparkle from the limestone rocks along this stretch of coast. For as long as anyone can remember, Jamaicans have favored Ocho Rios as their own escape from the heat and the crowds of Kingston.

**Dunn's River Falls** is an eye-catching sight: 600 feet of cold, clear mountain water splashing over a series of stone steps to the warm Caribbean. The best way to enjoy the falls is to climb the slippery steps. Don a swimsuit, take the hand of the person ahead of you, and trust that the chain of hands and bodies leads to an experienced guide. The leaders of the climbs are personable fellows who reel off bits of local lore while telling you where to step. ⊠ *Immediately off Main Rd. (A-1), between St. Ann's and Ocho Rios,* ☎ *809/974–2857.* ☞ *$5.* ☉ *Daily 9–5.*

The **Prospect Plantation** tour is the best of several offerings that delve into the island's former agricultural lifestyle. It's not just for specialists; virtually everyone enjoys the beautiful views over the White River Gorge and the tour by jitney (a canopied open-air cart pulled by a tractor) through a plantation with exotic fruits and tropical trees planted over the years by such celebrities as Winston Churchill and Charlie Chaplin. Horseback riding over 900 acres is available as is minigolf, and there's a pub on site. ⊠ *Hwy. A1, just west of downtown Ocho Rios,* ☎ *809/974–2058.* ☞ *$12.* ☉ *Daily 10:30–3:30; tours at 11, 1:30, and 3:30.*

The only major historic site in Ocho Rios is the **Old Fort,** built in 1777 as a defense against invaders from the sea. The original "defenders" spent much of their time sacking and plundering as far afield as St. Augustine, Florida, and sharing their bounty with the local plantation owners who financed their missions. Fifteen miles west is **Discovery Bay,** site of Columbus's landing, with a small museum of artifacts and Jamaican memorabilia.

Ocho Rios's newest attraction is the **Coyaba River Garden and Museum,** which features exhibits on Jamaica's many cultural influences (the national motto is "Out of Many One People"). A guided tour through the lush gardens introduces you to the flora and fauna of the island.

The museum covers the island's history from the time of the Arawak Indians up to the modern day. The complex includes a crafts and gift shop and a snack bar, and offers the Moonshine and Sunshine Festival, a dinner-entertainment package (by reservation only). ⊠ *Shaw Park Rd., Ocho Rios,* ☎ *809/974–6235.* ⛃ *$4.50.* ☉ *Daily 8–5.*

Other excursions of note are the one to Runaway Bay's Green Grotto Caves (and a boat ride on an underground lake); a ramble through the Shaw Park Botanical Gardens; a visit to Sun Valley, a working plantation with banana, coconut, and citrus trees; and a drive through Fern Gully, a natural canopy of vegetation filtered by sunlight (Jamaica has the world's largest number of fern species, more than 500).

**8** **Port Antonio.** Every visitor's presence in Port Antonio pays homage to the beginnings of Jamaican tourism. Early in the century the first tourists arrived here on the island's northeast coast, 133 miles east of Montego Bay, drawn by the exoticism of the island's banana trade and seeking a respite from the New York winters. The original posters of the shipping lines make Port Antonio appear as foreign as the moon, yet in time it became the tropical darling of a fast-moving crowd and counted Clara Bow, Bette Davis, Ginger Rogers, Rudyard Kipling, J. P. Morgan, and William Randolph Hearst among its admirers. Its most passionate devotee was the actor Errol Flynn, whose spirit still seems to haunt the docks, devouring raw dolphinfish and swigging gin at 10 AM.

Although the action has moved elsewhere, the area can still weave a spell. Robin Moore wrote *The French Connection* here, and Broadway's tall and talented Tommy Tune found inspiration for the musical *Nine* while being pampered at Trident.

For as long as anyone can remember, Port Antonio has been a center for some of the finest deep-sea fishing in the Caribbean. Dolphins (the delectable fish, not the lovable mammal) are the likely catch here, along with tuna, kingfish, and wahoo. In October the weeklong Blue Marlin Tournament attracts anglers from around the world. By the time enough beer has been consumed, it's a bit like the running of the bulls at Pamplona, except that fish stories carry the day.

A stroll through the town suggests a step into the past. **Queen Street,** in the residential Titchfield area, a couple of miles north of downtown Port Antonio, has several fine examples of Georgian architecture. **DeMontevin Lodge** (⊠ 21 Fort George St., on Titchfield Hill, ☎ 809/993–2604), owned by the Mullings family (the late Gladys Mullings was Errol Flynn's cook, and you can still get great food here), and the nearby **Musgrave Street** (the Craft Market is here) are in the traditional sea-captain style that one finds along coasts as far away as New England.

The town's best-known landmark is **Folly,** on the way to Trident, a Roman-style villa in ruins on the eastern edge of East Harbor. The creation of a Connecticut millionaire in 1905, the manse was made almost entirely of concrete. Unfortunately, the cement was mixed with seawater, and it began to crumble as it dried. According to local lore, the millionaire's bride took one look at her shattered dream, burst into tears, and fled forever. Little more than the marble floor remains today. Note that Folly becomes something of a ganja hangout after sundown and should be avoided then.

A good way to spend a day in Port Antonio is swimming in the deep azure water of the **Blue Lagoon.** Although there's not much beach to speak of, there is a water-sports center, changing rooms, and a soothing mineral pool, off to one side under the shade of a tree. Yummy, inexpensive, Jamaican fare is served at a charming waterside terrace restaurant, where you'll find a live jazz band performing on Saturday nights. ⌧ *1 mi east of San San Beach,* ☎ *809/993–8491. Restaurant serves lunch only Mon.–Wed., dinner only Thurs.–Sun.*

A short drive east from Port Antonio deposits you at **Boston Bay,** which is popular with swimmers and has been enshrined by lovers of jerk pork. The spicy barbecue was originated by the Arawaks and perfected by runaway slaves called the Maroons. Eating almost nothing but wild hog preserved over smoking coals enabled the Maroons to survive years of fierce guerrilla warfare with the English.

Some 6 miles northeast of Port Antonio in the village of Nonsuch are the **Athenry Gardens,** a 3-acre tropical wonderland, and the **Nonsuch Caves,** whose underground beauty has been made accessible by concrete walkways, railed stairways, and careful lighting. ⌧ *Athenry/Nonsuch,* ☎ *809/993–3740.* ⌫ *$5.* ⊘ *Daily 9–5.*

**12** **Port Royal.** Just south of Kingston, Port Royal was called "the wickedest city in the world"—before an earthquake tumbled it into the sea in 1692. The spirits of Henry Morgan and other buccaneers add a great deal of energy to what remains. The proudest possession of St. Peter's Church, rebuilt in 1726 to replace Christ's Church, is a silver communion plate said to have been donated by Morgan himself.

A ferry from the Square in downtown Kingston goes to Port Royal at least twice a day, and the town is small enough to see on foot. If you drive out to Port Royal from Kingston, you'll pass several sites of interest, including remains of old forts virtually covered over by vegetation, an old naval cemetery, which has some intriguing headstones, and a bit farther on, a monument commemorating Jamaica's first coconut tree, planted in 1863 (there's no tree there now, just plenty of cactus and scrub brush).

You can no longer down rum in Port Royal's legendary 40 taverns, but you can explore the impressive remains of **Fort Charles,** once the area's major garrison. On the grounds is the small **Fort Charles Maritime Museum** and **Giddy House,** an old artillery storehouse that gained its name after being permanently tilted by the earthquake of 1907. Nearby, in the graveyard of **St. Peter Church,** is the tombstone of Lewis Galdy who was swallowed up in the great earthquake of 1692, spewed into the sea, rescued, and lived another four decades in "Great Reputation." ⌧ *Fort Charles, Port Royal,* ☎ *809/967–8059.* ⌫ *J$60.* ⊘ *Daily 9:30–5.*

NEED A
BREAK?     **Gloria's Rendezvous** (⌧ 5 Queen St., ☎ 809/976–8066), the brightly painted, ramshackle eatery next to the Port Royal Police Station, is wildly popular with Kingston locals escaping the sultry city heat on weekends. Delectable grilled fish and chicken are the draw.

**9** **Rio Grande River.** Rafting on the Rio Grande (yes, Jamaica has a Rio Grande, too) is a must. This is the granddaddy of the river-rafting attractions, an 8-mile-long swift green waterway from Berrydale to Rafter's Rest. Here the river flows into the Caribbean at St. Margaret's Bay. The trip of about three hours is made on bamboo rafts pushed along by a raftsman who is likely to be a character. You can pack a picnic lunch and eat it on the raft or along the riverbank; wherever you lunch, a vendor of Red Stripe beer will appear at your elbow. A restaurant, bar, and souvenir shops are located at Rafter's Rest. The trip costs about $40 per two-person raft. (☞ Guided Tours *in* Jamaica A to Z, *below*).

❼ **Somerset Falls.** Eight miles west of Port Antonio is Somerset Falls, a sun-dappled spot crawling with flowering vines. You can climb the 400 feet with some assistance from a concrete staircase. A brief raft ride takes you part of the way. ✉ *Somerset Falls, no phone.* 🖫 *$2.* ⊙ *Daily 10–5.*

⓭ **Spanish Town.** Located 12 miles west of Kingston on A1, Spanish Town was the island's capital under Spanish rule. The town boasts the tiered Georgian **Antique Square,** the **Jamaican People's Museum of Crafts and Technology** (in the Old King's House stables), and **St. James,** the oldest cathedral in the Western Hemisphere. Spanish Town's original name was Santiago de la Vega, which the English corrupted to St. Jago de la Vega, both meaning St. James of the Plains. Contact the Jamaica National Heritage Trust (☎ 809/922–1287) for further information on this heritage town.

# Jamaica A to Z

## Arriving and Departing

BY PLANE

**Donald Sangster International Airport** (☎ 809/952–4001), in Montego Bay, is the most efficient point of entry for visitors destined for Montego Bay, Ocho Rios, Runaway Bay, and Negril. **Norman Manley International Airport** (☎ 809/924–8235), in Kingston, is best for visitors to the capital or Port Antonio.

**Air Jamaica Express** (☎ 809/952–5401 in Montego Bay, 809/923–8680 in Kingston), a new subsidiary of Air Jamaica, provides shuttle services on the island. Be sure to reconfirm your departing flight a full 72 hours in advance. **Air Jamaica** (☎ 809/952–4300 in Montego Bay or 800/523–5585) provides the most frequent service from U.S. cities, including New York, Philadelphia, Baltimore, Atlanta, Miami, and Orlando. **American Airlines** (☎ 809/952–5950 in Montego Bay, 809/924–8305 in Kingston, or 800/433–7300) flies nonstop daily from New York, Miami, and San Juan. **US Air** (☎ 800/428–4322) flies in from Baltimore and Charlotte. **Continental** (☎ 800/231–0856) flies in four times a week from Newark. **Northwest Airlines** (☎ 212/563–7200 or 800/225–2525) has daily direct service to Montego Bay from Minneapolis and Tampa. **Aeroflot** (☎ 800/995–5555) flies in from Havana. **Air Canada** (☎ 809/952–5160 or 800/776–3000) offers daily service from Toronto, Halifax, Winnipeg, and Montreal in conjunction with Air Jamaica. **British Airways** (☎ 809/952–3771 or 800/247–9297) connects the island with London.

## Currency

The Jamaican government abolished the fixed rate of exchange for the Jamaican dollar, allowing it to be traded publicly and subject to market fluctuations. At press time the Jamaican dollar was worth about J$40 to U.S.$1. Currency can be exchanged at airport bank counters, exchange bureaus, or commercial banks. Prices quoted are in U.S. dollars unless otherwise noted.

## Emergencies

**Police, Fire, and Ambulance:** Police and air-rescue ☎ 119; fire department and ambulance ☎ 110. **Hospitals: University Hospital** (✉ Mona, Kingston, ☎ 809/927–1620), **Cornwall Regional Hospital** (✉ Mt. Salem, in Montego Bay, ☎ 809/952–5100), **Port Antonio General Hospital** (✉ Naylor's Hill, Port Antonio, ☎ 809/993–2646), and **St. Ann's Bay Hospital** (✉ Near Ocho Rios, ☎ 809/972–2272). **Pharmacies: Jamaica Pegasus hotel** (✉ 81 Knutsford Blvd., Kingston, ☎ 809/926–3690), **McKenzie's Drug Store** (✉ 16 Strand St. in Montego Bay, ☎

809/952–2467), and **Great House Pharmacy** (✉ Brown's Plaza in Ocho Rios, ☎ 809/974–2352).

## Getting Around

BICYCLES, MOPEDS, AND MOTORCYCLES

The front desks of most major hotels can arrange the rental of bicycles, mopeds, and motorcycles. Daily rates run from about $45 for a moped to $70 for a Honda 550. Deposits of $100–$300 or more are required. However, we highly recommend that you *NOT* rent a moped or motorcycle. The strangeness of driving on the left, the less-than-cautious driving style that prevails on the island, the abundance of potholes, and the prevalence of vendors who will approach you at every traffic light are just a few reasons to skip cycles. If you want to venture out on your own, rent a car.

BUSES

Buses are the mode of transportation Jamaicans use most, and consequently buses are *extremely* crowded and slow. They're also not air-conditioned, and rather uncomfortable. Yet the service is fairly frequent between Kingston and Montego Bay and between other significant destinations. Schedule or route information is available at bus stops or from the bus driver.

CAR RENTALS

Traffic keeps to the left in Jamaica, and those who are unfamiliar with driving on the left will find that it takes some getting used to. Please note that driving in Jamaica is a chore and can be extremely frustrating (not the way to spend a vacation). You must constantly be on guard—for enormous potholes, people and animals darting out in the street, and aggressive drivers.

Jamaica has dozens of car-rental companies throughout the island. Because rentals can be difficult to arrange once you've arrived, you must make reservations and send a deposit before your trip. (Cars are scarce, and without either a confirmation number or a receipt you may have to walk.) You must be at least 21 years old to rent a car (at least 25 years old at several agencies), have a valid driver's license (from any country), and have a valid credit card. You may be required to post a security of several hundred dollars before taking possession of your car; ask about it when you make the reservation. Rates average $75–$100 a day. Best bets are **Avis** (☎ 800/331–1212 or 809/952–4543 in MoBay, 809/924–8013 in Kingston), **Hertz** (☎ 800/654–3131 or 809/979–0438 in MoBay), and **National** (☎ 800/328–4567 or 809/952–2769 in MoBay). In Jamaica, try the branch offices in your resort area or try **Island Car Rentals** (☎ 809/952–5771 in MoBay, 809/926–5991 in Kingston), **United Car Rentals** (☎ 809/952–3077), or **Jamaica Car Rental** (☎ 809/952–5586).

TAXIS

Some but not all of Jamaica's taxis are metered. If you accept a driver's offer of his services as a tour guide, be sure to agree on a price before the vehicle is put into gear. All licensed taxis display red Public Passenger Vehicle (PPV) plates. Cabs can be summoned by telephone or flagged down on the street. Rates are per car, not per passenger, and 25% is added to the metered rate between midnight and 5 AM. Licensed minivans are also available and bear the red PPV plates. JUTA is the largest taxi franchise and has offices in all resort areas.

TRAINS

At press time, rail service between Kingston and Montego Bay was suspended.

## Guided Tours

Half-day tours are offered by a variety of operators in the important areas of Jamaica. The best great-house tours include Rose Hall, Greenwood, and Devon House. Plantations to tour are Prospect, Barnett Estates, and Sun Valley. The Appleton Estate Tour uses a bus to visit villages, plantations, and a rum distillery. The increasingly popular waterside folklore feasts are offered on the Dunn's, Great, and White rivers. The significant city tours are in Kingston, Montego Bay, and Ocho Rios.

### AIR TOURS

**Helitours Jamaica Ltd.** (☎ 809/974–2265) offers helicopter tours of Jamaica, ranging from 15 minutes to an hour at prices that vary accordingly ($65–$225).

### LAND TOURS

**Blue Mountain Tours** (☎ 809/974–0635) offers a daylong downhill bicycle tour of the mountains, which coasts down from 5,060 feet through coffee plantations and rain forests. The cost is about $80 and includes lunch. **Maroon Tourist Attraction Co.** (☎ 809/952–4546) leads tours from Montego Bay to Maroon headquarters at Accompong, giving visitors a glimpse of the society of Maroons, descendants of fugitive slaves, who live in Cockpit Country. **Touring Society of Jamaica** (☎ 809/975–7158 in Ocho Rios or ☎ 809/944–8400, FAX 809/944–8408 in the Blue Mountains), operated by American Lynda Lee Burke, offers several eco-tours, from birding in the Blue Mountains to the natural history of Cockpit Country. **Valley Hikes** (☎ FAX 809/993–2543) in Port Antonio offers guided hikes up the Rio Grande Valley or a combination hiking/rafting trip.

### SEA TOURS

**Calico Sailing** (☎ 809/952–5860, FAX 809/979–0843) offers snorkeling trips and sunset cruises on the waters of MoBay; costs are $50 and $25 respectively. **An Evening on the Great River** (☎ 809/952–5047 or 809/952–5097) is a must for tour groups, yet fun nonetheless. The adventure includes a boat ride up the torch-lit river, a full Jamaican dinner, open bar, a native folklore show, and dancing to a reggae band. It costs around $60 per person with hotel pickup and return, less if you arrive via your own transport. Tours are offered Sunday through Thursday. **Martha Brae River Rafting** (☎ 809/952–0889) leads trips down the Martha Brae River, about 25 miles from most hotels in Montego Bay. The cost is just under $40 per raft (two per raft) for the 1½-hour river run. **Mountain Valley Rafting** (☎ 809/952–0527 or 809/952–6388) runs trips down the River Lethe, approximately 12 miles (about 50 minutes) southwest of Montego Bay. The trip is about $40 per raft (two per raft), lasting an hour or so, through unspoiled hillside country. Bookings can also be made through hotel tour desks. **Rio Grande Attractions Ltd.** (☎ 809/993–2778) guides raft trips down the Rio Grande River (☞ Exploring, *above*). The cost is $40 per raft. **South Coast Safaris Ltd.** (☎ 809/965–2513) has guided boat excursions up the Black River for some 10 miles (round-trip), into the mangroves and marshlands to see the alligators, birds, and plant life, aboard the 25-passenger *Safari Queen* and 25-passenger *Safari Princess*. **Undersea Tours MoBay** (☎ 809/922–1287) offers you a good look at MoBay's marine sanctuary without getting wet by booking passage ($35) on a semisubmersible craft.

### TOUR OPERATORS

Quality tour operators include **Caribic Tours** (☎ 809/952–4469), **Glamour Tours** (☎ 809/979–8415), **Greenlight Tours** (☎ 809/952–2650), and **SunHoliday Tours** (☎ 809/952–5629).

## Language

The official language of Jamaica is English. Islanders usually speak a patois among themselves, a lyrical mixture of pidgeon English, Spanish, and various African languages.

## Opening and Closing Times

Normal business hours for stores are weekdays 8–4, Saturday 8–1. Banking hours are generally Monday–Thursday 9–2, Friday 9–noon and 2:30–5.

## Passports and Visas

Passports are not required of visitors from the United States or Canada, but every visitor must have proof of citizenship, such as a birth certificate or a voter registration card (a driver's license is not enough). British visitors need passports but not visas. Each visitor must possess a return or ongoing ticket. Declaration forms are distributed in flight to keep customs formalities to a minimum.

## Precautions

Do not let the beauty of Jamaica cause you to relax the caution and good sense you would use in your own hometown. Never leave money or other valuables in your hotel room; use the safe-deposit boxes that most establishments make available. Carry your funds in traveler's checks, not cash, and keep a record of the check numbers in a secure place. Never leave a rental car unlocked, and never leave valuables, even in a locked car. Finally, resist the call of the wild when it presents itself as a scruffy-looking native offering to show you the "real" Jamaica. Jamaica on the beaten path is wonderful enough; don't take chances by wandering far from it. And ignore efforts, however persistent, to sell you a ganja joint. Carry along some insect repellent and a strong sunscreen to avoid natural hazards.

## Taxes and Service Charges

Hotels collect a 10% government consumption tax on room occupancy. The departure tax is J$500. Most hotels and restaurants add a 10% service charge to your bill. If not, a 10% to 20% tip is appreciated.

## Telephones and Mail

The area code for all Jamaica is 809. Direct telephone, telegraph, telefax, and telex services are available.

At press time, airmail postage from Jamaica to the United States or Canada was under J$1.50 for letters, J$1 for postcards.

## Visitor Information

Before you go, contact the **Jamaica Tourist Board** (⌧ 801 2nd Ave., 20th floor, New York, NY 10017, ☎ 212/856–9727, 800/233–4582, FAX 212/856–9730; 500 N. Michigan Ave., Suite 1030, Chicago, IL 60611, ☎ 312/527–1296, FAX 312/527–1472; 1320 S. Dixie Hwy., Suite 1100, Coral Gables, FL 33146, ☎ 305/665–0557, FAX 305/666–7239; 3440 Wilshire Blvd., Suite 1207, Los Angeles, CA 90010, ☎ 213/384–1123, FAX 213/384–1780; in Canada, 1 Eglinton Ave. E, Suite 616, Toronto, Ontario M4P 3A1, ☎ 416/482–7850, FAX 416/482–1730; in the U.K., 1–2 Prince Consort Rd., London, SW7 2BZ, ☎ 0171/224–0505, FAX 0171/224–0551).

In Jamaica, the main office of the **Jamaica Tourist Board** is in Kingston (⌧ 2 St. Lucia Ave., New Kingston, Box 360, Kingston 5, ☎ 809/929–9200). There are also JTB desks at both Montego Bay and Kingston airports and offices in Black River (☎ 809/965–2074), Montego Bay (☎ 809/952–4425), Negril (☎ 809/957–4243), Ocho Rios (☎ 809/974–2570), and Port Antonio (☎ 809/993–3051).

If you'd like to delve into the heart of Jamaica rather than simply explore her sybaritic pleasures, the tourist board will arrange for you to spend a little time with a local host family through the **Meet the People** program. They'll try to match interests, vocations, ages, whatever, so you'll have some common ground. There's no fee involved (other than for activities you and your hosts might select); this is the best way to come to know the warmth and good companionship the island has to offer.

# 15 Martinique

**T**HE ARAWAKS named Martinique *Madinina,* "Island of Flowers." Exotic wild orchids, frangipani, anthurium, jade vines, flamingo flowers, and hundreds of vivid varieties of hibiscus still grow on the island. But, these days, you are more likely to smell Chanel No. 5 than flowers. Martinique is a rich, highly developed island with a six-lane highway, the biggest shopping malls, and some of the finest restaurants in the Caribbean. Only in the mountainous north does nature run wild.

Updated by
Simon Worrall

Everything about Martinique, from the snappy new airport to the beautiful, old plantation houses, has style. Even the women working at the rental-car agencies look as though they are dressed for an evening at the opera. It's no surprise, then, that the island, along with Barbados, has one of the highest standards of living in the Caribbean. In their dealings with foreigners, the Martinicans are courteous, polite, and self-assured, qualities anchored in the privileged position that the island has enjoyed historically.

As Jamaica was the key to the British ruled islands, so Martinique was the administrative, social, and cultural center of the French West Indies. Unlike neighboring Guadeloupe, which the Martinicans look down on, Martinique was—and is—deeply attached to France. Martinique is not *like* France; it *is* France. While Guadeloupe was an island of merchants and shopkeepers, Martinique was a rich, aristocratic island, a place which gave birth to an Empress and saw the full flowering of plantation-house society with its servants and *soirées,* wine cellars and snobbery. At properties like the Leyritz Plantation or Habitation Clément one can still feel the echoes of that time.

The 425-square-mile island, the largest of the Windward Islands, was discovered by Columbus on his fourth voyage, in 1502. He came ashore at Le Carbet, pausing long enough to remark, "My eyes would never tire of contemplating such vegetation," and to put ashore a number of goats to provide fresh meat for future visits. But his eyes quickly tired of the snakes he saw slithering about in his newfound Eden, so he weighed anchor and put water between him and them, never to return.

Carib arrows, which had already defeated the peace-loving Arawaks, kept outsiders at bay until 1635, when Pierre Belain d'Esnambuc, a Norman nobleman and adventurer, landed with a group of 100 settlers at the mouth of the Roxelane River. The French promised the Caribs the western half of the island, but instead polished them off and imported African slaves to work their sugarcane plantations.

By the mid-17th century, sugar was making the island rich. Britain wanted to pluck her away from the French, and the two nations fought over the island until the early 19th century. In 1815, the island was ceded by treaty to France, and French it has remained ever since, becoming a *région* in 1974, a status not unlike that of an American state vis-à-vis the federal government. The Martinicans vote in French national elections and have all the benefits of France's social and economic systems. The island is governed by a prefect who is appointed by the French minister of the interior.

As on Guadeloupe, you'll need some French to feel truly at home here, though the locals are more forthcoming in English than on Guadeloupe. And as on Guadeloupe, smoking is ubiquitous—even on the dive boats!

**378**

Martinique

**KEY**

❶ Exploring Sites

㉕ Hotels and Restaurants

ATLANTIC OCEAN

㉖

N1

Ste-Marie
❶**12**

*Havre de la Trinité*

*Caravelle Peninsula*

❶**13**

㉜ Tartane

❶**14** *Pointe Caracoli*

㉛

La Trinité

㉚

N4

*Baie du Galion*

❶ Gros-Morne

Le Robert

*Havre du Robert*

N1

*Pte. de la Rose*

N1 ㊸
N1 ㊸

❶**16** Lamentin

**Lamentin International Airport**

㊺

❶**15** Le François ㊻

㊼

*Mt. Vauclin*

N6

N5 Ducos

Le Vauclin

㉔

D7

❶ Rivière-Salée
N5

D17 ⑳

*Rivière-Pilote*

N6

D18

D18A

Ste-Luce ㊺
D7 ㉑ ㊻

Le Marin

㉓

D18A

㊺㊻ ⑤⑧–㊽

*Pte. Figuier* ㊸ **Pte. Marin**

**Cap Chevalier**

D9

*Cul-de-Sac du Marin*

㉒

Ste-Anne

**Les Salines**

㊽–㊺

*Petrified Forest*

**Anse-Trabaud**

*Pte. d'Enfer*

*Pte. des Salines*

*St. Lucia Channel*

**Lodging**

Anse Caritan, **68**

Baie du Galion, **32**

Le Bakoua, **54**

La Batelière Hotel, **33**

Club Med/Buccaneer's Creek, **67**

Diamant Les Bains, **62**

Diamant-Novotel, **61**

Fregate Bleue, **46**

Habitation Lagrange, **26**

Les Ilets de l'Impératrice, **47**

Impératrice, **40**

Lafayette, **41**

Leyritz Plantation, **25**

Manoir de Beauregard, **69**

Le Marine, **63**

Martinique Cottages, **44**

Le Méridien Trois-Ilets, **53**

Novotel Carayou, **55**

La Pagerie, **50**

Relais Caraïbes, **64**

Rivage Hotel, **51**

La Riviera, **45**

Saint Aubin, **30**

Valmenière, **42**

# Lodging

Martinique's accommodations range from tiny inns called Relais Creoles to splashy tourist resorts and luxurious plantation houses. The majority of the hotels are clustered in Pointe du Bout and Anse-Mitan on the Trois-Ilets peninsula across the bay from Fort-de-France, Le Diamant, and Ste-Anne. Attractive packages are offered by many of the hotels, and it's a good idea to ask what's available when you call to reserve. Most of the major hotels include a large buffet breakfast in their rates, but they are generally bad. Look, instead, for a *petit déjeuner* of fresh fruit, croissants, baguettes, jam, and *café au lait*.

The **Villa Rental Service** (☎ 596/71–56–11, FAX 596/63–11–64) can assist with rentals of homes, villas, and apartments. Most are in the south of the island near good beaches and can be rented on a weekly or monthly basis.

| CATEGORY | COST* |
|---|---|
| $$$$ | over $240 |
| $$$ | $150–$240 |
| $$ | $85–$150 |
| $ | under $85 |

*\*All prices are for a standard double room for two with Continental breakfast, excluding $1.50 per person per night tax and 10% service charge.*

### Basse-Pointe

**$–$$**   ★   🏨 **Leyritz Plantation.** Sleeping on a former sugar plantation, in the antiques-furnished rooms of the manor house or cottages or in a renovated slave cabin, is certainly a novelty. Leyritz is isolated in the northern part of the island, on 16 acres of lush vegetation, with manicured lawns and stunning views of Mont Pelée. Nicest are the 10 cottage rooms, which have rough wood beams, mahogany four-poster beds, marble-top armoires, secretaries, and other antiques. The slightly larger former slave quarters have eaves, stone-and-stucco walls, more contemporary furnishings, and madras linens. Ironically, it's the newer bungalows that are cramped and lacking in individuality. Except for periodic invasions of cruise-ship passengers, it is very quiet here—a sharp contrast to the frenzied level of activity at the hotels in Pointe du Bout. You may not want to spend your entire vacation here, but it makes an interesting overnight stay while visiting the northern part of the island. There's free transportation to the beach, which is about 30 minutes away. ⊠ *Basse-Pointe 97218,* ☎ *596/78–53–92,* FAX *596/78–92–44. 67 rooms. Restaurant, bar, air-conditioning, pool, tennis court. DC, MC. CP, MAP.*

### Fort-de-France

**$$**   🏨 **Impératrice.** The slightly musty rooms of the Impératrice are in a 1950s five-story building that overlooks La Savane park in the heart of the city. The rooms in the front are either the best or the worst, depending upon your sensibilities: They are noisy, but they overlook the city's center of activity. All rooms have air-conditioning, TV, four-poster bed, and private bath and are decorated with bright Creole prints; 20 have balconies. Children under 8 stay free in the room with their parents, children 8–15 stay at a 50% discount. The hotel also has a popular sidewalk café. ⊠ *Fort-de-France 97200,* ☎ *596/63–06–82 or 800/223–9815; in Canada, 800/468–0023; in NY, 212/251–1800;* FAX *596/72–66–30. 24 rooms. Restaurant, bar, air-conditioning. AE, DC, MC, V. CP.*

**$$**   ★   🏨 **Valmenière.** If you have to fly in, have a meeting, and fly out, this brand new property, part of the Best Western group, is ideal. With its blue-tinted glass windows, high-tech elevator, and white tubular steel walkways, it would not be out of place in La Défense, Paris's business district. Perched on a hill between the airport and Fort-de-France, it is squeaky clean, efficient, and wired for work. The beds are king-size and the imported French mattresses are a boon for anyone suffering from backache. The suites are large, with a separate entrance to the living room, abundant cupboard space, and a desk. Three *chambres de bureau* (business rooms) have beds that can fold away, turning the room into a flexible office space. The hotel offers a full range of business services, from fax machines to conference rooms, and translation and secretarial assistance. There is also a good restaurant. For downtime, there is an exercise room in the basement and a pool and sunroof on the top floor. Only the views—an oil refinery, a landfill, and the island's main highway—remind you that the main purpose of the hotel is not leisure. ⊠ *Ave. des Arawaks, Fort-de-France 97200,* ☎ *596/75–75–75,* FAX *596/75–69–70. 113 rooms, 7 suites. Restaurant, bar, pool, exercise room, business services. AE, DC, MC, V. CP.*

$ ⊡ **Lafayette.** If you want to be in the heart of town, this is one of the few decent options. Owner Simone Broussillon is a mine of information and extremely helpful. Rooms are rather dark and old-fashioned, with heavy wood furnishings, teal linens, and floral curtains. All have TV and phone. At night, the street outside becomes one of the main promenades for Fort-de-France's *femmes de nuit.* ⊠ *5 rue de la Liberté, Fort-de-France 97200,* ☎ *596/73–80–50 or 800/223–9815,* FAX *596/60–97–75. 24 rooms. Bar, use of Le Bakoua hotel beach facilities. AE, DC, V. CP.*

## Lamentin

$ ⊡ **Martinique Cottages.** These garden bungalows set in the countryside have kitchenettes, terraces, cable TVs, and phones. La Plantation restaurant is a gathering spot for gourmets. It specializes in *nouvelle cuisine Creole,* with such inventive delicacies as yellow banana and *foie gras mille-feuille.* The beaches are a 15-minute drive away. The cottages are difficult to find; take advantage of the property's airport transfers. ⊠ *Lamentin 97232,* ☎ *596/50–16–09,* FAX *596/50–26–83. 8 rooms. Restaurant, kitchenettes. AE, MC, V. EP.*

## La Trinité

$$ ⊡ **Baie du Galion.** This new hotel, a member of the Best Western chain, is on the lovely, wild Presqu'île du Caravelle (Caravelle Peninsula). The medium-size rooms are furnished in a charming Creole style, with polished dark-wood furnishings and bright fabrics. All have air-conditioning, TV, phone, safe, fridge, and balcony; 50 also have kitchenette. Hiking is good in the adjacent nature reserve. The beach, though on the Atlantic, is relatively good for swimming, and the enormous pool is a focal point for guests. ⊠ *Anse Tartane 97220,* ☎ *596/58–65–30 or 800/223–9815,* FAX *596/58–25–76. 146 rooms. Restaurant, bar, air-conditioning, refrigerators, in-room safes, pool, tennis court. AE, MC, V. BP, MAP.*

$$ ⊡ **Saint Aubin.** This restored coral-colored colonial house, with pretty gables and intricate gingerbread trim, is in the countryside above the Atlantic coast. Each modern, if musty, room has wicker furnishings, air-conditioning, TV, phone, and private bath. Those on the top floor are larger and ideal for families; five second-floor rooms open onto a shared balcony with sweeping views of the sea. This is a peaceful retreat, and only 3 miles from La Trinité, 2 miles from the Spoutourne sports center and the beaches on the Caravelle Peninsula. The inn's restaurant, which serves estimable Creole fare, is closed during June and October. Owner Guy Foret is an engaging host. ⊠ *Box 52, La Trinité 97220,* ☎ *596/69–34–77 or 800/223–9815; in Canada, 800/468–0023; in*

NY, 212/840–6636, ⟨FAX⟩ 596/69–41–14. 15 double rooms. Restaurant, bar, air-conditioning, pool. AE, DC, MC, V. CP.

## Le Diamant

$$$$   🏨 **Diamant-Novotel.** This self-contained resort occupies half an island in an ideal windsurfing location. Just beyond the registration area, a footbridge spans a large pool on the way to the spacious guest rooms, each of which has a small balcony facing either the sea or the pool. Furnishings are cane and wicker painted pastel peach and green, and the floors are tile. The dining room is large and unromantic, set up to accommodate groups, but there is a pleasant terrace bar where a local band plays on most nights. A smaller, more formal restaurant is open during peak season. The four beaches on the 5-acre property are small. Scuba packages are offered. Children under 16 stay free with their parents. The staff speaks English and maintains a surprising level of enthusiasm and efficiency, given the hotel's size and the large number of tour groups. ✉ Le Diamant 97223, ☎ 596/76–42–42 or 800/221–4542, ⟨FAX⟩ 596/76–22–87. 180 rooms. 2 restaurants, 3 bars, air-conditioning, pool, beauty salon, 2 tennis courts, 4 beaches, dive shop, water-sports center, boutiques, car rental. AE, DC, MC, V. CP, MAP.

$$   🏨 **Diamant Les Bains.** For the last 30 years Hubert Andrieu and his
★ wife, Marie-Yvonne, have been doing everything they can to make people feel at home at this intimate, beachfront property. Andrieu, who trained locally and in Canada, is the chef, turning out fine, Creole dishes for the excellent, on-site restaurant. Marie-Yvonne manages the staff and the office. A few rooms are in the main house, above the restaurant. But most are in pretty, whitewashed chalets, surrounded by flowers and palm trees. The tile floors, cheerfully painted furniture, and white ceilings, together with the light breeze that always plays off the ocean, gives them the feeling of an old-fashioned, seaside hotel. The bungalows also each have a terrace screened by hibiscus bushes. The beach is a few yards away, and there is a (small) pool in the center of the property. For those who just want to rest and relax, this quiet, pretty hotel is the perfect spot—although you will need to speak some French to feel truly at home. ✉ Le Diamant 97223, ☎ 596/76–40–14 or 800/223–9815; in Canada, 800/468–0023; in NY, 212/251–1800; ⟨FAX⟩ 596/76–27–00. 24 rooms. Restaurant, bar, air-conditioning, refrigerators, pool, water-sports center. MC, V. CP, MAP. Closed Sept.

$$   🏨 **Le Marine.** Mini-apartments—one room with bed, kitchenette, and balcony—are in rows of pristine stucco buildings that progress down the hillside to the beach. The rooms are painted in mint, aqua, and periwinkle and decorated with bright abstract prints. The main building, which contains the restaurant, front desk, boutique, and flower shop, is 100 feet above the beach, and the pool is at the bottom of the hill, just above the beach. This arrangement is visually attractive, but the climb up the steps from the pool and beach to the main house and restaurant is strenuous. The hotel caters to French families on tour packages, and the high turnover and large-group clientele contribute to the wear and tear on facilities, although management works hard at maintenance. As at other Marine properties, the staff tends to be youthful and energetic, but things can get impersonal during high season. ✉ Pointe de la Chery 97223 (near Diamant), ☎ 596/76–46–00 or 800/221–4542, ⟨FAX⟩ 596/76–25–99. 149 rooms. Restaurant, 2 bars, kitchenettes, 2 pools (1 for children), 2 tennis courts, dive shop, free use of water-sports equipment at Diamant-Novotel, deep-sea fishing, boutique, flower shop. AE, DC, MC, V. CP, MAP.

$$   🏨 **Relais Caraïbes.** Of all the hotels on Martinique, this one comes clos-
★ est to having the individuality and authenticity of a country inn, as well as good food and attractive accommodations. A note of immediate chic

is struck in the thatched public rooms, awash in interior gardens, white wicker furnishings, and antiques ranging from bronze Indian elephants to African masks, culled from the world travels of owner Monsieur Senez. Twelve bungalows, decorated in a similar eclectic style, are spread over the manicured grounds, which offer views of the sea and Diamond Rock. Each has a bedroom, a small salon with a sofa bed, a kitchenette, and a bathroom. There are also three standard rooms in the main house, which have unusual touches like hand-painted headboards, straw birdcages, and Chinese fans. The pool is perched at the edge of a cliff that drops to the sea. The hotel is a mile off the main road, and you need a car to get around. The beach, however, is a short walk away. ✉ *Pointe de la Chery, Diamant 97223, ☎ 596/76–44–65 or 800/223–9815, FAX 596/76–21–20. 15 rooms. Restaurant, bar, kitchenettes, pool, scuba instruction, boating. AE, MC, V. CP, MAP.*

## Le François

**$$$** ⊡ **Fregate Bleue.** This is another of Martinique's distinctive inns. The
★ owner, Madame Yveline de Lucy de Fossarieu, left the management of Leyritz Plantation, because she wanted the quiet life. In 1991 she opened the Fregate Bleue, an eight-room bed-and-breakfast. The hotel is a member of a French association called Les Relais du Silence, whose primary criterion is that the hotel is quiet. The house itself is captivating, filled with light, plants, trompe l'oeil paintings, and hand-carved parrots. The rooms are delightful, their spaciousness accentuated by off-white furnishings, patterned carpets, and the occasional antique. Each also has a balcony, most of which overlook Les Ilets de l'Impératrice. (Two rooms and the small cottage have limited sea views.) All rooms have a small kitchenette and a modern bathroom with such niceties as bathrobes. Madame de Lucy serves *petit déjeuner* (breakfast) on the upstairs veranda, and dinners, when requested. The nearest restaurants are a 10-minute drive away, and you must negotiate a rutted road to get to the highway. The Fregate Bleue's pool is small, but the beaches of Le Francois and Le Vauclin are five minutes away. ✉ *Le François 97240 (5 mi south of Le François on Vauclin Rd.), ☎ 596/54–54–66 or 800/633–7411, FAX 596/54–78–48. 7 rooms. Kitchenettes, pool. AE, MC, V. BP.*

**$$$** ⊡ **Les Ilets de l'Impératrice.** If you have ever wanted to be marooned on a desert island, but have three meals a day cooked for you, a hammock to lie in, and all the rum punches you can handle, this is the place for you. Catharine Deneuve and Yves Montand shot *Le Sauvage* in a cove just below this weathered, Creole-style house, perched on the tiny island of Thierry. According to legend, the Empress Joséphine swam in the sandy pool just off the shore. The four rooms upstairs, with white painted wood walls and exposed beams, have rattan beds and furniture. Unfortunately, they do not have their own showers; guests use a communal one downstairs. Also downstairs is a large, wood-floor living room with antique furniture. A terrace offers superlative views of the ocean. This place is a magical spot to relax, though the service may not be that of a professionally run hotel. You might also find it a bit claustrophobic after a while, especially since you very much share the house with the people who run it. ✉ *Box 12, Le Francois 97240, ☎ FAX 596/65–82–30. 4 rooms. AE, MC, V. MAP.*

**$** ⊡ **La Riviera.** Three pretty whitewashed buildings with red tile roofs overlook Le François Bay and do indeed look as if they were transported straight from St. Tropez. All rooms have a balcony opening onto breathtaking water views. Decor is contemporary and fresh, mostly in floral patterns. Owner-manager Marie-Anne Prian and her husband, Jacques, speak English and are most helpful. The restaurant serves marvelous Continental-tinged Creole cuisine; try the blaff of sea urchins or the omelet flamed with aged rum. A long private pier makes La Riviera popular with yachties. ⊠ *Rte. du Club Nautique, Le François 97240,* ☎ *596/54–68–54,* FAX *596/54–30–43. 14 rooms. Restaurant, bar, air-conditioning, minibars, boating. AE, MC, V. CP, MAP.*

## Les Trois-Ilets

$$$$    🏨 **Le Bakoua.** Rooms here are relatively small, given the $275-a-night
★    tariff (higher if you're on the beach), but this elegant enclave *is* Martinique's chicest address, and the service is pampering. Accommodations are in three hillside buildings and a fourth on the man-made white-sand beach. The decor is cushy-cum-rustic, with polished hardwood furnishings, frilly floral linens, and white tile floors. All rooms have a balcony or patio; bathroom with hand-painted tile walls, marble vanity, and hair dryer; and the usual deluxe amenities. The beach is compact and adjoins that of the Méridien. The pool, referred to as a *piscine trompe de l'oeil,* is above the beach, and the water flows over one side, giving the impression that the pool is part of the ocean. Entertainment consists of live music and shows nightly, including dancing, limbo, and Friday-night performances of Les Grands Ballets de la Martinique. Most of the staff speaks commendable English. Be sure to inquire about special package deals. ⊠ *Box 589, Fort-de-France 97200,* ☎ *596/66–02–02 or 800/221–4542; in the U.K., 0171/730–7144;* FAX *596/66–00–41. 140 rooms, including 2 1-bedroom suites. 2 restaurants, bar, air-conditioning, minibars, pool, beauty salon, 2 tennis courts, water-sports center, boutique, flower shop. AE, DC, MC, V. CP, MAP.*

$$$$    🏨 **Le Méridien Trois-Ilets.** There is a great deal of activity here, even in the low season, much of it revolving around the always-congested pool and man-made beach. Unfortunately, the hotel has aged. Despite sporadic redecorations, the boxy, oddly configured rooms, done in blond woods and floral fabrics, remain patchworked with repairs. They are air-conditioned and have wall-to-wall carpeting, built-in hair dryers, TVs, and minibars. Some have balconies with a splendid view of the bay and of Fort-de-France. La Case Créole offers some of the better hotel dining on the island. The hotel staff speaks excellent English, the atmosphere is the island's most convivial, and there's live entertainment nightly. ⊠ *Trois-Ilets 97229,* ☎ *596/66–00–00 or 800/543–4300,* FAX *596/66–00–74; in NY, 212/245–2920. 295 rooms, 2 luxury suites, 4 1-bedroom suites. 2 restaurants, bar, air-conditioning, minibars, pool, 2 tennis courts, marina, water-sports center, duty-free shops, casino, tour desk, car rental. AE, DC, MC, V. BP, MAP.*

$$$    🏨 **Novotel Carayou.** Part of the giant Accord group, this property has been extensively renovated and is now one of the snappier resort hotels on the island. The three story, apartment-style buildings are not the most beautiful. but with their white, blue, and yellow trim they are cheerful and extremely clean. The best rooms are seaside. Others are grouped around the pool. Each has white tile floors and blue fabrics, as well as spacious bathrooms. The main restaurant, where guests are served breakfast, is up a flight of steps on a terrace built over the water, with views of Fort-de-France. The Café Creole, at the (rather cramped) beach, also serves light meals. For those seeking a busy, action-packed vacation the hotel offers a plethora of activities, from tennis (one rather poor court) to windsurfing, waterskiing, sailing, and paragliding, though not all these are included in the base rate. Up to two children (under age 16) can stay free, and for 150F per day the Club Ti-Pirate will take them off your hands. The service here is somewhat languid, the clientele mostly package tour groups from France. ⊠ *Trois-Ilets 97229,* ☎ *596/66–04–04,* FAX *596/66–00–57. 200 rooms, 1 suite.*

*Restaurant, bar, pool, tennis court, windsurfing, sailing, waterskiing, boutique, AE, MC, V. CP.*

**$$** 🏨 **La Pagerie.** La Pagerie looks as if it were plucked out of the Côte d'Azur and planted near the marina in Pointe du Bout. The hotel has small air-conditioned rooms and studios, all with private bath and trim little balcony, and some with kitchenette. The decor is handsome throughout, with dark-wood furnishings, planters, and lace curtains, but in recent years the property has become slightly run down. Although the hotel has no beach or water-sports activities, it is within a short stroll of the resort hotels, restaurants, and activity. Lunch and dinner are served alfresco by the pool. The lively, cheerful atmosphere has made it a favorite evening watering hole of local expatriates and the sailing crowd. ⊠ *Pointe du Bout 97229,* ☎ *596/66–05–30,* 🅵🅰🆇 *596/66–00–99; U.S. reservations, 800/221–4542; in NY, 212/757–6500. 98 rooms. Restaurant, bar, air-conditioning, pool. AE, MC, V. EP, MAP.*

**$** 🏨 **Rivage Hotel.** You get good value for your money at Maryelle and Jean Claude Riveti's small hotel. The place does have the air of a motor inn circa the Eisenhower years, but it's immaculately maintained, and the studios give you much more room than neighboring hotels at about a third of the cost. Each garden-view unit has a private bath and either a kitchenette (not always as clean as the rest of the property) or a minifridge. Breakfast and light meals are served in the friendly, informal snack bar. You should have no difficulty communicating: English, Spanish, and French are spoken. The beach is right across the road. ⊠ *Anse-Mitan 97229,* ☎ *596/66–00–53,* 🅵🅰🆇 *596/66–06–56. 17 rooms. Snack bar, air-conditioning, pool, beach, car rental. MC, V. EP.*

## Marigot

**$$$$** 🏨 **Habitation Lagrange.** It's worth flying to Martinique just to come
**★** here. Nowhere else on the island do you feel the style and elegance of the old plantation house society more than in this 19th-century manor house, set in a lush, fertile valley on the northeast coast. Everything here—from the Staffordshire "Unicorn" tableware in the dining room to the antique shaving mirrors and Hermès toiletries in the bathrooms—is done with impeccable taste. The story of Habitation Lagrange begins with a love affair. Once a rum distillery belonging to one of the island's leading families, the house fell into disrepair until Jean Louis de Lucy, who had grown up here, gave it as a gift to his wife, Isabella. It was renovated in 1990 and is now one of the most distinctive properties in the Caribbean. Accommodations are in four different buildings. Rooms in the main building have four-poster beds, mahogany floors, beautiful linens, and tall French windows opening onto a wraparound veranda. The bathrooms, with their wood-encased bathtubs and copper fittings, are exquisite. In the "Ecurie," which once served as the stables, are an additional three rooms. The original stone walls have been incorporated into the decor; parquet floors, huge windows, and canopy beds complete the picture. Two two-story buildings house 12 rooms with gabled ceilings, furnished with mahogany armoires and wicker chaise longues, and hung with chintz curtains. Dinner is served in the "ajouba," a long wooden structure open to the night breeze. The chef, Jean-Charles Brédas, is arguably Martinique's finest homegrown talent. *Gratin au lambis* (conch au gratin) and *tartane de sarde* (raw fish marinated in lime juice and served with green peppercorns and scallions) are just two of the delicacies he conjures. The wine list is one of the most extensive on the island. One hundred-year-old *figier maudite* trees, a profusion of flowers, and a babbling brook make the grounds a delight to ramble around. Be forewarned, though: The road to the house is bumpy and potholed. ⊠ *Marigot 97225,* ☎ *596/53–60–60,*

FAX *596/53–50–58. 17 rooms, 1 suite. Dining room, bar, pool, tennis court, library. AE, DC, MC, V. BP, MAP. Closed Sept.–mid-Oct.*

## Schoelcher

$$$–$$$$ ⊞ **La Batelière Hotel.** On a flower-filled, 5-acre property north of Fort-
★ de-France, this smart, resort hotel offers some of the island's largest rooms and by far its best tennis courts. It is extremely well run: Service is prompt, security intimidating (a veritable army of uniformed guards hovers about the main gate). Many rooms overlook the sea, and all have contemporary furniture, air-conditioning, direct-dial phone, cable TV, radio, and private balcony or patio. The restaurant, where breakfast is served, is on an airy terrace with great views of the ocean. One level below that is the semicircular pool and pool bar. Below that, down a flight of steps, is a small beach sheltered from the waves by a breakwater. Both a casino and disco are on the property. ⊠ *Schoelcher 97233,* ☎ *596/61–49–49 or 800/223–6510,* FAX *596/61–62–29. 192 rooms, 5 duplexes, 2 suites. 2 restaurants, 2 bars, air-conditioning, pool, 6 tennis courts, water-sports center, casino, disco, shopping arcade, conference rooms. AE, DC, MC, V. CP, MAP.*

## Ste-Anne

$$$ ⊞ **Anse Caritan.** This appealing property combines the amenities of a large hotel with the service and ambience of a more intimate one. It's nestled amid exquisite tropical gardens fronting a ribbon of champagne-colored sand. Management does its best to give the hotel an "island" feel. A large traditional fishing boat, or *gommier,* sits next to the pool; and rooms, though nothing exceptional in soft colors like periwinkle, mauve, and gray, have unusual touches like hand-painted leaves and bamboo on the walls. Rooms have air-conditioning, phones, safes, hair dryers, and a rough wood terrace or balcony, most with a sea view. The restaurant is known for its innovative Creole fare, and there's live music nightly. The staff is remarkably friendly and diligent. The Rasta gardener, for example, will pick herbs to soothe your sunburn, and the managers actually encourage guests' comments. ⊠ *Point des Salines, Ste. Anne 97227,* ☎ *596/76–74–12,* FAX *596/76–72–59. 96 rooms. Restaurant, bar, snack bar, air-conditioning, in-room safes, pool, water-sports center, dive shop, deep-sea fishing, disco. AE, MC, V. CP, MAP.*

$$$ ⊞ **Manoir de Beauregard.** Built in the early 18th century, this imposing plantation house was made into a hotel by the Saint-Cyr family in
★ 1928. For more than 60 years it was one of the best small hotels in Martinique, then, tragically, in 1990, it was ravaged by fire. Now it has risen like the proverbial phoenix from the ashes. The main building, with its 2-foot-thick stone walls and mullioned windows, feels like a medieval abbey. Where the nave would be is a drawing room with bentwood rockers, chandeliers, and checkerboard marble floors. On either side of the drawing room are two "aisles" with sloping, beamed roofs; one serves as the bar, which leads out onto a sunny terrace and a (small) L-shape pool, while the other has been turned into a re-created Creole dining room. The restaurant is across a small courtyard in a new, unattractive wooden building and serves such dishes as beef in a ginger sauce, shrimp with green pepper sauce, and other examples of *la nouvelle cuisine antillaise.* Three bedrooms are upstairs in the main building. They have beamed ceilings, antique furniture, four-poster beds, and rich linens. Other rooms are in a modern annex at the other side of the property. They are not so nice, but one is a gem: a circular tower room, with a four-poster bed, that was traditionally reserved for *les jeunes mariés* (honeymooners). All rooms have phones, TV, and air-conditioning. ⊠ *Chemin des Salines, Ste. Anne 97227,* ☎

*596/76–73–40,* FAX *596/76–93–24. 10 rooms. Restaurant, bar, air-conditioning, pool. AE, MC, V. CP.*

**$$–$$$** ☎ **Club Med/Buccaneer's Creek.** Occupying 48 landscaped acres, Martinique's Club Med is an all-inclusive village with plazas, cafés, restaurants, boutique, and a small marina. Air-conditioned pastel cottages contain twin beds and private shower bath. The only money you need spend here is for bar drinks, personal expenses, and excursions into Fort-de-France or the countryside. There's a white-sand beach, a plethora of water sports, and plenty of nightlife. ✉ *Pointe Marin 97180,* ☎ *596/76–72–72 or 800/258–2633; in NY, 212/750–1670;* FAX *596/72–76–02. 300 rooms. 2 restaurants, 2 bars, air-conditioning, 7 tennis courts, fitness and water-sports center, nightclub, disco. AE, MC, V. All-inclusive (except drinks).*

# Dining

It used to be argued that Martinique had the best food in all the Caribbean, but many believe this top-ranking position has been lost to some of the other islands of the French West Indies—Guadeloupe, St. Barts, even St. Martin. Nevertheless, Martinique remains an island of restaurants serving classic French cuisine and Creole dishes, its wine cellars filled with fine French wines. Hotel restaurants are predictably good—consult the lodging listings for more recommendations—but some of the best restaurants are tucked away in the countryside, and therein lies a problem. The farther you venture from tourist hotels, the less likely you are to find English-speaking folk. But that shouldn't stop you from savoring the cuisine. The local Creole specialties are *colombo* (curry), *accras* (cod or vegetable fritters), *crabes farcis* (stuffed land crab), *écrevisses* (freshwater crayfish), *boudin* (Creole blood sausage), *lambi* (conch), *langouste* (clawless Caribbean lobster), *soudons* (sweet clams), *blaff* (fish or shellfish plunged into seasoned stock), and *oursin* (sea urchin). The favorite local libation is *le 'ti punch,* a "little punch," concocted of four parts white rum, one part sugarcane syrup (some people like a little more syrup), and a squeeze of lime.

Most restaurants offer a prix fixe menu, often with several choices of entrées and wine, that represents tremendous value. For additional savings, pick up a copy of the *Ti Gourmet* booklet, available at the tourist office and larger hotels; most of the restaurants listed offer a free drink or discount upon presentation.

### What to Wear

As in Guadeloupe, people dress for dinner in casual resort wear. Men don't wear jackets but do wear collared shirts. Women typically wear light cotton sundresses. Nice shorts are fine for lunch, but at dinnertime beach attire is too casual for most restaurants.

| CATEGORY | COST* |
|---|---|
| $$$ | over $50 |
| $$ | $30–$50 |
| $ | under $30 |

*per person, excluding drinks*

### Anse-d'Arlets

**$–$$** ✕ **Tamarin Plage Restaurant.** The lobster *vivier* (tank) in the middle of the room gives you a clue to the specialty here, but there are other recommendable offerings as well. Fish soup or Creole boudin are good starters; then consider court bouillon, crayfish fricassee, or octopus. The beachfront bar is a popular local hangout. ✉ *Anse-d'Arlets,* ☎ *596/68–71–30. MC, V.*

$  ✕ **Bidjoul.** Many modest restaurants line the small side street that is actually Anse-d'Arlets's main drag. The street borders the water, and fishermen sail right up to the eateries with their latest catch. Bidjoul has a tiny dining room; opt for one of the tables set up under the canopy on the beach across the road. The salads (try the smoked salmon, or the *pêcheur,* with tuna, shrimp, crab, and rice) are huge, and the grilled fish as fresh as could be. So, too, is the fish at the neighboring restaurants, but the enthusiasm of Bidjoul's owner makes it stand out. It has become the popular gathering spot for watching the sun set into the Caribbean Sea. ✉ *Anse-d'Arlets,* ☎ *596/68–65–28. Reservations not accepted. MC, V.*

## Basse-Pointe

$$–$$$  ✕ **Leyritz Plantation.** The pride of Martinique is *the* place all the cruise
★ passengers head to as soon as they disembark. The restored 18th-century plantation has exquisite stone walls, the ambience of a country inn, and a dramatic view of Mont Pelée. The menu is mostly Creole, featuring boudin, chicken with coconut, curried dishes, and steaks. ✉ *Basse-Pointe,* ☎ *596/78–53–92. Reservations essential. MC, V.*

## Fort-de-France

$$$  ✕ **La Fontane.** Mango trees shade the wraparound veranda of this his-
★ toric, colonial-style house on the road to Balata, with distant views of Les Pitons de Carbet, a chain of volcanic hills, and Balata's wedding-cake cathedral. Inside you'll find Oriental rugs, fresh flowers, and a display of antiques that includes a handsome gramophone and a grandfather clock. Try *Le Bambou de la Fontane,* a salad of fish, tomato, corn, melon, and crayfish. Other options are cream soup with crab, lobster stewed with basil, *noisettes d'agneau* (medallions of lamb) with boletus mushrooms and mango, or the red snapper with lemon-lime sauce. For dessert, the *nuage de sorbet,* a medley of nine different homemade ice creams, is a treat. There is an excellent wine list, the espresso is *comme il faut,* and, at 95F, the lunch menu is a bargain. ✉ *Km 4, Rte. de Balata,* ☎ *596/64–28–70. Reservations essential. AE. Closed Sun.–Mon.*

$$$  ✕ **La Grande Voile.** Crisp white cloths, fine china and crystal, and lots
★ of windows overlooking the harbor give a formal air to this lovely dining room. Starters include chilled chicken-liver mousse, crayfish ravioli, and fresh steamed mussels. These can be followed with such dishes as lobster in Creole sauce or *filet de boeuf.* Finish off your feast with a memorable soufflé or guava mousse with raspberry sauce. The *menu dégustation* (a variety of sample-size portions) is an affordable way to savor the restaurant's specialties. Service is sometimes on the slow side. ✉ *Pointe Simon,* ☎ *596/70–29–29,* 𝖥𝖠𝖷 *596/61–85–02. AE, MC, V. Closed Sun.*

$$  ✕ **Le Coq Hardi.** Crowds flock here for the best steaks and grilled meats in town. You can pick out your own steak and feel confident that it will be cooked to perfection. Steak tartare is the house specialty, but tournedos Rossini (with artichoke hearts, foie gras, truffles, and Madeira sauce), entrecôte bordelaise, prime rib, and T-bone steaks are also on the menu. For dessert, there's a selection of sorbets, profiteroles, and pear Belle Hélène. ✉ *Km 0.6, rue Martin Luther King,* ☎ *596/71–59–64. AE, MC, V. No lunch Wed. and Sat.*

$$  ✕ **Le Planteur.** Chef Andre Charles Donatien, a Martinican with 30
★ years of experience in Paris and Fort-de-France, was recently voted one of the three best chefs on the island by a Parisian culinary institute. His passion is mixing French and Creole traditions. He uses "roucou"— a red seed in a fibrous pod once used by the Arawaks as body paint— as a food coloring in one of his specialties: red snapper in *sauce à belle doudou,* made with cream and tomatoes. Try, too, the delicious pump-

kin and shrimp soup or the spicy *Salade Tahitienne,* raw fish marinated in lime juice and coconut. Rose-color walls (which, the proprietor claims, make people drink more), antique hurricane lamps, and historic photos by Lois Hayot complement the food. ⊠ *1 rue de la Liberté,* ☎ *596/63–17–45. AE, MC. No lunch Sun.*

$ ✕ **Le Marie Sainte.** Warm wood paneling, exposed beams, colorfully
★ tiled tables, and bright napery create a homey ambience in this wildly popular lunchtime spot. It's worth waiting on the occasional line for the scrumptious *daube de poissons* (braised fish), crayfish, and banana beignets. ⊠ *160 rue Victor Hugo,* ☎ *596/70–00–30. AE, MC, V. Closed Sun. No dinner.*

$ ✕ **Le Second Soufflé.** This is heaven for vegetarians. The chef uses fresh
★ produce to make soufflés ranging from *aubergine* (eggplant) to *filet de ti-nain* (small green bananas) with chocolate sauce. He also whips up such nonsoufflé items as eggplant ragout and okra quiche. The food echoes the famous Voltaire line painted on the wall: "Tu ne possèdes rien si tu ne digères pas bien" ("You have nothing if you don't have good digestion.") Even the decor pays tribute to the Martinican table, with colorful murals of fruits and vegetables. ⊠ *27 rue Blénac,* ☎ *596/63–44–11. No credit cards. Closed weekends.*

### Lamentin

$$–$$$ ✕ **Le Verger.** An orchard is the setting for this green-and-white coun-
★ try house, not far from the airport. But you don't come for the locale— the food is the draw, and it's some of the very best on the island. Chef Bruno Hoang, who is also the owner's son, has many years of experience in Paris under his belt, plus an insider's knowledge of local, Creole traditions. He creates an oursin blaff that is justly renowned; to make it, you need 20 pounds of sea urchins (though it is only the eggs that are used); a rich broth of onion, spices, parsley, and white wine; and great patience. Pheasant, duck (try the perfect *magret* with green peppercorns), and other game are on the extensive menu. Classic French wines round out an excellent meal. Follow the signs for La Trinité; the entrance to the restaurant is on the right immediately after an Esso station. ⊠ *Pl. d'Armes,* ☎ *596/51–43–02. AE, DC, MC, V. Closed Sun.*

### Le Diamant

$$$ ✕ **Relais Caraïbes.** Parisian Jean Senez opened this individual bunga-
★ low colony *avec* restaurant, and spends enough time in Paris to gather original objets d'art for decor and for sale. Lunch or dinner choices include spicy chicken Antilloise, a half lobster in two sauces, fish fillet in a basil sauce, and fricassee of country shrimp. The crisply decorated dining room, awash in fresh flowers, commands a clear view of Diamond Rock. ⊠ *Pointe de la Chery, Diamant,* ☎ *596/76–44–65. AE, MC, V. Closed Mon.*

$$ ✕ **L'Écrin Bleu.** The breathtaking views of the sea and St. Lucia would be reason enough to visit this terrace eatery, but you hardly need more incentive than is provided by the delectable and affordable seafood. Choose your own lobster or try the salmon tartare, sea bream in spiced beurre blanc, swordfish with saffron, or conch *en feuilleté* (in puff pastry). The gourmet menu (260F) includes crayfish in ginger or saffron sauce, half a grilled lobster, and John Dory in sweet pepper sauce, not to mention dessert. ⊠ *Rte. des Anse-d'Arlets,* ☎ *596/76–41–92. AE.*

$–$$ ✕ **Le Diam's.** With its brightly lit, open-sided dining room (the sea is only a few yards away), this is one of the most pleasant places to eat on Le Diamant's main street. Lemon-color walls, art naïf, and bright yellow tablecloths decorate the restaurant, which recently won first prize in a local gourmet competition. Judging by the mahimahi with sugarcane sauce, salmon in tarragon sauce, and spicy *gambas* (large prawns),

it deserved to. For less demanding palates there are simpler dishes like
pizza and pasta, as well as a good *menu enfant* for 40F. If you are staying in the Diamant area and don't have a car, they will even come and
fetch you, and take you home—free! ⊠ *Pl. de l'Eglise,* ☎ *596/76–23–
28. AE, MC, V. Closed Tues. No lunch Wed.*

$     ✕ **Chez Christiane.** Don't be deceived by the seedy front bar (which
★     rocks during pool tournaments and free Friday rum tastings). The
back dining room is delightful, with bamboo walls, fresh flowers, and
local artist Roland Brival's imaginative paintings of local fauna (he adds
texture with shards of green glass). The Creole cuisine is magnificent.
The 70F menu might offer boudin, fried fish in caper sauce, and a *coupe
glacée* (sundae). Other top choices are a smoky callaloo soup (here called
*soupe verte aux crabes*), braised ray with ginger, and smoked chicken
colombo. ⊠ *Rue Diamant,* ☎ *596/76–49–55. No credit cards.*

## Le François

$$$   ✕ **La Maison de L'Îlet Oscar.** This bistro under the palms is not like any
other restaurant in Martinique. For starters, it is on an island, and to
get there you have to be fetched by fishing boat. The price of the boat
trip is included in the two seafood menus that the restaurant offers.
Though the food is decent enough, it is the ambiance that makes this
place special. The Creole house with beamed ceilings and tile floors was
won by the present proprietor in a poker game. It has four small rooms
where guests can spend the night (though rooms at its sister hotel, Les
Ilets de l'Impératrice [☞ Lodging *above,*] are better), but the young French
couple who have been running the place since 1995 focus on the restau-
rant. Tables are laid out at the water's edge under palapa-covered pavil-
ions. Before lunch, you will probably be taken to *La Beignoir de
Joséphine,* a shallow pool where, according to legend, Napoléon's ill-
fated wife would swim. ⊠ *Le François 97240,* ☎ *596/53–60–60.
Reservations essential. Dinner by appointment only. AE, MC, V.*

$     ✕ **Club Nautique.** While this little place is not going to turn up in *Ar-
chitectural Digest,* the food—which comes fresh daily out of the sea—
is exquisitely prepared. Have the house specialty drink, a *décollage* (it
means "takeoff" in French—and this potent herb-infused rum will have
you jetting sky high), then dig into turtle steak or charcoal-broiled lob-
ster. The restaurant is right on the beach, and boat trips depart from
here for snorkeling in the nearby coral reefs. ⊠ *Le François,* ☎
*596/54–31–00. AE, DC, MC, V. No dinner Sun.*

## Les Trois-Ilets

$$    ✕ **La Villa Creole.** The steak béarnaise, curries, conch, court bouillon,
★     and other dishes are all superb. However, the real draw here is owner
Guy Bruère-Dawson, a popular singer and guitarist who entertains during dinner. The setting is romantic at this very popular place, with ceiling fans whirring and oil lamps flickering on the tables. Ask to be seated
in the lush back garden. ⊠ *Anse-Mitan,* ☎ *596/66–05–53. Reservations essential. AE, DC, V. Closed Sun. No lunch Mon.*

$     ✕ **Au Poisson d'Or.** This typical Creole restaurant offers several ex-
cellent set menus. You might choose seafood callaloo, fried conch or
sea urchin, or scallops sautéed in white wine. The decor is attractive:
bamboo walls, straw thatching, madras napery, a veritable jungle of
potted plants, and clever paintings of seafood. The only drawback is
its position on the "wrong side" of the road, away from the beach.
Choose a table in the front area of the terrace to benefit from any passing breezes. ⊠ *Anse Mitan,* ☎ *596/66–01–80. Reservations not accepted. AE, MC. Closed Mon.*

$     ✕ **La Marina.** Beckoning red-and-white awnings and colorful murals
give this breezy terrace a cheerful atmosphere. Views are of the yachts
cruising in and out of their berths. Top choices include seafood risotto

and lambi fricassee. Tasty pizzas and salads are the best budget options. ⊠ *Pointe du Bout,* ☎ *596/66–02–32. AE, MC, V.*

## Morne-des-Esses

$$  ✕ **Le Colibri.** Jules Palladino, a large, gregarious man who clearly loves
★  his food, has established his culinary domain in this spot in the northwestern reaches of the island. Choice seating is at one of the seven tables on the cheerful back terrace. For starters, try *buisson d'écrevisses,* a pyramid of six giant freshwater crayfish accompanied by a tangy tomato sauce flavored with thyme, scallions, and tiny bits of crayfish. This is one of the few places to get traditional *cochon au lait* (suckling pig) and *gibier* (game), such as rabbit in prune sauce and tender, smoky *manicou* (cousin to the opossum). ⊠ *Morne-des-Esses,* ☎ *596/69–91–95. AE, MC, V. Closed Mon. off-season.*

## Ste-Anne

$$$  ✕ **Aux Filets Bleus.** In addition to dining at this open-air eatery on the beach, you can go for a swim and dance to live music on top of the underground lobster tank. The cheerful decor takes its cue from the surrounding waters, rippling in various shades of blue from azure to teal. Be sure to check out the astonishing, angry mural outside the restaurant, all upraised fists and Picasso-esque profiles, (à la *Guernica*). Fish soup, stuffed crab, and avocado vinaigrette are all good opening bids. In addition to an assortment of lobster entrées, there is grilled or steamed fish and octopus with red beans and rice. Prices are slightly above what you'd expect for basically straightforward cooking and beachfront ambience. ⊠ *Pointe Marin,* ☎ *596/76–73–42. AE, MC.*

$–$$  ✕ **La Dunette.** Dinner at this restaurant, in the small Ste-Anne hotel of the same name, is served on a plant-hung terrace overlooking the sea. Wrought-iron chairs and tables and bright blue awnings add to the refreshing garden atmosphere. Your choices for lunch or dinner include fish soup, grilled fish or lobster, snapper stuffed with sea urchin, conch fricassee, and several colombos and tandooris. There is a piano bar in the evening, and waterskiing is offered after lunch for those who scoff at digestion. ⊠ *Ste-Anne,* ☎ *596/76–73–90. MC, V.*

$–$$  ✕ **Poï et Virginie.** Facing the jetty in the center of Ste-Anne is this popular restaurant with bamboo walls, bright art naïf, ceiling fans, and colorful, fresh-cut flowers. It's had the honor of winning the *Clé d'Or Gault Millau* award. The menu is extensive—from meats to fish—but the specialty is the lobster and crab salad. Other noteworthy dishes are lemon chicken in coconut milk, tuna with green peppers, and crayfish in saffron. Lunchtime is busy, especially on weekends; get here soon after noon if you want a table facing the bay, with views of St. Lucia in the distance. ⊠ *Rue de Bord de Mer, Ste-Anne,* ☎ *596/76–72–22. AE, DC, MC, V. Closed Mon. No lunch Tues.*

## Ste-Luce

$$–$$$  ✕ **La Corniche.** It's a dizzying climb up to this charming small hotel, but once you catch your breath you can enjoy the fine vistas of emerald hills and sapphire sea and even finer fare. Start with the marinated kingfish with mustard sauce, then segue into a delicate, flaky John Dory with coconut sauce or juicy quail stuffed with passion fruit. ⊠ *Monésie, Ste-Luce,* ☎ *596/62–47–48. MC, V. Closed Mon. No dinner Sun.*

$$  ✕ **La Petite Auberge.** This country inn is hidden behind a profusion of tropical flowers, just across the main road from the beach. Fresh seafood is turned into such dishes as *filet de poisson aux champignons* (fish cooked with mushrooms), conch flamed in aged rum, crabe farci, and fresh langouste in a Creole sauce. Or sample *magret à la mangue* (duck breast with mango), veal stuffed with spinach, or entrecôte Creole. They're all winners. The inn has 12 guest rooms, all with rustic

decor (pink-and-white tile floors, wood paneling, hardwood beds, white wicker furnishings, floral linens), air-conditioning, balcony, and minifridge, for an unbeatable 330F a night EP. ✉ *Plage du Gros Raisins, Ste-Luce,* ☎ *596/62–59–70. AE, MC, V.*

## St-Pierre

$$  ✕ **Le Fromager.** This beautiful restaurant is perched high above St-Pierre,
★  with smashing views of the town's red roofs and the sea beyond from the breezy terrace. Dining inside is also pleasant, thanks to the gleaming ecru tile floors, white wicker, polished hardwood furnishings, lace tablecloths, old rum barrels, and potted plants. Superlative choices include crayfish colombo, marinated octopus, and duck fillet with pineapple. You may also opt for the 100F chef's choice menu, which might include avocado vinaigrette and sole sauce *pêcheur* (in a Creole sauce), as well as fruit or crème caramel. ✉ *On the road toward Fond St. Denis,* ☎ *596/78–19–07. AE, DC, MC, V.*

$  ✕ **La Factorérie.** The food is appealing and the views sweeping at this open-air restaurant alongside the ruins of the Eglise du Fort. Fresh vegetables from the nearby agricultural training school accompany grilled langouste, grilled chicken in a piquant Creole sauce, and the fresh catch of the day. This is a convenient spot to have lunch when visiting St-Pierre, but it is not worth a special trip. ✉ *Quartier Fort, St-Pierre,* ☎ *596/78–12–53. Reservations essential. AE, MC, V.*

## Trinité

$$  ✕ **Le Vieux Galion.** This seaside restaurant plays up the nautical theme, with a huge aquarium and murals of old sailing ships complementing fantastic Atlantic views. The crashing surf serenades diners on the terrace. Owner Jean-Pierre Maur does wonders with seafood. Especially memorable are grouper rouged with peppers, Tahitian *poisson cru* (marinated raw fish), and conch *à l'armoricaine* (with tomato, garlic, crème fraîche, and cognac). ✉ *Rte. du Tartane, Anse Bellune,* ☎ *596/58–20–58. AE, MC, V. Closed Wed.*

# Beaches

All of Martinique's beaches are open to the public, but hotels charge a fee for nonguests to use changing rooms and facilities. There are no official nudist beaches, but topless bathing is prevalent. Unless you're an expert swimmer, steer clear of the Atlantic waters, except in the area of Cap Chevalier and the Caravelle Peninsula. The soft, white-sand beaches are south of Fort-de-France; to the north the beaches are hard-packed gray volcanic sand.

**Anse-à-l'Ane** beach has picnic tables and a nearby shell museum. Cool off in the bar of the Le Calalou hotel. **Anse-Mitan** has golden sand and offers excellent snorkeling. Small, family-owned bistros are half hidden among palm trees nearby. **Anse-Trabaud** is on the Atlantic side, across the southern tip of the island from Ste-Anne. There is nothing here but white sand and the sea. **Diamant,** the island's longest beach (2½ miles), has a splendid view of Diamond Rock, but the waters are sometimes rough and the currents are strong. **Pointe du Bout** beaches are man-made, superb, and lined with luxury resorts, among them the Méridien and the Bakoua. **Pointe Marin** stretches north from Ste-Anne. A good windsurfing and waterskiing spot, it also has restaurants, campsites, sanitary facilities, and a 10F charge. Club Med occupies the northern edge. **Les Salines** is a 1½-mile cove of soft white sand lined with coconut palms. A short drive south of Ste-Anne, Les Salines is awash with families and children during holidays and on weekends but quiet and uncrowded during the week—even at the height of the winter season. This beach, especially the far end, is the most peaceful and beautiful.

## Outdoor Activities and Sports

### Bicycling

The **Parc Naturel Régional de la Martinique** (☎ 596/73–19–30) has designed biking itineraries off the beaten track. Bikes can be rented from **Funny** (☎ 596/63–33–05) and **Discount** (☎ 596/66–54–37). Mountain biking is popular in mainland France and now it has reached Martinique. VTT (Vélo Tout Terrain) bikes specially designed with 18 speeds to handle all terrains may be rented from **V.T.Tilt** (✉ Anse-Mitan, ☎ 596/68–16–75).

### Boating

For boat rentals and yacht charters, check with **ATM Yachts** (✉ Port de Plaisance du Marin, ☎ 596/74–98–17; in the U.S., 909/678–2250 or 800/227–5317), **Caraibes Evasion** (✉ Pointe du Bout Marina, ☎ 596/66–02–85), **Moorings Antilles Françaises** (✉ Port de Plaisance du Marin, ☎ 596/74–75–39), **Star Voyages** (✉ Marina Pointe du Bout, ☎ 596/68–16–75), and **Tropic Yachting** (✉ Marina Pointe du Bout, ☎ 596/66–03–85).

### Deep-Sea Fishing

Fish cruising these waters include tuna, barracuda, dolphinfish, kingfish, and bonito. For a day's outing on the 37-foot *Egg Harbor*, with gear and breakfast included, contact **Bathy's Club** (✉ Méridien, ☎ 596/66–00–00). Charters of up to five days can be arranged on Captain Réné Alaric's 37-foot *Rayon Vert* (✉ Auberge du Vare, Case-Pilote, ☎ 596/78–80–56). **Bleu Marine Evasion** (✉ Le Diamant, ☎ 596/76–46–00) also offers excursions.

### Golf

At **Golf de l'Impératrice Joséphine** (✉ Trois-Ilets, ☎ 596/68–32–81) there is an 18-hole Robert Trent Jones course with an English-speaking pro, fully equipped pro shop, a bar, and restaurant. A mile from the Pointe du Bout resort area and 18 miles from Fort-de-France, the club offers special greens fees for hotel guests and cruise-ship passengers.

### Hiking

Inexpensive guided excursions are organized year-round by the **Parc Naturel Régional de la Martinique** (✉ 9 blvd. Général de Gaulle, Fort-de-France, ☎ 596/73–19–30).

### Horseback Riding

Excursions and lessons are available at the **Black Horse Ranch** (✉ Near La Pagerie in Trois-Ilets, ☎ 596/66–00–04), **La Cavale** (✉ Near Diamant on the road to Novotel hotel, ☎ 596/76–22–94), **Ranch Jack** (✉ Near Anse-d'Arlets, ☎ 596/68–37–67), and **Ranch Val d'Or** (✉ Ste-Anne, ☎ 596/66–03–46).

### Sailing

Hobie Cats, Sunfish, and Sailfish can be rented by the hour from hotel beach shacks. Also check **ATM Yachts** (✉ Port de Plaisance du Marin, ☎ 596/74–98–17; in the U.S., 909/678–2250 or 800/227–5317), **Cercle Nautique de Schoelcher** (✉ Anse Madame, ☎ 596/61–15–21), **Club Nautique du Marin** (✉ Le François, ☎ 596/74–92–48), and **Hotel Frantour** (✉ Trois-Ilets, ☎ 596/66–04–04).

### Scuba Diving

To explore the old shipwrecks, coral gardens, and other undersea sites, you must have a medical certificate and insurance papers. Among the island's dive operators are **Bathy's Club** (✉ Méridien, ☎ 596/66–00–

00), **Club Subaquatique** (✉ Le Port, Case-Pilote, ☎ 596/78–73–75),
**Marine Hotel** (✉ Le Diamant, ☎ 596/76–46–00), **Okeonos Club** (✉
Le Diamant, ☎ 596/76–21–76), **Planete Bleue** (✉ La Marina, Trois-
Ilets, ☎ 596/66–10–01), and **Sub Diamant Rock** (✉ Novotel, ☎
596/76–42–42).

### Sea Excursions and Snorkeling
The glass-bottom boat **Seaquarium** (✉ Fort-de-France, ☎ 596/61–49–
49) and the semisubmersible **Aquascope** (✉ Pointe du Bout, ☎ 596/68–
36–09) conduct 45- to 60-minute excursions. A relatively new attraction
is the 50-passenger submarine **Mobilis** (✉ St-Pierre, ☎ 596/78–18–
18), which plunges to a depth of more than 300 feet in the waters surrounding St-Pierre, touring the many shipwrecks and the rainbow-hued
sea gardens that are found there. The hour-long voyage is like something out of Jules Verne and costs 350F. For information on other sailing, swimming, snorkeling, and beach picnic trips, contact **Affaires
Maritimes** (☎ 596/71–90–05).

### Sports Center
The **Anse-Spoutourne** (☎ 596/73–19–30), on the Caravelle Peninsula,
is an open-air sports and leisure center offering sailing, tennis, and other
activities.

### Tennis and Squash
In addition to its links, the **Golf de l'Impératrice Joséphine** (✉ Trois-
Ilets, ☎ 596/68–32–81) has three lighted tennis courts. There are also
two courts at **Le Bakoua** (☎ 596/66–02–02), six excellent courts at
**La Batelière Hotel** (☎ 596/61–64–52), seven courts (six lighted) at
**Club Med/Buccaneer's Creek** (☎ 596/76–74–52), two courts at **Diamant-Novotel** (☎ 596/76–42–42), one court at the **Leyritz Plantation**
(☎ 596/78–53–92), and two courts at **Le Méridien Trois-Ilets** (☎
596/66–00–00). Several other hotels have tennis courts that are available to nonguests when empty, including the **Primerêve Hotel** (☎
596/69–40–40), **Anchorage Hotel** (☎ 596/76–92–32), and **Le Marine** (☎ 596/76–46–00). For additional information about tennis on
the island, contact **La Ligue Régionale de Tennis** (✉ Petit Manoir,
Lamentin, ☎ 596/51–08–00). An hour's court time averages 50F for
nonguests. There are also three squash courts at the modern, aptly
named **Squash Hotel** (✉ 3 blvd. de la Marine, ☎ 596/63–00–34),
just outside Fort-de-France.

# Shopping

French fragrances and designer scarves, fine china and crystal, leather
goods, and liquors and liqueurs are all good buys in Fort-de-France.
Purchases are further sweetened by the 20% discount on luxury
items when paid for by traveler's checks or certain major credit
cards. Among local items, look for Creole gold jewelry, such as loop
earrings, heavy bead necklaces, and slave bracelets; white and dark
rum; and handcrafted straw goods, pottery, and tapestries. In addition, U.S. Customs allows you to bring some of the local flora into
the country.

### Shopping Areas
The area around the cathedral in Fort-de-France has a number of
small shops carrying luxury items. Of particular note are the shops on
rue Victor Hugo, rue Moreau de Jones, rue Antoine Siger, and rue Lamar-
tine. There's a Galleries Lafayette department store in downtown Fort-
de-France. On the outskirts of Fort-de-France, shopping malls include
Centre Commercial de Cluny, Centre Commercial de Dillon, Centre

Commercial de Bellevue, and more than 100 boutiques at La Galleria in Le Lamentin.

## Good Buys

### CHINA AND CRYSTAL

**Cadet Daniel** (⊠ 72 rue Antoine Siger, Fort-de-France, ☎ 596/71−41−48) sells Lalique, Limoges, and Baccarat. **Roger Albert** (⊠ 7 rue Victor Hugo, Fort-de-France, ☎ 596/71−71−71) carries crystal from all the major designers.

### FLOWERS

**Les Lelia Flor** (⊠ St. François, ☎ 596/54−44−73) sells a wide variety of flowers and plants. **MacIntosh** (⊠ 31 rue Victor Hugo, Fort-de-France, ☎ 596/70−09−50, and at the airport, ☎ 596/51−51−51) packages anthuriums, torch lilies, and lobster claws for shipment. **Les Petites Floralies** (⊠ 75 rue Blénac, Fort-de-France, ☎ 596/71−66−16) has a wide selection of flowers and plants.

### LOCAL HANDICRAFTS

Following the peeling roadside signs advertising *ateliers artisanales* (art studios) can yield unexpected treasures, many of them reasonably priced. **Art et Nature** (⊠ Ste-Luce, ☎ 596/62−59−19) features Joel Gilbert's unique wood paintings, daubed with 20−30 shades of earth and sand. **Atelier Ceramique** (⊠ just outside Le Diamant, ☎ 596/76−42−65) displays the crafts of owners and talented artists David and Jeannine England, who have lived in the Caribbean for more than a decade and are members of the small British expatriate community on the island. Whether or not you like their products—ceramics, paintings, and miscellaneous souvenirs—it's a rare chance to brush up on your English. **Galerie Arti-Bijoux** (⊠ 89 rue Victor Hugo, Fort-de-France, ☎ 596/63−10−62) has some unusual and excellent Haitian art—paintings, sculptures, ceramics, and intricate jewelry cases—at reasonable prices. **L'Eclat de Verre** (⊠ Hwy. N4, outside Gros Morne, ☎ 596/58−34−03) specializes in all manner of glittering glasswork. **La Paille Caraibe** (⊠ Morne des Esses, 596/69−83−74) is where you can watch the artisans at work at weaving straw baskets, mats, hats, and amphorae. **Le Poterie-Briqueterie des Trois-Ilets** (⊠ Trois-Ilets, ☎ 596/68−17−12) allows you to watch the creation of pots, vases, and jars patterned after ancient Arawak and Carib traditions. **Victor Anicet** (⊠ Monésie, ☎ 596/68−25−42) fashions lovely ceramic masks and vases.

### PERFUMES

**Airport minishops** sell the most popular scents at in-town prices, so there's no need to carry purchases around. **Roger Albert** (⊠ 7 rue Victor Hugo, Fort-de-France, ☎ 596/71−71−71) stocks such popular scents as Dior, Chanel, and Guerlain.

### RUM

One of the best rums on the island is the Vieux Rhum from the **JM distillery** (⊠ Macouba, ☎ 596/78−92−55). Rum can also be purchased at various other distilleries, including **Duquesnes** (⊠ Fort-de-France, ☎ 596/71−91−68), **St. James** (⊠ Ste-Marie, ☎ 596/69−30−02), **Clément** (⊠ Le François, ☎ 596/54−62−07), and **Trois Rivières** (⊠ Ste-Luce, ☎ 596/62−51−78).

# Nightlife and the Arts

The island is dotted with lively discos and nightclubs, but entertainment on Martinique is not confined to partying. Most leading hotels offer nightly entertainment in season, including the marvelous **Les Grand Ballets de Martinique,** one of the finest folkloric troupes in the Caribbean. In addition, many restaurants offer live combos, usually on weekends.

## Casinos

The **Casino Trois-Ilets** (⊠ Méridien, ☎ 596/66−00−30) is open from
9 PM to 3 AM Monday to Saturday. You must be at least 21 (with a picture ID) to enter, and there is a 70F admission charge (admission to
slot-machine room is free). Try your hand at American and French
roulette or blackjack.

## Discos

Your hotel or the tourist office can put you in touch with the current
"in" places. It's also wise to check on opening and closing times and
cover charges. For the most part, the discos draw a mixed crowd of
locals and tourists, the young and the not so young. Some of the currently popular places are **Blue Night** (⊠ 20 blvd. Allègre, Fort-de-France,
☎ 596/71−58−43), **La Cabane de Pêcheur** (⊠ Diamant-Novotel, ☎
596/76−42−42), **Le New Hippo** (⊠ 24 blvd. Allègre, Fort-de-France,
☎ 596/60−20−22), **L'Oeil** (⊠ Petit Cocotte, Ducos, ☎ 596/56−11−
11), **Le Sweety** (⊠ Rue Capitaine Pierre Rose, Fort-de-France, ☎
596/71−83−41), **VonVon** (⊠ Méridien, ☎ 596/66−00−00), and **Zipp's
Club** (⊠ Dumaine, Le François, ☎ 596/54−65−45).

## Jazz and Zouk

Currently the most popular music is zouk, which mixes Caribbean
rhythm and an Occidental tempo with Creole words. Jacob Devarieux
(Kassav) is the leading exponent of this style and is occasionally on
the island. More likely, though, you will hear zouk music played by
one of his followers at the hotels and clubs. Jazz musicians, like the
music, tend to be informal and independent. They rarely hold regular
gigs. The **Neptune** (⊠ Diamant, ☎ 596/76−25−47) is a hot spot for
zouk. In season, you'll find one or two combos playing at clubs and
hotels, but it is only at **Coco Lobo** (⊠ Fort-de-France, ☎ 596/63−63−
77), located next to the tourist office, that there are regular jazz sessions. For the last seven years Martinique has also hosted the Caribbean's
premiere **jazz festival.** It takes place in early December and, as well as
showcasing the best of the islands, has attracted such top American
performers as Branford Marsalis, Dizzy Gillespie, and Eddie Daniels.

## Other Music

**L'Amphore** (⊠ behind Le Bakoua hotel, ☎ 596/66−03−09) is a late-
night hangout with a popular piano bar. **Las Tapas** (⊠ 7 rue Garnier
Pages, Fort-de-France, ☎ 596/63−71−23) presents flamenco or salsa
and merengue bands. **La Villa Creole** (⊠ Anse-Mitan, ☎ 596/66−05−
53) is a charming bistro whose owner, Guy Dawson, entertains nightly
on the guitar—everything from Brel and Piaf to original ditties.

# Exploring Martinique

The north of the island will appeal to nature lovers, hikers, and mountain climbers. The drive from Fort-de-France to St-Pierre is impressive.
The route across the island, via Morne Rouge, from the Caribbean to
the Atlantic is spectacular. This is Martinique's wild side, a place of waterfalls, rain forest, and mountains. The highlight is *Mont Pelée.* The
south is the more developed half of the island. This is where the resorts
and restaurants are, as well as the casinos, shopping malls, and beaches.

*Numbers in the margin correspond to points of interest on the Mar-
tinique map.*

SIGHTS TO SEE

**⓫ Ajoupa-Bouillon.** This flower-filled, 17th-century village in the midst
of pineapple fields is the jumping-off point for two sites well worth
visiting: the **Saut Babin,** a 40-foot-high waterfall, half an hour's walk
from the village; and the **Gorges de la Falaise,** a river gorge where you

can swim. **Les Ombrages** botanical gardens has marked trails through the rain forest. ⊠ *Les Ombrages:* ☉ *Daily 8–4.*

**4** **Balata.** Two sites here are worth visiting: the **Balata Church,** an exact replica of Sacré-Coeur Basilica in Paris, built in 1923 to commemorate those who died in World War I; and the **Jardin de Balata** (Balata Gardens). Jean-Philippe Thoze, a professional landscaper and devoted horticulturist, spent 20 years creating this collection of thousands of varieties of tropical flowers and plants. There are shaded benches where you can relax and take in the panoramic views of the mountains. ⊠ *Rte. de Balata,* ☎ *596/72–58–82.* 🎫 *30F.* ☉ *Daily 9–5.*

**10** **Basse-Pointe.** Just south of this settlement on the Atlantic coast is a Hindu temple, one of the relics of the East Indians who settled in this area in the 19th century. The view of the eastern slope of Mont Pelée is lovely from here. But the highlight of Basse-Pointe is the estimable **Leyritz Plantation,** which has been a hotel for several years. When tour groups from the cruise ships are not swarming over the property, the rustic setting, complete with sugarcane factory and gardens, is delightful. Fans of the arcane can visit the plantation's **Musée de Poupées Végétales.** Where Rodin used marble, local artisan Will Fenton has used bananas, balisier (a tall grass), and other local plants to make dolls of famous French women—from Marie Antoinette to Madame Curie—all in extravagant period costumes. ⊠ *Musée de Poupées Végétales, Leyritz Plantation,* ☎ *596/78–53–92.* 🎫 *15F.* ☉ *Daily 9–5.*

**3** **Bellefontaine.** This colorful fishing village has pastel houses on the hillsides and beautifully painted gommier canoes (fishing boats made from the gum tree) bobbing in the water. Look for the house built in the shape of a boat.

**13** **Caravelle Peninsula.** Much of this peninsula, which thrusts 8 miles into the Atlantic Ocean, is under the auspices of the Regional Nature Reserve and offers places for trekking, swimming, and sailing. This is the home of **Anse-Spoutourne,** an open-air sports and leisure center operated by the nature reserve (☞ Outdoor Activities and Sports, *above*). Tartane has a popular beach with cool Atlantic breezes. The peninsula is also home to ☞ **Dubuc Castle.**

**19** **Diamond Rock.** A mile offshore from the small, friendly village of Le Diamant is this volcanic mound. In 1804, during the squabbles over possession of the island between the French and the English, the latter commandeered the rock, armed it with cannons, christened it HMS *Diamond Rock,* and proceeded to use it as a warship. For almost a year and a half, the British held the rock, bombarding any French ships that came along. The French got wind of the fact that the British were getting cabin fever on their isolated ship-island and arranged a supply of barrels of rum for those on the rock. The French easily overpowered the inebriated sailors, ending one of the most curious engagements in naval history.

NEED A BREAK? On the main drag of Le Diamant, with *les pieds dans l'eau* (its feet in the water), is **Pizza Pepe** (☎ 596/76–40–49). Here, you can order such creative pizzas as *oceanique* (crab, onions, olives) and Ingrid (crème fraîche, salmon, olives). You can also get a plate of roast chicken or grilled shark.

**14** **Dubuc Castle.** At the eastern tip of the ☞ **Caravelle Peninsula** are the ruins of this castle, once the home of the Dubuc de Rivery family, who owned the peninsula in the 18th century. According to legend, young

Aimée Dubuc de Rivery was captured by Barbary pirates, sold to the Ottoman Empire, became a favorite of the sultan, and gave birth to Mahmud II.

**㉑ Forêt de Montravail.** A few miles north of ☞ Ste-Luce, this is one of the best places in the south of the island for a short hike through tropical forest. There is also an interesting group of Carib rock drawings.

**❶ Fort-de-France.** With its superb setting on the Baie des Flamands and its historic fort, Martinique's capital, home to about one-third of the island's 360,000 inhabitants, should be a grand place. It isn't. The center of town is a warren of narrow streets (if you come by car you will find yourself sitting in endless gridlock). True, there are some good shops with Parisian wares (at Parisian prices) and lively street markets selling, among other things, human hair for wigs (starting price, 200F). But the heat, exhaust fumes, and litter tend to make exploring them a chore. At night, the city feels dark and gloomy, with little street life except for the extravagantly dressed *femmes de nuit* who openly parade the streets from 10 PM.

That said, there are interesting things to see here. The city's heart is **La Savane,** a 12½-acre landscaped park filled with tropical trees, fountains, and benches. It's a popular gathering place and the scene of promenades, parades, and impromptu soccer matches. Along the east side, there are numerous snack-wagons selling everything from hot dogs and barbecued chicken to delicious fresh-squeezed juices. A statue of Pierre Belain d'Esnambuc, leader of the island's first settlers, is upstaged by Vital Dubray's flattering white Carrara marble statue of the empress Joséphine, Napoléon's first wife. Sculpted in a high-waisted Empire gown, Joséphine gazes toward Trois-Ilets across the bay, where in 1763 she was born Marie-Joseph Tascher de la Pagerie. Unfortunately, the most imposing historic site, **Fort St. Louis,** which runs along the east side of La Savane, is the headquarters of the Captain of the Fleet Commanding the Antilles Guyane Navy, and cannot be visited. Unless, that is, you write to the officer in charge—*en français,* of course; no faxes, please. Near the harbor is a marketplace where high-quality local crafts are sold. Across from La Savane, you can catch the ferry for the beaches at Anse-Mitan and Anse-à-l'Ane and for the 20-minute run across the bay to the resort hotels of Pointe du Bout. The ferry is more convenient than a car for travel between Pointe du Bout and Fort-de-France.

Rue de la Liberté runs along the west side of La Savane. At the corner of rue de la Liberté and rue Perrinon is the **Bibliothèque Schoelcher,** the wildly elaborate Byzantine-Egyptian-Romanesque–style public library. It was named after Victor Schoelcher, who led the fight to free the slaves in the French West Indies in the 19th century. The eye-popping structure was built for the 1889 Paris Exposition, after which it was dismantled, shipped to Martinique, and reassembled piece by ornate piece at its present location. ⊠ *At corner of rue de la Liberté and rue Perrinon,* ☎ *596/70–26–67.* ☉ *Mon., Tues., and Thurs. 8:30–12:30 and 2–6; Wed. and Fri. 8–1; Sat. 8:30–noon.*

At the southern end of rue de la Liberté is the **Musée Départementale de Martinique,** which contains exhibits on the pre-Columbian Arawak and Carib periods, including pottery, beads, and part of a skeleton that turned up during excavations in 1972. One exhibit examines the history of slavery; costumes, documents, furniture, and handicrafts from the island's colonial period are on display. ⊠ *9 rue de la Liberté,* ☎ *596/71–57–05.* 🖅 *15F.* ☉ *Weekdays 8:30–1 and 2:30–5, Sat. 9–noon.*

**Rue Victor Schoelcher** runs through the center of the capital's primary shopping district, a six-block area bounded by rue de la République, rue de la Liberté, rue de Victor Severe, and rue Victor Hugo. Stores feature Paris fashions (at Paris prices) and French perfume, china, crystal, and liqueurs, as well as local handicrafts. Also on rue Victor Schoelcher you'll find the Romanesque **St-Louis Cathedral,** the sixth to be built on the site (the others were destroyed by fire, hurricane, or earthquake). This one dates from 1878 and has lovely stained-glass windows. A number of Martinique's former governors are interred beneath the choir loft.

| | |
|---|---|
| NEED A<br>BREAK? | **Couleur Café** (✉ corner rues Victor Severe and Gallieni, ☎ 596/71–54–41) is a hip, open-sided hangout, with a bamboo ceiling, African tapestries, and roughly painted turquoise counter and chairs. It's always jammed with gorgeous, impoverished young French people, who congregate to gossip, smoke, and scarf down fine salads, quiches, and *croque monsieurs* (open-faced ham and cheese sandwiches), every day from 10 AM to 2:30 PM. |

The Galerie de Biologie et de Géologie at the **Parc Floral et Culturel,** in the north-eastern corner of the city center, will acquaint you with the variety of exotic flora on this island. There's also an aquarium showing fish that can be found in these waters. The park contains the island's official cultural center, where there are sometimes free evening concerts. Wandering about the grounds, you'll run into musicians and artists, who may give you an impromptu lesson on playing the steel drum or working with driftwood. ✉ *Pl. Jose-Marti, Sermac,* ☎ *596/71–66–25.* ✍ *Grounds free; aquarium 35F; botanical/geological gallery 5F.* ☉ *Park daily dawn–10 PM; aquarium daily 9–7; gallery Tues.–Fri. 9:30–12:30 and 3:30–5:30, Sat. 9–1 and 3–5.*

The **Rivière Madame** meanders through the park and joins the bay at Pointe Simon. The river divides the downtown area from the ritzy residential district of Didier in the hills. Fronting the river, on avenue Paul Nardal, are the vibrantly noisy, messy, smelly vegetable and fish markets. One of the best shows in town occurs around 4 PM, when fishermen return with their catch, effortlessly tossing 100-pound bundles of rainbow-hued fish.

**⓯ Le François.** A sizable city of some 16,000 inhabitants, this is the main city on the Atlantic coast. Sadly, the old wooden buildings are being replaced by concrete. But the classic West Indian cemetery, with its black-and-white tiles, is still here. The town's greatest attraction, however, is the **Habitation Clément.** This is Martinique's Williamsburg, complete with Creole ladies in traditional dresses dotted picturesquely around the grounds. Built with the wealth generated by its rum distillery, it is one of the finest plantation houses in the Caribbean. Lovingly preserved in its original 18th-century splendor, it offers a unique glimpse into the elegance and privilege of the old plantation house society. Jacques Chirac visited. President Bush and François Mitterrand had a summit meeting here. Barbara Hendricks, the opera singer, loved it. The rum distillery is still operational (free tastings). The grounds contain a superb collection of historic trees. ✉ *Habitation Clément,* ☎ *596/54–62–07.* ☉ *Daily 9–6.*

Le François is also noted for its snorkeling. Offshore are the (privately owned) **Les Ilets de l'Impératrice** (☞ Dining and Lodging, *above*). The islands received that name because, according to legend, this is where Empress Joséphine would come to bathe in shallow basins, known as *fond blancs* because of their white-sand bottoms. Group boat tours leave from the harbor ($30 per person includes lunch and drinks). You can also haggle with a fisherman to take you out for a while on his boat to indulge in the uniquely Martinican custom of standing waist-deep in the calm water, sipping a 'ti punch, eating accras, and smoking. There is a lovely bay 6 miles farther along the coast at **Le Robert.**

⑯ **Lamentin.** There is nothing pretty about Lamentin. The multibillion-franc airport, which opened in 1995, is the most notable landmark. The rest of the town is a sprawling industrial and commercial zone. There is one reason to stop here, though, and that is to gawk at the Caribbean's biggest, fanciest shopping malls: **Euromarche** and the brand new **La Galleria,** a megamall housing 100 shops and boutiques where you can find everything from *pâté de foie gras* and Camembert to CD's and sunglasses.

⑨ **Macouba.** Named after the Carib word for fish, this village was a prosperous town in the 17th century, when tobacco made it rich. Today, its cliff-top location affords magnificent views of the sea, the mountains, and, on clear days, the neighboring island of Dominica. It is also the starting point for the island's most spectacular drive, the 6-mile route to **Grand-Rivière** on the northernmost point. From Grand-Rivière, you can trek 11 miles on a well-marked path that leads through lush tropical vegetation to the beach at Anse-Ceron on the northwest coast. Macouba is home to the **JM Distillery.** It produces the best *rhum vieux* (aged rum) on the island. A tour and samples are free. ⊠ *JM Distillery, on main road, Macouba,* ☎ *596/78–92–55.* ⊡ *Free.* ☉ *Weekdays 7 AM–noon and 1:30–3:30.*

NEED A BREAK?  Stop in at **Yva Chez Vava** (⊠ Rte. 1 on eastern edge of Grand-Rivière, ☎ 596/55–72–72) for a rum punch and a lunch of seafood and Creole dishes, including an excellent fish soup and a tasty fricassee of crayfish.

㉓ **Le Marin.** The yachting capital of Martinique is also known for its colorful August carnival and its Jesuit church. Built in 1766, the church is one of the oldest on the island. One mile out of town, a small road leads to picturesque **Cap Chevalier.**

⑦ **Le Morne Rouge.** This town, lying on the southern slopes of Mont Pelée, was destroyed by the volcano when it erupted in 1902. Today it's a popular resort spot, and offers hikers some of the most spectacular mountain scenery on Martinique. This is the starting point for a climb up the 4,600-foot mountain. But don't try it without a guide unless you want to get buried alive under pumice stones. The **Route de la Trace** (Route N3), which winds south of Le Morne Rouge to St-Pierre, used to be one of the main footpaths across the northern half of the island. It is steep and winding, but that didn't used to stop the *porteuses* of old: Balancing a tray, they would carry up to 100 pounds of provisions on their heads for the 15-hour trek to the Atlantic Coast. Today, the Route de la Trace is one of the Caribbean's great drives.

⑤ **Musée Gauguin.** Martinique was a brief station in Paul Gaugin's wanderings, but a decisive moment in the evolution of his art. He arrived from Panama in 1887 with friend and fellow painter Charles Laval and, having pawned his watch at the docks, rented a wooden shack on a hillside above this village. He only stayed seven months, before sickness and poverty drove him back to Paris, but the work he did here and on his return to France precipitated a change in his art. Indeed, he would later say that to understand him and his art one had to understand his Martinique period. Dazzled by the tropical colors and vegetation, Gaugin developed a style that directly anticipated his Tahitian paintings. This excellent museum is a labor of love on the part of local art historian, Maiotte Dauphite and a group of other Martinicans.

Though it has no originals (Gaugin's most famous Martinique painting, *Vegetation Tropicale,* is in the Royal Scottish Museum in Edinburgh), the museum has an excellent set of reproductions. Indeed, this is the only place you can see all of Gaugin's Martinique work under one roof. There are also interesting exhibits of letters and documents relating to the painter, and an exhibition of local costumes. Another major artist is also remembered here: the writer Lafcadio Hearn, who came to Martinique in the same year as Gaugin, on assignment for Harper's magazine. In his endearing book, *Two Years in the West Indies,* he provides the most extensive description of the island before ☞ St-Pierre was buried in ash and lava. ⊠ *Anse-Turin,* ☎ *596/78–22–66.* ▱ *15F.* ◷ *Daily 9–5:30.*

**⑱ Pointe du Bout.** This area is filled with resort hotels, among them the Bakoua and the Méridien. The Pointe du Bout marina is a colorful spot where a whole slew of boats are tied up. The ferry to Fort-de-France leaves from here. More than anywhere else on Martinique, Pointe du Bout caters to the vacationer. A cluster of boutiques, ice-cream parlors, and rental-car agencies forms the hub from which restaurants and hotels of varying caliber radiate. The beach at **Anse-Mitan** is one of the best on the island. At **Anse-à-l'Ane,** a little to the west of Pointe du Bout, there is a pretty white-sand beach complete with picnic tables. There are also numerous small restaurants and inexpensive guesthouse hotels here. Ten miles south of here is **Anse-d'Arlets,** a quiet backwater fishing village. You'll see fishermen's nets strung up on the beach to dry and pleasure boats on the water.

**⑧ Le Prêcheur.** This village was the childhood home of Françoise d'Aubigné, who later became the Marquise de Maintenon and the second wife of Louis XIV. **The Tomb of the Carib Indians** found here commemorates a sadder event. The site is actually a formation of limestone hills from which the last of the Caribs are said to have flung themselves to avoid capture by the Marquise's forebears.

**❷ Schoelcher.** It's pronounced "shell-cher" and is home of the University of the French West Indies and Guyana. La Batelière Hotel, noted for its sports facilities, is also here.

**❻ St-Pierre.** The rise and fall of St-Pierre is one of the most remarkable stories in the Caribbean. It is the island's oldest city, with a current population of about 6,000. But at the turn of this century, St-Pierre was a flourishing city of 30,000. It was known as the Paris of the West Indies. There were cabarets, cafés, and a cathedral. Warehouses climbed the hills. As many as 30 ships at a time stood at anchor. By 1902, it was the most modern town in the Caribbean, with electricity, phones, and a tram. In the spring of 1902, Mont Pelée began to rumble and spit out ash and steam. On May 2, it spewed out a river of lava that engulfed a factory, killing 25. City officials, however, ignored the warning, needing voters in town for an upcoming election. Shortly after 8 AM on May 8, 1902, two thunderous explosions rent the air. As it erupted, Mont Pelée split in half, belching forth a cloud of burning ash, poisonous gas, and lava that spewed down the mountain at 250 mph. With temperatures of more than 3,600°F, St-Pierre was instantly vaporized. Thirty thousand people were killed in two minutes. The Paris of the West Indies had become its Pompeii. One man survived, though. Of all the inhabitants of St-Pierre, he was probably the last person anyone would have expected to live—and the last many would have wanted to. His name was Cyparis and he was a prisoner in the town's jail. Though he was scorched by the heat, the thick walls of his underground cell saved him. He was later pardoned and for some years afterward was a sideshow attraction at the Barnum & Bailey Circus.

For those interested in the eruption of 1902, the **Musée Vulcanologique** is a must. It was established in 1932 by American volcanologist Franck Perret. His collection includes photographs of the old town, documents, and a number of relics—some gruesome—excavated from the ruins, including molten glass, melted iron, and contorted clocks stopped at 8 AM. ⊠ *St-Pierre,* ☎ *596/78–15–16.* 🖼 *15F.* ☉ *Daily 9–5.*

In the town itself, you can still see the ruins of the island's first church (built in 1640), the theater, the toppled statues, and Cyparis's cell. The Cyparis Express is a small tourist train that runs through the city, hitting the important sights with a running narrative (in French). ⊠ *Departs from Pl. des Ruines du Figuier,* ☎ *596/55–50–92.* 🖼 *30F.* ☉ *Runs every 45 mins, weekdays 9:30–1 and 2:30–5:30; call for exact times.*

**㉒ Ste-Anne.** A lovely white-sand beach and a Roman Catholic church are the highlights here. To the south is **Pointe des Salines,** the southernmost tip of the island and site of Martinique's best beach, **Les Salines,** 1½ miles of soft white sand. It's definitely *the* place for beach bums, and there is a lively scene here on weekends; *le topless* is almost *de rigeur.* Nearby is the **Petrified Forest,** known in French as the *Savane des Petrifications*. It's not a forest at all, but a field of petrified boulders formed into the shape of logs.

**㉑ Ste-Luce.** One of the prettiest fishing villages on the island, Ste-Luce has excellent beaches. To the east is **Pointe Figuier,** an excellent spot for scuba diving. On the way you will also find the **Ecomusée de Martinique,** despite its name more a historical than a natural museum. Holdings include artifacts from Arawak and Carib settlements through the plantation years. ⊠ *Anse Figuier,* ☎ *596/62–79–14.* 🖼 *15F.* ☉ *Tues.–Sun. 9–5.*

**⑫ Ste-Marie.** This town is home to about 20,000 Martinicans and is the commercial capital of the island's north. There is a lovely mid-19th-century church here, as well as the **Musée du Rhum,** operated by the St. James Rum Distillery. It is housed in a graceful galleried Creole house. Guided tours of the museum take in displays of the tools of the trade and include a visit to the distillery. And, yes, you may sample the product. ⊠ *Ste-Marie,* ☎ *596/69–30–02.* 🖼 *Free.* ☉ *Weekdays 9–6, weekends 9–1.*

**⑰ Les Trois-Ilets.** Named after the three rocky islands nearby, this is a lovely little village with a population of about 3,000. It's known for its pottery, straw, and woodwork and as the birthplace of Napoléon's Empress Joséphine. On the village square, you can visit the simple church where she was baptized Marie-Joseph Tascher de la Pagerie. The Martinicans have always been enormously proud of Joséphine, even though she reintroduced slavery on the island and most historians consider her to have been a rather shallow woman. A stone building that held the kitchen of the estate where she grew up is now home to the **Musée de la Pagerie.** (The main house blew down in the hurricane of 1766, when Joséphine was three.) It contains an assortment of memorabilia pertaining to Joséphine's life and loves (she was married at 16 in an arranged marriage to Alexandre de Beauharnais). There are family portraits; documents, including a marriage certificate; a love letter written to her in 1796 by Napoléon; and various antique furnishings, including the bed she slept in as a child. ⊠ *Trois-Ilets,* ☎ *596/68–38–34.* 🖼 *15F.* ☉ *Tues.–Sun. 9–5.*

The **Maison de la Canne** (at Pointe Vatable, as you leave town) will teach you everything you ever wanted to know about sugarcane. Exhibits take you through three centuries of sugarcane production, with displays of tools, scale models, engravings, and photographs. ⊠ *Trois-Ilets,* ☎ *596/68–32–04.* ▣ *15F.* ☉ *Tues.–Sun. 9–5:30.*

**㉔** **Le Vauclin.** The return of the fishermen shortly before noon each day is the big event in this important fishing port on the Atlantic coast. There is also an 18th-century church here, the Chapel of the Holy Virgin. Nearby is the highest point in the south, **Mt. Vauclin** (1,654 feet). A hike to the top will reward you with one of the best views on the island.

## Martinique A to Z

### Arriving and Departing

BY FERRY

The **Caribbean Express** (☎ 596/63–12–11) offers scheduled interisland service aboard a 128-foot, 227-passenger motorized catamaran, linking Martinique with Dominica, Guadeloupe, Les Saintes, and St. Lucia. For those who don't get seasick, it's an enormously pleasurable way to travel, with great views of the islands. Fares run approximately 25% below economy airfares. Sailings are not every day of the week for all destinations; check schedule.

BY PLANE

The most frequent flights from the United States are on **American Airlines** (☎ 800/433–7300), which has year-round daily service from more than 100 U.S. cities to San Juan. From there, the airline's American Eagle flies on to Martinique with a stop first at Guadeloupe. **Air France** (☎ 800/237–2747) flies direct from Miami and San Juan. **Air Canada** (☎ 800/776–3000) has service from Montréal and Toronto. **LIAT** (☎ 809/462–0700), with its extensive coverage of the Antilles, flies in from Antigua, St. Maarten, Guadeloupe, Dominica, St. Lucia, Barbados, Grenada, and Trinidad and Tobago. **Council Charter** (☎ 212/661–4546 or 800/765–6065) provides Saturday–Saturday flights out of New York's JFK, and offers flight-lodging packages.

FROM THE AIRPORT

You'll arrive at the new Lamentin International Airport, which is about a 15-minute taxi ride from Fort-de-France and about 40 minutes from the Trois-Ilets peninsula, the first of many resort areas on the southern beaches where most hotels are located.

### Currency

The currency used on Martinique is the French franc. At press time, the exchange rate was 4.60F to U.S. $1. U.S. dollars are accepted in some hotels, but for convenience, it's better to convert your money into francs. Banks give a more favorable rate than hotels. A currency exchange service that also offers a favorable rate is **Change Caraibes,** in the arrivals building at Lamentin International Airport (☎ 596/51–57–91), which is open weekdays 7 AM–9 PM and Saturday 8:30–2, and in Fort-de-France (⊠ rue Ernest Deproge, across from Tourist Office, ☎ 596/60–28–40), which is open weekdays 7:30–6 and Saturday 8–12:30. Note: Prices quoted here are in U.S. dollars unless indicated otherwise.

Major credit cards are accepted in hotels and restaurants in Fort-de-France and the Pointe du Bout areas; few establishments in the countryside accept them. There are ATMs at the airport and at branches of the Credit Agricole bank, which are on the Cirrus system, and also accept Visa and MasterCard. There is a 20% discount on luxury items paid for with traveler's checks or with certain credit cards.

### Emergencies

**Police:** ☎ 17. **Ambulance:** ☎ 70–36–48 or 71–59–48. **Fire:** ☎ 18.
**Hospital:** There is a 24-hour emergency room at **Hôpital La Meynard**

(✉ Châteauboeuf, just outside Fort-de-France, ☎ 596/55–20–00). **Pharmacies:** Pharmacies in Fort-de-France include **Pharmacie de la Paix** (✉ Corner rue Victor Schoelcher and rue Perrinon, ☎ 596/71–94–83) and **Pharmacie Cypria** (✉ Blvd. Général de Gaulle, ☎ 596/63–22–25).

## Getting Around

### BICYCLES AND MOTORBIKES

Bikes, scooters, and motorbikes are all popular. They can be rented in Fort-de-France from **Funny** (☎ 596/63–33–05), **T. S. Location Sarl** (☎ 596/63–42–82), or **Loca Scoot** (☎ 596/63–55–84); in St. Anne at **Huet** (☎ 596/76–79–66); and in St. Luce at **Vespa Marquis** (☎ 596/60–02–84).

### BUSES

Public buses are crowded and are not recommended for the timid traveler. But eight-passenger minivans (license plates bear the letters TC), are an inexpensive—and fun—means of transportation. In Fort-de-France, the main terminal for the minivans is at Pointe Simon on the waterfront. There are frequent departures from early morning until 8 PM; fares range from $1 to $5.

### CAR RENTALS

Unless you are at an all-inclusive resort, a car will be essential. With about 175 miles of well-paved and well-marked roads (albeit with international signs), Martinique is also a good place for driving. The Martinicans drive with aggressive abandon, but are surprisingly courteous and will let you into the flow of traffic. Country roads are mountainous with hairpin curves. Watch out, too, for *dos d'anes* (literally, donkey backs), speed bumps that are extremely hard to spot—particularly at night—but if you hit one you'll know about it. Streets in Fort-de-France are narrow and choked with traffic during the day. If you want a detailed map, the *Carte Routière et Touristique* is available at bookstores. A full tank of gas will get you all the way around the island with gallons to spare.

A valid U.S driver's license is needed to rent a car for up to 20 days. After that, you'll need an International Driver's Permit. U.K. visitors can use their EU licenses. Rates are about $60 per day (unlimited mileage), but always question agents closely. If you book from the United States at least 48 hours in advance, you can qualify for a hefty discount. Among the many agencies are **Avis** (☎ 596/70–11–60 or 800/331–1212), **Budget** (☎ 596/63–69–00 or 800/472–3325), and **Hertz** (☎ 596/60–64–64 or 800/654–3131).

### FERRIES

Weather permitting, *vedettes* (ferries) operate daily between Fort-de-France and the Marina Méridien in Pointe du Bout and between Fort-de-France and Anse-Mitan and Anse-à-l'Ane (all trips take about 25 minutes). The Quai d'Esnambuc is the arrival and departure point in Fort-de-France. At press time, the one-way fare was 16F; round-trip, 27F.

### TAXIS

Taxis are expensive. Rates are regulated by the government, but local taxi drivers are an independent lot, and prices often turn out to be higher than the minimum "official" rate. Martinique is considering introducing a metering system, but it's feared that this measure would further raise prices. At press time, it cost 50F just to get into a taxi and go a few hundred yards. From the airport to Fort-de-France was about 100F; from the airport to Pointe du Bout, about 225F. A 40% surcharge is in effect between 8 PM and 6 AM and on Sunday. This means that if you arrive at Lamentin at night, depending on where your hotel is, it may be cheaper to rent a car from the airport and keep it for 24 hours than to take a one-way taxi to your hotel. For a radio cab call ☎ 596/63–63–62 or 596/63–10–10.

## Guided Tours

For a personalized tour of the island, ask the tourist office to arrange a tour with an English-speaking taxi driver. There are set rates for tours to various points on the island, and if you share the ride with two or three other sightseers, the price will be whittled down.

**Madinina Tours** (⊠ 89 rue Blénac, Fort-de-France, ☎ 596/70–65–25) offers half- and full-day jaunts, with lunch included in the all-day outings. Boat tours are also available, as are air excursions to the Grenadines and St. Lucia. Madinina has tour desks in most of the major hotels. **Parc Naturel Regional de la Martinique** (⊠ 9 blvd. Général de Gaulle, Fort-de-France 97206, ☎ 596/73–19–30) organizes inexpensive guided hiking tours year-round. Descriptive folders are available at the tourist office.

## Language

Many Martinicans speak Creole, a mixture of Spanish and French. Try *sa ou fe* for hello. In major tourist areas you'll find someone who speaks English, but the courtesy of using a few French words, even if it is *Parlez-vous anglais?*, is appreciated. The people of Martinique are extremely courteous and will help you through your French. Even if you do speak fluent French, you may have a problem understanding the accent of the country people. Most menus are written in French, so a dictionary is helpful.

## Opening and Closing Times

Stores that cater to tourists are generally open weekdays 8:30–6, Saturday 8:30–1. Banking hours are weekdays 7:30–noon and 2:30–4.

## Passports and Visas

U.S. and Canadian citizens must have a passport (one that expired no more than five years ago is acceptable) or proof of citizenship, such as an original (not photocopied) birth certificate or a voter registration card accompanied by a government-authorized photo identification. British citizens are required to have a passport. In addition, all visitors must have a return or ongoing ticket.

## Precautions

Exercise the same safety precautions you would in any other big city. Don't leave jewelry or money unattended on the beach.

Beware of the *mancenillie* (manchineel) trees. These pretty trees with green fruits that look like apples are poisonous. Sap and even raindrops falling from the trees onto your skin can cause painful, scarring blisters. The trees have red warning signs posted by the Forestry Commission.

If you plan to ramble through the rain forest, be careful where you step. Fer de lances, and several other varieties of poisonous snake, exist on Martinique.

Except for the area around Cap Chevalier and the Tartane peninsula, the Atlantic waters are rough and should be avoided by all but expert swimmers.

## Taxes and Service Charges

A resort tax varies from hotel to hotel; the maximum is $1.50 per person per day. Rates quoted by hotels usually include a 10% service charge; some hotels add 10% to your bill. All restaurants include a 15% service charge in their menu prices.

## Telephones and Mail

To call Martinique station-to-station from the United States, dial 011 plus 596 plus the local six-digit number.

It is not possible to make collect calls from Martinique to the United States, but you can use a calling card. There are few coin telephone booths, and those are usually in hotels and restaurants. Most public telephones now use a Telecarte. Telecartes may be purchased from post offices, café-tabacs, and hotels.

To place an interisland call, dial the local six-digit number. To call the United States from Martinique, dial 19–1, area code, and the local number. For Great Britain, dial 19–44, area code (without the first zero), and the number.

Airmail letters to the United States cost 4.60F for up to 20 grams; postcards, 3.70F. For Great Britain, the costs are 4.40F and 3.60F, respectively. Stamps may be purchased from post offices, café-tabacs, and hotel newsstands.

## Visitor Information

For information contact the **French West Indies Tourist Board** (☎ 800/391–4909). You can also contact the **French Government Tourist Office, Martinique Promotion Bureau** (✉ 444 Madison Ave., New York, NY 10022, ☎ 212/757–1125; ✉ 9454 Wilshire Blvd., Beverly Hills, CA 90212, ☎ 310/271–2358; ✉ 676 N. Michigan Ave., Chicago, IL 60611, ☎ 312/751–7800; in Canada, ✉ 1981 McGill College Ave., Suite 490, Montréal, Québec H3A 2W9, ☎ 514/288–4264, or ✉ 1 Dundas St. W, Suite 2405, Toronto, Ontario M5G 1Z3, ☎ 416/593–4723 or 800/361–9099; in the U.K., ✉ 178 Piccadilly, London W1V 0AL, ☎ 0181/124–4123).

On Martinique, the **Martinique Tourist Office** (✉ Blvd. Alfassa, ☎ 596/63–79–60) is open Monday–Thursday 8–5, Friday 7:30–5, Saturday 8–noon. The office's free maps and booklets, *Choubouloute* and *Martinique Info,* are useful. The Tourist Information Booth at Lamentin International Airport is open daily until the last flight has landed.

# 16 Montserrat

Updated by
Pamela
Acheson

**M**ONTSERRAT IS ONE OF THE LEAST-DEVELOPED ISLANDS in the Eastern Caribbean. The population is only about 11,000 and the scenery here is rugged and dramatic. Although only 11 miles long and 7 miles wide, the island has three mountain ranges and there are also dramatic waterfalls, dense rain forests, and fertile fields rich with mango, coconut, papaya, and banana trees. All this makes the island a hiker's heaven and there are literally hundreds of trails, from easy beginner walks to arduous half-day trips that require a guide. Mountain biking has recently taken over the island and there is a training camp as well as numerous off-road mountain bike trails.

The highest point is Chance's Peak, which lies at the southern end of the island and rises to a height of 3,002 feet. Also in the southern hills is the volcano known as Galway's Soufrière. In 1995 the volcanic activity increased significantly and the southern end of the island was evacuated but the volcano has returned to its quieter state and residents have returned home. Visitors head here to wonder at the powerful sight of steam pouring from vents in the dramatic yellow-and-pink rock and the lush tropical vegetation circling the crater rim.

Montserrat is a small, friendly island that tends to attract independent travelers who want a low-key, away-from-it-all vacation. If you want to pump iron, drink piña coladas, and boogie till dawn, you'll probably be bored. If you like seclusion, nature, and peace and quiet, you'll love it.

There is only one white sand beach. The others range in color from beige to gray. The calm beaches are on the western side of the island and some of them are most comfortably reached by boat. The eastern, or Atlantic, coast is rockier, more windswept, and less fertile. Steep cliffs make most of the beaches on that side of the island inaccessible.

About a third of the island's population of 11,000 lives in the capital city of Plymouth, which faces the Caribbean on the southwest coast. Most of the villas and hotels are concentrated here in a small area, measuring about 5 miles by 2 miles. Look around and you'll find Montserrat's vegetation at it's most luxuriant. Hibiscus and bougainvillea, giant philodendron and avocado trees, mango trees, christophines (a kind of squash), and many other species all thrive on the terracelike hills that slope down to the water. There are also spectacular views across the Caribbean to Antigua's mysterious island of Rodondo and, a bit farther away, Nevis and St. Kitts, a sequence of hazy gray-blue peaks on the northwestern horizon.

Christopher Columbus sailed by the leeward coast of this Caribbean island in 1493, and, seeing the jagged mountains, he named it Montserrat, after the Santa Maria de Montserrate monastery near Barcelona, which is surrounded by similar terrain.

The Carib Indians who inhabited the island then were still there in 1632, when dissident Irish Catholics fleeing persecution arrived from nearby St. Kitts. These new settlers found a green and luxuriant island whose topography strongly resembled that of their native Ireland, prompting Montserrat's nickname, the Emerald Isle of the Caribbean. Today the Irish influence is much diminished. Still, your passport is stamped with a shamrock upon arrival, the phone book is loaded with Irish places and surnames, and St. Patrick's Day is celebrated enthusiastically (albeit to commemorate a major 18th-century slave uprising).

Actually, the African influence is more pronounced, thanks to Montserrat's comparatively low profile. Newborns are still given "jumbie" nicknames to fool the evil spirits, and the related jumbie dances, designed to ward off or propitiate those spirits, are lusty and vibrant. The rollicking Carnival, two weeks of merrymaking held during the Christmas season, is a riot of color in traditional authentic costumes.

Despite the fact that Montserrat built a $30 million seaport several years ago that is big enough to accommodate small cruise ships, the island still retains its peaceful, unhurried, completely nontouristy atmosphere. For now, the island is on the itinerary of only a few cruises, mostly the oversize sailing vessels. It remains to be seen what changes will occur as more and more ships come calling.

# Lodging

The number of hotels on Montserrat is limited, with the two largest—the Vue Point and Montserrat Springs—the island's only real resorts. Small hotels that cater to businesspeople, guest houses, and a few bed-and-breakfasts are also available. Be aware that most hotels are "tropical-breeze-cooled": Only a few have rooms that are air-conditioned. Most of Montserrat's hotels operate on the Modified American Plan (MAP).

Alternatively, there are many villas of all sizes available for rent. Villas are not only affordable here; given their comforts and conveniences, many consider them preferable to the hotels. You can even request the properties where your favorite rock stars—from Sting to Elton John—relaxed.

| CATEGORY | COST* |
|---|---|
| $$$ | over $145 |
| $$ | $75–$145 |
| $ | under $75 |

*All prices are for a standard double room for two in winter, excluding 7% tax and 10% service charge.*

## Hotels

**$$$**   ⊞ **Montserrat Springs Hotel and Villas.** Spacious air-conditioned rooms
★   in this, the largest of the island's hotels, are in one wing of the main building and in cottages scattered along the steep hillside sloping down to the beach. All rooms have excellent views of the water and Chance's Peak. The bright and airy decor is primarily cream and white. Rooms have private balconies and cable TV; suites have separate living rooms and full kitchens. The beautiful outdoor pool, at 70 feet long, is one of the largest in the Caribbean. From the terrace surrounding it, you can take in sweeping views of the ocean in one direction and Chance's Peak in the other. At the beach bar you can luxuriate in a whirlpool filled with piping-hot mineral water direct from a soufrière. The restaurant serves good West Indian and Continental cuisine (☞ Dining, *below*). ⊠ *Box 259, Plymouth,* ☎ *809/491–2481 or 800/253–2134,* 𝗙𝗔𝗫 *809/491–4070. 40 rooms, 6 suites. Restaurant, 2 bars, room service, large pool, 2 Jacuzzis (1 fresh water, 1 hot mineral–spring water), 2 tennis courts, exercise room, beach. AE, MC, V. EP, MAP.*

**$$–$$$**   ⊞ **Vue Pointe.** The moment you arrive here you feel as though both
★   the staff and the owners, Cedric and Carol Osborne, really care about your well-being. The gracious Monday-night cocktail parties that the Osbornes host at their house, with drinks, delicious homemade hors d'oeuvres, and good conversation, are a perfect example. (Cedric Osborne comes from one of the island's first families and is a mine of information about local goings-on.) The breeze-cooled accommodations include 12 rooms in the main building and 28 hexagonal rondavels that

Montserrat

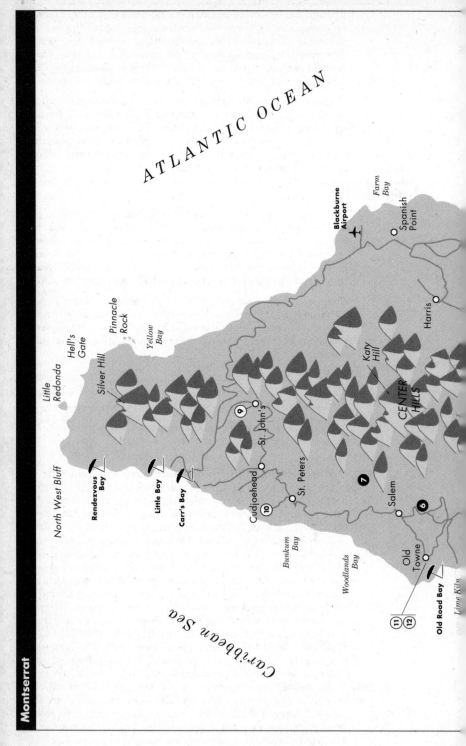

ATLANTIC OCEAN

Caribbean Sea

Blackburne Airport

Farm Bay

Spanish Point

Harris

Little Redonda

Hell's Gate

Pinnacle Rock

Silver Hill

Yellow Bay

North West Bluff

Rendezvous Bay

Little Bay

Carr's Bay

Cudjoehead

St. John's

⑨

St. Peters

⑩

Bunkum Bay

Woodlands Bay

Kay Hill

CENTER HILLS

Salem

⑦

⑥

Old Towne

Old Road Bay

⑪ ⑫

Lime Kiln

spill down to the gray-sand beach on Old Road Bay. Each rondavel has a large bedroom, cable TV, phone, hair dryer, minifridge, spacious bathroom, and most have great views of the ocean. In the main building a large lounge and bar overlook the pool; the Wednesday-night barbecue, with steel bands and other entertainment, is an event well attended by locals and guests alike. In the adjacent sea-view restaurant, you can have a candlelight dinner of local and international specialties (the chef is one of the most skilled on the island). A 150-seat conference center serves as a theater and disco. For water-sports enthusiasts, there is scuba diving, snorkeling, and fishing. ⊠ *Box 65, Plymouth,* ☎ *809/491–5210 or 800/235–0709,* 𝕱𝔸𝕏 *809/491–4813. 12 rooms, 28 rondavels. Restaurant, bar, pool, 2 tennis courts, shuffleboard, water-sports center, game room, gift shop. AE, MC, V. EP, MAP.*

$$   🏨 **Flora Fountain Hotel.** This is a hotel for people coming on business (only 35% of the clientele are tourists) or for those who appreciate an old, rambling hotel in the heart of town. The two-story structure is built around an enormous fountain that's sometimes lighted at night, with small tables scattered in the inner courtyard. There are 18 plainly decorated but adequate rooms, all with tile bath, air-conditioning, most with balconies. All rooms have phones but not all have TVs, so ask if it's important to you. The restaurant has a chef from Bombay who serves simple sandwiches and fine Indian dishes. Friday night's Indian buffet includes several meat and fish dishes, at least two kinds of rice, vegetable and pork dishes with spices, *raita* (a yogurt sauce), and *samosa* (spicy meat patties). Children under 12 stay free when sharing the room with an adult. ⊠ *Box 373, Church Rd., Plymouth,* ☎ *809/491–6092,* 𝕱𝔸𝕏 *809/491–2568. 18 rooms. Restaurant, bar. AE, D, MC, V. EP, CP, MAP.*

$–$$   🏨 **Providence Estate House.** On an island where it is almost impossi-
★   ble to find good bed-and-breakfast accommodations, this two-unit guest house, perched on a bluff high above the ocean with spectacular views of St. Kitts, Nevis, and Redonda, stands out. The present owners lovingly restored the former plantation house, and the beautiful stone-and-wood building, with a wraparound veranda, is now one of the finest examples of traditional Caribbean architecture on the island. The two guest rooms—one has a bath as well as a shower and is considerably larger—are on the ground floor and open directly onto the pool area, where gleaming water is edged with tiles from Trinidad. Both rooms have the original timbered ceilings and massive stone walls, which keep them cool in the summer, and are decorated with red quarry tiles and pastel fabrics. If there is any drawback to this idyll, it is the location. The nearest restaurant is 3 miles away in Belham Valley, and the nearest beach is a hike down the hillside. But the owners are willing to make evening meals on request, and they have also installed a kitchenette by the pool, where you can prepare your own meals. A large breakfast of eggs, oatmeal, and fruits from the garden (in season) is included in the room rate. ⊠ *Providence Estate House, Montserrat,* ☎ *809/491–6476,* 𝕱𝔸𝕏 *809/491–8476. 2 rooms. Kitchenette, pool, cable TV. No credit cards. CP.*

$   🏨 **Belham Valley Hotel.** On a hillside overlooking Belham Valley and the Belham Valley River, this hotel has a cottage and two apartments (a studio and a newer two-bedroom). All have a stereo, cable TV, a fully equipped kitchen, and a phone; none are air-conditioned. It's the restaurant here that's the big draw, with its lovely views and great food (☞ Dining, *below*). The beach is an eight-minute walk away. ⊠ *Box 409, Plymouth,* ☎ *809/491–5553. 3 units. Restaurant, maid service. AE, MC. EP.*

**$**  ⚏ **Lime Court Apartments.** Right in the center of town, opposite the Parliament building, you'll find this slightly run-down, large white colonial-style apartment building. The downstairs apartments tend to be dark and airless, and with the sound of the generator and the puttering of the fridges, not very peaceful. But the large, well-equipped, two-bedroom, two-bath "penthouse," up a flight of steps at the top of the building, has a fine view from its balcony of the town's red rooftops and the sea beyond. It can sleep two couples and is reasonable at $45 per night. All apartments have kitchenettes with a stove and microwave, and private bathrooms (showers only). ⊠ *Box 250, Parliament St., Plymouth,* ☎ *809/491–3656. 8 apartments. Maid service, cable TV. AE, MC, V. EP.*

## Villas and Condominiums

Luxury villas sprang up all over Montserrat in the 1980s, and there's a great range to choose from if you want a do-it-yourself vacation on the island. All the villa developments are on the west coast of the island, within 20 minutes of Plymouth by car. The majority are in the districts of Old Towne, Olveston, and Woodlands. The latter is particularly noteworthy for its magnificent views of the ocean and its steep hillsides covered in lush vegetation. Prices are high for just two people (a one-bedroom is around $1,000 per week) but become more reasonable when the cost can be split among more people. Two-bedroom villas with a pool range from $1,000 to $2,400 per week; three-bedroom villas from $1,500 to $2,500; and four-bedroom villas from $2,500 to $3,000. There are villas of all sizes that are the ultimate in luxury and exceed even these prices. Off-season rates are as much as 50% lower (and usually negotiable), and some excellent bargains can be picked up by summer travelers. All villas come with maid service.

⚏ **Caribbean Connection Plus** (☎ 203/261–8603, FAX 203/261–8295) is a Stateside reservation service for about 50 one- to four-bedroom villas and some condos. It also has an on-island representative to ensure that all goes well.

⚏ **Isles Bay Plantation** (⊠ Box 64, Plymouth, ☎ 809/491–5248, FAX 809/491–5016; in London, ☎ FAX 0171/482–1071), known locally as the Beverly Hills of Montserrat, has the crème de la crème of Montserrat's villas. Each house is set on approximately ½ acre of tropical landscaped gardens, has its own 40-foot pool, and is only a 10-minute walk from the beach.

⚏ **Montserrat Enterprises Ltd** (⊠ Box 58, Marine Dr., Plymouth, ☎ 809/491–2431 [ask for Mr. Edwards], FAX 809/491–4660) has 22 villas in Old Towne, Woodlands, and Isles Bay.

⚏ **Neville Bradshaw Agencies** (⊠ Box 270, Plymouth, ☎ 809/491–5270, FAX 809/491–5069) has a wide range of villas, mostly in Old Towne and Isles Bay.

⚏ **Shamrock Villas** (⊠ Box 180, Plymouth, ☎ 809/491–2431) are one- and two-bedroom apartments and town-house condominiums in a hillside development minutes from Plymouth.

# Dining

Despite its size, Montserrat offers a variety of dining options to fit all budgets. Most of the more inexpensive eateries are found in small cafés, some of which look like the proverbial hole-in-the-wall. Don't be deceived, as most offer delicious Caribbean home cooking. The island also has a lively assortment of rum shops—the Caribbean version of local bars—packed with islanders on Friday nights; you can join in and get a drink and a simple meal.

Montserrat's national dish is goatwater stew, made with goat meat and vegetables and similar to Irish stew. Goat meat is strong but tasty. Mountain "chicken" (actually enormous frogs) is also a great favorite. Yams, breadfruit, christophines (a kind of squash), limes, mangoes, papayas, and a variety of seafood are served in most restaurants. Home-brewed ginger beer, one of the finest traditional drinks of the West Indies, is widely available.

## What to Wear
In general, neat casual clothing is the norm at lunch and dinner. Beach attire is too casual. Although jackets are not required, shorts and jeans are not acceptable at the fancier restaurants for dinner.

| CATEGORY | COST* |
| --- | --- |
| $$$ | over $30 |
| $$ | $20–$30 |
| $ | under $20 |

*per person, excluding drinks and service. If the service charge is not added to the bill, leave a 10%–15% tip.*

$$$  ✕ **Montserrat Springs Hotel.** The split-level cathedral-ceilinged dining room, enclosed on three sides, faces a large pool and a sundeck, beyond which you can see the ocean. A menu of West Indian and Continental cuisine includes an excellent goatwater stew, local snapper with a Creole sauce, grilled tenderloin steak, and an excellent Spanish omelet. The Friday Barbecue and Sunday buffet brunch are extremely popular and reservations are a must. ⊠ *Richmond Hill, Plymouth,* ☎ *809/491–2481. AE, MC, V.*

$$$  ✕ **Vue Pointe.** Candlelit dining in the hillside hotel's restaurant over-
★     looking the sea makes for a very romantic evening. There is a nightly five-course table d'hôte menu, or you can order à la carte. West Indian–style mountain "chicken", kingfish, beef Wellington, and red snapper with Creole sauce are favorites. For dessert, it's hard to choose between the lime pie and the guava cheesecake. The Wednesday-night barbecue, accompanied by music from a steel band, is a popular island event. ⊠ *Old Towne,* ☎ *809/491–5210. AE, MC, V.*

$$–$$$  ✕ **Belham Valley Hotel.** Considered by many to be the best restaurant
★     on the island, this former private home offers intimate, elegant dining. The best tables are on the open-air terrace; hung with ferns and croton plants, it looks down over picturesque Belham Valley and the lights of Isle Bay Hill. The sound of tree frogs and the rhythm of the ocean mingle with the clink of glasses and the recorded music of Stan Getz, Astrud Gilberto, and other jazz greats. Hibiscus tumbles over stone walls and sprouts from table vases; ceilings and floors are timbered. The beautiful setting is accompanied by one of the best menus on the island. Start with conch fritters or liver pâté, and progress to Seafood Delight (sautéed lobster, red snapper, and sea scallops in a vermouth sauce) or stuffed red snapper. Scrumptious desserts are mango or lime mousse, lemon cake, and a tropical fruit sundae with a ginger sauce. At lunchtime, the offerings are lighter: omelets, salads, and sandwiches. A Chinese menu is offered for lunch and dinner on Thursdays. The wine list is extensive. ⊠ *Old Towne,* ☎ *809/491–5553. Reservations essential for dinner. AE, MC, V. No lunch weekends.*

$$  ✕ **Emerald Café.** Dining is relaxed at 10 tables inside and on the terrace, where there are white tables shaded by blue umbrellas. Burgers, sandwiches, salads, and grilled chicken and fish are served at lunchtime. For dinner you can order tournedos sautéed in spicy butter, broiled or sautéed Caribbean lobster, T-bone steak, mountain chicken diablo, and giant swordfish steaks. The Island Coconut Pie and other homemade pastries are superb. There's also an ample list of liqueurs and wines,

a full bar, and entertainment on weekends. ✉ *Wapping, Plymouth,* ☎ *809/491–3821. MC. No lunch Sun.*

**$$** ✗ **Oasis.** A 200-year-old stone house is the setting for this charming restaurant. You can dine indoors in the intimate bar and lounge, but most choose the outdoor patio, which looks out onto colorful tropical flowers. Calypso mountain chicken, jumbo shrimp Provençale, red snapper with lime butter, and grilled sirloin steak are house specialties. Owners Eric and Mandy Finnamore are also well known for their British-style fish-and-chips. ✉ *Wapping, Plymouth,* ☎ *809/491–2328. No credit cards. Closed Wed.*

**$** ✗ **Blue Dolphin.** This is the place to come for superb mountain chicken
★ served with fresh local vegetables, the house specialty. The inside here may be short on ambience—the chairs are Naugahyde, and the menu is scrawled on a blackboard without prices or descriptions—but the seductive aromas wafting from the kitchen announce that the Blue Dolphin serves some of the best food on the island, including luscious pumpkin fritters and mouthwatering lobster. This eatery, set on a hill, also has a fabulous view of the town and sea. ✉ *Amersham,* ☎ *809/491–3263. No credit cards.*

**$** ✗ **Evergreen Restaurant.** This casual spot in downtown Plymouth is a good choice for local chicken, pizzas, and hamburgers. There are daily specials and fresh pastries. ✉ *Plymouth,* ☎ *809/491–3514. No credit cards.*

**$** ✗ **Golden Apple.** In this large, galleried stone building, you'll be served huge plates of good, local cooking. The restaurant's specialty is goatwater stew, cooked on weekends only, outside over an open fire. Souse; *pelau* (chicken-and-rice curry); conch, stewed or curried; and mountain chicken are also excellent. Tables covered with cheerful red-and-white-checked tablecloths add to the relaxed atmosphere. There's also a grocery store attached. ✉ *Cork Hill,* ☎ *809/491–2187. No credit cards.*

**$** ✗ **Mrs. Morgan's.** Friday and Saturday are goatwater-stew days at Mrs. Morgan's, and from 11:30 onward you can join the carloads of locals who make the trek up here to the north of the island to eat their fill. Order yourself a hearty bowl of the stew, which costs only E.C.$8 (U.S.$3.50), and plunk yourself down at one of the four picnic tables in the simple, unadorned room. The stew is just the way it should be— with the flesh falling off the bone, brimming with dumplings and innards. If that doesn't sound appetizing, try the souse, baked chicken, or any of the other down-home specialties. ✉ *Airport Rd., St. John's,* ☎ *809/491–5419. No credit cards.*

**$** ✗ **Niggy's.** In his previous life, the owner was a British character actor
★ in Hollywood. That was before he decided to trade the smell of greasepaint and the roar of the crowd for a place behind the bar in this extremely popular restaurant (the British governor eats here regularly). The setting is a simple clapboard cottage with yellow bella flowers trailing over the gate, and the food, served at picnic-style benches under a trellis of flowering plants, is excellent and a good value. Try the grilled steaks and chops, shrimp scampi, or one of the pasta specials. Inside at the bar, you'll be regaled with tales of Hollywood, and the whole place feels like a set for a Caribbean remake of *Casablanca*. There's entertainment weekends, and for those who want to stay over, there are two simple but clean rooms in the back. The property is a 10-minute drive from the center of Plymouth. ✉ *Kinsale,* ☎ *809/491–7489. No credit cards. No lunch.*

**$** ✗ **Spreadeagle.** This is a tiny place that you'll be glad you found if you visit Galway's Soufrière or Great Alps Falls. Peter "Bobb," the owner, keeps beer on ice and serves all sorts of beverages and light snacks. ✉ *German's Bay,* ☎ *809/491–7503. No credit cards.*

$　✕ **Ziggy's.** John and Marcia Punter have moved their very popular
★　restaurant to the Belham Valley area. It's larger now but still simply
decorated and still almost always full. This remains one of the best bistros
on the island. The owners create magical cuisine out of all the fruits
and vegetables that grow on the island, including ginger, nutmeg,
yams, plantain, christophine, and coconuts. Despite the crowds, this
restaurant has retained their "one seating per evening" policy. ⊠ *Belham Valley,* ☎ *809/491–8282. No credit cards. Closed Wed.*

# Beaches

The sand on many of the **Montserrat beaches** often surprises visitors
because of it's color. Sand on the south coast is of volcanic origin; usually referred to as black, it's actually light to dark gray. On the northwest coast, the sand is beige or white.

### Northwest Coast
Good swimming waters can be found at **Carr's Bay,** a gray-sand beach,
which is generally calm.

Tucked between two hills is **Little Bay,** with a secluded, light gray
beach. Nearby reefs offer excellent diving but heavy swells are sometimes present. Although you can drive to this beach some prefer to take
a sailboat here.

**Rendezvous Bay** is Montserrat's only white-sand beach. It's a long, secluded beach that is good for swimming and walking. It is accessible
by boat or by a 45-minute hike over a hill.

### Southwest Coast
Picnic tables, changing rooms, and outside showers dress up **Fox's Bay,**
just outside of Plymouth. It's a gray-sand beach and there are numerous reefs just offshore. A bird sanctuary is nearby.

**Old Road Bay** is a long stretch of gray sand several miles north of Plymouth with a beach bar, water sports, and a dive shop. This is a calm
swimming beach with excellent snorkeling.

**Isles Bay,** several miles north of Plymouth, offers walkers a long stretch
of gray sand and a view of the island's only golf course.

**Sugar Bay,** to the south of Plymouth, is a beach of fine gray volcanic
sand. The Yacht Club overlooks this beach.

# Outdoor Activities and Sports

### Boating
**Captain Martin** (☎ 809/491–5738) takes guests out on his 46-foot trimaran for a full-day sail to the white-sand beach at **Rendezvous Bay**
for swimming and snorkeling at the nearby reef. The boat leaves about
10 AM and returns about 5 PM; the cost is $45 and includes an open
bar and snorkeling equipment. **Vue Pointe** hotel (☎ 809/491–5210)
offers sailing and snorkeling excursions to Rendezvous Bay, Little Bay,
and Carr's Bay. The cost is $25 a person and includes a sandwich lunch
and snorkeling equipment.

### Golf
The **Montserrat Golf Course** (☎ 809/491–5220), in the picturesque Belham Valley, is "slope rated" 116 by the USGA (in other words, it's incredibly hilly) and must be one of the few golf courses in the world
that can list gopher holes and iguanas among its hazards. The course
plays as a true 18-hole golf course, with 11 greens and 18 tees. Four

fairways run along the ocean. The rest are up hill and down dale. Watch out for the iguanas—they collect golf balls.

## Hiking

Three mountain ranges, rain forests, and volcanic sulphur springs provide numerous hiking opportunities. There are many trails; guides are suggested for the longer and more difficult ones. To hire a knowledgeable guide, contact Cecil Cassell at the **Montserrat Tour Guides Association** (☎ 809/491–3160), call the department of tourism, or ask at your hotel. Be sure to wear sturdy rubber-soled shoes.

## Mountain Biking

At **Island Bikes** (✉ Harney St., Plymouth, ☎ 809/491–5552, FAX 809/491–5552), Butch Miller and Susan Goldin, the bustling, can-do Americans who run the outfit, are self-confessed biking junkies and know the island like the backs of their own saddles. Rentals are $25 a day, $140 a week. The couple also conduct guided tours which include refreshments and a sag wagon for the faint of heart, offer van tours that drop 4 to 12 people off at a designated area (such as the top of Windy Hill), and can arrange bed-and-bike package tours. They sponsor two international cycle races each year and run the Island Bikes Mountain Bike Training Center, which offers off-road practice areas, downhill slalom areas, and numerous steep descent and ascent trails.

## Sailing, Snorkeling, and Scuba Diving

Snorkeling equipment is provided on the day cruises to the white-sand coves on the west coast; boats usually have an open bar. Arrangements can be made through the **Vue Pointe** hotel (☎ 809/491–5210) or **Captain Martin** (☎ 809/491–5738).

**Sea Wolf Diving School** (☎ 809/491–7807) in Plymouth and **Aquatic Discoveries** (☎ 809/491–3474), next to the Vue Pointe hotel, both offer one- or two-tank dives, night dives, and instruction from PADI-certified instructors. Costs are about $40 for a one-tank dive and $60 for a two-tank dive. Aquatic Discoveries also offers snorkel tours, whale-watching trips, and deep-sea-fishing excursions.

**Danny Water Sports** (☎ 809/491–5645), operating out of the Vue Pointe hotel, rents snorkel equipment and Windsurfers and also offers fishing, Sunfish sailing, and waterskiing.

## Spectator Sports

Cricket is the national passion. Cricket and soccer matches are held from February through June in **Sturge Park. Shamrock Car Park** is the venue for netball and basketball games. Contact the tourist board (☎ 809/491–2230) for schedules.

## Tennis

There are lighted tennis courts at the **Vue Pointe** hotel (☎ 809/491–5210), the **Montserrat Springs Hotel** (☎ 809/491–2481), and the **Montserrat Golf Club** (☎ 809/491–5220).

## Windsurfing

Contact **Danny Water Sports** (☎ 809/491–5645) to rent boards (about $10 per 45 minutes).

# Shopping

Montserrat's sea-island cotton is famous for its high quality, but, unfortunately, there is only a limited amount and it is not cheap. There are good buys on hand-turned pottery, straw goods, hand-screened prints, ceramic jewelry, and jewelry made from shells and coral. Montserratian stamps can be purchased at the post office or at the Philatelic Bureau, just across the bridge in Wapping. Two lip-smacking local food products are Cassell's hot sauce, available at most supermarkets, and Perk's Punch, an effervescent rum-based concoction manufactured by **J. W. R. Perkins, Inc.** (☎ 809/491–2596).

## Good Buys

### CLOTHES

The **Jus' Looking** (✉ George St., Plymouth, ☎ 809/491–4076; small branch at airport, open in afternoons only, ☎ 809/491–4040) boutique features "sculpted," hand-painted pillows from Antigua; painted and lacquered boxes from the Dutch West Indies; Sunny Caribbee's jams, jellies, and packaged spices from the British Virgin Islands (including an Arawak love potion and a hangover cure); special teas; and Caribelle Batik's line of richly colored fabrics, shirts, skirts, pants, and dresses. The shop also has an excellent selection of local poetry and history books.

**Montserrat Shirts** (✉ Parliament St., ☎ 809/491–2892) has a good selection of men's tropical cotton shirts, plus T-shirts and sandals for the whole family. They will custom screen T-shirts.

**Etcetera** (✉ John St., ☎ 809/491–3299) is a little shop carrying colorful, lightweight cotton batik dresses, plus hats, beachwear, and a small but fine selection of local crafts. (If you're lucky, you may see someone making a hat of coconut palm fronds.)

The **Montserrat Sea Island Cotton Co.** (✉ corner of George and Strand Sts., Plymouth, ☎ 809/491–7009), long famous for its cotton creations, has dresses, shirts, and other clothing items plus table linens, much of it made from local sea island cotton.

### CRAFTS

The **Tapestries of Montserrat** (✉ Parliament St., ☎ 809/491–2520), on the second floor of the John Bull Shop, offers a floor-to-ceiling display of hand-tufted creations—from wall hangings and pillow covers to tote bags and rugs—all with fanciful yarn adornments of flowers, carnival figures, animals, and birds. Owners Gerald and Charlie Handley will even help you create your own design for a small additional fee.

At **Carol's Corner** (✉ Vue Pointe hotel, ☎ 809/491–5210), Carol Osborne sells everything related to Montserrat—stamps, copper bookmarks, paintings, the *Montserrat Cookbook,* Frane Lessac's books of prose, as well as resortwear.

Drop by **Dutcher's Studio** (✉ Olveston, ☎ 809/491–5253) to see hand-cut, hand-painted objects made from glass, ceramics, and old bottles, and some very appealing ceramic jewelry. If Paula Dutcher is there, ask about the morning iguana feeding at her house. Anywhere from 5 to 50 reptiles converge on her lawn, sunning themselves and eating hibiscus from your hand.

**Island House** (✉ John St., ☎ 809/491–3938) stocks a fine collection of Haitian art, Caribbean prints, and clay pottery.

**Sunset Gallery** (✉ Parliament St., ☎ 809/491–5552) carries an excellent selection of local watercolors, prints, sculptures, and crafts.

# Nightlife

The hotels offer regularly scheduled barbecues and steel bands, and the small restaurants feature live entertainment in the form of calypso, reggae, rock, rhythm and blues, and soul.

**Niggy's** (✉ Kinsale, ☎ 809/491–7489) usually has a vocalist Friday and Saturday nights, and there is often live jazz on weekends. The **Yacht Club** (✉ Wapping, ☎ 809/491–2237) has live island music on Friday, while the **Plantation Club** (✉ Wapping, upstairs over the Oasis, ☎ 809/491–2892) is a lively late-night place with taped rhythm and blues, soul, and *soca* (Caribbean music). The **Inn on Sugar Bay** (✉ Sugar Bay, ☎ 809/491–5067) has local bands entertaining most evenings. **La Cave** (✉ Evergreen Dr., Plymouth, no phone), featuring West Indian–style disco and Caribbean and international music, is popular among the young locals. **Nepcoden** (✉ Weekes, no phone), with its ultraviolet lights, peace signs, and black walls, is a throwback to the '60s. In this cellar restaurant you can eat rotis or chicken for $6. **Colors** (✉ Fox's Bay, no phone) is one of the island's most popular nightclubs, with live bands and lots of dancing on weekends.

# Exploring Montserrat

*Numbers in the margin correspond to points of interest on the Montserrat map.*

SIGHTS TO SEE

**Bamboo Forest.** The most likely place to spot the Montserrat National Bird, *iaterus oberi*, or Montserrat oriole, found nowhere else on earth, is in the Bamboo Forest, a large tract of semi–rain forest inhabited by birds, frogs, and plants. It is home to many of the 100 species of birds that visit Montserrat. You will also see bromeliads, tulip and breadfruit trees, and a plethora of other tropical plants. Because no roads lead into the area and there are no marked paths, you are advised to go with a guide. The most knowledgeable guide is **Joseph Peters,** who will take you on a two- to three-hour tour and fill you in on the wildlife and botany. He can be reached at his home (☎ 809/491–6850) or via the Department of Tourism in Plymouth. You can also call the **Department of Agriculture** (☎ 809/491–2546). ✉ *South Soufrière Hills*

**6 Chance's Peak.** The island's highest point pokes up 3,002 feet through the rain forests. The climb to the top is arduous, but there are now 2,000 makeshift stairs (thanks to Cable & Wireless, who added the wooden stairs after Hurricane Hugo to ease access to their mountaintop radio tower). If you do make it to the top, what little breath you may have left will be taken away by the view, *if* the clouds have parted. (Go early in the morning, when the clouds are least likely to be there.) ✉ *Soufrière Hills via Old Fort Rd.*

**4 Fox's Bay Bird Sanctuary.** Green herons, yellow crowned night herons, rare blue herons, coots, egrets, mangrove cuckoos, and kingfishers plus many lizards and iguanas call this a 15-acre mangrove swamp home. The marked trail through the sanctuary begins right near Fox's Bay beach. ✉ *Grove Rd.*

**Galway's Plantation.** Montserrat's most intact historical site is the 1,300-acre plantation built in the late 17th century by the prosperous Irishmen John and Henry Blake, who came to Montserrat from Galway. It has been earmarked as an important archaeological site by the Smithsonian. Amateur archaeologists come here annually in the summer, and the sugar boiling house and parts of both a wind-driven and cattle-driven sugar mill have been partially restored. ✉ *Old Fort Rd.*

**7 Galway's Soufrière.** The most spectacular scene on Montserrat is probably a 13-acre area of boiling hot springs and fumaroles of gurgling, bubbling (and quite smelly) molten sulfur. Getting here involves both driving on a rugged road and a fairly strenuous half-hour hike and many people hire guides, which can be arranged through the

**Montserrat Tour Guides Association.** Everyone's heard the phrase "so hot you could fry an egg on it." Here your guide will almost certainly fry an egg to demonstrate the intense heat of the rocks. ⊠ *Soufrière Hills via Old Fort Rd.*

**8** **Great Alps Waterfall.** Montserrat's White River creates dramatic falls as it plunges 70 feet down a rocky mountain wall and splashes into a shallow pool at the Great Alps Waterfall. It's a moderately strenuous 30- to 45-minute hike through thick rain forests to get there and for a refreshing break, just step in the pool and let the waters cascade right over you. ⊠ *Old Fort Rd. at St. Patrick's Village.*

**3** **Montserrat Museum.** A restored sugar mill on Richmond Hill just north of town is a showcase for Montserrat history. Here you will find the museum, with its excellent collection of maps, historical records, artifacts (including some Arawak and Carib items), and all sorts of memorabilia pertaining to the island's growth and development. ⊠ *Richmond Hill,* ☎ *809/491–5443.* ⊡ *Free (donations accepted).* ☉ *Sun. and Wed. 2:30–5 (but call to be sure).*

**1** **Plymouth.** The islands biggest town is neat and clean, its narrow streets lined with trim Georgian structures built mostly of stones that came from Dorset as ballast on old sailing vessels. On the south side, a bridge over Fort Ghaut ("gut," or ravine) leads to Wapping, where most of the restaurants are located.

It's hard not to notice the residence of the governor of Montserrat, **Government House,** which is a frilly Victorian house, painted green with white trim and decorated with a shamrock. It dates from the 18th century and is set amidst extraordinarily lovely gardens. Although the public is not allowed inside, everyone is welcome to walk through the beautiful landscaping surrounding the building. ⊠ *Peebles St., no phone.* ⊡ *Free.* ☉ *Mon., Tues., Thurs., Fri. 10–noon.*

Great piles of local vegetables and fruits and vendors in brightly colored outfits mark the **Plymouth Market,** where islanders bring their produce on Friday and Saturday mornings. ⊠ *Parliament St.* ☉ *Fri., Sat. 7–noon.*

**2** **St. Anthony's Church.** Just north of town, this majestic structure built of gray stone is one of the prettiest churches on Montserrat. It was consecrated sometime between 1623 and 1666 and was rebuilt in 1730 following one of the many clashes between the French and the English in the area. Two silver chalices displayed in the church were donated by freed slaves after emancipation in 1834. ⊠ *Hwy. 2.*

**5** **St. George's Fort.** The fort itself is overgrown and in ruin but the great view of Plymouth from the hilltop is well worth the trip. You can hike or drive. ⊠ *Hwy 4.*

## Monserrat A to Z

### Arriving and Departing

BY PLANE

Although Antigua is not the only gateway, it's the best way to reach Montserrat. **BWIA** (☎ 800/538–2942) flies direct on Wednesday and Friday (plus Sundays in season) to Antigua from New York and on Monday, Wednesday, Thursday, and Friday from Miami; it also has regularly scheduled nonstop service from Toronto, Canada, and Heathrow Airport, London. **American Airlines** (☎ 800/433–7300) has connecting service from a number of U.S. cities through San Juan, Puerto Rico. **Air Canada** (☎ 800/776–3000) offers service from Toronto; **British Airways** (in Britain, ☎ 0181/897–4000; in the U.S., ☎ 800/247–9297) from Gatwick Airport, London; and **Lufthansa** (☎ 800/645–3880 in the U.S.) transports visitors from Frankfurt via Puerto Rico.

From Antigua's V. C. Bird International Airport, you can make your connections with **LIAT** (☎ 809/491–2533 or 800/253–5011) or **Montserrat Airways** (☎ 809/491–5342 or 809/491–6494) for the 15-minute flight to Montserrat.

You will land on the 3,400-foot runway at Blackburne Airport, on the Atlantic coast, about 11 miles from Plymouth.

FROM THE AIRPORT

Taxis meet every flight; the government-regulated fare from the airport to Plymouth is E.C.$29 (U.S.$11).

## Currency

The official currency is the Eastern Caribbean dollar (E.C.$), often called beewee. At press time, the exchange rate was E.C.$2.67 to U.S.$1. U.S. dollars are readily accepted, but you'll often receive change in beewees. Note: Prices quoted here are in U.S. dollars unless noted otherwise.

## Emergencies

**Police:** ☎ 999 or 809/491–2555.

**Hospital:** There is a 24-hour emergency room at **Glendon Hospital** (✉ Plymouth, ☎ 809/491–2552).

**Pharmacies: Lee's Pharmacy** (✉ Evergreen Dr., Plymouth, ☎ 809/491–3274) and **Daniel's Pharmacy** (✉ George St., Plymouth, ☎ 809/491–2908).

## Getting Around

CAR RENTALS

The island has more than 115 miles of paved (but potholed) roads. Unless you're uncomfortable about driving on the left, you won't have any trouble exploring. You'll need a valid driver's license, plus a Montserrat license, which is available at the airport or the Treasury Department on Strand Street in Plymouth weekdays 8:30–2:30. The fee is E.C.$30 (U.S.$12). Rental cars cost about $35–$40 per day. The smaller companies, whose prices are generally 10%–25% cheaper, will negotiate, particularly off-season. **Pauline Car Rentals** (✉ Plymouth, ☎ 809/491–2345) and **Jefferson's Car Rental** (✉ Dagenham, ☎ 809/491–2126) are local rental companies. Other agencies are **Reliable** (✉ Plymouth, ☎ 809/491–6990), and **Ethelyne's Car Rental** (✉ Plymouth, ☎ 809/491–2855).

MOUNTAIN BIKES

Montserrat is great mountain-bike country, with trails rated among the 50 best in the world. It's small, with relatively traffic-free roads and lots of challenging hills to try out all those gears. Potholes will present a constant challenge, as will the heat and steep gradients. Even so, biking is a great way to get around this island, where the majority of facilities, shops, and accommodations are concentrated in a small area on the west coast. (☞ Outdoor Activities and Sports, *above*).

TAXIS

Taxis, private vehicles, or the M11 (a play on the local registration numbers, meaning your own two legs) are the main means of transport on the island. Taxis are always available at the airport, the main hotels, and the taxi stand in Plymouth (☎ 809/491–2261). The Tourist Board publishes a list of taxi fares to most destinations. Be sure to agree with your driver on the fare in advance and know whether you have agreed to pay in E.C. or U.S.D.

### Guided Tours

Guides are recommended when you are heading to Mount Chance, Galway's Soufrière, and the Great Alps Falls. Prices for two people range from $10 to $30. Guides and tours can be arranged by calling Cecil Cassell, president of the **Montserrat Tour Guide Association** (☎ 809/491–3160, FAX 809/491–2052). Or you can call **John Ryner** (☎ 809/491–2190) and the aptly named **Be-Beep Taylor** (☎ 809/491–3787). Prices (fixed by the department of tourism) are E.C.$30 per hour (U.S.$12) or E.C.$130–$150 (U.S.$50–$58) for a five-hour day tour. Refreshments are extra. For further information, contact the Tourist Board.

### Language

It's English with more of a lilt than a brogue. You'll also hear a patois that's spoken on most of the islands.

### Opening and Closing Times

Most shops are open Monday to Saturday 8–4 and a good number close at noon on Wednesday and close other weekdays from noon–1. Banking hours vary slightly from bank to bank but are generally open at the minimum from Monday to Thursday 8–3 and Friday 3–5.

### Passports and Visas

U.S., Canadian, and British citizens only need proof of citizenship, such as a passport, a notarized birth certificate, or a voter registration card plus a photo ID, such as a driver's license. A driver's license by itself is *not* sufficient. All visitors must hold an ongoing or return ticket.

### Precautions

Ask for permission before taking pictures. Some residents may be reluctant photographic subjects, and they will appreciate your courtesy.

Most Montserratians frown at the sight of skimpily dressed tourists; do not risk offending them by strolling around town in short shorts and swimsuits (which are not acceptable even with a cover-up).

### Taxes and Service Charges

Hotels collect a 7% government tax and add a 10% service charge. Most restaurants add a 10%–15% service charge. If restaurants do not add the service charge, it's customary to leave a 10% or 15% tip. Taxi drivers should be given a 10% tip. The departure tax is E.C.$25 (about U.S.$9).

### Telephones and Mail

To call Montserrat from the United States, dial area code 809 and access code 491 plus the local four-digit number. International direct dial is available on the island; both local and long-distance calls come through clearly. To call locally on the island, you need to dial the seven-digit number, the first three digits of which are always 491.

Airmail letters and postcards to the United States and Canada cost E.C.$1.15 each. Montserrat is one of several Caribbean islands whose stamps are of interest to collectors. You can buy them at the main post office in Plymouth, which is open Monday, Tuesday, Thursday, Friday 8:15–3:55 and Wednesday, Saturday 8:15–11:25 AM.

### Visitor Information

You can get information about Montserrat through the **Montserrat Tourist Office** (✉ 775 Park Ave., Huntington, NY 11743, 516/425–0900) and the **Caribbean Tourism Organization** (✉ 20 E. 46th St., New York, NY 10017, ☎ 212/682–0435).

On Montserrat, the **Montserrat Tourist Board** (✉ Church Rd., Plymouth, ☎ 809/491–2230) is open weekdays 8–noon and 1–4.

# 17 Puerto Rico

Updated by
Jonathan Runge

**F**EW CITIES IN THE CARIBBEAN are as steeped in Spanish tradition as Puerto Rico's Old San Juan. Originally built as a fortress enclave, the old city has myriad attractions, including restored 16th-century buildings, museums, art galleries, bookstores, and 200-year-old houses with balustraded balconies of filigreed wrought iron overlooking narrow cobblestone streets. This Spanish tradition also spills over into the island's countryside, from its festivals celebrated in honor of various patron saints in the little towns to the *paradores,* inexpensive but accommodating inns whose concept originated in Spain.

Puerto Rico boasts hundreds of beaches with every imaginable water sport and acres of golf courses and tennis courts. It has, in San Juan's sophisticated Condado and Isla Verde areas, glittering hotels; flashy, Las Vegas–style shows; casinos; and frenetic discos. It has the ambience of the Old World in the seven-square-block area of the old city and in its quiet colonial towns. Out in the countryside lie its natural attractions, including the extraordinary, 28,000-acre Caribbean National Forest, more familiarly known as the El Yunque rain forest, with 100-foot-high trees (more than 240 species of them) and dramatic mountain ranges. You can hike through forest reserves laced with trails, go spelunking in vast caves, and explore coffee plantations and sugar mills. Having seen every sight on the island, you can then do further exploring on the islands of Culebra, Vieques, Icacos, and Mona, where aquatic activities, such as snorkeling and scuba diving, prevail.

Puerto Rico, 110 miles long and 35 miles wide, was populated by several tribes of Indians when Columbus landed on the island on his second voyage in 1493. In 1508, Juan Ponce de León, the frustrated seeker of the Fountain of Youth, established a settlement on the island and became its first governor, and in 1521, he founded Old San Juan. For three centuries, the French, Dutch, and English tried unsuccessfully to wrest the island from Spain. In 1897, Spain granted the island dominion status. In 1899, as a result of the Spanish American War, Spain ceded the island to the United States, and in 1917, Puerto Ricans became U.S. citizens. In 1952, Puerto Rico became a semiautonomous commonwealth territory of the United States.

If you're a U.S. citizen, you need neither passport nor visa when you land at the bustling Luis Muñoz Marín International Airport, outside San Juan. You don't have to clear customs, and you don't have to explain yourself to an immigration official. English is widely spoken, though the official language is Spanish.

## Lodging

Accommodations on Puerto Rico come in all shapes and sizes. Self-contained luxury resorts cover hundreds of acres. San Juan's high-rise beachfront hotels likewise cater to the cruise-ship and casino crowd; several target the business traveler. Out on the island, the government-sponsored paradores are lodgings modeled after Spain's successful parador system. Some are rural inns, some offer motel-style (no-frill) apartments, and some are large hotels. They are required to meet certain standards, such as proximity to a sightseeing attraction or beach and a kitchen serving native cuisine. Parador prices range from $50 to $125 for a double room. Reservations for all paradores can be made by calling 800/443–0266 in the United States, 787/721–2884 in San Juan, or 800/981–7575 elsewhere in Puerto Rico. They are a phenomenal bargain but tend to get noisy and raucous on weekends, when families descend from the cities for a minivacation.

Most hotels in Puerto Rico operate on the European Plan (EP). In some larger hotels, however, packages are available that include several or all meals, while others offer all-inclusive deals. Also, beware when booking hotels outside of San Juan that rates most often do not include airport transfers. Be sure to ask if the hotel offers transportation, the cost, and if advance arrangements are necessary.

| CATEGORY | COST* |
|----------|-------|
| $$$$ | over $225 |
| $$$ | $150–$225 |
| $$ | $75–$150 |
| $ | under $75 |

*All prices are for a standard double room for two, excluding 7% tax (9% for hotels with casinos) and 10%–15% service charge.*

## Old San Juan

**$$–$$$**   🏨 **Gallery Inn.** Owners Jan D'Esopo and Manuco Gandia restored this
★   rambling, classically Spanish house, one of the oldest private residences in the area, and turned it into an inn. It's full of quirky architectural details—winding, uneven stairs; private balconies; a music room with a Steinway grand piano; lots of public rooms, areas, and decks to hide out with a book; and small interior gardens. The rooms are individually decorated and have telephones but no televisions; most are air-conditioned. Among the best rooms are Terrasina and Jonathan (all the rooms are named after Jan's children and grandchildren). Views from the rooftop patio are some of the best in the old city—a panorama of the El Morro and San Cristóbal forts and the Atlantic. Galería San Juan, a small gallery and working studio in the inn, features work in various medias by Jan D'Esopo, Bruno Lucchesi, and Teresa Spinner—sculpture and silk screen prints fill nearly every nook and cranny of the inn. There's even a package available that combines a five-night stay with the creation of your portrait bust. There is no restaurant, but meals can be cooked for groups upon request. ✉ *204–206 Calle Norzagaray, 00901,* ☎ *787/722–1808,* 𝐅𝐀𝐗 *787/724–7360. 16 rooms and suites. Self-service bar. AE, MC, V. CP.*

## San Juan

**$$$$**   🏨 **Caribe Hilton International.** Built in 1949, this property occupies 17
★   acres on Puerta de Tierra. Rooms have been modernized and refurbished over the years and have a crisp, pastel decor and balconies with ocean or lagoon views; the higher the floor, the better the view. The Tower rooms, however, could use freshening up. Be sure to ask for a room in the main part of the hotel. Executive levels provide services such as private check-in and checkout, complimentary evening cocktails, and complimentary Continental breakfast for business travelers. The spacious atrium lobby—a hub of activity—is decorated with rose marble, waterfalls, and lavish tropical plants. Restaurants include Batey del Pescador for seafood and Peacock Paradise for Chinese cuisine. The hotel has San Juan's only private beach, complete with a boardwalk at its edge. ✉ *Box 1872, San Juan 00902,* ☎ *787/721–0303 or 800/468–8585,* 𝐅𝐀𝐗 *787/724–6992. 672 rooms and suites. 6 restaurants, air-conditioning, 2 pools, 6 tennis courts, exercise room, racquetball, squash, beach, casino, business services. AE, D, DC, MC, V. EP, MAP.*

**$$$$**   🏨 **Condado Plaza Hotel and Casino.** The Atlantic and the Condado Lagoon border this property. Two wings, appropriately named Ocean and Lagoon, are connected by an enclosed, elevated walkway over Avenida Ashford. Standard rooms have walk-in closets and separate

Pta. Agujereada
Pta. Borinquén
Bahía de Aguadilla
Pta. Gorda

Isabela

Puerto de Tortuguero
Cerro Gordo

2 — Quebradillas — Camuy — 22 — 13 Arecibo — Vega Baja
10
129 — Río Abajo Forest — Manatí — 2 — Maricao

14 Aguadilla
Aguada
23 15 Rincón — 115 — 27 28
24 — San Sebastián — 111 — 12
25 — Bahía de Añasco
26

Mayagüez
16 TO MONA ISLAND — 17 — 102 — 105 — Maricao — Adjuntas — Toro Negro Forest
29
30
31 — Cabo Rojo — 102 — 19 — 33 — Juana Díaz — Coamo — 41
32 — 18 — San Germán — Yáuco — 10 — 14 — 52
Joyuda Beach
Boquerón Beach — 20 — 101 — La Parguera — Guayanilla — Santa Isabel — Bahía de Rincón
Boquerón — 116 — Guánica
Bahía Salinas — Bahía Sucia — 34 — 35 — 22
Pta. Jagüey — 21 — Ensenada Las Pardas — Caña Gorda — 37 38 39 40 — Ponce

San Sebastián — 111

Utuado — 11 — Jayuya — 149 — 36

Caribbean Sea

N

0 — 20 miles
0 — 30 km

---

**Exploring**
Aguadilla, **14**
Arecibo Observatory, **13**
Bacardi Rum Plant, **3**
Barrilito Rum Plant, **2**
Bayamón, **4**
Boquerón, **20**

Las Cabezas de San Juan Nature Reserve, **7**
Cabo Rojo, **18**
Caguana Indian Ceremonial Park, **11**
Caparra Ruins, **1**
Caribbean National Forest (El Yunque), **5**
Culebra, **9**
Fajardo, **8**

Luquillo Beach, **6**
Mayagüez, **17**
Mona Island, **16**
Phosphorescent Bay, **21**
Ponce, **22**
Rincón, **15**
Río Camuy Cave Park, **12**
San Germán, **19**

Vieques, **10**

**Dining**
Anchor's Inn, **45**
Black Eagle, **26**
El Bohío, **31**
La Casona de Serafín, **30**
Horned Dorset Primavera, **27**

**KEY**

🚢 Ferry

❶ Exploring Sites

㉓ Hotels and Restaurants

Lazy Parrot, **25**
Lupita's, **37**
El Molino del Quijote Restaurante, **23**
Pastrami Palace, **24**
Restaurant El Ancla, **39**

**Lodging**
Casa del Francés, **50**

El Conquistador Resort and Country Club, **44**
Copamarina Beach Resort, **35**
Crow's Nest, **47**
Hacienda Tamarindo, **49**
Horned Dorset Primavera, **27**
Hotel Melia, **40**

Hyatt Dorado Beach, **43**
Hyatt Regency Cerromar Beach, **42**
Inn on the Blue Horizon, **48**
Lemontree Waterfront Cottages, **28**
Mayagüez Hilton and Casino, **29**
Palmas del Mar, **46**

Parador Baños de Coamo, **41**
Parador Boquemar, **32**
Parador Hacienda Gripiñas, **36**
Parador Oasis, **33**
Parador Villa Parguera, **34**
Ponce Hilton and Casino, **38**

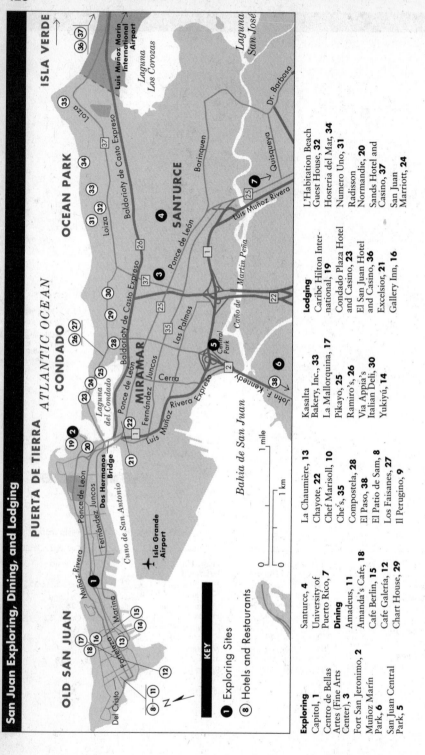

# San Juan Exploring, Dining, and Lodging

428

**Exploring**
Capitol, 1
Centro de Bellas
Artes (Fine Arts
Center), 3
Fort San Jeronimo, 2
Muñoz Marín
Park, 6
San Juan Central
Park, 5

Santurce, 4
University of
Puerto Rico, 7

**Dining**
Amadeus, 11
Amanda's Cafe, 18
Cafe Berlin, 15
Cafe Galería, 12
Chart House, 29

La Chaumière, 13
Chayote, 22
Chef Marisoll, 10
Che's, 35
Compostela, 28
El Paso, 38
El Patio de Sam, 8
Los Faisanes, 27
Il Perugino, 9

Kasalta
Bakery, Inc., 33
La Mallorquina, 17
Pikayo, 25
Ramiro's, 26
Via Appia's
Italian Deli, 30
Yukiyú, 14

**Lodging**
Caribe Hilton Inter-
national, 19
Condado Plaza Hotel
and Casino, 23
El San Juan Hotel
and Casino, 36
Excelsior, 21
Gallery Inn, 16

L'Habitation Beach
Guest House, 32
Hosteria del Mar, 34
Numero Uno, 31
Radisson
Normandie, 20
Sands Hotel and
Casino, 37
San Juan
Marriott, 24

**KEY**

Exploring Sites

Hotels and Restaurants

dressing areas. There are a variety of suites, including spa suites with oversize Jacuzzis, and a fully equipped business center. The Plaza Club floor has 24-hour concierge service and a private lounge, and guests there receive complimentary Continental breakfast, afternoon hors d'oeuvres, and evening coffee. The Ocean wing sits on a small strip of public beach, and there are two pools. This is the sister hotel of the El San Juan resort, and guests have access to all the facilities there via a complimentary shuttle bus (the bus will also drop passengers off in Old San Juan). Dining options include Tony Roma's (a branch of the American chain) and an informal restaurant poolside. ⊠ *999 Av. Ashford, Condado 00902,* ☎ *787/721–1000 or 800/468–8588,* 𝔽𝔸𝕏 *787/722– 7955. 589 rooms and suites. 7 restaurants, 3 bars, air-conditioning, 5 pools (1 saltwater), hot tub, 2 tennis courts, health club, water-sports center, casino, business services. AE, D, DC, MC, V. EP, MAP.*

**$$$$** ⊞ **El San Juan Hotel and Casino.** An immense chandelier illuminates
★ the hand-carved mahogany paneling, rose marble, and French tapestries in the huge lobby of this 12-acre resort on the Isla Verde beach. The casino is right off the lobby. You'll be hard pressed to decide if you want a suite in the main tower, with whirlpool bath and wet bar; a garden lanai room, with private patio and whirlpool bath; or a casita, with a sunken Roman bath. (Some of the tower rooms have no balcony or ocean view; be sure to check.) All rooms have CD player, three phones, TV with VCR, minibar, and walk-in closets with an iron and board. Dark rattan furnishings are complemented by rich carpets and tropical-print spreads and drapes. This luxurious hotel attracts a money-eyed mix of international business and leisure travelers. The posh Dar Tiffany restaurant, an oasis of potted palms, etched glass, and Tiffany lamps, serves impeccable Continental fare. The intimate, romantic La Piccola Fontana is one of San Juan's better Italian restaurants. Don't miss the informal rooftop bar; watching the sunset from here is a splendid end to a day of sightseeing. ⊠ *Av. Isla Verde, Box 2872, San Juan 00902,* ☎ *787/791–1000 or 800/468–2818,* 𝔽𝔸𝕏 *787/791–0390. 389 rooms. 5 restaurants, 8 bars, air-conditioning, minibars, accessible rooms for people with disabilities, no-smoking rooms, in-room VCRs, 2 pools (1 with swim-up bar), children's pool, 3 hot tubs, 3 tennis courts, health club, water-sports center, shops, casino, dance club, recreation room, concierge, business services, shuttle bus to Condado Plaza Hotel and Old San Juan. AE, DC, MC, V. EP, MAP.*

**$$$$** ⊞ **San Juan Marriott.** The red neon sign atop San Juan's newest hotel
★ is a beacon to its excellent Condado location. The hotel opened in January 1995 and has been the keystone to the revival of tourism in the Condado. Rooms have soothing pastel carpeting, flowered spreads, attractive tropical artwork on the walls, and balconies overlooking the ocean, the pool, or both. The staff has been well trained and is both courteous and friendly. Restaurants include Tuscany, for northern Italian cuisine, and the more casual La Vista, popular for dining alfresco. On weekends, there's live entertainment in the enormous lobby, which, combined with the persistent ringing of slot machines from the adjoining casino, makes the area quite noisy (rooms are soundproofed). Gorgeous Condado beach is right outside, as is a large pool area. The hotel's spa/gym is the best of any resort in Puerto Rico. ⊠ *1309 Av. Ashford, San Juan 00907,* ☎ *787/722–7000 or 800/228–9290,* 𝔽𝔸𝕏 *787/722– 6800. 510 rooms, 15 suites. 3 restaurants, 2 lounges, air-conditioning, no-smoking rooms, pool, beauty salon, hot tub, sauna, 2 tennis courts, health club, casino, video games, children's programs, business services, meeting rooms. AE, D, DC, MC, V. EP, MAP, FAP.*

**$$$$** ⊞ **Sands Hotel and Casino.** One of Puerto Rico's largest casinos glit-
★ ters just off the lobby, stunning artwork from around the world grace the public rooms, and a huge free-form pool lies between the hotel and

its beach. Rooms are air-conditioned and have tiny balconies (ask for one with an ocean view). The decor is basic tropical, with a green, peach, and white color scheme and white rattan furniture. The exclusive Plaza Club section is that rare executive level worth the added expense, offering garden suites, a masseuse, a small gym, and other enticements. ⊠ *187 Isla Verde Rd., Isla Verde 00979,* ☎ *787/791–6100 or 800/544–3008,* FAX *787/791–8525. 418 rooms. 4 restaurants, 2 lounges, air-conditioning, pool, water-sports center, casino, recreation room, concierge, business services. AE, D, DC, MC, V. EP.*

$$$  🏨 **Radisson Normandie.** This oceanfront, art-deco style hotel is a national landmark. It was built in 1939, in the shape of the fabled ocean liner of the same name. Rooms have minibars, cable TV, coffeemakers, and hair dryers; some have sunrooms. Additional frills and pampering can be found at the seventh-floor executive club, where you receive complimentary Continental breakfast and evening hors d'oeuvres. You can make reservations to use the tennis courts at the Hilton next door. ⊠ *Corner of Av. Muñoz Rivera and Av. Rosales, Puerta Tierra, Box 50059, San Juan 00902,* ☎ *787/729–2929 or 800/333–3333,* FAX *787/729–3083. 177 rooms. 2 restaurants, air-conditioning, lounge, pool, health club, jogging, scuba diving, snorkeling, boating, business services. AE, D, DC, MC, V. EP, MAP.*

$$  🏨 **Excelsior.** Located across the Condado Lagoon in Miramar, the Excelsior is off the beaten path in a commercial area of the city and is popular with business travelers. Room decor here is standard hotel fare, but the rates are a good value. Each room has a phone, fridge, and a private bath with a hair dryer; some have kitchenettes. Fine carpets adorn the corridors, and sculptures decorate the lobby. Augusto's, one of the hotel's restaurants, is highly respected for its international cuisine. Complimentary coffee, newspaper, and shoe shine are offered each morning. ⊠ *801 Av. Ponce de León, Miramar 00907,* ☎ *787/721–7400 or 800/223–9815,* FAX *787/723–0068. 140 rooms. 2 restaurants, cocktail lounge, air-conditioning, refrigerators, pool, exercise room, beach shuttle, free parking. AE, DC, D, MC, V. EP.*

$$  🏨 **Hosteria del Mar.** Right on the beach in Ocean Park, this small, white
★   inn/guest house is set in a residential neighborhood. It's a wonderful alternative to the hustle and bustle of the Condado or Old San Juan— you have to go down to the beach and look west to see the high-rises of the Condado looming in the distance. Rooms here are attractive and simple, with tropical prints and rattan furniture prevailing, and many have ocean views. Four apartments have kitchenettes. All accommodations are air-conditioned and come with cable TV and phones. The staff is courteous and helpful. A vegetarian-oriented restaurant is on the ground floor facing the trade winds and offers fabulous views of the wide beach in front. ⊠ *1 Calle Tapia, Ocean Park 00911,* ☎ *787/727–3302,* FAX *787/268–0772. 8 rooms, 4 apartments, 1 minisuite. Restaurant, air-conditioning. AE, DC, MC, V. EP.*

$$  🏨 **Numero Uno.** Several years ago, former New Yorkers Ester and Chris
★   Laube bought this three-story, red-roofed guest house on the beach, spruced it up, and turned it into a very pleasant and comfortable accommodation. It's set in a quiet residential neighborhood, right in the middle of the nicest beach on San Juan. The simple but clean rooms offer double, queen-, or king-size beds and most are air-conditioned or have ceiling fans. A walled-in patio provides privacy for sunning or hanging out by the small pool. On the other side of the wall, a wide, sandy beach beckons. Beach chairs and towels are provided to guests. A bar and small restaurant borders the pool. ⊠ *1 Calle Santa Ana, Ocean Park 00911,* ☎ *787/727–9687,* FAX *787/726–5010. 12 rooms. Restaurant, bar, pool. AE, MC, V. CP.*

**$–$$** 🏨 **L'Habitation Beach Guest House.** On the beach in Ocean Park is this
★ gay-oriented guest house with a definite French air. Owner Alain Tasca
is from Paris by way of Guadeloupe and Key West. He has established
a very relaxed ambience in this casual, eight-room accommodation.
Rooms are well-sized, simple, and comfortable and all have air-conditioning and cable TV. Chambermaid Natasha sees to it that everything is kept clean and in its place and will chase after offenders who
don't wash sand off their feet before entering the house. A bar and snack
bar sit in a corner of a palm-shaded, sandy patio between the guest
house and the beach. Beach chairs and towels are provided. Alain's margaritas will knock your sandals off. ✉ *1957 Calle Italia, Ocean Park
00911,* ☎ *787/727–2499,* 𝔽𝔸𝕏 *787/727–2599. 8 rooms. Bar, snack bar,
air-conditioning, private beach. AE, MC, V. CP.*

## Out on the Island

### CABO ROJO

**$–$$** 🏨 **Parador Boquemar.** You can walk to the Boquerón public beach (one
of the island's best) from this small parador at the end of Route 101.
Rooms are comfortable. Each has air-conditioning, TV, minifridge,
phone, and private bath and is decorated in the island uniform of tropical prints and rattan. Ask for a third-floor room with a balcony overlooking the water. La Cascada, a *mesón gastronomico,* is well known
for its superior, traditional native cuisine. On weekends, the lounge is
filled with live music. At press time, the parador was adding 20 new
rooms. ✉ *Box 133, Boquerón 00622,* ☎ *787/851–2158 or 800/443–
0266,* 𝔽𝔸𝕏 *787/851–7600. 64 rooms. Restaurant, lounge, air-conditioning,
refrigerators, pool, coin laundry across street. AE, D, DC, MC, V. EP.*

### COAMO

**$** 🏨 **Parador Baños de Coamo.** On Route 546, Km 1, northeast of Ponce,
this mountain inn is located at the hot sulfur springs that are said to be
the Fountain of Youth of Ponce de León's dreams. Rooms open onto
latticed wooden verandas and have a pleasing blend of contemporary
and period furnishings. All are air-conditioned and have private bath.
The parador can make arrangements for you to ride Puerto Rico's glorious, unique *paso fino* horses. ✉ *Box 540, 00769,* ☎ *787/825–2186
or 800/443–0266,* 𝔽𝔸𝕏 *787/825–4739. 48 rooms. Restaurant, lounge,
air-conditioning, pool, hot springs. AE, DC, MC, V. EP.*

### DORADO

**$$$$** 🏨 **Hyatt Dorado Beach.** The ambience is a bit more subdued at this resort than at its sister, the Cerromar Beach (☞ *below*), and guests can
take advantage of the facilities there. A variety of elegant accommodations
are in low-rise buildings scattered over 1,000 lavishly landscaped acres—
among the most beautiful in the Caribbean. Most rooms have private
patios or balconies, and all have polished terra-cotta floors, marble baths,
and air-conditioning. Upper-level rooms in the Oceanview Houses have
a view of the two half-moon beaches. ✉ *Rte. 693, 00646,* ☎ *787/796–
1234 or 800/233–1234,* 𝔽𝔸𝕏 *787/796–2022. 298 rooms. 3 restaurants,
2 lounges, air-conditioning, 2 pools, wading pool, spa, 2 18-hole Robert
Trent Jones golf courses, 7 tennis courts, health club, hiking, jogging,
water-sports center, bicycles, casino. AE, DC, MC, V. EP, MAP.*

**$$$$** 🏨 **Hyatt Regency Cerromar Beach.** One of the best sports-oriented resorts in the Caribbean, the family-oriented Cerromar has two Robert
Trent Jones golf courses, 14 tennis courts, a spa and health club, jogging and biking trails, a 900-foot river pool, a Jacuzzi in a man-made
cavern, a swim-up bar, and a three-story-high water slide. It's 22 miles
west of San Juan, right on the Atlantic. The modern seven-story hotel
is done up in tropical style. Rooms have tile floors, marble baths, air-
conditioning, and a king-size or two double beds. You'll find quieter

rooms on the west side, away from the pool activity. Guests at the Cerromar and its sister facility, the Hyatt Dorado Beach (☞ *above*) a mile down the road, have access to the facilities of both resorts, and colorful red trolleys make frequent runs between the two. Sushi Wong's serves delicious pan-Asian cuisine, and Medici's is a sophisticated northern Italian eatery. ✉ *Rte. 693, Km 11.8, 00646,* ☎ *787/796–1234 or 800/233–1234,* 𝖥𝖠𝖷 *787/796–4647. 506 rooms. 3 restaurants, 3 bars, sushi bar, air-conditioning, pool, spa, 2 18-hole Robert Trent Jones golf courses, 14 tennis courts, health club, hiking, jogging, bicycles, casino with live entertainment, dance club. AE, DC, MC, V. EP, MAP.*

### GUÁNICA

**$$$** 🏨 **Copamarina Beach Resort.** Sprawling across 18 acres between the
★ sea and the Guánica Dry Forest is this quiet, landscaped resort. The pool is the centerpiece of the property, surrounded by the open-air reception area, manicured lawns, the outdoor Las Palmas Cafe, the elegant Ballena restaurant and bar, and the building wings. The bay bottom on this section of beach is covered in seaweed, but secluded beaches with clear water can be found a few minutes' drive down the road. The spotless rooms have small terraces with water views, one queen-size or two double beds, TV, phone, and air-conditioning. The furniture is bleached-wood-and-rattan, and the bedspreads are the ubiquitous tropical print. Try the red snapper in the dining room, and stop in the bar for the bartender's straight-up margarita. Arrange a snorkeling excursion to Gilligan's Island, an offshore key. Kayaks, sailboats, paddleboats, and tennis rackets are some of the gear for rent. There are plans to add 55 rooms, 15 villas, and a convention center to the complex. ✉ *Rte. 333, Km 6.5, Caña Gorda, Gúanica, Box 805, 00653,* ☎ *787/821–0505 or 800/468–4553,* 𝖥𝖠𝖷 *787/821–0070. 70 rooms. 2 restaurants, 2 bars, air-conditioning, 2 pools, hot tub, 2 tennis courts, volleyball, scuba-diving packages, bicycles, gift shop, recreation room, meeting rooms. AE, D, DC, MC, V. EP.*

### HUMACAO

**$$$–$$$$** 🏨 **Palmas del Mar.** This luxurious resort community is on 2,750 acres
★ of a former coconut plantation on the sheltered southeast coast (about an hour's drive from San Juan). Two hotels, the 23-suite Palmas Inn and 100-room Candelero Hotel, are the centerpieces of the complex. In the rustic yet elegant Candelero, rooms are airy and spacious. Ask for a room on the third floor, where there are cathedral ceilings. The Palmas Inn suites, all with stunning sea or garden views, evoke luxurious Mediterranean villas, with pastel-pink connecting walkways, cobblestone plazas, and fountains adorned with hand-painted tile work. The resort includes private homes and condominium villas. ✉ *Box 2020, Rte. 906, 00792,* ☎ *787/852–6000 or 800/468–3331,* 𝖥𝖠𝖷 *787/852–6330. 100 rooms; 140 villas; 23 1-, 2-, and 3-bedroom suites. 10 restaurants, air-conditioning, pool, 18-hole Gary Player golf course, 20 tennis courts, equestrian center, exercise room, beach, sailing, scuba diving, marina, water-sports center, fishing, bicycles, casino. AE, DC, MC, V. EP, MAP.*

### JAYUYA

**$** 🏨 **Parador Hacienda Gripiñas.** Don't stay here if you're looking for a
★ beach vacation: The sea is more than 30 miles away. This white hacienda is for those looking for a romantic mountain hideaway. Polished wood and beam ceilings warm the interior. Large airy rooms are decorated with native crafts. Relaxation beckons at every turn: Rocking chairs nod in the spacious lounge, hammocks swing on the porch, and splendid gardens invite a leisurely stroll. Your morning coffee is grown on the adjacent working plantation, and its aroma seems to fill the grounds,

as does the chirp of the ubiquitous coquis (tree frogs). ✉ *Rte. 527, Km 2.5, Box 387, 00664,* ☎ *787/828–1717 or 800/443–0266,* FAX *787/721–4698. 19 rooms. Restaurant, lounge, pool, hiking. AE. EP.*

### LA PARGUERA

**$$** 🏨 **Parador Villa Parguera.** This parador is a stylish hotel on Phos-
★ phorescent Bay. Large, colorfully decorated rooms have TV, phone, air-conditioning, private bath, and balcony or terrace. A spacious dining room, overlooking the small swimming pool and the bay beyond, serves excellent native and international dishes. Children under 10 stay free in their parents' room. Ask about honeymoon packages. ✉ *Rte. 304, Box 273, Lajas 00667,* ☎ *787/899–3975 or 800/443–0266,* FAX *787/899–6040. 62 rooms. Restaurant, lounge, air-conditioning, salt-water pool, nightclub. AE, D, DC, MC, V. EP.*

### LAS CROABAS

**$$$$** 🏨 **El Conquistador Resort and Country Club.** This massive $250 mil-
★ lion complex is a world unto itself, divided into five self-contained hotels. It's perched dramatically atop a 300-foot bluff overlooking the Caribbean, the Atlantic, and the El Yunque rain forest. The architecture is a harmonious blend of Moorish and Spanish colonial: cobblestone streets, white stucco and terra-cotta buildings, open-air plazas with soaring arches and tinkling fountains, tiled benches, and gas lamps. Plants and colorful caged parrots decorate many of the open spaces. One of the five hotels, Las Olas, is actually built into the cliff face. In all of the hotels, the stylish, elegant decor in the large rooms runs toward the ubiquitous Caribbean rattan and pastels, spiced with native artwork. Each room has a seating area with couch, glass-top coffee table, desk, chairs, and entertainment center. Enormous bathrooms have sunken tub, long marble countertop, makeup mirror, and walk-in closet. Nice extras include dimmer switches on bedside lamps, well-stocked minibars, CD players, and VCRs. The hotel's beach is an offshore island, which you reach via shuttle boat. The pampering begins at LMM International Airport: The resort is the only one on the island to operate a private lounge and provide deluxe motor-coach transfers. The ride is a little over an hour. ✉ *Av. El Conquistador, Box 70001, Las Croabas 00738,* ☎ *787/863–1000 or 800/468–5228,* FAX *787/863–6586. 918 rooms and suites. 10 restaurants, 3 bars, lounge, air-conditioning, minibars, in-room VCRs, 5 pools, spa, 18-hole Arthur Hills golf course, 7 tennis courts, health club, 32-slip marina, scuba diving, water-sports center, fishing, shops, casino, nightclub, children's program, business services, convention center, car rental. AE, D, DC, MC, V. EP.*

### MAYAGÜEZ

**$$$–$$$$** 🏨 **Mayagüez Hilton and Casino.** Built on 20 acres about 2 miles north
★ of the city of Mayagüez, this pink stucco resort on the island's west coast is about a 2½-hour drive from San Juan. The superb Rotisserie restaurant is known for its lavish theme buffets and top-notch steaks and seafood. Rooms are air-conditioned and have minibar, TV, and telephone. The decor is typical tan-and-muted-pastel. Many rooms overlook the parking lot, although poolside rooms view the tropical gardens and Mayagüez harbor in the distance. The hotel caters mainly to businesspeople. ✉ *Rte. 2, Km 152.5, Box 3629, 00681,* ☎ *787/831–7575 or 800/445–8667; in Puerto Rico, 800/462–3954;* FAX *787/265–3020. 141 rooms, 3 suites, 10 junior suites. Restaurant, lounge, bar, air-conditioning, minibars, no-smoking rooms, Olympic-size pool, baby pool, hot tub, 3 tennis courts, exercise room, casino, dance club, playground, meeting rooms. AE, D, DC, MC, V. EP.*

## PONCE

**$$–$$$$**  🏨 **Ponce Hilton and Casino.** By far the biggest resort on the south coast, this cream-and-turquoise hotel, nestled amid 80 acres of landscaped gardens, caters to a corporate clientele. Completely self-contained, it offers three restaurants (La Hacienda's antiques mimic an old coffee plantation; the romantic and elegant La Cava has a working wine cellar and can be reserved for a private dinner), access to a public beach, casino, shopping arcade, pool, four tennis courts, a driving range, and a disco with pool tables and live music on weekends. Although the lobby has all the warmth of an airline terminal, the large guest rooms are attractive enough, decorated in sky blue, teal, and peach, and furnished with modern rattan. All have a minibar, safe, TV, phone, and balcony. The views are best from the fourth-floor rooms. A drawback is the hotel's location—a 10-minute cab ride from town. ⊠ *Rte. 14, Av. Santiago de los Caballeros, Box 7419, 00732,* ☎ *787/259–7676 or 800/445–8667,* FAX *787/259–7674. 156 rooms, 8 suites. 3 restaurants, 2 bars, in-room safes, minibars, pool, beauty salon, hot tub, driving range, 4 tennis courts, basketball, exercise room, Ping-Pong, volleyball, shops, casino, dance club, baby-sitting, business services, meeting rooms. AE, D, DC, MC, V. EP.*

**$–$$**  🏨 **Hotel Melia.** Set in the heart of Ponce and facing the Parque de Bom-
★ bas and the Ponce Cathedral, this family-owned hotel provides a wonderful, low-key base for exploring the marvelous turn-of-the-century architecture, museums, and landmarks of downtown Ponce. The lobby has an old-world feel, with high ceilings, tiled floors, and well-worn but charming decor (the plastic covers on the lobby lamp shades need to go, however). Rooms have standard, if somewhat dated, decor and have TVs, phones, and air-conditioning. Some of the rooms have balconies that overlook the park. Breakfast is served on the rooftop terrace, which offers pretty views of the city and mountains. ⊠ *2 Calle Cristina, Box 1431, 00733,* ☎ *787/842–0260,* FAX *787/841–3602. 80 rooms. Restaurant, bar, air-conditioning. AE, MC, V. CP.*

## RINCÓN

**$$$$**  🏨 **Horned Dorset Primavera.** The emphasis here is on privacy and re-
★ laxation. The Spanish neocolonial-style resort is tucked away amid lush landscaping overlooking the sea. The only sounds that you're likely to hear as you lounge on the long, secluded, narrow beach, are the crash of the surf and an occasional squawk from Pompidou, the enormous parrot in the lounge. Suites have private balconies and are exquisitely furnished with antiques, including handsome mahogany four-poster beds, dressers, and nightstands. Casa Escondido, opened in 1995, has eight rooms—some have their own plunge pool—and is designed as a typical turn-of-the-century Puerto Rican hacienda, with tile or wood floors, stately mahogany furnishings, private terraces, and black marble baths. There are no radios, televisions, or telephones in any of the resort's rooms. The elegant restaurant serves Continental cuisine in surroundings befitting royalty. A delightful Continental breakfast is served in the open-air lounge. The hotel is a member of the prestigious Relais & Châteaux group. Children under 12 are not permitted. ⊠ *Rte. 429, Km 3, Box 1132, 00743,* ☎ *787/823–4030 or 787/823–4050,* FAX *787/823–5580. 30 rooms. Restaurant, lounge, pool, library. AE, MC, V. EP.*

**$$**  🏨 **Lemontree Waterfront Cottages.** These sparkling, large apartments
★ sit right on the beach, with staircases from their decks to the sand. There are four units, each with a fully equipped kitchen, TV, telephone, and large deck with mahogany-topped wet bar and gas grill. The owner-managers, Mary Jeanne and Paul Hellings, have put their personal touches on the apartments. Paul creates all the detailed woodwork, and

Mary Jeanne designs the interiors. The bright tropical decor includes local artwork on the walls. There is one three-bedroom unit with two baths, one two-bedroom unit, and two newer one-bedroom units. The one-bedroom units have wooden cathedral ceilings and picture windows. The beach is small, but larger ones are close by. It's a 10-minute drive to downtown Rincón. ⊠ *Rte. 429, Box 200, Rincón,* ☎ *787/823–6452,* FAX *787/823–5821. 4 units. Kitchens, beach, weekly maid service, laundry service, linens provided. AE, MC, V.*

### SAN GERMÁN

$
★ ⊞ **Parador Oasis.** The Oasis, not far from the town's two plazas, was a family mansion 200 years ago; the lobby retains a taste of the house's history with peppermint-pink walls and white-wicker furniture. The older rooms are convenient—right off the lobby—but show their age. The newer rooms in the rear lack character but are functional, clean, and a little roomier. All have TV, phone, and air-conditioning. ⊠ *72 Calle Luna, Box 144, 00683,* ☎ *787/892–1100 or 800/443–0266,* FAX *787/892–1175. 52 rooms. Restaurant, lounge, air-conditioning, pool, hot tub, sauna, exercise room. AE, D, DC, MC, V. EP.*

### VIEQUES

$$$ ⊞ **Inn on the Blue Horizon.** Known for its restaurant, Cafe Blu, and its octagonal Blu bar, this small hotel sits on 20 windswept acres fronting the Caribbean. There are only three rooms, but at press time, owners and former New Yorkers James Weis and Billy Knight had plans to add more. Furnished with antiques, the rooms are sumptuous and lovely, as is the patio/lounge area. ⊠ *Rte. 996, Box 1556, 00765,* ☎ *787/741–3318. 3 rooms. Restaurant, bar, pool. AE, MC, V. CP.*

$$–$$$ ⊞ **Casa del Francés.** Self-professed curmudgeon Irving Greenblatt, a former Bostonian, runs this atmospheric if somewhat run-down guest house in a restored French sugar plantation great house. Rooms are rather plain but enormous, with vaulted 17-foot ceilings. The food is good, the pool inviting, the guests an eclectic mix, and Irving a true character who will regale you with horror stories of running a Caribbean hotel. The sightseeing boat for the phosphorescent bay leaves from here. ⊠ *Box 458, Esperanza 00765,* ☎ *787/741–3751,* FAX *787/741–2330. 18 rooms. Restaurant, bar, pool, snorkeling. AE, MC, V. EP, MAP (compulsory in season).*

$$–$$$ ⊞ **Hacienda Tamarindo.** Set on a windswept hill with sweeping views
★ of the Caribbean, the new Hacienda Tamarindo is the nicest place to stay on Vieques. Owners Burr and Linda Vail left Vermont to build this extraordinary small hotel—with a huge tamarind tree right in the middle! The rooms are all individually decorated but share excellent craftsmanship, like mahogany louvered doors, terra-cotta tiled floors, and custom-tiled baths. Some of the rooms have private terraces and hot tubs, and two are accessible to people with disabilities. Half of the rooms have air-conditioning, while the rest face the trade winds. All are furnished with an eclectic mix of art and antiques shipped from Vermont. A full American breakfast is served on the second-floor terrace. Guests can walk down the hill to the Inn on the Blue Horizon (☞ *above*) for lunch and dinner. Box lunches are available on request. Children under 12 are not permitted. ⊠ *Rte. 996, Box 1569, 00765,* ☎ *787/741–8525,* FAX *787/741–8525. 16 rooms. Honor bar, pool. AE, MC, V. FAP.*

$$ ⊞ **Crow's Nest.** Owner Liz O'Dell has made her simple but comfort-
★ able inn a very satisfying place to stay on Vieques. A Southerner by way of Massachusetts, Liz is a wealth of information and hospitality. She will arrange for you to do just about anything that's available on the island. Her 13-room lodging, set on 5 hilltop acres with pretty ocean views, is a great value. All rooms have kitchenettes and most are air-

conditioned. Liz provides beach chairs and coolers for guests—a thoughtful touch. There is a lounge with TV/VCR, and one of the island's best restaurants, also called the Crow's Nest, is on the premises. ✉ *Rte. 201, Km 1.6, Box 1521, 00765,* ☎ *787/741–0033,* ℻ *787/741– 1294. 13 rooms. Restaurant, bar, kitchenettes, pool, car rental. AE, MC, V. EP.*

## Villa and Apartment Rentals

Villa and condominium or apartment rentals are becoming increasingly popular in Puerto Rico, particularly outside San Juan. If you are traveling with several people, these are often a very affordable option. Call the tourist information office in the area where you are interested in staying, or try the options listed below.

If you're part of a large group or you'd like to investigate off-season rates at higher-end properties in the Isla Verde area of San Juan, contact **Condo World** (✉ 26645 W. Twelve Mile Rd., Southfield, MI 48034, ☎ 800/521–2980). For rentals out on the island, try **Island West Properties** (✉ Rte. 413, Km 1.3, Box 700, Rincón 00677, ☎ 787/823–2323, ℻ 787/823–3254). It has weekly and monthly vacation rentals that fall into the **$** to **$$** range. For rentals on Vieques, the person to talk to is Jane Sabin at **Connections** (✉ Box 358, Vieques, 00765, ☎ 787/741–0023 or 800/772–3050). Or try **Acacia Apartments** (✉ 236 Calle Acacia, Esperanza, Vieques, 00765, ☎ 787/741–1856).

# Dining

The quality of restaurants on the island is among the best in the Caribbean. In San Juan you'll find everything from Italian to Thai, as well as superb local eateries serving *comidas criollas* (traditional Caribbean-Creole meals). Many of San Juan's best restaurants, such as Pikayo, Chayote, and Augusto's, are located in small, lesser-known hotels. If you're staying in the capital, by all means venture out and sample the wealth of options available. Wherever you go, it is *always* a good idea to make reservations in the busy season, from mid-November through April.

Puerto Rican cooking emphasizes local vegetables: Plantains are cooked a hundred different ways—*tostones* (fried green), *amarillos* (baked ripe), and chips. Rice and beans with tostones or amarillos are basic accompaniments to every dish. Locals cook white rice with *habichuelas* (red beans), *achiote* (annatto seeds), or saffron; brown rice with *gandules* (pigeon peas); and *morro* (black rice) with *frijoles negros* (black beans). Garbanzos and white beans are served in many daily specials. A wide assortment of yams is served baked, fried, stuffed, boiled, mashed, and whole. *Sofrito*—a garlic, onion, sweet pepper, coriander, oregano, and tomato puree—is used as a base for practically everything.

Beef, chicken, pork, and seafood are all rubbed with *adobo,* a garlic-oregano marinade, before cooking. *Arroz con pollo* (chicken with rice), *sancocho* (beef and tuber soup), *asopao* (a soupy rice with chicken or seafood), and *encebollado* (steak smothered in onions) are all typical plates.

Fritters, also popular, are served in snack places along the highways as well as at cocktail parties. You may find *empanadillas* (stuffed fried turnovers), *surrullitos* (cheese-stuffed corn sticks), *alcapurias* (stuffed green banana croquettes), and *bacalaitos* (codfish fritters).

Local *pan de agua* is an excellent French loaf bread, best hot out of the oven. It is also good toasted and should be tried in the *Cubano* sandwich (roast pork, ham, Swiss cheese, pickles, and mustard).

Local desserts include flans, puddings, and fruit pastes served with native white cheese. Homegrown mangoes and papayas are sweet, and *pan de azucar* (sugar bread) pineapples make the best juice on the market. Fresh *parcha* (passion fruit), *guarapo* (sugarcane), and *guanabana* (a fruit similar to papaya) juice are also sold cold from trucks along the highway. Puerto Rican coffee is excellent served espresso-black or generously cut *con leche* (with hot milk).

To sample local cuisine, consult the listing of *mesones gastrónomicos* in the *¿Qué Pasa?* guide. These are restaurants cited by the government for preserving island culinary traditions and maintaining high standards.

The best frozen piña coladas are served at the Caribe Hilton and the Hyatt Dorado Beach, although local legend has it that the birthplace of the piña colada is the Gran Hotel El Convento. Rum can be mixed with cola (known as a *cuba libre*), soda, tonic, juices, water, served on the rocks, or even up. Puerto Rican rums range from light white mixers to dark, aged sipping liqueurs. Look for Bacardi, Don Q, Ron Rico, Palo Viejo, and Barilito.

## What to Wear
The dress code for restaurants in Puerto Rico varies greatly. The price category of a restaurant is usually a good indicator of its formality. For less expensive places, anything but beachwear is generally fine. Ritzier hotel dining rooms and expensive eateries will expect collared shirts for men and chic attire for women, although jacket and tie requirements are rare. However, Puerto Ricans enjoy dressing up for dinner, so chances are you'll never feel overdressed.

| CATEGORY | COST* |
|---|---|
| $$$$ | over $45 |
| $$$ | $30–$45 |
| $$ | $15–$30 |
| $ | under $15 |

*per person, excluding drinks and service*

## Old San Juan

**$$$$**  ✕ **Chef Marisoll.** Set off a Venetianesque courtyard surrounded by ornate balconies (you can dine inside or out), this dark-wooded, high-ceilinged restaurant serves gourmet international cuisine. Start with a small duck caesar salad or a cream of exotic wild mushroom soup. Then feast on a beef tenderloin or a fillet of salmon. For dessert, try Chef Marisoll's specialty, a crème caramel. ⊠ *202 Calle Cristo,* ☎ *787/725–7454. AE, D, MC, V. Closed Mon. No lunch Sun.*

**$$$$**  ✕ **Il Perugino.** The best Italian restaurant in Old San Juan, this small
★ and intimate eatery set in a 200-year-old building stresses attentive service and delicious Italian cuisine. Classic carpaccios, scallops with porcini mushrooms and other exotic salads, homemade pastas like black fettuccine with crayfish and baby eels, hearty main courses such as rack of lamb with red wine sauce and aromatic herbs, and desserts like a killer *tiramisù* make this a must for serious gourmets. An excellent wine cellar, housed in the former cistern, completes the experience. ⊠ *105 Calle Cristo,* ☎ *787/722–5481. AE, MC, V.*

**$$$–$$$$**  ✕ **La Chaumière.** Reminiscent of an inn in the French provinces, this intimate restaurant with black-and-white floors, heavy wood beams, and floral curtains serves onion soup, oysters Rockefeller, rack of lamb, scallops Provençale, and veal Oscar (layered with lobster and asparagus in béarnaise sauce) in addition to daily specials. ⊠ *367 Calle Tetuan,* ☎ *787/722–3330. AE, DC, MC, V. Closed Sun. No lunch.*

**$$–$$$**  ✕ **Amadeus.** In an atmosphere of gentrified Old San Juan, this charm-
★ ing restaurant offers a nouvelle Caribbean menu. The front dining room

is attractive—whitewashed walls, dark wood, white napery, ceiling fans, and a trendy, pretty crowd to match—but go through the outside passage to the back dining room where printed cloths, candles, and exposed brick make for even more romantic dining. The roster of appetizers includes buffalo wings and plantain mousse with shrimp. Chicken breast stuffed with sun-dried tomatoes, cheese ravioli with a goat-cheese-and-walnut sauce, and Cajun-grilled mahimahi are a few of the delectable entrées. ⊠ *106 Calle San Sebastián,* ☎ *787/722–8635. AE, MC, V. Closed Mon.*

$$–$$$ ✕ **Cafe Galería.** This stylish, airy restaurant, with marble floors, white walls, and dark wood accents, is centered around a skylit atrium. Chef Figueroa prepares Italian and international cuisine featuring fresh pastas and sauces (you mix and match), risottos, and seafood dishes as well as delicious local desserts like flan, *arroz con dulce* (rice pudding), and kiwi tart. ⊠ *205 Calle San Justo,* ☎ *787/725–0478. AE, MC, V. Closed Sun.*

$$–$$$ ✕ **La Mallorquina.** The oldest restaurant in Puerto Rico (it is said to date from 1848) is recommended more for its atmosphere than for its food. Pale pink walls and whirring ceiling fans are pleasant, and the nattily attired wait staff is friendly. The food is good but basic Puerto Rican and Spanish fare, such as asopao and paella. ⊠ *207 Calle San Justo,* ☎ *787/722–3261. AE, MC, V.*

$$–$$$ ✕ **Yukiyú.** The only Japanese restaurant in Old San Juan, it manages ★ to serve some of the best Japanese food in Puerto Rico under the supervision of Chef Igarashi. Those craving a sushi bar should beeline for this establishment, as sushi is a specialty, along with teppan yaki. ⊠ *311 Recinto Sur,* ☎ *787/721–0653. AE, MC, V.*

$$ ✕ **Amanda's Cafe.** This airy café, across from San Cristóbal on the north side of the city, offers seating inside or out with a view of the Atlantic and the old city wall. The cuisine is Mexican, French, and Caribbean, and the nachos, refreshing fruit frappés, and margaritas are the best in town. ⊠ *424 Calle Norzagaray,* ☎ *787/722–0187. AE, MC, V.*

$–$$ ✕ **El Patio de Sam.** A warm dark-wood and faux-brick interior and a wide selection of beers make Sam's a popular late-night gathering place. The menu is mostly steaks and seafood, with a few native dishes like asopao mixed in. Try the Samueles Special pizza—mozzarella, tomato sauce, beef, pepperoni, and black olives: It feeds two or three adults. The dessert flans melt in your mouth. ⊠ *102 Calle San Sebastián,* ☎ *787/723–1149. AE, D, DC, MC, V.*

$ ✕ **Cafe Berlin.** This casual café, bakery, and delicatessen has outdoor ★ seating overlooking the Plaza Colón. Tasty vegetarian fare prevails— try one of the creative salads. Nonvegetarian dishes are also available. The Cafe's pastries, desserts, fresh juices, and organic coffee are the perfect elixir to a day of touring Old San Juan. ⊠ *407 Calle San Francisco,* ☎ *787/722–5205. MC, V.*

## San Juan

$$$$ ✕ **Compostela.** Contemporary Spanish food and a serious 9,000-bottle ★ wine cellar are the draws to Compostela, a restaurant with a dark-wood interior and many plants. Specialties include mushroom pâté and Port *pastelillo* (meat-filled pastries), grouper fillet with scallops in salsa verde, rack of lamb, duck with kiwi sauce, and paella. This is a favorite restaurant with the local dining elite, and it is honored yearly in local competitions. ⊠ *106 Av. Condado, Santurce,* ☎ *787/724–6088. AE, DC, MC, V. Closed Sun.*

$$$$ ✕ **Pikayo.** Chef Wilo Benet is one of the darlings in the foodie firma-★ ment, thanks to his artful fusion of classic French, Caribbean Creole, and California nouvelle cuisine with definite Puerto Rican flair. The beautifully presented dishes, which change regularly, are a feast for the

eye as well as the palate. Your meal might consist of tostones stuffed with oven-dried tomatoes, followed by *monfongo* (spiced, mashed green plantains topped with saffron shrimp) or a hearty land-crab stew. More traditional and equally delicious dishes are also available. The decor is smartly contemporary, with lots of black-and-white accents and comfortable banquettes, and the service is very attentive. ⊠ *Tanama Princess Hotel, 1 Calle Joffre, Condado,* ☎ *787/721–6194. AE, MC, V. Closed Sun. and Mon. No lunch Sat.*

**$$$$** ✕ **Ramiro's.** Step into a soft sea green dining room for some imagi-
★ native Castilian cuisine. Chef-owner Jesus Ramiro is known for his artistic presentation: flower-shape peppers filled with fish mousse, a mix of seafood caught under a vegetable net, roast duckling with sugarcane honey, and, if you can stand more, a kiwi dessert sculpted to resemble twin palms. ⊠ *1106 Av. Magdalena, Condado,* ☎ *787/721–9049. AE, DC, MC, V. No lunch Sat.*

**$$$–$$$$** ✕ **Chayote.** Chef Alfredo Ayala, a champion of the latest trends in Puerto
★ Rican and Caribbean cuisine, has created a sensation with this restaurant. Slightly off the beaten path in Miramar, this elegant and chic eatery of earthen tones and contemporary Puerto Rican art is an "in" spot to eat among the San Juan cognoscenti. The chef fuses haute international cuisine with tropical panache. Appetizers include *sopas del dias* (soups of the day) made with local produce like yuca and yams, chayote stuffed with prosciutto, cheese and tomatoes in a tempura batter, and corn tamales with shrimp in coconut sauce. Half of the entrées on the menu are seafood dishes, including pan-seared tuna with Asian ginger sauce and black grouper fillet in a vegetable fricassee sauce with Gouda cheese fritters. Classic meat dishes like fillet of beef and rack of lamb are also available. The ginger flan and the almond floating island in rum custard sauce are musts for dessert. ⊠ *Hotel Olimpo Court, 603 Av. Miramar, Miramar,* ☎ *787/722–9385. AE, MC, V. Closed Sun.*

**$$$–$$$$** ✕ **Los Faisanes.** This Continental stunner is one of San Juan's most distinguished eateries. Mahogany doorways, faux-Tiffany lamps, crisp white and ecru napery, and Bernadaud china set a refined tone, carried through by the equally elegant cuisine. Feast on roast duck with guava and cinnamon, veal chops with scallion and mushroom sauce, and wonderfully light soufflés. ⊠ *1108 Av. Magdalena, Condado,* ☎ *787/725–2801. AE, MC, V.*

**$$$** ✕ **Chart House.** It's no secret that the graceful veranda of this restored Ashford mansion across from the Marriott is a perfect spot for cocktails, and a lively crowd gathers here in the evening. The upstairs open-air dining rooms are splashed with bright marine-themed artwork. The menu includes prime rib, steak, shrimp teriyaki, Hawaiian chicken, and the signature dessert: mud pie. ⊠ *1214 Av. Ashford, Condado,* ☎ *787/728–0110. AE, D, DC, MC, V. No lunch.*

**$$** ✕ **Che's.** Juicy *churrasco* (barbecued steaks), lemon chicken, and grilled sweetbreads are specialties at this casual Argentinean restaurant. The hamburgers are huge, and the french fries are fresh. The Chilean and Argentinean wine list is also decent. ⊠ *35 Calle Caoba, Punta Las Marias,* ☎ *787/726–7202. AE, D, DC, MC, V.*

**$** ✕ **El Paso.** This family-run restaurant serves genuine Creole food seasoned for a local following. Specialties include asopao, pork chops, and breaded *empanadas* (meat pastries). There's always tripe on Saturday and arroz con pollo on Sunday. ⊠ *405 Av. De Diego, Puerto Nuevo,* ☎ *787/781–3399. AE, DC, MC, V.*

**$** ✕ **Kasalta Bakery, Inc.** Make your selection from rows of display
★ cases offering a seemingly endless array of tempting treats. Walk up to the counter and order from an assortment of sandwiches (try the Cubano), meltingly tender octopus salad, savory *caldo gallego* (a soup jammed with fresh vegetables, sausage, and potatoes), cold drinks, strong

café con leche, and luscious pastries. ⊠ *1966 Calle McLeary, Ocean Park,* ☎ *787/727–7340. AE, MC, V.*

$    ✕ **Via Appia's Italian Deli.** The only true sidewalk café in the Condado, this eatery serves pizzas, sandwiches, cold beer, and pitchers of sangria. It is a good place to people-watch. The staff is somewhat grumpy, however. ⊠ *1350 Av. Ashford, Condado,* ☎ *787/725–8711. AE, MC, V.*

## Out on the Island

CABO ROJO

$$    ✕ **La Casona de Serafin.** This informal, ocean-side bistro is a *mesón gastronómique* and specializes in steaks, seafood, and Puerto Rican *criolla* (Creole) dishes. The indoor dining room has bleached walls, mahogany furniture, and subdued red napery. Try the tostones, asopao, and surrullitos, and follow up with the pumpkin-custard dessert. The somewhat dilapidated palm-fringed patio sits right on the beach, so you can listen to the waves lap the shore. ⊠ *Hwy. 102, Km 9,* ☎ *787/851–0066. AE, MC, V.*

$–$$    ✕ **El Bohio.** A local favorite, this informal restaurant 15 minutes south of Mayagüez serves steak and a variety of seafood—all cooked just about any way you want it. You can dine on the large, enclosed wooden deck that juts out over the sea or in the dining room inside. ⊠ *Hwy. 102, Playa Joyuda,* ☎ *787/851–2755. AE, DC, MC, V.*

FAJARDO

$–$$    ✕ **Anchor's Inn.** From the windows of this unadorned seaside eatery, you can watch the flotillas of brightly colored yachts and fishing boats in Fajardo harbor. The latter must head straight for the restaurant with their catch, for the seafood is as fresh and succulent as it gets. A *mesón gastronómico,* Anchor's Inn specializes in such Puerto Rican dishes as surrullitos, asopao, and lobster *mofongo* (green plantains stuffed with lobster). There are seven guest rooms upstairs. ⊠ *Rte. 987, Km 2.4,* ☎ *787/863–7200. AE, MC, V. Closed Tues.*

PONCE

$$    ✕ **Restaurant El Ancla.** The seafood and Puerto Rican specialties here are served with tostones, *papas fritas* (french fries), and garlic bread. The menu ranges from lobster and shrimp to chicken, beef, and asopao. The piña coladas, with or without rum, and the flan are especially good. ⊠ *Av. Hostos Final 9, Playa-Ponce,* ☎ *787/840–2450. AE, DC, MC, V.*

$    ✕ **Lupita's.** A fine mariachi band patrols the mezzanine and courtyard of this festive Mexican restaurant Thursday through Sunday nights. The handsome arched dining room has an Aztec decor, with ponchos and serapes hung on the walls for added color. The food—Mexican-American standards like nachos, tacos, and chicken mole—is quite good, the margaritas and shooters even better, and the ambience festive. ⊠ *Calle Isabel 60,* ☎ *787/848–8808. AE, MC, V.*

RINCÓN

$$$–$$$$    ✕ **Horned Dorset Primavera.** Tucked away on the west coast of the island in a posh hotel of the same name, this is the finest food you'll encounter outside of San Juan. Owners Harold Davies and Kingsley Wratten take their dining room very seriously. The menu is printed in two languages, French and Spanish, even though most of the clientele is American (the waiters save the day). Although tropical accents appear here and there, the cuisine is heavily Cordon Bleu–influenced: Filet mignon in a mushroom sauce, braised lamb in red wine, and grilled fish du jour are de rigueur here. A five-course, prix-fixe menu is available for $48 per person. ⊠ *Rte. 429, Km 3, Box 1132,* ☎ *787/823–4030 or 787/823–4050. AE, MC, V.*

**$$** ✕ **Black Eagle.** The inconsistent quality of the food here hasn't dimmed its status as a Rincón dining landmark. It's on the water's edge, and you dine on the veranda, listening to the lapping waves. The steak-and-seafood menu lists breaded conch fritters, a fresh fish of the day, lobster, and imported prime meats. ✉ *Hwy. 413, Km 1,* ☎ *787/823–3510. AE, DC, MC, V.*

**$$** ✕ **El Molino del Quijote Restaurante.** Amid beautifully landscaped gardens just off the beach, this festive, colorful restaurant with tile-topped tables and local artwork serves Spanish and Puerto Rican cuisine. Try the *bolas de pescado* (fish balls) appetizer and one of the paellas as an entrée, or combine several appetizers for a meal. The sangria is highly recommended. Two one-bedroom cabanas are available to rent. ✉ *Rte. 429, Km 3.3,* ☎ *787/823–4010. AE, MC, V. Closed Mon.–Thurs.*

**$–$$** ✕ **Lazy Parrot.** Highly regarded by locals in Rincón for its fresh mahimahi, filet mignon, and homemade desserts, this little restaurant is also an art gallery and guest house. Perched in the hills, with mountain and ocean views, this is great place to kick back and listen to the ever-present sound of the coquis. It's only open on weekends in the summer. ✉ *Rte. 413, Km 4.1, Barrio Puntas,* ☎ *787/823–5654. AE, MC, V. Closed Mon. in winter.*

**$** ✕ **Pastrami Palace.** A favorite ex-pat hangout, this friendly, small restaurant and lunch counter in downtown Rincón serves up American basics from omelets, pancakes, and sandwiches to homemade pies, ice cream, and excellent coffee. The colorful decor includes local artwork, and there's a small library for lunchtime reading. An outdoor café is called (groan) the Garden of Eatin. ✉ *Calle Parque,* ☎ *787/823–0102. No credit cards. No dinner.*

## Beaches

By law, all of Puerto Rico's beaches are open to the public (except for the Caribe Hilton's man-made beach in San Juan). The government runs 13 *balnearios* (public beaches), which have dressing rooms, lifeguards, parking, and in some cases picnic tables, playgrounds, and camping facilities. Admission is free, parking $1. Most balnearios are open 9–5 daily in summer and Tuesday through Sunday the rest of the year. Listed below are some major balnearios. You can also contact the Department of Recreation and Sports (☎ 787/722–1551 or 787/722–1771).

**Boquéron Beach,** on the southwest coast, is a broad beach of hard-packed sand fringed with coconut palms. It has picnic tables, cabin rentals, bike rentals, basketball court, minimarket, scuba diving, and snorkeling. **Isla Verde,** a white sandy beach bordered by huge resort hotels, offers picnic tables and good snorkeling, with equipment rentals nearby. Set near San Juan, it's a lively beach popular with city folk. **Luquillo Beach** is crescent-shaped and comes complete with coconut palms, picnic tables, and tent sites. Coral reefs protect its crystal-clear lagoon from the Atlantic waters, making it ideal for swimming. It's one of the largest and best-known beaches on the island, and it gets crowded on weekends. **Ocean Park,** a residential neighborhood just east of the Condado, is home to the prettiest beach in San Juan. Here you'll find a mile-long, wide stretch of fine golden sand and often choppy but very swimmable waters. Very popular on weekends with local college students, this is also one of the cities' two gay beaches (the other is in front of the Atlantic Beach Hotel). **Playa Flamenco,** one of the most beautiful beaches in the Caribbean, is on the north shore of Culebra. The 3-mile-long crescent has shade trees, picnic tables, and rest rooms. It is popular on weekends with day-trippers from Fajardo. During the winter, storms in the North Atlantic often create great waves for bodysurfing. **Playa Soni,** on the eastern end of Culebra, is a wide strand of sparkling white sand on a protected bay with calm waters. Views of the islets of Culebrita, Cayo Norte, and St. Thomas are stunning. As there are no facilities and little shade, bring lots of water and an umbrella. **Seven Seas Beach,** an elongated beach of hard-packed sand, is always popular with bathers. It has picnic tables and tent and trailer sites; snorkeling, scuba diving, and boat rentals are nearby. **Sun Bay,** a white-sand beach on the island of Vieques, has shade trees, picnic tables, and tent sites, and offers snorkeling and scuba diving. Boat rentals are nearby.

## Outdoor Activities and Sports

### Bicycling

The broad beach at Boquerón makes for easy wheeling. You can rent bikes at **Boquerón Balnearios** (✉ Rte. 101, Boquerón, Dept. of Recreation and Sports, ☎ 787/722–1551 or 787/722–1771). In the Dorado area on the north coast, bikes can be rented at the **Hyatt Regency Cerromar Beach** (☎ 787/796–1234) or the **Hyatt Dorado Beach** (☎ 787/796–1234). Bikes are for rent at many of the hotels out on the island, including the **Ponce Hilton** (☎ 787/259–7676) and the **Copamarina Beach Resort** (☎ 787/821–0505).

### Boating

Virtually all the resort hotels on San Juan's Condado and Isla Verda strips rent paddleboats, Sunfish, Windsurfers, kayaks, and the like. Contact **Condado Plaza Hotel Watersports Center** (☎ 787/721–1000, ext. 1361), the **El San Juan Hotel Watersports Center** (☎ 787/791–1000), or the **Caribe Hilton** (☎ 787/721–0303). Out on the island, your hotel will be able either to provide rentals or recommend rental outfitters.

### Fishing

Half-day, full-day, split charters, and big- and small-game fishing can be arranged through **Benitez Deep-Sea Fishing** (✉ Club Náutico de San Juan, Miramar, ☎ 787/723–2292), **Castillo Watersports** (✉ ESJ Towers, Isla Verde, ☎ 787/791–6195 or 787/726–5752), and **Caribe Aquatic Adventures** (✉ Radisson Normandie, ☎ 787/724–1882, ext. 240). Out on the island, try **Tropical Fishing Charters** (✉ El Conquistador, Fajardo, ☎ 787/863–1000 or 787/789–5564), **Dorado Marine Center** (✉ 271 Méndez Vigo, ☎ 787/796–4645), and **Parguera Fishing Charters** (✉ Lajas, ☎ 787/899–4698 or 787/382–4698).

### Fitness

While most hotels and resorts have some semblance of a gym for the buff-body crazed, three gyms in San Juan stand out for their superb equipment: **Le Spa Fitness Center** (✉ San Juan Marriott, ☎ 787/722–7000), **Muscle Factory** (✉ 1302 Ave. Ashford, ☎ 787/721–0717), and **Fitness City** (✉ 1959 Calle Loiza, Suite 401, Ocean Park, ☎ 787/268–7773).

### Golf

There are four beautiful Robert Trent Jones–designed 18-hole courses shared by the **Hyatt Dorado Beach** and the **Hyatt Regency Cerromar Beach** hotels (✉ Dorado, ☎ 787/796–1234, ext. 3238 or 3016). You'll also find 18-hole courses at the **Palmas del Mar resort** (✉ Humacao, ☎ 787/852–6000), the **Berwind Country Club** (✉ Río Grande, ☎ 787/876–3056), **Club Ríomar** (✉ Río Grande, ☎ 787/887–3964), the **El Conquistador** (✉ Fajardo, ☎ 787/863–1000, hotel guests only), and **Punta Borinquén** (✉ Aguadilla, ☎ 787/890–2987). The **Bahia Beach Plantation** (✉ Río Grande, ☎ 787/256–5600) is Puerto Rico's newest course. There are two 9-hole courses out on the island, one at the **Club Deportivo del Oeste** (✉ Cabo Rojo, ☎ 787/851–8880), and one at the **Aguirre Golf Club** (✉ Aguirre, ☎ 787/853–4052). The **Ponce Hilton** (✉ Ponce, ☎ 787/259–7676) has a driving range. Be sure to call ahead when you plan to play; public hours at these courses vary, and you should schedule a tee time.

## Hiking

Dozens of trails lace **El Yunque** (information is available at the Sierra Palm Visitor Center, Rte. 191, Km 11.6, ☎ 787/887–2875 or 787/766–5335). You can also hit the trails in **Río Abajo Forest** (south of Arecibo) and **Toro Negro Forest** (east of Adjuntas). Each reserve has a ranger station.

## Horseback Riding

Beach trail rides can be arranged at **Palmas del Mar Equestrian Center** (✉ Palmas del Mar, Humacao, ☎ 787/852–6000). **Hacienda Carabalí** (✉ Rte. 992, Km 4, Luquillo, ☎ 787/889–5820) offers beach riding and rain-forest trail rides.

## Sailing

Sailing instruction is offered by **Palmas Sailing Center** (✉ Palmas del Mar, Humacao, ☎ 787/852–6000, ext. 10310) and most of the large resort hotels. Trips are offered by **Caribe Aquatic Adventures** (✉ Radisson Normandie, ☎ 787/729–2929, ext. 240) and **Castillo Watersports** (✉ ESJ Towers, Isla Verde, ☎ 787/791–6195 or 787/726–5752). Rentals are available at many hotels around the island.

## Snorkeling and Scuba Diving

There is excellent diving off Puerto Rico's coast. Some outfits offer package deals combining accommodations with daily diving trips; check when making your arrangements. Escorted half-day dives range from $45 to $90 for one- and two-tank dives, including all equipment. Packages, which include lunch and other extras, start at $60. Night dives are often available at close to double the price. Snorkeling excursions, which include equipment rental and sometimes lunch, start at $25. Snorkel equipment rents at beaches for about $5.

Caution: Coral-reef waters and mangrove areas can be dangerous to novices. Unless you're an expert or have an experienced guide, avoid unsupervised areas and stick to the water-sports centers of major hotels.

Snorkeling and scuba-diving instruction and equipment rentals are available at **Boquerón Dive Shop** (✉ Main St., Boquerón, ☎ 787/851–2155), **Caribbean School of Aquatics** (✉ Taft #1, Suite 10F, San Juan, ☎ 787/728–6606), **Caribe Aquatic Adventures** (✉ Radisson Normandie, ☎ 787/729–2929, ext. 240), **Coral Head Divers** (✉ Palmas del Mar, Humacao, ☎ 787/852–6000 or 800/468–3331), **Dive Copamarina** (✉ Copamarina Beach Resort, R. 333, Guánica, ☎ 787/821–6009; hotel-dive packages available), **Island Queen** (✉ Rincón, ☎ 787/823–6301), **Parguera Divers Training Center** (✉ La Parguera, ☎ 787/899–4171), and **Viking Puerto Rico** (✉ Rincón, ☎ 787/823–7010).

## Spectator Sports

BASEBALL

The island's season runs October–February. Many major-league ballplayers in the United States got their start in Puerto Rico's baseball league, and some return in the off-season to hone their skills. Stadiums are in San Juan, Santurce, Ponce, Caguas, Arecibo, and Mayagüez; the teams also play once or twice in Aguadilla. Contact the tourist office for details or call **Professional Baseball of Puerto Rico** (☎ 787/765–6285).

HORSE RACING

Thoroughbred races are run year-round at **El Comandante Racetrack.** On race days the dining rooms open at 12:30 PM. ⊠ *Rte. 3, Km 15.3, Canóvanas,* ☎ 787/724–6060. ⏱ *Wed., Fri., Sun., holidays 12:30–6.*

## Surfing

The best surfing beaches are along the Atlantic coastline from Borinquén Point south to Rincón, where there are several surf shops. Surfing is best from November through April. Aviones and La Concha beaches in San Juan and Casa de Pesca in Arecibo are summer surfing spots and have nearby surf shops.

## Tennis

If you'd like to use the courts at a property where you are not a guest, call in advance for information about reservations and fees.

There are 17 lighted courts at **San Juan Central Park** (⊠ Calle Cerra exit on Rte. 2, ☎ 787/722–1646); 6 lighted courts at the **Caribe Hilton Hotel** (⊠ Puerta de Tierra, ☎ 787/721–0303, ext. 1730); 8 courts, 4 lighted, at **Carib Inn** (⊠ Isla Verde, ☎ 787/791–3535, ext. 6); and 2 lighted courts at the **Condado Plaza Hotel** (⊠ Condado, ☎ 787/721–1000, ext. 1775). Out on the island, there are 14 courts, 2 lighted, at **Hyatt Regency Cerromar Beach** (⊠ Dorado, ☎ 787/796–1234, ext. 3040); 7 courts, 2 lighted, at the **Hyatt Dorado Beach** (⊠ Dorado, ☎ 787/796–1234, ext. 3220); 20 courts, 4 lighted, at **Palmas del Mar** (⊠ Humacao, ☎ 787/852–6000, ext. 51); 3 lighted courts (and a practice wall) at the **Mayagüez Hilton** (⊠ Mayagüez, ☎ 787/831–7575, ext. 2150); 4 lighted courts at the **Ponce Hilton** (⊠ Ponce, ☎ 787/259–7676); and 4 lighted courts at **Punta Borinquén** (⊠ Aguadilla, ☎ 787/891–8778).

## Windsurfing

Many resort hotels rent Windsurfers to their guests, including the **El San Juan,** the **El Conquistador, Palmas del Mar,** the **Hyatts,** and the **Condado Plaza.** If your hotel doesn't provide them, they can probably help you make arrangements with a local outfitter.

# Shopping

San Juan is not a free port, and you won't find bargains on electronics and perfumes. You can, however, find excellent prices on china, crystal, fashions, and jewelry.

Shopping for local Caribbean crafts can be great fun. You'll run across a lot of tacky things you can live without, but you can also find some treasures, and in many cases you'll be able to watch the artisans at work. (For guidance, contact the Puerto Rico Tourism Company's Artisan Center, ☎ 787/721–2400, ext. 2201, or the Fomento Crafts Project, ☎ 787/758–4747, ext. 2291.)

Popular souvenirs and gifts include *santos* (small, hand-carved figures of saints or religious scenes), hand-rolled cigars, handmade *mundillo* lace from Aguadilla, Carnival masks (papier-mâché from Ponce and fierce *veijigantes* made from coconut husks in Loiza, an African-American enclave near San Juan), and fancy men's shirts called *guayaberas.* Also, some folks swear that Puerto Rican rum is the best in the world.

## Shopping Districts

**Old San Juan** is full of shops, especially on Cristo, Fortaleza, and San Francisco streets. **Plaza Las Américas,** south of San Juan, is the largest shopping mall in the Caribbean, with 200 shops, restaurants, and movie theaters. Other malls out on the island include **Plaza del Caribe** in Ponce, **Plaza del Carmen** in Caguas, and the **Mayagüez Mall.**

## Good Buys

### CLOTHING

You can get discounts on Hathaway shirts and Christian Dior clothing at **Hathaway Factory Outlet** (✉ 203 Calle Cristo, ☎ 787/723–8946). Discounts on Ralph Lauren apparel are found at the **Polo/Ralph Lauren Factory Store** (✉ 201 Calle Cristo, ☎ 787/722–2136). The **London Fog Factory Outlet** (✉ 156 Calle Cristo, ☎ 787/722–4334) offers reductions on men's, women's, and children's raincoats. People line up to enter **Marshalls** (✉ Plaza de Armas, ☎ 787/722–0874) in Old San Juan. Try the **Bikini Factory** (✉ 3 Palmar Norte, Isla Verde, ☎ 787/726–0016) for stylish men's and women's swimwear.

### JEWELRY

There is gold, gold, and more gold at **Reinhold** (✉ 201 Calle Cristo, ☎ 787/725–6878). For brand-name watches visit the **Watch and Gem Palace** (✉ 204 Calle San José, Old San Juan, ☎ 787/722–2136).

### LOCAL CRAFTS

For one-of-a-kind buys, head for **Puerto Rican Arts & Crafts** (✉ 204 Calle Fortaleza, Old San Juan, ☎ 787/725–5596). You should pay a visit to the **artisan markets** in Sixto Escobar Park (✉ Puerta de Tierra, ☎ 787/722–0369) and Luis Muñoz Marín Park (✉ Next to Las Américas Expressway west on Piñero Ave., Hato Rey, ☎ 787/763–0568). The **Haitian Gallery** (✉ 367 Calle Fortaleza, ☎ 787/725–0986) carries Puerto Rican crafts and a selection of folksy, often inexpensive paintings from around the Caribbean. In Ponce, consult the **Casa Paoli Center of Folkloric Investigations** (✉ 14 Calle Mayor, ☎ 787/840–4115).

### PAINTINGS AND SCULPTURES

**Corinne Timsit International Galleries** (✉ 104 Calle San Jose, Old San Juan, ☎ 787/724–1039) features work by contemporary Latin American painters. **DMR Gallery** (✉ 204 Calle Luna, Old San Juan, ☎ 787/722–4181) features handmade furniture by artist Nick Quijano. **Galería Botello** (✉ 208 Calle Cristo, Old San Juan, ☎ 787/723–2879; ✉ Plaza Las Américas, ☎ 787/754–7430) exhibits and sells antique *santos* (religious sculptures). **Galería Gotay** (✉ 212 Calle San Francisco, Old San Juan, ☎ 787/722–5726) carries contemporary art in many medias. Another gallery worth visiting is the **Galería San Juan** (✉ Gallery Inn, 204–206 Calle Norzagaray, Old San Juan, ☎ 787/722–1808), especially to view the sculptures of bronze artiste Jan D'Esopo.

# Nightlife and the Arts

*¿Qué Pasa?*, the official visitors' guide, has current listings of events in San Juan and out on the island. Also, pick up a copy of the *San Juan Star, Quick City Guide,* or *Sunspots,* and check with the local tourist offices and the concierge at your hotel to find out what's doing.

## Nightlife

Fridays and Saturdays are big nights in San Juan. Dress to party. Bars are usually always casual. However, if you try to go out in jeans, sneakers, and a T-shirt, you will probably be refused entry at most nightclubs or discos (except the gay ones), unless you look like a model.

### BARS

Calle San Sebastián in Old San Juan is lined with trendy bars and restaurants; if you're in the mood for barhopping, head in that direction—it's pretty crazy on weekend nights.

**Blue Dolphin** (✉ 2 Calle Amapola, Isla Verde, ☎ 787/791–3083) is a hangout where you can rub elbows with some offbeat locals and enjoy some stunning sunset happy hours. While strolling along the Isla Verde beach, just look for the neon blue dolphin on the roof—you can't miss it. **El Patio de Sam** (⊠ 102 Calle san Sebastián, Old San Juan, ☎ 787/723–1149) is an Old San Juan institution whose expatriate clientele claims it serves the best burgers on the island. The dining room is awash in potted plants and strategically placed canopies that create the illusion of dining on an outdoor patio. **Hard Rock Cafe** (253 Recinto Sur, Old San Juan, ☎ 787/724–7625), almost as common as McDonald's these days, is located in Old San Juan.

### CASINOS

By law, all casinos are in hotels, primarily in San Juan. The government keeps a close eye on them. Dress for the larger casinos tends to be on the more formal side, and the atmosphere is refined. The law permits casinos to operate noon–4 AM, but individual casinos set their own hours.

Casinos are located in the following San Juan hotels (☞ Lodging, *above*): **Condado Plaza Hotel, Caribe Hilton, Dutch Inn & Tower** (⊠ 999 Ashford Ave., Condado), **Sands, El San Juan, Holiday Inn Crowne Plaza** (⊠ Rte. 187, Isla Verde), and **Radisson Ambassador** (⊠ 1369 Ashford Ave., Condado). Elsewhere on the island, there are casinos at the **Hyatt Regency Cerromar** and **Hyatt Dorado Beach** hotels, and at **Palmas del Mar,** the **Ponce Hilton,** the **El Conquistador,** and the **Mayagüez Hilton.**

### DISCOS

Out on the island nightlife is hard to come by, but there are discos in the **Mayagüez** and **Ponce Hiltons.**

**Amadeus** (⊠ El San Juan Hotel, Isla Verde, ☎ 787/791–1000) is a flashy disco in Isla Verde that attracts a well-dressed local crowd who come here to impress their dates and shake it. **Club Ibiza** (⊠ La Concha Hotel, ☎ 787/721–6090) is the hot spot on Fridays, with an interesting, mixed crowd. At press time, the former site of the now-defunct Peggy Sue was being transformed into a new, glamorous club to be called **Egypt** (⊠ Robert Todd Ave., San Juan, ☎ 787/725–4664 or 787/725–4675). **Krash** (⊠ 1257 Av. Ponce de León, Santurce, ☎ 787/722–1390) plays the best dance music on the island; gay crowds flock here. **Lazers** (⊠ 251 Calle Cruz, ☎ 787/721–4479), with multilevels and a landscaped roof deck overlooking San Juan, attracts different crowds on different nights; Thursdays and Sundays are gay nights.

### NIGHTCLUBS

The Sands Hotel's **Players Lounge** brings in such big names as Joan Rivers, Jay Leno, and Rita Moreno. Try El San Juan's **El Chico** to dance to Latin music in a western saloon setting. The Condado Plaza Hotel's **La Fiesta Lounge** sizzles with steamy Latin shows. The **Casino Lounge** offers live jazz Wednesday through Saturday. The El Centro Convention Center offers the festive **Olé Latino** Latin revue (☎ 787/722–8433). **Houlihan's** (⊠ Ashford and Condado Aves., Condado, ☎ 787/723–8600) is a restaurant with an upstairs nightclub popular among the local party crowd. On weekends there is always a line of revelers on the sidewalk waiting to get in.

## The Arts

**LeLoLai** is a year-round festival that celebrates Puerto Rico's Indian, Spanish, and African heritage. Performances take place each week, moving from hotel to hotel, showcasing the island's music, folklore, and culture. Because it is sponsored by the Puerto Rico Tourism Company and major San Juan hotels, passes to the festivities are included in some packages offered by participating hotels. You can also purchase tickets to a weekly series of events for $10. Contact the El Centro Convention Center, 787/723–3135. Reservations can be made by telephoning 787/722–1513. **La Tasca del Callejon** (⊠ Calle Fortaleza 317, ☎ 787/721–1689) is renowned for its tapas bar and the cabaret show (usually including flamenco guitar) performed by its engaging, talented staff.

# Exploring Puerto Rico

*Numbers in the margin correspond to points of interest on the Old San Juan Exploring map.*

## Old San Juan

Old San Juan, the original city founded in 1521, contains authentic and carefully preserved examples of 16th- and 17th-century Spanish colonial architecture, some of the best in the New World. More than 400 buildings have been beautifully restored in a continuing effort to preserve the city. Graceful wrought-iron balconies, decorated with lush green hanging plants, extend over narrow streets paved with blue-gray stones (*adequines,* originally used as ballast for Spanish ships). The old city is partially enclosed by the old walls, dating from 1633, that once completely surrounded it. Designated a U.S. National Historic Zone in 1950, Old San Juan is chockablock with shops, open-air cafés, private homes, tree-shaded squares, monuments, plaques, pigeons, and people. The traffic is awful. Get an overview of the inner city on a morning's stroll (bearing in mind that this "stroll" includes some steep climbs). However, if you plan to immerse yourself in history or to shop, you'll need two or three days. You may want to set aside extra time to see El Morro and Fort San Cristóbal, especially if you're an aficionado of military history. UNESCO has designated each fortress a World Heritage Site; each is also a National Historic Site. Both are administered by the National Park Service; you can take one of its tours or wander around on your own.

SIGHTS TO SEE

**❼ Casa Blanca.** The original structure on this site, not far from the ramparts of El Morro, was a frame house built in 1521 as a home for Ponce de León. But Ponce de León died in Cuba, never having lived in it, and it was virtually destroyed by a hurricane in 1523, after which Ponce de León's son-in-law had the present masonry home built. His descendants occupied it for 250 years. From the end of the Spanish-American War in 1898 to 1966, it was the home of the U.S. Army commander in Puerto Rico. A museum devoted to archaeology is on the second floor. The lush surrounding gardens, cooled by spraying fountains, are a tranquil spot for a restorative pause. ⊠ *1 Calle San Sebastián,* ☎ *787/724–4102.* ☞ *$2.* ⊙ *Wed.–Sat. 9–noon and 1–4:30.*

**❸ La Casa de los Contrafuertes.** This building is also known as the Buttress House because wide exterior buttresses support the wall next to the San Jose Plaza. The house is one of the oldest remaining private residences in Old San Juan. Inside is the Pharmacy Museum, a re-creation of an 18th-century apothecary shop, and the Latin American Graphic Arts Museum and Gallery, which hosts occasional exhibitions. ⊠ *101 Calle San Sebastián, Plaza de San José,* ☎ *787/724–5477.* ☞ *Free.* ⊙ *Wed.–Sun. 9–4:30.*

**⓬ Casa del Libro.** This 18th-century building contains exhibits devoted to books and bookbinding. The museum's 5,000 books include many rare volumes. ⊠ *255 Calle Cristo,* ☎ *787/723–0354.* ☞ *Free.* ⊙ *Tues.–Sat. 11–4:30.*

**⓰ City Hall.** Called the *Alcaldía,* this structure was built between 1604 and 1789. In 1841, extensive renovations were done to make the Alcaldía resemble Madrid's city hall, with arcades, towers, balconies, and a lovely inner courtyard. A tourist information center and an art gallery are on the first floor. ⊠ *North side of Plaza de Armas,* ☎ *787/724–7171, ext. 2391.* ⊙ *Weekdays 8–4.*

**⑪ Cristo Chapel.** According to legend, in 1753 a young horseman, carried away during festivities in honor of the patron saint, raced down the street and plunged over the steep precipice. A witness to the tragedy promised to build a chapel if the young man's life could be saved. Historical records maintain the man died, though legend contends that he lived. Inside is a small silver altar, dedicated to the Christ of Miracles. ⊠ *Calle Cristo.* ⊙ *Tues. 10–3:30 and on most Catholic holidays.*

**⑥ Dominican Convent.** Built by Dominican friars in 1523, the convent often served as a shelter during Carib Indian attacks and, more recently, as headquarters for the Antilles command of the U.S. Army. Now home to the Institute of Puerto Rican Culture, the beautifully restored building contains an ornate 18th-century altar, religious manuscripts, artifacts, and art. The Institute also maintains a bookshop here. The convent is the intended future home of the city's museum of fine arts. Classical concerts are occasionally held here. ⊠ *98 Calle Norzagaray,* ☎ *787/721–6866.* ⊡ *Free.* ⊙ *Mon.–Sat. 9–5.*

**⑩ La Fortaleza.** Sitting on a hill overlooking the harbor, La Fortaleza, the Western Hemisphere's oldest executive mansion in continual use and official residence of the present governor of Puerto Rico, was built as a fortress. The original primitive structure, built in 1540, has seen numerous changes over the past four centuries, resulting in the present collection of marble and mahogany, medieval towers, and stained-glass galleries. Guided tours are conducted every hour on the hour in English, on the half hour in Spanish. ⊠ *Calle Recinto Oeste,* ☎ *787/721–7000, ext. 2211 or 2358.* ⊡ *Free.* ⊙ *Weekdays 9–4.*

**⊛ ① Fuerte San Felipe del Morro.** Sitting on a rocky promontory on the northwestern tip of the old city is "El Morro", a fortress built by the Spaniards between 1540 and 1783. Rising 140 feet above the sea, the massive six-level fortress covers enough territory to accommodate a nine-hole golf course. It is a labyrinth of dungeons, ramps and barracks, turrets, towers, and tunnels. Built to protect the port, El Morro has a commanding view of the harbor. Its small, air-conditioned museum traces the history of the fortress. Tours and a video show are available in English. ⊠ *Calle Norzagaray,* ☎ *787/729–6960.* ⊡ *Free.* ⊙ *Daily 9–5.*

**⑮ La Intendencia.** From 1851 to 1898, this handsome three-story neoclassical building was home to the Spanish Treasury; now it is the headquarters of Puerto Rico's State Department. ⊠ *Calle San José, at the corner of Calle San Francisco,* ☎ *787/722–2121, ext. 230.* ⊡ *Free. Tours at 2 and 3 in Spanish, 4 in English.* ⊙ *Weekdays 8–noon and 1–4:30.*

**⑤ Pablo Casals Museum.** This museum contains memorabilia of the famed cellist, who made his home in Puerto Rico for the last 16 years of his life. Manuscripts, photographs, and his favorite cellos are on display, in addition to recordings and videotapes of Casals Festival concerts (the latter shown on request). ⊠ *101 Calle San Sebastián, Plaza de San José,* ☎ *787/723–9185.* ⊡ *$1.* ⊙ *Tues.–Sat. 9:30–5:30.*

**⑳ Paseo de la Princesa.** This street down at the port is spruced up with flowers, trees, benches, and street lamps. Take a seat and watch the boats zip across the water.

**⑭ Plaza de Armas.** This is the original main square of Old San Juan. The plaza, bordered by calles San Francisco, Fortaleza, San José, and Cruz,

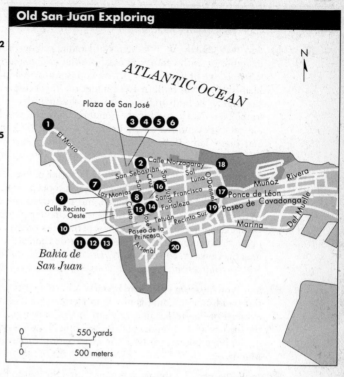

Old San Juan Exploring

has a lovely fountain with 19th-century statues representing the four seasons.

**NEED A BREAK?** La Bombonera (⊠ 259 Calle San Francisco, ☎ 787/722–0658), established in 1903, is known for its strong Puerto Rican coffee and *Mallorca*—a Spanish pastry made of light dough, toasted, buttered, and sprinkled with powdered sugar. Breakfast, for under $5, is served until 11. It's a favorite Sunday-morning gathering place in Old San Juan.

**⑰ Plaza de Colón.** This bustling square has a statue of Christopher Columbus atop a high pedestal. Originally called St. James Square, it was renamed in honor of Columbus on the 400th anniversary of the discovery of Puerto Rico. Bronze plaques in the base of the statue relate various episodes in the life of the great explorer. On the north side of the plaza is a terminal for buses to and from San Juan. ⊠ *On the pedestrian mall of Calle Fortaleza.*

**⑨ Plazuela de la Rogativa.** In this little plaza, statues of a bishop and three women commemorate a legend, according to which the British, while laying siege to the city in 1797, mistook the flaming torches of a *rogativa* (religious procession) for Spanish reinforcements and beat a hasty retreat. The monument was donated to the city in 1971 on its 450th anniversary. ⊠ *Caleta de las Monjas.*

**⑬ Popular Arts and Crafts Center.** Run by the Institute of Puerto Rican Culture, the center is located in a colonial building next door to the Casa del Libro (☞ *above*). The center is a superb repository of island craft work, some of which is for sale. ⊠ *253 Calle Cristo,* ☎ *787/722–0621.* 🎟 *Free.* ☉ *Mon.–Sat. 9–5.*

**⑱ San Cristóbal.** This 18th-century fortress guarded the city from land attacks. Even larger than El Morro, San Cristóbal was known as the

Gibraltar of the West Indies. ⊠ *Norzagaray Blvd.,* ☎ *787/729–6960.* ☞ *Free.* ⊘ *Daily 9–5.*

❹ **San José Church.** With its series of vaulted ceilings, this is a splendid example of 16th-century Spanish Gothic architecture. The church, which is one of the oldest Christian houses of worship in the Western Hemisphere, was built in 1532 under the supervision of the Dominican friars. The body of Ponce de León, the Spanish explorer who came to the New World seeking the Fountain of Youth, was buried here for almost three centuries before being removed in 1913 and placed in the San Juan Cathedral. ⊠ *Calle San Sebastián, Plaza de San José,* ☎ *787/725–7501.* ☞ *Free.* ⊘ *Mon.–Sat. 8:30–4; mass Sun. at 12:15 PM.*

❽ **San Juan Cathedral.** This great Catholic shrine of Puerto Rico had humble beginnings in the early 1520s as a thatch-topped wood structure. Hurricane winds tore off the thatch and destroyed the church. It was reconstructed in 1540, when the graceful circular staircase and vaulted Gothic ceilings were added, but most of the work on the church was done in the 19th century. The remains of Ponce de León are in a marble tomb near the transept. ⊠ *153 Calle Cristo,* ☎ *787/722–0861.* ⊘ *Weekdays 8:30–4; masses Sat. 7 PM, Sun. 9 AM and 11 AM, weekdays 12:15 PM.*

❷ **San Juan Museum of Art and History.** A bustling marketplace in 1855, this handsome building is now a modern cultural center that houses exhibits of Puerto Rican art. Multi-image audiovisual shows present the history of the island; concerts and other cultural events take place in the huge courtyard. ⊠ *Calle Norzagaray, at the corner of Calle MacArthur,* ☎ *787/724–1875.* ☞ *Free.* ⊘ *Tues.–Sun. 10–4.*

❿ **Tapia Theater.** This theater was named after the Puerto Rican playwright Alejandro Tapia y Rivera. Built in 1832 and remodeled in 1949 and again in 1987, the municipal theater is the site of ballets, plays, and operettas. Stop by the box office to find out what's showing. ⊠ *Calle Fortaleza at Plaza de Colón,* ☎ *787/722–0407.*

## San Juan

You'll need to resort to taxis, buses, públicos, or a rental car to reach the points of interest in "new" San Juan.

Avenida Muñoz Rivera, Avenida Ponce de León, and Avenida Fernández Juncos are the main thoroughfares that cross Puerta de Tierra, just east of Old San Juan, to the business and tourist districts of Santurce, Condado, and Isla Verde. Dos Hermanos Bridge connects Puerta de Tierra with Miramar, Condado, and Isla Grande. Isla Grande Airport, from which you can take short hops, is on the bay side of the bridge. On the other side of the bridge, the Condado Lagoon is bordered by Avenida Ashford, which threads past the high-rise Condado hotels and El Centro Convention Center, and Avenida Baldorioty de Castro Expreso, which barrels all the way east to the airport and beyond. Due south of the lagoon is Miramar, a primarily residential area with fashionable turn-of-the-century homes and a cluster of hotels and restaurants.

South of Santurce is the "Golden Mile"—Hato Rey, the city's bustling financial hub. Isla Verde, with its glittering beachfront hotels, casinos, discos, and public beach, is to the east, near the airport.

*Numbers in the margin correspond to points of interest on the San Juan Exploring, Dining, and Lodging map.*

SIGHTS TO SEE

❶ **Capitol.** In Puerta de Tierra is Puerto Rico's Capitol, a white marble building that dates from the 1920s. The grand rotunda, with mosaics and friezes, was completed a few years ago. The seat of the island's bicameral legislature, the Capitol contains Puerto Rico's constitution and is flanked by the modern buildings of the Senate and the House of Representatives. There are spectacular views from the observation plaza on the sea side of the Capitol. Pick up a booklet about the building from the House Secretariat on the second floor. Guided tours are by appointment only. ⊠ *Av. Ponce de León, Puerta de Tierra,* ☏ *787/721–6040, ext. 2458 or 3548.* ☑ *Free.* ⊙ *Weekdays 8:30–5.*

**3** **Centro de Bellas Artes.** Internationally acclaimed performers appear at the Fine Arts Center. This completely modern facility, the largest of its kind in the Caribbean, has a full schedule of concerts, plays, and operas. ⊠ *Corner of Av. De Diego and Av. Ponce de León, Box 41287, Minillas Station, Santurce 00940,* ☏ *787/725–7353.*

**2** **Fort San Jeronimo.** At the eastern tip of Puerta de Tierra, behind the splashy Caribe Hilton, this tiny fort is perched over the Atlantic like an afterthought. Added to San Juan's fortifications in the late 18th century, the structure barely survived the British attack of 1797. Restored in 1983 by the Institute of Puerto Rican Culture, it is now a military museum. At press time, however, the museum remained closed for repairs, and no reopening date had been announced, so visitors could only view the fort from the outside. ⊠ *Calle Rosales, Puerta de Tierra,* ☏ *787/724–5477.*

👋 **6** **Muñoz Marín Park.** This idyllic tree-shaded spot is dotted with gardens, lakes, playgrounds, and picnic areas. An aerial gondola connects the park with the parking area and provides a 6½-minute tour of the park. ⊠ *Next to Las Américas Expressway, west on Av. Piñero, Hato Rey,* ☏ *787/751–3353.* ☑ *Free; parking $1 per vehicle.* ⊙ *Tues.–Sun. 9–5.*

**5** **San Juan Central Park.** Southeast of Miramar, Avenida Muñoz Rivera skirts along the northern side of this mangrove-bordered park, a convenient place for jogging and tennis. The park was built for the 1979 Pan-American Games. ⊠ *Cerra St. exit on Rte. 2, Santurce,* ☏ *787/722–1646.* ☑ *Free.* ⊙ *Mon. 2–9:45, Tues.–Fri. 6:30 AM–9:45 PM, weekends 6:30 AM–6 PM.*

**4** **Santurce.** The area that lies between Miramar on the west and the Laguna San José on the east is a busy mixture of shops, markets, and offices. The classically designed **Sacred Heart University** is the home of the **Museum of Contemporary Puerto Rican Art**, which showcases the works of such modern masters as Rodon, Campeche, and Oller. ⊠ *Barat Bldg.,* ☏ *787/268–0049.* ☑ *Free.* ⊙ *Weekdays 9–5.*

NEED A
BREAK?

**Pescadería Atlántica** (⊠ 81 Calle Loiza, ☏ 787/726–6654) is a combination seafood restaurant and retail store. Stop in for a cool drink at the bar and a side dish of *calamares,* lightly breaded squid in a hot, spicy sauce.

**7** **University of Puerto Rico.** Río Piedras, a southern suburb of San Juan, is home to the University, located between Avenida Ponce de León and Avenida Barbosa. The university's campus is one of two sites for performances of the Puerto Rico Symphony Orchestra. Theatrical productions and other concerts are also scheduled here throughout the year. The **University Museum** has permanent archaeological and historical exhibits and occasionally mounts special art displays. ⊠ *Next to university's main entrance on Av. Ponce de León, Río Piedras,* ☏ *787/764–0000, ext. 2452.* ⊙ *Mon.–Wed. and Fri. 9–4:30, Thurs. 9–9, Sat. 9–3.*

The university's main attraction is the **Botanical Garden,** a lush forest of more than 200 species of tropical and subtropical vegetation. Footpaths lead to a graceful lotus lagoon, a bamboo promenade, an orchid garden, and a palm garden. ⊠ *Intersection of Rtes. 1 and 847 at entrance to Barrio Venezuela, Río Piedras,* ☎ *787/763–4408.* ☒ *Free.* ⊙ *Daily 9–4.*

## San Juan Environs

*Numbers in the margin correspond to points of interest on the Puerto Rico map.*

SIGHTS TO SEE

**❸ Bacardi Rum Plant.** Visitors can take a 45-minute tour of the bottling plant, museum, and distillery, which has the capacity to produce 100,000 gallons of rum a day. There is a gift shop. (Yes, you'll be offered a sample.) ⊠ *Rte. 888, Km 2.6, Cataño,* ☎ *787/788–1500.* ☒ *Free.* ⊙ *Tours every 20 mins Mon.–Sat. 9–10:30 and noon–4.*

**❷ Barrilito Rum Plant.** On the grounds are a 200-year-old plantation home and a 150-year-old windmill, which is listed in the National Register of Historic Places. ⊠ *Rte. 5.*

**❹ Bayamón.** In the central park, across from Bayamón's city hall, there are some historical buildings and a 1934 sugarcane train that runs through the park (☎ 787/798–8191), which is open daily 8 AM–5 PM. On the plaza, in the city's historic district, stands the 18th-century Catholic church of Santa Cruz and the old neoclassical city hall, which now houses the **Francisco Oller Art and History Museum.** ⊠ *Calle Santiago Veve,* ☎ *787/787–8620.* ☒ *Free.* ⊙ *Tues.–Sat. 9–4.*

**❶ Caparra Ruins.** In 1508, Ponce de León established the island's first settlement here. The ruins are that of an ancient fort. Its small **Museum of the Conquest and Colonization of Puerto Rico** contains historical documents, exhibits, and excavated artifacts. (You can see the museum's contents in less time than it takes to say the name.) ⊠ *Rte. 2, Km 6.6, Guaynabo,* ☎ *787/781–4795.* ☒ *Free.* ⊙ *Tues.–Sat. 8:30–4:30.*

## Out on the Island

Puerto Rico's 3,500 square miles is a lot of land to explore. While you can get from town to town via público, we don't recommend traveling that way unless your Spanish is good and you know exactly where you're going. The public cars stop in each town's main square, leaving you on your own to reach the beaches, restaurants, paradores, and sightseeing attractions. You'll do much better if you rent a car. Most of the island's roads are excellent. However, there is a tangled web of roads through the mountains, and they are not always well marked. It helps to buy a good road map.

*Numbers in the margin correspond to points of interest on the Puerto Rico map.*

EASTERN PUERTO RICO

**☖ ❼ Las Cabezas de San Juan Nature Reserve.** Opened in 1991, the reserve contains mangrove swamps, coral reefs, beaches, and a dry forest— all of Puerto Rico's natural habitats rolled into a microcosmic 316 acres. Nineteenth-century El Faro, one of the island's oldest lighthouses, is restored and still functioning; its first floor contains a small nature center that has an aquarium and other exhibits. The reserve is open, by reservation only, to the general public Friday–Sunday and to tour groups Wednesday and Thursday. Tours are given on request (in advance, by telephone) four times a day. ⊠ *Rte. 987, Km 5.8,* ☎ *787/722–5882; weekends, 787/860–2560.* ☒ *$5.*

**☖ ❺ Caribbean National Forest.** To take full advantage of the 28,000-acre El Yunque (as it's commonly known) rain forest, go with a tour. Dozens of trails lead through the thick jungle (it sheltered the Carib Indians for 200 years), and the tour guides take you to the best observation points, bathing spots, and waterfalls. Some of the trails are slippery, and there are occasional washouts.

However, if you'd like to drive there yourself, take Route 3 east from San Juan and turn right (south) on Route 191, about 25 miles from the city. The **Sierra Palm Visitor Center** (☎ 787/887–2875) is on Route 191, Km 11.6. Nature talks and programs at the center are in Spanish and English and by appointment only—another good reason to go with a tour group. The center is open daily 9–5 (until 4 in winter).

El Yunque, named after the good Indian spirit Yuquiyu, is in the Luquillo mountain range. The rain forest is verdant with feathery ferns, thick ropelike vines, white tuberoses and ginger, miniature orchids, and some 240 different species of trees. More than 100 billion gallons of rainwater fall on it annually. Rain-battered, wind-ravaged dwarf vegetation clings to the top peaks. (El Toro, the highest peak in the forest, is 3,532 feet.) El Yunque is also a bird sanctuary and the base of the rare Puerto Rican parrot. Millions of tiny, inch-long coquis can be heard singing (or squawking, depending on your sensibilities). ⊠ *For further information write Caribbean National Forest, Box B, Palmer, PR 00721 or call Catalina Field Office,* ☎ *787/887–2875 or 787/766–5335.*

**❾ Culebra.** This island off the east coast of Puerto Rico has lovely white-sand beaches, coral reefs, and a wildlife refuge. In the sleepy town of Dewey, on Culebra's southwestern side, check at the visitor information center at city hall (☎ 787/742–3291) about boat, bike, or car rentals. Don't miss **Playa Flamenco,** 3 miles north of Dewey, or **Playa Soni** on the eastern end of the island: They are two of the prettiest beaches in the Caribbean.

**❽ Fajardo.** This is a major fishing and sailing center with thousands of boats tied and stacked in tiers at its three large marinas. Boats can be rented or chartered here, and the *East Wind,* a 53-foot catamaran, can take you out for a full day of snorkeling, swimming, and sunning for $55 per person. Fajardo is also the embarkation point for ferries to the islands of Culebra (a $2.25 fare) and Vieques ($2). ⊠ *Rte. 3.*

**❻ Luquillo Beach.** One of the island's best and most popular beaches, Luquillo was once a flourishing coconut plantation. Coral reefs protect its calm, pristine lagoon, making it an ideal place for a swim. The entrance fee is $1 per car, and there are lockers, showers, and changing rooms, as well as stands selling savory Puerto Rican delicacies. The beach gets crowded on weekends, when it seems as if the whole world heads for Luquillo. ⊠ *Rte. 3, Km 35.4.* ⊠ *$1 per car.*

**❿ Vieques.** On this island off the east coast of Puerto Rico, is **Sun Bay public beach,** a gorgeous stretch of sand with picnic facilities and shade trees. **Red** and **Blue** beaches, located on the U.S. Marine/Camp Garcia base (open to the public 6 AM–6 PM), are superb for snorkeling and privacy. **Mosquito Bay** is best experienced on moonless nights, thanks to the millions of bioluminescent organisms that glow when disturbed—it's like swimming in a cloud of fireflies. Seventy percent of Vieques is owned by the U.S. Navy, ensuring it will remain unspoiled. The deserted beaches—Green, Red, Blue, Navia, and Media Luna— are among the Caribbean's loveliest; you might see a wild paso fino horse galloping in the surf. The **visitor information center** (☎ 787/741–5000) is in the fishing village of Esperanza. Both Vieques and Culebra (☞ *above*), parched in contrast to the lush eastern end of Puerto Rico, are havens for colorful "expatriates" escaping the rat race stateside.

This is pure old-time Caribbean: fun, funky, and unspoiled—the kind of getaway that is fast disappearing.

WESTERN PUERTO RICO

⓮ **Aguadilla.** In this area, somewhere between Aguadilla and Añasco, south of Rincón, Columbus dropped anchor on his second voyage in 1493. Both Aguadilla and **Aguada,** a few miles to the south, claim to be the spot where his foot first hit ground, and both towns have plaques to commemorate the occasion. ⊠ *Rte. 111.*

⓭ **Arecibo Observatory.** The town of Arecibo is home to one of the world's largest radar/radio telescopes. A 20-acre radar dish, with a 600-ton suspended platform hovering over it, sits in a 565-foot-deep sinkhole (karst fields, an alien landscape of collapsed limestone sinkholes, are the prevalent geology throughout this part of the island). You can take a self-guided tour of the observatory, where groundbreaking work in astronomy, including SETI (the search for extraterrestrial intelligence) continues. ⊠ *Rte. 625,* ☎ *787/878–2612.* ☒ *Free.* ☉ *Tues.–Fri. 2–3, Sun. 1–4:30.*

⓴ **Boquerón.** This tiny, funky, pastel village has sidewalk oyster vendors, bars, restaurants serving fresh seafood, and several of the standard T-shirt shops. There are also diving and snorkeling tours at the Boquerón Dive Shop on Main Street. Boquerón's balneario is one of the best beaches on the island. Parking is $1 per car, and two-room rustic cabins are for rent (☎ 787/724–2500, ext. 130 or 131). ⊠ *Rte. 101.*

⓲ **Cabo Rojo.** Once a pirates' hangout, this town is now a favorite resort area of Puerto Ricans. The area has long stretches of white-sand beaches on the clear, calm Caribbean Sea, as well as many seafood restaurants, bars, and hotels. There are also several paradores in the region. ⊠ *Rte. 102.*

⓫ **Caguana Indian Ceremonial Park.** This area was used 800 years ago by the Taíno tribes for recreation and worship. Mountains surround a 13-acre site planted with royal palms and guava. According to Spanish historians, the Taínos played a game similar to soccer, and in this park there are 10 courts bordered by cobbled walkways. There are also stone monoliths, some with colorful petroglyphs; a small museum; and a souvenir shop. ⊠ *Rte. 111, Km 12.3,* ☎ *787/894–7325.* ☒ *Free.* ☉ *Daily 9–4:30.*

⓱ **Mayagüez.** Puerto Rico's third-largest city has a population approaching 100,000. Although bypassed by the mania for restoration that saw Ponce and Old San Juan spruced up for the Columbus quincentennial, Mayagüez is graced by some lovely turn-of-the-century architecture, such as the landmark Art Deco Teatro Yagüez and the Plaza de Colón.

☾ North of town visit the **Mayagüez Zoo,** a 45-acre tropical compound that's home to about 500 animals. In addition to Bengal tigers, reptiles, and birds, there's a lake and a children's playground. ⊠ *Rte. 108 at Barrio Miradero,* ☎ *787/834–8110.* ☒ *$1; parking $1.* ☉ *Wed.–Sun. 9–4.*

⓰ **Mona Island.** Fifty miles west of Mayagüez in the turbulent shark-infested Mona Passage, Mona Island is nicknamed the Galápagos of the Caribbean, thanks to the plethora of endangered and unique indigenous species that call it home. The variety of marine and bird life is especially breathtaking. The coastline is rimmed with imposing limestone cliffs up to 200 feet high pocked with caves that are said to contain buried treasure; the many perfectly preserved Taíno hieroglyphs and rock paintings there are of great archaeological value.

Access to the island is only via private plane or boat. Very limited camping facilities are available on the pristine beaches. Call the Department of Natural Resources for information and camping reservations (☎ 787/723–1616 or 787/721–5495).

㉑ **Phosphorescent Bay.** The fishing village of **La Parguera,** an area of simple seafood restaurants, mangrove cays, and small islands, lies south of San Germán at the end of Route 304. This is an excellent scuba-diving area, but the main attraction is Phosphorescent Bay. Boats tour the bay, where microscopic dinoflagellates (marine plankton) light up like Christmas trees when disturbed by any kind of movement. The phenomenon can be seen only on moonless nights. Boats leave for the hour-long trip nightly between 7:30 and 12:30, depending on demand, and the trip costs $8 per person. You can also rent or charter a small boat to explore the numerous cays.

㉒ **Ponce.** From San Germán (☞ *below*), Route 2 traverses splendid peaks and valleys; pastel houses cling to the sides of steep green hills. The Cordillera Central mountains run parallel to Route 2 here and provide a stunning backdrop to the drive. East of Yauco, the road dips and sweeps right along the Caribbean and into Ponce.

Puerto Rico's second-largest city (population 300,000) underwent a massive restoration in preparation for its 300th anniversary, celebrated in 1996, of the city's first settlement.

The town's 19th-century style has been recaptured with pink marble-bordered sidewalks, gas lamps, painted trolleys, and horse-drawn carriages. You have not seen a firehouse until you've seen the red-and-black-striped **Parque de Bombas,** a structure built in 1882 for an exposition and converted to a firehouse the following year. The city hired architect Pablo Ojeda O'Neill to restore it, and it is now a museum of Ponce's history, which, not surprisingly, has a display of Fire Brigade memorabilia. ⊠ *Plaza Las Delicias,* ☎ *787/284–4141, ext. 342.* ☞ *Free.* ⊘ *Wed.–Mon. 9:30–6.*

Ponce's charm stems from a combination of neoclassical, Ponce Creole, and art-deco styles. The tiny streets lined with wrought-iron balconies are reminiscent of New Orleans's French Quarter. Stop in and pick up information about this seaside city at the columned **Casa Armstrong-Poventud,** the home of the Institute of Puerto Rican Culture and a Tourism Information Office, open weekdays 8–noon and 1–4:30 (use the side entrance). Stroll around the **Plaza Las Delicias,** with its perfectly pruned India-laurel fig trees, graceful fountains, gardens, and park benches. View **Our Lady of Guadalupe Cathedral** (masses are held daily), and walk down Calles Isabel and Christina to see turn-of-the-century wooden houses with wrought-iron balconies.

Two superlative examples of early-20th-century architecture house the **Ponce History Museum** (Museo de la Historia de Ponce), where 10 rooms of exhibits vividly re-create Ponce's golden years, providing especially fascinating glimpses into the worlds of culture, high finance, and journalism during the 19th century. ⊠ *53 Calle Isabel,* ☎ *787/844–7071.* ☞ *$3.* ⊘ *Mon. and Wed.–Fri. 10–5, weekends 10–6.*

Continue as far as Calles Mayor and Christina to the white stucco **La Perla Theater,** with its Corinthian columns. Be sure to allow time to visit the **Ponce Museum of Art** (Museo de Arte de Ponce). The architecture alone is worth seeing: The modern, two-story building designed by Edward Durell Stone (who designed New York's Museum of Modern Art) has seven interconnected hexagons, glass cupolas, and a pair of curved staircases. The collection includes late Renaissance and

Baroque works from Italy, France, and Spain, as well as contemporary art by Puerto Ricans. ⊠ *Av. Las Américas,* ☎ *787/848–0505.* 🎫 *$3.* ⊙ *Daily 10–5.*

Another fine museum is **Castillo Serrallés,** a splendid Spanish Revival mansion perched on El Vigía Hill, with smashing views of Ponce and the Caribbean. This former residence of the Serrallés family, owners of the Don Q rum distillery, has been restored with a mix of original furnishings and antiques that recall the era of the sugar barons, including a baronial dining room with heavy carved mahogany and wrought-iron doors. A short film details the history of the sugar and rum industries. The unusual, rather ugly 100-foot-tall cross (La Cruceta del Vigía) looming behind the museum is being restored; when finished (a completion date had not been set at press time), visitors will be able to climb to its observation tower. ⊠ *El Vigía Hill,* ☎ *787/259–1774.* 🎫 *$3.* ⊙ *Tues.–Sun. 10–5.*

There are two intriguing historical sights just outside the city. **Hacienda Buena Vista** is a 19th-century coffee plantation, restored by the Conservation Trust of Puerto Rico, with much of the authentic machinery and furnishings intact. Reservations are required for the 90-minute tours; tours in English are given on request (in advance) once a day. ⊠ *Rte. 10, Km 16.8, north of Ponce,* ☎ *787/722–5882 weekdays, 787/848–7020 weekends.* 🎫 *$5.* ⊙ *Wed.–Fri. open to tour groups; Fri.–Sun. open to public.*

The **Tibes Indian Ceremonial Center** is the oldest cemetery in the Caribbean. It is a treasure trove of pre-Taíno ruins and burials, dating from AD 300 to AD 700. Some archaeologists, noting the symmetrical arrangement of stone pillars, surmise the cemetery may have been of great religious significance. The complex includes a detailed re-creation of a Taíno village and a museum. ⊠ *Rte. 503, Km 2.7,* ☎ *787/840–2255.* 🎫 *$2.* ⊙ *Wed.–Sun. 9–4.*

**⑮ Rincón.** Located along Route 115, one of the island's most scenic areas of rolling hills dotted with pastel-colored houses, Rincón is perched on a hill and overlooks its beach, which was the site of the World Surfing Championship in 1968. Skilled surfers flock to Rincón during the winter, when the water is rough and challenging. The town is also increasingly popular with divers. Locals boast that the best diving and snorkeling in Puerto Rico (and some even say the Caribbean) is off the Rincón coast, particularly around the offshore island of Desecheo, a federal wildlife preserve. Whale-watching is another draw for this town; humpback whales winter off the coast from December through February. ⊠ *Rte. 115.*

**⑫ Río Camuy Cave Park.** This 268-acre reserve contains one of the world's largest cave networks. Guided tours take you on a tram down through dense tropical vegetation to the entrance of the cave, where you continue on foot over underground trails, ramps, and bridges. The caves, sinkholes, and subterranean streams are all spectacular (the world's second-largest underground river runs through here), but this trip is not for the claustrophobic. Be sure to call ahead; the tours allow only a limited number of people. ⊠ *Rte. 129, Km 18.9,* ☎ *787/898–3100 or 787/756–5555.* 🎫 *$10; parking $1.* ⊙ *Tues.–Sun. 8–4. Last tour starts at 3:50.*

**⑲ San Germán.** This quiet and colorful Old World town is home to the oldest intact church under the U.S. flag. Built in 1606, **Porta Coeli** (Gates of Heaven) overlooks one of the town's two plazas (where the townspeople continue the Spanish tradition of promenading at night). The church is now a museum of religious art, housing 18th- and 19th-century paintings and wooden statues. ⌖ *Rte. 102,* ☎ *787/892–5845.* ⌖ *Free.* ☉ *Tues.–Sun. 9–noon and 1–4.*

# Puerto Rico A to Z

## Arriving and Departing

### BY PLANE

The **Luis Muñoz Marín International Airport** (☎ 787/462–3147), east of downtown San Juan, is one of the easiest and cheapest destinations to reach in the Caribbean. The airport is the Caribbean hub for **American Airlines** (☎ 800/433–7300). American has daily nonstop flights from New York, Newark, Miami, Boston, Philadelphia, Chicago, Nashville, Los Angeles, Dallas, Baltimore, Hartford, Raleigh-Durham, Washington, D.C., and Tampa. **Continental** (☎ 800/231–0856) has nonstop service from Newark. **Delta** (☎ 800/221–1212) has nonstop service from Atlanta and Orlando, as well as connecting service from other major cities. **Northwest** (☎ 800/447–4747) has nonstop flights from Detroit and Minneapolis to San Juan. **TWA** (☎ 800/892–4141) flies nonstop from New York, Miami, and St. Louis. **United** (☎ 800/241–6522) flies nonstop from Miami, and Chicago. **USAir** (☎ 800/428–4322) offers nonstop flights from Philadelphia and Charlotte. Puerto Rico–based **Carnival Airlines** (☎ 800/437–2110) operates daily nonstop flights from New York, Newark, Miami, and Orlando to San Juan, Ponce, and Aguadilla. **Midway** (☎ 800/446–4392) flies nonstop from Raleigh/Durham. **Tower Air** (☎ 800/452–5531) flies nonstop from New York/JFK. **American Trans Air (ATA)** (☎ 800/382–5892) operates nonstop from Boston and Orlando.

Foreign carriers include **Air France** (☎ 800/237–2747), **British Airways** (☎ 800/247–9297), **BWIA** (☎ 800/327–7401), **Iberia** (☎ 800/772–4642), **LACSA** (☎ 800/225–2272), and **Lufthansa** (☎ 800/645–3880).

Connections between Caribbean islands can be made through **American Eagle** (☎ 800/433–7300), **Air Jamaica** (☎ 800/523–5585), **ANA** (☎ 800/693–0007), **LIAT** (☎ 800/468–0482), and **Sunaire Express** (☎ 800/595–9501).

### FROM THE AIRPORT

**Taxi Turisticos** (☞ Getting Around, *below*) charge set rates depending on the destination. Uniformed and badged officials help you find a cab at the airport and provide written information about fares. To Isla Verde, the fare is $8; to Condado, it's $12; to Old San Juan, it's $16. If you don't hail one of these cabs, you're at the mercy of the meter and the cabdriver. Other options are the **Airport Limousine Service** (☎ 787/791–4745), which provides minibus service to hotels in the Isla Verde, Condado, and Old San Juan areas at basic fares of $2.50, $3.50, and $4.50, respectively; the fares do vary, depending on the time of day and number of passengers. Limousines of **Dorado Transport Service** (☎ 787/796–1214) serve hotels and villas in the Dorado area for $15 per person.

## Currency

The U.S. dollar is the official currency of Puerto Rico.

## Emergencies

**Police, fire, and medical emergencies:** ☎ 911. **Hospitals:** Hospitals in the Condado/Santurce area with 24-hour emergency rooms are **Ashford Community Hospital** (⌖ 1451 Av. Ashford, ☎ 787/721–2160) and **San Juan Health Centre** (⌖ 200 Av. De Diego, ☎ 787/725–0202). **Pharmacies:** In San Juan, **Walgreens** (⌖ 1130 Av. Ashford, Condado, ☎ 787/725–1510) operates a 24-hour pharmacy; in Old San Juan, try

**Puerto Rico Drug Company** (✉ 157 Calle San Francisco, ☎ 787/725–2202). Walgreens operates more than 30 pharmacies on the island.

## Getting Around

If you are staying in San Juan, you can get around by walking, bus, taxi, or hotel shuttle. However, if you venture out on the island, a rental car is your best transportation option.

Roads in Puerto Rico are generally well marked; however, a good road map is helpful when traveling to more remote areas on the island. Some car-rental agencies distribute free maps of the island when you pick up your car. These maps lack detail and are usually out-of-date due to new construction. The simplest thing to do is head to the nearest gas station—most of them sell better maps. Good maps are also available at the **Book Store** (✉ 257 Calle San José, Old San Juan, ☎ 787/724–1815). Keep in mind that distances are posted in kilometers while road speed signs are in m.p.h.

### BUSES

The **Metropolitan Bus Authority (AMA)** (☎ 787/250–6064) operates *guaguas* (buses) that thread through San Juan. The fare is 25¢, and the buses run in exclusive lanes, *against the traffic* on major thoroughfares, stopping at magenta, orange, and white signs marked *Parada* or *Parada de Guaguas*. The main terminals are Covadunga parking lot and Plaza de Colón, in Old San Juan, and Capetillo Terminal in Rio Piedras, next to the central business district.

### CAR RENTALS

U.S. driver's licenses are valid in Puerto Rico for three months. All major U.S. car-rental agencies are represented on the island, including **Avis** (☎ 787/721–4499 or 800/331–1212), **Hertz** (☎ 787/791–0840 or 800/654–3131), **Budget** (☎ 787/791–3685 or 800/472–3325), and **National** (☎ 787/791–1805 or 800/328–4567). Local rental companies, sometimes less expensive, include **Caribbean Rental** (☎ 787/724–3980), **Charlie Car Rental** (☎ 787/728–2418 or 800/289–1227), and **L & M Car Rental** (☎ 787/725–8416). Prices start at about $30 (plus insurance), with unlimited mileage. Discounts are offered for long-term rentals, and insurance can be waived for those who rent with American Express or gold credit cards (be sure to check with your credit-card company before renting). Some discounts are offered for AAA or 72-hour advance bookings. Most car rentals have shuttle service to or from the airport and the pickup point. If you plan to drive across the island, arm yourself with a good map and be aware that there are many unmarked roads up in the mountains. Many service stations in the central mountains do not take credit cards. Speed limits are posted in miles, distances in kilometers, and gas prices in liters.

### FERRIES

The ferry between Old San Juan (Pier 2) and Cataño (☎ 787/788–1155) costs a mere 50¢ one-way. The ferry runs every half hour from 6 AM to 10 PM. The 400-passenger ferries of the **Fajardo Port Authority** (☎ 787/863–0852), which carry cargo as well as passengers, make the 90-minute trip between Fajardo and the island of Vieques twice on weekdays and three times on weekends ($2 one-way). They make the 90-minute run between Fajardo and the island of Culebra once a day Monday–Thursday and twice a day Friday–Sunday ($2.25 one-way).

### LINÉAS

*Linéas* are private taxis you share with three to five other passengers. There are more than 20 companies, each usually specializing in a certain region. Most will arrange door-to-door service. Check local yellow pages listings under Linéas de Carros. They're a cheaper method of transport and a great way to meet people, but be prepared to wait: They usually don't leave until they have a full load.

PLANES

From the Isla Grande Airport, you can take a **Vieques Air-Link** (☎ 787/722–3736) flight to Vieques ($30 one-way), or a **Flamenco Airways** (☎ 787/725–7707) flight to Culebra for ($25 one-way).

PÚBLICOS

*Públicos* (literally, "public cars"), with yellow license plates ending in "P" or "PD," scoot to towns throughout the island, stopping in each town's main plaza. These 17-passenger vans operate primarily during the day, with routes and fares fixed by the Public Service Commission. In San Juan, the main terminals are at the airport and at Plaza Colón on the waterfront in Old San Juan.

TAXIS

The Puerto Rico Tourism Company has recently instituted a much-needed and well-organized taxi program for tourists. Taxis painted white and sporting the *garita* (sentry box) logo and **Taxi Turístico** label charge set rates depending on the destination; they run from the airport or the cruise-ship piers to Isla Verde, Condado/Ocean Park, and Old San Juan, with rates ranging from $6 to $16. Metered cabs authorized by the **Public Service Commission** (☎ 787/751–5050) start at $1 and charge 10¢ for every additional tenth of a mile, 50¢ for every suitcase, and $1 for home or business calls. Waiting time is 10¢ for each 45 seconds. The minimum charge is $3. Be sure the driver starts the meter. You can also call **Major Taxicabs** (☎ 787/723–2460) in San Juan and **Ponce Taxi** (☎ 787/840–0088).

TROLLEYS

If your feet fail you in Old San Juan, climb aboard the free open-air trolleys that rumble and roller-coast through the narrow streets. Departures are from La Puntilla and from the marina, but you can board anywhere along the route.

## Guided Tours

Old San Juan can be seen either on a self-guided walking tour or on the free trolley. To explore the rest of the city and the island, consider renting a car. (We do, however, recommend a guided tour of the vast El Yunque rain forest.) If you'd rather not do your own driving, there are several tour companies you can call. Most San Juan hotels have a tour desk that can make arrangements for you. The three standard half-day tours (at $15–$30) are of Old and New San Juan; Old San Juan and the Bacardi Rum Plant; and Luquillo Beach and El Yunque rain forest. All-day tours ($25–$45) can include a trip to Ponce, a day at El Comandante Racetrack, or a combined tour of the city and El Yunque rain forest.

Leading tour operators include **Gray Line of Puerto Rico** (☎ 787/727–8080), **Normandie Tours, Inc.** (☎ 787/722–6308), **Rico Suntours** (☎ 787/722–2080 or 787/722–6090), **Tropix Wellness Tours** (☎ 787/268–2173), and **United Tour Guides** (☎ 787/725–7605 or 787/723–5578). **Cordero Caribbean Tours** (☎ 787/786–9114 or 787/780–2442 evenings) runs tours in air-conditioned limousines for an hourly rate.

## Language

Puerto Rico's official language is Spanish, and although English is widely spoken, you will probably want to take a Spanish phrase book along if you rent a car to travel around the island.

## Opening and Closing Times

Shops are open from 9 to 6 (from 9 to 9 during Christmas holidays). Banks are open weekdays from 8:30 to 2:30 and Saturday from 9:45 to noon.

## Passports and Visas

Puerto Rico is a commonwealth of the United States, and U.S. citizens do not need passports to visit the island. British citizens must have passports. Canadian citizens need proof of citizenship (preferably a passport).

## Precautions

San Juan, like any other big city and major tourist destination, has its share of crime, so guard your wallet or purse on the city streets. Puerto Rico's beaches are open to the public, and muggings can occur at night even on the beaches of the posh Condado and Isla Verde tourist hotels. While you certainly can and should explore the city and its beaches, using common sense will make your stay more secure and enjoyable. Don't leave anything unattended on the beach. Leave your valuables in the hotel safe, and stick to the fenced-in beach areas of your hotel. Always lock your car and stash valuables and luggage out of sight. Avoid deserted beaches at night.

## Taxes and Service Charges

The government tax on room charges is 7% (9% in hotels with casinos). Some hotels automatically add a 10%–15% service charge to your bill. In restaurants, a 15%–20% tip is expected. There is no departure tax.

## Telephones and Mail

Note that the area code for Puerto Rico changed from 809 to 787 as of March 1, 1996. Puerto Rico uses U.S. postage stamps and has the same mail rates (22¢ for a postcard, 32¢ for a first-class letter). Post offices in major Puerto Rican cities offer Express Mail next-day service to the U.S. mainland and to Puerto Rican destinations.

## Visitor Information

Before you go, contact the **Puerto Rico Tourism Company** (⊠ Box 6334, San Juan, PR 00914, ☎ 787/721–2400). From the States, you can call toll-free at ☎ 800/223–6530. Other branches: ⊠ 575 5th Ave., 23rd floor, New York, NY 10017, ☎ 212/599–6262, FAX 212/818–1866; ⊠ 3575 W. Cahuenga Blvd., Suite 560, Los Angeles, CA 90068, ☎ 213/874–5991, FAX 213/874–7257; ⊠ 901 Ponce de León Blvd., Suite 604, Coral Gables, FL 33134, ☎ 305/445–9112, FAX 305/445–9450. In the United Kingdom, contact the tourism office: ⊠ 11a W. Halkin St., London SW1X 8JL, ☎ 0171/333–0333.

On Puerto Rico, the government-sponsored **Puerto Rico Tourism Company** (⊠ Paseo la Princesa, Old San Juan, Puerto Rico 00902, ☎ 787/721–2400) is an excellent source for maps and printed tourist materials. Be sure to pick up a free copy of *¿Qué Pasa?*, the official visitors' guide.

Information offices are also found at **Luis Muñoz Marín International Airport** in Isla Verde (☎ 787/791–1014 or 787/791–2551) and **La Casita** (☎ 787/722–1709), near Pier 1 in Old San Juan. Out on the island, information offices are located in **Ponce** (⊠ Fox Delicias Mall, 2nd floor, Plaza Las Delicias, ☎ 787/840–5695), **Aguadilla** (⊠ Rafael Hernández Airport, ☎ 787/890–3315), **Cabo Rojo** (⊠ Rte. 100, Km 13.7, ☎ 787/851–7070), and in many towns' city halls on the main plaza. Offices are usually open weekdays from 8 to noon and 1 to 4:30.

# 18 Saba

**T**HIS 5-SQUARE-MILE FAIRY-TALE ISLE is not for everybody. If you're looking for exciting nightlife or lots of shopping, forget Saba, or make it a one-day excursion from St. Maarten. There are only a handful of shops on Saba, even fewer inns and eateries, and the island's movie theater closed with the arrival of cable. Saba has only 1,200 friendly but shy inhabitants; everyone knows everyone and crime is virtually nonexistent, as is unemployment. Beach lovers should also take note that Saba is an essentially beachless volcanic island: Steep cliffs ring the island and plummet sharply to the sea.

Updated by
Jonathan Runge

So, why Saba? Saba is a perfect hideaway, a challenge for hikers (Mt. Scenery rises to a height of 2,855 feet), a haven for seasoned divers, and, for Sabans, heaven on water. It's no wonder they call their island the Unspoiled Queen.

The capital of Saba (pronounced *say*-ba) is the Bottom, which sits in the bottom of a volcanic crater, hence the name. Meandering goats have the right of way on the Road (there's only one); chickens cross at their own risk. In tiny, toylike villages, flower-draped walls and neat picket fences border narrow paths. Tidy houses with red roofs and gingerbread trim are planted on the mountainside among the bromeliads, palms, hibiscus, orchids, and Norwegian pines. Saba may be one of the most picturesque islands in the Caribbean; it's certainly the most immaculate and has an enchanting fairy-tale air to it. Despite such modern additions as television sets (since 1965) and 24-hour electricity (installed in 1970), the island's uncomplicated lifestyle has persevered. Saban ladies still hand-embroider delicate Saba lace—a reminder of Saban gentility that has flourished since the 1870s—and brew the potent rum-based liquor, Saba Spice, sweetened with secret herbs and spices. Families still follow the generations-old tradition of burying their dead in their neatly tended gardens.

Saba is part of the Netherlands Antilles Windward Islands and is 28 miles—a 15-minute flight with a hair-raising landing—from St. Maarten. The island is a volcano that has been extinct for 5,000 years. Carib Indians may have lived here around AD 800. Columbus spotted the little speck in 1493, but somehow Saba remained uninhabited until the first Dutch settlers arrived from Statia in 1640. In the 17th, 18th, and early 19th centuries the French, Dutch, English, and Spanish vied for control of the island. Saba changed hands 12 times before permanently raising the Dutch flag.

Sabans are a hardy lot. To get from Fort Bay to the Bottom, the early Sabans carved 900 steps out of the mountainside. Everything that arrived on the island, from a pin to a piano, had to be hauled up. Those rugged steps remained the only way to travel until the Road was built by Josephus Lambert Hassell (a carpenter who took correspondence courses in engineering) in the 1940s. An extraordinary feat of engineering, the handmade road took 25 years to build. If you like roller coasters, you'll love the 9-mile, white-knuckle route, which begins at sea level in Fort Bay, zigs up to 1,968 feet, and zags down to 131 feet above sea level at the airport, constructed on the island's only flat point, called (what else?) Flat Point.

## Lodging

Like everything else on Saba, the hotel/guest houses are tiny and tucked into tropical gardens. The selection is limited, and because most restaurants are located in the guest houses, you would do well to take advantage of meal plans. Accommodations are invariably neat and quite reasonably priced. Saba has experienced a (relative) boom in hotel development of late, but is still very low-key compared to other islands. Dive packages are available with almost all accommodations, so be sure to ask.

| CATEGORY | COST* |
|---|---|
| $$$ | over $125 |
| $$ | $75–$125 |
| $ | under $75 |

*All prices are for a standard double room in high season, excluding 5% tax and 10%–15% service charge.*

## Hotels

**$$$** ★ ☎ **Captain's Quarters.** All the rooms here are spacious and airy, furnished with Victorian antiques (including canopied four-poster beds in most rooms), and decorated with floral print fabrics. Be advised that some of the older rooms on the street side can be somewhat noisy due to neighbors with loud TV sets. Two choice bedrooms are in the small main house, which was built by a Saban sea captain in 1832. Across the parking lot from the pool is a long bungalow unit holding six rooms; numbers 7 through 10 can easily sleep four. Two rooms with stunning views of the sea were added in 1994 in a building behind the bar, and a new dining area was added in 1996. Hibiscus, poinsettia, and papaya trees grace the grounds. ⊠ *Windwardside,* ☎ *599/4–62201,* FAX *599/4–62377; in NY,* ☎ *212/289–6031,* FAX *212/289–1931. 10 rooms. Restaurant, bar, pool. AE, MC, V. CP.*

**$$$** ★ ☎ **Willards of Saba.** This is the most luxurious and expensive place to stay on the island. Set on the side of a cliff with stunning panoramic vistas of the Caribbean, Willard's has the nicest pool (and it's heated) on the island and is the only hotel with a tennis court. Spacious rooms and bungalows are individually decorated, but all have tile floors, white walls, ceiling fans, rattan furniture, and a balcony. The three types of room—bungalow, luxury, and VIP—vary in size, furnishings, and whether the bathroom contains a tub or shower. Willards does not allow children younger than 14 due to its precarious perch. Some may find its location somewhat isolated and inconvenient to town, but others will relish the view and privacy. ⊠ *Box 515, Windwardside,* ☎ *599/4–62498 or 800/223–9815,* FAX *599/4–62482. 7 rooms. Restaurant, bar, fans, pool, hot tub, tennis court. AE, MC, V. EP, MAP.*

**$$** ☎ **Cottage Club.** Local brothers Dean and Mark Johnson run this property. Ten gingerbread bungalows, nestled amid rainbow-hued tropical gardens, have balconies overlooking either the water or the village of English Quarter. Interiors are large and breezy, with gleaming tile floors and high beamed ceilings. Pastel shell prints are used for drapes and spreads, and local art decorates the walls. Each bungalow has its own fully equipped kitchen, dining area, bath (shower only), balcony, telephone, and cable TV. The stone, colonial-style main house holds the reception area and is a showplace for antiques from the owners' collection, accented with potted plants and Saban-lace curtains. Bungalows 1, 2, and 6 have the best views. A pool, conference room, and small gym were slated for completion in June 1996. If you give the owners a shopping list, they'll stock your kitchen for you. ⊠ *Windwardside,* ☎ *599/4–62486 or 599/4–62386,* FAX *599/4–62476. 10 units. Grocery delivery, kitchens. MC, V. EP.*

**$$** ☎ **Gate House.** Two ex–New Yorkers run this six-room inn in the tiny village of Hell's Gate. The secluded location, between the airport and Windwardside, makes this somewhat of a getaway, even for Saba. Spacious rooms have whitewashed walls and tile floors and are deco-

ATLANTIC OCEAN

Flat
Pt.

Juancho E.
Yrausquin Airport

Cove Bay

Spring Bay

Core
Gut
Bay

SABA MARINE PARK

Cove of Rum
Bay

Great
Pt.

Hell's Gate

Windwardside

Mt.
Scenery

Mary's Point Mtn.

Troy
Hill

Torrens
Bay

Torrens Pt.

Well's Bay

Ladder
Bay

Ladder

**KEY**

- Cruise Ship
- Ferry
- ① Exploring Sites
- ⑨ Hotels and Restaurants

**Exploring**
The Bottom, **7**
Cove Bay, **2**
Flat Point, **1**
Fort Bay, **8**
Hell's Gate, **3**
Mt. Scenery, **4**
Well's Bay, **5**
Windwardside, **6**

**Dining**
Brigadoon Restaurant, **16**
Captain's Quarters, **13**
Gate House, **21**
In Two Deep, **9**
Lollipop's, **12**
Saba Chinese Bar & Restaurant, **14**
Scout's Place, **15**
Sunset Bar & Restaurant, **10**
Tropics, **18**
Willards of Saba, **20**

**Lodging**
Captain's Quarters, **13**
Cottage Club, **19**
Cranston's Antique Inn, **11**
Gate House, **21**
Juliana's, **17**
Scout's Place, **15**
Willards of Saba, **20**

TO ST. MAARTEN

rated with crisp pinstripe and checked fabrics and colorful art. Two units have kitchenettes. The restaurant off the lobby overlooks the sea and is creating an admiring buzz on the island. Chef Beverly changes the menu of local specialties daily; the prix fixe dinner is $20. ⊠ *Hell's Gate,* ☎ *599/4–62416; in U.S., 708/354–9641;* ⅀ *599/4–62529. 6 rooms. Restaurant. MC, V. CP, MAP.*

**$$**   🏠 **Juliana's.** Juliana and Franklin Johnson's comfortable, tidy studios have tile floors, light wood furnishings, and floral print spreads. One has a queen-size bed; the others have doubles or twins. There's also a 2½-room apartment (Flossie's Cottage) with a kitchenette, a living-dining room, and a bedroom, as well as a large porch facing the sea. Almost every window provides fabulous views of the Caribbean. Across the street is the pool, and the café, Tropics. ⊠ *Windwardside,* ☎ *599/4–62269; in U.S., 800/328–5285;* ⅀ *599/4–62389. 9 studios, 1 apartment, 1 2-bedroom cottage. Restaurant, pool. MC, V. EP.*

**$–$$**   🏠 **Scout's Place.** Accurately billed as "Bed 'n Board, Cheap 'n Cheerful," Scout's Place makes up in convenience and value what it lacks in luxury. Staying here puts you in the center of Windwardside, within walking distance of Sea Saba dive center. The four original rooms are extremely plain and have no hot water; two share a bath. Eleven newer rooms do have hot water (in private bathrooms), as well as four-poster beds and balconies. The restaurant serves a full breakfast. ⊠ *Windwardside,* ☎ *599/4–62205,* ⅀ *599/4–62388. 15 rooms, 13 with private bath. Restaurant, bar, pool, gift shop, car rental. MC, V. EP, CP.*

**$**   🏠 **Cranston's Antique Inn.** The six rooms of this slightly run-down spot are popular digs for the diving set. The shared baths are far from luxurious (dingy decor à la early '70s), but the rooms have attractive hardwood floors and are neatly decorated with pink or blue fabrics and dark wood antiques; most have four-poster beds. The pool bar is festive, and the Inner Circle disco is practically across the street. ⊠ *The Bottom,* ☎ ⅀ *599/4–63203. 6 rooms, 1 with private bath. Restaurant, bar, pool. D, MC, V. EP.*

### Apartment Rentals

Twelve apartments, cottages, and villas, all with hot water and modern conveniences, are available for daily, weekly, and monthly rentals. For a listing of all rental properties, check with the **Saba Tourist Office** (☎ 599/4–62231 or 800/722–2394). **WIMCO** (☎ 800/932–3222) rents the fabulous and palatial Haiku House for $2,000–$4,500 per week, as well as other villas.

# Dining

In most of Saba's restaurants you pretty much have to take potluck. If you don't like what's cooking in one place, you can check out the other restaurants. However, it won't take you long to run out of options, and it's tough to find gourmet cooking.

### What to Wear

Restaurants here are quite informal wherever you go. Shorts or a nice cover-up over your swimsuit are a good idea during the day. For dinner you may want to put on pants or a casual sundress, but you won't find any dress requirements. Nights in Windwardside can be cool due to the elevation.

| CATEGORY | COST* |
| --- | --- |
| **$$$** | over $25 |
| **$$** | $20–$25 |
| **$** | under $20 |

*\*per person for a three-course meal, excluding drinks and service*

**$$$** ✕ **Willards of Saba.** Stunningly set on a cliff high above Windward-side, Saba's most expensive restaurant has views of the sea a dizzying 2,000 feet below. The fusion menu of international and Asian cuisine includes such specialties as chicken adobo, Shanghai rolls, and fresh lobster. A unique touch is the restaurant's hot-lava stone grill, where you grill your seafood or meat as you like it and add the chef's sauces. Order one of the Bava wines from Italy; Willard's is the only restaurant in the Caribbean that offers them. Access to the restaurant is up a steep drive and only a few taxis will make the climb. Be sure to call the restaurant to arrange transport. ⊠ *Windwardside*, ☎ *599/4–62498. AE, MC, V.*

**$$–$$$** ✕ **Captain's Quarters.** At this newly renovated restaurant you can dine in comfort on a breezy terrace surrounded by flowers and mango trees. The chef artfully blends Dutch, Indonesian, French, and Creole cuisines. Try the chicken breast served in spicy Indonesian-style peanut sauce. The fish (whatever's fresh that day) is prepared with a variety of sauces, including lime butter. On Saturday night the owner takes over the grill and barbecues steaks, chicken, and fish. Service is pleasant but can be slow. ⊠ *Windwardside*, ☎ *599/4–62201. Reservations essential. AE, MC, V.*

**$$** ✕ **Tropics.** A black-and-white-checked tile floor, crisp black and white napery, and gleaming silver flatware create a chic, if not exactly tropical, atmosphere in this poolside restaurant. The entrées, a mix of Continental and West Indian dishes, can be on the bland side; stick with steak and simply prepared fresh seafood. Try the croquette appetizer: a spicy blend of meat lightly breaded and deep-fried. Call ahead for opening hours. ⊠ *Windwardside*, ☎ *599/4–62469. MC, V. Closed Sun.*

**$–$$** ✕ **Brigadoon Restaurant.** A local favorite, this open-front restaurant
★ on the first floor of a colonial building allows you to take in the passing action on the street—which doesn't mean a whole lot on Saba. Fresh fish grilled and served with a light Creole sauce is the specialty, but there are also chicken and steak dishes, lobster, and flavorful creations such as shrimp encrusted with salt and pepper. Monday night is Mexican night. ⊠ *Windwardside*, ☎ *599/4–62380. AE, D, MC, V. No lunch.*

**$–$$** ✕ **Gate House.** Slightly out of the way, on the road to the airport, this restaurant is run by two ex–New Yorkers. Caribbean cuisine reigns here, and the menu changes daily, making use of the freshest seafood, poultry, and meats, as well as local produce and herbs. ⊠ *Hell's Gate*, ☎ *599/4–62416. MC, V. Closed Wed. No lunch.*

**$–$$** ✕ **Lollipop's.** Owner Carmen was nicknamed Lollipop in honor of her sweet disposition. Sample her fine land crab, goat, and fresh grilled fish. Meals are served on the tranquil outdoor terrace, with its stonework and charming aqua-and-white trellis. If you make a reservation, Carmen will pick you up and drop you off at your hotel after dinner. ⊠ *St. John's*, ☎ *599/4–63330. No credit cards.*

**$–$$** ✕ **Scout's Place.** Chef and manager Diana Medero cooks up braised steak with mushrooms, curried goat, and chicken cordon bleu. You can also opt for a simple sandwich—the crab is best. Tables covered with flowered plastic cloths are arranged on a porch with stunning views of the water. Wednesday breakfast serves as the unofficial town meeting for expatriate locals. There is a lunch seating at 12:30 and a dinner seating at 7:30; only snacks and drinks are served during the rest of the day. ⊠ *Windwardside*, ☎ *599/4–62205. Reservations essential for scheduled seatings. MC, V.*

**$** ✕ **In Two Deep.** The owners of Saba Deep run this delightful harbor-side spot, with its stained-glass window and mahogany bar. The soups, sandwiches (especially the Reuben), and smoothies (try the lemon pucker) are excellent. The bar is plastered with humorous sayings, and customers are usually high-spirited—most have just come from a dive. It's open daily from 8 to 6. ✉ *Fort Bay,* ☎ *599/4–63438. MC, V.*

$    ✕ **Saba Chinese Bar & Restaurant.** In this plain little house with plastic tablecloths you can get, among other things, sweet-and-sour pork or chicken, cashew chicken, and curried dishes. ✉ *Windwardside,* ☎ *599/4–62268. No credit cards. Closed Mon.*

$    ✕ **Sunset Bar & Restaurant.** Artificial flowers and colorful place mats enliven this humble, homey place. Authentic Creole food—heavenly johnnycakes, bread tart pudding, and lip-smacking ribs—is served. ✉ *The Bottom,* ☎ *599/4–63332. No credit cards.*

## Outdoor Activities and Sports

### Boating
**Saba Deep** (☎ 599/4–63347) occasionally conducts one-hour, round-island cruises that include cocktails, hors d'oeuvres, and a marvelous view of the sunset.

### Deep-Sea Fishing
Saba is not a big fishing destination, but a few Sabans will take you out on their boats. Keep in mind that these are not big, fancy vessels. If you want to arrange a fishing trip, contact the Tourist Office or Saba Deep (☞ *above*), or ask your hotel to arrange it for you.

### Hiking
You can't avoid some hiking, even if you just go to mail a postcard. The big deal, of course, is Mt. Scenery, with 1,064 slippery steps leading up to the top.

For information about Saba's 18 recommended botanical hiking trails, check with the Tourist Office. Botanical tours are available upon request. A guided strenuous full-day hike through the undeveloped back side of Mt. Scenery costs about $50.

### Scuba Diving and Snorkeling
**Saba Deep** (☎ 599/4–63347, ℻ 599/4–63397) and **Sea Saba** (☎ 599/4–62246, ℻ 599/4–62362) will take you to explore Saba's 26 dive sites. Both offer rental equipment, SSI- (Scuba Schools International) and PADI-certified instructors, and dive packages that include accommodations anywhere on the island. **Wilson's Diving** (☎ 599/4–62541, ℻ 599/4–63334), in Fort Bay, specializes in shorter dive trips for day-trippers. For information on dive packages, call **Dive Saba Travel** (☎ 713/789–1396 or 800/883–7222) or **Go-Diving** (☎ 612/931–9101 or 800/328–5285).

## Shopping

### Gift Ideas
The island's most popular purchases are Saba lace and Saba Spice. The history of Saba lace (also called Spanish lace) goes back more than a century to Saban Gertrude Johnson, who attended a Caracas convent school where she learned the art of drawing and tying threads to adorn fine linens. When she returned home in the 1870s, she taught lace making to other Saban ladies, and the art has endured ever since. Every weekday Saban ladies display and sell their creations at the community center in Hell's Gate. Many also sell their wares from their houses; just follow the signs. Collars, tea towels, napkins, and other small items are relatively inexpensive, but larger items, such as tablecloths, can be pricey. You should also know that the fabric requires some care—it is not drip-dry. Although Saba Spice may *sound* as delicate as Saba lace

and the aroma is as sweet as can be, the base for the liqueur is 151-proof rum, and all the rest is window dressing.

## Shops

Saba's famed souvenirs can be found in almost every shop. While you're wandering around Windwardside (the streets here have no names), stop in at **Saba Tropical Arts** (☎ 599/4–62373), which sells silk-screened T-shirts and souvenirs. The **Square Nickel** (☎ 599/4–62477) is Saba's five-and-dime. The **Breadfruit Gallery** (☎ 599/4–62509) is an art gallery featuring local artist's work. **Around the Bend** (☎ 599/4–62519) carries island souvenirs and clothing. **The Little Shop** (☎ 599/4–62519) features bags and handmade items by Frieda. **Jobean Designs** (no phone) features handmade glass-bead jewelry as well as sterling silver and gold pieces. Most of the shops (with the exception of Around the Bend) are closed on Sunday. In the Bottom, the **Saba Artisan Foundation** (☎ 599/4–63260) turns out hand-screened fabrics that you can buy by the yard or already made into resort clothing for men, women, and children. It also sells printed T-shirts, spices, and clothing. Look also for the superlative *Saban Cottages: A Book of Watercolors,* sold at the Tourist Office and several stores.

# Nightlife

Guido's Pizzeria is transformed into the **Mountain High Club disco** (Windwardside, ☎ 599/4–62330)—there's even a mirrored disco ball suspended from the ceiling—on Friday and Saturday nights, and you can dance till 2 AM. Do the nightclub scene at the **Inner Circle** (✉ The Bottom, ☎ 599/4–62240), or just hang out at **Scout's Place** or the **Captain's Quarters.** Consult the bulletin board in each village for a listing of the week's events.

# Exploring Saba

Saba is a steep mountain set in the middle of the cobalt-blue Caribbean. Getting around the island means negotiating the narrow, twisting roadway that clings to the mountainside and rises from sea level to almost 2,000 feet. This is best left to an experienced taxi driver so you can enjoy the stunning views and verdant scenery that graces this tiny island.

*Numbers in the margin correspond to points of interest on the Saba map.*

SIGHTS TO SEE

❼ **The Bottom.** Sitting in a bowl-shape valley 820 feet above the sea, this town is the seat of government and the home of the lieutenant governor. The gubernatorial mansion, next to Wilhelmina Park, has fancy fretwork, a high-pitched roof, and wraparound double galleries. In 1993, Saba University opened a medical school in the Bottom, at which about 70 students are enrolled.

On the other side of town is the **Wesleyan Holiness Church,** a small stone building with white fretwork, dating from 1919. Stroll by the church, beyond a place called the Gap, to a lookout point where you can see the 400 rough-hewn steps leading down to **Ladder Bay.** Ladder Bay and Fort Bay were the two landing sites from which Saba's first settlers had to haul themselves and their possessions. Sabans sometimes walk down to Ladder Bay to picnic. Think long and hard before you do: It's 400 steps back *up* to The Road.

❷ **Cove Bay.** On the northeastern side of the island, a 20-foot-long strip of rocks and pebbles laced with gray sand is now the only place for sunning (and moonlit dips after a Saturday night out). There's a picnic area there, and a small tidal pool encircled by rocks for children to swim in.

**❶ Flat Point.** It is the only place on the island where planes can land. The runway here is among the world's smallest, measuring only 1,200 feet. Only STOL (Short Takeoff and Landing) prop planes dare land here, as each end of the runway drops off more than 100 feet into the crashing surf below.

**❷ Fort Bay.** The end of The Road is also the jumping-off place for all of the island's dive operations and the location of the St. Maarten ferry dock. The island's only gas station is here, a 277-foot deep-water pier that accommodates the tenders from ships. On the quay is a recompression chamber, one of the few in the Caribbean, and Saba Deep's dive shop; its snack bar, In Two Deep, is a good place to catch your breath while enjoying some refreshments and the view of the water.

**❸ Hell's Gate.** The island's main road makes 20 hairpin turns up over 1,000 vertical feet to Hell's Gate. **Holy Rosary Church,** poised on Hell's Gate's hill, is a stone church, which looks medieval but was built in 1962. In the **community center** behind the church, village ladies sell blouses, handkerchiefs, tablecloths, and tea towels embellished with the delicate and unique Saba lace. The same ladies make innocent-sounding Saba Spice, each according to her old family recipe. The rum-based liqueur will knock your socks off. The truly intrepid can venture to Lower Hell's Gate, where the **Old Sulphur Mine Walk** leads to bat caves (with typical sulfuric stench) that can—with caution—be explored.

**❹ Mt. Scenery.** Stone and concrete steps—1,064 of them—rise to the top of Mt. Scenery. The steps lead past giant elephant ears, ferns, begonias, mangoes, palms, and orchids up to a mahogany grove at the summit: six identifiable ecosystems in all. Helpful signs have been posted naming the trees, plants, and shrubs, and the Tourist Office can provide a field guide describing what you'll see along the way. On a cloudless day the view is spectacular. Have your hotel pack a picnic lunch, wear nonslip shoes, take along a jacket and a canteen of water, and hike away. The round-trip excursion will take about three hours and is best begun in the early morning.

**Saba Bank.** This fertile fishing ground 3 miles southwest of Saba is an excellent diving spot because of its coral gardens and undersea mountains. As other islands become "dived out," Saba is dedicated to preserving its marine life, which attracts more than 3,000 divers each year.

**Saba Marine Park.** Established in 1987 to preserve and manage the island's marine resources, the park circles the entire island, dipping down to 200 feet, and is zoned for diving, swimming, fishing, boating, and anchorage. One of the unique features of Saba's diving is the submerged pinnacles of land (islands that never made it) at about the 70-foot depth mark. Here all forms of sea creatures rendezvous. The information center offers talks and slide shows for divers and snorkelers and provides brochures and literature on marine life. (Divers are requested to contribute $2 a dive to help maintain the park facilities.) ⊠ *Harbor Office, Fort Bay,* ☎ *599/4–63295.* ☺ *Weekdays 8–5. Call first to see if anyone's around.*

**❺ Well's Bay.** Saba's famous, disappearing black-sand beach, located on the northwestern coast, is usually around for a few months in the summer. (The sand is washed in and out by rough winter surf.)

**❻ Windwardside.** The island's second-largest village, perched at an altitude of 1,968 feet, commands magnificent views of the Caribbean. Here, among the oleander bushes, you'll find rambling lanes and narrow alleyways winding through the hills and a cluster of tiny, neat houses and shops.

At the northern end of the village is the **Church of St. Paul's Conversion,** a colonial building with a red-and-white steeple. Just down the road is the **Saba Tourist Office,** where you can pick up brochures and books about Saba. You may want to spend some time browsing through the shops in town.

The **Saba Museum,** surrounded by lemongrass and clover, lies just behind the Captain's Quarters. There are small signs marking the way to the 150-year-old house that has been set up to look much as it did when it was a sea captain's home. Period pieces on display include a handsome mahogany four-poster bed with pineapple design, an antique organ, and, in the kitchen, a rock oven. You can also look at old documents, such as a letter a Saban wrote after the hurricane of 1772, in which he sadly says, "We have lost our little all." The first Sunday of each month, the museum holds croquet matches on its grounds; all-white attire is requested at this formal but fun social event. ⊠ *Windwardside, no phone.* ✉ *$1 donation requested.* ⊙ *Weekdays 10–4.*

NEED A BREAK?

**Tropics Café** (☎ 599/4-62469) is the place to rest your feet after walking up and down the steep hills of Windwardside. This small, poolside café serves up good burgers and sandwiches, to be enjoyed while taking in the sweeping view of the azure Caribbean, 1,500 feet below.

# Saba A to Z

## Arriving and Departing

### BY BOAT

*The Edge,* a high-speed ferry, leaves St. Maarten's Pelican Marina in Simpson Bay three times weekly at 9 AM and returns by 5 PM. The trip to Saba's Fort Bay takes an hour, and the round-trip fare is $60 (☎ 599/5–42640 in St. Maarten). If you take the watery way, however, you'll have lost more than an hour of sightseeing time on Saba.

### BY PLANE

Unless you parachute in, you'll arrive from St. Maarten via **Windward Islands Airways** (☎ 599/5–54210). The approach to Saba's tiny airstrip is the stuff of which nightmares are made. The strip is only a quarter mile long, but the STOL aircraft are built for it, and the pilot needs only half of it. Try not to panic; remember that the pilot knows what he is doing and wants to live just as much as you do. (If you're nervous, don't sit on the right. The wing just misses grazing the cliffside on the approach.) Once you've touched down on the airstrip, the pilot taxis an inch or two, turns, and deposits you just outside a little shoe box called the Juancho E. Yrausquin Airport.

### FROM THE AIRPORT

Taxis meet planes and take you to your destination.

## Currency

U.S. dollars are accepted everywhere, but Saba's official currency is the Netherlands Antilles florin (NAf; also called the guilder). The exchange rate fluctuates but is around NAf1.80 to U.S.$1. Prices quoted here are in U.S. dollars unless noted otherwise. **Barclays Bank** and **Commercial Bank** in Windwardside are the only banks on the island. Barclays is open weekdays 8:30–2; Commercial, 8:30–4.

## Emergencies

**Police:** ☎ 599/4–63237 in the Bottom, ☎ 599/4–62221 in Windwardside. **Hospital:** The **A. M. Edwards Medical Center** (✉ The Bottom, ☎ 599/4–63288) is a 10-bed hospital with a full-time physician. **Pharmacy:** The **Pharmacy** (✉ The Bottom, ☎ 599/4–63289).

## Getting Around

### CAR RENTALS

Saba's one and only road—The Road—is serpentine, with many a hairpin (read hair-raising) curve. However, if you dare to drive, cars can be rented at **Scout's Place** (✉ Windwardside, ☎ 599/4–62205) and at **Johnson's Rent A Car** (✉ Juliana's, Windwardside, ☎ 599/4–62469). A car rents for about $40 per day, with a full tank of gas and unlimited mileage. (If you run out of gas, call the island's only gas station, down at Fort Bay, ☎ 599/4–63272. It closes at noon.)

### HITCHHIKING

Carless Sabans get around the old-fashioned ways—walking and hitchhiking (very popular and safe). If you choose to get around by thumbing rides, you'll need to know the rules of The Road. To get a ride from the Bottom (which actually is near the top of the island), sit on the wall opposite the Anglican church; to catch a ride in Fort Bay, sit on the wall opposite Saba Deep dive center, where the road begins to twist upward.

## Guided Tours

All 12 of the taxi drivers who meet the planes at Yrausquin Airport also conduct tours of the island. The cost for a full-day tour is $8 per person with a minimum of four people. If you're just in from St. Maarten for a day trip, have your driver make lunch reservations for you at **Scout's Place** or the **Captain's Quarters** before starting the tour. After a full morning of sightseeing, your driver will drop you off for lunch, complete the tour afterward, and return you to Yrausquin in time to make the last flight back to St. Maarten. Guides are available for hiking; arrangements may be made through the tourist office.

## Language

Saba's official language is Dutch, but everyone on the island speaks English.

## Opening and Closing Times

Businesses and government offices on Saba are open weekdays 8 AM to 5 PM. Most shops are closed on Sunday.

## Passports and Visas

U.S. citizens need proof of citizenship. A passport is preferred, but a birth certificate or voter registration card will do (a driver's license will *not*). British citizens must have a British passport. All visitors must have an ongoing or return ticket.

## Precautions

Take along insect repellent, sunscreen, and sturdy, no-nonsense shoes that get a good grip on the ground.

## Taxes and Service Charges

Hotels collect a 5% government tax. Most hotels and restaurants add a 10%–15% service charge to your bill. You must pay a $2 departure tax when leaving Saba for either St. Maarten or St. Eustatius.

## Telephones and Mail

To call Saba from the United States, dial 011/599/4 followed by the five-digit number, which always begins with a 6. On the island, it is only necessary to dial the five-digit number. Telephone communications are excellent on the island, and you can dial direct long distance.

Airmailing a letter to the United States costs NAf1.30; a postcard, NAf.60.

## Visitor Information

For help planning your trip, contact, in the United States, the **Saba Tourist Office** (⊠ Box 6322, Boca Raton, FL 33427, ☎ 407/394–8580 or 800/722–2394, ⅻ 407/394–8588). In Canada, contact **New Concepts in Travel** (⊠ 2455 Cawthra Rd., Suite 70, Mississauga, Ontario L5A 3PI, ☎ 905/803–0131, ⅻ 905/803–0132).

On Saba, the amiable Glenn Holm is at the helm of the **Saba Tourist Office** (⊠ Windwardside, ☎ 599/4–62231, ⅻ 599/4–62350). It's open weekdays 8–noon and 1–5, and Sunday 10–2. The tourist office can help you make guest-house reservations.

Book reservations through a travel agent or over the telephone; mail can take a week or two to reach the island.

# 19 St. Barthélemy

**S**T. BARTHÉLEMY'S MAGIC lies in the way this tiny tropical isle blends the essence of the Caribbean with the essence of France. You can spend the day on a deserted beach lying under a palm tree, then choose from more than 50 excellent restaurants for an elegant evening meal. When you tire of the sun, you can easily drive all over the island, taking in the vistas and the soft breezes, and then stop off for an exquisitely prepared gourmet lunch. Or you can head to one of the three shopping areas for duty-free French perfumes and the latest in French fashion.

Updated by
Jonathan Runge

The island itself is a mere 8 square miles, with lots of hills and sheltered inlets. Gustavia, the only real town, wraps itself neatly around a lilliputian harbor. Red-roof bungalows dot the hillsides. And beaches that run the gamut from calm to "surfable," shell to fine white sand, and crowded to deserted encircle the island. The French cuisine here is tops in the Caribbean, and gourmet lunches and dinners are rallying points of island life. A French *savoir vivre* pervades, and the island is definitely for the style conscious—casual but always chic. A winter getaway for the rich and famous, St. Barts is no place for the beach bum or the shopping-mall sets.

Rothschild owns property and Rockefeller built an estate here, and for a long time the island, 15 miles from St. Martin in the French West Indies, was the haunt of the well heeled and well informed. Although the island still has cachet and remains largely a retreat for the wealthy, the tourist base has expanded in the last decade. Last year, even with Hurricane Luis, almost 200,000 visitors stopped by, including day-trippers from nearby islands and passengers from cruise ships that anchor just outside the harbor.

Longtime visitors speak wistfully of the old, quiet St. Barts. Although development *has* quickened the pace, the island has not been overrun with prefab condos or glitzy resorts. The largest hotel has fewer than 100 rooms, and the remaining rooms are scattered in about 40 small hotels around the island; no high-rises are allowed. The tiny airport accommodates nothing bigger than 19-passenger planes (and these only during daylight hours), and there aren't any flashy late-night attractions. Moreover, St. Barts is not a destination for the budget-minded. Development has largely been in luxury lodgings and gourmet restaurants.

When Christopher Columbus "discovered" the island in 1493, he named it after his brother, Bartholomeo. A small group of French colonists arrived from nearby St. Kitts in 1656 but were wiped out by the fierce Carib Indians who dominated the area. A new group from Normandy and Brittany arrived in 1694. This time the settlers prospered—with the help of French buccaneers, who took full advantage of the island's strategic location and well-protected harbor. In 1784 the French traded the island to King Gustav III of Sweden in exchange for port rights in Göteborg. He dubbed the capital Gustavia, laid out and paved streets, built three forts, and turned the capital into a prosperous free port. The island thrived as a major shipping and commercial center until the 19th century, when earthquakes, fire, and hurricanes brought financial ruin. Many residents fled for newer lands of opportunity, and in 1878 France agreed to repurchase its beleaguered former colony.

Today the island is still a free port and, as a dependency of Guadeloupe, is part of an overseas department of France. Dry, sunny, and rocky, St. Barts was never one of the Caribbean's "sugar islands" and thus never developed an industrial slave base. Most natives are descendants of those

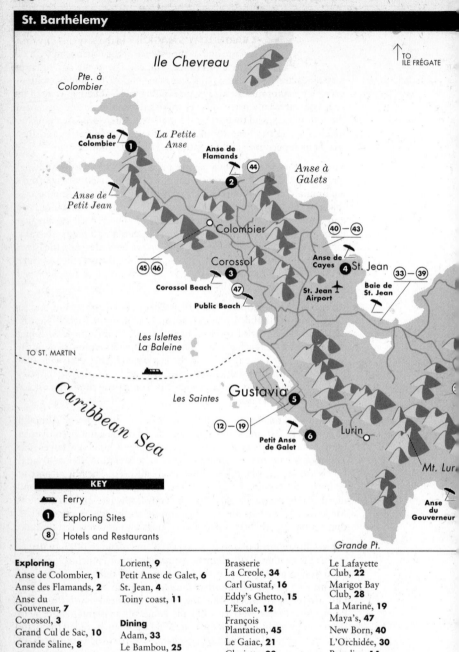

Ile Chevreau

Pte. à
Colombier

TO
ILE FRÉGATE

Anse de
Colombier **1**

La Petite
Anse

Anse de
Flamands

**44**

**2**

Anse à
Galets

Anse de
Petit Jean

Colombier

**40** — **43**

**45** **46**

Corossol

**3**

Anse de
Cayes

**4** St. Jean

**33** — **39**

Corossol Beach

St. Jean
Airport

Baie de
St. Jean

**47**

Public Beach

Les Islettes
La Baleine

TO ST. MARTIN

*Caribbean Sea*

Les Saintes

Gustavia

**5**

**12** — **19**

Petit Anse
de Galet

**6**

Lurin

Mt. Lur

Anse
du
Gouverneur

Grande Pt.

**KEY**

🛥 Ferry

**1** Exploring Sites

**8** Hotels and Restaurants

**Exploring**
Anse de Colombier, **1**
Anse des Flamands, **2**
Anse du
Gouveneur, **7**
Corossol, **3**
Grand Cul de Sac, **10**
Grande Saline, **8**
Gustavia, **5**

Lorient, **9**
Petit Anse de Galet, **6**
St. Jean, **4**
Toiny coast, **11**

**Dining**
Adam, **33**
Le Bambou, **25**

Brasserie
La Creole, **34**
Carl Gustaf, **16**
Eddy's Ghetto, **15**
L'Escale, **12**
François
Plantation, **45**
Le Gaiac, **21**
Gloriette, **23**

Le Lafayette
Club, **22**
Marigot Bay
Club, **28**
La Marine, **19**
Maya's, **47**
New Born, **40**
L'Orchidée, **30**
Paradiso, **14**

ATE

↑ TO
ILE TOC VERS

ATLANTIC OCEAN

Les Grenadiers

La Tortue

Pte. Milou   (30)

(31)   Lorient
Beach

Marigot   Marechal
Beach

(28) (27)

(22)—(26)

(10)
Grand
Cul de Sac

Marigot

Lorient

(9)

(32)

Mt. du
Grand Fond

(29)   Vitet   Petit
Cul de Sac

Toiny

Morne Vitet   (21)   (11)

(20)   Grande
Saline

(8)

Morne de
Grand Fond

Pt. à Toiny

. Lurin

Grande
Saline

Anse de
Grand Fond

N

se
u
rneur

(7)

Pt. du Gouverneur

| 0 | | 1 mile |
| --- | --- | --- |
| 0 | | 1 km |

Le Patio, **42**
Le Repaire, **13**
Le Rivage, **26**
Le Sapotillier, **17**
Le Tamarin, **20**
Topolino, **36**
Wall House, **18**
West Indies Café, **29**

**Lodging**
Carl Gustaf, **16**
Club La Banane, **31**
Eden Rock, **35**
El Sereno Beach
Hotel and Villas, **24**
Filao Beach, **37**
François
Plantation, **45**

Guanahani, **27**
Hostellerie des Trois
Forces, **29**
Hotel Christopher, **30**
Hotel Manapany
Cottages, **41**
Hotel St. Barth Isle
de France, **44**
Hotel Yuana, **43**

La Normandie, **32**
Le P'tit Morne, **46**
Le Toiny, **21**
Tropical Hotel, **38**
Village St. Jean, **39**

tough Norman and Breton settlers of three centuries ago. They are feisty, industrious, and friendly but insular. However, you will find many new, young French arrivals—predominantly from northwestern France—who speak English well.

You may hear some old-timers speak the old Norman patois of their ancestors or see the older women dressed in the traditional garb of provincial France. They have prospered with the tourist boom, but some are worried that the upward swing of prices may threaten business, especially tour groups and families. So far, though, this gem of an island continues to draw an ever-widening circle of fans.

Be aware that timing here is very important. A larger number of hotels and restaurants here have seasonal closings than on other islands. There are still some places open in August, but your selections will be more limited; places begin reopening at the end of October. Fortunately, the gorgeous beaches never close. The advantage of traveling in the off-season is enormous savings—sometimes half of the high-season rate.

In the fall of 1995, Hurricane Luis tore through St. Barts, causing major damage to some hotels and restaurants, but the island was virtually back to normal by the '95 Christmas season. Some establishments are gone for now: Castelets, Baie des Flamands, and the Pelican are closed until further notice. Others, like the Filao Beach, Taiwana, and Chez Francine have been rebuilt or relocated. Almost every business has been newly painted and, in many cases, refurbished, so the upside is that you'll notice a freshness to the island. Many beaches are wider than before, including Flamands and Gouverneur.

# Lodging

Expect to be shocked at the prices of accommodations. You pay for the privilege of staying on the island rather than for the hotel. Even at $500 a night, bedrooms tend to be small, but that does not detract from the lure of St. Barts for those who can afford it. Away from the beaches are a number of small hotels that are surprisingly reasonable, as well as a multitude of rental bungalows that offer less expensive accommodations, or, in the case of more luxurious villas, good value for the money. As a matter of fact, those in the know *always* rent villas, including celebrities, the rich and famous, and those who wish they were.

## Villas

On St. Barthélemy, "villa" is used generically to describe anything from a small cottage to a truly luxurious house with a cook, a maid, and a pool. You get what you pay for. In-season rates range from $900 to $25,000 a week. For the price of a moderately expensive hotel room, you can get a villa or a small cottage. If you get a group of friends together, you can get a villa with a number of rooms and a private pool for significantly less than it would cost for each person to stay in one of the expensive hotels. How to choose between a villa and a hotel? It may depend on whether you want the full kitchen that comes with a villa or would rather pay the sometimes expensive restaurant tabs to sample the island's exceptional food. Whether you stay in a villa or a hotel you will almost always want to rent a car, so be sure to figure this as part of your budget, no matter where you stay. *Reserve your villa as far in advance as possible.* Peak periods, like the holiday season, are usually booked solid by the previous summer. Cancellations do occur, so you may luck out, but the best plan is to reserve as soon as you can. The most desirable properties are always the first to go.

Villas can be rented through **Sibarth** (☎ 590/27–62–38), where Madame Lecour, the reigning queen of St. Barts's real estate, oversees more than 200 properties. **WIMCO** (☎ 800/932–3222), based in Newport, R.I., is the agency's representative in the United States. Its pleasant reservations agents are very knowledgeable about the properties. Rents range from $1,000 to $2,000 per week for one-bedroom villas, $1,600 to $7,000 for two- and three-bedroom villas. Larger villas rent from $9,000 to $19,000 per week. Another company, **Country Village Rentals–St. Barth's** (☎ 802/253–8777 or 800/320–8777, FAX 802/253–2144), based in Stowe, Vermont, also rents villas and distinguishes itself with a very friendly staff and a personal touch. Owner Doug Foregger, who represents more than 200 villas on the island, tries to match the customer with the perfect villa. Prices range from $700 to $25,000 per week.

## Hotels

Most hotels offer either the Continental (CP) or European (EP) meal plan, although the Modified American Plan (MAP) is sometimes available. Only the Hotel Christopher (☞ *below*) offers the Full American Plan (FAP), with all meals provided. Hotels may have as many as six different rate periods during a year. The highest rates are in effect from mid-December to early January, and hotels are booked far in advance for this holiday period. Rates used for the listings below are for the second highest period, early January through April—still in season, but not the holiday peak. At all other times, rates are usually lower. If you are flexible in your planning, you can save a good deal of money.

| CATEGORY | COST* |
|---|---|
| $$$$ | over $400 |
| $$$ | $300–$400 |
| $$ | $200–$300 |
| $ | under $200 |

*All prices are for a standard double room for two, excluding a 10%–15% service charge; there is no government room tax.*

$$$$ ★ 🏨 **Carl Gustaf.** Red-tile-roofed buildings spill down the hillside at this very expensive, small luxury resort at the head of Gustavia harbor. Each one- and two-bedroom suite looks out across a deck with a small private plunge pool, to spectacular views of the harbor, the quaint town of Gustavia, and the hilly coastline of the island. Units have spacious, air-conditioned, gleaming-white bedrooms and living rooms stylishly highlighted with nautical and tropical prints, plus rough marble floors, high ceilings, tiny but state-of-the-art kitchens, fax machine, two TVs, two stereos, VCR, minibar, and marble bath. The glittering nighttime view from the piano-bar lounge and elegant, open-air restaurant (known for its classic French cuisine) is one of the most spectacular on the island. ✉ *Box 700, rue des Normands, Gustavia 97133,* ☎ *590/27– 82–83 or 800/932–3222,* FAX *590/27–82–37. 14 1- and 2-bedroom suites. Restaurant, air-conditioning, kitchenettes, minibars, refrigerators, in-room VCRs, pool, sauna, health club. AE, DC, MC, V. CP.*

$$$$ 🏨 **El Sereno Beach Hotel and Villas.** The quiet, casual chic of this compact—some would say cramped—resort attract many repeat guests (although at these prices one may wonder why). The small, simply furnished rooms, with whitewashed walls and blue beams, have either a sea or garden view. They don't get much of a breeze, but they are air-conditioned and have a minifridge, satellite TV, telephone, and patio. High walls and plants provide privacy. The beach, with its exceptionally calm waters, is just steps away. There are also nine comfortably furnished one-bedroom, gingerbread-trimmed villas. The West Indies Café has replaced La Tocque Lyonnaise as the hotel's restaurant. ✉ *Box 19, Grand Cul de Sac 97133,* ☎ *590/27–64–80,* FAX *590/27–75–47. 20 rooms (3 sea-view),*

9 1-bedroom villas. 2 restaurants, bar, air-conditioning, pool, beach, water-sports center, shop. AE, DC, MC, V. EP.

$$$$ 🏨 **Filao Beach.** One of St. Barts's most popular beaches and excellent service win many repeat guests at this casual resort. Rooms are in two-unit bungalows—many completely rebuilt and redecorated after Hurricane Luis swept them away in 1995—set back from the beach amidst gardens. Although simple and smallish, they are brightly decorated with rattan furniture and pastel print fabrics; all have a patio, air-conditioning, TV, fridge, and hair dryer. Rooms closer to the beach rise accordingly in price, but the garden rooms are still only steps away from the sand. Bathrooms are compact but neat and fully stocked with toiletries. A restaurant, open for breakfast and lunch, is on the raised wooden deck that surrounds the pool. The bartender is well known for his killer cocktails. The hotel is a member of the prestigious Relais & Châteaux organization. ✉ *Box 667, St. Jean 97099,* ☎ *590/27–64–84 or 800/742–4276,* FAX *590/27–62–24. 30 rooms. Restaurant, bar, air-conditioning, refrigerators, pool. AE, MC, V. CP.*

$$$$ 🏨 **Guanahani.** This elegant 7-acre resort, the island's largest, is set between two beaches, one sheltered and one open to ocean waves. The lobby is a riot of color—deep greens, soothing blues, and rich plaids—and has a terrace where you can relax over a drink. Rooms and one-bedroom suites are in tightly clustered bungalows, expensively decorated with bright tropical fabrics and Georgian-style furniture. Some newer units are done in a stunning contemporary style, with wood floors and dark wood furniture, colorful walls, funky art and sculpture, a sunken seating area, and a partial curved wall between the sleeping and bath areas. Suites have either private pools or Jacuzzis. Units vary tremendously in terms of privacy, views, and distance from activities; there are just six rooms on the beach. To avoid disappointment, be sure to make your preference known when making your reservation. A poolside restaurant is open for breakfast and lunch. The more formal Bartolomeo is open for dinner and serves classic French cuisine in both an indoor dining room and outside in a tropical garden. ✉ *Box 609, Grand Cul de Sac 97098,* ☎ *590/27–66–60 or 800/223–6800,* FAX *590/27–70–70. 17 double rooms, some with ocean views; 39 deluxe rooms; 8 1-bedroom suites; 13 1-bedroom suites with private pool. 2 restaurants, 2 pools, beauty salon, hot tubs, 2 tennis courts, windsurfing, water-sports center. AE, MC, V. CP.*

$$$$ 🏨 **Hotel Manapany Cottages.** A ramshackle entry road ends at this luxury enclave of closely spaced units that stretch back from a narrow (although Hurricane Luis did widen the beach somewhat) and not very swimmable beach. Accommodations vary from rather snug St. Barts–style cottages and suites tucked into the hillside to much-in-demand beachfront suites with marble baths and four-poster beds. Bronze bodies ring the pretty but small pool, and outsiders drop in regularly to dine at the hotel's two restaurants. The atmosphere here is sophisticated and cosmopolitan, and there are many repeat guests. Airport transfers are complimentary. ✉ *Box 114, Anse des Cayes 97133,* ☎ *590/27–66–55 or 800/847–4249,* FAX *590/27–75–28. 32 cottages. 2 restaurants, 2 bars, pool, hot tub, tennis court, exercise room, water-sports center, shop. AE, D, DC, MC, V. CP.*

$$$$ 🏨 **Hotel St. Barth Isle de France.** This intimate luxury enclave, which
★ is on one of the island's prettiest beaches, lost its beachside pool and restaurant to Hurricane Luis (both were rebuilt over the summer of '96). Everything else is in tip-top shape, having been spruced up since the storm. Enormously spacious rooms and suites are either beachfront, in the two-story clubhouse, or across the street in bungalows facing gardens and one of the hotel's two pools. All units are decorated with mahogany furniture, island prints, and white cotton bedspreads. Each

has a patio or balcony, a private bath with two sinks and a tub, a minifridge, cable TV, and a phone. Some garden bungalows have a kitchenette. The restaurant serves breakfast and lunch, and you may opt for breakfast in your room. ⊠ *Box 612, Baie des Flamands 97098,* ☎ *590/27–61–81,* FAX *590/27–86–83. 12 rooms, 18 bungalows, 3 beach junior suites. Restaurant, bar, 2 pools, tennis court, exercise room, squash. AE, MC, V. CP.*

**$$$$** 🏨 **Le Toiny.** Luxury awaits at this comfortable little hideaway tucked
★ into the hillside at a remote end of the island. Twelve spacious, green-roofed villas, each with a private patio and pool (10 by 20 feet), are arranged for maximum privacy. Each is exquisitely appointed, with a massive four-poster mahogany bed and armoire, Chinese porcelain vases, Italian fabrics, and fine linens, and has a minibar, two TVs, VCR, hair dryer, fax, safe, stereo, air-conditioning, and three telephones. You can also request either a stair-stepper or a stationary bike. The bathroom has a walk-in shower as well as a tub. The elegant, alfresco restaurant, Le Gaiac, overlooks the Italian-tiled communal swimming pool and offers sweeping views of the distant ocean. A wonderful beach, Saline, is a 10-minute drive away. ⊠ *Anse de Toiny 97133,* ☎ *590/27–88–88 or 800/932–3222,* FAX *590/27–89–30. 13 villas. Restaurant, bar, air-conditioning, in-room safes, minibars, in-room VCRs, pool, fitness equipment, laundry. AE, DC, MC, V. CP.*

**$$$–$$$$** 🏨 **Club La Banane.** If you're looking for privacy, you may like this intimate hideaway, where guests keep pretty much to themselves. The nine unique units are decorated with plants, antique furniture, and a bit of whimsy. There are four-poster beds, sunken bath areas, all kinds of antiques, Haitian artwork, and unusual pottery. Rooms look out on dense tropical greenery. There are two small swimming pools (one with a waterfall), and it's a three-minute walk to the beach. The restaurant is open only to hotel guests for breakfast and lunch. Visitors come from around the island for dinner, served alfresco around the pool, and for the nightly after-dinner show in which the entire staff participates, including owner Jean-Marie Rivière, a Parisian cabaret producer. ⊠ *Quartier Lorient 97133,* ☎ *590/27–68–25,* FAX *590/27–68–44. 9 rooms. Restaurant, bar, 2 pools. AE, MC, V. CP.*

**$$$–$$$$** 🏨 **Eden Rock.** Set on a craggy bluff that abruptly splits St. Jean Beach is St. Barts's first hotel, opened in the '50s by Rémy de Haenen and just completely restored by the new owners from Britain, Jane and David Matthews. The six rooms have four-poster beds, tropical print fabrics, mosquito netting, sparkling silver fixtures, a minibar, and a stunning view of St. Jean Bay. The terra-cotta floors are original. You can breakfast in the restaurant or in your room. The spectacular open-air bar and French-Creole gourmet restaurant, which stretch along the top of the rock, are great places to enjoy the sea breeze and watch the frigate birds dive-bomb for fish. Construction was ongoing at press time to add some beachfront units and a beachfront bar-restaurant. A new windsurfing and water-sports center, Le Centre Nautique, is at the foot of the bluff. ⊠ *St. Jean 97133,* ☎ *590/27–72–94,* FAX *590/27–88–37. 6 rooms. Restaurant, bar, windsurfing, water-sports center. AE, MC, V. CP.*

**$$$–$$$$** 🏨 **Hotel Christopher.** Sofitel Resorts manages this full-service hotel. Four two-story colonial-style buildings overlooking the water (but not on the beach) hold beautifully furnished, air-conditioned rooms with panoramic views of St. Martin and nearby islets. Each room has a private terrace or balcony with sitting area, minifridge, and contemporary marble bath. Some bathrooms have small gardens: If the sight of a small lizard in here will ruin your vacation, ask for a bath sans greenhouse. There is a giant (4,500-square-foot) swimming pool—by far the largest on the island—with islands and footbridges. L'Orchidée serves French and Creole cuisine at dinner, and the poolside restaurant,

Le Mango, has a lunch menu that includes selections for the calorie-conscious. In season, there is a complimentary shuttle to St. Jean beach twice daily except Sunday. Many packages are available, so be sure to inquire when you book. ⊠ *Pointe Milou 97133,* ☎ *590/27–63–63 or 800/221–4542,* FAX *590/27–92–92. 40 suites. 2 restaurants, air-conditioning, room service, pool, exercise room. AE, DC, MC, V. EP, CP, MAP, FAP.*

**$$–$$$$** ⊞ **François Plantation.** A colonial-era graciousness pervades this elegant hillside complex of West Indian–style cottages. It's owned and managed by longtime island habitués Françoise and François Beret. Monsieur Beret is a passionate gardener, and the grounds are an intensely colorful display of tropical flowers and greenery. The smallish, air-conditioned rooms are dominated by the antique mahogany queen-size four-poster beds and decorated with brightly colored fabrics. Two units are larger and can accommodate an extra bed. All have minifridge, telephone, and TV. The pool is at the very top of a very steep hill, with magnificent views of the beach below, the hills of St. Barts, and nearby islets. You'll need a car to get to the beach and to go out for lunch (the restaurant is open only for breakfast and dinner); some packages include a rental car. ⊠ *Colombier 97133,* ☎ *590/27–78–82; in the U.S., 800/932–3222;* FAX *590/27–61–26. 4 garden- and 8 sea-view rooms. Restaurant, air-conditioning, pool. AE, MC, V. CP.*

**$$–$$$$** ⊞ **Hotel Yuana.** Green-roofed West Indian–style cottages are strung along a flowery hillside at this small complex overlooking Anse des Cayes. Appealing rooms have white walls, white tile floors, colorful tile baths, blue or peach painted wicker furniture, floral print fabrics, a kitchenette, and a wide terrace overlooking the ocean. Each unit has both a ceiling fan and air-conditioning, plus a TV/VCR and a phone. A 30-foot boat is available to rent. Airport transfers are included, package rates are available, and children under 12 stay free. ⊠ *Anse des Cayes 97133,* ☎ *590/27–80–84 or 800/645–6030,* FAX *590/27–78–45. 12 rooms. Bar, breakfast room, air-conditioning, fans, kitchenettes, in-room VCRs, pool. AE, MC, V. EP.*

**$–$$** ⊞ **Tropical Hotel.** This complex is straight up the hill from St. Jean Beach. Rooms are in a motel-like, one-story, L-shape building and open onto patios and views of either the ocean or thick tropical foliage. They are simple but well maintained and have air-conditioning, TV, telephone, and minifridge. White walls and furniture create an airy atmosphere. The main building houses reception, a TV/game room, and an appealing open-air bar and lounge. ⊠ *Box 147, St. Jean 97133,* ☎ *590/27–64–87,* FAX *590/27–81–74. 21 rooms. Bar, snack bar, air-conditioning, pool, recreation room. AE, MC, V. CP.*

**$–$$** ⊞ **Village St. Jean.** The second generation of the Charneau family now
★ runs this popular cottage colony, which has acquired a strong following over the years. The accent is on service and affordability, and this is one of the best values on the island. Cottages are spacious, although a bit sparsely furnished (except for the recently refurbished two-bedroom cottages), and have open-air kitchenettes and patios. There are also six hotel rooms without kitchenettes but with refrigerators. Rooms have been done over with elegant natural fabrics and dark wood furniture, including some teak pieces from Bali; some have beam ceilings and cheerful striped awnings, and most have king-size beds. Units have a variety of views, from full ocean to almost none; note that the units closest to the road are subject to the ongoing noise of minimoke engines struggling with the steep terrain. The open-air restaurant, Le Patio, serves excellent Italian fare. From the hotel it is an easy five-minute walk down to popular St. Jean Beach and to a variety of stores and restaurants (the walk back up is a bit more strenuous). ⊠ *Box 623, St. Jean 97098,* ☎ *590/27–61–39 or 800/633–7411,* FAX *590/27–77–*

96. *6 rooms, 20 cottages. Restaurant, bar, grocery, air-conditioning, pool, hot tub, boutique, library. AE, MC, V. EP.*

$ ★ **Hostellerie des Trois Forces.** This rustic, fairly isolated mountain-top inn is an idiosyncratic delight, with a string of tiny, gingerbread-trimmed West Indian–style cottages charmingly decorated according to astrological color schemes (Libra is soft blue; Leo, bright red; etc.). All have a minibar, a terrace with a breathtaking ocean view, and air-conditioning or a ceiling fan. Most have four-poster beds. The tinkle of chimes floats through the pleasant restaurant. Astrologer Hubert de la Motte (he's a Gemini, by the way) is the very personable owner and talented chef (along with Chef Bernard Calci), and he may even arrange a reading for you. The slogan of the rustic restaurant is Food Is Love. ⊠ *Morne Vitet,* ☎ *590/27–61–25,* ℻ *590/27–81–38. 8 rooms. Restaurant, bar, minibars, pool. AE, MC, V. EP.*

$ ★ **La Normandie.** This small, family-run, cozy hotel offers modestly furnished rooms that are about a five-minute walk from the beach and extremely inexpensive for the island (well under $100 per day)—probably one of the best values in St. Barts. All are air-conditioned, and some have TVs. There is a small pool. ⊠ *Lorient 97133,* ☎ *590/27–61–66,* ℻ *590/27–68–64. 8 rooms. Air-conditioning, pool. No credit cards. EP.*

$ ★ **Le P'tit Morne.** There is good value in these modestly furnished mountainside studios, each with a private balcony, air-conditioning, and panoramic views of the coastline below. Small kitchenettes are adequate for creating light meals or packing picnic lunches. The snack bar serves breakfast. It's relatively isolated here, and the beach is a 10-minute drive away. ⊠ *Box 14, Colombier 97133,* ☎ *590/27–62–64,* ℻ *590/27–84–63. 14 rooms. Snack bar, air-conditioning, kitchenettes, pool, library. AE, MC, V. CP.*

## Dining

The French reverence for food is evident everywhere on St. Barts, from the most expensive classic French restaurant to the simplest beach-side café. If you enjoy exquisitely prepared cuisine served at an enjoyable pace (and don't mind paying for it), then you've come to the right island. A la carte prices at the well-known French restaurants are very high, but many offer a prix fixe menu for a very reasonable price—a nice way to sample the cuisine. Lunch prices are usually cheaper than evening prices (with the infamous exception of Le Lafayette), and Italian, Creole, and French-Creole restaurants tend to be less expensive day and night. Beware that restaurants here typically charge for drinking water (a French custom), which comes by the bottle, both sparkling and flat, and costs about $4. *Accras* (salt cod fritters) with Creole sauce (minced hot peppers in oil), spiced christophine (a kind of squash), *boudin Créole* (a very spicy blood sausage), and a lusty *soupe de poissons* (fish soup) are some of the delicious and ubiquitous Creole dishes.

Reservations are always recommended; on weekend nights in season, they're essential almost everywhere.

### What to Wear
Jackets are rarely required and rarely worn, but this is a tony island and people here are fashionably dressed. Jeans are de rigueur when worn with a hip collared shirt or T-shirt. Shorts at the dinner table will label you *américain*. Think casual chic when planning your wardrobe and you'll be fine. If you're unsure, ask about the dress code when making reservations.

| CATEGORY | COST* |
|----------|-------|
| $$$$ | over $60 |
| $$$ | $45–$60 |
| $$ | $30–$45 |
| $ | under $30 |

*per person for a three-course meal, excluding drinks, service, and 4% sales tax*

**$$$$**  ✕ **Carl Gustaf.** Not even the sweeping views of the harbor can detract
★ from the sublime creations of Patrick Gateau. Monsieur Gateau, who trained at the Crillon in Paris, deftly weaves tropical influences into his classical cuisine. Among his standouts are warm goat-cheese salad, lobster spring rolls, lobster ravioli in shellfish cream sauce, and grilled swordfish steak with stewed aubergines, tomatoes, sweet peppers, and onions. You choose your dessert when you order your meal to allow time for it to be prepared. Look no further than the warm chocolate praline cake—it will reduce a chocolate lover to tears. The large, breezy, white dining room has an open-air terrace that overlooks Gustavia harbor. ⊠ *rue des Normands, Gustavia,* ☎ *590/27–82–83. AE, MC, V. No lunch Sun. in summer.*

**$$$$**  ✕ **François Plantation.** A flower-draped, lantern-hung arborway leads
★ to this elegant restaurant. Inside, mahogany tables and chairs are surrounded by beautiful plants. Chef Philippe Ruiz's cuisine *legère,* a lighter version of classic French cuisine, draws guests from all over the island; locals consistently rate it in their top three. Try his ravioli of goat cheese and foie gras, and move on to roasted sea bass spiced with vanilla or lamb fillet roasted in a light crust with basil and Gorgonzola cheese and served with sautéed fennel and tomato. You can also order the rare Coutancie beef: The cattle must drink three liters of beer and receive a 20-minute rubdown twice daily, among other strict guidelines, to qualify. Dessert specials include a remarkable warm dark chocolate tart served with vanilla ice cream. ⊠ *Colombier,* ☎ *590/27–78–82. Reservations essential. AE, D, MC, V. Closed Sept.–Oct. No lunch.*

**$$$**  ✕ **Le Gaiac.** Cool breezes waft through this open-air restaurant at the elegant, out-of-the-way Le Toiny hotel. Pale blue napery and blue canvas chairs beautifully complement the blue bay view. Chef Maxime Des Champs hails from France, and combines local ingredients with traditional French cooking techniques. Appetizers at lunch include duck carpaccio with coffee-flavored vinaigrette and a delicious chilled spicy mango soup. Entrées include club sandwiches, salads, and grilled fish and shellfish. The dinner menu expands with roast rack of lamb in a clay shell with thyme and honey, yellowtail snapper with lightly curried lentils and squash, and pigeon layered with red cabbage and sweet potato, and spiced with local herbs. Don't miss the fabulous buffet lunch on Sundays. ⊠ *Anse de Toiny,* ☎ *590/27–88–88. AE, DC, MC, V. Closed Sept.–mid-Oct. and Tues. in summer.*

**$$$**  ✕ **Le Lafayette Club.** Despite truly outrageous prices, this lunch-only, beachside bistro is such an in-season "in" spot that reservations are necessary if you want to eat between noon and 2. Expect to pay about $18 for a green salad with bacon and croutons or goat cheese and sliced tomatoes, $30 and up for grilled local fish, fillet of duck, and shrimp with fresh pasta. The grilled lobster entrée is a whopping $70. ⊠ *Grand Cul de Sac,* ☎ *590/27–62–51. No credit cards. Closed May–mid-Nov. No dinner.*

**$$$**  ✕ **L'Orchidée.** This elegant French-Creole restaurant with coral stucco walls and mahogany archways is in the Hotel Christopher. Have a seat in a casual captain's chair on the deck, amid the white napery and gleaming silver, and listen to the waves on the rocky shore. The staff is friendly and solicitous, the atmosphere romantic, and the food beautifully presented. Try grilled mahimahi with lime or chicken with curry-and-coconut sauce served with two kinds of mashed potatoes. A prix fixe menu is available for about $45. ⊠ *Hotel Christopher, Pointe Milou,* ☎ *590/27–63–63. AE, MC, V. No lunch.*

$$$ ✕ **Le Sapotillier.** Dining in this cozy boîte or in the courtyard under a
★ grand old sapodilla tree, you may feel like a guest in the owners' house—yet the food is anything but down-home. This long-established French and Creole restaurant serves such delicacies as frogs' legs, and snail lasagna with spinach, walnuts, and Roquefort sabayon. The sumptuous black-and white-chocolate mousse is a house favorite. ⊠ *rue de Centenaire, Gustavia,* ☎ *590/27–60–28. Reservations essential. MC, V. Closed May–mid-Oct. No lunch.*

$$–$$$$ ✕ **West Indies Café.** On the site of the former La Tocque Lyonnaise, this café is set on a terraced, outdoor pavilion overlooking the bay. Chef Yvan, hailing from St. Tropez and Paris, prepares French cuisine à la Provence; he's best known for his innovative cooking with beer. Try the veal kidneys with basil and beer sauce and the crispy pineapple with caramelized juice. ⊠ *El Sereno Beach Hotel and Villas, Grand Cul de Sac,* ☎ *590/27–64–80. AE, DC, MC, V. Closed June–Aug.*

$$–$$$ ✕ **Adam.** Vincent Adam, a graduate of the Culinary Academy of
★ France, opened this haute cuisine gem in the hills just off St. Jean beach. Dinner is served in the Creole-style house or in the garden. Many locals insist it's one of the top restaurants on the island. There are both an à la carte menu with wonderful choices and a very reasonable prix fixe menu (about $38). Offerings include lobster tabbouleh, salmon tartare with caviar and oysters, terrine of sweetbreads, and fillet of beef. Vegetarian selections are also available. ⊠ *St. Jean,* ☎ *590/27–93–22. AE, MC, V. No lunch.*

$$–$$$ ✕ **Le Bambou.** In the hills above Grand Cul du Sac is this small restaurant, formerly known as Le Flamboyant. The name change has also brought a change in cuisine—Asian fare is now served here. A Laotian chef, Monsieur Thao, prepares Vietnamese, Thai, and Chinese food. You can dine inside, but most guests opt for the breezy terrace with a fine view of the countryside and the sea in the distance. Reservations are not required, but they're a good idea if you want to sit outside. ⊠ *Grand Cul de Sac,* ☎ *590/27–75–65. MC, V. Closed Mon. No lunch.*

$$–$$$ ✕ **Marigot Bay Club.** Have a seat at the dark-wood bar or at a table on the beam-ceiling patio, and take in the views of the colorful sailboats moored in the bay. The owner of this casual spot loves to fish and often reels in the catch of the day himself. It might be grouper, tuna, red snapper, or yellowtail and is frequently served with a Creole sauce. Other specials here include lobster ravioli, conch sausages, codfish fritters, and steamed shark in a red pepper and butter sauce. Lunch is served in-season, except on Mondays. ⊠ *Marigot,* ☎ *590/27–75–45. Reservations essential. AE, MC, V. No lunch Mon.*

$$–$$$ ✕ **Maya's.** Locals, visitors, and celebs keep returning to pack this in-
★ formal, open-air restaurant, just outside of Gustavia on the north end of Public Beach. Relax in a colorful deck chair, and watch the boats in Gustavia's harbor as you contemplate the Creole, Vietnamese, and Thai menu. You choose from five selections for each of three courses. The menu changes nightly, but you might find christophine au gratin, several fresh salads, *canard à l'orange* (duck in orange sauce), salmon teriyaki, and shrimp curry. ⊠ *Public Beach,* ☎ *590/27–75–73. AE, D, MC, V. Closed Sun. and June–Oct. No lunch.*

$$–$$$ ✕ **Le Tamarin.** Always among the favorite restaurants of those who live
★ on St. Barts, this open-air eatery on the way to Saline Beach is famous for its French and Creole fusion cuisine and its resident parrot, Cooky. Relax in a hammock under the tamarind tree with a Ti Punch and then savor some of the house specialties including carpaccios of salmon, tuna,

and beef; fresh grilled lobster; and the renowned lemon tart and choco-late cake. ⊠ *Salines,* ☎ *590/27–72–12. AE, MC, V. Closed Mon. No dinner in summer.*

**$$–$$$** ✕ **Wall House.** Consistently excellent French cuisine is the hallmark of this restaurant on the far end of the far side of Gustavia's harbor. The interior is glistening white—shiny white wicker furniture, white tile floors, white tablecloths and walls—with pots of greenery here and there. Owner Gerard Began is unobtrusively on-site most evenings, and the staff is gracious and will make enthusiastic recommendations. Start with marinated salmon with dill, gazpacho, grilled mahimahi over sliced cucumbers, foie gras, or cold eggplant mousse. For your main course, try fillet of shark in lobster sauce, duck in cassis sauce with sautéed potatoes, or beef with pepper sauce. Three prix fixe menus offer excellent value. The lunch menu features lighter fare. ⊠ *Gustavia,* ☎ *590/27–71–83. AE, MC, V.*

**$–$$$** ✕ **Le Repaire.** This busy brasserie overlooks Gustavia's harbor and is a popular spot from early breakfast until the wee hours of the morn-ing (it's open from 6 AM to 1 AM). Grab a cappuccino, pull a captain's chair up to the front window, and watch cruise-ship passengers come off the boats to descend upon the town. The menu includes everything from cheeseburgers to foie gras and grilled fish and lobster. There is a billiards table and live music on weekends. ⊠ *quai de la République, Gustavia,* ☎ *590-27-72–48. MC, V. Closed Sun.*

**$–$$$** ✕ **Topolino.** This lesser-known but good (and reasonably priced) Ital-ian restaurant is set back from the road, within easy walking distance of St. Jean beach. Linen tablecloths, freshly cut flowers, and dim light-ing create a romantic evening atmosphere. The menu includes fresh seafood, grilled chicken and steaks, various veal dishes, a number of pasta choices, and thin-crusted pizzas. There is a happy hour from 6 to 7 and live entertainment almost every night. The wine list has a num-ber of fine, inexpensive choices. ⊠ *St. Jean,* ☎ *590/27–70–92. MC, V. No lunch.*

**$$** ✕ **New Born.** For authentic Creole cuisine, head down the bumpy road that leads to the Hotel Manapany. The dark-wood restaurant is some-what devoid of decoration except for a large aquarium in the back; ask for a table near it if you want to watch the sharks, turtles, and trop-ical fish swim while you eat. The fresh seafood is caught at the beach (just steps away) by owners Franky and David. This is the place to sam-ple such Creole specialties as accras, boudin, curried goat or shrimp, and salt cod salad. For dessert try the coconut custard or bananas flambé. ⊠ *Anse des Cayes,* ☎ *590/27–67–07. AE, MC, V. Closed Sun. in off-season. No lunch.*

**$$** ✕ **Le Patio.** Some of the best classic Italian food on the island is served
★ à la Creole by candlelight at this pleasant hillside restaurant, where you can dine inside or on the terrace. Entrées change weekly, but you may find grouper medallions rolled in black peppercorns with a light gin-ger and lime sauce or salmon fillet with both a mustard and a crushed tomato sauce, in addition to six or seven pasta offerings. The an-tipasto here is renowned. Children will enjoy holiday menus—such as red snapper in phantom sauce at Halloween. There are nice views of the bay, and the atmosphere is romantic and intimate. Service is un-hurried, despite the remarkably reasonable prices. There's a $36 prix fixe menu. ⊠ *Village St. Jean Hotel,* ☎ *590/27–61–39. MC, V. Closed Wed. and June. No lunch.*

**$–$$** ✕ **Eddy's Ghetto.** The combination of imaginatively prepared, mod-
★ estly priced fare—barbecued ribs (a house specialty), crab salad, ragout of beef, crème caramel—and a disarmingly fun-loving atmosphere has made Edward Stakelborough's open-air restaurant a hit. The crowd is

lively, and the wine list is impressive (but avoid the house white). ⊠ *Gustavia, just off rue du Général de Gaulle. No phone. No credit cards.*

$–$$  ✕ **L'Escale.** Great food, ambience, and views draw locals and visitors
★ alike to this open-air restaurant, at the water's edge on the far side of Gustavia's harbor. The varied menu includes a wide range of pasta (lasagna, tortellini, ravioli, and spaghetti with marinara, Bolognese, and other sauces), as well as fresh local fish, veal scallopini in an assortment of sauces, steak tartare, chicken, and 12 kinds of pizza. Many dishes are cooked in a wood-burning oven. ⊠ *Gustavia,* ☎ *590/27–81–06. Reservations essential. MC, V. No lunch.*

$–$$  ✕ **La Marine.** Mussels from France arrive on Thursday, and in-the-know islanders are there to eat them at the very popular dockside picnic tables. The lunch menu always includes fresh fish, hamburgers, and omelets; dinner adds more grilled meat and fish. ⊠ *rue Jeanne d'Arc, Gustavia,* ☎ *590/27–70–13. AE, MC, V.*

$–$$  ✕ **Paradiso.** Five kinds of homemade pasta and carpaccios are served each day at this friendly eatery in a historic Creole building. Specialties include fresh lobster medallions served on a bed of lentils, veal kidneys sautéed and served with a mustard sauce, and lamb filet mignon with rosemary. You can eat in the air-conditioned dining room or on the breezy terrace. ⊠ *rue du Roi, Gustavia,* ☎ *590/27–80–78. AE, MC, V. No lunch Sun.*

$–$$  ✕ **Le Rivage.** Bathing suits are acceptable attire at this popular and very
★ casual Creole establishment on the beach at Grand Cul de Sac. Delicious lobster salad, sandwiches, and fresh grilled fish are served at indoor and outdoor tables. The relaxed atmosphere and surprisingly low prices can make for an enjoyable meal, but the service gets frantic when the restaurant is busy. ⊠ *St. Barth Beach Hotel, Grand Cul de Sac,* ☎ *590/27–82–42. AE, MC, V.*

$  ✕ **Brasserie La Creole.** Right in the center of the St. Jean shopping arcade is this casual brasserie with indoor seating, a comfortable bar, and outdoor umbrella tables. Drop by in the morning for freshly baked croissants and magnificent coffee. At lunch try the *croque-monsieur,* a hot open-face sandwich of thin-sliced ham and Gruyère cheese. There is a full breakfast menu (the restaurant opens at 7 AM), and from noon until midnight, sandwiches, salads, and various beef, chicken, and fish entrées are served. ⊠ *St. Jean,* ☎ *590/27–68–09. AE.*

$  ✕ **Gloriette.** This beachside spot serves delicious local Creole dishes, such as crunchy accras and cassoulet of local lobster, as well as light salads. ⊠ *Grand Cul de Sac,* ☎ *590/27–75–66. AE, MC, V.*

## Beaches

There are nearly 20 *plages* (beaches) scattered around the island, each with a distinctive personality and all of them public. Even in season, it is possible to find a nearly empty beach. Topless sunbathing is common, but nudism is forbidden—although both Saline and Gouverneur are de facto nude beaches. Here are the main attractions:

**St. Jean** is like a mini Côte d'Azur—beachside bistros, bungalow hotels, bronze beauties, windsurfing, and lots of day-trippers. The reef-protected strip is divided by Eden Rock promontory, and there's good snorkeling west of the rock. **Lorient** is popular with St. Barts's families and surfers, who like its rolling waves. **Marigot** is a tiny, calm beach with good snorkeling along the rocky far end. Around the point from Marigot, next to the Guanahani Hotel, is tiny **Marechal Beach,** which offers some of the best snorkeling on the island. Shallow, reef-protected **Grand Cul de Sac** is especially nice for small children and windsurfers; it has excellent lunch spots and lots of pelicans. Secluded **Grande Saline,** with its sandy ocean bottom, is just about everyone's favorite beach and is great for swimmers. Despite the law, young and old alike go nude on this beach. It can get windy here, so go on a calm day. **Anse du Gouverneur** is even more secluded than Grande Saline—nude sunbathing takes place here, too—and equally beautiful, with good snorkeling and views of St. Kitts, Saba, and St. Eustatius. A five-minute walk from Gustavia is **Petit Anse de Galet** (Shell Beach), named after the tiny shells on its shore. **Public Beach** is an excellent place to enjoy the sunset and watch the boats. **Corossol Beach** is a top boat- and sunset-watching spot. The beach at **Colombier** is the least accessible but the most private; you'll have to take either a rocky footpath from La Petite Anse or brave the 30-minute climb down a cactus-bordered trail from the top of the mountain behind the beach. A lot of boaters favor this beach and cove for its calm anchorage. **Flamands** is the most beautiful of the hotel beaches—a roomy strip of silken sand, now even wider due to Hurricane Luis.

# Outdoor Activities and Sports

## Boating

St. Barts is a popular yachting and sailing center, thanks to its location midway between Antigua and St. Thomas. Gustavia's harbor, 13 to 16 feet deep, has mooring and docking facilities for 40 yachts. There are also good anchorages available at Public, Corossol, and Colombier. **Loulou's Marine** (☎ 590/27–62–74), a ship chandlery, is the place for yachting information and supplies. **Marine Service** (☎ 590/27–70–34) offers full-day outings on a 40-foot catamaran to the uninhabited Ile Fourchue for swimming, snorkeling, cocktails, and lunch; the cost is $96 per person. Marine Service also arranges deep-sea-fishing trips, with a full-day charter of a 30-foot crewed cabin cruiser running $800; an unskippered motor rental runs about $260 a day. You can also take an hour's cruise on the glass-bottom boat *L'Aquascope* by contacting Marine Service. **OcéanMust Marina** (☎ 590/27–62–25), located in Gustavia, offers all kinds of boat charters. **St. Barth Caraibes Yachting** (☎ 590/27–52–48), in Gustavia, can charter any type of boat you require.

## Diving and Deep-Sea Fishing

Deep-sea fishing can be arranged through **Marine Service** (☎ 590/27–70–34), **St. Barth Caraibes Yachting** (☎ 590/27–52–48), or **Océan-Must Marina** (☎ 590/27–62–25). Marine Service also operates a PADI-certified diving center, with scuba-diving trips for about $50–$80 per person, gear included. The CMAS-certified **Club La Bulle** (☎ 590/27–62–25) and PADI-certified **St. Barth Plongée** (☎ 590/27–54–44), both in Gustavia, are other scuba options.

## Horseback Riding

Laure Nicolas leads two-hour excursions in the morning and afternoons for $35 per person from **Ranch des Flamands** (⊠ Anse des Flamands, ☎ 590/27–80–72).

## Tennis

If you wish to play tennis at a hotel at which you are not a guest, be sure to call ahead to inquire about fees and reservations. There are two lighted tennis courts at the **Guanahani** (☎ 590/27–66–60), **Le Flamboyant Tennis Club** (☎ 590/27–75–65), and the **Sports Center of Colombier** (☎ 590/27–61–07). There is one lighted court each at the **Hotel Manapany Cottages** (☎ 590/27–66–55), the **Taiwana** (☎ 590/27–65–01), and the **St. Barth Isle de France** (☎ 590/27–61–81), which also has the island's only squash court.

## Windsurfing

Windsurfing fever has definitely caught on here. Boards can be rented for about $20 an hour at water-sports centers along St. Jean and Grand Cul de Sac beaches. Lessons are offered for about $40 an hour at **St. Barth Wind School** (⊠ St. Jean, ☎ 590/27–71–22), **Le Centre Nautique** (⊠ Eden Roc, St. Jean, ☎ 590/27–72–94) and at **Wind Wave Power** (⊠ St. Barths Beach Hotel, ☎ 590/27–60–70), which also has parasailing.

# Shopping

St. Barts is a duty-free port, and there are especially good bargains in jewelry, porcelain, imported liquors, and French perfumes, cosmetics, and designer resort wear.

## Shopping Areas

Shops are clustered in **Gustavia, La Savane Commercial Center** (across from the airport), and **La Villa Créole,** an appealing shopping complex in St. Jean. A gourmet supermarket, **Match,** is located across from the airport, as is **Unic Plus,** another supermarket with a good selection of fruits, veggies, and meats. Two other supermarkets worth checking out are **Sodexa** located in La Villa Créole and **MonoShop** in Marigot.

## Good Buys

CLOTHES

A number of boutiques in all three shopping areas carry the latest in French and Italian sportswear and haute couture fashion items. The price tags may astound you (even after you convert the francs to dollars you may still be in high three figures), but these prices are actually well below the Paris price for the same item, and so they are considered bargains by some. Shops to look for include Stéphane & Bernard, Libertine, Hermès, Gucci, Cartier, Gianni Versace, and Black Swan, all of which are in Gustavia and have branches either across from the airport or in St. Jean or both; but there are many other stores and boutiques to be found. At both St. Jean's La Villa Créole and La Savane (across from the airport), it is worth working your way from one end of the shopping complex to the other.

ISLAND CRAFTS

Stop in Corossol to pick up some of the intricate straw work—wide-brim beach hats, mobiles, handbags—that the ladies of Corossol create by hand. In Gustavia, look for hand-turned pottery at **St. Barts Pottery** (☎ 590/27–62–74). You'll see coral and exotic shell jewelry at the **Shell Shop** (no phone). Superb local skin-care products are available at **Ligne de St. Barth** (☎ 590/27–82–63) in Lorient. Gustavia also has a market, **Le 'Ti Marché,** dedicated to art and crafts handmade on the island. Open every day except Sunday, the market is set up in stalls on the corner of rue du Roi Oscar II near the city hall. The much-sought-after Belou's P line of aromatic oils is available here. For details call 590/27–83–72 or the tourist office.

WINE AND GOURMET SHOPS

Wine lovers will enjoy **La Cave** (⊠ Marigot, ☎ 590/27–63–21), where an excellent collection of French vintages is stored in temperature-controlled cellars. Also check out **La Cave du Port Franc** (☎ 590/27–65–27), on the far side of the harbor and at Public, for vintage wines, contemporary paintings, and objets d'art.

For exotic groceries or picnic fixings, stop by one of St. Barts's fabulous gourmet delis, **La Rotisserie** (☎ 590/27–63–13), on rue du Roi Oscar II (branches in St. Jean and Pointe Milou).

# Nightlife

For an island of its petite size, St. Barts offers a surprising amount of things to do at night, notably on weekends. There are many special places to go for cocktail hour, and some of the hotels and restaurants provide late-night fun.

**American Bar** (☎ 590/27–86–07), at L'Escale restaurant, is an after-dinner hangout for the retro-hip; there's a 1968 Cadillac Eldorado outside and lots of neon inside. **Bar de l'Oublie** (☎ 590/27–70–06), where the young French who work on the island gather for drinks, gets hopping late-night. **Carl Gustaf** (☎ 590/27–82–83) lures those in search of quiet conversation and some gentle piano music at the day's end. It's also Gustavia's best sunset-watching spot. **Club La Banane** (☎ 590/27–68–25) has a popular *après-dîner* cabaret show nightly. **Feel-ing** (☎ 590/27–88–67) is one of the island's hot spots for dancing. An indoor dance floor and spacious outdoor bar/patio make this a fun place to hang out. The disco is located in the hills above Gustavia, just past the Santa Fe Restaurant. **Guanahani** (☎ 590/27–66–60) has a piano bar. **La Licorne** (☎ 590/27–83–94), in Lorient, is very hot with a local crowd and only open on Saturday night. **Manapany** (☎ 590/27–66–55) has a piano bar. **Le Petit Club** (☎ 590/27–66–33), in Gustavia, is the place to head for real late-night dancing. **Le Repaire** (☎ 590/27–72–48), in Gustavia, lures a crowd for cocktail hour. **Le Select** (☎ 590/27–86–87), in Gustavia, is St. Barts's original hangout, and has a boisterous garden where the barefoot boating set gathers for a brew.

# Exploring St. Barthélemy

Getting around this hilly and very picturesque isle is easy on the excellent and well-marked roads. Since St. Barts is small, you can rent a Jeep or moke at the airport and see the entire island in half a day.

*Numbers in the margin correspond to points of interest on the St. Barthélemy map.*

SIGHTS TO SEE

**❶ Anse de Colombier.** At the end of Flamands Road, a rocky footpath leads to the island's most remote beach. A 25-minute hike around a rocky promontory leads to a pretty beach and cove, popular with boaters.

**❷ Anse des Flamands.** This wide beach has small hotels, including the St. Barth Isle de France, and many rental villas. From here you can take a brisk hike to the top of the now-extinct volcano that is believed to have given birth to St. Barts. From the peak are gorgeous views of the islands.

**❼ Anse du Gouverneur.** Legend has it that pirate's treasure is buried at this, one of St. Barts's most beautiful beaches. The road here from Gustavia supplies some spectacular vistas. If the weather is clear, you will be able to see the islands of Saba, St. Eustatius, and St. Kitts from the beach.

NEED A BREAK?   The hilltop **Sante Fe Restaurant** (✉ Morne Lorne, at the turnoff to Gouverneur's Beach, ☎ 590/27–61–04) is a popular spot for sunsets and American-style hamburgers.

**❸ Corossol.** The island's French provincial origins are most evident in this two-street fishing village with a little rocky beach. Residents speak an old Norman dialect, and some of the older women still wear traditional garb—ankle-length dresses, bare feet, and starched white sunbonnets called *quichenottes* (kiss-me-not hats). The women don't like to be photographed. However, they are not shy about selling you some of their handmade straw work—handbags, baskets, broad-brim hats, and delicate strings of birds—made from lantana palms. The palms were introduced to the island 100 years ago by foresighted Father Morvan, who planted a grove in Corossol and Flamands, thus providing the country folk with a living that is still pursued today. Here, too, is the **Inter Oceans Museum,** which features more than 7,000 seashells from around the world. ☎ 590/27–62–97. ☒ 20F. ☉ *Daily 9–5.*

❿ **Grand Cul de Sac.** A winding road passes through the mangroves, ponds, and beach of Grand Cul de Sac, where there are plenty of water-sports concessions and excellent beachside restaurants, including the West Indies Cafe and the ultra-chic Le Lafayette Club (☞ Dining, *above*).

❽ **Grande Saline.** The big salt ponds of Grande Saline are no longer in use, and the place looks desolate, but climb the short hillock behind the ponds for a surprise—the long arc of **Anse de Grande Saline.**

❺ **Gustavia.** With just a few streets on three sides of its tiny harbor, Gustavia is easily explored in a two-hour stroll. Here you will find excellent shopping, many restaurants and cafés, and a museum. Remember that most shops close from noon to 2, so you might want to combine shopping with an enjoyable lunch at one of the restaurants overlooking the harbor.

A good place to park your car is rue de la République, where flashy catamarans, yachts, and sailboats are moored. If you haven't gotten a map or have some questions, head to the **tourist office** on the pier, where you can pick up an island map and a free copy of *St. Barth Magazine,* a monthly publication on island happenings. If you feel like stopping for a café au lait, a croissant, or a drink, settle in at either **Bar de l'Oubli** or **Le Select,** two cafés just a few steps away.

As you stroll through the little streets, you will notice that plaques sometimes spell out names in both French and Swedish, a reminder of the days when the island was a Swedish colony. Small shops along rue du Roi Oscar II, rue de la France, rue du Bord de Mer, and rue du Général de Gaulle sell French perfumes, the latest in French and Italian designer wear for men and women, resort wear, crystal, gold jewelry, and other luxury items.

On the far side of the harbor known as Le Pointe is the charming **Municipal Museum,** where you will find watercolors, portraits, photographs, and historic documents detailing the island's history as well as displays of the island's flowers, plants, and marine life. ☎ 599/27–89–07. ☒ 10F. ☉ *Mon.–Thurs. 8:30–12:30 and 2:30–6, Fri. 3–6, Sat. 9–11.*

❾ **Lorient.** Site of the first French settlement, Lorient is one of the island's two parishes, and a restored church, historic headstones, a school, post office, and gas station mark the spot. Lorient Beach has royal palms and rolling waves.

One of St. Barthélemy's treasured secrets, **Le Manoir,** is in Lorient. The 1610 Norman manor was painstakingly shipped from France and reconstructed here in 1984 by the charming Jeanne Audy Rowland in tribute to the island's Viking forebears. The tranquil surrounding courtyard and garden contain a waterfall and a lily-strewn pool. Madame Rowland graciously allows visitors. The manor guest rooms and its cottage are also available at a very reasonable daily or weekly rate (☎ 590/27–79–27), "but you must have an artist's soul," she requests sweetly and earnestly. It also helps if you speak some French.

**❻ Petit Anse de Galet.** Just south of Gustavia, this quiet little *plage* is also known as Shell Beach because of the tiny shells heaped ankle-deep in some places.

**❹ St. Jean.** Brimming with bungalows, bistros, sunbathers, and windsurfing sails, the half-mile crescent of sand at St. Jean is the island's most popular beach. Informal restaurants are scattered here and there along the shore, and windsurfers skim along the water, catching the strong trade winds. If you walk as far to the west as possible, you can get a close look at the little planes taking off from the airport. For respite from the sun, cross the street near Eden Rock and you will find many branches of Gustavia boutiques and several restaurants.

**⓫ Toiny coast.** Over the hills beyond Grand Cul de Sac is this much-photographed coastline. Drystone fences crisscross the steep slopes of Morne Vitet along a rocky shoreline that resembles the rugged coast of Normandy.

NEED A
BREAK?

**Chez Pompi** (✉ Petit Cul de Sac, ☎ 590/27–75–67), on the road to Toiny, is a delightful cottage straight from a Cézanne painting. Pompi (aka Louis Ledee) is an artist of some repute, whose naive, slightly abstract artwork clutters the walls of his tiny studio. You can browse and chat with the amiable Monsieur Pompi while enjoying his fine Creole and country French cuisine. The gallery is open daily (except Sundays) from 9 to 6 .

# St. Barthélemy A to Z

## Arriving and Departing

### BY BOAT

Catamarans leave Philipsburg in St. Maarten at 9 AM daily, arriving in Gustavia's harbor around 11 AM. These are one-day, round-trip excursions (about $50, including open bar), with departures from St. Barts at 3:30 PM. If there's room, one-way passengers ($25) are often taken as well. The seas can be choppy, and it is not uncommon for passengers to get seasick. Contact **Bobby's Marina** in Philipsburg (☎ 599/5–23170) for reservations. The *St. Barth Express* (☎ 590/27–77–24) sails leaves from Gustavia at 7:30 AM for the trip to Philipsburg (Bobby's Marina), and Marigot (Port la Royale); it leaves Marigot at 3:30 PM for the return trip (stopping at Philipsburg). **St. Barth Yachting Service** (☎ 590/27–64–49), **Marine Service** (☎ 590/27–70–34), and **Océan-Must Marina** (☎ 590/27–62–25) in Gustavia have boats for private charter.

### BY PLANE

The principal gateway from North America is St. Maarten's Juliana International Airport. Although it is only 10 minutes by air to St. Barts, the last two may take your breath away. Don't worry when you see those treetops out your window. You're just clearing a hill before dropping down to the runway. Flights leave at least once an hour between 7:30 AM and 5:30 PM on either **Windward Islands Airways** (☎ 590/27–61–01 or 599/5–54210) or **Air St. Barthélemy** (☎ 590/87–73–46 or 599/5–3150). **Air Guadeloupe** (☎ 599/5–4212 or 590/87–53–74) offers daily service from Espérance Airport in St. Martin, the French side of the same island. Air Guadeloupe also has direct flights to St. Barts from Guadeloupe and San Juan, while **Air St. Thomas** (☎ 590/27–71–76) operates daily flights between St. Barts and both St. Thomas and San Juan. You must reconfirm your return interisland flight, even during off-peak seasons, or you may very well lose your reservation.

FROM THE AIRPORT

Airport taxi service costs $5–$15 (to the farthest hotel). Since the cabs are unmetered, you may be charged more if you make stops on the way. Cabs meet some flights, and a taxi dispatcher (☎ 590/27–66–31) is there some of the time, but if you plan to rent a car, which most people do, it's really easiest to do it at the airport. Many hotels offer free pickup and drop-off.

## Currency

The French franc is legal tender. Figure about 5F to the U.S. dollar. U.S. dollars are accepted in most establishments, but you may receive change in francs. Credit cards are accepted at most shops, hotels, and restaurants. Note: Prices quoted here are in U.S. dollars unless indicated otherwise.

## Emergencies

**Hospital: Gustavia Clinic** (☎ 590/27–60–35) is on the corner of rue Jean Bart and rue Sadi Carnot. For the doctor on call, dial 590/27–76–03. **Pharmacies:** There is a pharmacy in Gustavia on quai de la République (☎ 590/27–61–82) and one in St. Jean at the La Savane Commercial Center (☎ 590/27–66–61).

## Getting Around

CAR RENTALS

Most people opt to rent cars. There are excellent beaches, restaurants, and vistas all around the island. Beware the steep, curvy, haphazardly paved roads; get a map; and check the rental car's brakes before you drive away. The most common—and by far the most fun—rental car is the minimoke, a small open-air vehicle with a bumper-car feel. **Avis** (☎ 590/27–71–43), **Budget** (☎ 590/27–67–43), **Hertz** (☎ 590/27–71–14), and **Europcar** (☎ 590/27–73–33) are represented at the airport, among others. Check with several of the rental counters for the best price. All accept credit cards. You must have a valid driver's license, and in high season there may be a three-day minimum (or no cars available). During peak periods, like Christmas week and February, be sure to arrange for your car rental ahead of time. Your choices will most likely be limited to minimokes, Suzuki Jeeps, and open-sided Gurgels (VW Jeep)—all with stick shift only, which rent in season for about $50 a day, with unlimited mileage and limited collision insurance. A few hotels have their own car fleets, and a car should be rented at the time you make your room reservation. The choice of vehicles may be limited, but many hotels offer 24-hour emergency road service, which most rental companies do not. There are only two gas stations on the island, one near the airport and one in Lorient. They are not open on Sunday or after 5 PM, but you can use the one near the airport with a credit card at any time.

HITCHHIKING

Hitching rides is a popular, legal, and interesting way to get around; it is widely practiced in the more heavily trafficked areas on the island.

MOTORBIKES

Motorbike companies rent motorbikes, scooters, mopeds, and mountain bikes. Motorbikes go for about $30 per day and require a $100 deposit. Call **Rent Some Fun** (☎ 590/27–70–59).

TAXIS

Taxis are expensive and not particularly easy to arrange, especially in the evening. There are two taxi stations on the island, in Gustavia and at the airport. You may also arrange cab service by calling 590/27–66–31 or 590/27–75–81. There is a flat rate of 25F for rides up to five minutes long. Each additional three minutes is 20F. Fares are 50% higher from 8 PM to 6 AM and on Sunday and holidays.

## Guided Tours

Tours are by minibus or taxi. There are three tours offered by the tourist office (approximately 45 minutes, 1 hour, or 1½ hours in length); these are less expensive—about $10 per person for the shortest one—than private tours. A private five-hour island tour costs about $100 per vehicle (three–four people); an hour-long tour costs about $40 for up to three people and $50 for up to eight people. Itineraries are negotiable.

Tours can be arranged at hotel desks, through the tourist office, or by calling any of the island's taxi operators (☎ 590/27–66–31 in Gustavia or ☎ 590/27–75–81 at the airport). If you don't speak French, be sure to request a driver whose English is good. **St. Barth's Services** (☎ 590/27–56–26, FAX 590/27–56–81) can arrange customized tours as well as take care of virtually any other needs you may have, including airline ticketing, maid service, private parties, etc. Helicopter tours are offered by **Trans Helico Caraibes** (☎ 590/27–40–68) for about $65 per person.

## Language

French is the official language, though a Norman dialect is spoken by some longtime islanders. Most hotel and restaurant employees speak some English—at least enough to help you get or find what you need.

## Opening and Closing Times

Businesses and offices close from noon to 2 during the week and are closed on Saturday and Sunday. Shops are generally open weekdays 8:30–noon and 2–5, and Saturday 8:30 to noon. Some of the shops across from the airport and in St. Jean also open on Saturday afternoon and until 7 PM on weekdays. The banks are open weekdays 8–noon and 2–3:30.

## Passports and Visas

U.S. and Canadian citizens need either a passport (one that expired no more than five years ago will suffice) or a notarized birth certificate with a raised seal accompanied by photo identification. A valid passport is required for stays of more than three months. British and other EU citizens need a national identity card. All visitors need a return or ongoing ticket.

## Precautions

Roads are frequently unmarked, so be sure to get a map. Instead of road signs, look for signs pointing to a destination. These will be nailed to posts at all crossroads. Roads are narrow and sometimes very steep, so check the brakes and gears of your rental car *before* you drive away. St. Barts drivers seem to be in some kind of unending grand prix and keep their minimokes (the car of choice on this island) maxed out at all times. Prepare yourself for cars charging every which way, making sudden changes in direction while honking wildly, and backing up at astonishingly high speeds. They pause for no one. Some hillside restaurants and hotels have steep entranceways and difficult steps that require a bit of climbing or negotiating. If this could be a problem for you, ask about accessibility ahead of time.

## Taxes and Service Charges

A 10F departure tax is charged for departure to other French islands, and a 16F departure tax is charged to all other destinations. Some hotels add a 10%–15% service charge to bills; others include it in their tariffs. Many restaurants include a 15% service charge in their published prices. Be sure to ask if service is included. It is especially important to remember this when your credit-card receipt is presented to be signed with the tip space blank (just draw a line through it), or you could end up paying a 30% service charge. Most taxi drivers own their vehicles and do not expect a tip.

### Telephones and Mail

To phone St. Barts from the United States, dial 011–590 and the local six-digit number. To call the United States from St. Barts, dial 19–1, the area code, and the local number. For St. Martin, dial just the six-digit number; for St. Maarten, dial 3 plus the five-digit number. For local information, dial 12. Public telephones do not accept coins; they accept Telecartes, a type of prepaid credit card that you can purchase from the post offices at Lorient, St. Jean, and Gustavia, as well as at the gas station next to the airport. Making an international call with a Telecarte is less expensive than making the call from your hotel.

Mail is slow. It can take up to three weeks for correspondence between the United States and the island. Post offices are in Gustavia, St. Jean, and Lorient. It costs 3.10F to mail a postcard to the United States, 3.90F to mail a letter.

### Visitor Information

Information can be obtained by writing the **French West Indies Tourist Board** (⊠ 610 5th Ave., New York, NY 10020) or by calling France-on-Call at 900/990–0040 (50¢ per minute). You can also write to or visit the U.S. branches of the **French Government Tourist Office** (⊠ 444 Madison Ave., 16th floor, New York, NY 10022; ⊠ 9454 Wilshire Blvd., Suite 303, Beverly Hills, CA 90212; ⊠ 645 N. Michigan Ave., Suite 3360, Chicago, IL 60611), and write, visit, or call the branches in Canada (⊠ 1981 McGill College Ave., Suite 490, Montréal, Québec H3A 2W9, ☎ 514/288–4264; ⊠ 30 St. Patrick St., Suite 700, Toronto, Ontario M5T 3A3, ☎ 416/593–4723) and the United Kingdom (⊠ 178 Piccadilly, London W1V OAL, ☎ 0171/629–9376).

The **Office du Tourisme** (☎ 590/27–87–27, ℻ 590/27–74–47) is in a white- and blue-trimmed building on the Gustavia pier; the people who work there are most eager to please. Hours are Monday through Friday from 8:30 to 6 and Saturday from 9 to noon.

# 20 St. Eustatius

Updated by
Jonathan Runge

**T**HE FLIGHT APPROACH to the tiny Dutch island of St. Eustatius, commonly known as Statia (pronounced *stay*-sha) in the Netherlands Antilles, is almost worth the visit itself. In the distance looms the Quill, an extinct volcano that encloses a stunning primeval rain forest within its crater. Although Statia is a dry island, the higher elevations are alive with untended greenery and abloom with flowers—bougainvillea, oleander, and hibiscus.Little 12-square-mile Statia, past which Columbus sailed in 1493, prospered almost from the day the Dutch Zeelanders colonized it in 1636. In the 1700s, a double row of warehouses crammed with goods stretched for a mile along the bay, and there were sometimes as many as 200 ships tied up at the duty-free port. The island was called the "Emporium of the Western World" and "Golden Rock." There were almost 8,000 Statians on the island in the 1790s (today, there are about 1,700). Holland, England, and France fought one another for possession of the island, which changed hands 22 times. In 1816, it became a Dutch possession and has remained so to this day.

During the American War of Independence, when the British blockaded the North American coast, food, arms, and other supplies for the American revolutionaries were diverted through the West Indies, notably through neutral Statia. (Benjamin Franklin had his mail routed through Statia to ensure its safe arrival in Europe.) On November 16, 1776, the brig-of-war *Andrew Doria,* commanded by Captain Isaiah Robinson of the Continental Navy, sailed into Statia's port flying the Stars and Stripes and fired a 13-gun salute to the Royal Netherlands standard. Governor Johannes de Graaff ordered the cannons of Fort Oranje to return the salute, and that first official acknowledgment of the new American flag by a foreign power earned Statia the nickname America's Childhood Friend. In retaliation, British admiral George Rodney attacked and destroyed the island in 1781. Statia has yet to recover its prosperity, which, ironically, ended partly because of the success of the American Revolution: The island was no longer needed as a transshipment port, and its bustling economy gradually came to a stop.

Statia is in the Dutch Windward Triangle, 178 miles east of Puerto Rico and 35 miles south of St. Maarten. Oranjestad, the capital and only "city" (note quotes), is on the western side facing the Caribbean. The island is anchored at the north and the south by extinct volcanoes, like the Quill, that are separated by a central, dry plain.

Statia is a playground for hikers and divers. Colorful coral reefs and myriad ancient ships rest on the ocean floor alongside 18th-century warehouses that were slowly buried in the sea by storms. Much of the aboveground activity has to do with archaeology and restoration; students from William and Mary's College of Archaeology converge on the island each summer, the University of Leiden in the Netherlands has a pre-Columbian program, and the island's Historical Foundation is actively engaged in restoring Statian landmarks. Statia is also a way station for oil, with a 16-million-barrel storage bunker encased in the Boven, an extinct volcano on the northern end of the island. On any given day, there will be several oil tankers at anchor waiting to give or receive the liquid gold.

Most visitors will be content with a day visit from nearby St. Maarten, exploring some of the historical sights and enjoying a meal at B's Garden Restaurant. Those who stay longer tend to be collectors of unspoiled islands with a need to relax and a taste for history. Perhaps the locals are the best reason to visit this island. Statians are warm, welcoming,

498

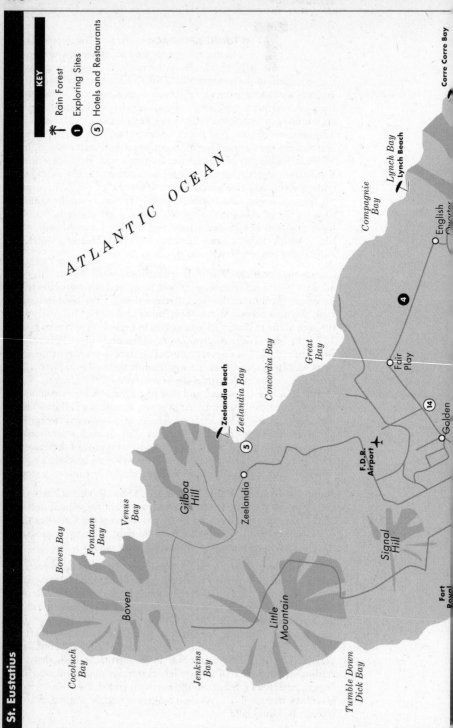

St. Eustatius

ATLANTIC OCEAN

**KEY**
🌿 Rain Forest
① Exploring Sites
⑤ Hotels and Restaurants

Boven Bay
Cocoluch Bay
Fontaan Bay
Venus Bay
Boven
Jenkins Bay
Gilboa Hill
Little Mountain
Tumble Down Dick Bay
Zeelandia Beach
Zeelandia Bay
⑤
Zeelandia
Concordia Bay
Great Bay
Compagnie Bay
Lynch Bay
Lynch Beach
F.D.R. Airport
Signal Hill
Fort Royal
Fair Play
④
⑭
Golden
English Quarter
Corre Corre Bay

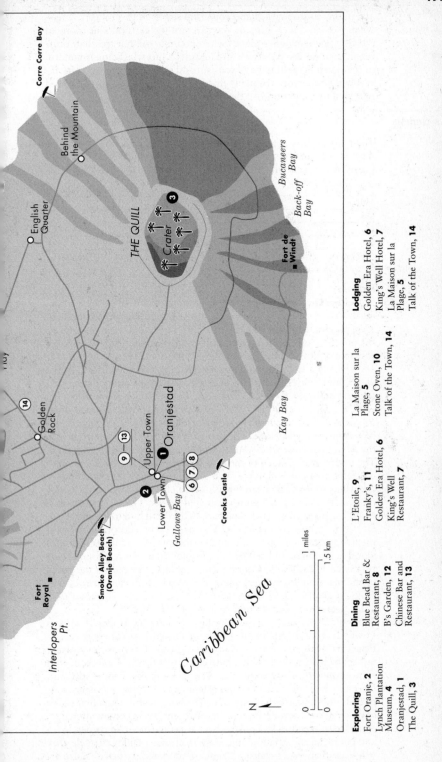

**Exploring**
Fort Oranje, **2**
Lynch Plantation
Museum, **4**
Oranjestad, **1**
The Quill, **3**

**Dining**
Blue Bead Bar &
Restaurant, **8**
B's Garden, **12**
Chinese Bar and
Restaurant, **13**

L'Etoile, **9**
Franky's, **11**
Golden Era Hotel, **6**
King's Well
Restaurant, **7**

La Maison sur la
Plage, **5**
Stone Oven, **10**
Talk of the Town, **14**

**Lodging**
Golden Era Hotel, **6**
King's Well Hotel, **7**
La Maison sur la
Plage, **5**
Talk of the Town, **14**

and happy to stop and chat. People still say hello to strangers here—when passing drivers beep or wave, return the gesture. This is one of the very few remaining islands where tourists will not feel that locals resent their perceived wealth and luxurious lifestyle. Statia is mindful of the potential gold mine of tourism and is making the necessary investments to restore the many historical buildings and forts, expand pier facilities, and improve the tourism infrastructure.

## Lodging

There are no luxury accommodations on Statia; as a rule, cheerful is the best you can expect. Many of the properties include breakfast, making most of them quite affordable.

| CATEGORY | COST* |
| --- | --- |
| $$$$ | over $125 |
| $$$ | $100–$125 |
| $$ | $75–$100 |
| $ | under $75 |

*All prices are for a standard double room for two, excluding 7% tax and 10%–15% service charge.*

### Hotels

**$$**   🏨 **Golden Era Hotel.** This harbor-front hotel is in need of some sprucing up. Rooms are air-conditioned and motel-modern, with minifridges, TVs, phones, and simple, well-worn furniture. All have little terraces, but only half have a full or partial view of the sea; the rest look out over concrete or down onto the roof of the restaurant. There is little that is aesthetically attractive about this hotel, but at least it is central, by the water, and enjoys a cheerful clientele and an accommodating and friendly staff. ⊠ *Bay Rd., Box 109, Lower Town, Oranjestad,* ☎ *599/38–2345 or 800/223–9815,* ℻ *599/38–2445. 19 rooms, 1 suite. Restaurant, bar, air-conditioning, saltwater pool. AE, MC, V. EP.*

**$$**   🏨 **La Maison sur la Plage.** The main attraction of this isolated area is the Atlantic, whose wild waters slap the 2-mile crescent of gray sand. The undertow for much of the strip here can be dangerous, but there is a safer area a few minutes' walk down the beach. The hotel's cozy lobby has well-worn rattan furnishings, a checkerboard on the coffee table, and shelves filled with weathered books. There's a stone-and-wood bar, and a *très* French dining room bordered by a trellis and greenery. Owners Therese and Michel Viali are slowly redecorating each of the five spartan cottages with pastel print spreads and drapes, natural wood furnishings, and ceiling fans. Rooms do not have phones; some rooms have TV/VCRs. Continental breakfast is served on the porch of the main building, overlooking the water. ⊠ *Zeelandia Rd., Box 157, Zeelandia,* ☎ *599/38–2256,* ℻ *599/38–2831. 10 rooms with bath. Restaurant, bar, lounge, fans, pool, MC, V. CP.*

**$–$$**   🏨 **King's Well Hotel.** Perched on the cliffs between Upper Town and
  ★   Lower Town, this small hotel offers nine rooms, two of which are efficiencies. Four rooms have water views, and all rooms are pleasant but sparsely furnished, with a balcony, minifridge, TV, and bath with shower only; there are no phones. The back rooms are more spacious, offer the best views, have ceiling fans, and feature queen-size waterbeds—well worth the extra $20. The hotel is still in the first stages of renovation; a new dining area, more rooms, and a combination pool and Jacuzzi were under construction at press time. The owners, Win and Laura, an expatriate couple, hope to attract a sailing clientele; they will lease their yacht-charter license to interested parties and also arrange sailing lessons. They also plan to open a small health spa, with massage and skin treatments. The restaurant serves a complimentary

Continental breakfast, as well as lunch and dinner. ⊠ *Bay Rd., Lower Town, Oranjestad,* ☎ ℻ *599/38–2538. 9 rooms. Restaurant, bar. D, MC, V. CP.*

**$–$$** 🏨 **Talk of the Town.** Four tidy cottages with red roofs and coral trim
★ surround the pool. They contain simple but bright rooms decorated with locally handcrafted furnishings, dark carpeting, beamed ceilings, floral spreads, and local art. All rooms have air-conditioning, gleaming white baths with shower only, cable TV, and direct-dial phone. There is a swimming pool, a deck with lounge chairs, and a restaurant downstairs. The hotel is on the road between the airport and town, an excellent choice for those who don't need a water view. Breakfast is included. Children under 12 stay free. ⊠ *L. E. Saddlerweg,* ☎ *599/38– 2236,* ℻ *599/38–2640. 18 rooms, 2 with kitchenettes. Restaurant, bar, air-conditioning, pool. MC, V. CP.*

### Apartment Rentals

Statia has only a handful of apartments, though a spate of small developments and guest houses have gone up recently to meet demand. As a general rule, figure $50 and under per night and don't expect much beyond a bathroom and kitchenette. Check with the tourist office for information about apartment rentals on the island.

## Dining

The variety of cuisines here is surprising, given the size of the island. Besides the traditional West Indian fare, you can find French and Chinese cuisine. Don't come to Statia, however, for the cuisine or quality of the restaurants. Your best bet is to eat local-style, that is, West Indian, and keep your expectations simple. All restaurants are very casual, but do cover up your beachwear.

| CATEGORY | COST* |
|---|---|
| $$$ | over $25 |
| $$ | $15–$25 |
| $ | under $15 |

*per person for a three-course meal, excluding drinks and service*

**$$$** ✕ **La Maison sur la Plage.** The three top attractions here are the view
★ of the Atlantic, the French fare, and Therese, the grande dame of the place, who's a kick. The two chefs (one is the owner; the other is well known in St. Barts restaurant circles) prepare some of the finest cuisine on the island. For dinner, start with the escargots and move on to the veal terrine with mushrooms and an herb sauce, served with a pastry top, or try the lamb medallions broiled with Roquefort cheese. ⊠ *La Maison sur la Plage hotel, Zeelandia,* ☎ *599/38–2256. MC, V.*

**$$–$$$** ✕ **King's Well Restaurant.** "Good food, cold drinks and easy prices" reads the hand-painted sign at this breezy terrace eatery overlooking the sea, run by a fun-loving expatriate couple, Win and Laura. The steaks are from Colorado, the lobster is fresh, and the *rostbraten* (roast beef) and schnitzels are authentic—one of the owners is German. ⊠ *Bay Rd., Lower Town, Oranjestad,* ☎ *599/38–2538. MC, V.*

**$$** ✕ **B's Garden.** This patio spot in the courtyard next to the tourist of-
★ fice serves sandwiches and burgers—good enough to satisfy any homesick American—at lunch, and local cuisine, such as baked snapper with shrimp sauce and tenderloin steak with green peppercorn sauce, at dinner. The courtyard is surrounded by the beautiful old stone fort and government buildings. ⊠ *Oranjestraat, Upper Town,* ☎ *599/38– 2733. No credit cards. Closed Sun. No dinner Mon.*

**$$** ✕ **Golden Era Hotel.** The restaurant and bar of this establishment are somewhat stark, but the Creole food is excellent and the large dining room is right on the water. Popular Sunday-night buffets—a steal at

$14—are served outside by the pool and ocean, with a local band providing entertainment. ⊠ *Golden Era Hotel, Bay Rd., Lower Town, Oranjestad,* ☎ *599/38–2345. AE, MC, V.*

**$$**   ✕ **Talk of the Town.** Breakfast, lunch, and dinner are served at this pleasant restaurant midway between the airport and town. Pink tablecloths, an abundance of hanging plants, and softly seductive calypso music in the background weave a romantic spell. Local, Continental, and American dishes are offered, with seafood (predictably) the standout. Try the curried shrimp or the filet mignon. ⊠ *L. E. Saddlerweg, near Upper Town,* ☎ *599/38–2236. AE, D, MC, V.*

**$–$$**   ✕ **Blue Bead Bar & Restaurant.** A friendly Dutch expatriate couple runs
★       this restaurant with spectacular water views—don't miss a sunset cocktail here. Meals are served on a cheery bright blue- and yellow-trimmed veranda decked with potted plants; the fare runs the gamut of influences: West Indian, Indonesian, Dutch, and American. The daily specials are recommended, as is anything made with chef-owner Phil's own saté sauce—a spicy, peanutty heaven. A steel band plays here on Saturday nights; the bar swings long after the kitchen closes. ⊠ *Bay Rd., Lower Town,* ☎ *599/38–2873. No credit cards.*

**$**   ✕ **Chinese Bar and Restaurant.** Owner Kim Cheng serves up tasty Asian and Caribbean dishes—*Bamigoreng* (Indonesian chow mein), pork chops Creole—in hearty portions at his unpretentious establishment. Dining indoors can be slightly claustrophobic, but just ask your waitress if you may tote your Formica-top table out onto the terrace. She'll probably be happy to lend a hand and then serve you under the stars. ⊠ *Prinsesweg, Upper Town, Oranjestad,* ☎ *599/38–2389. No credit cards.*

**$**   ✕ **L'Etoile.** West Indian dishes, such as spicy stuffed land crab and goat meat, are served at this simple snack bar–restaurant. You can also order hot dogs, hamburgers, and spareribs. ⊠ *Heiligerweg, Upper Town, Oranjestad,* ☎ *599/38–2299. No credit cards.*

**$**   ✕ **Franky's.** Come here for good local barbecue: ribs, chicken, lobster,
★       and fish served later than at most other places on Statia. Try the bullfoot soup and goat-water stew. The less adventurous can get pizza on the weekend, when there is live music. ⊠ *Ruyterweg, Upper Town, Oranjestad,* ☎ *599/38–2575. No credit cards.*

**$**   ✕ **Stone Oven.** A Spanish couple runs this cozy little eatery, offering such West Indian specialties as goat-water stew. You can eat either indoors in the little house or outside on the palm-fringed patio. ⊠ *16A Feaschweg, Upper Town, Oranjestad,* ☎ *599/38–2543. No credit cards.*

# Beaches

Beachcombing is a sport for the intrepid: The beaches are pristine but tiny, unmaintained, and occasionally rocky. Sand is mainly volcanic black (actually varying shades of gray). The nicest strands are on the Atlantic side, but the surf is generally too rough for swimming. It is possible (but not recommended) to hike around the coast at low tide, though a car is advised to reach the more remote Atlantic stretches.

A big deal on the beaches here is searching for Statia's famed blue glass beads. Manufactured in the 17th century by the Dutch West Indies Company, the blue glass beads were traded for rum, slaves, cotton, and tobacco. They were also awarded to faithful slaves or included as a part of the groom's settlement by the bride's father. Although they are found only on Statia, some researchers believe that it was beads like these that were traded for Manhattan. They're best unearthed after a heavy rain, but as the locals chuckle, "If you find one, it's a miracle, man."

**Smoke Alley Beach** (also called **Oranje Beach**) is the nicest and most accessible. The beige-and-black-sand beach is on the Caribbean, off Lower Town, and is relatively deserted until late afternoon, when the locals arrive. A 30-minute hike down an easy, marked trail behind the Mountain Road will bring you to **Corre Corre Bay** and its gold-sand cove. Two bends north of Corre Corre Bay, **Lynch Bay** is somewhat protected from the wild swells. On the Atlantic side, especially around Concordia Bay, the surf is rough and there is sometimes a dangerous undertow, making beaches in this area better for sunning than swimming. **Zeelandia Beach** is a 2-mile strip of black sand on the Atlantic side. A dangerous undertow runs here, but a small section is considered okay for swimming. Plans are being made to construct a breakwater to make the area safer for swimming. As is, it's a lovely and deserted stretch for sunning, walking, and wading.

## Outdoor Activities and Sports

### Fishing

**Golden Rock Dive Center** (☎ FAX 599/38–2964) offers full- and half-day sportfishing trips for $500 and $350, respectively, including gear and bait.

### Hiking

Trails range from the easy to the "Watch out!" The big thrill here is the Quill, the 1,968-foot extinct volcano with its crater full of rain forest. Give yourself two to three hours to make the climb and the return. The tourist office has a list of 12 marked trails and can put you in touch with a guide (whose fee will be about $20). Wear layers: It can be cool on the summit and steamy in the interior. It is rumored that monkeys have taken up residence in the rain forest.

### Scuba Diving

Statia has more than 30 dive sites, including **Barracuda Reef,** where barracudas swim around colorful coral walls, and **Double Wreck,** where coral has taken on the shape of the two disintegrated ships. **Dive Statia** (☎ 599/38–2435, FAX 599/38–2539), a fully equipped and PADI-certified dive shop offering certification courses, is operated by Rudy and Rinda Hees out of a warehouse just down the road from the Old Gin House. Several hotels offer dive packages with Dive Statia, including the Golden Era, Kings Well, and Talk of the Town. Courses are also available in underwater photography, night diving, and multilevel diving. Statia's other dive shop is the **Golden Rock Dive Center** (☎ FAX 599/38–2964) another PADI facility.

### Snorkeling

Crooks Castle has several stands of pillar coral, giant yellow sea fans, and sea whips. Jenkins Bay and Venus Bay are other favorites with snorkelers. For equipment rental, contact **Dive Statia** (☎ 599/38–2435). Equipment rentals are $5–$10; trips are about $20.

### Spectator Sports

Cricket and soccer matches are played at the sports complex in Upper Town. Statia hosts teams from other Caribbean islands on weekends; admission is free. Call the office of the sports coordinator (☎ 599/38–2209) for schedules.

### Tennis

There's a lone tennis court at the **community center** (☎ 599/38–2249) that's lighted at night. It has changing rooms, but you'll have to bring your own rackets and balls. The cost is $2 (check with the tourist office for more information). Volleyball and basketball are also played here.

# Shopping

Though shopping on Statia is duty-free, it is also somewhat limited. A handful of shops do offer unusual items, however. **Mazinga Gift Shop** on Fort Oranjestraat in Upper Town (☎ 599/38–2245) is a small department store of sorts. It has duty-free jewelry, cosmetics, and liquor, in addition to beachwear, sports gear, stationery, film, books, and magazines. The **Paper Store** (✉ Van Tonningenweg, Upper Town, ☎ 599/38–2208) sells magazines, a few books, and stationery supplies. Check out the **Fun Shop** (✉ Van Tonningenweg, Upper Town, ☎ 599/38–82253) for toys and souvenirs.

# Nightlife

Statia's five local bands stay busy on weekends. **Talk of the Town** (☎ 599/38–2236) is the place to be for live music on Sunday night. **Cool Corner** (☎ 599/38–2523), a tiny corner bar in the heart of town, across from the St. Eustatius Historical Foundation Museum, is a lively after-work and weekend hangout. The **Exit Disco** (☎ 599/38–2543), at the Stone Oven restaurant, has dancing on weekends and occasionally hosts live bands. Sometimes the **community center** (☎ 599/38–2249) has a dance. Crowds are found all weekend at **Franky's Place** (☎ 599/38–2575), in the heart of town on the Ruyterweg. It's West Indian fare is very popular. The **Lago Heights Club and Disco** (no phone), at the shopping center in Chapelpiece, is known to all as Gerald's and has dancing and a late-night barbecue.

# Exploring St. Eustatius

Statia is an arid island consisting of a valley between two mountain peaks. Most everything to see lies in the valley, making touring the island easy. From the airport, you can rent a car or take a taxi and be in historic Oranjestad in minutes; those who want to hike the Quill, Statia's highest peak, can drive to the trailhead in under 15 minutes.

*Numbers in the margin correspond to points of interest on the St. Eustatius map.*

SIGHTS TO SEE

❹ **Lynch Plantation Museum.** Also known as the Berkel Family Plantation, this museum, out in Lynch Bay, is the only domestic museum in the Dutch Caribbean. It consists of two one-room buildings, set up as they were almost 100 years ago. There's a remarkable collection preserving this family's history—family pictures, Bibles, spectacles, a sewing machine, original furniture, and some farming and fishing implements give a detailed perspective of life in Statia. Ismael Berkel guides tours of the houses, and if you ask, he may proudly show you his two medals of honor from the Dutch royal families for his conservation efforts. Be sure to sign the guest register. You'll need either a taxi or a car to visit, and it's well worth the trouble. ✉ *Lynch Bay; call tourist office at* ☎ *599/38–2209 to arrange tour.* 🎟 *Free; donations accepted.*

❶ **Oranjestad.** Statia's capital and only town sits on the western coast facing the Caribbean. It's a split-level town: Upper Town and Lower Town. History buffs will enjoy poking around the ancient Dutch Colonial buildings, which are being restored by the historical foundation. Both Upper Town and Lower Town are easily explored on foot. At the **tourist office,** which is right at the entrance to Fort Oranje, you can pick up maps, brochures, and friendly advice, as well as a listing of 12 marked hiking trails. You can also arrange for guides and guided tours.

**❷** With its three bastions, **Fort Oranje** has clutched these cliffs since 1636. In 1976, Statia participated in the U.S. bicentennial celebration by restoring the old fort, and now the black cannons point out over the ramparts. In the parade grounds a plaque, presented in 1939 by Franklin D. Roosevelt, reads, "Here the sovereignty of the United States of America was first formally acknowledged to a national vessel by a foreign official." The post office used to be in the fort but burned in 1991. There are plans under way to rebuild the structure to house boutiques and restaurants.

In the center of Upper Town is the award-winning **St. Eustatius Historical Foundation Museum.** It's set in the Doncker house, a lovely building with slim columns and a high gallery. British admiral Rodney set up his headquarters here during the American Revolution, while he was stealing everything from gunpowder to port in retaliation for Statia's gallant support of the fledgling country. The house, acquired by the foundation in 1983 and completely restored, is Statia's most important intact 18th-century dwelling. Exhibits trace the island's history from the 6th century to the present. The basement exhibit details Statia's pre-Columbian history with the results of archaeological digs on the island. Statia is the only island thus far where ruins and artifacts of the Saladoid, a newly discovered tribe, have been excavated. ⊠ *12 Van Tonningenweg,* ☎ *599/38–2288.* ▣ *$2.* ☉ *Weekdays 9–5, weekends 9–noon.*

The **Dutch Reformed church,** on Kerkweg (Church Way), was built in 1775. It has been partially restored and has lovely stone arches facing the sea. Ancient tales can be read on the gravestones in the 18th-century cemetery adjacent to the church. On Synagogepad (Synagogue Path) off Kerkweg, is **Honen Dalim** ("She Who Is Charitable to the Poor"), one of the Caribbean's oldest synagogues. Dating from 1738, it is now in ruins but is slated for restoration by groups from the United States and Holland.

| | |
|---|---|
| NEED A BREAK? | The **Cool Corner** (☎ 599/38–2523), just up from the tourist office, is a cool spot to have a beer and catch up on island gossip. Inexpensive Chinese food is also available. It's open Monday to Saturday 7 AM–2 AM. For sandwiches, pizzas, or pastries, wander over to the **Sandbox Tree Bakery** (☎ 599/38–2469) just behind the synagogue on Kerkweg. It's open weekdays 5:30 AM–7 PM and Saturday 5:30 AM–1 PM. |

**Lower Town** sits below Fort Oranjestraat (Fort Orange St.) and some steep cliffs and is reached from Upper Town on foot via the zigzagging, cobblestone Fort Road or by car via Van Tonningenweg. Warehouses and shops that in the 18th century were piled high with European imports are now either abandoned or simply used to store local fishermen's equipment and house Dive Statia. The **Old Gin House,** a restored 18th-century cotton mill, on the land side of Bay Road, was the best hotel on Statia but is now closed and at press time was on the market. The palms, flowering shrubs, and park benches along the water's edge are the work of the historical foundation members. All along the beach are the crumbling ruins of 18th-century buildings, dating from Statia's period of prosperity. The sea, which has slowly advanced since then, now surrounds many of the ruins, making for fascinating snorkeling.

**❸** **The Quill.** This 1,968-foot-high extinct volcano encloses a primeval rain forest within its crater. Hikers will want to head here to see giant elephant ears, ferns, flowers, wild orchids, fruit trees, wildlife, and birds hiding in the trees. The volcanic cone rises in the southern sector of the island, 3 miles south of Oranjestad on the main road. Local boys go up to the Quill by torchlight to catch delectable sand crabs. You can join them and ask your hotel to prepare your catch for dinner. The tourist board will make arrangements.

## St. Eustatius A to Z

### Arriving and Departing

BY PLANE

**Windward Islands Airways** (⊠ Winair, ☎ 599/5–54210) makes the 20-minute flight from St. Maarten five times a day, the 10-minute flight from Saba daily, and the 15-minute flight from St. Kitts twice a week. Be sure to confirm your flight a day or two in advance, as schedules can change abruptly.

FROM THE AIRPORT

Planes put down at the **Franklin Delano Roosevelt Airport,** where taxis meet all flights and charge about $3.50 for the drive into town. There's an Avis outlet at the airport, should you decide to rent a car.

### Currency

U.S. dollars are accepted everywhere, but legal tender is the Netherlands Antilles florin (NAf), also referred to as guilders, and you shouldn't be surprised to receive change in them. The exchange rate fluctuates but is about NAf1.75 to U.S.$1. Prices quoted here are in U.S. dollars unless noted otherwise.

### Emergencies

**Police:** ☎ 599/38–2333. **Hospital: Queen Beatrix Medical Center** (⊠ 25 Prinsesweg, ☎ 599/38–2211 and 599/38–2371) has a full-time licensed physician on duty.

### Getting Around

To explore the island (and there isn't very much), car rentals are available through the **Avis** (☎ 599/38–2421 or 800/331–1212) outlet at the airport. **Rainbow Car Rental** (☎ 599/38–2811) has several Hyundais for rent. **Brown's** (☎ 599/38–2266) and **Lady Ama's Services** (☎ 599/38–2451) rent cars and Jeeps. Statia's roads are pocked with potholes and the going is slow and bumpy. Goats and cattle have the right of way.

### Guided Tours

All 10 of Statia's taxis are available for island tours. A full day's outing costs $35 per vehicle, usually including airport transfer.

The **St. Eustatius Historical Foundation Museum** (☎ 599/38–2288) sells a sightseeing package, which includes a guided walking tour, a booklet detailing the sites on the tour, and museum admission. The tour begins in Lower Town at the Marina and ends at the museum. You can take the tour on your own with the book (there are corresponding numbered blue signs on most of the sites), but a guide may prove more illuminating.

### Language

Statia's official language is Dutch (it's used on government documents), but everyone speaks English. Dutch is taught as the primary language in the schools, and street signs are in both Dutch and English.

### Opening and Closing Times

Most offices are open weekdays 8–noon and 1–4 or 5. **Barclays Bank** is open weekdays 8–2; **Windward Islands Bank** is open Monday–Thursday 8:30–noon and 1–3:30, Friday 8:30–noon and 2–4:30. Both are in Upper Town.

## Passports and Visas

All visitors must have proof of citizenship. A passport is preferred, but a birth certificate or voter registration card will do. (A driver's license will *not* do.) British citizens need a valid passport. All visitors need a return or ongoing ticket.

## Taxes and Service Charges

Hotels collect a 7% government tax and a 10%–15% service charge. Most restaurants add a 10%–15% service charge. The departure tax is $5 for flights to other islands of the Netherlands Antilles and $10 to foreign destinations. In addition, you'll probably be asked to contribute your leftover guilders to the latest cause.

## Telephones and Mail

Statia has microwave telephone service to all parts of the world. To call Statia from the United States, dial 011–599/38 + the local number. When calling interisland, dial only the four-digit number. Direct dial is available. There are two pay phones on the island, one near the airport and one in Landsradio. Airmail letters to the United States are NAf1.30; postcards, NAf.60.

## Visitor Information

For help planning your trip, contact the **Statia Tourist Office** (⊠ Box 6322, Boca Raton, FL 33427-6322, ☎ 407/394–8580 or 800/722–2394, FAX 407/394–8588), which is very willing to advise you on any aspect of planning a trip to Statia.

Once on the island, the **tourist board** (⊠ 3 Fort Oranjestraat, ☎ FAX 599/38–2433), at the entrance to Fort Oranje, can provide you with a map and help arrange guided tours. Office hours are weekdays 8–noon and 1–5.

# 21 St. Kitts and Nevis

Updated by
Jordan Simon

**F**OR YEARS, VISITORS TO ST. KITTS AND NEVIS have tended to be self-sufficient types who know how to amuse themselves and appreciate the warmth and character of country inns. The Frigate Bay area of St. Kitts is the only area with a few larger hotels and condominium developments, while the Four Seasons opened a resort in 1991 on tiny Nevis.

Mountainous St. Kitts, the first English settlement in the Leeward Islands, crams some stunning scenery into its 65 square miles. Vast, brilliant green fields of sugarcane sweep down to the sea. The island is fertile and lush with tropical flora and has some fascinating natural and historical attractions: a rain forest, replete with waterfalls, thick vines, and secret trails; a central mountain range, dominated by the 3,792-foot Mt. Liamuiga, whose crater has been long dormant; and Brimstone Hill, the Caribbean's most impressive fortress, which was known in the 17th century as the Gibraltar of the West Indies.

The island is home to 35,000 people and hosts some 60,000 visitors annually. The shape of St. Kitts has been variously compared to a whale, a cricket bat, and a guitar. It's roughly oval, 19 miles long and 6 miles wide, with a narrow peninsula trailing off toward Nevis, 2 miles southeast across the strait.

The island is known as the mother colony of the West Indies because it was from here that the English settlers sailed to Antigua, Barbuda, Tortola, and Montserrat and the French dispatched colonizing parties to Martinique, Guadeloupe, St. Martin, St. Barts, La Désirade, and Les Saintes. The French, who inexplicably brought a bunch of monkeys with them as pets, arrived on St. Kitts a few years after the British. As rich in history as it is fertile and lush with tropical flora, St. Kitts is just beginning to develop its tourism industry, and this quiet member of the Leeward group has that rare combination of natural and historic attractions and fine sailing, island hopping, and water-sports.

In 1493, when Columbus spied a cloud-crowned volcanic isle during his second voyage to the New World, he named it *Nieves,* the Spanish word for "snows." It reminded him of the snowcapped peaks of the Pyrenees. Nevis (pronounced *Nee*-vis) rises out of the water in an almost perfect cone, the tip of its 3,232-foot central mountain smothered in clouds. It's even less developed than its sister island, St. Kitts.

Nevis is known for its natural beauty—long beaches with white and black sand, lush greenery—for a half dozen mineral spa baths, and for the restored sugar plantations that now house small, charming inns. In 1628, settlers from St. Kitts sailed across the 2-mile channel that separates the two islands. At first they grew tobacco, cotton, ginger, and indigo, but with the introduction of sugarcane in 1640, Nevis became the island equivalent of a boomtown. As the mineral baths were drawing crowds, the island was producing an abundance of sugar. Slaves were brought from Africa to work on the magnificent estates, many of them nestled high in the mountains amid lavish tropical gardens.

The restored plantation homes that now operate as inns are both islands' most sybaritic lures for the leisurely life. There is plenty of activity for the energetic—mountain climbing, swimming, tennis, horseback riding, snorkeling. But the going is easy here, with hammocks for snoozing, lobster bakes on palm-lined beaches, and candlelit dinners in stately dining rooms and on romantic verandas. Each inn, run by British or American expatriates, has its own distinct ambience, thanks to the delightful, often eccentric owners.

**Exploring**
Basseterre, **1**
Black Rocks, **7**
Bloody Point, **2**
Brimstone Hill, **5**
Middle Island, **4**
Romney Manor, **3**
Sandy Point Town, **6**

**Dining**
Arlecchino, **19**
Ballahoo, **15**
Chef's Place, **17**
Fisherman's Wharf, **16**
Georgian House, **20**
Golden Lemon, **8**
Olivee's, **14**
PJ's Pizza, **29**
Patio Restaurant, **24**
Rawlins Plantation, **9**
Royal Palm, **11**
Turtle Beach Bar and
Grill, **30**
White House, **13**

**Lodging**
Bird Rock Beach
Resort, **22**
Colony's Timothy
Beach Resort, **25**
Fairview Inn, **10**
Fort Thomas Hotel, **18**
Frigate Bay Beach
Hotel, **23**
Golden Lemon, **8**
Horizons Villas
Resort, **26**
Jack Tar Village
Beach Resorts
and Casino, **27**
Morgan Heights
Condominiums, **12**
Ocean Terrace Inn, **16**
Ottley's Plantation
Inn, **11**
Palms Hotel, **21**
Rawlins Plantation, **9**
Sun 'n Sand Beach
Village, **28**
White House, **13**

**St. Kitts**

Willett's Bay
Dieppe Bay
Sandy Bay
St. Paul's
Sadlers
Tabernacle
Newton Ground
NORTH WEST RANGE
Mt. Liamuiga
Cay
Sandy Point Town
Pump Bay
Verchild's Peak
SOUTH EAST RANGE
Half–Way Tree
Middle Island
Old Road Town
Challengers
Caribbean Sea

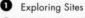

**KEY**
🛥 Ferry
**1** Exploring Sites
**8** Hotels and Restaurants

0 — 10 miles
0 — 15 km

N

A T L A N T I C   O C E A N

Nicola
Town
⑪
*Hermitage
Bay*
Cayon
Keys
l's
⑫
⭢ **Conaree Bay**
*Monkey
Hill*
⑬
**Golden Rock
Airport** ✈
*Muddy
Pt.*
㉗
㉘
㉙
⑭
❶ Basseterre ㉒
⭢ **North Frigate Bay**
*Basseterre
Bay*
⑮-㉑
⭢ **North Friar's Bay**
⭢ **Frigate
Bay**
㉓-㉖
**South Friar's
Bay**
**Sandbank
Beach** ⭢
*Mosquito
Bluff*
*St. Anthonys
Peak*
*Great
Salt
Pond*
㉚
*Turtle
Bay*
**White House Bay** ⭢
**Cockleshell Bay** ⭢
*Major's
Bay*
**Banana
Bay**
*Nag's
Head*

TO NEVIS

ATLANTIC OCEAN

Nevis

Huggins Bay

Eden Brown

Long Haul Bay

Newcastle Beach

Newcastle

Newcastle Airport

Nevis Peak

The Narrows

Mosquito Bay

Oualie Beach

Cotton Ground

Pinney's Beach

TO ST. KITTS

513

N

Caribbean Sea

Charlestown

Zion

Morning Star

Fig Tree

Gingerland

Saddle Hill

White Bay

Red Cliff

Dogwood Pt.

Long Pt.

5 miles

5 km

**KEY**

Ferry

❶ Exploring Sites

⑩ Hotels and Restaurants

**Exploring**
Bath Springs, 2
Charlestown, 1
Eden Brown Estate, 5
Fort Ashby, 7
Hurricane Hill, 6
Nelson Museum, 3
Nelson Spring, 8

St. John's Church, 4
St. Thomas Anglican Church, 9

**Dining**
Callaloo, 15
Eddy's Bar and Restaurant, 12

Four Seasons Resort, 11
Golden Rock, 20
Hermitage Plantation Inn, 17
Miss June's, 16
Montpelier Plantation Inn, 18

Mt. Nevis Hotel, 22
Muriel's Cuisine, 14
Nisbet Plantation Beach Club, 21
Oualie Beach, 24
Prinderella's, 26
SunShine's, 10
Tequila Sheila's, 27

Unella's, 13

**Lodging**
Four Seasons Resort Nevis, 11
Golden Rock, 20
Hermitage Plantation Inn, 17

Hurricane Cove Bungalows, 25
Montpelier Plantation Inn, 18
Mt. Nevis Hotel/Condominiums, 22
Nisbet Plantation Beach Club, 21
Old Manor Estate, 19

Oualie Beach Hotel, 24
Yamseed Inn, 23

Nevis is linked with St. Kitts politically. The two islands, together with Anguilla, achieved self-government as an Associated State of Great Britain in 1967. In 1983, St. Kitts and Nevis became a fully independent nation. Nevis papers sometimes run fiery articles advocating independence from St. Kitts, and the sister islands may separate someday. However, it's not likely that a shot will be fired, let alone one that will be heard around the world.

Fortunately, early reports of widespread devastation after 1995 Hurricanes Luis and Marilyn were greatly exaggerated; both islands suffered minimal damage in comparison to many other Antilles.

# ST. KITTS

## Lodging

St. Kitts has an appealing variety of places to stay—beautifully restored plantation inns, full-service hotels, condominium complexes, simple beachfront cottage colonies, and an all-inclusive hotel. There are also a number of guest houses and self-catering condominiums available.

| CATEGORY | COST* |
|---|---|
| $$$$ | over $275 |
| $$$ | $200–$275 |
| $$ | $125–$200 |
| $ | under $125 |

*All prices are for a standard double room for two, excluding 7% tax and 10% service charge.*

### Hotels

$$$$   🖼 **Golden Lemon.** Arthur Leaman, a former decorating editor of *House*
★   *and Garden,* created and runs this internationally famous, quiet retreat at the isolated north end of the island. The eight rooms in the restored 17th-century great house are each different and impeccably decorated. There are canopied, wrought-iron, and four-poster beds swaddled in mosquito netting, armoires, chaise longues, rocking chairs, and a variety of stunning fabrics in delectable shades from mango to raspberry. You can also stay in a one- or two-bedroom town house with a wraparound terrace and kitchenette (some have a private pool). These are decorated with an eclectic yet harmonious blend of West Indian crafts, antiques, and artwork culled from Arthur's world travels. The cool, dark, well-appointed bar and lounge offer a peaceful respite from the bright sun, and the restaurant is one of the best on the island. A gray-sand beach, guarded by rusty cannonballs and shaded by spindly, elegant palms, offers views of St. Martin shimmering in the distance. The hotel allows no children under 18. ✉ *Box 17, Dieppe Bay,* ☎ *809/465–7260 or 800/633–7411,* 🟥 *809/465–4019. 32 rooms and suites. Restaurant, pool, tennis court, duty-free shop. AE, MC, V. MAP.*

$$$$   🖼 **Ottley's Plantation Inn.** This former sugar plantation has been trans-
★   formed into a spectacularly elegant inn. Nestled at the foot of Mt. Liamuiga, on 35 manicured acres that border a rain forest, it has views that sweep out to the wild Atlantic. The beautifully restored, 18th-century, English colonial–style great house and cut-stone cottages hold 15 guest rooms. The spacious rooms, many with high ceilings and white wood floors, are decorated with an eclectic mix of white wicker, antiques, and floral print fabrics. The cottages, with exquisite old tile and stonework and English country house decor, are honeymoon heaven. The 65-foot, spring-fed pool stretches out from the remaining walls of the sugar factory, with an open-air bar at one end and the alfresco

Royal Palm restaurant along one side. Take a stroll on the property's rain-forest trail. The engaging owners or their (grown) kids are always available to dispense advice and good cheer. ☒ *Box 345, Ottley's,* ☎ *809/465–7234 or 800/772–3039,* ℻ *809/465–4760. 15 rooms. Restaurant, bar, pool, shuttle to beach/town. AE, MC, V. MAP.*

$$$$ 🏨 **Rawlins Plantation.** Another former sugar plantation, this lovely inn
★ is fairly isolated, on 12 acres at the northern end of the island (the notoriously bumpy, rutted dirt access road emphasizes the wilderness feel). The views are spectacular: on one side of the inn, lush greenery climbs to the peak of Mt. Liamuiga; on the other side, the Caribbean sea stretches out to the island of Statia. Hammocks are slung among the pear and almond trees, and the plantation's original copper syrup vats crop up everywhere you look. Ten rooms, each with bath, are scattered across the grounds in various restored buildings of the old estate (including the original sugar mill), and each is unique. You'll find mahogany four-poster beds, wicker chairs, hardwood floors, and fabrics in soft pastel prints. Some, however, might consider the furnishings a bit spare. There is no air-conditioning, but all units have ceiling fans and good cross ventilation. The restaurant, well known on the island for its Continental-Caribbean cuisine, is decorated with antiques. This is a great place to get away from it all. ☒ *Box 340, Mt. Pleasant,* ☎ *809/465–6221 or 800/346–5358,* ℻ *809/465–4954. 10 rooms. Restaurant, pool, tennis court, croquet, complimentary laundry service. AE, MC, V. MAP.*

$$$$ 🏨 **White House.** Three radiant acres of flowering gardens and manicured lawns surround this small, secluded property in the foothills above Basseterre. There are views of the Caribbean in the distance, but you'll have to take a ten-minute ride in the hotel's shuttle to get to the beach. The 18th-century plantation great house has been beautifully restored, and the stable and carriage house have been rebuilt. You'll be greeted by the fierce posturing of the house English bulldogs (they're actually lambs), then by the gracious owners, Janice and Malcolm Barber. The tasteful, uncluttered bedrooms have hardwood floors and are individually decorated with 19th-century antiques, mahogany beds (many are four-poster), and Laura Ashley fabrics. There is no air-conditioning, but all rooms have ceiling fans. ☒ *Box 436, St. Peter's,* ☎ *809/465–8162 or 800/223–1108,* ℻ *809/465–8275. 10 rooms. Restaurant, bar, pool, tennis court, croquet, laundry service, shuttle to beach/town. AE, MC, V. MAP.*

$$$–$$$$ 🏨 **Horizons Villas Resort.** These gleaming new coral-white-and-jade villas, most affording stunning views of the Caribbean and/or Atlantic, are meticulously maintained. The smaller one-bedroom villas boast an enormous terrace the size of a New York studio apartment; the larger three-bedroom units include a private plunge pool. All offer every conceivable amenity, from full kitchen (including dishwasher, and thoughtful touches like mugs left in the freezer) and huge bathtubs fit for a Roman emperor to washer/dryer, VCR, and CD player. The individually owned and decorated units favor soothing pinks, olive, teal, and taupe tones, with rattan and blond wood furnishings, vivid local artwork, and immaculate white tile floors. The pool/grill area is uncommonly pleasant, Frigate Bay Beach is a two-minute walk down the hill, and the golf course is a short drive away. A new restaurant opened in the spring 1996 and 28 more villas are scheduled for completion by 1997. ☒ *Box 1143, Basseterre,* ☎ *809/465–0584 or 800/830–9069,* ℻ *809/465–0785. 46 units (only a few in rental pool at any given time). Restaurant, grill, pool, complimentary Continental breakfast and greens fees. AE, D, MC, V.*

**$$–$$$** 🏨 **Jack Tar Village Beach Resorts and Casino.** A lively atmosphere pervades this appealing all-inclusive resort, whose motto could well be "moderate prices, but nothing in moderation." Sports of all sorts are available, and each day has a schedule of recreational activities and contests. Two pools are a nice touch: One is for the volleyball and water aerobics crowd, the other for those who want a quiet, relaxing dip. Nightly live entertainment, a disco, and the island's only casino keep the action going late into the night. Guest rooms are freshly decorated with floral linens, boating prints, and jade carpets; all rooms were thoroughly renovated following Hurricanes Luis and Marilyn. Each room has a small terrace or balcony. There are no water views from any of the rooms (unless you count water hazards on the golf course, or a sliver of ocean from some top floor rooms.) The restaurants are noted for their theme buffets, as well as for solid Continental and Creole fare. ✉ *Box 406, Frigate Bay,* ☎ *809/465–8651 or 800/999–9182,* 𝐅𝐀𝐗 *809/465–8651. 240 rooms, 2 suites. 2 restaurants, bars, 2 pools, beauty salon, massage, spa, access to golf course, 4 tennis courts, basketball, exercise and aerobics classes, minigym, shuffleboard, Ping-Pong, scuba lessons, water-sports center, shops, casino, disco, child care. AE, D, DC, MC, V. All-inclusive.*

**$$** 🏨 **Bird Rock Beach Resort.** Perched on a bluff overlooking its own poky beach, a few miles from the airport and downtown, this rather plain-looking resort has been expanding every year, with a dive shop and casual beach grill added in 1995. Two-story buildings contain air-conditioned rooms and suites with balcony and ocean view. Suites also have kitchenettes. The tile-floored rooms are simply furnished with rattan and wicker furniture, floral fabrics, and paintings of birds. An informal alfresco dining room turns out Continental favorites with local ingredients. There is particularly excellent snorkeling and diving in the waters just off the resort's golden-sand cove. Golf and the larger Frigate Bay beaches are just five minutes away. The staff is most hospitable and the invigorating mix of young Europeans on a budget and divers from around the world give Bird Rock an international flavor and flair. ✉ *Box 227, Basseterre,* ☎ *809/465–8914 or 800/621–1270,* 𝐅𝐀𝐗 *809/465–1675. 38 units. Restaurant, beach grill, 2 bars, 2 pools (one with swim-up bar), tennis court, dive shop, gift shop, shuttle service to golf. AE, DC, MC, V. EP, MAP.*

**$$** 🏨 **Colony's Timothy Beach Resort.** If you don't mind trading a bit of atmosphere for modern comfort at a good price, this could well be the ideal spot for a beach-oriented vacation. The management is attentive and friendly at this casual hotel, set at the end of Frigate Bay beach, overlooking the Caribbean. Simple beige stucco buildings hold comfortable, adequately furnished rooms and suites. Larger units have kitchens and multiple bedrooms, and every room has air-conditioning. Opt to stay in one of the original buildings, which sit right on the beach; they have better views than the most recent additions and are larger and airier. You can choose from a wide variety of sports activities. Greens fees for the nearby golf course are included in the room rate. The hotel's Coconut Cafe is a local favorite; however, rates are based on EP (no meals), so you are free to sample the cuisine around St. Kitts as well. ✉ *Box 81, Frigate Bay,* ☎ *809/465–8597 or 800/838–5375,* 𝐅𝐀𝐗 *809/465–7723; Colony Reservations Worldwide, 800/777–1700. 60 rooms. Restaurant, pool, water-sports center. AE, MC, V. EP.*

**$$** 🏨 **Fairview Inn.** The main building of this old, quiet, and rather simple inn is an 18th-century great house, with graceful white verandas and Oriental rugs on hardwood floors. The rooms are in little cottages sprinkled around the backyard, in the shadow of a looming mountain. They're tiny and have functional motel furnishings, with either twin or double beds, private patios, and have private baths with showers or bathtubs. Some have air-conditioning, some fans, some neither. Those in the converted stables have the most character, with exposed stone walls. Banks of yellow allemanda climb the trellises surrounding the pool, which has an ocean view. Alas, despite the property's faded charm and ambience, and the grandiose ambition of the owner to transform it into a more elite resort, the price/value ratio is not what it should be. The restaurant serves superb West Indian cuisine. ⊠ *Box 212, Basseterre,* ☎ *809/465–2472 or 800/223–9815,* FAX *809/465–1056. 30 rooms. Restaurant, 2 bars, pool. AE, D, MC, V. EP, MAP.*

$$ 🏨 **Frigate Bay Beach Hotel.** The third fairway of the island's golf course adjoins this property (guests here get discounts on greens fees), and the two nearby beaches—Caribbean and Atlantic—are reached by complimentary shuttle buses (the Caribbean beach is also easily reached by following the path from the far end of the pool, along the edge of the golf course). The whitewashed, air-conditioned buildings contain standard rooms as well as condominium units with fully equipped kitchens. There are hillside and poolside units; the latter are preferable for their nicer views and fresher ambience. Rooms and condos have beige or navy tile floors and are decorated with floral linens and sailing prints. All have ceiling fans and sliding glass doors leading to a terrace or balcony. There's an Olympic-size pool with swim-up bar and a terraced restaurant overlooking the pool, where raucous buffet theme nights with live music are the rule. Packages of all sorts are available. ⊠ *Box 137, Basseterre,* ☎ *809/465–8935 or 800/468–3750,* FAX *809/465–7050. 64 rooms. Restaurant, bar, pool. AE, D, MC, V. EP, MAP.*

$$ 🏨 **Ocean Terrace Inn.** Referred to locally as OTI, this is a rarity: a stylish, ★ intimate business hotel. The main building—which houses the fancier restaurant, reception, a pool with a swim-up bar, and many of the rooms—is set high on a hill overlooking the ocean, amid lovingly tended gardens dotted with gazebos. Even the bar areas are distinctive, with African masks, aquariums, screeching birds, and brilliantly back-lit murals of cavorting dancers and drummers. One- and two-bedroom condos are farther down the hill but also have water views. All are air-conditioned and are handsomely decorated in rattan and bright fabrics. Fisherman's Wharf, on the waterfront at the bottom of the hill, is a casual seafood restaurant. The hotel's Pelican Cove Marina has its own fleet of boats that you can take out or charter. There is a daily shuttle to nearby beaches. New ownership plans to expand over the next few years, but vows to retain the hotel's cozy appeal. ⊠ *Box 65, Basseterre,* ☎ *809/465–2754 or 800/524–0512,* FAX *809/465–1057. 54 units. 2 restaurants, 2 bars, 2 pools, outdoor hot tub, water-sports center, fleet of boats, 2 boutiques. AE, MC, V. EP, MAP.*

$$ 🏨 **Sun 'n' Sand Beach Village.** This simple complex is on the beach at North Frigate Bay, on the Atlantic side of the island. Studios in two-story buildings and two-bedroom, self-catering units in pretty, Antillean-style wood-and-stucco cottages stretch back from the beach. Decor is simple and tropical, with rattan furnishings, island prints and batiks, and beige tile floors. Studios are air-conditioned; each has twin or queen-size beds, bath with shower, and a private terrace. The cottages have a convertible sofa in the living room and a fully equipped kitchen; there's a window air conditioner in the bedroom and a ceiling fan in the living room. ⊠ *Box 341, Frigate Bay,* ☎ *809/465–8037 or 800/223–6510,* FAX *809/465–6745. 32 studios, 18 2-bedroom cottages. Restaurant, bar, grocery, pool, children's pool, 2 tennis courts, beach, gift shop. AE, D, MC, V. CP, MAP.*

$–$$ 🏨 **Fort Thomas Hotel.** The Canadian owners of this hotel, which has long been popular with business travelers and tour groups, have sunk a great deal of money into much-needed renovations. In fact, their ambitious five-year expansion hopes to add a casino, amphitheater, nightclub, man-made beach, gym, dive shop, and villa complex. The original hotel is built on the site of an old fort, on a hillside overlooking Basseterre and the harbor. Unfortunately, the cannons anchoring the driveway and a few ramparts scattered about the grounds near the pool are the only reminders of its storied past. The building resembles an antiseptic stateside motel, but the owners have softened it by adding "colonial" touches like gingerbread trim and arched picture windows. The rooms are spacious, with seashell colors and wicker furnishings. The second-floor rooms have far better views and are worth the minimal surcharge. Individually owned third-floor "penthouses" are available to rent as well. There's a free shuttle bus to the Frigate Bay beaches, and the hotel is walking distance to town and the stores at Pelican Mall. The pool has great views of Basseterre and the ocean, which can also be enjoyed from canopied porch swings and gingerbread gazebos. ⊠ *Box 407, Basseterre,* ☎ *809/465–2695,* FAX *809/465–7518. 64 rooms. Restaurant, bar, pizzeria, pool, putting green, tour desk, gift shop, game room. AE, D, MC, V. EP, MAP.*

**$–$$** ▥ **Morgan Heights Condominiums.** A laid-back atmosphere and reasonable prices are found at this complex along the Atlantic (although not on the beach), 10 minutes from Basseterre. The rooms are clean and comfortable, with simple contemporary white wicker furniture and ceramic tile floors. All are air-conditioned with covered patios that overlook the water. The buildings are along a main highway and can be somewhat noisy during the day. The Atlantic Club serves excellent local cuisine and piña coladas with a punch. ⊠ *Box 536, Basseterre,* ☎ *809/465–8633,* FAX *809/465–9272. 5 2-bedroom units that can be rented as 1-bedroom units and individual hotel rooms. Restaurant, pool, beach shuttle. AE, D, MC, V. EP.*

**$** ▥ **Palms Hotel.** This delightful all-suites hotel has a prime location right
★ in Palms Arcade for those wishing to explore Basseterre. Air-conditioned units are decorated mainly in corals and teals, with bright throw rugs, pastel floral linens and art deco–style fixtures, including elaborate chandeliers. Even the smaller junior suites contain cable TVs, minifridges, coffeemakers, and phones. Drawbacks? The nearest beach is a 10-minute drive, and the central location means it can be rather noisy (under no circumstances rent during Carnival or other major festivals if you crave peace). ⊠ *Box 64, The Circus, Basseterre,* ☎ *809/465–0800,* FAX *809/465–5889. 10 units. Bar, shops. AE, MC, V.*

# Dining

St. Kitts restaurants range from funky little beachfront bistros to small, elegant plantation dining rooms; there is an interesting variety of cuisine to sample, most tinged, one way or another, with the flavors of the Caribbean. Many restaurants offer a variety of West Indian specialties that are popular on St. Kitts, such as curried mutton, Arawak chicken (seasoned chicken, rice, and almonds served on breadfruit leaf), pepper pot, and honey-glazed garlic spareribs.

## What to Wear

Dress is casual at lunch (but no bathing suits!) throughout the island. Dinner, although not necessarily formal, definitely calls for long pants and sundresses.

| CATEGORY | COST* |
|---|---|
| $$$$ | over $40 |
| $$$ | $30–$40 |
| $$ | $20–$30 |
| $ | under $20 |

*per person, excluding drinks and service. There is no sales tax on St. Kitts.*

**$$$$** ✕ **Golden Lemon.** Owner Arthur Leaman creates the recipes himself
★ for the West Indian, Continental, and American dishes served in his
hotel, and he never repeats them more than once in a two-week period. The evening begins with cocktails and hors d'oeuvres on the patio.
The three-course dinner, with its fixed menu, is served in a tasteful room,
with crystal chandeliers, white rattan furnishings, and antiques. Arched
doorways welcome the island breezes. The longtime Kittitian chef, Trevor
Browne, makes delicious pumpkin soup, chicken with peanut sauce,
and lobster medallions Creole. The patio, lush with bougainvillea and
ferns, is a popular spot for Sunday brunch, which can include banana
pancakes, rum beef stew, and curried conch fritters. ⊠ *Dieppe Bay*,
☎ *809/465–7260. Reservations essential. AE, MC, V.*

**$$$$** ✕ **Patio Restaurant.** In their flower-filled home, Joan and Peter Mal-
lalieu prepare, with the help of their staff, a full à la carte menu with
complimentary wine and liqueur. Try the flame-broiled mahimahi with
shrimp, or treat yourself to a sampling of traditional local dishes, including *conki* (a coconut side dish) and pepper pot. Piña colada gâteau
and tropical fruit mousses make for tempting desserts. ⊠ *Frigate Bay
Beach*, ☎ *809/465–8666. Reservations essential. MC, V.*

**$$$$** ✕ **Rawlins Plantation.** Elegant dinners are served in a lovely room with
★ fieldstone walls and high vaulted ceilings. The fixed-price, four-course
dinner ($40 per person) changes nightly but always emphasizes local
ingredients. Dishes may include christophine or pumpkin-and-coconut
soup, smoked snapper and watercress salad, shrimp ceviche with coriander and sour oranges, or lobster in puff pastry with tarragon sauce.
The guava and lime parfaits and chocolate terrine with passion-fruit sauce
are delicious. The bountiful lunch buffet ($24) offers such items as bread-
fruit salad, flying fish fritters, and *bobote* (ground beef, eggplant, spices,
curry, and homemade chutney). ⊠ *Mt. Pleasant*, ☎ *809/465–6221.
Reservations essential by noon. AE, MC, V. No dinner Sun.*

**$$$$** ✕ **Royal Palm.** Set beside the pool at Ottley's Plantation, this is a
★ restaurant to experience at night, under the latticed roof, gazing across
manicured lawns to the lights of the elegantly restored great house.
Pamela Yahn, a graduate of the prestigious Culinary Institute of America, is the island's most creative and assured chef. Her menu is an eclectic mix of California-Caribbean dishes, with some classic Italian,
French, and Chinese items. Start with baked brie or Creole pumpkin
soup, then have grilled sea scallops with Kittitian salsa or lobster *bam-
baya* (sautéed with ginger, tamarind, key lime juice, shallots, garlic, and
sun-dried tomatoes). For dessert, try banana fritters *l'antillaise* (spiced
and fried in rum) or mango mousse with raspberry sauce. The presentation is just as artful and appetizing. This is the island's merriest
dining spot, in no small part due to co-owners Art and Ruth Keusch.
Art serenades diners with a twinkle in his eye, while Ruth comically
rolls her eyes. The combination of superb food and warm bonhomie
they offer is unbeatable. ⊠ *Ottley's Plantation Inn*, ☎ *809/465–
7234. Reservations essential. AE, D, MC, V.*

**$$$$** ✕ **White House.** Lunch is served on the garden terrace; romantic dinners, complete with candlelight and crystal, are served either in the elegant, antiques-filled dining room or outside under a marquee tent. The
chef prepares a four-course dinner each night, which may include
pumpkin or crab soup, Cornish game hen with banana stuffing, or fresh
broiled local seafood. Many of the ultrafresh ingredients are cultivated
in owner Janice Barber's gardens. Afternoon tea is also served here.
⊠ *St. Peter's*, ☎ *809/465–8162. Reservations essential. AE, MC, V.*

**$$$–$$$$** ✕ **Georgian House.** Janice and Malcolm Barber, owners of the delightful
★ White House, took over and thoroughly reinvigorated this once-tired
institution, occupying a magnificent 1750 brick-and-fieldstone town
house with gorgeous parquet floors. Enjoy drinks in the courtyard, be-

fore repairing to the sumptuous dining area. Everything is comme il faut almost to a fault: Bernadaud and Wedgwood china, crisp white napery, candles gleaming in oversized glass vases, vaulting floral arrangements, high-back mahogany chairs. The fare is equally elegant without being pretentious. The main menu changes weekly, but among the signature dishes are conch scallopini, a well-nigh perfect rack of lamb, and snapper brilliantly complemented by shrimp and sesame sauce. The prices aren't stratospheric, given the quality and refined atmosphere; even the wine list is carefully considered and reasonably priced. The Georgian House offers an unbeatable combination of classic haute cuisine, classical music, and classy ambience. ⊠ *South Independence Sq.,* ☎ *809/465–4049. AE, MC, V. Closed Sun. No lunch.*

**\$\$–\$\$\$** ✕ **Fisherman's Wharf.** Part of the Ocean Terrace Inn (head straight rather than up the hill to the hotel's main building), this extremely casual waterfront eatery is decorated in swaggering nautical style, with rustic wood beams, rusty anchors, cannons, and buoys. Try the excellent conch chowder, followed by fresh grilled lobster or other shipshape seafood, and finish off your meal with a slice of the memorable banana cheesecake. The tables are long, wooden affairs and it's generally lively, especially on weekend nights. ⊠ *Fortlands, Basseterre,* ☎ *809/465–2754. AE, MC, V. No lunch.*

**\$\$–\$\$\$** ✕ **Olivee's.** Robert Cramer and Ian Smith have converted their tradi-
★       tional West Indian home, filled with antiques acquired on their extensive travels, into the island's most charming, convivial eatery. Drinks are served on the hillside terrace, set amid fragrant tropical gardens with smashing views of Basseterre and the Caribbean. Robert is the maître d'; Ian, the chef. The prix fixe menu is \$20–\$40 depending on your entrée and includes delectable homemade sourdough bread. Among Ian's savory Continental selections, delicately spiced with island flair, are saltfish fritters with red pepper coulis, sweet potato pâté, herb-stuffed chicken breast in kumquat glaze, and grilled lime-marinated swordfish with guava and red onion relish. Most of the fruits and vegetables are organically grown on the property. The bittersweet chocolate torte with gooseberry sauce is sublime. You can choose from their well-considered wine list. Sunday brunch is also served. Olivee's also functions as a B&B, with two rooms, priced at \$65 and \$75 a night, beautifully furnished with antiques, local crafts, and beds swaddled in mosquito netting. ⊠ *Upper Buckley's, Basseterre,* ☎ *809/465–3662. AE, MC, V. Restaurant closed May 15–Nov. 15.*

**\$\$** ✕ **Arlecchino.** The shaded courtyard of this breezy trattoria is a pleasant place to while away the afternoon or evening. Enjoy the sublime minestrone, fresh pastas (try the spaghetti in conch sauce), creative pizzas (the picante—salami and chilies—is as hot as the name promises), and excellent veal Parmigiana, then top off the meal with the best cappuccino and cannolis on St. Kitts. ⊠ *Cayon St., Basseterre,* ☎ *809/465–9927. AE, MC, V. Closed Sun.*

**\$–\$\$** ✕ **Turtle Beach Bar and Grill.** Simple but scrumptious cuisine has made this informal restaurant a popular daytime watering hole. Taste treats include honey-mustard ribs, calypso chicken, coconut-shrimp salad, and grilled, stuffed lobster. The glorified shack is on an isolated beach at the south end of the South East Peninsula Road; just look for the signs. Business cards from around the world plaster the bar, and the room is brightly decorated with a small sailboat, colorful crusted bottles dredged from the deep, and painted wooden fish, turtles, and toucans. You can rent a kayak, Windsurfer, or mountain bike here to help you work off your meal, snorkel, look out for green vervet monkeys and hawksbill turtles, or schedule a deep-sea fishing trip. ⊠ *Turtle Beach,* ☎ *809/469–9086. AE, MC, V. No dinner Sun.–Thurs.*

**$** ✕ **Ballahoo.** This second-floor terrace restaurant is in the heart of downtown, overlooking the Circus. It draws a crowd of locals and tourists for breakfast, lunch, and dinner. Lilting calypso and reggae on the sound system, whirring ceiling fans, potted palms, and colorful island prints create the appropriate tropical ambience. Specialties include conch simmered in garlic butter, madras beef curry, lobster and shrimp in a light creamy sauce, and (it's true) a rum and banana toasted sandwich. ✉ *Fort St., Basseterre,* ☎ *809/465–4197. AE, MC, V. Closed Sun.*

**$** ✕ **Chef's Place.** Inexpensive West Indian meals are the draw here, as well as the best eavesdropping—the clientele runs toward local cops and middle-level government paper-pushers. Try the local version of jerk chicken (moister than usual) or the goat stew. The best seats are outside on the wide white veranda. ✉ *Upper Church St., Basseterre,* ☎ *809/465–6176. No credit cards. Closed Sun.*

**$** ✕ **PJ's Pizza.** "Garbage pizza" may not sound too appetizing, but this pie, topped with everything but the kitchen sink, is a favorite here. You can also choose from 10 other varieties of pizza or create your own. Sandwiches and other Italian standards are available (lasagna is a house specialty). Finish your meal with delicious, moist rum cake. This casual spot borders the golf course and is open to cooling breezes. The atmosphere is always boisterous. ✉ *Frigate Bay,* ☎ *809/465–8373. AE, MC, V. Closed Mon. and Sept.*

## Beaches

All beaches on the island are free and open to the public, even those occupied by hotels. The powdery white-sand beaches are all in the Frigate Bay area of the island or on the lower peninsula.

Two of the island's best are the twin beaches of **Banana Bay** and **Cockleshell Bay,** which together cover more than 2 miles at the southeastern tip of the island. Several large hotels, including the Banana Bay and Casablanca, were abandoned in the early stages of development—their skeletal structures marring an otherwise idyllic scene.

**Conaree Bay** on the Atlantic side is a narrow strip of gray-black sand where the water is good for body surfing. There are no facilities here.

Snorkeling and windsurfing are good at **Dieppe Bay,** a black-sand beach on the north coast, where the Golden Lemon hotel is located.

Locals consider the Caribbean side of **Friar's Bay** the island's finest beach. You can haggle with fishermen here to take you out snorkeling off the eastern point. The waters on the Atlantic side are rougher, but the beach itself has a wild, desolate beauty.

**Frigate Bay,** on the Caribbean, features talcum-powder-fine sand, while on the Atlantic side, **North Frigate Bay** is 4 miles wide and a favorite with horseback riders (☞ Outdoor Activities and Sports, *below*).

A tiny dirt road, virtually impassable after heavy rains, leads to **Sandbank Beach** on the Atlantic side. The shallow coves are protected here, making it ideal for families, and it's usually deserted.

**White House Bay** is rocky, but the snorkeling, taking in several reefs surrounding a sunken tugboat, is superb.

## Outdoor Activities and Sports

### Boating

Sunfish and Hobie Cats can be rented at **Tropical Surf** (✉ Turtle Bay, ☎ 809/469–9086) and **Mr. X Watersports** (✉ Frigate Bay, ☎ 809/465–4995).

### Deep-Sea Fishing

Angle for yellowtail snapper, wahoo, mackerel, tuna, dolphin, shark, and barracuda with **Tropical Tours** (☎ 809/465–4167) and **Captain Redbeard Boat Charters** (☎ 809/465–0482).

### Golf

The **Royal St. Kitts Golf Club** (☎ 809/465–8339) is an 18-hole championship course in the Frigate Bay area.

### Hiking

Trails in the central mountains vary from easy to don't-try-it-by-yourself. Monkey Hill and Verchild's Peak are not difficult, although the Verchild's climb will take the better part of a day. Don't attempt Mt. Liamuiga without a guide. You'll start at Belmont Estates on horseback, then proceed on foot to the lip of the crater at 2,600 feet. You can go down into the crater, clinging to vines and roots. **Greg Pereira** (☎ 809/465–4121), whose family has lived on St. Kitts for well over a century, takes groups on half-day trips into the rain forest and on full-day hikes up the volcano and through the grounds of a private 250-year old great house, followed by excursions down canyons and past petroglyphs. He and his staff provide a running, overflowing commentary of fascinating historical, folkloric, and botanical tidbits, as well as refreshing fruit juices (with CSR [Cane Spirit Rothschild], the local firewater). **Kriss Tours** (☎ 809/465–4042) takes small groups into the crater, through the rain forest, and to Dos d'Anse Pond on Verchild's Mountain. Oliver Spencer takes hikers **Off the Beaten Track** (☎ 809/465–6314) to the ruins of a fragrant, abandoned coffee plantation taken over by sprawling banyan trees.

### Horseback Riding

Frigate Bay and Conaree Beach are great for riding. Guides from **Trinity Stable** (☎ 809/465–3226) will lead you into the hills at a leisurely gait. **Royal Stables** (☎ 809/465–2222) offers sunset beach rides and tours into the rain forest on horseback.

### Parasailing, Waterskiing, and Windsurfing

**Turtle Tours** (☎ 809/469–9086) at Turtle Bay rents Windsurfers, surfboards, kayaks, and boogie boards. **Fantasy Parasailing** (Frigate Bay, ☎ 809/465–8930) will have you flying as high as 600 feet above the turquoise waters.

### Scuba Diving and Snorkeling

Kenneth Samuel of **Kenneth's Dive Centre** (☎ 809/465–7043 or 809/465–2670) is a PADI-certified dive master who takes small groups of divers with C cards to nearby reefs. Auston MacLeod, a PADI-certified dive master–instructor and owner of **Pro-Divers** (☎ 809/465–3223), offers resort and certification courses. He also has Nikonos camera equipment for rent. **Mr. X Watersports** (☎ 809/465–4995) arranges various snorkeling trips, as well as waterskiing and sailing.

There are more than a dozen excellent dive sites on St. Kitts, all with a variety of sea life and color. **Coconut Tree Reef,** one of the largest in the area, includes sea fans, sponges, and anemones. **Black Coral Reef** features the rare black coral tree. **Brassball Wreck** is a shallow-water wreck, good for snorkeling and photography. **Redonda Bank** is an extensive area of reef that's just beginning to be explored. The shallow **Tug Boat** is a good spot for snorkelers, who will spot everything from gliding rays to darting grunts and jacks. **Bloody Bay Reef** is noted for its network of underwater grottoes daubed with purple anemones, siena bristle worms, and canary yellow sea fans that seem to wave you in.

## Sea Excursions

**Leeward Island Charters** (☎ 809/465–7474) offers day and overnight charters on two catamarans—the 47-foot *Caona* and the 70-foot *Spirit of St. Kitts*. Day sails are from 9:30 to 4:30 and include barbecue, open bar, and snorkeling equipment. **Tropical Tours** (☎ 809/465–4167) offers moonlight cruises on the 52-foot catamaran *Cileca III* and glass-bottom-boat tours. *Jazzie II* (☎ 809/465–3529) is another glass-bottom boat that cruises the southeastern coast, with free snorkeling equipment. *Tropical Dreamer* (☎ 809/465–8224) is another catamaran available for day and sunset cruises. For the ultimate underwater trip, call **Blue Frontier Ltd.** (☎ 809/465–4945); owner Lindsey Beck will take you for a half-hour ride off Frigate Bay in his two-man submarine.

## Spectator Sports

**Cricket** matches are played in Warner Park from January to July, **soccer** from July to December, **softball** from January to August. Contact the tourist board (☞ Visitor Information *in* St. Kitts and Nevis A to Z, *below*) for schedules.

## Tennis

There are four lighted courts at **Jack Tar Village Beach Resorts** (☎ 809/465–8651), two lighted courts at **Sun 'n' Sand Beach Village** (☎ 809/465–8037), as well as one court each at **Bird Rock Beach Resort** (☎ 809/465–8914), the **Golden Lemon** (☎ 809/465–7260), and **Rawlins Plantation** (☎ 809/465–6221).

# Shopping

St. Kitts has limited shopping, but there are a few duty-free shops where you can find some good buys in jewelry, watches, perfume, china, and crystal. Excellent paintings and sculptures can be found at several galleries around the island. Among the island crafts, the best-known are the batik fabrics, scarves, caftans, and wall hangings of Caribelle Batik. There are also locally produced jams, jellies, herb teas, and handcrafts of local shell, straw, and coconut. And CSR (Cane Spirit Rothschild) is a "new cane spirit drink" that's distilled from fresh sugarcane right on St. Kitts.

## Shopping Districts

Most shopping plazas are in downtown Basseterre near the Circus. Some shops have tiny branches in other areas, particularly in Dieppe Bay. **Palms Arcade** is on Fort Street, near the Circus. The **Pelican Mall** has 26 stores, a restaurant, tourism offices, and a bandstand. This shopping arcade is designed to look like a traditional Caribbean street. **Shoreline Plaza** is next to the Treasury Building, right on the waterfront in Basseterre. **TDC Mall** is just off the Circus in downtown Basseterre.

## Good Buys

ISLAND CRAFTS AND GIFTS

**Caribelle Batik** (✉ Romney Manor, ☎ 809/465–6253) sells batik wraps, T-shirts, dresses, wall hangings, and the like.

**Island Hopper** (✉ The Circus, ☎ 809/465–2905) is a good place for island crafts, especially wood carvings, pottery, and textiles, as well as humorous T-shirts and trinkets.

**Music World** (✉ The Circus, ☎ 809/465–1998) offers a vast selection of island rhythms—lilting soca and zouk, pulsating salsa and merengue, wicked hip-hop, and mellow reggae and calypso.

**Palm Crafts** (✉ Palms Arcade, ☎ 809/465–2599) sells a variety of goodies, including savory Caribbean jams and jellies, clingy resort wear, and hand-painted ceramic ware.

**Plantation Picture House** (✉ Fort St., ☎ 809/465–7740) showcases the enchanting silk pareus, jewelry, prints, and papier-mâché works of Kate Spencer (who also has a studio just outside the Rawlins Plantation).

**Rosemary Lane Antiques** (✉ 7 Rosemary La., ☎ 809/465–5450) occupies a beautifully restored 18th-century town house and is crammed with superlative, affordable antiques and objets d'art from throughout the Caribbean. They will gladly ship any purchases.

**Spencer Cameron Art Gallery** (✉ N. Independence Sq., ☎ 809/465–1617) has historical reproductions of Caribbean island charts and prints, in addition to owner Rosey Cameron's popular Carnevale clown prints and a wide selection of exceptional artwork by Caribbean artists. They will mail anywhere, so you don't have to lug home something that catches your eye.

**Splash** (✉ TDC Plaza, Bank St., ☎ 809/465–9279) carries colorful beachwear by local designers.

IMPORTS

**Slice of the Lemon** (✉ Palms Arcade, ☎ 809/465–2889) carries fine perfumes but is better known for its elegant jewelry.

**TDC** (✉ TDC Plaza, on Bank St., ☎ 809/465–2511) carries fine china and crystal, along with cameras and other imports.

# Nightlife

Most of the Kittitian nightlife revolves around the hotels, which host folkloric shows and calypso and steel bands.

## Casinos

The only game in town is at the **Jack Tar Village Beach Resorts and Casino** (☞ Lodging, *above*), where you'll find blackjack tables, roulette wheels, craps tables, and one-armed bandits. Dress is casual, and play continues till the last player leaves. Note: You do not need to purchase Jack Tar passes to play, even though the casino entrance is in the hotel lobby.

## Discos and Live Music

On Saturday night head for the **Turtle Beach Bar and Grill** (✉ Turtle Bay, ☎ 809/469–9086), where there is a beach dance-disco. Play volleyball into the evening, then dance under the stars into the night. At **J's Place** (✉ across from Brimstone Hill, ☎ 809/465–6264), you dance the night away with locals on Friday and Saturday. **Reflections Night Club** (☎ 809/465–6000), upstairs at Flex Fitness Center, is a hot Kittitian nightspot. It's open Tuesday through Sunday from 9 until well past midnight. Cover charge is E.C.$10 Thursday, Friday, and Saturday nights. Another disco popular with locals is the **Cotton House Club** (✉ Canada Estate, no phone), open weekends from 10 PM. Weekends, **Kool Runnins** (✉ Morris Paul Dr., Pond Industrial Site, ☎ 809/466–5665) serves up jerk chicken, *roti* (East Indian burrito), and goat-water stew, to the accompaniment of live local bands in an open-air gazebo. The hot spot for happy hour (free eats and occasional live music) is the tropical bar **Stonewalls** (✉ Princes St., Basseterre, ☎ 809/465–5248). **Bayembi Cultural Entertainment Bar and Cafe** (✉ just off The Circus, ☎ 809/466–5280) looks like a United Nations garage sale, and the ambience is definitely Peace Corps hip, with jazz guitar sets Wednesdays, karaoke Saturdays, joyous Happy Hours daily, and even poetry readings. It also offers light snacks and local artwork for sale.

# Exploring St. Kitts

Main Road traces the perimeter of the large, northwestern part of the island, through seas of sugarcane that encircle the island's mountain range, past breadfruit trees and old stone walls. Villages with tiny houses of stone and weathered wood are scattered throughout the island. The drive back to Basseterre around the other side of the island is a pleasant one, through small, neat villages with centuries-old stone churches and pastel-colored cottages. The most spectacular stretch of scenery is on the splendid $12 million Dr. Kennedy Simmonds Highway to the tip of the South East Peninsula. Reminiscent of California's famed Highway 1, this ultrasleek modern road twists and turns through the undeveloped grassy hills that rise between the calm Caribbean sea and the windswept Atlantic. You can see the main sights of the capital city in a half hour or so; allow three to four hours for an island tour.

*Numbers in the margin correspond to points of interest on the St. Kitts map.*

SIGHTS TO SEE

**❶ Basseterre.** Set in the southern part of the island, the capital city of St. Kitts is an easily walkable town. It is graced with tall palms, and although many of the buildings appear run-down and in need of paint, you will find interesting shopping areas, excellent art galleries, and some beautifully maintained houses.

The octagonal **Circus** was built in the style of London's famous Piccadilly Circus. Duty-free shops can be found along the streets and courtyards leading off from it.

There are lovely gardens on the site of a former slave market at **Independence Square.** The square is surrounded on three sides by 18th-century Georgian buildings. ⊠ *Off Bank St.*

**St. George's Anglican Church** is a handsome stone building with a crenellated tower which was originally built by the French in 1670 and called Nôtre Dame. The British burned it down in 1706 and rebuilt it four years later, naming it after the patron saint of England. Since then, it has suffered fire, earthquake, and hurricanes and was once again rebuilt in 1859. ⊠ *Cayon St.*

**❼ Black Rocks.** This series of lava deposits was spat into the sea ages ago when the island's volcano erupted. They have since been molded into fanciful shapes by centuries of pounding surf. ⊠ *On the Atlantic coast, just outside the town of Sadlers, in Sandy Bay.*

**❷ Bloody Point.** French and British soldiers joined forces here in 1629 to repel a mass Carib attack. ⊠ *Outside village of Challengers.*

**❺ Brimstone Hill.** This well-restored 38-acre fortress is the most important historic site on St. Kitts. From the parking area it's quite a steep walk up to the top of the fort, but it's well worth it if military history and/or spectacular views interest you. After routing the French in 1690, the English erected a battery on top of Brimstone Hill, and by 1736 there were 49 guns in the fortress. In 1782, 8,000 French troops lay siege to the fortress, which was defended by 350 militia and 600 regular troops of the Royal Scots and East Yorkshires. A plaque in the old stone wall marks the place where the fort was breached. When the English finally surrendered, the French allowed them to march from the fort in full formation out of respect for their bravery. (The English afforded the French the same honor when they surrendered the fort a mere year later.) A hurricane did extensive damage to the fortress in 1834, and in 1852 it was evacuated and dismantled. The beautiful stones were carted away to build houses.

The citadel has been partially reconstructed and its guns remounted. A seven-minute orientation film recounts the fort's history and restoration. You can see what remains of the officers' quarters, the redoubts, barracks, the ordnance store, and the cemetery. Its museums display, among other things, pre-Columbian artifacts, a collection of objects pertaining to the African heritage of the island's slaves (masks, ceremonial tools, etc.), weaponry, uniforms, photographs, and old newspapers. In 1985, Queen Elizabeth visited Brimstone Hill and officially opened it as part of a national park. There's a splendid view from here that includes Montserrat and Nevis to the southeast, Saba and Statia to the northwest, and St. Barts and St. Maarten to the north. Nature trails snake through the tangle of surrounding hardwood forest and savannah (a fine spot to catch the green vervet monkeys skittering about). ✉ *Main Rd., Brimstone Hill.* 🎟 *$5.* ⊙ *Daily 9:30–5:30.*

NEED A BREAK?  **J's Place** (☎ 809/465-6264), across from the entrance to Brimstone Hill, is ideal for a drink, a sandwich, or a full West Indian meal, including a sensational lobster salad.

❹ **Middle Island.** Thomas Warner, the "gentleman of London" who brought the first settlers to St. Kitts, died here in 1648 and is buried beneath a green gazebo in the churchyard of St. Thomas Church.

**Old Road Town.** This site marks the first permanent English settlement in the West Indies, founded in 1624 by Thomas Warner. Take the side road toward the interior to find some well-preserved **Carib petroglyphs**, testimony of even older habitation. ✉ *Main Road, west of Challengers.*

❺ **Romney Manor.** This house is set in 6 acres of gardens, with exotic flowers, an old bell tower, and a 350-year-old saman tree (sometimes called a rain tree). Inside, at **Caribelle Batik** (☞ Shopping, *above*), you can watch artisans hand-printing fabrics by a 2,500-year-old Indonesian process known as *batik*. Look for signs indicating a turnoff for Romney Manor near Old Road Town.

❻ **Sandy Point Town.** This quaint village contains West Indian–style raised cottages and features a Roman Catholic church with lovely stained-glass windows.

# NEVIS

## Lodging

With the exception of the Four Seasons Resort, most hotels on Nevis are beautifully restored manor or plantation houses. Typically, the owners of the inn live there with their families. Visitors are received warmly and graciously, almost like friends, and it is easy to begin thinking you have been personally invited down for a visit. In the evening, before dinner, it is common for the family, inn guests, and those visitors who have come to eat at the restaurant to gather in a drawing room or on a terrace for cocktails and to exchange stories of the day. Most of the inns operate on the Modified American Plan (MAP) and offer a free shuttle to their private stretch on Pinney's Beach.

| CATEGORY | COST* |
| --- | --- |
| $$$$ | over $300 |
| $$$ | $225–$300 |
| $$ | $150–$225 |
| $ | under $150 |

*All prices are for a standard double room for two, MAP, excluding 7% tax and 10% service charge.

**$$$$** 🏨 **Four Seasons Resort Nevis.** The 196-room property manages to com-
★ bine world-class elegance with West Indian ambience and hospitality.
On a stunning stretch of Pinney's Beach, with a spectacular view of
St. Kitts in the distance, the hotel offers a complete range of water activities, along with clay and all-weather tennis courts, a free-form
pool, a challenging 18-hole golf course designed by Robert Trent Jones
II, and a full-service health club. Spacious guest rooms are richly furnished with mahogany armoires and headboards and cushioned rattan sofas and chairs, and have large indoor and veranda seating areas,
which can be used for private dining. Rooms have both ceiling fans and
air-conditioning, ice maker, fully stocked refrigerated bar, and a
cable TV/VCR. There are two outstanding restaurants, one of which
is fairly formal (although jacket and tie are not required). Special activities for children are scheduled regularly. There are usually good-
value sports and romantic packages, even during the high season. ✉
*Box 565, Charlestown,* ☎ *809/469–1111; in the U.S., 800/332–
3442; in Canada, 800/268–6288;* 🖷 *809/469–1112. 196 rooms. 2
dining rooms, pub, casual outdoor dining, pool, 18-hole golf course,
10 tennis courts, aerobics, fitness center, beach, water sports, catamaran
rentals, 2 boutiques, baby-sitting, children's program, laundry service
and washer/dryers, car rental. AE, D, MC, V. EP, MAP, FAP.*

**$$$$** 🏨 **Nisbet Plantation Beach Club.** From the manor house of this 18th-
★ century plantation you can see the beach at the end of a long avenue
of coconut palms, and from the bar you look out over an old sugar
mill covered with hibiscus, cassia, frangipani, and flamboyants. Well-
maintained Nisbet offers a range of accommodations, from plantation-
style cottages to lanai suites, all simply but tastefully appointed in
whitewashed wicker and rattan and tropical prints. They all are situated along an avenue of palm that leads to a blinding white-sand beach
and the ocean. ✉ *Newcastle Beach,* ☎ *809/469–9325; in the U.S.,
800/344–2049;* 🖷 *809/469–9864. 38 rooms. 2 restaurants, 2 bars,
beach, pool, tennis court, croquet, snorkeling, boutique, laundry. AE,
MC, V. EP, MAP.*

**$$$** 🏨 **Hermitage Plantation Inn.** A 250-year-old great house—said to be
★ the oldest wooden house on the island—houses the restaurant and forms
the core of this appealing inn set in the hills. The duplex guest cottages
are some of the prettiest accommodations on the island. Rooms are
furnished with antiques, including four-poster canopy beds (mostly king-
size), and have patios or balconies, ceiling fans, phones, and minifridges;
some also have lovely views of the distant ocean, and some have full
kitchens. Also available is a two-bedroom replica of a manor house,
with its own pool. The beach is 15 minutes away, and if you haven't
got a car, transportation will be arranged. Many guests simply relax
in a hammock or spend the day by the pool at this peaceful retreat (a
member of the prestigious Romantik Hotels group). What really makes
the Hermitage special is vivacious owners Maureen and Richard
Lupinacci, who will quickly introduce you to Nevisian society: high,
low, and always lively. ✉ *St. Johns, Fig Tree Parish,* ☎ *809/469–3477,*
🖷 *809/469–2481. 12 suites. Restaurant, bar, pool, tennis court, horse-
back riding, free beach shuttle. AE, MC, V. EP, MAP.*

**$$$** 🏨 **Montpelier Plantation Inn.** Iron gates provide a majestic entrance
to this intimate and charming inn, a member of the prestigious Romantik
Hotels group, set on 100 beautifully landscaped hillside acres. Reception, evening cocktails, and dinner take place in and around the great
house—an imposing fieldstone structure furnished with antiques. Accommodations are in simple cottages scattered along the hillside. Each
cottage contains one or two rooms, has two patios, and is adequately
but sparely furnished. Rooms have Italian ceramic tile floors and large
bathrooms; a few have marvelous four-poster beds. The pool is large

and pretty (a gorgeous mural decorates one of the pool area's walls), but beach lovers can head (via complimentary transportation) to Pinney's Beach, where the estate has a 3-acre private section of beach and a pavilion. Guests come not for the amenities so much as for the incomparable air of quiet unpretentious elegance. Owners James and Celia Gaskell downplay their royal connections (Princess Di stays here); James prefers to talk about his extensive organic gardens. Montpelier is the most civilized hostelry on Nevis. ⊠ *Box 474, Charlestown,* ☎ *809/469–3462 or 800/243–9420,* FAX *809/469–2932. 17 rooms. Restaurant, bar, pool, tennis court, beach (away from hotel). AE, MC, V. Closed late Aug.–early Oct. BP, MAP.*

**$$** 🏨 **Golden Rock.** Co-owner Pam Barry runs this inn, which was built by her great, great, great grandfather over 200 years ago. She has decorated the 16 units with four-poster beds of mahogany or bamboo, native grass rugs, straw and glass-bottle lamps, metal paintings, bamboo beds, brilliantly hued wooden fish, basketry, rocking chairs, and bright French floral-print fabrics. All rooms have a private bath and a patio. The restored sugar mill is a two-level suite (with a glorious wood-and-bamboo staircase), and the old cistern is now a spring-fed swimming pool. The charming rooms recently received much-needed refreshing. The estate covers 150 mountainous acres and is surrounded by 25 acres of lavish tropical gardens, including a sunken garden. Enjoy the Atlantic view and cooling breeze from the bar. The Saturday-night West Indian buffet is very popular December through June. Barry also organizes historical and nature hikes. ⊠ *Box 493, Gingerland,* ☎ *809/469–3346 or 800/223–9815,* FAX *809/469–2113. 16 rooms, 1 suite. Restaurant, bar, pool, tennis court, educational activities. AE, MC, V. EP, MAP.*

**$$** 🏨 **Mt. Nevis Hotel/Condominiums.** Air-conditioned standard rooms and suites at this hotel are done up with handsome white wicker furnishings, southwestern pastel fabrics, glass-top tables, and colorful island prints. Suites have full, modern kitchens and dining areas; all units have a balcony, direct-dial phone, minifridge, cable TV, and VCR. The main building houses the casual restaurant and bar, which open onto a terrace that overlooks the pool and provides a view of St. Kitts in the distance. Shuttle service is provided to the water-sports center at Newcastle Beach, replete with a boutique and outdoor restaurant-bar. The hotel also has its own ferry, which is used for moonlight cruises when it's not taking passengers to and from St. Kitts. The Mt. Nevis is the perfect choice for those seeking contemporary accommodations with typical Nevisian warmth, yet without the stratospheric prices of the Four Seasons. ⊠ *Box 494, Newcastle,* ☎ *809/469–9373 (collect),* FAX *809/469–9375. 32 rooms. Restaurant, bar, pool, beach club, water sports, boutique. AE, D, MC, V. EP, MAP.*

**$$** 🏨 **Old Manor Estate.** Vast tropical gardens surround this restored sugar plantation in the shadow of Mt. Nevis. The outbuildings, such as the smokehouse and jail, have been imaginatively restored, and the old cistern is now the pool. Many of the enormous guest rooms have high ceilings, gorgeous stone or tile floors, marble vanities, exposed wood beams, king-size four-poster beds, and colonial reproductions; some units, however, are a bit gloomy and dark, with old-fashioned dowdy madras settees and soiled carpets. The air throughout is one of faded, slightly shabby elegance, but new ownership has embarked on an ambitious five-year plan to brighten everything up. They also plan to lighten the fare at the well-respected Cooperage restaurant, an old stone dining room whose elegantly rustic setting mirrors its stolid, solid Continental fare. There's transportation to and from the beach. The hotel is not recommended for children under 12. ⊠ *Box 70, Charlestown,* ☎ *809/469–*

*3445; in the U.S., 800/223–9815 or 800/892–7093; FAX 809/469–3388. 14 rooms. 2 restaurants, 2 bars, pool. AE, MC, V. EP, MAP.*

**$$** ★ ⌂ **Oualie Beach Hotel.** Every few years this beachside spot builds a few more charming West Indian–style cottages, and there are now 22 rooms, including air-conditioned deluxe rooms with mahogany four-poster canopy beds and marble vanities. All rooms look across the water to stunning views of neighboring St. Kitts. The rooms are bright, airy, and tastefully furnished and all have refrigerator, cable TV, phone, and safe. Studio units have a full kitchen. There is a full dive shop here offering NAUI-certified instruction, and dive packages are available. Sunfish and Windsurfers may be rented, and the hotel has introduced Skimmer waterborne rowing machines. Ironically, Hurricanes Luis and Marilyn actually expanded the already lovely tawny beach. Breakfast, lunch, and dinner are served at an informal restaurant and bar. ⊠ *Oualie Beach,* ☎ *809/469–9735,* FAX *809/469–9176. 22 rooms. Restaurant, bar, dive center, water-sports. AE, D, MC, V. EP, MAP.*

**$–$$** ⌂ **Hurricane Cove Bungalows.** Don't be deceived by the ramshackle exterior of these cottages clinging precariously to a hill overlooking lovely Tamarind Bay. The interiors are charmingly rustic, with hand-carved wood furnishings and gleaming tile floors. All have full kitchens and an enclosed patio with breathtaking ocean views (save for one cottage, far in the back). Several have private pools. The postage-stamp-size hotel pool is in the foundation of a 250-year-old fort. The beach is a three-minute walk away. ⊠ *Tamarind Bay,* ☎ FAX *809/469–9462. 10 1-, 2- and 3-bedroom bungalows. Pool. MC, V.*

**$** ⌂ **Yamseed Inn.** A very rough access road leads to this pale yellow bed-and-breakfast overlooking St. Kitts, tucked away from resort and plantation hotels on its own private patch of white sand. Friendly innkeeper Sybil Siegfried offers four rooms in her house, nestled amid beautiful grounds (Sybil's an avid gardener). Chirping hummingbirds welcome you into the stylish reception area. Each room has a private bath and is handsomely appointed with a mahogany bed, wood-panel ceiling, throw rugs, white-tile floors, and antiques. Breakfast includes delicious homemade muffins and grated coconut muesli. The only flaw in paradise is Yamseed's location near the airport, which puts it in the flight path (fortunately, air traffic isn't busy). ⊠ *On the beach, Newcastle,* ☎ *809/469–9361. 4 rooms. 3-night minimum. No credit cards. BP.*

# Dining

Dinner options on Nevis include the elegance of the dining room at the Four Seasons Resort, intimate dinners at plantation guest houses (where the menu is often set), and a variety of more casual eateries. Seafood is ubiquitous, and there are many places in which to sample excellent West Indian fare.

### What to Wear

As in St. Kitts, dress is casual at lunch, although beach attire is unacceptable. Dress pants or a sundress is apropos for dinner; men may even want to don a jacket in season at some of the inns and at the Four Seasons Resort.

| CATEGORY | COST* |
|---|---|
| **$$$$** | over $40 |
| **$$$** | $30–$40 |
| **$$** | $20–$30 |
| **$** | under $20 |

*per person, excluding drinks and service.*

**\$\$\$\$**   ✕ **Four Seasons Resort.** This elegant dining room, paneled in imported South American hardwood, has tables set with glistening silver and china, and graceful, 12-foot-high doors that open to the breezes and sweeping views of Pinney's Beach and the sea beyond. Cuisine is nouvelle with a Caribbean flair—Antiguan wahoo baked in a banana leaf with coconut milk; curry and scotch bonnet broth; and pan-seared local red snapper with mango salsa and bitter orange sauce. There is a weekly Caribbean buffet with a full steel band. ⊠ *Pinney's Beach,* ☎ *809/469–1111. Reservations essential. AE, D, MC, V.*

**\$\$\$\$**   ✕ **Miss June's.** Dinner with Miss June Mestier, a lady from Trinidad, ★   could never be called ordinary. While she prepares the fare, her son serves drinks—from Miss June's secret rum punch to a very proper martini—to the guests (limited to 20) on the veranda. Promptly at 8:30 everyone heads to the dining room, where several tables are set with fine if mismatched china and crystal. The first course is a soup of Miss June's creation, usually something spicy; the second course, fresh fish prepared in some exotic local style, followed by salad. "Now that you've had your dinner," Miss June announces, "it's time to have fun!" as guests turn to the buffet table laden with at least 18 dishes. Selections change nightly but always include curries; local vegetable dishes; meats like leg of lamb in champagne orange sauce, chicken simmered in coconut milk, or ribs in mauby (a bark distillation) and pineapple; and seafood— all adapted by Miss June from Trinidadian recipes. Wine flows freely throughout (this is truly an all-inclusive meal at $65). At the end, Miss June will join you for coffee and brandy; she won't kick you out, but you may be asked to turn the lights out when you leave—regretfully. No wonder several guests invite Miss June to stay with them whenever she's abroad. ⊠ *Jones Bay,* ☎ *809/469–5330. Reservations essential. MC, V.*

**\$\$\$\$**   ✕ **Nisbet Plantation Beach Club.** The antiques-filled dining room in the ★   great house at Nisbet—an oasis of polished hardwood floors, mahogany and cherrywood furnishings, and stone walls—has long been a popular place for lunch and dinner. There are also tables on the screened-in veranda, where there's a view down the palm-tree-lined fairway to the sea. The five-course menu is unusually varied for Nevis. A combination of Continental and Caribbean cuisines is prepared with many local ingredients. Sumptuous choices include sautéed scallops on angel-hair pasta in cinnamon sauce, chilled avocado and apricot soup, roast quail stuffed with herb duxelles in raspberry sauce, grilled red grouper in lemongrass sauce, and banana and Tia Maria mousse in a chocolate shell. Lighter fare (sandwiches, salads, hamburgers) is served at lunch at the beach restaurant, Coconuts. ⊠ *Nisbet Plantation,* ☎ *809/469–9325. Reservations essential. AE, MC, V.*

**\$\$\$**   ✕ **Golden Rock.** Tables are draped in pink and arranged in a romantic, dimly lit room whose fieldstone walls date back to when this was a plantation house. Enchanting Eva Wilkin originals grace the walls (be sure to admire the mural behind the bamboo bar). Local Nevisian cuisine is the specialty here; chicken in a raisin curry, grilled local snapper with *tania* (a type of tuber) fritters, and green papaya pie are house favorites. ⊠ *Golden Rock,* ☎ *809/469–3346. Reservations essential. AE, MC, V. Closed Sun.*

**\$\$\$**   ✕ **Hermitage Plantation Inn.** After cocktails in the antiques-filled parlor, ★   dinner is served at one long table on the outside veranda. The four-course preset menu might include carrot and tarragon soup, red snapper in ginger sauce, fried conch steak, and a rum soufflé. The conversation is always lively, thanks to witty, gregarious owners Maureen and Richard "Loopy" Lupinacci. ⊠ *Hermitage Plantation,* ☎ *809/469–3477. Reservations essential. AE, MC, V. Personal checks accepted.*

**$$$** ✕ **Montpelier Plantation Inn.** Genial owners James and Celia Gaskell
★   preside over an elegant evening. Cocktails and hors d'oeuvres are
served amid the antiques in the parlor of the great house. Dinner is by
candlelight on the white terrace. Cream of avocado and coconut soup,
lobster, red snapper, chicken calypso, sirloin steak bordelaise, and
roast beef and Yorkshire pudding are some of the choices on the ster-
ling menu. Many of the fresh ingredients are homegrown in the ex-
tensive gardens. ⊠ *Montpelier Plantation,* ☎ *809–469–3462.*
*Reservations essential. AE, MC, V. Closed late Aug.–early Oct.*

**$$$** ✕ **Mt. Nevis Hotel.** The airy 60-seat dining room, where white wicker
tables are draped with coral napery and set with fine china and silver,
opens onto the terrace and pool. During the day, there is a splendid
view of St. Kitts in the distance. The menu is one of the island's most
creative, thanks to head chef Jeff de Barbieri. Starters include grilled
portobello mushrooms with goat cheese and black olives in sherry vinaigrette, and lobster bisque. Entrées may include yellowtail fragrant
with coriander, mango and ginger; penne with smoked chicken, shi-
itakes, and roast peppers; or veal chop stuffed with spiced walnuts in
caper sauce. ⊠ *Mt. Nevis Hotel/Condominiums, Newcastle,* ☎
*809/469–9373. AE, D, MC, V.*

**$–$$** ✕ **Oualie Beach.** This low-key, casual bar and restaurant on Oualie
Bay is the perfect stop for authentic Nevisian fare with French flair after
a long day on the beach. Try the delicious homemade soups, including ground-nut or breadfruit vichyssoise. Then move on to Creole
conch stew, lobster crepes, or chicken breasts stuffed with spinach. The
atmosphere is rollicking on weekends, with live music and local crowds.
⊠ *Oualie Beach,* ☎ *809/469–9735. AE, D, MC, V.*

**$–$$** ✕ **Prinderella's.** This casual open-air restaurant enjoys a stunning set-
ting on Tamarind Bay, with views across the channel to St. Kitts. A
lovely mural behind the bamboo bar suffices for decor. Seafood is the
obvious specialty, although the English owners, Ian and Charlie
Mintrim, do a proper shepherd's pie and roast beef with Yorkshire pudding. Yachties (it has a great anchorage) buzz around the bar, there's
wonderful snorkeling right around the point, and Friday brings a boisterous happy hour, with free finger food like salmon mousse, hummus,
and chicken wings. Ask Charlie to tell you the story behind the restaurant's name; it features Prinderella, a cince, and a gairy frogmother.
You'll want a bouble dourbon when she's finished. ⊠ *Jones Bridge,*
☎ *809/469–1291. AE, MC, V. Closed Mon. June–Sept. (Mon.–Wed.*
*in Oct., Nov., and Apr. 15–May).*

**$** ✕ **Callaloo.** This simple but stylish eatery, run by genial Abdul Hill who
learned to cook with typical French/Creole flair on St. Martin, is another local standout. Delicious rotis make a quick, cheap lunch. Or
opt for the yummy grilled kingfish in lemon butter, conch Creole, curried goat or ribs, all served with generous side portions of rice and beans,
salad, and provisions. ⊠ *Government Rd. and Main St., tel. 809/469–*
*5389. AE, D, MC, V. Closed Sun.*

**$** ✕ **Eddy's Bar and Restaurant.** Colorful flags flutter from the veranda
★   of this second-story restaurant, overlooking Charlestown's Memorial
Square in the center of Charlestown. A local artist designed the tablecloths and bright, boldly colored wall hangings. You'll find fine stir-
fries and local West Indian specialties, such as cream of cauliflower soup
and tender, crispy conch fritters with just the right amount of sass in
the sauce. Eddy's mom, Eulalie Williams, makes the terrific hot sauce,
which you can buy at the Main Street Supermarket down the street.
Stop by between 5 and 8 on Wednesday for happy hour; drinks are
half price, snacks are free. ⊠ *Main St., Charlestown,* ☎ *809/469–5958.*
*AE, MC, V. Closed Thurs., Sun., and Sept.*

$ ✕ **Muriel's Cuisine.** Hanging plants, local still lifes, and table vases dress
★ up this simple eatery. Three meals are served daily, except Sunday. Bountiful entrées come with mounds of rice and peas and fresh vegetables,
a side salad, and garlic bread. The subtly spiced jerk chicken would
pass muster in many a Jamaican kitchen, and the goat-water and beef
stew are fabulous: full-bodied and fragrant with garlic and coriander.
Muriel St. Jean is the gracious hostess. Her restaurant attracts a very
local clientele—women in hair curlers and young men who come to
flirt shyly with the waitresses. ⊠ *Upper Happy Hill Dr., Charlestown,*
☎ *809/469–5920. AE, D, MC, V. Closed Sun.*

$ ✕ **SunShine's.** Everything about this palm-thatched beach shack is
colorful and larger-than-life, including the rastaman SunShine himself.
Flags from around the world—Bavaria to Brazil—drape the lean-to;
the clientele is almost as international, including such celebrities as Woody
Allen, Robert Plant, Alan Alda, and Wayne Gretzky (who wandered
over unsuspectingly from the adjacent Four Seasons). They found picnic tables splashed with bright Rasta sunup to sunset colors; nothing
has been left unpainted, including the palm trees. Fishermen literally
cruise right up to the grill with their catch; you might savor lobster
rolls, conch fritters, curried conch, or snapper Creole. Try the lethal
house specialty, the Killer Bee. As SunShine boasts in his take on the
rum punch, "One and you're stung, two you're stunned, three it's a
knockout." ⊠ *Pinney's Beach, no phone. No credit cards.*

$ ✕ **Tequila Sheila's.** This rustic corrugated tin-and-wood shack sits
right on a beach with glorious views of St. Kitts (management even provides chaise longues). The hybrid Pacific Rim/California menu is written daily on a blackboard; you might find anything from cheeseburgers
with eggplant pepper relish to tequila lime chicken. It's regular events
like Sunday Beach Party Brunch or Saturday Night Fever discos, however, that lasso locals and tourists alike. ⊠ *Cades Bay,* ☎ *809/469–*
*1633. MC, V. Closed Mon. No lunch Tues.*

$ ✕ **Unella's.** The atmosphere is nothing fancy—just simple tables set
on a second-floor porch overlooking the waterfront in Charlestown—
but the fare is good West Indian. Stop here for exceptional lobster (more
expensive than the rest of the menu), curried lamb, island-style spare
ribs, and steamed conch, all served with local vegetables, rice, and peas.
Unella opens shop around 9 in the morning, when locals and boaters
appear waiting for their breakfast; she stays open all day. ⊠ *Water-*
*front, Charlestown,* ☎ *809/469–5574. No credit cards.*

## Beaches

All the beaches on the island are free to the public. There are no changing facilities, so you'll have to wear a swimsuit under your clothes. If
you're doing a cab tour, you may arrange with your driver to drop you
off at the beach and pick you up later.

**Newcastle Beach** is by Nisbet Plantation (☞ Lodging, *above*). Popular among snorkelers, it's a broad beach of soft, white sand shaded by
coconut palms at the northernmost tip of the island, on the channel
between St. Kitts and Nevis.

**Oualie Beach,** at Mosquito Bay, just north of Pinney's, is a black-sand
beach where **Oualie Beach Club** (☎ 809/469–9518) can mix you a
drink and fix you up with water-sports equipment.

**Pinney's Beach** is the island's showpiece beach. It's almost 4 miles of
soft, golden sand lined with a magnificent grove of palm trees, and it's
on the calm Caribbean Sea. The palm-shaded lagoon is a scene right
out of South Pacific. The Four Seasons Resort is now here, and sev-

eral of the mountain inns have private cabanas and pavilions on the beach; it is, nevertheless, a public beach.

## Outdoor Activities and Sports

### Boating

Hobie Cats and Sunfish can be rented from **Oualie Beach Club** (☎ 809/469–9518). **Newcastle Bay Marina** (✉ Newcastle, ☎ 809/469–9395) has Phantom sailboats, a 23-foot KenCraft powerboat, and several inflatables with outboards available for rent. **Frank Morse** (✉ Oualie Beach, ☎ 809/469–9735) has a 65-foot aluminum sloop, *Never Say Never,* on which he takes guests for day sails.

### Deep-Sea Fishing

The game here is kingfish, wahoo, grouper, tuna, and yellowtail snapper. If you want local expertise, call **Captain Valentine Glasgow** (☎ 809/469–1989), who has a 31-foot Ocean Master, *Lady James,* to take you in search of the big ones. **Jans Travel Agency** (☎ 809/469–5578) arranges deep-sea fishing trips.

### Golf

Duffers doff their hats to the beautiful, impeccably maintained Robert Trent Jones II-designed 18-hole championship course at the **Four Seasons** (☎ 809/469–1111).

### Hiking

The center of the island is Nevis Peak, which soars up to 3,232 feet, flanked by Hurricane Hill on the north and Saddle Hill on the south. If you plan to scale Nevis Peak, a daylong affair, it is highly recommended that you go with a guide. Your hotel can arrange it for you; you can also ask the hotel to pack a picnic lunch. Both the **Nevis Academy** (☎ 809/469–2091, FAX 809/469–2113), headed by David Rollinson, and **Top to Bottom** (☎ 809/469–5371) offer eco-rambles (slower tours) and hikes. Three-hour rambles or hikes are $20 per person, $30 for the more strenuous climb up Mt. Nevis.

### Horseback Riding

You can arrange for mountain-trail and beach rides through **Cane Gardens** (☎ 809/469–5648).

### Scuba Diving and Snorkeling

The village of Jamestown was washed into the sea around Fort Ashby; the area is a popular spot for snorkeling and diving. Reef-protected Pinney's Beach offers especially good snorkeling. Try **Scuba Safaris** (✉ Oualie Beach, ☎ 809/469–9518) or **Nevis Water Sports** (✉ Oualie Beach, ☎ 809/469–9690) for everything from a resort course to full certification.

### Spectator Sports

Grove Park is the venue for **cricket** (January–July) and **soccer** (July–December). Your hotel or the tourist board can fill you in on dates, times, and grudge matches of particular interest between Kittitians and Nevisians.

One of the Caribbean's most endearing, unusual events is the occasional "Day at the Races" sponsored by the **Nevis Turf and Jockey Club** (☎ 809/469–3477). The races, which attract a "pan-Caribbean field" (as the club likes to boast), are held on a wild, windswept course overlooking the "white horses" of the Atlantic. Last-minute changes and scratches are common, and a party atmosphere prevails.

## Tennis

There are 10 tennis courts at the **Four Seasons Resort Nevis** (☎ 809/469–1111), two at **Pinney's Beach Hotel** (☎ 809/469–5207), and one court each at **Nisbet** (☎ 809/469–9325), **Montpelier Plantation** (☎ 809/469–3462), and **Golden Rock** (☎ 809/469–3346).

## Water Sports

**Montpelier Plantation** (☎ 809/469–3462) has a 17-foot Boston whaler for scuba, snorkeling, and waterskiing trips. Snorkeling and waterskiing trips can also be arranged through **Oualie Beach Club** (☎ 809/469–9518) and **Newcastle Bay Marina** (☎ 809/469–9395). Windsurfers can also be rented at both places.

## Windsurfing

For windsurfing, **Winston Crooke** (☎ 809/469–9615) rents equipment and teaches classes. A two-hour beginner's class is $40 per person. If you rent equipment only, it's $12 an hour per person. **Windsurfing Nevis** (✉ Oualie Beach Hotel, ☎ 809/469–9682) also offers top-notch instructors and equipment.

# Shopping

Nevis is certainly not the place for a shopping spree, but there are unique and wonderful surprises here, notably the island's stamps, batik and hand-embroidered clothing.

**Caribco Gifts** (✉ Main St., ☎ 809/469–1432) is a cheaper alternative for T-shirts, candles, and pottery emblazoned with Nevis logos.

Local items of note are the batik caftans, scarves, and fabrics found in the Nevis branch of **Caribelle Batik** (✉ in the Arcade of downtown Charlestown, ☎ 809/469–1491).

For more than 50 years Dame Eva Wilkins painted island people, flowers, and landscapes. An Eva Wilkins mural hangs over the bar at the Golden Rock (☞ Dining, *above*). Her originals sell for $100 and up, and prints are available in some of the local shops. The **Eva Wilkin Gallery** (Clay Ghaut, Gingerland, ☎ 809/469–2673) occupies her former light-filled atelier; the terraces afford understandably inspiring ocean views. If the paintings, drawings, and prints are out of your price range, consider buying the lovely note cards based on her designs.

**Knick Knacks** (✉ The Courtyard, off Main St., Charlestown, ☎ 809/469–5784) showcases top local artisans, including Marvin Chapman (stone and wood carvings) and Jeannie Rigby (exquisite dolls). They also sell whimsical hats, beach wraps, and pottery.

Beekeeping is a buzzing biz on Nevis, and you'll find beeswax candles (which burn longer than the regular wax variety) and the fragrant, tropically flavored honey at many stores. Quentin Henderson, the affable head of the **Nevis Beekeeping Cooperative,** will even arrange trips (by appointment only) to various hives and his Beehouse to demonstrate the procedures. (✉ Gingerbread, ☎ 809/469–5521, ext. 2086)

The **Nevis Handicraft Co-op Society** (☎ 809/469–5509), next door to the tourist office, offers work by local artisans, including clothing, ceramic ware, woven goods, and homemade jellies.

Nevis is known for the quality of its joiners, including **Paintfield Hill and Sons** (✉ Morning Hill, ☎ 809/469–2499), whose superlative hardwood furniture can be shipped.

Stamp collectors should head for the **Philatelic Bureau,** just off Main Street opposite the tourist office. St. Kitts and Nevis are famous for their decorative, and sometimes lucrative, stamps. An early Kittitian stamp recently brought in $7,000.

Kate Spencer's lovely island paintings and silk scarves and pareus are on sale at the **Plantation Picture House** (⊠ Main St., Charlestown, ☎ 809/469–5694).

For dolls and baskets handcrafted in Nevis, visit the **Sandbox Tree** (☎ 809/469–5662) in Evelyn's Villa, Charlestown. Among other items available here are hand-painted chests. This is an appealing shop even if you are only browsing.

## Nightlife

In season, it is usually easy to find a local calypso singer or a steel or string band performing at one of the hotels on weekends. You can count on entertainment at the **Four Seasons Resort** (☎ 809/469–1111) on both Friday and Saturday nights. On Friday night the Shell All-Stars steel band entertains in the gardens at **Old Manor Estate** (☎ 809/469–3445). The **Golden Rock** (☎ 809/469–3346) brings in David Freeman's Honeybees String Band to jazz things up for the Saturday-night buffet. You can have dinner and a dance on Wednesday night at **Pinney's Beach Hotel** (☎ 809/469–5207). **Oualie Beach Hotel** (☎ 809/469–9735) throws a popular Saturday-night buffet with live string band and masquerade troupe. **Eddy's Bar and Restaurant** (☞ Dining, *above*) holds raucous West Indian nights with theme buffet and live string band Friday and Saturday.

Apart from the hotel scene, there are a few places where young locals go for late-night calypso, reggae, and other island music. **Club Trenim** (⊠ On Government Rd. in Charlestown, no phone) has disco dancing starting at 8:30 every night except Tuesday. **Dick's Bar** (⊠ Brickiln, no phone) has live music or a DJ on Friday and Saturday evenings.

## Exploring Nevis

The main road of Nevis makes a 20-mile circuit, with various offshoots bumping and winding into the mountains. You can tour Charlestown, the capital city, in a half hour or so, but you'll need three to four hours to explore the entire island.

*Numbers in the margin correspond to points of interest on the Nevis map.*

SIGHTS TO SEE

**❷ Bath Springs.** The springs and the ruins of **Bath Hotel,** built by John Huggins in 1778, sustained recent hurricane damage, but both were expected to reopen by late 1996. The springs, with temperatures of 104–108°F, emanate from the hillside. Huggins's 50-room hotel, the first hotel in the Caribbean, was adjacent to the waters. Eighteenth-century accounts reported that a few days of imbibing and immersing in these waters resulted in miraculous cures. It would take a minor miracle to restore the decayed hotel to anything like grandeur—it closed down in the late 19th century—but the spring house has been partially restored, and some of the springs are still as hot and restorative as ever. Bathing costs $2. ⊙ *Weekdays 8–noon and 1–3:30, Sat. 8–noon.*

**❶ Charlestown.** About 1,200 of the island's 9,300 inhabitants live in the capital of Nevis. The town faces the Caribbean, about 12½ miles south of Basseterre in St. Kitts. If you arrive by ferry, as most people do, you'll walk smack onto Main Street from the pier. Although it is true that tiny Charlestown, founded in 1660, has seen better days, it's easy to imagine how it must have looked in its heyday. The buildings may be weathered and a bit worse for wear now, but there is still evidence of past glory in their fanciful galleries, elaborate gingerbread, wood shutters, and colorful hanging plants. The stonework building with the clock tower houses the **courthouse** and **library**. A fire in 1873 severely damaged the building and destroyed valuable records; the current building dates from the turn of the century. You're welcome to poke around the second-floor library, which is one of the coolest places on the island. The little park opposite the courthouse is **Memorial Square**, dedicated to the fallen of World Wars I and II. ⊠ *Corner of Prince and William Sts., no phone.* ☉ *Mon.–Sat. 9–6.*

| | |
|---|---|
| NEED A BREAK? | Drop into the **Courtyard Cafe** (⊠ across the street from the tourist office, ☎ 809/469–5685), Caribbean Confections's lush, foliage-filled outdoor restaurant, for coffee and homemade pastries. There are also sandwiches, peanut-butter cookies, and popcorn. |

The **Alexander Hamilton Birthplace**, which contains the **Museum of Nevis History,** is on the waterfront, covered in bougainvillea and hibiscus. This Georgian-style house is a reconstruction of the statesman's original home, which was built in 1680 and is thought to have been destroyed during an earthquake in the mid-19th century. Hamilton was born here in 1755. He left for the American colonies 17 years later to continue his education; he became secretary to George Washington and died in a duel with political rival Aaron Burr. The **Nevis House of Assembly** sits on the second floor of this building, and the museum downstairs contains Hamilton memorabilia and documents pertaining to the island's history, as well as fascinating displays on island geology, politics, and cuisine. ⊠ *Low St., no phone.* ☜ *$2.* ☉ *Weekdays 8–4, Sat. 10–1.*

**⑤ Eden Brown Estate.** This government-owned mansion, built around 1740, is known as Nevis's haunted house, or, rather, haunted ruins. In 1822, apparently, a Miss Julia Huggins was to marry a fellow named Maynard. However, on the day of the wedding the groom and his best man had a duel and killed each other. The bride-to-be became a recluse, and the mansion was closed down. Local residents claim they can feel the presence of "someone" whenever they go near the old house. You're welcome to drop by; it's free.

**⑦ Fort Ashby.** Overgrown with tropical vegetation, this site overlooks the place where the settlement of Jamestown fell into the sea after a tidal wave hit the coast in 1680. Needless to say, this is a favored target of scuba divers. ⊠ *1½ mi southwest of Hurricane Hill, on Main Rd.*

**⑥ Hurricane Hill.** From here is a splendid view of St. Kitts. ⊠ *West of Newcastle Airport.*

**③ Nelson Museum.** This collection merits a visit for the memorabilia of Lord Nelson, including letters, documents, paintings, and even furniture from his flagship. Nelson was based in Antigua but returned often to court, and eventually to marry, Frances Nisbet, who lived on a 64-acre plantation here. ⊠ *Bath Rd.,* ☎ *809/469–0408.* ☜ *$2 ($1 if admission paid to Nevis History Museum).* ☉ *Weekdays 9–4, Sat. 10–1.*

**⑧ Nelson Spring.** The spring's waters have considerably decreased since the 1780s, when young Captain Horatio Nelson periodically filled his ships with fresh water here.

**④ St. John's Church.** Among the records of this church built in 1680 is a tattered, prominently displayed marriage certificate that reads: "Horatio Nelson, Esquire, to Frances Nisbet, Widow, on March 11, 1787." ⊠ *Fig Tree.*

**❾ St. Thomas Anglican Church.** The island's oldest church was built in 1643 and has been altered many times over the years. The gravestones in the old churchyard have stories to tell, and the church itself contains memorials to the early settlers of Nevis.

# ST. KITTS AND NEVIS A TO Z

## Arriving and Departing

BY BOAT

The 150-passenger government-operated ferry MV *Caribe Queen* makes the 45-minute crossing from Nevis to St. Kitts twice daily except Thursday and Sunday. The schedule is a bit erratic, so confirm departure times with the tourist office. Round-trip fare is $8. An air-conditioned, 110-passenger ferry, MV *Spirit of Mount Nevis,* makes the run twice daily Thursday and Sunday. The fare is $12 round-trip. Call **Nevis Cruise Lines** (☎ 809/469–9373) for information and reservations. Sea-taxi service between the two islands is operated by dive master **Kenneth Samuel** (☎ 809/465–2670) and by Auston MacLeod of **Pro-Divers** (☎ 809/465–3223) for $20 (summer), $25 (winter).

BY PLANE

**American** (☎ 800/433–7300) and **Delta** (☎ 800/221–1212) fly from the United States to Antigua, St. Croix, St. Thomas, St. Maarten, and San Juan, Puerto Rico, where connections to St. Kitts (and to a lesser extent, to Nevis) can be made on regional carriers such as **American Eagle,** part of the American Airlines system (☎ 800/433–7300); **LIAT** (☎ 809/465–2511); and **Windward Island Airways** (☎ 809/465–0810). LIAT has two flights daily between St. Kitts and Nevis. **British Airways** (☎ 800/247–9297) flies from London to Antigua, and **Air Canada** (☎ 800/776–3000) flies from Toronto to Antigua. **Air St. Kitts–Nevis** (☎ 809/465–8571), **Nevis Express** (☎ 809/469–9756), and **Carib Aviation** (in St. Kitts, ☎ 809/465–3055; in Nevis, 809/469–9295; FAX 809/469–9185) are reliable air-charter operations providing service between St. Kitts and Nevis and other islands.

FROM THE AIRPORT

Taxis meet every flight at both island's airports. The taxis are unmetered, but fixed rates, in E.C. dollars, are posted at the airport and at the jetty. On St. Kitts the fare from the airport to the closest hotel in Basseterre is E.C.$16; to the farthest point, E.C.$56. On Nevis some sample fares are from the ferry slip to Nisbet Plantation, E.C.$36, and to Golden Rock, E.C.$30. From the airport, the rates are, respectively, E.C.$17 and E.C.$40. (The current exchange rate is E.C.$2.60 for U.S.$1.) Be sure to clarify whether the rate quoted is in E.C. or U.S. dollars. There is a 50% surcharge for trips made between 10 PM and 6 AM.

## Currency

Legal tender is the Eastern Caribbean (E.C.) dollar. At press time, the rate of exchange was E.C.$2.60 to U.S.$1. U.S. dollars are accepted practically everywhere, but you'll usually get change in E.C. dollars. Prices quoted here are in U.S. dollars unless noted otherwise. Most large hotels, restaurants, and shops accept major credit cards, but small inns and shops often do not. It's always a good idea to check current credit-card policies before you turn up with only plastic in your pocket.

## Emergencies

**Police:** ☎ 911. **Hospital:** There is a 24-hour emergency room at the **Joseph N. France General Hospital** (⊠ Basseterre, ☎ 809/465–2551) and at

**Alexandra Hospital** (⊠ Charlestown, ☎ 809/469–5473). **Pharmacies:** In St. Kitts, **Skerritt's Drug Store** (⊠ Fort St., ☎ 809/465–2008) is open Monday–Wednesday 8–5, Thursday 8–1, Friday 8–5:30, and Saturday 8–6; **City Drug** (⊠ Fort St., Basseterre, ☎ 809/465–2156) is open Monday–Wednesday and Friday–Saturday 8–7; Thursday 8–5, Sunday 8–10 AM; and **City Drug** (⊠ Sun 'n' Sand, Frigate Bay, ☎ 809/465–1803) is open Monday–Saturday 8:30–8, Sunday 8:30–10:30 AM and 4–6 PM. In Nevis, **Evelyn's Drugstore** (⊠ Charlestown, ☎ 809/469–5278) is open weekdays 8–5, Saturday 8–7:30, and Sunday 7 AM–8 PM; the **Claxton Medical Centre** (⊠ Charlestown, ☎ 809/469–5357) is open Monday–Wednesday and Friday 8–6, Thursday 8–4, Saturday 7:30–7, and Sunday 6–8 PM.

## Getting Around

### BUSES

A privately owned minibus circles St. Kitts. Check with the tourist office (☞ Visitor Information, *below*) about schedules.

### CAR RENTALS AND SCOOTERS

You'll need a local driver's license, which you can get by presenting yourself, your valid driver's license, and E.C.$30 (U.S.$12) at the police station on Cayon Street in Basseterre. (In Nevis, the car-rental agency will help you obtain a local license at the police station.) The license is valid for one year.

In St. Kitts, try **Avis** (☎ 809/465–6507), which has the best selection of Suzuki and Daihatsu jeeps, **Budget** (809/466–5585), **Delise Walwyn** (☎ 809/465–8449), and **Sunshine** (☎ 809/465–2193). **Economy Car** (☎ 809/465–8449) also rents scooter bikes. **TDC Rentals** (☎ 809/465–2991) has a wide selection of vehicles and the best service. Car rentals start at about $35 per day for a compact. At press time, the price of gas was $2 per gallon. Remember to drive on the left!

You may not want to drive in Nevis. The island's roads are pocked with crater-size potholes; driving is on the left, and, to make it more difficult, you may be given a right-drive vehicle. Pigs, goats, and cattle crop up out of nowhere to amble along the road, and if you deviate from Main Street, you're likely to have trouble finding your way.

**TDC Rentals, Ltd.** (⊠ Charlestown, ☎ 809/469–5690), known for its exceptional service, rents a wide range of vehicles, has offices on St. Kitts, and offers a three-day rental that includes a car on both islands. **Avis** (⊠ Stoney Grove, ☎ 809/469–1240) provides Suzuki Jeeps and Nissan cars. **Nisbett Rentals Ltd.** (⊠ Charlestown, ☎ 809/469–9211) rents cars, minimokes, and Jeeps. None of these companies charge for mileage, and all of them accept major credit cards.

### TAXIS

Taxis rates are government-regulated, and the rates are posted at the airport, the dock, and in the free **Traveller** tourist guide. There are fixed rates to and from all the hotels and to and from major points of interest. In St. Kitts, you can call the **St. Kitts Taxi Association** (☎ 809/465–8487, after hours, ☎ 809/465–7818). In Nevis, taxi service (☎ 809/469–5621, after dark, 809/469–5515) is available at the airport, by the dock in Charlestown, as well as through arrangement with your hotel.

## Guided Tours

The taxi driver who picks you up will probably offer to act as your guide to the island. Each driver is knowledgeable and does a three-hour tour for $50. He can also make a lunch reservation at one of the plantation restaurants, and you can incorporate this into your tour. In Nevis,

Fitzroy "Teach" Williams (☎ 809/469–1140) is particularly recommended. You can also stop by the St. Kitts/Nevis Department of Tourism in Basseterre or the front desk of your hotel to arrange for a tour.

In St. Kitts, **Tropical Tours** (☎ 809/465–4167) can run you around the island and take you to the rain forest. **Kriss Tours** (☎ 809/465–4042) and **Greg's Safari** (☎ 809/465–4121) specialize in rain-forest and volcano tours. Also try **Addy's Nature Tours** (☎ 809/465–8069) for still more rain-forest and volcano adventures and **Kantours** (☎ 809/465–2098) for general island tours.

In Nevis, **All Seasons Streamline Tours** (☎ 809/469–5705 or 809/469–1138, FAX 809/469–1139) has a fleet of air-conditioned, 14-seat vans and uniformed drivers to take you around the island at a cost of $75 for three hours. Another tour option is **Jan's Travel Agency** (✉ Arcade, Charlestown, ☎ 809/469–5578), which arranges half- and full-day tours of the island. You can also stop by the Nevis Tourist Office (☞ Visitor Information, *below*) to pick up a copy of the Nevis Historical Society's self-guided tour of the island.

## Language
English with a strong West Indian lilt is spoken here.

## Opening and Closing Times
Although shops used to close for lunch from noon to 1, more and more establishments are remaining open Monday–Saturday 8–4. Some shops close earlier on Thursday. Hours vary somewhat from bank to bank but are typically Monday–Thursday 8–3 and Friday 8–5. **St. Kitts & Nevis National Bank** is also open Saturday 8:30–11.

## Passports and Visas
Although it is always wiser to travel in the Caribbean with a valid passport, U.S. and Canadian citizens need only produce proof of citizenship in the form of a voter registration card or birth certificate (a driver's license will not suffice). British citizens must have a passport; visas are not required. A return or ongoing ticket is mandatory.

## Precautions
Visitors, especially women, should not jog on long, lonely roads.

## Taxes and Service Charges
Hotels collect a 7% government tax and add a 10% service charge to your bill. In restaurants, a tip of 15% is appropriate. The departure tax is $10. There is no departure tax from St. Kitts to Nevis, or vice versa. Taxi drivers typically receive a 10% tip.

## Telephones and Mail
To call St. Kitts from the United States, dial area code 809, then access code 465, 466, 468, or 469 and the local four-digit number. Caribbean Phone Cards, which can be purchased in denominations of $5, $10, and $20, are handy for making local phone calls, calling other islands, and accessing USADirect lines. To make an intra-island call, simply dial the seven-digit number. Warning for both islands: Many private lines and hotels charge access rates if you use your ATT, Sprint, or MCI phonecards; there's no regularity, and it can be frustrating. Avoid using the widely advertised **Skantel** (☎ 800/877–8000), which ostensibly allows you to make credit-card calls; rates are usurious and they usually freeze an outrageous amount for up to week on your credit card until they finally put through the exact bill.

Airmail letters to the United States and Canada cost E.C.80¢ per half ounce; postcards require E.C.50¢. Mail takes at least 7–10 days to reach the United States. St. Kitts and Nevis issue separate stamps, but each honors the other's. The beautiful stamps are collector's items, and you may have a hard time pasting them on postcards.

## Visitor Information

Contact the **St. Kitts & Nevis Tourist Board** (✉ 414 E. 75th St., New York, NY 10021, ☎ 212/535–1234 or 800/582–6208, 🆇 212/734–6511), **St. Kitts & Nevis Tourist Office** (✉ 11 Yorkville Ave., Suite 508, Toronto, Ontario M4W 1L3, ☎ 416/921–7717, 🆇 416/921–7997), and **St. Kitts & Nevis Tourist Office** (✉ 10 Kensington Ct., London W8 5DL, ☎ 0171/376–0881, 🆇 0171/937–3611).

In St. Kitts, contact **St. Kitts/Nevis Department of Tourism** (✉ Pelican Mall, Bay Rd., Box 132, Basseterre, ☎ 809/465–2620 or 809/465–4040, 🆇 809/465–8794) and the **St. Kitts–Nevis Hotel Association** (✉ Box 438, Basseterre, ☎ 809/465–5304, 🆇 809/465–7746).

The **Nevis Tourist Office** (☎ 809/469–5521) is on Main Street in Charlestown. The office is open Monday and Tuesday 8–4:30 and Wednesday–Friday 8–4.

# 22 St. Lucia

Updated by
Jane E. Zarem

**C**ONTRARY TO POPULAR FOLKLORE, Columbus never set foot on St. Lucia; until a few years ago, neither did most Americans. A boom in all-inclusive resort construction has been drawing increasing droves of Yankees—a bit to the dismay of Brits and Europeans who've cherished this lush, tropical paradise for decades. St. Lucia, a 238-square-mile island toward the southern end of the Windwards, has honey-colored sand beaches and posh hotels in the north. In the south, striking natural attractions dominate: The Pitons (Petit and Gros), the island's twin peaks, rise straight out of the sea to more than 2,400 feet; a dense rain forest blankets much of the topography; and bubbling sulfur springs gurgle at the mouth of a low-lying volcano that erupted thousands of years ago and now produces highly acclaimed curative waters.

Because of its natural beauty, St. Lucia is often referred to as "the Helen of the West Indies." The coastline is familiar to sailors and divers alike—the reefs near the Pitons are especially sought-after scuba sites. In between the populous north and the gorgeous south a tortuously winding road passes through lush valleys, rain forest, banana plantations, secluded bays, and small villages. Marigot Bay, whose claim to fame is having been the filming location for *Doctor Doolittle,* is on the west coast and is one of the Caribbean's prettiest bays. The village of Choiseul, on the south coast, is an important arts center, maintaining Carib traditions and nurturing local talent.

In its less secluded regions, St. Lucia is noticeably sophisticated, hosting not only Carnival in February but also a world-renowned Jazz Festival in late spring. Another St. Lucian festival, National Day, celebrates December 13, 1502—even though historians now think the island was sighted in 1499 by Juan de la Cosa, Columbus's navigator. In any case, the island's true first inhabitants, the Arawaks, paddled up from South America sometime before AD 200. The warlike Caribs followed and conquered around AD 800 and were still here when the first Europeans attempted to set up camp.

In 1605, 67 English settlers bound for Guiana were blown off course and landed near Vieux Fort. Within a few weeks the Caribs had killed all but 19, who escaped in a canoe. Another group of English settlers dropped by 30 years later but were met with a similar lack of hospitality. Finally, the French signed a treaty with the Caribs in 1660 and took control of the island.

Thus began a 150-year period of battles between the French and the English that saw a dizzying 14 changes in power before the British took permanent possession in 1814. During those battle-filled years, Europeans colonized the island. They developed sugar plantations, using slaves from West Africa to work the fields. By 1838, when slaves were emancipated, more than 90% of the island consisted of African descendants. This is still largely true of today's 140,000 St. Lucians.

On February 22, 1979, St. Lucia became an independent state within the British Commonwealth of Nations, with a resident governor-general appointed by the queen. Still, there are many relics of French occupation, notably in the island patois—spoken everywhere—the Creole cuisine, and the names of the places and the people.

St. Lucia's coal industry began on the island in 1883; until about 1920, Castries, the capital, was a leading coal port in the West Indies. Sugarcane became the next major money crop, followed by bananas during the 1960s. Today, the tourism industry is running neck and neck with bananas, particularly since the banana-growing countries of the small Caribbean are now having to compete for a share of the European market. The importance of tourism pleases the savvy St. Lucians, who are working hard to avoid ruining their island with opportunistic overbuilding—as has happened on some other islands. They are also diversifying their agriculture in order to strengthen their economy further by reducing imports. Consequently, there is a tangible solidity to St. Lucia, an optimism that is reflected in general friendliness as well as in a startling number of spectacular new hotels and resorts.

# Lodging

St. Lucia is beginning to rival Jamaica in the number of all-inclusives and resorts dotting the island. Additionally, a few small and inexpensive lodgings have popped up around Rodney Bay, offering bright, clean modern suites at bargain prices. Virtually all the development is along the calm Caribbean coast, either around Soufrière to the south or, more commonly, between Castries and Cap Estate in the north.

Fortunately, there is not a glut of resorts or hotels in any one price range or catering to any one type of tourist. You'll find some that draw principally Europeans; others, Americans. Some are lavish; others, laid-back and less costly. Some have all-inclusive meal plans; just as many are MAP or EP. And many offer wedding packages: St. Lucian law requires residence for only three days to acquire a marriage license.

Just about every resort has friendly, accommodating service and is either in a fairly secluded cove or along an unspoiled beach. Consider spending the last night or two of your stay at one of the lodgings in Soufrière, about 45 minutes from Hewanorra International Airport, or at the Skyway Inn, just across the street from the airport. The foremost complaint of visitors to St. Lucia is the 90-minute, topsy-turvy drive between hotels in the north and Hewanorra in the south.

About 35 small, comparatively inexpensive hotels and inns are represented by a marketing group called the **Inns of St. Lucia** (✉ 20 Bridge St., Castries, St. Lucia, ☎ 809/452–4599, ℻ 809/452–5428). For private villa rentals, contact **Tropical Villas** (✉ Box 189, Castries, St. Lucia, ☎ 809/452–8240, ℻ 809/450–8089).

| CATEGORY | COST* |
|---|---|
| $$$$ | over $350 |
| $$$ | $200–$350 |
| $$ | $125–$200 |
| $ | under $125 |

*All prices are for a standard double room for two, excluding 8% tax and 10% service charge.*

## Castries and the North End

$$$$ ★ 🏨 **LeSPORT.** Boredom will never strike at this unique and beautiful resort, which is not easy to pigeonhole. Though crowned by the Oasis—a $3.5 million temple to well-being that looks like a sun-bleached Moorish palace—it is not entirely a spa; and despite its name, it's no jock's hotel. Health nuts will be very happy here, and you can experiment with the spa cuisine; but it is also possible to eat enormous quantities of the chef's excellent meals and accomplish nothing but the acquisition of a dangerous suntan on the perfect U-shaped beach. Most guests laze around in white robes awaiting thalassotherapy—seawater beauty treatments that LeSPORT (and its Grenadian sister, LaSOURCE) pioneered—before throwing themselves into one of the 30-something things-to-do (archery, tai chi, fencing, waterskiing, scuba, tennis, volleyball etc., etc.) coordinated by the charming Charles Simon

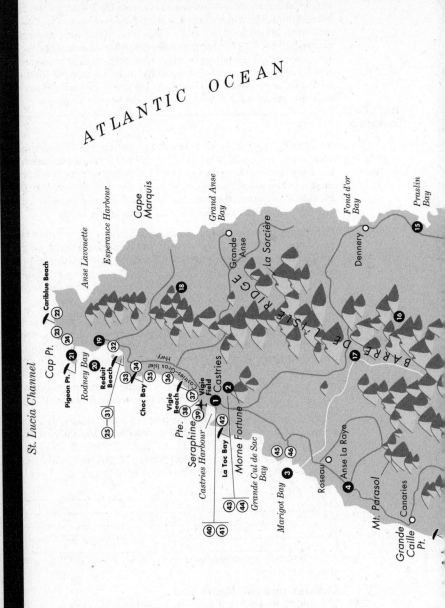

ATLANTIC OCEAN

St. Lucia Channel

Cap Pt.

Cariblue Beach

Anse Lavouette

Esperance Harbour

Cape Marquis

Grand Anse Bay

Fond d'or Bay

Praslin Bay

Grande Anse

La Sorcière

Dennery

Pigeon Pt.

Rodney Bay

Reduit Beach

BARRE DE L'ISLE RIDGE

Choc Bay

Castries–Gros Islet Hwy.

Castries

Vigie Field

Vigie Beach

Pte. Seraphine

Castries Harbour

Morne Fortune

Grande Cul de Sac Bay

La Toc Bay

Marigot Bay

Roseau

Anse La Raye

Mt. Parasol

Grande Caille Pt.

Canaries

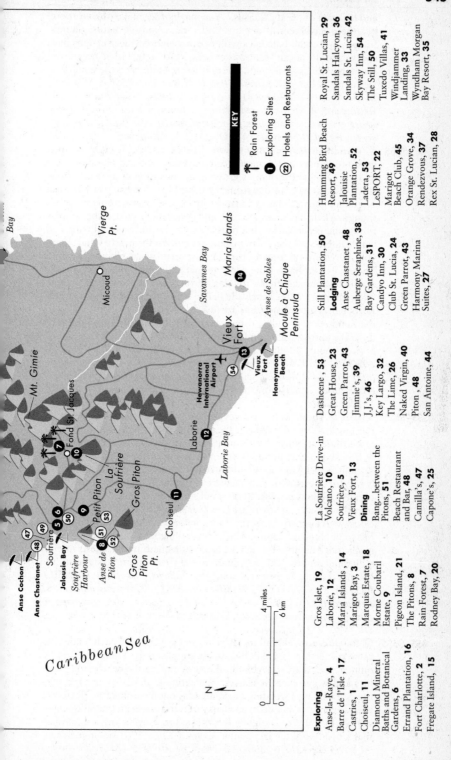

545

**KEY**

&#10033; Rain Forest

&#9312; Exploring Sites

&#9313; Hotels and Restaurants

*Caribbean Sea*

N

0 ___ 4 miles
0 ___ 6 km

Mt. Gimie

Bay

*Vierge Pt.*

Micoud

Savannes Bay

*Maria Islands*

Anse de Sables

Moule à Chique Peninsula

Fond St. Jacques

Soufrière

Anse Cochon

Anse Chastanet

Jalousie Bay

Soufrière Harbour

Petit Piton

La Soufrière

Gros Piton

Anse de Piton

Gros Piton Pt.

Choiseul

Laborie

Laborie Bay

Vieux Fort

Hewanorra International Airport

Vieux Fort

Honeymoon Beach

**Exploring**
Anse-la-Raye, **4**
Barre de l'Isle , **17**
Castries, **1**
Choiseul, **11**
Diamond Mineral
Baths and Botanical
Gardens, **6**
Errand Plantation, **16**
Fort Charlotte, **2**
Fregate Island, **15**

Gros Islet, **19**
Laborie, **12**
Maria Islands , **14**
Marigot Bay, **3**
Marquis Estate, **18**
Morne Coubaril
Estate, **9**
Pigeon Island, **21**
The Pitons, **8**
Rain Forest, **7**
Rodney Bay, **20**

La Soufrière Drive-in
Volcano, **10**
Soufrière, **5**
Vieux Fort, **13**

**Dining**
Bang...between the
Pitons, **51**
Beach Restaurant
and Bar, **48**
Camilla's, **47**
Capone's, **25**

Dasheene , **53**
Great House, **23**
Green Parrot, **43**
Jimmie's, **39**
J.J.'s, **46**
Key Largo, **32**
The Lime, **26**
Naked Virgin, **40**
Piton, **48**
San Antoine, **44**

Still Plantation, **50**

**Lodging**
Anse Chastanet , **48**
Auberge Seraphine, **38**
Bay Gardens, **31**
Candyo Inn, **30**
Club St. Lucia, **24**
Green Parrot, **43**
Harmony Marina
Suites, **27**

Humming Bird Beach
Resort, **49**
Jalouisie
Plantation, **52**
Ladera, **53**
LeSPORT, **22**
Marigot
Beach Club, **45**
Orange Grove, **34**
Rendezvous, **37**
Rex St. Lucian, **28**

Royal St. Lucian, **29**
Sandals Halcyon, **36**
Sandals St. Lucia, **42**
Skyway Inn, **54**
The Still, **50**
Tuxedo Villas, **41**
Windjammer
Landing, **33**
Wyndham Morgan
Bay Resort, **35**

and his team of "Body Guards." You may not see much of your room, but these have central air, queen-size beds, marble baths, phones, fridges, and small balconies with ocean views; costlier versions have cool marble floors and four-poster beds. Thirty refurbished oceanfront rooms have bigger balconies. The only disappointment is the small, low-tech gym. ⊠ *Box 437, Cariblue Beach,* ☎ *809/450–8551 or 800/544–2883,* ℻ *809/452–0368. 100 rooms, 2 suites, 1 plantation house. Restaurant, 2 bars, air-conditioning, 3 pools, beauty salon, hot tub, sauna, tennis court, aerobics, exercise rooms, dance classes, water-sports center, bicycles, boutique. AE, DC, MC, V. All-inclusive.*

**$$$$**　　🏨 **Wyndham Morgan Bay Resort.** The expanding Wyndham Hotel group took over this property from the French-owned Hotel Pullman in 1992. The landscaping is growing up, beautifying the eight three-story blocks that fan out from the central pool-restaurant-bar area. Nothing's going to change the mostly partial sea views from the rooms, though. Their balconies are tiny, and decor the usual Caribbean pale florals and peach wicker, but beds are king-size and especially firm and comfortable, and there's an ingenious angle on the mirrors that shows you your entire self from the back (always useful where bikinis are worn). There's everything for the party animal and sportif type, with drinks and entertainment freely flowing—from early morning aerobics to midnight pizza at the beachside Palm Grill—to the delight of a largely European crowd. Americans are just discovering Wyndham, although the hundred new rooms being planned will probably speed the process. The narrow, gray-sand beach with cloudy water is the biggest disappointment. ⊠ *Box 2216, Gros Islet,* ☎ *809/450–2511,* ℻ *809/450–1050. 340 rooms. 2 restaurants, 2 bars, beach grill, air-conditioning, pool, hot tub, sauna, 4 tennis courts, aerobics, archery, exercise room, water-sports center, boutique, game room. AE, D, MC, V. All-inclusive.*

**$$$–$$$$**　　🏨 **Club St. Lucia.** Set on 50 acres at the northernmost point of St. Lucia, this bustling, friendly resort is the island's largest. Of the all-inclusives, this is the least expensive; it's not particularly luxurious. It caters mostly to Brits, but tennis enthusiasts come here to be close to the adjacent St. Lucia Racquet Club (☞ Outdoor Activities and Sports, *below*), which is free for guests. Others come here to get hitched; expect to see three to five weddings per day. Rooms and suites are in bungalows scattered over the hillside, and there are two beaches. Accommodations are spacious, with king-size beds, tile floors, patios, and air-conditioning in all but some standard rooms, which have ceiling fans. Live entertainment is scheduled nightly. Though the food is adequate at best, guests receive a discount and free transportation to the Great House Restaurant (☞ Dining, *below*). ⊠ *Box 915, Smugglers Village, Castries,* ☎ *809/450–0551 or 800/777–1250,* ℻ *809/450–0281. 352 rooms and suites. Restaurant, 2 bars, pizza parlor, pool, hot tub, tennis courts, water-sports center, minimart, shops, disco, laundry service, transport to stables. AE, DC, MC, V. All-inclusive.*

**$$$–$$$$**　　🏨 **Rendezvous.** This all-inclusive resort on Malabar Beach, under the same ownership as LeSPORT, is for couples only. Things tend to be quite active, with volleyball in the pool and on the beach, and aerobics and water exercise classes. The activities desk can arrange anything, including a wedding. Accommodations have pink marble floors, king-size four-poster beds, a balcony or terrace, and air-conditioning—but no TVs. There is nightly live music for dancing and a piano bar that's open until the last couple leaves. ⊠ *Box 190, Malabar Beach,* ☎ *809/452–4211 or 800/544–2883,* ℻ *809/452–7419. 84 rooms, 8 suites, 8 cottages. 2 restaurants, 3 bars, air-conditioning, 2 pools, 2 hot tubs, sauna, 2 tennis courts, exercise room, water-sports center, dive shop, catamaran, bicycles. AE, MC, V. All-inclusive.*

**$$$–$$$$** ⊞ **Royal St. Lucian.** This classy resort, facing beautiful Reduit Beach, caters
★ to your every whim. The colonnaded reception area is stunning—an Italian palazzo with vaulted atrium, cool marble walls, a gurgling fountain, and a sweeping grand staircase. The russet-roofed white buildings form a "U" in the pristine landscaped grounds. The large, rambling pool has Japanese-style bridges, a natural rock waterfall, and a swim-up bar. The split-level suites are sumptuous (maybe the best on the island), with a separate sitting area, luxurious bathroom, large patio or balcony, a soothing pastel color scheme, cable TV, air-conditioning, three phones, a minibar, and a jet shower. Guests, many of whom are European, may use the tennis and water-sports facilities at the adjacent sister property, the Rex St. Lucian. Not the most authentic Caribbean experience in St. Lucia, the food, service, and decor are, nevertheless, stellar. ⊠ *Box 977, Castries,* ☎ *809/452–9999 or 800/225–5859,* ℻ *809/452–9639. 98 suites. 3 restaurants, 2 bars, air-conditioning, pool, snorkeling, meeting facilities. AE, DC, MC, V. EP, MAP.*

**$$$–$$$$** ⊞ **Sandals St. Lucia.** Sandals, the all-inclusive, couples-only chain of
★ resorts, debuted here in April 1993 and has been a smashing success. This secluded 155-acre property, one of two Sandals resorts on the island, is a 10-minute drive south of Castries and Vigie Airport. The list of perks here goes on and on: private plunge pools, a ¼-acre swimming pool, a lovely beach, a nine-hole golf course, floodlit tennis courts, an outstanding fitness center, etc. There's no shortage of restaurants either; take your choice of Asian, Continental, French, southwestern, or Caribbean cuisine. Guest rooms and suites, done in mahogany furnishings with king-size four-poster beds, all have air-conditioning, hair dryers, direct-dial telephones, and cable TV. Suites have concierge service. Most important, guests, who are mostly American, seem to have a blast—thanks in part to a young, raucous, and fun-loving staff. No tipping is allowed. ⊠ *La Toc Rd., Castries,* ☎ *809/452–3081,* ℻ *809/453–7089. 213 rooms, 60 suites. 5 restaurants, 5 bars, air-conditioning, pool, 9-hole golf course, 5 tennis courts, health club, beach, water-sports center. AE, DC, MC, V. All-inclusive.*

**$$$** ⊞ **Sandals Halcyon.** This Sandals all-inclusive beachfront resort for couples only—one of two Sandals resorts on the island—is at Choc Bay, 10 minutes north of Castries and Vigie Airport. Somewhat quieter and more low-key than its sister resort, there's still a lot of activity and enthusiasm on the part of both guests and staff. All rooms are surrounded by lovely gardens and are attractively decorated with mahogany furniture, king-size four-poster beds with bright print spreads, and white tile floors. Rates vary depending on the view and proximity to the beach. The sea here is generally calm, and guests enjoy a wide range of water sports and other activities—exercise equipment, nightly entertainment, and more. A shuttle runs hourly between the two Sandals resorts, so guests at either can "stay at one, play at two." Sandals Halcyon has four restaurants, serving Italian, Caribbean, and International cuisine at dinner; sumptuous buffet breakfasts and lunches; and light food and snacks all day long. Seaside weddings take place often here, and it's a popular honeymoon hotel—although couples who vacation here represent all age groups. ⊠ *Box GM 910, Choc Bay, Castries,* ☎ *809/453–0222,* ℻ *809/451–8435. 180 rooms. 3 restaurants, 3 bars, snack bar, air-conditioning, pool, 2 tennis courts, basketball, health club, volleyball, Ping-Pong, shuffleboard, beach, water-sports center. AE, DC, MC, V. All-inclusive.*

**$$$** ⊞ **Windjammer Landing.** This sun-kissed resort, with sweeping views of one of St. Lucia's prettiest bays, fulfills anyone's beachcombing fantasies. White stucco villas crowned with tile alternate with a porticoed reception area and thatch-hut public rooms. Villas are huge and tastefully decorated in the ubiquitous island pastels and rattan furnishings.

You can arrange to have dinner prepared and served in your villa. The ambiance is rustic simplicity with painted natural wood timbers, tile floors, wicker chairs, and straw mats. A people mover transports guests up the steep hill from the main building and shops to their villas. A waterfall connects two bi-level pools; many of the villas have private plunge pools, as well. ✉ *Box 1504, Labrelotte Bay, Castries,* ☎ *809/452–0913,* 🖷 *809/452–9454. 131 1-, 2-, 3-, and 4-bedroom villas. 4 restaurants, 2 bars, picnic meals, air-conditioning, 2 pools, tennis, scuba diving, snorkeling, windsurfing, sailing, waterskiing, 3 boutiques, laundry. AE, MC, V. EP, MAP.*

$$ 🏨 **Harmony Marina Suites.** Your suite may have a view of the pool or Rodney Bay Marina, but don't fear—Reduit Beach is only 200 yards away. The 22 suites have air-conditioning, large bathroom with hair dryer, a red-tile balcony or terrace, and wet bar; four also have kitchenettes. The eight VIP suites have additional 10-foot sundecks, a whirlpool bath, a four-poster bed, Australian sheepskin throw rugs, but no kitchen. A rarity: The terrace furniture is comfortable, cushioned chaise longues. This is a nice alternative to the megaresort scene, and the adjacent minimarket—one of the best-stocked on the island— makes the kitchenette suites ideal for long-term stays. ✉ *Box 155, Castries,* ☎ *809/452–8756,* 🖷 *809/452–8677. 30 suites. Restaurant, bar, air-conditioning, refrigerators, pool, hairdresser, boating, fishing, baby-sitting, laundry service. MC, V. EP, MAP.*

$$ 🏨 **Marigot Beach Club.** On one of the most beautiful hideaway bays on the island, this is a quiet spot 9 miles south of Castries and not too far from the mountains and sights around Soufrière. Guest quarters climb the steep hillside that forms a backdrop for the resort, and a tram transports guests up and down. Studios and one-bedroom apartments have kitchenettes and private patios that overlook the water. Marigot Bay is a favorite of yachtspeople, so the boating activity—mostly sailboats—adds atmosphere. The resort has an excellent water-sports center, where you can arrange diving and snorkeling trips, windsurfing, kayaking, waterskiing, or sailing excursions. The lovely beach, shaded by coconut palms, looks like one you'd see in the South Seas. Club Paradis, the open-air waterfront bar and restaurant, offers a wide selection of Caribbean and Continental fare. ✉ *Box 101, Marigot Bay, Castries,* ☎ *809/451–4974,* 🖷 *809/451–4973. 44 units. Restaurant, bar, pool, beach, water-sports center, shops. MC, V. EP, MAP.*

$$ 🏨 **Rex St. Lucian.** The broad, white, informal lobby, with potted plants and upholstered sofas, leads to the gardens, pool area, and beach. Rooms are spread out over considerable acreage (this was once two hotels), some facing Reduit Beach, some set among the gardens. They are attractively decorated and have double or king-size beds, clock radios, direct-dial phones, and patios or terraces. Standard rooms don't have air-conditioning or tubs; they have ceiling fans and showers. Rooms accessible to people with disabilities are available, and executive suites are especially suitable for business guests. Two restaurants—the Hummingbird and the Flamingo—are on site, and the hotel offers nightly entertainment. Guests (the clientele is largely European) also can stroll to several restaurants and nightspots in the Rodney Bay Marina area. ✉ *Box 512, Reduit Beach, Castries,* ☎ *809/452–8351,* 🖷 *809/452–8331. 260 rooms. 2 restaurants, 3 bars, ice-cream parlor, pool, beauty salon, 2 tennis courts, dive shop, water-sports center, boutiques, shopping plaza, laundry service and dry cleaning. AE, DC, MC, V. EP, MAP.*

$$ 🏨 **Tuxedo Villas.** This pristine-white apartment complex set around a tiny swimming pool in a peaceful corner close to Reduit Beach is a good value. Each of the small but comfortable units has a living room, dining room, kitchen, and one or two bedrooms with private bath and air-conditioning. Two-bedroom, two-bath villas have kitchens that

are well equipped with full-size fridge-freezers, glass-topped bamboo tables and breakfast bars, and patios. There's nothing exciting here, but everything works, everything's spotless, and the staff is friendly. ⊠ *Box 419, Castries,* ☎ *809/452–8553,* FAX *809/452–8577. 10 apartments. Restaurant, bar, air-conditioning, pool. AE, MC, V. EP.*

$ 🏨 **Auberge Seraphine.** New in 1995, this impressive small inn overlooks Vigie Cove and is minutes from Vigie Airport, Pointe Seraphine, and downtown Castries. Accommodations are spacious, cheerful, and bright, and most have a view of the cove and Vigie Yacht Marina. A broad clay-tiled sundeck—the center of activity—surrounds a small pool. The popular restaurant offers fine Caribbean, French, and Continental cuisine; the management is proud of its well-stocked wine cellar. One child (age 2–12) stays free when sharing a room with two adults. ⊠ *Box 309, Ville Ville Bay, Pointe Seraphine, Castries,* ☎ *809/453–2073,* FAX *809/451-7001. 22 rooms Restaurant, bar, pool, meeting facilities. AE, MC, V. EP, MAP.*

$ 🏨 **Bay Gardens.** Conveniently located on the south side of Rodney Bay
★ and 7 miles north of Castries, this compact resort is an easy walk from beautiful Reduit Beach, several popular restaurants and nightclubs, and the marina. Shuttle service to the beach is free. Bay Gardens is new (it opened in late 1995), modern, and colorful. The lime-green building is studded with flower gardens that will be more impressive as they mature. Guest rooms surround a courtyard with a double serpentine pool and Jacuzzi. Air-conditioned rooms are furnished with white wicker furniture and colorful print spreads in tropical colors, and each has a balcony or patio. Executive rooms also have a trouser press and whirlpool bath. Eight self-contained apartments with kitchenettes and separate sitting rooms cater especially to families. Spices restaurant offers a varied menu, along with a weekly barbecue, Caribbean buffet, and Sunday brunch. One child (age 2–12) stays free when sharing a room with two adults. ⊠ *Box 1892, Rodney Bay, Castries,* ☎ *809/452–8060,* FAX *809/452–8059. 45 rooms, 8 apartments. Restaurant, bar, ice-cream parlor, air-conditioning, 2 pools, beauty parlor, shop, meeting facilities. AE, MC, V. EP, MAP.*

$ 🏨 **Candyo Inn.** This small pink hotel, in the heart of Rodney Bay, is one of the best buys in the Caribbean. It's a five-minute walk from beaches and several good restaurants, and it has a small pool and a lanai decked with the usual plastic lawn furniture and potted palms. An outdoor bar near the pool serves drinks and snacks. The two-story building and its lush green grounds are carefully looked after and spotless. All rooms have air-conditioning, veranda, white-tile floors, and white contemporary furniture with floral upholstery. The eight suites have kitchenettes, larger sitting areas, and tubs; they're worth the extra $15 a night. A small atrium lobby has a convenience shop. The staff is delightful. ⊠ *Box 386, Rodney Bay,* ☎ *809/452–0712,* FAX *809/452–0774. 4 rooms, 8 suites. Bar, air-conditioning, pool. AE, MC, V. EP.*

$ 🏨 **Green Parrot.** The hillside setting is the draw at this small hotel, set high above Castries and the harbor on Morne Fortune. The motel-like rooms have a patio, air-conditioning, and vanity. A free bus scoots you to town and the beach; the hotel also arranges excursions to Anse Jambette, a private beach, for swimming and snorkeling. The Green Parrot restaurant, open to the public, is internationally acclaimed for its cuisine. ⊠ *Box 648, the Morne, Castries,* ☎ *809/452–3399,* FAX *809/453–2272. 62 rooms. Restaurant, bar, pool, beach shuttle, shop, cabaret. AE, MC, V. EP, MAP.*

$ 🏨 **Orange Grove Hotel.** Up a long hill, off the road to Windjammer Landing, is this recently renovated hilltop hotel. The rooms—large, light, and clean—are packed with all the conveniences you'd expect at a larger resort. Standard rooms have showers; superior rooms and suites have bath and shower. All have tropical prints and Caribbean-style rattan furniture, as well as separate sitting areas and balconies or patios overlooking the hillside. And although you're away from the beach, you are welcome to use the beach facilities at Club St. Lucia 15 minutes away; free transportation is available. Its Café Clementine serves West Indian and International cuisine. The hotel is getting to be better known among Americans. ⊠ *Box GM 702, Castries,* ☎ *809/452–9040,* ℻ *809/452– 8094. 51 rooms, 11 suites. Restaurant, bar, air-conditioning, pool, beauty salon, shop, beach shuttle. AE, MC, V. EP, MAP.*

## Soufrière Area

$$$$   ⊞ **Jalousie Plantation.** This all-inclusive resort opened amid contro-
★      versy over its location—a dramatic setting between the Pitons (many locals felt the land shouldn't have been developed). More than 100 brown wooden cottages tumble down the steep hillside, but the environment-conscious owners have managed to screen them with dense tropical vegetation so they are virtually invisible from a distance. The setting, originally a coconut plantation, is absolutely spectacular. The main building, Jacquot Great House, is midway down the hill and has restaurants, lounges, and shops. A broad front lawn leads to a large oval pool, an open-air restaurant, a dock with water-sports facilities, and a private gray-sand beach. People movers come along every five minutes to shuttle guests up and down the steep hillside. Large cottage suites have a separate sitting room and an enormous bathroom with an extra shower. All rooms have air-conditioning, elegant dark-wood furniture, plenty of closet space, and a complimentary stocked refrigerator. The full-service spa, perched high on the hill, has seven full-time therapists; each guest is entitled to one or two complimentary treatments, depending on length of stay. Sports and exercise facilities are extensive, and there's a wealth of entertainment and other diversions available. ⊠ *Box 251, Soufrière,* ☎ *809/459–7666 or 800/392–2007,* ℻ *809/459–7667. 102 cottages, 12 suites. 4 restaurants, 3 bar-lounges, air-conditioning, pool, spa, 3-hole golf course, 4 tennis courts, horseback riding, squash, scuba diving, snorkeling, windsurfing, sailing, waterskiing, deep-sea-fishing charters, pro shop, boat shuttle to Soufrière and Castries. AE, DC, MC, V. All-inclusive.*

$$$–$$$$   ⊞ **Anse Chastanet Hotel.** If you invest in one of the Hillside Premium
★          or Deluxe rooms (Numbers 7 and 14) here, you are in for a slice of heaven. Nick Troubetskoy, the Canadian owner-architect, designed each to meld into the tropical mountainside, with louvered wooden walls open to stunning Piton and Caribbean vistas or to the deep shady green of the forest. Each has a terra-cotta-tiled floor, madras cotton fabrics, chunky wood furniture, great circles of upside-down baskets acting as lamp shades (small yellow birds like to rest on these), and truly covetable burlap and carved wood artwork; none have a phone or TV. Most rooms have an irresistible quirk. Number 14B has a tree growing in the bathroom; Number 7F has a vast bathroom, its shower completely open to the panorama of the Pitons. Other rooms (the "Superior" Numbers 5S and 6S) are mostly octagonal gazebos, with the same decor but far less space, and less privacy in some cases. This is a magical setting— another world—as long as you're fit to climb the 100 steps from the gray-sand beach up to the mid-level restaurant and then the rooms. Good food and great scuba are the attractions: Divers come from the earth's four corners to peep at these reefs, and the French executive chef has raised the hotel's already high standards of cuisine. ⊠ *Box 7000, Soufrière,* ☎ *809/459–7000,* ℻ *809/454–7067. 36 rooms and 12 suites. 2 restaurants, 2 bars, tennis court, dive shop, water-sports center. AE, DC, MC, V. EP, MAP.*

**$$$-$$$$**
**★**  ⊞ **Ladera.** This quiet, elegantly rustic hideaway is nestled high in the mountains amid lush botanical gardens overlooking the Pitons, the Caribbean sea, and Jalousie Plantation. It is one of the most sophisticated and unusual small resorts in the Caribbean—a home away from home for rock stars, corporate VIPs, and honeymooners. Most guests are American, and many stay here for the last night or two at the end of a longer vacation spent at a larger resort up north. The villas and suites are stylishly furnished with a harmonious blend of French colonial antiques and local crafts, and have a completely open wall that provides a dazzling, unobstructed view of the Pitons. Most units have small plunge pools, and one has a Jacuzzi. Guests can use the tennis courts at Jalousie Plantation for an hourly fee. Daily shuttle service to Soufrière and Anse Chastanet Beach is provided. An MAP plan is available, and the Dasheene Restaurant (☞ Dining, *below*) is considered by many to be the best on the island. Certainly the view is! Transfers to Hewanorra are complimentary for guests staying four nights. ⊠ *Box 255, Soufrière,* ☎ *809/459–7323. 6 villas, 13 suites. Restaurant, bar, pool, gift shop. AE, MC, V. MAP.*

**$**
**★**  ⊞ **Humming Bird Beach Resort.** This charming little resort is at the northern edge of Soufrière, right on the bay and within view of the Pitons. Rooms are in small seaside cabins adjoined by a maze of wooden decking. Most rooms have breathtaking views of the Pitons. The decor is attractive but simple; a primitive motif is emphasized by African sculptures. Two rooms each have a dark mahogany four-poster bed hung with a sheer mosquito net drape; the cool breezes of the trade winds will lull you to sleep without any annoying bug bites spoiling the atmosphere. Most rooms have private modern baths; two rooms and a suite have a shared bathroom. The two-bedroom country cottage—with sitting room, kitchenette, and a spectacular Piton view—is suitable for a family or two couples vacationing together. The Lifeline Bar and Restaurant is a favorite hangout of locals and expatriates. ⊠ *Box 280, Soufrière,* ☎ *809/454–7232,* FAX *809/459–7033. 9 rooms, 1 suite, 1 2-bedroom cottage. Restaurant, bar, pool, boutique. D, MC, V. EP, MAP.*

**$**  ⊞ **Skyway Inn.** If you're staying in the north but have an early-morning flight to catch from Hewanorra, this is the ideal place to stay. It's just 100 yards from the airport and minutes from Vieux Fort and its beaches. The inn is clean and comfortable. There's an open-air restaurant and bar on the roof and a pool down below. A free shuttle runs to both the beach and the airport. You don't want to spend a week here, but as far as airport hotels go, it's quite impressive. ⊠ *Box 353, Vieux Fort,* ☎ *809/454–7111,* FAX *809/454–7116. 44 rooms. Restaurant, bar, gift shop, meeting room, beach and airport shuttle. AE, MC, V.*

**$**  ⊞ **The Still.** One name, two very different resorts: At The Still Plantation, about a five-minute walk inland from Soufrière, there are one- and two-bedroom modern self-catering apartments with sitting rooms and kitchenettes, as well as studios with no kitchens. The restaurant here is well-known for its excellent Caribbean cuisine. There's a swimming pool and boutique. The Still Beach Resort, at the northern end of Soufrière Bay, has just three one-bedroom apartments and two studios that are right on the black-sand beach; they have a commanding view of the Pitons. There's a restaurant at the beach resort, as well, but most units have a kitchenette and all have a beachfront patio, where you can dine alfresco. If hiking and nature walks are more important than a beach, the plantation is the better choice; it's en route to Diamond Falls, the volcano, and rain forest. If you prefer sand and sea to pool and gardens, choose the beach resort. Guests at one can use the facilities of the other. ⊠ *Box 246, Soufrière,* ☎ *809/459–5179 or 809/459–7224,* FAX *809/459–7301. 13 apartments, 6 studios. 2 restaurants, 2 bars, pool, beach, gift shops. MC, V. EP.*

# Dining

If you stop by the Castries market (☞ Exploring St. Lucia, *below*) on a Friday or Saturday, you'll see the riches produced in this fertile volcanic soil. Mangoes, plantains, breadfruits, limes, pumpkins, cucumbers, papaya (pawpaw), yams, christophines (a green, squashlike vegetable), and coconuts are among the fruits and vegetables that appear on menus throughout the island. Every menu lists the catch of the day (usually flying fish, kingfish, or dolphinfish) along with the ever-popular lobster. And you may see the national dish—saltfish and green fig—a concoction of dried, salted white fish and boiled green banana, which is definitely an acquired taste. More usual Eastern Caribbean standards include callaloo, stuffed crab back, curried chicken or goat, and *lambi* (conch). Chicken, pork, and barbecues are also popular here. Most of the meats are imported—beef from Argentina and Iowa, lamb from New Zealand. The French influence is strong in St. Lucian restaurants, and most chefs cook with a Creole flair. With the increase in tourism, a broader mix of cuisines has become available, particularly in Castries and the Rodney Bay area.

## What to Wear

Dress on St. Lucia is casual but conservative. Nice shorts are usually fine during the day, but locals frown on bathing suits in restaurants and other public places. In the evening, things are casually elegant, but even the fanciest places expect only a collared shirt for men and a dress for women.

| CATEGORY | COST* |
|---|---|
| $$$$ | over $40 |
| $$$ | $25–$40 |
| $$ | $15–$25 |
| $ | under $15 |

*per person, excluding drinks and service*

## Castries Area

**$$$$**  ✕ **San Antoine.** High on the Morne, with splendid views of Castries
★    below and Martinique in the distance, this historic building was originally the great house of the San Antoine Hotel, built in the late 1800s, destroyed by fire in 1970, and restored soon after. The hotel once hosted literary luminary Somerset Maugham. Now the restored building is one of the most elegantly appointed restaurants on the island, and the cuisine is arguably the best. Try the superbly grilled fish, caramelized filet steak Robert, or honey roast rack of lamb; all entrées are served with a selection of fresh vegetables. You may dine à la carte or opt for the five-course prix-fixe dinner. Complimentary taxi service is available for parties of four or more. ⊠ *Old Morne Rd, south of Castries,* ☎ *809/452–4660. AE, MC, V. Closed Sun.*

**$$$**  ✕ **Green Parrot.** The Green Parrot comes complete with sommelier and
★    crisp napery. The menu of local and international dishes, prepared by Chef Harry (who was trained at London's prestigious Claridge's hotel), always includes a lot of seafood. There's lively entertainment—a belly dancer on Wednesday night and limbo night on Saturday—but the real reason to dine here is the view over Castries and the harbor. This is a hot spot for locals and tourists alike. ⊠ *The Morne, Castries,* ☎ *809/452–3399. Reservations essential. Jacket required. AE, MC, V.*

**$$–$$$**  ✕ **Jimmie's.** This popular, open-air, mom-and-pop-cozy restaurant and bar perched above the bay makes a relaxing daytime stop and becomes a romantic dinner spot when the harbor lights twinkle below. Appetizers on the seafood-dominated menu include a great Creole stuffed crab, while a wise choice of entrée is the special seafood platter with samplings from every part of the day's catch. All entrées come with several local vegetables—pumpkin, black beans, christophines, greens—plus garlic bread. Dessert lovers had better be in a banana mood, since the menu lists about 10 options—every single one, from fritters to ice cream, made with St. Lucian "figs." ⊠ *Vigie Marina, Vigie Cove, Castries,* ☎ *809/452–5142. Reservations not accepted. AE, MC, V.*

$$–$$$ ✕ **Naked Virgin.** Tucked away in the quiet Castries suburb of Marchand (just opposite the local post office—keep asking), this pleasant hangout offers terrific Creole cuisine and mellow music, and every couple leaves with a free T-shirt. The owner, Paul John, has worked in many of the island's major hotels; his rum concoction, the Naked Virgin, could be the best punch you've ever tasted. You can try one, with his compliments, with your dinner. Shrimp Creole and fried flying fish are highly recommended. You'll also find duck à l'orange, stuffed Cornish game hen, and T-bone steak on the menu. ⊠ *Marchand Rd., Castries,* ☎ *809/452–5594. AE, MC, V.*

$ ✕ **J. J.'s.** Not only are the prices right here, but the food is some of the best on the island. Superbly grilled fish with fresh vegetables is tops. The welcome is friendly and the atmosphere is casual; tables are set on a terrace above the road. On Friday nights the music blares, and the locals come to hang out and dance in the street. ⊠ *Marigot Bay Rd. (3 mi before the bay), Marigot,* ☎ *809/451–4076. Reservations not accepted. No credit cards.*

## Rodney Bay and the North End

$$$$ ✕ **Great House.** From this romantic spot, perched on a hill overlooking Anse Becune Bay, you can enjoy views of the water and of Martinique in the distance. The restaurant is run by the owners of Club St. Lucia, and guests there are given a discount and free transportation. Traditional French dishes have Creole overtones, as in the appetizer of pumpkin and potato soup and entrées like lime-grilled dorado fillet, Antillean shrimp sautéed in a Creole sauce, and broiled sirloin with thyme butter and sweet potato chips. The menu changes nightly. Come to the Great House—voted "Best Restaurant on St. Lucia" in 1995—to enjoy the sunset, first-class service, and elegant setting. ⊠ *Cap Estate,* ☎ *809/450–0450 or 809/450–0211. AE, DC, MC, V. No lunch.*

$$–$$$ ✕ **Capone's.** The tropics meet the Jazz Age in this restaurant. In a setting of black-and-white tile floors, a polished wood bar, and a player piano, waiters and waitresses dressed like gangsters serve rum drinks called Valentine's Day Massacre and Mafia Mai Tai. Your check is delivered in a violin case. The pasta is fresh, and the meat dishes include *osso buco alla Milanese* (veal knuckle) and chicken rotisserie. The **Pizza Parlour** (◷ 11 AM–midnight) turns out burgers and sandwiches, as well as pizza. ⊠ *Rodney Bay, across from Rex St. Lucian hotel,* ☎ *809/452–0284. AE, MC, V. Closed Mon. No lunch.*

$$ ✕ **The Lime.** The Lime is a favorite place for "liming" (hanging out). A
★ casual bistro with lime-colored gingham curtains, straw hats decorating the ceiling, and hanging plants, it offers a businessman's three-course lunch and a buffet of local dishes, like callaloo and lambi. Starters may include homemade pâté or stuffed crab back. Entrée choices may be medallions of pork fillet with the chef's special orange-and-ginger sauce, stewed lamb, or fish fillet poached in white wine and mushroom sauce. The prices are reasonable, which is perhaps why expatriates and locals gather here in the evenings. Next door is Late Lime's, the nightclub where the crowd moves when the evening starts turning into morning. ⊠ *Rodney Bay,* ☎ *809/452–0761. MC, V. Closed Tues.*

$–$$ ✕ **Key Largo.** Brick-oven gourmet pizzas are the specialty at this casual eatery at Rodney Bay Marina, across the lagoon from Rodney Bay's many hotels. You're welcome simply to stop in for an espresso or cappuccino, but the popular Pizza Key Largo—topped with shrimp, artichokes, and what seems like a few pounds of mozzarella—is tough to pass up. ⊠ *Rodney Bay,* ☎ *809/452–0282. MC, V.*

## Soufrière Area

$$$$ ✕ **Dasheene Restaurant and Bar.** Part of the striking Ladera resort (☞
★    Lodging, *above*), Dasheene is a small, casual mountaintop retreat with breathtaking views of the Pitons and the clear Caribbean sea between them. This is some of the best food in St. Lucia—Caribbean specialties with new American and Continental accents. Appetizers on a frequently changing menu may include smoked kingfish crepes and spicy seafood gazpacho. Typical entrées are tuna steak with coconut-avocado cream sauce and chicken breast with a mango or a pecan-and-peanut sauce. For dessert, the chocolate crème brûlée flambé takes about five minutes to cool down but is well worth the wait. There's live entertainment many nights, and soft, jazzy background music otherwise. This is a favorite dinnertime spot for those celebrating an anniversary or other special event—try to arrive in time to watch the sunset. ⊠ *Soufrière,* ☎ *809/459–7323. AE, DC, MC, V.*

$$$ ✕ **Piton Restaurant and Bar.** Too many cooks spoil the broth? Not here
★   on two terraces—one magically suspended among the trees, the other a spacious rooftop—at the wonderful mountainside Anse Chastanet resort (☞ Lodging, *above*), where the French executive chef, Jacky Rioux, works with a St. Lucian maestro to invent sublime variations on local dishes. The menus might include a creamed conch soup *en croute* (with a latticed puff-pastry lid), roast grouper stuffed with lobster mousse, dolphinfish poached in coconut milk with a lime sauce, and—the best local food joke you'll ever taste—"St. Lucian apple pie," made not with apples but with candied, spiced christophines and served with passion-fruit ice cream. Between them, these chefs cater to every culinary fantasy. Be prepared to hike up a couple of dozen stairs to get to the restaurant. ⊠ *Anse Chastanet, 2 mi north of Soufrière,* ☎ *809/459–7000. AE, DC, MC, V.*

$$ ✕ **Beach Restaurant and Bar.** This open-air lunch spot on the beach at the Anse Chastanet resort (☞ Lodging, *above*) is the perfect place to break from a day of diving, boating, or sunbathing. The West Indian cuisine is delicious, and many specialties are prepared right before your eyes on a barbecue grill. The *rotis* (Caribbean-style turnovers) here are the best on the island, served with homemade mango chutney you could eat by the jar. Try also the island pepper pot—pork, beef, or lamb simmered for many hours with local veggies and spices; or a good old tuna melt in case you're homesick. Dessert always features an unusual flavor of ice cream. There's always a young and lively crowd here, and although the restaurant caters mostly to the resort's guests, everyone is quite welcome. Mainly, lunch is served; but on Tuesday and Friday nights, the beach barbecue/Creole buffet is very popular. ⊠ *Anse Chastanet, Soufrière,* ☎ *809/459–7000. AE, DC, MC, V.*

$$ ✕ **Still Plantation.** For visitors to Diamond Falls, lunching at the Still is a good option. The two dining rooms in this attractive restaurant seat up to 400 people, so it is a popular stop for tour groups and cruise passengers. The emphasis is on Creole cuisine using local foods—christophines, breadfruits, yams, callaloo—and seafood, but there are also pork chops and beef dishes. All fruits and vegetables used in the restaurant are produced organically on the estate. ⊠ *Soufrière,* ☎ *809/459–5179. MC, V.*

$–$$ ✕ **Bang . . . between the Pitons.** The eccentric Brit Colin Tennant (a.k.a. Lord Glenconner), founder of the glamorous hideaway island of Mustique, came to St. Lucia to open his dream resort between the Pitons, over which he lost control (it's a long story). The resort became Jalousie Plantation, but Tennant stayed on to open this wickedly cute spoof on a Jamaican jerk joint, with ice-cream-colored paintwork, assorted wooden chairs and cushion-strewn booths, a cerise velvet-draped stage for music, and a buzz like the early days of Mustique—when Jagger was young, but beware—this place closes at whim. ⊠ *On waterfront next to Jalousie Plantation, south of Soufrière,* ☎ *809/459–7864. No credit cards.*

$ ✕ **Camilla's.** Tiny, second-floor Camilla's is pretty in pink, somewhat under-ventilated on a hot night (apart from the two balcony tables), but friendly as anything. The menu is admirably simple and all local—you can have today's catch curried, Creole-style, or grilled with lemon sauce; there's barbecue chicken with garlic sauce and fries; or lobster salad. There's also a list of tropical cocktails bigger than the entire restaurant! ⊠ *12 Boulevard St., Soufrière,* ☎ *809/459–5379. AE.*

## Beaches

Beaches are all public, and many are flanked by hotels, where you can rent water-sports equipment and have a rum punch. On the other hand, some are difficult to reach because they abut resort property. There are also secluded beaches, accessible only by water, to which hotels can arrange boat trips. Don't swim along the windward (east) coast; the Atlantic waters are rough and sometimes dangerous.

**Anse Chastanet.** At the resort of the same name, just north of Soufrière, this palm-studded, gray-sand beach has a backdrop of green hills, brightly painted fishing skiffs bobbing at anchor, and the island's best reefs for snorkeling and diving. The wooden gazebos of the hotel are nestled among the palms, with a dive shop, restaurant, and bar on the beach (☞ Dining and Lodging, *above*). **Anse Cochon.** An uncrowded cove south of Anse-la-Raye, this black-sand beach is most easily reached by boat. The waters are superb for swimming and snorkeling. **Anse des Pitons.** South of Soufrière in Jalousie Bay, this black-sand beach sits directly between the Pitons and is accessible through Jalousie Plantation (☞ Lodging, *above*) or by boat; it offers great snorkeling and diving. **Honeymoon Beach.** Just west of Vieux Fort, this is a sandy escape. **Pigeon Point.** Part of the Pigeon Island National Historic Park (⊠ E.C.$10), Pigeon Point has a small beach and a restaurant; it's a great place for picnicking and swimming. **Reduit Beach.** A long stretch of beige sand next to Rodney Bay is home to the Rex St. Lucian—which offers numerous water sports—and the luxurious Royal St. Lucian. Many feel Reduit (pronounced *red–wee*) is the finest beach on the island. **Vieux Fort.** At the southernmost tip of St. Lucia, Vieux Fort has a long secluded stretch of white sand and waters protected by reefs.

## Outdoor Activities and Sports

Most hotels offer Sunfish, water skis, snorkeling gear, and other non-motorized water-sports equipment free to guests and for a fee to nonguests. Rodney Bay in the north and Marigot Bay on the west coast are the two boating centers. The waters around Anse-la-Raye and Anse Chastanet are the most popular sites for diving and snorkeling.

## Boating

Bareboat or crewed yachts are available for charter through **Destination St. Lucia Ltd.** (✉ Rodney Bay, ☎ 809/453–8531), **Moorings Yacht Charter** (✉ Marigot Bay, ☎ 809/451–4357 or 800/535–7289), **Sunsail Stevens** (✉ Rodney Bay, ☎ 809/452–8648), and **Trade Wind Yacht Charters** (✉ Rodney Bay, ☎ 809/452–8424).

## Deep-Sea Fishing

Among the sea creatures in these waters are dolphinfish, Spanish mackerel, barracuda, kingfish, and white marlin. For half- or full-day fishing excursions, contact **Captain Mike's** (✉ Vigie Bay Marina, ☎ 809/452–0216 or 809/452–7044) or **Mako Watersports** (✉ Rodney Bay Marina, ☎ 809/452–0412).

## Fitness Centers

If your resort lacks the kind of equipment you'd expect for what you're paying—and many do—try the **St. Lucia Racquet Club** (✉ Club St. Lucia, Cap Estate, ☎ 809/450–0551), which has Nautilus equipment, exercise machines, and aerobics and step classes. It's the best gym on the island. **Body Inc.** (✉ Gablewoods Mall, ☎ 809/451–9744) is a well-equipped gym and aerobics studio. Day passes are also available to **Jalousie Plantation** (✉ Soufrière, ☎ 809/459–7666) and **LeSPORT** (✉ Cap Estate, ☎ 809/450–8551), which have excellent spa facilities.

## Golf

The golf courses on St. Lucia are scenic and good fun, but they're not professional caliber.

**Sandals St. Lucia** (✉ La Toc Rd., Castries, ☎ 809/452–3081) has a nine-hole course for guests. Greens fees are $15–$20 for 18 holes, club rental an additional $10, and a caddy is required. **St. Lucia Golf Club** (✉ Cap Estate, ☎ 809/452–8523) is the island's only golf course (nine holes) open to the public. A $49.50 package includes 18 holes of golf, cart, and club rental.

## Hiking

The island is laced with trails, but you should not attempt the challenging peaks on your own. Your hotel, the tourist board, or the **Forest and Land Department** (☎ 809/450–2231 or 809/450–2078) can give you information about finding a guide. The **St. Lucia National Trust** (☎ 809/452–5005), established to preserve the island's natural and cultural heritage, offers hiking tours to several areas, including Pigeon Island, the Maria Islands, and Fregate Island. Full-day excursions, including lunch, cost about $40 per person and are available through hotels or ground tour operators.

## Horseback Riding

For trail rides and excursions, contact **International Riding Stables** (✉ Gros Islet, ☎ 809/452–8138), **Jalousie Plantation** (✉ Soufrière, ☎ 809/459–7666), **North Point Riding Stables** (✉ Cap Estate, ☎ 809/450–8853), or **Trim's Riding School** (✉ Cas-en-Bas, ☎ 809/452–8273). The cost is about $30 per half hour.

## Jogging

Jog on the beach by yourself or team up with the **Roadbusters** (Jimmy James at ☎ 809/452–5112 or evenings at 809/452–4790). They meet near Vigie Field Tuesday and Thursday evenings and Sunday mornings.

## Parasailing

Contact the **Rex St. Lucian** hotel (✉ Rodney Bay, ☎ 809/452–8351).

## Scuba Diving

**Scuba St. Lucia** (☎ 809/459–7355) is a PADI five-star training facility, with a dive shop at Anse Chastanet (one of the most highly regarded dive sites anywhere) and at the Rex St. Lucian hotel. Daily beach and boat dives, resort courses, underwater photography, and day trips are offered. Dive trips can also be arranged through **Buddies Scuba** (✉ Vigie Marina, Castries, ☎ 809/452–5288), **Dive Jalousie** (✉ Soufrière, ☎ 809/459–7666), **Dolphin Divers** (✉ Rodney Bay Marina, ☎ 809/452–9485), the **Moorings Scuba Centre** (✉ Marigot Bay, ☎ 809/451–4357), and **Windjammer Diving** (✉ Castries, ☎ 809/452–0913).

## Sea and Snorkeling Excursions

Several yachts take passengers on day sails to Soufrière and the Pitons for about $70 per person. From Vigie Cove, Castries, sail on the 140-foot **Brig Unicorn** (☎ 809/452–6811), used in the filming of the TV miniseries *Roots*; the 56-foot catamarans **Endless Summer I** and **II** (☎ 809/450–8651); **Surf Queen** (☎ 809/452–8232), a trimaran; and **Calypso Queen** (☎ 809/452–8232), a motor yacht. From Pigeon Island, Rodney Bay, sail on a 56-foot luxury cruiser, the **MV Vigie** (☎ 809/452–8232).

Sea and snorkeling excursions can be arranged through **Mako Watersports** (☎ 809/452–0412), **Captain Mike's** (☎ 809/452–0216 or 809/452–7044), or through your hotel.

## Spectator Sports

Cricket and soccer, the two national pastimes, are played at Mindoo Philip Park in Marchand, 2 miles east of Castries. The **St. Lucia Racquet Club** (☎ 809/450–0551), which hosted the Davis Cup in 1994, is the site of regional tennis events, the most important being the St. Lucian Open in early December. Contact the tourist board (☎ 809/452–4094) for specific information regarding schedules.

## Squash

**Jalousie Plantation** (✉ Soufrière, ☎ 809/459–7666) has one court available to nonguests. **St. Lucia Racquet Club** (✉ adjacent to Club St. Lucia, Cap Estate, ☎ 809/450–0551) has a court and a pro who gives lessons and holds clinics; it is not air-conditioned. **St. Lucia Yacht Club** (✉ Rodney Bay, ☎ 809/452–8350), at the north end of the island, has one court.

## Tennis

**Jalousie Plantation** (✉ Soufrière, ☎ 809/459–7666) has four lighted courts open to nonguests for a $20-per-hour fee. **St. Lucia Racquet Club** (✉ adjacent to Club St. Lucia, ☎ 809/450–0551) is one of the top tennis facilities in the Caribbean—probably the best in the Lesser Antilles. Apart from hosting many tour events, its seven flood-lit courts are in perfect shape, the pro shop is extensive, and the staff knowledgeable.

## Waterskiing

Contact **Waves** (✉ Choc Beach, ☎ 809/451–3000). Rentals are also available at some hotels.

## Windsurfing

Most of the major resorts have Windsurfers and instruction available and will accommodate nonguests for a fee. Reduit Beach and Vieux Fort have the best wind; in the fall, from August to October, the wind loses strength island-wide. **Island Windsurfing Ltd.** (✉ Anse de Sables Beach, Vieux Fort, ☎ 809/454–7400) offers board hire and instruction. The **Rex St. Lucian hotel** (✉ Rodney Bay, ☎ 809/452–8351) is the local agent for Mistral Windsurfers. Also contact **Marigot Bay Resort** (⊠ Marigot Bay, ☎ 809/453–4357).

# Shopping

As tourism is increasing in St. Lucia, so are the options for shopping. The island's best-known products are the unique hand-silk-screened and hand-printed designs of Bagshaw Studios, which are designed, printed, and sold only on St. Lucia. You can also bring home native-made wood carvings, pottery, straw hats and baskets, and locally grown cocoa, coffee, and spices.

## Shopping Areas

In **Castries,** the market and vendor's arcade are well worth a visit. William Peter Boulevard, the capital's main shopping street, is where the locals shop. You can find many of the same items at craft stands and at gift shops at virtually every resort.

Die-hard shoppers will be happy at the duty-free shops at **Pointe Seraphine,** a Spanish-style complex by the harbor, where 23 shops sell designer perfumes, china and crystal, jewelry, watches, leather goods, liquor, and cigarettes. Native crafts are also sold in the shopping center. Be sure to bring your passport and airline ticket to get duty-free prices.

**Gablewoods Mall** (⊠ Gros Islet Hwy., north of Castries) has about 35 shops selling groceries, spirits and wines, jewelry, clothing, local crafts, foreign newspapers, books, music, and household goods.

## Good Buys

### DUTY-FREE

Pointe Seraphine and Hewanorra International Airport are the only places on the island where you can purchase goods duty-free. In Pointe Seraphine, look for:

**Images** (☎ 809/452–6883) stocks designer perfumes. **Little Switzerland** (☎ 809/452–7587) carries fine china and crystal. **Meli's Boutique** (☎ 809/452–7587) has leather handbags, jewelry, crystal, and perfumes. **A Touch of Class** (☎ 809/452–7443) is the place for Caribbean literature and local souvenirs.

### FABRICS AND CLOTHING

**Bagshaw Studios** (⊠ La Toc Rd., La Toc Bay, ☎ 809/452–7570; also at Vigie Airport, Pointe Seraphine, and Marigot Bay) sells silk-screened fabrics, clothing, and table linens in wildly tropical colors and intricate designs that are instantly recognizable. Bagshaw's products make the most distinctive St. Lucian gifts, since they are not exported. **Batik Studio** (⊠ Humming Bird Beach Resort, Soufrière, ☎ 809/459–7232) offers superb sarongs, scarves, and wall panels created by Joan Alexander, the proprietress of the hotel. **Caribelle Batik** (⊠ Old Victoria Rd., the Morne, Castries, ☎ 809/452–3785) creates batik clothing and wall hangings; visitors are welcome to watch the craftspeople at work. **Sea Island Cotton Co.** (⊠ Bridge St., Castries, ☎ 809/452–3257 and Gablewoods Mall ☎ 809/452–3674) sells quality T-shirts, Caribelle Batik clothing, and other resort wear, as well as souvenir items.

### MUSIC

Take home a cassette recording of the band you've been dancing to every night from **Jeremies** (⊠ 83 Brazil St., Castries, ☎ 809/452–5079). **Sights 'n Sounds** (⊠ 46 Micoud St., Castries, ☎ 809/451–9600; and Gablewoods Mall, ☎ 809/451–7300) sells recorded music at two locations.

NATIVE CRAFTS

**Artsibit Gallery** (✉ corner Brazil and Mongiraud Sts., ☎ 809/452–7865) exhibits and sells artwork by top St. Lucian artists. **Choiseul Art & Craft Centre** (✉ La Fargue, ☎ 809/454–3226) stands among the remnants of the last Carib presence in St. Lucia. The center has a huge selection of handmade Amerindian basketware and pottery, as well as sculpture and bas-reliefs carved from local woods. The quality is excellent, and prices are reasonable. **Eudovic Art Studio** (✉ Morne Fortune, ☎ 809/452–2747) is a workshop and studio where trays, masks, and figures carved from local mahogany, red cedar, and eucalyptus wood are made, displayed, and sold. **Made in St. Lucia** (✉ Gablewoods Mall, ☎ 809/453–2788) is a fabulous shop that sells only items that are made on the island of St. Lucia. You'll find sandals, shirts, hot sauces, costume jewelry, carved wooden objects, steel drums, clay cooking pots, original art, and other quality items at fair prices. **Noah's Arkade** (✉ Jeremie St., Castries, and Pointe Seraphine, ☎ 809/452–2523) has hammocks, wood carvings, and straw mats, baskets, and hats. Also for sale are island-inspired books and maps of St. Lucia. **Vendor's Arcade** (✉ Jeremie St., Castries), across from the market, is a maze of stalls and booths where you'll find handmade wood carvings and other handicrafts among the T-shirts and costume jewelry.

SPICES

At the **market** in Castries, local vendor's sell beautiful fruits and vegetables which, alas, you can't import to the United States. But you can bring home the spices, such as cocoa, turmeric, ginger, peppercorns, cinnamon, nutmeg, mace, and vanilla essence. You can find a variety of bottled hot pepper sauces for sale. Prices are a fraction of what you'd spend in the supermarket back home.

STAMPS

The **St. Lucia Philatelic Bureau,** at the General Post Office (✉ Bridge St., Castries, ☎ 809/452–2671) supplies collectors and stamp dealers throughout the world with the beautiful and sought-after commemoratives issued by the St. Lucia government.

# Nightlife and the Arts

## Nightlife

The large, all-inclusive hotels feature nightly entertainment—island music, calypso singers, and steel-band jump-ups, as well as disco, karaoke, and even talent shows and toga parties. Many offer entertainment packages, including dinner, to nonguests.

GROS ISLET

On Friday nights, sleepy Gros Islet becomes sin city, like Bourbon Street during Mardi Gras, as the entire village is transformed into a street fair. At the far end of the street, mammoth stereos loudly beat out sounds as locals and strangers let their hair down. It can get rowdy, so it's best to travel in a group and keep your wits about you. But then Friday night is *the* night to jump. Worried about crashing the party? Just roll down your window and ask: You'll know if you're invited.

**Banana Split** (✉ St. George's St., ☎ 809/450–8125) offers entertainment and special theme nights, with a perpetual "spring break" atmosphere. **The Captain's Cellar** (✉ Pigeon Island, ☎ 809/450–0253) is a cozy pub that features live jazz on weekends. **Golden Apple** (✉ Grande Rivière, ☎ 809/450–0634), a lively restaurant and bar with a party atmosphere, is probably one of the best spots for meeting locals.

Another Friday-night street scene and a popular alternate venue for liming can be found just before you enter Marigot Bay. The music is supplied by **J. J.'s** (☎ 809/451–4076), and the popular fare is curried goat. More and more locals are choosing to come here instead of the Gros Islet happening, which is becoming more touristy.

A number of nightspots are at Rodney Bay, and they jump on weekends. Most have a cover charge of E.C.$15–$20.

**A-Pub** (☎ 809/452–8725) is a lounge in an A-frame building overlooking Rodney Bay. **Bistro** (☎ 809/452–9494) is where young boaters tie up for drinks, chess, darts, and backgammon. **Capone's** (☎ 809/452–0284) is an art deco place right out of the Roaring '20s, with a player piano and rum drinks. **Charthouse** (☎ 809/452–8115) has a popular bar, jazz on stereo, and live music on Saturday. **Green Parrot** (✉ The Morne, ☎ 809/452–3399) is in a class all by itself. Chef Harry Edwards hosts the floor show, which features limbo dancers—Harry has been known to shimmy under the pole himself. There are also belly dancers. Dress semiformally for this great fun. **Indies** (☎ 809/452–0727) is a disco where you can dance to Caribbean and international rhythms Tuesdays through Saturdays from 10 PM on; dress is casual, though smart—no hats or sandals; no shorts or sleeveless shirts for men. **The Lime** (☎ 809/452–0761) is a particular favorite of the locals, with dance music and local entertainment every night but Tuesdays.

## The Arts

**Derek Walcott Theatre.** This small, open-air theater in the ruins of an old Cap Estate plantation house seats just 200 people for monthly productions of music, dance, and drama, as well as Sunday Brunch programs. The Trinidad Theatre Workshop also presents an annual performance here. For schedule and ticket information, contact the Great House Restaurant (✉ Cap Estate, ☎ 809/450–0551 or 809/450–0450, FAX 809/450–0451).

# Exploring St. Lucia

One road encircles the island, so it's impossible to get lost. The road, however, snakes through mountains with hairpin turns, sheer drops, dizzying elevations, and is often full of potholes. It takes about three hours to drive the whole loop from Castries, down the West Coast Road, back up the East Coast, and across the Barre de l'Isle Ridge. And that's with no stops. Even under ideal conditions, it's a tiring drive, so plan to stop several times along the way.

The West Coast Road from Castries to Soufrière has undergone a widening and major face-lift that began in 1992 and was completed in 1995. It still has steep hills and sharp turns, but it's pothole-free (so far), well-marked, and incredibly scenic. South of Castries, the road climbs Morne Fortune, cuts through a huge banana plantation (more than 127 different varieties of bananas, often called "figs," are grown on the island), and passes by small fishing communities. The area just north of Soufrière is the island's breadbasket where most of the mangoes, breadfruit, tomatoes, limes, and oranges are grown. In the mountainous region, you'll see Mt. Parasol and Mt. Gimie (pronounced "Jimmy"), St. Lucia's highest peak, which rises to 3,117 feet. As you approach Soufrière, you'll have several opportunities for spectacular views of the Pitons. The landscape changes dramatically as you travel from the Pitons to modern Hewanorra International Airport on the southeast tip of the island. The terrain starts with steep mountainside with dense vegetation, progresses to undulating hillsides that form a backdrop for tiny coastal fishing villages, and finally the small hills become rather flat. Anyone arriving at Hewanorra and staying at a resort near Soufrière will have a chance to travel along the South Coast Road, a nonstop journey of about an hour. A road leads up the East Coast from Vieux Fort through the villages of Micoud and Dennery on the Atlantic coast. Don't be fooled by the road's smooth start; it gets bumpier and bumpier as you progress and twists and turns through mountains and villages. The reward, however, is an opportunity to see some absolutely breathtaking scenery. The fierce Atlantic pounds against rocky cliffs, and dense vegetation covers the mountainsides—mostly acres and acres of bananas and coconut palms. Anyone who arrives at Hewanorra and stays at a resort near Castries will get two opportunities—coming and going—to travel along the East Coast Road, a 90-minute, 33-mile, stomach-churning journey each way. The area north of Castries is the most developed part of the island and is easy and safe to navigate. Of far more interest to the hedonist than to the historian, it features some of the island's best beaches and resort hotels. One of the island's most important historical sites, however, is at the island's northwestern tip.

*Numbers in the margin correspond to points of interest on the St. Lucia map.*

SIGHTS TO SEE

**❹ Anse-la-Raye.** The beach here is a colorful sight, with fishing nets hanging on poles to dry and brightly painted fishing boats bobbing in the water. The fishermen of Anse-la-Raye still make canoes by the old-fashioned method of burning out the center of a log.

**⓱ Barre de l'Isle Forest Reserve.** Barre de l'Isle Ridge divides the eastern and western halves of St. Lucia. A mile-long trail cuts through the Forest Reserve; four lookout points provide panoramic views of the island. Visible in the distance are Mount Gimie, the Caribbean Sea and the Atlantic coast, immense green valleys, and tiny east-coast communities. The reserve is about a half hour from Castries. It takes about an hour to walk the trail, and another hour to climb Mt. La Combe ridge. Permission of the Forest & Lands Department (☎ 809/450–2231 or 809/450–2078) is required to access the trail; a naturalist or forest officer guide will accompany you.

**❶ Castries.** On the northwest coast, Castries is a busy commercial city of about 60,000 on the shore of a sheltered bay surrounded dramatically by green Morne Fortune. The city's charm lies entirely in its liveliness, since practically all the colorful old colonial buildings were razed by four great fires between 1796 and 1948. Ships carrying bananas, coconut, cocoa, mace, nutmeg, and citrus fruits for export leave from **Castries Harbour,** one of the busiest ports in the Caribbean.

Cruise ships dock across the harbor at **Pointe Seraphine,** about a 20-minute walk or short cab ride from the city center—or you can take the shuttle boat that operates when ships are in port. Spanish-style Pointe Seraphine has 33 mostly upscale duty-free shops, a tourist information center where you can get island maps, a taxi stand, and car-rental agencies. This is the starting point for many island tours.

**Derek Walcott Square** is a green oasis ringed by Brazil, Laborie, Micoud, and Bourbon streets. Formerly Columbus Square, it was renamed in 1993 after St. Lucian poet Derek Walcott—one of two Nobel laureates from the island, the other being the late economist Sir Arthur Lewis. Some of the 19th-century buildings that managed to survive fire, winds, and rains can be seen on Brazil Street, the southern border of the square. At the corner of Laborie and Micoud streets there is a 400-year-old **saman tree.** A favorite local story is of the English botanist who came to St. Lucia many years ago to catalog the flora. Awestruck by this huge old tree, she asked a passerby what it was. "Massav," he replied, and she gratefully jotted that down in her notebook, unaware that "massav" is patois for "I don't know." Directly across the street is the Roman Catholic **Cathedral of the Immaculate Conception,** which was built in 1897.

At the corner of Jeremie and Peynier streets, a new, clean, open-air produce **market** with a brilliant orange roof recently opened and is full of excitement and bustle. The market is open every day but is most lively on Friday and Saturday mornings, when farmers bring their produce to town.

Just south of downtown, next to Sandals St. Lucia resort, the **Bagshaw Studios** combines the opportunity to see how original tropical prints are processed into colorful silk-screened fabrics and to shop for fashions and household items created on site. ⊠ *La Toc Rd., La Toc Bay,* ☎ *809/452–7570.* ⊠ *Free.* ☉ *Weekdays 8:30–5, Sat. 8:30–4, Sun. 10–1; weekend hours are extended if a cruiseship is in port.*

NEED A BREAK?    Stop for refreshment at **Chez Paul** (⊠ Derek Walcott Sq., Castries, ☎ 809/452-3022), set in the courtyard of one of the last remaining authentic colonial buildings in Castries.

⓫ **Choiseul.** This coastal town, in the southwest of the island, is home to wood-carving and pottery shops. At the turn of the road past the Anglican Church, built in 1846, a bridge crosses the River Dorée, so named because the riverbed is blanketed with fool's gold. In La Fargue, just to the south, the **Choiseul Art & Craft Centre** (☎ 809/459–3226) sells superb traditional Carib handicrafts, including pottery, wickerwork, and braided khuskhus grass mats and baskets.

❻ **Diamond Mineral Baths and Botanical Gardens.** Louis XIV provided funds in 1713 for the construction of these baths, fed by an underground flow of water from the sulfur springs, for his troops to "fortify them against the St. Lucian climate." It is claimed that Josephine Bonaparte bathed in the original bath when she was a young girl visiting her father's plantation in Soufrière. During the Brigand's War, just after the French Revolution, the baths were destroyed. The site was excavated in 1932, and two of the baths were restored. Today, you can see the waterfall and walk through the beautifully kept botanical gardens before slipping into your swimsuit for a dip in the steaming curative waters. ⊠ *Soufrière Estate, Soufrière,* ☎ *809/452–4759 or 809/454–7565.* ⊠ *E.C.$5.* ☉ *Daily 10–5.*

⓰ **Errard Plantation.** Near the village of Dennery, this family-operated cocoa plantation provides an excellent opportunity to see a working agricultural estate. Tours can be arranged by your hotel or booked through a tour guide service.

❷ **Fort Charlotte.** Begun in 1764 by the French as the *Citadelle du Morne Fortune,* Fort Charlotte was completed after 20 years of battling and changing hands. Its old barracks and batteries have now been converted to government buildings and local educational facilities, but you can drive around and look at the remains, including redoubts, a guardroom, stables, and cells. At the end of the road you can also walk up to the Inniskilling Monument, a tribute to one of the most famous battles, fought in 1796, when the 27th Foot Royal Inniskilling Fusiliers wrested the Hill of Good Fortune from the French. At the Military Cemetery, which was first used in 1782, faint inscriptions on the tombstones tell the tales of the French and English soldiers who died here. Six former governors of the island are buried here, as well. From this vantage point on the top of Morne Fortune, you'll see Martinique to the north and the twin peaks of the Pitons to the south.

**⑮ Fregate Island Nature Reserve.** A mile-long trail encircles the preserve, which you reach from the small fishing village of Praslin. A natural promontory provides a lookout where you can view the two small islets, Fregate Major and Fregate Minor, and—with luck—the migratory frigate birds that nest here in the summer. Guided tours, which include a ride in an Amerindian-style canoe to a tiny island for a picnic lunch and swim, are arranged through the St. Lucia National Trust (⊠ Box 595, Castries, ☎ 809/452–5005 or 809/453–1495, FAX 809/453–2791).

**⑲ Gros Islet.** North of the lagoon, Gros Islet (pronounced "grow zeelay") is a quiet little fishing village. But on Friday nights, Gros Islet springs to life with a wild and raucous street festival ("jump up") to which everyone is invited (☞ Nightlife, *above*).

**⑫ Laborie.** This is the prototypical St. Lucian fishing village, little changed over the centuries. You can stop to buy some local bread and fresh fish.

**⑭ Maria Islands Nature Reserve.** Two tiny islands in the Atlantic, off the southeast coast, comprise the reserve, which has its own interpretive center. The 25-acre Maria Major and 4-acre Maria Minor, its little sister, are inhabited by rare species of lizards and snakes that share their home with frigate birds, terns, doves, and other wildlife. There's a small private beach for swimming and snorkeling; bring a picnic. ⊠ *Moule à Chique,* ☎ *809/454–5014.* ☎ *E.C.$3 Wed.–Sat.; E.C.$.50 Sun.* ☉ *Wed.–Sun. 9:30–5.*

**③ Marigot Bay.** A few miles south of Castries, this is one of the most beautiful natural harbors in the Caribbean. In 1778, British admiral Samuel Barrington sailed into this secluded bay within a bay and covered his ships with palm fronds to hide them from the French. Today, this resort community is a great favorite of yachtspeople. Parts of the movie *Doctor Doolittle* were filmed here more than 30 years ago. You can charter a yacht, swim, snorkel, or simply mingle with the yachting crowd at one of the bars. A 24-hour ferry connects the two sides of the bay.

NEED A BREAK? Stop for a rum punch and lunch and soak up the atmosphere at the open-air **Café Paradis** (⊠ Marigot Beach Club, Hurricane Hole, Marigot, ☎ 809/451–4974), a happy haunt of boaters.

**⑱ Marquis Estate.** If you want a close-up of a working plantation and are willing to get a little wet and muddy in the process, you can tour the island's largest one. The 600-acre Marquis Estate (☎ 809/452–3762) is located at Marquis Bay, on the north Atlantic coast. The estate began as a sugar plantation. Now it produces bananas and copra (dried coconut processed for oil) for export, as well as a number of other tropical fruits and vegetables for local consumption. St. Lucia Representative Services Ltd. (☞ Guided Tours, *below*) conducts the tour, and will pick you up at your hotel in an air-conditioned bus. You may tour the estate by bus or by horseback, and a river ride to the coast and lunch at the plantation house is included. Self-drive or private taxi tours are not permitted. Wear your most casual clothes, and be prepared to rough it.

**⑨ Morne Coubaril Estate.** This 250-acre coconut and cocoa plantation, the first major estate established in St. Lucia, has a rich French history that dates back to 1713, when Crown land was granted to three St. Lucian brothers by King Louis IV. Authentic 18th-century plantation life is explained, as a guide escorts you along an original mule-carriage pathway and through a typical reconstructed "village." The tropical flowers and foliage are thick and beautiful. You'll see how cocoa, copra, and manioc were processed in the days before mechanization. This is a fascinating half-hour ecotour. There's a small gift shop, where you can purchase freshly made cocoa, straw items, and hand-carved wooden pieces. If you wish to have lunch, a Creole buffet is available at The Pitt for E.C.$25 per person. ⌧ *Soufrière*, ☎ *809/459–7340*. ▧ *E.C.$15.* ☉ *Daily 9–5.*

**Morne Fortune.** Just to the south of Castries, Morne Fortune forms a striking backdrop for the capital. With a name that translates to "Hill of Good Luck," this mountain has, ironically, seen more than its share of bad luck over the years—including devastating hurricanes and those four fires that leveled Castries. The drive to Morne Fortune from Castries will take you past the **Government House,** on Government House Road, the official residence of the governor-general of St. Lucia and one of the island's few remaining examples of Victorian architecture.

**㉑ Pigeon Island.** Jutting out on the northwest coast, Pigeon Island is now connected to the mainland by a causeway that was built several years back. Tales are told of the pirate Jambe de Bois (Wooden Leg), who used to hide out here. This 44-acre hilltop island, a strategic point during the struggles for control of St. Lucia, is now a national landmark, with a small beach with calm waters for swimming and snorkeling, restaurants, and picnic areas. Scattered around the grounds are ruins of barracks, batteries, and garrisons dating from 18th-century French and English battles. In the Interpretation Centre, a multimedia display unfolds the ecological and historical significance of this island. ⌧ *Pigeon Island, St. Lucia National Trust,* ☎ *809/450–8167 or 809/452–5005,* ℻ *809/453–2791.* ▧ *E.C.$10.* ☉ *Daily 9–5.*

**❽ The Pitons.** These incredible mountains have become the symbol of St. Lucia. For the best land view, take the road south out of Soufrière for a magnificent look at these twin peaks, which rise precipitously out of the azure Caribbean. The perfectly shaped pyramidal cones, covered with thick tropical vegetation, were formed by lava from a volcanic eruption 30 million to 40 million years ago. They are not identical twins since—confusingly—Petit Piton, at 2,619 feet, is rather taller than Gros Piton (2,461 feet), though "Gros" is, indeed, broader. Gros Piton is currently the only one recommended to climb, though the way up even the shorter Piton is one very tough trek and requires the permission of the Forest and Lands Department (☎ 809/450–2231 or 809/450–2078) and a knowledgeable guide.

**❼ Rain Forest.** The Edmund Forest Reserve, part of the dense tropical rain forest that covers about 10% of the island, is most easily accessible from the east of Soufrière on the road to Fond St. Jacques. A trek through the lush landscape can take from three hours to a full day. The permission of the Forest & Lands Department (☎ 809/452–2231 or 809/452–2078) is required to access the trails, and the department provides a naturalist or forest officer guide. You'll also need plenty of stamina. The views of mountains, valleys, and the sea beyond are spectacular. It takes an hour or so to reach the forest from the north end of the island.

**❷⓪ Rodney Bay.** About 15 minutes north of Castries, the body of water named for Admiral Rodney is an 80-acre, man-made lagoon surrounded by hotels and many popular restaurants. The Rex St. Lucian and Royal St. Lucian hotels are in this area, as is the Rodney Bay Marina—one of the Caribbean's premier water-sports centers. The Rodney Bay Ferry makes the trip between the marina and the shopping complex hourly, 9–4, for $4 round-trip.

**⑤ Soufrière.** The town of Soufrière, which dates from the mid-18th century, was the French colonial capital. It was named for the nearby volcano and has a population of about 9,000 people. The harbor is the deepest on the island, accommodating smaller cruise ships that nose right up to the wharf. A nearby jetty contains an excellent small-crafts center. The **Soufrière Tourist Information Centre** (⊠ Bay St., ☎ 809/459–7200) provides information about area attractions.

**⑩ La Soufrière Drive-in Volcano.** Your nose will note this volcano's sulfur springs—more than 20 pools of black, belching, smelly, sulfurous waters and multicolored sulfur and assorted other mineral deposits baking and steaming on the surface. Actually, you don't drive in; you walk—behind your guide, whose service is included in admission—around a fault in the substratum rock, which makes for a fascinating 20-minute experience, but one that can be stinky on a hot day. ⊠ *Bay St., Soufrière,* ☎ *809/459–5500.* ☜ *E.C.$3.* ☉ *Daily 9–5.*

**⑬ Vieux Fort.** St. Lucia's second-largest city is the location of Hewanorra International Airport. From the **Moule à Chique Peninsula,** the southernmost tip of the island, you can see all of St. Lucia to the north and St. Vincent 21 miles south. Looking straight down, you can see where the clear waters of the Caribbean blend with the bluer Atlantic waters.

NEED A
BREAK?

**Sandy Beach Restaurant and Bar** (⊠ Vieux Fort, ☎ 809/454–7416) is right on the beach and specializes in light lunches. It's a popular place for families on weekends and holidays.

## St. Lucia A to Z

### Arriving and Departing

BY PLANE

There are two airports on the island. Wide-body planes use modern Hewanorra International Airport, on the southern tip of the island. Vigie Field, a small airport in Castries, services interisland and charter flights.

**American** (☎ 809/454–6777 or 800/433–7300) has nonstop service to Hewanorra from New York on Saturday and Sunday and daily service through San Juan from New York and most major other U.S. cities. **American Eagle** flights from San Juan land at Vigie Field. **Air Canada** (☎ 809/452–3051 or 800/776–3000; in Canada, 800/268–7240) has direct weekend service from Toronto. **British Airways** (☎ 809/452–3951 or 0181/897–4000) has direct service from London to St. Lucia. **BWIA** (☎ 809/452–3778 or 800/327–7401) has direct service from Miami, New York, and London. **Helenair** (☎ 809/452–7196) flies into Vigie from Grenada, St. Vincent, and other islands in the eastern Caribbean. **LIAT** (☎ 809/452–3051 or 809/462–0701) services the island with small island-hoppers that fly into Vigie, linking St. Lucia with Barbados, Trinidad, Antigua, Martinique, Dominica, Guadeloupe, and other islands.

FROM THE AIRPORT

Taxis are unmetered, and the government's list of suggested fares is not binding. Negotiate with the driver *before* you get in, and be sure that you both understand whether you've agreed upon E.C. or U.S. dollars. The drive from Hewanorra to Castries takes about 75 minutes and costs about $50. From Vigie Field, the 10–20 minute ride to most resorts in the north costs $10–$15. Many resorts include airport transfers in their rates.

Some visitors to St. Lucia opt for the expensive but quick means of helicopter transportation. The cost for the 15-minute flight from Hewanorra to Castries is $90 per person, including luggage; for the 10-minute flight to Soufrière, it costs $75 per person. There are helipads at Pointe Seraphine, Windjammer Landing, Jalousie Plantation, and several other locations. Contact **Eastern Caribbean Helicopters** (⊠ Pointe Seraphine, ☎ 809/453–6952 or 809/454–7313) or **St. Lucia Helicopters** (⊠ Pointe Seraphine, ☎ 809/453–6950, FAX 809/452–1553).

## Currency
The official currency is the Eastern Caribbean dollar (E.C.$). Figure about E.C.$2.65 to U.S.$1. U.S. dollars are readily accepted, but you'll usually get change in E.C. dollars. Major credit cards and traveler's checks are widely accepted. Prices quoted in this chapter are in U.S. dollars unless indicated otherwise.

## Emergencies
**Police:** ☎ 999. **Fire and Hospital:** ☎ 911. Hospitals with 24-hour emergency rooms are **Victoria Hospital** (⊠ Hospital Rd., Castries, ☎ 809/452–2421), St. Lucia's largest hospital; **St. Jude's Hospital** (⊠ Vieux Fort, ☎ 809/454–7671), a privately endowed hospital run by nuns; **Soufrière Hospital** (☎ 809/459–7258); and **Dennery Hospital** (☎ 809/453–3310). **Pharmacies:** Try **Williams Pharmacy** (⊠ Bridge St., Castries, ☎ 809/452–2797) or **M & C's Drugstore** (⊠ Bridge St., Castries, ☎ 809/452–2811; Gablewoods Mall, Gros Islet Hwy., north of Castries, ☎ 809/451–7808).

## Getting Around
### BUSES
This is an inexpensive and colorful, though not always dependable, means of transportation. There is no published bus schedule, although they run until approximately 10 PM. The fare from Castries to the north end of the island is E.C.$1.50; from Castries to the southern end (Vieux Fort), E.C.$7. Minivans cruise the island and, like taxis, will stop when hailed. You can also catch a minivan in Castries, at the corner of Micoud and Bridge streets.

### CAR RENTALS
Driving in St. Lucia is on the left, British-style, and the roads are often deeply potholed. Almost two-thirds of the island's 500 miles of road are not paved at all; you may wish to think twice about driving.

To rent a car, you must be 25 years or older and hold a valid driver's license and a credit card. You must buy a temporary St. Lucian license either at an airport or at police headquarters (Bridge St., Castries); however, most resorts have a branch office of a major rental agency, which will obtain the temporary license for you. The license costs $12 and is valid for three months. Car-rental rates begin at about $50 per day for a jeep and $75 for a car with standard transmission, with discounts for weekly rentals. Gasoline is expensive: E.C.$6.00 per gallon.

Car-rental agencies include **Avis** (⊠ Pointe Seraphine, ☎ 809/452–2700; Hewanorra, ☎ 809/454–6325; and Vigie, ☎ 809/452–2046), **Budget** (⊠ Castries, ☎ 809/452–0233 or Hewanorra, ☎ 809/454–5311), **Hertz** (⊠ Castries, ☎ 809/452–0679; Hewanorra, ☎ 809/454–9636; or Vigie, ☎ 809/451–7351), **National** (⊠ Castries, ☎ 809/450–8721; Hewanorra ☎ 809/454–6699; or Vigie, ☎ 809/452–3050). Local agencies are **C. T. L. Rent-A-Car** (⊠ Rodney Bay Marina, ☎ 809/452–0732), **Cool Breeze Jeep/Car Rental** (⊠ Hewanorra, ☎ 809/454–7898;

Soufrière, ☎ 809/459–7729), and **S. L. Y.'s Car Rentals** (✉ Castries, ☎ 809/452–2057).

FERRIES

The **Rodney Bay Ferry** (✉ Box 672, Castries, ☎ 809/452–0087, FAX 809/452–8816) has ferry service twice daily from Rodney Bay (right by the Lime restaurant) to Pigeon Island. The round-trip fare is $40 and includes lunch and the entrance fee to Pigeon Island. Snorkel equipment can be rented for $12.

TAXIS

Taxis are always available at the airport, the harbor, and in front of the major hotels, but they are expensive and do not have meters. Determine the fare and the currency being quoted before you get into the cab.

## Guided Tours

BY AIR

**Eastern Caribbean Helicopters** (☎ 809/453–6952) and **St. Lucia Helicopters** (☎ 809/453–6950) provide sightseeing tours of the island. The 10-minute North Island Tour ($45 per person) leaves from Pointe Seraphine, in Castries, and flies up the west coast to Pigeon Island, then back down via the Atlantic coastline. The 20-minute South Island Tour ($80 per person) starts at Pointe Seraphine and circles picturesque Marigot Bay, Soufrière, and the majestic Pitons before returning inland over the volcanic hot springs and tropical rain forest.

BY LAND AND SEA

**Barnards Travel** (✉ Micoud St., Castries, ☎ 809/452–1615) offers a full range of half- and full-day island tours, as well as excursions to Dominica, Martinique, St. Vincent, and the Grenadines. **St. Lucia Representative Services Ltd.** (☎ 809/452–3762) has half- and full-day island tours, as well as excursions to a number of neighboring islands. **Sunlink International** (☎ 809/452–8232) offers a variety of half- and full-day tours, as well as day trip to the Grenadines aboard a 60-foot catamaran. **Taxi drivers** generally know the island and can give you a full tour—and often an excellent one, since government-sponsored training programs were introduced in 1994. Expect to pay $20 per hour plus tip for up to four people.

## Language

The official language is English, but you'll also hear the local French Creole patois.

## Opening and Closing Times

Shops are open weekdays 8 or 8:30–4, Saturday 8–noon. Hotel shops and some mall stores are open Sunday afternoon. Banks are open Monday–Thursday 8–3, Friday 8–5, and, at a few branches in Rodney Bay, Saturdays 9–noon.

## Passports and Visas

U.S., Canadian, and British citizens whose stay does not exceed six months must produce a valid passport (or a birth certificate or other proof of citizenship along with a photo ID) and a return or ongoing ticket.

## Precautions

Bring along insect repellent to ward off mosquitoes and sand flies. Be aware that sea urchins live among the rocks on the coastline; should one's long black spines lodge under your skin, don't try to pull them out. Apply an ammonia-based liquid and the spine will retreat, allowing you to ease it out. Manchineel trees have poisonous fruit and leaves that can cause skin blisters on contact. Even raindrops falling off the trees can cause blisters; these trees are usually marked when on hotel property. Do not swim on the rough Atlantic side of the island.

## Taxes and Service Charges

Hotels and restaurants collect an 8% government tax. Hotels and most restaurants add a 10% service charge. Taxi drivers appreciate a 10% tip; porters and bellhops, 75¢ per bag. The airport departure tax is $11 or E.C.$27.

## Telephones, Electricity, and Mail

The area code for St. Lucia is 809. You can make direct-dial overseas and interisland calls from St. Lucia, and the connections are excellent.

Electric voltage is 220/240 AC, 50 cycles, with a square three-pin plug; American appliances require an adapter and/or transformer. A few hotels have 110 AC voltage capability available to guests.

The General Post Office is on Bridge Street, Castries (☉ Weekdays, 8:30–4). All towns and villages have sub-offices. Postage for airmail letters to the United States, Canada, and Great Britain is E.C.95¢ for up to 1 ounce. Postcards are E.C.75¢ to the United States and Canada, E.C.85¢ to Great Britain.

Courier service is available to and from the island via Federal Express (Box 1255, Castries, ☎ 809/452–1230 or 809/452–1388) and UPS (20 Bridge St., Castries, ☎ 809/452–5898 or 809/452–5428).

## Visitor Information

Contact the **St. Lucia Tourist Board** (✉ in the U.S. and Canada, 820 2nd Ave., 9th floor, New York, NY 10017, ☎ 212/867–2950 or 800/456–3984, FAX 212/370–7867; in the U.K., 421A Finchley Rd., London NW3 6HJ, ☎ 0171/431–4045, FAX 0171/437–7920).

In St. Lucia, the **St. Lucia Tourist Board** is based at the Pointe Seraphine duty-free complex on Castries Harbor (✉ Box 221, Castries, ☎ 809/452–4094 or 809/452–5968, FAX 809/453–1121). The office is open weekdays 8–4:30. There are also offices in downtown Castries (✉ Jeremie St., ☎ 809/452–2479), Soufrière (✉ Bay St., ☎ 809/459–7200), at Vigie Field (☎ 809/452–2595), and at Hewanorra International Airport (☎ 809/454–6644).

# 23 St. Martin/ St. Maarten

**T**HERE ARE FREQUENT NONSTOP FLIGHTS from the United States to St. Martin/St. Maarten, so you don't have to spend half your vacation getting here—a crit-

Updated by
Jonathan Runge

ical advantage if you have only a few days to enjoy the sun. The 37-square-mile island is home to two sovereign nations, St. Maarten (Dutch) and St. Martin (French), so you can experience two cultures for the price of one. However, the Dutch side has lost most of its European flavor.

The island is ideal for people who like to have lots of things to do. Whatever can be done in or on the water—snorkeling, windsurfing, waterskiing—is available here; there is golf and tennis as well. Especially on the French side, there are enough good-quality restaurants for serious diners to try a different one each night, even on a two-week stay. The duty-free shopping is as good as anywhere else in the Caribbean. There's an active nightlife, with discos and casinos. Day trips can be taken by ship or plane to the nearby islands of Anguilla, Saba, St. Eustatius, and St. Barthélemy. There are hotels for every taste and budget—from motel-type units for the package tour trade to some of the most exclusive resorts in the Caribbean. The standard of living is one of the highest in the Caribbean, so the islanders can afford to be honest and to treat visitors as welcome guests. If you wander even slightly off the beaten track, you'll find friendly and opinionated locals willing and eager to share their insider knowledge. Corruption and crime, which had been on the rise, have decreased dramatically in the '90s, thanks to an exemplary cooperative effort between the two governments.

On the negative side, St. Martin/St. Maarten has been thoroughly discovered and exploited; unless you stay in an exclusive resort, you will often find yourself sharing beachfronts with tour groups or conventioneers (the exception being some of the beaches in Terres Basses on the French side). Yes, there is gambling, but the table limits are so low that hard-core gamblers will have a better time gamboling on the beach. As is often the case in the Caribbean, the island infrastructure has not kept pace with development. There are plans to expand marina, airport, and road services, but meanwhile you will probably run into congestion at the airport and seemingly endless traffic on the roads.

In the fall of 1995, Hurricane Luis ripped through the island, causing major damage, but at press time everything was virtually back to normal.

## Lodging

Until recently, the Dutch side commanded all the big, splashy resorts. The casinos are still to be found exclusively on the Dutch side—gambling is illegal on the French side. However, St. Martin is having something of a building boom, especially in the area around Nettlé and Orient bays. All the hotels on the French side have an English-speaking staff. There are also small inns and Mediterranean-style facilities on both sides of the island. Many hotels offer enticing packages and you'll save substantially if you travel off-season; the downside of this is that many hotels and restaurants are closed for recovering from the winter onslaught. In general, the French resorts are more intimate, but what the Dutch properties lack in ambience, they compensate for in clean, functional, comfortable rooms with all the "extras." Most of the larger Dutch resorts feature time-share annexes; the units are often available for rental for those who prefer the condo lifestyle at comparable rates.

Worth noting on the French side is a coalition of seven small inns called Les Hôtels de Charme. They are dedicated to providing "warmth, individual attention, and homey feeling," with rates that range from $ to $$; some include breakfast. The participating hotels are Alizéa, Panoramic Privilege, L'Hoste, Blue Beach, Hotel du Golf, Chez Martine, and the Sunrise Hotel. For information on any of these inns, call 800/468–6796 in the United States or 590/87–33–44 in St. Martin.

As a rule, rooms on the beach or with a sea view command the highest prices. Most properties are EP or CP (the latter usually only in season), though meal plans are sometimes available.

Both sides of the island offer a wide variety of homes, villas, condominiums, and housekeeping apartments. Information in the United States can be obtained through **WIMCO** (⌧ Box 1461, Newport, RI 02840, ☎ 800/932–3222), **Caribbean Home Rentals** (⌧ Box 710, Palm Beach, FL 33480, ☎ 407/833–4454), **Jane Condon Corp.** (⌧ 211 E. 43rd St., New York, NY 10017, ☎ 212/986–4373), and **St. Maarten Villas** (⌧ 707 Broad Hollow Rd., Farmingdale, NY 11735, ☎ 516/249–4940). On the island, contact **Carimo** (☎ 590/87–57–58), which has some truly fabulous villas for rent in the tony and desirable Terres Basses section of the island, or **St. Martin Rentals** (☎ 599/5–54330; in the U.S., ☎ 800/872–8356).

| CATEGORY | COST* |
|---|---|
| **$$$$** | over $300 |
| **$$$** | $225–$300 |
| **$$** | $150–$225 |
| **$** | under $150 |

*All prices are for a standard double room for two in high season, excluding 5% tax (Dutch side), a taxe de séjour (set by individual hotels on the French side), and a 10%–15% service charge.*

## Dutch Side

**$$$$**    🏨 **Port de Plaisance.** Heavily damaged by Hurricane Luis in September of 1995, this resort on Simpson Bay Lagoon was closed at press time. Repairs are under way and Port de Plaisance was scheduled to reopen in October. Interiors of the 88 luxurious studios and one- and two-bedroom apartments are done in soothing pink and beige. Views are of either the lagoon or the resort's own marina. One of the two pools is carved out of rock and has a majestic waterfall. The spa offers every imaginable beauty treatment, from seaweed wraps to aromatherapy, and the sports facilities are equally extensive. The casino's marble entrance is dominated by a stunning 25-foot bronze statue of a mermaid astride four dolphins. The one drawback is the lack of a beach or even a beach shuttle. ⌧ *Box 2089, Cole Bay,* ☎ *599/5–45222 or 800/732–9479,* FAX *599/5–42315. 88 apartments. 2 restaurants, 5 bars, air-conditioning, kitchens, in-room VCRs, 2 pools, hot tub, spa, 7 tennis courts, health club, boating, marina, shops, nightclub, car rental. AE, D, DC, MC, V. EP.*

**$$$**    🏨 **Maho Beach Hotel & Casino.** Despite losing an entire wing to Hurricane Luis, this pink-and-white self-contained megaresort was up and running for last year's winter season. It is scheduled to be completely restored by late 1996. The spacious rooms, which have either sea or garden views, have private balconies, cathedral ceilings and light pastel and deep ocean-colored decors. The trick is to get a room far enough away from the airport's landing strip (those behind the main lobby are the quietest). Restaurants include excellent Italian dining at Tiberio, burgers and live music at Cheri's Café, and beachside Middle Eastern food at Orient Express. The hotel complex is home to both the island's largest casino, the Casino Royal (☞ *Nightlife and the Arts, below*), and its largest pool. Unfortunately the service can't keep up

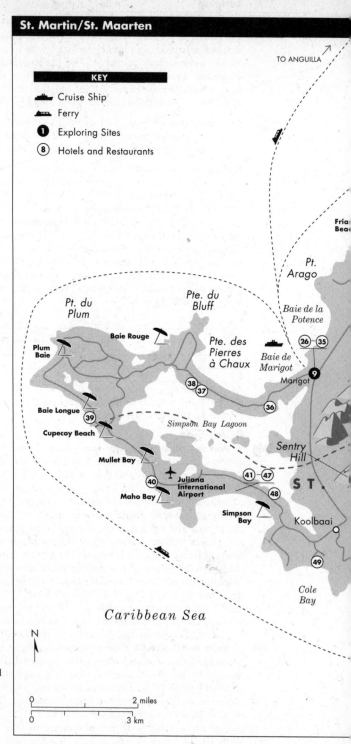

**St. Martin/St. Maarten**

KEY

🚢 Cruise Ship
⛴ Ferry
❶ Exploring Sites
⑧ Hotels and Restaurants

TO ANGUILLA

Fria
Bea

Pt.
Arago

Pte. du
Bluff

Pt. du
Plum

Baie de la
Potence

Baie Rouge

Pte. des
Pierres
à Chaux

Plum
Baie

Baie de
Marigot

㉖–㉟

❾

Marigot

㊲㊳

㊱

Baie Longue

㊳

Simpson Bay Lagoon

Cupecoy Beach

Sentry
Hill

Mullet Bay

㊶–㊸

S T.

㊵

Juliana
International
Airport

㊸

Maho Bay

Simpson
Bay

Koolbaai

Caribbean Sea

㊾

N

Cole
Bay

0 _____ 2 miles
0 _____ 3 km

with the sprawl, and you may be neglected as the staff struggles to meet guest needs. ✉ *Maho Bay,* ☎ *599/5–52115 or 800/223–0757,* 𝔽𝔸𝕏 *599/5–53180. 600 rooms, 29 suites. 10 restaurants, 3 bars, 3 pools, hot tub, spa, 3 tennis courts, health club, water sports, 75 shops, casino, dance club, baby-sitting, car rental. AE, D, MC, V. EP, MAP.*

**$$$** 🏨 **Pelican Resort & Casino.** Walk into the reception area and be greeted by gaming tables. On the lower level is a sales office enticing you to buy into this hotel-condo complex. An assortment of white stucco buildings house the resort's apartments, suites, and deluxe studios, all of which have a sweeping view of the Caribbean. The resort has 1,400 feet of beach (though it's not great for swimming because of the seaweed) and its own 60-foot catamaran, *El Tigre,* which is available for charters. ✉ *Simpson Bay,* ☎ *599/5–42503 or 800/626–9637,* 𝔽𝔸𝕏 *599/5–42133. 660 suites and studios. 2 restaurants, grocery, 4 bars, kitchens, 8 pools, 6 tennis courts, health spa, water-sports center, casino, medical center, playground, car rental. AE, D, DC, MC, V. EP.*

**$$–$$$** 🏨 **Horny Toad Guesthouse.** This is one of the most charming proper-
★ ties on the island, thanks to the caring touch of owners Bette and Earle Vaughn, who keep things immaculate. Each of the eight apartments on the beach is individually decorated, and the blue-and-white sun terrace duplicates the patterns of delft china. There is a barbecue area for guests, but no restaurant. ✉ *Box 397, Simpson Bay,* ☎ *599/5–54323, or 800/417–9361, ext. 3013,* 𝔽𝔸𝕏 *599/5–53316. 2 studios, 6 1-bedroom apartments. Barbecue, library. No credit cards. EP.*

**$$–$$$** 🏨 **La Vista.** On this intimate property, Antillean buildings are connected by brick walkways lined with riotous hibiscus and bougainvillea. All accommodations are suites with a private balcony, and guests have the use of the facilities at the adjacent Pelican Resort. ✉ *Box 40, Pelican Key,* ☎ *599/5–43005 or 800/365–8484,* 𝔽𝔸𝕏 *599/5–43010. 24 suites. Restaurant, air-conditioning, pool, tennis available at Pelican Resort, horseback riding. AE, MC, V. EP.*

**$$–$$$** 🏨 **Oyster Pond Beach Hotel.** The refined elegance of this hotel is quite
★ out of character with the rest of St. Maarten. Two towers with Moorish arches and stone walls surround a courtyard. There are split-level suites and standard rooms, all with terra-cotta floors, a secluded balcony or terrace, and pastel French cottons. A newer building offers larger rooms with balconies facing the sea. The hotel is a one-minute walk from Dawn Beach, which is excellent for snorkeling, though not for sunbathing or swimming. The dining room opens onto the Atlantic Ocean, and the pool is perched right at the water's edge. A PADI-certified dive shop is on the premises. Breakfast is included. ✉ *Oyster Pond, Box 239, Philipsburg,* ☎ *599/5–22206, 599/5–23206, or 800/777–1700,* 𝔽𝔸𝕏 *599/5–25695. 40 rooms, 20 suites. Restaurant, bar, air-conditioning, fans, saltwater pool, dive shop, water-sports center, car rental. AE, D, MC, V. BP.*

**$$** 🏨 **Great Bay Beach Hotel & Casino.** One of the island's few properties offering an all-inclusive rate as well as a room-only rate, this resort, a 10-minute walk from the center of Philipsburg, has its own stretch of beach and terrific views of the bay. The bustling open-air lobby, with striped awnings overlooking the sea, is more striking than the average rooms which are furnished in typical muted pastels. You do get a private balcony or terrace with an ocean or mountain view. A list of activities is posted each morning, and the hotel staff can arrange virtually any type of island excursion or sport. ✉ *Box 910, Philipsburg,* ☎ *599/5– 22446 or 800/223–0757,* 𝔽𝔸𝕏 *599/5–23859. 285 rooms, 10 1-bedroom suites. 2 restaurants, 3 bars, 2 pools, beauty salon, tennis court, exercise room, beach, water-sports center, gift shop, casino, nightclub, car rental. AE, DC, MC, V. EP, All-inclusive.*

**$–$$** ☷ **Holland House Beach Hotel.** This is a centrally situated hotel, with the shops of Front Street at its doorstep and mile-long Great Bay Beach as its backyard. Each room has muted-pastel spreads and drapes and a balcony; most have kitchenettes. Ask for a beach view. The delightful open-air restaurant overlooking the water serves reasonably priced dinners, and the indoor-outdoor patio lounge is a popular spot to watch the sunset. ✉ *35 Front St., Box 393, Philipsburg,* ☎ *599/5–22572 or 800/223–9815,* FAX *599/5–24673. 54 rooms, 6 suites. Restaurant, lounge, air-conditioning, gift shop, activities desk, meeting room. AE, D, DC, MC, V. EP.*

**$** ☷ **Passangrahan Royal Guest House.** It's entirely appropriate that
★ the bar here is named Sidney Greenstreet. This is the island's oldest inn, and it looks like a set for an old Bogie-Greenstreet film. The green-and-white building was once Queen Wilhelmina's residence and the government guest house. Wicker peacock chairs, balconies shaded by tropical greenery, and a broad tile veranda are some of the hallmarks of this guest house. There are no TVs or phones in the rooms, and you're offered just a sliver of Great Bay Beach. ✉ *15 Front St., Box 151, Philipsburg,* ☎ *599/5–23588,* FAX *599/5–22885. 30 rooms, 1 suite. Restaurant, bar. AE, MC, V. EP.*

**$** ☷ **Seaview Hotel & Casino.** This is another good buy on Front Street and Great Bay Beach. The air-conditioned, twin-bed rooms are very modest, cheerful, and clean. Ten of the rooms look out on the courtyard, where breakfast is sometimes served; four rooms face the sea. Children under 12 stay free. ✉ *59 Front St., Box 65, Philipsburg,* ☎ *599/5–22323 or 800/223–9815; in NY, 212/545–8469; in Canada, 800/468–0023;* FAX *599/5–24356. 45 rooms. Breakfast room, air-conditioning, casino. AE, D, MC, V. EP.*

## French Side

**$$$$** ☷ **Le Meridien L'Habitation Le Domaine.** There are better bargains on the island, yet this bustling resort remains wildly popular with tour groups and families. There are 1,600 feet of white-sand beach and a slew of sports facilities, but no matter where you stay on the compound, few units boast an ocean view, the service is polite but impersonal, and French Muzak is annoyingly omnipresent. The setting is pleasant enough—at the end of a white-knuckle road, amid beautifully landscaped gardens on enchanting but windless Marcel Cove. All the rooms, suites, and apartments have balconies, and the one-bedroom apartments on the marina have fully-equipped kitchens and private patios. A couple of two-story buildings dubbed Le Domaine contain rooms and suites that are smaller and pricier but brighter and more tropical. Guests have free access to the facilities of Le Privilège Resort & Spa (☞ *below*). La Belle France is a typically solid and *très cher* gourmet restaurant. ✉ *Box 581, Anse Marcel 97150,* ☎ *590/87–33–33 or 590/87–78–80; in the U.S., 800/543–4300;* FAX *590/87–30–38. 400 rooms, 82 suites. 4 restaurants, 4 bars, air-conditioning, refrigerators, 2 pools, miniature golf, 6 tennis courts, aerobics, racquetball, squash, beach, watersports center, 100-slip marina, boutiques, disco, car rental. AE, DC, MC, V. EP.*

**$$$$** ☷ **La Samanna.** This secluded hotel looks as if it were transported to
★ St. Martin from Morocco. La Samanna is set in a tropical garden on a slope overlooking the ravishing Baie Longue beach. Red hibiscus is everywhere. Studios and one- and two-bedroom villas all have a private patio and small luxuries such as potpourri and fresh flowers. The decor is stunning: cool mint, apricot, and teal fabrics; unusual ceramic work; painted tiles; and clever variations on traditional Caribbean wicker and rattan. The restaurant is one of the island's finest. ✉ *Box 159, Marigot 97150,* ☎ *590/87–51–22 or 800/854–2252,* FAX *590/87–87–*

*86. 25 rooms, 30 1-bedroom suites, 30 2-bedroom suites. Restaurant, lounge, minibars, pool, 3 tennis courts, exercise room, water-sports center, boutique, TV room, library. AE. CP.*

$$$$  🏨 **Le Privilege Resort & Spa.** So heavy was the damage from Hurricane Luis, that this resort, which is all of three years old, had to be virtually rebuilt. The result is a sparkling new Le Privilege, perched above Anse Marcel and Le Meridien L'Habitation. Those into the spa life will take advantage of all kinds of treatments available, from massage to lymphatic drainage. Rooms and suites are spacious and very comfortably furnished, with tile floors, marble baths, and such thoughtful touches as CD players and in-room safes. There is a free shuttle service down to the beach and the resort's excellent marina. ⊠ *Anse Marcel 97150,* ☎ *590/87–38–38 or 800/874–8541,* FAX *590/87–44–12. 40 rooms and suites. 3 restaurants, bar, in-room safes, in-room VCRs, 2 pools, beauty salon, spa, 6 tennis courts, health club, racquetball, squash, marina, sailing, scuba diving, windsurfing, fishing, nightclub. AE, MC, V. CP.*

$$$–$$$$  🏨 **Esmeralda Resort.** It may look like a Sun Belt housing development, but the interiors of these deluxe villas are tastefully decorated. The 51 rooms and suites in 15 villas can be combined any way you like, from studio to five-bedroom palatial digs. Each villa has a private pool, and all the rooms have a private terrace. L'Astrolabe has a reputation for excellent French cuisine. ⊠ *Box 541, Orient Bay,* ☎ *590/87–36–36 or 800/622–7836,* FAX *590/87–35–18. 15 villas. 5 beach restaurants, indoor restaurant, kitchenettes, 15 pools, 2 tennis courts, water-sports center, gift shop. AE, D, MC, V. CP.*

$$–$$$$  🏨 **Green Cay Village.** Set high above Orient Beach facing the trade winds,
★     this villa/hotel is a great choice for small groups or families. Part of the Orient Bay Resort complex, Green Cay offers spacious one-, two-, and three-bedroom villas, each with its own private pool, large deck, fully equipped kitchen, and outdoor dining patio. Daily maid service is included. Although all villas have plenty of privacy, those highest on the hill enjoy the most seclusion, as well as the most stunning views. Breakfast is served by the pool for a reasonable fee, and guests have charge privileges at all Orient Bay Resort restaurants and bars. ⊠ *B.P. 3006, Parc Baie Orientale 97064,* ☎ *590/87–38–63 or 800/932–3222,* FAX *590/87–39–27. 16 villas. Charge privileges at all Orient Bay resort restaurants and bars, kitchens, room service, in-room VCRs, pools, tennis and water sports available at Orient Bay Resort. AE, MC, V. EP.*

$$$  🏨 **Grand Case Beach Club.** This informal condo complex is situated on Grand Case's crescent-shape beach, with another "secret" strand of sand a two-minute walk away. Damaged by Hurricane Luis, the club was closed at press time but undergoing a complete restoration—including new furnishings and new decor—and was scheduled to reopen in April 1996. Studios and one- and two-bedroom apartments all have balconies or patios; the 62 oceanfront units are much in demand. The kitchen at the aptly named Café Panoramique restaurant has been upgraded since it spirited chef Alain Billard away from Le Bec Fin. ⊠ *Box 339, Grand Case 97150,* ☎ *590/87–51–87 or 800/223–1588,* FAX *590/87–59–93. 40 studios, 33 1- and 2-bedroom apartments. Restaurant, lounge, air-conditioning, kitchenettes, tennis court, catamaran, billiards, car rental. AE, MC, V. CP.*

$$–$$$  🏨 **Captain Oliver's.** This property straddles the St. Maarten/St. Mar-
★     tin border: Stay in France, and dine in the Netherlands. The bungalows are a good bargain and a good way to avoid the hustle and bustle of St. Maarten. The small hotel faces a beautiful horseshoe-shape bay; bungalows have a view of the bay or garden. The exceptionally clean, fresh rooms have a patio/deck; sail-and-stay packages can be arranged by the

friendly and helpful staff. ⊠ *Oyster Pond 97150,* ☎ *590/87–40–26 or 800/223–9862,* 𝔽𝔸𝕏 *590/87–40–84. 50 rooms. Restaurant, snack bar, air-conditioning, kitchenettes, minibars. AE, DC, MC, V. CP.*

$$–$$$ 🎟 **Pavillon Beach Hotel.** Every room and suite at this small hotel faces the sea and has a private balcony. The spacious studios and one-bedroom suites are decorated in warm pastel colors and have tile floors and elegant rattan furniture. Bathrooms come with a hair dryer and shower but no tub. From the ground-level rooms, you can walk right onto the beach through sliding wooden shutters. The managers, Paul and Marie-Florence, are wonderfully warmhearted and helpful. ⊠ *Plage de Grand Case, RN 7, Grand Case 97150,* ☎ *590/87–96–46 or 800/223–9815,* 𝔽𝔸𝕏 *590/87–71–04. 17 rooms. Kitchenettes. MC, V. EP.*

$–$$$ 🎟 **Mont Vernon.** This hotel was heavily damaged by Hurricane Luis and was closed at press time but scheduled to reopen in July 1996. Gingerbread work decorates this rambling hotel, which sits on a bluff overlooking Orient Bay. It's rather a sprawling eyesore when seen from the beach. All rooms have a private balcony. The rooms in the buildings on the crest facing the ocean have the best views and are slightly larger than the others. The other choice rooms are in the buildings by the pools and beach. This is a big resort that lures package-tour groups as well as business seminars. ⊠ *Baie Orientale, BP 1174, 97062,* ☎ *590/87–62–00 or 800/223–0888,* 𝔽𝔸𝕏 *590/87–37–27. 394 suites. 2 restaurants, 2 bars, pool, 2 tennis courts, exercise room, snorkeling, windsurfing, shops, car rental. AE, DC, MC, V. CP, MAP.*

$$ 🎟 **Alizéa.** The view of Orient Bay from this Mont Vernon hill setting is stunning. There is a path to the beach (a 10-minute walk). An open-air feeling pervades the hotel, from its terrace restaurant—the food is superb—to the 26 guest apartments done up with contemporary light-wood furnishings. Rooms vary in style and design, but all are tasteful and each has a kitchenette and a large private balcony. ⊠ *Mont Vernon 25, 97150,* ☎ *590/87–33–42,* 𝔽𝔸𝕏 *590/87–41–15. 8 1-bedroom bungalows, 18 studios. Restaurant, bar, kitchenettes, pool. AE, D, MC, V. CP.*

$$ 🎟 **Anse Margot.** This quiet, thoroughly French property is one of the many hotels that line the stretch of land between the sea and Simpson's Bay, known as Baie Nettlé. The rooms here are in eight three-story town-house buildings. All units have a private balcony with either a garden or beach view. Upholstery, drapes, and spreads are a brown-and-coral geometric print. There is a stretch of beach along Simpson Bay that's good for sunbathing but not swimming; you may prefer the Nettlé beach across the street. A complimentary breakfast buffet is served in the open-air Entre Deux Mers, one of the better hotel restaurants. It's about a five-minute drive to Marigot. ⊠ *Box 979, Baie Nettlé 97150,* ☎ *590/87–92–01 or 800/742–4276,* 𝔽𝔸𝕏 *590/87–92–13. 96 rooms, 35 1-bedroom suites. Restaurant, bar, 2 pools, hot tub, water-sports center, gift shop, meeting room. AE, D, DC, MC, V. BP.*

$–$$ 🎟 **Hôtel l'Atlantide.** This small hotel has four sun-drenched units, ranging in size from a studio to a two-bedroom suite. Private balconies overlook Grand Case Bay and the beach. The decor is airy, with gleaming white tile floors, and crisp pastel-striped or floral upholstery. There's no restaurant or bar, but the village of Grand Case is known for its lively restaurant scene. ⊠ *BP 5140, Grand Case 97150,* ☎ *590/87–09–80,* 𝔽𝔸𝕏 *590/87–30–09. 4 units. No credit cards. EP.*

$–$$ 🎟 **Hôtel L'Esplanade Caraïbes.** Opened in 1992, this complex still
★ sparkles as if brand-new. It's built on a hillside overlooking Grand Case Bay, a three-minute walk from the beach. Two curved stone staircases with inlaid tile and brick lead up from the bougainvillea beds to the open-air reception area. The standard suites are large, with private balconies and gleaming wood ceilings; some have an office alcove with a desk. Duplexes have elegant cathedral ceilings and mahogany staircases, as well

as an extra half bath, an upstairs loft bedroom; upholstery throughout is striped with muted pinks and corals. There is no restaurant at the hotel, but Grand Case's roster of gourmet spots is just a short walk away. ✉ *Box 5007, Grand Case 97150,* ☎ *590/87–06–55,* FAX *590/87–29–15. 24 units. Pool, deep-sea-fishing boat for rent. AE, D, MC, V. EP.*

**$–$$** ⬛ **Marine Hotel Simson Beach.** This sprawling complex may be the best
★ buy on the Nettlé Bay hotel strip. Rooms and duplex suites are cheerfully decorated, most have a view of the water, and all have a kitchenette and balcony. Budget-conscious Europeans love this place because of the many extras, like a huge breakfast buffet and nightly local entertainment. There are shuttles (not complimentary) to Marigot, Philipsburg, and beaches. ✉ *Box 172, Nettlé Bay,* ☎ *590/87–54–54,* FAX *590/87–92–11. 120 studios, 45 1-bedroom duplexes. Restaurant, bar, grocery, kitchenettes, pool, tennis court, beach, dive shop, watersports center, bicycles, activity center, gift shop, coin laundry, car rental. AE, DC, MC, V. CP.*

**$** ⬛ **Golden Tulip St. Martin.** This resort, in the somewhat isolated Cul de Sac area, opened in early 1994. Heavily damaged by Hurricane Luis, the hotel was closed at press time but scheduled to reopen in April 1996. It offers a luxury feel for a budget price. Clusters of blue bungalows with white gingerbread trim, each housing a suite, are spread out along the water. Each unit has a kitchenette and a porch facing the sea. The interiors are spacious, with white tile floors and pretty floral upholstery fabrics. ✉ *BP 5240, Cul de Sac 97072,* ☎ *590/87–89–98 or 800/344–1212,* FAX *590/87–35–14. 94 units. Restaurant, bar, poolside snack bar, kitchenettes, minibars, 5 pools, horseback riding, sailing, windsurfing, deepsea fishing, boutique, baby-sitting. AE, DC, MC, V. EP.*

**$** ⬛ **Hevea.** This small white guest house with smart striped awnings is
★ across the street from the beach in the heart of Grand Case. The rooms are dollhouse small but will appeal to romantics. There are beam ceilings, washstands, and carved-wood beds with lovely white coverlets and mosquito nets. The five rooms, studios, and apartment are on the terrace level; two studios and one apartment are on the garden level. Hotel guests can get a special "house" dinner at the delightful gourmet restaurant for $30. ✉ *163 blvd. de Grand Case, Grand Case 97150,* ☎ *590/87–56–85 or 800/423–4433,* FAX *590/87–83–88. 8 units. Restaurant. MC, V. EP.*

**$** ⬛ **La Residence.** The downtown location and soundproof rooms of this
★ Marigot hotel make it a popular place for business travelers. All the accommodations have a balcony, dark rattan furniture and tile floors. You've a choice among single or double rooms, some with mezzanine loft beds. The intimate restaurant offers a good $28 three-course menu. You'll have to take a cab to get to the beach. ✉ *rue du Général de Gaulle, Marigot 97150,* ☎ *590/87–70–37 or 800/223–9815,* FAX *590/87–90–44. 21 rooms. Restaurant, lounge, minibars, sundry shop. AE, D, MC, V. MAP, CP.*

**$** ⬛ **Le Royale Louisiana.** Located in downtown Marigot in the boutique shopping area, this upstairs hotel has white and pale green galleries that overlook the flower-filled courtyard. There's a selection of twin, double, and triple duplexes and you can reach the nearest beach by a 20-minute walk or by taxi. ✉ *rue du Général de Gaulle, Box 476, Marigot 97055,* ☎ *590/87–86–51,* FAX *590/87–96–49. 68 rooms. Restaurant, snack bar, air-conditioning, beauty salon. AE, MC, V. CP.*

## Dining

It may seem that this island has no monuments. Au contraire, there are many of them, all dedicated to gastronomy, making St. Martin one of the best Caribbean islands for gourmets. You'll scarcely find a touch of Dutch; the major influences are French and Italian. This season's "in" eatery may be next season's remembrance of things past, as things do have a way of changing rapidly. The generally steep prices reflect both the island's high culinary reputation and the difficulty of obtaining fresh ingredients. Not surprisingly, the hotel restaurants on the French side are usually more sophisticated, but at prices that would make almost anyone but a Rockefeller go Dutch. In high season, *be sure to make reservations,* and call to cancel if you can't make it. Many restaurants close completely or just for lunch during August, September, and into October. We've tried to note all seasonal closings, but since not all restaurants have official policies, it's a good idea to call ahead during the off-season. Hurricane Luis only temporarily affected the restaurant business. All establishments listed below were back to normal by the start of the '95–'96 winter season, most freshened up with new coats of paint, decks, and furnishings.

## What to Wear

Appropriate dining attire on this island ranges from swimsuits to sport jackets. You can often tell by the price category—the more expensive a restaurant is, the more dressed up you should get. For men, a jacket and khakis or jeans will take you anywhere; for women, dressy pants, a skirt, or even fancy shorts will be acceptable almost everywhere. Jeans are de rigueur in the less formal and more trendy eateries. In the listings below, dress is casual (and chic, of course) unless otherwise noted, but ask when making reservations if you're unsure.

| CATEGORY | COST* |
|---|---|
| $$$$ | over $50 |
| $$$ | $35–$50 |
| $$ | $25–$35 |
| $ | under $25 |

*per person for a three-course meal, excluding drinks and service*

DUTCH SIDE

**$$$$** ✕ **Felix.** This classy yet casual little beachside eatery serves dinner by candlelight. At lunchtime, take a dip at Simpson Bay Beach (you can come here in your swimsuit as long as you're not wet) before feasting on salad Felix (an imaginative concoction of bananas, sweet potatoes, and avocado), rack of lamb Provençale, or steak au poivre. The restaurant is on the road to the Pelican Resort. ⊠ *Pelican Key,* ☎ *599/5–42797. AE, D, DC, MC, V. No dinner Wed.*

**$$$** ✕ **Le Bec Fin.** To reach the well-known upstairs restaurant, you stroll through a flowery courtyard. The rotation of chefs here has unfortunately lead to inconsistency in the quality of the classical French cuisine. Starters include vol-au-vent (pastry) bursting with escargots in fennel cream sauce and tagliatelle with shrimp in ginger. Fish, such as red snapper fillet in rum butter sauce, is your best bet for a main course. The meringue swan with mint ice cream is delightful to the eye and the palate. The breezy downstairs café annex serves breakfast and lunch with great crepes (try the seafood) and salads. ⊠ *119 Front St., Philipsburg,* ☎ *599/5–22976. AE, MC, V.*

**$$$** ✕ **Oyster Pond Beach Hotel.** A more genteel evening on St. Maarten
★ is hard to find. A delightful terrace with wonderful sea views is decked with fine linens and china and fresh flowers. Lobster medallions dancing in a truffle, tomato, and basil sauce; fillet of red snapper in sauce piquant; and sweet, billowy dessert soufflés are specialties. The hotel's guests have priority in this romantic dining room, so you should reserve well in advance. ⊠ *Oyster Pond,* ☎ *599/5–22206 or 599/5–23206. Reservations essential. AE, MC, V.*

**$$$**   ✕ **Le Perroquet.** A cool green-and-white West Indian–style house over-looking a lagoon is the peaceful setting for this restaurant. Chef Pierre Castagna prepares exotic specialties, such as grilled breast of ostrich in a bordelaise sauce. ✉ *Airport Rd., Simpson Bay,* ☎ *599/5–44339. AE, MC, V. Closed Mon.*

**$$$**   ✕ **Saratoga.** The handsome mahogany-outfitted dining room in the
   ★ Yacht Club's stucco and red tile building has views of the Simpson Bay Marina. The menu changes daily, according to the whim of owner and chef John Jackson, who trained at the Culinary Institute of America; everything is flown in fresh. He dubs his cuisine "freestyle creative contemporary," merrily borrowing from various influences, from Asian to southwestern. You might start with Malpeque oysters with balsamic-horseradish sauce or seven-seaweed salad with sea beans, daikon, and sesame, then segue into crispy fried roundhead snapper in fermented black bean sauce or grilled chicken breast in a cumin-Gouda crust. The wine list is admirably balanced and reasonably priced, with 10–12 wines offered by the glass. ✉ *Simpson Bay Yacht Club, Airport Rd.,* ☎ *599/5–42421. Reservations essential in season. AE, MC, V. Closed Sun. No lunch.*

**$$$**   ✕ **Spartaco.** Every element of the northern Italian cuisine served in this 200-year-old stone plantation house is either homemade or imported from Italy. Some of the specialties are black angel-hair pasta with shrimp and garlic; swordfish baked with pink peppercorns and rosemary, served over linguine; and veal Vesuviana, with mozzarella, oregano, and tomato sauce. ✉ *Almond Grove, Cole Bay,* ☎ *599/5–45379. AE, MC, V. Closed Mon.*

**$$–$$$**   ✕ **Antoine.** Enjoy a romantic evening at this elegant, airy terrace overlooking Great Bay; it's new location is on Front Street, across from the Galaxy Cinema. Candles glow on tables set with crisp blue and white napery and gleaming silver, and the sound of the surf drifts up from the beach. You might start your meal with French onion soup or lobster bisque, then move on to steak au poivre, duck in brandy sauce with cherries, or lobster thermidor. Pastas and Creole specials are also available. For dessert, try the sublime Grand Marnier soufflé. ✉ *Front St., Philipsburg,* ☎ *599/5–22964. Reservations essential in high season. AE, MC, V. Closed Sun.*

**$$**   ✕ **L'Escargot.** A lovely 19th-century house wrapped in verandas is home to one of St. Maarten's oldest classic French restaurants. Starters include frogs' legs in garlic sauce and crepes filled with caviar and sour cream. There is also, of course, a variety of snail dishes. For an entrée, try grilled red snapper with red wine and shallot sauce or *canard de l'escargot* (crisp duck in pineapple and banana sauce). There's a fun cabaret Wednesday night; you don't have to pay the cover charge if you come for dinner. ✉ *84 Front St., Philipsburg,* ☎ *599/5–22483. AE, MC, V.*

**$–$$**   ✕ **Wajang Doll.** Indonesian dishes are served in the garden of this West Indian–style house. *Nasi goreng* (fried rice) and red snapper in a sweet soy glaze are standouts, but the specialty is *rijsttafel*, a traditional Indonesian meal of rice accompanied by 15 to 20 different dishes. ✉ *137 Front St., Philipsburg,* ☎ *599/5–22687. AE, MC, V. Closed Sun. No lunch.*

**$**   ✕ **Chesterfield's.** Casual lunches of burgers and salads and more elaborate Continental dinners are served at this informal, nautically themed restaurant at the marina. The dinner menu includes French onion soup, roast duckling with fresh pineapple and banana sauce, and several different preparations of shrimp. The Mermaid Bar is a popular spot with yachtsmen. ✉ *Great Bay Marina, Philipsburg,* ☎ *599/5–23484. No credit cards.*

**$** ✕ **Harbour Lights.** This modest family-run spot is in a historic building built in 1870. The decor is warm, with peach and coral walls and sea-foam-green tablecloths. Choose among excellent *rotis* (roasts) and pilafs and even better, stewed or curried chicken, meats, and seafood. Try one of the knockout cocktails made with the local guavaberry liqueur. Tables on the second-floor balcony overlook Back Street and make for pleasant alfresco dining. ⊠ *30 Back St., Philipsburg,* ☎ *599/5–23504. AE, MC, V.*

**$** ✕ **Shiv Sagar.** Authentic East Indian cuisine, emphasizing Kashmiri and ★ Mogul specialties, is served in this small mirrored room fragrant with cumin and coriander. Marvelous tandooris and curries are offered, but try one of the less-familiar preparations like *madrasi machi* (red snapper cooked in a blend of hot spices). A large selection of vegetarian dishes is also offered. There's a friendly open-air bar out front. ⊠ *3 Front St., Philipsburg,* ☎ *599/5–22299. AE, D, DC, MC, V. Closed Sun.*

**$** ✕ **Turtle Pier Bar & Restaurant.** Chattering monkeys and squawking ★ parrots greet you at the entrance to this classic Caribbean hangout, teetering over the lagoon and festooned with creeping vines. There are 200 animals in this informal zoo, but that's nothing compared to the menagerie hanging out at the bar during happy hour. The genial owner, Sid Wathey, whose family is one of the island's oldest, and his American wife, Lorraine, have fashioned one of the funkiest, most endearing places in the Caribbean, with cheap beer on draft, huge American breakfasts, all-you-can-eat ribs dinners for $9.95, and live music several nights a week. ⊠ *Airport Rd.,* ☎ *599/5–52230. No credit cards.*

## French Side

**$$$$** ✕ **Chez Martine.** A charming, globe-trotting French couple, Eliane and ★ Jean-Pierre, have made this small hotel into a personable hostelry with an excellent French restaurant. Dine by the water's edge in an intimate room with polished silverware, blue glassware, and white napery. The chef, Thierry de Launay, studied under Joël Robuchon. You might begin with superb velvety seafood consommé, then segue into roast lamb on a bed of eggplant and spinach in corn sauce or lobster in puff pastry; the homemade duck-liver pâté also claims a loyal following. There are two prix fixe menus: one without wine at $60, and one with selected wines for each course at $89. The wine list has several very drinkable wines for under $20. ⊠ *140 blvd. Grand Case, Grand Case 97150,* ☎ *590/87–51–59. DC, MC, V. No lunch off-season.*

**$$$$** ✕ **La Samanna.** This restaurant has an exquisite setting in the celebrated hotel; you'll dine by candlelight on a tented terrace surrounded by bougainvillea. The clientele is chic, international, and often famous. Innovative chef Mark Ehrler (from Maxim's in Paris and New York) might seduce the palate with seafood risotto, sautéed snapper over Creole black sausage, or roasted lamb chops with seasonal salad and chickpeas sprinkled with fruity cold-press olive oil. Three kinds of caviar are served with blinis and chilled Absolut. Dinner for two (with wine) can easily set you back $175. The superb wine cellar holds more than 25,000 bottles. ⊠ *Baie Longue,* ☎ *590/87–51–22. Reservations essential. Jacket. AE, DC, MC, V.*

**$$$$** ✕ **Le Santal.** The approach to this dazzler, through a working-class suburb of Marigot, is forbidding. The exterior appears ramshackle, but the interior is transformed by soft lighting, china, and crystal. Specialties of the house include lobster soufflé on a bed of spinach and eggplant, foie gras sautéed in cassis, and lacquered duck. The owners also run the excellent Jean Dupont and Asia, but this is their showplace. Reservations are not required, but they're highly recommended if you want to eat at one of the five tables by the water. ⊠ *Sandy Ground,* ☎ *590/87–53–48. AE, MC, V. No lunch.*

**$$$–$$$$** ✕ **Le Poisson d'Or.** Feast in this posh popular place on a constantly chang-
★ ing menu of dishes such as sautéed foie gras with pear and walnut cream
sauce or smoked lobster in champagne sauce. The setting is a restored
stone house, with a huge veranda holding 20 tables. The space doubles
as a gallery exhibiting works of top-notch Caribbean artists. ⊠ *rue d'An-
guille, Marigot,* ☎ *590/87–72–45. AE, MC, V. No lunch.*

**$$$–$$$$** ✕ **Rainbow.** In a town of splendid seaside boîtes, this is one of the best.
★ The cobalt blue and white decor of the split-level dining room is strik-
ingly simple, and the atmosphere, created by lapping waves and mur-
muring guests, is highly romantic. Fleur and David are the stylish,
energetic hosts, and chef Mario Tardif is from one of the world's gas-
tronomic capitals, Québec City. Try his shrimp and scallop fricassee with
Caribbean chutney, duck *magret* (breast meat served with its skin), grilled
swordfish, or sautéed veal scallopini with capers, garlic, and chives. Dishes
are dressed with fanciful touches like red cabbage crisps. Finish the meal
off with sublime orange, honey, and ginger soufflé. ⊠ *Grand Case,* ☎
*590/87–55–80. AE, MC, V. Closed Sun. No lunch.*

**$$$–$$$$** ✕ **La Vie En Rose.** This bustling restaurant is right off the pier, about
a 30-second stroll from the tourist information office. The menu is clas-
sic French with an occasional Caribbean twist—fillet of swordfish
sautéed in a passion-fruit butter sauce, freshwater crayfish in puff pas-
try. Appetizers include a delightful warm smoked salmon with pota-
toes and chives and lobster salad spiced with a touch of ginger. Save
room for chocolate mousse cake topped with vanilla sauce. The ground-
floor tearoom and pastry shop serve an excellent luncheon with wine
for $20. In season, you may make dinner reservations up to one month
in advance. ⊠ *rue de la République, Marigot,* ☎ *590/87–54–42.
Reservations essential in season. AE, D, DC, MC, V. No credit cards
at lunch. No lunch Sun.*

**$$$** ✕ **Alizéa.** Many claim that this elegant terrace restaurant offers the best
★ cuisine on the island. French chef Laurent Guyon trained with Roger
Verge from the famous Moulin de Mougins. The prix fixe menu is an
excellent value at $40. Sample the homemade foie gras with red wine
jelly or roasted sea scallop appetizers. Entrées include mahimahi with
fennel and sweet potatoes, and beef tenderloin with stewed shallots in
red wine sauce. There are several vegetarian selections. You won't go
wrong with the crème brûlée with honey and vanilla for dessert. ⊠
*Hotel Alizéa, Mont Vernon,* ☎ *590/87–41–20. AE, DC, MC, V.*

**$$$** ✕ **Le Tastevin.** A chic pavilion, with tropical plants, ceiling fans, and
water views, provides an elegant dining setting. Owner Daniel Passeri,
a native of Burgundy, also founded the homey Auberge Gourmande
across the street. The menu here is more ambitious, including foie gras
in Armagnac sauce, duck breast in banana-lime sauce, and red snap-
per fillet with curry and wild-mushroom sauce. ⊠ *Grand Case,* ☎
*590/87–55–45. Reservations essential in season. AE, DC, MC, V. No
credit cards at lunch.*

**$$–$$$** ✕ **Maison sur le Port.** Watching the sunset from the palm-fringed ter-
race is not the least of the pleasures in this old West Indian house sur-
rounded by romantically lit garden fountains. Try the sautéed duck fillet
in passion-fruit sauce or red snapper with beurre blanc. There are also
three-course fixed-price menus at $21.50 and $29. Chef Jean-Paul
Fahrner's imaginative salads are lunchtime treats. There is a children's
menu with burgers and chicken sandwiches. ⊠ *On the port, Marigot,*
☎ *590/87–56–38. AE, D, MC, V. Closed Sun.*

**$$–$$$** ✕ **Le Pressoir.** Many say that presentation is everything. Combine that
★ with excellent food in a charming West Indies house, where the bill
won't break the bank, and you have a great restaurant. French and
Creole fusion cuisine reigns; go for the fresh local fish prepared with

tropical fruit glazes and sauces. The crème brûlée is superb. ⊠ *Grand Case,* ☎ *590/87–76–62. AE, MC, V.*

**$$** ✕ **Le Marocain.** This exotic oasis in the middle of Marigot resembles a pasha's posh digs, with lush potted plants, intricate mosaics, hand-painted tiles, and wood carvings. The food is as colorful and enticing as the decor, with wonderfully perfumed *tajines* (casseroles of chicken or meat) and *pastillas* (fragrant pastries filled with spices, raisins, and meat or chicken) among the standouts. ⊠ *rue de Hollande, Marigot,* ☎ *590/87–83–11. AE, MC, V.*

**$$** ✕ **Mini Club.** This popular eatery, on an upstairs terrace nestled amid coconut palms, has the feel of a tree house. Dining here is always pleasant, but come on Wednesday and Saturday nights when there's a sumptuous buffet of more than 30 dishes—salads, roast pork, suckling pig, beef, fish, lobster—all for $40 per person, with wine. There is also a $25 prix fixe menu at lunch and dinner. Standard menu selections include poached fish in Creole sauce and steak béarnaise. ⊠ *rue d'Anguille, Marigot,* ☎ *590/87–50–69. AE, MC, V.*

**$–$$** ✕ **Bistrot Nu.** For simple, unadorned fare at a reasonable price, this
★ may be the best spot on the islands. Traditional brasserie-style food—coq au vin, fish soup, snails, pizza, and seafood—is served in a friendly atmosphere. The place is enormously popular; its tables are packed until it closes at 2 AM. ⊠ *rue de Hollande, Marigot,* ☎ *590/87–97–09. MC, V. Closed Sun.*

**$–$$** ✕ **Don Camillo da Enzo.** Country-style decor and excellent service distinguish this small eatery. Both northern and southern Italian dishes are served. Some favorites are the carpaccio, green gnocchi in Gorgonzola cream sauce, and veal medallions in marsala sauce. ⊠ *Port La Royale, Marigot,* ☎ *590/87–52–88. AE, MC, V.*

**$–$$** ✕ **La Plaisance.** The cool strains of jazz waft through this lively open-air brasserie as you sample terrific salads (try the Niçoise or *landaine*—duck, smoked ham, croutons, and fried egg), pizzas (wonderful lobster), pastas (garlic and basil pistou), and fresh grilled seafood at unbeatable prices. This is one of several fine ultracasual eateries at Port La Royale, all offering simple, appetizing food, fixed-price menus, and happy hours. ⊠ *Port La Royale, Marigot,* ☎ *590/87–85–00. AE, MC, V.*

**$** ✕ **Yvette's.** The attempts at romance couldn't be more endearing:
★ Classical music plays softly, and the tiny, eight-table room is a symphony in Valentine red, from the curtains, tablecloths, and roses to the hot pepper sauce. Yvette herself couldn't be more down-home, nor her food more delicious. Plates are piled high with lip-smacking Creole specialties, such as *accras* (spicy fish fritters), stewed chicken with rice and beans, and conch and dumplings. This is the kind of place that is so good you're surprised to see other tourists—but word gets around. ⊠ *Orleans,* ☎ *590/87–32–03. AE (5% surcharge).*

## Beaches

The island's 10 miles of beaches are all open to the public. Beaches occupied by resort properties charge a small fee (about $3) for changing facilities, and water-sports equipment can be rented in most of the hotels. You cannot, however, enter the beach via the hotel unless you are a paying guest or will be renting equipment there. Some of the 37 beaches are secluded, and some are located in the thick of things. Topless bathing is virtually de rigueur on the French side, where the beaches are generally better than on the Dutch side. If you take a cab to a remote beach, be sure to arrange a specific, clearly understood time for your driver to return to pick you up. Don't leave valuables unattended on the beach or in your rental car, even in the trunk.

Hands down, **Baie Longue** is the best beach on the island. It's a beautiful, mile-long curve of white sand on the westernmost tip of the island. This is a good place for snorkeling and swimming, but beware of a strong undertow when the waters are rough. You can sunbathe in the buff, though only a few do. There are no facilities. **Baie Rouge** is one of the most secluded beaches on the island. This little patch of sand is at the base of high cliffs and is backed by private homes rather than by hotels. Some rate it the prettiest beach on the island. The waves here can be rough. There's a small snack and soda stand at the beach's entrance. **Cupecoy Beach** is a small shifting arc of white sand fringed with eroded limestone cliffs, just south of Baie Longue on the western side of the island, near the Dutch-French border. On the eastern part of the beach swimwear is worn, but farther west, sun worshipers start shedding their attire. This section is also the island's gay beach. There are no facilities, but a truck is often parked at the entrance, with a vendor who sells cold sodas and beers. You have to approach the **Dawn Beach–Oyster Pond** area through the grounds of the Dawn Beach Hotel. The long white-sand beach is partly protected by reefs (good for snorkeling), but the water is not always calm. When the waves come rolling in, this is the best spot on the island for bodysurfing. **Ilet Pinel** is a little speck off the northeast coast with about 500 yards of beach where you can have picnics and privacy. There are no facilities. Putt putts (small boats) are available to take you from French Cul de Sac and Orient Beach. Ecru-color sand, palm and sea-grape trees, calm waters, and the roar of jets lowering to nearby Juliana International Airport distinguish the beach at **Maho Bay.** Concession stand, beach chairs, and facilities are available. At **Mullet Bay,** the powdery white-sand beach is crowded with guests of the Mullet Bay Resort (which was closed at press time). **Orient Beach** is the island's best-known "clothes-optional" beach—it's on the agenda for voyeurs from visiting cruise ships. You can enter from the parking area. The nude section is to the right on the southern end of the beach. Farther down toward the middle of the beach is the Orient Bay Resort, with several restaurants, bars, water sports, and chaises (with food and beverage service) for rent. Beyond Baie Longue is **Plum Baie,** where the beach arcs between two headlands and the occasional sunbather discloses all. **Simpson Bay** is a long half moon of white sand near Simpson Bay Village, one of the last undiscovered hamlets on the island. In this small fishing village you'll find refreshments, a dive shop for water-sports equipment rentals, and neat little ultra-Caribbean town homes.

# Outdoor Activities and Sports

All the resort hotels have activities desks that can arrange virtually any type of water sport.

## Boating

Motorboats, speedboats, sailboats, and Waverunners can be rented at **Lagoon Watersports** (⌧ Mullet Bay Resort, ☎ 599/5−52801), **Caribbean Watersports** (⌧ Nettlé Bay, ☎ 590/87−58−66), and **Caraibes Sport Boats** (⌧ Marina Port la Royale, ☎ 590/87−89−38).

**Sun Yacht-Charters** (☎ 800/772−3500), based in Oyster Pond, has a fleet of 50 Centurion sailboats for hire. The cost of a week's bareboat charter for a 36-foot Centurion with six berths is $2,850 in peak winter season. Also in Oyster Pond, the **Moorings** (☎ 590/87−32−55 or 800/535−7289) has a fleet of Beneteau yachts, and bareboat and crewed catamarans. **Dynasty** (☎ 590/87−85−21), in Marigot's Port la Royale Marina, offers an excellent fleet of Dynamique yachts, ranging in size from 47 to 80 feet.

### Deep-Sea Fishing

Angle for yellowtail, snapper, grouper, marlin, tuna, and wahoo on half- or full-day deep-sea excursions. Prices usually include bait and tackle, instruction for novices, and an open bar. Contact **Bobby's Marina** (⊠ Philipsburg, ☎ 599/5–22366), **Lee Deepsea Fishing** (⊠ Philipsburg, ☎ 599/5–44233, 599/5–44234, or 599/5–70747), or **Sailfish Caraibes** (⊠ Port Lonvilliers, ☎ 590/87–31–94 or 590/27–40–90).

### Fitness

**L'Aqualigne** (☎ 599/5–42426), on the Dutch side at the Pelican Resort, is a health spa with gym, sauna, and beauty treatments, including manicures, facials, and massages. **Fitness Caraibes** (☎ 590/87–35–81) is a toning center at Nettlé Bay. **Future Fitness Center** (☎ 590/87–90–27), in Marigot, has decent free-weight equipment as well as machines and aerobics. **Le Privilège** (☎ 590/87–37–37), a sports complex at Anse Marcel above Le Meridien L'Habitation, has a full range of exercise equipment and the island's best spa.

### Golf

**Mullet Bay Resort** (☎ 599/5–52801) has an 18-hole championship course. Surprisingly, this is the only course on the island. Greens fees are $90 for 18 holes, $50 for 9 holes. The course remains open, even though the resort was closed at press time.

### Horseback Riding

Rides can be arranged through your hotel, or you can contact **Crazy Acres Riding Center** (⊠ Wathey Estate, Cole Bay, ☎ 599/5–42793), **Bayside Riding Club** (⊠ Orient Bay, ☎ 590/87–36–64), **O.K. Corral** (⊠ Oyster Pond, ☎ 590/87–40–72), or **Caid & Isa** (⊠ Anse Marcel, ☎ 590/87–45–70). All the outfits offer beach rides and can accommodate different skill levels.

### Jetskiing and Waterskiing

On the Dutch side, rent equipment through the **Divi Little Bay Resort**'s water-sports activity center (☎ 599/5–22333). On the French side, try **Orient Bay Watersports** (☎ 590/87–40–75) or **Laguna Watersports** (☎ 590/87–91–75) at Nettlé Bay.

### Parasailing

On the French side, **Orient Bay Watersports** (☎ 590/87–40–75) offers parasailing rides on Orient Bay.

### Running

The **Road Runners Club** meets Wednesday in the parking lot of the Raoul Illidge Sportscomplex for a 5 PM Fun Run and Sunday at 6:45 AM in the parking lot of the Pelican Resort for a 2K–15K run. For more information, contact Dr. Frits Bus at 599/5–22467 or Ron van Sittert at 599/5–22842.

### Scuba Diving

The water temperature here is rarely below 70°F, and visibility is usually excellent. There are many diving attractions, both right around the island and around numerous offshore islands. On the Dutch side is Proselyte Reef, named for the British frigate HMS *Proselyte,* which sank south of Great Bay in 1801. In addition to wreck dives, reef, night, and cave dives are popular. Off the northeast coast of the French side, dive sites include Ilet Pinel, for good shallow diving; Green Key, with its vibrant barrier reef; and Tintamarre, for sheltered coves and underwater geologic faults.

On the Dutch side, SSI- (Scuba Schools International) and PADI-certified dive centers include **Trade Winds Dive Center** (⊠ Bobby's Marina, ☎ 599/5–75176), **St. Maarten Divers** (⊠ Philipsburg, ☎ 599/5–22446),

**Leeward Island Divers** (⊠ Simpson Bay, ☎ 599/5–42268), **Ocean Explorers Dive Shop** (⊠ Simpson Bay, ☎ 599/5–45252), and **Pelican Dive Adventures** (⊠ Pelican Resort Marina, ☎ 599/5–42503, ext. 1553). On the French side, **Lou Scuba** (⊠ Marine Hotel Simson Beach, Nettlé Bay, ☎ 590/87–16–61) is a PADI-certified dive center. **Blue Ocean** (⊠ Marigot, ☎ 590/87–89–73) is PADI and CMAS certified. **Octoplus** (⊠ Grand Case Blvd., ☎ 590/87–20–62) is a complete dive center.

## Sea Excursions

You can take a daylong picnic sail to nearby islands or secluded coves aboard the 45-foot ketch **Gabrielle** (☎ 599/5–23170), or the sleek 76-foot catamaran **Golden Eagle** (☎ 599/5–22167). The 50-foot catamaran **Bluebeard II** (☎ 599/5–52898), moored in Simpson Bay, sails around Anguilla's south and northwest coasts to Prickly Pear, where there are excellent coral reefs for snorkeling and powdery white sands for sunning. The **Lady Mary** (☎ 599/5–53892) sails around the island each evening from La Palapa Center on Simpson Bay; $65 per person includes dinner, open bar, and live calypso music. It's tremendous fun. The **Laura Rose** (☎ 599/5–70710) offers a variety of half- and full-day sails.

The luxurious 75-foot motor catamaran **White Octopus** (☎ 599/5–24096 or 599/5–23170) makes the run to St. Barts, departing at 9 AM from Bobby's Marina or Captain Oliver's Marina and returning at 5 PM.

In St. Martin, sailing, snorkeling, and picnic excursions to nearby islands can be arranged through **Orient Bay Watersports** (⊠ Club Orient, ☎ 590/87–40–75), **Le Meridien L'Habitation** (☎ 590/87–33–33), **La Belle Creole** (☎ 590/87–66–00), and **La Samanna** (☎ 590/87–51–22).

## Snorkeling

Coral reefs teem with marine life, and clear water allows visibility of up to 200 feet. Some of the best snorkeling on the Dutch side can be had around the rocks below Fort Amsterdam off Little Bay Beach, in the west end of Maho Bay, off Pelican Key, and around the reefs off Dawn Beach and Oyster Pond. On the French side, the area around Orient Bay, Green Key, Ilet Pinel, and Flat Island (or Tintamarre) is especially lovely for snorkeling and should soon be officially classified a regional underwater nature reserve. Arrange rentals and trips through **Ocean Explorers** (☎ 599/5–45252) and **Orient Bay Watersports** (☎ 590/87–40–75).

## Tennis

If you want to play tennis at a hotel at which you are not a guest, be sure to call ahead to find out whether they allow visitors. You'll probably need to make reservations, and there's usually an hourly fee. There are three courts at the **Pelican Resort** (☎ 599/5–42503); three lighted courts at the **Divi Little Bay Beach Resort** (☎ 599/5–22333); three lighted courts at the **Maho Beach Hotel** (☎ 599/5–52115); six lighted courts at **Le Privilège** (Anse Marcel, ☎ 590/87–38–38), which also has four squash and two racquetball courts; 14 courts (seven lighted) at **Port de Plaisance** (☎ 599/5–45222); two lighted courts at the **Mont Vernon Hotel** (☎ 590/87–62–00); one lighted court at the **Marine Hotel Simson Beach** (☎ 590/87–54–54); 14 courts at **Mullet Bay Resort** (☎ 599/5–52801); and nine lighted court each at the **Grand Case Beach Club** (☎ 590/87–51–87) and the **Coralita Beach Hotel** (☎ 590/87–31–81).

## Windsurfing

Rental and instruction are available at **Divi Little Bay Beach Resort** (☎ 599/5–22333, ext. 186) and **Orient Bay Watersports** (☎ 590/87–40–75). The **Nathalie Simon Windsurfing Club** (☎ 590/87–48–16) offers rentals and lessons in Orient Bay.

# Shopping

About 180 cruise ships call at St. Maarten each year, and they do so for about 500 reasons. That's roughly the number of duty-free shops on the island.

Prices can be 25%–50% below those in the United States and Canada on French perfumes, liquor, cognac and fine liqueurs, cigarettes and cigars, Swedish crystal, Finnish stoneware, Irish linen, Italian leather, German cameras, European designer fashions, Swiss watches, plus thousands of other things you never knew you wanted. But check prices before you leave home, especially if you live in the New York City area—Manhattan's prices (including mail order) for cameras and electronic equipment are hard to beat anywhere. If you're shopping for electronics in Philipsburg, try negotiating for a lower price. Competition is fierce, and some stores will bargain if you pay cash. In general, you will find more fashion on the French side in Marigot, although stalwarts like Polo Ralph Lauren and Benetton have Philipsburg outlets. You will also find Marigot to be a much more pleasant place to shop and stroll.

St. Maarten's best-known "craft" is its guavaberry liqueur, made from rum and the wild local berries (not to be confused with guavas) that grow only on this island's central mountains.

Prices are quoted in florins, francs, and dollars; shops take credit cards and traveler's checks. Most shopkeepers, especially on the Dutch side, speak English. (If more than one cruise ship is in port, avoid Front Street. It's so crowded you won't be able to move.) Although most merchants are reputable, there are occasional reports of inferior or fake merchandise passed off as the real thing. As a rule of thumb, if you can bargain excessively, it's probably not worth it.

## Shopping Areas

In St. Maarten: **Front Street,** Philipsburg, is one long strip lined with sleek boutiques and colorful shops. **Old Street,** near the end of Front Street, has 22 stores, boutiques, and open-air cafés. There is a slew of boutiques in the **Mullet** and **Maho** shopping plazas, as well as at the **Plaza del Lago,** at the Simpson Bay Yacht Club complex.

In St. Martin: Wrought-iron balconies, colorful awnings, and gingerbread trim decorate Marigot's smart shops, tiny boutiques, and bistros in the **Marina Port La Royale** complex and on the main streets, **rue de la Liberté** and **rue de la République.**

## Good Buys

**Carat** (⌧ Marigot, ☎ 590/87–73–40, and Philipsburg, ☎ 599/5–22180) sells china and jewelry. **La Cave du Savour Club** (⌧ Marigot, ☎ 590/87–58–51) is the place to pick up a bottle of wine for your picnic. **H. Stern** (⌧ Philipsburg, ☎ 599/5–23328) specializes in colorful jewelry and elegant watches. **Havane** (⌧ Marigot, ☎ 590/87–70–39) sells designer fashions. **La Romana** (⌧ Front St., Philipsburg, ☎ 599/5–22181) stocks designer fashions. **Lil' Shoppe** (⌧ Philipsburg, ☎ 599/5–22177) carries eel-skin wallets, handbags, perfumes, and a large selection of swimwear. **Lipstick** (⌧ Marina Port la Royale, ☎ 590/87–73–24; Marigot, ☎ 590/87–53–92; Philipsburg, ☎ 599/5–26051) carries an enormous selection of perfume and cosmetics (including sunscreen). **Little Europe** (⌧ Philipsburg, ☎ 599/5–24371) sells fine jewelry, along with crystal and china. **Little Switzerland** (⌧ Marigot, ☎ 590/87–50–03, and Philipsburg, ☎ 599/5–23530) sells fine crystal, china, perfume, and jewelry. **New Amsterdam Store** (⌧ Philipsburg, ☎ 599/5–22787) handles designer fashions, fine linens, and porcelain. **Oro de Sol** (⊠ Marigot, ☎ 590/87–56–51) carries jewelry and watches, as well as perfume, cosmetics, and Cuban cigars. **Yellow House** (⊠ Philipsburg, ☎ 599/5–23438) carries perfumes, cosmetics, and gifts.

### Island Specialties

**ABC Art Gallery** (⊠ Marigot, ☎ 590/87–96–00) exhibits the work of local artists. **Galerie Lynn** (⊠ 83 blvd. de Grand Case, ☎ 590/87–77–24) sells stunning paintings and sculptures. **Gingerbread Galerie** (⊠ Port La Royale, ☎ 590/87–73–21) specializes in Haitian art. **Greenwith Galleries** (⊠ Philipsburg, ☎ 599/5–23842) specializes in Caribbean art. **Minguet** (⊠ Rambaud Hill, ☎ 590/87–76–06) carries pictures by the artist Minguet depicting island life. **Le Poisson D'Or** (⊠ Marigot, ☎ 590/87–72–45) restaurant houses a gallery featuring the work of local artists. **Shipwreck Shop** (⊠ Philipsburg, ☎ 599/5–22962; ⊠ Port La Royale, ☎ 590/87–27–37) stocks Caribelle batik, hammocks, handmade jewelry, the local guavaberry liqueur, and herbs and spices.

# Nightlife

To find out what's doing on the island, pick up any of the following publications: *St. Maarten Nights, What to Do in St. Maarten, St. Maarten Events,* or *St. Maarten Holiday*—all distributed free in the tourist office and hotels. *Discover St. Martin/St. Maarten,* also free, is a glossy magazine that includes articles about the island's history and the latest on shops, discos, restaurants, and even archaeological digs.

Each of the resort hotels has a Caribbean spectacular one night a week, replete with limbo and fire dancers and steel bands.

Casinos are the main focus on the Dutch side, but there are discos that usually start late and keep on till the fat lady sings.

### Bars and Nightclubs

**Bamboo Cocktail Bar** (⊠ rue de la Liberté, Marigot, ☎ 590/29–01–00) is the place for karaoke fans. **Le Bar de la Mer** (⊠ Market Square, Marigot, ☎ 590/87–81–79) on the harbor is a popular gathering spot in the evening (it's open 'til 2). **Cheri's Cafe** (⊠ across from the Maho Beach Hotel & Casino, ☎ 599/5–53361) is a local institution, with cheap food and great live bands. **Coconuts Comedy Club** (⊠ Maho Plaza, ☎ 599/5–52115) headlines top comedy acts Sunday through Friday. **David's** (⊠ rue de la Liberté, Marigot, ☎ 590/87–51–58) is run by an expatriate Brit; its raucous Tuesday and Friday trivia nights are legendary. **News Music Cafe** (⊠ Airport Rd., Simpson Bay, ☎ 599/5–42236) is a friendly spot where you can order food into the wee hours. **Surf Club South** (☎ 590/87–50–40), just east of Grand Case, is American-owned and comes complete with road signs from the Garden State Parkway posted at the entrance. **Turtle Pier Bar & Restaurant** (⊠ Airport Rd., ☎ 599/5–52230) always hops with a lively crowd.

### Casinos

All the casinos have craps, blackjack, roulette, and slot machines. You must be 18 years old or older to gamble. The casinos are located at the **Great Bay Beach Hotel, Divi Little Bay Beach Resort, Pelican Resort, Mullet Bay Resort, Seaview Hotel,** and the **Coliseum** (⊠ Cay Bay Hill, ☎ 599/5–25629) in Philipsburg; **Port de Plaisance**; and **Casino Royal at Maho Beach** (which produces the splashy Paris Revue Show).

### Discos

**Amnesia** (⊠ Maho Beach Hotel & Casino, ☎ 599/5–22962), formerly La Luna, is Maho's disco, popular with young people. Like the Amnesia in Ibiza, it sometimes features "foam" dancing. **L'Atmo 2000** (⊠

Marina Royale, Marigot, no phone), formerly the Copacabana, is where French nationals and locals flock for salsa and soca on Fridays. It's open every night but Monday. **L'Aventure** (⊠ Front de Mer, Marigot, ☎ 590/87–01–97) attracts a young crowd of locals, French nationals, and gays who gyrate to the latest house music. It's open every night but Sunday.

## Exploring St. Martin/St. Maarten

St. Martin/St. Maarten's roads are in very good condition and are generally well marked. Beware of traffic congestion, especially in and around Phillipsburg and Marigot.

*Numbers in the margin correspond to points of interest on the St. Martin/St. Maarten map.*

SIGHTS TO SEE

**⑥ French Cul de Sac.** Just north of Orient Beach is where you'll find the French colonial mansion of St. Martin's mayor nestled in the hills. Little red-roof houses look like open umbrellas tumbling down the green hillside. The scenery here is glorious, and the area is great for hiking. There is a lot of construction, however, as the surroundings are slowly being developed, including a hideous eyesore of the Mont Vernon Hotel that looks like a hospital. From the beach here, shuttle boats make the five-minute trip to **Ilet Pinel**, an uninhabited island that's fine for picnicking, sunning, and swimming.

**⑧ Friar's Beach.** This small, picturesque cove between Marigot and Grand Case attracts a casual crowd of locals. A small snack bar, **Kali's**, owned by a welcoming gentleman wearing dreadlocks, serves refreshments. A bumpy tree-canopied road leads inland to **Pic du Paradis**, at 1,278 feet the highest point on the island, affording breathtaking vistas of the Caribbean.

**⑦ Grand Case.** The most picturesque town on the island is set in the heart of the French side on the beach at the foot of green hills and pastures. Though it has only one mile-long main street, it's known as the "Restaurant Capital of the Caribbean": More than 20 restaurants serve French, Italian, Indonesian, and Vietnamese fare, as well as fresh seafood. The budget-minded love the "lolos"—stands along the waterfront selling savory barbecue (they were destroyed by Hurricane Luis, but at press time were being rebuilt). Grand Case Beach Club is at the end of this road and has two beaches where you can take a short dip.

**② Guana Bay Point.** North of Philipsburg off Sucker Garden Road, Guana Bay Point offers a splendid view of the island's east coast, tiny deserted islands, and petite St. Barts, which is anything but deserted.

**⑨ Marigot.** This town is a wonderful place to tarry awhile if you are a shopper, a gourmet, or just a Francophile. Marina Port La Royale is the shopping complex at the port, but rue de la République and rue de la Liberté, which border the bay, are also filled with duty-free shops, boutiques, and bistros. The harbor area has a new crafts pavilion selling everything from handmade crafts to fish so fresh they're still mad. You are likely to find more creative and fashionable buys in Marigot than in Philipsburg. There is less bustle here, and the open-air cafés are tempting places in which to stop for a rest. Unlike Philipsburg, Marigot does not die at night, so you may wish to stay into the evening. Across the parking lot, on the pier road leading to the ferries for Anguilla, is the helpful **French tourist office**, where you can pick up the usual assortment of free maps and brochures. Just north of town there is a shopping complex on the inland side of the main road. At the back of it is **Match** (☎ 590/87–92–36), the largest supermarket on the French side, carrying a broad selection of tempting picnic makings—from country pâté to foie gras—and a vast selection of wines.

NEED A
BREAK? With a roguish glint in his eye, owner Roger Drovin proclaims the melt-in-your-mouth croissants at **Cafe Terrasse Mastedana** (✉ rue de la Liberté, no phone) to be "zee best." This humble little establishment along the main road by Port La Royale, bedecked with pennants from around the world, is perfect for a light breakfast or snack.

**Orient Beach,** the island's best-known nudist beach, is in the northeast part of the island on the French side and is reached by a rough, bumpy dirt road. Hurricane Luis blew down the "naturist" resort there, although at press time it was being rebuilt and should be open for the '96-'97 winter season. The hurricane also made the beach much wider and sandier, the silver lining of such a devastating storm. This is wind-surfing heaven, with a couple of rental shops on the beach to take advantage of the steady onshore trade winds.

NEED A
BREAK? Stop in at the **Bikini Beach Bar and Restaurant** (☎ 590/87–43–25) for the best calamari you've ever tasted. Daily specials of French and Creole cuisine tempt the palate as the trades cool you off under the striped awning. Beach chaises and umbrellas are for rent with food and beverage service available at your chaise. A lively bar with great tunes is an option for the sun-drenched and burned.

**⑤ Orléans.** North of Oyster Pond and the Etang aux Poissons (Fish Lake) is the oldest settlement on the island, which is also known as the French Quarter. Noted local artist Roland Richardson makes his home here. He opens his **studio** to the public on Thursday from 10 to 6, or by appointment (☎ 590/87–32–24). He's a proud islander ready to share his wealth of knowledge about the island's cultural history.

**④ Oyster Pond.** Just north of Dawn Beach on Sucker Garden Road is the legendary point where two early settlers, a Frenchman and a Dutchman, allegedly began to pace in opposite directions around the island to divide it between their respective countries. Local legend maintains that the obese sweaty Hollander stopped frequently to refresh himself with gin—the reason that the French side is nearly twice the size of the Dutch. (The official boundary marker is on the other side of the island.)

**① Philipsburg.** The Dutch capital of St. Maarten stretches about a mile along an isthmus between Great Bay and the Salt Pond, and has three more or less parallel streets: Front Street, Back Street, and Pondfill. Front Street has been recobbled, cars are discouraged from using it, and the pedestrian area has been widened. Shops, restaurants, and casinos vie for the hordes coming off the cruise boats. Little lanes called *steegjes* connect Front Street with Back Street, which is considerably less congested because it has fewer shops.

**Wathey Square** is in the middle of the isthmus on which Philipsburg sits. The square bustles with vendors, souvenir shops, and tourists. Directly across the street from the square is a striking white building with a cupola. It was built in 1793 and has since served as the commander's home, a fire station, and a jail. It now serves as the town hall, courthouse, and the post office, and was beautifully restored in 1995. The streets surrounding the square are lined with hotels, duty-free shops, fine restaurants, and cafés, most of them in pastel-colored West Indian cottages gussied up with gingerbread trim. Narrow alleyways lead to arcades and flower-filled courtyards where there are yet more boutiques and eateries. The pier just off the square is a good spot to view Great Bay and the beach that stretches alongside it for about a mile.

The **Simart'n Museum** hosts rotating cultural exhibits and a permanent historical display entitled "Forts of St. Maarten/St. Martin," featuring artifacts ranging from Arawak pottery shards to articles salvaged from the wreck of HMS *Proselyte.* ⊠ *7 Front St., Philipsburg,* ☎ *599/5–24917.* ⚏ *$1.* ◷ *Mon.–Sat. 10–4.*

🍤 ❸ **St. Maarten Zoological and Botanical Garden.** This ambitious development, the labor of love of a local policeman, features plants and animals indigenous to the Caribbean basin and South America, including coatimundis, ocelots, peccaries, and boa constrictors. The two large walk-through aviaries, petting zoo, and playground should delight children of all ages. Hurricane Luis caused extensive damage to the gardens, but repairs were under way at press time; call ahead. ⊠ *Arch Rd., Madame Estate,* ☎ *599/5–32030.* ⚏ *$4.* ◷ *Weekdays 9–5, weekends 10–6.*

**Sucker Garden Road.** This road runs north of Philipsburg through spectacular scenery—soaring mountains, turquoise waters, quaint West-Indian houses, and wonderful views of St. Barts. The paved roller-coaster road eventually leads down to **Dawn Beach,** one of the island's best snorkeling beaches.

**Terres Basses.** This area of the island incorporates the coastline from Sandy Ground, just south of Marigot, to Cupecoy Beach, a small but beautiful beach of sandstone cliffs and coves, on the Dutch side. Some of the island's nicest beaches are found in this region: **Baie Rouge, Plum Baie,** and **Baie Longue** cling to its westernmost point. They are all accessible down bumpy but short dirt roads and perfect for swimming and picnicking. Also found here is Baie Nettlé, with its many reasonably priced hotels, and the Mediterranean-style village resort of **La Belle Creole,** commanding Pointe du Bluff.

# St. Martin/St. Maarten A to Z

## Arriving and Departing

### BY BOAT

Motorboats zip several times a day from Anguilla to the French side at Marigot, three times a week from St. Barts. Catamaran service is available daily from the Dutch side to St. Barts on the **White Octopus** (☎ 599/5–24096 or 599/5–23170). The high-speed ferry **Edge** (☎ 599/5–22167) slaps across from Saba three times a week.

### BY PLANE

There are two airports on the island. **L'Espérance** (☎ 590/87–53–03) on the French side is small and handles only island-hoppers. Jumbo jets fly into **Princess Juliana International Airport** (☎ 599/5–4211) on the Dutch side.

The most convenient carrier from the United States is **American Airlines** (☎ 800/433–7300), with daily nonstop flights from New York and Miami, as well as connections from more than 100 U.S. cities via its San Juan hub. **Continental Airlines** (☎ 800/231–0856) has several flights a week from Newark. **LIAT** (☎ 809/462–0701) has daily service from San Juan and several Caribbean islands including Antigua, the BVIs, and St. Kitts. **ALM** (☎ 800/327–7230) has daily service from Aruba, Bonaire, Curaçao, the Dominican Republic, and from Atlanta and Miami via Curaçao. **BWIA** (☎ 800/327–7401) offers service from Trinidad and Barbados. **Air Martinique** (☎ 596/51–08–09 or 599/5–4212) connects the island with Martinique twice a week. **Windward**

**Islands Airways** (Winair, ☎ 599/5–4230), which is based on St. Maarten, has daily scheduled service to Anguilla, Saba, St. Barts, St. Eustatius, St. Kitts/Nevis, and St. Thomas. **Air Guadeloupe** (☎ 599/5–4212 or 590/87–53–74) has several flights daily to St. Barts and Guadeloupe from both sides of the island. **Air St. Barthélemy** (☎ 590/87–73–46 or 599/5–3150) has frequent service between Juliana and St. Barts. Tour and charter services are available from Winair and **St. Martin Helicopters** (Dutch side, ☎ 599/5–4287).

## Currency

Legal tender on the Dutch side is the Netherlands Antilles florin (guilder), written NAf; on the French side, the French franc (F). The exchange rate fluctuates, but in general it is about NAf1.78 to U.S.$1 and 5F to U.S.$1. On the Dutch side, prices are usually given in both NAf and U.S. dollars, which are accepted all over the island, as are credit cards. Note: Prices quoted here are in U.S. dollars unless otherwise noted.

## Emergencies

**Police:** Dutch side (☎ 599/5–22222), French side (☎ 590/87–50–10). **Ambulance:** Dutch side (☎ 599/5–22111), French side (☎ 590/87–50–06). **Hospital: St. Maarten Medical Center** (✉ Cay Hill, ☎ 599/5–31111) is a fully equipped hospital. **Pharmacies:** Open Monday–Saturday 7–5, and include the **Central Drug Store** (✉ Philipsburg, ☎ 599/5–22321), and **Pharmacie du Port** (✉ Marigot, ☎ 590/87–50–79).

## Getting Around

Although there are other means of transportation, we recommend renting a car. You'll find it's needed to explore the island fully and visit a variety of beaches and restaurants.

### BUSES

One of the island's best bargains at 80¢ to $2, depending on your destination, buses operate frequently between 7 AM and 7 PM (less often 7–10 PM) and run from Philipsburg through Cole Bay to Marigot. There are no official stops: You just stand by the side of the road and flag the bus down. Exact change is preferred though not required, and drivers don't accept bills over $5.

### CAR RENTALS

You can book a car at Juliana International Airport, where all major rental companies have booths. If you don't have a reservation and aren't exactly sure who to rent from, be prepared for an onslaught of hawkers, most of whom represent local companies, shouting that they have newer cars with more features and better prices. The upside of this is that prices tend to go down the longer your wait. Depending on demand, you can get a car as low as $25 a day. There are also rentals at every hotel area. Rental cars, in general, are inexpensive—approximately $35–$45 a day for a subcompact car. All foreign driver's licenses are honored, and major credit cards are accepted. If you opt for collision coverage, most policies still require a $500 or more deductible. Check with your credit card company about coverage. **Avis** (☎ 800/331–1212), **Budget** (☎ 800/472–3325), **Dollar** (☎ 800/800–4000), **Hertz** (☎ 800/654–3131), and **National (Eurocar)** (☎ 800/328–4567) all have offices on the island. Scooters rent for $22–$37 a day at **Rent 2 Wheels** (✉ Nettlé Bay, ☎ 590/87–20–59).

### TAXIS

Taxi rates are government regulated, and authorized taxis display stickers of the St. Maarten Taxi Association. There is a taxi service at the Marigot port near the Tourist Information Bureau. Fixed fares apply from Juliana International Airport and the Marigot ferry to the various hotels and around the island. Fares are 25% higher between 10 PM and midnight, 50% higher between midnight and 6 AM.

## Guided Tours

A 2½-hour taxi tour of the island costs $35 for one or two people, $10 for each additional person. Your hotel or the tourist office can arrange it for you. Best bets are **St. Maarten Sightseeing Tours** (✉ Philipsburg, ☎ 599/5–22753) and **Calypso Tours** (✉ Philipsburg, ☎ 599/5–42858), which offer, among other options, a three-hour island tour for $17 per person. You can tour in deluxe comfort with **St. Maarten Limousine Service** (☎ 599/5–24698) for $40–$50 per hour; there's a three-hour minimum. Fully equipped Lincoln Continentals accommodate up to six people and are furnished with stereo, fully stocked bar, and air-conditioning. The limo service also offers transportation to and from Juliana airport at rates ranging from $30 to $65 one-way. (This includes one hour of waiting time free of charge for late arrivals.) On the French side, **R&J Tours** (✉ Colombier, ☎ 590/87–56–20) will show you the island; prices vary with the number of people and the itinerary; a three-hour tour for one person is $15.

**Ocean Explorers Sea Walk.** Uniquely designed helmets enable you to breathe normally underwater as guides point out the profusion of riotously colored marine life in Simpson Bay. Swimming ability is not required, just curiosity and a bathing suit. The walk is led four times daily and costs $35 per person. ✉ *Simpson Bay,* ☎ *599/5–45252.*

## Language

Dutch is the official language of St. Maarten, and French is the official language of St. Martin, but almost everyone speaks English. If you hear a language you can't quite place, it's Papiamento, a Spanish-based Creole of the Netherlands Antilles.

## Opening and Closing Times

Shops on the Dutch side are open Monday–Saturday 8–noon and 2–6; on the French side, Monday–Saturday 9–noon or 12:30, and 2–6. Some of the larger shops on both sides of the island open Sunday and holidays when the cruise ships are in port. Some of the small Dutch and French shops set their own capricious hours.

Banks on the Dutch side are open Monday–Thursday 8:30–3:30 and Friday 8:30–4:40. French banks are open weekdays 8:30–1:30 and 2–3 and close afternoons preceding holidays.

## Passports and Visas

U.S. citizens need proof of citizenship. A passport (valid or not expired more than five years) is preferred. An original birth certificate with raised seal (or a photocopy with notary seal) or a voter registration card is also acceptable. All visitors must have a confirmed room reservation and an ongoing or return ticket. British and Canadian citizens need valid passports.

## Taxes and Service Charges

On the Dutch side, a 5% government tax is added to hotel bills. On the French side, a *taxe de séjour* (visitor's tax) is tacked on to hotel bills (the amount differs from hotel to hotel, but the maximum is $3 per day, per person). Departure tax from Juliana airport is $5 to destinations within the Netherlands Antilles and $10 to all other destinations. It will cost you 15 French francs to depart by plane from l'Espérance Airport or by ferry to Anguilla from Marigot's pier.

In lieu of tipping, service charges are added to hotel bills all over the island and, by law, are included in all menu prices on the French side. On the Dutch side, most restaurants add 10%–15% to the bill.

Hotels on the Dutch side add a 15% service/energy charge to the bill. Hotels on the French side add 10%–15% for service.

Taxi drivers expect a 10% tip.

## Telephones and Mail

To call the Dutch side from the United States, dial 011–599 + local number; for the French side, 011–590 + local number. To phone from the Dutch side to the French, dial 06 + local number; from the French side to the Dutch, 011–5995 + local number. Keep in mind that a call from one side to the other is an overseas call, not a local call.

At the Landsradio in Philipsburg, there are facilities for overseas calls and an AT&T USADirect telephone, where you are directly in touch with an AT&T operator who will accept collect or credit-card calls.

On the French side, it is not possible to make collect calls to the United States, and there are no coin phones. If you need to use public phones, go to the special desk at Marigot's post office and buy a Telecarte (it looks like a credit card), which gives you 40 units (it takes 120 units to cover a five-minute call to the United States) for around 31F or 120 units for 93F. There is a public phone on the side of the tourist office in Marigot where you can make credit-card calls: The operator takes your credit-card number (any major card) and assigns you a PIN (Personal Identification Number), which you can then use to charge calls to your card.

Calls from anywhere on the island to the United States cost $4 per minute.

Letters from the Dutch side to the United States and Canada cost NAf1.30; postcards, NAf.60. From the French side, letters up to 20 grams, 4.10F; postcards, 3.50F.

## Visitor Information

For information about the Dutch side, contact the **tourist office** on the island directly (☎ 599/5–22337), or, in New York, contact the **St. Maarten Tourist Office** (✉ 675 3rd Ave., Suite 1806, New York, NY 10017, ☎ 212/953–2084, ᴙ 212/953–2145). In Canada, contact **St. Maarten Tourist Information** (✉ 243 Ellerslie Ave., Willowdale, Toronto, Ontario M2N 1Y5, ☎ 416/223–3501, ᴙ 416/223–6887). Information about French St. Martin can be obtained by writing the **French West Indies Tourist Board** (✉ 610 5th Ave., New York, NY 10020) or by calling France-on-Call at 900/990–0040 (50¢ per minute). You can also write to or visit the U.S. branches of the **French Government Tourist Office** (✉ 444 Madison Ave., 16th floor, New York, NY 10022; ✉ 9454 Wilshire Blvd., Suite 303, Beverly Hills, CA 90212; ✉ 645 N. Michigan Ave., Suite 3360, Chicago, IL 60611), and write, visit, or call the Canadian and U.K. offices (✉ 1981 McGill College Ave., Suite 490, Montréal, Québec H3A 2W9, ☎ 514/288–4264; ✉ 30 St. Patrick St., Suite 700, Toronto, Ontario M5T 3A3, ☎ 416/593–4723; ✉ 178 Piccadilly, London W1V OAL, ☎ 0171/629–9376).

On the Dutch side, the **tourist information bureau** is on Cyrus Wathey (pronounced "watty") Square in the heart of Philipsburg, at the pier where the cruise ships send their tenders. The administrative office is on Walter Nisbeth Road 23 (Imperial Building) on the third floor. ☎ 599/5–22337. ☉ *Weekdays 8–noon and 1–5; closed holidays.*

On the French side, there is the very helpful **tourist information office** on the Marigot pier. ☎ 590/87–57–21, ᴙ 590/87–56–43. ☉ *Weekdays 8:30–1 and 2:30–5:30, Sat. 8–noon; closed holidays and afternoon preceding holiday.*

# 24 St. Vincent and the Grenadines

Updated by
Jane E. Zarem

**T**HE MOUNTAINOUS ISLAND OF ST. VINCENT and a string of 32 lush islands and cays in the Grenadines comprise one nation called St. Vincent and the Grenadines—often abbreviated SVG. This group of islands is the southernmost of the Windwards, except for Grenada and Trinidad and Tobago. St. Vincent, only 18 miles long and 11 miles wide, is located just over 13° north of the equator; its Grenadines line up like a tadpole tail for 45 miles to the southwest. Each of the islands is, in a different way, a refuge for the demanding escapist, who will be hard put to find all-inclusive resorts, glitzy disco clubs, and duty-free shopping malls; rather, these islands are rich in natural beauty.

St. Vincent's major export is bananas, and these plants, along with coconut palms and breadfruit trees, crowd more of the island than the 107,000-person population does. This has obvious charm for the nature lover, who can spend weeks hiking St. Vincent's not always well-paved trails, perhaps sighting the rare St. Vincent parrot in the Vermont Valley, or climbing the Caribbean's most active volcano, La Soufrière, which last erupted in 1979. Below sea level, snorkeling and scuba landscapes are similarly exciting, both off St. Vincent and around the Grenadines.

Despite its unspoiled beauty, most people don't linger long in St. Vincent; they use it simply as a stop-off en route to their preferred Grenadine. That has a lot to do with the beaches, which are narrow and mostly black—in contrast to the Grenadines' picture-postcard expanses of powdery white sand. But St. Vincent deserves more than a pass-through. It has spectacular scenery, cascading waterfalls, a rugged coastline, and a fascinating history.

Although these islands have their share of the poor and unemployed, the superfertile soil allows everyone to grow enough food to eat and trade for necessities. Since tourists aren't looked upon as meal tickets, beggars are few. Recent progress (improved roads, Bequia's new airport), however, has its price: It is no longer entirely safe to hike alone along forest trails, and petty theft has become a reality.

Historians believe that in 4300 BC, long before King Tut ruled Egypt, the Ciboney Indians inhabited St. Vincent. Unhampered by passports and political unrest, the Ciboney made their way to Cuba and Haiti, leaving St. Vincent to the Arawaks. Columbus sailed by in 1492, while the Arawaks were involved in intermittent skirmishes with the bellicose Caribs. Though Columbus never actually stopped on St. Vincent, Discovery Day (or St. Vincent and the Grenadines' Day) is still commemorated on January 22.

Declared a neutral island by French and British agreement in 1748, St. Vincent became something of a political football in the years that followed. Ceded to the British in 1763, it was captured by the French in 1779 and restored to the British by the Treaty of Versailles in 1783. By the 19th century, St. Vincent was quite sure it was more British than French; on October 27, 1979, it gained independence from Great Britain.

In contrast to their colorful history, the Grenadines seem timeless, as free from politics as the beaches are free from debris and crowds. Nine miles south of St. Vincent is Bequia, the first and largest of the Grenadine Islands. Its Admiralty Bay is one of the finest anchorages in the Caribbean. With superb views, snorkeling, hiking, and swimming, the island has much to offer the international mix of backpackers and luxury-yacht owners who frequent its shores.

A two-hour sail (or 10-minute flight) south is the private island of Mustique. More arid than Bequia, Mustique does not need to tout itself to tourists, least of all those hoping for a glimpse of the rich and famous (Princess Margaret, Mick Jagger, David Bowie) who own houses here. The appeal of Mustique is seclusion and privacy.

Just over 3 square miles, Canouan is an unspoiled island that offers travelers an opportunity to relax, snorkel, and hike.

The tiny island of Mayreau has 182 residents and one of the area's most beautiful beaches. The Caribbean is often mirror-calm, yet just yards away on the southern end of this narrow island is the rolling Atlantic surf.

John Caldwell has spent 20 years turning Palm Island from a mosquito-infested mangrove swamp into a small island paradise. The Caldwell family also hosts day-tripping cruise passengers who come to lounge on the wide white beaches, which are dotted and fringed with palm trees.

Union Island isn't really a place for landlubbers: The island caters almost exclusively to French sailors, who keep very much to themselves. Surface transport is limited, and to see the island you need a boat. You won't find the laid-back friendliness of the other Grenadines here.

Petit St. Vincent is another private luxury-resort island, reclaimed from the jungle by manager Haze Richardson. It's actually possible to spend your entire vacation in one of the resort's widely spaced stone houses without ever seeing another human being.

Numerous yachts and catamarans can be chartered for day sails from any of the Grenadines to the tiny uninhabited Tobago Cays. Avid snorkelers claim that the cays have some of the best hard and soft coral formations found outside the Pacific Ocean. The beaches here are perfect for secluded picnics.

# ST. VINCENT

## Lodging

Luxury resorts may require booking about six months in advance, but most St. Vincent hotels can squeeze you in with far less notice. There's a bit of a lull in January, between Christmas week and the February rush, when rooms are sometimes available on a day's notice. Many hotels offer MAP (Modified American Plan, with breakfast and dinner included).

| CATEGORY | COST* |
|---|---|
| $$$$ | over $200 |
| $$$ | $130–$200 |
| $$ | $80–$130 |
| $ | under $80 |

*All prices are for a standard double room for two, excluding 7% tax and 10% service charge.*

### Kingstown

$ 🏨 **Cobblestone Inn.** Downtown in the city, as Vincentians call Kingstown, this former sugar warehouse, built in 1814 of local stone, has a delightful, sunny interior courtyard and arched passageways that lead to most rooms. A popular rooftop bar-restaurant serves breakfast and soup-salad-burger lunches. All the rooms have exposed stone walls, rattan furniture, and small, sparkling bathrooms. Many are rather dark, with a faint, not unpleasant, dungeonlike smell that emanates from the stones. Number 5 at the front is lighter and bigger than most of the other rooms but noisier, too. Downstairs you'll find Basil's Restaurant

*ATLANTIC OCEA*

Colonarie Bay
Sans Souci

Grant's Bay

Yambou Head

Biabou

Mesopotamia

Argyle

Stubbs Bay

Milligan Cay

Greiggs

Yambou R.

Calliaqua

Mt. St. Andrew

Glen

Indian Bay

Villa

Calliaqua Beach

Kingstown

Arnos Vale Airport

Kingstown Bay

Layou

Buccament Bay

Questelle's Bay

TO BEQUIA

2 miles

3 km

N

**KEY**

🚢 Ferry
① Exploring Sites
⑮ Hotels and Restaurants

**Exploring**
Barrouallie, **4**
Black Point Tunnel, **10**
Colonarie, **11**
Falls of Baleine, **6**
Fort Charlotte, **2**

Fort Duvernette, **14**
Georgetown, **9**
Kingstown, **1**
Layou, **3**
Mesopotamia, **12**
Montreal Gardens, **13**

Owia, **7**
Rabacca Dry River, **8**
Wallilabou Bay, **5**

**Dining**
Aggie's, **20**
Basil's Bar and Restaurant, **18**

Dolphins, **21**
French Restaurant, **26**
Lime N' Pub, **27**
The Valley, **15**
Vee Jay's Rooftop Dining Club, **22**

Young Island, **25**

**Lodging**
Beachcombers, **30**
Cobblestone Inn, **17**
Emerald Valley Resort, **15**

Grand View Beach Hotel, **24**
Heron Hotel, **19**
Indian Bay Beach Hotel and Apartments, **23**
Lagoon Marina and Hotel, **31**

Petit Byahaut, **16**
Sunset Shores Beach Hotel, **28**
Umbrella Beach Hotel, **29**
Young Island, **25**

**The Grenadines**

*Caribbean Sea*

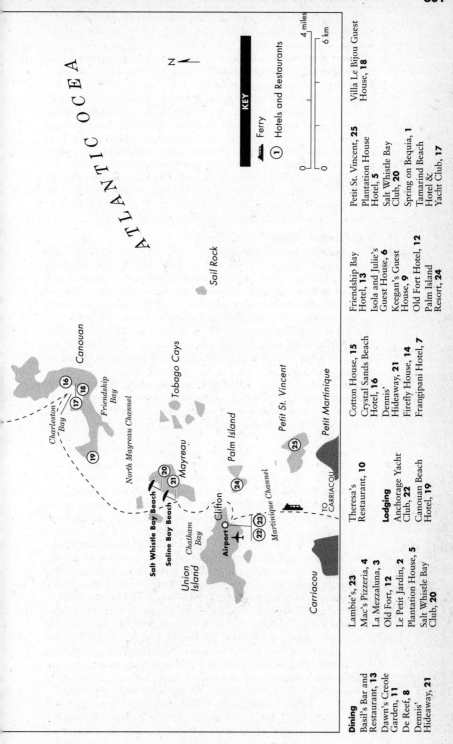

ATLANTIC OCEAN

N

**KEY**

⛴ Ferry

① Hotels and Restaurants

0 ———————— 4 miles
0 ———————— 6 km

Canouan

Friendship
Bay

Charleston
Bay

North Mayreau Channel

Mayreau

Tobago Cays

Palm Island

Petit St. Vincent

Petit Martinique

Sail Rock

TO
CARRIACOU

Martinique Channel

Union
Island

Chatham
Bay

Clifton

Airport

Salt Whistle Bay Beach

Saline Bay Beach

Carriacou

**Dining**
Basil's Bar and
  Restaurant, **13**
Dawn's Creole
  Garden, **11**
De Reef, **8**
Dennis'
  Hideaway, **21**

Lambie's, **23**
Mac's Pizzeria, **4**
La Mezzaluna, **3**
Old Fort, **12**
Le Petit Jardin, **2**
Plantation House, **5**
Salt Whistle Bay
  Club, **20**

Theresa's
  Restaurant, **10**

**Lodging**
Anchorage Yacht
  Club, **22**
Canouan Beach
  Hotel, **19**

Cotton House, **15**
Crystal Sands Beach
  Hotel, **16**
Dennis'
  Hideaway, **21**
Firefly House, **14**
Frangipani Hotel, **7**

Friendship Bay
  Hotel, **13**
Isola and Julie's
  Guest House, **6**
Keegan's Guest
  House, **9**
Old Fort Hotel, **12**
Palm Island
  Resort, **24**

Petit St. Vincent, **25**
Plantation House
  Hotel, **5**
Salt Whistle Bay
  Club, **20**
Spring on Bequia, **1**
Tamarind Beach
  Hotel &
  Yacht Club, **17**

Villa Le Bijou Guest
  House, **18**

and an array of shops selling local craftwork and fashions. ⊠ *Box 867, Kingstown, St. Vincent,* ☎ *809/456–1937. 19 rooms. Restaurant, bar, air-conditioning. AE, D, MC, V. CP.*

$    🏨 **Heron Hotel.** Steps away from the Grenadines wharf, on the second floor above a Georgian plantation warehouse that now contains shops but once provided lodgings for the plantation bosses, the Heron caters mostly to stopover island-hoppers. It has managed to retain an old-fashioned atmosphere: Rooms are straight out of a '50s boardinghouse, with thin, wine-red or navy carpets; billowing faded floral drapes; single beds; bentwood chairs; and tiny cream-color bathrooms. They fan out from a palm-filled central courtyard, with tables set on a veranda for breakfast (light lunches, drinks, and West Indian dinners are also available). There's also a corner TV lounge with black floorboards, two giant ficus plants, and rows of wooden armchairs. ⊠ *Box 226, Kingstown, St. Vincent,* ☎ *809/457–1631,* 𝙵𝙰𝚇 *809/457–1189. 12 rooms. Dining room, lounge, air-conditioning. MC, V. CP.*

## Villa Beach Area

$$$$  🏨 **Grand View Beach Hotel.** The Sardine family's turn-of-the-century
★    cotton plantation great house is now Tony and Heather Sardine's beautiful hotel, perched on a lookout point just east of Indian Bay. It manages to have both great facilities and down-home charm. Most of the simple white-walled rooms with hardwood floors enjoy the sweeping vista toward the Grenadines, and all have air-conditioning or fan, direct-dial phones, and satellite TV. A "Luxury Level" has big ocean-facing terraces and a pair of honeymoon suites with king-size beds and whirlpool tubs. A good restaurant serves West Indian and Continental dishes. Sailboats, Windsurfers, and snorkeling equipment are complimentary. ⊠ *Box 173, Villa Point, St. Vincent,* ☎ *809/458–4811,* 𝙵𝙰𝚇 *809/457–4174. U.S. agent: Charms Caribbean Vacations,* ☎ *800/ 223–6510. 19 rooms. Restaurant, pool, massage, sauna, tennis court, health club, squash, water-sports center nearby, reading room. AE, MC, V. CP, MAP.*

$$$$  🏨 **Young Island.** A mere 200 yards from Villa beach lies a 25-acre is-
★    land populated by prosperous couples who dream of being shipwrecked on a tropical island but don't want to get their feet wet. You arrive by ferry, are handed a rum punch crowned with a hibiscus blossom, and are conducted to one of 29 houselets. Each has its own patio; rattan, palm-weave, and cane decor; and a bathroom that opens into an open-air, but private, shower; as well as a plunge pool, if you're in Number 6 or 10. Keys are optional, but you have a wall safe; phones are nonexistent, but messages are brought promptly; and there's dual voltage. "Superior" accommodations are lower down, among the tumbling masses of flamboyant, nutmeg, almond, mango, ferns, coffee, breadfruit, etc., etc., while the more expensive deluxe and luxury cottages, with sitting area, are high over the sea; all are exactly halfway between the Swiss Family Robinson's tree house and the Ritz. The landscape conceals a lagoon pool, shaded hammocks, and beach (it's tiny, but white-sand) loungers, plus various bird families. Watch hummingbirds over a Creole French toast breakfast (made with banana bread) on your terrace, and you may feel like you've taken a five-minute boat to heaven. ⊠ *Box 211, Young Island,* ☎ *809/458–4826,* 𝙵𝙰𝚇 *809/457– 4567. U.S. agent: Ralph Locke Islands, Box 800, Waccabuc, NY 10597,* ☎ *914/763–5526 or 800/223–1108. 29 rooms. Restaurant, 2 bars, in-room safes, refrigerators, saltwater pool, tennis court, scuba diving, water-sports center, yacht charters. AE, D, MC, V. MAP, FAP.*

$$$   🏨 **Sunset Shores Beach Hotel.** This U-shape, lemon-color low rise is the nearest thing on St. Vincent to a corporate hotel, which is not very near at all. There's a Caribbean news update board in the lobby, con-

ference facilities for 100, and the Lions tend to hold their roisterous meetings here; but other than that, you won't be bothered by men in suits. All rooms overlook the large-enough pool in the center of the U, which faces the sea at Indian Bay. Superior rooms have patios, carpets, and TVs, and really are superior to the rest. The poolside Sunrunner Bar is nicely placed opposite the sunset. ⊠ *Box 849, Villa Beach, St. Vincent,* ☎ *809/458–4411,* FAX *809/457–4800. 32 rooms. Restaurant, 2 bars, air-conditioning, pool, Ping-Pong, water-sports center nearby, meeting rooms. AE, D, MC, V. EP, MAP.*

$ ★ ▦ **Beachcombers.** At Villa, next to Sunset Shores, Flora and Richard Gunn have built a tiny and darling village on their sloping lawns, with a pair of chalet buildings containing the guest rooms, an open-terraced bar-restaurant, and the reception area, which includes a shop and a library. Their daughter Cheryl, who studied cooking in London, is the chef; daughter Beverley, who studied hotel management in Switzerland, runs the hotel. You could eat breakfast off the floor of any bedroom here, such is the standard of housekeeping, though some rooms are prettier than others. Numbers 1–3 are prime, since they face the sea; 1 and 3 ($5 extra) have small kitchens; 4–6 are in back of these, overlooking the Mango Tree Lounge and garden. The other building, containing rooms 7–12, faces the "Bridal Bridge" (they do weddings) and the garden's frenzy of flowers and has a communal red-tile terrace in front. Bathrooms lack tubs, but this is an insignificant privation when the welcome is this warm and the rates this low. There's a brand-new, fully equipped spa, which Flora uses for her other career—as beauty and massage therapist. Yes, this is the only Vincentian B&B featuring top-class aromatherapy, reflexology, facials, sauna, steam, and Turkish bath. ⊠ *Box 126, Villa Beach, St Vincent,* ☎ *809/458–4283. 14 rooms. Restaurant, bar, fans, sauna, spa, steam room, Turkish bath, shop. AE, MC, V. BP.*

$ ▦ **Indian Bay Beach Hotel and Apartments.** This pretty, two-story building sits on Indian Bay, with its small, sheltered, somewhat rocky white-sand beach that appeals to snorkelers. It's just a stone's throw from the action at Villa Beach. The simple apartments have either one or two bedrooms; the best overlook the bay, with use of a large terrace on top of the restaurant, A La Mer—an airy space with white-trellised arches and a sapphire-blue awning, which holds a barbecue with live steel-band music on Friday nights. Both baby-sitting and lower weekly rates are available, making this spot especially nice for families. ⊠ *Box 538, Kingstown, St. Vincent,* ☎ *809/458–4001,* FAX *809/457–4777. 14 apartments. Restaurant, bar, air-conditioning, kitchenettes, beach, water sports nearby. AE, MC, V. EP, CP, MAP.*

$ ▦ **Umbrella Beach Hotel.** If you're prepared to sacrifice gorgeous bedroom decor for the sake of your pocketbook but still want to be well located, this very simple cluster of small apartment rooms may fit the bill. All are clean but have shower-only bathrooms and are dark and plain, with white walls, red marble-chip floors with a rush mat, and plastic chairs at a small Formica table. Steps away are Villa Beach, across from Young Island (ask permission to take the ferry over), the Lime N' Pub, and French Restaurant, where you could spend the cash you saved on the room. ⊠ *Villa Beach, St. Vincent,* ☎ *809/458–4651,* FAX *809/457–4930. 9 rooms. Fans, kitchenettes, beach and water sports nearby. MC, V. EP.*

## Elsewhere on St. Vincent

$$$ ▦ **Petit Byahaut.** Sort of a Young Island for those with Swiss Family Robinson fantasies who *do* want to get their feet wet, this 50-acre valley resort accommodates its guests in tents, albeit permanent, wood-floored, 10-by-13-foot tents, complete with private deck, queen-size

beds, and solar-heated showers. This adults' camp is accessible only by boat, which collects you from Kingstown (rates include this, as well as all meals), and there is a selection of other boats to play with once you're settled in, along with scuba and snorkeling equipment. On the grounds are a big, black-sand beach, hammocks, and some interesting Carib Indian artifacts. There's a boutique, excursions are easily arranged, and that's about the extent of the facilities, but then, you don't stay here unless you're reasonably adventuresome and interested in seclusion. ⊠ *Petit Byahaut Bay, St. Vincent,* ☎ FAX *809/457–7008. 7 tents. Restaurant, bar, scuba diving, snorkeling, beach, ferry service. MC, V. FAP.*

**$$** 🏨 **Lagoon Marina and Hotel.** The only hotel overlooking sheltered Blue
★ Lagoon Bay may well be the friendliest hotel on the island. Thanks to its full-service yacht marina, complete with the best-equipped marine shop in St. Vincent, there are usually seafaring types liming in the terrace bar, and plenty of yacht traffic to watch from your big, comfortable balcony with its two couches. Sliding patio doors lead onto these from the high wood-ceilinged, carpeted rooms; you can practically dive into the sea from Numbers 1–9, which hang over the wooden quay and face the sunset; 10–20 overlook the narrow, curved black-sand beach. Basic wooden furniture, twin beds, rather dim lighting, tiled bathrooms, and ceiling fans provide an adequate level of comfort; about half the rooms have air-conditioning (for a few dollars extra), but don't expect luxury. Sloping garden grounds contain a secluded two-level pool and the St. Vincent Dive Experience Headquarters, and there's a pretty, candlelit terrace restaurant. ⊠ *Box 133, Blue Lagoon, St. Vincent,* ☎ *809/458–4308,* FAX *809/457–4716. U.S. agent: Charms Caribbean Vacations,* ☎ *800/742–4276. 19 rooms. Restaurant, bar, pool, beach, scuba diving, scuba diving, snorkeling, windsurfing, boating, sailing, yacht marina, yacht charter, conference room. AE, V. EP.*

**$–$$** 🏨 **Emerald Valley Resort.** The rural, rain-forested Penniston Valley, a half-hour drive from Kingstown, is the unlikely setting for the Grenadines' only casino, which is, equally improbably, attached to this recently renovated family-friendly 5-acre resort. Two pairs of Brits toiled for two years to bring a run-down property up to very high standards. The 12 chalets have locally made wood-frame king-size or twin beds, stone-floored terraces, and (stoveless) kitchenettes. In the garden grounds are an outdoor bar, a two-level pool bisected by a wooden bridge and diving platform, a stage for local bands on weekends, two tennis courts (pro lessons available), a new golf course, and the pretty Valley restaurant (☞ Dining, *below*). What you don't get, of course, is a beach, and the nearest groceries are in Kingstown, but the Vermont Nature Trail is 2½ miles away, and you can gamble till the small hours if bored. ⊠ *Penniston Valley, Box 1081, St. Vincent,* ☎ *809/456–7140,* FAX *809/456–7145. 12 chalets. Restaurant, 2 bars, air-conditioning, fans, kitchenettes, in-room VCRs, pool, 9-hole golf course, 2 tennis courts, croquet, volleyball, casino. AE, MC, V. EP.*

## Dining

West Indian food is the way to go in St. Vincent. You'll enjoy interesting local fare that is reasonably priced at all but the most expensive hotels. Dishes include callaloo (spinachlike) soup, curry goat, *rotis* (turnovers filled with curried potatoes and meat or conch), seasonal seafood (lobster, kingfish, snapper, and dolphinfish), local vegetables (such as christophines, breadfruit, dasheen, and eddoes), and exotic fruit (from sugar apples and soursop to pineapple and papaya). Fried chicken and burgers are available everywhere, but look for the "imported beef" note on the menu; local beef is not aged, so it tends to be extremely chewy. The local lager, Hairoun, is brewed at Camden Park, on the leeward coast, according to a German recipe.

## What to Wear

Restaurants on St. Vincent are, for the most part, very casual. In Kingstown, the closest thing on the island to a city, you may want to dress a little more formally—maybe put on a pair of khakis—but none of the places listed below require a jacket or tie. On the Grenadines ultracasual is fine everywhere.

| CATEGORY | COST* |
|----------|-------|
| $$$ | over $20 |
| $$ | $10–$20 |
| $ | under $10 |

*per person, excluding drinks and 7% sales tax*

**$$$** ✕ **Basil's Bar and Restaurant.** This air-conditioned restaurant, downstairs in the Cobblestone Inn, is owned by the infamous Basil of Mustique but has little else in common with that laid-back Grenadine glitterati hangout. This is the Kingstown power-lunch venue, serving a daily buffet of local fish dishes, plus seafood pasta and chicken poached in fresh ginger and coconut milk, to local businessmen and yachties for about $12 an entrée. The bar can get lively in the evenings, when dinner tables are candlelit. There's a Chinese buffet on Fridays. ✉ *Bay St., Kingstown,* ☎ *809/457–2713. AE, MC, V.*

**$$$** ✕ **French Restaurant.** Referred to as "The French," this Caribbean in-
★ stitution on Villa Beach, facing Young Island, is where everyone goes when they're feeling posh—especially when in a lobster mood, since they have a state-of-the-art lobster pool on the terrace. You can watch the staff fish for your supper. As befits a place run by a couple from Orléans, most dishes are the Gallic version of local cuisine. Stuffed crab back, for instance, comes in a shell of pastry, not crab; steak—*au poivre*, with garlic butter, or béarnaise—is imported; onion soup and lemon tart are comme il faut; and bread is warm, fresh—a real baguette. At the inside bar, complete with an eccentric, giggling barman, frothy cocktails and Martinique-style tea punch are served to yachties who hang out here in the winter season. ✉ *Villa Beach,* ☎ *809/458–4972. AE, V.*

**$$$** ✕ **The Valley.** This pretty terrace hung with fishing nets is part of the Emerald Valley Resort—which includes the only casino in St. Vincent and the Grenadines. And if it's Saturday (also some Fridays), a local band serenades diners. The pride of the kitchen is river lobster, retrieved from the Vermont River, which runs through this area. Other dishes are a local–international mix: tomato, mozzarella, and basil salad; baked red snapper with coconut stuffing; broiled *poussin* (young chicken) with local herbs. Get directions if you're driving, and call first—the restaurant has an unpredictable tendency to be closed. ✉ *Penniston Valley,* ☎ *809/456–7140. AE, MC, V.*

**$$$** ✕ **Young Island.** Five-course chef's-choice dinners of seafood, roast pig, beef, and chicken tend to be heavy and old-fashioned, but fare is lighter at the Lucullan Tuesday buffets and at the Saturday barbecues, when a steel band makes it an event. Lunch is served buffet- or barbecue-style on the beach daily and features seafood, fresh fruits, salads, and cold cuts, with an assortment of fresh breads. Pink-clothed tables are secreted individually in palm-thatched huts dotted around the beach, with more in the stone-floored terrace dining room; they're romantically candlelit at night. ✉ *Young Island,* ☎ *809/458–4826. Reservations essential. AE, MC, V.*

**$–$$** ✕ **Dolphins.** Sandwiched between the Lime N' Pub and The French
★ is this welcome addition to the villa scene. The well-traveled, Scottish-born father-and-son owners insist on fresh local ingredients for

everything on the menu. And from the kingfish, snapper, lobster, conch, and shrimp to the dressing on the chef's salad, nothing is bottled, canned, or artificial. Sit on the large covered terrace or take up residence in the bar, with its separate menu, old-fashioned Naugahyde booths, and barkeep who mixes a mean punch. Local musicians play (Friday and Saturday), and the work of local artists, including that of former classical violinist and owner Austin Patterson, decks the walls. Dolphins is also the pioneer of St. Vincent home delivery, so note the number if you're staying nearby. ⊠ *Villa Beach,* ☎ *809/457–4337. MC, V.*

**$–$$** ✕ **Lime N' Pub.** Although this sprawling, waterfront, indoor-outdoor restaurant and bar is named after the *pursuit* of liming, its decor happens to feature a great deal of virulent green, which could prove painful after several cocktails! An eclectic all-day menu caters to burger and pizza eaters, as well as seafood fans, and even provides for hybrid diners if they're brave enough to order the smoked sailfish pizza. Rotis and coconut shrimp go down well with a bottle of Hairoun. The mood is casual during the day, romantic and candlelit at night. Shop before dinner at the swimwear-and-batik boutique, or stay late and dance on weekends, when the place resembles a singles bar. ⊠ *Villa Beach, opposite Young Island,* ☎ *809/458–4227. AE.*

**$–$$** ✕ **Vee Jay's Rooftop Dining Club.** This local restaurant above Roger's Photo Studios (have your pix developed while you eat), nearly opposite the Cobblestone Hotel, offers downtown Kingstown's best port view from beneath its green corrugated plastic roof. Among "authentic Vincie cuisine" specials chalked on the blackboard are mutton or fish stew, chicken or vegetable rotis, curried goat, or not remotely Vincie sandwiches and burgers, which can be authentically washed down with mauby (a bittersweet drink made from tree bark—an acquired taste), linseed, peanut punch, sorrel cordials, or a cocktail. Lunch is buffet-style. ⊠ *Upper Bay St., Kingstown,* ☎ *809/457–2845. Reservations essential for dinner. AE, MC, V. Closed Sun.*

**$** ✕ **Aggie's.** Opposite the Sardine Bakery on Grenville, the Kingstown shopping street, is this casual bar and restaurant, with a swimming-pool-blue ceiling and trellised arches. It serves local seafood dishes, like conch souse and kingfish steak, delicious pumpkin or callaloo soup, rotis, baked chicken leg, and salads, right up to midnight. They'll even pack it up to take out. There's a Friday happy hour from 4 to 6. ⊠ *Grenville St., Kingstown,* ☎ *809/456–2110. No credit cards.*

# Beaches

Most of the white-sand beaches are just south of Kingstown; black-sand beaches ring the rest of the island. No beach has lifeguards, so even experienced swimmers are taking a risk.

**Buccament Bay,** which is good for swimming, is a tiny black-sand beach on the west coast. The exposed Atlantic coast is dramatic, but the water is rough and unpredictable. The windward side of the island has no beachfront facilities. **Indian Bay,** adjacent to Villa Beach, has white sand but is slightly rocky. **Questelle's Bay** (pronounced keet-*ells*), on the westward (leeward) coast north of Kingstown and next to the Camden Park Industrial Site, has a black-sand beach. **Villa Beach** is the island's main beach (although it's hardly big enough to merit such a title); it's on the west coast, south of Kingstown and is small and safe, with dive shops nearby.

# Outdoor Activities and Sports

## Hiking

**Buccament Valley** contains two well-marked trails, including the Vermont Trail, where you may be lucky enough to see the rare St. Vincent parrot, *Amazona guidingii,* for which a 5 AM start is recommended. **Dorsetshire Hill,** about 3 miles from Kingstown, rewards you with a sweeping view of city and harbor; picturesque Queen's Drive is nearby. **La Soufrière,** the queen of climbs, is St. Vincent's active volcano (which last erupted, appropriately enough, on Friday the 13th in 1979). Approachable from both windward and leeward coasts, this is *not* a casual excursion for inexperienced walkers. Climbs are all-day affairs. You'll need stamina and sturdy shoes for this climb of just over 4,000 feet. Be sure to check the weather before you leave; hikers have been sorely disappointed when they reached the top and found the view completely obscured by enveloping clouds. A Land-Rover and guide can be arranged through your hotel (or ☞ Guided Tours *in* St. Vincent and the Grenadines A to Z, *below*). The four-wheel-drive vehicle takes you past Rabacca Dry River through the Bamboo Forest. From there it's a two-hour hike to the summit. You can arrange in advance to come down the other side of the mountain to the Châteaubelair area. **Mount St. Andrew,** on the outskirts of Kingstown, is a pleasant climb on a well-marked trail through a rain forest.

## Sailing and Charter Yachting

You may wish to charter a sailboat or catamaran (bareboat or complete with captain, crew, and cook) to weave you around the Grenadines for a day or a week. Boats of all sizes and degrees of luxury are available. Hotels can recommend charter yachts. The **Lagoon Marina and Hotel** (☎ 809/458–4308) in the Blue Lagoon area of St. Vincent has 44-foot crewed sloops from $200 per day.

## Water Sports

The constant trade winds are perfect for windsurfing, and 80-foot visibility on numerous reefs means superior diving. Many experienced divers find St. Vincent and Bequia far less crowded and nearly as rich in marine life as Bonaire and the Caymans; snorkeling in the Tobago Cays is among the world's best. Dive operations are small and often less luxurious than on other islands, but they are competent and professional. Many offer three-hour beginner "resort" courses, full certification courses, and excursions to nearby reefs, walls, and wrecks. Dive shops are on St. Vincent, Bequia, Canouan, Petit St. Vincent, Mustique, Union, and Palm islands. Most dive shops and larger hotels also rent Sunfish, Windsurfers, and snorkel gear. Depending on the weather, Young Island has some of the area's most colorful snorkeling. If you're not a guest at this private island resort, phone for permission to take the ferry and rent equipment from the resort's water-sports center (☞ Lodging, *above*).

**Dive St. Vincent** (⊠ Young Island Dock, Villa Beach, ☎ 809/457–4714, FAX 809/457–4928) is where NAUI instructor Bill Tewes and his staff offer beginner and certification courses and trips to the Falls of Baleine. A single-tank dive is about $50. **St. Vincent Dive Experience** (⊠ Lagoon Marina Hotel, ☎ 809/456–9741), run by NAUI instructor Perry Hughes, offers all levels of training and certification, plus night dives, snorkeling, and tours. A single-tank dive is about $40.

# Shopping

## Local Crafts

**Noah's Arkade** (⊠ Bay St., Kingstown, ☎ 809/457–1513) sells appealing local crafts (batik, baskets) and resort wear. **St. Vincent Crafts-**

**men Center** (✉ James St., Kingstown, ☎ 809/457–1288), in the north-west end of the city, sells grass floor mats and other woven items, as well as batik cloth, carved wooden dolls, and framed artwork. **Sprott Bros.** (✉ Bay St., Kingstown, ☎ 809/457–1121) carries colorful garments and crafts designed and made by Vincentians.

### Luxury Goods

St. Vincent isn't a duty-free port, although a few shops sell luxury goods at duty-free prices. Price and selection, however, don't come close to the values available on other Caribbean islands. Swiss watches, crystal, china, and jewelry can be found in Kingstown at **Stecher's Jewelers & Gift Shop** (✉ In the Cobblestone Arcade on Bay St., ☎ 809/457–1142; at the airport ☎ 809/458–4587), at **Voyager** (✉ Halifax St., ☎ 809/456–1686), and at **Y De Lima** (✉ Bay and Egmont Sts., ☎ 809/457–1681).

# Nightlife

Don't look for fire-eaters and limbo demonstrations on St. Vincent. Nightlife here consists mostly of Friday-night hotel barbecue buffets and jump-ups, so called because the lively steel-band and calypso music makes listeners jump up and dance.

**The Attic** (✉ 1 Melville St., above Kentucky Fried Chicken, Kingstown, ☎ 809/457–2558), a jazz club with modern decor, features international artists and steel bands. There is a small cover charge; call ahead for hours and performers. **Emerald Valley Casino** (✉ Penniston Valley, ☎ 809/456–7140) has the homey atmosphere of an English pub but offers bar, food, and all the gaming of Vegas—three roulette tables (the only single-zero ones in the Caribbean), three blackjack, one Caribbean stud poker, one craps, five video slots, three slots—and is open Wednesday to Monday 9 PM–3 AM, until 4 AM on Saturday. **Touch Entertainment Centre** (✉ Grenville St., Kingstown, ☎ 809/457–1825), in the heart of Kingstown, is a dance hall with disco music on Fridays and live music on Saturdays. It attracts a local crowd of mostly young people. There's a small cover charge. **Young Island** (✉ Young Island, ☎ 809/458–4826) hosts sunset cocktail parties with hors d'oeuvres once a week on Fort Duvernette, the tiny island behind the resort. On that night, 100 steps up the hill are lit by flaming torches, and a string band plays. Reservations are necessary for nonguests.

# Exploring St. Vincent

Kingstown's shopping and business district, cathedrals, and sights can easily be seen in a half day, with another half day for the Botanical Gardens. Outlying areas and the Falls of Baleine each require a full day; trips to La Soufrière and the Vermont Trail are major undertakings, requiring a very early start and a full day's strenuous hiking. Island maps are in the "Discover SVG" booklet, available everywhere. The coastal roads of St. Vincent offer panoramic views and insights into the island way of life. The Leeward Highway follows the scenic Caribbean coastline; the Windward Highway follows the more dramatic Atlantic coast.

*Numbers in the margin correspond to points of interest on the St. Vincent map.*

SIGHTS TO SEE

❹ **Barroualie.** This used to be an important whaling village; the inhabitants of Barroualie (pronounced *bar*-relly) now earn their livelihoods trawling for blackfish.

⓾ **Black Point Tunnel.** In 1815, with the help of Carib and African slaves, Colonel Thomas Browne drilled this 350-foot-long tunnel through volcanic rock to facilitate the transportation of sugar from estates in the north to the port in Kingstown. The tunnel links Grand Sable with Byera Bay, just north of Colonarie.

⓫ **Colonarie.** In the hills behind the town are hiking trails. Signs on the trails are limited, but the local people are helpful with directions.

❻ **Falls of Baleine.** They're impossible to get to by car but an absolute must to see on an escorted all-day boat trip or by chartered boat from Villa Beach or the Lagoon Marina (☞ Outdoor Activities and Sports, *above*). The ride to the falls offers scenic island views. When you arrive, be prepared to climb from the boat into shallow water to get to the beach. Local guides help visitors make the easy five-minute sneakers-and-swimsuit trek to the falls. Swim in the freshwater pool, climb under the 63-foot falls (they're chilly), and relax in this Garden of Eden.

❷ **Fort Charlotte.** Built in 1806 to keep Napoleon at bay and named for the wife of King George III, the fort sits on Berkshire Hill, 636 feet above sea level, with cannons and battlements perched on a dramatic promontory overlooking the city and the Grenadines to the south, Lowman's Beach and the calm east coast to the north. The fort saw little military action. Nowadays it is the island's women's prison. Next to it, and visible from the water, is the old leper's colony.

⓮ **Fort Duvernette.** This tiny island juts up like a loaf of pumpernickel bread behind Young Island. Take the *African Queen*–style ferry for a couple of E.C. dollars from the dock at Villa Beach near Kingstown (call the boatman from the phone on the dock), and set a time for your return (60–90 minutes is plenty for exploring). Views from the 195-foot summit are terrific, but you'll have to climb the 100 or more steps carved into the mountain to get there. Entering the little overgrown house is not for the squeamish; expect to encounter (harmless) bats. Rusting cannons from the early 1800s are still here, aimed not toward seagoing invaders but defending against marauding Caribs.

❾ **Georgetown.** Halfway up the island's east coast, amid coconut groves and the long-defunct Mount Bentinck sugar factory, this is St. Vincent's second-largest city.

❶ **Kingstown.** The capital city and port of St. Vincent is on the island's southwestern coast. It is very much a working city, with no concessions made to tourists, or to cruise-line day-trippers. The **harbor** is far more likely to be hosting a freighter than a passenger ship, but what few gift shops there are can be found nearby, on and around Bay Street. Here you will also find the **financial complex,** a cool-looking, tall structure built in 1992, of which the island is inordinately proud. Among other official offices, the tourist office is located here.

Grenadines Wharf, along the Bayfront at the southeast end of town, is busy with schooners loading supplies for the Grenadines. Nearby, several 19th-century buildings are built of bricks used as ballast in vessels that returned to Europe with holds filled with sugar and molasses.

The most exciting thing to do in Kingstown is to browse among the infinite varieties of tropical fruits and vegetables at the **Kingstown Market,** in the center of town on Upper Bay Street, just one block from the waterfront. Produce is laid out in the outdoor section; around the square there are dozens of stalls where you can buy inexpensive homemade meals, drinks, ice cream, bread and cookies, clothing, trinkets, and even get a haircut. Though the bustle is greatest on Saturdays before 11 AM, there is usually a crowd all day long. Be sure to visit the indoor **fish**

**market,** too. This was a gift from the Japanese people, who also donated ecological deep-sea-fishing lessons, plus a sister market on Union Island.

St. Vincent is known worldwide for its particularly beautiful and colorful commemorative stamps, which are illustrated with tropical flowers, undersea creatures, and local architecture. You can purchase stamps at the **Philatelic Bureau,** on Lower Bay Street, as well as at the **post office,** on Halifax Street, east of Egmont.

**St. George's Cathedral,** a yellow Anglican church built in the early 19th century, is on Grenville Street, west of the Methodist Church. The dignified Georgian architecture includes simple wood pews, an ornate chandelier, and stained-glass windows. The markers in the cathedral's graveyard recount the history of the island. Across the street is **St. Mary's Roman Catholic Cathedral,** built in 1823 and renovated in the 1930s. The renovations resulted in a strangely appealing blend of Moorish, Georgian, and Romanesque styles applied to black brick.

A few minutes away by taxi or bus is St. Vincent's famous **Botanical Gardens.** Founded in 1765, it is the oldest botanical garden in the Western Hemisphere. Captain Bligh—of *Bounty* fame—brought the first breadfruit tree to this island to feed the slaves. You can see a direct descendant of this tree among the mahogany, rubber, and teak trees in the gardens. Several rare St. Vincent parrots live in the small aviary on the well-kept grounds. Local guides offer their services for $2–$4 an hour. ⊠ *c/o Minister of Agriculture, Kingstown,* ☎ *809/457–1003.* ☞ *Free.* ⊘ *Daily 6–6.*

The tiny **National Museum** inside the entrance to the Botanical Gardens houses a series of maps tracing the migrations of the Ciboney, the very first Vincentians, who arrived on the island around 4000 BC. The pre-Columbian Indian clay pottery on exhibit was found by Dr. Earle Kirby, St. Vincent's resident archaeologist and the museum's director. Dr. Kirby's historical knowledge is as entertaining as it is extensive, and a visit here is much enhanced by his annotations. ⊠ *Botanical Gardens,* ☎ *809/456–1787.* ☞ *$1.* ⊘ *Wed. 9:45–noon, Sat. 4–6.*

**③ Layou.** Just beyond this small fishing village, about 45 minutes north of Kingstown, are petroglyphs (rock carvings) left by the Caribs 13 centuries ago. If you're seriously interested in archaeological mysteries, you'll want to arrange a visit (through the Tourist Board) with Victor Hendrickson, who owns the land. For E.C.$5, Hendrickson or his wife will meet you and escort you to the site.

**⑫ Mesopotamia.** The rugged, ocean-lashed scenery along St. Vincent's windward coast is the perfect counterpoint to the lush, calm west coast. The Mesopotamia Valley offers a breathtaking panoramic view that is unsurpassed in this part of the Caribbean; you'll see dense forests, streams, and banana plantations. Blue plastic bags cover the fruit—particularly important for export—to protect it from wind and insect damage. Coconut, breadfruit, sweet corn, peanuts, and arrowroot also grow in the rich soil here, which is why the area is nicknamed "the breadbasket of St. Vincent." The valley is surrounded by mountain ridges, including 3,181-foot Grand Bonhomme Mountain.

**⑬ Montreal Gardens.** The extensive collection of exotic flowers, trees, and spice plants may not be as well maintained as Kingstown's Botanical Gardens, but the aroma of cocoa powder and nutmeg wafting on the cool breeze is enticing. And because it is high up in the mountains north of Mesopotamia, there are magnificent views across ridges and valleys to the sea. Spend an hour with well-informed guides or wander on your

**$$$**   🏨 **Spring on Bequia.** Spring is nestled in green hills overlooking groves of tall palms and grazing goats. It's about a mile above town (a pretty walk, though you may want to take a taxi back uphill), and the nearest beach, lovely but too shallow for serious swimming and occasionally seaweedy, is a 10-minute stroll away. The large wood-and-stone rooms attract upscale travelers who want serenity and seclusion. The airy veranda bar is the site of manager Candy Leslie's deservedly famous Sunday curry lunch (reservations essential). ⊠ *Spring Bay, Bequia, St. Vincent,* ☎ *809/458–3414. U.S. agent: Spring on Bequia,* ⊠ *Box 19251, Minneapolis, MN 55419,* ☎ *612/823–1202. 10 rooms. Restaurant, bar, pool, tennis court. AE, D, MC, V. EP.*

**$$–$$$**   🏨 **Friendship Bay Hotel.** This sprawling white house, with large terraces and sweeping views, is on a hill that rises above another group of pretty, coral stone accommodations close to the beach. Friendship offers a beautiful curve of white-sand beach and tropical plant-filled grounds and, on Saturday nights around the Mau Mau Beach Bar, one of the liveliest barbecue and jump-ups in the Caribbean. This is distinguished from the hundreds of beach bars you have known by its swing seats, cleverly built to keep you upright even after potent rum punches. ⊠ *Box 9, Bequia, St. Vincent,* ☎ *809/458–3222,* ℻ *809/458–3840. 27 rooms. Restaurant, 2 bars, tennis court, dive shop, water-sports center, boutique. AE, MC, V. CP.*

**$$–$$$**   🏨 **Old Fort Hotel.** A stunning setting on a cliff above the Atlantic, in a stone estate house built by the French 200 years ago, singles out this property from the others and endows its rooms with some of the most panoramic Grenadine vistas around, plus cooling trade-wind breezes that obviate the need for air-conditioning. There are only six rooms here, all done up like a cross between Captain Bligh's cabin and a Provençal farmhouse, with chunky hardwoods and exposed stone. This modest size, and the fact that the nearest beach, Ravine, is nearly 500 feet below and a bit too rough for swimming, makes the Old Fort a getaway destination rather than a lazy vacation base. Fortunately, the restaurant (☞ Dining, *below*) is excellent, because it's a trek into town. ⊠ *Mt. Pleasant, Bequia, St. Vincent,* ☎ *809/458–3440,* ℻ *809/458–3824. 6 rooms. Restaurant, bar, hiking. MC, V. EP, MAP.*

**$–$$**   🏨 **Frangipani Hotel.** The Frangipani has gained the status of venerable
★   institution partly because its owner, St. Vincent Prime Minister James Mitchell, lives here on Bequia. Surrounded by flowering bushes, the garden units are built of stone, with private verandas and baths. Four simple, less-expensive rooms are in the main shingle-sided house, only one with a private bath. A two-bedroom house with a patio and another apartment with a large bedroom and kitchen are nearby. String bands appear on Mondays, with folksingers on Friday nights during tourist season. The Thursday-night steel-band jump-up at the beachfront bar is a must; the bar, with its huge, white-painted wooden armchairs facing the sunset, is probably the nicest around. ⊠ *Box 1, Bequia, St. Vincent,* ☎ *809/458–3255,* ℻ *809/458–3824. 13 rooms. Restaurant, bar, water-sports center, yacht excursions, boutique. MC, V. EP.*

**$**   🏨 **Isola and Julie's Guest House.** Right on the water in Port Elizabeth, these two separate buildings share a small restaurant and bar. Furnishings are spare and simple, but the rooms are airy and light, with private baths (some have hot water!), and the food is great. ⊠ *Box 12, Bequia, St. Vincent,* ☎ *809/458–3304, 809/458–3323, or 809/458–3220. 25 rooms. Restaurant, bar. No credit cards. MAP.*

**$**   🏨 **Keegan's Guest House.** If you want budget beach accommodations with a quiet, friendly atmosphere, look no further. On Lower Bay, this *very* simple place offers family-style West Indian breakfasts and dinners for its guests. Rooms 3, 4, and 5 have a shared bath and are cheaper, although there is no hot water to be found (you really do get used to own along the narrow paths. ⊠ *Montreal,* ☎ *809/458–5452.* ⊠ *Free.* ⊙ *Daily 8–4.*

**❼ Owia.** The Carib village of Owia, two hours from Kingstown on the island's far northeast coast, is the home of many of the indigenous people of St. Vincent. It is also the location of the Owia Arrowroot Processing Factory. Used for generations to thicken sauces and flavor cookies, arrowroot is now in demand as a finish for computer paper. Close to the village is the Owia Salt Pond, where you can take a dip before the long ride back to Kingstown.

**❽ Rabacca Dry River.** Looking every bit like a moonscape, this rocky gulch just past the village of Georgetown was carved out of the earth by the lava flow from the 1902 eruption of La Soufrière. The trail to the rim of the volcano, a two-hour ascent, begins here.

**❺ Wallilabou Bay.** You can stop to sunbathe, swim, and have a picnic or simple lunch at the yacht services building at Wallilabou (pronounced wally-la-*boo*) Bay. There are no showers, but a small waterfall is a short, lovely stroll away.

# THE GRENADINES

The Grenadines are wonderful islands to visit for fine diving and snorkeling opportunities, good beaches, and unlimited chances to laze on the beach with a picnic, waiting for the sun to set so you can go to dinner. Travelers seeking privacy, peace and quiet, or active water sports and informal socializing will be happy on a Grenadine, though which one may take some trial and error—these islands are by no means interchangeable.

## Bequia

Just 9 miles south of St. Vincent's southwestern shore, Bequia (pronounced *beck*-wee) is the largest of the Grenadine Islands. Sandy beaches surround the island, and picturesque Admiralty Bay is a favorite anchorage for yachtspeople. Boat-building, whaling, and fishing have been the industries here for generations. A range of lodging possibilities and some nightlife attracts visitors who want to stay awhile. Regular and frequent ferry service from St. Vincent makes the island a favorite for day trips.

### Lodging

For price information on hotels, *see* the price chart in the Lodging section of St. Vincent, *above.*

**\$\$\$\$** 🏨 **Plantation House Hotel.** You can't help but pass by the pale peach
**★** Plantation House when strolling to Princess Margaret or Lower Bay beaches. Set in 10 grassy acres of manicured gardens, dotted with palms, hammocks, loungers, and a raised pool, the five-room main house is appended by 17 garden cabanas, plus three deluxe beachfront rooms. Since the current Dutch/Austrian husband-and-wife managers took over in 1994, just about everything has been redone and made gorgeous, with rattan and wicker decor in all rooms and also in the cabanas. The bar may be *the* Bequia social center due to the presence of the French chef (☞ *Dining, below*). ⊠ *Box 16, Admiralty Bay, Bequia, St. Vincent,* ☎ *809/458–3425,* 🖷 *809/458–3612. U.S. agent: E & M Assoc.,* ⊠ *211 E. 43rd St., New York, NY 10017,* ☎ *800/223–9832. 8 rooms, 17 cabanas. 2 restaurants, bar, air-conditioning, minibars, pool, tennis courts, scuba diving, snorkeling, windsurfing, boating, waterskiing, boutique. AE, MC, V. MAP.*

it). ⊠ *Bequia, St. Vincent,* ☎ *809/458–3254 or 809/458–3530. 11 rooms. Dining room. No credit cards. MAP.*

## Dining

Dining on Bequia ranges from West Indian to gourmet cuisine, and it's consistently good. Barbecues at Bequia's hotels mean spicy West Indian seafood, chicken, or beef, plus a buffet of side dishes and sweet desserts. Restaurants are occasionally closed on Sundays; phone to check.

For price information on restaurants, *see* the price chart in the Dining section of St. Vincent, *above.*

**$$$** ✕ **Old Fort.** Otmar and Sonja Schaedle restored this mid-1700s building overlooking the Atlantic to its bougainvillea-shaded, stone-arched, candlelit beauty and continue to serve food good enough to attract non-hotel guests up the recently paved road. Try a tuna steak or char-grilled whole snapper, accompanied by fresh, homemade bread and a curry of pigeon peas. ⊠ *Old Fort Hotel, Mt. Pleasant,* ☎ *809/458–3440. Reservations essential. MC, V.*

**$$$** ✕ **Le Petit Jardin.** The chef at this chalet-style restaurant prepares
★ gourmet lobster and fish with West Indian ingredients and according to French recipes. If you're missing your prime rib, the house specialty is steak imported from the United States, which you can wash down with a bottle from the longer-than-average wine list. ⊠ *Port Elizabeth,* ☎ *809/458–3318. Reservations essential. No credit cards.*

**$$$** ✕ **Plantation House.** This refurbished, fancy hotel has a fancy chef to match, who earned the ultimate French accolade of a Michelin star in a previous job. Dinner is served nightly (except Saturday) at the hotel's Verandah restaurant, where menu selections reflect a Continental theme with local flair. On Saturday evenings, a barbecue buffet is presented at the hotel's other restaurant, The Green Flash. The buffet includes a variety of barbecued meats and fish, salads, vegetable dishes, and an excellent array of pastries prepared by a local pastry chef. A resident pianist plays during dinner hours at the Verandah and a local band provides entertainment at the Saturday barbecues. ⊠ *Plantation House Hotel, Admiralty Bay,* ☎ *809/458–3425. AE, MC, V.*

**$–$$$** ✕ **De Reef.** This duo of a restaurant and a café on Lower Bay is the essential feeding station for long, lazy beach days, with the restaurant taking over when the café closes at dusk, as long as you've made reservations. For lunch or dinner, conch, lobster, whelks, and shrimp are treated the West Indian way, and the mutton curry is famous. For breakfast (from 7 AM), or light lunch, the café bakes its own breads, croissants, coconut cake, and cookies and blends fresh juices to accompany them. ⊠ *Lower Bay,* ☎ *809/458–3484. Reservations essential for dinner. No credit cards.*

**$$** ✕ **La Mezzaluna.** This is an incongruously traditional Italian trattoria, owned by its Roman chef and useful for city dwellers with pasta-withdrawal symptoms. Here, ravioli is more likely to be stuffed with local lobster than spinach and ricotta, but eggplant parmigiana, beef carpaccio, and *grissini* (Italian bread sticks) they've got. ⊠ *Above Port Elizabeth,* ☎ *809/457–3080. No credit cards. Closed Tues.*

**$–$$** ✕ **Dawn's Creole Garden.** The walk up the hill is worth it for the delicious West Indian lunches and dinners, especially the Saturday-night barbecue buffet and the major five-course, two-entrée dinners, including the fresh christophine and breadfruit accompaniments that Dawn's is known for. There's a wonderful view and live guitar entertainment most Saturday nights. ⊠ *At the far end of Lower Bay beach,* ☎ *809/458–3154. Dinner reservations essential. No credit cards.*

**$–$$** ✕ **Mac's Pizzeria.** The island's best lunches and casual dinners are en-
★ joyed amid fuchsia bougainvillea on the covered outdoor terrace over-

looking the harbor. Choose from mouthwatering lobster pizza, quiche, pita sandwiches, lasagna, home-baked cookies, and muffins. ⊠ *On the beach, Port Elizabeth,* ☎ *809/458–3474. Reservations essential for dinner. No credit cards.*

**$–$$**    ✕ **Theresa's Restaurant.** On Monday nights, Theresa and John Ben-
★    nett offer a rotating selection of enormous and tasty Greek, Indian, Mexican, or Italian buffets. West Indian dishes are served at lunch and dinner
the rest of the week. ⊠ *At the far end of Lower Bay beach,* ☎ *809/458–
3802. Reservations essential for dinner. No credit cards.*

## Beaches

**Friendship Bay** can be reached by land taxi and is well equipped with
windsurfing and snorkeling rentals and an outdoor bar. **Hope Beach,**
on the Atlantic side, is accessible by a long taxi ride (about E.C.$20—
every driver knows how to get there) and a mile-long walk downhill
on a semipaved path. Your reward is a magnificent beach and total
seclusion, and—if you prefer—nude bathing. Be sure to ask your taxi
driver to return at a prearranged time. Bring your own lunch and
drinks; there are no facilities. Swimming can be dangerous because of
rough waters. **Industry Bay** boasts towering palm groves, a nearly secluded beach, and a memorable view of several uninhabited islands.
The tiny, three-room Crescent Bay Lodge is here; its huge bar offers
drinks and late lunches (☎ 809/458–3400). **Lower Bay,** a wide, palm-
fringed beach that can be reached by taxi or by hiking beyond Princess
Margaret Beach, is an excellent location for swimming and snorkeling; wear sneakers, not flip-flops. Facilities for windsurfing and snorkeling are here, as well as the De Reef restaurant. **Princess Margaret
Beach,** which is quiet and wide and has a natural stone arch at one
end, is a half-hour walk over rocky bluffs from the Plantation House
Hotel. Though it has no facilities, this is a popular spot for swimming,
snorkeling, or simply relaxing under palms and sea-grape trees.

## Outdoor Activities and Sports

### SCUBA DIVING AND SNORKELING

Of Bequia's two dozen dive sites, the best are Devil's Table, a shallow
dive rich in fish and coral; a sailboat wreck nearby at 90 feet; the 90-
foot drop at the Wall, off West Cay; the Bullet, off Bequia's north point
for rays, barracuda, and the occasional nurse shark; the Boulders for soft
corals, tunnel-forming rocks, thousands of fish; and Moonhole, shallow
enough in places for snorkelers to enjoy. For snorkeling on your own,
take a water taxi to the bay at Moonhole and arrange a pickup time.

**Dive Bequia** (⊠ At the Plantation House Hotel, Box 16, Bequia, ☎
809/458–3504, FAX 809/458–3886) and **Sunsports** (⊠ At the Gingerbread Complex, Box 1, Bequia, ☎ 809/458–3577, FAX 809/457–3031)
offer one- and two-tank dives, night dives, and certified instruction,
plus snorkel excursions and equipment rental.

### TENNIS

Tennis courts are located at four island hotels: **Frangipani Hotel** (⊠
Admiralty Bay, ☎ 809/458–3255), **Friendship Bay Hotel** (⊠ Friendship Bay, ☎ 809/458–3222), **Plantation House Hotel** (⊠ Belmont
Beach, ☎ 809/458–3425), and **Spring On Bequia** (⊠ Spring Bay, ☎
809/458–3414).

## Shopping

All Bequia's shops are in the capital, Port Elizabeth, and are open weekdays 10:30–5 or 6, Saturdays 10:30–noon.

### BEST BUYS

**Bequia Bookshop** (⊠ Opposite the dinghy dock, ☎ 809/458–3905)
has an exhaustive selection of Caribbean literature, plus cruising guides

and charts, beach novels, souvenir maps, and exquisite scrimshaw and hand-carved whalebone penknives. **Crab Hole** (✉ Admiralty Bay, ☎ 809/458–3290) sells hand-printed and batik fabric, clothing, and household items. You can see the fabrics being created in the workshop out back. **Local Color** (✉ Port Elizabeth, ☎ 809/458–3202), above the Porthole restaurant, has an excellent and unusual selection of handmade jewelry, wood carvings, and resort clothing. **Mauvin's Model Boat Shop** (✉ ¼ mile down the road to the left of main dock, no phone) is where you can buy handmade model boats (you can even special-order a replica of your own yacht). Bequia is renowned for its model boatbuilders. **Melinda's By Hand** (✉ Port Elizabeth, ☎ 809/458–3409) sells hand-painted cotton and silk clothing and accessories. **Solana's** (✉ Port Elizabeth, ☎ 809/458–3554) offers attractive beachwear, saronglike pareus, and handy plastic beach shoes.

## Nightlife
Along with the various jump-ups at hotels, the nearest thing to a nightclub is **Harpoon Saloon** (✉ Port Elizabeth, ☎ 809/458–3272) clearly visible above the bay to port side as you sail into Bequia; it regularly hosts local bands.

## Bequia A to Z
### ARRIVING AND DEPARTING
The MV *Admiral I* and the MV *Admiral II* motor ferries leave Kingstown for Bequia Monday through Friday at 9 AM, 10:30 AM, 4:30 PM, and, depending on availability, 7 PM. Saturday departures are at 12:30 PM and 7 PM; Sunday, 9 AM and 7 PM. Schedules are subject to change, so be sure to check times upon your arrival. All scheduled ferries leave from the main dock in Kingstown. The trip takes 60 minutes and costs $4.

The MV *Snapper* mail boat travels south on Saturdays, Mondays, and Thursdays at about 10:30 AM, stopping at Bequia, Canouan, Mayreau, and Union, and returns north on Tuesdays and Fridays, departing Bequia at 11 AM. The cost is about $4.

Weekday service between St. Vincent and Bequia is also available on the island schooner *Friendship Rose,* which leaves St. Vincent at about 12:30 PM. The *Discover St. Vincent and the Grenadines* booklet, available in hotels and at the airport, includes current interisland schedules.

**Mustique Airways** (☎ 809/458–4380 or 809/458–4818) flies into Bequia's airport daily from Barbados. The **Bequia shuttle** operates four days a week between St Vincent, Bequia, and Canouan. **LIAT** (☎ 809/458–4841 or 800/253–5011) offers day-trip airfare to any three Grenadines and back to St. Vincent for around $200.

### EMERGENCIES
**Police:** ☎ 809/456–1955. **Medical Emergencies:** ☎ 999. **Hospital:** Bequia Hospital (☎ 809/458–3294).

### GUIDED TOURS
To see the views, villages, and boat-building around the island, hire a taxi (Gideon, ☎ 809/458–3760, is recommended) and negotiate the fare in advance.

Water taxis, available at any dock, will also take you by Moonhole, a private community of stone homes with glassless windows, some decorated with bleached whale bones. The fare is about $11.

For those who prefer sailboats to motorboats, Arne Hansen and his catamaran *Toien* can be booked through the **Frangipani Hotel** (☎ 809/458–3255). Day sails to Mustique run $35–$40 per person, including drinks. An overnight snorkel-sail trip to the Tobago Cays costs about $150 for two people, including breakfast and drinks.

VISITOR INFORMATION
The **Bequia Tourism Board** (☎ 809/458–3286) is located on the main dock at Port Elizabeth and is open daily 9–12:30 and 1:30–4 (except for Saturday afternoons).

# Canouan

Goat-herding is still a career possibility here. This tiny island—just 3½ miles long and 1¼ miles wide—does have a modern airstrip, however, with night landing equipment. Canouan also claims some of the finest white-sand beaches in the Caribbean. Walk, loaf, swim, dive, or snorkel—these are your options.

## Dining and Lodging

For price information, *see* the price charts in the Dining and Lodging sections of St. Vincent, *above*.

**$$$$**  ✕🏠 **Canouan Beach Hotel.** This hotel, perched on a tongue of beach poking out from the southwest end of the island, attracts French tourists, who dominate at any time of year. Simple white cottages have patios. Catamaran day sails weekdays and live music twice a week are offered here. ⊠ *Canouan, St. Vincent,* ☎ *809/458–8888,* 𝖥𝖠𝖷 *809/458– 8875. 43 rooms. Restaurant, bar, air-conditioning, driving range, tennis court, scuba diving, snorkeling, windsurfing, marina. AE, MC, V. MAP, All-inclusive.*

**$$$$**  ✕🏠 **Tamarind Beach Hotel & Yacht Club.** This attractive hostelry on a sparkling white-sand beach is Canouan's newest. Guest rooms are located in three large two-story buildings that face the beach. The rooms have natural wood walls and are decorated with rattan furniture and louvered wooden doors that open onto spacious balconies and a beautiful Caribbean vista. Ceiling fans join with the trade winds to keep you cool. At the Palapa Restaurant, on the beach, an Italian chef prepares fascinating Caribbean cuisine, grilled meats and fish, as well as pizzas and pasta, which you can enjoy alfresco. ⊠ *Charlestown, Canouan, St. Vincent,* ☎ *809/458–8044 or 800/223–1108,* 𝖥𝖠𝖷 *809/458–8851. 48 rooms. Restaurant, bar, beach bar, fans, dive shop, snorkeling, windsurfing, sailing, fishing. No credit cards. FAP.*

**$$–$$$**  ✕🏠 **Crystal Sands Beach Hotel.** A local family runs this extremely simple place on Charleston Bay. Cottages share a connecting door for larger groups and have private baths and patios. There's a fine beach and a veranda bar and dining area. If you take the mail boat from Kingstown (☞ Arriving and Departing *in* Bequia A to Z, *above*), pack light and be prepared to climb from the large ferry into a small rowboat to get to shore. ⊠ *Canouan, St. Vincent,* ☎ *809/458–8015. 10 rooms. Bar, dining area, snorkeling, fishing. No credit cards. EP.*

**$$–$$$**  ✕🏠 **Villa Le Bijou Guest House.** This place is up the hill and only a 10-minute walk from Friendship Bay (15 minutes from the airstrip; pack light—taxis are rarely available). Accommodations border on the primitive, and the electricity is often on vacation, but the view is stunning. ⊠ *M. de Roche, Villa La Bijou, Canouan, St. Vincent,* ☎ *809/458– 8025. 6 rooms. No hot water in the shared baths. Dining area, snorkeling, windsurfing, sailing. No credit cards. MAP.*

## Outdoor Activities and Sports

SCUBA DIVING AND SNORKELING
Tony Alongi, the owner/operator of **Dive Canouan** (⊠ Box 530, Tamarind Beach Hotel, ☎ 809/458–8044 or 809/458–8234, 𝖥𝖠𝖷 809/458–8851), offers dive and snorkel packages that include tours

to the Tobago Cays, south of Canouan. You can also take a resort or certification course.

### Nightlife

Surprise: There's a bar and disco on weekends at **Villa Le Bijou Guest House** (☞ Dining and Lodging, *above*).

## Mayreau

Privately owned Mayreau (pronounced my-*row*) is minuscule—just 1½ square miles. Farm animals outnumber citizens. Except for water sports and hiking, there's not much to do, and visitors like it that way. This is the perfect place for a meditative or vegetative vacation. To get here, take a boat from Union Island.

### Dining and Lodging

For price information, *see* the price charts in the Dining and Lodging sections of St. Vincent, *above*.

**$$$$** ✕🏨 **Salt Whistle Bay Club.** Set far back from the water, Mayreau's only hotel is so cleverly hidden that sailors need binoculars to be sure it's there at all. Each roomy stone cottage, with a name like Oleander or Ivora, has a round-stone, hot-water shower that looks like a large, medieval telephone booth. You can dry your hair on the breezy, shared second-story veranda atop each two-room building. The outdoor dining area has stone tables covered by thatched palms where you can enjoy turtle steak, duckling, lobster, and à la carte lunches. There used to be a jump-up, but guests preferred peace and quiet. ✉ *Write Salt Whistle Bay Club, Management Offices, 1020 Bayridge Dr., Kingston, Ontario, Canada K7P 2S2,* ☎ *800/263–2780 in the U.S.; outside the U.S., call collect 613/634–1963;* 🖷 *800/263–2780 in the U.S.; outside the U.S., 613/384–6300. In the Caribbean, marine radio VHF channel 68; boat phone 493–9609. 10 cottages, 4 suites. Restaurant, bar, snorkeling, windsurfing, catamaran charter. No credit cards. FAP.*

**$–$$** ✕🏨 **Dennis' Hideaway.** Dennis (who plays the guitar two nights a week) is a charmer, the food is great, the drinks are strong, and the view is heaven. The rooms are clean but very simple: a bed, nightstand, chair, and a place to hang some clothes. ✉ *Saline Bay,* ☎ *809/458–8594. 7 rooms. Restaurant. No credit cards. EP.*

### Beaches

**Saline Bay Beach** is beautiful, but there are no facilities. The mail boat's tender stops at the dock here. **Salt Whistle Bay Beach** takes top honors—it's one of the Caribbean's prettiest. The beach is an exquisite half-moon of powdery white sand, shaded by perfectly spaced palms and flowering bushes, with the rolling Atlantic a stroll away.

### Outdoor Activities and Sports

HIKING

Hike 25 minutes over Mayreau's mountain (wear shoes; bare feet or flip-flops are a big mistake) to a good photo opportunity at the stone church atop the hill and stunning views of the Cays. Then have a drink at Dennis' Hideaway and enjoy a swim at Saline Bay Beach.

SCUBA DIVING AND SNORKELING

**Grenadines Dive** (☎ 809/458–8138 or 809/458–8122; ☞ Outdoor Activities and Sports, Union Island, *below*) can arrange scuba-diving trips. **Undine Potter** (✉ Salt Whistle Bay Club, ☎ 800/263–2780 from the U.S.; in the Grenadines, marine radio VHF channel 16 or 68) will arrange day trips with charter yachts to the cays or nearby islands for swimming and snorkeling. The Salt Whistle Bay's snorkel equipment has seen better days; you may want to buy or rent your own before you arrive.

# Mustique

Trendsetter Princess Margaret put this 3- by 1½-mile former copra, cotton, and sugarcane estate on the map after Colin Tennant (now Lord Glenconner) bought it. The company he formed in 1968 to develop Mustique into the glamorous hideaway island it is now has 37 shareholders and a House Rentals Department that must be contacted about a year in advance to rent the royal holiday home, Balliceaux, or another of the 40-odd luxury villas that pepper the northern half of the island. Some house owners keep their villas empty in their absence, including Mustique's two most glittering habitués, Mick Jagger and David Bowie. Their villas are concealed behind Brobdingnagian fences, but anyone who insists on star-gawking will get to see whoever's "on island" at Basil's Bar, the island's social center, sooner or later.

Next to his bar, in a cluster of candy-colored houses that don't quite qualify as a town, Basil also runs a boutique crammed with clothes and accessories imported and specially commissioned from all over the world, a cornucopian delicatessen to feed residents fresh Brie and Moët, and an antiques shop stocked with fabulous pieces for those fabulous houses. There's also a fish market, a grocery warehouse, a gas station—and a police station with nothing much to do. To some, that adds up to paradise; others *hate* it, but you pays yer money, you takes yer choice!

## Lodging

For price information on hotels, *see* the price chart in the Lodging section of St. Vincent, *above.*

**$$$$**   **Cotton House.** The island's only hotel centers on the stone-and-coral
★    former estate warehouse, originally converted by the late Oliver Messel (the great British theater designer-decorator-architect, who was to Mustique as Haussmann was to Paris). The whole place has undergone a complete overhaul under the aegis of utterly charming supermanager Warren Francis and his wonderful wife Gilly, transforming what had sunk into an expensively underwhelming hostelry back to a hotel in the world's top rank. The 18th-century plantation house was used to store cotton, sugar, and rum. Along with the stone mill, which is now the hotel boutique, it is the oldest structure on Mustique. The wraparound wooden veranda functions as lounge, bar, tea terrace, restaurant, and social center. Breakfast is taken around the hilltop pool, in Messel's outrageous ruined Scottish castle folly. Off the pool path are baby cottages containing junior suites (Numbers 9–11), which, with their breezy walk-through layouts, are the cutest of the three room types. The deluxe suites (12–16) are mere steps away from the main house but have nothing but this and their size to recommend them over the fantastic quartet of deluxe rooms in high-up Battowia House. These have balconies perched over Mustique's northern coast, with a particularly gorgeous view from corner Room 6, and come in at around $225 a night less than a deluxe suite—as do the two beach rooms (Numbers 21 and 22). Decor is sophisticated but faithful to Messel's vision of Caribbean simplicity and light, with white walls and ceiling fans, antiques, and rattan furniture. Bathrooms have marble fittings, and rooms have dressing areas, French windows, desks—and perfect peace. In addition to the restaurant, there's a beach bar with a weekly barbecue. Airport transfers and an island tour are included, as are water sports, tennis, and a driver to chauffeur you to Basil's or the beach. ⊠ *Box 349, Mustique, St. Vincent,* ☎ *809/456–4777 or 800/447–7462,* 𝖥𝖠𝖷 *809/456–5887.*

*10 rooms, 10 suites. Restaurant, bar, fans, minibars, pool, 2 tennis courts, horseback riding, scuba diving, snorkeling, windsurfing, sailing, boutique, library, airport shuttle. AE, D, MC, V. FAP.*

**$–$$**   🏠 **Firefly House.** Tiny and charming with just five rooms, this is the island's only budget choice, but it's still well located, above Britannia Bay, and the rooms have private baths, and picnic equipment, plus, for $5 extra, air-conditioning. "You don't have to be rich and famous to enjoy Mustique" says the Firefly flier, but the sensitive and/or paranoid may suffer a poor-relations complex staying here. ⊠ *Mustique, Box 349,* ☎ *809/456–3414. 5 rooms. Bar, refrigerators, scuba diving, snorkeling, windsurfing, sailing. No credit cards. CP.*

VILLA RENTALS

Renting one of Mustique's privately owned villas is not as expensive as it seems at first glance, since rates include a full staff, with cook but no groceries, laundry service, and a vehicle or two; rates are per house, not per person. Houses range from simple rusticity—if you can call ensuite bathrooms for every bedroom, at least one phone line, probably a pool, cable TV, VCR, CD player, and even fax, rustic—to extravagant, expansive, faux-Palladian follies with resident butler; but all are designer-elegant and immaculately maintained. Rates start at $2,800 a week for the two-bedroom Pelican Beach off-season and go way up to $12,000 a week for the palatial five-bedroom, five-person staff, two-Jeep, one-Jacuzzi Blackstone, during winter. Princess Margaret's three-bedroom place is surprisingly modest, at a mere $3,300 a week in summer. ⊠ *House Rentals Dept., Mustique Co. Ltd., Box 349, St. Vincent and the Grenadines,* ☎ *809/458–4621,* 𝖥𝖠𝖷 *809/456–4565. 43 villas. AE, DC, MC, V. FAP.*

## Dining

For price information on restaurants, *see* the price chart in the Dining section of St. Vincent, *above.*

**$–$$$**   ✕ **Basil's Bar and Restaurant.** Basil's is the only place to be seen on
★   Mustique, and only partly because it *is* the only place on Mustique, apart from the more formal, quieter Cotton House. Resembling many a beachside terrace restaurant, with its wooden deck built over the waves, palm-roofed at the edges with a central bar and dance floor open to the stars, there's something about the atmosphere that hints at happenings. Well, you never know who you may run into. . . . The food is simple and good—mostly fish hauled out of the water a hundred yards away, homemade ice cream, burgers and salads, great French toast, the usual cocktails, and many unusual wines. The Wednesday barbecue is the regular party night, and there's live music Mondays. ⊠ *Britania Bay,* ☎ *809/458–4621. AE, MC, V.*

## Beaches

**Macaroni Beach** is Mustique's most famous stretch of sand, offering surfy swimming (no lifeguards, so be careful), powdery white sand, a few palm huts for shade, and picnic tables on a grassy garden. From the northern coast, working west, **L'Ansecoy, Endeavour,** and **Britannia bays** are also fine, and much calmer, the last being the best for day-trippers, with Basil's Bar adjacent for lunch. Farther south, **Gelliceaux Bay,** by the Cotton House, provides the best snorkeling beach.

## Outdoor Activities and Sports

Water-sports facilities are available at the Cotton House, and most villas have equipment of various sorts. There's a communal tennis court for those whose villa lacks its own, a cricket ground for the Brits, and motorbikes for trail-riding around the bumpy roads for rent at $45 per day.

HORSEBACK RIDING

The best sport to indulge in on Mustique is horseback riding, since this is one of the few islands where you can rent a fine horse. Rides leave Monday–Saturday at 8 and 9 AM, 3 and 4 PM from the **Equestrian Centre** (✉ Macaroni Bay, ☎ 809/458–4316), and rates are $40 per hour.

SCUBA DIVING AND SNORKELING

Scuba is best arranged through **Dive Mustique** (✉ Mustique Island, ☎ 809/458–4621).

# Palm Island

A private speck of land, Palm Island has wide white-sand beaches and one very casual resort. Access is through Union Island, 1 mile to the west; you're picked up by the resort launch for the 10-minute boat ride to Palm Island.

## Lodging

For price information on hotels, *see* the price chart in the Lodging section of St. Vincent, *above*.

**$$$$** 🏨 **Palm Island Resort.** A seafarer was shipwrecked, stranded on a desert island, reunited with his new wife, had two sons, found a swamp-ridden, mosquito-infested jungle called Prune Island, and toiled with his family for 25 years to turn it into a resort. This is no Judith Krantz novel, it's how Palm Island came to be, and you can read all about it over tea, delivered at 4 PM to your cabana terrace. In the better, newer cabanas (Numbers 11–18), you'll enjoy a private sunset view from your room-width patio doors, over the northwest facing Casuarina Beach. If you got an older room (Numbers 1–6 and 19–22), you will lack both big windows and much in the way of privacy, and you may also tire of the pink-and-green color scheme that is overdue for retirement. Bathrooms aren't the greatest, with dribbly but scenic outdoor showers in the newer cabanas, scant towels, and the same marble-chip floors as in the bedroom in all, but balanced against that is a collective and genuine warmth in the staff, which has people coming back year after year. The food is important when you're a captive audience; the island buffets and full-service dinners here are just fine, and the pastry chef has made breakfast worth getting up for. Adjacent to the hotel is a separate yacht club where you can go for the only change of scene apart from a jog on "Highway 90" (1.25 miles around), or a day sail to the Tobago Cays. Windsurfers, Sunfish, and floating mats are complimentary. Leave your fancy clothes at home—this is a really casual place. And plan on busy, active days. Nightlife is practically nil but for Wednesday and Saturday barbecues with calypso music—in season. You could view this as a cut-rate Petit St. Vincent. ✉ *Palm Island, St. Vincent,* ☎ *809/458–8824,* 🖷 *809/458–8804. U.S. agent: Paradise Found,* ☎ *800/776–7256. 24 rooms, 15 self-catering villas. Open-air bar-restaurant, grocery, tennis court, jogging, scuba diving, snorkeling, windsurfing, boating, fishing, recreation room, baby-sitting. AE, MC, V. FAP.*

# Petit St. Vincent

This is the southernmost of St. Vincent's Grenadines. Like the others, it is ringed with white-sand beaches and covered with beautiful tropical foliage. Guests are treated royally at the island's one classy, secluded resort. To get here, you fly into Union island where the PSV motor launch will meet you.

## Lodging

For price information on hotels, *see* the price chart in the Lodging section of St. Vincent, *above*.

**$$$$** ⌂ **Petit St. Vincent.** This is a very special 113-acre private island, where you can indulge shipwreck fantasies without foregoing the frozen mango daiquiri at sunset, room-service breakfast, the skills of a great chef, and so on. There are only 22 houses on PSV, with bedroom, sitting room, and one or two bathrooms in a U-shape around a big, partly covered wooden deck. Floors are tiled and grass matted, walls are of stone, and—on two sides—glass, with patio doors that slide away entirely, giving you trade winds for a lullaby. Despite their rustic appearance, with copra matting vanities and cobblestoned shower stalls, bathrooms conceal the Grenadines' best toiletries, robes, beach bags, towels, and an iron, and they have American-style 110-volt, two-prong outlets, so you don't need transformers. No house is more than a five-minute walk from dinner, yet each is completely private, with a sweet system of flags and bamboo mailbox to convey whims to the staff (who outnumber guests two to one), since there are no phones. Hoist your red flag, and nobody *dreams* of approaching; hoist the yellow, and you can have lunch or dinner, tea or drinks, a ride to the jetty, or a picnic for a day on the "West End" promptly delivered. Some prefer the houses that fringe the windward beach (Numbers 6–11), others like the distant trio high up on the bluff (Numbers 1–3), and still others swear by the three perched above the Atlantic surf (Numbers 20–22), with stone steps to the beach. All benefit from the soft white strand that encircles the island, as well as from the hiking paths, water sports, tennis court, and fitness trail. Also available are day trips to neighboring Mopion—a.k.a. Petit St. Richardson, after visionary owner Haze Richardson. You'll probably meet him, along with a selection of his seven yellow Labradors—the happiest dogs in the world. ⌂ *PSV, Box 12506, Cincinnati, OH 45212, ☎ 513/242–1333, 800/654–9326, or 809/458–8801. 22 houses. No credit cards. Closed Sept. and Oct. FAP.*

# Union

Gorgeous from a distance, the island's Mount Parnassus soars 900 feet into the air. Union is a popular stopping-off point for yachtspeople and visitors heading to some of the smaller islands, but it doesn't offer the charm or friendliness of other Grenadines. The main town, Clifton Harbour, is small and rather commercial. Union's airstrip is right behind the Anchorage Yacht Club.

## Lodging

For price information on hotels, *see* the price chart in the Lodging section of St. Vincent, *above*.

**$$–$$$** ⌂ **Anchorage Yacht Club.** Between the airstrip and what little beach there is are rooms and bungalows with concealed outdoor showers and terraces facing the water, all comfortably furnished, with water sports and yacht chartering galore for entertainment. The full-service marina creates a cosmopolitan buzz around the place and in the enormous bar-café area in front, where all three meals are served. There's also a pizza and sandwich counter, and a jump-up on Mondays for all those sailors who got stranded here. ⌂ *Union, St. Vincent, ☎ 809/458–8221, FAX 809/458–8365. 10 rooms, 6 bungalows. Restaurant, bar, air-conditioning, water-sports center, boating. AE, MC, V. CP.*

## Dining

For price information, *see* the price chart in the Dining section of St. Vincent, *above*.

**$$**  ✕ **Lambie's.** On the main street in Clifton, Lambie's offers good conch Creole; the restaurant's walls are made from their shells. There's steel-band music every night in season. ⊠ *Clifton,* ☎ *809/458–8549. No credit cards.*

### Beaches
The beach around Clifton Harbour is narrow, unattractive, rocky, and shadeless. Other beaches have no facilities and are virtually inaccessible without a boat; the desolate but lovely Chatham Bay offers good swimming.

### Outdoor Activities and Sports
SCUBA DIVING
**Grenadines Dive** (☎ 809/458–8138 or 809/458–8122, ℻ 809/458–8122), run by NAUI instructor Glenroy Adams, is the local operation, including Tobago Cays trips and wreck dives at the *Purina,* a sunken World War I English gunship.

### Union Visitor Information
The **Union Island Tourist Bureau** (☎ 809/458–8350), located at the airstrip behind the Anchorage Yacht Club, is open daily from 8–12 and 1–4.

# ST. VINCENT AND THE GRENADINES A TO Z

### Arriving and Departing
BY PLANE
Most U.S. visitors fly via **American Airlines** (☎ 800/433–7300) into Barbados, Grenada, or St. Lucia, then take a small plane to St. Vincent's E.T. Joshua Airport or to Bequia, Mustique, Canouan, or Union. (Other destinations in the Grenadines require a boat ride on either a scheduled ferry, a chartered boat, or your hotel's launch.) Other airlines that connect with interisland flights are **BWIA** (☎ 800/538–2942), **British Airways** (☎ 800/247–9297), **Air Canada** (☎ 800/776–3000), and **Air France** (☎ 800/237–2747).

**LIAT** (Leeward Islands Air Transport, ☎ 809/462–0700; in NY, 212/251–1717; elsewhere in the U.S., 800/253–5011), **Air Martinique** (☎ 809/458–4528), **Carib Express** (☎ 809/456–5075), **Mustique Airways** (☎ 809/458–4380), and **SVG AIR** (☎ 809/456–5610, ℻ 809/458–4697) fly interisland. Delays are common but usually not outrageous.

FROM THE AIRPORT
Taxis and buses are readily available at E.T. Joshua Airport and are available, but rarer, on those Grenadine islands with airstrips. A taxi from the airport to Kingstown will cost about $7.50 (E.C.$20); bus fare is less than 50¢. If you have a lot of luggage, it might be best to take a taxi—buses (actually minivans) are short on space, since they are usually full of people.

### Currency
Although U.S. and Canadian dollars are accepted at all but the smallest shops, Eastern Caribbean currency (E.C.$) is preferred everywhere. At press time, the exchange rate was fixed at E.C.$2.67 to U.S.$1; hotels and shops generally give a rate of E.C.$2.50–$2.60 to U.S.$1. Price quotes are normally given in E.C. dollars; however, especially when you negotiate taxi fares, be sure you know which type of dollar you're agreeing on. Note: Prices quoted here are in U.S. dollars unless indicated otherwise.

## Emergencies

**Police:** ☎ 809/457–1211. **Hospital: Kingstown General Hospital** (☎ 809/456–1185). **Pharmacies:** In Kingstown, **Deane's** (✉ Middle St., ☎ 809/456–2877), **Medix Pharmacy** (✉ Grenville St., ☎ 809/456–2989), or **People's Pharmacy** (✉ Bedford St., ☎ 809/456–1170); on Bequia, **People's Pharmacy** (✉ Port Elizabeth, ☎ 809/458–3936).

## Getting Around

### BUSES

Public buses are really privately owned, brightly painted minivans with names like "Easy Na," "Irie," and "Who to Blame." Bus fares run E.C.$1–$6 on St. Vincent; for the 10-minute ride from Kingstown to Villa Beach, for example, the fare is E.C.$1.50. Buses operate all day long until about midnight, and routes are indicated on a sign in the windshield. Just wave from the road, and the driver will stop for you; pay the man by the door on the way out, with the correct change in EC$ coins, if possible. In Kingstown, buses leave from the Terminus in Market Square; they serve the entire island. Smaller islands in the Grenadines also have taxi-vans and pickup trucks with benches in the back and canvas covers for the occasional rain shower.

### CAR RENTALS

Rental cars cost about $50 per day with some free miles. Using a credit card avoids a $300 cash deposit. Gasoline costs $2.50 per gallon. One road winds its way around the perimeter of the island, so it's impossible to get lost. Be sure to drive on the left, and honk your horn before you enter blind curves out in the countryside—you'll encounter plenty of steep hills and hairpin turns. Although major improvements are being made, roads are not always well marked or maintained. Unless you already have an international driver's license, you'll need to purchase a temporary local license for E.C.$40. Licenses are available at the airport, at the police station on Bay Street, or at the Licensing Authority on Halifax Street.

Among the rental firms are **David's Auto Clinic** (✉ Sion Hill, just south of Kingstown, ☎ 809/456–4026), **Kim's Rentals** (✉ Grenville St., Kingstown, ☎ 809/456–1884), **Star Garage** (✉ Grenville St., Kingstown, ☎ 809/456–1743), **Sunshine Rentals** (✉ Arnos Vale, ☎ 809/456–5380), and **Unico Auto Rentals,** (✉ At the airport, ☎ 809/456–5744).

### TAXIS

Taxi fares are set by the government. Between Kingstown and the hotels and restaurants at Villa Beach, the one-way fare is E.C.$15–$20. To hire a taxi by the hour, the rate is E.C.$40.

## Guided Tours

Tours can be arranged informally through taxi drivers, who double as knowledgeable guides. Your hotel or the tourism board will recommend a driver, or call Kelvin Harry (☎ 809/457–1316), president of the Taxi Driver's Association. He'll send one of the Association's members, identifiable by a round yellow-and-blue decal on the taxi windshield. Always settle the fare first, in either U.S. or E.C. dollars. The average cost is E.C.$40 per hour.

**Austin and Chris Patterson** (✉ Villa, ☎ 809/457–4337), father and son, of Dolphins Restaurant, have four-wheel-drive Jeeps, a ketch, a speedboat, and inns all over the island. Tours include navigation of the Mesopotamia Valley underwater river, and a day sail to their secret deserted island, plus the usual journey to the volcano and falls; tours come complete with locally cooked lunches—plus lots of insider knowledge. **Baleine Tours** (✉ Villa, St. Vincent, ☎ 809/457–4089) offers scenic coastal trips to the Falls of Baleine, as well as charters to Bequia and

Mustique, deep-sea fishing trips, and snorkeling excursions. **Dive St. Vincent** (✉ Young Island Dock, Villa Beach, St. Vincent, ☎ 809/457–4714) offers a day trip to Baleine that includes a scenic voyage along the coast, snorkeling, and swimming at a black-sand beach. **Grenadine Travel Co.** (✉ Arnos Vale, St. Vincent, ☎ 809/458–4818) arranges air, sea, and land excursions throughout the islands. **Sam's Taxi Tours** (✉ Cane Garden, ☎ 809/456–4338) arranges hiking tours to La Soufrière Volcano and scenic walks along the Vermont Nature Trails.

## Language
English is spoken everywhere in the Grenadines, often with a Vincentian dialect.

## Opening and Closing Times
Stores and shops in Kingstown are open weekdays 8–4. Many close for lunch from noon to 1 or so. Saturday hours are 8–noon. Banks are open weekdays 8–1, 2, or 3; Fridays until 5. The branch of National Commercial Bank of St. Vincent at the airport is also open Saturday 7–5.

## Passports and Visas
U.S., Canadian, and U.K. travelers need proof of citizenship (e.g., passport, birth certificate, or voter's registration card). Other nationals must have a valid passport. All visitors must hold return or ongoing tickets. Visas are not required.

## Precautions
There's relatively little **crime** here, but don't tempt fate by leaving your valuables lying around or your room or car unlocked. **Insects** can be a minor problem on the beach during the day, but when hiking and sitting outdoors in the evening, you'll be glad you brought industrial-strength mosquito repellent. Beware of the **manchineel tree,** whose little green apples look tempting but are toxic. Even touching the sap of the leaves will cause an uncomfortable rash, and you should not shelter beneath them during rainstorms. Most trees on hotel grounds are marked with signs; on more remote islands, the bark may be painted red. Hikers should watch for brazilwood trees/bushes, which look and act similar to poison ivy. When taking **photos** of market vendors, private citizens, or homes, be polite enough to ask permission first, and expect to give a gratuity for the favor. **Sea urchins** are spiny black sea creatures that sit on the sand in shallow water. If you happen to step on one, you can put away your dancing shoes. It's painful! Rubbing a little lime—or an ammonia-based liquid—on the wound may help.

## Taxes and Service Charges
The departure tax from St. Vincent and the Grenadines is $7.50 (E.C.$20). Restaurants and hotels charge a 7% government tax; if a 10% service charge is included in your bill, no additional tip is necessary.

## Telephones and Mail
The area code for St. Vincent and the Grenadines is 809. Local information is 118; international is 115. From St. Vincent and most Grenadines, you can dial direct to other countries. When you dial a local number from your hotel in the Grenadines, you can drop the 45 prefix. Pay phones are best operated by the prepaid phonecard available from stores and usable in several Caribbean islands. The General Post Office, on Halifax St. in Kingstown, is open daily from 8:30 to 3 and Saturdays from 8:30 to 11:30. Mail between St. Vincent and the United States may take about two weeks. Airmail postcards cost E.C.90¢; airmail letters cost E.C.$1.80 an ounce.

## Visitor Information

Before you go, contact the **St. Vincent and the Grenadines Tourist Office** (In the U.S.: ✉ 801 2nd Ave., 21st floor, New York, NY 10017, ☎ 212/687–4981 or 800/729–1726, FAX 212/949–5946; ✉ 6505 Cove Creek Pl., Dallas, TX 75240, ☎ 214/239–6451, FAX 214/239–1002; in Canada: ✉ 32 Park Rd., Toronto, Ontario M4W 2N4, ☎ 416/924–5796, FAX 416/924–5844; in the United Kingdom: ✉ 10 Kensington Court, London W8 5DL, ☎ 0171/937–6570, FAX 0171/937–3611). Ask for their visitor's guide, which is filled with useful, up-to-date information.

On St. Vincent, the **St. Vincent Board of Tourism** (✉ Upper Bay St., ☎ 809/457–1502, FAX 809/456–2610) is in the new financial complex, close to the port. It's open Monday to Friday from 8 to noon and 1–4:30. There's also a Tourist Information Desk (☎ 809/458–4685) at E. T. Joshua Airport.

# 25 Trinidad and Tobago

Updated by
Edie Jarolim

**T**HE TWO-ISLAND REPUBLIC OF TRINIDAD AND TO-
BAGO is the southernmost link in the Antillean island
chain, lying some 9 miles off the coast of Venezuela
and safely outside the path of all those devastating Caribbean hurricanes. Both Trinidad and Tobago are more geologically akin to continental South America than they are to the other Caribbean islands:
Tobago's Main Ridge and Trinidad's Northern Range are believed to
represent the farthest reaches of the Andes mountain range. But although
the two islands are linked geographically and politically, in some ways
they could not be more dissimilar.

Trinidad's growth arose out of oil prosperity—it remains one of the
largest petroleum producers in the Western Hemisphere—which made
it a prime destination for business travelers. They enjoyed the sophisticated shopping, restaurants, and hotels in the nation's lively capital,
Port-of-Spain, partying late into the night to the syncopated steel-
band sounds that originated in Trinidad.

The economy slumped along with oil prices in the mid-1980s, but
Trinidad is now recovering with an influx of small businesses. Port-
of-Spain is still one of the most active commercial cities in the West
Indies, and the cultural scene is as vital as ever, especially during the
country's riotous Carnival. The capital hosts around 51,000 of Trinidad's
1.3 million residents—Africans, Indians, Americans, Europeans, and
Asians, each with their own language and customs (the official language
is English, however). But you have to leave Port-of-Spain to find a good
beach and to enjoy the island's natural attractions, and there are currently few accommodations in a nonurban setting that offer more
than bare-bones comfort.

It is Tobago, 22 miles away, that affords tourists the lazier life and seaside lodgings that most of them seek. Unspoiled rain forests and coral
reefs and a largely undeveloped coastline have made the smaller island
an ideal getaway for nature lovers, divers, and privacy-seekers. However, tourism is being promoted heavily and new hotels are being built;
without careful control, Tobago could lose the idyllic quality that led
Daniel Defoe to depict it as the quintessential desert island in *Robinson Crusoe.*

Trinis tend to think of Tobagonians as country bumpkins, lacking in
sophistication and culture. Residents of Tobago pride themselves on
their friendliness, and consider their city cousins a bit too aloof. As a
visitor, you would be hard-pressed to make such distinctions: What you're
likely to notice, instead, is that although both islands are very welcoming,
they remain relatively free of the hustling of tourists that's found
around much of the Caribbean.

Columbus reached these islands on his third voyage, in 1498. Three prominent peaks around the southern bay of Trinidad prompted him to name
the land La Trinidad, after the Holy Trinity. Trinidad was captured by
British forces in 1797, ending 300 years of Spanish rule. Tobago's history is more complicated. It was "discovered" by the British in 1508.
The Spanish, Dutch, French, and British all fought for it until it was
ceded to England under the Treaty of Paris in 1814. In 1962, both islands—T&T, as they're commonly called—gained their independence
within the British Commonwealth, finally becoming a republic in 1976.

North Pt.

Man of War Bay

Little Tobago

Charlotteville

Castara Bay

Hillsborough Bay

Rockley Bay

TOBAGO

Plymouth

Scarborough

Pigeon Pt.

**Crown Pt. Airport**

ATLANTIC

Galera Pt.

Sans Souci

Saline Bay

Matura Bay

Mt. Oropuche

Madamas Bay

Valencia

Main Road

Churchill Roosevelt Hwy.

**Piarco Airport**

Eastern

Chupara Pt.

Uriah Butler Hwy

Maracas Bay

Port-of-Spain

Caribbean Sea

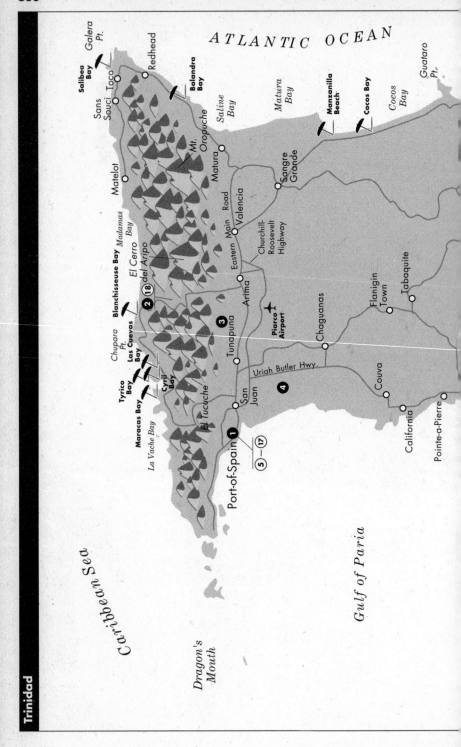

ATLANTIC OCEAN

*Caribbean Sea*

*Galera Pt.*

*Guataro Pt.*

**Salibea Bay**
Sans Souci
Redhead
Toco

**Balandra Bay**
*Saline Bay*

*Matura Bay*

**Manzanilla Beach**

**Cocos Bay**
*Cocos Bay*

Matelot

Mt. Oropuche

*Madamas Bay*

**Blanchisseuse Bay**
*Oropuche*

El Cerro del Aripo

*Chupara Pt.*
**Las Cuevas Bay**

**Tyrico Bay**
**Cyril Bay**

**Maracas Bay**

*La Vache Bay*

El Tucuche

El Tucuche

San Juan

Matura

*Saline Bay*

Valencia

Eastern Main Road

Churchill-Roosevelt Highway

Arima

Sangre Grande

Piarco Airport

Tunapuna

Uriah Butler Hwy.

Chaguanas

Flanigin Town

Tabaquite

Couva

California

Pointe-a-Pierre

Port-of-Spain

2 (18)

3

1

4

5 — (17)

*Dragon's Mouth*

*Gulf of Paria*

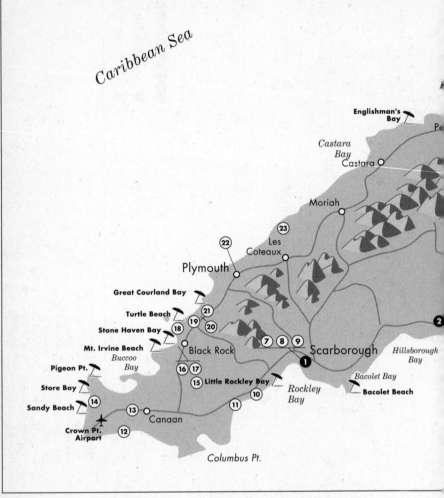

*Caribbean Sea*

Englishman's Bay

*Castara Bay*

Castara

Moriah

23

22   Les Coteaux

Plymouth

**Great Courland Bay**

**Turtle Beach**   21   19

**Stone Haven Bay**   18   20

**Mt. Irvine Beach**   7   8   9   **Scarborough**

*Buccoo Bay*   Black Rock   1   *Hillsborough Bay*

**Pigeon Pt.**   16   17   *Bacolet Bay*

**Store Bay**   15   **Little Rockley Bay**   **Bacolet Beach**

**Sandy Beach**   14   10   *Rockley Bay*

**Crown Pt. Airport**   13   Canaan   11

12

*Columbus Pt.*

| Exploring | Dining | Rouselle's, **9** | Grafton Beach Resort, **17** |
|---|---|---|---|
| Charlotteville, **5** | Blue Crab, **8** | | Le Grand Courlan, **20** |
| Flagstaff Hill, **4** | Cocrico Inn, **22** | **Lodging** | Kariwak Village, **12** |
| Fort King George, **2** | Dillon's, **13** | Arnos Vale Hotel, **23** | Mt. Irvine Bay Hotel, **16** |
| Scarborough, **1** | Kariwak Village, **12** | Blue Horizon Resort, **15** | Ocean Point, **11** |
| Speyside, **3** | Mount Marie, **7** | Blue Waters Inn, **6** | Palm Tree Village, **10** |
| | Ocean View, **17** | Coco Reef Resort, **14** | |
| | Papillon, **18** | | |

The Sisters

Bloody Bay

Parlatuvier

Parlatuvier

Pigeon Peak

North Pt.

Lover's Beach

Man O'War Bay

Charlotteville

**5**

**4**

**3**

⑥

Speyside

St. Giles Island

Bird of Paradise Island

Little Tobago

Delaford

King's Bay

Roxborough

Carapuse Bay

ATLANTIC OCEAN

Mt. St. George

**2**

orough ay

N

**KEY**

**1** Exploring Sites

⑥ Hotels and Restaurants

0        4 miles
0        6 km

Plantation Beach Villas, **21**

Rex Turtle Beach Hotel, **19**

# TRINIDAD

## Lodging

Trinidad accommodations range from charming guest houses to tony hotels; most of the acceptable establishments, however, are within the vicinity of Port-of-Spain, far from any beach. Carnival week is one of two times in the year for which you should book reservations far in advance (the other is Christmas); expect to pay twice the price charged the rest of the year.

Most places offer breakfast and dinner for an additional flat rate (MAP), but on the whole these plans mean less variety than you'll get if you strike out for meals on your own.

The number of private homes in Trinidad offering bed-and-breakfast accommodations is growing each year. Contact the **Trinidad and Tobago Bed and Breakfast Co-operative Society** (⊠ Box 3231, Diego Martin, ☎ FAX 809/627–2337).

| CATEGORY | COST* |
| --- | --- |
| $$$$ | over $175 |
| $$$ | $100–$175 |
| $$ | $60–$100 |
| $ | under $60 |

*All prices are for a standard double room for two, excluding 15% tax and 10% service charge.*

**$$$–$$$$**  **Trinidad Hilton and Conference Center.** Perched above the Gulf of
★ Paria and Queen's Park Savannah, and set on landscaped gardens, the Hilton is extremely stylish. It stretches out horizontally across the hilltop, and gently moves down the hillside: You take the elevator *down* to your room. The design, with its gleaming dark wood and tropical landscaping, is lovely, and each of the rooms has a balcony, which either opens to a fine view of Queen's Park, the city, and the sea beyond, or overlooks the inviting Olympic-size swimming pool. The hotel has its shortcomings: Rooms are somewhat generically decorated and vary quite a bit in upkeep and amenities, the route to the pool is labyrinthine, and service is somewhat erratic (you might find your bed unmade when you return from sightseeing in the afternoon). That said, this hotel is the most upscale and has the most amenities in the city. ⊠ *Lady Young Rd., Box 442, Port-of-Spain,* ☎ *809/624–3211; in the U.S., 800/445–8667;* FAX *809/624–4485. 394 rooms. 2 restaurants, 3 bars, air-conditioning, pool, 2 tennis courts, drugstore, gift shops, meeting rooms, car rental, taxi service. AE, DC, MC, V. EP.*

**$$$**  **Holiday Inn.** Proximity to the port and Independence Square is both the draw and the drawback of this hotel. From any upper floor room you'll have a lovely pastel panorama of the old town and of ships idling in the Gulf of Paria, and you're within walking distance of the downtown sights and shops. But with the action comes traffic: Independence Square is clogged with people and cars throughout the day. Rooms are done in standard international mode, complete with hair dryers, a rarity on Trinidad. La Ronde, a revolving rooftop bistro, offers a striking view of the city at night. ⊠ *Wrightson Rd., Box 1017, Port-of-Spain,* ☎ *809/625–3366; in the U.S., 800/465–4329;* FAX *809/625–4166. 235 rooms, 2 suites. Restaurant, air-conditioning, pool, beauty salon, exercise room, shops, baby-sitting, laundry service, business services, car rental, taxi service. AE, DC, MC, V. BP.*

**$$**  **Hotel Normandie.** Built by French Creoles in the 1930s on the ruins
★ of an old coconut plantation, the gracious Normandie has touches of Spanish, English colonial, and even postmodern architecture. It's set

back from residential St. Ann's Road, adjoining an artsy mall of crafts shops and galleries. The standard rooms, set around a pretty court-yard with a pool, have wood floorboards and fittings, noisy but effi-cient air-conditioning, and very little light. The 13 larger loft rooms are far better: For $25 more, you get a towering duplex with a bigger bathroom (the fact that two children under 12 can stay free makes them perfect for families). Service is friendly and efficient. La Fantasie (☞ Dining, *below*) provides room service until 11 PM. ⊠ *10 Nook Ave., Box 851, St. Ann's, Port-of-Spain,* ☎ FAX *809/624–1181. 61 rooms. Restaurant, bar, café, air-conditioning, pool, gallery, shops, meeting rooms, car rental, taxi service. AE, DC, MC, V. EP, MAP.*

$$  🖭 **Kapok Hotel.** This well-run hotel, quiet and convenient to fine shopping, is good value for the price. The rooms, done in greys and pinks, are spacious and sunlit, with rattan furniture and Polynesian prints the colors of highlighting markers. Front ones are best for the view over the Savannah, and even better are the studios—with kitchenette—for the same price as a room. Parents will appreciate the hotel's coin-op-erated laundry and ironing room, and kids will enjoy the lively menagerie of birds, fish, and monkeys that live by the pool. The hotel's Cafe Sa-vanna was recently sacrificed to a room expansion, but the Tiki Vil-lage (☞ Dining, *below*) remains popular with locals. ⊠ *16–18 Cotton Hill, St. Clair, Port-of-Spain,* ☎ *809/622–6441 or 800/344–1212,* FAX *809/622–9677. 94 rooms, including 6 suites and 9 studios. Restau-rant, air-conditioning, pool, beauty salon, shops, business services, taxi service. AE, DC, MC, V. EP.*

$–$$  🖭 **La Maison Rustique.** This little bed-and-breakfast in a gingerbread house is a charmer, and it has a great location, near Queen's Park Sa-vannah amid other wonderful Victorian homes. Rooms in the garden cottage are the nicest, but all rooms are clean and serviceable. Some are air-conditioned, and a few have private baths. The proprietor, Maureen Chin-Asiong, is a hotel school graduate and lists the Wilton School of Cake Decorating in Chicago among her credits. She not only serves good breakfasts—popovers, croissants, quiche—but also whips up afternoon tea, snacks, and picnic baskets. There's a five-night Car-nival package for $500. ⊠ *16 Rust St., St. Clair, Port-of-Spain,* ☎ FAX *809/622–1512. 7 rooms (3 with private bath). No credit cards. BP.*

$  🖭 **Alicia's House.** The Govias managed to keep the family atmosphere when they converted their home for guests, so all here is welcoming and reassuring, if not fancy. The enormous, breezy lounge has squashy sofas, round tables, cane chairs, a piano, and a tank of fish; it leads into the dining area, where you may take breakfast, and other meals if you order ahead. Rooms vary greatly in size and amenities; the large Admiral Rooney (a local flower) offers a garden-view desk and a giant bathtub, while the little Back Room has a private spiral staircase to the pool. Some of the furnishings, bed coverings, and curtains have seen better days, but rates are very reasonable and include such extras as a hot tub and a water cooler by the pool, 14-channel U.S. cable TV, air-conditioning, private bathrooms, and phones in every room. Alicia's House is a 10-minute walk from the Savannah and close to the Nor-mandie and the Hilton hotels. ⊠ *7 Coblentz Gardens, St. Ann's, Port-of-Spain,* ☎ *809/623–2802 or 809/624–8651; toll-free from airport, 223;* FAX *809/622–8560. 17 rooms. Dining room, lounge, air-condi-tioning, pool, hot tub, laundry facilities. AE, MC, V. EP, CP, MAP.*

$  🖭 **Asa Wright Nature Centre.** Bird-watchers and nature photogra-
★  phers are frequently among the guests at this handsome lodge. Built in 1908, it's set in a lush rain forest (about 90 minutes east of Port-of-Spain) populated by nearly 200 species of birds. There are impressive views of the verdant Arima Valley and the Northern Range from the veranda, where tea is served each afternoon. Just inside is an elegant,

comfortable lounge with black painted floorboards, bookcases, antiques, and ornithological memorabilia. The two huge bedrooms that abut this share its romantic atmosphere, with fans turning slowly on tall ceilings, hardwood closets, and antique beds. All other rooms are in modern lodges near the house, simply outfitted with wood floors, motel-style furniture, and private covered terraces. You'll feel you're miles from anywhere, and, actually, you are, so you'll need the three meals a day and evening rum punch that are included in the rates. Airport transfers cost $40. (For more information about the center, *see* Exploring, *below.*) ⊠ *Box 4710, Arima, Trinidad,* ☎ *809/667–4655,* ⅎ𝔸𝕏 *809/667– 0493. 24 rooms, 1 bungalow. Dining room, lounge, guided field trips, gift shop, airport shuttle. No credit cards. FAP.*

$  ⊞ **Carnetta's House.** When Winston Borrell retired as director of tourism for Trinidad and Tobago, he and his wife, Carnetta, opened up their suburban two-story house to guests. One guest room is on the upper floor, the same level as the lounge and terrace dining room. The other four are on the ground floor, with the choice room, Le Flamboyant, opening onto the garden's patio. All rooms have a private bathroom with shower, telephone, radio, and TV. And, although there is air-conditioning, cool breezes usually do the trick. Unfortunately, the doors need to be shuttered at night for security reasons. Winston is a keen gardener, and his garden has a sampling of plants that are a fascinating introduction to tropical flowers and herbs. Carnetta uses the herbs in her cooking, and she can prepare some of the best dinners that you may find in Port-of-Spain. Equally important is the fund of information that both Carnetta and Winston can offer on what to see and do in Trinidad and the necessary arrangements they can make to do it. ⊠ *28 Scotland Terr., Andalusia, Maraval, Port-of-Spain,* ☎ *809/628–2732,* ⅎ𝔸𝕏 *809/628–7717. 5 rooms. Dining room, lounge, air-conditioning, laundry facilities, car rental, airport shuttle. AE, DC, MC, V. EP, BP, MAP.*

$  ⊞ **Monique's.** Mike and Monique Charbonné really *like* having guests,
★ as they have been proving for over a decade. Rooms are sizable and spotless, and most are bright. Numbers 25 and 26 are enormous and can sleep up to six; they're darker than the other rooms, but each has a little sunken red stone patio where you can soak up some sun. Breakfast and dinner are available in the parlorlike dining room. The airy, marble-floored lounge is a great place to hang out—with the hosts often as not. Mike sometimes organizes a picnic to the couple's 100-acre plantation near Blanchisseuse. ⊠ *114 Saddle Rd., Maraval, Port-of-Spain,* ☎ *809/628–3334 or 809/628–2351,* ⅎ𝔸𝕏 *809/622–3232. 26 rooms. Dining room, air-conditioning, common room with TV. AE. EP, MAP.*

$  ⊞ **Tropical.** Crazy-paved steps take you into a pretty reception area with a clicking ceiling fan, murmuring TV, pea-green Lloyd Loom chairs, white arches, and white wrought-iron gates shielding a central, cloisterlike courtyard. That's about it for the grounds, except for the small pool. Rooms, too, are spartan, if psychedelic, with their fuchsia-and-tomato drapes, bedcovers, and shower curtains. Most are big, and all have air-conditioning. Big pluses are the excellent restaurant-bar and club attached, serving local food, and the low rates. ⊠ *6 Rookery Nook, Maraval, Port-of-Spain,* ☎ *809/622–5815,* ⅎ𝔸𝕏 *809/622–3174. 13 rooms. Restaurant, bar, air-conditioning, pool, nightclub. AE. EP.*

# Dining

There's a distinctively Creole touch to T&T cuisine, but ask what Creole seasoning is and you'll hear a different answer from each person you ask. The herbs and spices used on the islands range from fresh bay leaves (bright green, not dried) to nutmegs from the trees and a variety of peppers. The cooking also uses a lot of guava, plantain, and local fish and meat. Asian, Indian, African, French, and Spanish influences, among others, can be tasted, often in a single meal. Indian food is a favorite: *Rotis* (East Indian sandwiches) are served as a fast food; a mélange of curried meat or fish and vegetables frequently makes an appearance; and a wide selection of *vindaloos* (spicy hot meat, vegetable, and seafood dishes) and poori can be had. Crab lovers will find large blue-backs curried, peppered, and served with tomatoes, and used in callaloo soup (a national treasure made of green dasheen leaves mixed with okra, coconut milk, and crabmeat). Shark-and-bake is the sandwich of choice, made of lightly seasoned, fried shark meat.

In addition to excellent Creole fare, good Italian food and other European cuisines can now be had in Trinidad. Hotel restaurants, of course, cater to a less adventuresome market.

No Trinibagan dining experience can be complete, of course, without a rum punch with fresh fruit and the legendary Angostura Bitters, made by the same local company that produces the excellent Old Oak rum, but watch out for the fiendish sugar content. Light, refreshing Carib beer is the local lager; dark-beer aficionados can try Royal Extra Stout (R.E.). Local chocolate, found in supermarkets, is made in squares and often flavored with bay leaf and nutmeg.

## What to Wear

The restaurants of Trinidad and Tobago are informal: You won't find any jacket and tie requirements. Beachwear, however, is a little too casual for most places. A nice pair of shorts is apropos for lunch; for dinner, you'll probably feel most comfortable in a pair of slacks or a casual sundress.

| CATEGORY | COST* |
| --- | --- |
| $$$ | over $25 |
| $$ | $15–$25 |
| $ | under $15 |

*per person, excluding drinks, service, and 15% tax*

$$$ ✕ **La Boucan.** Trinidadian dancer Geoffrey Holder painted the large mural of a social idyll in the Savannah that dominates one wall of this room at the Hilton. A more leisurely Trinidad is also reflected in the old-fashioned charm of silver service, uniformed waiters, soft lighting, pink tablecloths, and the serenade of a grand piano. The menu is international, including steaks, seafood grills, and other simple preparations, but you can also find such local specialties as callaloo soup, shrimp Creole, and West Indian chicken curry (these dishes are served mild unless you assure your waiter you want them spicy). Afternoon tea, served Wednesday through Friday from 4 to 6, is a treat. ⊠ *Trinidad Hilton, Lady Young Rd., Port-of-Spain,* ☎ *809/624–3211. AE, DC, MC, V.*

$$–$$$ ✕ **Solimar.** In a series of dimly lit, plant-filled eating areas, Chef Joe Brown offers a menu that tries to travel the world in one meal: You might enjoy shrimp tempura, Irish smoked salmon, Hawaiian barbecued mahimahi, Greek salad, linguine Alfredo, or Zwiebel schnitzel, all while listening to John Denver singing "I think I'd rather be a cowboy." Best bets are the day's specials—seafood mixed grill, perhaps, followed by double chocolate mousse with crème de cacao. Solimar is popular with expat types and tends toward careful casualness. ⊠ *6 Nook Ave., St. Ann's,* ☎ *809/624–6267. AE, DC, MC, V.*

$$ ✕ **La Fantasie.** The Hotel Normandie's restaurant is done up in lovely Caribbean Art Deco, the clean lines of the design complemented by

deep peach, mauve, and other vibrant island colors. La Fantasie pioneered *cuisine nouvelle créole,* and many of the dishes are lighter versions of local fare made with a French flair. Seafood is the best bet—grilled snapper stuffed with shrimp in tart tomato sauce, perhaps. The air-conditioning is blissfully glacial, but on cooler nights it's nice to dine outside on the terrace, gazing at the moon through the palms. ⊠ *Hotel Normandie, 10 Nook Ave., St. Ann's, Port-of-Spain,* ☎ *809/624–1181. AE, DC, MC, V.*

**\$\$** ✕ **Tiki Village.** Cosmopolitan Port-of-Spainers are as passionate about their Asian food as New Yorkers and San Franciscans are. Everyone touts their favorite, but this capacious eatery, a serious (nonkitsch) version of Trader Vic's, is the most reliable. It's high under the rafters atop the Kapok Hotel, sun-lit during the day and affording good views of an electrified Trinidad at night. Fine Asian food is served, including, on weekends and public holidays, a very popular dim sum, where dishes such as pepper squid and tofu stuffed with fish are ordered in tasting-size portions. ⊠ *Kapok Hotel, 16–18 Cotton Hill, St. Clair,* ☎ *809/622–6441. AE, DC, MC, V.*

**\$\$** ✕ **Veni Mange.** The best lunches in town are served inside this small
★ stucco house, decorated with paintings by local artists. It's difficult to find but well worth the effort. Credit Allyson Hennessy—a Cordon Bleu–trained cook who has become a celebrity of sorts because of a TV talk show she hosts—and her friendly and flamboyant sister-partner, Rosemary Hezekiah. The creative Creole menu changes daily; starters might include cream of pumpkin soup, and for a main course you could find stewed oxtail with banana fritters and stewed lentils. There's always a vegetarian entrée option, too. Homemade desserts are divine. Now if only we could convince the sisters to stay open more than one night a week for dinner! ⊠ *13 Lucknow St., St. James, Port-of-Spain,* ☎ *809/622–7533. AE, MC, V. No dinner Thurs.–Tues.*

**\$–\$\$** ✕ **Rafters.** Behind a stone facade with a green tin awning and wooden doors stands a pub that has become an urban institution. Once it was a rum shop; currently it's a bar and a restaurant. The pub is the center of activity, especially Friday night. In late afternoons the place begins to swell with Port-of-Spainers ordering from the tasty selection of burgers, barbecues, and burritos. The Seafood Sampler platter (seasonal fin and shellfish, including shrimp and conch) is served with baked potato and tartar sauce for about \$8 (TT\$45). In the evening an unexpectedly romantic candlelit restaurant with a mostly Continental menu opens in another part of the delightful old building. ⊠ *6A Warner St., Port-of-Spain,* ☎ *809/628–9258. AE, DC, MC, V.*

**\$** ✕ **Wazo Deyzeel.** "Oiseaux des îles"—get it?—is adored by all for its setting, high up in the hills of St. Ann, with Port-of-Spain spread out below; its live bands and dancing on weekends; its friendliness; and its prizewinning cocktails (the cucumber-lime-rum-syrup Wazo Combo is essential); as well as for its food. The Thursday-night all-you-can-eat Caribbean buffet might include grouper, flying fish, red snapper, macaroni pie, *cou-cou* (cornmeal and coconut dumplings), *bhajia* (East Indian spinach fritters), and savory pumpkin pie, and at about \$10 is probably the best bargain in the city. Friday, Saturday, and Sunday nights you could go for a seafood platter or a beef pot roast, all cooked by three Jamaican ladies. Candy-color director's chairs, white walls, a big, open-air terrace for admiring the view, wining (a naughty dance style), and liming (hanging out) set the tone. ⊠ *Carib Way, 23 Sydenham Ave., St. Ann's,* ☎ *809/623–0115. MC, V. Closed Mon.–Wed.*

# Beaches

Although Trinidad is not the beach destination Tobago is, it has its share of fine shoreline, spread out along the North Coast Road within an hour's drive of Port-of-Spain. The drive to the beaches of the east coast takes several hours. To get there you must take the detour road to Arima, but "goin' behind God's back," as the Trinis say, rewards the persistent traveler with gorgeous vistas and secluded beaches.

**Balandra Bay,** sheltered by a rocky outcropping, is popular among body-surfers.

**Blanchisseuse Bay,** on the North Coast Road, is a narrow, palm-fringed beach. Facilities are nonexistent, but the beach is ideal for a romantic picnic. You can haggle with local fishermen to take you out in their boats to explore the coast.

**Las Cuevas Bay,** on the North Coast Road, is a narrow, picturesque strip of sand named for the series of partially submerged and explorable caves that ring the beach. A food stand offers tasty snacks, and vendors hawk fresh fruit across the road. There are basic changing and toilet facilities. It's less crowded here than at nearby Maracas Bay (☞ *below*), and seemingly serene, although, as at Maracas, the current can be treacherous.

**Manzanilla Beach** has picnic facilities and a postcard-pretty view of the Atlantic, though its water is occasionally muddied by the Orinoco River, which flows in from South America. The road here, nicknamed the Cocal, is lined with stately palms whose fronds vault like the arches at Chartres. This is where many well-heeled Trinis have vacation homes.

**Maracas Bay** is a long stretch of sand with a cove and a fishing village at one end. It's *the* local favorite, so it can get crowded on weekends. Parking sites are ample, and there are snack bars and rest-room facilities. Try a shark-and-bake (a deep-fried shark sandwich, served in a pita-type bread with hot sauce and cilantro-garlic salsa) from one of the huts ranged along the road at Maracas. Patsy's is considered the best. Wash it down with a grenadillo (like a giant passion fruit) juice from the stand on Patsy's right, if it's available.

**Marianne Beach** is the quietest and prettiest of all, with a natural freshwater lagoon at the east end. Pay Vincent James TT$3 to park on his land; you can also rent the three-room first floor of the house you see for about $13—it's very basic (☎ 809/674–7145 after 1 PM).

**Salibea Bay,** just past Galera Point, which juts toward Tobago, is a gentle beach with shallows and plenty of shade—perfect for swimming. Snack vendors abound in the vicinity.

**Tyrico Bay** is a small beach lively with surfers who flock here to enjoy the excellent surfing. The strong undertow may be too much for some swimmers.

# Carnival

Trinidad always seems to be either anticipating, celebrating, or recovering from a festival, the largest of which is Carnival. Occurring each year between February and early March, Trinidad's version of the pre-Lenten bacchanal is reputedly the oldest in the Western Hemisphere; there are festivities all over the country, but the most lavish is in Port-of-Spain. Not as overwhelming as its rival in Rio or as debauched as Mardi Gras in New Orleans, Trinidad's Carnival has the warmth and character of a massive family reunion.

Carnival is about extravagant costumes. Colorfully attired troupes—called *mas*—that sometimes number in the thousands march to the beat set by the steel bands. You can visit the various mas "camps" around the city where these elaborate getups are put together—the addresses are listed in the newspapers—and perhaps join one that strikes your fancy. Fees run anywhere from $35 to $100; you get to keep the costume. Children can also parade in a Kiddie Carnival that takes place on Saturday morning a few days before the real thing.

Carnival is also a showcase for performers of calypso, music that mixes dance rhythms with social commentary, sung by characters with such evocative names as Shadow, the Mighty Sparrow, and Black Stalin. As Carnival approaches, many of these singers perform nightly in calypso tents scattered around the city. You can also visit the pan yards of Port-of-Spain, where steel orchestras, such as the Renegades, Desperadoes, Catelli All-Stars, Invaders, and Phase II, rehearse their calypso arrangements. Most can be heard practically year-round.

Carnival officially lasts only two days, from *J'ouvert* (sunrise) on Monday to midnight the following day. If you're planning to go, it's a good idea to arrive in Trinidad a week or two early to enjoy the preliminary events. For several nights before Carnival, costume makers display their talents, and the steel bands and calypso singers perform in competitions in the grandstands of the old racetrack in Queen's Park, where the Calypso Monarch was crowned until 1993, when the Dimanche Gras festivities moved to the National Stadium in the Cruise Ship Complex at the Port. At J'ouvert, the city starts filling with metal-frame carts carrying steel bands, flatbed trucks hauling sound systems, and thousands of revelers who squeeze into the narrow streets. Finally, at the stroke of midnight on "Mas Tuesday," Port-of-Spain's exhausted merrymakers go to bed. The next day everybody's back to business.

## Outdoor Activities and Sports

### Bird-Watching

Trinidad and Tobago ranks among the top 10 countries in the world in terms of the number of species of birds per square mile—more than 600 altogether, many living within pristine rain forests, lowlands and savannahs, and fresh- and saltwater swamps. If you're lucky, you might spot the collared trogon, blue-backed manakin, or rare white-tailed Sabrewing hummingbird. Restaurants often hang feeders outside their porches, as much to keep the birds away from your food as to provide a chance for observation.

Bird-watchers can fill up their books with notes on the variety of species to be found in Trinidad at the **Asa Wright Nature Centre** and the **Caroni Bird Sanctuary** (☞ Exploring, *below*), and the **Pointe-à-Pierre Wild Fowl Trust** (☒ 42 Sandown Rd., Pt. Cumana, ☎ 809/637–5145), located on 26 acres within the unlikely confines of a petrochemical complex; you must call in advance for a reservation at Pointe-à-Pierre. **Winston Nanan** (☎ 809/645–1305) runs highly recommended bird-watching tours to nearby Guayana and Venezuela.

### Deep-Sea Fishing

The islands off the northwest coast of Trinidad offer excellent waters for deep-sea fishing; the ocean here was a favorite angling spot of Franklin D. Roosevelt. Members of the **Trinidad and Tobago Yacht Club** (☒ Bayshore, ☎ 809/637–4260) may be willing to arrange a tour.

### Golf

The best golf course in Trinidad is the 18-hole **St. Andrew's Golf Club** (☒ Moka, Maraval, ☎ 809/629–2314), just outside Port-of-Spain.

## Tennis

The following private tennis courts allow nonmembers or nonresidents to play: the **Trinidad Hilton** (☎ 809/624–3211), the **Trinidad Country Club** (⊠ Long Circular Rd., Maraval, ☎ 809/622–3470), and the **Tranquility Square Lawn Tennis Club** (⊠ Victoria Ave., Port-of-Spain, ☎ 809/625–4182).

# Shopping

Good buys on the islands include such duty-free items as Angostura Bitters and Old Oak or Vat 19 rum, all widely available throughout the country.

### Duty Free

**Stecher's** (⊠ Trinidad Hilton, ☎ 809/624–3322; ⊠ Long Circular Mall, St. James, ☎ 809/622–0017) is a familiar name for those seeking to avoid taxes on fine perfumes, electronics, and jewelry; you can arrange to have your purchases delivered to the airport the day of your departure. **Y. de Lima** (⊠ High St., ☎ 809/655–8872; ⊠ West Mall, Western Main Rd., St. James, ☎ 809/622–7050) sells traditional luxury duty-free items.

### Fabric

Thanks in large part to Carnival costumery, there's no shortage of fabric shops on the islands. The best bargains for Asian and East Indian silks and cottons can be found in downtown Port-of-Spain, on **Frederick Street** and around **Independence Square.**

### Local Crafts

The tourism office can provide an extensive list of local artisans who specialize in everything from straw and cane work to miniature steel pans.

**Bonga!** (⊠ Ellerslie Plaza, Cotton Hill, behind the Kapok Hotel, ☎ 809/624–8819) stocks smart T-shirts, carryalls, shorts, and bathing suits. **Poui Boutique** (⊠ Ellerslie Plaza, Cotton Hill, behind the Kapok Hotel, ☎ 809/622–5597) has stylish hand-done wax batik clothing and Ajoupa ware, an attractive local terra-cotta pottery. **Craft Boutique** (⊠ Corner of Adam Smith Sq. S and Murray St., Woodbrook, ☎ 809/627–2736) is located in Monica Monceaux's house, a delight in gingerbread wood tracery. Almost every inch of the house is utilized by Monica and her craftspeople, who make carnival and folk dolls, Christmas ornaments (even those for the Hilton tree), crocheted picture frames, preserves, and dozens of other items in merry disarray. **The Market** (⊠ Nook Ave., adjoining the Hotel Normandie, ☎ 809/624–1181) is a collection of shops that specialize in indigenous fashions, crafts, jewelry, basketwork, and ceramics. Among them, the **Craft Shop** (☎ 809/623–0377) carries goods more imaginative than its name, including beautiful metallic wall sconces and mirrors.

### Malls

**Ellerslie Plaza** (⊠ On Cotton Hill behind the Kapok Hotel, no phone) is an attractive outdoor mall well worth browsing. You can drop by for a snack at the Patisserie or lunch at the stylish Gourmet Club. A fine design clothing shop, **Meiling** (☎ 809/628–6205) features cottons in ecru or white and smart little girls' dresses with shirred tops. **Long Circular Mall** (⊠ Long Circular Rd., St. James, ☎ 809/622–4925) has upscale boutiques that will keep you occupied window-shopping. Check out the handcrafted jewelry at the **Signature Collection** (☎ 809/622–9945), with its pricey but one-of-a-kind pieces.

## Records

**Rhyner's Record Shop** (✉ 54 Prince St., ☎ 809/623–5673; ✉ Piarco International Airport duty free, ☎ 809/669–3064) is where to go for the best selection of calypso and soca music.

## Nightlife and the Arts

When Nobel prize–winning poet Derek Walcott returns home to Trinidad, he often gives readings or gets involved in one of the productions of the thriving local theater. There are several excellent theaters in Port-of-Spain. Consult local newspapers for listings.

Trinidadian culture doesn't end with music, but it definitely begins with it. Although both calypso and steel bands are best displayed during Carnival, the steel bands play at clubs, dances, and fêtes throughout the year. There's no lack of nightlife in Port-of-Spain, and spontaneity plays a big role—look for the handwritten signs announcing the "pan yard" where the next informal gathering of steel drum bands is going to be. A type of music that's popular right now is "sweet Parang," a mixture of Spanish patois and calypso sung to tunes played on a string instrument much like a mandolin.

**Blue Iguana** (✉ main street, Chaguanas, no phone) is the place to go for lively late-night action. It's about 20 minutes west of town in Chaguanas, so get a party together from your hotel and hire a cab. It opens at 10 PM, Wednesday through Sunday. **Cricket Wicket** (✉ 149 Tragarete Rd., ☎ 809/622–1808), a popular watering hole with a cupola-shape bar in the center, is a fine place to hear top bands, dance, or just sit and enjoy the nocturnal scenery. **Mas Camp Pub** (✉ Corner of Ariapata Ave. and French St., Woodbrook, ☎ 809/623–3745) is Port-of-Spain's most comfortable and dependable nightspot. Along with a bar and an ample stage where a DJ or live band reigns, there's also an open-air patio. The kitchen dishes up hearty, reasonably priced Creole lunches, and if one of the live bands strikes your fancy, chances are you can buy a cassette of their music here. **Moon Over Bourbon Street** (✉ Southern Landing, Westmall, Westmoorings, ☎ 809/637–3448) has comedy or music most nights, plus long, long happy hours. **Pelican** (✉ 2–4 Coblentz Ave., St. Ann's, ☎ 809/627–6271), an English-style pub, gets increasingly frenetic as the week closes, with a singles bar atmosphere. **Smokey & Bunty** (✉ Western Main Rd. and Dengue St., St. James, no phone) is where to collect gossip over a beer. It calls itself a sports bar but is really just the essential liming corner. **Wazo Deyzeel** (✉ 23 Sydenham Ave., St. Ann's, ☎ 809/623–0115) is the current fave with a mixed age group for its music, dancing, drinking, views, and great food cooked by three Jamaican ladies. It's closed Monday–Wednesday.

## Exploring Trinidad

The intensely urban atmosphere of Port-of-Spain belies the tropical beauty of the countryside surrounding it. It is truly stunning, but you will need a car, and three to eight hours (if you stop at any of the northern beaches [☞ Beaches, *above*]) to see all there is to see. Begin by circling the Savannah—seemingly obligatory to get almost anywhere around here—to Saddle Road, in the residential district of Maraval. After a few miles the road begins to narrow and curve sharply as it climbs into the Northern Range and its undulating hills of lush, junglelike foliage. Stop at the Lookout on North Coast Road, and have Keith Davis sing you a hilarious calypso, complete with any biographical details you give him. (He's not allowed to ask, but a few T&T dollars are appreciated—and deserved.) From the town of Blanchisseuse, en route to the Asa Wright Nature Centre, the road winds through canyons of moist, verdant foliage, towering palms, mossy grottoes, and "big bamboo"—so large that a calypso song was written about it. In this tropical rain forest, keep an eye out for vultures, parakeets, hummingbirds, toucans, and, if you're lucky, maybe red-bellied, yellow-and-blue macaws.

*Numbers in the margin correspond to points of interest on the Trinidad map.*

## Port-of-Spain

❶ Be sure to bring along lots of film—the renewed charms of **Port-of-Spain** are well worth photographing. Most sightseeing tours begin at the port. If you're planning to explore by foot, which will take two to four hours, start early in the day; by mid-afternoon the port area can be hot and as packed as Calcutta. You'll want to end up on a bench in the Queen's Park Savannah, sipping a cool coconut water bought from one of the vendors operating out of a flatbed truck. For about 50¢, he'll lop the top off a green coconut with a deft swing of the machete and, when you've finished drinking, lop again, making a bowl and spoon of coconut shell for you to eat the young pulp—the texture of a boiled egg white. According to Trinis, "It'll cure anyt'ing dat ail ya, mon."

SIGHTS TO SEE

☾ **Emperor Valley Zoo and the Botanical Gardens.** The cultivated expanse of parkland just north of the Savannah is the site of the president's and prime minister's official residences. A meticulous lattice of walkways and local flora, the parkland was first laid out in 1820 for Governor Woodford and is a model of what a tropical garden should be. In the midst of this serene wonderland is the zoo, leisurely apportioned on 8 acres and largely featuring birds and animals of the region—from the brilliantly plumed scarlet ibis to slithering anacondas and pythons; wild parrots breed in the area and can be seen (and heard) in the surrounding foliage. The zoo draws a quarter of a million visitors a year and more than half of them are children, so admission is priced accordingly—a mere TT$1.50 for under-12s. ⊠ *Botanical Gardens, Port-of-Spain,* ☎ *809/622–3530.* ⌑ *TT$3.* ☉ *Daily 9:30–6.*

**Frederick Street.** Port-of-Spain's main shopping drag, starting north from the midpoint of Independence Square, is a market street of scents—corn roasting and Indian spices—and crowded shops.

**Independence Square.** Across Wrightson Road from the south side of King's Wharf, this is not a square at all: It's a wide, dusty thoroughfare crammed with pedestrians, car traffic, taxi stands, and peddlers of everything from shoes to coconuts—not a pleasant walk for lone females. Flanked by government buildings and the familiar twin towers of the Financial Complex (familiar because it adorns one side of all T&T dollar bills), the square is gloriously chaotic, loud, and confusing. On the south side of Independence Square, the **Cruise Ship Complex,** full of duty-free shops, forms an enclave of international anonymity with the Holiday Inn. On the eastern end of the square is the **Cathedral of the Immaculate Conception,** built by the sea in 1832, but subsequent landfill around the port gave it an inland location. The imposing Roman Catholic structure is made out of stone from nearby Laventille.

**King's Wharf.** Though it is no longer as frenetic as it was during the oil boom of the 1970s, the town's main dock entertains a steady parade of cruise and cargo ships, a reminder that the city started from this strategic harbor. It's on Wrightson Road, the main street along the water on the southwest side of town.

**Magnificent Seven.** A series of astonishing buildings constructed in a variety of 19th-century styles flanks the western side of the Savannah. Notable among them are **Killarney,** patterned (loosely) after Balmoral Castle in Scotland, with an Italian-marble gallery surrounding the ground floor; **Whitehall,** constructed in the style of a Venetian palace by a cacao-plantation magnate and currently the office of the prime minister; **Roomor,** a flamboyantly baroque colonial-period house with a preponderance of towers, pinnacles, and wrought-iron trim that suggests an elaborate French pastry; and the **Queen's Royal College,** in German Renaissance style, with a prominent tower clock that chimes on the hour.

**National Museum and Art Gallery.** It's worth heading over to the southeast corner of the Savannah, if only to see the Carnival exhibits, the Amerindian collection and historical re-creations, and the fine 19th-century paintings of Trinidadian artist Cazabon. ⊠ *117 Upper Frederick St.,* ☎ *809/623–5941 or 809/624–6477.* ⊡ *Free.* ⊙ *Tues.–Sat. 10–6.*

**Queen's Park Savannah.** If the downtown port area is the pulse of Port-of-Spain, the great green expanse roughly bounded by Maraval Road, Queen's Park West, Charlotte Street, and Saddle Road is the city's soul. Its 2-mile circumference is a popular jogger's track. On the west side of the Savannah, you'll see a garden of architectural delights: the elegant lantern-roof **George Brown House,** what remains of the **Old Queen's Park Hotel,** and the Magnificent Seven (☞ *above*). The racetrack at the southern end of the Savannah is no longer a venue for horse racing, but it is still the setting for music and costume competitions during Carnival and, when not jammed with calypso performers, tends toward quietude. The northern end of the Savannah is devoted to plants. A rock garden, known as the **Hollow,** and a fishpond add to the rusticity.

---

NEED A
BREAK?

Two blocks south of the Savannah, and one block west to Rust Street, stop for tea and pastries (or even an American breakfast) at **La Maison Rustique** (☎ 809/622–1512), a pretty white house set amid tropical gardens. It's also a pleasant bed-and-breakfast.

---

☼ **Water Park.** The water park at the Valley Vue Hotel is open to nonguests and has the biggest, wettest slides in the West Indies—three 400-foot chutes leading to a shallow pool. ⊠ *Ariapita Rd., St. Ann's,* ☎ *809/624–0940.* ⊡ *TT$20.* ⊙ *Daily 10–6.*

**Woodford Square.** At Prince and Frederick streets, the square has served as the site of political meetings, speeches, public protests, and occasional violence. It's dominated by the magnificent **Red House,** a Renaissance-style building that takes up an entire city block. Trinidad's House of Parliament takes its name from a paint job done in anticipation of Queen Victoria's Diamond Jubilee in 1897. The original Red House was burned to the ground in a 1903 riot, and the present structure was built four years later. The chambers are open to the public.

The view of the south side of the square is framed by the Gothic spires of **Trinity,** the city's Anglican Cathedral, consecrated in 1823; its mahogany-beam roof is modeled after that of Westminster Hall in London. On the north is the impressive **public library** building, the **Hall of Justice** and **City Hall.**

## Out on the Island

➋ **Asa Wright Nature Centre.** Its nearly 500 acres are covered with plants, trees, and multihued flowers, and the surrounding acreage is atwitter with more than 170 species of birds, from the gorgeous blue-green mot-

mot to the rare nocturnal oilbird. If you stay for two nights or more (☞ Lodging, *above*), the oilbirds' breeding grounds in Dunston Cave are included among the sights along the center's guided hiking trails. Those who don't want to hike can relax on the veranda of the inn and watch the diversity of birds that swoop about the porch feeders—an armchair bird-watcher's nirvana. This stunning plantation house looks out to the Arima valley, as lush and untouched as the earth offers. Even if you're not staying over, book ahead for lunch (TT$37.50) on Monday through Saturday or for a noontime Sunday buffet (TT$62.50). ⊠ *90-mins from Port-of-Spain; look for a fork in the road about ½-hr outside the town of Blanchisseuse; take the right, signposted to Arima, and drive another ½ hr on this road (and a very sharp right at the green hut),* ☎ *809/667–4655.* ⚏ *$6.* ☉ *Daily 9–5. Guided tours at 10:30 and 1:30; reservations essential.*

**④ Caroni Bird Sanctuary.** This large swamp with mazelike waterways is bordered by mangrove trees, some plumed with huge termite nests. In the middle of the sanctuary are several islets that are home to Trinidad's national bird, the scarlet ibis. Just before sunset the ibis arrive by the thousands, their richly colored feathers brilliant in the gathering dusk, and, as more flocks alight, they turn their little tufts of land into bright Christmas trees. It's not something you see every day. Bring a sweater and insect repellent for your return trip.

Across from the sanctuary's parking lot sits a sleepy canal with several boats and guides for hire; the smaller boats are best. The fee is usually about $6–$15. The only official tour operator is Winston Nanan (☞ Guided Tours *in* Trinidad and Tobago A to Z, *below*); phone or write him in advance for reservations. ⊠ *½ hr from Port-of-Spain; take Churchill Roosevelt Hwy. eastbound to the Uriah Butler southbound; turn right and in about 2 mins, after passing the Caroni River Bridge, follow sign for Sanctuary, no phone.* ⚏ *Free.*

**③ Lopinot Complex.** It's said that the ghost of the French count, Charles Joseph de Lopinot, prowls his former home on stormy nights. Lopinot came to Trinidad in 1800 and chose this magnificent site to plant cocoa. His restored estate house has been turned into a museum; a guide is available from 10 to 6. This is one of the main centers for Parang, a beautiful string-based folk music, which has become Trinidad's equivalent of Christmas carols. ⊠ *Take the Eastern Main Rd. from Port-of-Spain to Arouca; look for sign that points north, no phone.* ⚏ *Free.* ☉ *Daily 6–6.*

# TOBAGO

## Lodging

On Tobago, there are a few modest lodgings in the towns, but the trend is toward seaside resorts, many of them appealingly low key. If you're staying on the east side of Tobago, accommodations with meal plans are almost essential because of the dearth of restaurants.

For bed-and-breakfast accommodations contact the **Trinidad and Tobago Bed and Breakfast Co-operative Society** (⊠ Box 3231, Diego Martin, ☎ 🅵🅰🆇 809/627–2337) or the **Tobago Bed and Breakfast Association** (⊠ c/o Federal Villa, 1-3 Crooks River, Scarborough, ☎ 809/639–3926, 🅵🅰🆇 809/639–3566).

For price information on hotels, *see* the price chart *in* the Lodging section of Trinidad, *above.*

$$$$   ⊞ **Arnos Vale Hotel.** It's always been the most romantic spot on Tobago. The sprawling Mediterranean design encompasses lush Tobagonian horticulture spread across 400 acres on the northeast coast of
Tobago. The charming suites and rooms are individually decorated in
tiny floral prints with rattan furniture and green tile floors. In any event,
they'll remain in their wonderful location, in white stucco cottages set
on a hill that descends, through a series of winding paths, to a secluded
beach, pool, and bar. The elegant hilltop restaurant, with antique
pieces, iron-lattice tables, a chandelier, and a hand-painted piano, has
a crescent-shape patio that offers a sweeping view of the sea. Italian
tour groups generally book half the rooms; the other half is available
for general booking. ⊠ *Arnos Vale, Box 208, Scarborough,* ☎ *809/639–
2881,* ℻ *809/639–4629. 35 rooms, 3 suites. Restaurant, bar, air-conditioning, pool, 2 tennis courts, beach, dive shop, snorkeling, gift shop,
dance club. AE, DC, MC, V. EP.*

$$$$   ⊞ **Coco Reef Resort.** One of Tobago's two new resorts, this should also
be among the best if the service matches the hotel design and the setting (it was just about to open when we visited). Elements of Caribbean,
Colonial, and Mediterranean architecture blend in an abundance of
arches, tiles, and fretwork flourishes; harsh angles have been eliminated
to create a soothing space. The room decor makes use of lots of cool
tiles, too, along with pretty wall stencils and hand-crafted wicker furniture. Coco Reef is well placed, near Pigeon Point and Store Bay, and
has its own small beach, Coco Bay. With its concierge, social director,
water sports, and arcade with tony boutiques, this place is likely to attract an active international set who are used to being pampered. ⊠
*Box 434, Scarborough,* ☎ *809/639–8571 or 800/221–1294,* ℻
*809/639–8574 or 305/639–2717 (reservations). 96 rooms, 39 suites.
2 restaurants, 2 bars, air-conditioning, pool, beauty salon, spa, 2 tennis courts, health club, baby-sitting, Jeep rental. AE, D, DC, MC, V.
CP, MAP.*

$$$$   ⊞ **Grafton Beach Resort.** If any hotel has the action on Tobago, it's
★   the Grafton. Yet it's stretched out languidly along the shore under the
tall palms, and so it's possible, with sea-view rooms, to feel away
from it all. This sparkling complex has the most international ambience of any Tobago hotel, from the huge, lobby-bar-restaurant-pool
area to the top-class in-room facilities. Rooms are furnished with solid
teak pieces, and have cool terra-cotta-tile floors. The Neptune seafood
restaurant and the bar, where local folk shows and bands perform nightly,
are perched, cruise-liner-style, above and around the bigger-than-
average pool, with the Ocean View restaurant (☞ Dining, *below*) to
one side. A walkway leads directly to a fine beach, with a bar. You can
learn to scuba, play squash, work out in the fitness room, and go canoeing, sailing, windsurfing, or surfing—all inclusive in the rates. ⊠
*Black Rock, Tobago,* ☎ *809/639–0191,* ℻ *809/639–0030. 99 rooms,
2 suites. 2 restaurants, 3 bars, air-conditioning, pool, sauna, exercise
room, squash, beach, windsurfing, scuba training, boating, dance club,
live entertainment, shops. AE, DC, MC, V. EP, MAP.*

$$$$   ⊞ **Le Grand Courlan.** There's been a lot of hoopla about this new hotel,
under the same ownership as—and right next door to—the Grafton
(☞ *above*) but aiming for a more upscale clientele. It wasn't yet complete when we were there, but it promises all kinds of amenities to jus-
tify the highest prices on the island (starting at more than $400 a night
for a standard—termed "deluxe"—room). The restaurant's hand-
carved furnishings looked classy and the personalized stationary for
each guest is a nice touch, but the overall design and the sample room
were no great shakes. Perhaps it's unfair to judge a place that wasn't
open; still, before you shell out the big bucks, you'd be better off staying elsewhere and checking out this neighboring property yourself. ⊠

*Box 25, Scarborough, Tobago,* ☎ *809/639–0191 or 800/467–4464,*
FAX *809/639–0030. 68 rooms, 10 suites. 2 restaurants, 2 bars, health
bar, pool, spa, health club, squash, dive shop, windsurfing, boating,
shops, convention center. AE, DC, MC, V. EP, MAP.*

**$$$$**   🏨 **Mt. Irvine Bay Hotel.** The advantage of this low-key hotel is golf—
on the 18-hole, par-72, 127-acre International Championship course—
for which guests get special rates. The main-house bedrooms aren't so
special, although all amenities are on tap. If you're looking for romance,
one of the 51 cottages, set in an arc around the main building and offering private patios, are worth the extra cost. A 17th-century mill is
the focal point of the main restaurant, and there are two more restaurants besides—a dressy French one, Le Beau Rivage, and the Jacaranda.
You can swim up to the bar at the largest of the island's hotel pools,
play tennis on two floodlit courts, and take the private trail across the
road to the beach, where there's another bar. The grounds are lovely
and the golf is great—it's too bad the service is not always up to par.
✉ *Mt. Irvine Bay, Box 222, Tobago,* ☎ *809/639–8871,* FAX *809/639–
8800 or 800/742–4276. 107 rooms, 5 suites, 51 cottages. 3 restaurants, 2 bars, air-conditioning, pool, beauty parlor, sauna, spa, 18-hole
golf course, 2 tennis courts, shops, convention center. AE, DC, MC,
V. EP, CP, MAP.*

**$$$$**   🏨 **Plantation Beach Villas.** Nestled on a hillside above a palm-fringed
beach and right next door to a bird sanctuary, these lovely pink and
white villas are comfortably furnished in plantation style—four-poster
beds, rocking chairs, louvre doors, and lots of West Indian fretwork.
If you're traveling with a group or a large family, the price is quite reasonable: Each two-story villa has three bedrooms (one air-conditioned,
two with ceiling fans) and three baths, as well as a teak veranda with
a view of the sea. Cleaning service and linens are included, and a cook
can be provided on request. This is a very convenient choice in a serene
and elegant setting. ✉ *Stonehaven Bay, Blackrock (write to Box 1020,
Port-of-Spain, Trinidad),* ☎ FAX *809/639–0455 or* ☎ *800/742–4276
(reservations). 6 villas. Beach bar, air-conditioning, full kitchens, pool,
laundry facilities. MC, V.*

**$$$**   🏨 **Blue Waters Inn.** If your dream of the tropics is a simple place as
★   close to the waves as possible, this is for you. The inn is set amid 46
acres of greenery, including massive gnarled beach plum trees that seem
to hold up the complex. A good 90-minute drive from Scarborough
and up a bumpy driveway bring you to this beach hotel and its villas
on the northeast Atlantic coast, with Little Tobago and Bird of Par-
adise island across Bateaux Bay. Rooms are fairly standard, in pleas-
ant beach motel mode, but you're guaranteed the sounds of waves all
night. The bungalows have one or two bedrooms, living room, and
kitchen. There are only small stores in the area; if you don't want to
shop in Scarborough before you set out, you can fax ahead to request
the provisions you'd like your room stocked with. But the freshest fish
are to be had daily at the restaurant, and the lively bar will keep you
occupied with its array of exotic drinks. This is an ideal spot for divers,
bird-watchers, and beach loungers alike. ✉ *Bateaux Bay, Speyside, To-
bago,* ☎ *809/660–4341 or 800/742–4276 (reservations),* FAX *809/660–
5195. 31 rooms, 4 apartments, 3 bungalows. Restaurant, bar, tennis
court, beach, kayaking, windsurfing, dive instruction, car rental. AE,
MC, V. EP, CP, MAP, FAP.*

**$$$**   🏨 **Rex Turtle Beach Hotel.** If you're taking the kids, this may be your
★   ideal hotel: There's baby-sitting and many planned activities for chil-
dren (on holidays they go all out to entertain the little ones, with hundreds of little lanterns for a Hindu festival and lights climbing way up
the skyscraper palm trees at Christmas). Although it was built in 1971,
this sprawling beachfront property is very well maintained. Rooms are

attractive, with typical Tobagonian teak ceilings, wooden louvre doors, and brightly colored bedspreads; all have garden and ocean views. The family annex room is an especially good deal, offering a small extra bedroom for $21 more. Turtle Beach's popularity is not hard to understand: The relaxed atmosphere, evening entertainment, array of complimentary water sports, and lovely grounds are all appealing. As the name suggests, turtles use this beach to lay their eggs from February through June; you can request a wake-up call (perhaps at 2 or 3 AM) if you want to watch. ⊠ *Great Courland Bay (write to Box 201, Scarborough, Tobago),* ☎ *809/639–2851 or 305/471–6170 (U.S. reservations),* FAX *809/639–1495. 125 rooms. Restaurant, 2 bars, coffee shop, pool, 2 tennis courts, lawn tennis, volleyball, water-sports center, bicycles, gift shop. AE, DC, MC, V. EP, MAP.*

**$$** ⊞ **Kariwak Village.** There are many return guests to Allan and Cyn-
★   thia Clovis's charming and reasonably priced cabana village. You enter a bamboo, raw teak, and coral stone lobby and bar area. Outside, in a bamboo pavilion, is the highly respected restaurant (☞ Kariwak Village *in* Dining, *below*). Nine large, round, palm-thatched cabanas, each containing two bedrooms, are in a semicircle around a pretty pool. Rooms are simple and air-conditioned, with loft-height dark-wood ceilings, carpeted floors, and wicker armchairs; each has a separate bathroom and dressing area and a little terrace outside the patio doors. Lush flora makes a fairly small site seem more spacious, and an herb-and-vegetable garden out back, which furnishes Cynthia's kitchen with ingredients, provides a place for a stroll. Great rum punches and local bands playing on weekends make this a favored liming spot. It's very near the airport, Store Bay, and Pigeon Point. ⊠ *Crown Pt., Tobago (write to Box 27, Scarborough, Tobago),* ☎ *809/639–8442,* FAX *809/639–8441. 18 rooms. Restaurant, bar, air-conditioning, pool, shuttle service to beach. AE, DC, MC, V. EP, MAP.*

**$$** ⊞ **Palm Tree Village.** Across the rural old coast road from Little Rockley Bay, a five-minute drive from Scarborough, this place offers peace and quiet with a useful array of facilities. Choose either a "superior room," facing the beach, with a hardwood floor and furniture, or a two- or four-bedroom villa set back from the Atlantic in the manicured, but barely landscaped, grounds. "Standard rooms," in cottages close to the main building, have small lounge areas and plenty of windows, but these—in a confusing lineup of packages and plans—are usually only available at TT$ rates to locals. Try negotiating for one, though. There can be a forlorn feeling here, perhaps due to the lack of trees on site, the narrowness of the 2-mile-long beach (except at low tide), or the tininess of the pool. ⊠ *Box 327, Little Rockley Bay, Scarborough,* ☎ *809/639–4347,* FAX *809/639–4180. 18 villas, 20 "superior rooms," 36 "standard rooms." Bar, pub, pool, tennis court, horseback riding, beach, snorkeling, piano room, dance club, conference center. AE, DC, MC, V. EP, MAP.*

**$–$$** ⊞ **Blue Horizon Resort.** "Resort" is a misnomer for this compact red-roofed apartment complex set above the Mt. Irvine golf course, since all it offers in the way of facilities are a small pool, which the apartments overlook, a barbecue pit, and an under-stocked minimart. However, it does offer peace and quiet and sunset views from the deluxe apartments, which are a far better deal than the first-floor, viewless standards. Another advantage is the spaciousness of the rooms, and parents can observe their children in the pool from each unit. Decor is basic—small, straight-backed plaid sofas and chairs around the satellite TV are the only lounge furniture—with kitchens and bathrooms. Deluxe apartments have spiral staircases leading to galleried lofts that children will adore—though little ones could easily fall from them. Balconies overlook each other, except for that of the single "luxurious" apartment, with an extra bedroom and tons of space. This is a good budget pick for families. ✉ *Jacamar Dr., Mt. Irvine, Tobago,* ☎ *809/639–0433,* FAX *305/592–4935. 13 apartments. Pool, minimart, airport shuttle. AE, MC, V. EP.*

$–$$   🏨 **Ocean Point.** A resort in miniature, this friendly "condo hotel" is complete with tiny kitsch fountain, a quartet of parakeets and Raj the macaw, a barbecue pit, and a palm-thatched bar-restaurant (East Indian food is the specialty) at one end of a child-size, kidney-shape pool. Five studios with five split-level loft apartments above them constitute the living quarters, all sparkly white with pine fittings and terra-cotta floors, big showers in the bathrooms, plus an inviting hammock on the balcony (upstairs) or porch (downstairs). Lofts offer views of the sunrise over the ocean. The studios face the pool, and the noise can be annoying during the day. (Little Rockley beach is a minute's walk away, but it's narrow and rocky—not the best for sunbathing.) A 10-minute drive takes you to Store Bay. A free shuttle to the airport and supermarket is provided. Dive packages are available. ✉ *Milford Rd., Lowlands, Tobago,* ☎ FAX *809/639–0973. 5 studios, 5 apartments. Restaurant, bar, air-conditioning, kitchenettes, pool, airport and supermarket shuttles. AE, DC, MC, V. EP.*

# Dining

Macaroni pie and chicken is Tobago's Sunday dinner favorite, perhaps with fried plantain or potatoes. Oil Down tastes better than it sounds: It's a gently seasoned mixture of boiled breadfruit and salted beef or pork flavored with coconut milk. Mango ice cream or a sweetly sour tamarind ball makes a tasty finish. You may want to take home some hot pepper sauce or chutney to a spice-loving friend or relative.

For price information on restaurants, *see* the price chart *in* the Dining section of Trinidad, *above.*

$$–$$$   ✕ **Dillon's.** Stanley Dillon's other career as a fishing-charter operator
★   guarantees the freshest catch at his seafood restaurant by the airport. White walls hung with local art, red plaid tablecloths, and a silver service wait staff create a soothing atmosphere halfway between homey and posh. The menu mixes traditional favorites, such as shrimp cocktail, French onion soup, lobster thermidor, and surf and turf, with callaloo, stuffed kingfish, chunky fish broth, and other Creole dishes. Get here early on weekends, before the line stretches to the runway. ✉ *Airport Rd. near Crown Pt.,* ☎ *809/639–8765. AE, MC, V.*

$$–$$$   ✕ **Ocean View.** Grafton Beach Resort's main restaurant is a large open terrace overlooking the Caribbean, but with a clearer view of the hotel pool, bar, and evening's entertainment than of the waves. Four times a week, you can enjoy an all-you-can-eat dinner buffet, which might include char-grilled chicken, steak and pork, Creole dolphinfish, curried blue crab, any number of root vegetables, spaghetti, *pelau* (rice and peas), cauliflower with cheese, a salad bar, and an array of desserts: You'll wish you'd remembered to pack the Tums. ✉ *Grafton Beach Resort, Black Rock,* ☎ *809/639–0191. AE, DC, MC, V.*

$$   ✕ **Cocrico Inn.** A café with a bar against one wall, the Cocrico offers delectable home cooking. The three rotating chefs use fresh fruits and vegetables grown in the neighborhood. They zealously guard their recipes, including a marvelous cou-cou and lightly breaded, subtly spiced grouper. There is nothing fancy here, just warm and delicious food and cool air-conditioning. ✉ *Corner of North and Commissioner Sts., Plymouth,* ☎ *809/639–2661. AE, V.*

$$   ✕ **Kariwak Village.** Recorded steel-band music plays gently in the
★   background at this romantic candlelit spot. In a bamboo pavilion cre-

ated to resemble an Amerindian round hut, Cynthia Clovis orchestrates a very original four-course menu. Changing daily, the choices may include christophine soup, curried green fig, kingfish with shrimp sauce, and coconut cake. Whatever it is, it will be full of herbs and vegetables freshly picked from Cynthia's own organic garden, and home-baked breads. It's a treat for vegetable lovers, because Kariwak knows how to honor the simple squash and green beans. The nonalcoholic drinks are wonderful, even the iced coffee, which is more like a frozen coconut cappuccino. Saturday buffets, with live jazz or calypso, are a Tobagonian highlight. ⊠ *Kariwak Village, Crown Pt.,* ☎ *809/639–8442. AE, DC, MC, V.*

**$$** ✕ **Papillon.** Named after one of the proprietor's favorite books, this seafood restaurant is a homey room with an adjoining patio. Lobster Buccoo Bay is marinated in sherry and broiled with herbs. Seafood casserole au gratin means chunks of lobster, shrimp, fish, and cream, all seasoned in ginger wine. Baby shark is marinated in rum and lime. Or you can just enjoy some good broiled chicken or pork cutlets with pineapple. Papillon is one good reason for staying at the Old Grange Inn next door, owned by the same Trinidadian family. ⊠ *Buccoo Bay Rd., Mt. Irvine,* ☎ *809/639–0275. AE, DC, MC, V.*

**$$** ✕ **Rouselle's.** An enchanting terrace high above Scarborough Bay with
★ a big, congenial bar, Rouselle's was just a liming spot until friends and regulars demanded proper food. Bet they didn't expect food this good. The small menu dons different accessories rather than changing completely, so you may find grouper, broiled and served with a fresh Creole sauce and several vegetables—garlicky green beans, carrots with ginger, a raw bok choy salad, and potato croquette with spices and celery; dolphinfish with white wine sauce; or lobster, which is very hard to procure, steamed just so. Whatever there is, you can trust that it'll be delicious. A sizable *amuse-gueule* (appetizer), hot garlic bread, plus dessert (save room for pineapple pie or homemade ice cream) are included in the entrée price. Don't forgo the Rouselle's punch: The recipe's a secret, but the lovely, welcoming co-owners, Bobbie and Charlene, will probably let you in on it. ⊠ *Old Windward Rd., Bacolet,* ☎ *809/639–4738. Lunch by reservation only. AE, MC, V.*

**$–$$** ✕ **Blue Crab.** Alison Sardinha is Tobago's most ebullient and kindly
★ hostess, and her husband, Ken, one of its best chefs. He cooks "like our mothers cooked," serving the local food with heavy East Indian influence, a bit of Portuguese, and occasionally Asian, too. There might be kingfish, *katchowrie* (spiced split pea patties, a little like falafel), curry chicken, or long-cooked suckling pig. There's always a callaloo, differently flavored on different days, fine rotis and cou-cou, and sometimes a "cookup"—pelau-type rice, with *everything* in it. The place is officially open only on Wednesday and Friday nights, but Miss Alison will open up on other evenings (and for weekend lunches, too) even for one table, if you call in the morning. The setting, on a wide, shady terrace overlooking the bay, is just about perfect, and there's a bar for cocktails. Two guest rooms (the front one's a beauty) in the Sardinhas' home are also available. If you want to see the joy of Caribbean cooking in one presentation, ask Alison how to make one of the dishes: Her expressions, gestures, and advice should be exported. They epitomize the joy of living. ⊠ *Robinson St. at Main St., Scarborough,* ☎ *809/639–2737. AE, MC, V.*

**$** ✕ **Mount Marie.** If you want to find a spotlessly clean, air-conditioned restaurant in Scarborough that serves good local and international fare, look no further. The menu changes according to what's available at the market but usually includes pasta and seafood dishes. The place is owned by the local police pension fund and managed by the very stylish and efficient Petunia Thomas. Best of all, it's a real bargain. ⊠

*Mt. Marie, near Rockley Bay harbor just off Claude Noel Hwy.,* ☎
*809/639–2014. AE, MC, V.*

## Beaches

Traveling to Tobago without sampling the beaches is like touring
France's Burgundy region without drinking the wine. You'll not find
manicured, country-club sand here, but those who enjoy feeling as though
they've landed on a private desert island will relish the untouched quality of these shores.

**Bacolet Beach** is a dark-sand beach that was the setting for the films
*Swiss Family Robinson* and *Heaven Knows, Mr. Allison.*

**Englishman's Bay** is a charming beach; what's more, it's completely
deserted.

**Great Courland Bay,** near Fort Bennett, is a long stretch of clear, tranquil water. The sandy beach—one of Tobago's longest—is home to several glitzy hotels. A recently built marina attracts the yachting crowd.

**King's Bay Beach,** surrounded by steep green hills, is the most visually
satisfying of the swimming sites off the road from Scarborough to Speyside—the bay hooks around so severely that you feel as if you're swimming in a lake. The crescent-shape beach is easy to find because it's
marked by a sign about halfway between Roxborough and Speyside.
Just before you reach the bay there is a bridge with an unmarked turnoff
that leads to a gravel parking lot; beyond that, a landscaped path
leads to a waterfall with a rocky pool where you can refresh yourself.
You may meet enterprising locals who'll offer to guide you to the top
of the falls, a climb that you may find not worth the effort.

**Little Rockley Bay** is just west of Scarborough (take Milford Road off
the main highway). The beach is craggy and not much good for swimming, but it is quiet and offers a pleasing view of Tobago's capital across
the water.

**Lover's Beach** is so called because of its pink sand and because it is so
secluded: You have to hire a local to take you there by boat.

**Man O' War Bay,** in Charlotteville, is flanked by one of the prettiest
fishing villages in the Caribbean. You can lounge on the sand and purchase the day's catch for your dinner.

**Mt. Irvine Beach,** across the street from the Mt. Irvine Bay Hotel, is an
unremarkable setting, but it has great surfing in July and August; the
snorkeling is excellent too. It's also ideal for windsurfing in January
and April. There are picnic tables surrounded by painted concrete
pagodas and a snack bar.

**Parlatuvier,** on the north side of the island, is best approached via the
road from Roxborough. The beach here is a classic Caribbean crescent, a scene peopled by villagers and local fishermen.

**Pigeon Point** is the stunningly beautiful locale inevitably displayed on
Tobago travel brochures. Although the beach is public, it abuts part
of what was once a large coconut estate, and you must pay a token
admission (about TT$10) to enter the grounds and use the facilities.
The beach is lined with towering royal palms, and there's a food stand,
a few gift shops, a diving concession, and paddleboats for rent. The
waters are calm.

**Sandy Beach,** along Crown Point, is abutted by several hotels. You won't
lack for amenities around here.

**Stone Haven Bay** is a gorgeous beach that's across the street from Grafton
Beach Resort, a luxury hotel complex.

**Store Bay,** where boats depart for Buccoo Reef, is probably the most
socially convivial setting in the area. The beach is little more than a
small sandy cove between two rocky breakwaters, but, ah, the food
stands here: six shacks licensed by the tourist board to local ladies, fea-

turing roti, pelau, and the world's messiest dish, crab and dumplings. Miss Jean's (☎ 809/639–0563) is the most popular; try Miss Esmie's crab, though.

**Turtle Beach** is named for the turtles that lay their eggs here at night between February and June. (If you're very quiet, you can watch; the turtles don't seem to mind.) It's set on Great Courland Bay (☞ *above*).

## Outdoor Activities and Sports

### Bird-Watching

The naturalist **David Rooks** (☎ 809/639–4276) offers walks inland and trips to offshore bird colonies. Call Pat Turpin (☎ 809/660–4327) or Renson Jack (☎ 809/660–5175) at **Pioneer Journeys** for information about their 6½-hour bird-watcher tours of Bloody Bay Rain Forest.

### Deep-Sea Fishing

**Dillon's Fishing Charter** (✉ Pigeon Point, ☎ 809/639–8765) is the best for whole- and half-day trips for kingfish, barracuda, wahoo, dolphinfish, blue marlin, etc. Trips start at $165 for four hours, including equipment.

### Golf

The 18-hole course at the **Mt. Irvine Golf Club** (✉ Mt. Irvine Bay Hotel, ☎ 809/639–8871) has been ranked among the top five in the Caribbean.

### Nature Preserves

Eco-consciousness is strong on both islands and especially on Tobago, where the rain forests of the Main Ridge were set aside for protection in 1764, creating the first such preserve in the Western Hemisphere. Natural areas now include Little Tobago and St. Giles Islands, both major seabird sanctuaries. In addition, the endangered leatherback turtles maintain breeding grounds on some of Tobago's leeward beaches.

### Scuba Diving

An abundance of fish and coral thrive on the nutrients of South America's Orinoco River, which are brought to Tobago by the Guayana current. There are many good spots to submerge, including Crown Point, St. Giles Islands, and off the west coast, but it's the waters off Speyside that draw scuba-diving aficionados from around the world. You can get information, supplies, and instruction at **AquaMarine Dive Ltd.** (✉ Blue Waters Inn, ☎ 809/660–4341), **Dive Tobago** (✉ Pigeon Pt., Box 53, Scarborough, ☎ 809/639–0202), **Man Friday Diving** (✉ Charlotteville, ☎ 809/660–4676), **Tobago Dive Experience** (✉ Grafton Beach Resort, ☎ 809/639–0191, ext. 39 or 800/544–7631), and **Tobago Marine Sports Ltd.** (✉ Crown Point Beach Hotel, ☎ 809/639–0291).

### Snorkeling

Tobago offers many wonderful spots for snorkeling. Although the reefs around Speyside are becoming better known, **Buccoo Reef** is easily still the most popular—perhaps too popular. Over the years the reef has been damaged by the ceaseless boat traffic and by the thoughtless visitors who take pieces of coral for souvenirs. Even so, it's still a trip worth experiencing, particularly if you have children. Daily 2½-hour tours by flat, glass-bottom boats let you snorkel at the reef, swim in a shallow lagoon pool, and take a look at Coral Gardens, where fish and coral are yet untouched. The trip costs about $8, and masks, snorkeling equipment and reef shoes are provided. Departure is at 11 AM from Pigeon Point. Most of the scuba-diving companies also arrange snorkeling tours. There is also good snorkeling by the beach near the **Arnos Vale Hotel** and the **Mt. Irvine Bay Hotel**.

### Tennis

**Rex Turtle Beach** (☎ 809/639–2851), **Mt. Irvine** (☎ 809/639–8871), and the **Blue Waters Inn** (☎ 809/660–4341) allow nonmembers and nonresidents to play.

## Shopping

The souvenir-bound will do better in Trinidad than they will in Tobago, but determined shoppers should manage to ferret out some things to take home: Scarborough has the largest collection of shops, and Burnett Street, which slopes sharply from the port to St. James Park, is a good place to browse.

### Local Crafts

**Cotton House** (⊠ Bacolet St., Scarborough, ☎ 809/639–2727) is a good bet for jewelry and imaginative batik work. Paula Young runs her shop like an art school. You can visit the upstairs studio; if it's not too busy, you can even make a batik square at no charge. **Forro's** (⊠ Wilson Rd., across from the Scarborough market, Scarborough, ☎ 809/639–2979; ⊠ Crown Point Airport, Tobago, no phone) sells it's own fine line of homemade tamarind chutney, lemon or lime marmalade, hot sauce, and guava or golden apple jelly. Mrs. Eileen Forrester, wife of the Anglican priest at St. David's in Plymouth, supervises a kitchen full of good cooks who boil and bottle the condiments and pack them in little straw baskets. Most jars are small, easily carried, and very inexpensive. **Souvenir and Gift Shop** (⊠ Port Mall, Scarborough, ☎ 809/639–5632) stocks straw baskets and other crafts.

## Nightlife and the Arts

People will tell you there's no nightlife on Tobago. Don't believe them. Whatever you do the rest of the week, don't miss the huge impromptu party, affectionately dubbed Sunday School, that gears up after midnight on all the street corners of Buccoo and breaks up around dawn. Pick your band, hang out for a while, then move on. In downtown Scarborough on weekend nights, you can also expect to find competing sound systems blaring at informal parties that welcome extra guests. In addition, "Blockos" (spontaneous block parties) spring up all over the island; look for the hand-painted signs. Tobago also has Harvest parties on Sunday, when a particular village opens its doors to visitors for hospitality. These occur throughout the year and are a great way to meet the locals.

**Bonkers** (⊠ Store Bay local road, Crown Point, tel. 809/639–7173), a hot new bar and disco with a castaway theme (watch out—the DJ may make you walk the plank into the pool) draws a younger crowd. The music ranges from jazz and reggae to soca (calypso with a political bite). More sedentary types might consider coming on games night, when chess and domino players take the floor. **Grafton Beach Resort** (⊠ Black Rock, ☎ 809/639–0191) has some kind of organized cabaret-style event every night. Even if you hate that touristy stuff, check out Les Couteaux Cultural Group, who do a high-octane dance version of Tobagonian history. **Kariwak Village** (⊠ Crown Pt., ☎ 809/639–8442) has hip hotel entertainment, frequented as much by locals as tourists, on Friday and Saturday nights—almost always one of the better local jazz/calypso bands. **Rex Turtle Beach Hotel** (⊠ Great Courland Bay, ☎ 809/639–2851) hosts Les Couteaux Cultural Group (☞ *above*) and other similar shows on Wednesday and Sunday. **Starting Gate** (⊠ Shirvan Rd., Mt. Irvine, ☎ 809/639–0225), a casual indoor-outdoor pub, is the venue for frequent party-discos.

# Exploring Tobago

A driving tour of Tobago, from Scarborough to Charlotteville and back, can be done in about four hours, but you'd never want to undertake this spectacular, and very hilly, ride in that time. Plan to spend at least one night at the Speyside end of the island and give yourself a chance to enjoy this largely untouched country and seaside at leisure. The Blue Waters Inn (☞ Lodging, *above*) is open for meals and for overnighting; it's about as close to the sea as you can get without swimming.

*Numbers in the margin correspond to points of interest on the Tobago map.*

### SIGHTS TO SEE

**❺ Charlotteville.** This delightful fishing village is enfolded in a series of steep hills. Fishermen here announce the day's catch (usually flying fish, redfish, or bonito) by sounding their conch shells. A view of Man O' War Bay with Pigeon Peak, Tobago's highest mountain, behind it at sunset is an exquisite treat for the eye. The underwater cliffs and canyons at the nearby **St. Giles Islands** draw divers to this spot where the Atlantic meets the Caribbean. ⊠ *Take the Windward Rd. inland across the mountains from Speyside.*

**❹ Flagstaff Hill.** One of the highest points of the island sits at the northern tip of Tobago. Surrounded by ocean on three sides and with a view of the hills, Charlotteville, and St. Giles Islands, this was the site of an American military lookout and radio tower during World War II. It's an ideal spot for a sunset picnic.

**❷ Fort King George.** On Mt. St. George, a few miles east of the town of Scarborough, Tobago's best-preserved historic monument clings to a cliff high above the ocean. Fort King George was built in the 1770s and operated until 1854. It's hard to imagine that this lovely, tranquil spot commanding sweeping views of the bay and landscaped with lush tropical foliage was ever the site of any military action, but the prison, officer's mess, and several stabilized cannons attest otherwise.

Just to the left of the tall wooden figures dancing a traditional Tobagonian jig is the former barrack guardhouse, now home to the small **Tobago Museum.** Exhibits include a variety of weapons along with pre-Columbian artifacts found in the area; the fertility figures are especially interesting. Upstairs are maps and photographs of Tobago past. Be sure to check out the gift display cases for the perversely fascinating jewelry made from embalmed and painted lizards and sea creatures; you might find it hard to resist a pair of bright yellow shrimp earrings. ⊠ *84 Fort King George, Scarborough,* ☎ *809/639–3970.* 🎫 *TT$5.* ☺ *Weekdays 9–5.*

In addition to the museum, a **Fine Arts Centre** at the foot of the fort complex features the work of local artists.

---

**NEED A BREAK?**   After touring the fort, head for the **Old Donkey Cart House** (⊠ Bacolet St., ☎ 809/639–3551), 2 miles south of Scarborough, a green-and-white colonial house with an outdoor terrace—the perfect spot to relax with a glass of Rhine wine or German beer.

---

**❶ Scarborough.** Nestled around Rockley Bay on the island's leeward hilly side, this town is near the airport and is a popular cruise ship port, but it conveys the feeling that not much has changed here since the area was settled two centuries ago. It may not be one of the pastel-color, delightful cities of the Caribbean, but Scarborough does have its charms, including an array of interesting little shops. Note the red and yellow Methodist Church on the hillside, one of Tobago's oldest churches.

❸ **Speyside.** At the far reach of the windward coast of Tobago, this small fishing village has a few lodgings and restaurants. Glass-bottom boats operate between Speyside and **Little Tobago Island,** one of the most important seabird sanctuaries in the Caribbean. Divers are drawn to the unspoiled reefs in the area and to the strong possibility of spotting giant manta rays. The approach to Speyside from the south affords one of the most spectacular vistas of the island.

NEED A BREAK?
**Jemma's Sea View Kitchen** (☎ 809/660–4066), along the main road in Speyside, offers tasty West Indian meals served in a house on stilts by the ocean. You'll find nothing fancy here, just delicious Tobagonian home cooking, including a wondrous baked chicken, and great views.

# TRINIDAD AND TOBAGO A TO Z

## Arriving and Departing

### BY BOAT

The Port Authority maintains ferry service every day except Saturday between Trinidad and Tobago, although flying is preferable, because the sea can be very rough. The ferry leaves once a day, and the trip takes about five hours. Round-trip fare is TT$60. Cabins, when available, run TT$160 (one-way, double occupancy). Tickets are sold at offices in Port-of-Spain (☎ 809/625–3055) and at Scarborough, in Tobago (☎ 809/639–2417). The new *Condor Express* (☎ 809/627–8473 for information), which takes only 2½ hours to go between the islands, also operates every day except Saturday. The price is TT$100 round-trip.

### BY PLANE

There are daily direct flights to Trinidad's Piarco Airport, about 30 minutes east of Port-of-Spain, from New York and Miami, and frequent direct flights from Toronto and London on **BWIA** (☎ 809/669–3000 or 809/664–4268), Trinidad and Tobago's national airline. In the fall of 1995, BWIA initiated direct service to Tobago's Crown Point Airport from New York's JFK and from Miami International. BWIA also offers flights to Port-of-Spain from other cities in the Caribbean. BWIA flights from Trinidad to Tobago take about 15 minutes and depart 6 to 10 times a day. **American** (☎ 809/664–4661) offers direct flights from Miami to Trinidad. **Air Canada** (☎ 809/664–4065) flies nonstop to Trinidad from Toronto. There are numerous flights to Port-of-Spain from other Caribbean cities on **LIAT** (☎ 809/623–1837 or 809/623–1838). LIAT also has service from the eastern Caribbean islands to Tobago. **Air Caribbean** (☎ 809/623–2500) has 15-minute flights from Trinidad to Tobago that depart several times a day.

Package tours aren't generally touted as heavily as they are for other Caribbean islands, but there are bargains to be had, especially around Carnival. One particularly good tour operator is **Pan Caribe Tours** (✉ Box 3223, Austin, TX 78764, ☎ 512/266–7995 or 800/525–6896, FAX 512/266–7986). BWIA also has a variety of Caribbean tours.

### FROM THE AIRPORT

Taxis are readily available at Piarco Airport. The fare to Port-of-Spain is set at $20 ($30 after 10 PM), to the Hilton at $24. By car, take Golden Grove Road north to Arouca, then follow Eastern Main Road west for about 10 miles to Port-of-Spain. In Tobago, the fare from Crown Point Airport to Scarborough is fixed at $8, to Speyside at $36.

## Currency

The Trinidadian dollar (TT$) has been devalued twice in recent years. The current exchange rate is about TT$5.50 to U.S.$1. The major hotels in Port-of-Spain have exchange facilities whose rates are comparable to official bank rates. Trinidad's best rate is found at the Hilton. Most businesses on the island will accept U.S. currency if you're in a pinch. Note: Prices quoted here are in U.S. dollars unless indicated otherwise.

## Emergencies

**Police:** ☎ 999. **Fire and Ambulance:** ☎ 990. **Hospitals: Port-of-Spain General Hospital** (✉ 169 Charlotte St., ☎ 809/623–2951), **Tobago County Hospital** (✉ Fort St., Scarborough, ☎ 809/639–2551). **Late-Night Pharmacies: Bhaggan's** (☎ 809/627–4657) is at Charlotte and Oxford streets near the Port-of-Spain General Hospital; **Ross Drugs** (☎ 809/639–2658) is in Scarborough. For a complete list of other pharmacies, check the T&T Yellow Pages.

## Getting Around

CAR RENTALS

It's not worth renting a car if you are staying in Port-of-Spain, where the streets are often jammed with traffic and drivers who routinely play "chicken" with one another; taxis are your best bet. If you're planning to tour Trinidad, however, it's worth your while to get some wheels. As befits one of the world's largest exporters of asphalt, Trinidad's roads are generally good, although you may encounter roadwork in progress as major resurfacing is done. In the outback, roads are often narrow, twisting, and prone to washouts in the rainy season. Inquire about conditions before you take off, particularly if you're heading toward the north coast. Never drive into downtown Port-of-Spain during afternoon rush hour.

In Tobago you might be better off renting a Jeep than relying on taxi service, which is much more expensive. A four-wheel-drive vehicle is far better and safer than a car, because many roads, particularly in the interior, or on the far coast near Speyside and Charlotteville, are bumpy, pitted, winding, and/or steep (though the main highways are smooth and fast).

Various tours are also offered by rental agencies on both islands, and rates are negotiable. All agencies require a credit-card deposit, and in season you must make reservations well in advance of your arrival. Figure on paying $40–$60 per day. Don't forget to drive on the left.

Trinidad has a **Thrifty** (✉ Piarco International Airport, ☎ 809/669–0602) office. Reliable local companies include **Auto Rentals** (✉ Piarco International Airport, ☎ 809/669–2277), with many other locations, and **Lord Kalloo Car Rental and Taxi Service** (✉ Piarco International Airport, ☎ 809/669–5673; ✉ 32 Ariapata Ave., ☎ 809/622–9073).

In Tobago, **Thrifty** is represented at the Rex Turtle Beach Hotel (☎ 809/639–8507). Other options are **Rattan's Car Rentals** (✉ Crown Point Airport, ☎ 809/639–8271) or **Singh's Auto Rentals** (✉ Grafton Beach Resort, ☎ 809/639–0191, ext. 53).

TAXIS

Taxis in Trinidad are easily identified by their license plates, which begin with the letter H. Passenger vans, called Maxi Taxis, pick up and drop off passengers as they travel and are color coded according to which of the six areas they cover (yellow for Port-of-Spain, blue for Tobago). They are easily hailed day or night along most of the main roads near Port-of-Spain. For longer trips you will need to hire a private taxi. Taxis are not metered; many routes have fixed rates, though they are not always observed, particularly at Carnival. Pick up a rate sheet from the tourism office. On the whole, the drivers are honest, friendly, and informative, and the experience of riding in a Maxi Taxi with a souped-up sound system during Carnival is worth whatever fare you pay.

## Guided Tours

Almost any taxi driver in Port-of-Spain will be willing to take you around the town and to the beaches on the north coast. It costs around $70 for up to four people to go Maracas Bay beach, plus $20 per hour extra if you decide to go farther; you may be able to haggle for a cheaper rate. For a complete list of tour operators and sea cruises, contact the tourism office.

**Tobago Travel** (✉ Box 163, Scarborough, ☎ 809/639–8778, FAX 809/639–8786), the most experienced tour operator on Tobago, offers a wide array of travel services. **Travel Centre** (✉ 44-58 Edward St., Port-of-Spain, ☎ 809/623–5096, FAX 809/623–5101) is one of Trinidad's best tour operators. Their office is also American Express's card-member service office, for check-cashing and other matters. **Winston Nanan** (✉ Nanan Bird Sanctuary Tours, 38 Bamboo Grove #1, Uriah Butler Hwy., Valsayn, ☎ 809/645–1305) is the only official tour operator at the Caroni Bird Sanctuary (☞ Exploring Trinidad, *above*); phone or write him in advance for reservations.

## Language

The official language is English, although there is no end of idiomatic expressions used by the loquacious Trinis. You will also hear smatterings of French, Spanish, Chinese, and Hindi. (Trinidad's population is about one-quarter Indian.)

## Opening and Closing Times

Most shops open Monday–Friday 8–4:30, Saturday 8–noon; malls stay open later during the week and operate all day Saturday. Banking hours are Monday–Thursday 8–2 and Friday 8–noon and 3–5.

## Passports and Visas

Citizens of the United States, the United Kingdom, and Canada who expect to stay for less than six weeks may enter the country with a valid passport. A visa is required for longer stays.

## Precautions

Insect repellent is a must during the rainy season (June–December) and is worth having around anytime. Trinidad is only 11 degrees north of the equator, and the sun here can be intense; bring a strong sunblock.

## Taxes and Service Charges

Restaurants and hotels add a 15% value-added tax (VAT). Many also add a 10% service charge to your bill. If the service charge is not added, you should tip 10%–15% of the bill for a job well done. The airport departure tax is TT$75.

## Telephones and Mail

The area code for both islands is 809. For telegraph, telefax, teletype, and telex, contact **Textel** (✉ 1 Edward St., Port-of-Spain, ☎ 809/625–4431). Faxes can be sent from major hotels.

Postage for first-class letters to the United States is TT$2.25; for postcards, TT$2.

## Visitor Information

For advance information, there's a new **Travel Trade Hotline** (☎ 800/748–4224 in the U.S.). You can also contact offices of the **Tourism and Industrial Development Company of Trinidad and Tobago Ltd. (TIDCO)** (In the U.S., ✉ 7000 Boulevard E, Guttenberg, NJ 07093, ☎ 201/662–3403 or 201/662–3408, FAX 201/869–7628; in the U.K., ✉ International House, 47 Chase Side, Enfield, Middlesex, EN2 6NB2, ☎ 0181/367–5175, FAX 0181/367–9949; in Canada, ✉ Taurus House, 512 Duplex Ave., Toronto, Ontario M4R 2E3, ☎ 416/484–4864, FAX 416/484–8256).

In Trinidad, information is available from **TIDCO** (✉ 10–14 Phillips St., Port-of-Spain, ☎ 809/623–1932, FAX 809/623–3848; Piarco Airport, ☎ 809/664–5196). For Tobago, contact the **Tobago Division of Tourism** (✉ N.I.B. Mall, Level 3, Scarborough, ☎ 809/639–2125, FAX 809/639–3566), or drop in at its information booth at Crown Point Airport (☎ 809/639–0509).

# 26 Turks and Caicos Islands

Updated by
JoAnn
Milivojevic

**T**HE TURKS AND CAICOS ISLANDS are relatively unknown except to scuba divers and aficionados of
beautiful beaches, who religiously return to these waters year after year. Miles-long, soft, sparkling white-sand beaches
ring the flat islands, and offshore, pristine reefs overflow with a variety fish, crustaceans, and coral, making for excellent snorkeling and
scuba diving. The islands' slogan, "Beautiful by Nature," reflects its
tranquillity and natural wonders.

It is claimed that Columbus's first landfall was on Grand Turk. First settled by the English more than 200 years ago, the British Crown Colony
of Turks and Caicos is renowned in two respects: Its booming banking
and insurance institutions lure investors from the United States and elsewhere, and its offshore reef formations entice divers to the world of colorful marine life surrounding its more than 40 islands and small cays,
only eight of which are inhabited. The total landmass is 193 square miles;
the population of the eight inhabited islands and cays is some 12,350.

The Turks and Caicos are two groups of islands in an archipelago lying
575 miles southeast of Miami and about 90 miles north of Haiti. The
Turks Islands include Grand Turk, which is the capital and seat of government, and Salt Cay, with a population of about 200. According to
local legend, these islands were named by early settlers who thought
the scarlet blossoms on the local cactus resembled the Turkish fez.

Approximately 22 miles west of Grand Turk, across the 7,000-foot-deep
Christopher Columbus Passage, is the Caicos group, which includes South,
East, West, Middle, and North Caicos and Providenciales. South Caicos,
Middle Caicos, North Caicos, and Providenciales (nicknamed Provo)
are the only inhabited islands in this group; Pine Cay and Parrot Cay
are the only inhabited cays. "Caicos" is derived from *cayos,* the Spanish word for cay, and is believed to mean "string of islands."

Around 1678, Bermudians, lured by the wealth of salt in these islands,
began raking salt from the flats and returning to Bermuda to sell their
crop. Despite French and Spanish attacks and pirate raids, the Bermudians persisted and established a trade that became the bedrock of the
Bermudian economy. In 1766 Andrew Symmers settled here to hold
the islands for England. Later, Loyalists from Georgia obtained land
grants in the Caicos Islands, imported slaves, and continued the lifestyle
of the pre–Civil War American South.

Today, the government has devised a long-term development plan to
improve the visibility of the Turks and Caicos in the Caribbean tourism
market. Providenciales, in particular, is well under way as a tourist destination and also as an offshore financial center and company regis-
trant. Mass tourism on the scale of some other island destinations,
however, is not in the cards; government guidelines promote a "quality, not quantity," policy toward tourism, including conservation
awareness and firm restrictions on building heights and casino construction. Without a port for cruise ships, the islands remain uncrowded and peaceful.

## Lodging

Hotel accommodations are available on Grand Turk, North Caicos,
South Caicos, Pine Cay, and Provo. There are also some small, non-
air-conditioned guest houses on Salt Cay and Middle Caicos. Accommodations range from small island inns to the splashy Club Med
Turkoise to the luxury Grace Bay Club in Providenciales. Because of

the popularity of scuba diving here, virtually all the hotels have dive shops and offer dive packages. Dive packagers offering air-hotel-dive packages include **Dive Provo** (☎ 800/234–7768) and **Undersea Adventures** (☎ 800/234–7768). Most of the medium and large hotels offer a choice of EP and MAP. People who don't rent a car or scooter tend to eat at their hotels, so MAP may be the better option. Another option favored by many visitors, particularly families, is renting a self-contained villa or private home; contact the **Ministry of Tourism** (☎ 809/94–62321) three to six months in advance for more information. Please note that the government hotel tax does not apply to guest houses with fewer than four rooms.

| CATEGORY | COST* |
|---|---|
| **$$$$** | over $250 |
| **$$$** | $170–$250 |
| **$$** | $110–$170 |
| **$** | under $110 |

*All prices are for a standard double room for two in winter season, excluding 7% tax and 10%–15% service charge. Please note that some hotels are now charging 8% tax.*

## Grand Turk

**$$–$$$** 🏨 **Guanahani Beach Hotel.** One of the finest stretches of beach on the island belongs to this hotel; the palm-tree-lined property is popular with honeymooners. Fully renovated by new owners in 1994, the rooms have pale ceramic tile floors and bright, primary-color Caribbean print bedspreads and curtains. Every room has an ocean view, two double beds, and a full bathroom. A crewed yacht is available to rent for day trips or romantic moonlight rides. ✉ *Box 178,* ☎ *809/94–62135,* FAX *809/94–61460. 16 rooms. Restaurant, 2 bars, pool, dive packages with Blue Water Diving, 35-foot yacht, gift shop. MC, V.*

**$$** 🏨 **Hotel Kittina.** This family-owned hostelry, the largest hotel on Grand
★ Turk, is split in two by the town's main drag. On one side, comfortable, lodge-style rooms and sleek balconied suites with kitchens sit on a gleaming white-sand beach. Across the street, the older main house holds a lively dining room and rooms that ooze island atmosphere. Behind the house are the pool and garden. All rooms and suites are air-conditioned and have tile floors. Be sure to catch the occasional Friday-night poolside barbecue. ✉ *Duke St., Box 42,* ☎ *809/94–62232 or 800/548–8462,* FAX *809/94–62877. 43 rooms, 2 suites. 2 restaurants, 2 bars, air-conditioning, room service, pool, dive shop, windsurfing, boating, bicycles, scooters, boutique, baby-sitting, travel services. AE, MC, V. EP, MAP.*

**$** 🏨 **Coral Reef Resort.** One- and two-bedroom units here have complete kitchens, air-conditioning, and contemporary furnishings. The resort is a short drive from town, and the beach is a few steps from your door. ✉ *Box 10,* ☎ *809/94–62055,* FAX *809/94–62911. 18 units. Restaurant, bar, air-conditioning, pool, tennis court, mini–fitness center, water sports arranged with dive operations, boutique. AE, MC, V. EP, MAP.*

**$** 🏨 **Ocean View Hotel.** A white picket fence, slightly worn wood and rattan furniture, and hand-stenciled walls and doors give this popular hotel a home-sweet-home atmosphere. Guest rooms are individually decorated and have cool tile floors and clean white walls. Hearty homemade meals are served in the breezy dining area, and the lively bars stay open until midnight or until the last person goes home (whichever comes later). The beach is right across the street. ✉ *Box 97,* ☎ *809/94–62517. 14 rooms, 3 suites. Restaurant, 2 bars, horseback riding, dive packages with Sea Eye Diving and Omega Diving, bicycles. AE, D, MC, V. MAP.*

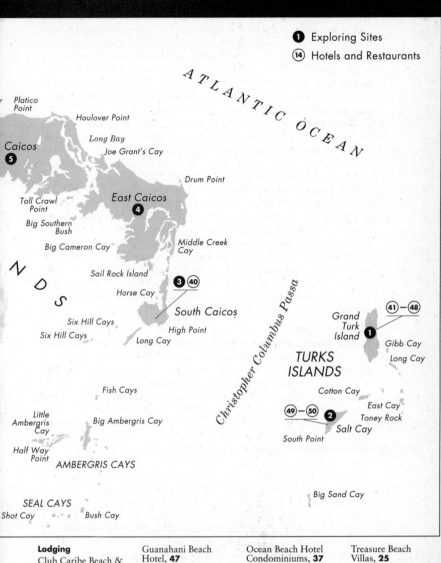

● Exploring Sites
⑭ Hotels and Restaurants

ATLANTIC OCEAN

Platico Point
Haulover Point
Long Bay
Joe Grant's Cay
Caicos ❺
Drum Point
Toll Crawl Point
East Caicos ❹
Big Southern Bush
Big Cameron Cay
Middle Creek Cay
N D S
Sail Rock Island
Horse Cay
❸ ㊵
South Caicos
Six Hill Cays
Six Hill Cays
High Point
Long Cay
Grand Turk Island ❶
㊶—㊽
Gibb Cay
Long Cay
TURKS ISLANDS
Christopher Columbus Passa
Fish Cays
Cotton Cay
East Cay
Little Ambergris Cay
Big Ambergris Cay
㊾—㊿ ❷
Toney Rock
Salt Cay
Half Way Point
South Point
AMBERGRIS CAYS
SEAL CAYS
Big Sand Cay
Shot Cay
Bush Cay

**Lodging**

Club Caribe Beach & Harbour Hotel, **40**
Club Med Turkoise, **23**
Club Vacanze Prospect of Whitby Hotel, **36**
Coral Reef Resort, **41**
Erebus Inn Resort, **27**
Grace Bay Club, **24**

Guanahani Beach Hotel, **47**
Hotel Kittina, **43**
Island Princess, **20**
JoAnne's B&B, **38**
Le Deck Hotel & Beach Club, **21**
Meridian Club, **35**
Mount Pleasant Guest House, **50**

Ocean Beach Hotel Condominiums, **37**
Ocean Club, **31**
Ocean View Hotel, **48**
Pelican Beach Hotel, **39**
Salt Raker Inn, **42**
Sandals, Turks and Caicos, **34**

Treasure Beach Villas, **25**
Turk's Head Inn, **45**
Turquoise Reef Resort & Casino, **22**
Turtle Cove Inn, **26**
Windmills Plantation, **49**

**$**   🏨 **Salt Raker Inn.** Across the street from the beach, this galleried house was the home of a Bermudian shipwright 180 years ago. The rooms and suites are not elegant but are individually decorated and have a homey atmosphere, and each has air-conditioning and a minifridge. The three garden rooms are desirable for their screened porches and ocean views. ✉ *Duke St., Box 1,* ☎ *809/94–62260,* FAX *809/94– 62817. U.K. reservations, 44 Birchington Rd., London NW6 4LJ,* ☎ *0171/328–6474. 10 rooms, 2 suites. Restaurant, bar, air-conditioning, dive packages with Blue Water Diving, bicycles. AE, D, MC, V. EP.*

**$**   🏨 **Turk's Head Inn.** Built in 1850 by a prosperous salt miner, this classic Bermudian building has had incarnations as the American Consulate and as the governor's guest house (the queen reportedly took a room here on her last visit to the island). Now run by a Frenchman known as Mr. X, the inn has acquired a strong European flavor. A plethora of Brits and other expat Europeans make it their stomping ground. The seven distinctive rooms, which have ceiling fans and air-conditioning, are lovingly furnished with antiques and island artifacts, and the owner's own drawings and detailed maps adorn many of the walls. In the front courtyard, an oversize hammock provides the perfect vantage point from which to admire the well-tended garden. The beach is only a few strides away. The bar and restaurant area bustle at night. ✉ *Duke St., Box 58,* ☎ *809/94–62466,* FAX *809/94–62825. 7 rooms, 1 self-contained apartment. Showers only. Restaurant, bar, air-conditioning, dive packages with Sea Eye Diving. AE, MC, V.*

## North Caicos

**$$$**  🏨 **Club Vacanze Prospect of Whitby Hotel.** An Italian resort chain, Club
★   Vacanze, took over this secluded retreat in 1994. Miles of beach are yours for sunbathing, windsurfing, or snorkeling. Spacious guest rooms are simple but elegant; in true getaway fashion, they lack TVs and radios. The restaurant here is quite good. ✉ *Kew Post Office, North Caicos,* ☎ *809/94–67119,* FAX *809/94–67114. 28 rooms, 4 suites. Restaurant, bar, pool, tennis court, dive shop, windsurfing, baby-sitting, travel services. AE, MC, V. EP, MAP.*

**$$**  🏨 **Ocean Beach Hotel Condominiums.** This unpretentious place provides family-style accommodations on a 10-mile stretch of sheltered beach. The spacious units, each with kitchenette, all face the ocean. Cool and constant trade winds, invited in through large sliding glass doors, replace the need for air-conditioning. The hotel offers an intimate lifestyle away from the fray. ✉ *Whitby, North Caicos,* ☎ *809/94–67113 or 800/710–5204; in Canada, 905/336–2876;* FAX *809/94–67386. 10 units. Restaurant, bar-lounge, bicycles, fishing, car rental. MC, V. MAP.*

**$$**  🏨 **Pelican Beach Hotel.** This hotel has large rooms done in pastels and dark wood trim. Ask to stay on the second floor, where rooms have high wood ceilings and fabulous ocean views. Ceiling fans and constant sea breezes keep you cool. ✉ *Whitby, North Caicos,* ☎ *809/94–67112,* FAX *809/94–67139. 14 rooms, 2 suites. Restaurant, bar, fishing. MC, V.*

**$**   🏨 **JoAnne's B&B.** This no-frills, charming bed-and-breakfast on the beach is the perfect spot for those seeking peace and quiet. Rooms are light and airy with cool, white tile floors. Two friendly dogs escort you to the sea and trot along with you as you shell and sun on a very private stretch of beach. The owner, a former Peace Corps worker, also runs Papa Grunts, an excellent restaurant nearby. Her island stories entertain and delight. Faxing is the best way to make reservations. ✉ *Whitby, North Caicos,* ☎ FAX *809/94–67301. 3 rooms. Scooters. MC, V.*

## Pine Cay

**$$$$** 🏨 **Meridian Club.** High rollers vacation in high style on this privately
★   owned 800-acre island. Club guests enjoy an unspoiled cay with 2½ miles of soft white sand and a 500-acre nature reserve with tropical

landscaping, freshwater ponds, and nature trails that lure bird-watchers and botanists. A stay here is truly getting away from it all, as there are no air conditioners, telephones, or TVs. The accommodations range from spacious rooms with king-size beds (or twin beds on request) and patios to one- to four-bedroom cottage-homes that range in decor and amenities from rustic to well appointed. There's also a "round room" cottage and two ocean-view atrium units that are separated by a lovely interior garden. Rooms in the main complex run over $485 a night for two in winter and include all meals. Cottage homes start at $3,000 a week EP. ⊠ *Pine Cay,* ☎ *800/225–4255; in NY, 800/331–9154;* FAX *809/94–65128. 12 rooms, 13 cottage-homes. Restaurant, bar, pool, tennis court, windsurfing, sailing, bicycles. No credit cards. EP, AP.*

## Providenciales

$$$ ☷ **Club Med Turkoise.** This lavish $23 million resort is one of the most sumptuous of all Club Med's villages. One-, two-, and three-story bungalows line a mile-long beach, and all the usual sybaritic pleasures are here. This club is especially geared toward couples, singles aged 28 and over, and divers. The one-price-covers-all-except-drinks package includes all the diving, water sports, and daytime activities you can handle. ⊠ *Providenciales,* ☎ *809/94–65500 or 800/258–2633; in NY, 212/750–1684 or 212/750–1687;* FAX *809/94–65501. 298 rooms. 3 restaurants, bar, snack bar, pool, 8 tennis courts, exercise room, beach, water-sports center, dive center, fishing, bicycles, boutique, disco, nightly entertainment, TV/video room, library. AE, MC, V. All-inclusive (except for drinks).*

$$$ ☷ **Grace Bay Club.** Staying at this Swiss-owned, Mediterranean-style
★ resort is a little like being the guest of honor of a very gracious host with unbeatable taste. The suites, which all feature a breathtaking view of Grace Bay's stunning turquoise waters, are tastefully furnished with rattan and pickled wood. Mexican-tile floors are elegantly appointed with throw rugs from Turkey and India. If you choose to take advantage of the myriad activities (from diving to golf to individually planned and catered picnics on surrounding islands), you will be expertly provided for; but the main attraction here is natural beauty. Relax and enjoy a getaway that is peaceful, invigorating, and wonderfully pampering. ⊠ *Box 128, Providenciales,* ☎ *809/94–65050 or 800/677–9192,* FAX *809/94–65758. 22 suites. Restaurant, bar, pool, hot tub, 2 tennis courts, beach, water sports, video/book library. AE, MC, V. EP, MAP.*

$$$ ☷ **Sandals, Turks and Caicos.** A row of giant palm trees lines the approach to this new, elegant pink-and-white resort, which was added to the Sandals chain at press time. Stroll among the lush tropical landscaping, take a dip in the free-form lap pool, and dine in one of the delicious restaurants—there are plenty of sports and activities to work off the extra calories. You'll be suffiently pampered with bar service that extends to the beach. Luxurious accommodations combined with white-glove service make this all-inclusive resort a truly relaxing experience. ⊠ *Grace Bay,* ☎ *809/94–68000 or 800/726–3257. 200 rooms. 3 restaurants, pool, hot tub, 2 tennis courts, exercise room, waters ports, dive center.*

$$$ ☷ **Turquoise Reef Resort & Casino.** Oversize oceanfront rooms have
★ rattan furniture and a rich Caribbean color scheme. Furnished with a king or two double beds, all rooms are air-conditioned and have a color TV and ceiling fan, and either a terrace or a patio. The island's only casino is here. Guests enjoy a free daily-activities program that includes pool volleyball and children's treasure hunts. ⊠ *Box 205, Provo,* ☎ *809/94–65555,* FAX *809/94–65522. 228 rooms. 3 restaurants, 3 bars, air-conditioning, room service, pool, hot tub, 2 tennis courts, exercise room, beach, dive shop, water-sports facility, boutiques, duty-free*

*shop, casino, dance club, live nightly entertainment, baby-sitting, travel services. AE, MC, V. EP, MAP.*

**$$** 🏨 **Le Deck Hotel & Beach Club.** This 27-room pink hostelry was built
★ in classic Bermudian style around a tropical courtyard. It offers clean rooms with a tile floor, color TV, phone, and air-conditioning. Le Deck is especially popular with divers, and its atmosphere is informal and lively with a mostly thirty-something-and-over crowd. ✉ *Box 144, Grace Bay, Provo,* ☎ *809/94–65547,* FAX *809/94–65770. 27 rooms, including 2 suites. Restaurant, bar, air-conditioning, pool, beach, water sports, boutique. AE, D, MC, V. EP, CP, AP, MAP.*

**$$** 🏨 **Island Princess.** Wood walkways at this hotel lead up to and around the rooms, which are situated in two wings. All rooms have cable TV and a private balcony. This is a great little hotel for families. It's on the beach, the restaurant serves excellent Italian and Caribbean food, and there's nightly entertainment. ✉ *The Bight,* ☎ *809/94–64260,* FAX *809/94–64666. 80 rooms. Restaurant, bar, 2 pools, water-sports center, boating, recreation room, playground. AE, D, MC, V. MAP.*

**$$** 🏨 **Ocean Club.** "Escape the Stress of Success" is the slogan for this luxury beachfront suite resort, which was completing its renovations at press time. It's situated on Grace Bay's 12-mile stretch of pristine beach, a short walk away from Provo's only golf course. The all-suite accommodations range from efficiency studios to deluxe versions with ocean view, full screened balcony, kitchen, dining room, and living room. The refreshing decor is mostly wicker. Third-floor rooms have striking slanted ceilings, and all but efficiency accommodations include washer and dryer. Efficiency suites fall into our $ category. ✉ *Box 240, Providenciales,* ☎ *809/94–65880 or 800/742–4276,* FAX *809/94–65845. Restaurant, bar, pool, 18-hole golf course, tennis court, exercise room, dive shop, duty-free shop, playground. AE, MC, V.*

**$$** 🏨 **Treasure Beach Villas.** These one- and two-bedroom modern, self-catering apartments have fully equipped kitchens and ceiling fans. You may want a car or bike (Treasure Beach has rentals) to reach the grocery store or restaurants; bus service is limited. Provo's 12 miles of white sandy beach is just outside your door, and the hotel can organize fishing, snorkeling, and scuba expeditions. ✉ *The Bight,* ☎ *809/94–64211,* FAX *809/94–64108; in the U.S., Box 8409, Hialeah, FL 33012. 8 single, 10 double rooms. Pool, tennis court. AE, D, MC, V. EP.*

**$$** 🏨 **Turtle Cove Inn.** A marina, a free-form pool, a dive shop with equipment rentals and instruction, and lighted tennis courts attract the sporting crowd to Turtle Cove. There's a free boat shuttle to the nearby beach and snorkeling reef. All rooms have a TV, phone, and air-conditioning, and eight also have minifridges. A handful of good restaurants are within walking distance. ✉ *Providenciales,* ☎ *809/94–64203 or 800/887–0477,* FAX *809/94–64141. 30 rooms, 1 suite. 2 restaurants, 2 bars, air-conditioning, 2 tennis courts, pool, dive shop, marina, bicycles. AE, MC, V. EP.*

**$–$$** 🏨 **Erebus Inn Resort.** This resort sits on a cliff overlooking Turtle Cove
★ and has wonderful views of the marina and the Caribbean beyond. All units have two double beds, modern wicker furnishings, and original island artwork, including some lovely and unique Haitian wall hangings. Rooms in the older chalet cost under $110 a night (double occupancy) in winter. For those preferring creature comforts, we recommend the units in the newer section ($$); each has air-conditioning, cable TV, and phone. Frequent bus shuttles take guests to a nearby beach. The restaurant and bar, always one of Provo's liveliest spots, has a menu of French and Caribbean cuisine. Five affordable restaurants are within walking distance, as are a shopping center and several dive operations. ✉ *Turtle Cove, Box 238, Providenciales,* ☎ *809/94–64240,* FAX *809/94–*

64704. *30 rooms. Restaurant, bar, 2 pools (1 saltwater), 2 tennis courts, aqua-aerobics, exercise room, baby-sitting. AE, MC, V. EP, MAP.*

## Salt Cay

**$$$$** ⭐ 🏨 **Windmills Plantation.** The attraction here is the lack of distraction: no nightlife, no cruise ships, no crowds, and no shopping. Owner-manager-architect Guy Lovelace and his interior designer wife, Patricia, built the hotel as their version of a colonial-era plantation. The great house has four suites, each with a sitting area, four-poster bed, ceiling fans, and a veranda or balcony with a view of the sea. All are furnished in a mix of antique English and wicker furniture. Four other rooms are housed in two adjacent buildings. Room rates, which during the height of winter run from $415 a night and up for two people, include snorkeling equipment, three meals, and unlimited bar drinks, wine, and beer. ⊠ *Salt Cay,* ☎ *809/94–66962 or 800/822–7715,* 🅵🅰🆇 *809/94–66930. 4 rooms, 4 suites. Restaurant, bar, pool, horseback riding, 2½-mile nature trail, beach, snorkeling, fishing, library. AE, MC, V. AP.*

**$–$$** 🏨 **Mount Pleasant Guest House.** This simple, somewhat rustic hotel offers guests inexpensive lodging at a remote location. Not all rooms have private baths. ⊠ *Salt Cay,* ☎ *809/94–66927. 7 rooms. Restaurant, bar, horseback riding, scuba diving, bicycles, library. MC, V.*

## South Caicos

**$–$$** 🏨 **Club Caribe Beach & Harbour Hotel.** Cockburn Harbour, the only natural harbor in the Turks and Caicos Islands, is the perfect setting for this hotel. The 16 beachfront villas, which can be rented as studios or as one-, two-, or three-bedroom apartments, have cool tile floors and kitchenettes equipped with minifridge and microwave. Half of the rooms don't have air-conditioning, but they get a nice breeze around the clock. The 22 harbor rooms are smaller than the others but have air-conditioning. There's a dive shop with a full-time instructor. ⊠ *Box 1, South Caicos,* ☎ *809/94–63444 or 800/722–2582,* 🅵🅰🆇 *809/94–63446. 38 rooms. Restaurant, bar, dive shop, windsurfing, bicycles. AE, D, MC, V. EP, MAP.*

# Dining

Like everything else on these islands, dining out is a very laid-back affair, which is not to say that it is cheap. Because of the high cost of importing all edibles, the cost of a meal is usually higher than that of a comparable meal in the United States. A 7% government tax and a 10% service charge are added to your check. Reservations are not required. Dress is casual throughout the island.

| CATEGORY | COST* |
|---|---|
| **$$$** | over $25 |
| **$$** | $15–$25 |
| **$** | under $15 |

*per person for a three-course meal, excluding drinks, service, and 7% sales tax*

## Grand Turk

**$$** ✕ **Salt Raker Inn.** Starters at this rustic, informal patio restaurant include tomato and mozzarella salad and melon with ginger. Lobster in cream and sherry sauce, barbecued steak, and seafood curry are oft-ordered entrées. For dessert, try the tasty apple pie. The Sunday dinner and sing-along is popular. ⊠ *Salt Raker Inn, Duke St.,* ☎ *809/94–62260. AE, D, MC, V.*

**$$** ✕ **Sandpiper.** Candles flicker on the Sandpiper's terrace, set beside a flower-filled courtyard. The leisurely pace here creates a relaxing setting to experience such blackboard specialties as lobster, filet mignon, seafood platter, or pork chops with applesauce. ⊠ *Hotel Kittina, Duke St.,* ☎ *809/94–62232. AE, D, MC, V.*

$–$$   ✕ **Turk's Head Inn.** The menu changes daily at this lively restaurant, touted by many residents as the best on the island. Some staples include escargots, pâté, and a handful of other delectables, including local grouper fingers perfectly fried for fish-and-chips. Look for lobster, quiche, steaks, and homemade soups on the blackboard menu. You may not want to leave after your meal—come nightfall, the inn's bar is abuzz with local gossip and mirthful chatter. ✉ *Turk's Head Inn, Duke St.,* ☎ *809/94–62466. AE, MC, V.*

$   ✕ **Regal Begal.** Drop by this popular local eatery for native specialties such as cracked conch, minced lobster, and fish-and-chips. The atmosphere is casual and the decor unmemorable, but the portions are large and the prices easy on your wallet. ✉ *Hospital Rd.,* ☎ *809/94–62274. No credit cards.*

$   ✕ **Water's Edge.** Relaxed waterfront dining awaits you at this pleasantly rustic eatery. The limited menu covers the basics with a twist—from barbecued grouper to a fresh seafood crepe. A kids' menu is also available. The food is authentic and filling, and the view at sunset breathtaking, but the irresistible homemade pies are enough to justify a visit. ✉ *Duke St.,* ☎ *809/94–61680. MC, V. Closed Mon.*

### Providenciales

$$$   ✕ **Gecko Grille.** Gourmet dining can be enjoyed either indoors amid tropical hand-painted murals or out on the garden patio. The menu features creative dishes such as almond cracked conch with a lime *rémoulade* (a cold, mayonnaise-based sauce), and grilled pork chops marinated in papaya juice. Portions are quite large, so either share or bring a hearty appetite. ✉ *At the Ocean Club Resort, Grace Bay,* ☎ *809/94–65880. AE, MC, V.*

$$$   ✕ **The Terrace.** The cuisine here has a Euro-Caribbean flair, and the menu changes according to the freshest ingredients available. You can make a meal from such delicious starters as freshly baked tomato-and-goat-cheese tarts, lobster bisque, and simmered mussels. Main courses include roast rack of lamb, and fresh conch encrusted with pecans. Top it all off with a classic crème brûlée. ✉ *Turtle Cove,* ☎ *809/94–64763. AE, MC, V. Closed Sun.*

$$–$$$   ✕ **Alfred's Place.** Austrian owner Alfred Holzfeind caters to an Amer-
★   ican palate with an extensive menu featuring everything from prime rib to chicken salad. The alfresco lounge is a popular watering hole for locals and tourists alike. ✉ *Turtle Cove,* ☎ *809/94–64679. AE, D, MC, V. Closed Mon. July–Oct.*

$$–$$$   ✕ **Anacaona.** This exquisitely designed restaurant offers a true gourmet
★   dining experience minus the tie, the air-conditioning, and the attitude. Located at the equally impressive Grace Bay Club, this is Caribbean-Continental open-air dining at its best. Start with a bottle of fine wine from the extensive cellar, then enjoy a three- or four-course meal of the chef's light but flavorful cooking, which combines traditional French recipes with fresh seafood and Caribbean fruits, vegetables, and spices. Oil lamps on the tables, gently circulating ceiling fans, and a natural soundtrack of the breeze, the ocean, birds, and even a few neighboring frogs all add to the Eden-like environment. ✉ *Grace Bay Club,* ☎ *809/94–65050. AE, MC, V.*

$–$$   ✕ **Dora's.** This popular local eatery serves up island fare—turtle, shredded lobster, spicy conch chowder—seven days a week, from 7 AM until the last person leaves the bar. Plastic print and lace tablecloths, hanging plants, and Haitian art add to the island ambience. Soups ($4) come with homemade bread, and entrées such as fish-and-chips, conch Creole, and grilled pork chops come with a choice of vegetable. Be sure to come early for the packed Monday- and Thursday-night all-you-can-eat $20 seafood buffet. The price includes round-trip transportation to your hotel. ⊠ *Leeward Hwy.,* ☎ *809/94–64558. No credit cards.*

**$–$$** ✕ **Fast Eddie's.** Plants festoon this cheerful restaurant, which is across from the airport. Broiled turtle steak, fried grouper fingers, and other island specialties are joined on the menu by old American standbys such as cheeseburgers and cherry pie. Wednesday evening there's a $20 ($10 for children) all-you-can-eat seafood buffet. Friday is prime rib and live music night. Free transportation to and from your hotel is provided. ⊠ *Airport Rd.,* ☎ *809/94–13175. MC, V.*

**$–$$** ✕ **Hong Kong Restaurant.** A no-frills place with plain wood tables and chairs, the Hong Kong offers dine-in, delivery, or take-out. The menu includes lobster with ginger and green onions, chicken with black-bean sauce, sliced duck with salted mustard greens, and sweet-and-sour chicken. ⊠ *Leeward Hwy.,* ☎ *809/94–65678. V. No lunch Sun.*

**$** ✕ **Banana Boat.** Buoys and other sea relics deck the walls of this brightly painted casual restaurant situated on the wharf. Grilled grouper, lobster-salad sandwiches, conch fritters, and a refreshing conch salad are among the menu options. Excellent tropical drinks include the house specialty, the rum-filled Banana Breeze. ⊠ *Turtle Cove,* ☎ *809/94–15706. AE, MC, V.*

**$** ✕ **Caicos Cafe.** There's a pervasive air of celebration in the uncovered outdoor dining area of this popular eatery. Choose from a selection of local and American cuisine, including lobster sandwiches, hamburgers, and a variety of excellent salads. ⊠ *Across from the Turquoise Reef,* ☎ *809/94–65278. AE. No lunch Sun.*

**$** ✕ **Hey, José.** Frequented by locals, this restaurant claims to serve the
★ island's best margaritas. Customers also return for the tasty Tex-Mex treats: tacos, tostados, nachos, burritos, fajitas, and José's special-recipe hot chicken wings. Creative types can build their own pizzas. ⊠ *Central Square,* ☎ *809/94–64812. AE, MC, V. Closed Sun.*

**$** ✕ **Pub on the Bay.** If beachfront dining is what you're after, it doesn't get much better than this. Located in the Blue Hill residential district, a five-minute drive from downtown Provo, this restaurant serves fried or steamed fish, oxtail stew, barbecue ribs, chicken, various sandwiches, and even turtle steak. There is no air-conditioning inside the restaurant, so you may as well cross the street to one of three thatched roof "huts," which stand quite literally on the beach. ⊠ *Blue Hill Rd.,* ☎ *809/94–15309. AE, MC, V.*

**$** ✕ **Top O' the Cove Gourmet Delicatessen.** You can easily walk to this tiny café on Leeward Highway from the Turtle Cove and Erebus Inns. Don't be put off by the location in the Napa Auto Parts plaza—the restaurant's interior is not at all garagelike! You can order breakfast, deli subs, sandwiches, salads, and cool soft-swirl frozen yogurt. You can also get a gourmet cup of coffee to go. It's open every day but Christmas and New Year's from 7 AM to 3:30 PM. ⊠ *Leeward Hwy.,* ☎ *809/94–64694. No credit cards.*

# Beaches

There are more than 230 miles of beaches in the Turks and Caicos Islands, ranging from secluded coves to miles-long stretches. Most beaches are soft coralline sand. Tiny uninhabited cays offer complete isolation for nude sunbathing and skinny-dipping. Many are accessible only by boat.

**Big Ambergris Cay,** an uninhabited cay about 14 miles beyond the Fish Cays, has a magnificent beach at Long Bay. **East Caicos,** an uninhabited island accessible only by boat, has a beautiful 17-mile beach along its north coast. **Governor's Beach,** a long white strip on the west coast of Grand Turk, is one of the nicest beaches on this island. The north and east coasts of North Caicos are bordered by great beaches for swimming, scuba diving, snorkeling, and fishing. **Three Mary's Cays** has excellent snorkeling with a friendly ancient barracuda named Old Man. **Pine Cay,** a private upscale retreat, has a 2½-mile strip of beach—among the most beautiful in the archipelago. A fine white-sand beach stretches 12 miles along the northeast coast of **Providenciales.** There are good beaches at **Sapodilla Bay;** for excellent close-to-shore snorkeling there's a reef near the White House off Penn's Road.

There are superb beaches on the north coast of **Salt Cay. Big Sand Cay,** 7 miles to the south of Salt Cay, is known for its excellent beaches. Only in **South Caicos** are the beaches small and unremarkable, but the vibrant reef makes it a popular destination for divers.

## Outdoor Activities and Sports

### Bicycling

Provo has a few steep grades to conquer, but they're short, and there's little traffic. Bikes can be rented at the **Island Princess** (☎ 809/94–64260) hotel at the Bight for $10 a day, through **Turtle Inn Divers** (✉ Turtle Cove Inn, ☎ 809/94–15389) for $12 a day and $60 a week, or at the **Turquoise Reef Resort & Casino** (✉ Grace Bay, ☎ 809/94–65555) for $14 a day. In Grand Turk on Duke Street, both the **Salt Raker Inn** (☎ 809/94–62260) and the **Hotel Kittina** (☎ 809/94–62232) rent bikes for $10 per day, $40 per week.

### Boat Rentals

You can rent a boat with a private captain for a half or full day of sportfishing through **J&B Tours** (✉ Provo, ☎ 809/94–65047) or **Porpoise** (✉ Salt Cay, ☎ 809/94–66927) for about $300 a day. **Dive Provo** (✉ Turquoise Reef Resort, Provo, ☎ 809/94–65040) rents small sailboats for $20 per hour and provides beginning instruction for $40 for up to two hours. Sailing not your bent? Try open-cockpit ocean kayaking, available at Dive Provo for $10 per hour for one and $15 per hour for two.

### Fishing

**Silver Deep** (✉ Provo, ☎ 809/94–15595) will take you out for half- or full-day bonefishing or bottom fishing expeditions, bait and tackle included. The same outfit will arrange half- or full-day deep-sea fishing trips in search of shark, marlin, kingfish, sawfish, wahoo, and tuna, with all equipment furnished. Deep-sea, bone-, and bottom fishing are also available aboard the *Sakitumi* (☎ 809/94–64203 or 809/94–64393).

### Golf

A 6,529-yard golf course opened on Providenciales in late 1991. **Provo Golf Club** (☎ 809/94–65991) has an 18-hole, par-72 championship course, designed by Karl Litten, that is sustained by a desalination plant producing 250,000 gallons of water a day. The turf is sprinkled in green islands over 12 acres of natural limestone outcroppings, creating a desert-style design of narrow "target areas" and sandy waste areas—a formidable challenge to anyone playing from the championship tees. Fees are $65 plus $15 for a mandatory electric cart. A pro shop, driving ranges, and a restaurant and bar round out the club's facilities.

### Horseback Riding

Horses roam lazily around the main roads on Grand Turk. While there is no organized riding program, most hotels will make arrangements for their guests, and rates can be negotiated with individual owners.

## Parasailing

A 15-minute flight is available for $45 at either **Dive Provo** (⊠ Turquoise Reef Resort, Provo, ☎ 809/94–65040 or 800/234–7768) or **J&B Tours** (⊠ Leward Marina, ☎ 809/94–65047).

## Scuba Diving

Diving is the top attraction here. (All divers must carry and present a valid certificate card before they'll be allowed to dive.) These islands are surrounded by a reef system of more than 200 square miles—much of it unexplored. Grand Turk's famed wall drops more than 7,000 feet and is one side of a 22-mile-wide channel called the Christopher Columbus Passage. From January through March, an estimated 6,000 eastern Atlantic humpback whales swim through this passage en route to their winter breeding grounds. There are undersea cathedrals, coral gardens, and countless tunnels. Among the operations that provide instruction, equipment rentals, underwater video equipment, and trips are **Sea Eye Divers** (⊠ Grand Turk, ☎ 809/94–61407), **Blue Water Divers** (⊠ Salt Raker Inn, Grand Turk, ☎ 809/94–62432), **Off the Wall Divers** (⊠ Grand Turk, ☎ 809/94–62159), **Dive Provo** (⊠ Turquoise Reef Resort, Provo, ☎ 809/94–65040 or 800/234–7768), **Flamingo Divers** (⊠ Provo, ☎ 809/94–64193), **Provo Turtle Divers** (⊠ Provo, ☎ 809/94–64232), and **Porpoise Divers** (⊠ Salt Cay, ☎ 809/94–66927).

Note: A modern hyperbaric/recompression chamber is located on Provo in the **Menzies Medical Centre** (☎ 809/94–64242) on Leeward Highway. Divers in need on Grand Turk are airlifted to Provo—a 30-minute flight.

## Sea Excursions

The *Ocean Outback* (☎ 809/94–64080), a 70-foot motor cruiser, has barbecue-and-snorkel cruises to uninhabited islands. Both the 37-foot catamaran *Beluga* (☎ 809/94–15196, $39 per half day) and the 56-foot trimaran *Tao* (☎ 809/94–65040) run sunset cruises, as well as sailing and snorkeling outings. A full-day outing on the *Tao* is $59 per person, including snorkel rental and lunch. For $20 per person, **Dive Provo** (⊠ Ramada Turquoise Reef Resort, ☎ 809/94–65040 or 800/234–7768) gives two-hour glass-bottom-boat tours of the spectacular reefs. **Turtle Inn Divers** (⊠ Turtle Cove Inn, ☎ 809/94–15389) offers full-day Sunday excursions for divers for $64.50 per person ($25 per person for nondivers and snorkelers). The *Turks and Caicos Aggressor* (☎ 504/385–2628 or 800/348–2628, FAX 504/384–0817) offers luxury six-day dive cruises with full accommodations.

## Snorkeling

**Dive Provo** (⊠ Provo, ☎ 809/94–65040 or 800/234–7768), **Blue Water Divers** (⊠ Salt Raker Inn, Grand Turk, ☎ 809/94–62432), and **Provo Turtle Divers** (⊠ Provo, ☎ 809/94–64232) all provide rentals for about $10 and trips for $20. **Sea Eye Diving** (⊠ Grand Turk, ☎ 809/94–61407) offers equipment and trips, as well as diving packages and instruction.

## Spectator Sports

Cricket is the most popular game in town. The season runs from July through August. Tennis, basketball, softball, and darts are other local favorites. You're welcome to join in. Inquire at the tourist board (☎ 800/241–0824) for a list of events.

## Tennis

On Provo, there are two lighted courts at **Turtle Cove Inn** (☎ 809/94–64203), eight courts (four lighted) at **Club Med Turkoise** (☎ 809/94–65500), two courts at the **Turquoise Reef Resort** (☎ 809/94–65555), two lighted courts at the **Erebus Inn** (☎ 809/94–64240), one court at

**Treasure Beach Villas** (☎ 809/94–64211), and two lighted courts at **Grace Bay Club** (☎ 809/94–65050). On Grand Turk, the **Coral Reef Resort** (☎ 809/94–62055) has one lighted court. There is also one court at the **Meridian Club** (✉ Pine Cay, ☎ 800/225–4255) and one court at the **Club Vacanze Prospect of Whitby Hotel** (✉ North Caicos, ☎ 809/94–67119).

### Waterskiing
Waterskiers will find the calm turquoise water ideal for long-distance runs. **Dive Provo** (✉ Turquoise Reef Resort, Provo, ☎ 809/94–65040) charges $35 for a 15-minute run.

### Windsurfing
Rental and instruction are available at the **Club Vacanze Prospect of Whitby Hotel** (✉ North Caicos, ☎ 809/94–67119) and **Dive Provo** (✉ Turquoise Reef Resort, Provo, ☎ 809/94–65040).

## Shopping

Shopping is limited to hotel gift shops, airports, and occasional street vendors, except on Provo, where new shops and franchises open every month. Most of these stores can be found in five main shopping complexes: Market Place, Central Square, Caribbean Place, all on Leeward Highway; Turtle Cove Landing, in Turtle Cove; and the newest complex, Ports of Call, in Grace Bay. Delicate baskets woven from the local top grasses and small metalworks are the only crafts native to the Turks and Caicos, and they are sold in many shops.

The **Bamboo Gallery** (✉ Market Place, Provo, ☎ 809/94–064748) sells all types of Caribbean art, from vivid Haitian paintings to wood carvings and local metal sculptures. **Greensleeves** (✉ Central Square, Provo, ☎ 809/94–64147) is the place to go for paintings by local artists, island-made rag rugs, baskets, jewelry, and sisal mats and bags. **Mama's Gifts** (✉ Ports of Call, Provo, ☎ 809/94–13338) sells hand-woven and embroidered straw baskets, handbags, hats, and shell and wood jewelry. **Maison Creole** (✉ Grace Bay, Provo, no phone) sells unique Caribbean arts and crafts including painted metal sculptures, furniture, carved wood masks, canes, and bowls. **Pelican's Pouch/Designer I** (✉ Turtle Cove Landing, Provo, ☎ 809/94–64343) displays resort wear, sandals, Provo T-shirts, perfumes, and gold jewelry on the ground floor; head upstairs for basketry, sculpture, and watercolors. **Paradise Gifts/Arts** (✉ Central Square, Provo, ☎ 809/94–64637) has a ceramics studio on the premises; in addition to ceramics, jewelry, T-shirts, and paintings by local artists are sold here. **Royal Jewels** (✉ Leeward Hwy., Provo, ☎ 809/94–64885; ✉ Turquoise Reef Resort, Provo, ☎ 809/94–65311; ✉ Airport, Provo, ☎ 809/94–65311) sells gold and jewelry, designer watches, and perfumes—all duty free.

## Nightlife

On Provo, the newest hot spot is **Casablanca** (✉ next to Club Med, ☎ 809/94–65449), a Monte Carlo–style nightclub complete with mirrors and a decked-out crowd. **Disco Elite** (✉ Airport Rd., ☎ 809/94–64592) has strobe lights and an elevated dance floor. A full band plays native, reggae, and contemporary music on Thursday night at the **Erebus Inn** (✉ Turtle Cove, ☎ 809/94–64240). **Le Deck** (✉ Grace Bay, ☎ 809/94–65547) offers one-armed bandits every night. Locals frequent **Smokey's on the Beach** (✉ near Le Deck hotel, ☎ 809/94–13466), a lively restaurant-bar that, as the name suggests, is right on the beach, and a great place to watch the sunset. A lively lounge can be found at the **Turquoise Reef Resort** (✉ Grace Bay, ☎ 809/94–65555), where a musician plays to the mostly tourist crowd. **Port Royale** (✉ Turquoise Reef Resort, ☎ 809/94–65508) is the island's only gambling casino. **Bacchus** (✉ opposite Turquoise Reef Resort, ☎ 809/94–65214) is open Thursday, Friday, and Saturday night for drinks and dancing.

On Grand Turk, Xavier Tonneau (a.k.a. Mr. X) leads sing-alongs in his bar at the **Turk's Head Inn** (✉ Duke St., ☎ 809/94–62466) almost every night. There's folk and pop music at the **Salt Raker Inn** (✉ Duke St., ☎ 809/94–62260) on Wednesday and Sunday nights. Night owls can head over to the **Lady** (✉ at the former naval base, no phone) for dancing. The **Rack Room** (✉ Back Salina, ☎ 809/94–61802) has a DJ, occasional live local bands, and gaming.

## Exploring the Turks and Caicos Islands

Pristine beaches with vistas of turquoise waters, small local settlements, historic ruins, and native flora and fauna are among the sights to be seen on these islands. Keep an eye out for fruit-bearing trees like lime, papaya, and custard apple. Birds to look for include the great blue heron, the woodstar humming bird, and the squawking Cuban crow. It's hard to get lost on the islands, as there aren't many roads; given the low amount of traffic, motor scooters can be a fun way to explore.

*Numbers in the margin correspond to points of interest on the Turks and Caicos Islands map.*

### Grand Turk

Fewer than 4,000 people live on this 7½-square-mile island. Diving is definitely the big deal here. Grand Turk's Wall, with a sheer drop to 7,000 feet, is well known to divers.

**❶ Cockburn Town.** The buildings in this, the colony's capital and seat of government, reflect the 19th-century Bermudian style of architecture. The narrow streets are lined with low stone walls and old street lamps, now powered by electricity. Horses and cattle wander around as if they owned the place, and the occasional donkey cart clatters by, carrying a load of water or freight. In one of the oldest native stone buildings in the islands, the **Turks & Caicos National Museum** houses the Molasses Reef wreck of 1513, the earliest shipwreck discovered in the Americas. The natural-history exhibits include artifacts left by African, North American, Bermudian, French, Hispanic, and Taino settlers. An impressive addition to the museum is the coral reef and sea-life exhibit, faithfully modeled on a popular dive site just off the island. ☎ 809/94–62160. ➲ $5. ☉ Mon.–Tues. and Thurs.–Fri. 9–4, Wed. 9–6, Sat. 10–1.

NEED A
BREAK?
The **Pepper Pot** (no phone) is a little blue shack at the end of Front Street where Peanuts Butterfield makes her famous conch fritters.

### Salt Cay

Only 200 people live on this tiny 2½-square-mile dot of land. There's not much in the way of development, but there are splendid beaches on the north coast. Salt sheds and salt ponds are silent reminders of the days when the island was a leading producer of salt. February through March, whales pass by on the way to their winter breeding grounds. Scuba divers can dive the Endymion, a recently discovered 140-foot wooden-hulled British warship that sank in 1790.

**❷ Balfour Town.** What little development there is on Salt Cay is found in this town. It's home to the Windmills Plantation hotel, the Mount Pleasant Guest House, and a few stores.

## South Caicos

The 8½-square-mile island was once an important salt producer; today it's the heart of the fishing industry. Spiny lobster and queen conch are found in the shallow Caicos bank to the west and are harvested for export by local processing plants. The bonefishing here is some of the best in the West Indies. At the northern end of the island are fine, white-sand beaches; the south coast is great for scuba diving along the drop-off; and there's excellent snorkeling off the windward (east) coast, where large stands of elkhorn and staghorn coral shelter a variety of small tropical fish.

**❸ Cockburn Harbour.** The best natural harbor in the Caicos chain is home to the South Caicos Regatta, held each year in May.

## East Caicos

**❹ East Caicos.** Uninhabited and accessible only by boat, East Caicos has a magnificent 17-mile beach stretching along its north coast. The island was once a cattle range and the site of a major sisal-growing industry.

## Middle Caicos

Since telephones are a rare commodity here, the boats that dock here and the planes that land on the little airstrip provide the island's 270 residents with their main connection to the outside world. **J&B Tours** offer boat tours from Provo to the mysterious caves (☞ Outdoor Activities and Sports, *above*).

**❺ Conch Bar Caves.** The largest (48 square miles) and least developed of the inhabited Turks and Caicos Islands, Middle Caicos is home to limestone caves with eerie underground lakes and milky-white stalactites and stalagmites. Archaeologists have discovered Arawak and Lucayan Indian artifacts in the caves and the surrounding area.

## North Caicos

The beaches of North Caicos, a 41-square-mile island, are superb for shelling and lolling, and the waters offshore offer excellent snorkeling, bonefishing, and scuba diving (there are no scuba outfitters on the island, so divers will have to make arrangements with dive shops on Provo).

**❼ Flamingo Pond.** This is a regular nesting place for the beautiful pink birds. They tend to wander out in the middle of the pond, so bring binoculars to see them better.

**❻ Kew.** The ruins of old plantations can be seen in this settlement, which includes a small post office, school, and church, set among lush tropical trees bearing limes, papayas, and custard apples. To visit Kew is to gain a better understanding of what life is like for many native islanders.

**❽ Sandy Point.** Getting to this settlement is half the fun, as you rattle along dirt and stone-filled roads. You'll pass salt flats where you'll very likely see flamingos standing around in the shallow waters. They're shy birds, so bring binoculars to see them better. A secluded cove here provides excellent snorkeling.

## Pine Cay

**❾ Pine Cay.** One of a chain of small cays connecting North Caicos and Provo, 800-acre Pine Cay is privately owned and under development as a planned community. It's home to the exclusive Meridian Club resort, playground of jet-setters, and its 2½-mile beach is the most beautiful in the archipelago. The island has a 3,800-foot airstrip and electric carts for getting around.

## Providenciales

In the mid-18th century, so the story goes, a French ship was wrecked near here and the survivors were washed ashore on an island they gratefully christened La Providentielle. Under the Spanish, the name was changed to Providenciales.

About 6,000 people live on Provo, a considerable number of whom are expatriate U.S. and Canadian businesspeople and retirees. Provo's 44 square miles are by far the most developed in the Turks and Caicos. With its rolling ridges and 12-mile beach, the island is a prime target for developers. More than two decades ago a group of U.S. investors, including the DuPonts, Ludingtons, and Roosevelts, opened up this island for visitors and those seeking homesites in the Caribbean. In 1990 the island's first luxury resort, the Turquoise Reef Resort & Casino, opened, and with it, the island's first gourmet Italian restaurant. The luxurious Ocean Club, a condominium resort at Grace Bay, was also completed in 1990 and was followed by the upscale Grace Bay Club resort in 1992. The newest luxury resort is the Royal Bay, which opened in 1995. Competition created by the new resorts spurred many of the older hotels to undertake much-needed renovations.

**⓫ Downtown Provo.** Near Providenciales International Airport, the downtown of Provo is a cluster of stone and stucco buildings in a strip mall that house car-rental agencies, law offices, boutiques, banks, and other businesses.

NEED A
BREAK?
    Stop in at **Fast Eddie's** (✉ Airport Rd., ☎ 809/94–64075), a casual eatery, for a drink and a platter of seafood.

**⓾ Island Sea Center.** On the northeast coast, this is the place to learn about the sea and its inhabitants. Here you'll find the **Caicos Conch Farm,** a major mariculture operation where the mollusks are farmed commercially. The farm's tourist facilities include a video show, boutique, and a "hands-on" tank. A geodesic dome, housing natural-history exhibits, was severely damaged in a 1993 fire, but reopened in 1995. Established by the PRIDE Foundation (Protection of Reefs and Islands from Degradation and Exploitation), the **JoJo Dolphin Project,** named after a 7-foot-long male bottlenose dolphin who cruises these waters and enjoys playing with local divers, is also here. You can watch a video on JoJo and learn how to interact with him safely if you see him on one of your dives. ✉ *Island Sea Center* ☎ *809/94–65330, Caicos Conch Farm* ☎ *809/94–65849.* ✆ *$6.* ☉ *Mon.–Sat. 9–5.*

## West Caicos

Accessible only by boat, this island is uninhabited and untamed, and there are no facilities whatsoever. A glorious white beach stretches for a mile along the northwest point, and offshore diving is among the most exotic in the islands. A wall inhabited by countless species of large marine life begins ¼ mile offshore. If you do tour West Caicos, take along several vats of insect repellent. It won't help much with the sharks, but it should fend off the mosquitoes and sand flies. Be advised, too, that the interior is overgrown with dense shrubs, including manchineel.

**⓭ Molasses Reef.** It is rumored to be the final resting place of the *Pinta,* which is thought to have been wrecked here in the early 1500s. Over the past few centuries numerous wrecks have occurred in the area between West Caicos and Provo, and author Peter Benchley is among the treasure seekers who have been lured to this island.

**⓬ Northwest Reef.** The site offers great stands of elkhorn coral and acres of staghorn brambles. But this area is only for experienced divers. The wall starts deep, the currents are strong—and there are sharks in the waters.

# Turks and Caicos Islands A to Z

## Arriving and Departing

### BY BOAT

Because of the superb diving, three live-aboard dive boats call regularly. Contact the **Aquanaut** (c/o See & Sea, ☎ 800/348–9778), the **Sea Dancer** (c/o Peter Hughes Diving, ☎ 800/932–6237), or the **Turks and Caicos Aggressor** (c/o Aggressor Fleet, ☎ 504/385–2628 or 800/348–2628, FAX 504/384–0817).

### BY PLANE

**American Airlines** (☎ 800/433–7300) flies daily between Miami and Provo. **Turks & Caicos Islands Airlines** (☎ 809/94–64255) is the only regularly scheduled carrier that flies between Provo, Grand Turk, and other outer Turks and Caicos islands. Many air charter services also connect the islands (☞ Guided Tours, *below*).

### FROM THE AIRPORT

Taxis are available at the airports; expect to share a ride. Rates are fixed. A trip between Provo's airport and most major hotels runs about $15. On Grand Turk, a trip from the airport to town is about $5; from the airport to hotels outside town, $6–$11.

## Currency

The unit of currency is U.S. dollars.

## Emergencies

**Police:** Grand Turk, ☎ 809/94–62299; Providenciales, ☎ 809/94–64259; North Caicos, ☎ 809/94–67116; South Caicos, ☎ 809/94–63299. **Hospitals:** There is a 24-hour emergency room at **Grand Turk Hospital** (⊠ Hospital Rd., ☎ 809/94–62333) and at **Providenciales Health-Medical Center** (⊠ Leeward Hwy., ☎ 809/94–64201). **Pharmacies:** Prescriptions can be filled at the **Government Clinic** (⊠ Grand Turk Hospital, ☎ 809/94–62040) and at the **Providenciales Health-Medical Center** in Provo (⊠ Leeward Hwy., ☎ 809/94–64201).

## Getting Around

### BUSES

On Provo, shuttle buses operated by **Executive Tours** (☎ 809/94–64524) run from the hotels into town every hour, Monday through Saturday 9 AM–6 PM. Fares are $2 each way. A new public bus system on Grand Turk charges 50¢ one-way to any scheduled stop.

### CAR RENTALS

Local rental agencies on Provo are **Turks & Caicos National** (☎ 809/94–64701), **Provo Rent-A-Car** (☎ 809/94–64404), **Rent A Buggy** (☎ 809/94–64158), and **Turquoise Jeep Rentals** (☎ 809/94–64910); on Grand Turk, **Dutchie's Car Rental** (☎ 809/94–62244). Rates average $40 to $65 per day, plus a $10-per-rental-agreement government tax. To rent cars on South Caicos, check with your hotel manager for rates and information.

### FERRIES

Ferries are available between some islands; check with local marinas. The only government ferry (no phone) runs between Grand Turk and Salt Cay.

### SCOOTERS

You can scoot around Provo by contacting **Scooter Bob's** (☎ 809/94–64684) or the **Honda Shop** (☎ 809/94–64397). On Grand Turk, contact **Kittina Scooter Rental** (☎ 809/94–62232). On North Caicos, contact **North Caicos Scooter Rentals** (☎ 809/94–67301). Rates generally start at $25 per day for a one-seater and $40 a day for a two-seater, plus a one-time $5 government tax, plus gas.

TAXIS

Taxis are unmetered, and rates, posted in the taxis, are regulated by the government. In Provo, call the Provo taxi association (☎ 809/94–65481).

## Guided Tours

A **taxi** tour of the islands costs between $25 and $30 for the first hour and $25 for each additional hour. On Provo, contact **Paradise Taxi Company** (☎ 809/94–13555). **Turtle Tours** (☎ 809/94–65585) offers a variety of bus and small-plane tours. You can also fly to Middle Caicos, the largest of the islands, for a visit to its mysterious caves or to North Caicos to see the ruins of a former slave plantation. If you want to island hop on your own schedule, air charters are available through **Blue Hills Aviation** (☎ 809/94–15290), **Flamingo Air Services** (☎ 809/94–62109 or 809/94–64933), and **SkyKing** (☎ 809/94–15464).

## Language

The official language of the Turks and Caicos is English.

## Opening and Closing Times

Most offices are open weekdays from 8 or 8:30 till 4 or 4:30. Banks are open Monday–Thursday 8:30–2:30, Friday 8:30–12:30 and 2:30–4:30.

## Passports and Visas

U.S. citizens need some proof of citizenship, such as a birth certificate (original or certified copy), plus a photo ID or a current passport. British subjects must have a current passport. All visitors must have an ongoing or return ticket.

## Precautions

Petty crime does occur here, and you're advised to leave your valuables in the hotel safe-deposit box. Bring along a can of insect repellent: The mosquitoes and no-see-ums can be vicious.

If you plan to explore the uninhabited island of West Caicos, be advised that the interior is overgrown with dense shrubs that include manchineel, which has a milky, poisonous sap that can cause painful, scarring blisters.

In some hotels on Grand Turk, Salt Cay, and South Caicos, there are signs that read, "Please help us conserve our precious water." These islands have no freshwater supply other than rainwater collected in cisterns, and rainfall is scant. Drink only from the decanter of fresh water your hotel provides; tap water is safe for brushing your teeth or other hygiene uses.

## Taxes and Service Charges

Most hotels collect a 7%–8% government tax; all add a 10%–15% service charge to your bill. Restaurants collect a 7% government tax and add a 10% service charge to your bill. Taxi drivers expect a token tip. The departure tax is $15.

## Telephones and Mail

You can call the islands direct from the United States by dialing 809 and the number. To call home from Turks and Caicos, dial direct from most hotels, from some pay phones, and from **Cable and Wireless,** which has offices in Provo (☎ 809/94–64499) and Grand Turk (☎ 809/94–62200), open Monday–Thursday 8–4:30 and Friday 8–4. You must dial 0, followed by the country code (1 for U.S. and Canada; 44 for U.K.), area code, and local number.

Postal rates for letters to the United States, Bahamas, and Caribbean
are 50¢ per half ounce; postcards, 35¢. Letters to the United Kingdom
and Europe, 65¢ per half ounce; postcards, 45¢. Letters to Canada,
Puerto Rico, and South America, 65¢; postcards, 45¢.

## Visitor Information

For tourist information, contact the **Turks and Caicos Islands Tourist
Board** (☎ 800/241–0824). The **Caribbean Tourism Organization** (⊠
20 E. 46th St., New York, NY 10017, ☎ 212/682–0435) is another
source of information. In the United Kingdom, contact **Morris-Kevan
International Ltd.** (⊠ International House, 47 Chase Side, Enfield Middlesex EN2 6NB, ☎ 0181/367–5175).

On Grand Turk, the **Government Tourist Office** (⊠ Front St., Cock-
burn Town, Grand Turk, ☎ 809/94–62321; ⊠ Turtle Cove Landing,
Provo, ☎ 809/94–64970) is open Monday–Thursday 8–4:30 and
Friday 8–5.

# 27 The U.S. Virgin Islands

*St. Thomas, St. Croix, St. John*

Updated by
Lynda Lohr

T IS THE COMBINATION of the familiar and the exotic in the U.S. Virgin Islands that defines this "American Paradise" and explains much of its appeal. The effort to be all things to all people—while remaining true to the best of itself—has created a sometimes paradoxical blend of island serenity and American practicality in this U.S. territory 1,000 miles from the southern tip of the U.S. mainland.

The postcard images you'd expect from a tropical paradise are here: Stretches of beach arc into the distance and white sails skim across water so blue and clear it stuns the senses; red-roof houses add their spot of color to the green hillsides' mosaic, along with the orange of the flamboyant tree, the red of the hibiscus, the magenta of the bougainvillea, and the blue stone ruins of old sugar mills; and towns of pastel-tone European-style villas, decorated by filigree wrought-iron terraces, line narrow streets climbing up from a harbor.

Those images remain despite the arrival of Hurricane Marilyn in September 1995. Mother Nature bounced quickly back, filling the hillsides with explosions of green. Repairs to the infrastructure have been a bit slower, but should be back in good order by the end of 1996.

The other part of the equation are all those things that make it so easy and appealing for Americans to visit this cluster of islands. The official language is English, the money is the dollar, and the U.S. government runs things. There's cable TV, Pizza Hut, and McDonald's. There's unfettered immigration to and from the mainland, and investments are protected by the U.S. flag. Visitors to the U.S.V.I. have the opportunity to delve into a "foreign" culture while anchored by familiar language and landmarks.

Your destination here will be St. Thomas (13 miles long); its neighbor St. John (9 miles long); or, 40 miles to the south, St. Croix (23 miles long). A pro/con thumbnail sketch of these three might have it that St. Thomas is bustling (hustling), the place for shopping and nightlife (commercial glitz and overdevelopment); St. Croix is more Danish, picturesque, and rural (more provincial and duller, particularly after dark); and St. John is matchless in the beauty of its National Park Service—protected land and beaches (a one-town island mostly for villa vacationers or campers). Surely not everything will suit your fancy, but chances are that among the three islands you'll find your own idea of paradise.

## Lodging

The U.S.V.I. has lodging options to suit any style, from luxury five-star resorts to casual condominiums and national-park campgrounds.

On St. Thomas, guest houses and smaller hotels are not typically on the beach, but they offer pools and shuttle service to nearby beaches (St. Thomas is not a walking island), and the several historic inns above town have a pleasing island ambience. In keeping with its small-town atmosphere and more relaxed pace, St. Croix offers a good variety of more moderately priced small hotels and guest houses, which are either on the beach or in a rural setting where a walk to the beach is easy. Accommodations on St. John defy easy categorization. The national-park and private campground sites start bare and progress through standing tents, tent cabins, and small cottages. At the other end of the spectrum are luxury retreats of understated elegance that offer rest and relaxation of a high—and pricey—order.

The prices below reflect rates during high season, which generally runs from December 15 to April 15. Rates are 25% to 50% lower the rest of the year.

| CATEGORY | COST* |
|----------|-------|
| $$$$ | over $200 |
| $$$ | $150–$200 |
| $$ | $100–$150 |
| $ | under $100 |

*All prices are for a standard double room, excluding 8% accommodations tax.*

## St. Thomas

**$$$$**   🏨 **Bolongo Inclusive Beach Resort.** This 77-room beachfront resort also includes the 40-room Bolongo Villas next door and the six-room Bolongo Inn across the street. Hit hard by Hurricane Marilyn, it recovered quickly. All resort rooms have efficiency kitchens and balconies, and are just steps from a strand of white beach. The oceanfront villas feature minisuites, and one-, two-, and three-bedroom units with full kitchens and large balconies, right on the ocean, with beautiful views. The inn's rooms are air-conditioned with private baths. The resort offers a choice of all-inclusive or semi-inclusive plans, which means you'll pay less if you want fewer activities. ✉ *50 Estate Bolongo, 00802,* ☎ *809/775–1800 or 800/524–4746,* FAX *809/775–3208. 123 units, from hotel rooms to 1- to 3-bedroom villas. 2 restaurants, 3 pools, 3 tennis courts, health club, shuffleboard, volleyball, beach, nightclub. AE, D, DC, MC, V.*

**$$$$**   🏨 **Grand Palazzo.** Hurricane Marilyn closed this luxury resort, but it's
★   scheduled to reopen in September 1996. This premier luxury resort resembles a villa in Venice and offers stunning ocean views through the lobby's French doors. Guest rooms, in six buildings that fan out from the main villa, are spacious and so luxuriously furnished with European fabrics, they just might tempt you to stay inside. When you do venture out, you'll find elegance everywhere, from the beautiful pool to the gourmet restaurant and the casual alfresco lunch area. A multilingual staff, classical music, and 24-hour room service add to the sophisticated atmosphere. ✉ *Great Bay Estate, 00802,* ☎ *809/775–3333 or 800/545–0509,* FAX *809/775–4444. 152 rooms. 2 restaurants, 3 bars, pool, 4 tennis courts, health club, beach. AE, D, DC, MC, V.*

**$$$$**   🏨 **Marriott's Frenchman's Reef and Morning Star Beach Resorts.**
★   Sprawling, luxurious, and on a prime harbor promontory east of Charlotte Amalie like a permanently anchored cruise ship, these two resorts are St. Thomas's full-service American superhotels. All rooms are spacious and furnished with contemporary furniture in soft pastels. Many Frenchman's Reef rooms have glorious ocean and harbor views, but a few look out over the parking lot. Morning Star rooms are more luxurious, in buildings tucked among the foliage that stretches along the fine white sand of Morningstar Beach; the sound of the surf can lull you to sleep. In addition to enjoying various snack and sandwich stops and a raw bar, you can dine alfresco on American or gourmet Caribbean fare, or oceanfront at the Tavern on the Beach. There's also a lavish buffet served overlooking the sparkling lights of Charlotte Amalie and the harbor. Live entertainment and disco, scheduled activities for all ages, branches of several duty-free shops, and a shuttle boat to town make having fun easy. This is a property you don't have to leave. ✉ *Box 7100, 00801,* ☎ *809/776–8500 or 800/524–2000,* FAX *809/776–3054. 517 rooms, 18 suites. 6 restaurants, 6 bars, 2 snack bars, 2 pools, 4 tennis courts, beach, tours. AE, D, DC, MC, V.*

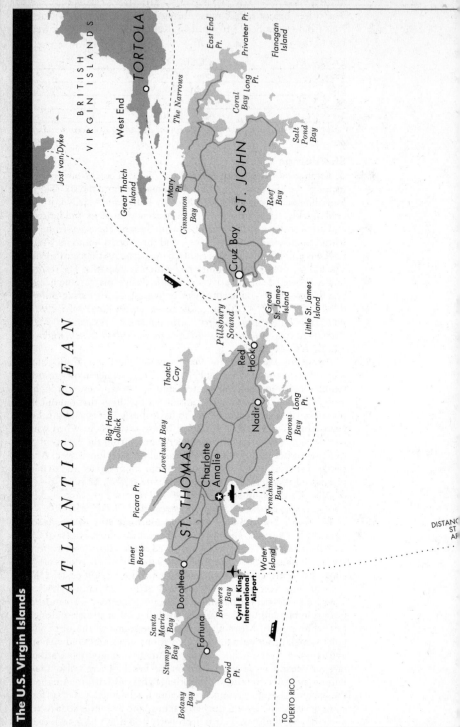

**The U.S. Virgin Islands**

ATLANTIC OCEAN

BRITISH VIRGIN ISLANDS

TORTOLA

Jost van Dyke

West End

Great Thatch Island

The Narrows

East End Pt.

Privateer Pt.

Flanagan Island

Coral Bay Long Pt.

ST. JOHN

Salt Pond Bay

Mary Pt.

Cinnamon Bay

Cruz Bay

Reef Bay

Pillsbury Sound

Great St. James Island

Little St. James Island

Thatch Cay

Red Hook

Big Hans Lollick

Loveland Bay

Nadir

Bovoni Bay Long Pt.

Inner Brass

Picara Pt.

ST. THOMAS

Charlotte Amalie

Frenchman Bay

Santa Maria Bay

Dorothea

Water Island

Stumpy Bay

Fortuna

Brewers Bay

Cyril E. King International Airport

DISTANC
ST
AF

David Pt.

Botany Bay

TO PUERTO RICO

## St. Thomas

Outer Brass

Picara Pt.

Inner Brass

Tropaco Pt.

Vluck Pt.

Magens Bay

Hull Bay

Stumpy Pt.

Santa Maria Bay

Magens Bay

Stumpy Bay

Crown Mt.

9 7

Target Pt.

Bordeaux Bay

Dorthea

Signal Hill

8

West Cay

Botany Bay

Fortuna Hill

Brewers Beach

Contant 34

Frenchtown

Fortuna

10

Barents Bay

Perseverance Bay

Brewers Bay

Cyril E. King International Airport

Altona 35 36 37

St. T Har

Fortuna Bay

David Pt.

Red Pt.

Crown Bay

Hassel Island

Lindbergh Beach

Water Island

Limestone Bay

Caribbean Sea

TO PUERTO RICO

TO ST. CROIX

**Exploring**
Charlotte Amalie, **1**
Clinton Phipps Racetrack, **3**
Coral World at Coki Point, **5**
Drake's Seat, **7**
Estate St. Peter Greathouse Botanical Gardens, **8**
Havensight Mall, **2**
Mountain Top, **9**
Red Hook, **4**
Reichhold Center for the Arts, **10**
Tillett Gardens, **6**

**Dining**
Alexander's Cafe, **36**
Blackbeard's Castle, **16**
Blue Marlin, **23**
Chart House, **37**
Entre Nous, **14**
Eunice's Terrace, **31**
Hard Rock Café, **19**
Hotel 1829, **12**
Il Cappucino, **20**
Little Bopeep, **15**
Romanos, **32**

Tickles Dockside Pub, **25**
Virgilio's, **13**
Zorba's Cafe, **17**

**Lodging**
Admiral's Inn, **35**
Blackbeard's Castle, **16**
Bolongo Inclusive Beach Resort, **22**
Grand Palazzo, **24**
Hotel 1829, **12**
Island View Guest House, **34**
Marriott's Frenchman's Reef and Morning Star Beach Resorts, **21**

## St. Croix

TO
ST. THOMAS

Hams
Bluff

Davis
Bay

Cane Bay

Salt
River
Bay

Hams Bay

Mt. Eagle

80

La
R

**4**

Annaly

**21**

Blue Mt.

75

Northside Rd.

**19**

**18**

**22** Rain
Forest

Mahogany Rd.

**5**

63

**6**

St. George
Hill

Northside Rd.

Sunny
Isle

Christia

**2**

Frederiksted

**7**

Kingshill

**23** **24** **25**

Centerline Rd.

70

64

**8**

West End
Salt Pond

Alexander Hamilton
Airport

Sandy
Point

66

Melvin H. Evans Hwy.

Krause
Pt.

Cane
Bay

Long Pt.
Bay

Long Pt.

### KEY

Cruise Ship

**1** Exploring Sites

**9** Hotels and Restaurants

*Caribbean Sea*

**Exploring**
Cane Bay, **3**
Christiansted, **1**
Estate Mount
Washington
Plantation, **4**
Fredriksted, **7**
Judith's Fancy, **2**
Mt. Pellier Domino
Club, **5**
St. Croix Leap, **6**
St. George Village
Botanical Gardens, **8**

**Dining**
Blue Moon, **23**
Camille's, **10**
Great House at Villa
Madeleine, **16**
Harvey's, **14**
Kendricks, **13**
Le St. Tropez, **26**
Top Hat, **11**

**Lodging**
Buccaneer, **15**
Club St. Croix, **17**
Cormorant Beach
Club and Villas, **18**
The Frederiksted, **24**
Hibiscus Beach
Hotel, **19**
Hotel Caravelle, **9**
Pink Fancy, **12**
Sprat Hall, **22**
Villa Madeleine, **16**
Waves at Cane
Bay, **20**
Westin Carambola
Beach Resort, **21**

Buck Island

Buck Island Beach

Long Reef

Christiansted Harbor

Green Cay

Pull Pt.

Coakley Bay

Teague Bay

Cramer Park

Cottongarden Pt.

Tamarind Reef Beach

19
18
e Rd.
17
9
14

15

East End Rd.

82

Reef Beach

Sugarloaf Hill

Pt. Udall (East Pt.)

Gallow's Bay

16

Isaac Bay

Grapetree Bay

isti̇ansted

1

Recovery Hill

Prospect Hill

South Side Rd.

Grass Pt.

Robin Bay

62

Great Pond Bay

South Side Rd.

Milord Pt.

Manchenil Bay

Canegarden Bay

60

N

0                    2 miles
0                    3 km

# St. John

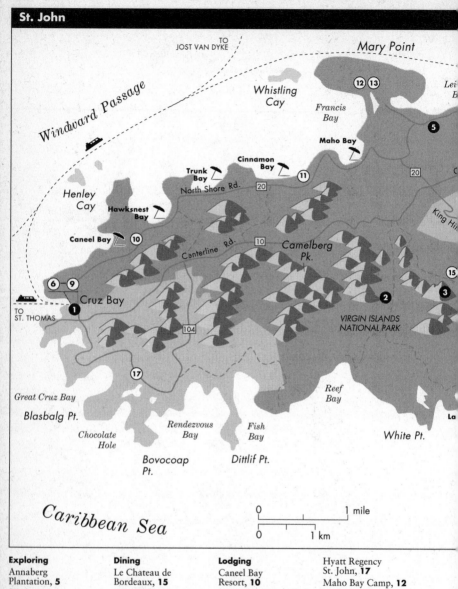

TO JOST VAN DYKE

Mary Point

Windward Passage

Whistling Cay

Francis Bay

Lei B

⑫ ⑬

⑤

Maho Bay

Henley Cay

Cinnamon Bay

Trunk Bay

⑪

North Shore Rd.  20

Hawksnest Bay

20

King Hil

Caneel Bay  ⑩

Canterline Rd.  10

Camelberg Pk.

⑮

⑥ ⑨

Cruz Bay

②

③

①

VIRGIN ISLANDS NATIONAL PARK

TO ST. THOMAS

104

⑰

Great Cruz Bay

Reef Bay

Blasbalg Pt.

Chocolate Hole

Rendezvous Bay

Fish Bay

White Pt.

La

Bovocoap Pt.

Dittlif Pt.

Caribbean Sea

0 ——— 1 mile
0 ——— 1 km

**Exploring**
Annaberg Plantation, **5**
Bordeaux Mountain, **3**
Coral Bay, **4**
Cruz Bay, **1**
Reef Bay Trail **2**

**Dining**
Le Chateau de Bordeaux, **15**
Ciao Mein, **17**
Ellington's, **8**
Fish Trap, **6**
Paradiso, **7**
Shipwreck Landing, **14**

**Lodging**
Caneel Bay Resort, **10**
Cinnamon Bay Campground, **11**
Estate Concordia, **16**
Gallows Point Suite Resort, **8**
Harmony, **13**

Hyatt Regency St. John, **17**
Maho Bay Camp, **12**
Raintree Inn, **9**

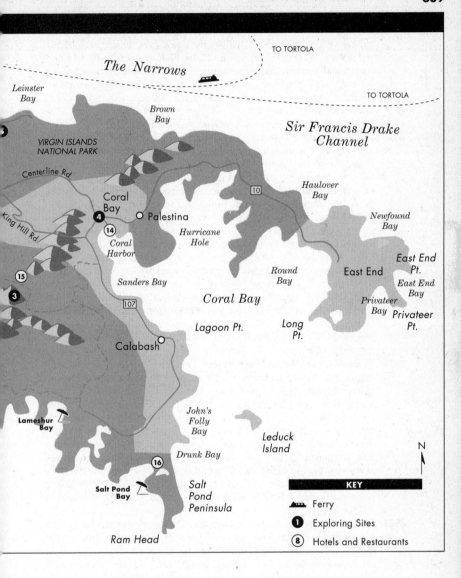

The Narrows

TO TORTOLA

TO TORTOLA

Leinster
Bay

Brown
Bay

Sir Francis Drake
Channel

VIRGIN ISLANDS
NATIONAL PARK

Centerline Rd

Coral
Bay

**4**

**14**

Coral
Harbor

Palestina

Hurricane
Hole

Haulover
Bay

Newfound
Bay

10

King Hill Rd

**15**

**3**

Sanders Bay

107

Round
Bay

East End

East End
Pt.

East End
Bay

Coral Bay

Privateer
Bay

Privateer
Pt.

Lagoon Pt.

Long
Pt.

Calabash

Lameshur
Bay

John's
Folly
Bay

Drunk Bay

Leduck
Island

N

**16**

Salt Pond
Bay

Salt
Pond
Peninsula

Ram Head

**KEY**

Ferry

**1** Exploring Sites

**8** Hotels and Restaurants

$$$$   ☒ **Pavilions & Pools.** This small hotel will be closed until December
★      1996, thanks to Hurricane Marilyn. When it reopens, simple, tropi-
       cal-cool decor and privacy will set the mood here, where each island-
       style room has its own very private 22-by-14-foot or 18-by-16-foot pool
       and a small sunning deck. The unpretentious accommodations include
       air-conditioning, telephones, full kitchens, and VCRs. Water sports are
       available at Sapphire Beach on the adjacent property. ☒ *6400 Estate
       Smith Bay, 00802,* ☎ *809/775–6110 or 800/524–2001,* FAX *809/775–
       6110. 25 rooms. Restaurant, private pools. AE, MC, V.*

$$$$   ☒ **Point Pleasant Resort.** Expect to find lovingly preserved natural veg-
★      etation and a wonderful nature trail when this resort finishes Hurri-
       cane Marilyn repairs in October 1996. Stretching up a steep, tree-filled
       hill from Smith Bay, affording a great view of St. John and Drake's Pas-
       sage to the east and north, this resort offers a range of accommoda-
       tions, from simple bedrooms to multiroom suites. Units are in a number
       of buildings hidden among the trees, and all have striking views. The
       air-conditioned rooms have balconies, and all rooms have kitchens. Three
       appealing, nice-size pools surrounded by decks are placed at different
       levels on the hillside. Although there are water sports here, the "beach"
       is almost nonexistent; guests are granted beach privileges at next door's
       Renaissance Grand Beach Resort, a one-minute walk away. Every
       guest gets four hours' free use of a car daily. (You need only pay the
       $9.50 per day insurance cost.) ☒ *6600 Estate Smith Bay, No. 4,
       00802,* ☎ *809/775–7200 or 800/524–2300,* FAX *809/776–5694. 134
       rooms. 2 restaurants, bar, 3 pools, tennis court, exercise room, beach.
       AE, D, MC, V.*

$$$$   ☒ **Renaissance Grand Beach Resort.** This resort's zigzag architectural
       angles spell luxury, from the marble atrium lobby to the one-bedroom
       suites with private whirlpool baths. The beach is excellent, and there's
       a fitness center with Nautilus machines. The lobby is often populated
       by those lucky business types whose companies favor the resort as a
       convention-and-conference center. Daily organized activities for chil-
       dren include iguana hunts, T-shirt painting, and sand-castle building.
       This tends to be a very busy hotel, with lots of people in the restau-
       rants and on the beach. ☒ *Smith Bay Rd., Box 8267, 00801,* ☎
       *809/775–1510 or 800/322–2976,* FAX *809/775–3757. 297 rooms. 2
       restaurants, snack bar, 2 pools, 6 tennis courts, beach, fitness center.
       AE, D, DC, MC, V.*

$$$$   ☒ **Sapphire Beach Resort and Marina.** On a clear day the lush green
★      mountains of the neighboring B.V.I. seem close enough to touch from
       this resort on one of St. Thomas's prettiest beaches. There's excellent
       snorkeling on the reefs to each side of the beach. This is a quiet retreat
       where you can nap while swinging in one of the hammocks strung be-
       tween the palm trees in your front yard; but on Sunday the place rocks
       with a beach party. All units have fully equipped kitchens, air-condi-
       tioning, telephones, and satellite TV. Children are welcome and may
       join the Little Gems Kids Klub. Children under age 12 sleep in their
       parents' accommodations at no extra charge and eat free (when with
       their parents) at the Seagrape Restaurant. ☒ *Box 8088, 00801,* ☎
       *809/775–6100 or 800/524–2090,* FAX *809/775–4024. 171 rooms. 3
       restaurants, 2 bars, 4 tennis courts, beach. AE, MC, V.*

$$$$   ☒ **Wyndham Sugar Bay Plantation Resort.** From afar, this large clus-
       ter of bulky white buildings looks rather overwhelming, but the hotel
       has lots to offer. Most rooms overlook water and some have great views

of the British Virgin Islands. All units have balconies and are spacious and comfortable, with contemporary furnishings and such amenities as hair dryers and coffeemakers. The beach is small for a property of this size, but there's a giant pool with waterfalls, all manner of water sports, tennis courts and a tennis stadium, and plenty of other diversions for people of all ages. Children under 19 stay free in the same room as their parents. ⊠ *6500 Estate Smith Bay, 00802,* ☎ *809/777–7100 or 800/927–7100,* FAX *809/777–7200. 300 rooms. Restaurant, bar, 3 pools, 2 tennis courts, health club, beach, snorkeling. AE, D, DC, MC, V.*

**$–$$$$** 🏨 **Hotel 1829.** This historic Spanish-style inn is popular with visiting
★ government officials and people with business at Government House down the street. It's on Government Hill, just at the edge of Charlotte Amalie's shopping area. Rooms, on several levels (no elevator), range from elegant and roomy to quite small but are priced accordingly, so there's one for every budget. Author Graham Greene is said to have stayed here, and it's easy to imagine him musing over a drink in the small, dark bar. The gourmet terrace restaurant (☞ Dining, *below*) is a romantic spot for dinner. The rooms have refrigerators, TVs, and air-conditioning. There's a tiny, tiny pool for cooling off. ⊠ *Box 1567, 00801,* ☎ *809/776–1829 or 800/524–2002,* FAX *809/776–4313. 15 rooms. Restaurant, bar, pool. AE, D, MC, V.*

**$$$** 🏨 **Blackbeard's Castle.** This small and very popular hillside inn is laid out around a tower from which, it's said, Blackbeard kept watch for invaders on the horizon. It's an elegantly informal kind of place, where guests while away Sunday morning with the *New York Times.* Stunning views (especially at sunset) of the harbor and Charlotte Amalie can be had from the gourmet restaurant (☞ Dining, *below*), the large freshwater pool, and the outdoor terrace, where locals come for cocktails. Charlotte Amalie is a short walk down the hill, and beaches are a short taxi ride away. Rates include Continental breakfast. ⊠ *Box 6041, 00804,* ☎ *809/776–1234 or 800/344–5771,* FAX *809/776–4321. 20 rooms. Restaurant, bar, pool. AE, D, DC, MC, V.*

**$$** 🏨 **Sign of the Griffin.** If it's a house party you have in mind, you might want to consider these privately owned, furnished one- and two-bedroom homes with great views on a hillside 500 feet above Tutu Bay. Each house has a fully equipped kitchen, telephone, private garden, and covered terrace. You'll need a car to get around from here. Maid service is provided weekdays, and for stays of three weeks or more, you'll receive a 10% discount. ⊠ *Box 11668, 00801,* ☎ *809/775–1715. 5 houses. No credit cards.*

**$$** 🏨 **Villa Blanca Hotel.** Above Charlotte Amalie on Raphune Hill is this secluded hotel, surrounded by an attractive garden and with modern, balconied rooms with rattan furniture, kitchenettes, cable TVs, and ceiling fans (six have air-conditioning). All the rooms have eastern views of Charlotte Amalie's harbor as well as partial westerly views of Drake's Channel and the B.V.I. ⊠ *Box 7505, 00801,* ☎ *809/776–0749 or 800/231–0034,* FAX *809/779–2661. 14 rooms. Pool. AE, D, DC, MC, V.*

**$$** 🏨 **Villa Santana.** Built by General Santa Anna of Mexico circa 1857,
★ the villa still provides a panoramic view of the Charlotte Amalie harbor along with plenty of age-old West Indian charm. This St. Thomas landmark, close to town, has villa-style rooms. Dark wicker furniture, white plaster and stone walls, shuttered windows, cathedral ceilings, and interesting nooks contribute to the feeling of romance and history. Villas La Torre and La Mansion are split-level with spiral staircases, and all units have full kitchens and either four-poster or cradle beds. Rooms are kept cool by ceiling fans and natural trade winds and do

not have telephones. ✉ *Denmark Hill, 00802,* ☎ 𝔽𝔸𝕏 *809/776–1311. 5 rooms. Pool. AE.*

**$**   🏨 **Admiral's Inn.** This charming inn stretches down a hillside on the point of land known as Frenchtown, just west of Charlotte Amalie. All rooms have wonderful views of either the town and the harbor or the ocean; the four ocean-view rooms have private balconies and refrigerators. All units have rattan furniture; cream- or teal-color bedspreads, vertical blinds; coral, teal, and cream carpeting; and large, tiled vanity areas. The rocky shoreline is perfect for snorkeling. The inn's man-made pool is surrounded by a large wooden deck; there's bar service, and Continental breakfast is included. ✉ *Villa Olga, 00802,* ☎ *809/774–1376 or 800/544–0493,* 𝔽𝔸𝕏 *809/774–8010. 13 rooms. Restaurant, bar, pool. AE, D, MC, V.*

**$**   🏨 **Island View Guest House.** This clean, simply furnished guest house rests amid tropical foliage on the south face of 1,500-foot Crown Mountain, the highest point on St. Thomas. As a result it has one of the most sweeping views of Charlotte Amalie harbor available from its pool and shaded terrace, where complimentary breakfast is served. All rooms have some view of the water, but on the balconies of the six newer rooms (all with air-conditioning and a ceiling fan), perched on the very edge of the hill, you feel suspended in midair. ✉ *Box 1903, 00801,* ☎ *809/774–4270 or 800/524–2023,* 𝔽𝔸𝕏 *809/774–6167. 13 rooms with bath, 2 rooms share bath. Pool. AE, MC, V.*

## St. Croix

**$$$$**   🏨 **Buccaneer.** If you want a self-contained tropical beach resort, this
★    300-acre property is the place for you. A palm tree–lined main drive leads to the large pink hotel at the top of a hill, and a number of smaller guest cottages, shops, and restaurants are scattered throughout the property's rolling, manicured lawns. Stroll through the elegant lobby, with its green-and-white marble checkerboard floor, into the open-air terrace, where guests can relax and take in the view. Most of the guest rooms in this former sugar plantation have been renovated to incorporate eye-catching marble or colorful tile floors; four-poster beds and massive wardrobes of pale wood, pastel fabrics, and locally produced artwork, along with such modern conveniences as refrigerators and cable TVs, are the furnishings. Spacious bathrooms are noteworthy for their marble bench showers and double sinks. ✉ *Box 25200, Gallows Bay 00824,* ☎ *809/773–2100 or 800/225–3881. 150 rooms. 4 restaurants, in-room safes, 2 pools, spa, golf, 8 tennis courts, water sports center, jogging, 3 beaches. AE, D, DC, MC, V.*

**$$$$**   🏨 **Cormorant Beach Club and Villas.** Breeze-bent palm trees, hammocks, the thrum of North Shore waves, and a blissful sense of respected privacy rule here. The open-air public spaces are filled with tropical plants and comfy wicker furniture in cool peach and mint-green shades. Ceiling fans and tile floors add to the atmosphere at this top-shelf resort, which resembles a series of connected Moorish villas. The beachfront rooms are lovely, with dark wicker furniture, pale-peach walls, white-tile floors, and floral-print spreads and curtains; all rooms have a patio or balcony and telephone, cable TV, and electronic safes. Bathrooms stand out for their coral rock–wall showers, marble-top double sinks, and brass fixtures. Morning coffee and afternoon tea are set out daily in the building breezeways. The airy, high-ceiling restaurant is one of St. Croix's best. The hotel offers a variety of meal plans including an all-inclusive package with free drinks. ✉ *4126 La Grande Princesse, Christiansted 00820,* ☎ *809/778–8920 or 800/548–4460,* 𝔽𝔸𝕏 *809/778–9218. 34 rooms, 4 suites, 14 2- and 3-bedroom villas. Restaurant, bar, pool, 2 tennis courts, croquet, beach, snorkeling. AE, DC, MC, V.*

**$$$$**   ⊞ **Villa Madeleine.** Since this exquisite hotel opened in 1990 it has earned
★   a reputation as one of St. Croix's best. The main building was patterned
after a turn-of-the-century West Indian plantation great house. Richly
upholstered furniture, Oriental rugs, teal walls, and whimsically painted
driftwood set the mood in the billiards room, in the austere library and
sitting room, and at Cafe Madeleine, the resort's highly praised Continental restaurant; all are straight from the pages of *Architectural Digest*. The great house sits atop a hill, on which private guest villas are
scattered in both directions, affording views of the north and south
shores. The villas' decor is modern tropical, with rattan and plush cushions, and many bedrooms have bamboo four-poster beds. Each villa
has a full kitchen and a private swimming pool. Special touches in the
rooms include pink-marble showers and, in many cottages, hand-
painted floral borders along the walls, done in splashy tropical colors.
⊠ *Box 3109, 00822,* ☎ *809/778–7377 or 800/548–4461,* FAX *809/773–
7518. 43 villas. Restaurant, bar, private pools, tennis court, billiards,
library, concierge. AE, D, DC, MC, V.*

**$$$$**   ⊞ **Westin Carambola Beach Resort.** The 26 quaint, two-story red-
★   roof villas, including one that's wheelchair accessible, are connected
by lovely arcades hacked from the luxuriant undergrowth. The rooms
are identical; the only difference is the view—ocean or garden. Decor
is Laura Ashley–style English country house, with rocking chairs and
sofas upholstered in soothing floral patterns, terra-cotta floors, rough-
textured ceramic lamps, and mahogany ceilings and furnishings. All
have private patios and huge baths (showers only). The two-bedroom
suite, with its 3-foot-thick plantation walls and large patio, is the *perfect* Caribbean family dwelling. There are two fine restaurants (the Sunday buffet brunch is legendary for its munificent table), an exquisite
ecru beach, and lots of quiet nooks for a secluded drink. ⊠ *Box 3031,
Kingshill,* ☎ *809/778–3800 or 800/228–3000,* FAX *809/778–1682. 151
rooms, 2-bedroom cottage. 2 restaurants, deli, pool, 4 tennis courts,
library. AE, D, DC, MC, V.*

**$$–$$$**   ⊞ **Sprat Hall.** This 20-acre seaside Frederiksted property is a restored
1670 plantation estate, the oldest in the U.S.V.I. The homey, antiques-
filled great house (no smoking, please) has guest rooms that hark back
to more genteel days, with high-standing four-poster beds, antique furniture, bowls of fresh-cut bougainvillea and ginger thomas. Rooms and
cottages are spread out all over the estate. The two family cottages are
rather dingy and not in the same class as the great-house rooms. One
of the great-house rooms has air-conditioning. There are extensive horseback riding facilities here, and a complimentary Continental breakfast
is served daily. ⊠ *Box 695, Frederiksted 00841,* ☎ *809/772–0305. 9
rooms, 8 suites, 1 1-bedroom cottage, 2 2-bedroom cottages. Restaurant, horseback riding, beach. AE.*

**$$–$$$**   ⊞ **Waves at Cane Bay.** Owners Kevin and Suzanne Ryan have done
★   wonders with this 25-year-old property since purchasing it in 1989.
The two peach-and-mint-green buildings house enormous, balconied
guest rooms done in cream and soft pastel prints, all with kitchens or
kitchenettes; although, there's also the option, on Tuesday through Saturday, of dining in the restaurant. The small inn caters to couples and
to divers who take advantage of the fine reef located just offshore. The
hotel is rather isolated, and its beachfront is rocky, but Cane Bay
Beach is right next door and there is a small patch of sand at poolside
for sunbathing. The pool itself is unusual, having been carved from the
coral along the shore: The floor and one wall are concrete, but the seaside wall is made of natural coral, and the pool water is circulated as
the waves crash dramatically over the side, creating a foamy whirlpool
on blustery days. ⊠ *Box 1749, Kings Hill 00851,* ☎ *809/778–1805*

*or 800/545–0603. 12 rooms, 8 with air-conditioning, 1 suite. Restaurant, bar, in-room safes, pool, snorkeling. AE, MC, V.*

**$$** 🏨 **Club St. Croix.** Popular with honeymooners, this condominium resort's studio, one-, and two-bedroom apartments are spacious and bright. Indian-print throw rugs and cushions complement the bamboo furniture and rough, white-tile floors; the modern decor is further highlighted by glass-top tables and mirrored closet doors. Penthouses have loft bedrooms reached by spiral staircases, and studios enlist Murphy beds in the sitting rooms. Every room has a full kitchen and a sundeck, with waterfront views of Christiansted and Buck Island. On the beach you'll find a poolside restaurant and bar and a dock. Although the rooms are well kept, more thorough attention would benefit the grounds. ✉ *Estate Golden Rock, Christiansted 00820,* ☎ *809/773–4800 or 800/524–2025,* 🖷 *809/778–4009. 54 rooms. Water sports. AE, D, MC, V. EP.*

**$$** 🏨 **Hibiscus Beach Hotel.** This affordable, appealing property is set on the same stretch of palm tree–lined beach as its sister hotel, the Cormorant. Guest rooms at the Hibiscus Beach are divided among five two-story pink buildings, each named for a tropical flower. Most have views of the oceanfront, thanks to the staggered placement of the buildings at strategic angles, but request a room in the Hibiscus building—it's closest to the water. Rooms have welcome amenities such as cable TV, safe, and minibar, and are tastefully furnished: White tiled floors and white walls are brightened with pink-striped curtains; bright, flowered bedspreads; and fresh-cut hibiscus blossoms. Bathrooms are clean but nondescript—both the shower stalls and the vanity mirrors are on the small side. Every unit has a roomy balcony that faces the sea. The staff is friendly and helpful, and the manager's party in the open-air bar-restaurant is a pleasant gathering. ✉ *Box 4131, La Grande Princesse 00820-4441,* ☎ *809/773–4042,* 🖷 *809/773–7668. 37 rooms. Restaurant, minibar, in-room safes, pool, snorkeling. AE, D, MC, V.*

**$$** 🏨 **Hotel Caravelle.** The charming three-story Caravelle is an excellent bet for moderately priced lodging in Christiansted. All rooms have refrigerators, television, and telephones. They're decorated in tasteful dusky blues and whites, with floral-print bedspreads and curtains as well as vaulted ceilings. Baths are clean and new, though the unique tile in the showers is a holdover from when the hotel was built in 1968. Superior rooms overlook the harbor, but most rooms do have some sort of ocean view. Owners Sid and Amy Kalmans are friendly and helpful. The fine Banana Bay Club, a casual terrace eatery serving seafood and Continental cuisine, is also on the premises. ✉ *44 A Queen Cross St., 00820,* ☎ *809/773–0687 or 800/524–0410,* 🖷 *809/778–7004. 43 rooms, 1 2-bedroom suite. Restaurant, bar, pool, meeting room. AE, D, DC, MC, V.*

**$** 🏨 **The Frederiksted.** Don't be put off by the neat but unprepossessing exterior: This modern four-story inn is your best bet for lodging in Frederiksted. In the inviting, outdoor tile courtyard, the glass tables and yellow chairs of the hotel's bar and restaurant crowd around a small freshwater swimming pool. Yellow-striped awnings and tropical greenery create a sunny, welcoming atmosphere. Steps at one side of the courtyard lead to the second floor's main desk and sundeck. The bright, pleasant guest rooms are outfitted with bar refrigerators and microwaves and are decorated with light-color rattan furniture and print bedspreads. Bathrooms are on the small side but are bright and clean. The nicest rooms are those with an ocean view; these are also the only rooms that have a bathtub in addition to a shower. ✉ *20 Strand St., 00840,* ☎ *809/772–0500 or 800/524–2025,* 🖷 *809/772–0500 ext. 147. 40 rooms. Restaurant, bar, pool. AE, D, DC, MC, V.*

**$** ⚏ **Pink Fancy.** This homey, restful place is a few blocks west of the cen-
★ ter of town in a much less touristy neighborhood. The oldest of the four
buildings here is a 1780 Danish town house, and old stone walls and
foundations enhance the setting. The inn's efficiency rooms are basic
but clean and well tended; all have hardwood floors, tropical-print fabrics, and wicker furniture. The hotel is laid out around the pool, where
pink-and-white awnings throw shade over the patio, hammock, and small
bar. Complimentary breakfast and cocktails are included in room rates.
✉ *27 Prince St., 00820,* ☎ *809/773–8460 or 800/524–2045,* FAX
*809/773–6448. 13 rooms. Bar, pool. AE, MC, V.*

## St. John

**$$$$** ⚏ **Caneel Bay Resort.** This 170-acre peninsula resort was a Rockresort
★ for many years, and it has maintained its atmosphere of quiet, unassuming elegance. The hotel closed when Hurricane Luis hit just before
Hurricane Marilyn in September 1995, but should reopen by October
1996. There are no crowds, no loud groups at the bar (in fact, there
are no bars, just lounges where you may sit at tables and order beverages), and no glitz. Visitors return year after year—some weeks in
February are booked a year in advance. Attention is paid to every detail, and the grounds are immaculately maintained. The flamboyant trees
here even seem to shed their blossoms neatly. The property has seven
beaches and three restaurants, one in a restored 18th-century sugar mill.
The spacious rooms have simple interiors and no telephone or TV.
Jackets are requested for men (during winter season) in restaurants after
6 PM. ✉ *Box 720, Cruz Bay 00830,* ☎ *809/776–6111 or 800/928–
8889,* FAX *809/693–8280. 168 rooms. 3 restaurants, 11 tennis courts,
fitness room, 7 beaches, water sports. AE, MC, V. EP, MAP, FAP.*

**$$$$** ⚏ **Hyatt Regency St. John.** This 34-acre property at Great Cruz Bay
shuns the weathered, old-money elegance of Caneel and lays on the
gloss and glitz to the point that even the landscaping looks freshly polished. It's a beautiful place: The grounds are positively iridescent, and
the pool area is a sybarite's delight, with waterfalls and islands and a
poolside bar. Spacious, well-appointed guest rooms line the beach and
encircle the pool, while some suites and luxurious town houses are set
back slightly from the water. The hotel suffered damage when Hurricane Marilyn swept through in September 1995, especially the beachfront rooms, but all was put back to normal by mid-1996. Try the on-site
Ciao Mein restaurant or the fabulous Sunday brunch buffet down by
the beach. There are morning, afternoon, and evening children's programs that include beach games, stargazing, island tours, and arts and
crafts. ✉ *Box 8310, Great Cruz Bay 00830,* ☎ *809/693–8000 or
800/233–1234,* FAX *809/779–4985. 285 rooms. 3 restaurants, pool, 6
tennis courts, fitness room, beach, marina, water sports. AE, DC,
MC, V. EP, MAP.*

**$$$** ⚏ **Gallows Point Suite Resort.** These soft-gray buildings with peaked
roofs and shuttered windows are clustered on the peninsula south of
the Cruz Bay ferry dock. The garden apartments have sky-lighted, plant-
filled showers big enough to frolic in. The upper-level apartments have
loft bedrooms and better views. There's no air-conditioning; harbor-
side villas get better trade winds but are noisier. Daily maid service is
included in the rates. Ellington's restaurant bridges the entranceway.
✉ *Box 58, Cruz Bay 00831,* ☎ *809/776–6434 or 800/323–7229,* FAX
*809/776–6520. 60 rooms. Restaurant, pool, tiny beach, snorkeling.
AE, DC, MC, V. EP.*

**$$–$$$** ⚏ **Estate Concordia.** The newest brainchild of Stanley Selengut, the de-
veloper of Maho Bay Campgrounds, these environmentally correct stu-
dios and duplexes are located on 51 oceanfront acres on remote Salt Pond
Bay. Energy is wind- and solar-generated (even the ice maker is solar-

powered). ⊠ *Salt Pond Bay, 00830,* ☎ *809/693–5855. 9 condominium units, 5 tents. Pool, short drive to beach. No credit cards.*

**$$**   🏨 **Harmony.** Nestled in the tree-covered hills adjacent to the Maho Bay Campground is another Selengut ecotourism resort. The spacious, two-story units here have your Caribbean basics—decks, sliding glass doors, living-dining areas, and great views—but staying here is definitely a learning experience. Buildings are constructed from recycled materials and energy comes entirely from wind and sun. You can use your unit's laptop computer to monitor your electricity consumption, sure to be lowered by the energy-saving appliances. Tile floors, undyed organic cotton linens, and South American handicrafts create a look to match the ideals. ⊠ *Box 310, Cruz Bay 00830,* ☎ *809/776–6240,* ☎ *800/392–9004. 12 units. Self-service restaurant, beach down the hill. No credit cards.*

**$$**   🏨 **Maho Bay Camp.** Eight miles from Cruz Bay, this private campground is a lush hillside community of tent cottages (canvas and screens) linked by boardwalks, stairs, and ramps that also lead down to the beach. The 16-by-16-foot shelters have beds, dining table and chairs, electric lamps (and outlets), propane stove, ice cooler, kitchenware, and cutlery. The camp has the chummy feel of a retreat and is very popular, so book well in advance. ⊠ *Cruz Bay 00830,* ☎ *809/776–6240, 212/472–9453, or 800/392–9004 for reservations. 114 tent cottages. Restaurant, barbecue areas, commissary, bathhouses (showers, sinks, toilets), beach, water sports. No credit cards.*

**$–$$**   🏨 **Cinnamon Bay Campground.** Tents, cottages with four one-room units in each cottage, and bare sites are available at this National Park Service location surrounded by jungle and set at the edge of big, beautiful Cinnamon Bay Beach. The tents are 10 by 14 feet, with flooring, and come with living, eating, and sleeping furnishings and necessities; the 15-by-15-foot cottages have twin beds. Bare sites, which come with a picnic table and a charcoal grill, can be reserved up to eight months in advance. You can reserve by phone with a credit card. The bare sites are cheap—at press time they were $17 a site—but, if you're thinking of this option for budgetary reasons alone, be warned: The tent sites and cottages range from around $75 to $105 in season for two people per night. Security is minimal so be careful with your belongings. ⊠ *Box 720, Cruz Bay 00830-0720,* ☎ *809/776–6330 or 800/539–9998. 44 tents, 40 cottages, 26 bare sites. Cafeteria, commissary, bathhouses (showers, toilets), beach, water sports. AE, MC, V.*

**$–$$**   🏨 **Raintree Inn.** If you want to be right in the center of the action in town and bunk at an affordable island-style place, go no farther. The dark-wood rooms, some with air-conditioning, have a simple, tropical-cabin decor. Lower-floor rooms are very small. Three efficiencies have kitchens and a comfortable sleeping loft—which you have to climb an indoor ladder to reach. The Fish Trap restaurant is next door. This is a no-smoking property. ⊠ *Box 566, Cruz Bay 00831,* ☎ FAX *809/693–8590 or 800/666–7449. 11 rooms. AE, D, MC, V. EP.*

## Dining

Just about every kind of cuisine you can imagine is available in the U.S.V.I. The beauty and freedom of the islands have attracted a cadre of professionally trained chefs who know their way around fresh fish and local fruits. If you are staying in a large hotel, you will pay prices similar to those in New York City or Paris—in other words, dining out is usually expensive.

St. Thomas is the most cosmopolitan of the islands and has the most visitors, so it is not surprising that the island also has the largest number and greatest variety of restaurants. St. Croix restaurants are both more relaxed and, in some ways, more elegant. Dining on St. John is, in general, more casual; the emphasis is on simple food prepared to order and served in an informal setting at reasonable prices.

## What to Wear

Restaurants in the U.S.V.I. are relaxed and informal. During the day, many people eat in their beach attire. In the evening, however, shorts and T-shirts are inappropriate for the nicer restaurants and luxury resorts. Pants and collared shirts, for men and women, are usually appropriate at such establishments.

| CATEGORY | COST* |
|---|---|
| $$$$ | over $35 |
| $$$ | $25–$35 |
| $$ | $15–$25 |
| $ | under $15 |

*per person for a three-course meal, excluding drinks and service*

## St. Thomas

**$$$$** ✕ **Blackbeard's Castle.** This romantic hillside restaurant is one of St.
★ Thomas's best. Diners here have a spectacular view of Charlotte Amalie and the harbor as they dine alfresco on such gourmet delights as tournedos of beef with fried green tomatoes or macadamia-nut-crusted mahimahi with pineapple salsa and plantain chips. Lunch offerings include excellent soups, sandwiches, and several pasta dishes. The à la carte Sunday brunch is immensely popular. ⊠ *Blackbeard's Castle, Charlotte Amalie,* ☎ *809/776–1234. AE, D, DC, MC, V.*

**$$$$** ✕ **Entre Nous.** The view here, from high over Charlotte Amalie's harbor, is as exhilarating as the dining is elegant. In the evening, you can watch the light-bedecked cruise ships pull slowly out of the harbor while deciding among such main courses as rack of lamb, Caribbean lobster, veal, and Chateaubriand. ⊠ *Bluebeard's Castle, Charlotte Amalie,* ☎ *809/774–4050. AE, MC, V. No lunch.*

**$$$$** ✕ **Hotel 1829.** You'll dine by candlelight flickering over stone walls and pink table linens at this restaurant on the terrace of the hotel. The menu and wine list are extensive, from Caribbean rock lobster to rack of lamb. Many items, including a warm spinach salad, are prepared tableside, and the restaurant is justly famous for its dessert soufflés, made of chocolate, Grand Marnier, raspberry, or coconut, to name a few. ⊠ *Government Hill, near Main St., Charlotte Amalie,* ☎ *809/776–1829. Reservations essential. AE, D, MC, V. No lunch.*

**$$$$** ✕ **Romanos.** Inside this huge old stucco house in Smith Bay is a de-
★ lightful surprise: a spare, elegant setting and superb northern Italian cuisine. Owner Tony hasn't advertised since the restaurant opened in 1988, and it is always packed. Try the pastas, either with a classic sauce or one of Tony's unique creations, such as a cream sauce with mushrooms, prosciutto, pine nuts, and Parmesan. ⊠ *97 Smith Bay,* ☎ *809/775–0045. MC, V. Closed Sun. No lunch.*

**$$$$** ✕ **Virgilio's.** This intimate, elegant hideaway serves the best northern
★ Italian cuisine on the island. Eclectic groupings of paintings and prints cover the two-story-high brick walls. Come here for superb minestrone; perfectly cooked capellini with fresh tomatoes and garlic; spaghetti peasant style (a rich tomato sauce with mushrooms and prosciutto); exquisite fresh fish, veal, and chicken dishes; and a host of daily specials. Maître d' Regis is on hand day and night, welcoming customers and helping the very gracious staff. Don't leave without having a Virgilio's cappuccino, a chocolate-and-coffee drink so rich it's like dessert. ⊠ *Main St., Charlotte Amalie,* ☎ *809/776–4920. AE, MC, V. Closed Sun.*

**\$\$\$** ✕ **Blue Marlin.** Dockside dining at its friendliest is the trademark of this open-air restaurant close to the St. John ferry dock at Red Hook. The clientele is a mix of sailors and fishers who work on the docks along with tourists waiting for the ferry. The menu emphasizes fish, chicken, and steak cooked without heavy sauces and oils. ⊠ *Red Hook,* ☎ *809/775–6350. AE, MC, V.*

**\$\$–\$\$\$** ✕ **Alexander's Cafe.** This charming restaurant is a favorite with the people in the restaurant business on St. Thomas—always a sign of quality. Local media types and wine aficionados (the always-changing wine list offers the best value on the island) are often among the crowd that packs this place. Alexander is Austrian, and the schnitzels are delicious and reasonably priced; pasta specials are fresh and tasty. Save room for strudel. Next door is Alexander's Bar & Grill, serving food from the same kitchen but in a more casual setting and at slightly lower prices. ⊠ *24A Honduras,* ☎ *809/776–4211. AE, D, MC, V. Closed Sun.*

**\$\$–\$\$\$** ✕ **Chart House.** In an old great house on the tip of the Frenchtown peninsula, this restaurant has a superb view. The menu includes fresh fish and teriyaki dishes, lobster, and Hawaiian chicken; there's also a large salad bar. ⊠ *Villa Olga, Frenchtown,* ☎ *809/774–4262. AE, D, DC, MC, V.*

**\$\$** ✕ **Little Bopeep.** Inside this unpretentious restaurant just outside Char-
★ lotte Amalie is some of the best West Indian food on the island. Try the curried chicken, conch in Creole sauce, sweet potato stuffing, and fried plantains. ⊠ *Barbel Plaza,* ☎ *809/774–1959. AE, MC, V.*

**\$\$** ✕ **Tickles Dockside Pub.** The Crown Bay location has been a locals' choice
★ for years, but this second branch of the casual, alfresco restaurant, just off the docks, is a welcome addition to East End. Enjoy sandwiches, ribs, and chicken (served with generous portions of french fries) while you watch the iguanas beg for table scraps—and bring your camera! ⊠ *American Yacht Harbor, Bldg. D,* ☎ *809/775–9425. MC, V.*

**\$\$** ✕ **Zorba's Cafe.** Tired of shopping? Summon up one last ounce of energy and head up Government Hill to Zorba's. Sit and have a cold beer or bracing iced tea in the 19th-century stone-paved courtyard surrounded by banana trees to replenish. Greek salads and appetizers, moussaka, and an excellent vegetarian plate top the menu. ⊠ *Government Hill, Charlotte Amalie,* ☎ *809/776–0444. AE, MC, V. No lunch Sun.*

**\$–\$\$** ✕ **Eunice's Terrace.** This excellent West Indian cook is justly famous. Her roomy, two-story restaurant has a bar and a menu of native dishes, including callaloo (a West Indian soup), conch fritters, fried fish, local sweet potato, fungi, and green banana. ⊠ *Rte. 38, near Renaissance Grand Beach Resort and Coral World, Smith Bay,* ☎ *809/775–3975. AE, MC, V.*

**\$–\$\$** ✕ **Hard Rock Cafe.** A hot spot from the day it opened, this waterfront restaurant is pretty much like its namesakes around the world. Rock-and-roll memorabilia dominate the decor, and the menu is full of hamburgers, sandwiches, salads, and great desserts. Doors open at 11 AM and stay open until 2 AM, and there's always a wait during prime meal-times. ⊠ *International Plaza on the Waterfront,* ☎ *809/777–5555. AE, MC, V.*

**\$–\$\$** ✕ **Il Cappuccini.** In the lower courtyard of the Taste of Italy shopping area is this quiet indoor-outdoor café that serves a variety of sandwiches (including an excellent Italian ham sandwich) and pasta dishes. ⊠ *A Taste of Italy, 4–5 Back St.,* ☎ *809/775–1090. AE, MC, V. No dinner.*

## St. Croix

**\$\$\$\$** ✕ **Great House at Villa Madeleine.** This elegant restaurant, part of the Villa Madeleine resort nestled in the hills on St. Croix's East End, serves such diverse cuisine as chicken alla Bolognaise, swordfish medallions sautéed with green tomato and asparagus, and a number of fine beef dishes. The wine list is extensive. ⊠ *Teague Bay (take Rte. 82 out of Christiansted and turn right at the Reef Condominiums)*, ☎ 809/778–7377. AE, D, DC, MC, V. Closed Sun.

**$$$$** ✕ **Kendricks.** This restaurant, a longtime favorite with locals, moved
★ its great food and tranquil ambience to Gallows Bay. At the upstairs restaurant, waiters in bow ties dote on customers seated at tables laid with crisp linens and fine china. The menu is stylish Continental, and dishes are lovingly presented. Try the lobster spring rolls with warm ginger and soy butter to start, or the silken cream of shiitake soup. Move on to the house specialty, roasted pecan-crusted pork loin with ginger mayonnaise, or the grilled rack of lamb with roasted garlic and fresh thyme sauce. At their downstairs café, look for lighter fare and a jazz band. ⊠ *12 Chandlers Wharf, Gallow's Bay*, ☎ 809/773–9199. AE, MC, V. Closed Sun.

**$$$** ✕ **Top Hat.** Owned by a delightful Danish couple, this restaurant has
★ been in business since 1970 serving international cuisine with an emphasis on Danish specialties—roast duck stuffed with apples and prunes, *frikadeller* (savory meatballs in a tangy cocktail sauce), fried Camembert with lingonberries, and smoked eel. The old West Indian structure, complete with gingerbread trim, is nicely accented in gray, white, and pink. The photographs on the walls are the work of owner and European-trained chef Hans Rasmussen. ⊠ *52 Company St.*, ☎ 809/773–2346. AE, D, MC, V. Closed May–Aug. and Sun. No lunch.

**$$** ✕ **Blue Moon.** This terrific little bistro, popular for its live jazz on Friday nights, has an eclectic, often-changing menu that draws heavily on Asian, Cajun, and French influences. Try the delicious seafood chowder or luna pie (veggies and cheese baked in phyllo dough) as an appetizer; the sweet-potato ravioli in mushroom sauce as an entrée; for dessert, the chocolate mint napolean is heavenly. ⊠ *17 Strand St.*, ☎ 809/772–2222. AE. Closed Mon. and July–Sept.

**$$** ✕ **Le St. Tropez.** A ceramic-tiled bar and soft lighting add to the Mediterranean atmosphere at this pleasant bistro, tucked into a courtyard off Frederiksted's main thoroughfare. Diners, seated either inside or on the adjoining patio, enjoy French fare such as salads, brochettes, and grilled meats in delicate sauces. The menu changes daily, often taking advantage of fresh local seafood. ⊠ *67 King St.*, ☎ 809/772–3000. AE, D, MC, V. Closed Sun.

**$** ✕ **Camille's.** This tiny, lively spot, whose warm, exposed brick walls are splashed with colorful island prints, is perfect for lunch or a light supper. Sandwiches and burgers are the big draw here, though the daily seafood special, often wahoo or mahimahi, is also popular. ⊠ *Corner of Company and Queen Cross Sts.*, ☎ 809/773–2985. No credit cards. Closed Sun.

**$** ✕ **Harvey's.** The plain, even dowdy room contains just 12 tables, and plastic, flowered tablecloths constitute the sole attempt at decor. But who cares? The delicious local food ranks among the island's best. Daily specials such as mouthwatering goat stew and melting whelks in butter, served with heaping helpings of rice, fungi, and vegetables, are listed on the blackboard. Genial owner Sarah Harvey takes great pride in her kitchen, bustling out from behind the stove to chat and urge you to eat up. ⊠ *11B Company St.*, ☎ 809/773–3433. No credit cards. Closed Sun. No dinner.

## St. John

**$$$–$$$$** ✕ **Ciao Mein.** In this classy restaurant (i.e., no shorts or collarless shirts), column A and column B give you transcultural choices: Chinese and Italian. Order from one side of the menu for such delights as Szechuan sesame noodles or wok-roasted duck. From the other side, you can have delicious pasta, calamari, or veal saltimbocca, and amaretto cheesecake. And, of course, you can certainly mix your dishes. ✉ *Hyatt Regency,* ☎ *809/693–8000. AE, MC, V. Closed Mon. No lunch.*

**$$$** ✕ **Ellington's.** Extending onto the second-story veranda of the Gallows Point Suite Resort's central building, Ellington's is a peaceful, appealing spot. The outside tables are particularly quiet and romantic. The menu is Continental, with chicken, fish, and steak dishes. You might start with the jumbo shrimp cooked in sweet coconut and served with a mango sauce, or the seafood chowder. Entrées include sea scallops and pesto, swordfish scampi, filet mignon, and fresh lobster. Save room for dessert, perhaps the banana chocolate chip cake or the white chocolate brownie. ✉ *Gallows Point Suite Resort,* ☎ *809/693–8490. AE, MC, V.*

**$$$** ✕ **Le Chateau de Bordeaux.** The best view you're going to find to dine
★ by is on the terrace here or in the air-conditioned dining room (go at sunset). The rustic cabin is magically transformed into an elegant, ultraromantic aerie by wrought-iron chandeliers, lace tablecloths, and antiques. The innovative preparations appeal equally to the eye and the palate. You might start with velvety carrot soup, perfectly contrasted with roasted chilies. Segue into the rosemary-perfumed rack of lamb with a honey-dijon-nut crust in a shallot-and-port-wine sauce, or the macadamia-coated salmon with crème fraîche dill glaze. Don't miss the whelks, which are done to perfection. ✉ *Rte. 10, just east of Centerline Rd.,* ☎ *809/776–6611. DC, MC, V.*

**$$$** ✕ **Paradiso.** Come here for good Italian food. This popular place, on
★ the upper level of Mongoose Junction, is open to the breezes and also has an outdoor terrace lined with tables. There are nightly pasta and fish specials as well as classic veal and chicken dishes. ✉ *Mongoose Junction,* ☎ *809/693–8899. AE, MC, V. No lunch.*

**$$** ✕ **Fish Trap.** There are several rooms here, all open to the breezes, and
★ all busy with happy diners. This local favorite serves up six kinds of fresh fish nightly, along with tasty appetizers, such as conch fritters and Fish Trap chowder. The menu also includes steak, pasta, chicken, and hamburgers. ✉ *Downtown, Cruz Bay,* ☎ *809/693–9994. AE, D, MC, V. Closed Mon. No lunch.*

**$** ✕ **Shipwreck Landing.** Start with a house drink, perhaps a fresh-squeezed concoction of lime, coconut, and rum, then move on to hearty taco salads, fried shrimp, teriyaki chicken, and conch fritters. The birds keep up a lively chatter in the bougainvillea that surrounds the open-air restaurant, and there's live music on Sunday nights in season. ✉ *Coral Bay,* ☎ *809/693–5640. MC, V.*

## Beaches

All beaches on these islands are open to the public, but often you will have to walk through a resort to reach them. Once there, you'll find that resort guests may have access to lounge chairs and beach bars that are off limits to you; for this reason, you may feel more comfortable at one of the beaches not associated with a resort. Whichever one you choose, remember to remove your valuables from the car.

### St. Thomas
**Coki Point Beach,** next to Coral World, is a popular snorkeling spot for cruise-ship passengers; it's common to find a group of them among the reefs on the east and west ends of the beach. If Coral World has reopened when you visit, you can use its lockers and changing rooms. **Magens Bay** is usually lively because of its spectacular arc of white sand, more than a half mile long, and its calm waters—two peninsulas protect it. The bottom is flat and sandy, so this is a place for sunning and

swimming rather than snorkeling. At **Morningstar Beach,** close to Charlotte Amalie, many young residents show up for bodysurfing or volleyball. This pretty curve of beach fronts the Morning Star section of the Marriott's Frenchman's Reef Hotel. Snorkeling is good here near the rocks. From **Sapphire Beach** there is a fine view of St. John and other islands. Snorkeling is excellent at the reef to the right or east, near Pettyklip Point. All kinds of water-sports gear are for rent. The condo resort at **Secret Harbour** doesn't at all detract from the attractiveness of this covelike East End beach. Not only is it pretty, it is also superb for snorkeling—go out to the left, near the rocks. **Hull Bay,** on the north shore, faces Inner and Outer Brass cays and attracts fishermen and beachcombers. It is open to rough Atlantic waves and is the only place to surf on the island.

## St. Croix

**Buck Island** and its reef, which is under environmental protection, can be reached only by boat; nonetheless, a visit here is a must on any trip to St. Croix. Its beach is beautiful, but its finest treasures are those you can see when you plop off the boat and adjust your face mask, snorkel, and flippers. The waters are not always gentle at **Cane Bay,** a breezy north-shore beach, but the scuba diving and snorkeling are wondrous, and there are never many people around. Just swim straight out to see elkhorn and brain corals. Less than 200 yards out is the drop-off or so-called Cane Bay Wall. South of Frederiksted, try the beach at the **On the Beach Resort**; palm trees can provide plenty of shade for those who need it, and there is a fine beachside restaurant for a casual lunch on weekends. **Rainbow Beach,** the beach at the West End Beach Club, has a bar, water sports, and volleyball. **Tamarind Reef Beach** is a small but attractive beach east of Christiansted. Both Green Cay and Buck Island seem smack in front of you and make the view arresting. Snorkeling is good. There are several popular West End beaches along the coast north of Frederiksted.

## St. John

**Caneel Bay** is actually seven white-sand beaches on the north shore, six of which can be reached only by water if you do not care to traipse across the hotel's lush grounds. The main beach (ask for directions at the gatehouse) provides easy access to the public. **Cinnamon Bay,** a long, sandy beach facing beautiful cays, serves the adjoining national-park campground. Facilities (showers, toilets, commissary, restaurant, beach shop, gift shop, small museum, kayak and windsurfing rentals) are open to all. There's good snorkeling off the point to the right, and rental equipment is available. **Hawksnest Beach** is becoming more popular every day; it's narrow and lined with sea-grape trees. There are rest rooms, cooking grills, and a covered shed for picnicking. It's popular for group outings and is the closest beach to town, so it is often fairly crowded. **Salt Pond Bay,** on the southeastern coast of St. John, is a scenic area to explore, next to Coral Bay and rugged Drunk Bay. This beach is for the adventurous. It's a short hike down a hill from the parking lot, and the only facility is an outhouse. The beach is a little rockier here, but there are interesting tide pools and the snorkeling is good. Take special care to leave nothing valuable in the car, because reports of thefts are numerous here. **Trunk Bay** is probably St. John's most-photographed beach and the most popular spot for beginning snorkelers because of its underwater trail. It's the St. John stop for cruise-ship passengers who choose a snorkeling tour for the day, so if you're looking for seclusion, check cruise-ship listings in *St. Thomas This Week* to find out what days the lowest number are in port. There are changing rooms, a snack bar, picnic tables, a gift shop, telephones, small lockers, and snorkeling equipment for rent.

# Outdoor Activities and Sports

### Fishing

In the past quarter-century, some 20 world records, many for blue marlin, have been set in the waters surrounding the Virgin Islands, most notably at St. Thomas's famed North Drop. To book a boat from St. Thomas or St. John, call the **Charter Boat Center** (☎ 809/775–7990 or 800/866–5714) or **American Yacht Harbor** (☎ 809/775–6454). On St. Croix, contact **Cruzan Divers** (☎ 809/772–3701), **Captain Bunny's** (☎ 809/778–6987), or **Ruffian Enterprises** (✉ St. Croix Marina, ☎ 809/773–6011 day, 809/773–0917 night).

### Golf

On St. Thomas, scenic **Mahogany Run** (☎ 809/775–5000), with a par-70, 18-hole course and a view of the B.V.I., lies to the north of Charlotte Amalie and has the especially tricky "Devil's Triangle" trio of holes. On St. Croix, the **Buccaneer's** (☎ 809/773–2100) 18-hole course is conveniently close to (east of) Christiansted. More spectacular is the course at **Westin Carambola Beach Resort** (☎ 809/778–5638), in the valleyed northwestern part of the island, designed by Robert Trent Jones. The **Reef Club** (☎ 809/773–8844), at the northeastern part of the island, has nine holes.

### Horseback Riding

At Sprat Hall on St. Croix, near Frederiksted, Jill Hurd runs **Paul and Jill's Equestrian Stables** (☎ 809/772–2880 or 809/772–2627) and will take you clip-clopping through the rain forest, along the coast, or on moonlit rides. Costs range from $50 to $75 for the three-hour rides.

### Sailing/Boating

The U.S.V.I. constitutes one of the biggest charter-boat fleet bases in the Western Hemisphere. You can go through a broker to book a private sailing vessel with crew or contact a charter-boat company directly. Among brokers for the U.S.V.I., **Blue Water Cruises** (✉ Box 1345, Camden, ME 04843, ☎ 800/524–2020) has an excellent worldwide reputation. Charter-boat companies on St. Thomas include **Island Yachts** (✉ 6100 Red Hook Quarter, Suite 4, 00802, ☎ 809/775–6666 or 800/524–2019), in Red Hook. On St. Croix, the **Annapolis Sailing School** (✉ Box 3334, 601 6th St., Annapolis, MD 21403, ☎ 410/267–7205 or 800/638–9192) offers one-week live-aboard cruises leaving from Christiansted.

#### SMALL POWERBOAT RENTALS

This is an interesting—and surprisingly affordable—way to see the islands. **Club Nautico** (✉ American Yacht Harbor, St. Thomas, 00802, ☎ 809/779–2555) and **Nauti Nymph** (✉ American Yacht Harbor, St. Thomas 00802, ☎ 809/775–5066) both have a variety of 21- to 27-foot boats.

#### DAY SAIL CHARTER COMPANIES

The following businesses can effortlessly book you on a submarine ride, a parasail boat, a kayak trip, a Jet Ski ride, a Hobie Cat sail, or a half-day inshore light-tackle fishing excursion. They get customer feedback on a daily basis and know exactly what type of boats and crew they are booking. They will be happy to answer any questions.

On St. Thomas, call the **Charter Boat Center** (✉ 6300 Smith Bay 16-3, 00802-1304, ☎ 809/775–7990).

On St. Croix, try **Mile-Mark Charters** (✉ Box 3045, 59 King's Wharf, Christiansted 00822, ☎ 809/773–2628 or 800/523–3483, FAX 809/773–7400). **Big Beard's Adventure Tours** (✉ Box 4534, Pan Am Pavilion,

Christiansted 00822, ☎ 809/773–4482) runs trips to Buck Island and beach barbecues using two catamarans, one with a glass bottom. **Buck Island Charters** (✉ Box 25273, Gallows Bay 00824, ☎ 809/773–3161) with Captain Heinz's trimaran, the *Teroro II*, departs for full- or half-day Buck Island trips from Green Cay Marina.

On St. John, **Connections** (✉ Box 37, 00831, ☎ 809/776–6922) represents a dozen of the finest local boats; many of its employees have actually worked on the boats they book. **Proper Yachts** (✉ Box 1570, 00831, ☎ 809/776–6256) has a fleet of luxury day-sail boats.

## Scuba Diving/Snorkeling

There are numerous dive operators on the three islands, and some of the hotels offer dive packages. Many of the operators listed below also offer snorkeling trips; call individual operators for details.

### ST. THOMAS

**Aqua Action Watersports** (✉ 6501 Red Hook Plaza, Suite 15, 00802, ☎ 809/775–6285) is a full-service, PADI five-star shop with all levels of instruction. They also rent sea kayaks and Windsurfers.

**Chris Sawyer Diving Center** (✉ 6300 Estate Frydenhoj 00802-1411, Suite 29, ☎ 809/775–7320 or 800/882–2965; locations at Compass Point, American Yacht Harbor, and the Renaissance Grand Beach Resort) is a five-star PADI facility as well as a NAUI certification center offering instruction up to dive master. It specializes in dives to the 310-foot RMS *Rhone*.

**Seahorse Dive Boats** (✉ Crown Bay Marina, 00802, Suite 505, ☎ 809/774–2001) is a PADI five-star operation and does both day and night dives on local wrecks and reefs.

**Underwater Safaris** (✉ Box 8469, 00801, ☎ 809/774–1350) is conveniently located in Long Bay at the Ramada Yacht Haven Marina—which is also home to the U.S.V.I. charter-boat fleet. It is a PADI five-star dive operation that specializes in Buck Island dives to the wreck of the World War I cargo ship *Cartenser Sr.*

### ST. CROIX

**Anchor Dive** (✉ Salt River Marina, Box 5588, Sunny Isle 00823, ☎ 809/778–1522) has wall and boat dives.

**Dive Experience, Inc.** (✉ Box 4254, 1 Strand St., Christiansted 00822-4254, ☎ 809/773–3307 or 800/235–9047) is a PADI five-star training facility providing the range from certification to introductory dives.

**Dive St. Croix** (✉ 59 King's Wharf, Box 3045, Christiansted 00820, ☎ 809/773–3434 or 800/523–3483, FAX 809/773–7400) takes divers to walls and wrecks—more than 50 sites—and offers introductory, certification, and PADI, NAUI, and SSI C-card completion courses. It has custom packages with five hotels. Dive St. Croix is the only dive operation on the island allowed to run dives to Buck Island.

**V.I. Divers, Ltd.** (✉ Pan Am Pavilion, Christiansted 00820, ☎ 809/773–6045 or 800/544–5911) is a PADI five-star training facility with a 32-foot dive boat and hotel packages.

### ST. JOHN

**Cruz Bay Watersports Co., Inc.** (✉ Box 252, 00830, ☎ 809/776–6234 or 800/835–7730, FAX 809/693–8720) is a PADI five-star diving center with two locations in Cruz Bay. Owner-operators Patty and Marcus Johnston offer regular reef, wreck, and night dives aboard three custom dive vessels.

**Low Key Water Sports** (✉ Box 716, 00830, ☎ FAX 809/693–8999), at the Wharfside Village, offers PADI certification and resort courses, one- and two-tank dives, wreck dives, and specialty courses.

**St. John Watersports** (✉ Box 1570, 00830, ☎ 809/776–6256) is a five-star PADI center in the Mongoose Junction shopping mall.

## Tennis

### ST. THOMAS

Most hotels rent time to nonguests. For reservations call **Bluebeard's Castle Hotel** (☎ 809/774–1600, ext. 196), **Frenchman's Reef Tennis Courts** (☎ 809/776–8500, ext. 444), **Sapphire Beach Resort** (☎ 809/775–6100, ext. 2131), **Renaissance Grand Beach Resort** (☎ 809/775–1510), or **Wyndham Sugar Bay** (☎ 809/777–7100). All of the above courts have lights and are open into the evening. **Grand Palazzo** (☎ 809/775–3333), **Limetree Tennis Center** (☎ 809/774–8990), and **Mahogany Run Tennis Club** (☎ 809/775–5000) are expected to open when the properties reopen (☞ Lodging, *above*). **Bolongo Inclusive Beach Resort** (☎ 809/775–1800, ext. 486) has courts for the use of guests only. There are two public courts at **Sub Base** (next to the Water and Power Authority), open on a first-come, first-served basis. The lights are on here until 8 PM.

### ST. CROIX

The public courts found in Frederiksted and out east at Cramer Park are in pretty questionable shape: It's better to pay the fees to play at the many hotel courts around the island.

There are a pro, a full tennis pro shop, and eight courts (two lighted) at the **Buccaneer Hotel** (☎ 809/773–2100); a resident pro and four courts (two lighted) at the **Westin Carambola Beach Resort** (☎ 809/778–3800); three lighted courts at **Club St. Croix** (☎ 809/773–4800); a pro, pro shop, and two courts at **St. Croix by the Sea** (☎ 809/778–8600); and two courts at the **Chenay Bay Beach Resort** (☎ 809/773–2918).

### ST. JOHN

**Caneel Bay Resort** (☎ 809/776–6111) has 11 courts (none lighted) and a pro shop. The **Hyatt Regency** (☎ 809/776–7171) has 6 lighted courts and a pro shop. The **public courts** near the fire station are lighted until 10 PM and are available on a first-come, first-served basis.

# Shopping

## St. Thomas

Most people would agree that St. Thomas lives up to its self-described billing as a shopper's paradise. Even if shopping isn't your idea of paradise, you still may want to slip in on a quiet day (check the cruise-ship listings—Monday and Saturday are usually the least crowded) to check out the prices. Among the best buys are liquor, linens, imported china, crystal (most stores ship), and jewelry. The sheer volume of jewelry available makes this one of the few items for which comparison shopping is worth the effort.

Most stores take major credit cards. There is no sales tax in the U.S.V.I., and shoppers can take advantage of the $1,200 duty-free allowance per family member. Shoppers also get an additional 5% discount on the duty on the next $1,000 worth of goods, but remember to save your receipts.

### SHOPPING DISTRICTS

The prime shopping area in Charlotte Amalie is between Post Office and Market squares and consists of three parallel streets running east to west (Waterfront, Main Street, and Back Street) and the alleyways connecting them. **Vendors Plaza,** on the waterfront at Emancipation Gardens, is a centralized location for all the vendors who used to clog the sidewalks with their merchandise.

**Havensight Mall,** next to the cruise-ship dock, has parking and many of the same stores as Charlotte Amalie, though it's not as charming. West of town, the pink-stucco **Nisky Center** is more of a hometown shopping center than a tourist area, but there's a bookstore (next to a bakery and yogurt shop), as well as a bank, gift shops, and clothing stores.

Out east, at Red Hook, **American Yacht Harbor** is a waterfront shopping arcade with branches of some of the Charlotte Amalie stores as well as a deli, a candy store, and a few restaurants.

### ART GALLERIES

**A. H. Riise Caribbean Print Gallery** (⊠ Riise's Alley off Main St., ☎ 809/776–2303). Haitian and Virgin Islands art are displayed and sold here, along with art books and the exquisite botanical prints and note cards from MAPes MONDe.

**The Gallery** (⊠ Veteran's Dr., ☎ 809/776–4641). Inside the waterfront branch of Down Island Traders (and owned by the same people), the Gallery carries Haitian art along with works by a number of Virgin Islands artists. Items on display include oil paintings, metal sculpture, wood carvings, painted screens and boxes, figures carved from stone, and oversize papier-mâché figures. Prices range from $50 to $5,000.

**Van Renselaer Art Gallery** (⊠ Al Cohen Mall, ☎ 809/774–4598) features owner Corrine Van Renselaer's own artwork plus the best from the island's many artists. Look for watercolors, batik, paintings, ceramics, and oils.

**Mango Tango** (⊠ Al Cohen Plaza at Raphune Hill, ☎ 809/777–3995) represents a variety of U.S.V.I. artists and some from neighboring islands as well. A framing service is also available.

### BOOKS AND MAGAZINES

**Dockside Bookshop** (⊠ Havensight Mall, Bldg. IV, ☎ 809/774–4937). This place is packed with books for children, travelers, cooks, and historians, as well as a good selection of paperback mysteries, best-sellers, art books, calendars, and art prints. It carries a selection of books written in and about the Caribbean and the Virgin Islands, from literature to chartering guides to books on seashells and tropical flowers. There's no markup here.

**Education Station Books** (⊠ Wheatley Center, ☎ 809/776–3008). There is no markup at this full-service bookstore that concentrates on Caribbean literature and black American and African history. There's also a large cookbook selection, a music section featuring jazz and "world beat" tapes from Africa, and prints by local artists. In addition, you can buy and sell used books of all types here. Visit **Education Station Ltd.,** just next door, for children's books.

**Island Newsstand** (⊠ Grand Hotel in Charlotte Amalie) and **Magazines** (⊠ Fort Mylner Shopping Center near Tillett Gardens). These two shops have the largest selection of magazines and newspapers on St. Thomas. Expect to pay about 20% above stateside prices.

### CAMERAS AND ELECTRONICS

**Boolchand's** (⊠ 31 Main St., ☎ 809/776–0794; ⊠ Havensight Mall, ☎ 809/776–0302) sells a variety of brand-name cameras as well as audio and video equipment.

**Royal Caribbean** (✉ 2 locations on Main St., ☎ 809/776–4110; ✉ Havensight Mall, ☎ 809/776–8890) has attractive prices on some cameras and accessories; portable cassette players are usually good buys here.

### CHINA AND CRYSTAL

**A.H. Riise Gift Shops** (✉ Riise's Alley off Main St.; ✉ Havensight Mall; ☎ 809/776–2303) carry Waterford, Wedgwood, Royal Crown, and Royal Doulton at good prices.

**English Shop** (✉ Waterfront, ☎ 809/776–5399; ✉ Havensight Mall, ☎ 809/776–3776) sells china and crystal from major European and Japanese manufacturers.

**Little Switzerland** (✉ Locations at Main St., Emancipation Park, Havensight Mall, and American Yacht Harbor, ☎ 809/776–2010) carries crystal from Lalique, Baccarat, Waterford, Riedel, and Orrefors, and china from Villeroy & Boch and Wedgwood, among others.

### CLOTHING

**G'Day** (✉ Waterfront at Royal Dane Mall, ☎ 809/774–8855). Everything in this tiny shop is drenched in the bright colors of Australian artist Ken Done, Scandinavian artist Sigrid Olsen, and items by Cotton Fields—swimwear, resort wear, accessories, and umbrellas.

**Janine's Boutique** (✉ A-2 Palm Passage, ☎ 809/774–8243) has women's and men's dressy and casual apparel from European designers and manufacturers, including the Louis Feraud collection, and select finds from Valentino, Christian Dior, YSL, and Pierre Cardin.

**Java Wraps** (✉ Royal Dane Mall, ☎ 809/774–3700) specializes in Indonesian batik creations and offers a complete line of beach coverups, swimwear, and leisure wear for women, men, and children.

**Local Color** (✉ Hibiscus Alley, ☎ 809/774–3727) sells cool cotton T-shirts and other casual clothing with the designs of St. Thomas artist Kerry Topper. Brightly printed sundresses, shorts, and shirts by Jams; big-brim straw hats dipped in fuchsia, turquoise, and other tropical colors; and unique jewelry are also for sale here.

### CRAFTS AND GIFTS

The **Caribbean Marketplace** (✉ Havensight Mall, Bldg. III, ☎ 809/776–5400) is the place to look for Caribbean handicrafts, including Caribelle batiks from St. Lucia; bikinis from the Cayman Islands; Sunny Caribee spices, soaps, teas from Tortola; and coffees from Trinidad.

The **Cloth Horse** (✉ Fort Mylner Shopping Center, ☎ 809/779–2222) has signed pottery from the Dominican Republic; wicker furniture and household goods from the island of Hispaniola; and pottery, rugs, and bedspreads from all over the world.

**Down Island Traders** (✉ Veteran's Dr., ☎ 809/776–4641) deals in hand-painted calabash bowls ($10); finely printed Caribbean note cards; jams, jellies, spices, and herbs; herbal teas made of rum, passion fruit, and mango; high-mountain coffee from Jamaica; and a variety of handicrafts from throughout the Caribbean.

**Pampered Pirate** (✉ 4 Norre Gade, ☎ 809/775–5450) carries island-made dolls, Christmas ornaments, prints and paintings along with its other gift items.

### FOOD

**Gourmet Gallery** (✉ Sub Base, ☎ 809/776–8555) has an excellent and reasonably priced wine selection, as well as condiments, cheeses, and specialty ingredients for everything from tacos to curries to chow mein.

For fruits and vegetables, go to the **Fruit Bowl** (✉ Wheatley Center, ☎ 809/774–8565). **Marina Market** (✉ Across from Red Hook ferry, ☎ 809/779–2411) offers the islands' freshest meats and seafoods as well as various sundries. There are also **supermarkets** at Sub Base, Four Winds, Tutu Park Mall, and the Havensight area.

JEWELRY

**A.H. Riise Gift Shop** (✉ Riise's Alley off Main St.; Havensight Mall; ☎ 809/776–2303) is St. Thomas's oldest and largest shop for luxury items, with jewelry, pearls, ceramics, china, crystal, flatware, perfumes, and watches.

**Amsterdam Sauer** (✉ 14 Main St., ☎ 809/774–2222) displays many fine one-of-a-kind designs.

**Cardow's** (✉ 3 stores on Main St., ☎ 809/776–1140; 1 at Frenchman's Reef Hotel, ☎ 809/774–0434; 2 at Havensight Mall, ☎ 809/774–0530 or 774–5905) offers an enormous "chain bar" more than 100 feet long, where you're guaranteed 30%–50% savings off U.S. retail prices or your money will be refunded within 30 days of purchase.

**Cartier** (✉ 30 Trompeter Gade, ☎ 809/774–1590) has fantastically beautiful and fantastically priced items as well as a surprising number of affordable ones.

**Colombian Emeralds** (✉ 1 store on Main St., 1 on the waterfront, and 1 at Havensight Mall; ☎ 809/774–3400) offers set and unset gems of every description, including high-quality emeralds.

**H. Stern** (✉ 3 stores on Main St., ☎ 809/776–1939; ✉ Havensight Mall, ☎ 809/776–1223; ✉ Frenchman's Reef, ☎ 809/774–7658) is one of the most respected names in gems.

**Irmela's Jewel Studio** (✉ Tolbod Gade, ☎ 809/774–5875) has long offered some of the Caribbean's most exquisite gems.

**Little Switzerland** (✉ Main St., Emancipation Gardens, Havensight Mall, all ☎ 809/776–2010; ✉ American Yacht Harbor, ☎ 809/777–3100) is the sole U.S.V.I. distributor for Rolex watches. The store also does a booming mail-order business.

**Opals of Australia** (✉ Drake's Passage, ☎ 809/774–8244) offers a wide variety of these iridescent wonders.

LEATHER GOODS

**Gucci** (✉ Riise's Alley off Main St., ☎ 809/774–7841; ✉ Havensight Mall, ☎ 809/774–4090) sells the traditional insignia-designed items for men and women.

**Leather Shop** (✉ Main St., ☎ 809/776–3995; ✉ Havensight Mall, Bldg. II, ☎ 809/776–0040) has big names at big prices: Fendi and Bottega Veneta are prevalent. However, there are also reasonably priced purses, wallets, and briefcases.

**Traveler's Haven** (✉ Havensight Mall, ☎ 809/775–1798) sells leather bags, backpacks, vests, and money belts.

**Zora's** (✉ Norre Gade across from Roosevelt Park, ☎ 809/774–2559) specializes in fine leather sandals made to order; they're sold alongside made-only-in-the-Virgin-Islands backpacks, briefcases, and "fish" purses in durable, brightly colored canvas.

LINENS

**Shanghai Linen** (✉ Waterfront, ☎ 809/776–2828) does a brisk trade in linen.

**Mr. Tablecloth** (⊠ Main St., ☎ 809/774–4343) has a friendly staff who will help you choose from a floor-to-ceiling array of linens.

**A.H. Riise Liquors** (⊠ Riise's Alley off Main St.; Havensight Mall; ☎ 809/776–2303) offers a large selection of liquors, cordials, wines, and tobacco, including rare vintage cognacs, Armagnacs, ports, and Madeiras. They also stock imported cigars, fruits in brandy, and barware from England.

**Al Cohen's Discount Liquor** (⊠ Across from Havensight Mall, Long Bay Rd., ☎ 809/774–3690) is a warehouse-style store with a large wine department.

MUSIC

**Parrot Fish Records and Tapes** (⊠ Back St., ☎ 809/776–4514) stocks standard stateside tapes and compact discs, along with a good selection of music by Caribbean artists, including local groups. For a catalog of calypso, soca, steel band, and reggae music, write to Parrot Fish, Box 9206, St. Thomas 00801.

**Modern Music** (⊠ Across from Havensight Mall, ☎ 809/774–3100; ⊠ Nisky Center, ☎ 809/777–8787; ⊠ Four Winds Plaza, ☎ 809/775–3310) has the latest stateside and Caribbean CD and cassette releases, plus oldies, classical, and new-age music.

PERFUMES

**Sparky's** (⊠ Main St., ☎ 809/776–7510) is staffed by impeccably turned-out salesclerks who can give you a facial and makeup lesson.

**Tropicana Perfume Shoppes** (⊠ 2 Main St., ☎ 809/774–0010 or 809/774–1834) has the largest selection of fragrances for men and women in all of the Virgin Islands.

SUNGLASSES

**Fashion Eyewear** (⊠ Garden St., ☎ 809/776–9075), tucked into a tiny building, is an even tinier shop that sells sunglasses priced from $40 to $450. They'll also copy the prescription from your current glasses and make new clear-lens glasses or sunglasses in a few hours.

TOYS

**Land of Oz** (⊠ Royal Dane Mall, ☎ 809/776–7888) has a huge selection of toys fashioned by European craftsmen that include Royal Doulton collector dolls, Brio wood trains, German nutcrackers, and English wood sailboats.

## St. Croix

Although St. Croix doesn't offer as many shopping opportunities as St. Thomas, the island does have an array of smaller stores with unique merchandise. In Christiansted, the best shopping areas are the **Pan Am Pavilion** and **Caravelle Arcade** off Strand Street and along **King and Company streets.**

BOOKS

The **Bookie** (⊠ 1111 Strand St., Christiansted, ☎ 809/773–2592) carries paperback novels, stationery, newspapers, and greeting cards. Stop in for the latest local gossip and events.

CHINA AND CRYSTAL

**Little Switzerland** (⊠ Hamilton House, 1108 King St., Christiansted, ☎ 809/773–1976), the St. Croix branch of a Virgin Islands institution, features a variety of Rosenthal flatware, Lladro figurines, Waterford and Baccarat crystal, Lalique figurines, and Wedgwood and Royal Doulton china.

At the **Royal English Shop** (✉ 5 Strand St., Frederiksted, ☎ 809/772–4886) Royal Doulton, Royal Worcester, Spode, Royal Albert, Havilland, Bernardaud china cost significantly less than on the mainland. Store hours vary, depending on the cruise-ship schedule, so call ahead.

CLOTHING

**Caribbean Clothing Company** (✉ 41 Queen Cross St., Christiansted, ☎ 809/773–5012) features contemporary sportswear by top American designers as well as Bally shoes for men.

**From the Gecko** (✉ 1233 Queen Cross St., ☎ 809/778–9433) offers the hippest buys on St. Croix, from superb batik sarongs to hand-painted scarves.

**Java Wraps** (✉ 51 Company St., Christiansted, and Pan Am Pavilion, ☎ 809/773–3770) sells Indonesian batik cover-ups and resort wear for men, women, and children, and fine home furnishings from around the world.

**Tribal Threadz** (✉ 52 C Company St., Christiansted, ☎ 809/773–2883) stocks urban island wear by Karl Kani, No Fear, and many more popular lines—for contemporary guys and gals.

**Skirt Tails** (✉ Pan Am Pavillion, Christiansted, ☎ 809/773–1991) has hand-painted batik and washable silk clothing in a rainbow of colors, perfect for vacations in the tropics. The store carries swimwear, sarongs, pant and short sets, and flowy dresses.

CRAFTS AND GIFTS

**American West India Company** (✉ 1 Strand St., Christiansted, ☎ 809/773–7325) offers a range of goods from around the Caribbean, including Jamaican allspice and Haitian metalwork.

**Green Papaya** (✉ Caravelle Arcade No. 15, Christiansted, ☎ 809/773–8848) sells handcrafted furniture and accessories for the home with attention to the unusual. Asian baskets and lovely wrought-iron lamps and hurricanes with handblown teardrop lanterns are among its selection of goods from all over the world.

**Folk Art Traders** (✉ 1B Queen Cross St. at Strand St., Christiansted, ☎ 809/773–1900) has energetic owners who travel to Haiti, Jamaica, Guayama, and elsewhere in the Caribbean to find the treasures sold in their shop, including baskets, masks, pottery, and ceramics.

JEWELRY

**Colombian Emeralds** (✉ 43 Queen Cross St., Christiansted, ☎ 809/773–1928 or 809/773–9189) specializes—of course—in emeralds, including some that are under $100, and also carries diamonds, rubies, sapphires, and gold. A branch store, **Jewelers' Warehouse** (☎ 809/773–5590), is across the street. The chain, the Caribbean's largest jeweler, offers certified appraisal and international guarantees.

**Crucian Gold** (✉ 57A Company St., Christiansted, ☎ 809/773–5241), in a small courtyard in a West Indian–style cottage, carries the unique gold creations of St. Croix native Brian Bishop.

**Sonya's** (✉ 1 Company St., Christiansted, ☎ 809/778–8605) is the home of the island's signature hook bracelet, which was designed by owner Sonya Hough.

LIQUOR

**Harborside Market and Spirits** (✉ 59 King's Wharf, Christiansted, ☎ 809/773–8899) has a good selection of liquor at duty-free prices in its conveniently located shop.

**Woolworth's** (⊠ Sunny Isle Shopping Center, Centerline Rd., ☎ 809/778–5466) carries a huge line of discount, duty-free liquor.

**Frontier Duty Free** (⊠ 53AB Company St., Christiansted, ☎ 809/773–3663 or 800/408–3337) has a full line of perfumes, along with cosmetics, leather goods, and liquors at duty-free prices.

**St. Croix Perfume Center** (⊠ 1114 King St., Christiansted, ☎ 809/773–7604) offers an extensive array of fragrances, including all the major brands.

## St. John

Because of the island's many natural wonders, travel literature about St. John often all but overlooks the pleasures of shopping there. But the blend of luxury items and handicrafts found in the shops on St. John makes for potentially excellent shopping opportunities. With several levels of cool, stone-wall shops, set off by colorfully planted terraces and courtyards, Mongoose Junction is one of the prettiest malls in the Caribbean. Wharfside Village, on the other side of Cruz Bay, is a painted-clapboard village with shops and restaurants.

# Nightlife

Nightlife in the U.S.V.I. is a spontaneous affair. Although there are many tourist-oriented cultural shows that can make for a fun night out—including broken-bottle dancing at various hotels—socializing is what the evenings are about. Most of the music scene is in small clubs with dance floors.

## St. Thomas

NIGHTSPOTS

**Barnacle Bill's** (☎ 809/774–7444), Bill Grogan's Crown Bay landmark with the bright red lobster on its roof, is a musicians' home away from home.

**Castaways** (☎ 809/774–8446) is the watering hole and dance floor for the crews, owners, and those chartering the boats anchored at Yacht Haven.

**Club Z** (☎ 809/776–4655), still one of the hottest spots on the island, is a disco-style club located on Contant Hill, with a spectacular view of glittering harbor lights to enjoy on the terrace between dances.

**Sugar's Nightclub at the Old Mill Complex** (☎ 809/776–3004), located in—you guessed it—an old mill, is a rock-till-you-drop late-night spot Thursday through Sunday. Whatever the tunes, the place is lively, and there's a small dance floor, as well as a good sound system.

JAZZ AND PIANO BARS

You'll find piano bars at **Entre Nous** at Bluebeard's Castle Hotel (☎ 809/776–4050) and **Randy's Bistro** at Al Cohen Mall on Raphune Hill (☎ 809/777–3199). "Gray, Gray, Gray" plays piano at both. An island favorite, he's been around for years and shouldn't be missed.

## St. Croix

Christiansted has a lively and eminently casual club scene near the waterfront. At **Mango Grove** (⊠ 53 King St., ☎ 809/773–0200) you'll hear live guitar and vocals in an open-air courtyard with a bar and Cinzano umbrella–covered tables. Easy jazz can be heard in the courtyard bar at **Indies** Saturday evenings (⊠ 55–56 Company St., ☎ 809/692–9440). To party under the stars in a very, very informal setting, head to the **Wreck Bar** (☎ 809/773–6092), on Christiansted's Hospital

Street, for crab races as well as rock and roll. . **Hotel on the Cay** (⊠ Protestant Cay, ☎ 809/773–2035) has a West Indian buffet on Tuesday nights that features a broken-bottle dancer and Mocko Jumbie. On Thursday nights, the **Cormorant** (⊠ La Grande Princesse, ☎ 809/778–8920) throws a similar event. The **2 Plus 2 Disco** (⊠ 17 La Grande Princesse, ☎ 809/773–3710) spins a great mix of calypso, soul, disco, and reggae, with live music on weekends.

Although less hopping than Christiansted, Frederiksted restaurants and clubs have a variety of weekend entertainment. **Blue Moon** (⊠ 17 Strand St., ☎ 809/772–2222), a waterfront restaurant, is the place to be for live jazz on Friday 9 PM–1 AM. Head up to Mahogany Road to the **Mt. Pellier Domino Club** (⊠ 50 Mt. Pellier, ☎ 809/772–9914) for local bands Friday through Sunday.

### St. John

Some friendly hubbub can be found at the rough-and-ready **Backyard** (☎ 809/693–8886), *the* place for sports watching as well as grooving to Bonnie Raitt et al. There's calypso and reggae on Wednesday and Friday at **Fred's** (☎ 809/776–6363). **Etta's** at the Inn at Tamarind Court (☎ 809/776–6378) serves up a blend of jazz and rock on Friday.

Notices on the bulletin board across from the U.S. post office and on telephone poles will keep you posted on special events: comedy nights, movies, and the like.

# Exploring St. Thomas

St. Thomas is only 13 miles long and less than 4 miles wide, but it's an extremely hilly island, and even an 8- or 10-mile trip could take several hours. Don't let that discourage you, though, because the ridge of mountains that runs from east to west through the middle, and separates the Caribbean and Atlantic sides of the island, offers spectacular vistas and is a lot of fun to explore—especially in a Jeep and with lots of time. The best views come on the North Side, but the others are all something to write home about. Look for glimpses of St. Croix some 40 miles to the south. Watch out for wandering cows and goats when you get up into the hills. Don't hesitate to take an unexpected turn off the main road—after all, discovery is what vacations are all about.

You'll find plenty of restaurants and watering holes spread out around the island, so food and drink won't be far no matter where you travel.

*Numbers in the margin correspond to points of interest on the St. Thomas map.*

### Charlotte Amalie

**❶** This tour of historic (and sometimes hilly) **Charlotte Amalie** and environs is on foot, so wear comfortable shoes, start early, and stop often to refresh. A note about the street names: In deference to the island's heritage, the streets downtown are labeled by their Danish names. Locals will use both the Danish name and the English name (such as Dronnigen's Gade and Main Street).

**All Saints Anglican Church.** Built in 1848 from stone quarried on the island, the church has thick, arched window frames lined with the yellow brick that came to the islands as ballast aboard merchant ships. The merchants left the brick on the waterfront when they filled their boats with molasses, sugar, mahogany, and rum for the return voyage. The church was built in celebration of the end of slavery in the Virgin Islands in 1848. It took a bad blow when Hurricane Marilyn hit, but will be rebuilt. ⊠ *Domini Gade,* ☎ *809/774–0217.* ◷ *Mon.–Sat. 6 AM–3 PM.*

**Cathedral of St. Peter and St. Paul.** This building was consecrated as a parish church in 1848 and serves as the seat of the territory's Roman Catholic diocese. The ceiling and walls of the church are covered in the soft tones of murals painted in 1899 by two Belgian artists, Father Leo Servais and Brother Ildephonsus. The San Juan–marble altar and side walls were added in the 1960s. ⊠ *Lower Main St.,* ☎ *809/774– 0201.* ◷ *Mon.–Sat. 8–5.*

**Crystal Palace.** Now a private home, the palace is so named because it was the first building on the island to have glass windows. ⊠ *Corner of Bjerge Gade and Crystal Gade.*

**Danish Consulate Building.** Built in 1830, it housed the Danish Consulate until the Danish West Indian Co. sold its properties to the local government in 1992. It now serves as home to the territory's governor. ⊠ *Take the stairs north at the corner of Bjerge Gade and Crystal Gade to Denmark Hill.*

**Dominus House.** A yellow-brick building dating to 1854, it is typical of 19th-century West Indian architecture. Today it houses restaurants. ⊠ *Government Hill.*

**Dutch Reformed Church.** Founded in 1744 and burned in 1804, it was rebuilt to its austere loveliness in 1844. The unembellished cream-color hall exudes peace—albeit monochromatically. The only touches of another color are the forest-green shutters and carpet. It suffered extensive damage when Hurricane Marilyn hit, but should be rebuilt by 1997. ⊠ *Corner of Nye Gade and Crystal Gade,* ☎ *809/776–8255.* ◷ *Weekdays 9–5. Call ahead; doors are sometimes locked.*

**Educators Park.** A peaceful place amid the town's hustle and bustle, it has memorials to three famous Virgin Islanders: educator Edith Williams, J. Antonio Jarvis (a founder of the V.I. *Daily News*), and educator and author Rothchild Francis, for whom Market Square is named. The last gave many speeches from this location. ⊠ *Main St. across from U.S. Post Office.*

**Emancipation Garden.** Across from Fort Christian, this garden honors the freeing of slaves in 1848. Today the gazebo's smooth floor is used for official ceremonies and is a preferred picnic location for clerks from nearby shops and offices as well as visitors. ⊠ *Between Tolbod Gade and Fort Christian.*

**Enid M. Baa Public Library.** The library is a large pink building typical of the 18th-century town houses common to the north side of Main Street. The merchants' homes were built across from the brick warehouses, with their stores downstairs and living quarters upstairs. The library was the home of St. Thomas merchant and landowner Baron von Bretton. It's the first recorded fireproof building. Its high-ceiling, cool, stone-floor interior is perfect for an afternoon of browsing through the historic-papers collection or just sitting in the breeze by an open window reading the daily paper. ⊠ *Main St.*

**Fort Christian.** St. Thomas's oldest standing structure, this monument anchors the shopping district. It was built 1672–87, and now carries a U.S. national landmark status. The clock tower was added in the 19th century. This remarkable redoubt has, over time, been used as a jail, governor's residence, town hall, courthouse, and church. It now houses a museum featuring artifacts of U.S.V.I. history, natural history, and turn-of-the-century furnishings. There is a spectacular view from the roof. ✉ *Waterfront Hwy. just east of shopping district,* ☎ *809/776–4566.*

**Frederick Lutheran Church.** This historic church features a massive mahogany altar. The pews, each with its own door, were once rented to families of the congregation. Lutheranism is the state religion of Denmark, and, when the territory was without a minister, the governor—who had his own elevated pew—would fill in. ✉ *Norre Gade,* ☎ *809/776–1315.* ☉ *Mon.–Sat. 9–4.*

**Frenchtown.** Popular with tourists for its several bars and restaurants, Frenchtown also serves as home to the descendants of immigrants from St. Barthelemy (St. Barts.) You can watch them pull up their boats and display their catch of the day along the waterfront. The harbor here has an abundance of yellowtail, parrot fish, and oldwife nearly as colorful as the fishers' small boats. You may see a number of people cleaning fish on the jetty or rubbing elbows at the Maison Noel bar. If you want to get a feel for the residential district of Frenchtown, walk west to some of the town's winding streets, where the tiny wood houses have been passed down from generation to generation. ✉ *Turn south off Waterfront Hwy. at the U.S. Post Office.*

**Government House.** Built as an elegant home in 1867, it now serves at governor's office. The first floor is open to the public. The staircases are of native mahogany, as are the plaques hand-lettered in gold with the names of the governors appointed and, since 1970, elected. Brochures detailing the history of Government House are available, but you may have to search for them. Look behind or under the guest book to the left of the entrance.

The three murals at the back of the lobby were painted by Pepino Mangravatti in the 1930s as part of the U.S. government's Works Projects Administration (WPA). The murals depict Columbus's landing on St. Croix during his second voyage in 1493; the transfer of the islands from Denmark to the United States in 1917; and a sugar plantation on St. John.

To tour the second floor you will have to be accompanied by the deputy administrator. You can call ahead to make an appointment for a tour, or you can take a chance that the officials will be in. It's worth the extra effort it takes to visit the second floor if for no reason other than the view from the terrace. Imagine the affairs of state of a colonial time being conducted in the hush of the high-ceiling, chandeliered ballroom. In the reception room are four small paintings by Camille Pissarro, but unfortunately they are hard to appreciate because they are enclosed in frosted-glass cases. More interesting, and visible, is the large painting by an unknown artist that was found in Denmark and depicts a romanticized version of St. Croix; the painting was purchased by former governor Ralph M. Paiewonsky, who then gave it to Government House. ✉ *Government Hill,* ☎ *809/774–0001.* ☉ *Weekdays 8–5.*

**Grand Hotel.** This imposing building stands at the head of Main Street. Once the island's premier hotel, it now houses offices and shops. ✉ *Tolbod Gade at Norre Gade.*

**Hassel Island.** East of Water Island in Charlotte Amalie Harbor, it is part of the Virgin Islands National Park and houses the ruins of the British military garrison (built during a brief British occupation of the U.S.V.I. during the 1800s) and the remains of a marine railway (where ships were hoisted onto land to the ship repair yard). Also on Hassel Island is the shell of the hotel that writer Herman Wouk's fictitious character, Norman Paperman, tried to turn into his own paradise in the book *Don't Stop the Carnival*. Presently there is no transportation to the island and nothing to service visitors once they arrive.

**Hotel 1829.** Dating from the same year, it was built as a guest house. Its bright coral walls accented with fancy black wrought iron, Hotel 1829 has a darkly cool and romantic bar and a dining terrace where gourmet food is served, both with an exquisite harbor view framed by tangerine-color bougainvillea. ⊠ *Government Hill.*

**Legislature Building.** Its pastoral-looking lime-green exterior conceals the vociferous political wrangling of the Virgin Islands Senate going on inside. Built originally by the Danish as a police barracks, the building was later used to billet U.S. Marines, and much later it housed a public school. Visitors are welcome to sit in on sessions in the upstairs chambers. ⊠ *Waterfront across from Fort Christian,* ☎ *809/774–0880.* ⊙ *Daily 8–5.*

**Market Square.** Formally called Rothchild Francis Square, it's a good place to stop for fresh fruit snacks. A cadre of old-timers sell papaya, taina roots, and herbs. Sidewalk vendors offer a variety of African fabrics and artifacts, tie-dyed cotton clothes at good prices, and fresh-squeezed fruit juices. ⊠ *Turn north off Main St. at Strand Gade.*

**Memorial Moravian Church.** Built in 1884, it was named to commemorate the 150th anniversary of the Moravian Church in the Virgin Islands. ☎ *809/776–0066.* ⊙ *Weekdays 8–5.*

**99 Steps.** A staircase "street" built by the Danes in the 1700s, leads to the residential area above Charlotte Amalie and a small hotel. If you count the stairs as you go up you'll discover, as have thousands before you, that there are more than 99. ⊠ *Look for the steps heading north from Government Hill.*

NEED A BREAK?     You might want to stop at **Blackbeard's Castle** at the top of 99 stairs for some of the island's best food and a swim—the pool is open to daytime customers. As you lunch on the terrace, you can take in the view of Charlotte Amalie and the harbor.

**Pissarro Building.** Home to several shops, it was the birthplace of French Impressionist painter Camille Pissarro. ⊠ *Main St.*

**Queen's Street.** It is a hike to this quaint street, but you will find it is even quieter and more removed than Government Hill below. The homes are privately owned except for Blackbeard's Castle, now a hotel. Its tower was built in 1679 and is believed to have been used by the notorious pirate Edward Teach. ⊠ *Top of 99 Steps.*

**Roosevelt Park.** A good spot to people-watch, you'll see members of the local legal community head to the nearby court buildings while you rest on the park benches. The small monument on the south side of the park is dedicated to U.S.V.I. war veterans. ⊠ *Norre Gade.*

**Savan.** A neighborhood of small streets and small houses, it was first laid out in the 1700s as the residential area for a growing class of "free coloreds," a middle class of artisans, clerks, and shopkeepers. You'll find a row of Rastafarian shops along the first block and a restaurant that sells pâté, a delicious turnover-type pastry stuffed with meat or vegetables. ⊠ *Turn north off lower Main St. onto General Gade.*

**Seven Arches Museum.** Located in a restored West Indian home built about 1800, you'll find historic furnishings, cannonballs, and gas lamps. Behind the house is a quaint West Indian cottage. ☎ 809/774–9295. 🖃 *$5 suggested.* ⊙ *Tues.–Sun. 10–3 or by appointment.*

**Synagogue of Beracha Veshalom Vegmiluth Hasidim.** The synagogue's Hebrew name translates as the Congregation of Blessing, Peace, and Loving Deeds. The small building's white pillars contrast with rough stone walls, as does the rich mahogany of the pews and altar. The sand on the floor symbolizes the exodus from Egypt. Since the synagogue first opened its doors in 1833, it has held a weekly Sabbath service, making it the oldest synagogue building in continuous use under the American flag and the second oldest (after the one on Curaçao) in the Western Hemisphere. 🖃 *15 Crystal Gade,* ☎ *809/774–4312.* ⊙ *Weekdays 9–4.*

**Tortola Wharf.** Catch the *Native Son* and other ferries to the B.V.I. There's an upstairs restaurant where you can watch the Charlotte Amalie Harbor traffic as you enjoy an iced tea. 🖃 *Waterfront Hwy.*

**U.S. Post Office.** While you buy your postcard stamps, contemplate the murals of waterfront scenes by *Saturday Evening Post* artist Stephen Dohanos. His art was commissioned as part of the WPA in the 1930s. 🖃 *Tolbod Gade and Main St.*

**V.I. Visitor's Information Center.** Tucked away in the block between the U.S. Post Office and the waterfront, you'll find a hospitality lounge complete with bathrooms and a place to stash your luggage if you want to shop on your way to the airport. This useful spot was under reconstruction at press time, but should be completed by winter 1997. 🖃 *Tolbod Gade across from Emancipation Garden.*

**Vendors Plaza.** Merchants sell everything from T-shirts to African attire to leather goods that may carry name brands but aren't. Look for local art among the ever-changing selections at this busy market. 🖃 *West of Fort Christian at the Waterfront.*

**Water Island.** Look about a quarter of a mile out in Charlotte Amalie Harbor for a view of this island. It was once a peninsula of St. Thomas, but a channel was cut through so U.S. submarines could get to their base in a bay just to the west, known today as Sub Base. Today private residents live on the island.

## The South Shore and East End

🔄 ***Atlantis* Submarine.** Probably the only way any of us are going to go 150 feet underwater, this submarine carries 46 passengers on a two-hour ride; it's air-conditioned and there's a surface vessel that maintains constant radio contact. While submerged, you may see stingrays, turtles, colorful coral, and more fish than any aquarium ever imagined. Watch for the remains of the *Michelle,* and an occasional lemon shark. 🖃 *Havensight Mall,* ☎ *809/776–5650.* 🖃 *$72.*

❸ **Clinton Phipps Racetrack.** Try your luck at the scheduled races held here, especially on local holidays. Be prepared for large crowds; it's a popular sport. 🖃 *Rte. 30 at Nadir,* ☎ *809/775–4555.*

**Coki Point.** Snorkel the reefs at its eastern and western ends. You may want to dash in for a swim or just do some people-watching while nibbling on a meat pâté, which you can buy from one of the vendors. Don't leave valuables unattended in your car or on the beach at Coki Point. 🖃 *Turn north off Rte. 38.*

**Compass Point.** Home to a fair-size marina and several shops and restaurants that cater to boaters, the area is a good spot to while away an afternoon. It's fun to park your car for a walk around the colorful area. And it's easy to engage the boaters—many sailed here from points around the globe—in conversation. You'll find everything from burgers to German fare at the area's restaurants.✉ *Turn south off Red Hook Rd. at the well-marked entrance road just east of Independent Boat Yard.*

☝ ❺ **Coral World at Coki Point.** At press time, this was temporarily closed until repairs are completed on the damages caused by Hurricane Marilyn. When it opens Coral World will again be home to a three-level underwater observatory (call ahead for shark-feeding times), the world's largest reef tank, and an aquarium with more than 20 TV-size tanks providing capsulated views of life in the waters of the Virgin Islands and around the world. Coral World's staff will answer your questions about the turtles, iguanas, parrots, and flamingos that inhabit the park, and there's a restaurant, souvenir shop, and the world's only underwater mailbox, from which you can send postcards. ✉ *Turn north off Smith Bay Rd. at the sign,* ☎ *809/775–1555.*

❷ **Havensight Mall.** If you're not up for the crowds on Main Street, do your shopping here. Just about all the major stores have branches here to cater to cruise-ship passengers who disembark nearby. It is also where you'll find the offices for *Atlantis* submarine, and the Dockside Book Shop, a bookstore with stateside prices instead of hotel markups. ✉ *Rte. 30 at Havensight.*

**Paradise Point Tramway.** Fly skyward in a gondola straight up the hill to Paradise Point, a scenic overlook with breathtaking views of Charlotte Amalie and the harbor. There's bar, a restaurant, and several shops. ✉ *Rte. 30 at Havensight,* ☎ *809/774–9809.* 💲 *$10.* ☉ *Daily 7:30–4:30.*

❹ **Red Hook.** A busy shopping area, it has grown from a sleepy little town connected to the rest of the island only by dirt roads (or by boat) to an increasingly self-sustaining village. There are several small branches of some Charlotte Amalie shops, including Little Switzerland, at the newly expanded American Yacht Harbor. There is also a deli and candy store. Tickles Dockside Pub and Mackenzie's Restaurant both serve burgers, salads, and sandwiches. There are more restaurants, two small grocery stores, and a few shops spread up and down the busy road. Visit with the fishing and sailing charter crews tending their boats along the docks. And for some real local ambience, you might stop for a beer at the Warehouse Bar.

Park your car in the public lot or the private lot across the street—about $5 for the entire day—for a ferry trip to St. John, only 20 minutes by boat, but light years away in ambience. The ferry leaves at 6:30 AM, 7:30 AM, and on the hour until midnight.

❻ **Tillett Gardens.** Clustered in this complex in a booming local shopping area, you'll find a colony where local artisans craft stained glass, pottery, gold jewelry, and ceramics. Tillett's paintings and silk-screened fabrics are also on display and for sale. The gardens encircle a shaded courtyard with fountains and Polli's, an outdoor Mexican restaurant. ✉ *Rte. 38 across from Four Winds Shopping Center.*

**Virgin Islands National Park Headquarters.** This park facility consists of a dock, a small grassy area with picnic tables, and a visitor center where maps and brochures are available. ✉ *Turn east off Rte. 32 at the sign,* ☎ *809/775–6238.*

## North Shore, Center Island, and West

**Brewer's Beach.** Popular with the students at the nearby University of the Virgin Islands, it is a long strand of powdery beach. If you're hungry, trucks selling lunch, snacks, and drinks often park along the road. ✉ *Rte. 30 across the runway from the airport.*

**Department of Agriculture.** If you buy a plant, be sure to stop here to get the plant's roots sprayed for diseases and to get a certificate to present to U.S. customs when you leave the territory. ✉ *Rte. 40.*

**❼ Drake's Seat.** Sir Francis Drake was supposed to have kept watch over his fleet and looked for enemy ships of the Spanish fleet from this vantage point. Magens Bay and Mahogany Run are to the north, with the B.V.I. and Drake's Passage to the east. Off to the west are Fairchild Park, Mountain Top, Hull Bay, and smaller islands such as the Inner and Outer Brass islands. The panoramic vista is especially breathtaking (and romantic) at dusk, and if you arrive late in the day you'll miss the hordes of day-trippers on taxi tours who stop at Drake's Seat to take a picture and buy a T-shirt from one of the many vendors. By afternoon the crowd thins and most of the vendors are gone. ✉ *Rte. 40.*

**❽ Estate St. Peter Greathouse Botanical Gardens.** Perched on a mountainside 1,000 feet above sea level, with views of more than 20 other islands and islets, is this unusual spot where you can wander through a gallery displaying local art, sip a complimentary rum or virgin punch while looking out at the view, or follow a nature trail that leads through nearly 200 varieties of tropical trees and plants, including an orchid jungle. ✉ *Rte. 40, St. Peter Mountain Rd.,* ☎ *809/774–4999.* ✏ *$8.* ☉ *Mon.–Sat. 9–4:30.*

**Hull Bay.** You may come across the fishing boats and homes of the descendants of settlers from the French West Indies who fled to St. Thomas more than 200 years ago. If you have the opportunity to engage them in conversation, you will hear speech patterns slightly different from those of other St. Thomians. Hull Bay, with its rougher Atlantic surf and relative isolation, is one of the best surfing spots on St. Thomas. ✉ *Rte. 37.*

**Hull Bay Hideaway.** This is a place to take a break from the rigors of sightseeing. You will find a rustic beach bar offering camping facilities, albeit severely primitive ones. (Bring lots of insect repellent.) Stop by on a Sunday afternoon and sip a beer while you listen to rock and roll played by the local dentist and his band. ✉ *Rte. 37.*

**Magens Bay Beach.** Popular with tourists and locals, this is the island's busiest beach. It's often listed among the world's most beautiful beaches, and on weekends and holidays it hops with groups partying under the sheds. There's also an outdoor bar, bathhouses, a nature trail, and a snack bar. ✉ *Take Rte. 35 till it ends at the admission booth.* ✏ *Small admission charge.*

**Mahogany Run Golf Course.** Designed by Tom Fazio, the golf course overlooks the Caribbean sea. It features the "Devil's Triangle," a three-hole challenge that often stumps even the best golfers. The road in to the golf course was once bordered by centuries-old mahogany trees cleared to build the golf course (before they were cleared to build their namesake). ✉ *Rte. 42,* ☎ *809/777–5000.*

**❾ Mountain Top.** Don't forget to stop for a banana daiquiri and spectacular views from the observation deck more than 1,500 feet above sea level. There are also a number of shops selling everything from Caribbean art to nautical antiques, ship models, and T-shirts. ✉ *Head north off Rte. 33.*

**❿ Reichhold Center for the Arts.** This open-air amphitheater has its more expensive seats covered by a roof. It offers an eclectic selection of events ranging from local beauty pageants to traveling theater groups. Schedules vary so check the local paper to see what's on when you're in town. ⊠ *Rte. 30 across from Brewers Beach,* ☎ *809/693–1559.*

**Sapphire Beach.** If you're on St. Thomas at full moon, grab the champagne (and the bug spray) and head to this popular spot for the moonrise. The moon rises out of the sea, illuminating the beach in a most romantic light. ⊠ *Rte. 38.*

## Exploring St. Croix

St. Croix is a big island, as the Virgin Islands go, and a study in contrasting beauty. The island is not as hilly as St. Thomas or St. John; a lush rain forest envelops the northwest, the East End is dry and barren, and palm-lined beaches with startlingly clear aquamarine water ring the island. The island's capital, Christiansted and it's other major town, Frederiksted, are both named after Danish Kings, with tin-roofed, 18th-century buildings in pale yellow, pink, and ocher. There's lots of interesting spots spread out between the towns and to the east of Christiansted.

*Numbers in the margin correspond to points of interest on the St. Croix map.*

❶ **Christiansted** is an historic, Danish-style town that always served as St. Croix's commercial center. While trade in the 1700s and 1800s concerned sugar, rum, and molasses, today it's the home to law offices, tourist shops, and restaurants. Many of the structures, which are built from the harbor up into the gentle hillsides, date from the 18th century.

☾ **Buck Island Reef National Monument.** This is a must-see on any visit to St. Croix. Located off the northeast coast, it is reached only by boat. Charter boat trips leave daily from the Christiansted Waterfront or from Green Cay Marina, about 2 miles east of Christiansted. Check with your hotel for their recommendations. The island's pristine beaches are just right for sunbathing, but there's enough shade for those who don't want to fry. The spectacular snorkeling trail set in the reef allows visitors the opportunity for a close-up study of coral formations and tropical fish. The crew members give special attention to novice snorkelers and children. A hiking trail to Buck Island's highest point offers spectacular views of the reef below and St. John to the north. ⊠ *Northshore,* ☎ *809/773–1460.*

**D. Hamilton Jackson Park.** When you're tired of sightseeing, stop here for a rest. It's named for a famed labor leader, judge, and journalist who started the first newspaper not under the thumb of the Danish crown. ⊠ *Between Fort Christianvaern and the Danish Customs House.*

**Danish Customs House.** Built in 1734, this building houses the National Park Service offices. It also served as the island's post office and later a library. ⊠ *King St.* ☾ *Weekdays 8–5, weekends and holidays 9–5; closed Dec. 25, Easter, and Thanksgiving.*

**Fort Christiansvaern.** This large yellow structure dominates the harbor front. In 1749 the Danish built the fort to protect the harbor, but the structure was repeatedly damaged by hurricane-force winds and was partially rebuilt in 1771. It is now a National Historic Site and the best preserved of the five remaining Danish-built forts in the Virgin Islands. ⊠ *Box 160, Christiansted 00821,* ☎ *809/773–1460.* 🎟 *$2 (includes admission to Steeple Building, below).* ☾ *Weekdays 8–5, weekends and holidays 9–5; closed Dec. 25, Easter, and Thanksgiving.*

**Government House.** One of the town's most elegant buildings, it was built as a home for a Danish merchant in 1747. The building today houses U.S.V.I. government offices. Slip into the peaceful inner courtyard to admire the still pools and gardens. A sweeping staircase leads visitors to a second-story ballroom, still the site of official government functions. ⊠ *King St.,* ☎ *809/773–1404.*

**The Market.** Named after Christian "Shan" Hendricks, it was built in 1735 as a slave market. Today farmers and others sell their goods under the wood-and-galvanized-aluminum structure every Wednesday and Saturday 8–5. ⊠ *Company St.*

**Post Office.** Built in 1749, it once housed the Danish West India & Guinea Company warehouse. The Danish Customs House and the post office building were once one structure. ⊠ *Church St.*

**Scale House.** Now the visitor's bureau, the building was constructed in 1856. It once served as a scale house, where goods passing through the port were weighed and inspected. ⊠ *King St.,* ☎ *809/773–0495.*

**Steeple Building.** Built by the Danes in 1753, it was the first Danish Lutheran church on St. Croix. It is now a National Park museum and contains exhibits documenting the island's Indian habitation. There is also an extensive array of archaeological artifacts, a handful of displays concerning the African-American experience, and exhibits on the architectural development of Christiansted on St. Croix, the early history of church, and Alexander Hamilton, the first secretary of the U.S. Treasury, who grew up in St. Croix. ⊠ *Box 160, Christiansted 00822,* ☎ *809/773–1460.* 🖙 *$2 (includes admission to Fort Christiansvaern).* ☉ *Tues.–Thurs. (if the Park has enough staff to open it) 9–11, 1–4. Call ahead to check.*

## Outside Christiansted and Points East

**Cramer's Park.** This territorial beach on northeast coast is very popular with locals. It's a spot for beach picnics and camping on long weekends. ⊠ *Rte. 82.*

**Point Udall.** This rocky promontory, the easternmost point in the United States, juts into the Caribbean Sea. The climb to this point, by a rutted dirt road, may be slow, but it's worth the effort. On the way back, look for "The Castle," an enormous mansion atop the cliffs that resembles a cross between a Moorish mosque and the Taj Mahal. It was built by an extravagant recluse known only as the Contessa. ⊠ *Rte. 82.*

## Between Christiansted and Frederiksted

A drive through St. Croix's country side is trip back in time. Ruins of old plantations, many bearing whimsical names bestowed by early owners, dot the landscape. When you get to Slob, you may think you're passing by a spot where some messy soul lived. Not so. Long ago it was a low-lying area, or slob.

The roads west are fairly flat, making for an easy drive. While the traffic moves quickly—by island standards—on the main roads, don't hesitate to poke around down some side lanes to see what there is to see.

**❸ Cane Bay.** This is one of St. Croix's best launches for scuba diving, and you may see a few wet-suited, tank-backed figures near the small stone jetty making their way out to the drop-off (a bit farther out there is a steeper drop-off to 12,000 feet). ⊠ *Rte. 80.*

This is the site of the popular Picnic in Paradise, the gourmet delicatessen, restaurant, and beach club located just past Cane Bay on the sea side of the road. Pick up their popular quiche, pasta, or salad to take to the beach for lunch, or dine alfresco at one of their outdoor tables. ⊠ *Rte. 80,* ☎ *809/778–1212.*

➍ **Estate Mount Washington Plantation.** Several years ago, while surveying the property, the owners discovered the ruins of a historic sugar plantation buried beneath the rain-forest brush. The grounds have since been cleared and opened to the public. A free, self-guided walking tour of the animal-powered mill, rum factory, and other ruins is available daily, and the antiques shop located in the old stables is open on Saturdays. ⊠ *Rte. 63; watch for sign,* ☎ *809/772–1026.*

☙ **Estate Whim Plantation Museum.** The lovingly restored estate, with a windmill, cook house, and other buildings, will give you a true sense of what life was like on St. Croix's sugar plantations in the 1800s. The oval-shape great house has high ceilings, antique furniture, decor, and utensils well worth seeing. Notice its fresh and airy atmosphere—the waterless stone moat around the great house was used not for defense but for gathering cooling air. The apothecary exhibit is the largest in all the West Indies. You will also find a museum gift shop. This is a great place for your kids to stretch their legs on the spacious grounds. ⊠ *Rte. 70, Box 2855, Frederiksted 00841,* ☎ *809/772–0598.* ⊡ *$5.* ☉ *Mon.–Sat. 10–4.*

➋ **Judith's Fancy.** This historic site is home to ruins of an old great house and the tower left from a 17th-century château that was once home to the governor of the Knights of Malta. The "Judith" comes from the first name of a woman buried on the property. From the guardhouse at the entrance to the neighborhood, follow Hamilton Drive past a number of St. Croix's loveliest homes. At its conclusion, Hamilton Drive overlooks Salt River Bay, where Christopher Columbus anchored in 1493. A skirmish between members of Columbus's crew and a group of Arawak-speaking Indians resulted in the first bloody encounter between Europeans and West Indians. The peninsula on the east side of the bay is named for the event: Cabo de las Flechas (Cape of the Arrows). On the way back, make a detour left off Hamilton Drive onto Caribe Road, for a close look at the neighborhood's ruins. ⊠ *Turn north onto Rte. 751 off Rte. 75.*

**Mt. Eagle.** This is St. Croix's highest peak, at 1,165 feet. Leaving Cane Bay and passing North Star beach, follow the beautiful coastal road that dips briefly into the forest, then turn left. There is no street sign, but you'll know the turn: The pavement is marked with the words "The Beast" and a set of giant paw prints. The hill you're about to climb is the location of the infamous Beast of the America's Paradise Triathlon, an annual St. Croix event in which participants must bike up this intimidating slope. ⊠ *Rte. 69.*

➎ **Mt. Pellier Domino Club.** This sprawling palm-frond and bamboo hut, nestled in the rain forest, sells cold drinks, fried chicken, pork chops, and johnnycakes. But the real attraction is Miss Piggy, a beer-guzzling sow who scurries across her pen like Pavlov's dogs at the sound of a beer can opening. (Actually, she's switched to nonalcoholic beer for her health!) ⊠ *Mahogany Rd., Rte. 76.*

**Rain Forest.** This is a not-to-be missed site. A thick tangle of turpentine and mahogany trees in places forms a canopy over the road. ⊠ *Rte. 76.*

**St. Croix by the Sea Hotel.** This hotel has one of the most spectacular sea views on St. Croix. Stroll through the lobby and outside to the 154-foot ocean-fed swimming pool, the largest saltwater pool in the

Caribbean. The view of Christiansted and Buck Island, to the east, is terrific. ✉ *Turn north off Rte. 75 onto Rte. 751; watch for sign.*

**6** **St. Croix Leap.** Located in the heart of the rain forest, this is a workshop where you can purchase handsome articles of mahogany, saman, or thibet wood crafted by local artisans. ✉ *Rte. 76,* ☎ *809/772–0421.*

**8** **St. George Village Botanical Gardens.** At this 17 acre-estate, you'll find lush and fragrant flora amid the ruins of a 19th-century sugarcane plantation village. You'll see miniature versions of each ecosystem on St. Croix, from a semiarid cactus grove to a verdant rain forest. Turn north off Route 70 at sign for gardens. ✉ *Box 3011, Kingshill 00851-3011,* ☎ *809/692–2874.* 🎫 *$5.* 🕐 *Daily 9–4; closed holidays.*

**Salt River Bay National Historical Park and Ecological Preserve.** This joint national and local park was dedicated in November 1993. In addition to such sites of cultural significance as a prehistoric ceremonial ball court and burial site, it encompasses a biodiverse coastal estuary that hosts the largest remaining mangrove forest in the U.S.V.I., a submarine canyon, and several endangered species, including the hawksbill turtle and roseate tern. At present, few sites are of more than archaeological interest to laypeople, but plans call for a museum, interpretive walking trails, and a replica of a Carib village. ✉ *Rte. 75 to Rte. 751.*

**Salt River Marina.** This lush lagoon is home to the Anchor Dive Shop and a couple of casual eateries catering to yachties. The road that veers to the left behind the marina leads to the beach where Columbus landed. ✉ *Tradewinds Rd. at Rte. 80,* ☎ *809/778–1522.*

**Sandy Point Beach.** A ritual that began millions of years ago is played out annually between March and June. That's when the majestic leatherback turtles come ashore to lay their eggs. These creatures, which can weigh up to 800 pounds and are of an older species than the dinosaurs, are oblivious to onlookers when they lay their eggs in the sand. With only the moonlight to guide them, Earthwatch volunteers patrol the beach nightly during the turtles' nesting season to protect the eggs from predators and poachers. The beach is a federal wildlife preserve and is closed to the public at night, but the Earthwatch volunteers in conjunction with the St. Croix Environmental Association will take groups of up to 10 people with them. ✉ *Rte. 66, west on unpaved road,* ☎ *809/773–1989.*

## Frederiksted

**7** **Frederiksted,** St. Croix's other town, was founded in 1751. It's noted less for its Danish than for its Victorian architecture that dates from after the uprising of former slaves and the great fire of 1878. A single long cruise-ship pier juts into the sparkling sea. A stroll around will take you no more than an hour. There are several restaurants and bars, so you won't go hungry.

**Apothecary Hall.** Built in 1839, this is a good example of 19th-century architecture. ✉ *King Cross St.*

**Fort Frederik.** In 1848 the slaves of the Danish West Indies were freed by Governor General Peter van Scholten as he stood on the fort's ramparts. The fort, completed in 1760, houses a number of interesting historical exhibits as well as an art gallery. ✉ *Waterfront,* ☎ *809/772–2021.* 🎫 *Free.* 🕐 *Weekdays 8:30–4:30.*

**Market Place.** Stop here for fresh fruits and vegetables sold early in the morning, just as they have been for more than 200 years. ✉ *Queen St.*

**St. Croix Aquarium.** The tanks are home to an ever-changing variety of local sea creatures. ⊠ *Strand St.,* ☎ *809/772–1345.* ☉ *Wed.–Sun. 11–4.* ☞ *$3.*

**St. Patrick's Church.** This Roman Catholic church was built in 1843 of coral. ⊠ *Prince St.*

**St. Paul's Episcopal Church.** This church is a mixture of classic and Gothic Revival architecture, built in 1812. ⊠ *Prince St.*

**Visitor's Center.** Right on the pier, it once served as a Customs House. Built at the end of the 1700s, the two-story gallery was added in the 1800s. ⊠ *Waterfront,* ☎ *809/772–0357.*

| | |
|---|---|
| NEED A BREAK? | If you're hungry as you head out of town, stop about ½ mile north at the seaside **La Grange Beach Club** for a yummy salad or sandwich and then enjoy a swim at the beach. ⊠ *Rte. 63,* ☎ *809/772–5566.* |

# Exploring St. John

St. John may be small, but the roads are narrow and wind up and down steep hills, so don't expect to get anywhere in a hurry. Bring along your swimsuit for stops at some of the most beautiful beaches in the world.

*Numbers in the margin correspond to points of interest on the St. John map.*

❺ **Annaberg Plantation.** Partially restored by the Park, this reminder of the days when the island courted agriculture instead of tourists was built in the 1780s. As you stroll around, look up at the steep hillsides and imagine cutting sugarcane against that grade in the hot sun. Slaves, Danes, and Dutchmen toiled here to harvest the sugarcane that produced sugar, molasses, and rum for export. There are no official visiting hours, no charge for entry, and no official tours, although some well-informed taxi drivers will show you around. Occasionally artisans provide free demonstrations of various island crafts, while local ladies bake luscious johnnycakes (the Caribbean Egg McMuffin). For more information on talks and cultural demonstrations, contact the St. John National Park Service Visitors Center (⊠ Leinster Bay off the North Shore Rd., ☎ 809/776–6201).

❸ **Bordeaux Mountain.** At 1,277 feet, this is St. John's highest peak. Stop for a moment hereabouts and you'll find bay trees. Crackle a leaf from one, and you'll get a whiff of the spicy aroma that you may recognize from the bay rum for which St. John is famous. Follow the dirt road from the cluster of shops at the overlook to Picture Point, a worthwhile drive. ⊠ *Centerline Rd./Rte. 10.*

**Caneel Bay Resort.** Laurence Rockefeller bought this lush property from the Danish West India Company in the 1950s. He bought more acreage along the north shore and donated all of it to the U.S. government as a national park. Caneel Bay Beach (home of two friendly stingrays that have been fed by snorkelers) is reached by parking in the Caneel parking lot and walking through the grounds (ask for directions). Visitors are welcome at the three restaurants and other designated areas. ⊠ *North Shore Rd./Rte. 20,* ☎ *809/776–6111.*

**Cinnamon Bay.** The snorkeling around the point to the right is good unless the waves are up—look for the big angelfish and the swarms of purple triggerfish that live here. The national-park campground is at Cinnamon Bay and includes a snack bar, bathhouse, boutique, restaurant, general store, water-sports equipment rental, and self-guided museum. Across the road from the beach parking lot is the beginning of the two Cinnamon Bay hiking trails: Look for the ruins of a sugar mill to mark the trailhead. The nature trail here takes you on a flat circle through the woods, following signs that identify the flora. The other trail heads all the way up to Centerline Road. ✉ *North Shore Rd./Rte. 20.*

**❹ Coral Bay.** The island's second town is named for its shape rather than for its underwater life. (The word *coral* comes from *krawl*, Danish for "corral.") The community at the dry, eastern end of the island is the ultimate in laid-back style. It's quiet, neighborhoody, local, and independent. The small wood-and-stucco West Indian homes here house everyone from families born here to newer residents who offer palm readings and massage. This is a place to get away from it all. ✉ *At end of Centerline Rd./Rte. 10.*

**❶ Cruz Bay.** Start at the town dock for a leisurely stroll through the streets of this colorful, compact town: There are plenty of shops through which to browse, along with a number of watering holes where you can stop to take a breather.

**Hawksnest Beach.** If this gorgeous bay looks familiar, you've seen it in Alan Alda's film *Four Seasons.* It's a popular locals beach. ✉ *North Shore Rd./Rte. 20.*

**Hurricane Hole.** This vast body of water features tiny bays where boats ride out hurricanes in safety. The road meanders past with drop-dead views. It's only a 15- to 20-minute ride from Coral Bay, where Taino Indians are believed to have first settled on the island 2,000 years ago. At Haulover Bay, only a couple hundred yards separate the Atlantic Ocean from the Caribbean. ✉ *East End Rd.*

**National Park Service Visitors Center.** The Park rangers will answer questions and provide you with brochures about park hikes and activities. The center also has a good book section with volumes about the islands' flora and fauna. ✉ *North Shore Rd./Rte. 20 in Cruz Bay,* ☎ *809/776–6201.*

**Peace Hill.** You can see forever from this gorgeous spot along the North Shore. A five-minute uphill walk from the parking lot takes you past the ruins of an old sugar mill to a grassy spot perfect for picnics. The white pile of stones is all that remains of *Christ of the Caribbean,* a statue erected in 1953 by Colonel Julius Wadsworth and donated, along with 9 acres of land, to the national park in 1975. The statue was another one of the Hurricane Marilyn's casualties. ✉ *North Shore Rd./Rte. 20.D/rd*

**❷ Reef Bay Trail.** Hike down to Reef Bay by yourself or on a hike led by a National Park Service ranger. The rangers identify the trees and plants on the hike down, fill you in on the history of the Reef Bay Plantation, and tell you about the carvings you'll find in the rocks at the bottom of the trail. The National Park Service provides a boat ($10) to take you back to Cruz Bay, saving you the uphill return climb (☞ Guided Tours, *below*). ✉ *Centerline Rd./Rte. 10.*

**Salt Pond.** A remote beach only about 1 foot above sea level is a good stop if you'd like a break from driving. It's well worth it to hike the trail south to the spectacular cliffs of Ram Head. In any case you or your rented car can't proceed much farther on here without venturing onto a truly rocky road that heads west. Be sure at least to get a view of Lameshur Bay, one of the best snorkeling places on St. John and an area once used for underwater training by the U.S. Navy. ✉ *Rte. 107.*

**Trunk Bay.** The most popular beach on St. John sports a beautiful beach with an underwater trail that's good for beginner snorkelers. It's usually packed with cruise-ship tourists over for the day from St. Thomas. ⊠ *North Shore Rd./Rte. 20.*

---

# U.S. Virgin Islands A to Z

## Arriving and Departing

### BY BOAT

Some 20 cruise lines, ranging from floating budget hotels to small luxury yachts taking only 100 passengers, stop at St. Thomas, St. John, or St. Croix.

Virtually every type of ship and major cruise line calls at St. Thomas; only a few call at St. Croix and St. John. One of these ports is usually included as part of a ship's eastern Caribbean itinerary. Many of the ships that call at St. Thomas also call at St. John or offer an excursion to that island. For a cruise aboard an ocean liner, contact **Cunard Line** (⊠ 555 5th Ave., New York, NY 10017, ☎ 800/528–6273), **Dolphin Cruise Lines** (⊠ 901 South America Way, Miami, FL 33132, ☎ 800/222–1003), **Holland America Line** (⊠ 300 Elliot Ave. W, Seattle, WA 98119, ☎ 800/426–0327), **Norwegian Cruise Lines** (⊠ Box 025403, Miami, FL 33102, ☎ 800/327–7030), **Princess Cruises** (⊠ 10100 Santa Monica Blvd., Los Angeles, CA 90067, ☎ 800/421–0522), **Royal Caribbean Cruise Line** (⊠ 1050 Caribbean Way, Miami, FL 33132, ☎ 800/327–6700), or **Royal Cruise Lines** (⊠ 1 Maritime Plaza, San Francisco, CA 94111, ☎ 800/622–0538). For a cruise aboard a luxury yacht, contact **Renaissance Cruises** (⊠ 1800 Eller Dr., Suite 300, Box 350307, Fort Lauderdale, FL 33335-0307, ☎ 800/525–2450) or **Seabourn Cruise Line** (⊠ 55 Francisco St., San Francisco, CA 94133, ☎ 800/929–9595).

Increasingly popular are cruises aboard oversize sailboats. Although the sails on these rather odd-looking ships are more often cosmetic than functional, the ships usually offer a more relaxed itinerary and stop at less-traveled anchorages. Itineraries and ship deployments change frequently, so contact your cruise line or travel agent for the latest scheduled sailings. **Windstar Cruises** (⊠ 300 Elliot Ave. W, Seattle, WA 98119, ☎ 800/258–7245) stops in St. John. You can experience a **Club Med** (☎ 800/258–2633) all-inclusive vacation on the sea aboard *Club Med I,* a 617-foot ship with seven computerized sails that Club Med bills as the largest sailing ship in the world. The ship sails out of Martinique on seven-day winter cruises (it's in St. Thomas for one day) and spends summers in the Mediterranean. **Windjammer Barefoot Cruises** (⊠ Box 190120, Miami Beach, FL 33119-0120, ☎ 800/327–2601) sails from the nearby British Virgin Islands to neighboring islands on cruises of 6- to 13-day durations.

### BY PLANE

One advantage of visiting the U.S.V.I. is the abundance of nonstop flights that can have you at the beach in three to four hours from most East Coast departures. You may fly into the U.S.V.I. direct on **Delta** (☎ 800/221–1212) and from Baltimore on Delta and on **USAir** (☎ 800/622–2025). **American** (☎ 800/474–4884) flies direct from Miami, New York, Raleigh–Durham, and San Juan. Another option is to pick up a local flight from San Juan on **American Eagle** (☎ 800/474–4884).

## Currency

The U.S. dollar is the medium of exchange here.

## Emergencies

**Police:** Dial ☎ 911.

**Hospitals:** The emergency room of **St. Thomas Hospital** (☎ 809/776–8311) in Sugar Estate, Charlotte Amalie, is open 24 hours a day. In Christiansted there is the **Governor Juan F. Luis Hospital and Health Center** (✉ 6 Diamond Ruby, north of Sunny Isle Shopping Center, on Rte. 79, ☎ 809/778–6311) or the **Frederiksted Health Center** (✉ 516 Strand St., ☎ 809/772–1992). On St. John contact the **Myrah Keating Smith Community Health Center** on Centerline Road (✉ Susanaberg, ☎ 809/693–8900) or call an emergency medical technician directly (☎ 809/776–6222).

**Air Ambulance: Bohlke International Airways** (☎ 809/778–9177) operates out of the St. Croix airport. **Air Ambulance Network** (☎ 800/327–1966) also serves the area from Florida.

**Coast Guard:** For emergencies on St. Thomas or St. John, call the **Marine Safety Detachment** (☎ 809/776–3497) from 7 to 3:30 weekdays; on St. Croix, call 809/778–2692. If there is no answer, call the **Rescue Coordination Center** (☎ 809/729–6770 or 809/729–6800, ext. 140–145) in San Juan, open 24 hours a day.

**Pharmacies: Sunrise Pharmacy** is open at Red Hook (☎ 809/775–6600). **Kmart** operates a pharmacy inside its Tutu Park Mall (☎ 809/777–3854). On St. Croix, try **People's Drug Store, Inc.** in Christiansted (☎ 809/778–7355) and **Sunny Isle Shopping Center** (☎ 809/778–5537) or **D & D Apothecary Hall** (☎ 809/772–1890) in Frederiksted. On St. John, the **St. John Drug Center** (☎ 809/776–6353) is in Cruz Bay.

## Getting Around
### BY BUS
Public buses are not the quickest way to get around on the islands, because service is minimal, but the deluxe mainland-size buses on St. Thomas and St. Croix make public transportation a very reasonable and comfortable way to get from east and west to town and back (on St. Thomas there is no service north). Fares are $1 between outlying areas and town and 75¢ in town. St. John has no public bus system, and residents rely on the kindness of taxi vans and safari buses for mass transportation.

### CAR RENTALS
Any U.S. driver's license is good for 90 days here; the minimum age for drivers is 18, although many agencies won't rent to anyone under the age of 25. Driving is on the left side of the road (although your steering wheel will be on the left side of the car). Many of the roads are narrow and the islands are dotted with hills, so there is ample reason to drive carefully. Jeeps are particularly recommended on St. John, which has well-paved main roads but many dirt side roads.

On St. Thomas, you can rent a car from **ABC Rentals** (☎ 809/776–1222 or 800/524–2080), **Anchorage E-Z Car** (☎ 809/775–6255 or 800/524–2027), **Avis** (☎ 809/774–1468), **Budget** (☎ 809/776–5774), **Cowpet Car Rental** (☎ 809/775–7376 or 800/524–2072), **Dependable** (☎ 809/774–2253 or 800/522–3076), **Discount** (☎ 809/776–4858), **Hertz** (☎ 809/774–1879), **Sea Breeze** (☎ 809/774–7200), **Sun Island** (☎ 809/774–3333 or 800/233–7941), or **Thrifty** (☎ 809/776–7282).

On St. Croix, call **Atlas** (☎ 809/773–2886 or 800/426–6009), **Avis** (☎ 809/778–9355), **Budget** (☎ 809/778–9636), **Caribbean Jeep & Car** (☎ 809/773–4399), **Fair Auto Rental** (☎ 809/773–5031), **Olympic** (☎ 809/773–2208 or 800/344–5776), and **Thrifty** (☎ 809/773–7200).

On St. John, call **Avis** (☎ 809/776–6374), **Cool Breeze** (☎ 809/776–6588), **Hertz** (☎ 809/776–6695), **O'Connor Jeep** (☎ 809/776–6343),

**St. John Car Rental** (☎ 809/776–6103), or **Spencer's Jeep** (☎ 809/776–6628).

BY FERRY

Ferries ply two routes between St. Thomas and St. John—either between the Charlotte Amalie waterfront and Cruz Bay or between Red Hook and Cruz Bay. The schedules for daily service between Red Hook, St. Thomas, and Cruz Bay, St. John are as follows: Ferries leave Red Hook weekdays 6:30 and 7:30 AM, and all week long hourly 8 AM to midnight. They leave Cruz Bay for Red Hook hourly 6 AM to 10 PM and at 11:20 PM. The 15- to 20-minute ferry ride is $3 one-way.

BY TAXI

Taxis of all shapes and sizes are available at various ferry, shopping, resort, and airport areas on St. Thomas and respond quickly to a call.

In Charlotte Amalie, taxi stands are across from Emancipation Gardens (in front of Little Switzerland behind the post office) and along the waterfront. Away from Charlotte Amalie, you'll find taxis available at all major hotels and at such public beaches as Magens Bay and Coki Point, as well as at the Red Hook ferry dock. Calling taxis will work, too, but allow plenty of time.

Taxis on St. Croix, generally station wagons or minivans, are a phone call away from most hotels and are available in downtown Christiansted, at the Alexander Hamilton Airport, and at the Frederiksted pier during cruise-ship arrivals. Rates, set by law, are prominently displayed at the airport, and drivers are required to show a rate sheet if passengers request it. Try the **St. Croix Taxi Association** (☎ 809/778–1088) at the airport and **Antilles Taxi Service** (☎ 809/773–5020) or **Cruzan Taxi and Tours** (☎ 809/773–6388) in Christiansted.

On St. John buses and taxis are the same thing: open-air safari buses. Technically the safari buses are private taxis, but everyone uses them as an informal bus system. They congregate at the Cruz Bay Dock, ready to take you to any of the beaches or other island destinations; you can also pick them up anywhere on the road by signaling.

## Guided Tours

On St. Thomas, the **V.I. Taxi Association City-Island Tour** (☎ 809/774–4550) gives a two-hour tour aimed at cruise-ship passengers that includes stops at Drake's Seat and Mountain Top. **Tropic Tours** (☎ 809/774–1855 or 800/524–4334) offers half-day shopping and sightseeing tours of St. Thomas by bus six days a week for $20 per person, and full-day snorkeling tours to St. John every day for $60 per person (including lunch). It picks up at all the major hotels. Bird-watching, whale-watching, and a chance to wait hidden on a beach while the magnificent turtles come ashore to lay their eggs are all open to visitors. Write the **St. Croix Environmental Association** (⊠ Box 3839, St. Croix 00822, ☎ 809/773–1989) or **EAST** (Environmental Association of St. Thomas–St. John) (⊠ Box 12379, St. Thomas 00801, ☎ 809/776–1976) for more information on hikes and special programs, or check the community calendar in the *Daily News* for up-to-date information.

Van tours of St. Croix are offered by **St. Croix Safari Tours** (☎ 809/773–6700) and **St. Croix Transit** (☎ 809/772–3333). The tours, which depart from Christiansted and last about three hours, start at $25 per person. One of the best ways to see the rain forest and hills of the west end may be a tour by horseback with **Paul and Jill's Equestrian Stable** (☎ 809/772–2880 or 809/772–2627).

On St. John, stop at the taxi stand in the Cruz Bay Park for tours of the island. The park service also gives a variety of guided tours on- and off-shore. For more information, or to arrange a tour, contact the **St. John National Park Visitor Center** (✉ Cruz Bay, ☎ 809/776–6201).

## Language

English, often with a Creole or West Indian lilt, is what's spoken on these islands.

## Opening and Closing Times

On St. Thomas, Charlotte Amalie's Main Street–area shops are open weekdays and Saturday 9–5. Havensight Mall shops (next to the cruise-ship dock) hours are the same, though some shops sometimes stay open until 9 on Friday, depending on how many cruise ships are staying late at the dock. You may also find some shops open on Sunday if a lot of cruise ships are in port. American Yacht Harbor stores are open weekdays and Saturday 9–6. St. Croix store hours are usually weekdays 9–5, but you will definitely find some shops in Christiansted open in the evening. On St. John, store hours are reliably similar to those on the other two islands, and Wharfside Village shops in Cruz Bay are often open into the evening.

## Passports and Visas

No proof of citizenship is required for U.S. citizens entering the U.S.V.I. However, you may need proof of citizenship to return to the U.S. mainland. Canadian citizens are required to present some proof of citizenship—if not a passport, then a birth certificate—to enter. If you are arriving from the U.S. mainland or Puerto Rico, you need no inoculation or health certificate.

Britons need a valid passport to enter the U.S.V.I. (✉ £15 for a standard 32-page passport, £30 for a 94-page passport). You do not need a visa for the U.S.V.I. if you are visiting either on business or pleasure, are staying fewer than 90 days, have a return ticket or ongoing ticket, are traveling with a major airline (in effect, any airline that flies from the United Kingdom to the United States), and complete visa waiver I-94W, which is supplied either at the airport of departure or on the plane.

## Precautions

Crime exists here, but not to the same degree that it does in larger cities on the U.S. mainland. Still, it's best to stick to well-lit streets at night and use the same kind of street sense (don't wander the back alleys of Charlotte Amalie after five rum punches, for example) that you would in any unfamiliar territory. If you plan on carrying things around, rent a car, not a Jeep, and lock possessions in the trunk. Keep your rental car locked wherever you park. Don't leave cameras, purses, and other valuables lying on the beach while you're off on an hour-long snorkel, whether at the deserted beaches of St. John or the more crowded Magens and Coki beaches on St. Thomas.

## Taxes and Service Charges

An 8% tax is added to hotel rates. Departure tax for the U.S.V.I. is included in the cost of your airplane ticket. Some hotels and restaurants add a 10% or 15% service charge to your bill, generally only if you are part of a group of 15 or more. There is no sales tax in the U.S.V.I.

## Telephones and Mail

The area code for all the U.S.V.I. is 809, and there is direct dial to the mainland. Local calls from a public phone cost 25¢ for each five minutes. On St. John the place to go for any telephone or message needs is **Connections** (☎ 809/776–6922). On St. Thomas, it's **Islander Services** (☎ 809/774–5302), behind the Greenhouse Restaurant in Charlotte Amalie, or **East End Secretarial Services** (☎ 809/775–5262, FAX

809/775–3590), upstairs at the Red Hook Plaza. On St. Croix, visit **AnswerPLUS** (✉ 5005B Chandlers Wharf, Gallows Bay, ☎ 809/773–4444) or **Worldwide Calling** (head of the pier in Frederiksted, ☎ 809/772–2490).

The main U.S. post office on St. Thomas is near the hospital, with branches in Charlotte Amalie, the Tutu Mall, and Frenchtown; there's a post office at Christiansted, Gallows Bay, Sunny Isle, and Frederiksted on St. Croix, and at Cruz Bay on St. John. Postal rates are the same as elsewhere in the United States: 32¢ for a letter, 20¢ for a postcard to anywhere in the United States, 50¢ for a ½-ounce letter mailed to a foreign country.

## Visitor Information

Information about the United States Virgin Islands is available through the U.S.V.I. **Government Tourist Offices** (✉ 225 Peachtree St., Suite 760, Atlanta, GA 30303, ☎ 404/688–0906, FAX 404/525–1102; ✉ 500 N. Michigan Ave., Suite 2030, Chicago, IL 60611, ☎ 312/670–8784, FAX 312/670–8789; ✉ 3460 Wilshire Blvd., Suite 412, Los Angeles, CA 90010, ☎ 213/739–0138, FAX 213/739–2005; ✉ 2655 Le Jeune Rd., Suite 907, Coral Gables, FL 33134, ☎ 305/442–7200, FAX 305/445–9044; ✉ 1270 Avenue of the Americas, Room 2108, New York, NY 10020, ☎ 212/332–2222, FAX 212/332–2223; ✉ 900 17th Ave. NW, Suite 500, Washington, DC 20006, ☎ 202/293–3707, FAX 202/785–2542; ✉ 1300 Ashford Ave., Condado, Santurce, Puerto Rico 00907, ☎ 809/724–3816, FAX 809/724–7223; ✉ 3300 Bloor St., Suite 3120, Center Tower, Toronto, Ontario, Canada M8X 2X3, ☎ 416/233–1414, FAX 416/233–9367; ✉ 2 Cinnamon Row, Plantation Wharf, York Pl., London SW11 3TW, ☎ 0171/978–5262, telex 27231, FAX 0171/924–3171).

You can also call the **Division of Tourism**'s toll-free number (☎ 800/878–4463).

The **U.S. Virgin Islands Division of Tourism** has an office in St. Thomas (✉ Box 6400, Charlotte Amalie 00804, ☎ 809/774–8784, FAX 809/774–4390). The **visitor center** in Charlotte Amalie across from Emancipation Garden is expected to open by winter 1997. There's also a **visitor information** kiosk at Havensight Mall, in St. Croix (✉ Box 4538, Christiansted, U.S.V.I. 00822, ☎ 809/773–0495) and on the pier (✉ Strand St., Frederiksted, U.S.V.I. 00840, ☎ 809/772–0357), and in St. John (✉ Box 200, Cruz Bay, U.S.V.I. 00830, ☎ 809/776–6450).

# INDEX

✗ = *restaurant*, ⌘ = *hotel*

# NOTES

*Escape to ancient cities and exotic*

*islands*  *with CNN Travel Guide, a*

*wealth of valuable advice. Host Valerie Voss will take you*

*to all of your favorite destinations,*

*including those off the beaten path.*

*Tune into your passport to the world.*

# CNN TRAVEL GUIDE

SATURDAY 12:30 PM ET    SUNDAY 4:30 PM ET

# Fodor's Travel Publications

*Available at bookstores everywhere, or call 1–800–533–6478, 24 hours a day.*

## Gold Guides
### U.S.

Alaska

Arizona

Boston

California

Cape Cod, Martha's
Vineyard, Nantucket

The Carolinas & the
Georgia Coast

Chicago

Colorado

Florida

Hawai'i

Las Vegas, Reno,
Tahoe

Los Angeles

Maine, Vermont,
New Hampshire

Maui & Lāna'i

Miami & the Keys

New England

New Orleans

New York City

Pacific North Coast

Philadelphia & the
Pennsylvania Dutch
Country

The Rockies

San Diego

San Francisco

Santa Fe, Taos,
Albuquerque

Seattle & Vancouver

The South

U.S. & British Virgin
Islands

USA

Virginia & Maryland

Washington, D.C.

### Foreign

Australia

Austria

The Bahamas

Belize & Guatemala

Bermuda

Canada

Cancún, Cozumel,
Yucatán Peninsula

Caribbean

China

Costa Rica

Cuba

The Czech Republic
& Slovakia

Eastern &
Central Europe

Europe

Florence, Tuscany
& Umbria

France

Germany

Great Britain

Greece

Hong Kong

India

Ireland

Israel

Italy

Japan

London

Madrid & Barcelona

Mexico

Montréal &
Québec City

Moscow, St.
Petersburg, Kiev

The Netherlands,
Belgium &
Luxembourg

New Zealand

Norway

Nova Scotia, New
Brunswick, Prince
Edward Island

Paris

Portugal

Provence &
the Riviera

Scandinavia

Scotland

Singapore

South Africa

South America

Southeast Asia

Spain

Sweden

Switzerland

Thailand

Tokyo

Toronto

Turkey

Vienna & the Danube

## Fodor's Special-Interest Guides

Caribbean Ports
of Call

The Complete Guide
to America's
National Parks

Family Adventures

Gay Guide
to the USA

Halliday's New
England Food
Explorer

Halliday's New
Orleans Food
Explorer

Healthy Escapes

Kodak Guide to
Shooting Great
Travel Pictures

Net Travel

Nights to Imagine

Rock & Roll Traveler
USA

Sunday in New York

Sunday in
San Francisco

Walt Disney World,
Universal Studios
and Orlando

Walt Disney World
for Adults

Where Should We
Take the Kids?
California

Where Should We
Take the Kids?
Northeast

Worldwide Cruises
and Ports of Call

# Fodor's
## Special Series

**Affordables**

Caribbean

Europe

Florida

France

Germany

Great Britain

Italy

London

Paris

**Fodor's Bed & Breakfasts and Country Inns**

America

California

The Mid-Atlantic

New England

The Pacific Northwest

The South

The Southwest

The Upper Great Lakes

**The Berkeley Guides**

California

Central America

Eastern Europe

Europe

France

Germany & Austria

Great Britain & Ireland

Italy

London

Mexico

New York City

Pacific Northwest & Alaska

Paris

San Francisco

**Compass American Guides**

Arizona

Canada

Chicago

Colorado

Hawaii

Idaho

Hollywood

Las Vegas

Maine

Manhattan

Montana

New Mexico

New Orleans

Oregon

San Francisco

Santa Fe

South Carolina

South Dakota

Southwest

Texas

Utah

Virginia

Washington

Wine Country

Wisconsin

Wyoming

**Fodor's Citypacks**

Atlanta

Hong Kong

London

New York City

Paris

Rome

San Francisco

Washington, D.C.

**Fodor's Español**

California

Caribe Occidental

Caribe Oriental

Gran Bretaña

Londres

Mexico

Nueva York

Paris

**Fodor's Exploring Guides**

Australia

Boston & New England

Britain

California

Caribbean

China

Egypt

Florence & Tuscany

Florida

France

Germany

Ireland

Israel

Italy

Japan

London

Mexico

Moscow & St. Petersburg

New York City

Paris

Prague

Provence

Rome

San Francisco

Scotland

Singapore & Malaysia

Spain

Thailand

Turkey

Venice

**Fodor's Flashmaps**

Boston

New York

San Francisco

Washington, D.C.

**Fodor's Pocket Guides**

Acapulco

Atlanta

Barbados

Jamaica

London

New York City

Paris

Prague

Puerto Rico

Rome

San Francisco

Washington, D.C.

**Mobil Travel Guides**

America's Best Hotels & Restaurants

California & the West

Frequent Traveler's Guide to Major Cities

Great Lakes

Mid-Atlantic

Northeast

Northwest & Great Plains

Southeast

Southwest & South Central

**Rivages Guides**

Bed and Breakfasts of Character and Charm in France

Hotels and Country Inns of Character and Charm in France

Hotels and Country Inns of Character and Charm in Italy

Hotels and Country Inns of Character and Charm in Paris

Hotels and Country Inns of Character and Charm in Portugal

Hotels and Country Inns of Character and Charm in Spain

**Short Escapes**

Britain

France

New England

Near New York City

**Fodor's Sports**

Golf Digest's Best Places to Play

Skiing USA

USA Today The Complete Four Sport Stadium Guide

**Fodor's Vacation Planners**

Great American Learning Vacations

Great American Sports & Adventure Vacations

Great American Vacations

Great American Vacations for Travelers with Disabilities

National Parks and Seashores of the East

National Parks of the West

ce

ces

R

**BRITISH VIRGIN
ISLANDS**
Tortola
Virgin Gorda

**CAYMAN ISLANDS**
Grand Cayman

**CURAÇAO**
Willemstad

**DOMINICA**
Roseau

**HAITI**
Port-au-Prince

**JAMAICA**
Kingston
Montego Bay
Negril
Ocho Rios
Port Antonio

**MARTINIQUE**
Fort de France

**ST. MAARTEN**
Philipsburg

**ST. VINCENT**
Kingstown

**TURKS & CAICOS**
Providenciale

**U.S. VIRGIN ISLANDS**
St. Croix
St. Thomas

**Travel**

http://www.americanexpress.com/travel

**American Express Travel Service Offices are found
in central locations throughout the Caribbean.**